Central Africa
a travel survival kit

Alex Newton

Central Africa – a travel survival kit

2nd edition

Published by
    Lonely Planet Publications
    Head Office: PO Box 617, Hawthorn, Vic 3122, Australia
    Branches: PO Box 2001A, Berkeley, CA 94702, USA
                      12 Barley Mow Passage, Chiswick, London W4 4PH, UK

Printed by
    Singapore National Printers Ltd, Singapore

Photographs by

Geoff Crowther (GC)	Hal Frantz (HF)	Greg Herriman (GH)
Barry Hewlitt (BH)	Joan La Rosa (JL)	Alex Newton (AN)
Jane Siegel (JS)	Tony Wheeler (TW)	Karen Woodbury (KW)

Front cover: Lion cub, Joe Van Os, The Image Bank
Back cover: Pottery vendor, Mora, Northern Cameroun (AN)

First Published
    May 1989

This Edition
    January 1994

**Although the authors and publisher have tried to make the information as
accurate as possible, they accept no responsibility for any loss, injury or
inconvenience sustained by any person using this book.**

National Library of Australia Cataloguing in Publication Data

Newton, Alex
    Central Africa – a travel survival kit.

    2nd ed.
    Includes index.
    ISBN 0 86442 138 9.

    1. Africa, Central – Guidebooks.
    I. Title. (Series : Lonely Planet travel survival kit)

916.704

text © Alex Newton 1994
maps © Lonely Planet 1994
photos © photographers as indicated 1994
climate charts compiled from information supplied by Patrick J Tyson, © Patrick J Tyson, 1994

Alex Newton

Raised in Madison, Georgia, Alex Newton was one of the many Americans affected in the 1960s by John Kennedy's challenge to join the Peace Corps. Following almost three years' service in Guatemala as an agricultural advisor and four years on Wall St as a lawyer, he studied French and development economics and ended up in Africa, where he has spent seven years working on development assistance programs. After crossing the Sahara to visit every country in Central and West Africa, and discovering that no-one is spared the hassles of visiting this area, Alex decided to write a guidebook that addressed the needs of every kind of traveller to Central Africa. This is the second edition of *Central Africa – a travel survival kit*. He has also written Lonely Planet's Guide to *West Africa*. Now living in Dhaka and always keen on meeting interesting people, he bids travellers passing through Bangladesh to look him up.

From the Author

This book is dedicated to my mother, Polly Newton. By your thoughtfulness and zest for living, you have inspired not just me but all those around you to value friends, contribute where you can and make the most of life.

My foremost thanks go to my wife, Betsy Wagenhauser, for her support. Month after month, even on those nights when I was typing until 3 am, she never complained; how can I thank her enough? (She'd probably say 'Just give me those royalties, baby!')

Special thanks also go to Fernando Molina of Quito, Ecuador, for his wonderful drawings of Central African masks; to the National Museum of African Art in Washington, DC which provided a number of the photographs as did Hal Frantz (Equatorial Guinea), Bob Macke (Gabon), Barry Hewlitt (Central African Republic) and Joan La Rosa (gorilla photos); to the Peace Corps volunteers of Gabon who, led by Scott Foust as the 'chef du fun' sent piles of information and maps on Gabon; to Joe Hindman, the Peace Corps Director in Chad, for showing me the 'in' spots of N'Djamena and starting me on the right track in northern Cameroun and southern Chad; to Janet McIntyre of Norfolk, UK, for invaluable information on Kisangani; to Peace Corps leader Jason Kary for his hospitality in Moundou; to David Stanley of Canada for his invaluable comments on the 1st edition; to Peace Corps volunteer Kelly Briles of Greensburg, Pennsylvania, for his detailed information and map of Sarh; and last but certainly not least to François Pahud of Crissier, Switzerland for saving my life in a dark alley of Kinshasa's Cité district, and for sending me information on southern Zaïre.

Thanks finally to all the people who sent in letters. They include:

Malcolm Aikman (AUS), Linda Baskey (USA), Beth Blue USA), A Y Brooks (UK), Robert Casimaty (AUS), Hayley Cavill (UK), Tony Chamberlain (UK), Trudy Chamberlain (UK), Herma Darmstadt (NL), Mark Davidson (UK), Jonathan Duddles (AUS), Scott Foust (USA), Gordon Glanz (C), Suzy Gornall (UK), Steve Halteman (USA), Bruce Hayes (USA), Dylan Hayes (UK), Gordon Heitzeberg (USA), Phyllis Jansyn (Cam), John Kelly (USA), Besdel Knudsen (DK), Jan Kucera (USA), Tony Leisner (USA), Chuck Ludlam (USA), Robert Lukesch (A), Bob Newman (AUS), Martin Nienbuis (NL), Brian O'Day (USA), Anders Olsson (S), Penny & Rachel (UK), Jordi Raich (SP), Laurence & Odile Bancod Reynolds (F), David Sacco (USA), Michael

Sheehan (USA), Laura Silvani (Sp), Manfred Stanek (A), Lisa Steeley (USA), Martin Storey (USA), Christina Taylor (UK), Soan Thung (NL), Wendy Turnbull (SA), and J W Vanderwaal (NL).

A – Austria, AUS – Australia, C – Canada, Cam – Cameroun, DK – Denmark, F – France, NL – the Netherlands, SA – South Africa, Sp – Spain, UK – United Kingdom, USA – United States of America

From the Publisher

This edition of Central Africa was edited by Miriam Cannell and Simone Calderwood. Sally Woodward was responsible for the design, mapping and illustrations, and Margaret Jung designed the front cover. Thanks to Vyvyan Cayley for proofreading, to Sharan Kaur, Adrienne Costanzo and Kay Waters for copy-editing, and to Chris Klepp for providing the title page photo.

Warning & Request

Things change – prices go up, schedules change, good places go bad and bad places go bankrupt – nothing stays the same. So if you find things better or worse, recently opened or long since closed, please write and tell us and help make the next edition better.

Your letters will be used to help update future editions and, where possible, important changes will also be included in a Stop Press section in reprints.

We greatly appreciate all information that is sent to us by travellers. Back at Lonely Planet we employ a hard-working readers' letters team to sort through the many letters we receive. The best ones will be rewarded with a free copy of the next edition or another Lonely Planet guide if you prefer. We give away lots of books, but, unfortunately, not every letter/postcard receives one.

Contents

INTRODUCTION 11

FACTS ABOUT THE REGION 14

Geography 14   Economy 19   Religion 33
Climate 14   People 20   Language 35
National Parks 17   Music 23
Government 18   Social Customs 28

FACTS FOR THE VISITOR 36

Visas 36   Electricity 50   Highlights 74
Customs 41   Books 50   Food 75
Money 42   Maps 56   Drinks 78
When to Go 46   Film & Photography 56   Markets 78
What to Bring 47   Health 58   Things to Buy 79
Cultural Events & Holidays 48   Dangers & Annoyances 71
Post & Telecommunications 49   Activities 72

GETTING THERE & AWAY 83

Air 83   Crossing the Sahara 90
Land 88   Sea 96

GETTING AROUND 98

Air 98   Truck 101   Bicycle 103
Train 99   Bus 101   Local Transport 104
Bush Taxi 100   Car 101

CAMEROUN 106

Facts about the Country 106   Air 121   Bamenda 175
History 106   Bus 121   Around Bamenda 179
Geography 110   Train 121   Ring Road 179
Climate 110   Bush Taxi 122   **Eastern Cameroun** 181
Government 110   Car 122   Bertoua 181
Economy 111   Bicycle 123   Batouri 182
Population & People 111   **Yaoundé** 123   Garoua-Boulaï 182
Music 112   Around Yaoundé 136   Meiganga 182
Language 113   **Douala** 137   N'Gaoundal, Tibati & Banyo 182
Facts for the Visitor 114   **Southern Cameroun** ...150   **Northern Cameroun** 183
Visas & Embassies 114   Kribi 150   N'Gaoundéré 183
Documents 116   Around Kribi 153   Bénoué & Bouba Ndjida
Customs 116   Ebolowa 153   National Parks 188
Money 116   Ambam 155   Garoua 189
Business Hours & Holidays 116   **Western Cameroun** 155   Around Garoua 193
Post & Telecommunications 117   Limbe 155   Maroua 193
Photography 117   Buea & Mt Cameroun 159   Around Maroua 199
Health 117   Kumba 162   Mokolo 200
Dangers & Annoyances 117   Korup National Park &   Around Mokolo 201
Food 118   Mundemba 164   Rumsiki 202
Getting There & Away 118   Mamfé 165   Around Rumsiki 203
Air 118   Foumban 166   Mora 203
Land 119   Bafoussam 169   Around Mora 204
Sea 120   Around Bafoussam 173   Waza National Park 205
Getting Around 121   Dschang 174   Kousseri 206

CENTRAL AFRICAN REPUBLIC 207

Facts about the Country 207	Photography 217	Kembé 239
History 207	Health..............................217	Bangassou 239
Geography 210	Dangers & Annoyances 217	**The North** **239**
Climate 211	**Getting There & Away** **217**	Kaga Bandoro 239
Government........................211	Air 217	Kabo 240
Economy.............................212	Land 218	Sido 240
Population & People................212	River 220	St Floris &
Music 213	**Getting Around** **221**	Bamingui-Bangoran Parks......241
Language 214	Air 221	N'Délé 242
Facts for the Visitor **214**	Bus & Truck.........................221	Birao.............................242
Visas & Embassies 214	Canoe 221	**The West & South-West** .. **243**
Documents............................215	**Bangui** **221**	Bossembélé 243
Customs...............................216	Around Bangui 233	Bouar.............................244
Money.................................216	**The East**..............................**234**	Around Bouar 246
Business Hours & Holidays 216	Sibut................................234	Carnot............................246
Post & Telecommunications....216	Bambari 236	Berbérati 246
Time....................................217	Mobaye 238	Dzanga-Sangha Reserve 247

CHAD 251

Facts about the Country 252	Time.................................263	**The South**...........................**280**
History 252	Photography 263	Sarh................................280
Geography 256	Health..............................263	Entertainment.....................283
Climate 257	Dangers & Annoyances 263	Zakouma National Park 284
Government........................257	**Getting There & Away** **264**	Sido 284
Economy.............................257	Air 264	Koumra 285
Population & People................258	Land 264	Moundou 285
Music 259	**Getting Around** **266**	**The East** **288**
Language 260	Air 266	Abéché 288
Facts for the Visitor **260**	Bus 266	Around Abéché 289
Visas & Embassies 260	Truck................................266	**The North** **289**
Documents............................262	Car...................................267	Fada...............................289
Customs...............................262	**N'Djamena** **267**	Moussoro 290
Money.................................262	Around N'Djamena 278	Faya...............................290
Business Hours & Holidays 262	Linia Market 279	Tibesti Mountains 290
Post & Telecommunications....263	Lake Chad & Douguia...........279	

THE CONGO.. 292

Facts about the Country 292	Photography 302	Pointe-Noire.......................321
History 292	Health..............................302	Around Pointe-Noire 329
Geography 296	Dangers & Annoyances 302	Loubomo (Dolisie)................329
Climate 297	Food 302	Nyanga 333
Government........................297	**Getting There & Away** **303**	Mbinda 333
Economy.............................298	Air 303	Sibiti..............................333
Population & People................298	Land 303	Kinkala & Matoumbou 333
Arts & Culture......................298	Sea & River 304	**The Centre & The North** .. **334**
Language 299	**Getting Around** **305**	Djambala 334
Facts for the Visitor **299**	Air 305	Oyo................................334
Visas & Embassies 299	Minibus............................305	Owando 334
Documents............................301	Train................................305	Makoua 335
Customs...............................301	Car...................................305	Ouesso 336
Money.................................301	Riverboat...........................306	Bomassa 336
Business Hours & Holidays 301	**Brazzaville** **306**	Impfondo..........................337
Post & Telecommunications....301	Around Brazzaville................320	
Time....................................302	**The West**............................**321**	

EQUATORIAL GUINEA 338

Facts about the Country 338
History 338
Geography 341
Climate 341
Government...........................342
Economy................................342
Population & People................343
Arts & Culture 343
Language 343
Facts for the Visitor 344
Visas & Embassies 344
Documents.............................344
Customs.................................344
Money....................................345

Business Hours & Holidays ... 345
Post & Telecommunications... 345
Time......................................345
Photography..........................345
Health....................................346
Dangers & Annoyances 346
Getting There & Away 346
Air...346
Land......................................346
Sea..347
Getting Around 348
Air...348
Bush Taxi 348
Car..348

Boat.......................................348
Bioko Island 348
Malabo 348
Around Malabo......................355
Luba 355
Around Luba..........................356
Rio Muni (The Mainland) 357
Bata 357
Mbini.....................................361
The Southern Border.............361
Evinayong.............................362
Ebebiyin................................362

GABON 365

Facts about the Country 365
History 365
Geography 368
National Parks 369
Climate 370
Government...........................370
Economy................................370
Population & People................371
Education 371
Religion.................................371
Arts & Culture 371
Language 372
Facts for the Visitor 372
Visas & Embassies 372
Documents.............................374
Customs 374
Money....................................375
Business Hours & Holidays 375
Post & Telecommunications....375
Time......................................376

Film & Photography 376
Health....................................376
Food 377
Getting There & Away 377
Air...377
Land......................................378
Sea..379
Getting Around 379
Air...379
Minibus, Bush Taxi & Truck .. 379
Train......................................380
Boat.......................................380
Libreville 381
Around Libreville 396
The Coast 398
Port-Gentil 398
Iguéla & Setté Cama..............405
Cocobeach.............................405
The Western Interior........ 406
Ndjolé....................................406

Lambaréné.............................407
Around Lambaréné.................412
Mouila...................................413
N'Dendé.................................413
Tchibanga..............................414
The North & East 415
Bitam.....................................415
Oyem.....................................415
Makokou 418
Around Makokou....................419
Booué 419
Réserve de la Lopé................421
The South-East 422
Lastoursville...........................422
Koulamoutou 424
Moanda 425
Franceville 427
Around Franceville 433
Okondja.................................433

SÃO TOMÉ E PRÍNCIPE.. 434

Facts about the Country 434
History 434
Geography 436
Climate 437
Government...........................437
Economy................................437
Population & People................438
Arts & Culture 439
Language 439
Facts for the Visitor 439

Visas & Embassies...................439
Documents 440
Customs..................................440
Money....................................440
Business Hours & Holidays ... 440
Post & Telecommunications... 440
Time......................................440
Photography...........................441
Health.....................................441
Dangers & Annoyances 441

Getting There & Away 441
Air...441
Sea..441
Getting Around 442
Air...442
Bus & Taxi 442
Boat.......................................442
São Tomé 442
Around São Tomé 448
Príncipe 450

ZAÏRE... 452

Facts about the Country 452
History 452
Geography 458
Climate 459
Government...........................459
Economy................................460

Population & People................461
Arts & Culture 461
Music 463
Language 463
Facts for the Visitor 464
Visas & Embassies...................464

Documents 467
Customs..................................467
Money 467
Business Hours & Holidays.... 468
Post & Telecommunications ... 469
Time......................................469

Photography............................469	Kolwezi....................................503	**Eastern Zaïre.................... 518**
Health 469	Mbuji-Mayi..............................504	Bukavu 518
Dangers & Annoyances..........469	Kananga 504	Parc National de
Food 470	Ilebo 505	Kahuzi-Biéga 526
Getting There & Away...... 470	Kikwit 505	Goma.......................................528
Air..470	**Northern Zaïre................. 506**	Gisenyi 534
Land 471	Gbadolite.................................506	Rutshuru 536
Sea 472	Businga 507	Butembo 537
Getting Around................. 472	Zongo 507	Beni..539
Air..472	Gemena.....................................507	Kasindi 541
Major Routes 473	Binga 508	Komanda 541
Car 477	Lisala..508	Bunia 541
Boat..478	Bumba......................................508	**Parc National de**
Western Zaïre 480	Buta 509	**Virunga 541**
Kinshasa 480	Kisangani 509	Volcano Hikes 543
Around Kinshasa 497	Kisangani to Bukavu 514	Virunga Gorillas &
Mbanza-Ngungu.......................497	Ikela 514	Chimpanzees...........................544
Matadi......................................498	Mbandaka 514	Rwindi Plains 547
Boma..498	Around Mbandaka 515	Ishango....................................548
Muanda.....................................498	Epulu 515	Ruwenzori Mountains.............549
Central & Southern Zaïre 499	Isiro 516	Mt Hoyo 553
Lubumbashi..............................499	Garamba National Park 517	

INDEX 555

Maps 555	Text 555

Map Legend

BOUNDARIES

— · — · — · —	........International Boundary
— · · — · · —	...............Internal Boundary
+·+·+·+·+·+·+	....National Park or Reserve
- - - - - - -	........................The Equator
· · · · · · · ·	........................The Tropics

SYMBOLS

◉	NATIONAL	...................National Capital
●	PROVINCIAL	........Provincial or State Capital
●	Major	...............................Major Town
●	Minor	...............................Minor Town
■		..........................Places to Stay
▼		...........................Places to Eat
✉		...............................Post Office
✈		......................................Airport
i		....................Tourist Information
⊖		.............Bus Station or Terminal
66		.............Highway Route Number
⚲ ✝ 🕌 ✝		...... Mosque, Church, Cathedral
∴		.........................Temple or Ruin
✚		.....................................Hospital
※		......................................Lookout
⚑		.... Camping Area
⋒		...........................Picnic Area
⌂		.......................Hut or Chalet
▲		......................Mountain or Hill
⊢■⊣		.......................Railway Station
═		..........................Road Bridge
⧻		.........................Railway Bridge
⇒ ⇐		...........................Road Tunnel
⇢ ⇠		..........................Railway Tunnel
⌢⌢⌢		...................Escarpment or Cliff
⌣		....Pass
⊓⊔⊓⊔		.............Ancient or Historic Wall

ROUTES

────────	.......Major Road or Highway
- - - - - - -	.........Unsealed Major Road
────────	......................Sealed Road
- - - - - - -	.....Unsealed Road or Track
════════	..........................City Street
+++++++++++	.............................Railway
━━●━━	...............................Subway
- - - - - - -	......................Walking Track
- - - - - - -	.........................Ferry Route
⊬⊬⊬⊬⊬⊬⊬	........Cable Car or Chair Lift

HYDROGRAPHIC FEATURES

	....................River or Creek
	..............Intermittent Stream
	........Lake, Intermittent Lake
	...........................Coast Line
	......................................Spring
	...............................Waterfall
	..................................Swamp
	...............Salt Lake or Reef
	..................................Glacier

OTHER FEATURES

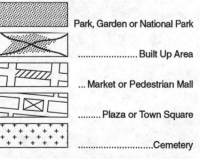

Park, Garden or National Park

.....................Built Up Area

... Market or Pedestrian Mall

.........Plaza or Town Square

...........................Cemetery

Note: not all symbols displayed above appear in this book

Introduction

Travellers are drawn to East Africa by its incomparable wildlife and scenery. West Africa offers a real opportunity to experience the essence of Black African culture – the art, the music, the markets. Central Africa combines the best of both worlds. Chad, northern Cameroun and northern Central African Republic, are clearly reminiscent of West Africa. The stunning costumes of the peoples of this region help to make the markets the most colourful in Central Africa. The people, mostly Muslim, live in hamlets scattered about the hot and dusty landscape, a bleak setting broken up by huge baobab trees which often appear to be growing upside-down.

Village life has changed very little over the centuries. Traditional roles are still very much a part of Central Africa, with decision making and hunting being left to the men,

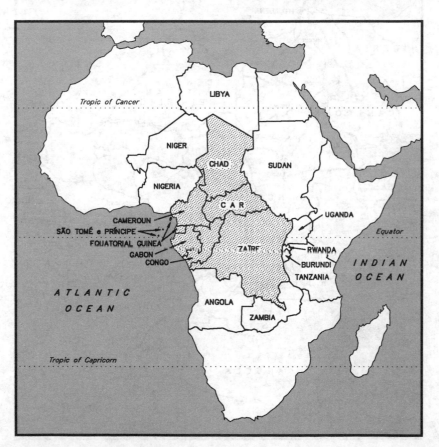

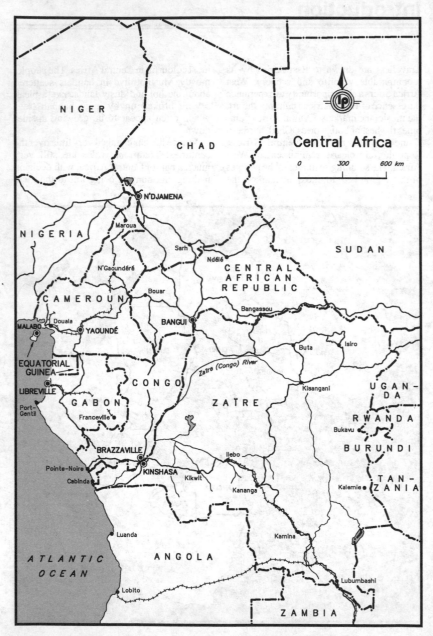

while the women tend to the children, work in the fields or prepare food. At night-time, the low beat of drums can often be heard, interrupted only by the occasional hyena calling his mate.

This is an area of stark beauty. Rumsiki in Cameroun, an area André Gide considered one of the 10 most beautiful on earth, has huge basalt outcrops creating a surreal, almost lunar landscape.

For a small fee the village sorcerer will predict your future in a ritualistic ceremony. Not far away is one of the better game parks in Africa, where during the hot season it is not unusual to see 300 or so elephants gathered around a single pond drinking to cool off. Further north on the edge of the desert at Lake Chad, you'll see fishers tossing their nets being eyed by hippos wallowing in the cool muddy waters.

The rest of Central Africa is totally different. Thick rainforests are traversed by the worst roads in Africa. Small Pygmy camps crop up here and there throughout the jungle. Because of the incredibly dense vegetation preventing the growth of urban centres, this was the most undeveloped area in Africa at the beginning of the 20th century. This is Tarzan country, where Albert Schweitzer set up his famous hospital over 70 years ago. Just crossing Zaïre overland can still take up to three weeks or more. Gabon, the richest country per capita in Black Africa, still has only about 400 km of asphalt roads outside the major cities and towns. The major cities, however, are some of the most modern in Africa, in part because three of Black Africa's six richest countries (Gabon, Cameroun, Congo) are here. As is the case with many of the wealthier 'Third World' nations, the relative affluence of these countries is oil based.

One of the most incredible sights is the snowcapped Ruwenzori mountain range in eastern Zaïre, with the third-highest peak in Africa. What's unusual in this exceedingly wet area is the spectacular flora. At 3000 metres, giant heather plants grow up to a height of 4.5 metres (compared to only 60 to 90 cm in other parts of the world), flower stems as broad as a man's arm, blue lobelia plants over three metres high (five to 10 cm elsewhere), and an undulating carpet of brilliantly coloured moss which seems to grow everywhere. Eastern Zaïre and neighbouring Rwanda and Uganda are also the home of the continent's last remaining mountain gorillas. A gorilla family in the jungle mountains is an unforgettable sight.

For the African music buff, Zaïre and Cameroun are undoubtedly the places to be. The Latin-sounding Zaïrian Congo music is the most popular throughout Africa. Any night in Kinshasa, you can hear live bands, some of them internationally renowned. Cameroun's makossa music is likewise heard all over West and Central Africa.

If it's African art you're interested in, you can't do better than Central Africa. The art of Zaïre, the Congo and eastern Cameroun is generally accepted as being among the finest on the continent. The Luba masks from Zaïre, with bug-like eyes and protruding nose and mouth, are so popular that they are sold all over West and Central Africa.

What is just as interesting, however, is simply mixing with people in the markets and villages. The best way to penetrate African culture is to make a friend. A friend will take you to his or her village, introduce you to the family, show you the bars with the best music in town, tell you when you're getting 'ripped off' and how to accomplish tasks in the best way.

Facts about the Region

GEOGRAPHY

Central Africa has a little of everything – flat lands, vast rainforests, hills and mountains. The major mountains are:

Tibesti mountain range
    northern Chad; travel to the area still requires
    special permission
Mt Cameroun (4100 metres)
    western Cameroon
Bioko Island's mountains
    Equatorial Guinea
Mt Hoyo (1450 metres)
    eastern Zaïre
Nyamulagira volcano (3056 metres)
    Zaïre
Nyiragongo volcano (3470 metres)
    Zaïre
Ruwenzori range
    Zaïre; Elizabeth Peak (5119 metres) is the third
    highest in Africa

In the rainy Ruwenzori range, known as the Mountains of the Moon, there are plants and flowers literally 15 to 20 times taller than similar varieties elsewhere in the world.

The principal hilly areas, typically rising to about 1000 metres and good for hiking, are in western Cameroun around Bamenda (a very popular area for hiking), northern Cameroun between Rumsiki and Mora and the Pic de Mindif, south of Maroua (probably the most challenging rock formation for serious rock-climbers), most of São Tomé, the central plateau of Congo particularly Léfini Park, and the lower areas of eastern Zaïre. Lubumbashi, in far southern Zaïre, is also a beautiful area with rolling hills.

Above all, Central Africa is famous for its rainforests, which are the most extensive in the world outside the Amazon basin. Some 80% of all tropical rainforests in Africa are in the Congo basin, which drains into the Zaïre (Congo) River – an area half the size of the USA. This is Pygmy territory as well.

In terms of total area, Zaïre dominates, with a larger rainforest area than all the other Central African countries combined. In per-centage terms, however, about 75% of Gabon and 60% of the Congo are covered in rainforests. Zaïre (primarily the north) and Equatorial Guinea both have about 45%, while about a third of Cameroun (primarily the south) and a small area in south-western Central African Republic (CAR) are dense rainforest areas. Fortunately, the rate of deforestation is not high except in Cameroun where the rate (.8% annually) is about half that of Brazil. For travellers, the rainforests are a mixed blessing because while they are wonderful to experience, the roads are mostly dirt and often in horrendously muddy conditions during the rainy season.

CLIMATE

Heat

Most people think Central Africa is very hot. Look at the average temperatures (in centi-grade) of the following cities:

City	Temperature	
	July	August
Washington	30	29
Rome	31	31
Tokyo	28	30
Singapore	31	30
Kinshasa (Zaïre)	27	29
Douala (Cameroun)	28	29
Lagos (Nigeria)	28	28
Cairo (Egypt)	35	35

In most of Central Africa high humidity is the problem, not heat. The only areas that get really hot are near the desert (Chad, northern Cameroun) and only from March to May does it get noticeably hotter. Put your face in front of a hair dryer and you'll know what it's like riding in a car with the windows down in Chad during this period. At least it's dry heat. While Chad and northern Cameroun can easily have temperatures 15°C hotter than average from March to May, many people prefer this to the humidity.

Rain

In Central Africa the weather pattern is erratic because of the equator. It cuts Central Africa almost in half – running just below Libreville, splitting Gabon in two, and through northern Zaïre near Kisangani and the Ruwenzori mountains. Douala (Zaïre), Yaoundé (Cameroun) and Bangui (the CAR) are all about 4° north of the equator, while Kinshasa, Brazzaville and Pointe-Noire are roughly 4° south of the equator.

As a gross simplification, Central Africa has two heavy rainy seasons: May to October above the equator and October to May south of the equator (with the heaviest rains falling mid-January to May). The rainy season north of the equator is the dry season south of the equator.

As an example of why this is a gross simplification, take the example of Yaoundé, which has two rainy seasons, March to June and September to November. It's fairly dry from July to August when you'd expect it to be rainiest. On the other hand, in Douala, only about 200 km due west, the rainy season is when you'd expect it – May to October. If possible, avoid visiting Yaoundé and Douala during the wet season. The sun rarely shines and most dirt roads, except for the main arteries, become impassable.

At or near the equator, rain tends to fall more heavily and all year round, slightly letting up in July to August in some areas, such as Libreville (Gabon).

In Chad and northern Cameroun, the skies are not continually overcast during the rainy season (mid-June to September). Indeed, many travellers prefer the rainy season in these two areas. The sun is not incessantly beating down, and temperatures are a little lower.

The main problem during the rainy season is travelling upcountry. Whereas in West Africa, most major roads upcountry are all-weather, in Central Africa this is not the case. Many of the dirt roads, even major routes, are passable only with 4WD vehicles, and the driving times are doubled. Without a 4WD vehicle, you may have no hope of reaching some of those more remote spots. This is true even in the dry areas such as Chad and northern Cameroun. In late July on the edge of the Sahara, you can find yourself surrounded by lake-size puddles of water that refuse to be absorbed by the lifeless soils.

People on tours shouldn't be concerned because 4WD vehicles are invariably used. Independent travellers who expect to do a lot of upcountry travel during rainy periods should bring patience, humour and a good book.

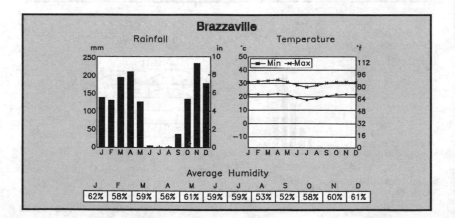

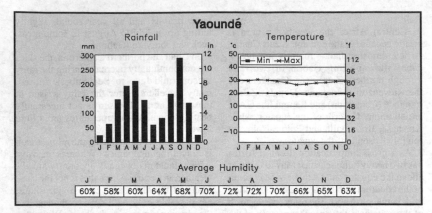

Yaoundé

Rainfall

Temperature

Average Humidity

J	F	M	A	M	J	J	A	S	O	N	D
60%	58%	60%	64%	68%	70%	72%	72%	70%	66%	65%	63%

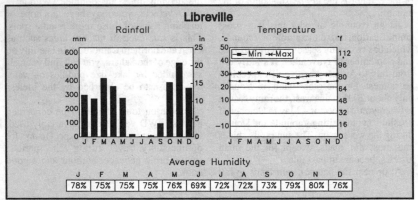

Libreville

Rainfall

Temperature

Average Humidity

J	F	M	A	M	J	J	A	S	O	N	D
78%	75%	75%	75%	76%	69%	72%	72%	73%	79%	80%	76%

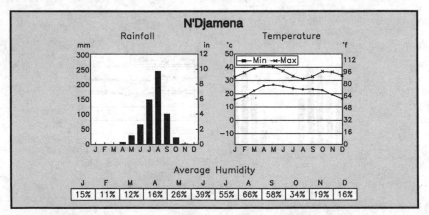

N'Djamena

Rainfall

Temperature

Average Humidity

J	F	M	A	M	J	J	A	S	O	N	D
15%	11%	12%	16%	26%	39%	55%	66%	58%	34%	19%	16%

The Harmattan

The November to February period may be a little cooler north of the equator, but December to February is the time of the harmattan winds when the skies in northern Central Africa are grey from the sands blown south from the Sahara. On bad days, visibility can be reduced to one km, or occasionally even less, resulting in aeroplane delays or cancellations. If you take a trip to the beautiful hilly area of western Cameroun in December, for example, you'll get none of the views that make them so popular, especially with hikers.

The harmattan usually begins in late November or early December and lasts several months. The worst part is usually over by around mid-February, although in the Sahel (the sub-Sahara area consisting mostly of sand and scattered large trees) the skies remain hazy until the first May rains. Fortunately, some days are fairly clear, so most travellers don't get too troubled by the harmattan. However, people with contact lenses should be prepared for problems. Photography nuts are going to be disappointed with hazy results and professional photographers may end up shooting themselves if they come during this period.

NATIONAL PARKS

The main problem with national parks in Central Africa isn't their lack of animals, it's their remoteness. Only one park, Réserve de la Lopé in Central Gabon, can be reached by public transport within one day of the capital city.

You can see elephants, lions, giant eland, bongos, buffalos, wart hogs, baboons, monkeys, chimpanzees, crocodiles, birds galore, various species of antelope, and hippos in many of the parks, and giraffes in some of the more northerly parks. In Waza National Park in northern Cameroun, herds of up to 300 elephants are frequently found at the principal water holes in the hot season (March to May). Even in East Africa, seeing herds of this size is quite rare. Most of the elephants in Central Africa, however, are forest elephants and are hidden throughout the rainforests of the Congo basin. Little is known about them but they make up an estimated third of the continent's total elephant population. They are not as big as the elephants in the savannah areas, have smaller, rounder ears and tusks that grow straight or even downwards.

The star attraction of Central Africa, however, is the gorilla, particularly the mountain gorilla families in eastern Zaïre – don't miss seeing them if you have the time and money (a permit costs more than US$100). As of 1993, Zaïre was the only place where you could go to see them as the gorilla sanctuaries in Rwanda were closed due to political trouble in the northern areas of that country. There are also many more lowland, chimpanzee-like gorillas throughout the Congo basin but none of their families have been habituated to humans, so seeing them is very difficult.

The major national parks in Central Africa are:

Djomba Gorilla Sanctuary
This sanctuary, in eastern Zaïre bordering Rwanda, is a four-hour drive by private vehicle or taxi north of Goma, and open year-round.
Dzanga-Sangha Reserve
In south-western Central African Republic (the CAR), this reserve is a two-day trip by public transport (a one-day trip by private vehicle) west from Bangui, and open year-round.
Garamba National Park
This park, in north-eastern Zaïre bordering Sudan, is a four-day drive by private vehicle north-east from Kisangani.
Kahuzi-Biéga Gorilla Sanctuary
This sanctuary in eastern Zaïre is an hour's drive north-east of Bukavu and is open year-round.
Korup National Park
This park in south-western Cameroun bordering Nigeria, is a two-day trip by public transport, (one day by private vehicle) from Douala, and is open year-round.
Réserve de la Lopé
This reserve in central Gabon is a five-hour train ride east of Libreville, and is open year-round.
St Floris National Park
This park in north-eastern CAR is one or two days' journey by private vehicle (or by chartered plane) north-east of Bangui; it's open from 1 December to 30 May.

Virunga National Park
  This park in eastern Zaïre, bordering Uganda, is a short day's drive from Goma north to the main lodge; it's open year-round.
Waza National Park
  In northern Cameroun, this park is a two-hour drive north of Maroua and is open from 15 November to 15 June.

If you're interested in seeing rainforests, the best areas are Dzanga-Sangha Reserve and, less organised and less accessible, the contiguous area in the Congo just to the south, east of Bomassa. Pygmy guides are necessary and available in both areas.

GOVERNMENT

The end of the Cold War has had an amazing impact on African politics. Previously, African dictators could justify single-party politics on the theory that Africa was different and what worked in the West wasn't necessarily the best system for Africa.

In reality, that logic was a facade for tyranny, and throughout the '80s, fewer and fewer African intellectuals were claiming with any conviction that a single-party government was democratic or that it was authentically African. But with the people of Eastern Europe throwing out their long-term dictators, not only the African intellectuals but also the masses of Africans have begun looking at their own leaders and wondering what right these men have to stay in power so long without periodical public approval. So, partly as a result of the end of the Cold War, the seeds of democracy have sprung up like flowers after the first rains in the Sahara. Through much of Central Africa, ordinary people are now far more willing than in the past to criticise their governments openly. Travellers too can feel freer to talk about politics in Zaïre, São Tomé, the Congo, Gabon and Cameroun where the changes have been most notable.

The USA through the World Bank, and the French government, not surprisingly, are playing a major role in all this. The World Bank, never very forthright, seems to be demanding an end to single-party rule in exchange for more assistance. The French, hoping to prevent revolution, are also applying pressure for political reform on all of the French-speaking countries – hence the nickname 'Paristroika'.

Congo and São Tomé, both with a long history of autocratic government, have surprisingly become the two major laboratories for democracy in Central Africa. Recently, the leaders of both countries were thrown out of office in the first free and open elections.

Although leaders in the other Central African countries don't like what's happening, they're being forced to embrace the new democracy if they wish to remain in power. As a result, every country in Central Africa except Chad has allowed opposition parties to operate freely and openly but, as of 1993, only in Cameroun has the president been forced into a contested election. In 1992, Paul Biya, Cameroun's leader who, by some well-documented accounts, has amassed a fortune in billions of US dollars since coming to power in 1982, won in a hotly contested election that many observers think was rigged.

Zaïre is a special case. As of mid-1993, the situation was literally out of control and very dangerous. Every few months, soldiers were going on rampages and looting cities, claiming they hadn't been paid for months. Among those killed was the French ambassador. President Mobutu, residing on a yacht in the middle of the Zaïre River for protection (or far away from his home town), was hanging on for his political life. He continued to control key elite army units and the treasury but all other government institutions and much of the army were controlled by a transitionary, parliamentary government that has been fighting since late 1991 to wrest control from the continent's most infamous dictator.

In short, multiparty politics has become the public cry of the '90s, and it will be interesting to see what develops. Greater economic prosperity, unfortunately, does not seem to be a likely outcome, at least in the short term.

ECONOMY
The Bad News

Overall, the economic situation in Central Africa is pretty bleak. Four of the world's 20 poorest countries (based on incomes) are here, including the world's poorest – Zaïre. The other three are Equatorial Guinea, the Central African Republic (CAR) and Chad, which has progressed from being the poorest to the fifth poorest.

A much better indicator of the situation, however, is the United Nations' human-development index of countries (based on life expectancy, adult literacy and purchasing power). According to this, Chad, Equatorial Guinea and the CAR, all with life expectancies lower than 50 years and adult literacy rates under 40%, are among the world's 20 least developed countries, with Zaïre significantly higher on the scale because of its higher life expectancy (53 years) and adult literacy rate (71%).

The situation is worst in Chad partly because of the recent 20-year civil war and, because of the unreliable rainfall. A 50% drop in rainfall may mean a zero harvest; the same in rainy Zaïre would not have nearly the same effect. However, the situation has visibly improved since the end of the war with Libya in the late '80s; most Arab families can once again afford to have their one daily luxury – a small glass of tea in the shade after a meal.

For Central African countries, with the exception of São Tomé and Chad where Western donors are pumping millions of US dollars into various projects, the economic situation is not improving. To the contrary, some countries are worse off now than at the time of independence. The classic example is Zaïre which was an 'upper-middle income' country in West-Central Africa at the time of independence and is now the poorest country in terms of income. President Mobutu's well publicised excesses during the '70s and the recent political turmoil are the reasons. By helping to keep him in power with generous aid, the US government should also take some of the blame.

Another economic disaster is Equatorial Guinea, due almost single-handedly to Macias Nguema, a little known African ruler who was every bit the equal of Idi Amin, if not worse. In 1976, Amnesty International called his regime the most brutal in the world. Virtually every Spanish expatriate in the country left shortly after he took over in the late '60s, ensuring the country's economic demise.

Bokassa, the president who declared the CAR an empire and spent over US$20 million on his coronation as 'emperor', put the country through a similar nightmare from which it is only slowly recovering.

In São Tomé, while living conditions are not so bad (in West and Central Africa, it ranks No 3 on the human development scale, following only Gabon and Cape Verde), personal incomes are about on a similar par with those in Chad because it has never recovered from the full-scale exodus of the Portuguese following independence.

Even though some of the Central African countries were self-sufficient in food production at independence, today every country in the region except Cameroun is a net importer of food. Except in the case of Chad, drought has had nothing to do with this because Central Africa is the rainiest area on the continent. With leaders such as Bokassa, Mobutu, Macias Nguema and Biya, Central Africa clearly has had a disproportionate share of corrupt leaders; much of the blame rests with them.

The Good News

There are some real success stories in Central Africa; Gabon and Cameroun are the well known examples. The three wealthiest countries in West and Central Africa on a per capita basis are all in Central Africa – Gabon (US$3000), the Congo (US$1000) and Cameroun (US$900). While per capita incomes are a poor way to compare living conditions, they provide a basis for comparing relative performance over the years. Here's how the top countries in Central and West Africa, based on per capita incomes, stack up now compared to 30 years ago:

1961	1992
Gabon	Gabon
Liberia	the Congo
Ghana	Cameroun
Côte d'Ivoire	Côte d'Ivoire
Sengal	Ghana
the Congo	Senegal
Sierra Leone	Cape Verde
Zaïre	Mauritania
Cameroun	Guinea
the CAR	Nigeria

Oil is the reason Gabon, the Congo and Cameroun have done so well. However, with the drop in oil prices, all of the oil-producing countries went into a significant slump during the the l980s and are now only slowly recovering. What happens to these economies when the oil dries up is anybody's guess, but for the moment, oil continues to fuel their economies.

During the '60s and '70s, the Côte d'Ivoire, the 'economic miracle' of West Africa, had the model economy in Africa. Cameroun, however, has had the highest growth rate in Africa since independence and by the mid-80s had surpassed the Côte d'Ivoire in per capita income. Like the Côte d'Ivoire, Cameroun's success has come primarily from agriculture (coffee, cocoa, rubber, timber, cotton) and oil – the critical plus. However, since the mid-80s, the economy has declined significantly and crime has risen. Ghana, which has had the highest growth rate in Africa since 1983, has taken over as the region's model economy. These three countries are the only countries in Central and West Africa that are net exporters of food.

It is Gabon, however, that has made big profits, almost all from oil. In Africa, only Libya has a higher per capita income – South Africa is third. But Gabon has only 1.2 million people. If being in the Third World is primarily determined on the basis of per capita income, it's not clear that Gabon deserves the title of a Third World country. However, when you look at its poor health care system and low life expectancy (52 years), it's simple to see that oil money can't change things overnight.

PEOPLE

One of the most startling things about the people of Central Africa is the extent of ethnic diversity. Gabon, a country of little more than one million people, has 43 dialects and almost as many tribal groups. Most of the other Central African countries are just as complex in their ethnic make-up. The colonial powers chose to ignore this multitude of races. For example, today the area of the Fang people constitutes three countries instead of one. Central Africa is overflowing with many such remnants from the colonial days.

Such is the legacy of the Europeans that some countries have one or two tribes which clearly predominate, whereas other countries are made up of minorities which are often linguistically and culturally incompatible. In Cameroun, for example, the largest ethnic group, the Bamiléké, represent only 15% of the total population.

This pattern is repeated throughout Africa. The result is that Africans of the same nationality often have difficulty communicating with one another. In many cases, the only way is by means of French or English, but a lot of Africans do not speak either. Go to the market in N'Djamena (Chad), for instance, and you'll be hard-pressed to find a vendor who speaks the official language – French.

For the traveller, this makes life both interesting and frustrating. Each group has its own special characteristics. For example in northern Cameroun, the Kirdi people are mostly farmers who are famous for their cliff dwellings and their intensive agriculture, whereas the Fulani people, who live in the same area, herd animals for their livelihood.

Some groups are better known than others. Descriptions of 11 of the better known ethnic groups in Central Africa follow. Most groups are located in one country; a few such as the Pygmy and the Fang people live in a number of countries.

Bamiléké

The largest ethnic group in Cameroun, the Bamiléké (bam-ee-lay-kay) live in the west around Bafoussam, the most densely populated area of the country. The Bamiléké are famous for their masks made entirely from beads and their woodcarvings which, in contrast to more stylised African art forms, are recognisable by their freer forms and rough finish. One of their most humorous dance masks shows a person with huge oval eyes under an elongated glove-shaped brow, accompanied by a big toothy grin.

If you're in western Cameroun, don't miss seeing one of the Bamiléké chiefs' compounds (*chefferies*), the most elaborate in Central Africa. The one at Bandjoun near Bafoussam, for example, has large buildings with tall thin sculptured columns like totem poles, elaborately carved doorways, and bamboo walls with fancy geometric designs.

Bamoun

The Bamoun (bah-moun) live in the same area as the Bamiléké people and their capital city is Foumban. They are especially renowned for their royal dynasty and also for their artwork, particularly their woodcarvings. The royal dynasty is one of the longest in Africa – 18 successive kings since 1394. Unlike so many African groups whose pre-colonial history is known only by word of mouth, the Bamoun have kept their sultans' personal belongings for many centuries. These are well preserved in the Sultan's Museum in the Palais Royal, a major tourist attraction in Cameroun.

Fang

Constituting over half the population of Gabon and most of the mainland population of Equatorial Guinea, the Fang sculptors are reputed to be the best in Africa. The paradox is that while Fang artists were masters of form and capable of expressing sensuous humanism, the Fang warriors were among the fiercest in Africa, with cannibalism reputedly being practised by some. Unfortunately, with the onslaught of the colonial powers in the 20th century, the Fang almost completely lost their artistic talents.

Fulani

The origin of the Fulani (fou-lan-ee), or Foulbé, is not certain, though it appears that they migrated centuries ago from Egypt and may even be of Jewish origin. They are usually tall, elegant and thin with aquiline noses, long dark hair, oval faces and light complexions. Some are so fair that they could be mistaken for Caucasian. The Fulani women are noted for their bright robes, elaborate hairdos and outrageously large gold earrings.

For centuries, these people have been cattle raisers throughout northern Central Africa and West Africa. While some combine farming with cattle raising, others are nomadic cattle herders who live in the pastoral zone and subsist entirely from raising livestock. A typical arrangement is for farmers to purchase cattle as a form of investment and turn them over to the Fulani to tend in return for occasional sacks of rice. Fulani herders can recognise every single animal in herds of 300 cattle and more.

Kirdi

The Kapsiki, Fata, Bata, Mafa, Guidar, Mofou and Podoko people inhabit the rocky mountainous areas of northern Cameroun and are known collectively as the Kirdi (keer-dee). The name, meaning 'infidels', was given to them by the Muslims who considered them uncivilised because they were animists. The Kirdi are mostly farmers, content to live simply with very few material possessions, and are a very interesting, hard-working people with the most fascinating, picturesque villages in all of Central Africa.

After being driven into their hilltop refuges by the Muslims centuries ago, the Kirdi built round dwellings with tall, pointed grass-covered roofs on the sides of rocky cliffs. From afar, their villages in the Mandara mountains (Mora, Mokolo, Mabas, Tourou) have a fairyland, 'hobbit-like' appearance and are a major tourist attraction. Some village chiefs have scores of wives and one chief is known to have over 100 offspring. The Kirdi practice a type of animism in which priests and sorcerers play particularly important roles.

Kongo

Although most of the Kongo people live in Zaïre, they also live in the Congo and Angola. At one stage they had one of the most powerful kingdoms in all of Central Africa, reaching its height around the mid-16th century, before being almost annihilated by the Portuguese.

Their dialect, Kikongo, is the most widely spoken language in western Zaïre, and their art is some of the finest in the Congo basin area. Kongo art is characterised by its realism and the typically natural poses of the human figures, usually with open mouths and often seated in relaxed positions.

A common theme is a mother and child. Fetishes, too, are extremely important in Kongo art – usually animals or human figures pierced with scores of nails or pieces of metal, giving the fetish its magical power and the sculpture a devilish air.

Kuba

The Kuba people (Bakuba is the plural form) live in central Zaïre, near Kananga, and are a tribe of virtuoso carvers whose artistic influence has been disproportionate to their small numbers. The Kuba kingdom flourished back in the 17th century during the reign of their 93rd king, Balongongo, whose ornate royal gown reputedly weighed 75 kg.

He became a cultural hero by introducing cassava, palm oil, tobacco, raffia and embroidery to the area. His wooden statue in the British Museum is the oldest art object from Central Africa. Kuba art is predominantly geometric and includes an unusually wide assortment of objects, such as masks with raffia cloth, a variety of wooden cups, boxes, game boards, tobacco pipes, combs, stools, charms, spoons and beds.

Luba

One of the largest ethnic groups in Zaïre, the Luba (plural Baluba), is found in southeastern Zaïre in the Shaba region, north of Lubumbashi. Many of the men working in the all-important copper mines in Shaba are Luba, and their dialect, Tshiluba, is the most widely spoken language in southern Zaïre. They are known for being the most prolific artists in Zaïre. Luba masks with huge bug-like eyes and ornate geometrical designs are sold all over Central Africa.

Pygmy

The original inhabitants of the African rainforests, the Pygmies are famous for their short stature (averaging about 120 cm or four feet in height) and adaptation to life in the rainforest. The men are primarily hunters, using bows with poisoned tips and they always work in groups, frequently with the assistance of dogs. They are also gatherers, collecting honey, nuts, roots and other foods native to the forest. The women also gather food and fish and in many places grow peanuts, which is a communal affair, involving women and girls down to the age of four.

The children are highly valued and are frequently passed to each member around the camp; therefore they get to know all the band at an early age. Unfortunately, mortality among children is very high; those who survive into adulthood seem to carry with them extraordinary immunities. Still, few survive beyond 50 years of age. Pygmies are very communal; for example in some tribes such as the Efe, when a nursing mother must leave the camp for short periods of time, she will often leave her child with another lactating woman for breast-feeding.

Due to their basically nomadic existence, Pygmies are scattered throughout the tropical forests in the Congo basin, including eastern Gabon and the Congo, the southwestern region of the Central African Republic (CAR), southern Cameroun and northern Zaïre. They move about in small groups, generally only settling in any one place for a short time while other groups have permanent settlements. With a culture still largely intact, Pygmies are also known for their spontaneous dancing and drumming, usually at night around a fire.

Sara

In southern Chad, the people are non-Muslim Black Africans. The largest group is the Sara who are concentrated in the area surrounding Sarh; they account for roughly a third of Chad's population. While the majority are farmers, they also occupy most of the civil service and higher military positions. The practice of elongating the lips was common among the Sara women. The purpose of this practice was not to enhance their appearance but to make themselves unattractive to the slave traders.

Toubou

The Toubou people are indigenous Saharans, numbering about 150,000, who live in far northern Chad. Like the Arabs with whom they are sometimes confused, they are Muslims, but unlike the Arabs, they do not consider themselves to be descendants of Mohammed. Rather, they consider themselves to be from a certain locality; Toubou means 'man from Tibesti'.

The Toubou are herders and nomads. They are fiercely independent, very clannish and heroic warriors; they started Chad's civil war back in the mid-60s partly because they weren't well represented in the government. Libya became their ally and used this as an excuse to invade Chad, eventually taking over the war completely.

MUSIC

One of the more interesting aspects of African culture is the music and dancing. Because it takes a while to get used to, few travellers get interested in this side of African life. It's a shame as, after all, the origin of much of our pop music can be traced back to Africa. Moreover, Central and West African music is extremely popular. Among Africans, the pop music from Central and West Africa dwarfs the popularity of music from the rest of Africa.

Most travellers don't know a lot about

Drums

Central and West African music. Sometimes, the music on the radio may sound similar and without knowing who is singing or what country the music is from, the whole music scene may seem incomprehensible. The best idea is to read an authoritative book on music before travelling to Central Africa; see the Books section in the Facts for the Visitor chapter.

Outside of Africa, it's not easy to find record stores which have extensive collections of African music except in France where Central and West African music is extremely popular these days. Several music stores outside Africa with a good range of African music are:

France
    Afric Music, Rue Plantes, 75014 Paris; metro stop Alesia (☎ (01) 4542-4352)
UK
    Stern's African Record Centre, 116 Whitfield St, Covent Garden, London W1P 5RW; it has a catalogue with over 1000 titles (☎ (071) 387-5550)
    Collet's Record Shop, 70 New Oxford St, London (☎ (071) 636- 3224)
    Discurio International Record Store , 9 Shepherd St, London W1 (☎ (071) 493-6030)
USA
    African Record Centre Ltd, 2343 7th Ave, New York (☎ (212) 281-2717)
    Rizzoli Bookstore, 712 Fifth Ave, New York
    Folkway Records, 701 Seventh Ave, New York (☎ (212) 586-7260)
    Kilimanjaro Music Store; corner of Florida Ave and California St, NW, Washington, DC 20009 (at the famous Kilimanjaro Club) (☎ (202) 462-8200)

Once you're in Central Africa, it's easy to find records and cassettes (but not CDs) of Central and West African music but most cassettes are of poor quality and records marked stereo are usually mono. Since many record stores do the recordings themselves, an alternative to buying cheap cassettes on the street is listening to some of their records and then having them record your selections (they usually allow you to pick individual songs) on a high-quality cassette. They rarely charge over US$4.

Traditional Music

When people talk about African music, there are really two types – the traditional village music and the modern pop music. Despite the rising international popularity of the latter, the former remains the musical mainstay for the vast majority of Africans. But traditional music is much harder for foreigners to appreciate. For one thing, very few of the instruments have scales. Rhythm has precedence over melody. To the uninitiated, it may sound monotonous and repetitive when in fact there is a lot going on.

Historically, traditional music has been the prerogative of only one social group, the *griots*. They are the villages' entertainers as well as oral historians and genealogists. At a wedding, for instance, it's usually a griot who does the entertaining. Yet despite their widely admired talents, they rarely enjoy personal esteem and are in one of the lowest social orders along with shoemakers and weavers. People often fear them because they know too many secrets.

Traditional music also serves a social purpose. Not only does each social occasion have its own type of music but there are different kinds of music for women, young people, hunters, warriors, etc.

The griots play and make their own instruments using local materials, such as gourds, animal skins, horns, etc. Included in this group are, foremost, drums and stringed instruments. A quick visit to almost any museum in Africa will give you a good idea of the variety. Nowhere is there a more imaginative assortment of drums than in Africa – cylindrical, kettle and frame drums as well as goblet and hourglass-shaped drums. There is a certain mystical aspect to musical instruments in Africa, as though they were alive with their own language of sounds. The fact that goats are the most talkative animals and their skins are used almost exclusively in making drums is no coincidence. One reason, perhaps, for the variety of drums is that they serve not only as musical instruments but for communication as well. The drums used for long distance messages are often made from the trunks of trees and can easily weigh several hundred kg.

Stringed instruments also come in as many varying forms as drums, starting with a one-string lute. *Kalimbas* (African thumb-pianos) are also popular all over Central Africa. There are also wind instruments, most notably flutes. Fulani shepherds are reputed to play the most beautiful flute music; their flutes are simply made from a length of reed. Flutes are also made from millet stalks, bamboo and gourds. If you're looking for something a little unique to collect but light and inexpensive, flutes are a good buy.

Other wind instruments include animal tusk horns and trumpets made from gourds, metal, shells or wood. They are found all over Central Africa and take a slightly different form in each area.

Unfortunately, hearing traditional African music in Central Africa is quite difficult

A Short History of African Pop Music

It all started about 90 years ago with the coming of the colonial era. Africans for the first time were introduced to music with ballads. The influence came from three sources. First, there were the Africans who were forced to become members of regimental bands associated with the forts. The music they played was typically European – polkas, marches and the like. Second, there was the impact of the Christian religious groups with their hymns. Finally, with the increasing trade with Europe, sailors from all over the world brought not only their favourite songs, but also instruments such as guitars, harmonicas and accordions. It may seem a little weird seeing a small accordion in some remote village, for instance, but you may.

Ghana was the richest country in the area and, not surprisingly, was where this influence was felt the most. What emerged was a Westernised form of music called highlife. The Western influence was greater in the dance bands which played to the Black elite in the cities than those which played in the hinterland. The latter combined acoustic guitars with rattles, drums and the like and developed a type of highlife that was substantially different from that of the dance bands. During WW II, Allied troops were stationed in West Africa resulting in the spread of other new musical ideas, especially the then-popular swing music. After the war, there were bands with sizeable repertoires, including calypso sounds. They began touring West Africa igniting the highlife fire everywhere, but at the same time continuing to assimilate foreign musical styles. Black music from across the Atlantic had a big impact, especially jazz, soul and, more recently, reggae.

Further south in Léopoldville and Brazzaville, there was another movement going on. During WW II, radio stations began popularising the early Cuban rumba stars, and new 'Congo bars' were popping up. The music was predominantly acoustic with solo guitars accompanied by small brass ensembles. Bottles struck like gongs provided the rhythmic accompaniment. However, the indigenous musical traditions of the Congo basin, called *le folklore*, remained the heart of the music, as it does today.

A decisive turning point was the arrival of the electric guitar and amplification. Large orchestras emerged in the early '50s, many elaborating on traditional rumba patterns such as the popular Zaïrian band African Jazz featuring Dr Nico and OK Jazz led by Franco, also Zaïrian and Africa's all-time most influential musician.

In the late 1960s when President Mobutu of Zaïre began his well-known 'Authenticité' movement, new orchestras began experimenting with some of the North American rhythms while still remaining faithful to traditional sounds at the same time. The result was enormously successful, producing a deluge of new orchestras that have dominated the African musical scene since.

As a result of all this assimilation, a variety of musical styles can be heard throughout Central and West Africa. African groups have incorporated African rhythms and developed their own unique sounds, with the result that African music is now having an impact on Western music. The hottest music in France today is Afro-pop, a cultural melee in which African talking drums and Latin rhythms meet Western technology. For years, Paris has been the mecca for African stars who have quit Dakar or Kinshasa for the West; the problem is that their recordings, once recorded in Africa for Africans, are now recorded in Paris and directed more at international audiences, arguably losing some authenticity in the process. ■

unless you stay in a village for some days. For books about traditional music, see the Books section in the Facts for the Visitor chapter.

Pop Music

Turn on the radio and if the song is African, there's a 50% chance it is Congolese/Zaïrian, a 25% chance it is Camerounian and, if you are not in the Congo, Cameroun or Zaïre, a 25% chance it is a local group/singer. That's stretching things a bit because musical tastes vary a good deal throughout Black Africa. However, if there's any one music that you'll hear just about everywhere, it's unquestionably the modern Congo sound from Zaïre and the Congo. Hearing it for the first time, you may think it's Latin as there's a lot of Latin influence in African popular music. Indeed, African pop music is an incredible mish-mash of traditional, Latin and Black American music with elements of American jazz and rock.

One of the more interesting things to do while wandering in any major city is to go into a record shop and ask to hear some of the local recording stars. There's no better way to learn the different styles, and maybe you will buy something. Each country chapter lists the most popular local recording stars.

As for hearing live African music, the sad fact is that there are few groups which perform on a regular basis. The best place by far is Kinshasa's famous Cité district, which is renowned for its numerous clubs with regular bands. Unfortunately, it's dangerous now because of the turmoil in Zaïre and many bands have left the country. Other cities where groups play on a regular basis are Brazzaville, Bangui, Libreville, São Tomé. Even some small towns, such as Bambari (the CAR) and Owando (the Congo), have nightclubs with regular bands.

In Central Africa, the most popular music is Congo and *makossa* music. Music from neighbouring Nigeria, particularly Afrobeat, can also be heard on occasion in the western, English-speaking area of Cameroun but generally not anywhere else. In northern Cameroun and Chad, you may hear popular Sahelian music from West Africa.

Congo Music The Congo music from Zaïre and neighbouring Congo continues to be at the top of all the pop charts throughout Black Africa. Indeed, it is the only music which is truly pan-African, its appeal stretching from Senegal to Zimbabwe. It has some of the best dance music and the various musicians are always introducing new instrumentation and elements from other styles while still retaining the basic rumba framework. So if it sounds Latin, it's probably Zaïrian. If not, it's probably from neighbouring Congo or Gabon. The two biggest stars, both legends in their own time, are Franco of *OK Jazz* (who recently died of AIDS) and Tabu Ley or Rochereau as he is also called.

Other leading musicians/groups include the following. Male: Langa Langa Stars, Sam Mangwana, Bella Bella, Kanda Bongo Man, Papa Wemba, Dr Nico (deceased), Pierre Moutouari and Pamelo Mounka (both from the Congo), and Akédengué (Gabon). Female: M'Bilia Bel, Abeti, M'Pongo Love (who died of AIDS) Tshala Muana (all from Zaïre) and Nayanka Bell (Côte d'Ivoire).

Makossa Music Cameroun's distinct makossa music has become so popular in recent years that it now follows only Congo music in popularity throughout much of Central Africa. It's a fusion of Camerounian highlife and soul, and strongly influenced by Congo music, with great use of the electric guitar. Like Congo music, the irresistible rhythms make you want to dance which is why it is so popular. Recognising it, however, requires a little structured listening. The biggest star is still Manu Dibango, whose hit *Soul Makossa* in the mid-70s put makossa music onto the African musical scene. Today his music, which is constantly evolving, is more jazz than makossa and is definitely not for dancing. Francis Bebey and Isadore Tamwo are also extremely popular, while Sam Fan Thomas is Cameroun's king of makassi, a lighter sound than makossa. Other makossa stars include Sammy Njondji, Moni Bile, Toto Guillaume and Ekambi Brillant.

Sahelian Music The sophisticated blend of old and new music played today by groups from Senegal has emerged as the hottest African music on the international scene. What distinguishes this music perhaps is the greater use of traditional instruments, the drum, the harp-like kora and the balafon, along with guitars and horns.

This jazz-inspired music is recorded mostly in Paris and, unlike most other Black African music, is directed perhaps more at the international market than the African market. The two worldwide superstars are Youssou N'Dour (leader of Super Étoile band) and Touré Kunda, both Senegalese, followed by Mory Kanté of Guinea. Youssou N'Dour is the leading exponent of *mbalax* music from Senegal, a Wolof term denoting drum-based music featuring a solo on the sabar drum. His drumming found its way on to Paul Simon's *Graceland* album.

My favourite is Touré Kunda, whose music tends towards the acoustic side and is grounded in drums, vocals, koras and balafons along with electric guitars and synthesisers. Mory Kanté, another leading musician on the Afro-Parisian scene, is the undisputed king of the kora and loved by the French but his jazzed up version bears little resemblance to what you hear in the villages.

There are some lesser known musicians from Senegal, including Thionne Seck and the highly acclaimed groups Super Diamono from the Cassamance and Xalam. The latter

has thrilled jazz festival audiences worldwide with their fusion of electronic funk, jazz, blues and African music.

The neo-traditional music of Mali bears a certain resemblance to Senegalese pop. The Malian superstar is Salif Keita, known for his stunning voice, fluent guitar and sax solos. His music has an unmistakably Islamic sound as does that of other Malian stars such as Fanta Damba, the long-standing Super Rail Band, Boncana Maiga and Toumani Diabaté, famous for his fast, percussive attack on the kora. Blues lovers should check out recordings by Malian Ali Farka Touré, who has performed with John Lee Hooker. His blues guitar work and gravelly singing are probably the closest thing to African blues.

Afro-Beat Music A fusion of African music, jazz and soul, Afro-beat along with juju is the most popular music today in Nigeria. The undisputed king of Afro-beat is Fela Anakulapo Kuti. Fela went to the USA in the late '60s and was greatly influenced by James Brown and Black American politics. He took Brown's jazz and mixed it with the many cultural intricacies of his own African music and developed a politicised Afro-Beat.

The instruments used by his orchestra are mainly non-African: guitars, trumpets, saxophones and electric pianos as well as drums. Yet the sounds are substantially African inspired. Fela Kuti's lyrics are always controversial and frequently political, so he has never been popular with the politicians. In

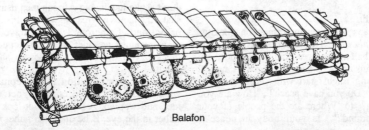

Balafon

1977, the military government burned his communal compound in the Kalakuta Republic, on the outskirts of Lagos and in 1984, they detained him on spurious currency smuggling charges, sentencing him to five years in prison. The outcry was loud and, following a change of government in 1986, he was released.

Another Afro-beat Nigerian musician is Sonny Okosun, the granddaddy of Afro-reggae. His politicised jungle rock music is a fusion of highlife, Santana rock and reggae, and his 1978 hit *Fire in Soweto* was a massive hit throughout West Africa.

Juju Music Juju music had its origins in Nigerian Yoruba music. The highlife bands began playing it in 1930s. The Nigerian civil war gave rise to the popularity of juju music. Many members of the highlife bands went east to Biafra, contributing greatly to highlife's decline in the west of Nigeria. So the Yoruba turned to juju. The music is characterised by tight vocal harmonies and sophisticated guitar work, backed by traditional drums and percussion. Today, it is one of the most popular music styles in Nigeria but its international appeal, including that in Central Africa, has evaporated. The leading Yoruba musicians are Sonny Ade, Shina Peters and, to a lesser extent, Ebenezer Obey.

SOCIAL CUSTOMS
The saying is that people go to East Africa to see the animals and West and Central Africa to see the people. Knowing the social customs takes on added importance in Central Africa, not only to avoid embarrassing situations but to enhance possibilities of getting to know people.

Greetings
Africans place great importance on greetings (*les salutations*). Sometimes this ritual lasts up to half a minute, especially in the northern Muslim areas of Central Africa. A typical greeting might start with 'Peace be unto you', 'Do you have peace?', 'How are you doing?' to 'Where are the people of your compound?', 'Is your body in peace?',

'Thanks be to God'. The typical African greetings go into all kinds of inquiries about the family, one's health, work, the weather, etc. Even if one is at death's door, the answer is always that things are fine.

In the cities, the traditional greetings may give way to shorter greetings in French or English. In either case, it's a social blunder to get down to business immediately or to walk past an adult in a house without greeting them.

If you can learn the ritual in the local language, you will be an incredible hit. Even if you can't, all it takes is a few words and you will find many friends. The unfortunate part is that many countries have four or five major languages and often another 20 or so minor ones. At least they'll know you're making the effort. A few phrases in the most popular local language are given in Facts about the Country sections in the individual country chapters.

The emphasis on greetings makes the handshake important. It's a soft handshake, not the Western knuckle cracker. Not to shake a man's hand when entering and leaving a social or business gathering is a real gaffe. In social settings you must go around the room, greet everyone and shake hands with the men. You do the same when you leave. In most areas, men and women don't shake hands unless the woman extends her hand first. In the French-speaking countries the thrice-kissed cheek greeting (starting with the left) is the norm for friends and even casual acquaintances of the opposite sex.

Women have traditionally been considered less important than men and for this reason they tend to show deference to men in their greetings. As noted, they usually don't shake hands, but African men usually shake the hands of Western women. In Chad or northern Cameroun, women travellers may encounter an elder who, in strict compliance with the Koran, refuses to shake hands.

Another consideration is eye contact, which is usually avoided, especially between men and women. A boy does not look his father in the eye. If he does, his father will be suspicious. Some eye contact is perfectly OK as long as it doesn't develop into a gaze. So if you're accustomed to looking people in the eye and associate this with honesty, remember that this is not the case in Africa.

Begging

In Africa, the only social security system for the great majority of people is the extended family. There is no government cheque to help the unemployed, sick or old. Many beggars are cripples or lepers. Nevertheless, because of the support of the extended family, as well as the general respect that Africans give to their elders, there are remarkably few beggars considering how poor Central Africa is.

For travellers, the point to remember is that Africans do not look down on beggars. Almsgiving is one of the pillars of Islam, something to remember in Chad and northern Cameroun. Travellers with foresight should keep small change on them for this purpose. They're not asking for a lot, usually a coin equivalent to US five or 10 cents. If you don't have any, just say 'next time' (la prochaine fois) and they'll usually go on.

Gifts

One great annoyance for most travellers is people everywhere approaching them and asking for hand-outs (le cadeau). They are not beggars because they only prey upon foreigners. Particularly in areas most frequented by travellers, hordes of kids as well as adults will approach you with their hands out saying, 'cadeau, cadeau'. You may be approached by a guy who will take you a block to point out the place that you may be looking for, and then ask for a cadeau. The girl at the bar may want a cadeau for just talking. Everybody's looking for a cadeau from foreigners. One of the benefits of travelling in remote areas is that this will be far less of a problem.

My strong recommendation is to follow local custom and not your emotions. In general, Africans never offer gifts to strangers unless they appear to be truly destitute or they have rendered a significant service.

Walking a block with you would not be a significant service but helping you for 10 minutes to find a room at night would probably warrant a tip. Africans would rebuff anybody else looking for a hand-out. By giving in, you only encourage the recipient to prey upon the next traveller. The problem is now so out of hand that it is a major complaint of many travellers. For some African men, this trade of preying on travellers is a living, particularly for those who hang around hotels. Even if some children seem undernourished, by giving them pieces of candy or money, this isn't going to help them in the long run and, instead, can do a lot of harm. Save your money for the truly destitute and ignore the rest.

On the other hand, in Central Africa it takes very little time to make friends. Africans frequently are very open and friendly towards foreigners and even after a few minutes of talking they may consider you a friend. They might even offer you a meal or a bed for the night. In instances such as this, a small gift would be customary. Even if nothing is offered, once you have established even a short-time relationship with an African, you should be aware that giving is very important in African society. You are expected to give gifts to those above you in the social hierarchy, or to respected people. It's not so much a case of reciprocity, rather, it's that if Allah or fate have been good to you, you should be willing to spread some of this good fortune around. Since non African foreigners are thought to be rich, they're expected to be generous. It's something you have to keep in mind everywhere you go.

If you're travelling near the desert, for example, take some tobacco with you for the men with whom you might strike up a brief friendship. Perfume makes an excellent gift for either sex, at least in northern Central Africa. You'll find yourself rewarded many times over. Similarly, the smart businessperson will bring small items from his or her country to show appreciation. One of the best gifts of all is a photograph, and it may even be worth bringing a cheap Polaroid as a second camera. Try to assess the situation and determine whether the person is being genuinely friendly or merely looking for a cadeau.

On a different note, Africans tend to expect tips in situations where it would not be customary in other countries. For instance, if you ask someone for directions to the bus station and rather than explaining verbally, the person walks three blocks with you to the station. Chances are the person may ask for a cadeau. This can be annoying particularly when the rendered assistance is quite minimal, but remember that in Africa, most people have no choice but to seize upon any opportunity to make money. Rendering favours is one of them. If you're not prepared to offer a tip, don't accept favours of any significance.

Bribery

Bribery, or 'dashing' (matabiche in Zaïre) in Central Africa is an annoyance that travellers are constantly faced with everywhere they go. From the minute you get off the plane or cross the border, you are likely to be confronted with a request for a bribe. For instance, a customs official may ask you to come into a small room for a body search and then ask if you have something for them.

My strong recommendation is to state as unequivocally as possible that you are not going to give them anything, and to say the same each time they repeat the request. In virtually all cases, they will back down and let you through. Many travellers think if they don't offer something, the official will trump up some excuse not to let them through. This is a tremendous mistake because it only encourages them to do the same to the next traveller. If only one in 20 travellers gives something, that's enough to provide the encouragement.

Occasionally the requests are accompanied by threats, typically threatening to deny entrance into the country. It is usually just a bluff lasting several minutes, and most travellers who are old hands in Africa have learned to be firm in their refusals to pay anything. So do the same, and in those rare instances where officials proceed to carry out their threat, you always have the option of backing down. In my last trip to Central Africa, very few border officials asked for bribes, and I didn't ever have to give in.

A traveller whose documents are not all in order is obviously in a much more vulnerable position and the previously mentioned advice may not work. It helps to know the regulations, however, because sometimes officials trump up totally fictitious ones in order to create a bribe situation. Zaïrian officials are notorious in this respect. Resist the temptation to explode in such instances because Africans everywhere react very negatively to outbursts. The point is that the chances are still good of getting away without giving a bribe.

In some instances, there seems to be no alternative to bribery, particularly in situations where officials are slow in processing documentation, such as a visa extension request. Sometimes they deliberately cause the delays so as to increase their chances of receiving a bribe, and sometimes the process is just normally slow. Offering a small gift to speed up the process may be your only option. If the borders have closed, offering a small gift for 'overtime' may open them up for you.

Dress

In general, Africans place great importance on clothing (les costumes), allocating a huge portion of their non-food budget on clothing. Western informality is definitely not the norm, although it is making a few inroads with the young in the bigger cities. Visitors to northern Central Africa are in for a real treat because Africans dress with a regal quality.

In Chad and northern Cameroun, both men and women often wear long costumes. For men, this is an embroidered robe-like garment reaching the ground, with pants and a shirt underneath. The woman's boubou is similarly regal, long and embroidered. They are invariably worn at important occasions, and sometimes at work or on market day or holidays.

For day wear, women have a loose top and

a length of cloth *(pagne)* around the waist for a skirt; this is made from the colourful cotton prints you see everywhere. The same wax or wax look-alike cloth is used in making men's casual clothes, which look like pyjamas. Because the designs are so distinctively African, it's initially surprising to learn that much of the better quality cloth actually comes from the Netherlands. Yet the most authentic cloths are the handmade design fabrics, such as the tie-dye, indigo wood-block prints and batiks, which are produced in individual cottage-type establishments.

As African clothing is conservative, it is not surprising that in the more traditional areas, especially Chad and northern Cameroun, shorts worn by either sex and tight pants worn by women are considered offensive. This may seem like a double standard because African women often go bare breasted in the villages, yet they would be ridiculed for wearing tight pants. It's all a bit confusing, but women should keep in mind that clothes should not be revealing or suggestive. For men, standards are less strict.

It is different in the big cities such as Yaoundé (Cameroun). You'll see everything from the latest Parisian fashions to the most traditional outfits. Yet you will not see shorts being worn by either sex (unless jogging) or African women wearing pants in the big cities of Chad and northern Cameroun. In the villages, women travellers might wish to purchase some colourful wrap-around pagnes or wear very loose-fitting long pants with socks.

Food & Etiquette

In the villages, African food is eaten with the hands, as well as in African-style homes in the cities. Visitors will usually be offered a spoon, if there is one. A bowl of rice and a bowl of sauce will be placed on the ground and those eating will sit around on a mat and dig in, but never before washing their hands. It is usually polite to take off your shoes.

The head of the household will distribute meat and vegetables to the visitors. Take a handful of rice or other staple and part of the sauce or meat, then form a ball – this is the hard part – and eat. Don't shy away; it's usually a lot of laughs for everyone. It won't be pleasant the first time getting your hands all gooey but remember, a wash basin is always passed around afterwards. You may even grow to like this way of eating because of the increased 'family' feeling that it fosters.

As with the Arabs, only the right hand is used in forming the ball of food because of the ancient practice of using the left hand for personal toiletries. A violation of this rule will cause a silent turmoil. Just because you're a tourist won't make much difference. Eating with the left hand would be as offensive to Africans as a stranger drinking from your glass would be to you.

Social Events

Much of African life centres around special events, such as weddings, baptisms, funerals, holidays and village celebrations *(fêtes)*. If you get an invitation, by all means accept. Just be sure to bring your dancing shoes because, except at funerals, there will probably be dancing. At baptisms, guests bring gifts for both the mother and the father – a small amount of money is perfectly acceptable. There will be a ceremony followed by a meal.

Weddings At weddings there is likely to be an official ceremony at the mayor's office followed by eating and dancing at someone's home. The wedding is only the culmination of a week of activities involving visits to relatives, meals, and the exchange of gifts; only relatives and the closest friends are invited to the ceremony.

Marriage is such an expensive affair for the groom that many African men cannot afford to get married before their late 20s or 30s. Gifts to the bride's family can easily cost several hundred dollars in sheep, money and the like – not exactly peanuts in an area of the world where incomes of US$200 a year are typical. Still, in traditional society men who could afford more than one wife usually would marry more. (The Koran allows up to four.) Despite what you may hear to the contrary from African men, the first wives definitely don't like the custom of multiple wives. On the other hand, there's not much they can do except go to their families, where they're unlikely to be welcomed with open arms if the husband's only 'sin' was taking a second wife.

Fêtes Other celebrations of particular interest to foreigners are the village fêtes. They may range from something fairly common, such as celebrating the end of the harvest, to something a little different, such as honouring the dead. There's usually traditional African dancing. Don't worry – you won't be asked to join in. If there's modern African music, however, you can expect to do some dancing.

Each fête is a little unique; elaborate dances with masks are typical. Seeing a village fête is very difficult because there are

not as many in Central Africa as there are in West Africa. So if you get the chance by no means pass it up. The country chapters mention a few of the more important celebrations.

Sport

Soccer is Africa's most popular sport, more so since the strong showing by Cameroun in the 1990 World Cup matches. Cameroun's star player, Milla, is now one of the continent's top sports idols. Seeing a game of football is easy as there are games almost every Sunday in the major cities.

The biggest sports events in Africa are probably the Africa Cup football matches held every even year in the spring. People are glued to their radios and TVs.

In Cameroun, the major running race is the Mt Cameroun race held annually on the last Sunday of January. There's also the Brazza-

Mankala

If you like games of intellectual challenge, one of the first things you should do upon arriving in Africa is to learn mankala – a game similar to backgammon. The game goes by many different names, including *mankala* in Zaïre, *woaley* or *awalé* in the Côte d'Ivoire and *ayo* in Yoruba (Nigeria). For starters, buy a mankala board. Most are rectangular, about a half-metre long with two rows of six cups each. Some boards also have a cup at one or both ends for storing captured peas (48 come with the game).

Even if games aren't your bag, you won't find a better way to meet Africans, especially if you're having trouble communicating. Mankala is a major pastime of Africans of all ages and has been since it originated in Egypt thousands of years ago. While it is designed for two people, teams are also possible. Finding an opponent is rarely difficult – opening the board amongst onlookers is usually all that's required.

The basics of play are not difficult, but mastering the game requires time. In Africa, one thing you will find is time, whether waiting for a bush taxi or simply cooling off in a bar or under a shade tree. There are several versions of the game played by different ethnic groups and varying in complexity. So don't be surprised if your opponent's rules are slightly different from those explained here.

Starting Play All mankala boards have 12 cups and 48 peas. Four peas are placed in each cup. The first player starts by picking up all the peas from any cup on his/her side of the board and dropping them one at a time in each consecutive cup to the right, counterclockwise.

Capturing Peas A player scores by capturing peas; the winner is the one who captures the most. A player captures peas only when the last pea dropped falls in a cup on the opponent's side containing only one or two peas. When that happens, the player picks up all the peas in that cup and stores them for counting at the end of the game.

In a well-executed move, a player may capture peas not only from the last cup but also from the next-to-the-last cup if it, like the last cup, contains only one or two peas (prior to the move).

The player may also capture peas from the third-to-the-last cup if it too contains only one or two peas. The same is true of the fourth-to-last cup, etc. For instance, if the last pea falls into a

ville to Pointe-Noire car rally during the first week of April in the Congo.

RELIGION

Before the Christians and Muslims began making inroads into Africa about 500 and 1000 years ago respectively, the only religions in Africa were the traditional ones, virtually all of which were animistic and involved ancestor worship.

Christianity is now the major religion in every Central African country except Chad, where Islam holds a slight edge over animism, and the Central African Republic, where Christians and animists are of roughly equal numbers. To some extent, this is a little misleading because many adherents of Christianity follow at least some animist practices as well.

Outside the northern two-thirds of Chad and northern Cameroun where Muslims pre-dominate and pockets of northern CAR, you'll find almost no followers of Islam in Central Africa. That's why it's so unusual that the president of Gabon, a country with a Muslim population of less than 1%, professes to be a follower of Islam.

Traditional Religions

Each ethnic group in Africa has its own religion, so there are literally hundreds of traditional religions in Central Africa. However, there are some factors common to all of them.

As throughout the world, superstition plays a major role. Good magic keeps away evil spirits. The religious men (sometimes called *marabouts* in the north) are the ones who tell fortunes, give advice on how to avoid danger, and dispense charms. They are frequently seen around the markets, usually with bags full of fetishes such as birds' skulls

---

cup with one or two peas and, say, the three cups immediately preceding it similarly contained only one or two peas prior to the move, the player would capture all the peas in all four cups.

End of Game The game ends when player A has no peas left on his/her side and player B must play at least twice consecutively in order to reach the opponent's side of the board. (In that instance, if player B has various alternative moves but only one will allow him to get to A's side of the board, he has no option – he must make that move in order to keep the game going.) Ending up with no peas does not mean you win the game, although it is beneficial in the scoring.

Scoring Each player counts the peas he/she has captured plus any peas remaining on the opponent's side of the board. Since there are 48 peas, any peas over 24 constitute a point. If, for example, your total is 30 peas (your opponent will have 18 peas), you will receive six points and your opponent zero. A match is whatever you decide – three games, 100 points, two hours, etc.

Rules The major rules of the game are as follows:

• Moves are always left to right, counterclockwise.
• A move is made by picking up all of the peas from any cup on your side of the board and dropping them one by one (and only one) in each consecutive cup to the right.
• A player is entitled to only one move at a time. (In some versions, the player continues until a cup is 'captured.')
• A cup of peas may be 'captured' only when the last pea in a move falls in a cup (a) on your opponent's side of the board and (b) with only one or two peas in it prior to the move. (In some versions, it makes no difference on which side of the board the last pea falls. In other versions, the last pea must fall in a cup with three peas.)
• To capture multiple cups of peas, each preceding cup must similarly contain only one or two peas prior to the move. If, for example, the last two cups contain two peas and the third-to-the last cup contains three peas and the fourth-to-the last cup contains two peas, you would capture the peas only from the last cup and the next-to-the last cup. (In some versions, multiple captures are not allowed.) ∎

and shells. The charms worn around the neck are called *grisgris* (gree-gree) and are found all over northern Central Africa and all over West Africa. If the charm hasn't been blessed by one of these religious men, it's worthless.

Virtually all traditional religions are animistic and accept the existence of a supreme being as well as reincarnation. The creator is considered to be too exalted to be concerned with humans but there are numerous lesser deities with whom one can communicate, usually through sacrifices, as well as deified ancestors. There are no great temples or written scriptures, and beliefs and traditions are handed down by word of mouth.

The lesser deities, who act as intermediaries between the creator and mortals, are frequently terrifying and correspond with natural phenomena or diseases. Africans pray to these deities in order to gain good health, bountiful harvests and numerous children. It would not be unusual to see an African offering a few ritualistic words to one of the deities before taking libations. Many of the village celebrations are in honour of one or more deities.

Ancestors play a particularly strong role in African religions. Their principal function is to protect the tribe. They are also the real owners of the land, and while you can enjoy it during your lifetime, you cannot sell it or harm it without incurring their wrath. Ethnic groups are usually broken down into clans, which include all individuals who can trace their origins to a particular ancestor. Each has its own taboos in relation to its protective genies.

Islam

In the early 7th century in Mecca, Mohammed received the word of Allah (God) and called on the people to turn away from pagan worship and submit to the one true God. His teachings appealed to the poorer levels of society and angered the wealthy merchant class. By 622 AD, life had become sufficiently unpleasant for Mohammed and his followers that they were forced to flee to Medina (Saudi Arabia). This migration, the Hejira, marks the beginning of the Islamic calendar, year 1 AH or 622 AD. By 630 AD they had gained a sufficient following to return and take Mecca. Mohammed died in 632 but within two decades most of Arabia was converted to Islam.

Muslims began infiltrating Africa about a thousand years ago. The Berbers from Morocco, for example, began raiding the Sahelian areas, bringing about the demise of West Africa's first major kingdom, the empire of Ghana. By the 1300s, many African rulers, particularly in the Sahel including Chad and northern Cameroun, had adopted Islam, at least in part. The second great West African kingdom, the empire of Mali, was almost always ruled by Muslims and Timbuktu became a major centre of Islamic teaching.

Islamic penetration through the coastal forests was quite another matter. Even today there are not many followers of Islam in Central Africa.

Islam is the Arabic word for submission and underlies the duty of all Muslims to submit themselves to Allah. The Five Pillars of Islam are the basic tenets which guide Muslims in their daily lives. These tenets are the *shahada*, *salah*, *zakat*, *ramadan* and the *hadj*.

The shahada – 'There is no God but Allah and Mohammed is his prophet' – is the basic profession of faith and the fundamental tenet of Islam. Salah is the call to prayer when Muslims must face Mecca and pray five times a day – at dawn, midday, mid-afternoon, sunset and nightfall. Zakat is the act of giving alms to the poor and needy. Ramadan is the ninth month of the Muslim calendar when all Muslims must fast from dawn to dusk. It commemorates the month when the Koran was revealed to Mohammed. The hadj is the pilgrimage to Mecca and it is the duty of every Muslim who is fit and can afford it to make the pilgrimage at least once in their lifetime.

Islamic Customs It is worthwhile remembering a few basic points lest you commit some social error, or miss out on some of the goings on. Whenever you visit a mosque, take off your shoes. In some mosques, women are not allowed to enter; in others, there may be a separate entrance since men and women pray separately. If you have a taxi driver or guide for the day, he may need to do his prayer ritual. Be on the lookout for signs he may express indicating he wants a few moments off, particularly around midday, late afternoon and sunset.

Despite the Islamic proscription against alcohol you may have heard that some Muslims drink like fish. Even so, it's impolite to drink alcohol in their presence unless they show approval. If a Muslim man refuses to shake hands with a woman, remember he's only following the Koran so don't take offence.

There are some important Islamic holidays, during which time little gets done (see the Cultural Events & Holidays section in the Facts for the Visitor chapter.)

LANGUAGE

Of the eight countries in Central Africa, French is the official language in Chad, the CAR, Cameroun, Gabon, Congo, Zaïre, Spanish in Equatorial Guinea, and Portuguese in São Tomé.

Some say it's an awful legacy of the colonial period that the official languages are non-African. However, to choose one of the many local languages for the official language would be politically disastrous. Moreover, few would be able to speak it. For African languages, see the Language section in Facts about the Country in the individual country chapters.

Facts for the Visitor

VISAS

French, German and Swiss travellers are exempted from having to get visas to certain Central African countries. Visitors from France and Germany do not require visas for the Central African Republic (CAR), Chad and Gabon, and while visas to the Congo are not required in principle, they are required in practice, especially for those arriving overland. Germans also do not require visas to visit Cameroun, while Swiss travellers are only exempt from having to get a visa for the CAR.

In addition to sending one to four photographs, embassies of some Central African countries in Europe and North America (Cameroun, Gabon, Zaïre) require that you show proof of intention to leave the country by possessing a return airline ticket or at least an airline ticket with a flight out of the country. They'll accept a photocopy of the airline ticket, so don't send the ticket itself. If it is lost in the mail you may not be reimbursed for quite a while.

If you buy a one-way airline ticket to Africa or travel overland, chances are you won't have any significant problems. During my last trip to Central Africa, only the Camerounian Embassy in Gabon asked if I had an onward airline ticket. Camerounian and Gabonese embassies in some West Africa countries occasionally make the same demand, but most do not. So the simple solution is to move on and get the visa in another country.

Central African embassies in Europe and North America have stricter visa requirements than those in neighbouring countries in Africa; some may even demand to see a recent bank statement demonstrating sufficient funds or a letter from your travel agent. If you can't produce or afford what they request, consider getting the visa in Africa. Many people travelling on the cheap try to procure the majority of their visas in Africa for this reason. It's worth keeping in mind.

The main problem is that visas are often more expensive to buy in Central Africa.

One quirk is that some embassies will issue visas of only very short duration. You may find, for instance, that the French Embassy in Niamey, which represents the Central African Republic in Niger, issues CAR visas for stays of only two days. Don't worry because it's easy to get an extension in Bangui. The other quirk, exit visas, are no longer required in any Central African country.

Occasionally, an embassy may refuse to issue you a visa if you are not a resident of the country where you're trying to get the visa. What's bizarre is that the same embassies in other African countries usually do not have the same requirement, so the easiest solution is often to get the visa elsewhere. You'll definitely encounter this problem with the Zaïrian embassies in Brazzaville (Congo) and Washington, DC (USA) and with quite a few Camerounian embassies, including those in Brussels (Belgium), The Hague (The Netherlands) and Abidjan (Côte d'Ivoire). On rare occasions, the embassies that impose this requirement will drop it if you present them with a *note verbale* from your embassy; the Zaïrian Embassy in Brazzaville is not one of those. A note verbale is a letter from an embassy or consulate stating that you are a citizen of that country, includes your passport number and requests that you be issued a tourist visa so that you can visit the country for a certain period of time. For an example of a note verbale (in French), see the Visas section in the Gabon chapter.

Some embassies in Africa routinely request a note verbale from your embassy even if you're a resident of the country – a definite problem if your country doesn't have an embassy or honorary consul. In that case, if you happen to be from a Commonwealth country, they will usually accept such a letter issued by the embassy or honorary consulate of another Commonwealth country.

For years, most African countries have refused to issue visas in passports with South African visas but this is generally no longer the case.

The cost of visas varies considerably. In the USA, for example, they vary from nothing for a visa to São Tomé, US$12.50 for one to Chad, US$44 for a Camerounian visa and US$50 for a one-month multiple-entry visa to Zaïre. In Africa, visa charges are sometimes much higher. This is particularly true in the case of Zaïre. Zaïrian embassies throughout most of Africa charge US$72 for a simple one-month single-entry visa (US$130 for a one-month multiple-entry visa!). In the case of the Congo, if you're organising a visa from the USA, a single-entry visa to the Congo for a stay of up to three months costs US$15 in Washington compared to US$100 for one obtained in Cameroun.

Multiple-Entry Visas

In addition to single-entry visas, some embassies issue multiple-entry visas, allowing you to re-enter many times during a given period. If you wish to take the 20-minute ferry from Brazzaville (Congo) to Kinshasa (Zaïre) you'll need a multiple-entry visa to re-enter the Congo.

Embassies of Chad, São Tomé and Equatorial Guinea do not issue multiple-entry visas. Embassies of Zaïre, Gabon, Cameroun, Congo and the CAR do issue them. They invariably cost more than single-entry visas. Many embassies in Europe and elsewhere will not tell you about the availability of multiple-entry visas unless you ask. Once in Africa, travellers sometimes regret not having asked because plans frequently change, sometimes requiring a second entrance into the same country.

Finally, in Gabon the border officials (not those at Libreville airport) used to demand proof of a hotel reservation. This old requirement has long been dropped but in the unlikely event that an official should try to raise this obstacle, you can be sure that he's just looking for a bribe.

Visa Agencies

A good tip if you need visas to a number of Central African countries, is to take a little time tripping around to all the embassies in your home country. In the UK and the USA, there are businesses that will do this for you, as travel agencies generally do not offer this service. In the telephone directory, they're usually listed under passport or visa services.

Shop around because fees vary considerably. Reliability and speed, however, are sometimes more important than price. Alpha Visa Service, for example, twice failed to send me some visa forms that I'd requested and failed to notify me that they wouldn't be able to get half the visas that I'd requested before my departure.

The agency will send you the application forms and you must return them with your passport, passport-sized photographs (usually two or three for each visa) and, for some countries such as Cameroun and Zaïre, a photocopy of your airline ticket. Businesses rely heavily on these agencies, and many travellers who have used them wouldn't do it any other way. Still, if you only need one or two visas, it may be quicker to do it yourself.

One word of warning: start the process early. Count on two weeks for them to send you the applications, one week per visa requested, and one week to send the passport back to you, ie about seven weeks in advance if you need, say, four visas. Give them lots of time but not too much otherwise the visa will expire before you arrive in the country.

Following is a list of several agencies in the USA which offer this service; prices do not include the embassy fee:

AAT Visa Services
  3417 Haines Way, Falls Church, VA 22041; US$15 per visa, less professional than other services (☎ (703) 820-5612)
Embassy Visa Service
  1519 Connecticut Ave, NW, Suite 300, Washington, DC 20036; US$31 per visa, best service available (☎ (202) 387-0300)

International Visas
LA World Trade Center, 350 S Figueroa St, Suite 185, Los Angeles, CA; US$20 per visa plus US$13 mailing costs (☎ (213) 625-7175)
Travel Agenda
119 West 57th St, Suite 1008, New York, NY 10019; US$13.50 per visa (☎ (212) 265-7887)

In the UK, the following agencies will organise visas for visits to several Central African countries:

Hogg Robinson Ltd
7 Butler Place (near Victoria railway station), London SW1H OQD (☎ (071) 222-8835)
Sterling House, 19 High Holborn (near Chancery Lane underground station), London EC1N 2JS (☎ (071) 242-7541)
119-123 Kingsway (opposite Holborn underground station), London WC2B 6PT; £10 per visa (☎ (071) 404-5454)
Thames Consular Services
363 Chiswick High Rd, London W4 4HS (☎ (071) 995-2492)
The Visa Service
2 Northdown St, Kings Cross, London N1 9BG (two minutes' from Kings Cross railway station); £10 for the first visa and £17 for each subsequent one (☎ (071) 833-2709; fax 833-1857)
The Visa Shop
at Trailfinders Travel, 194 Kensington High St, London W4; £12 per visa (☎ (071) 938-3848)

Central African Embassies Overseas
The cities listed below have diplomatic missions in the following Central African countries. For information about Central African embassies in African countries, see the later Obtaining Visas in Other African Countries section.

Athens (Greece)
Zaïre
Berlin (Germany)
Zaïre
Bern (Switzerland)
Cameroun, the CAR, Zaïre
Bonn (Germany)
Cameroun, the CAR, Chad, Congo, Gabon, Zaïre
Brazilia (Brazil)
Zaïre
Brussels (Belgium)
Cameroun, the CAR, Chad, Congo, Gabon, São Tomé, Zaïre
Buenos Aires (Argentina)
Zaïre

Geneva (Switzerland)
Gabon, Cameroun (consulate)
The Hague (The Netherlands)
Cameroun, Zaïre
Lisbon (Portugal)
São Tomé, Zaïre
London (UK)
Cameroun (visas for UK residents only), Gabon, São Tomé (honorary), Zaïre
Madrid (Spain)
Cameroun, Gabon, Equatorial Guinea, Zaïre
Marseilles (France)
Cameroun (consulate)
New Delhi (India)
Zaïre
New York (USA)
Equatorial Guinea, São Tomé
Ottawa (Canada)
Cameroun, the CAR, Gabon, São Tomé (in Montreal – honorary), Zaïre
Paris (France)
All countries except São Tomé
Rio de Janerio
Cameroun
Rome (Italy)
Cameroun, the CAR, Congo, Gabon, Zaïre
Stockholm (Sweden)
Zaïre
Sydney (Australia)
Cameroun (honorary)
Tel Aviv (Israel)
Zaïre
Tokyo (Japan)
Cameroun, the CAR, Gabon, Zaïre
Vienna (Austria)
Zaïre
Washington (USA)
Cameroun, the CAR, Chad, Congo, Gabon, Zaïre

Australia In Australia the only place where a visa to any of these countries might be obtained is through a French diplomatic mission, whether it be the embassy in Canberra or one of the consulates in Sydney or Melbourne. The exception is Cameroun; see the Cameroun chapter for details.

USA Central African embassies in the USA are as follows:

Cameroun
2349 Massachusetts Ave, NW, Washington, DC 20008 (☎ (202) 265-8790, 265-2400)
The CAR
1618 22nd St, NW, Washington, DC 20008 (☎ (202) 483-7800)

Chad
    2002 R St, NW, Washington, DC 20009 (☎ (202) 462-4009)
Congo
    4891 Colorado Ave, NW, Washington, DC 20011 (☎ (202) 726-5501)
Equatorial Guinea
    57 Magnolia Ave, Mt Vernon, New York (☎ (914) 667-4330)
Gabon
    2034 20th St, NW, Washington, DC 20009 (☎ (202) 797-1000)
São Tomé
    801 2nd Ave, Suite 1504, New York, New York 10017 (☎ (212) 687-8389)
Zaïre
    1800 New Hampshire Ave, NW, Washington, DC 20009 (☎ (202) 234-7690/1)

UK In the UK the addresses of Central African embassies are:

Cameroun
    84 Holland Park, London W11 3SB (☎ (071) 727-0771/4)
Gabon
    48 Kensington Court, London W8 (☎ (071) 937-5285)
São Tomé (Honorary)
    42 North Ordley St, London W1A 4PV (☎ (071) 499-1995; fax 629-6460)
Zaïre
    26 Chesham Place, London SW1X 8HH (☎ 071) 235-6137/8)

France In France the addresses of Central African embassies are:

Cameroun
    73 Rue d'Auteuil, 75016 Paris (☎ (1) 4651-8900)
Congo
    37 bis Rue Paul Valéry, 75016 Paris
Equatorial Guinea
    6 Rue Alfred de Vigny, 75008 Paris
Gabon
    26 bis Ave Raphaël, 75016 Paris (☎ (1) 2224-7960)
Zaïre
    32 Cours Albert Première, 75008 Paris (☎ (1) 4225-5750/4)

Obtaining Visas In Africa

If you'll be travelling through Central Africa for over three months, there's no way you can get all your visas beforehand. Most tourist visas to Central African countries are valid for a maximum of two or three months from the date of issue, sometimes less. Try to obtain as many as possible outside of Africa because getting them in Africa is sometimes difficult and usually more expensive.

If you cannot get all the visas you need, be selective and get the ones that are more difficult to obtain in Africa. Visas that are easy to obtain are those to Chad, the CAR and Zaïre (which has more embassies than any other Central African country but charges significantly higher fees in Africa than elsewhere). Visas to Chad and the CAR can be obtained anywhere in East Africa. Most French embassies in Africa (but rarely outside Africa) have authority to issue visas to Chad and the CAR except in the few countries where those countries have their own diplomatic missions. (Note that Portuguese embassies generally do not have authority to issue visas to São Tomé.)

Nevertheless, visas to the CAR as well as to Gabon and Cameroun present special problems. In the case of the CAR, which has its own embassies throughout most of Central Africa, there is a maddening requirement – applicable to Australians, New Zealanders, the Irish and some other nationalities (but not Britons, Canadians, Americans or Germans) – that the embassy must first obtain prior approval by telex from Bangui, a process that can take up to a week, sometimes more.

In the case of Gabon, in several (but not all) Central and West African countries including the Congo and Cameroun, the Gabonese Embassy won't issue a visa without first sending a telex to Libreville, a process that takes one or two weeks. So, if possible, definitely get a Gabonese visa at home.

As for Cameroun, visas are fairly easy to obtain if you'll be arriving from a neighbouring country although in Gabon, the Camerounian Embassy insists that you have an onward airline ticket. On the other hand, Camerounian visas are impossible to obtain anywhere in East Africa (except through the French Embassy in Nairobi), and are often quite difficult to obtain in West Africa (Nigeria excepted).

The following list shows in which African cities you can get Central African visas:

Cameroun
Abidjan (Côte d'Ivoire), Addis Ababa (Ethiopia), Algiers (Algeria), Bangui (the CAR), Bata (Equatorial Guinea), Brazzaville (Congo), Calabar (Nigeria), Cairo (Egypt), Dakar (Senegal), Kinshasa (Zaïre), Lagos (Nigeria), Libreville (Gabon), Malabo (Equatorial Guinea), Monrovia (Liberia), Nairobi (Kenya) c/o French Embassy, N'Djamena (Chad)

The CAR
Abidjan (Côte d'Ivoire), Algiers (Algeria), Brazzaville (Congo), Cairo (Egypt), Dakar (Senegal), Kinshasa (Zaïre), Khartoum (Sudan), Lagos (Nigeria), Libreville (Gabon), N'Djamena (Chad), Rabat (Morocco), Yaoundé (Cameroun) and most other African capital cities c/o French embassies

Chad
Algiers (Algeria), Bangui (the CAR), Brazzaville (Congo), Cairo (Egypt), Cotonou (Benin), Khartoum (Sudan), Kinshasa (Zaïre), Lagos (Nigeria), Libreville (Gabon), Malabo (Equatorial Guinea), Yaoundé (Cameroun)

Congo
Algiers (Algeria), Bangui (the CAR), Cairo (Egypt), Conakry (Guinea), Kinshasa (Zaïre), Libreville (Gabon), Luanda (Angola), Yaoundé (Cameroun)

Equatorial Guinea
Addis Ababa (Ethiopia), Calabar (Nigeria), Douala (Cameroun), Lagos (Nigeria), Las Palmas (Canary Islands), Libreville (Gabon), Rabat (Morocco), Yaoundé (Cameroun)

Gabon
Abidjan (Côte d'Ivoire), Algiers (Algeria), Bangui (the CAR), Brazzaville (Congo), Cairo (Egypt), Dakar (Senegal), Kinshasa (Zaïre), Lagos (Nigeria), Lomé (Togo), Luanda (Angola), Malabo (Equatorial Guinea), São Tomé (São Tomé), Yaoundé (Cameroun)

São Tomé
Libreville (Gabon), Luanda (Angola)

Zaïre
Abidjan (Côte d'Ivoire), Addis Ababa (Ethiopia), Algiers (Algeria), Bangui (the CAR), Brazzaville (Congo), Bujumbura (Burundi), Cairo (Egypt), Conakry (Guinea), Cotonou (Benin), Dakar (Senegal), Harare (Zimbabwe), Kampala (Uganda), Khartoum (Sudan), Kigali (Rwanda), Lagos (Nigeria), Libreville (Gabon), Lomé (Togo), Luanda (Angola), Monrovia (Liberia), Nairobi (Kenya), N'Djamena (Chad), Yaoundé (Cameroun)

Obtaining Visas at a Border/Airport The only place in Central Africa where you can obtain a tourist visa is at the border in northern Cameroun across from N'Djamena (Chad) where you can obtain a Chadian visa. Coming from nearby Maiduguri (northeastern Nigeria), at the Camerounian border you can also get a transit visit for Cameroun.

If you reside in, and your flight originates in, a country that doesn't have a Chadian or Camerounian embassy, there's an excellent chance that you'll be issued a visa at the airports in N'Djamena (Chad), Douala and Yaoundé (Cameroun). This is particularly true in N'Djamena; the Chadian police are the most easy-going in Central Africa and will almost certainly take you to the foreign ministry for a visa.

In Douala, the police will question you much more thoroughly but if your case is iron-clad, they'll issue you a Camerounian visa at the airport (most likely at the foreign ministry if you arrive at Yaoundé's new international airport). But this is risky because if they're not convinced, they'll put you on the next plane out at your expense.

Elsewhere in Central Africa, if you arrive at an airport without a visa, your chances of obtaining a visa are fairly poor. I met one traveller who had done this in five West and Central African countries and had always got in, but your chances in Central Africa are generally poorer than in West Africa where travellers are more common. Regardless, this will not work if you're flying from outside Africa because the airlines won't let you on the plane without a visa. But in Africa, airlines virtually never ask to see travellers' visas to the country of destination. I certainly recommend against travelling without visas but if you decide to take the risk, make sure that you look decent, have ample funds and have a good story as to why you couldn't get a visa.

Foreign Embassies in Central Africa
The following countries have embassies, high commissions or consulates in Central Africa:

Algeria
    Cameroun, Zaïre
Argentina
    Zaïre
Austria
    Zaïre
Belgium
    Cameroun, Congo, Gabon, Zaïre, the CAR (honorary)
Brazil
    Zaïre
Canada
    Cameroun, Zaïre
Côte d'Ivoire
    Cameroun, the CAR, Gabon, Zaïre
Denmark
    Congo (honorary)
Egypt
    Cameroun, the CAR, Chad, Congo, Zaïre
France
    all countries except São Tomé
Germany
    Cameroun, the CAR, Chad, Congo, Gabon, Zaïre
Greece
    Congo (honorary), Cameroun, Zaïre
India
    Zaïre
Italy
    Cameroun, Congo, Gabon, Zaïre
Japan
    Gabon, the CAR, Zaïre
Netherlands
    Cameroun, Zaïre, Congo (honorary), the CAR (honorary), Gabon (honorary)
Nigeria
    Every country except São Tomé
Portugal
    São Tomé, Congo (honorary)
Senegal
    Cameroun, Gabon
Spain
    Equatorial Guinea, São Tomé, Cameroun, Gabon (honorary)
Sweden
    Zaïre
Switzerland
    Cameroun, Zaïre, Congo (honorary)
Sudan
    Chad, the CAR, Zaïre
UK
    Cameroun, Zaïre, the CAR (honorary), Gabon (honorary)
USA
    all countries except São Tomé (which is covered by the US Embassy in Gabon)

Australia has no diplomatic representation in Central Africa. British and Canadian embassies will look after the needs of Aussies in the event that they require help of some kind.

CUSTOMS
Exporting Art
Art which is authentic and valuable cannot be exported under the laws of most African countries. Since very little art purchased by nonexperts fits this description, it's more a matter of being hassled by customs than doing something illegal.

Don't expect to travel upcountry and find something really valuable. With the exception of Zaïre, most of the museum-quality stuff has already been purchased. Also, knowing the difference between the real thing (ie old and used) and a forgery requires seeing and handling thousands of pieces. No book or sixth sense will enable you to bypass this process.

In Cameroun, exporting antiques is forbidden, and bribe-hungry officials have been known to declare obvious tourist art as antiques. Protect yourself with receipts from handicraft stores, or certificates signed by a museum chief.

Note that most countries, including Australia, Canada, the USA, Japan and virtually all countries in Europe, now prohibit the importation of ivory. In Australia, anything made from animal or plant matter is synonymous with the plague to Australian customs and any such items will certainly be fumigated, if not confiscated. It is wise to check the customs regulations first.

Importing Currency
Hard Currency There are no limits on the amount of foreign currency that you may import into Central African countries, but if you'll be importing a large amount, say over US$2000, you should declare this upon arrival. This is especially true in the Congo which enforces its currency exportation laws quite vigorously. It could also be the case in Cameroun since the police do everything possible to create bribe situations.

One of the biggest mistakes many travellers make is not bringing lots of French francs with them. In letter after letter, travellers speak of the problem of exchanging other currencies as well as travellers' cheques outside the capital cities. You'll need hard currency for emergencies because cashing travellers' cheques and using credit cards is difficult in Central Africa and often impossible in rural areas.

Even in Zaïre (in the areas near the Congo and the CAR) and São Tomé, French francs and CFA are often preferred to dollars or pounds. In CFA countries, banks in rural areas often won't touch dollars because they don't know the official exchange rate for that day. CFA and French francs, on the other hand, exchange 50 to one everywhere, and banks usually charge no commission for the exchange. Most stores will also accept French francs.

Local Currency Importing CFA francs into a CFA-zone country is never a problem, but importing the Zaïrian currency into Zaïre is severely restricted. In Zaïre, it is illegal to take more than about the equivalent of US$5 in zaïres, and any violation of the restrictions can cause major problems. Since the currency is very bulky and the exchange rates in Zaïre are almost invariably better inside the country, there is little reason to take this risk.

Exporting Currency
Except in the case of the Congo, taking CFA francs out of a CFA-zone country is virtually never a problem unless you are exporting large quantities, ie over US$1000 worth. The exact rules, however, are unclear. In many CFA countries, tourists are theoretically supposed to be able to take out more than local business people, and the limit is supposed to be higher if you're travelling to another CFA country. However, most border officials don't have a clue as to what the rules are. If you should run into problems, playing the ignorant tourist should help. Exporting other currencies from CFA countries is also not a problem.

Only in the Congo is the rule crystal clear and strictly enforced. The limit there is CFA 25,000 and you will probably be searched. If more than CFA 25,000 is found on you, it will definitely be confiscated.

For the exporting of currency from non-CFA countries, Zaïre is the only country which has strict rules; see the introductory Money section in the Zaïre chapter. You should have no problems in São Tomé.

MONEY
CFA 50 = FFr 1

The principal currency of the region is the CFA (Communauté Financielle Africaine) franc. Every Central African country except São Tomé and Zaïre uses the CFA franc.

By linking the value of the CFA franc to the French franc and exchanging them freely, Central Africa has a hard currency. This has eliminated the possibility of a black market and allowed travellers to go from one CFA country to the next without exchanging money. This is a mixed blessing, however, because the CFA is grossly over-valued, making Central Africa one of the most expensive regions in the developing world. It is also virtually impossible for Central African countries to export anything other than petroleum.

Even though the CFA is hard currency, exchanging CFA in other countries isn't easy. In East Africa, the banks seem very suspicious of it and generally won't accept it. In the USA, even the largest banks won't accept it. In short, the CFA is hard currency only in Central and West Africa and France.

Another hitch is that there are actually two CFAs – the Central African CFA and the West African CFA. The latter is used in Benin, Burkina Faso, Côte d'Ivoire, Mali, Niger, Senegal and Togo. There's usually not too much difficulty exchanging one for the other at a bank or at a major hotel in Central and West Africa, but don't expect street moneychangers to do the same.

Black Market
The only Central African country with a black market (or 'parallel market') is Zaïre. See the Facts for the Visitor section in the Zaïre chapter for more information.

You might also be asked to fill out a currency declaration form in Zaïre. These were abolished in Zaïre during the '80s but have occasionally appeared at Kinshasa airport and at the Kinshasa to Brazzaville ferry crossing. If you enter Zaïre through Kinshasa and are asked to fill out one of these forms declaring all your money, be aware that you may be hassled when leaving if you changed any of your money on the street. You won't be able to prove that all your money was exchanged at banks. The officials may make threats so as to intimidate you into offering a bribe. To avoid this possibility, when entering the country hide a small amount of hard currency where no-one can find it. If customs officials find it, they'll certainly confiscate it and may even detain you, especially if you hide a large amount. On my last trip, customs officials at Kinshasa airport didn't ask to see my declaration form and that seems to be the norm these days, but there's no guarantee you'll be so lucky.

Exchanging Money at the Airport
Don't expect to be able to change your money at every airport. If you can, don't hesitate to do so – the exchange rate is usually as good as the banks in the city centre. There are banks at the international airports in Brazzaville, Douala, Kinshasa, Libreville, and Yaoundé. Even in these cities, you'll sometimes find the airport banks closed. Don't worry as there are always taxi drivers who'll accept dollars or French francs, but don't expect the best exchange rate in town. In non-CFA countries (Zaïre and São Tomé), drivers prefer to be paid in hard currency.

Credit Cards
The most widely accepted credit card is American Express (AE), followed by Diners Club (D) and Visa (V). Carte Blanche (CB), MasterCard (MC) and Eurocard (EC) are much less accepted. As for restaurants, only some of the expensive ones accept credit cards.

As for obtaining cash with a credit card, American Express and Diners Club offer this service at their offices and, in the case of American Express, it's a very convenient way to get travellers' cheques denominated in French francs while you're travelling. However, very few banks in Central Africa offer this service to credit card owners and none do in Chad, the CAR, Equatorial Guinea or São Tomé. (For overseas assistance call American Express in the USA (☎ (202) 783-7474) collect.)

Using other credit cards such as Visa to obtain cash is also difficult. In several large cities such as Yaoundé and Libreville, there are a few banks where you can do this but not with every Visa card. In CFA countries, the banks that offer this service usually do so only with Visa cards issued by French banks. Travellers' cheques are a far preferable way to obtain cash in the big cities.

Travellers' Cheques
Travellers to Central Africa are constantly dismayed at how difficult it is to cash travellers' cheques anywhere outside the capital cities. There are banks in all the Central African capitals that readily accept travellers' cheques denominated in US dollars, UK pounds or German marks. However, service is slow, especially in Zaïre, and commissions are often ridiculously high, sometimes 5% or more. But outside the capital cities, cashing travellers' cheques is impossible in Chad, São Tomé, the CAR and Equatorial Guinea (with the possible exception of French-franc denominated cheques in Berbérati and Bata), almost impossible in Zaïre, difficult in Gabon (Port-Gentil excepted) and the Congo (Pointe-Noire excepted). It is only easy in Cameroun. If you're lucky and find a bank that accepts travellers' cheques, you may have to wait until the afternoon when they know the day's exchange rate.

In Central Africa, as few banks outside the capital cities accept travellers' cheques it doesn't matter what denomination of currency your cheques are in. Nevertheless, you'll be better off in Cameroun, Gabon and possibly the Congo bringing travellers' cheques denominated in French francs.

Moreover, you'll avoid having to shop around for the best exchange rates plus exchange transactions will usually be faster and transaction fees less.

It's well worth the effort scouting around to find a bank that sells them or an American Express agency that has travellers' cheques denominated in French francs. If you have no success, one solution is to bring all your money in cash, preferably French francs, and convert most of it to French franc travellers' cheques immediately upon arrival.

American Express and Thomas Cook are probably the best travellers' cheques. In Central Africa you'll find more banks will accept them than other kinds, and you'll be reimbursed faster if you lose them, even on weekends. American Express has representatives in Douala, Libreville and Brazzaville. American Express has a refund centre for Africa in Britain (☎ (44) 273-571600).

There are usually at least one or two banks in the largest capital cities that will accept Citicorp, Barclays Bank and Bank America travellers' cheques but elsewhere, you'll find few banks will. Citibank and Barclays Bank have branches in Gabon and Zaïre; Citibank is the slowest to reimburse, and on weekends, all you'll get is a recorded message. With others you may wait weeks, particularly if the issuing bank has no branch where you are. Just finding which bank, if any, is the correspondent bank is a big enough problem. If you lose your proof of purchase slip, getting reimbursed will take much longer – easily two weeks. Make photocopies of the purchase slip with numbers and put them in various bags and give one to your travelling companion.

You will of course need to bring some cash in small bills (preferably French francs) for emergencies. One drawback of bringing lots of cash is that it often has a lower exchange rate than for travellers' cheques. The banks' commission for exchanging foreign currency in cash (French francs excepted) is sometimes the same as for travellers' cheques.

Transferring Money
Transferring money can take weeks, and problems are often encountered. The bank may deny receiving money which has actually arrived. If money is wired, arrange for the forwarding bank to send a separate confirmation with full details. You can then go into the African bank with proof that your money has been sent.

Foreign Banks
The following foreign banks have branches in the Central African cities listed below:

Banque de Paris et des Pays-Bas
    Libreville, Kinshasa
Barclays Bank
    Kinshasa, Libreville
Citibank
    Kinshasa, Libreville, Port-Gentil
Crédit Lyonnais
    Bafoussam, Douala, Garoua, N'Gaoundéré, Yaoundé
Grindlays
    Kinshasa
Standard Chartered Bank
    Douala, Yaoundé

Costs
The primary complaint of most travellers to Central Africa is the high cost, particularly in comparison to other areas of the developing world. Hotels and restaurants, for example, are two to four times more expensive than those in most of South America. This is because the CFA is way over-valued and the culprit is France which refuses to devalue it. However, as of mid-1993, costs were headed downward as the French franc (and thus the CFA) was significantly devalued relative to most major currencies.

Budget Travel On my last trip through Central Africa, I stayed mostly at the cheapest hotels and averaged CFA 4000 (or about US$16 in mid-1993) for a room. Most of the beds had a single clean sheet, about half the rooms had fans, and maybe 20% of the hotels had bucket showers. Only occasionally did the bathroom rate a 'filthy'. Couples should budget about 25% more per room. Always inquire, however, about what's meant by a single; in many cheap hotels a single is a room with only one bed (frequently queen sized) and a double is a room with two beds.

To save money, consider spending more time in Zaïre, which is by far the cheapest country, and except for the occasional flare-ups, is still reasonably safe outside Kinshasa. Travelling there costs a quarter what it does in most CFA countries. In eastern Zaïre, for instance, it's not so difficult to find hotels for CFA 1000 (US$3.50) a night. However, rooms at that price tend to be somewhat grubby. The difference in the cost of food is not so great. A large Primus beer, for example, costs US$0.60 in Zaïre and $1.40 in neighbouring Congo.

As for meals, if you stick to African food and drink water, eating can average about US$1.50 to US$2 a meal. Adding merely one soft drink per meal, however, can raise this average by 40%. Adding a large beer can raise it up to 80%! So take a water container and purification tablets everywhere; they'll pay for themselves in a day or two. A more realistic bare minimum budget for meals, however, would be US$8 a day. In most countries this will include buying breakfast on the street, two simple African meals on the street, a large beer, a Coke and peanuts for snacking. Eating African street food does not mean eating poorly. The best African food is usually sold on the streets and because the women usually simmer it for hours on end, your only worry should be the germs on the plates and utensils.

If you want Western food, even in the cheapest restaurants you'll be hard-pressed to keep the average down to US$7 a meal. In a few of the larger cities, it's fairly easy to live off Lebanese *chawarmas* (lamb and vegetables in pita bread with sauce), which cost CFA 500. An alternative is surviving off simple street food, such as beef brochettes, bread and butter, peanuts and cassava chips. In the morning and evening, in many cities you'll see men serving Nescafé coffee, bread, butter and scrambled eggs on benches along the streets. If you eat your breakfast at these places instead of restaurants, it shouldn't average more than US$1.25.

There are considerable differences in transport costs between countries. The most expensive countries by far in this respect are the Congo, Gabon and the CAR; the cheapest are Cameroun and Zaïre. In Gabon, Libreville to Lambaréné (232 km) costs CFA 8000 by minivan; in Cameroun, N'Gaoundéré to Garoua (296 km) costs CFA 3000 in a five-seat car.

Hitching rides on the major routes is sometimes fairly easy and sometimes not. Many drivers will expect you to pay them, so straighten this out at the beginning. Most travellers take trucks, buses or bush taxis, of which there are various types. Considerable price differences exist among them. In descending order of cost, there are five-seat sedans, Peugeot 504 station wagons, buses and vans, and pick-up trucks. For example, in Cameroun, you can save 25% by taking a minivan instead of a Peugeot station wagon but the waiting and riding time can easily be 50% more.

Mid-Range Travel Travellers staying in first-class accommodation should expect to pay US$100 to US$150 a night for a single in major cities, but a very decent two or three-star hotel with a good restaurant and frequently a nice view and a pool will cost about 50% less.

As for meals, many countries in West Africa are so poor that only a small percentage of the locals can afford to eat at restaurants so many restaurants cater to foreigners and serve only continental cuisine. They are usually expensive, particularly if some of the ingredients are flown in from Europe. Eating relatively modestly in a restaurant in a major city can easily cost US$50 for two, sometimes a lot more.

Finding relatively inexpensive restaurants is not always easy. While they may increase the likelihood of getting stomach problems, the actual risk will be minimal if you stick to food like meat and rice and stay away from raw vegetables and fruits. Even in relatively expensive cities such as Yaoundé, for example, virtually every expatriate has frequented a *maison de poulet* (chicken house) where you can get excellent braised chicken, rice and a Coke for about US$11.

As for travelling around, renting a car can easily cost US$200 a day. Going from one city to another, taking a Peugeot 504 station wagon at the car park is much cheaper and you can make the trip more comfortable by renting two seats instead of one. For excursions out of town, consider hiring an all-day taxi instead of renting a car. The cost will usually be lower, there'll be less hassle, and if you are fortunate enough to get a good driver, chances are you'll see more interesting sites and learn a lot more.

Tipping
Tipping is a problem in Africa because there are few clear rules applicable to all people. Africans are not in the habit of tipping but a small amount of tipping is expected from wealthier Africans. Tipping to most Africans is related to the concept of a cadeau (gift); rich people are expected to give gifts. Almost all foreigners are considered to be rich, therefore a cadeau is expected unless the person obviously looks like a backpacker. Anyone staying at a fancy hotel would be expected to tip but there would not be the same expectation from a backpacker staying at a cheap hotel.

Expect to tip 10% of the bill at the better restaurants but check the bill closely to see if service is included (it frequently is at restaurants and hotels in French-speaking Africa). At the other end of the scale are the African restaurants with almost all African clientele – tipping is not expected from anyone. There's a grey area between these two classes of restaurants. Tipping in the mid-range restaurants is rarely expected from Africans and those who are obviously backpackers, but tipping may be expected from expats and almost always from wealthier tourists. Even the wealthier Africans will sometimes tip at all-African restaurants, not so much because it's expected but because it's a show of status.

In taxis, tipping is generally not the rule but well-heeled travellers in larger cities with numerous foreigners (eg Douala and Libre-ville) are expected to tip about 10% of the fare, except for rides in shared taxis where tipping never occurs.

In areas where the locals are unaccustomed to foreigners (ie most of Central Africa), travellers need to be keenly aware of the possible consequences of their actions. You should try to be as unobtrusive as possible and follow local customs to the tee, ie avoid tipping and offering small gifts unless this is the custom. If you're unsure of what the custom is, ask. Gestures such as tipping may seem innocuous but they can have the unwanted effect of encouraging the locals to view foreigners as a source of income and creating, eventually, a dependency relationship, chipping away at their long established culture. While there are no hard and fast rules, one way to view your actions is to reflect on what might be the result if a thousand tourists did exactly what you do – food for thought anyway.

WHEN TO GO
Rain is the major factor to consider in choosing when to travel to Central Africa because the upcountry roads, mostly dirt, become extremely muddy, making travel difficult if not impossible. Because the equator runs through the middle of Central Africa, the rain pattern in the south tends to be just the opposite of that in the north. The best time to travel in northern Central Africa tends to be the worst time to travel in southern Central Africa.

In Chad, Cameroun, Equatorial Guinea and most of the CAR, the best time to travel is November to April. You should be aware, however, that in Chad and northern Cameroun, midday temperatures over 40° C (104°F) are the norm from March to May.

In Gabon and São Tomé, where it rains virtually all year round, with a slight dry spell in July and August, try to avoid the heavy rainy season from January to May.

In most of Zaïre and the Congo, there's a dry spell from June to September and sometimes a very short dry spell around Christmas time, making these months the best times to travel. The time to avoid is February to mid-

May, which is the heavy rainy season everywhere except in the far north of these two countries. In the far north rain tends to fall all year round. Near Bangui (the furthest point north), the dry season is from November to February.

Another consideration for some people is whether the national parks will be open. Waza park in northern Cameroun is open from 15 November to 15 June, St Floris park in north-eastern CAR is open approximately 1 December to 15 May. In the rest of Central Africa, the parks are open all year round. In Zaïre, the best viewing time for most parks, including Virunga, is from June to September. November 15 also marks the beginning of the best period, lasting 3½ months, for climbing Mt Cameroun.

WHAT TO BRING
Clothes
Travel light as this will give you space for souvenirs and clothes. Keep your attire simple to avoid standing out like a sore thumb – that only makes you easy prey for hustlers. Buy things as you go. Women, for instance, can leave long dresses at home and buy the long, flowing African dresses sold everywhere.

Shorts are useful for the beaches and travelling upcountry, but women should not wear them anywhere in public, even in modern cities such as Yaoundé. One suggestion is to bring several wrap-around skirts to put on over your shorts as needed. Men can wear shorts anywhere, but doing so will only accentuate the differences with the locals, especially in northern Cameroun and most of Chad where Muslims predominate.

Pants are acceptable everywhere, but in Muslim areas, Western women usually find it easier to develop a good rapport with African women if they wear similar clothes, ie long dresses. This is particularly true in the villages. The men's second-hand jeans market throughout Central Africa, by the way, is fabulous.

A light sweater is advisable in the December to February period, particularly the further north you go. Those crossing the desert in the winter months should bring a heavy sweater.

Essential Items
Medical kit – see the health section later in this chapter

Tampons, sanitary napkins & contraceptives – often impossible to find outside major cities

Suntan lotion – you'll use less than you think; it's frequently available but usually not the kind you want

Foreign currency – hide at least US$100 worth of hard currency on you, preferably French francs (easier to exchange) and make sure no-one will ever find them

Passport photos – bring lots as you'll need two or three for every visa and visa extension. Visa-type photos are readily obtainable everywhere if you run out.

Photocopy of critical documents – copies of your passport (including relevant visas), airline ticket, credit cards and health certificate are useful and can speed up the replacement process if you lose them. Also, a photocopy of your passport and visa is useful whenever you have to leave your passport at an embassy to get a visa.

Recommended Items
French francs travellers' cheques – much easier to exchange in Central Africa (Zaïre and São Tomé excepted) than travellers' cheques in other currencies

Washbasin plug & soap powder – useful when washing clothes

Mosquito repellent

Iodine tablets or crystals – handy whenever bottled water is not available; iodine tablets are not recommended for pregnant women.

Water tech water purifier – self contained cup which purifies six ounces of water in 15 seconds (minimum of 400 litres); much easier to use than iodine tablets or crystals. Write to Water Technologies Corp, Box 2495, Ann Arbor, MI 48106, USA.

Map – Michelin's map of Central Africa (No 155) is far superior to others. For northern and western Cameroun, northern CAR and all of Chad, you'll also need the Michelin map for West Africa. Finding either in Central Africa is frequently difficult.

Money pouch

Day pack

Vitamin tablets

Film & photographic accessories – variety of speeds of film (1000 ASA is best for gorilla shots); lighting conditions vary considerably

Polaroid camera – use instant photos instead of money for gifts; used selectively, these will be much more appreciated (Africans love photographs, but usually have few of themselves.)

Alarm clock – hotel staff cannot always be relied upon to wake you up

International Drivers' Licence – some rental agents will not accept licences from other countries

French phrasebook – don't expect to find one easily in Central Africa

Small calculator – this can facilitate bargaining in the market immeasurably, especially if you don't speak French

Business cards – important in Central Africa; Africans like to make friends and giving someone your card is an indication you want to keep in contact. These cards can even be useful in dealing with police.

Rope, ice axe & crampons – for experienced climbers planning to scale the highest mountains of the Ruwenzori range (ie the glacial area above 4500 metres)

For Budget Travellers

Cassettes – Africans love Western music with a good beat; hard-core blues and complicated jazz go over like a bad joke. You can be sure bus and taxi drivers and many other Africans with cassette players will want to hear your music for a change. They also make good souvenirs for African friends you make along the way.

Blank cassettes – If you wish to record African music during your trip, you'll have a very difficult time finding high-quality blank cassettes, so bring them with you.

Plastic rain poncho – easier to carry than an umbrella, and doubles as a ground mat

Sleeping bag liner – useful for camping, or when a hotel's sheets are unbearably dirty

Camping gear – a good way to cut the high costs of travel in Central Africa; there are many rural areas where camping is the only form of accommodation

Student ID – student ID can occasionally be useful for obtaining discounts, particularly in Zaïre

CULTURAL EVENTS & HOLIDAYS

A consideration when planning your itinerary is to take note of the special events occurring throughout the year. The more important ones are in the following list and discussed more fully in the country chapters (*approximate dates).

1 January
New Year's Day is celebrated all over Africa

26 January*
Mt Cameroun Race. Held on the last Sunday in January, this race up and down Mt Cameroun is the continent's toughest.

March*
Mardi Gras in São Tomé is one of the country's major celebrations, with colourful street parades leading up to Lent. It can occur anywhere from late February to early April.

15 March*
Feast of Ramadan, or end of Ramadan (see the table at the end of this section). This is the second major Islamic holiday, celebrated in Chad, northern and western Cameroun, and northern CAR and Gabon following the annual 30-day Muslim fast. Especially interesting are the celebrations in Foumban (western Cameroun).

3-4 April*
The Trans-Congo car rally from Brazzaville to Pointe-Noire is Central Africa's biggest auto race and is held in the first week of April.

20 May
Cameroun National Festival, the country's major non-religious holiday.

23 May*
Tabaski or Id al Kabir (see the table for estimated dates) is the major Muslim holiday and is celebrated in Chad, northern and western Cameroun, northern CAR and Gabon. Tabaski is particularly interesting in Maroua (northern Cameroun).

15 August
Congo's Independence Day, the country's major holiday.

17 August
Gabon National Festival

11-18 November
Nso Cultural Week, held in Kumbo, a town on the Ring Rd in western Cameroun. The festival features wild-horse racing through the streets.

20 December
Colourful festival in Bafat, near Bamenda in Cameroun.

25 December
Christmas is celebrated in all Central African countries.

Islamic Holidays

There are some very important Islamic holidays when almost all of northern Central Africa's commercial life comes to a stop. Since the Islamic calendar is based on 12 lunar months with 354 or 355 days, these holidays are always about 11 days earlier than the previous year. The exact dates depend on the moon and are only announced about one day in advance.

This table lists the estimated dates for the major Muslim events for 1994 to 1996.

Event	1994	1995	1996
Id al Fitr	15 Mar	4 Mar	22 Feb
Tabaski	23 May	12 May	1 May
Mohammed's Birthday	20 Aug	9 Aug	29 Jul

End of Ramadan (Id al Fitr) Ramadan is the ninth month of the Islamic lunar-based calendar (the year is usually 354 days). During the entire 30-day month, Muslims are supposed to fast during the daylight hours. The fast is sometimes referred to as *le carême*. Muslims who do the carême (many do not, particularly those living in the cities) are usually weak during the afternoon because they are not allowed to eat or drink (except for athletes, pregnant women, and a few other exceptions) from sunrise to sunset. Work hours usually end around 1 or 2 pm.

You might think that people would lose weight during this period, but some actually gain weight because of the huge meals served after sunset and before sunrise. In general, it's a very festive time and people go more frequently to the mosque and visit friends at night.

The end of Ramadan is the second most important Muslim holiday – celebrated by a feast known as the Feast of Ramadan or the Small Feast, beginning on the evening of the 30th day. The centre of attraction is usually a roasted sheep, or possibly a goat.

Tabaski (Id al Kabir) Also known as the Great Feast, Tabaski is the most important celebration in northern Central Africa. On this day, Muslims kill a sheep to commemorate the moment when Abraham was about to sacrifice his son in obedience to God's command, only to have God intercede at the last moment and substitute a ram instead. It also coincides with the end of the pilgrimage (hadj) to Mecca. In the preceding two weeks, sheep prices can jump by 50% or more.

One-third of the sacrificed animal is supposed to be given to the poor, one-third to friends, and one-third for the family. Those who cannot afford a sheep are really embarrassed – most will do anything to scrape up the money. If you can manage to get an invitation, you'll be participating in what is, for most northern Central Africans, the most important and festive day of the year. Usually a two-day public holiday, it mainly involves attending the mosque for several hours, lots of eating, and visiting friends.

Mohammed's Birthday This occurs almost three months after Tabaski and is also widely celebrated.

POST & TELECOMMUNICATIONS
Post
Mail service in Africa bears the brunt of many jokes, but the reality is that the service is fairly reliable in most of Central Africa – it just takes a while getting there. From the USA, the usual delivery time is three to six weeks depending on the town's size and remoteness. From Europe, the delivery time is slightly less. However, considerable delays can occur just frequently enough to

---

The Hadj
Ask a Muslim what he's going to do with any profits from a development assistance project and he's likely to tell you that he'll use it to finance a pilgrimage to Mecca. All Muslims who are of good health and have the means are supposed to make the pilgrimage at least once in their life.

Those who do the pilgrimage receive the honorific title of Hadj for men, and Hadjia for women. For some, this can involve a lifetime of savings, usually several thousand dollars. It's not unusual for families to save up and send one member. Before the aeroplane, it used to involve a journey overland of a year or longer, sometimes requiring stops on the way to earn money. So if you meet someone with the prefix Hadj or Hadjia, you may appreciate the honour that is bestowed on them by the community. ∎

make it impossible to rely on the mail for matters involving critical time constraints.

The poste restante in most capital cities is fairly reliable; check the Post & Telecommunications sections in the country chapters for more details. Ask people to write you as follows: Joe DOE, Poste Restante, PTT, Yaoundé, Cameroun. To avoid getting your letters misfiled, it is very important that letters sent to you have your surname spelt in capital letters, and if you have a name with an apostrophe, make sure the sender drops the apostrophe, eg OLEARY, not O'LEARY (otherwise likely to be filed under L). American Express has a much more reliable poste restante service. Even if you aren't a cardholder, if you have their travellers' cheques you can have letters sent to you at their offices, eg Douala, Libreville and Brazzaville. Addresses of American Express offices are given in Information sections for each country chapter.

Contrary to what you may hear, it's rare that governments open mail; however, postal workers have been known to rip off stamps and resell them, especially in poverty-stricken Zaïre. So if you're mailing a letter from Central Africa, make sure you see the postal clerk frank your postage stamps.

The most expensive countries to send letters from are the Congo (CFA 250 per letter or postcard) and Gabon; Zaïre is the cheapest. Courier service is an alternative; DHL, which has the most offices, is located in many of the major cities of Central Africa.

Telephone

Telephone connections between Africa and Europe and the USA have improved greatly in recent years because international calls now go by satellite in virtually every country. Calling from Africa to Europe or North America is not nearly as difficult as it used to be even a few years ago. The main problem is still the high cost; it's about seven times more expensive calling from Africa to Europe or North America than vice versa, and there are no reduced rates at night. The other problem is the waiting time, which is often minutes but occasionally hours depending on the locality and time of day.

Calls between African countries, however, are sometimes relayed through Europe, in which case the reception is usually bad – *if* you can get a call through.

ELECTRICITY

The electricity supply throughout Central Africa is 220 volts. Plugs are usually two round pins, like those in Europe.

BOOKS

Except for several commercial reference books, the following list of books is limited to those that are available in paperback and can be purchased at bookshops or obtained by mail. Take several books with you! An art book, in particular, will be handy for reference purposes.

History
Africa *African Civilization Revisited: From*

Antiquity to Modern Times (Africa World, Trenton, New Jersey, 1990), by Basil Davidson, is an engaging book which builds on Davidson's earlier eight-part documentary series on the history of Africa for British TV.

A Short History of Africa (Cambridge University Press, 1988), by J D Fage & Roland Oliver, is also a very good paperback.

Africa Since 1800 (Cambridge University Press, 1981), by Roland Oliver & Anthony Atmore, is the last of a trilogy, the others are *Africa in the Iron Age* and *The African Middle Ages 1400-1800*. The book involves three parts: the pre-colonial period up to 1875, followed by the partition and colonial rule, and finally the roads to independence taken by different African territories, including the post independence decades.

Modern Africa (Longman, 1983) by Basil Davidson, focuses on African history since 1900. *The African Genius: An Introduction to African Social & Cultural History* (Little Brown & Co, Boston, 1990) is also by Basil Davidson.

For history books, contact Longman Publishers. In the UK, their address is Longman House, Harlow, Essex CM20 2JE England, and Addison-Wesley/Longman, Reading, MA 01867 or try Cambridge University Press, The Edinburgh Bldg, Shaftesbury Rd, Cambridge CB2 2RU. In the USA, contact Longman Publishers at 510 North Ave, New Rochelle, NY 10801; it publishes the most titles. Ask Longman for its free history and African studies catalogues.

Central & West Africa *Contemporary West African States* (Cambridge University Press, 1989), by Donald O'Brien, is recommended if you're looking for a thorough, if colourless, country by country account of conditions and events in contemporary Central Africa. It covers Cameroun and Chad plus six countries in West Africa.

West Africa: An Introduction to Its History (Longman, 1977), by Michael Crowder, covers West Africa and parts of Central Africa.

The Revolutionary Years: West Africa

Since 1800 (Longman, 1981), by J B Webster & A A Boahen, gives a more in-depth treatment of west and central African history.

Aspects of Central African History (Heinemann, 1968), edited by T Ranger, is a collection of 15 essays that complements other introductory histories of the area. Another book is *Topics of West African History* (Longman, 1986) by Adu Boahen.

The River Congo (Harper & Row, New York, 1977), by Peter Forbath, recounts the history of the kingdom of the Kongo to the birth of Zaïre.

Art & Culture
African Art in Cultural Perspective (W W Norton & Co, London and New York, 1985), by William Bascom is an excellent book focusing on sculpture and covering Central and West Africa region by region. There are 261 illustrations among 288 pages.

African Art (W W Norton & Co, 1988), by Frank Willett, is a superb introductory book on African art and provides a wider perspective than Bascom's book. I recommend taking along this paperback or Bascom's; the art will make a lot more sense and you'll develop a more critical eye.

A Short History of African Art (Penguin, New York, 1987), by Gillon Werner, is good for its historical perspective.

African Arts is a superb quarterly magazine published by the African Studies Centre (UCLA, Los Angeles, CA 90024), with good photography and well-researched articles. An annual subscription costs US$20.

African Textiles (Icon Editions, Harper & Row, New York, 1989), by John Picton & John Mack, is a bulky book with numerous photographs and is the best on the subject.

African Hairstyles (Heinemann Educational Books, 1988), by Esi Sagay, is a publication loaded with photographs of fascinating hairstyles from all parts of the continent.

Beads from the West African Trade by Picard African Imports (9310 Los Prados Lane, Carmel, CA 93923) is a six-volume paperback collection, each about 40 pages and focusing on a different category of beads, such as chevrons, millefiori beads, etc.

Music

African Rock (Obelisk Press, 384 pages, 1989), by Chris Stapleton & Chris May, is a highly recommended introduction to non-traditional African music of all kinds. In the USA, it is available through Original Music, 418 Lasher Rd, Tivoli, New York 12583. In the UK, Paladin Press publishes it under the title *African All Stars: the Pop Music of a Continent*.

The Da Capo Guide to Contemporary African Music (Da Capo Press, New York, 1988), also available from Original Music, is another good introduction. It has some errors but is unbeatable if you're looking for a musician-by-musician guide with short country-by-country surveys. The section on Central African musicians and countries is quite good. In the UK, it is published by Pluto Press under the name *Stern's Guide to Contemporary African Music*.

African Music, A People's Art (Lawrence Hill & Co, Westport, 1984), by Francis Bebey, is another excellent paperback on the traditional music of francophone Africa. At the end of the book Bebey, a Camerounian, gives a selective discography with extensive recordings from six Central African countries and eight West African countries.

The Music of Africa (1987), a four-record anthology of modern African music by Hilton Fyle of BBC fame. This section may also help to demystify the music scene. It's followed by a reference section of the best-known recording artists. A second step would be getting on the mailing list of Original Music (☎ (914) 756-2767), Box 190, Lasher Rd, Tivoli, New York 12583, USA. It has a catalogue of African music (cassettes and CDs) and books on African music, with prices and an explanation of the significance of each.

For a listing of music shops, see the Music section in the Facts about the Region chapter.

Fiction

Cameroun and the Congo are the only two countries in Central Africa that have produced any well-known novelists. Four prominent writers are Mbella Dipoko, Ferdinand Oyono, Kenjo Jumbam and Mongo Beti. Dipoko's *Because of Women* (1969) is a delicately told story of a river-man who quarrels with his pregnant wife over another woman. Oyono's *Houseboy* (1966) and *The Old Man and the Medal* (1969) are scathing short stories about colonial insensitivity, while Jumban's *The White Man of God* (1980) is about a boy growing up in a Camerounian village which is seriously divided when a white missionary arrives.

The most famous Camerounian novelist, however, is Mongo Beti; his books include *Mission to Kala* (1964), *The Poor Christ of Bomba* (1971) and *King Lazurus* (1970). The first, one of his funniest, is about a man sent off to retrieve a villager's wife who has run off with a man from another tribe; the second is about a French priest's attempts to convert an entire village to Catholicism and the ironic consequences which follow. The third is another cynical story concerning missionaries. All seven of these paperbacks are available from Heinemann.

The Laughing Cry by Henri Lopes (available through Readers International, Box 959, Columbia, LA 71418, USA), written by a Congolese, has been described by the Washington Post as 'satirical, tender, bawdy, savage and filled with love and hope'. He also has a book of short stories, *Tribaliks: Contemporary Congolese Stories* (Heinemann, 1988).

For other novels about life in Africa, refer to Western writers or to those from neighbouring Nigeria.

A Bend in the River (Random House, New York, 1989), by V S Naipaul, is a tale that takes place in Zaïre. *Talking Drums* (John Murray Publishers, London), by Shirley Deane, is a novel about Cameroun, focusing on village life near Yaoundé.

Things Fall Apart (Heinemann Educational Books, 1958), by Nigeria's Chinua Achebe is one of the most famous novels by an African writer. This classic has sold over a million copies and is definitely worth reading. *Anthills of the Savannah* also by

Chine Achebe (Doubleday, New York and London, 1988) is a humorous and satirical anatomy of political disorder and corruption in a fictional African country resembling Nigeria. It is Achebe's most recent novel and was a finalist for the 1987 Booker Prize in the UK and has been highly praised.

The Interpreter (Heinemann Educational Books, 1986), by Wole Soyinka, is one of two books written by this author from Nigeria who won the Nobel Prize for Literature, only the fifth person from a Third World country to win the prize. He is primarily a playwright and *A Dance of the Forests*, *The Man Died*, *Opera Wonyosi* and *A Play of Giants* are some of his more well-known plays. Heinemann publishes a number of his works. A man with a social vision who doesn't mind lambasting those in power, he uses a language which is far from simple, which is why relatively few Nigerians have read his works.

Reading the African Novel (Heinemann, 1987) by Simon Gikandi, and *Journeys Through the French African Novel* (Heinemann, 1990) by Mildred Mortimer, are two of the best works of criticism of the African novel.

For novels by African writers, look out for the African Writers Series (270 titles) published by Heinnemann Publishers. In the UK, contact Heinemann Educational Books at 22 Bedford Square, London WC1B 3HH (☎ (071) 637-3311). In the USA, contact them at 70 Court St, Portsmouth, NH 03801, USA (☎ (603) 778-0534).

Politics & Economics

If you're interested in understanding the roots of Africa's problems, check out Haskell Ward's recently published book, *African Development Reconsidered*. The theme that echoed most consistently through the conversations he had with Africans was that things work only when Africans feel they have done things for themselves and that Africa's lack of self-reliance lies at the heart of its problems. The systems imposed upon them following independence by well-meaning Western advisors have had very little to do with African needs; Africa's resulting dependence today on the West encompasses virtually every area of life. It's something to think about as you travel around.

For some truly fascinating and provocative reading touching on a number of topics, I highly recommend Blaine Harden's new book, *Africa: Dispatches From a Fragile Continent* (W W Norton & Co, New York, 1990). He examines why African political leadership has failed its people, but Harden believes there's hope. He also believes that African values still endure and are what make the continent a joy.

Squandering Eden (The Bodley Head, London, 1988), by Mort Rosenblum & Doug Williamson, is an easy-to-read and up-to-date book on Africa. Imbued with a non-patronising concern for the welfare of Africans and the African continent, it explores the theme that broad-based stable development should be the goal for all Africans, and that this is dependent on building a working relationship between African landholders and managers and their environment.

The Africans (Random House, New York and Seattle, 1984), by David Lamb, is a best-selling portrait of modern-day Africa, rich in political and social detail. The analysis lacks depth, but for entertainment it's unbeatable. Lamb, who has been twice nominated for the Pulitzer Prize, spent four years travelling to 46 countries, talking to both guerrilla leaders and presidents, and catching midnight flights to report about coups in little-known countries.

Political Economy of Africa (Longman, 1981), edited by David Cohen & John Daniel, is a selection of readings, some with a leftist viewpoint.

Ecology

Africa in Crisis (New Society Publications, Philadelphia, 1986), by Lloyd Timberlake, focuses on the political and environmental factors contributing to drought and famine in Africa and the roles that international aid organisations and African leaders have played in recent environmental disasters.

African Silences (Random House, New York, 1991), by Peter Matthiessen, focuses on Matthiessen's journeys through Zaïre, Gabon, the Central African Republic and parts of West Africa. The most compelling part of this deeply gripping, beautifully written book is his foray with other researchers to make estimates of the number of elephants in the Central African region; the count proved to be smaller than feared.

Travel

Travels in West Africa (1897, reprinted by Beacon Press, Boston, 1988), by Mary Kingsley, is a true classic. It's an engaging travelogue that details this flamboyant woman's two trips through Gabon during the 1890s. Her travels involved sailing up the Ogooué River, crossing 150 km of dense rainforest, dealing with the Fang (reputedly a dreaded cannibalistic tribe at the time) and gathering fish specimens for a museum and all the time facing every calamity with fortitude and good humor.

One Dry Season: In the Footsteps of Mary Kingsley (Alfred Knopf, New York, 1990), by Caroline Alexander, is an engaging book by an intrepid Rhodes Scholar who in 1987 retraced Mary Kingsley's travels in Gabon.

Impossible Journey: Two Against the Sahara (Penguin, New York, 1987), by Michael Asher, is an enthralling account of the first successful west-to-east crossing of the Sahara. Written by a former SAS Englishman travelling with his new Ethiopian bride, it recounts their adventure on camel-back starting in Mauritania and passing through Chad before ending at the Nile. Problems plague them throughout the journey, including dodging bullets in the Sudan.

Through the Dark Continent (Harper & Row, New York, 1878), by Henry Stanley, is the great classic describing Stanley's historic journey down the Zaïre River in the 1870s.

Cookbooks

The Africa News Cookbook (Viking Penguin Inc, New York, and Middlesex, UK, 1985), by Africa News Service Inc, is one of the few African cookbooks in print. This book covers the entire continent and each recipe has been carefully chosen to ensure that all ingredients are obtainable in the West.

A Safari of African Cooking (Broadside Press, Detroit, 1988), was written by a Ghanian, Bill Odarty, and provides 106 recipes, some from Central African countries (Zaïre and Chad).

Magazines

West Africa (West Africa Publishing Co, London), a weekly magazine, has a high reputation for the accuracy of its news.

Jeune Afrique (Le Groupe Jeune Afrique, Paris) is a popular weekly French-Language magazine which covers both Central and West African and world events, from an African perspective.

New African (IC Publications, London & New York), has a reputation for accurate and balanced reporting, with a mix of politics, financial and economic analysis, features on social and cultural affairs, plus country and topic surveys.

Africa News, not found readily on the newsstands, focuses on crucial issues in Africa and is probably the most consistently reliable source of information about Africa in a magazine format. It also has a research centre with over 4000 books mostly on Africa, over 150 periodicals, and 40 cabinets of newspaper clippings, press releases and reports, some quite old. The centre's address is Box 3851, Durham, NC 27702 (☎ (919) 286-0747).

Africa Business (IC Publications, London & New York) is a monthly magazine providing a wide variety of news items, commentaries and feature articles.

Africa (Africa Journal Ltd, London), also a monthly magazine, covers African business, economics and politics.

Economic Digest (Middle East Economic Digest, London) is the best weekly, providing business news, economic analyses and forecasts.

Africa Confidential (Miramoor Publications, London), an expensive twice-monthly publication, is unquestionably the best in giving the inside scoop.

Reference Books

Africa South of the Sahara (Europa Publications, London) is an expensive, respected reference book published annually with over 1100 pages of economic and commercial data, by country.

Africa Contemporary Record (Holmes & Meier, London), published annually, is even more detailed.

Africa Review (Walden Publishing Ltd, Essex, UK, and Alabama, USA) is a more concise (about 235 pages) and affordable (US$85) annual digest of economic and commercial data on African countries, along with general information on the African business environment.

Overseas Bookshops

Bookstores in Central Africa are listed under the individual country chapters. Don't expect to be able to pick up many interesting English books but those in French are abundant, particularly in Yaoundé, Douala and Libreville.

UK One of the country's truly outstanding travel bookshops is Blackwell's in Oxford; check it out. In London, Foyle's (☎ (071) 437-5660; 113 Charing Cross Rd, London WC2H OEB), one block from Cambridge Circus, claims to be the world's largest bookshop. Ask for their Africana section. Their travel section is not good. Waterstone's (☎ (071) 434-4291), next door to Foyle's, is much better for maps and travel guides.

Even better for maps, with a fairly good selection of travel guides as well, is Stanfords (☎ (071) 836-1321), 12 Long Acre St, Covent Garden, London WC2P. It is the official outlet for the Department of Overseas Surveys (DOS maps) and has maps for individual countries in Africa. If you will be driving, buy your maps here.

Africa Bookcentre at the Africa Centre (☎ (071) 240-6649), 38 King St, Covent Garden, London WC2 8JT, has a small book

department and is a good place to get practical first-hand information on Africa. The centre, which is a good place to meet people, also has a reading room open to the public with newspapers and magazines plus exhibitions, cinema, etc. Three other excellent London travel bookshops are The Travel Bookshop (☎ (071) 229-5260) at 13 Blenheim Crescent, London W11; Daunt Books (☎ (071) 224-2295) at 83 Marylebone High St, London W1M 4AL; and The Travellers Bookshop (☎ (071) 836-9132) at 25 Cecil Court, London WC2N 4EZ.

USA In New York City, your best bets for maps and travel guides are Travellers Bookstore (☎ (212) 664-0995), 22 West 52nd St; and Complete Traveller Bookstore (☎ (212) 685-9007), 199 Madison Ave at 35th St. Two stores with good Africana sections are Barnes & Noble (☎ (212) 807-0099), 105 5th Ave at 18th St; and Liberation Book Store (☎ (212) 281-4615), 421 Lenox Ave, corner of 131st St, Harlem.

In Washington, DC, the best store for travel books and maps is Travel Books Unlimited (☎ (301) 951-8533), 4931 Cordell Ave, Bethesda, MD. Downtown, The Map Store (☎ (202) 628-2608), 1636 Eye St, NW, carries Michelin maps of Africa.

In Chicago, The Savvy Traveller (☎ (203) 263-2100), 50 E Washington St, is the city's best-stocked source of guidebooks as well as other travel literature and paraphernalia.

On the West Coast, three stores specialising in travel are Travel Market (☎ (415) 421-4080), 130 Pacific Ave Mall, Golden Gateway Commons, San Francisco; Travel Bookstore (☎ (213) 660-2101), 1514 N Hillhurst, Los Angeles, three blocks east of Hollywood and Vermont; and Phileas Fogg's (☎ (800) 533-3644), 87 Stanford Shopping Center, Palo Alto. Travel Centres of the World, (Box 1788, Hollywood, CA 90078) specialises in travel guides and hard-to-get, detailed maps. Ask them to send you their catalogue.

Canada In Montreal, one of the best travel book stores is Librairie Ulysee (☎ 843-7135) at 1208 St-Denis, Montreal H2X 3JS. Another excellent one is Quillan Travel Store, 4B, 112-11 Ave, SE Calgary, Alberta T2G 0X5. It sells books, maps, videos and travel accessories by mail. Ask for their free travel catalogue indicating your destination. Another is The Travel Bug (☎ (604) 737-1122), 2667 W. Broadway, Vancouver, BC V6K 2G2. It carries many series and will sell by phone or mail. ITMB Publishing (☎ (604) 687-3320), 736A Gransville St, Vancouver, BC V6Z 1G3, has lots of scarce country road maps, but most are from other parts of Africa.

France One of the two largest travel bookshops in France is L'Astrolabe (☎ (01) 4285-495), 46 Rue de Provence, 75009 Paris (metro: Chaussée d'Antin). It has a huge selection of travel books and maps and lots of notices posted by people buying and selling gear and looking for travel partners. The other biggie is Ulysse (☎ (01) 4329-5210), 35 Rue St-Louis en Ile, 75004 Paris (metro: Pont Marie), which is the oldest travel bookshop in Paris and open Tuesday to Sunday from 10 am to 8 pm. Its selection of books is also vast, particularly the section on the Sahara.

Gilbert Joseph (☎ (01) 4325-5716), 26 Blvd St Michel, 75006 Paris (metro: St Michel) also has an excellent selection of maps and travel guides. Hachette Évasion (☎ (01) 4634-8952), 77 Blvd St-Germain, 65006 Paris, has some books not found at Gilbert Joseph. For a late night travel bookshop, try Librairie du Voyageur (☎ (01) 4633-3873) at 3 Rue Blainville, 75005 Paris. It's open every day from 11 am to 11 pm.

If you can't find the maps you want at any of these stores, try the Institut Géographique National. It has an excellent retail shop at 107 Rue la Boétie, 75008 Paris. The selection includes quite recent maps of many former French colonies.

For bookshops about Africa, try Présence Africaine (☎ (01) 4354-1588) several blocks from Gilbert Joseph at 25 bis Rue des Écoles, 75005 Paris. It specialises in serious literature and other books on Africa, many by African authors, but has no travel guides. On the same street (16 Rue des Écoles) you'll find L'Harmattan (☎ (01) 4326-0452), which, with Présence Africaine, are the two best bookshops in Paris focusing primarily on Africa.

Elsewhere in Europe In Holland, your best bet may be Geografische Boekhandel (☎ (020) 121-901), Overtoom 136, 1054 HN Amsterdam. In Germany, try Daerr Expeditionservice GmbH (☎ (089) 903-1519), Hauptstrasse 26, D-8011 Kirchheim/Munich, Ortsteil Heimstetten.

In Belgium, head for Peuples et Continents (☎ 511-2775) at 11 Rue Ravenstein, 1000 Brussels. It's the oldest travel bookshop in Belgium and still the best.

In Switzerland, there are excellent travel bookshops in the three largest cities: La Librairie du Voyageur (☎ 214544) at 8 Rue de Rive, zone 1204 in Geneva; Travel Bookshop (☎ 343883) at 11 Seitergraben, zone 8801 in Zurich; and Atlas Librairie de Voyage (☎ 229044) at 31 Schauplatzgasse, zone 3011 in Bern. They all carry English-language travel books.

Australia In Melbourne the International Bookshop (☎ (03) 614-2859), 2nd Floor, 17 Elizabeth St, probably has the largest selection of books on Africa. In Sydney try Gleebooks (☎ (02) 660-2333), 191 Glebe Point Rd, Glebe.

MAPS

For regional maps, Michelin (No 155 covers most of Central Africa) is definitely the best. If you'll be climbing the Ruwenzori mountains in eastern Zaïre, bring along a copy of *Ruwenzori – Map & Guide* by Andrew Wielochowski (c/o the author, 32 Seamill Park Crescent, Worthing 3N11 2PN, UK, 1989).

FILM & PHOTOGRAPHY
Permits

There are a few peculiarities about taking photographs in Africa. One is photo permits. Most Central African countries, including Cameroun, have dropped the requirement but they are still required in Zaïre, Chad and apparently Equatorial Guinea. Even in those countries, most expats prefer to use discretion rather than going through the hassle of getting one.

As for video cameras, most countries treat them like regular cameras. However, in a few countries such as Equatorial Guinea you may run into problems. The governments' concern is that you may be a commercial film maker, in which case special permission is required virtually everywhere. If you wear a Hawaiian shirt and look like a tourist, you may be more convincing.

Be aware that no-one may photograph militarily sensitive installations anywhere in Central Africa. Depending on the country, this may include most or all government buildings (even post offices!), airports, harbours, the Presidential Palace, the ministry of defence buildings, dams, radio and TV stations, bridges, railroad stations and factories. In short, any photos that might aid a potential coup d'etat. Photographing police officers or military personnel is a major blunder. The problem for tourists is that prohibited areas are rarely put in writing or stated in specific terms. When in doubt, ask first.

In Cameroun, an extra limitation is that you cannot photograph anything potentially embarrassing to the government, such as beggars and deformed people. Other countries prohibit photographs of local religious services. The rules change from country to country. In 'progressive' Cameroun, for example, taking a photo of the Presidential Palace would probably result in confiscation of the offending camera followed by a couple of days of intense interrogation for the photographer.

Photographing People

Every respect must be shown for others' customs and beliefs. In some places the camera lens may be seen as taking away something personal. As for objects, some are sacred and should be treated as such. The golden rule is to ask permission first – and take no for an answer. In some instances,

dress may be important and wearing long pants and removing your shoes in mosques, for instance, may make it more likely that your guests won't object.

While many Africans are sensitive to having their pictures taken, there are also many who enjoy being the subject of photos, especially if you are friendly. There are very few things more valuable to Africans than photographs of the family, relatives and friends. Your promise to send them one will be taken seriously; moreover, it is one of the most appreciated, and yet inexpensive, ways to express your friendship. The great pity is that maybe only one in 10 travellers actually sends that promised photo.

You can make a hit in Africa by bringing along an inexpensive Polaroid camera as a second camera. Despite the poverty everywhere, an instant photo of themselves is valued far more than money. In some instances, it may be the only photo that they have. Imagine a household of 10 or 15 people without even a photo of the head of the household! If you do this, however, you should be keenly aware of the potential impact on future travellers. You don't want to contribute to creating a situation where the locals come to expect foreigners to be carrying Polaroids – in some areas of the world this has happened! For this reason, reserve your Polaroid for situations where you have developed a true friend, not the five-minute acquaintance.

Paying for pictures is highly controversial and I discourage it. Travellers need to be aware of the potential cultural ramifications of their decision on the locals and on future travellers. Don't let your sympathy for Africans' poverty blind you. Will paying affect their future actions and expectations and how they view foreigners? In areas rarely visited by foreigners (ie, most of Central Africa), concerns of this nature are always of extreme importance. By paying for pictures you may be helping to create a situation where the locals come to expect – and beg for – a gift.

On the other hand, in areas visited by thousands of tourists every year such as Foumban and Rumsiki in Cameroun (the only two areas in Central Africa that might fall under this category), if the damage has already been done and Africans ask for a gift (most will), paying will have far less impact. Even in those cases, you'll be showing more respect by talking with your subjects a little before asking permission to take a photograph; some may even forego asking for anything. For instance, if you want to take shots of some crafts people, try chatting to them and take an interest in what they're doing. They may then be delighted if you take a few pictures for free. If they still want a gift, keep it modest.

Photographic Equipment

Film in Africa is expensive – US$7 to US$18 a roll – and only the most widely used film is sold. Also, light conditions vary widely, so bring all the film you'll need and a variety of ASAs (100, 200, 400); for shooting gorillas, 1000 ASA film is best. In Africa, you'll find lots of 100 ASA film and some 200 ASA, but rarely 400 ASA. That's because the sunlight in Africa is frequently very intense. During the rainy season, 200 ASA film is more useful and 400 ASA is probably the best in the rainforest areas.

As for equipment, bring everything with you, especially extra batteries and cleaning equipment. Dust and dirt can get into your equipment, making it filthy in no time. A filter is also a good idea.

Finally, some airports have fairly old model X-ray machines for checking baggage which may not be safe for film. Although many airports now have the newer film-safe models, some travellers bring protective lead bags – they're fairly inexpensive. Those with high-speed film (1000 ASA and higher) may also want to bring protective bags because even the film-safe models are safe only for slow-speed film. Also, the machines have a cumulative effect on the film, so if during your trip you'll be passing your film several times through X-ray machines, they could eventually affect the film. In general, however, I wouldn't worry because I've not yet met a customs official in Africa who wouldn't allow me to carry the film separately to avoid the X-ray.

Photography Tips

For two or three months starting in December, the Harmattan winds cover the skies in northern Central Africa with fine dust particles from the desert. Visibility can on occasion be reduced to one or two km. If photography is a primary reason for visiting Central Africa and northern Central Africa is of particular interest, pick a time other than between the beginning of December and mid-February. In eastern Zaïre, the hazy dry period is June to mid-September.

All too often, pictures of Africans come out with the faces too dark and with little or no detail. The easiest solution is to use a flash. Alternatively, if you use a light metre, the general rule is to open up one or 1½ stops from what the metre reads.

HEALTH

Travel health depends on your predeparture preparations, your day-to-day health care while travelling and how you handle any medical problem or emergency that does develop. While the list of potential dangers can seem quite frightening, with a little luck, some basic precautions and adequate information, few travellers to Central Africa experience more than upset stomachs.

Travel Health Guides

There are a number of books on travel health:

Staying Healthy in Asia, Africa & Latin America, (Moon Publications, USA). This is probably the best all-round guide to carry as it's compact, very detailed and well organised.

Travellers' Health (Oxford University Press), by Dr Richard Dawood, is a comprehensive, easy to read, authoritative and highly recommended book although it's rather large to lug around.

Where There is No Doctor (Hesperian Foundation), by David Werner, is a very detailed guide intended for someone, like a Peace Corps worker, going to work in an undeveloped country, rather than for the average traveller.

Travel with Children (Lonely Planet Publications), by Maureen Wheeler, has basic advice on travel health for children.

Predeparture Preparations

Health Insurance A travel insurance policy to cover theft, loss and medical problems is a wise idea. There are a wide variety of policies and it pays to shop around because prices and coverage vary considerably; your travel agent may also have recommendations. The international student travel policies handled by STA or other student travel organisations are usually good value. Typical costs are UK£70 for 45 days. Check the small print:

• Some policies specifically exclude 'dangerous activities' which can include scuba diving, motorcycling, even trekking. If these activities are on your agenda you don't want that sort of policy.
• You may prefer a policy which pays doctors or hospitals direct rather than you having to pay now and claim later. If you have to claim later make sure you keep all documentation. Some policies ask you to call back (reverse charges) to a centre in your home country where an immediate assessment of your problem is made.
• Check if the policy covers ambulances or an emergency flight home. If you have to stretch out you will need two seats and somebody has to pay for it!

In the USA, check the policies offered by: STA (☎ (800) 777-0112); Travel Assistance International (☎ (800) 222-8472), 1133 15th St, NW, Suite 400, Washington, DC 20008; Travel Insurance Services (☎ (800) 937-1387), Box 299, Walnut Creek, CA 94596; and Travel Guard International (☎ (800) 782-5151), 1100 Center Point Dr, Stevens Point, WI 54481.

In the UK, try STA; Marcus Hearn (65/66 Shoreditch High St, London E1 6JL); and Trailfinders (☎ (071) 938-3366), 46 Earls Court Rd, London W8 6EJ and 194 Kensington High St, London W8 7RJ (☎ (071) 938-3444).

Medical Kit A small, straightforward medical kit is a wise thing to carry. In many countries if a medicine is available at all it will generally be available over the counter and the price will be much cheaper than in the West. A possible kit list includes:

• Aspirin or panadol – for pain or fever.
• Antihistamine (such as Benadryl) – useful as a decongestant for colds, allergies, to ease the itch from insect bites or stings or to help prevent motion sickness.
• Antibiotics – useful if you're travelling well off the beaten track but they must be prescribed and you should carry the prescription with you.*
• Kaolin preparation (Pepto-Bismol) – for mild stomach upsets.
• Imodium or Lomotil – for more severe diarrhoea.
• Rehydration mixture – for treatment of severe diarrhoea, this is particularly important if travelling with children.
• Antiseptic such as Bacetracin, mercurochrome and antibiotic powder or similar dry sprays – for cuts and grazes.
• Calamine lotion – to ease irritation from bites or stings.
• Bandages and Band-aids – for minor injuries.
• Scissors, tweezers and a thermometer – mercury thermometers are prohibited by airlines.
• Insect repellent, sun block, Chapstick, water purification tablets and, if you'll be travelling in the Sahel, salt tablets and petroleum jelly.
• Your prescription medications – store in separate bags in case one is lost or stolen.

* Ideally antibiotics should be administered only under medical supervision and should never be taken indiscriminately. Overuse of antibiotics can weaken

your body's ability to deal with infections naturally and can reduce the drug's efficacy on a future occasion. Take only the recommended dose at the prescribed intervals and continue using the antibiotic for the prescribed period, even if the illness seems to be cured earlier. Antibiotics are quite specific to the infections they can treat; stop immediately if there are any serious reactions and don't use them at all if you are unsure if you have the correct one.

If you must buy drugs during your trip, buy them from a pharmacy that appears in good condition (many are listed in the country chapters) because the storage conditions in some are not the best. Also be sure to check the expiry date on any drugs you purchase. It's possible that drugs which are no longer recommended or have been banned in the West are still being dispensed in many Third World countries.

Health Preparations Make sure you're healthy before you start travelling. If you are embarking on a long trip make sure your teeth are OK because in some areas of Central Africa, a visit to the dentist would be the last thing you'd want.

If you wear glasses bring a spare pair and your prescription. Losing glasses can be a real problem although in many major cities you can get new spectacles made up quickly, cheaply and competently.

If you require a particular medication take an adequate supply as it may not be available locally or under a brand name no-one recognises. Take the prescription, with the generic rather than the brand name, as it will make getting replacements easier. It's a wise idea to have the prescription with you to show you legally use the medication as some pharmacies may require it for certain drugs.

Immunisations Vaccinations provide protection against diseases you might meet along the way. With few exceptions, virtually all countries in Central Africa require that you bring an International Health Certificate with a record of your vaccinations; it's available from your physician or health department.

Plan ahead for getting your vaccinations since some of them require an initial shot followed by a booster while some vaccinations should not be given together. Most travellers from Western countries will have been immunised against various diseases during childhood but your doctor may still recommend booster shots against measles or polio – diseases still prevalent in many developing countries. The period of protection offered by vaccinations differs widely and some are contraindicated in pregnancy.

In the USA, the Center for Disease Control has established a special hotline (☎ (404) 332-4559) for international travellers information, giving details on its recommendations for all sorts of vaccinations, by region. It is easier and cheaper to reach this 24-hour number at a low-toll time, including weekends.

In London, travellers can get all required vaccinations except, possibly, rabies at the Hospital for Tropical Diseases at 4 St Pancras Way, London NW1 0PE (easy bookings and friendly staff) as well as at Trailfinders Immunisation Centre (☎ (071) 938-3999) at 194 Kensington High St. The latter sells first-aid kits too (£13).

A yellow fever vaccination is required to enter most Central African countries and, to a lesser extent, a cholera vaccination although its effectiveness is doubtful. You will also need to take hepatitis and typhoid shots, and anti-malarial tablets. In addition, vaccinations for TB, tetanus, meningitis and polio are recommended for those planning to stay in Central Africa for a while and those travelling on the cheap who may encounter fairly unsanitary conditions.

Yellow Fever Every country in Central Africa requires a yellow fever vaccination, but about half of them waive the requirement if you're arriving directly from North America or Europe. Airport health officials, however, are sometimes unaware of this exemption, so get one anyway. Protection lasts 10 years. In some countries you have to go to a special yellow fever vaccination centre. Regardless of where you get the vaccination, you will need to start the injections about three weeks prior to departure. Vaccination is contraindicated in pregnancy but if you must travel to a high risk area it is probably advisable; check with your doctor. If you're coming from Australia, you'll also need your proof of vaccination to re-enter Australia, but in Europe and North America, there's apparently no such requirement.

Cholera The list of countries requiring a cholera vaccination is constantly in flux as the list tends to expand whenever there's a cholera outbreak in the region. In some countries you must have one if you're coming from an infected area (ie the rest of Africa). The vaccination is not very effective, only lasts six months and is contraindicated for pregnancy.

Tetanus & Diptheria Boosters are necessary every 10 years and protection is highly recommended.

Typhoid This vaccine is advised and will give you protection for three years. It is available in tablet form as well as injection.

Infectious Hepatitis (Hep A) Gamma globulin is not a vaccination but a ready-made antibody which has proven very successful in reducing both the chances of hepatitis infection and its severity should you get it. Because it may interfere with the development of immunity, it should not be given until at least 10 days after administration of the last vaccine needed and as close as possible to departure because its effectiveness decreases rapidly. Even after three months it has lost over 50% of its effectiveness and by six months it's totally worthless. For this reason, getting a shot every four months is better than waiting for six.

A hepatitis A vaccine (brand name Harvix) is now available which provides 100% protection for 12 months (with a course of two injections) or for 10 years (if you also have a third, booster injection).

Basic Rules

Care in what you eat and drink is the most important health rule; stomach upsets are the most likely travel health problem but the majority of these upsets will be relatively minor. Don't become paranoid; trying the local food is part of the experience of travel after all.

Water The number one rule is *don't drink the water* and that includes ice. If you don't know for certain that water is safe always assume the worst and either boil or purify it. The latter is easier as water is sold on the streets everywhere in convenient, see-through plastic bags, which you can purify in a water container. An alternative is to buy mineral water, available in every capital city in Central Africa and quite frequently even in the smaller cities and towns. The typical supermarket price is about US$1.35 per litre;

hotels will sell it for up to three times that amount.

Take care with fruit juice, particularly if water may have been added. Milk should be treated with suspicion as it is often unpasteurised. Boiled milk is fine if it is kept hygienically and yoghurt is always good. Tea or coffee should also be OK since the water should be boiled.

Water Purification The simplest way of purifying water is to thoroughly boil it. Technically this means for 10 minutes, something which happens very rarely! Simple filtering will not remove all dangerous organisms so if you cannot boil water it should be treated chemically. Chlorine tablets (Halazone, Puritabs, Steritabs or other brand names) will kill many but not all pathogens (in particular, giardia and amoebic cysts). Iodine is much more effective in purifying water and is available in tablet form (such as Potable Aqua) but follow the directions carefully and remember that too much iodine can be harmful. Iodine is contraindicated for pregnancy.

You can also use tincture of iodine (2%) or iodine crystals. Two drops of tincture of iodine per litre or quart of clear water is the recommended dosage which should then be left to stand for 30 minutes. After having tried all three methods, I now much prefer the crystals. Kept in a one-ounce glass container filled with water, the crystals last for months (they do not dissolve) and work faster. With tablets, you must wait for them to dissolve, then remember to shake the container, and then wait 10 to 15 minutes before drinking.

Iodine loses its effectiveness if exposed to air or damp so keep it in a tightly sealed container. Flavoured powder will disguise the taste of treated water and is a good idea if you are travelling with children.

If for some reason you may have to drink untreated water, there are two things to remember. First, most water in African cities and towns comes from potable sources. Second, the risk is less in the dry season. The problem is that the water can become contaminated in the pipes. African water systems operate under low pressure so that seepage of sewerage and waste into the pipes is quite possible. This is a much bigger problem during the rainy season.

Food Salads and fruit should be washed with purified water or peeled where possible. It's rare to find a restaurant that soaks its vegetables in an iodine solution. Hotels like the Meridien simply import their vegetables from Europe, but this doesn't avoid potential contamination through handling. Taking vitamin tablets may resist the temptation to eat raw vegetables.

Thoroughly cooked food is safest but not if it has been left to cool or if it has been reheated. Take great care with shellfish or fish and avoid undercooked meat. Ice cream is usually OK if it is a reputable brand name but beware of street vendors, and of ice cream that has melted and been refrozen. If a place looks clean and well-run and the vendor also looks clean and healthy then the food is probably safe. In general, places that are packed with travellers or locals will be fine; empty restaurants are questionable.

In some respects, eating at restaurants may be more risky than eating on the street with your hands. (The opposite is true when street food is eaten with plates and utensils.) Street food is usually safe because the ingredients are purchased daily. (In restaurants, you never know how long fish has been in the refrigerator, and how many power blackouts there have been.)

Nutrition If you don't like African food, if you're travelling hard and fast and therefore missing meals, or if you simply lose your appetite, you can soon start to lose weight and place your health at risk.

Make sure your diet is well balanced. If you eat African food, you don't have to worry because it's very well balanced nutritionally, particularly if you supplement it with fruit. In addition, peanuts and boiled eggs are sold on the street and are a safe way to get protein. Fruit you can peel (bananas, oranges or mangoes for example) are always safe and a good source of vitamins. Try to eat plenty of grains (rice) and bread. If you find you're not eating enough, it's a good idea to take vitamin and mineral supplements.

In the Sahel make sure you drink enough; don't rely on feeling thirsty to indicate when you should drink. Not needing to urinate or very dark yellow urine is a danger sign. Always carry a water bottle with you on long trips. There are people everywhere selling water in plastic bags; put this in your bottle and add the purification tablets. Excessive sweating can lead to loss of salt and therefore muscle cramping. Salt tablets can help but they're not a preventative. Adding additional salt to your food can help and it's available virtually everywhere in Central Africa.

Personal Hygiene Many health problems can be avoided by taking care of yourself. Wash your hands frequently, as it's quite easy to contaminate your own food. Clean your teeth with purified water rather than straight from the tap. Keep out of the sun when it's hot. Avoid potential diseases by dressing sensibly. You can get worm infections through bare feet. You can avoid insect bites by covering bare skin when insects are

---

Vital Signs

A normal body temperature is 37°C, more than 2°C higher is a 'high' fever. A normal adult pulse rate is 60 to 80 per minute (children 80 to 100, babies 100 to 140). You should know how to take a temperature and a pulse rate. As a general rule the pulse increases about 20 beats per minute for each 1°C rise in fever.

Respiration rate (breathing) is also an indicator of illness. Count the number of breaths per minute, between 12 and 20 is normal for adults and older children (up to 30 for younger children, 40 for babies). People with a high fever or serious respiratory illness (like pneumonia) breathe more quickly than normal. More than 40 shallow breaths a minute usually means pneumonia. ■

around or by using insect repellents. Seek local advice regarding bilharzia in rivers and lakes. In situations where there is no information, don't go in.

Medical Problems & Treatment

Potential medical problems can be broken down into several areas. First there are the climatic considerations – problems caused by extreme temperatures. Then there are diseases and illnesses caused by poor sanitation, insect bites or stings, animal or human contact. Simple cuts, bites or scratches can also cause problems.

Self-diagnosis and treatment can be risky, wherever possible seek qualified help. This book gives advice on the best hospitals or clinics in each town. An embassy can also usually advise a good place to go. So can four-star hotels although they often recommend doctors with four-star prices. This is when that medical insurance really comes in useful! In some places, standards of medical attention are so low that for some ailments the best advice is to get on a plane and go to Yaoundé or Libreville.

Climatic & Geographical Considerations

Sunburn In Central Africa you can get sunburnt even through cloud. Use a sunscreen and take extra care to cover areas which don't normally see sun – your feet for example. A hat provides added protection and use zinc cream or some other barrier cream for your nose and lips. Calamine lotion is good for mild sunburn.

Heat Exhaustion Dehydration or salt deficiency can cause heat exhaustion. Take time to acclimatise to the hotter temperatures and make sure you get sufficient liquids. Salt deficiency is characterised by fatigue, lethargy, headaches, giddiness and muscle cramps and in this case salt tablets may help. Vomiting or diarrhoea can deplete your liquid and salt levels.

Heat Stroke This serious, sometimes fatal, condition can occur if the body's heat regulating mechanism breaks down and the body temperature rises to dangerous levels. Long, continuous periods of exposure to high temperatures can leave you vulnerable to heat stroke and you should avoid excessive alcohol or strenuous activity when you first arrive in a hot climate.

The symptoms are feeling unwell, not sweating very much or at all and a high body temperature (39 to 41°C). Where sweating has ceased, the skin becomes flushed and red. Severe, throbbing headaches and lack of coordination will also occur and the sufferer may be confused or aggressive. Eventually the victim will become delirious or convulse. Hospitalisation is essential but meanwhile get the victim out of the sun and give them as much bland fluids to drink as they will tolerate; remove their clothing, cover them with a wet sheet or towel and then fan continually. Be careful not to cool them down too rapidly. If they start to shiver, their core body temperature will rise still further rather than decrease.

Fungal Infections Fungal infections are more of a problem along the coast of Central Africa than in the Sahel and even there, only during the rainy season. They are most likely to occur on the scalp, between the toes or fingers (athlete's foot), in the groin (jock itch or crotch rot) and ringworm on the body. You get ringworm (which is a fungus infection, not a worm) from infected animals or by walking on damp areas, like shower floors.

To prevent fungal infections wear loose clothes, avoid synthetic fibres, wash frequently and dry carefully and wear thongs or sandals into the shower. If you do get an infection, wash the infected area daily with a disinfectant or medicated soap and water and rinse and dry well. Apply an anti-fungal powder like the widely available Tinaderm. Try to expose the infected area to air or sunlight as much as possible and wash all towels and underwear in hot water and change them often.

Diseases of Insanitation

Diarrhoea A change of water, food or climate can all cause the runs but more serious is diarrhoea due to contaminated food or water. You may think that diarrhoea is inevitable, but there are in fact many short term visitors to Central Africa who never get it. It's water – not meat, noodles, rice or African dishes such as *foutou* (mashed plantains) – that is likely to give you diarrhoea. It's also not just drinking water – your Coke and fries may be safe but not the glass or utensils.

Despite all your precautions you may still have a bout of mild travellers' diarrhoea but a few rushed toilet trips with no other symptoms is not indicative of a serious problem. Moderate diarrhoea, involving half a dozen loose movements in a day, is more of a nuisance. Dehydration is the main danger with any diarrhoea, particularly for children, so fluid replenishment is the number one treatment. You'll also need to replace lost minerals in the body, particularly potassium.

Drink large quantities of un-sugared liquids such as tea, bouillon soup and bottled water. A good preparation is: the juice of one orange and a quarter teaspoon of salt together with 250 ml of water. The flow of fluids will also help relieve pains from muscle cramps as well as help to wash out whatever is down there. With severe diarrhoea a rehydrating solution is necessary to replace minerals and salts. You should stick to a bland diet as you recover. Soup, bread, soda biscuits and un-sugared oatmeal (easy to find) are all good.

For normal cases of bacterial diarrhoea, drugs are not recommended except, perhaps, Pepto-Bismol. It's also effective as a diarrhoea preventative. Four tablets a day will reduce your chance of illness significantly. However, it shouldn't be taken for more than three weeks. Lomotil or Imodium can be used in more severe cases; they bring relief from the symptoms although they do not actually cure it. Only use these drugs if absolutely necessary – for example, if you *must* travel – and never take more than the recommended dose. For children, Imodium is preferable. Do not use these drugs if you have a high fever or are severely dehydrated. Antibiotics can be very useful in treating severe diarrhoea especially if it is accompanied by nausea, vomiting, stomach cramps or mild fever.

Giardia This intestinal parasite is present in contaminated water and the symptoms are stomach cramps, nausea, bloated stomach, watery, foul-smelling diarrhoea and frequent gas. Giardia can appear several weeks after you have been exposed to the parasite, the symptoms may disappear for a few days and then return; this can go on for several weeks. Metronidazole known as Flagyl is the recommended drug but should only be taken under medical supervision.

Dysentery This serious illness is caused by contaminated food or water and is characterised by severe diarrhoea, often with blood or mucus in the stool. There are two kinds of dysentery. Bacillary dysentery is characterised by a high fever and rapid development; headache, vomiting and stomach pains are also symptoms. It generally does not last longer than a week, but it is highly contagious.

Amoebic dysentery is more gradual in developing, has no fever or vomiting but is a more serious illness. It is not a self-limiting disease but will persist until treated and can recur and cause long-term damage to the digestive system. The prescribed treatment is Flagyl or Fasigyn (a four-day treatment) followed by a new medicine, Humatin, for seven days.

A stool test is necessary to determine which type of dysentery you have. If you don't know which kind you've got or whether you've even got dysentery, you'll do better with a wide-spectrum antibiotic. A good one is sulfamethoxazole (brand names Bactrin and Septra in the USA). In French Central Africa, a very effective French drug available locally is Ercefuryl. If that's not available, try Centercine. Beware of needle-happy doctors. Africans tend to have an overly high regard for medicines administered by needles and most doctors comply. Medicine taken in pill form is usually just as effective, and safer, with no risk of acquiring AIDS.

Top :   African man (JS)
Bottom :   African woman (JS)

Top :　Flamingoes (GH)
Bottom Left :　Lion (GH)
Bottom Right :　Baboon (TW)

Cholera The cholera vaccine is largely ineffective. The US State Department, for example, no longer gives the shot to any of its overseas employees – even where there's a cholera epidemic! Take it anyway (or at least get your International Health Certificate stamped) because you don't want to take the risk of being jabbed with a dirty needle at the airport or border station. It's a disease that is largely avoided by drinking boiled not local water, so even in areas where there have been recent severe outbreaks (such as Peru and Ecuádor), the number of foreigners getting the disease has been minuscule.

The disease is characterised by a sudden onset of acute diarrhoea with 'rice water' stools, vomiting, muscular cramps, and extreme weakness. It's possible to lose as much as 10% of your body weight within a day through diarrhoea and vomiting. You need medical help, but the initial treatment is always the same: dehydration salts. If there is an appreciable delay in getting to hospital then begin taking tetracycline. This drug should not be given to young children or pregnant women.

Viral Gastroenteritis This is not caused by bacteria but, as the name suggests, a virus and is characterised by stomach cramps, diarrhoea, sometimes vomiting, sometimes a slight fever. All you can do is rest and drink lots of fluids.

Hepatitis Hepatitis A is the most common form of this disease and is spread by contaminated food or water. The symptoms are fever, chills, headache, fatigue, feelings of weakness and aches and pains. This is followed by loss of appetite, nausea, vomiting, abdominal pain, dark urine, light coloured faeces and jaundiced skin; the whites of the eyes may turn yellow. In some cases there may just be a feeling of being unwell, tired, no appetite, aches and pains and the jaundiced effect. You should seek medical advice, but in general there is not much you can do apart from rest, drink lots of fluids, eat lightly and avoid fatty foods. People who have had hepatitis must forego alcohol for

six months after the illness as hepatitis attacks the liver and it needs that amount of time to recover.

Hepatitis B, which used to be called serum hepatitis, is spread through sexual contact, especially male homosexual activity, and through skin penetration (eg dirty needles and blood transfusions). Avoid having your ears pierced, tattoos done or injections where you have doubts about the sanitary conditions. The symptoms and treatment of type B are much the same as type A but gamma globulin as a prophylactic is only effective against type A. There is now a vaccine available for hepatitis A (brand name Harvix) which provides protection for 12 months, or 10 years (if you choose a booster injection as well). There is also a very effective vaccine against Hepatitis B, given as a course of three injections over a six-month period, which is an option for those who know their travel plans well in advance of their trip. The course offers protection for about five years.

Typhoid Typhoid fever is another gut infection that travels the faecal-oral route, ie contaminated water and food are responsible. Vaccination against typhoid is not totally effective and it is one of the most dangerous infections so medical help must be sought.

The early symptoms are like so many others, you may feel like you have a bad cold or flu on the way, headache, sore throat, a fever which rises a little each day until it is around 40°C or more. Pulse is often slow for the amount of fever present and gets slower as the fever rises, unlike a normal fever where the pulse increases. There may also be vomiting, diarrhoea or constipation.

In the second week the high fever and slow pulse continue and a few pink spots may appear on the body along with trembling, delirium, weakness, weight loss and dehydration. If there are no further complications, the fever and symptoms will slowly go during the third week. However, you must get medical help before this as common complications are pneumonia (acute infection of the lungs) or peritonitis (burst appendix) and typhoid is very infectious.

The fever should be treated by keeping the person cool and dehydration should also be watched for. Chloramphenicol is the recommended antibiotic but there are fewer side affects with ampicillin.

Worms These parasites are most common in rural, tropical areas and a stool test when you return home is not a bad idea. They can be present on unwashed vegetables or in undercooked meat and you can pick them up through your skin by walking in bare feet. Infestations may not show up for some time, and although they are generally not serious, if left untreated they can cause severe health problems. A stool test is necessary to pinpoint the problem and medication is often available over the counter.

Diseases Spread by People & Animals

Tetanus This potentially fatal disease is found in undeveloped tropical areas and is difficult to treat but is preventable with immunisation. Tetanus occurs when a wound becomes infected by a germ which lives in the faeces of animals or people so clean all cuts, punctures or animal bites. Tetanus is known as lockjaw and the first symptom may be discomfort in swallowing, stiffening of the jaw and neck, then painful convulsions of the jaw and whole body.

Rabies Rabies is found in many countries and is caused by a bite or scratch by an infected animal. Dogs are noted carriers, but other animals such as monkeys can also put you at risk. Any bite, scratch or even lick from a mammal should be cleaned immediately and thoroughly. Scrub with soap and running water then clean with an alcohol solution. If there is any possibility that the animal is infected, medical help should be sought immediately. Even if the animal is not rabid, all bites should be treated seriously as they can become infected or can result in tetanus. A rabies vaccination is now available and should be considered if you are

in a high-risk category, eg cave explorers (bat bites) or people working with animals.

Meningococcal Meningitis Sub-Saharan Africa is considered the 'meningitis belt' and the meningitis season falls at the time most people would be attempting the overland trip across the Sahara – the northern winter before rains come. This very serious disease attacks the brain and can be fatal. A scattered blotchy rash, fever, severe headache, sensitivity to light and neck stiffness which prevents forward bending of the head are the first symptoms and death can occur within a few hours so immediate treatment is important.

Treatment is large doses of penicillin given intravenously, or, if that is not possible, intramuscularly, ie in the buttocks. Vaccination offers good protection for over one year but you should also check for reports of current epidemics.

Tuberculosis Although this disease is widespread in Central Africa, it is not a serious risk to travellers. Young children are more susceptible than adults and vaccination is a sensible precaution for children under 12 travelling in endemic areas. TB is commonly spread by coughing or by unpasteurised dairy products from infected cows. Milk that has been boiled is safe to drink and the souring of milk to make *lait caillé* (soured milk, available in the Sahel) or yoghurt kills the bacilli.

Bilharzia (Schistosomiasis) Bilharzia or 'schisto' is a disease caused by tiny blood flukes. The worms live in snails found on the edge of lakes or slow-moving rivers (there are few fast-flowing rivers in Central Africa). Inside the snail, they multiply and emerge as free-swimming creatures that, like heat-seeking missiles, home in on humans and other mammals in the water. In as little as five minutes, they can bore painlessly through the skin. Once inside you, most of the blood flukes take up residence in the intestines, where they produce eggs for seven to 30 years. Because most eggs are eliminated (and start the cycle over again), the disease frequently doesn't cause problems other than malnourishment. However, if the eggs end up in the liver or spleen, they can disrupt blood flow and cause the organs to swell. In that case, the disease will be mildly painful and have a very debilitating effect over the years.

Anyone in the mud or shallow water along the edge of a lake or river is vulnerable, which is why you should never enter any freshwater in Central Africa except that which is known to be safe. Even brief contact can lead to infection, so if you fall in accidentally, towel yourself off as quickly and as briskly as possible. However, don't let this scare you from missing out on every opportunity for a cooling dip; ask beforehand. Since the disease requires a human host to complete the cycle, rivers in uninhabited areas, such as remote parks, are at low risk.

The first indication is a tingling and sometimes a light rash around the area where the fluke entered. Weeks later, when the worm is busy producing eggs, a high fever may develop. A general feeling of being unwell may be the first indication but once the disease is established, abdominal pain and blood in the urine are other signs. For a mild case, there may be no clear signs at all, which is why anyone living overseas for a few years must get checked for bilharzia upon return. There is no vaccine and until recently, the only cure was a dangerous treatment with strong dosages of arsenic which killed the worms but, hopefully, not the person. Now a new drug, praziquantel (brand name Biltracide in the USA), clears it up with a single dose of pills.

Diptheria Diptheria can be a skin infection or a more dangerous throat infection. It is spread by contaminated dust contacting the skin or by the inhalation of infected cough or sneeze droplets. Frequent washing and keeping the skin dry will help prevent skin infection. A vaccination is available to prevent the throat infection.

Sexually Transmitted Diseases Sexually transmitted diseases (STDs) are rampant in Africa, even in the lowly populated Sahel. Health officials estimate that 25% of the people in that region, for example, have venereal disease. Among prostitutes it can reach as high as 100% in some areas. Numerous studies confirm that in Africa it is men seeking commercial sex who carry infections from one prostitute to another and eventually their wives and girlfriends. The problem is so serious in Africa that STDs cause far more deaths in women than AIDS does (another STD) in men, women and children combined.

Sexual contact with an infected sexual partner spreads these diseases and while abstinence is the only 100% preventative, use of a condom is also effective. Gonorrhoea and syphilis are the most common of these diseases, and sores, blisters or rashes around the genitals, and discharges or pain when urinating are common symptoms. Symptoms may be less marked or not observed at all in women. The symptoms of syphilis eventually disappear completely but the disease continues and can cause severe problems in later years. Treatment of gonorrhoea and syphilis is by antibiotics.

AIDS AIDS (Sida in French and Spanish) is devastating the adult population of Black Africa. In 1990, the World Health Organisation estimated that the number of adult AIDS cases in Africa was more than half of the world total. It is already one of the leading causes of death in many areas of the continent. A principal reason that AIDS is so deadly in Africa is that STDs, which are rampant in Africa, greatly facilitate transmission of the AIDS virus. One recent study shows that if one partner has AIDS and either partner has a lesion caused by an STD, the chances of getting the virus in a single sexual act are about 40% if a condom isn't used!

As of 1993, the CAR, Zaïre and the Congo were in a list of the 12 African countries with the highest incidence of AIDS. The disease has spread all over Central Africa, the risk being greater in cities than in rural areas, although the difference is diminishing. In

Africa, AIDS is transmitted primarily by heterosexual contact. Many if not most of the prostitutes in the largest Central African cities, such as Kinshasa and Douala, have it. Just avoiding sex with prostitutes is not enough, however, because Africans from all walks of life are known to carry the virus.

Compounding the problem is the presence of a different strain of AIDS virus – HIV-2. Strangely, the highest rate of people testing positive for this virus occurs in isolated Guinea-Bissau, but it is beginning to spread elsewhere. Equally perplexing, it has produced far fewer cases of AIDS than HIV-1, possibly because it doesn't usually cause AIDS. However, some experts speculate that it may have a longer incubation period and just hasn't started producing the disease yet.

Other than sex, the major way of contracting AIDS in Africa is through blood transfusions and injections. Finding safe blood is difficult in Africa because most countries don't screen blood for transfusions and embassies tend to be poor sources of information unless you can get to a medical person. As for injections, avoid them. At a minimum, make sure that a new syringe is used. Buy one from a pharmacy or bring one with you.

There is currently no cure for AIDS. Using condoms is a good preventative but abstinence is the most effective.

Insect Borne Diseases

Malaria Malaria is probably the most serious disease in Africa, yearly affecting about one in five Africans and killing about one million. Most Africans can't afford the preventative treatment, which is why a typical African farmer may have malaria for a quarter of his life.

It is spread by mosquito bites and is usually not fatal. However without treatment, malaria can develop more serious, potentially fatal effects. Moreover, there is a rare type of malaria (falciparum) that is fatal and death can occur in a day or two if not treated immediately. It does not produce immediate symptoms, which is why some travellers have died from it after returning to their homes where doctors, unfamiliar with the disease, incorrectly diagnosed it as a severe flu.

Diagnosing malaria is not easy because it can mimic the symptoms of other diseases, particularly the flu – high fever, lassitude, headache, pains in the joints, and chills. As a rule, the onset is sudden, with a violent, shaking chill followed by a rapid rise in temperature. A headache is common. After several hours of fever, profuse sweating occurs. Even Peace Corps nurses who have seen it many times have difficulty diagnosing malaria, so you should be a little sceptical if someone is 100% certain you've got it. The only sure way to diagnose malaria is by thorough examination of blood smears, but this cannot be done everywhere.

Anti-malarial drugs do not actually prevent the disease but suppress its symptoms. Chloroquine (brand name Aralen in the USA and Nivaquine in France and Central Africa) is the usual malarial prophylactic and consists of a 500-mg tablet taken once a week for two weeks prior to travel, weekly during your trip and six weeks after you return. Chloroquine is quite safe for general use, side effects are minimal and it can be taken by pregnant women. It's also effective for treatment but in larger doses. Most travellers take anti-malarial drugs religiously at first but after arriving in Africa become progressively blasé about it; only an estimated 10% follow this regimen to its conclusion – a mistake.

Unfortunately there is now a strain of the fatal falciparum malaria (plasmodium falciparum) which is resistant to chloroquine and within the last few years, cases have been reported in virtually every Central African country. So cholorquine is no longer completely effective. Fortunately, a new malaria drug, mefloquine (brand name Mefloquin in Europe and Larium in the USA), which is highly effective against chloroquine-resistant malaria, has been approved in most of Europe and, since 1990, in the USA. Its side effects are minimal and are no worse than those of chloroquine. They include, in rare cases, hallucinations, dizziness, nausea, fainting, premature contractions of the heart and vertigo. The primary disadvantage is that it cannot be taken by pregnant women, children weighing less than 15 kg, those taking heart/blood medications and those with a history of epilepsy or a significant psychiatric disorder. Mefloquin should be taken once a week. In the USA, physicians who are not able to find a supply can call ☎ (800) 526-6367 for information.

For those who are intolerant to mefloquine or for whom mefloquine is contraindicated, there are three alternative drugs which are effective to varying degrees against chloroquine-resistant malaria. The best alternative is doxycycline (brand name, Vibramycin in the USA), a tetracycline-based drug which must be taken daily. It cannot, however, be taken by pregnant women or children below age eight, and it causes hypersensitivity to sunlight so sun-burn must be avoided (ie use sun block). For those unable to take mefloquine or doxycycline, the recommendation is proguanil (brand name, Paludrine in the USA), which is weaker than chloroquine and has almost no known side effects. It should be taken daily (200 mg) along with 500 mg of chloroquine weekly; together, they are about two-thirds as effective as mefloquine. Both of these drugs are considered safe in pregnancy and in small children. A final alternative is Fansidar. Because it has so many bad side effects, it is now recommended only for emergency treatment. Moreover, it cannot be taken by pregnant women or people sensitive to sulphur.

All of these drugs act only to suppress malaria; they do not prevent it. The trick to avoiding malaria is not only avoiding mosquitoes but to make the mosquito avoid you, ie not wearing fragrances (perfume, aftershave lotion, etc), avoid dark clothing (they seem drawn to dark colours), cover bare skin and use a good repellent. Fortunately, African mosquitoes are active only at night, so they are less of a nuisance than many travellers expect. Mosquito nets on beds offer protection, as does a burning mosquito coil. The risk of infection is higher in rural areas and during the wet season.

Sleeping Sickness (Trypanosomiasis) In parts of tropical Africa, tsetse flies can carry this disease, which causes physical and mental lethargy. The tsetse fly is about twice the size of the common fly. The main problem is that it kills horses and cattle, leaving large areas of Central Africa with few or no such animals. Swelling at the site of the bite, which occurs five or more days later, is the first sign of infection followed by fever within two to three weeks. Even in areas where tsetse flies are amply present, the risk of infection to short-term visitors is virtually nil, and the illness responds well to medical attention.

Yellow Fever This disease is endemic in Central Africa. The viral disease is transmitted to humans by mosquitoes and the initial symptoms are fever, headache, abdominal pain and vomiting. There may appear to be a brief recovery before it progresses to more severe complications including liver failure. There is no medical treatment apart from keeping the fever down and avoiding dehydration but yellow fever vaccination gives good protection for 10 years and is an entry requirement for Central African countries.

Typhus Typhus is spread by ticks, mites or lice and begins as a bad cold, followed by a fever, chills, headache, muscle pains and a body rash. There is often a large painful sore at the site of the bite and nearby lymph nodes are swollen and painful.

As the name suggests, tick typhus is spread by ticks and trekkers may be at risk from cattle or wild-animal ticks. A strong insect repellent can help and serious walkers in tick areas should consider having their boots and trousers treated.

Bites
Snake Bite Snakes exist almost everywhere in Central Africa but it's rare to hear of a traveller getting bitten. The treatment is as follows: keep the victim calm and still, wrap

the bitten limb tightly, as you would for a sprained ankle, and attach a splint to immobilise it. Then seek medical help. Tourniquets and sucking out the poison are now comprehensively discredited.

Bedbugs & Lice Bedbugs live in various places particularly dirty mattresses and bedding. Spots of blood on bedclothes or on the wall around the bed can be read as a suggestion to find another hotel. Bedbugs leave itchy bites in neat rows. Calamine lotion may help.

Lice all cause itching and discomfort and make themselves at home in your hair (head lice), your clothing (body lice) or in your pubic hair (crabs). They get to you by direct contact with infected people or sharing combs, clothing and the like. Powder or shampoo treatment will kill the lice and infected clothing should then be washed in very hot water.

Other African Maladies

You already know the source of the rumours why you should never go swimming in a lake or a river because you might go blind (from 'oncho', also called 'river blindness' but known more formally as onchocerciasis) or come down with some weird African disease that over a period of time ages you by about 20 years (schisto).

But another malady is the guinea worm. It grows to a meter's length inside the body, then emerges through a skin blister on the leg and is typically extracted by wrapping the worm around a matchstick and carefully pulling it out – over a month's period! Fortunately foreign travellers are usually not at risk.

· You may have also heard that if your clothes aren't ironed or dried in a clothes drier, you'll get worms. It's true. A wet piece of clothing hanging outside to dry is the tumba fly's favourite place to deposit her eggs. If they are not ironed, the eggs will become larvae and bore into your skin. Often a small white spot can be seen at the site of the lesion. Fortunately, the larva always stays just below the surface of the skin. Even

many old African hands don't know how simple the treatment is – put petroleum jelly over the wound to suffocate the worm. It will come out, although a little push may be necessary. Left untreated, these worms become the twice the size of a grain of rice and are quite painful and more difficult to extract.

Foot Problems If you'll be travelling in the desert and you wear sandals, the soles of your feet may get very dry and hard and, as a result, begin cracking. The French call this *le croco*. If this happens, you'll have to change to shoes and socks or use petroleum jelly. If you wait until the cracks go very deep, they can be amazingly painful and become infected. Fortunately petroleum jelly is sold everywhere in Africa.

Women's Health

Gynaecological Problems Poor diet, low resistance due to the use of antibiotics for stomach upsets, and even contraceptive pills can lead to vaginal infections when travelling in hot climates. Keeping the genital area clean, wearing cotton underwear and skirts or loose-fitting trousers will help to prevent infections.

Yeast infections, characterised by a rash, itch and discharge can be treated with a vinegar or even lemon juice douche (ie diluted with water) or with yoghurt. Nystatin suppositories are the usual medical prescription. Trichomonas is a more serious infection with a discharge and a burning sensation when urinating. Male sexual partners must also be treated and if a vinegar-water douche is not effective, medical attention should be sought. Flagyl is the prescribed drug.

Pregnancy Most miscarriages occur during the first three months of pregnancy so this is the most risky time to travel. The last three months should also be spent within reasonable distance of good medical care as quite serious problems can develop at this time. Pregnant women should avoid all unnecessary medication, but vaccinations and malarial prophylactics should still be taken where possible. Additional care should be taken to prevent illness and particular attention should be paid to diet and nutrition.

DANGERS & ANNOYANCES
Mugging
Central Africa used to be one of the safer places in the Third World, and certainly safer than most large cities in the USA. This is no longer the case in four of the countries – Zaïre, Cameroun, the CAR and the Congo. Muggings, not just thefts, in the largest cities in these countries is now a major concern. One contributing factor is that Central Africans, excluding people in Chad and northern Cameroun, drink enormous amounts of alcohol. Warding off sometimes belligerent drunks is a major problem in Zaïre, Gabon, the CAR and the Congo. On the other hand, muggings are almost unheard of in São Tomé, Equatorial Guinea and Chad, and theft is rare except in N'Djamena (Chad).

Walking around Douala (Cameroun), Yaoundé (Cameroun), Brazzaville (the Congo) or Bangui (the CAR) at night is tantamount to inviting a mugging or theft – even more so in Kinshasa. Elsewhere, thieves, not muggers, are the major concern. Travellers are continually being robbed on trains in Zaïre, for example, and increasingly in the city centre of N'Djamena (Chad). The worst that usually happens, however, is a loss of money and papers. Except in Kinshasa, it's still fairly rare to hear of thieves carrying guns, but in the larger cities they are increasingly carrying knives.

On a scale of one to 10 in terms of danger, Douala, Yaoundé, Brazzaville and Bangui would rate seven, three or four for Libreville and less for the remaining cities. Kinshasa (Zaïre) is a special case. It would rate beyond the scale. As long as the situation in Zaïre remains in turmoil, avoid Kinshasa. This includes changing airlines in Kinshasa because taking a cab from the airport to the city centre at night is very risky. Even during the day, people have been dragged out of waiting cars at intersections and killed on the spot. It's far safer to change airlines in nearby Brazzaville. Most people in Kinshasa,

including the locals, simply do not go out at night. Elsewhere in Zaïre, the security situation is generally not so bad. Still, just about anywhere in the country, especially in major cities such as Lubumbashi, Kisangani and Goma, major disturbances can and occasionally do arise, sometimes severe enough to receive international press coverage.

Theft
By any standard, theft is a major problem in virtually all large Central African cities. In Kinshasa, the situation is definitely life-threatening. In some other large cities, as previously noted, theft is accompanied by muggings or the threat of armed violence frequently enough that one must definitely be concerned about those possibilities as well. Women are even more vulnerable.

Many thefts are due to the traveller's lack of foresight. The most common error is forgetting what you've got on. Avoid the temptation of wearing that new gold necklace or watch. Even seasoned veterans in Africa slip up, going to risky areas with jewellery and watches, even passports bulging out of their shirt pockets. Frequently, it's because at the beginning of the evening they didn't expect to end up in the hot district of town. Purse-snatching in the market and near the entrance to restaurants and nightclubs is fairly common everywhere. At nightclubs, you can't dance with your purse and leaving it at the table only invites theft.

My advice is to leave your purse or wallet behind. Either hide your money, take a small pouch bag which can be worn at all times, or wear clothing with lots of pockets – and leave most of your money, passports, IDs, credit cards, even watches at the hotel. It's surprising how few travellers use hotel safety boxes!

The police are less likely to hassle you if you carry a photocopy of your passport but if they do, the worst that usually happens is you have to fetch it or pay a bribe. Better that than to risk having your passport stolen. It's rare to find an expatriate, for example, who carries around a passport except when going upcountry.

A final suggestion is to hire someone to accompany you when walking around a risky area. It's usually not too difficult to find a kid hanging around who wouldn't mind picking up a bit of money warding off potential molesters.

Sexual Harassment

A frequent complaint of Western women living in Africa, particularly single women, is sexual harassment. You may have an 'admirer' who won't go away, or a border official may abuse you verbally. Rape, on the other hand, is statistically insignificant, perhaps in part because Black African societies are not repressive sexually.

One reason for such harassment is that Western women are frequently viewed as being 'loose'. Dress is sometimes a factor. Although you'll see African women in Western clothes in the larger, more modern cities of Central Africa, most still dress conservatively, usually wearing long skirts. When a visitor wears something significantly different from the norm, she will draw attention. In the mind of the potential sexual assailant, she is dressing peculiarly. He may think she's asking for 'peculiar' and aggressive treatment.

In general, the problem of dress is easy to resolve; look at what other women are wearing and follow suit. Long pants are usually not a problem but long dresses are much better. If you want to wear shorts, bring along a wrap-around skirt to cover them when you're in public. Going braless is ill-advised.

If you're in an uneasy situation, my advice is to act prudish – stick your nose in a book. Another method is to invent an imaginary husband who will be arriving shortly either in the country or at that particular spot. Or, if you are travelling with a male companion, introduce him as your husband.

Legal Problems

Travellers should be aware that if they get into serious legal problems, there is one US law firm in Central Africa that may be able to help – Mitchell, Friedlander & Gittleman (128 Ave Uganda, Kinshasa 1, Zaïre, ☎ 30659; fax 27730; telex 21340), which has its headquarters in Washington, DC (☎ (202) 835-0720). Staffed with US and Zaïrian attorneys, they are involved primarily in commercial law, helping companies set up operations and the like. Even outside Zaïre, they can assist in civil and criminal matters by recommending lawyers in other Central African countries and working collaboratively with them.

ACTIVITIES

One of the secrets of meeting people in Africa is to look for activities in which they're involved. Sport is one way to meet Africans but you've got to be a little selective. You're not going to find many Africans on sailboards or on the golf links. Football (soccer), basketball and tennis, on the other hand, are favourite African sports. Also, hiking and cycling are excellent ways to meet Africans in small villages.

Hiking & Rock-Climbing

Most of Central Africa is rainforest, presenting lots of opportunities for bush whacking in flat areas but not so many for hiking in areas with views. There are, however, several hilly, non-jungly areas that are great for hiking. The two most popular areas are northern Cameroun between Rumsiki and Mora and eastern Cameroun around Bamenda. Another good hiking area, rarely visited, is the mountainous area in the southern third of Bioko Island, Equatorial Guinea.

In Central Africa there are also mountain-climbing possibilities. The most popular and accessible mountain for climbing is Mt Cameroun (4070 metres), an hour's ride west of Douala. A greater challenge and far more spectacular, however, are the snowcapped Ruwenzori mountains in remote eastern Zaïre, the highest mountain range in Africa. They are nicknamed the 'Mountains of the Moon' in part because of their snowcapped peaks which tower just above the tropical forests. The highest point, Elizabeth Peak (5119 metres) on Mt Stanley, is the third-highest peak in Africa (Kilimanjaro and Mt Kenya are higher).

To the south closer to Lake Kivu are the active volcanoes of Nyiragongo (3470 metres) and Nyamulagira (3056 metres). They offer some wonderful views of Lake Kivu and the Ruwenzoris and are climbed quite frequently by travellers. Another major volcano is the 3106-metre Mt Malabo on Bioko Island in Equatorial Guinea but it's rarely climbed, in part because government permission is required before it can be visited.

The best place for technical rock-climbing is northern Cameroun, particularly Mindif which is south of Maroua. There's a huge rock 'La Dent de Mindif' jutting up out of nowhere that is so difficult to climb as to attract, reportedly, a Japanese TV network to film an ascent by a Japanese team. Two other rock formations with sheer walls requiring ropes, etc to scale are the protruding rock just north of Rumsiki and another at Hadjer el Hamis, on the eastern side of Lake Chad. Both have routes of varying difficulty.

Of the 10 better hiking and climbing areas in the following list, only the first five are frequently visited:

1. Ruwenzori mountains, eastern Zaïre
2. Nyiragongo and Nyamulagira volcanoes, eastern Zaïre
3. Mt Cameroun west of Douala, Cameroun
4. Area between Rumsiki and Mora, northern Cameroun
5. Area north-east of Bamenda, western Cameroun
6. Mt Malabo, Bioko Island, Equatorial Guinea
7. Mountainous area in the southern third of Bioko Island, Equatorial Guinea
8. Lac Bleu and Léfini Park, central Congo
9. Sangha Reserve, south-western CAR (involves days of stalking wildlife with Pygmy guides)
10. Rainforest area east of Bomassa, northern Congo (also involves stalking wildlife with Pygmy guides)

Cycling

It's fairly rare to see foreigners travelling around Central Africa on bicycles but on my latest trip, I met one in the CAR who was on his way from Kenya to Sudan via Central Africa. In many ways riding a bike is the best way to travel. Cyclists tend to make contact with locals much more easily than do other travellers. The appearance of a lone foreigner entering a village on a bicycle creates much more attention than the same individual hopping off a bus. And of course you see a lot more of the countryside.

The roads in much of Central Africa are not the best but most countries are connected by all-weather dirt roads. The main problems are the long distances and rain. The best time to ride a bike north of the equator is in the dry winter period from mid-October through February. South of the equator, June to September is the best time. People in villages and small towns are occasionally willing to rent their bicycles for the day to travellers; the market is a good place to ask.

Anyone in the UK considering doing some serious cycling in Central Africa should contact and/or join The Cyclist's Touring Club, Cotterail House, 69 Meadow Godalming, Surrey, GU7 3HS; it has lots of good information for members only, including information on crossing the Sahara by bicycle. Cyclists in the USA should contact the International Bicycle Fund, 4887 Columbia Dr South, Seattle, Washington 98108, USA. A low-budget, socially-conscious organisation, it conducts two annual, two-week bicycle tours in Cameroun, one in the west and one in the north, usually in December. It also publishes a book specifically on cycling in Africa, as well as information on cycling in Cameroun.

Soccer & Basketball

Bring along a deflated football (soccer) for a village family, a boy or group, and you'll be the hit of the day. If you want to play, the universities and municipal stadiums are by far the best places to find a game.

After soccer, basketball is Africa's second most popular sport and for travellers it's one of the best ways to meet Africans because foreigners are usually warmly welcomed in friendly matches.

Hash House Harriers

This is a jogging group of sorts which started back in 1939 when a bunch of Aussies in Malaysia began meeting to run through rice paddies and anywhere else so as to build up a thirst for drinking more beer. It's now an international organisation; in Central Africa there are groups only in Cameroun (Yaoundé, Douala, Bamenda and Garoua).

The runs, typically once a week on a Saturday or Monday, are not so tough as to prohibit non-joggers from participating. They run through African villages, through corn fields and in the hills, sometimes on city streets – anywhere. Since the starting point changes on each run, the only way to find the Hash is to ask around the expatriate community or call the British Embassy or marine guards at the US Embassy. But beware – the beer-drinking rituals afterwards are as important as the run.

Tennis, Squash & Swimming

You'll find tennis courts and swimming pools in many cities with populations over 100,000 and occasionally in smaller cities as well; Zaïre is the exception as there are many large cities without pools or tennis courts. Most facilities are at the major hotels and even if you're not a guest, you can usually use them – for a small price, of course. Squash is only available in Gabon (Libreville, Port-Gentil) and Zaïre (Kinshasa).

Golf

The best course in Central Africa is in Yaoundé; the greens are dark sand but the mountainous setting is quite impressive. The only other cities with golf courses, all with sand greens, are Libreville, Brazzaville, Kinshasa and Bangui.

Fishing

For most travellers, deep-sea fishing is prohibitively expensive, costing well over US$100 a day per person. For those still interested, the countries where most deep sea fishing enthusiasts head for are the Congo and Gabon. Tarpon is the major attraction. Charter boats are available in Libreville and Pointe-Noire. The season for tarpon in these countries is December to February. Surf-casting is also popular in the Congo south of Pointe-Noire.

The major agencies offering special fishing trips are located in Paris:

Au Coin de Pêche
  50 Ave de Wagram, 75017 Paris; its prices are lower (☎ (01) 4227-2861, 4227-4168)
Jet Tours
  Departement Chasse et Pêche, 19 Ave de Tourville, 75007 Paris; it offers one-week fishing trips to Gabon. Prices range from about 10,000 to 20,000 FF depending on the numbers, with a maximum of four (☎ (01) 4602-7022, 4705-0195)
Orchape
  6 Rue d'Armaille, 75007 Paris (☎ (01) 4380-3067, 4754-7857; telex 640771).

Other Water Sports

Sailboards are available for rent only in Libreville (Gabon) and Pointe-Noire (Congo). There are sailing clubs in some cities along the coast, but renting a boat is virtually impossible except in Pointe-Noire, where Hobie Cats are available from the local club. The only place noted for diving is Praia das Conchas on São Tomé; scuba equipment is available for rent.

HIGHLIGHTS

There are a number of factors to consider when planning an itinerary, particularly if you intend to travel to several countries. Basically, there are two environments – the hot tropics which cover most of the area, and the dry savannah area of northern Cameroun, the southern half of Chad, and northern CAR. Cameroun and the CAR are the only two countries with both environments. Although there is desert in northern Chad, just north of N'Djamena, very few travellers see that area because of the logistical difficulties; the great distances in getting there are, to say the least, daunting.

At the great risk of creating controversy, I have given my own assessment of 15 places in Central Africa that travellers seem to find the most fascinating. Fortunately, these areas are not yet overrun with travellers although some receive far more than others. Just don't lose sight of the fact that while Central Africa certainly has an abundance of natural beauty which rivals anything in East Africa, the people are more interesting than things and places.

Some environments are unique and particularly interesting; the Ruwenzori mountains of eastern Zaïre and the Rumsiki area of northern Cameroun are examples. These places are all discussed in detail in the country chapters. My list of the top places, most of which are in Zaïre and Cameroun, follows (random order):

Ruwenzori mountains
    eastern Zaïre (mountain-climbing)
Virunga National Park
    eastern Zaïre; includes Djomba Gorilla Sanctuary
Rumsiki area
    northern Cameroun; includes Mora and Maroua (famed for their markets), the much-photographed Pic de Rumsiki and great walking in the Mandara mountains
Sangha Wildlife Reserve
    south-western CAR; contiguous with virgin rainforest and Pygmy area in northern Congo, east of Bomassa
São Tomé Island
    beautiful beaches, excellent snorkelling
Western Cameroun
    includes Foumban (Bamoun chief's compound), Bamenda (hiking and camping) and Ring Rd
Zaïre and Oubangui Rivers
    Zaïre (river-boat trips)
Tibesti mountains
    northern Chad; generally inaccessible, but spectacular desert scenery

Runners-up include (random order):

Lake Kivu area
    eastern Zaïre; includes Nyamulagira and Nyiragongo volcanoes and Kahuzi-Biéga Gorilla Sanctuary
Waza Game Park
    northern Cameroun; (game-viewing)
Bioko Island
    particularly the mountainous southern region (mountain-climbing)
Kribi Beach
    south-western Cameroun
Mt Cameroun-Limbe area
    south-western Cameroun; (hiking and climbing)
Pygmy areas
    particularly around Epulu and Mt Hoyo, eastern Zaïre
Lubumbashi area
    southern Zaïre

FOOD

The food is definitely one of the most interesting aspects of Central African culture. One of the biggest mistakes many travellers make to Central Africa is to not get interested in African food. You may see women on the streets cooking mysterious globs with strange looking sauces in huge pots and decide, by looks alone, to write off African food.

In some cities such as Pointe-Noire (Congo), one of the 'in' places of many expatriates (never reputed for their willingness to take risks) is an African restaurant. African food is also usually safer than Western food because it's usually cooked much longer (sometimes all day) and the ingredients, except for the staple (rice, etc), are invariably fresh that day. Restaurant food, on the other hand, may have been sitting in a refrigerator for some time. Safety-wise, I'd pick African food any day.

If a sensitive stomach is your problem, don't worry. If you stick, at least initially, to less exotic dishes you'll be fine. I've yet to meet a traveller who didn't like, for instance, *Senegalese poulet yassa* or braised chicken or fish dishes from one of Yaoundé's chicken houses. My mother, who has the most sensitive stomach in the world, can testify to this. African food is by no means always hot. Dishes with peanut sauce are usually quite mild. The quality of food is fairly consistent throughout Central Africa. Except in northern Chad, rainfall is generally more than adequate everywhere, producing a wide variety of food and spices. Gabon is unique in that many of the cooks in African restaurants are not Gabonese, so the best African restaurant food in that country tends to be non-Gabonese.

The best place to find good African food is at somebody's home. The second-best place is frequently on the street corners where many women earn their reputations as terrific cooks. In general, the more varied the ingredients, the better. This also increases the cost slightly. The inferior cooks are those who skimp on the ingredients so that they can charge slightly lower prices to attract customers.

African restaurants are a mixed bag. The expensive ones usually cater to foreigners and, with few exceptions, should be avoided. Many of the best places are no-name holes-in-the-wall, hardly deserving to be called restaurants. Ask the locals to recommend the best place in town. The best usually cost only marginally more than the worst, so you might as well look for the best. The search is half the fun. It's important to remember that seafood may not be fresh at inland restaurants in which case it is best avoided. If you're a lover of fish dishes, order them when you're in a place close to the coast, or eating at the top restaurants in inland towns.

The great variety of ingredients is what makes African food interesting. Africans eat very well if they have enough money to buy lots of ingredients. If you want to sample the best, make friends with an African woman

Sauces

Sauces are the heart of African cuisine and each country has its own specialities. The spices commonly found in Cameroun, for example, can differ widely from those in Zaïre. Because groundnuts (peanuts) are grown almost everywhere in Central Africa, groundnut sauce is fairly common. Peanut butter can be used as the main ingredient. As for desserts, they are not a part of traditional African cuisine, however, fresh fruits are sometimes eaten afterwards.

Many of the African sauces are difficult to duplicate outside Africa for lack of the proper spices. Four recipes and a drink which require no special ingredients are listed below.

Fish/Chicken with Mwamba Sauce (Zaïre)

fish or one chicken
3-4 cups of water or stock
2 medium onions
½ green pepper
2 hot chillies, crushed, or 1 teaspoon cayenne pepper
several celery leaves
2 cloves garlic
½ teaspoon nutmeg
1 small tin tomato paste
1½ cups peanut butter
½ cup oil
1 teaspoon salt

Fry the oil until it starts to change colour, then add vegetables and fry until brown. Add nutmeg and tomato paste and cook for another two minutes. Pour the water or stock in a saucepan, add the fried mixture, salt and peanut butter, then bring to boil, stirring constantly. Separately, braise your fish or chicken, then add to the sauce and gently boil until the sauce thickens (about one hour). Serve with rice. Serves four to six.

Okra & Greens (Gabon)

16 okra
450 grams turnip/collard greens
1 finely chopped onion
½ cup palm (or pine) nuts
4 hot chilli peppers, crushed
2 dessertspoons oil
salt to taste

This is a hot side dish; you may want to reduce the peppers or use two teaspoons cayenne pepper instead. Any greens will do. Sauté onions until golden brown. Add remaining ingredients plus ¼ cup water. Cover skillet and simmer until tender (roughly 20 minutes). Serves four to six.

and then give her some money (what you would have spent in a restaurant) to make a meal. You won't be imposing because she can make a terrific meal and, at the same time, feed not only you but whoever else she normally feeds. If you're curious about African ingredients and spices, accompany her to the market. Most African food is quite hot, but as you get closer to the desert, you'll find fewer hot dishes.

If someone tells you they don't like African food, it's more likely due to the texture or excessive pepper than to the taste. The pepper can sometimes be controlled as the hot sauce is frequently offered as a side dish. As for the texture, a number of African dishes are made with okra (*gombo*) – the result is a slimy concoction. In the rural environment you may be eating local style (with your hands) in which case it's like

Spinach Stew (the CAR)
2 lb (900 grams) spinach
2 small onions, finely chopped
2 peeled tomatoes
1 green bell pepper, chopped
2 hot chillis, crushed, or 1 teaspoon cayenne pepper
1/3 cup peanut butter
2 dessertspoons oil
1 teaspoon salt

Sauté the onions in oil until golden brown then stir in remaining ingredients, except for peanut butter, and simmer for five minutes. Thin the peanut butter with several tablespoons of warm water to make a paste, then add to the pot and cook another 15 minutes or so. If it begins to stick add small amounts of water. Serve with rice. Serves six.

Groundnut Stew (Central African Style)
l chicken, cut into pieces
1 pint (600 ml) chicken stock
2 large onions, chopped
3 or 4 fresh tomatoes
2 cups okra
2 hot chillies, crushed, or 1 teaspoon cayenne pepper
2½ cm piece of ginger, crushed
3/4 cup peanut butter
1/3 cup oil
1 teaspoon salt

Cut the chicken into cubes. In a large heavy pot, brown chicken in hot oil, then add stock, onions and seasonings, cover and boil for 20 minutes then reduce the heat. In another pan, boil the tomatoes and okra. Then add this and remaining ingredients to the stew and bring to a boil, stirring vigorously to avoid sticking. Reduce the heat and simmer until chicken is well done. Serve with rice. Serves four.

Ginger Beer
ginger (12 pieces)
1 unpeeled pineapple
2 litres boiling water
sugar to taste

Beat ginger, add pineapple with peeling, pour boiling water over, let stand overnight, then strain, add sugar and chill. ■

dipping your hand into a bowl of raw eggs. There are any number of staples with which this can be eaten. One is banana *foutou*; another is *fufu*. The former is basically a glob of mashed plantains (cousins of the banana) and cassava, the latter a glob of fermented cassava. (Picture mashed potatoes mixed with gelatin and very sticky.) You grab a portion (with your right hand) and dip it in the sauce while forming a ball.

If you're turned off by slimy okra, you won't be the only one. Lots of people who love African food aren't particularly fond of it either. There is a much greater variety of African dishes than most foreigners come across. Because okra dishes (*eg sauce gombo avec viande*) are plentiful on the streets, it's easy to get the false impression that there's not much else.

African food typically consists of a staple plus some kind of sauce. The preferred staple everywhere is rice; it is also more expensive because much of it has to be imported. Cassava, however, is more common and cheaper. It's cooked and mashed into a sticky white mound resembling bread dough. Eaten with a tasty sauce, it can be surprisingly good.

DRINKS
Alcohol
While African cuisine is not everybody's cup of tea, everybody agrees that African beer is good by any standard. It is certainly better than the watery stuff in the USA and cheaper than that in Europe. It's even good in remote places, such as Chad. There may be a war going on there, but the Gala brewery keeps putting it out. In all there are roughly a dozen different beers brewed in Central Africa, about half coming from Cameroun.

In Zaïre, tourists say that Primus beer is as good as or better than what they're accustomed to drinking at home. Part of the reason may be that the brewery in Zaïre is partially owned by Heineken. While everyone has their own favourite beer, the best in Central Africa are reputed to be Gala and Primus.

Unfortunately alcoholism is a serious problem in Central Africa, especially in

Gabon and Equatorial Guinea. Gabonese spend an estimated 12% of their disposable incomes on alcohol and it appears to be even higher in Equatorial Guinea.

In Zaïre, the CAR, Congo and southern Cameroun, beer halls are everywhere. In Central Africa, being able to hold your liquor is the first thing every Peace Corps volunteer must learn. And you've got to learn to start drinking at 8 am!

Home-made brew is popular everywhere, even in Muslim areas. Two of the most popular are palm wine, which tends to be whitish in colour, and banana wine, which is clearer; both are drunk in villages throughout the rainforest areas of Central Africa. You'll see them sold in jugs along the roads. Palm wine is made from juice tapped from palm oil trees. It contains yeast and is allowed to ferment overnight. Closer to the Sahara where the climate becomes too dry for palm oil and banana trees, the cheaper millet beer is drunk.

Nonalcoholic Drinks
Ginger Beer There's one non-alcoholic drink, loosely called ginger beer (in English), that is consumed so much throughout all of Africa that it could almost be called the continental drink of Africa. It's made with so much ginger that it burns the throat and is too strong for many foreigners. In remote villages they may have nothing else to offer you. The name changes from area to area and ethnic group to ethnic group. Be wary, however, as the water is frequently contaminated because it's not distilled and rarely boiled.

MARKETS
In Central Africa, the most colourful markets tend to be in the northern half, particularly in Cameroun (eg Yaoundé, Foumban, Maroua and weekly markets in some of the smaller towns such as Mora) and Chad, most notably N'Djamena and the Sunday market in Linia. But you won't be wasting your time at some of the lesser markets. Those in small towns frequently offer a surprisingly large variety

of items, some not found in the larger markets, and can be quite fun.

Hassling

Most travellers love the markets, but a few find them extremely intimidating or annoying experiences – people grabbing you by the arm and not-so-gently pulling you over to the stall *pour voir seulement* (just to see). This is more of a problem in West Africa than Central Africa; still, it does occasionally occur in the larger markets such as in Yaoundé and in Bangui. Theft in these markets is also a major problem. If you're hesitant about the larger markets, start with the smaller ones.

As for strategies in dealing with overly persistent traders, if you are really not looking for anything in that section, say no and move on. If they keep pulling you and you find it really offensive, let them know in no uncertain terms – if your actions are clear, they'll stop most of the time. The problem is that one tends to get mad and ends up not seeing much. My recommendation is to go along with the flow. Head towards the stall so they no longer have any reason to pull you. Give things a good look and leave from there. Above all, try to view it as a game.

Bargaining

Bargaining, of course, is the name of the game. Most travellers expect the initial price to be three times the 'real' price. This is usually true, but not always. With African cloth sold by the yard, for example, you can expect little or no lowering of the price. The same is true of gold and silver. If the lady tells you the price and you come back with an offer one-third that amount, don't be surprised if she becomes extremely annoyed, folds up the material and refuses to talk further. Try to get a feel for prices beforehand. Ask knowledgeable locals or check out one of the hotel shops; prices in the market are typically half those in the stores.

Posting Your Purchases

No-one likes to lug around souvenirs, so mail them back. Shipping is actually fairly reliable. Purchases not exceeding US$25 in value that are mailed to the USA enter duty-free, and you may bring with you goods worth up to US$400 in value without paying duty. This also includes all mailed purchases.

Keep in mind that many developed countries do not charge duty on goods from underdeveloped countries to help them improve their export trade. In the USA, under the Generalised System of Preferences (GSP), goods from most countries of Central Africa are exempt from duty. The major exceptions to this are textiles and shoes; gold, silver and jade have certain restrictions in terms of duty-free treatment.

For information on exporting ivory and antiques, see the Customs section earlier in this chapter.

THINGS TO BUY

If you like art, particularly masks and wooden statues, there is a greater selection of such art in Central and West Africa than in the rest of Africa.

Masks are as imaginative, and frequently amusing or terrifying, as anything you've dreamed. You can buy silver and gold jewellery as well as beads at prices far below what you'd pay elsewhere, and there is a fascinating assortment of spears, musical instruments, agricultural tools, etc. These are just some of the reasons you might get hooked on African art. Yet African art is an acquired taste.

Two suggestions: before arriving, buy a book on African art (see the Books section earlier in this chapter) and, after arriving, go to an art museum (almost every capital city has one) or a good art shop. In Yaoundé, for example, go to the Musée d'Art Camerounais at the Benedictine monastery near the Mt Fébé hotel; it has some of the finest woodcarvings in Central Africa. In Libreville, see the museum near the US Embassy. Then you'll have some standard of comparison.

There's also a maturing process regarding taste – what you may find interesting at first may not appeal to you later. You're likely to get tired of the cheaper, mass-produced items very quickly. So when travelling, it's a good idea to save shopping for the latter part of the trip.

Knowing the context in which an object is used is important in terms of both appreciation and in detecting artificially used or aged pieces. Unlike Western art, almost all African art has a use. Masks, for instance, are for dances. Half the interest in a piece is sometimes knowing just how it is used. A knife may seem like any other knife until you learn, for example, that it's used only for circumcision. I know one couple who collect the small pieces of woven jewellery (called *caches sexes*) which cover peoples' private parts.

Woodcarving

Masks are sold all over Central Africa and are not cheap unless mass-produced. Other wooden objects include charms, African game boards, carved doors, latches, figurines and boxes. Each area has its own specialities.

Africans are extremely clever when it comes to artificially ageing wooden objects and making them appear used. Even museum curators can be fooled by a mark made by

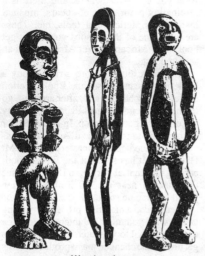
Woodcarvings

sandpaper rather than normal wear. Furthermore, after learning that 'old' for most wooden objects usually means nothing older than 40 to 50 years (they deteriorate rapidly in Africa unless specially protected), you may wonder what all the fuss over age is about anyway.

What's old and used will invariably bring a much higher price than what's new. But that doesn't mean all pieces made today are aesthetically inferior (although most are); they just don't have the wear. In a totally different category are most of the wooden carvings sold on the streets today. They are mass-produced and rubbish. Purchasing them only encourages the artisans to churn out more. Why not save your money and buy a single decent piece, thereby encouraging the artists to do quality work?

Prices of pieces that are not mass produced, like all art, can be pretty subjective. The only way to learn the price range is to ask knowledgeable locals or expatriates, or visit a fancy store and then bargain for one-third to one-half less at the local market (beware, however, the quality may be inferior).

Two major concerns with all wooden objects from Central Africa are cracking and beetles. Buy a new woodcarving and you may find it cracked by the time you get home. New wood must be dried slowly. Wrapping in plastic bags with a small water tray enclosed is one technique. If you see tiny bore marks with white powder everywhere, it means the powder post beetle (frequently confused with termites) is having a fiesta. There are three remedies – zap the buggers in a microwave oven, stick the piece in the freezer for a week, or drench it with lighter fluid.

Gold & Silver

In Central Africa, gold and silver are sold by the gram and the art work is included in the price. The artistry is decent but not exceptional and most people are more than pleased with the results. Prices have been very stable over the past decade, gold selling for around CFA 4500 (US$16) a gram and silver for around CFA 500 (US$2) a gram (more if the quality is superior). Despite what you may hear to the contrary, prices vary little from country to country. Quality is not a serious problem with gold, so getting cheated with the carats is fairly rare. The jewellers want you to return, and just because you don't speak French doesn't mean they won't believe you're a long-term resident. If you do get cheated, some countries have laws and you can return the goods.

With silver, quality is a major problem and this is why some people prefer to stick with the more expensive gold. The problem is that silver in most of Central Africa is not sterling. It tends to tarnish quickly, so that it has to be cleaned fairly regularly.

Painting
Painting is not an indigenous African art form. Nevertheless, in Kinshasa and Brazzaville, there are several well-established schools of art where you can pick up some interesting, good quality oil paintings, many with geometric designs, by young professors. See the individual country chapters for more details.

Beads
For Africans, beads are often more than simple adornment. They are used to create objects representing spiritual values vital to the community and can play major roles in community rituals such as birth, circumcision, marriage and death. Like all African art objects, they can acquire more importance than may be initially appreciated.

You'll find beads all over Central Africa but not to the same extent as in West Africa. In the markets, they are sold by the string, with one type of bead per string, while in the shops you can sometimes find ready-made necklaces with a variety of beads. The markets in Cameroun, particularly Yaoundé and Maroua, are some of the best. Several hundred major bead styles are sold in Africa, including a variety of glass beads and shells. Prices vary considerably and some beads are quite expensive. Most travellers don't realise that you can go to the market and have a necklace made to order. The vendors will usually string them for you on the spot.

The most common of all African beads is the glass bead, which was quite rare in Africa until the arrival of Europeans. Highly decorative beads from Venice featuring flowers, stripes and mosaic designs appealed particularly to the Africans' love of bright colour. Intrigued by the Venetian beads, some African artisans began making their own. Although Africans knew how to make glass before the arrival of Europeans, they found it easier to use discarded European bottles and medicine jars, which they pulverised into a fine powder. Many glass beads are tiny and sold by the pound, hence their name of pound beads. Today, the Nupe of Bida in central Nigeria, for example, wind molten glass on long iron rods to make beads and bracelets.

However, many of the beads you'll see in African markets, particularly the chevron beads, still come from Europe.

A variety of other elements are used in making beads, particularly cowrie shells in Central Africa but also amber, coral, copal, amazonite, silver, gold and brass. Poorer women sometimes have to make do with cheaper elements, such as plastic beads and imitation amber beads.

For publications on African beads, contact Picard African Imports (☎ (408) 624-4138), 9310 Los Prados Lane, Carmel, CA 93923, USA. They have six pamphlets for sale.

Malachite Jewellery
All over Central Africa you'll find beautiful dark green malachite jewellery, which comes from the southern Shaba region of Zaïre. The price is as low as you'll find anywhere in the world and it makes an excellent substitute for ivory.

Baskets
Because of their bulkiness, baskets are not a hot souvenir item with travellers. Some of the best are found in western Cameroun.

Sandstone
Sandstone is not something you'll find in

most of Central Africa. However, in Gabon there's heaps of it, occasionally well carved.

Gourds

The northern regions of Central Africa abound in gourds, sometimes carved with interesting designs. Those from Cameroun are the best.

Leather & Reptile Skins

The best place for leather goods is northern Cameroun, particularly Maroua. As for reptile skins, avoid items made from crocodile skins because crocodiles are being slaughtered on a massive scale in Africa and worldwide, and many countries including the USA have laws prohibiting the importation of items made from such skins.

Ivory

After years of witnessing the wholesale slaughter of the elephant, the world finally came to its senses in 1990. In that year almost 100 countries began honouring an international ban on ivory trade, including Australia (long before the ban), Canada, the USA, Japan and virtually all European countries, among others. The ban has been amazingly effective. Within a year, ivory prices (from US$70 to US$100 a pound before the ban) had tumbled by as much as 80%. In the USA, for example, imports have dropped to near zero and the market has virtually collapsed.

Again taking the USA as an example, under the ban it is illegal to bring ivory into the country (including elephant products gained from sport hunting), but not illegal to buy and sell ivory in the USA. Two exceptions are: antique ivory over 100 years old (significant documentary proof is required), and sport-hunted trophies provided proper permits are obtained. The first exception makes sense; the latter does not. Violating the law can land you in jail.

The ban came none too late. During the '80s, the African elephant declined in numbers by at least 50%, or about 80,000 annually. Most of this was done by poachers financed by intermediaries. Showing incredible loyalty and care to kin, elephants prefer to stay in groups, making them vulnerable to poachers, who pick off entire families at a time.

Since 1973, Kenya and Uganda, for example, have lost 89% of their elephants, the number declining from about 160,000 to 17,500. In 1988, the Burundi government in a single catch uncovered 100 metric tons of illegal ivory poached from some 11,000 elephants in neighbouring countries! In some West African countries, poachers have virtually wiped out the entire elephant population. In Central Africa, there are still large herds of forest elephants in some of the most pristine rainforest areas. However, the larger elephants found in the plains have been slaughtered unmercifully, particularly in Chad where they are on the point of extinction, and in Zaïre and the CAR where their numbers are a small fraction of what they were just 15 years ago.

With so many excellent substitutes for ivory, it's a wonder why it has been so difficult to wean people off ivory. Two substitutes are bone and wart hog tusk; both age very nicely. Unfortunately, the bone is sometimes from an elephant, in which case it's just as bad.

A third substitute is plastic which is almost indistinguishable from ivory, even to experts! The only sure way to tell the difference is to put it under a flame or, better, touch it with a lighted cigarette. Plastic will melt and bone will be scorched. Ivory, on the other hand, will not scorch but can be discoloured if the flame is left too long.

Finally, there's malachite jewellery from Zaïre. With the ban and all these alternatives, you shouldn't be tempted to buy ivory, although you definitely will see it still being sold all over Central Africa. ■

Getting There & Away

AIR

To/From the USA

There is no direct service from New York or any city in the USA to anywhere in Central Africa. You have the choice of flying via Europe or West Africa. Most people prefer flying via Europe because connections are usually faster, the selection of airlines and routes is much greater, and the price is usually the same.

The only two airlines with direct service from New York to West Africa are Air Afrique (☎ (800) 456-9192) and Nigeria Airways (☎ (212) 935-2700). Air Afrique (which as of 1991 had never had a fatal accident and appears to have maintained that record up to now) is a better airline, but Nigeria Airways flights from the USA and the UK are also quite good, giving Air Afrique strong competition. Air Afrique has twice-weekly flights stopping in Dakar (Senegal) and Abidjan (Côte d'Ivoire). Nigeria Airways has three flights a week to Lagos (Nigeria). From those West African cities you can make connections to virtually any capital city in Central Africa.

Chad, São Tomé and Equatorial Guinea are unusual in that there are clearly preferred routes. To get to Chad, the cheapest route is via Paris, connecting with one of the two to four weekly flights (depending on the season) to N'Djamena on Air France/UTA or Air Afrique.

The most convenient way to get to São Tomé is flying to Lisbon and connecting with the twice-weekly service to São Tomé on TAP (Air Portugal). Otherwise, you'll have to fly to Libreville (Gabon) and connect with one of the four weekly flights to São Tomé on Equatorial International Airlines.

For Equatorial Guinea, the most convenient way is on Iberia Airlines (☎ (800) 772-4642), which offers a service from New York to Madrid and one flight a week from Madrid to Malabo. Otherwise you could fly from Europe to Douala (Cameroun) and

connect with one of the four weekly flights from there to Malabo (and on to Bata) on Cameroun Airlines, Equato Guineana de Aviation or Air Affairs Afrique.

For the Central African Republic, you can take an Air Afrique flight from New York to Bangui, changing in Abidjan. A return economy fare is US$2700 and a 45-day excursion fare is about US$2080.

Fares Regular economy fares to and within Africa seem expensive but on a per-km basis are fairly standard for the industry. The problem is that there is not an array of special fares as in North America or Europe. If you fly to Africa on a full-fare economy ticket, consider buying only a one-way ticket because you can buy the return fare in local currency for about one-third less than the fare in dollars! However, if you're planning on getting visas in your home country, be warned that this could complicate things, as a few embassies in Europe and the USA (eg Cameroun, Zaïre and Gabon) still require travellers to have an onward airline ticket. Check the visa requirements of the Central African embassies in your country before you buy a one-way ticket.

Regular listed fares from New York to Central African capital cities are all the same – about US$1400 one-way economy and US$2100 return excursion (slightly higher during the high season, 15 May to 14 September). So even though Kinshasa (Zaïre), for example, is over 1000 km further south than Douala (Cameroun), the fares are the same, and it makes no difference whether you go via Europe or West Africa.

Most travellers to Africa take advantage of the airlines' three special round-trip fares – APEX, excursion and youth fares. Excursion fares are usually about a third less than normal economy fares. They also offer far more flexibility than the cheapest APEX fares, which are not actually available for any Central African destination. On the other hand, there are APEX fares for flights from New York to many West African cities, including Lagos (Nigeria), which is only 700 km west of Douala (Cameroun). The APEX fare from New York to Lagos on Nigeria Airways is US$1081 (45-day return restriction), and the return fare from Lagos to Douala is about US$300 – a saving of about US$700 compared to the low-season excursion fare (US$2078) from New York to Douala via Lagos on Air Afrique. If you are flexible with your destination, definitely check Nigeria Airways.

Travellers from 12 to 23 years of age can take advantage of Air Afrique's youth fare, which is US$1354 to most capital cities in Central Africa. The real advantage is that there are fewer restrictions – a minimum advance purchase requirement (at least five days) and no 45-day return restriction.

A final factor to consider is the seasonal variation in prices. During the summer months, fares are typically US$200 to US$300 higher. For information, call or write to Farefinders (☎ (213) 652-6305), 251 S Robertson, Beverly Hills, CA 90211, which is a travel service that digs out the cheapest flights on a daily basis. It sifts through a maze of computer figures to compile the best deal, with no charge or obligation, and can also make reservations.

Discount Agencies Virtually all discount agencies place small ads in the Sunday travel section of local newspapers, especially the *New York Times* and the *Los Angeles Times*. There are only a few specialising in travel to Africa; some of the best are:

Airlink Travel
50 East 42nd St, Suite 1804, New York, NY 10017 (☎ (212) 867-7770)
Costa Azul Travel
955 S Raymond Ave, Los Angeles, CA 90006 (☎ (800) 332-7202; (213) 384-7200)
International Travel Specialists
210 Eye St, NE, Washington, DC 20002 (☎ (800) 444-6064; (202) 547-5220/1)
Lan Si-Aire Travel
303 5th Ave at 31st St, New York, NY 10016 (☎ (212) 889-5478)

Maharaja Travels
393 5th Ave at 37th St, New York, NY 10016 (☎ (800) 223-6862; (212) 213-2020)
Magical Holidays
501 Madison Ave, New York, NY 10022 (☎ (800) 228-2208; (212) 486-9600)
Pan Express Travel
25 West 39th St, Suite 705, New York, NY 10018 (☎ (212) 719-9292, 719-2937)
Spector Travel of Boston
31 St James Ave, Boston, MA 02116 (☎ (800) 879-2374; (617) 338-0111)
STA
(☎ (800) 777-0112)
Travel Home
104 East 40th St, Suite 504, New York, NY 10016 (☎ (212) 867-9700)
US Travel Systems
45 West 34th St, Suite 404, New York, NY 10001 (☎ (212) 465-8600)

These discount agencies, called 'consolidators', are equivalent to London's bucket shops. They now have a quasi-legitimate stature and are generally quite reliable. They undercut their competitors by buying large blocks of tickets at discount prices. It pays to call numerous agencies because their rates vary considerably. Most of them offer special round-trip fares on Air Afrique to many Central African capital cities, but prices vary considerably according to the length of stay.

Two of the best are Maharaja and Spector Travel of Boston (formerly Bock Travel). These companies offer special return fares to cities in Central Africa for at least one-third less than the excursion fare. At the time of writing, Spector Travel, for example, offers return flights from New York or Boston to N'Djamena (Chad), Bangui (the CAR) or Brazzaville (Congo) for US$1269 and to Libreville (Gabon) and Douala (Cameroun) for US$1299 and US$1349, respectively. These fares, which are not available in December, have a three-week or 45-day return restriction; those with a six-month return restriction are about US$350 higher, ie New York to Brazzaville (or Kinshasa) for US$1599.

Maharaja's fares are similar, eg US$1450 from New York to Douala on Air Afrique with a four-month return restriction. Magical Holidays and STA fares are slightly higher, mostly with 45-day to four-month return restrictions. Magical Holidays, for example, charges US$1669 return from New York to Douala on the Belgian airline, Sabena during the low season (15 September to 14 May) and US$1921 during the high season; the maximum stay is 45 days.

If you wish to stay longer than four months, it may pay to fly to London or Amsterdam and buy a ticket from a bucket shop. This would also allow you to combine a trip to Africa with a trip to Europe. Unfortunately, some bucket shops are too understaffed to respond to mail, but you can always call. The only way to make a reservation is to pay for the ticket, which can be done by mail. Except during the Christmas holiday season, you'll be taking little risk by waiting until you get to London or Amsterdam to buy your ticket; the chances of getting a flight within a day or two are usually good. The wise will call first, however.

As for getting to Europe, the cheapest way is to act as a courier but you have to travel light. Round-trip fares from New York to Europe as a courier are about US$400 in the summer season. If interested, subscribe to Travel Unlimited, Box 1058, Allston, MA 02134. A monthly publication which costs US$25 a year, it is filled with detailed information on courier agencies around the world, including fare listings by agencies. Three among many in the USA are Courier Travel Service (☎ (800) 922-2359), Now Voyager (☎ (212) 431-1616) and UTL Travel (☎ (415) 583-5074).

Those willing to travel to Europe on the spur of the moment should try stand-by brokers. Five among many are Stand-buys (☎ (800) 255-0200), Vacations to Go (☎ (800) 338-4962), Airhitch (☎ (212) 864-2000), Moments Notice (☎ (212) 486-0503), and Boston-based Last Minute Travel (☎ (617) 267-9800).

To/From Canada
There are no direct flights from Canada to Central or West Africa, so most Canadians fly via Europe or connect with a flight out of New York to West Africa.

APEX and excursion fares are also available on regularly scheduled flights to Europe from Canada. In addition, there are bucket shops in Montreal and Toronto that operate like those in New York and elsewhere in the USA. In particular, there are some very cheap flights from Montreal to Paris. Also, Nation Air has some good deals on one-year open return tickets between Hamilton (near Toronto) and London. The cost is about C$285 one way and C$500 return. Nation Air also has flights from Hamilton to Brussels.

To/From the UK
Full Fares Full-fare economy tickets to Africa seem terribly expensive but the cost per km is fairly standard on a worldwide basis. London to Douala, for example, costs about £1500 return. The cheapest fares, APEX, are usually not available. Excursion fares are also cheaper than full-fare economy tickets but limit the passenger to a stay of, usually, 25 or 30 days. The excursion fare from London to Douala, for example, is about UK£1000, 19 days minimum and 30 days maximum stay. Nigeria Airways offers a good deal. Return London-Lagos is £972 economy (one-year maximum stay) and £878 excursion (25-day maximum stay). So unless you're purchasing a ticket through a bucket shop, flying through Lagos may be cheaper. Don't rely on these prices, however, because airlines are constantly changing not only their fares but also the terms and restrictions.

Another alternative is the London to Kinshasa (Zaïre) flight. It is significantly cheaper than the flight from London to Brazzaville (Congo) across the river. However, as of mid-1993, the security situation in Kinshasa was very bad. See the Zaïre chapter for more information.

Discount Fares It's usually much cheaper to purchase tickets from a discount agency than from the airlines directly and the savings can be as much as 50%. In London (and Amsterdam), there are two distinct kinds of travel agencies. The first kind are the well-known ones like Thomas Cook which offer virtually no fare reductions unless you press them for their 'concession' tickets or go on one of their all-inclusive tours. The second group, known colloquially as bucket shops, offer rock-bottom prices on major airlines. These agencies are small operators (usually three to five people) and for the most part are quite reliable. They get their name from the fact that the airlines sell them a 'bucket' of tickets at a discount, and the savings are passed on to the passengers.

Typical return fares offered by bucket shops from London to cities along the Central African coast range from about UK£500 to UK£775. There's no advance purchase requirement and return dates can be changed. Many bucket shops also offer cheap one-way fares.

Which airline you choose, how long you stay and when you fly (the Christmas season and 15 May to 14 September are generally the high seasons) all affect the ticket price. Aeroflot is usually the cheapest and you'll have to spend at least a night in Moscow, but at the airline's expense. Air Zaïre is also relatively cheap, but in terms of safety and service, is the worst airline connecting Europe with Central Africa. If you insist on flying on a European airline, it'll sometimes cost you UK£50 or so more. As for the length of stay, round-trip tickets with a 30 or 45-day maximum return restriction are about UK£70 to UK£100 cheaper than those with the return portion valid up to one year. African World Travel Services, for example, charges UK£690/765 (45-day/one-year return restrictions) from London to Kinshasa on Sabena, and US£599/690 (low season/high season) on Ethiopian Airlines to Kinshasa with a one-year return restriction. A London to Douala ticket is cheaper from most bucket shops; for example from about UK£500/570 with 45-day/one-year return restrictions.

Some people think that because the tickets are so cheap, there must be something fishy going on. It's not true, as the great majority of bucket shops are quite reliable. The problem is that every now and then one goes bust, giving a black eye to the overall reputation of bucket shops. Shopping around for the better ones takes time but some of them are listed here.

It's important to see at least three or four agencies because they don't all deal with the same airlines. Some agencies refuse to deal with Aeroflot, claiming it is too unreliable. Consequently, you'll find a wide variation in prices and availability of flights to a particular destination.

As for youth fares, STA (☎ (071) 937-7996), 74 Old Brompton Rd, London SW7, offers special fares for those under 26 years of age but many of their fares are no lower than those offered by bucket shops.

The Air Travel Advisory Bureau (☎ (071) 636-5000) is a free travel advisory service that can be very helpful. They refer inquirers to only reputable bucket shops but not always to the cheapest.

The following bucket shops appear to be reliable, well established and some of them will even respond by mail to inquiries:

African Travel Centre (ATC)
  4 Medway Ct, Leigh St, London WC1 9QX; consolidator for KLM and other airlines (☎ (071) 387-1211)
African Travel Systems (ATS)
  6 North End Parade, London W14 0SJ (☎ (071) 602-5091/2)
African World Travel Services (AWTS)
  Radnor House, 93 Regent St, London W1R 7TG; agency for almost all airlines serving Central Africa from London; offers one-way fares (☎ (071) 734-7181/2)
Afro-Asian Travel Ltd
  Linen Hall, 162 Regent St, London W1R JTB; agency for most airlines serving Central Africa (☎ (071) 437-8255/6)
AZAT Travel
  3 Tottenham St, London W1P 9PV; agency for most airlines serving Central Africa (☎ (071) 580-4632)
Cruxton Travel
  (☎ (081) 868- 0942, 868-2055)
Euro Asean Travel Ltd
  35 Kensington Park Rd, London W11 2EU; responds immediately and informatively to letter inquiries (☎ (071) 221-0900)
Hogg Robinson Ltd
  106 Bishopsgate, London EC2 4AX; consolidator for many airlines rather than a bucket shop (☎ (071) 628-3333)

London Student Travel
52 Grosvenor Gardens, London SW1 0AG; fares appear to be the lowest, eg £218 (one way) from London to Lagos, £432 return (☎ (071) 730-8111)
Pioneer Travel
47-51 Wharfdale Rd, London N1 9SE (☎ (071) 837-5267)
Super Fare Travel
231 Oxford St, London W1R 1AD (☎ 071) 734-7927)
Trailfinders Ltd
46 Earls Court Rd, London W8 6EJ and 194 Kensington High St W8 7RJ; is one of the best and deals with most airlines except Aeroflot; check out its magazine *Trailfinder* (☎ (071) 937-5400, 938-3366, 938-3444)
The World Sports Supporters Club
40 James St, London W1M 5HS; well-known, reliable agency unique in selling tickets on flights originating in Africa (☎ (071) 935-9107)

Warning: Tickets from bucket shops sell out much more quickly for flights in December and January than during the rest of the year. Also, reservations cannot be made without full payment.

To/From France

Excursion fares from Paris usually come with a 30-day maximum stay restriction. However, Air Afrique offers excursion fares originating in New York which allow young travellers to stay in Central Africa for up to three months. Young people may find flying from Paris advantageous because Air France/UTA and Air Afrique offer a youth fare (ages 12 to 23) with a one-year return restriction for about 40% less than the regular economy round-trip fare. There are direct flights from Paris to Libreville (Gabon) with Sabena, Air France/UTA, Air Afrique, Swissair, Air Gabon and Royal Air Maroc.

The special fares offered by travel agencies in France are, in general, as good as those offered in London. However, most of them limit you to a maximum stay of 30 days. Some agencies offer special round-trip fares valid for a year; the typical price is about 25% higher than that with the 30-day restriction.

French travel agencies offering special fares are:

FUAJ
Federation of Youth Hostels, 10 Rue Nôtre Dame-de-Lorette, 75009 Paris; offers special fares to young people and organised tours (☎ (01) 4285-5540)
GO Voyages
22 Rue de l'Arcade, 75008 Paris. This agency offers 20 to 25% reductions on the normal seven-to 30-day excursion rates, plus return tickets valid up to a year for 25 to 50% more. Most departures are from Paris and Brussels and some from London (☎ (01) 4266-1818).
Jeunes Sans Frontières
31 Quai des Grands-Augustins, 75002 Paris. This agency offers similar fares with the usual four-week return restriction and limited cancellation rights (☎ (01) 4329-3550).
Nouvelles Frontières
74 Rue de la Federation, 75015 Paris. This agency offers return fares to Douala (Cameroun) and Brazzaville (Congo) for about 5000 FF and 7200 FF, respectively. Many of its special fares, however, have a limited stay (one to four weeks), and limited cancellation rights. Ask about its reduced hotel rates and excursions (☎ (01) 4273-2525).
OTU
137 Blvd St-Michel, 75005 Paris. This is a university tourist organisation offering special fares to students and young people (☎ (01) 4329-1288).
Uniclam
63 Rue Monsieur-le-Prince, 75006 Paris. This agency has some unbeatable fares. Tickets can be purchased to Camcroun, the Congo and the CAR and most are for one year. Prices are about 600 FF less if the trip does not exceed four weeks. Flights during peak periods, such as Christmas, have a surcharge of about 700 FF. The agency also offers package deals including hotels (☎ (01) 4329-1236).

To/From Belgium

There is a weekly flight from Brussels to Yaoundé (Cameroun) with Sabena and a 30-day excursion fare to Kinshasa (Zaïre). Air Zaïre also has six flights a week to Kinshasa. Travel agents to try in Brussels include:

Acotra
51 Rue de la Madeleine, Madgelenasteenweg, 1000 Brussels. This agency offers special prices to teachers, and students under 31 years of age; destinations include Brazzaville, Kinshasa and Lagos (☎ (02) 512-8607; fax (02) 512-3974).

CJB
  6 Rue Mercelis, 1050 Brussels. CJB has special
  fares for students and young people (☎ (02) 511-
  6407).
Uniclam
  1 Rue de la Sablonnière, 1000 Brussels. This
  agency offers the same fares as Uniclam in Paris
  (☎ (02) 218-5562).
Nouvelles Frontières
  21 Rue de La Violette, 1000 Brussels. This
  agency offers the same fares as Nouvelles
  Frontières in Paris (☎ (02) 511-8013).

To/From the Netherlands

Flying Aeroflot to Brazzaville is still one of
the cheapest ways of flying to Central Africa
from Amsterdam. It is about Dfl950 for a
one-way ticket and Dfl1750 for a round-trip
ticket with a one-year return restriction.
Interflug also offers advantageous excursion
fares, for example, Dfl1954 to Brazzaville
with a two-month return restriction. The
excursion fare on Sabena's flights to Kinshasa,
which are normally well booked, is Dfl2430
with a 30-day return restriction.

To/From Germany

In Munich, ARD (☎ (089) 759-2609/45) at
89 Königwieserstrasse, 8 Munich 71,
specialises in cheap air fares to Africa. Its
lowest fares usually have a 35-day return
restriction; those with a one-year return
restriction are about 50% more expensive.
Lufthansa has a weekly flight from Frankfurt
to Douala (Cameroun).

To/From Other European Countries

From Zürich or Geneva, Swissair has two
weekly flights to Yaoundé. From Rome,
Cameroun Airlines has a weekly service to
Douala and Air Zaïre has one weekly flight
to Kinshasa. From Madrid, Air Iberia has one
weekly service to Malabo (Equatorial
Guinea) via the Canary Islands. A return
economy fare is about US$1000. From
Lisbon, TAP (Air Portugal) offers twice-
weekly, 12-hour flights to São Tomé and
Kinshasa with stops in Dakar (Senegal) and
Abidjan (Côte d'Ivoire).

To/From Australia

There are no direct flights from Australia to
Central Africa. The basic options are to fly
via East Africa or Europe. There are now
some interesting round-the-world (RTW)
fares with Qantas and Continental, allowing
you to stop in Nairobi and Harare. Otherwise, the three basic options are to fly
round-trip via East Africa, North Africa or
Europe.

The only direct flight to continental Africa
is with Qantas to Harare but at A$2442 return
(90-day maximum stay) from Perth this is
one of the most expensive options. There are
no cheap flights to Central Africa from
Zimbabwe.

A better option is to fly to Nairobi and then
pick up a return ticket to Central Africa from
there. This usually involves flying to Singapore and connecting with another flight to
Nairobi.

Ethiopian Airlines provides a weekly
service from Bangkok (Thailand) to
N'Djamena (Chad).

The high cost of flying to Africa makes
flying via Europe a viable alternative. A low-
season ticket to Europe costs around A$1700
return and you can then buy a bucket-shop
ticket to Central Africa in London, Amsterdam or Paris.

The most important thing is to shop
around. Travel agencies offer different
flights and prices, airlines occasionally have
special deals, and it is best to get as many
quotes as possible before deciding. A good
place to start looking is STA or Flight
Centres International; both have offices in all
major cities.

Departure Tax

In a number of countries in Central Africa,
the airport tax is included in the ticket price.
In other countries, the tax is levied at the
airport when you're leaving. If you're not
prepared, you may have to cash a US$50 bill
to pay a US$10 tax.

LAND
Truck Expeditions

There are numerous companies in Britain

and some on the Continent which take travellers across the Sahara desert to Central and East Africa via West Africa. They usually go through Niger, Nigeria, Chad, Cameroun, the CAR and Zaïre en route to Kenya.

These trips take one to five months and are not for everybody. Truck breakdowns and border closings requiring drastic changes in itinerary are warnings that shouldn't be taken lightly. The overland vehicles are invariably huge remodelled trucks, usually old Bedford army transport trucks, with velveteen seats which take 10 to 20 people.

The price is very reasonable considering the distance covered and the time involved. The adventure tour agency, Tracks, for example, offers a seven-week, one-way trans-Saharan trip from London to Douala (Cameroun) for US$1875; the food and camp-site kitty is extra, usually UK£12 per week. The classic London-Nairobi trip via Central Africa now costs about US$3250, plus US$20 a week for kitty.

Encounter Overland offers a 16-week, one-way trip through 14 countries from London to Nairobi (and back) via West and Central Africa for about this amount as does Tracks (15 weeks) and many other British companies. In Germany, Explorer offers a 15-week trip to Nairobi via West and Central Africa for DM 5260.

These trips offer the opportunity to see just about every kind of environment that Africa has to offer at a very reasonable price. The disadvantage is that they involve a lot of time in a fairly slow truck. Most days are spent riding from sunup to sundown; the rest of the time is spent eating, setting up tents and cots, cooking and performing designated duties.

The quality of the trip leaders varies considerably. A group that I saw passing through Cameroun had just passed near Rumsiki, an area with spectacular almost knife-like mountains jutting out of the ground. The famous French novelist, André Gide, considered this spot to be one the most beautiful in the world. There's hardly a tourist brochure on Cameroun without at least one picture of the area. Yet neither the trip leader nor anyone in the group had ever even heard of

it. So be sure that you meet your trip leader before signing up; a bad one can ruin the whole trip. For those with a little time these trips offer a safe way to see Africa and an unforgettable adventure at a cheap price.

Most of the British companies offering such trips advertise in *Time Out*, *LAM*, *Southern Cross* and the Saturday edition of the *Guardian* overseas travel section, all published in London. There are about 10 or 20 small travel companies in England offering such trips; those in the USA are usually representatives of these companies. In Germany, they advertise in *Abenteuer & Reisen* and *Tours*. The following companies are the most well known:

USA & Canada
Adventure Center
    5540 College Ave, Oakland, CA 94618 (☎ (800) 227-8747)
Himalayan Travel
    Box 481, Greenwich, CT 06836; represents Tracks in London (☎ (800) 225-2380)
Safari-Center International
    (☎ (800) 223-6046)
WestCan Treks
    17 Hayden St, Toronto, Ontario M4Y 2P2 (☎ (403) 439-0024)
Wilderness Travel
    801 Allston Way, Berkeley, CA 94710 (☎ (800) 247-6700)

UK
Encounter Overland
    267 Old Brompton Rd, London SW5 (☎ (071) 370-6845)
Exodus Expeditions
    9 Weir Rd, Balham, London SW12 0LT (☎ (081) 675-5550; fax (081) 673-0779)
Guerba Expeditions
    101 Eden Vale Rd, Westbury, Wiltshire BA13 3QX (☎ (0373) 82-6611/7046)
Hobo Trans-Africa
    Wissett Place, Halesworth, Suffolk IP19 8HY (☎ (0986) 873124)
Long Haul Expeditions
    56 Bohun Grove, East Barnet, Herts (☎ (081) 440-4848)
Phoenix Overland
    28 Drayton Green Rd, West Ealing, London W13 8RY (☎ (081) 840-4303)
Tracks
    12 Abindon Rd, London W8 6AF (☎ (071) 937-3028)

Germany

Explorer
 Hüttenstrasse 17, 4000 Düsseldorf 1 (☎ (0211) 370011; fax (0211) 377079)
Lama Expedition
 Roderbergweg 106, 6000 Frankfurt/Main 60 (☎ (069) 447897)
Travel Overland
 Nordenstrasse 42, 8000 Munich 33 (☎ (089) 21-8353)
Ticket-Shop
 Theresienstrabe 66, 8000 Munich 2 (☎ (089) 280850)
West African Travel
 Wilhelm Leuscher Strabe 228, 6103 Griesheim (☎ (06155) 63336)

Belgium & Switzerland

Caravanes de Jeunesse Belge
 6 Rue Mercelis, Brussels 1050 (☎ (02) 511-6406)
Jerrycan Expedition
 Rue Sautter 23, 1205 Geneva, Switzerland (☎ (022) 469282)

Australia

Peregrine Adventures
 7/428 George St, Sydney (☎ (02) 231-3588)
Adventure World
 73 Walker St, North Sydney 2060 (☎ (02) 956-7766)
Africa Travel Centre
 Level 12, 456 Kent St, Sydney 2000 (☎ (02) 267-3048)
Africa Wildlife Safaris
 259 Coventry St, South Melbourne, Victoria 3025 (☎ (03) 696-2899)

Crossing the Sahara

The first crossing of the Sahara by automobile was made in 1922 when a group of French people in five Citroën trucks made the north-south crossing in 20 days. Now the trip is done all the time but it's still high adventure. From November to early March, temperatures are fairly tolerable.

The desert offers lots of surprises. One you've probably heard about is how cold it can get at night. Another is that it's not all sand dunes like you may have seen in the film, *Lawrence of Arabia*. On the contrary, huge sand dunes are seen only occasionally on the most popular routes. You'll see spectacular mountains in some areas, hard flat sand in other areas, and lots of rocks in still other areas, with an oasis now and then to clean your dirty body and perk up your spirits.

Each environment offers its own special memories. Don't be surprised if you see a camel caravan or two, with a princess perched on a fancy saddle with flowing white material draped over four posts to shield her from the sun. When you see this, you'll know you're really there. If you meet a few Tuaregs (nomadic Berber people of the Sahara) in the middle of nowhere, there's nothing to worry about even though they used to be famous fighters and to this day would no more be seen without their swords than cowboys used to be without their guns.

Why do people get a charge out of crossing the Sahara desert? For a motorcyclist it's the challenge and thrill of crossing 1500 km of flat sand at cruising speeds of 120 km/h or more, with side trips off the beaten path to areas few non-nomads have ever seen. To others, flat sand offers only boredom.

It's the side trips, such as into the rocky Aïr mountains, that create the most lasting memories. Or maybe it's just the incredible vastness, the stillness, the wind, being in the middle of nowhere and the surprise of seeing anything resembling life, whether another vehicle, a bush, or a nomad appearing from the middle of nowhere and seemingly going to nowhere. I have never met anyone who regrets having taken the trip, despite temperatures of up to 50°C, inevitable problems with the vehicle, canned food and no place to take a crap without everyone seeing you.

Despite what you may have heard and read, the trip is not particularly dangerous if the minimum precautions are observed. It's done all the time, even by motorcyclists, who frequently go off the main routes and chart their own course. One warning, however, concerns crossing the Sahara during the hottest period, June to August. Only a few vehicles cross then and if you're hitchhiking, be prepared for some long waiting periods. Those driving will have their equipment and provisions inspected by the Algerian police. If you don't seem prepared, they may not allow you to cross.

Books The best English-language book from a logistical standpoint is the *Sahara Handbook* (1987) by Simon & Jan Glen. It's a goldmine of information on equipment, routes and techniques. You can get a copy from Roger Lascelles Publishers (☎ (081) 847-0935) at 47 York Rd, Brentford, Middlesex, UK TW8 0QP. Lascelles also publishes *Overland and Beyond* (1981) by Jonathan & Theresa Hewat; this anecdotal account of a transcontinental journey will give you a good idea of what you'll be up against in the Sahara and beyond. Also see the Books section in the Facts for the Visitor chapter.

Niger Route The Algiers-Tamanrasset-Agadez route, called the Route du Hoggar, is by far the most popular, especially for those headed to Central Africa; consequently, it's also the safest. (The other more westerly route through Mali, the Route du Tanezrouft, is described in *West Africa – a travel survival kit* and, more thoroughly, in *Morocco, Algeria & Tunisia – a travel survival kit*, both published by Lonely Planet.) For better or worse, the Hoggar route is paved except for about 500 km. If your vehicle breaks down in the unpaved section, you are fairly assured of being able to hitch a ride if necessary. It's 1975 km between Algiers and Tamanrasset, another 835 km to Agadez, and 1020 km more to Niamey, for a total of 3830 km.

The straight driving time to Central Africa (Chad or Cameroun) is only 10 or 11 days (four days from Algiers to Tamanrasset, three days more to Arlit, two more to Zinder and another one or two to the border of Chad or Cameroun). If possible, don't rush the trip as you may regret it afterwards. Allowing three to four weeks would be far more desirable. Nonetheless, those people who do rush the trip still thoroughly enjoy it. **Agadez** is one of the most fascinating desert towns in West Africa, and there are fabulous mountains along the way, making this one of the most interesting areas in all of West Africa. However, getting to and from the mountains requires a detour of at least a few days. The Hoggar mountains are north-east of Tamanrasset; the Aïr mountains are accessible from Agadez.

The road is paved between Algiers and Tamanrasset but north of Tamanrasset it is in terrible condition for long stretches, making travel very slow. The real 'crossing', however, is the sandy stretch between Tamanrasset and Arlit, just 598 km. Try to time your departure so that you can spend the night in **Gara Eckar**, an area about 260 km south of where the paved road ends and 60 km north of In Guezzam. You'll know you're there when you see the magnificent outcrops of wind-eroded sandstone rocks – ideal for photographs in the late afternoon or early morning.

From the Niger border control post at Assamakka to Agadez, you have the choice of going via Arlit or the old camel route via **Tegguidam Tessoumi**. The latter route is much less travelled but allows you to see the salt evaporation ponds at Tegguidam Tessoumi, where camels are loaded with salt for transport to northern Nigeria and elsewhere.

Don't worry too much about getting lost. The unpaved section has clearly visible stakes every few km, so it's fairly difficult to lose your way, although it sometimes happens. Count on three to four days from Tamanrasset to Agadez. In Tamanrasset, you must pass by the police and through customs. As for petrol, there are stations in Tamanrasset and in Arlit and you must have enough jerry cans to make the 598 km between the two, but bear in mind that you will use more petrol than normal. There is a petrol station (and water) at the border post, In Guezzam, but you cannot rely on the petrol supply as it is often limited and the army gets priority.

Hitchhiking Hitchhiking is not difficult except during the hottest part of the year, June to August. If you can't pay, the only people likely to pick you up are other foreigners, as truckers always want payment. You must, however, be prepared to wait a few days. It's easier finding free rides in trucks between Algiers and In Salah than further south. If you get a ride in a truck, don't expect to get away cheaply – CFA

25,000 or US$100 (dinars are usually not accepted) for the Tamanrasset-Agadez crossing is typical.

The waiting point for southbound travellers is Tamanrasset. For northbound travellers it is usually Agadez, sometimes Arlit. Anticipate waiting anywhere from a day or two in Tamanrasset in winter to a week in the summer. In Tamanrasset, the best places to catch a truck going south are the customs post and the gas station; you can also try restaurants, such as the Restaurant de la Paix.

Women travellers will have fewer hassles if there are other travellers in the vehicle. For example, there's safety in numbers against border officials who sometimes have nothing better to do than to get drunk and try to seduce women.

Travellers have varying experiences at Assamakka with the officials on both sides of the border. They treat most travellers politely or indifferently; the days when they acted like swine, demanding huge bribes, are largely but not completely over. As at all border crossings, the way you treat the customs and police officials can make a lot of difference to their reaction to you. Neat, clean 'border clothes' and tidy hair can work wonders. Friendliness and flattery can help too, so make a point of shaking every official's hand and being friendly. Also, you might bring along some cigarettes. Handing over money or expensive items only makes it far more difficult for other travellers.

Between Arlit and Niamey and between Tamanrasset and Algiers, you can hitch or take a bus. There are daily buses from Algiers to Ghardaia, Ghardaia to In Salah, and In Salah to Tamanrasset. There are also flights from Algiers-Tamanrasset, but getting seats is frequently difficult. Although many travellers hitchhike, it is not a totally safe way of getting around.

Algerian Formalities Algerian visas are not required for citizens of Denmark, Finland, Ireland, Italy, Norway, Spain, Sweden and Switzerland. People of other nationalities including Britons, who were previously exempted, must now get visas. (In London,

the Algerian Embassy issues visas in 48 hours; the cost is an extortionate UK£35 for Britons, UK£5 for others.) If you travel from south to north through Algeria, you can get a visa easily at the Algerian Embassies in Niamey, Yaoundé or Lagos. All of them issues visas either the same day or within 24 hours.

Going north-south, you are well advised to get your Algerian visa before leaving Europe. They are not available on arrival at the border, port or airport; the embassy in Tunis is currently issuing visas only to Tunisian residents, and the situation in Morocco can be equally tenuous. In Algiers, you can get visas to Niger and Mali within 24 hours, although they may direct you to their consulates in Tamanrasset. When going south to Niger, you no longer need to get an exit visa from the police in Tamanrasset; they'll give it to you at the border.

You must change the equivalent of about US$100 at the Algerian border regardless of how long you stay. This can make a short trip through Algeria expensive. Don't expect to be able to re-convert the local currency (dinar) into hard currency at the border. There is a substantial black market that brings as much as three times the official rate. Be sure to keep every bank receipt, otherwise you'll have serious problems at the border when leaving.

In Algiers, you can get visas to the following countries at their respective embassies: Cameroun (☎ 788195), 35 Rue J Apremont, Bouzaréah; Chad (☎ 606637), 18 Chemin Ahmed Kara, Cité des DNC, Hydra; Congo (☎ 583888), 107 Lot Cadat, Djenane Ben Omar, Kouba; Gabon (☎ 780264), 30 Rue Ali El-Hamadya, Bouzaréah; Niger (☎ 788921), 54 Rue du Vercors, Rostomya, Bouzaréah; Nigeria (☎ 593298), 77 Cité des PTT, Hydra; and Zaïre (☎ 580679), 104 Lot Cadat, Djenane Ben Omar, Kouba.

There are camp grounds all along the major routes in Algeria and many travellers use them exclusively. For more information, including the sights and best deals, on Algeria as well as Tunisia and Morocco, see Lonely Planet's *Morocco, Algeria & Tunisia – a travel survival kit*.

Equipment A complete medical kit is indispensable for motorcyclists and highly recommended for everybody else. See the Medical Kit section in the Facts for the Visitor chapter.

From December to February, you'll need warm clothing at night as near-freezing temperatures are not unusual. During the rest of the year, except from May to August, it can still get chilly at night, so bring a sweater. You'll need a sleeping bag/mat for the same reason, also sunglasses and a hat. Pick up a *chèche*, the cotton cloth that Tuaregs wrap around their heads. It can be useful to help prevent dehydration and it keeps the sand out of your eyes. Plastic bags are very handy since sand gets into everything. If you are crossing by motorcycle, consider bringing some facial mist spray. Some motorcyclists swear by it, saying they wouldn't think of crossing the desert again without this short-lived luxury.

If you're driving, don't wait until arriving in Algeria to get 20-litre jerry cans. They cost about 10 times as much in Algeria as they do in Britain. Count on using at least twice as much petrol per km as usual.

Metal sand ladders (*plaques de desensablement*) are indispensable. You can buy them along the way, but they become much more expensive south of Ghardaia. You'll also need a compass and a mirror, two good spare tyres, a three-ton hydraulic jack with wide supporting board, and a fire extinguisher – overheated engines have been known to catch on fire.

As for water, count on at least seven litres per person per day, more if you're riding a bike. Obviously, it's best to have an extra supply. For cooking bring a kerosene stove. In French West and Central Africa, kerosene is *petrole* and usually not difficult to find because most petrol stations in French West and Central Africa have a single pump labelled petrole.

You are permitted to bring in duty-free one bottle of scotch or two bottles of wine per person, plus a carton of cigarettes. Hold firm if custom officials say you cannot bring in liquor. They want it desperately. Alcohol, even Algerian wine, is not sold anywhere in Algeria except at major hotels, and then only to tourists at exorbitant prices. Naturally, the Algerians want this forbidden fruit. So don't be surprised if a border official asks if you have any to sell. The selling price of whisky is the equivalent of a night at a good hotel in town. Wine, on the other hand, is much less valuable. Cigarettes make such good presents that you should consider bringing some even if you don't smoke.

In London you can get everything you need (sand ladders, jerry cans, shovels with a large blade, tow rope, tyre pumps, puncture repair kits, etc) at Brownchurch Landrovers Ltd (☎ (071) 729-3606), 308 Hare Row, off Cambridge Heath Rd, London E2 9BX. In Nice, try the Off-Road Centre (☎ (93) 82-1977) at 107 Ave Cyrille Besset.

If you're heading south-north instead of north-south, you'll find just about everything you need in Arlit. Everything imaginable is sold here. Finally, a few non-essentials that experienced overland travellers highly recommend are a short-wave radio, binoculars for viewing the wildlife, welding rods (local workshops don't always have them), a logbook and French franc bills (easily exchanged).

Vehicle Type What one usually reads and hears is that a 4WD vehicle is required for crossing the Sahara. This is crap. The Sahara has been crossed in all kinds of vehicles including bicycles. I crossed it in a 10-year-old Volkswagon van without problem; others have crossed in more inappropriate vehicles. You are likely to see as many Peugeot 504

station wagons as Toyota Land Cruisers and you'll undoubtedly see a few Deux Cheveaux as well.

This is not to say that a Toyota Land Cruiser or the equivalent isn't preferable; you will probably need a 4WD vehicle for driving on the rugged muddy roads throughout Central Africa, particularly in Zaïre and the Congo. However, for crossing the Sahara a 4WD is not essential. Indeed, it can be worthless in the sand because it's speed, not traction, that will stop you from getting stuck. If you do get stuck, use sand ladders to get out. The main advantage of a Land Cruiser in the desert is its high clearance.

The point is that just about every vehicle under the sun has been used at one time or another to cross the desert, and yours will make it too if it's in good condition and you drive carefully in the soft spots.

Vehicle Documents There are a number of important documents you will need for crossing the Sahara, including an International Drivers' Licence.

International Drivers' Licence Many countries in Central Africa will recognise your regular drivers' licence but get an International Drivers' Licence anyway because in some countries, such as Nigeria, your regular licence will not be legally sufficient. Even in those countries where it is, don't expect the local African police to know this. They may not have seen a licence like yours and may doubt its validity. Finally, for those who get into trouble with the law, having two licences will allow you a certain amount of liberty if the police take your international licence and tell you to report somewhere.

International Drivers' Licences are valid for only one year. In the USA, they are obtainable from any office of the Automobile Association of America (AAA). All you need is two 4 cm x 4 cm passport photographs, a drivers' licence and US$10; they're issued on the spot. It can all be done by mail if you send them a photocopy of your licence. Contact the AAA (☎ (202) 331-3000), 1133 21st St, NW, Suite 110, Washington, DC

20036. In the UK, both the AA (☎ (071) 930-9559), Automobile Association Overseas Operations Department, 30-31 Haymarket, London SW1 4YZ and the RAC (☎ (081) 686-2314/2525), Royal Automobile Club, Box 8, 3-5 Lansdowne Rd, Croydon, Surrey CR9 2JH issue them; the cost is UK£3.

Car Insurance Almost no country in Africa will allow you to drive without third-party automobile insurance – a green card (*carte verte*). Getting insurance in Europe is next to worthless because coverage does not extend below about 20° latitude north (ie only Algeria, Morocco, Tunisia, Libya, Egypt).

Whether or not you have a carte verte, some countries in Central Africa may require you to buy insurance locally. You can usually buy it at the border or in the closest major town. In Algeria, it's very cheap – about 65 dinar for 10 days. In Niger, you can buy it at or near the border. The cost is about US$1 per day and may be valid for some countries in Central Africa. Many Europeans travelling on the cheap simply take their regular insurance card along and count on the fact that the border guards won't look at the back or read the small print to see which countries the insurance is valid for. In Nigeria and some other countries, this assumption often proves correct.

The following companies/organisations issue insurance:

UK
    Campbell Irvine Ltd, 46 Earls Court Rd, London W8 6EJ (☎ (081) 937-9903, 937-6981)
France
    Automobile Club de l'Ile de France, 14 Ave de la Grande Armée, 75017 Paris
Germany
    ADAC, Am Westpark 8, 8000 Munich 70 (☎ (089) 76 761)
    Bundersalle 9-30, Berlin 31

Carnet de Passage A *carnet de passage en douane*, or *triptyque*, is a temporary import/export document for a vehicle and allows you to bring a car into a country without paying the normal customs duty or lodging a deposit with customs. It is intended to ensure that you don't sell your vehicle en route without paying duty. If the vehicle is not exported when you leave, the country can obtain payment of the duty from the issuing organisation and eventually you.

Carnets are issued by automobile associations in many countries but not in the USA, so Americans must get theirs in Europe. In Britain, RAC and AA both issue them. In Germany, they're issued by ADAC and AVD (Lyonerstrasse 16, 6000 Frankfurt 71). In France, they're issued by the Automobile Club de l'Ile de France.

In all of these countries including France, getting a carnet is no problem; AAA members usually get a discount. However, if you're a foreigner or have a vehicle with foreign licence plates, they may demand that you be a member of the automobile association in your country before they'll issue you a carnet. All of them demand a guarantee. There are two types – bank guarantees and insurance company guarantees. For a bank guarantee, you must put up collateral equal to the estimated amount of the duty. The cost is frequently prohibitive. In Australia, for example, the AAA requires a bank guarantee equal to 300% of the value of the vehicle!

Insurance companies, on the other hand, demand much less up-front money. They will issue a bond upon payment of a refundable premium equal to a small percentage of the estimated amount of the duty. If the company must pay on a claim, it has the right to collect the same from you. (If you purchase a double indemnity bond, which costs twice as much, the insurance company will waive the right to recover against you.) In the UK, the AA uses Alexander Howden Ltd (☎ (071) 623-5500), 8 Devonshire Square, London EC2M 4PL; their premium is only 3% and is good for one year (you can't get a price reduction by asking for a lesser period of coverage). A bond takes about a week to get.

There was a time when a carnet posed a major problem for travellers in Central and West Africa. Those days have passed. While most countries in Africa require a carnet, Algeria, Morocco and Tunisia do not. In some countries, such as Mali and Niger, you may find they can be purchased at the border. This means that you can drive from Europe to Central Africa without getting one beforehand, regardless of which route across the Sahara you choose. Many motorcyclists don't bother with carnets and seem to experience no significant problems. Vehicle owners, however, should definitely get them so as to avoid the problems of having to buy one each time you cross a new border.

Even with a carnet, in Algeria (which doesn't require a carnet) you will have to pay double the new value of your vehicle if your car dies in the desert and you leave it there – Algerian authorities will assume you sold it! So if your car is a heap or you come without tools to repair it, you'll be taking a big risk.

Selling Vehicles Most new or used automobiles can be sold in Africa for about the same price or a little more than in Europe. Previously, they could be sold for a nice profit; those days have long since passed as there are so many people selling cars, and consequently, driving prices down. Also, in West and Central Africa there are far more foreigners selling vehicles than buyers looking for vehicles for the return journey back to Europe.

To sell your vehicle, you will have to turn it over to customs who will not release it until the prospective purchaser pays the duty; even then, the buyer may have to bribe someone. The paperwork is less in Benin, making it one of the more attractive places to sell automobiles. In Niger, temporarily imported vehicles cannot be sold unless the owner has resided there for at least two months. Left-hand drive Peugeot 504s and non-diesel Mercedes 280S are the easiest to sell but not those with fuel-injected engines. As for large motorcycles, Douala, Yaoundé and Libreville are the best markets in Central Africa. If you do sell your vehicle, make sure you discharge the carnet correctly in the country where you sell it; otherwise on arrival home you risk receiving a bill for unpaid import duty from your automobile association.

For those not lucky enough to find a buyer, the last alternative is to ship it back. If you don't want it stripped, put it in a container. This can be expensive; from Pointe-Noire (Congo), for example, you must pay the cost of an entire container, not less, ie about US$2500. However, it is sometimes possible to save money by being flexible about where you pick it up because prices to various ports in Europe may vary considerably. Douala is the best port in Central Africa for shipping. Those using the Swiss Nautilus Line have reported satisfaction with the service.

SEA
To/From the USA
From North America, the only shipping company that has fairly regular passenger-carrying freighters plying between the USA and West and Central Africa appears to be Lykes Lines. Their freighters typically leave from New Orleans; itineraries vary but may include Dakar (Senegal), Monrovia, Abidjan (Nigeria), Tema (Ghana) and Douala (Cameroun). Other than this, there appear to be only vessels chartered for a particular shipment. While they might accept a passenger or two, you'd have to go down to the docks to find out about them. For general information and inquiries, contact the Freighter Travel Club of America listed below or Carolyn's Cruises (☎ (415) 897-4039) 32 Garner Drive, Novato, CA 94947.

There are several newsletters loaded with information on freighters:

Ford's Freighter Guide
19448 Londelius St, Northbridge, CA 91324. This is published twice a year, costs US$7.95 and lists more than 30 freighter companies and their itineraries.
Freighter Cruise Service Newsletter
5925 Monkland Ave, Montreal, Quebec H4A 1G7 (☎ (514) 481-0447). This is a free thrice-yearly newsletter (one of the best) with freighter schedules including those to Africa.
Freighter Space Advisory
This is published twice monthly by Freighter World Cruises (☎ (818) 449-3106), 180 South Lake Ave, Pasadena, CA 91101. The annual subscription fee is US$22.

Freighter Travel News
This is a monthly newsletter published by the Freighter Travel Club of America, Box 12693, Salem, OR 97309. The US$18 subscription fee includes club membership and an information service.
Traveltips
This is published six times a year by Traveltips Cruise & Freighter Travel Association, 163-07 Depot Rd, PO Box 188, Flushing, NY 11358 (☎ (718) 939-2400). The US$15 annual membership fee includes a subscription to the magazine.

To/From Europe
From Europe, there are still a few romantics who occasionally hop a freighter, but they tend to have a few extra shekels. A typical trip from Europe (eg, from Antwerp in Belgium) takes about 13 days to the Côte d'Ivoire and 17 days to Zaïre.

Of the lines serving Central Africa, you cannot do better than the Swiss Nautilus Line (☎ (061) 237940), c/o Keller Shipping AG, Holbeinstrasse 68, 4002 Basel; c/o Socopao, Quai de la Marine 5, Douala; and c/o Transcap in Abidjan. Its freighters, which are reportedly quite clean, leave from Genoa and Marseilles to Point-Noire (Congo), stopping at Dakar, Tema, Lagos (Nigeria) and Douala (Cameroun). Nautilus charges about 2200 Swiss francs (about US$1500) one way to the Congo (about 875 Swiss francs to Dakar); the price includes meals. If you're shipping a vehicle, count on paying about 50 to 75% extra for the vehicle, depending on its length and weight.

From Antwerp (Belgium), you can take Compagnie Maritime Zaïroise (CMZ) or Compagnie Maritime Belge (CMB), both of which offer fortnightly cargo services to Matadi (Zaïre), calling at Le Havre, Lisbon, Dakar, Abidjan and, sometimes, Douala and Pointe-Noire. The trip takes about 15 days and it costs about 2000 Belgian francs (BF) for a single-berth crew cabin per day. CMB has two cargo ships, the *Esprit* and the *Quellin*, with limited passenger accommodation; fares start at 2500/2000 BF per day, respectively. CMZ has a passenger boat, the *Kananga*, with single fares starting from 60,000 BF, as well as cheaper cargo boats

Top : Painting from the Poto-Poto Art School, Brazzaville, Congo (AN)
Bottom : Chief's chairs from the Sultan's Museum at the Chefferie de Bandjoun, eastern Cameroun (AN)

Top : School children in a parade, the CAR (BH)
Bottom : Boys playing, the CAR (BH)

with fares starting around 2000 BF per day (ie about 30,000 BF for the entire journey). In Belgium, contact CMB (☎ (03) 223-2111; telex 72304) at St Katelijnevest 61, B-2000, Antwerp.

From Hamburg or Rotterdam, Polish Ocean Lines runs a twice-monthly service to the Congo, with 10 stops. The London agent is Gydnia America Shipping Lines Ltd (☎ (071) 253-9561), 238 City Rd, London EC1V 2QL. In Rotterdam, contact Pakhold-Rotterdam BV (☎ 302911) Box 544, Van Weerden Poelmanweg 25-31.

In the UK, call Lloyds Shipping (☎ (0206) 772277) and ask for its 'loading list'. You may find that the only shipping company with service to Central Africa is Grimaldi Lines (Eagle House, 109 Jermyn St, London SW1Y 6ES, ☎ (071) 930-5683), which has two freighters leaving every three or four weeks from Tilbury (London's port city) for Lagos and Douala; each can accommodate up to 65 passengers. Another possibility is UK West African Line (☎ (071) 247-5445) which has freighters from Tilbury to Lagos and even though it doesn't cater to passengers, there's often room for one or two on one of its freighters. Nigerian Shipping Lines also has cargo liners to Lagos, but it no longer offers passenger accommodation.

For more information, consult the monthly ABC Shipping Guide, available from World Travel Centre c/o Reed Travel Group (☎ (0582) 60-0111), Church St, Dunstable, Beds LU5 4HB, UK. For brochures and bookings, see Weider Travel (☎ (071) 836-6363) at Charing Cross Shopping Concourse, The Strand, London.

Getting Around

AIR

African Airlines

African airlines have been described by readers of the *African Economic Digest* as frightening, unreliable, dangerous, unpleasant, unpredictable, uncaring, overbooked, impertinent and dirty. Few travellers realise, however, that as of 1991, Air Afrique was one of only 28 airlines in the world that had never had an accident fatality.

Service varies greatly even with the same airline, but to be fair it can be excellent. On the other hand it can be as organised as a cattle car. There's some correlation between service and safety, but not always. The real concern is the quality of the maintenance operations. Foreign pilots operating in Africa say it varies greatly. Most of the airlines are serviced routinely in Europe and many have contracts with foreign airlines which provide the pilots and maintenance personnel. There is, then, usually an element of quality control. In general, airlines worldwide are about eight times safer now than in 1960, and the same applies to airlines flying in Africa.

So despite the horror stories you may hear, in general you need not worry about flying on African airlines. Try to take one of the better airlines although in many instances you may have no choice. If the American ambassador wants to get from Malabo to Douala, he or she will take the local airline – and so will you. Don't be terribly surprised if, on occasion, you have to wait at the airport for half a day or longer (never go to the airport without a good book and several magazines), or during the flight they're doing things to keep the door from coming off, or the luggage is stuffed in the back blocking an emergency exit. These things happen every now and then. When you do have a choice, the following list of airlines in descending order of quality (safety and service) is intended to give you some basis for choosing:

1 *Ethiopian Airlines, Air Afrique, Air Gabon and Cameroun Airlines*
   This is the order rated by the readers of *African Economic Digest*.
2 *Equatorial International Airlines*
   Serves São Tomé and provides an excellent service. It also seems to have the best reputation of all the airlines offering primarily inter-Africa service.
3 *Nigeria Airways, Lina Congo and Scibé-Airlift*
   Nigeria Airways' service to Lagos from London and New York is excellent and punctual, but on its inter-Africa routes, Nigeria Airlines has one of the worst reputations of any airline in West and Central Africa. You can board without knowing whether there's really a seat for you. In terms of safety, however, Nigeria Airways seems to be superior to those airlines in category four.
   The service on Lina Congo is quite good but its safety record in recent years has been marred by several accidents. Scibé-Airlift is the best airline serving cities within Zaïre. Foreigners take these airlines all the time, especially when there's no alternative. Many are flown by European pilots.
4 *Air Tchad, Air Zaïre and Equato Guineana de Aviation (EGA)*
   These are almost entirely local operations and are at the bottom of the barrel, but you may have no choice. Air Zaïre's international flights should be avoided because repair problems and delays are frequent. It has the worst reputation of any airline with international flights in Central Africa, and even within Zaïre it's not the best. Air Tchad's two decrepit planes are periodically serviced in Europe, so there is some quality control.

Changing Tickets

Tickets written by Nigeria Airways are not accepted by other airlines unless written outside Africa, ie paid for in hard currency. If you buy a ticket on Nigeria Airways in Douala, for example, and want it endorsed to another airline, it won't happen. The same is probably true of tickets on Air Zaïre as well.

Confirming Reservations

You must reconfirm your reservation in person before the flight, otherwise you won't have a reserved seat even if the ticket says 'OK'. Telephone reconfirmations are never accepted because your ticket must be stamped. The regulations say to reconfirm within 72 hours of the flight – that means not later than 72 hours. You can usually reconfirm up to a week in advance, sometimes more. If you reconfirm within less than 72 hours, you will more than likely find that your reservation is still valid. Even the day of the flight is usually not too late unless the flight is full, in which case your reservation may be cancelled. If someone will reconfirm for you, don't forget that they'll need your ticket. Flight schedules change frequently so maybe it's just as well that tickets must be reconfirmed.

If you're put on the waiting list, don't panic. Despite the general perception that African airlines overbook, they usually don't, so your chances of getting on are frequently good. It's usually not how far up the waiting list you are that counts, but who gets to the check-in counter first. The standard check-in time is two hours before flight departure; get there even earlier if you're on the waiting list. The check-in line will probably resemble a rugby scrum, so look immediately for a young man (a 'friend') who'll assist you – it's worth every cent.

Airport Hassles

For all too many travellers, the most harrowing experiences are at the airport. Kinshasa airport probably has the worst reputation and N'Djamena airport the best. Checking in can be a nightmare. You don't have to have been in Saigon the day it fell to know what it was like getting on the last plane out. In Africa it's like that on every flight. It's rare that the good person who respects the queue doesn't get on the plane, but it's just frequent enough to cause many people, Africans and foreigners alike, to lose their civility.

There is a way out of this, however. Find one of the enterprising young men who makes a living by getting people checked in. They rarely rip you off. If they take your baggage, they're not going to run away because they know they'll be nabbed by the police the next time they show up for 'work'. Which doesn't mean you should go

have a *pastis* (a popular drink in Central Africa) while they perform their magic. It will only cost you a dollar or two, more when you don't have a confirmed seat, and don't be surprised if the guy behind the counter insists you show your appreciation to him as well. So don't worry about these guys; it's the taxi drivers who are much more likely to rip you off.

All of the above is usually worse in the case of big airports such as Kinshasa or Brazzaville, but it can happen in the smaller ones as well. Sometimes you have no choice but to get in there and fight your way to the counter; just remember that if you choose not to, you'll still probably get on. One of the advantages of being on a tour is that you avoid this hassle. You lose some of what makes a trip to Central Africa truly an adventure, but a lot of people would just as soon not make it too much of an adventure.

Warning Try to avoid arriving at Kinshasa airport at night as thefts and muggings have occurred to taxi passengers going from the airport to the city centre. If you can't change your arrival time, organise a ride in one of the large airport buses which are quite safe.

Fares

Flying in Africa is expensive because distances are fairly long and you can't get anything cheaper than the round-trip excursion fare (two-thirds of the standard economy fare). To get this special round-trip fare, you must stay at least seven days. But take a four-day trip from, for example, Libreville to Brazzaville (750 km) and you'll pay the full economy fare both ways (about US$600 return). In Zaïre, you may be able to pay in zaïres and get a slightly cheaper fare by taking one of the small private airlines such as BAL. For more information about the costs of flights in Africa, see the Getting There & Away sections in the individual chapters.

TRAIN

Most people on the Central African cocktail circuit ridicule the African trains to the extent that you may conclude the idea is best forgotten. You're likely to find, however, that your informant has never taken one. Most of what you hear is second-hand and third-hand information. Moreover, the stories of the good rides rarely get told. In Pointe-Noire, for example, you may be told the Brazza Chou-Chou never arrives on time. Many travellers, however, are more than pleased with the service, especially if they have a bed (couchette).

Cameroun, Gabon, the Congo and Zaïre all have trains. Gabon's Transgabonais, Libreville to Franceville, is the newest with air-con and a restaurant but no sleeping compartments. The overnight trains of Cameroun and the Congo both have couchettes with fresh bed linen which cost about CFA 3500 more than 1st class. The Camerounian train usually doesn't have a restaurant but the Congo's does, only it's usually too crowded to get a seat.

The dilapidated trains in Zaïre are another matter. Robbery is a major problem on all of them. But if you want to travel overland in Zaïre, taking the train may seem like a luxury compared with going by road. Distances are so long in Zaïre and the trains so slow that you may literally be on one for four or five days. Taking a truck could be slower still and more expensive.

Below is a summary of the possibilities; the country chapters give the specifics. The best trains in Central Africa in descending order are:

Gabon
    Libreville to Franceville (12 hours)
Congo
    Brazzaville to Pointe Noire (12 hours)
Cameroun
    Ngaoundéré to Yaoundé (12 hours)
    Yaoundé to Douala (3½ hours)
    Douala to Kumba/Nkongsamba (8 hours)
Zaïre
    Kinshasa to Matadi (9 hours)
    Ilebo via Kananga to Lubumbashi (5 days)
    Lubumbashi via Kamina to Kalemie (4 days)
    Lubumbashi via Kamina to Kindu (5 days)

BUSH TAXI

You may think that bush taxis (*taxis de brousse*) are those beat-up old vehicles that take three hours to fill up and are packed like sardines, with an accident rate you'd just as soon not know about. The answer is yes, but not for all bush taxis. There's usually some correlation between the quality of the vehicles and the wealth of the country. Comparing bush taxis in Cameroun and Equatorial Guinea, for example, is like equating diamonds and glass. Those in Equatorial Guinea are generally in terrible condition; those in Cameroun may be relatively new. So just because it's a bush taxi doesn't mean the trip will be unbearable.

It's also not true that the waiting time is always long. For well-travelled routes such as Douala to Yaoundé and Garoua to Maroua (Cameroun), the waiting time is usually no more than 15 to 30 minutes. On the other hand, going from Bangui to Bouar (the CAR) could involve a half day's wait or more, especially if you arrive at the wrong time. In most cases, 6 to 8.30 am is the best time to catch bush taxis, though in some towns they leave earlier than 6 am.

Bush taxis are almost always located at a bush taxi station (*gare routière*). Just remember that the larger cities often have several, one for each major road leading out of town.

Bush taxis, however, can be quite dangerous. The better the roads, the more the danger. That's because this allows the drivers to drive like maniacs, which they all do. Don't sit there like most people with your eyes shut; pay him extra to go more slowly or say you have a heart problem. For the adventurous and those on-the-cheap, bush taxis are the only way to travel. Travellers on higher budgets should not write them off. If a well-driven route is chosen, such as Yaoundé to Douala or Yaoundé to Bafoussam, chances are that the experience will produce a few good stories to tell back home and some cherished memories.

There are three classes of overland transport that could come under the title 'bush taxi'; the Peugeot 504s, the minibuses and the pick-up trucks.

Peugeot 504

These cars, all of them assembled in Nigeria, are quite comfortable when relatively new and not packed like sardines (more than eight including driver). Usually, all it takes to change a nightmare to a pleasant ride is to buy an extra seat. The only country with lots of them is Cameroun. In other Central African countries, minibuses and pick-up trucks predominate. If you want to charter a Peugeot all to yourself, the price is easy to calculate if all you're doing is going from A to B and back. Take the price of one seat and multiply it by the number of available seats and then do the same for the return portion. Don't expect to pay any less just because you're saving the driver the time and hassle of looking for other passengers – time is not money in Africa.

Minibus

In Central Africa, minibuses (and larger school-type buses) are much more common than Peugeot 504s; when both are available, the minibuses are usually 25% cheaper. They may or may not be comfortable, depending mainly on how stuffed with people they are. The big disadvantage is that they are always a little slower and have longer waits at police checks because of the larger number of passengers to search. The cost of minibuses varies in Central Africa; the cheapest are in Cameroun (and Zaïre to the extent that they exist at all) and the most expensive by far are in Gabon, the Congo and the CAR. To give you an idea, the 296-km stretch from Ngaoundéré to Garoua (Cameroun) costs CFA 3000 while in Gabon, the Libreville to Lambaréné route (232 km) costs CFA 8000.

Pick-Up Truck

With wooden seats down the sides, covered pick-ups (*âches*) are definitely 2nd class, but often the only kind of bush taxi available. These trucks are invariably stuffed with not only people, but probably a few chickens as well, and your feet may be higher than your waist because they are resting on a sack of millet. The ride is guaranteed to be unpleasant unless you and your companions adopt

the African attitude, in which case each time your head hits the roof as the truck descends into yet another big pothole, a roar of laughter will ring forth instead of a cry of sympathy. There's nothing like African humour to change an otherwise miserable trip into a tolerable, even enjoyable experience.

TRUCK

You'll find yourself taking trucks a lot in Central Africa. While not falling under the general title of bush taxi, they are frequently the only mode of transport available, such as in Chad, the Congo and many parts of Zaïre. Drivers almost invariably demand payment and the amount will be about what you'd pay for a bush taxi. The individual country chapters give the details.

The chances of getting stuck in the mud on a jungle road are very high during the rainy season but then that's what travelling overland in Central Africa is all about.

BUS

The only places you'll find large buses operating are in Chad between N'Djamena and Sarh, and in south-western Cameroun, from Yaoundé to Douala and Yaoundé via Bafoussam to Bamenda. Those in Cameroun are large and modern and are by far the most comfortable way to travel; they also leave on fixed schedules and cost no more than bush taxis. Those on the N'Djamena to Sarh route are much older and usually crammed with people but they're the only form of public transport available for this route.

CAR

Central Africa has by far the worst roads in Africa. The only countries with a good network of paved roads are Cameroun, São Tomé and Equatorial Guinea (Bioko Island only). Everywhere else you'll be driving mainly on dirt roads; fortunately, with the exception of Zaïre and the Congo, the principal arteries are usually fairly well maintained. If you're planning to travel a lot by road, the location of the principal routes is a major consideration. Some dirt roads are all-weather while others are not and you can't necessarily tell this from the Michelin road map. The worst roads are in Zaïre and the Congo; for those two countries, a 4WD vehicle is indispensable. Everywhere else you can make do with 2WD on the main routes.

Few travellers drive as far south as Brazzaville or Kinshasa because you cannot get from there to the CAR or eastern Zaïre except by riverboats (which carry vehicles but at an enormous cost), and driving southeast to Lubumbashi is much tougher than crossing the Sahara.

As for travelling times, the major routes/times are as follows. A 'day' means seven to 10 hours driving time in a private vehicle, eight to 14 hours in a bush taxi.

Yaoundé to: Douala (three hours), Kribi (four hours), Bangui (three days), Maroua (2½ days), Libreville (two days, three by bush taxi), Bata (two days), Lagos (three days).

N'Djamena to: Sarh (one day), Abéché (two days), Maroua (four to five hours), Maiduguri (five hours), Kano (two days).

Brazzaville to: Owando (one day), Pointe-Noire (two days), Libreville (four to five days).

Kinshasa to: Matadi or Kikwit (one day), Lubumbashi (two weeks), Kisangani (by boat only – 10 to 12 days).

Bangui to: Mobaye (one day), Sarh (one to 1½ days), N'Gaoundéré (two days), Kisangani (about five days), Goma (10 to 12 days if the road is not too muddy – a big if).

Bukavu to: Goma (one day), Kigali (one day), Bujumbura (five hours), Nairobi (four days).

Car Rental

Renting a car in Central Africa is ridiculously expensive. You can easily spend in one day what you'd pay in the USA for a one-week

rental of the same model. For those still interested, there are car-rental agencies in every capital city except Malabo and São Tomé. In most countries, the city's major hotel will have one. There is little difference in price between car-rental agencies except in large cities where there may be a number of small operators.

If the small operators charge less, it's usually because the vehicles are older and sometimes not well maintained. While you can sometimes get a good deal, the problem is that you can never be sure about the car's condition. If you can't afford to be stuck in the middle of nowhere with a broken down vehicle, stick with Hertz, Avis and Eurocar. As in the USA and Europe, you will usually need to have a credit card to guarantee payment, or put down a large deposit. Nowhere in Central Africa may you take a rental car across a border and only in Cameroun may you leave it in another city (the surcharge is about US$200). In most cities, except in Cameroun, you are required to hire one of the agencys' chauffeurs if you take a vehicle outside the city.

Hertz, Eurocar and Avis are all well represented in Central Africa, but they are not the only ones. Avis, Hertz and Eurocar brochures sometimes fail to include some of their more obscure representatives. Their locations are listed in most of the country chapters.

Before you rent a car, consider whether you might not be better off hiring a taxi by the day. If your rental car breaks down, it's your problem instead of the taxi driver's and if you don't speak French and you're in a French-speaking country, the headache will be greater. You may, for instance, find yourself stuck on the road after getting the wrong type of fuel. Also, the chances of finding some remote spot or the African nightclub that you're looking for may be slim, especially if you don't speak French. More importantly, if you get a friendly driver, chances are he'll show you some things you'd never otherwise see, maybe his home for example.

Since Cameroun is where travellers are

most likely to rent a vehicle, the following table compares typical prices of rental cars there (which are much lower than in Gabon and the Congo) to those of all-day taxis (highly negotiable, anywhere from CFA 15,000 to CFA 20,000 plus fuel if you bargain well). All the fares are in CFA:

Distance	Toyota Corolla	Taxi
100 km	CFA 26,500	CFA 18,000
200 km	CFA 40,000	CFA 23,000
300 km	CFA 52,500	CFA 28,000

These prices with Avis in Cameroun include petrol and all costs (CFA 13,000 per day, CFA 100 per km, insurance and tax) but not a chauffeur (required in many countries). Note that for a day's drive of just 300 km, you'll pay about US$200. So if you rent a car to travel around Cameroun for a week, you'll probably end up paying roughly US$1400. In Gabon and the Congo, where rental costs are about 80% higher, the amount would be about US$2500 for the same mileage!

Taxi Rental The major problem with hiring taxis by the day is that many taxi drivers have never done it before. If you are planning to stay within the city limits, the price should include petrol and coming to an agreement shouldn't be too difficult. The problem comes when you want to travel outside the city. In that case, if you try to negotiate a price including petrol, you'll be asking for trouble. The driver will reduce the speed to a slow trot and complain incessantly every time you take even the most minor detour. His attitude will ruin your trip, no joke. Agree on a fixed rate plus petrol which doesn't require an estimate of petrol consumption. If you change your itinerary, it won't matter to the driver because you're the one paying for the petrol.

Still, it's not always easy to negotiate because he may never have done this before and may not speak English or French very well. The solution is to go to the nearest major hotel and explain to the doorman what you want and then ask him explain it to the driver. Once this is settled, your only other

problem is calculating the petrol usage. If his petrol meter is not working, you're asking for an argument at the end of the day. Get another driver!

The second major problem with hiring a taxi is that it is more likely to break down than a rental car. More than one weekend trip has been ruined when the taxi broke down miles out of the capital city and couldn't be quickly repaired – and no refund. The lesson is to inspect the car beforehand; if you hear a lot of rattling, choose another.

BICYCLE
If you'll be bringing a bicycle, also bring spokes, tubes, brake pads, cables, a spare tyre, a chain, a puncture kit and a decent set of tools as Western cycle parts are not available anywhere in Central Africa. Also, you need to work out a way to carry at least four or more litres of water comfortably as the heat can get intense and distances between villages can be great. Because long distances tend to be a major drawback to riding a bike in Central Africa, consider starting off in Cameroun because the distances there between major points of interest are not so great. For more information on cycling, see the Activities section in the Facts for the Visitor chapter.

BOAT
In Zaïre and the Congo, one of the more popular ways of travelling upcountry is by steamer. Riverboat trips include all the way from Kinshasa to Kisangani (Zaïre) on the Zaïre River; from Brazzaville to Ouesso (the Congo) via the Congo and Sangha rivers; as well as from Brazzaville to Bangui (the CAR) via the Congo and Ubangui rivers. (You can also, obviously, travel in the opposite direction for each of these trips.)

These steamers resemble floating villages more than boats, and taking one can be quite an adventure. They are also a cheap way to travel if you go deck class, but catching them can involve long waits (up to a month), particularly in Zaïre where the schedules have been disrupted by the political and economic turmoil in the country. See the Getting There

& Away sections under Zaïre, the Congo and the CAR chapters for more information.

LOCAL TRANSPORT
Bus
You'll find well-developed bus systems in Kinshasa, Brazzaville, Pointe-Noire, Libreville, Douala and Yaoundé. Shared taxis, however, are often almost as cheap and pass by much more frequently, so you'll probably find yourself taking them rather than buses except, perhaps, in Kinshasa where the distances are fairly great and Libreville where buses are much cheaper.

Taxi
Taxis in Central Africa do not have meters so bargaining is almost always required, especially at the airport and at major hotels. Typical fares are given in the country chapters. Fares have been very stable over the last few years, so be a little suspicious if the quoted price is much higher. If you can't speak French, be content if you pay no more than a 25% premium. The price always includes luggage unless you have a particularly bulky item. Also, fares invariably go up somewhere between 9 pm and midnight; the country chapters specify the time, but don't be surprised if the driver lies and tells you an earlier hour.

Don't expect bargaining to be automatic with taxis. Fares for going to and from most airports into town is fixed by law. Some taxi drivers at airports, however, totally disregard the fixed rates and generally act as though they received their training in New York. Still, many drivers in other cities are honest and will quote you the correct fare. The problem is how to tell whether the quoted fare is the correct one. Ask an airport official.

Keep in mind that there are two standards for calculating taxi fares – one when you hop in a cab with other people going in the same direction, and another when you 'charter' (as they frequently say in English-speaking Africa) one to yourself. (In French-speaking countries, the word *déplacement* is sometimes used.)

From the hotels, the rate is always the charter rate, plus there's usually a 50 to 100% premium on top of that to cover their waiting time. When you hail a cab on the streets in the city centre, it's not always easy to know which rate you're being offered, so be sure to clarify it.

In most of the large cities taxis are thicker than flies during the day and even in most medium-sized cities they are quite plentiful, but at night-time they seem to turn into pumpkins, even in the largest cities such as Kinshasa and Brazzaville. In some cities there are taxi *gares* where taxis wait for people wanting a charter, or there will be certain streets which are heavily frequented by taxis. If you're still having problems at night finding a taxi, the major hotel in town is invariably a place to pick up one. The problem is that it may take an exhaustive walk to get there. So maybe you should consider looking for a young man who'd like to earn some pocket money to find you one. All too many visitors to Africa are so intimidated by Africans or the language barrier that they don't make use of people willing at every step of the way to make your stay much more pleasant – at a cost of less than the price of a doughnut. And you don't have to speak French to say 'taxi' to a young man, he'll usually get the message.

Warning: Drivers tend to be sleepy from 18-hour work days and may race along at hair-raising speeds, particularly in the big cities. The sheep will say nothing, while the rest will raise their voices to intolerable levels – which language makes no difference.

ADVENTURE TOURS
Most of the agencies specialising in African adventure trips skip over Central Africa. However, there are several which do include it:

From the USA In the USA, Sobek (☎ (209) 736-2666/4524) Box 1089, Angels Camp, CA 95222, offers a 12-day adventure in eastern Zaïre looking for gorillas as does the American Museum of Natural History

(☎ (800) 462-8687 and (212) 769-5700), which includes the gorilla sanctuaries in Rwanda on its itinerary.

To join a cycling group, contact the International Bicycle Fund (☎ (206) 628-9314) at 4887 Columbia Dr South, Seattle, WA 98108. A nonprofit organisation dedicated to fostering increased use of bicycles for public transport, it sponsors two, two-week bicycle trips every December in Cameroun, one in the west (US$1090) and one in the north (US$1290).

For trips focusing on unique cultural experiences, there are several organisations that can be recommended. One is Spector Travel of Boston (previously listed under US discount agencies). Another is the African American Studies Program (☎ (312) 443-0929), 120 South LaSalle St, Suite 1144, Chicago, Ill 60603. It offers study/travel programmes intended to increase your awareness of the many cultures in Africa. Prices range from US$995 to US$2685 including air fares.

A third is Henderson Tours (☎ (800) 241-4644), 931 Martin Luther King Dr NW, Atlanta, GA 30314. It specialises in Black heritage tours covering 11 countries from Senegal to Gabon. A typical two-week trip costs about US$1800 plus air fares.

Two others are African Holidays (☎ (800) 528-0168), Box 36959, Tuscon, AZ 85740; and Magical Holidays (☎ (800) 228-2208), 501 Madison Ave, New York, NY 10022, which sponsors African heritage and cultural tours.

From the UK In the UK, the Travel Bug (☎ (061) 721-4202) in Manchester offers three-week tours of Zaïre which include a visit to some Pygmy settlements; prices start at UK£670 plus air fares. Two others are Ecosafaris (☎ (071) 370-5032), 146 Gloucester Rd, London SW7 4SZ, which has wildlife safaris to Zaïre among other places; and Equatoria (☎ (0367) 52830; telex 445787), 7 Oak St, Lechlade, Glos GL7

3AX, which sponsors gorilla safaris in Zaïre as well as walking trips and budget truck camping there.

From France In France, try Nouvelles Frontières (☎ (01) 4273-2525) at 74 Rue de la Federation, 75015 Paris; Visages du Monde (☎ (01) 4587-0404) at 26 Rue Poliveau, 75005 Paris; or Explorator (☎ (01) 4266-6624; fax 4266-5389) at 16 Place de la Madeleine, 75008 Paris. All three are involved in a wide assortment of adventure trips.

Uniclam (☎ (01) 4329-1236), 63 Monsieur le Prince, 75006 Paris, has special nine-day tours of western and northern Cameroun for 11,130 FF. Fives times a year, Terres d'Aventure (☎ (01) 4329-9450) at 16 Rue St-Victor, 75005 Paris, sponsors an exciting 24-day trip of eastern Zaïre including visits to the gorillas, climbing the Ruwenzori mountains and Nyiragongo volcano and visiting Pygmy settlements, for 22,850 FF including air fares from Paris.

From Elsewhere in Europe In Belgium, you could try Explorado (☎ (02) 648-2269), 61 Ave Legrand, 1050 Brussels, which specialises in isolated adventure trips. In the Netherlands, try Strichting Explorer (☎ (020) 255-434) Manixstraat 403, 1017 PJ Amsterdam.

In Germany, there is Sliva Expeditionen (☎ (0211) 379064), Postfach 548, 8000 Munich 33, which conducts expeditions in various West African countries, possibly expanding to Central Africa as well; Afrika Tours Individueil (☎ (089) 596081), Schwanthalerstrasse 22, 800 Munich 2; Minitrek Expeditionen (☎ (06221) 401443), Bergstrasse 153, 6900 Heidelberg 1, Germany; and Explorer (☎ (0211) 370011), Hüttenstrasse 17, 4000 Düsseldorf.

In Switzerland, try Jerrycan Expedition (☎ (022) 469282), Rue Sautter 23, 1205, Geneva.

Cameroun

Twenty-five years ago, eight countries in West and Central Africa had GNPs higher than Cameroun's. By the mid-80s, Cameroun was third, behind Gabon and the Congo, surpassing even the Côte d'Ivoire. Since then, the economy has gone downhill, due to falling oil prices, gross mismanagement of public-sector enterprises and incredible corruption at the highest levels, while crime has skyrocketed. Still, Cameroun remains one of the richest countries in Black Africa. Much of this wealth comes from oil, but agriculture is the cornerstone of the economy as Cameroun is one of a handful of African countries that is able to feed itself. Sound economic policies implemented before the present government took control is the reason.

Travellers are in luck. In the north, there are hobbit-like villages perched on rocky cliffs, each house like a miniature medieval fortress. Nearby is the land of the Kapsikis with its great basalt outcrops. Then there is Waza National Park, one of the best game reserves in Central Africa.

In the south-west, you could climb Mt Cameroun, the highest mountain in Central Africa outside the Ruwenzori mountain range in eastern Zaïre. It's also easily accessible. Other possibilities include hiking in the scenic mountains around Bamenda, and relaxing at a mountain resort in Dschang, which, at 1400 metres, has an average temperature of 22°C, making it a sort of Camerounian Baden-Baden.

In Foumban you can see the unusual royal palace of the Bamoun tribe displaying the personal belongings of 18 consecutive royal dynasties dating back to the 14th century, then browse through more than 20 artisan shops. You can follow this with a trip to Bandjoun where you can see the most impressive chief's compound in Central Africa and the best example in western Cameroun of Bamiléké architecture.

Finally, there is the beautiful coastal

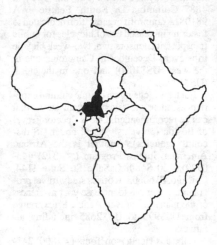

region around Kribi where there are long, isolated beaches of squeaky, white sand.

Facts about the Country

HISTORY
During most of the colonial period, France and Britain split up Cameroun, causing severe unification problems when independence came. There's not even a single official language; Cameroun is unique in Africa in that both French and English play that role. This, plus the fact that ethnically Cameroun has one of Africa's least homogeneous populations, makes it all the more amazing that until recently, Cameroun has had one of the most stable governments in Africa.

Little is known about Cameroun before 1472 when the Portuguese arrived, exclaiming 'Camarões, camarões' in amazement at

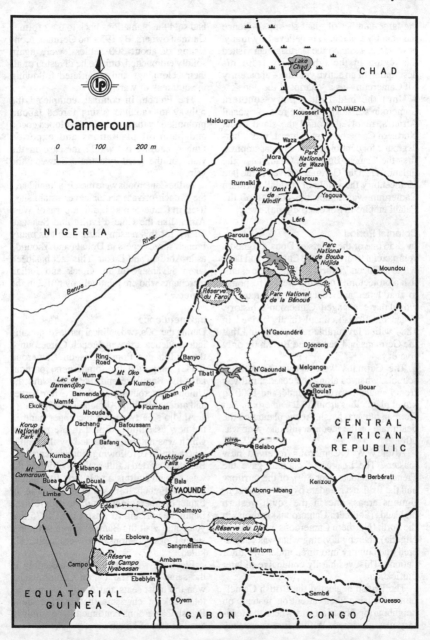

the large number of giant shrimps – hence the country's name. It is believed by many, however, that Hanno the Carthaginian visited the region in the 6th century from his description of an active volcano – apparently Mt Cameroun – as a 'chariot of the gods'.

Until the mid-19th century southern Cameroun's history, like the rest of coastal Africa's, revolved around the slave trade. Northern Cameroun, by contrast, was a battleground for control by various great empires, first the Kanem-Bornu in Chad, later the Fulani. When the Germans arrived in the late 19th century the whole of 'feudal' northern Cameroun was under the control of the Fulani empire in Sokoto (Nigeria).

Colonial Period
In 1856 one of the chiefs of Douala signed a commercial treaty with the English, and later wrote to Queen Victoria inviting her to establish a protectorate over the area. A response to that letter and repeated other requests would have changed Cameroun's history. When the British consul finally arrived in 1884 with a favourable reply, he found that the Germans had beaten the British by only five days.

The Germans were active. They built schools, wharves along the coast, a railway from Douala towards Yaoundé, and 1000 sq km of plantations around Mt Cameroun. But German rule was harsh. At one plantation the death rate of the labourers in one year was 20%.

After WW I Cameroun received new masters. The League of Nations gave the French a mandate over 80% of the territory and the British a mandate over two non-contiguous areas, one in the south-western highlands (Southern Cameroons) and one in the north (Northern Cameroons, now part of Nigeria), thereby dividing what was considered one country into three under two tutor nations. This was hardly conducive to later unification.

The British neglected the British Cameroons, focusing their attention instead on neighbouring Nigeria from where the territory was governed. Within five years they

had sold the plantations back to their former German owners. By 1939 the Germans, consisting of about 300 settlers, were again solidly entrenched, only to be divested of all their belongings and repatriated following the outbreak of war.

The French, in contrast, completed the railway to Yaoundé (using forced labour, prohibited by the mandate), developed cocoa and palm-oil plantations and exported timber, causing a fivefold increase in the value of the territory's trade between the wars.

As the Cameroons were merely a 'mandate', the French private sector never established itself in Cameroun as it did in parts of West Africa like the Côte d'Ivoire and Senegal. Today, for this reason, there aren't as many French shopkeepers in Douala and Yaoundé as in Abidjan and Dakar. This fact has been taken advantage of by Greek and Indian merchants who are relatively plentiful in the region.

Independence
During the '50s, two political parties espousing independence arose in French Cameroun – the Union des Populations du Cameroun (UPC) supported by southerners, particularly the Bamiléké and the Bassa; and the Union Camerounaise, led by a northerner and ardent Muslim, Ahmadou Ahidjo.

Ahidjo's party gained the upper hand in the new assembly, formed in the mid-50s, which was naturally resented by the southerners. In 1960, following independence, the Bamiléké started a full-scale rebellion in the west around Bafoussam. It took five battalions of French troops and a squadron of fighter bombers eight months to suppress the Bamiléké uprising (it wasn't until 1975 that you could visit the Bamiléké area without a special pass). Thousands were ruthlessly killed.

Elections were held for the assembly in the same year. The Union Camerounaise won the most seats and Ahidjo, despite his total lack of charisma, became president. British Cameroons continued to be administered as part of Nigeria.

In 1961 both parts of British Cameroons held a referendum to decide whether to join in what they thought would be a loose federation with the new country. Southern Cameroons voted in favour of federation while Northern Cameroons voted against, preferring to become part of Nigeria. For the next 11 years, French Cameroun and Southern British Cameroons existed as East Cameroun and West Cameroun, with two assemblies. In 1972 they voted to merge as a single 'republic' with one assembly.

Ahidjo

Ruling with an exceedingly tight rein and crushing all opposition, Ahidjo continued as president and was re-elected without opposition in 1975, the year Paul Biya, a southerner and a Christian, was installed as the country's first prime minister. Ahidjo gave other southerners important positions in the government but power rested with a small clique of northern Muslim 'barons' close to him.

Ahidjo was an archetypal political strongman if not an inspirational leader. Preoccupied with control, the autocratic ruler required all key government officials to give him an oath of personal loyalty, especially on public ceremonial occasions, and banned all political parties other than his own; he even banned all ethnic associations. Political dissent was simply not tolerated and his secret service was highly efficient. During Ahidjo's reign some 10,000 to 30,000 people were thrown into jail as political prisoners – a remarkably high number for a country which at that time had only seven million inhabitants. By the mid-1970s the threat of armed rebellion had long since gone, nonetheless the state of emergency declared during the 1960 Bamiléké uprising remained in effect as did newspaper censorship.

Economically, Ahidjo acted cautiously, avoiding the massive borrowing that today is sinking the economies of so many developing nations. Instead of investing in show projects and putting most of the money in infrastructure, he stressed agriculture, education, primary health care and roads. Today

the school enrolment level is 70%, one of the highest in Africa. After years of investing in agriculture, Cameroun has become a model for other African countries and is self-sufficient in food with a wide range of agricultural commodities for export. Admittedly, Ahidjo did have some luck on the way. In 1978 the country began pumping oil, making major investment initiatives possible.

To his great credit, Ahidjo had united the country and kept corruption and the problems associated with tribal rivalry within tolerable limits. Then in 1982 he suddenly and unexpectedly announced his resignation. His hand-picked successor was Paul Biya. Biya was his own man and started weeding many of the old 'barons' out of the government, systematically replacing them with people of his own tribe, the Beti. At this point, Ahidjo may have had second thoughts. In 1983, he was accused of masterminding an unsuccessful coup attempt, was forced into exile and sentenced to death *in absentia*.

In 1984 the northern barons, seeing their protected interests slipping away, recruited a group of northern army officers to stage a coup. The surprise was so great that they almost succeeded, but after two days of fighting and 70 casualties, Biya was back in control (and was re-elected unopposed in 1988).

In 1986 Cameroun made front-page news around the world when Lake Nyos, a small, remote volcanic lake just off the scenic Ring Rd in the country's mountainous western region, mysteriously began spewing a dense, lethal mixture of carbon dioxide gas and hydrogen sulphide gas into the night air. The next morning the countryside surrounding the lake was littered with dead cows, dogs, cats and other animals. As for the inhabitants in the villages surrounding the lake, only about 10% of them awoke that morning; the remainder, about 2000 people, were asphyxiated in their sleep. (Researchers say that the lake's gas supply is slowly rebuilding and that a similar event is likely to reoccur at any time.)

GEOGRAPHY

Geographically, Cameroun is the most diverse country in Central and West Africa, if not the entire continent. There are three major zones: the northern savannah area, the southern and eastern rainforests, and the smaller western hill region near Nigeria that was once British Cameroons.

In the west around Bafoussam and Bamenda, the rich volcanic soils have permitted much higher rural population densities than elsewhere. The western anglophone region, which is coffee and cocoa country, accounts for 22% of the country's population but only 10% of its total area. In the hot, dry north, which is semidesert in the northernmost stretches, are Lake Chad, the major game parks including Waza park, rocky escarpments including the Mandara mountains to the west of Maroua, and the broad Bénoué River flowing by Garoua and eventually into the Niger River.

The rainy south is covered with thick rainforests. Because of the underdeveloped road system in the south-eastern region, few travellers venture there. In remote pockets, there are still small hunting bands of Pygmies and, hopefully, a few remaining lowland gorilla families.

CLIMATE

The extremes in rainfall are astounding – from barely enough rainfall to support agriculture in the extreme north near Chad, to over 5000 mm (200 inches) in the south-

west around the 4070-metre Mt Cameroun. There is no single rainfall pattern. In the north the rainy season is from June to September. In the south and around Douala, light rains in March and April are followed by heavy rains from May to mid-November. There is much less rainfall in Yaoundé than in Douala but the pattern is the same except that in July and August, when Douala is virtually flooded, Yaoundé has a dry spell.

GOVERNMENT

In 1990, furious with Biya's inept handling of the economy and squandering of public funds, the Cameroun people (in particular the anglophones of western Cameroun) began to openly accuse the government of mismanagement and excessive corruption. They formed a new party, the Social Democratic Front (SDF). Using machine guns, government forces dissolved the initial meeting in Bamenda, leaving behind 12 dead and many injured.

The government's heavy-handed tactics backfired, igniting the founding of many other political parties, including the National Union for Democracy and Progress (UNDP); within a year there were 30 political parties and at least 10 truly independent newspapers. Mass demonstrations followed, especially in western Cameroun, and frequently ended in shootings. Within a year over 200 people had been killed, including many extra-judicial killings, and many others were imprisoned. The government hid the gross human rights

Logging

Environmentally, the major cause of concern is rainforest destruction, the main culprits being commercial logging followed by shifting agriculture. The rate of destruction, about .8% annually, is about half that of Brazil and by far the highest in Central Africa. Initially, most of the logging was along the coast extending towards Yaoundé; now it is penetrating areas of eastern and southern Cameroun. In western Cameroun, the Kilum mountain forests in the Bamenda highlands are the last large forests in that area. Half of the forests there were destroyed during the '70s and '80s but with the help of the Worldwide Fund for Nature (WWF) efforts are now underway to preserve the remainder, including replanting deforested areas.

The WWF is also working with the government to maintain Korup National Park, which is to the south-west in a fairly inaccessible area along the Nigerian border. The area is truly outstanding as the rainforests there are believed to harbour a greater variety of plant and animal life endemic to rainforests than any other rainforest area in Africa. ■

violations from public scrutiny by refusing to let representatives of any international human rights organisations enter the country. In some instances, the demonstrators ended up lynching those who had fired on them, so the armed forces soon became very cautious.

By opening the way to multiparty politics, Biya probably thought he could defuse matters; it didn't work. Instead, the opposition parties pressed him to call a national conference to draft a new constitution. All too aware of the revolutionary impact of similar conferences elsewhere in francophone Africa (in Benin the leader was deposed), Biya flatly refused, offering instead to create a new prime minister post. The parties retaliated by calling on the population to strike and use all forms of nonviolent civil disobedience. The response was overwhelming, especially in western Cameroun. Off and on during 1991, following the Bafoussam *villes mortes* (ghost town) plan of action, most offices, shops and markets in the western provinces were closed on weekdays and most taxis didn't run; even the port of Douala was virtually shut down for several months. Bandits took advantage of the anarchic situation, robbing residents and tourists alike and blackmailing car drivers.

Biya responded by installing military rule in seven of the country's 10 provinces. However, with so many political parties and pioneering independent newspapers (led by *Le Messager* of Douala) in flagrant opposition to the government, he finally had no choice but to call for immediate parliamentary elections, the first multiparty polls in over 30 years. The various opposition parties led by the UNDP won 52% of the seats, and a month later, in early 1992, the new prime minister, Simon Achidi Achu, announced a new coalition government. Later that year, on short notice Biya called for presidential elections and won over the scattered unprepared opposition, causing widespread rioting in western Cameroun, especially around Bamenda. What the future holds is far from clear, but as long as Biya continues to pilfer the treasury and mismanage the economy, his position will remain shaky.

ECONOMY

During the first part of the '80s, Cameroun was the success story of Central and West Africa, with real growth averaging 5 to 6% annually and average per-capita incomes reaching their peak in 1986, at around US$1100. Since then, with the drop in prices of oil, coffee, cocoa and cotton, the economy has been in a protracted recession, with no end in sight. Previously, the high oil revenues masked the gross inefficiencies of public enterprise; more recently, oil losses have, astonishingly, exceeded the government's total oil revenue. Teachers, doctors and other professionals have had to swallow salary reductions and, as in many poor countries like the CAR, are sometimes unpaid for months on end. Crime has risen by leaps and bounds; Yaoundé and Douala are now two of the most dangerous cities in Central Africa. The only thing the country can boast about is its agricultural production; the world's fifth-largest producer of cocoa, with earnings from coffee that are frequently even higher, it is still one of the few countries in Black Africa that is a net exporter of food.

Only Biya and his cronies seem to be doing well. He has by many accounts amassed one of the largest illicit fortunes in Africa (around US$6 billion according to some French magazines). Then there are the huge sums allegedly squandered by some of his ministers and friends.

POPULATION & PEOPLE

Forming the boundary between West and Central Africa, Cameroun is about the size of Spain with one-third of its people – about 12 million. It's easily the most densely populated country in Central Africa but compared to neighbouring Nigeria, where the population density is five times greater, it doesn't seem overly crowded. Douala, with over a million inhabitants, is the largest city.

The array of ethnic groups and languages in Cameroun is bewildering. With more than 130 ethnic groups, it is one of the most ethnically diverse countries in Africa. These tribes are not being overwhelmed by the 20th century. Strongly hierarchical, some are tenaciously managing to hold on to their traditions. Tribal leaders are not just called *chefs* (chiefs); the Bamoun call them *sultans*; the Bamiléké, *fons*; and the Fulani, *lamidos*.

The Bamiléké, centred around Bafoussam, are the most populous group in the western highlands. The Bamoun, another well-known tribe, are in the area around nearby Foumban. Around Yaoundé you'll find mostly Ewondo, and in the north mostly Fulani and Kirdi.

Traditionally, the Bamiléké women do the hard farm work, while the men tend to the animals and look after the cocoa and coffee plantations. Today the men are perhaps more famous as traders, and as so many have migrated to Douala the Bamiléké constitute over a third of the city's inhabitants, more than the city's original inhabitants, the

Douala. Forming a middle class of transport entrepreneurs and heavily involved in the import-export business, the Bamiléké control the city's economy.

In their homeland, you'll get a different picture – a people with a strong sense of tradition and a complex sociopolitical structure centred on independent chiefdoms. Unlike the Bamoun, who give allegiance to a single person, the sultan, the Bamiléké have about 80 *chefferies*, each strongly independent and very hierarchical. Below the *fon* is a council of dignitaries called the *mkem* and each member has responsibility for a secret society, such as the *kamveu*, which in turn is responsible for preserving the rituals. You can see these chefferies in the highlands, the one in Bandjoun being the most photographed.

For more about Cameroun, read Shirley Deane's new book *Talking Drums* (John Murray Publishers). She gives some insight into village life near Yaoundé.

The north is Muslim Fulani country. Whereas the south has been in contact with the Western world for over 500 years, until the 20th century the north was part of quasi-feudal Fulani kingdoms centred in Nigeria and tradition and resistance to outside influences remain strong. If you're in Cameroun at the time of the Muslim feast of Tabaski, head for Maroua. You'll see how strongly the Fulani hold to tradition. Partially for this reason, development here is going more slowly; for example, there are far fewer children are in school.

Most northerners, however, are neither Muslim nor Fulani. These people are known collectively as Kirdi, the Fulani word for pagan. They are the tribes the Fulani drove into the inhospitable rocky areas near Nigeria. You'll see them when you visit Rumsiki, Mokolo and Mora. They are even more alienated from the rest of Cameroun than are the Fulani of the north. Life expectancy among the Kirdi is only about 30 years.

MUSIC

The music of Cameroun is among the most popular in Africa, and the biggest name is still Manu Dibango. Now a true African superstar, he brought international fame to Camerounian *makossa*, the country's unique contribution to African pop music, with the release in 1973 of his album 'Soul Makossa', a worldwide dance-floor hit. Since then, he has gone beyond makossa and today most of his music is heavily influenced by jazz and electric pop; as a result, his international appeal is at least as great as his appeal in Cameroun. The sax-playing musician and composer is an intellectual and his sophisticated jazz of today is definitely not for everyone, nor is it for dancing, which is why it's seldom played on Camerounian radio. It's great for listening however, so don't leave without a recording.

Today, the king of Camerounian makossa music is Sam Fan Thomas. Other long-time favourite makossa singers are Moni Bile and guitarist Toto Guillaume, and their music, like Thomas', is definitely for dancing. Another is singer/instrumentalist Francis Bebey, who is certainly the most versatile of Camerounian musicians and master of a variety of styles. He uses the thumb piano, African flute, percussion and electric bass to draw on the whole range of African music, not just makossa, from traditional vocal styles and classical guitar to rumba and soukous bass. Newer makossa stars include Ndedi Eyango, Ndedi Dibango, Hoigene Ekwalla and female stars Bell Anjoh and Charlotte Nbango.

Son of a national hero and religious martyr, Eboa Lotin, my personal favourite, is a fabulous guitar player from western Cameroun. Lotin has a husky, sweet voice which meshes perfectly with gentle makossas for bass, drums, synth and acoustic guitar, producing some highly unusual and distinguishable sounds. As is the case with Manu Dibango's music, his is for listening, not dancing – which is unusual for Cameroun.

In the Yaoundé area, you are likely to hear some *bikutsi* music over the radio; it hasn't yet received international status but it's good for dancing. The biggest star is M'Barga Soukouss, who sings in Ewonde as do the other bikutsi singers.

LANGUAGE

Both French and English are the official languages, though French is more widely spoken. You won't hear much English, for example, in Douala or Yaoundé. Most government personnel, however, understand both. English is the principal non-African language in only 10% of the country – two provinces in the far western area bordering Nigeria, including the towns of Bamenda, Mamfé and Kumba. Pidgin, or bush English, is the conversational language in these provinces and widely understood even in the francophone provinces. Knowing a little will help immensely in bargaining and getting to know the people.

Cameroun has more African languages than just about any country in Africa. Five of the major ones are Bamiléké (spoken in the western highlands and around Douala), Ewondo (around Yaoundé), Bamoun (around Foumban), and Fulfulde and Arabic (in the north).

Greetings & Civilities in Ewondo
Good morning
bem-bay keh-REE
Good evening
bem-bay ahn-gouh-GEE
How are you?
oun-VUOY?
Thank you
ah-boun-ghan
Goodbye
oh-kell-em-VUOY

Greetings & Civilities in Bamiléké
Good morning
ZEL-ay
Good evening
oh-VOY
Response
YAH-lay
How are you?
YAH-may-lie?
I'm fine
yah-may-NOHK
Thank you
guh-pay-NO

Goodbye
oom-boh

Greetings & Civilities in Bamoun
Good morning/evening
may-SHAH-shoe
Response
aan
How are you?
peu-SAH-nay?
I'm fine
moh-ong-gham-DEE
Thank you
EYE-you-ah
Goodbye
MOH ou-ay-NAY

Facts for the Visitor

VISAS & EMBASSIES
Camerounian Visas
Everyone needs a visa except Germans and certain Africans. If you reside in a country without a Camerounian embassy or can prove that you have been away from your home country for more than three months, it is possible to get a visa at the airport in Douala. However, officials are very strict in enforcing the requirements and may insist you show them an official letter stating why you couldn't get a visa. If they're not convinced, you'll be forced to leave on one of the next flights out. Moreover, if you're coming directly from Europe and you don't have a visa, the airlines won't even let you on the plane. On the other hand, you need no visa if you're merely in transit and have a flight out within 24 hours.

The Camerounian Embassy in Washington, DC (☎ (202) 265-2400) requires two photos, US$44 and proof of a return airline ticket, while the one in London (☎ (071) 727-0771/4) issues visas in 24 hours, requires two photos, UK£26 and, possibly, proof of a return ticket. In both cases, the visas are valid for three months from the date of issue and good for three-month stays. Embassies elsewhere in Europe may also ask you to produce a round-trip ticket or a letter from your bank showing sufficient funds.

You can get visas to Cameroun fairly easily in all neighbouring countries, but in Libreville (Gabon) and Lagos (Nigeria) the Camerounian embassies insist that applicants have an onward airline ticket. In Nigeria, you can avoid this hassle by getting one in Calabar. The Camerounian Consulate there charges the equivalent of about CFA 2500 in *naira* for visas and requires two or three photos; visas valid for stays up to three months are usually issued in 24 hours, sometimes 48 hours.

Elsewhere in Africa, getting visas to Cameroun can be quite difficult as there aren't many embassies and some of them, such as the one in Abidjan (Côte d'Ivoire), only issue visas to residents. If you'll be crossing the Sahara on your way here, your best bet is Nigeria or Chad as there is no Camerounian embassy in Niger and getting a visa from the Camerounian Embassy in Algeria can take weeks. Cameroun has no embassies in East Africa but in Kenya you can get a visa to Cameroun from the French Embassy; this appears to be the only country in Africa where Cameroun has granted a French embassy such authority.

Visa Extensions As for visa extensions, you can obtain them in Yaoundé as well as in any of the regional capitals, usually without problem and without great cost. Prices vary. In Ebolowa, for example, you can get a six-week extension for CFA 2750 (same-day service) while in other areas the cost is CFA 5000 (and typically 24-hour service). Avoid getting one in Yaoundé as immigration officials there are known to hassle travellers.

Other African Visas
The CAR The CAR Embassy, which is open weekdays from 8 am to 1 pm, issues visas valid for three months from the date of issue which permit visits of up to one month's duration; bring CFA 10,000 and two photos. The process normally takes 24 hours. However, for people of certain nationalities (Australians, New Zealanders and the Irish

but not Britons, Americans, Germans or the French) the process normally takes about a week because the embassy will ask you to send a telex to Bangui requesting authorisation to enter the CAR; the telex office is on Ave Jaffre opposite the post office in Yaoundé and a response takes at least four days.

Chad Chadian visas are available at the border post in Kousseri and from the Chadian Embassy in Yaoundé. The embassy, which is open weekdays from 7.30 am to noon and from 2.30 to 6 pm and gives 24-hour service, requires two photos and CFA 5000 for a one-month visa.

Congo Visas to the Congo cost CFA 25,000 and are valid for up to two months, depending on what you request. Open weekdays from 7.30 am to 1.30 pm, the embassy requires two photos and gives 24-hour service.

Equatorial Guinea The Equatorial Guinea Embassy in Yaoundé is open weekdays from 8 am to 2 pm and gives same-day service for visas if you come fairly early in the morning with two photos, CFA 10,000 plus CFA 2500 for a telex announcing your arrival; your passport can be retrieved in the early afternoon. The Equatorial Guinea Consulate in Douala issues visas with the same requirements.

Gabon The Gabonese Embassy is open weekdays from 8 am to noon and from 3 to 6 pm. One-month visas to Gabon cost CFA 20,000; also bring two photos and an extra CFA 5000 for a telex to Libreville requesting visa approval. Responses usually take at least a week.

Ghana & Kenya The British Embassy in Yaoundé and British Consulate in Douala issue three-month visas to Kenya and transit visas to Ghana for CFA 16,500. If you're headed for Kenya, you can save money by getting a two-week visa at Nairobi airport or any Kenyan border (US$10 and renewable).

Nigeria You can get visas to Nigeria at the Nigerian Embassy in Yaoundé or the Nigerian Consulate in Douala. The embassy's visa section is open Mondays, Wednesdays and Fridays from 9 am to 12.30 pm and gives 48-hour service. Visas are valid for one-month stays and you must bring three photos. Visa fees vary greatly but are similar to those of other Nigerian embassies in Africa: Australians CFA 6046, Austrians CFA 2418, Belgians CFA 7585, Britons CFA 9331, Danes CFA 5670, Dutch CFA 1170, French CFA 2528, Germans CFA 4304, Italians CFA 3612, Japanese CFA 985, Spanish CFA 1505, Swedes CFA 2709 and Swiss CFA 4515. For Americans, Canadians, Finns and the Irish, visas are free.

Senegal The Senegalese Embassy, which is open weekdays from 8 am to noon and from 3 to 6 pm, charges CFA 3250 for one-month visas and more for those of longer duration. It gives 24-hour service and requires two photos.

Zaïre Visas to Zaïre are very expensive and cost the same in Yaoundé as elsewhere in Central Africa. Single/multiple-entry visas cost CFA 23,500/38,000 for one-month stays, CFA 43,000/56,000 for two-month stays, and CFA 62,500/71,000 for three-month stays. Open weekdays from 7.30 am to 2.30 pm, the Zaïrian Embassy also requires two photos and gives same-day service.

Other Countries The British Embassy issues three-month visas to Sierra Leone, Gambia, Kenya, Zambia, Malawi, Uganda, Zimbabwe and Botswana for CFA 16,500 each. The consular section of the French Embassy, which is open for visa service Monday to Saturday from 8 am to noon, issues visas to the Côte d'Ivoire (the embassy has closed), Togo and Burkina Faso, but not to Niger (its embassy has also closed). I was told that in addition to CFA 10,000 and two photos I would have to bring a copy of an airline ticket and a telex confirming a hotel reservation! Check this nonsense because no other French diplomatic mission in Africa seems to require such; alternatively, try the French Consulate in Douala.

Camerounian Embassies

Cameroun has embassies in Addis Ababa, Abidjan, Algiers, Bangui, Berne, Bonn, Brazzaville, Brussels, Cairo, Dakar, The Hague, Kinshasa, Lagos, Libreville, London, Madrid, Malabo, Monrovia, N'Djamena, Ottawa, Paris, Rio de Janeiro, Rome, Tokyo and Washington. There are also consulates in Calabar (Nigeria) and Geneva and an honorary one in Australia (8/47 Milson Rd, Cremorne, NSW 2090, (☎ (2) 909-2530).

Foreign Embassies

For a full list of foreign embassies, see the Information section under Yaoundé.

DOCUMENTS

Everyone needs a passport and an International Health Certificate with proof of having received a yellow fever vaccination within the past 10 years. Motorists must have a *carnet de passage en douane*. When travelling outside the major cities, you should carry your passport as there are police roadblocks all over the country. In town, carry your passport or at least a photocopy of it as police occasionally ask travellers to see their papers.

CUSTOMS

Importing currency is not a problem but you may not export more than CFA 25,000 if you're leaving the CFA zone. If you're travelling to countries within the CFA zone (Cameroun, the CAR, Chad, Congo, Equatorial Guinea and Gabon) there's no limit. However, officials don't always know the rules or are seeking bribes. Some officials say, for example, that CFA 200,000 is the limit within the CFA zone. Customs officials often ask to see travellers' money upon leaving, so if you'll be exporting CFA in excess of the above amounts, I would advise declaring your money on arrival.

MONEY

US$1   =   CFA 280
UK£1   =   CFA 425

The unit of currency is the Central African CFA. West African CFA can easily be exchanged at the banks for Central African CFA. Major stores in Yaoundé and Douala will occasionally accept West African CFA if you're purchasing something, also major hotels in those cities, but generally not those elsewhere. If you have money transferred to a local bank, you must get permission from customs to receive it in foreign currency, otherwise, you'll have to take it in CFA.

The best banks for changing money are usually Crédit Lyonnais and Standard Chartered Bank, both foreign banks; their service is relatively fast and their rates and commissions are usually better than those at the other major banks. Cameroun's major banks include the Banque Internationale pour l'Afrique Occidentale (BIAO), the Banque Internationale pour le Commerce et l'Industrie du Cameroun (BICIC) and the Société Générale de Banques au Cameroun (SGBC).

BUSINESS HOURS & HOLIDAYS

Business and government hours are weekdays from 8 am to noon and 2.30 to 5.30 pm, and Saturdays from 8 am to 1 pm. Banks are open weekdays from 7.30 to 11.30 am.

Public Holidays

The country's major holiday is National Day. In the north, especially Maroua, Tabaski is the major celebration.

1 January (New Year's Day)
11 February (Youth Day)
End of Ramadan
Good Friday
1 May (Labour Day)
Ascension Thursday
20 May (National Day)
Tabaski
15 August (Assumption Day)
Mohammed's Birthday
10 December
25 December (Christmas Day)

POST & TELECOMMUNICATIONS

If you're getting mail sent to you via poste restante (CFA 250 per letter), you'll receive it quicker in Douala than in Yaoundé. Mail at either place is held for only two weeks or so.

The Intelcam telephone, fax and telex centres (at the post office in Douala and next to it in Yaoundé) are very efficient for international calls but for domestic calls the waiting time can be quite lengthy as the queues are often long.

For three-minute calls to the UK/USA the charge is CFA 4500/6000! However, it's reportedly possible to make one-minute international calls, enough time to give the receiver your telephone number for a reverse call (it's much cheaper to make a call to Cameroun than from it). Most major hotels have telex and fax facilities as well.

TIME

Time in Cameroun is GMT plus 1, so when it's noon in Cameroun, it's 11 am in London and 6 am in New York (remember to add an hour during daylight-saving time).

PHOTOGRAPHY

Photo permits are no longer required in Cameroun. However, picture-taking of sensitive and strategic areas, such as the Presidential Palace, airports, ports, bridges, railway stations, military and telecommunications installations, or any other public building, is not permitted without a special permit. The problem is that police in Cameroun are often looking for bribes and they have a lot of discretion in determining what's 'sensitive' or 'strategic'; they may interpret such so broadly that it's difficult not to break the law. Moreover, officials in the provinces may not know the rules and may still ask to see an 'authorisation' saying you don't need a photo permit. Regardless, taking photos while out of the sight of police is still the best rule.

To be on the safe side, professional photographers should consider going to the Ministry of Information & Culture in one of the regional capitals (the permit will be valid for that region only) or in Yaoundé (valid for the entire country) and get a written statement that they have the right to take photos.

HEALTH

A yellow fever vaccination is required. In Cameroun, clinics are usually better than hospitals. In Yaoundé, the two best clinics are Polyclinique André-Fouda (☎ 222464) on Route de Ngousso north-east of the railway station, and Clinique St Marthe (☎ 223109). You'll find several good pharmacies on Ave Kennedy in Yaoundé; the best by reputation is Pharmacie Française (☎ 221476) at the corner of Aves Kennedy and Ahidjo. Pharmacie de l'Intendance (☎ 233812) is another on Ave Kennedy.

In Douala, the best clinic is the Polyclinique de Douala (☎ 421840) on Rue Njo-Njo in Bonapriso. Two of the best pharmacies are Pharmacie du Centre (☎ 421430) at 38 Blvd de la Liberté, and Pharmacie des Portiques (☎ 421444) nearby on Blvd Ahidjo.

DANGERS & ANNOYANCES

The security situation in Cameroun has deteriorated significantly in recent years. In Douala and Yaoundé, travellers get robbed every day, especially outside the banks and at the markets and *gare routières* (bus stations) where conditions are usually very crowded and perfect for robberies. Carrying any kind of luggage will mark you as a visitor, increasing your vulnerability considerably. In a single day while carrying a bag in Yaoundé, I was the victim of three attempted robberies. Arriving at the big city stations, you'll be immediately surrounded by hoards of pushy young men trying to grab your luggage and guide you to a particular bus or taxi; some of them, however, are actually thieves and before you know it your bag or wallet will be gone. If you arrive by taxi at one of the city's large gare routières, you might consider offering the driver a good tip, say CFA 200, to find you a vehicle while you wait inside the taxi and then have him carry your luggage to it while you hold firmly to your other possessions. Needless to say, walking around at night anywhere in Douala or Yaoundé is extremely risky and unwise.

The police in Cameroun are probably the worst in Central Africa, for they are even more corrupt and stop vehicles more frequently than those in the CAR, and are not timid about asking for bribes. They put up roadblocks everywhere, mostly just outside cities, and will stop you and, almost invariably, find something you've done wrong. If you don't offer a bribe, you risk being detained for a number of hours. If you don't have your passport, for example, don't be surprised if they detain you while someone else goes to fetch it. For this reason, it is a good idea to carry your passport (or at least photocopies of the first few pages and your Cameroun visa) everywhere.

FOOD

Cameroun has some of the best food in Central Africa. Consequently, you'll also find it in areas outside the country, such as in Gabon. One of the main ingredients is manioc leaves, which usually translates as *feuille* on menus. (Theoretically, any plant leaf could be feuille, but in most cases it's manioc leaves.) Manioc produces some of the best sauces in Central African cooking, and are invariably based in palm or peanut oil. *Sauce feuille viande* simply means that the sauce comes with meat; *sauce feuille avec poisson* is a less common variation with fish.

Antother very common sauce is one made from okra *(gombo)*; hence *sauce gombo* or *sauce de gombo avec crevettes* (with shrimp). Tomato-based sauces are also common *(sauce de tomate)*.

As in all African cooking, sauces in Cameroun are accompanied by rice *(riz)* or, more traditionally, a thick mashed potato-like substance which comes in at least three, slightly different forms – *couscous*, *pâte* (pronounced 'paht') or *fufu* – any of which can be made of rice, corn, manioc, plantains or bananas. Hence, you might see *pâte de riz* on the menu (more common in the north) or corn pâte (more common in western

Cameroun. Around Yaoundé, the women make a special pâte from peanuts called *ntomba nam* which is eaten with meat.

As in the case of pâte, corn-based couscous is more common in the south while riz-based couscous is more common in the north, and in no way do they resemble Moroccan couscous.

Similarly, fufu can be made from a variety of starches or grains, frequently cassava, plantain or corn. All of these staple dishes are traditionally eaten with the hands (the right one only), but in restaurants large spoons are frequently offered to foreign visitors.

You won't find much bush meat on the menu except near the rainforested southern border, which is just as well because these animals are becoming rare in Cameroun, more so than in other Central African countries. Bush meat includes porcupine *(porc-pic)*, crocodile, monkey *(singe)*, wart hog *(phacochère)*, bush pig *(sanglier)*, boa constrictor *(boa)* and antelope *(gazelle)*.

Getting There & Away

AIR

The only international flights from Europe to Yaoundé are on Swissair, twice weekly from Zurich and Geneva. The remaining flights are all to Douala, including daily flights from Paris on either Air France or Cameroun Airlines and one flight a week from Brussels (Sabena), Rome (Cameroun Airlines), Geneva and Zurich (Swissair), Frankfurt (Lufthansa) and Moscow (Aeroflot). The cheapest flights from London are on Aeroflot via Moscow with a ticket purchased from a bucket shop.

From the USA, you could take a flight to Paris and connect with one of the daily flights to Douala or, usually less expensive, you could take Air Afrique or Nigeria Airways from New York and transfer in Dakar (Senegal), Abidjan (Côte d'Ivoire) or Lagos (Nigeria). From Lagos there are five flights a week, on either Air Afrique or Cameroun Airlines. From East Africa, you can fly direct twice-weekly from Nairobi on Cameroun Airlines.

There are good connections between Douala and most Central African countries, including five flights a week to/from Malabo (Equatorial Guinea) on either Equator Guineana de Aviation (EGA) or Cameroun Airlines; four weekly flights to Libreville (Gabon) on either Cameroun Airlines or Air Gabon; three weekly flights to/from Brazzaville (Congo) on Cameroun Airlines or Air Afrique; and two flights a week to/from Kinshasa (Zaïre) on Cameroun Airlines or Air Gabon; two flights to Bangui (the CAR) on Cameroun Airlines or Air Afrique; and two flights to N'Djamena (Chad) on Cameroun Airlines or Unitair.

As for Cameroun Airlines, you have to wonder whether they couldn't have come up with a better symbol than something that looks like a paper aeroplane. Regardless, its international service is good; by reputation it's one of the four or five best airlines in Black Africa.

LAND
Train
If you're headed to Yaoundé from the CAR, you can save time by heading north-west from the border crossing (Garoua-Boulaï) and catching the train at N'Gaoundal (250 km by good road) instead of heading south-west from the border to catch it at Belabo (350 km by bad road).

Most Africans catch it at Belabo because the train fare is about 40% less. If you're staying overnight in Bouar (the CAR) and leave early the next morning, with luck you can make it to N'Gaoundal before 9.30 pm or so when the train passes.

Bush Taxi
To/From Chad N'Djamena to N'Gaoundéré normally takes 1½ to two days by bush taxi (about CFA 9000). Most travellers take the overnight train on the N'Gaoundéré to Yaoundé stretch. You'll find a bridge crossing between Kousseri and N'Djamena and the Chadian border there closes punctually at 5.30 pm.

To/From Nigeria Going to/from Nigeria, you'll find many taxis on the Maroua to Maiduguri stretch in the north. Once inside Nigeria, taxis fill up in minutes and go like the bomb was about to drop. The most popular crossing, however, is in the south via Ekok and Mamfé. The road between Mamfé and the border is so bad in the rainy season that drivers sometimes demand more money than usual; it is also very bad between Mamfé and Bamenda.

To/From the CAR If you're headed to the Central African Republic, you can take the train from Yaoundé to Belabo (CFA 5640/2770 in 1st/2nd class) and catch a bush taxi from there to Bertoua and the border at Garoua-Boulaï, or, less travelled, to Bertoua, Batouri and Berbérati, the more southerly route. Another option is taking a bus from Yaoundé to Bertoua; however, few travellers do this because the train is faster and more comfortable. The roads on all of these routes are dirt and in bad condition. Those in the CAR are generally better and connections are reasonably good.

To/From Gabon & Equatorial Guinea There are lots of bush taxis and minibuses headed south from Yaoundé to Ebolowa (CFA 1500); the trip takes about 2½ hours. From there to the southern border normally takes another five hours or so. From Ebolowa the road points south to Ambam; most minibuses and pick-up trucks depart in the morning. In Ambam the road splits, the easterly route heading for Bitam, Oyem and Libreville (Gabon) and the westerly route heading for Ebebiyin and Bata (Equatorial Guinea). On both routes you'll find a ferry to take you across the Ntem River which is only about 70 metres wide and flows east to west about 10 km south of Ambam. The ferries cross back and forth every hour and if they're not operating, you can always take a *pirogue* (canoe). From either river crossing it's another half hour or so to the border where you should have no problem finding vehicles headed for Ebebiyin (just two km across the border) or Bitam (30 km).

Car

The routes from Lagos (Nigeria) to Douala (1250 km) or Kano (Nigeria) to Douala (1360 km) via the southern border crossing at Ekok (Cameroun) both take two or three days. The road is paved the entire distance within Nigeria. In Cameroun, the scenic Mamfé to Douala road is now paved most of the way and is in much better condition than the 205-km Mamfé to Bamenda road, which becomes almost impassable during the rainy season, from June to September.

The drive south from N'Djamena (Chad) to N'Gaoundéré takes 1½ days on a good asphalt road. From there it's another two days to Yaoundé or Douala via Bafoussam, which is the preferred route.

Yaoundé to Bangui (the CAR) via Garoua-Boulaï is 1200 km and normally takes 2½ to three days. Most of the route is all-weather dirt road.

Yaoundé to Libreville (Gabon) via Oyem, which is also 1200 km, is paved for only about a quarter of the distance; the trip can be done in two very long days during the dry season, but 2½ to three days is more typical. In Gabon, the roads get very muddy and dangerously slippery during the rainy season from October until May, but bulldozers do a good job of keeping them passable year-round.

The road to Equatorial Guinea is the same as that to Gabon as far as Ambam (200 km from Yaoundé), where the road splits. Either way you must cross the Ntem River south of Ambam by ferry. Yaoundé to Bata can be driven in one very long day during the dry season; however, two easy days with a night in Ebebiyin is more typical. The dirt section of this route (Ebolowa to Bata) is fairly well maintained even during the rainy season.

SEA

To/From Europe

Douala is the best port in Central Africa for catching freighters to Europe; one of the principal companies is Grimaldi Lines. Others include Compagnie Maritime Zaïroise and Compagnie Maritime Belge, which have freighters ploughing between Europe and Zaïre, often stopping in Douala. If you're headed to Zaïre, check them out as the fare is reportedly less than the cost of flying. For a berth, contact the maritime travel agencies listed in the Douala section. In Europe contact Cameroun Shipping Lines (☎ (1) 4293 5070; telex 640016), 38 Rue de la Liège, 75008 Paris, or its German agency, Unimar Seatransport (☎ 30060; telex 216-2116) Box 106226, D 2000 Hamburg 1.

To/From Calabar (Nigeria)

Various boats plough back and forth every day between Oron (near Calabar) and Idenao (near Limbe). There are two classes of boats. One is a small speedboat which is fairly reliable, takes about four hours and costs up to CFA 10,000, depending on the number of passengers. The other is a large cargo boat, often loaded down with smuggled goods. These boats are cheaper (typically less than US$10 in naira) and for this reason are preferred by the locals. However, they are much more unreliable, usually take longer, and you cannot be certain where they'll drop you as this often depends on where the cargo is headed. If they drop you on a beach seemingly in the middle of nowhere, you might miss the nearest immigration station, in which case you could get hassled later by immigration officials. Moreover, the Nigerian and Camerounian navies are always on the lookout for boats with smuggled goods and if they stop your boat, you could find your trip significantly delayed and you might be hassled by police.

If you're heading from Cameroun to Nigeria, you have the choice of taking a bush taxi from Limbe to Idenao (CFA 1000), some 48 km to the north-west, and looking for a boat from there to Oron, or taking a bush taxi from Kumba to Ekondo Titi (CFA 1300), some 50 km to the west, and looking for a speedboat headed for Ikang, which is 25 km south-east of Calabar by road.

If you're heading from Calabar to Cameroun, you can take a ferry from Calabar south-west across the Cross River to Oron; there are two every day in either direction, departing Calabar at 8.30 am and 1.30 pm

and Oron at 11 am and 4 pm. The 20-km trip
takes 1½ hours and costs the equivalent of
about US$1 a person. Coming from Calabar,
you may have to stay overnight in Oron as
you may well find that all the vessels have
left by the time you arrive.

Alternatively, you could take a bush taxi
from Calabar to Ikang, a 45-minute trip.
There's a big sign at the ferry office in Ikang
indicating that the speedboat for Ekondo Titi
leaves at 8 am but in reality it can leave at
any time up to around 3 pm. You must go to
immigration and the police before leaving.
The trip to Ekondo Titi takes three or four
hours and there are police checks along the
way; you're sure to be asked for bribes by
both Nigerian and Camerounian police but
don't give in. If the ferry arrives in Ekondo
after 6 pm, Camerounian customs officials
are likely to refuse landing rights until the
next morning unless the passengers pay a
large bribe. There's no bank in Ekondo, so
you'll have to change money on the street.
From Ekondo it's not so difficult to find
minibuses headed east to Kumba but the road
is very bad.

Getting Around

AIR
Cameroun Airlines offers up to six flights a
day between Douala and Yaoundé. Between
Cameroun Airlines and Unitair, a new, primarily domestic airline, there are flights
every day from Douala and Yaoundé to
Maroua and Garoua, five times a week to
N'Gaoundéré, and once or twice a week to
Bafoussam, Bamenda, Batouri and Bertoua.
Fares are not cheap; one way from Maroua
to Yaoundé costs CFA 44,950, and from
Maroua to Douala costs CFA 51,150. Ask
about weekend excursion fares and student
discounts; Cameroun Airlines, for example,
offers such on its domestic flights.

BUS
There are now large modern buses on two of
the most heavily travelled routes: Yaoundé

to Douala and Yaoundé to western
Cameroun (Bafoussam, Bamenda, Foumban
and Dschang). These buses are much more
comfortable than bush taxis, just as fast, run
to set schedules and, unlike bush taxis, are
generally not stopped along the way by
police. From Yaoundé they take about three
hours to Douala (CFA 2500), 4¼ hours to
Bafoussam (CFA 2500) and six hours to
Bamenda, Dschang or Foumban (CFA
3500). To be sure of a seat you need to reserve
at least a few hours in advance; however,
there are so many companies that you can
usually arrive at the bus departure point and
find an empty seat without great difficulty.
Fortunately, the various bus companies all
have their offices in the same area, so looking
around for the next departure is easy.

TRAIN
If you're travelling to northern Cameroun,
consider taking the train. It's cheap, much
quicker than driving or taking a bush taxi,
and fairly decent. There's one train a day, the
Gazelle du Nord, which leaves nightly in
either direction from N'Gaoundéré and
Yaoundé, with onward connections to/from
Douala. The train has sleeping compartments but is not air-con and has no dining
car. You may have a choice between a compartment with two berths and four berths; the
former is only slight more expensive. Fares
from Yaoundé to N'Gaoundéré are CFA
11,600/6750 in 1st class/2nd class. For a
couchette (berth), you must pay an additional CFA 1750 above the 1st-class fare;
some cars have two-berth cabins, others have
four berths. Pillows, blankets and linen are
provided. The trains usually leave quite
punctually; the trip is supposed to take 11
hours but 12 or 13 hours is more typical. The
timetable, however, is constantly changing.

Reservations for a couchette can only be
made on the day of departure. You can buy
drinks and snacks from vendors. Second
class is crowded and uncomfortable and you
must get to the railway station two hours in
advance to be guaranteed a seat.

There are three other lines besides
Yaoundé to N'Gaoundéré: Yaoundé to

Douala, Douala to Kumba and Douala to Nkongsamba. The Douala to Yaoundé stretch has been rebuilt; there are four departures daily in either direction and on the better trains the trip now takes only about four hours. The 1st-class carriages on this run are very comfortable with air-con and TV plus there's a dining car. Second class isn't so bad either but it's quite crowded. Fares are CFA 3500/1900 in 1st class/2nd class.

In great contrast, the trains running north from Douala to Kumba and Nkongsamba are old and decrepit; just to Kumba (144 km by road) the trip can take eight hours or more. Taking one of these trains is mostly for the adventure.

BUSH TAXI

Bush taxis are usually Peugeot 504s or minivans and are frequently in good condition. The drivers, however, tend to go at life-threatening speeds, especially on well-maintained paved roads where fatal accidents are a daily occurrence. Bush taxis are relatively inexpensive in Cameroun compared to those elsewhere in the CFA zone; they cost about CFA 10 per km on many long paved routes and up to CFA 14 per km on some shorter paved routes. N'Gaoundéré to Garoua (296 km) costs CFA 3000 (CFA 10.1 per km), Douala to Bafoussam (266 km) costs CFA 2500 to CFA 3000 (CFA 9.4 to 11.1 per km) and Yaoundé to Ebolowa (110 km) is CFA 1500 (CFA 13.6 per km).

Luggage fees are extra and subject to negotiation; though are usually between 15 and 25% of the fare, depending in part upon the size of the baggage. Fares on dirt roads tend to be more expensive per km, and the fares in a Peugeot 504 are sometimes slightly higher than in a minibus. Especially in the north, the vehicles leave early in the morning. Between Douala and Yaoundé you can get them any time of the day, and there's little waiting time, but large buses are more popular and just as fast.

CAR

Cameroun has by far the cheapest petrol prices in Central Africa, with a litre of petrol costing CFA 195, and a litre of diesel CFA 165. Nigerian black-market petrol is cheaper, from about CFA 150 (red-coloured 'ordinary') to CFA 170 (white-coloured 'super'); the former is dirtier and many drivers refuse to use it. You'll see it being sold in large glass jars along the roads all over the country, more so the closer you get to Nigeria.

Many of the major arterial roads in Cameroun are paved and in good condition. However, there are some major routes that are still not paved, including Yaoundé to N'Gaoundéré, Foumban to N'Gaoundéré and the Nigerian border through Mamfé to Bamenda. Driving on these roads, especially during the rainy season, can be tortuous as they are in terrible condition.

Cameroun has been late in acquiring good roads. It wasn't until the mid-1980s that the most important link in the country, Douala to Yaoundé, was finally paved. The country clearly has sufficient resources from petroleum to finance the paving of the remaining links, but gross mismanagement by the government has made the going painfully slow.

The preferred route from Douala or Yaoundé north to N'Gaoundéré is now via Bafoussam, Banyo and Tibati. About 40% of the 833-km route between Bafoussam and N'Gaoundéré is paved; the remaining unpaved sections are in fairly bad condition. For this reason, the normal driving time from either Douala or Yaoundé to Maroua in the far north is three days. You can also put your vehicle on the Yaoundé to N'Gaoundéré train for about CFA 70,000, but virtually no-one does.

Car Rental

Avis is the country's leading car-rental agency, with representatives in Yaoundé, Douala and several of the smaller cities such as Garoua, Maroua and Bafoussam. Avis will allow you to pick up the car in one town and drop it off in another, but the drop-off charge is typically at least CFA 50,000. You'll also find Hertz in Yaoundé and some smaller operators in the largest cities but the latters' vehicles tend to be older, less reliable, and not as well maintained.

Generally speaking, renting a car in Cameroun is quite expensive (but less so than in most other CFA countries), with costs at around US$1400 per week if you average about 300 km per day. You can easily spend in one day what you'd pay in the USA for a one-week rental of the same model, which is why most travellers prefer hiring a taxi by the day. Moreover, if the car breaks down, it's his problem, not yours. Typical car-rental prices in Cameroun for the cheapest models are CFA 13,000 per day, CFA 100 per km, plus insurance and tax. At these rates and including the price of petrol, you can count on about CFA 26,500/40,000/52,500 per day if you average 100/200/300 km per day. In comparison, you should expect to pay about CFA 18,000/23,000/28,000 for an all-day taxi.

BICYCLE

Cameroun is a great country for cycling as many of the roads are paved or all-weather dirt. Mile-for-effort, the best areas are the south-west and the far north. Every year in December, the International Bicycle Fund (☎ (206) 628-9314), 4887 Columbia Dr South, Seattle, WA 98108, USA, sponsors two back-to-back trips, a two-week one in south-western Cameroun and a two-week one in northern Cameroun. The all-inclusive tour cost is approximately US$1100 for each segment plus air fares.

Yaoundé

Set in verdant hills some 750 metres above the sea, Yaoundé was a clear choice over Douala for the 'honour' of colonial capital. The cooler, almost European climate was more amenable to the newly transplanted Parisian overlords. Today's travellers likewise almost invariably prefer Yaoundé over Douala and it remains unique among capital cities in Central and West Africa for its hilly environment. If you take a taxi to the Mt Fébé area on the northern outskirts of town, you'll be surprised how cool the climate can be. No wonder the Benedictine monks built their monastery here.

Many people used to think of Yaoundé as a fairly sleepy city, at least in comparison to Douala, but now with close to 900,000 inhabitants (mostly Ewondo) and modern buildings dotting the landscape including a new airport, sports arena and Hilton Hotel, Yaoundé is beginning to shake off that reputation. The African sections of the city are as colourful and full of activity as any you'll find in Central Africa. Unfortunately, a rapidly increasing crime rate has tarnished the city's reputation in recent years to the point where many travellers are only too happy to leave.

Orientation

First-timers to Yaoundé are usually a little baffled by the street pattern, or lack thereof. Sprawled over undulating hills, the city has only a few streets that aren't snake-like, all in the compact central area which can be covered on foot. Ave Kennedy, the nearby circular Marché Central and the post office are all useful landmarks.

Ave Kennedy is a major hub of commercial activity. At one end is Place John Kennedy and the Centre Artisanal, the large tent-like structure where you'll find all sorts of Camerounian handicrafts; at the other end on Ave Ahidjo is Score supermarket, a Yaoundé institution. On both those streets as well as Avc Monseigneur Vogt and Ave de l'Indépendance you'll find many of the city's major shops, banks, bookshops, travel agencies, cinemas, bars and restaurants.

The centre of town – but not the commercial hub – is Place Ahmadou Ahidjo; the post office faces it. If you take the wide Blvd du 20 Mai northward, you'll come to the landmark Hilton Hotel and Rond-Point du Blvd 20 Mai. The administrative district (or Quartier du Lac) where many government buildings are located is just to the west thereof. If you head further north from that rond-point for about three km, past Carrefour Nlongkak, you'll be in Bastos, a major

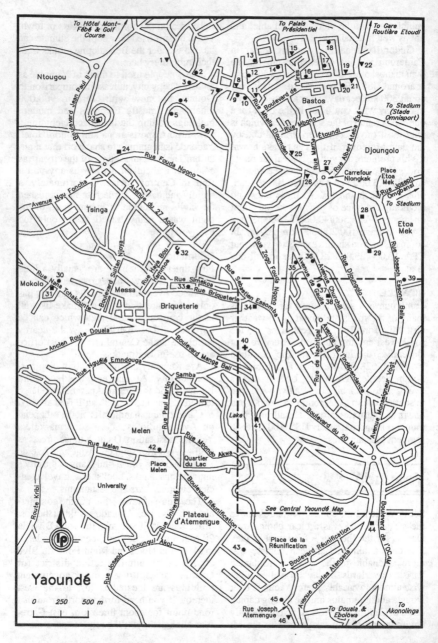

To Hôtel Mont-Fébé & Golf Course

To Palais Présidentiel

To Gare Routière Etoudi

Ntougou

Bastos

Djoungolo

Etoa Mek

Tsinga

Mokolo

Messa

Briqueterie

Melen

Place Melen

Quartier du Lac

University

Plateau d'Atemengue

Lake

Place de la Réunification

To Stadium (Stade Omnisport)

To Stadium

To Douala & Ebolowa

To Akonolinga

Boulevard Jean Paul II

Rue Fouda Ngono

Avenue Ngi Fonchà

Avenue du 27 Aoit

Rue Haya Bou Hamoa

Boulevard Sultan Njoya

Rue Simekoa

Rue Briqueterie

Rue Nana Tchakounte

Rue Mballa Eloumden

Boulevard de l'Ures

Rue Mbono

Rue Mana

Rue Albert Ateba Ebè

Rue Joseph Omgbansi

Rue Zogo Fouda Ngono

Rue Sébastien Essomba

Rue Djoungolo

Rue Joseph Essono Balla

Avenue de Gaulle

Avenue Churchill

Rue de Nachtigal

Avenue de l'Indépendance

Boulevard Manga Bell

Rue Paul Martin

Rue Moondo Akwa

Rue Melen

Rue Nguélé Emndouga

Ancien Route Douala

Boulevard Réunification

Rue Université

Rue Joseph Tchoungui Akoi

Boulevard du 20 Mai

Avenue Monseigneur Vogt

Boulevard Réunification

Avenue Charles Atangana

Boulevard de l'OCAM

Rue Joseph Atemengue

Route Kribi

Samba

Carrefour Nlongkak

Place Etoa Mek

Étoundi

See Central Yaoundé Map

Yaoundé

0   250   500 m

■ PLACES TO STAY

24 Hôtel Relaxe
27 Hôtel Idéal
28 Foyer International de l'Église
   Presbytérienne
29 Hôtel des Nations
31 Hôtel le Progrès
34 Hôtel Aurora
38 Hôtel Indépendance
41 Hôtel des Députés
44 Hôtel Impérial

▼ PLACES TO EAT

1 Restaurant le Coq Hardi
8 Café Central
9 Snack-Bar le Grille
11 Restaurant Chinois Chez Nous
15 Restaurant le Romarin
19 Restaurant l'Asiana
21 Restaurant le Bambou Village
22 Le Refuge Snack-Bar
25 Restaurant Samovar
26 Restaurant le Bec Fin
35 La Grande Muraille de Chine
46 Restaurant les Grilladins

OTHER

2 Swiss Embassy
3 Liberian Embassy
4 EEC Offices
5 Equatorial Guinea Embassy
6 Belgian Embassy
7 BAT Cameroun
10 Chadian Embassy
12 Senegalese Embassy
13 Spanish Embassy
14 Zaïrian Embassy
16 Gabonese Embassy
17 Moroccan Embassy
18 Congolese Embassy
20 CAR Embassy
23 Palais de Congrés
30 Marché de Mokolo
32 Grande Mosquée
33 Rex Cinéma
35 German Embassy
36 British Embassy
37 Socatour Travel Agency & British
   Council
39 Supermarché Tigre
40 Hôpital Central
42 Musée d'Art Nègre
43 Camp Militaire
45 French Embassy

embassy area and posh residential quarter named after the cigarette factory. Several km beyond you'll pass the huge Chinese-built Maison de la Culture and, nearby, the Presidential Palace on the northern outskirts of town, eventually arriving at the Benedictine monastery and, just beyond, the deluxe Hôtel Mont-Fébé. This last landmark is set on a hill over 1000 metres high, with a golf course below; the view of the city is unbeatable.

Three of the liveliest African quarters are Messa, Mokolo, and Briqueterie (also called Le Quartier), which is the main Muslim quarter and dominated by the Grande Mosquée. These three contiguous quarters are roughly two to three km north-west of the centre, beyond the hospital and are areas with cheap lodgings, street food and small bars with names such as 'Chasse-cafard' and 'La Parole de Dieu'. The unlicensed chicken houses here and elsewhere around town serve the best grilled chicken this side of Abidjan (Côte d'Ivoire). To the south thereof is Quartier Melen where the university and the Musée d'Art Nègre are located.

Information

Tourist Office The Secrétariat d'État du Tourisme (☎ 224411) is in the city centre at Place Ahidjo, opposite the post office.

Money The main banks for changing money are Crédit Lyonnais and Société Générale de Banques au Cameroun (SGBC) (☎ 234125) on Ave Monseigneur Vogt; BIAO (☎ 23-4135) and Banque pour le Commerce et l'Industrie (BICIC) (☎ 234130) on Ave Kennedy (also Ave Ahidjo); Banque de Paris et des Pays-Bas; and Standard Chartered Bank just south of Place de l'Indépendance.

Post & Telecommunications The main post office is in the heart of town at Place Ahidjo. To make telephone calls and send faxes, go to Intelcam across the street. You can also make local calls from the public telephones outside the post office.

Foreign Embassies Most of the embassies

are in Quartier Bastos, about three km north
of the central area:

Algeria
    (☎ 230655)
Belgium
    Immeuble de Mban, near EC offices (☎ 222788;
    telex 8314)
Central African Republic (the CAR)
    100 metres off Rue Albert Ateba Ébé (☎ 225155)
Chad
    Rue Mballa Eloumden (☎ 230624)
Congo
    Near Moroccan and CAR embassies (☎ 232458)
Equatorial Guinea
    Near the Belgian Embassy and EC offices
    (☎ 224149)
Gabon
    Just off Blvd de l'URSS, near the Zaïrian
    Embassy (☎ 222966)
Italy
    (☎ 223376)
Liberia
    Rue Mballa Eloumden (☎ 231296, 232631)
Morocco
    Near the Gabonese Embassy (☎ 225092)
Senegal
    Blvd de l'URSS, near the Zaïrîan Embassy
    (☎ 220308)
Spain
    Blvd de l'URSS, near the Senegalese Embassy
    (☎ 224189)
Switzerland
    Rue Mballa Eloumden (☎ 232896, 233052)
Zaïre
    Blvd de l'URSS, near the Senegalese Embassy
    (☎ 225103)

Many of the remaining foreign embassies are
in or near the central area including:

Canada
    Immeuble Stamatiades, Ave de l'Indépendance
    (☎ 230203, 221822; telex 8209)
France
    Rue Joseph Atemengué near the Place de la
    Réunification (☎ 234013, 220233; telex 8233)
Germany
    Ave de Gaulle (☎ 230056; telex 8412)
Netherlands
    Immeuble Le Concorde, Ave 27 Août (☎ 220544;
    telex 8237)
Nigeria
    Off Ave Monseigneur Vogt, near Marché du
    Mfoundi (☎ 223455)
UK
    Ave Churchill near Hôtel Indépendance (☎ 220-
    796/545; telex 8200)

USA
    Rue de Nachtigal, near Place de l'Indépendance
    (☎ 234014; fax 230753; telex 8223)

Other countries with embassies in Yaoundé
include Benin (☎ 233498), Brazil
(☎ 231957), Greece (☎ 223936), Israel
(☎ 221644), Sweden (☎ 233854) and
Tunisia (☎ 223368).

Cultural Centres The American cultural
centre (☎ 231633) is on Rue de Nachtigal
near the US Embassy. It has copies of the
International Herald Tribune as well as
various English-language magazines. The
British Council, which is a block north of
Place de l'Indépendance on Ave de Gaulle,
also has a library as does the Goethe Institut
(☎ 233874) on Ave Kennedy and the nearby
French cultural centre on Ave Ahidjo, near
the end of Ave Kennedy.

Travel Agencies For tours, one of the best
travel agencies is Socatour (☎ 233219; telex
8766) on Ave de Gaulle, just north of Place
de l'Indépendance. It offers various all-
inclusive tours of western and northern
Cameroun and rents cars as well. For airline
reservations, try Antoniades Travel Agency
(ATA) (☎ 231488) in the city centre on Rue
Goker. Others agencies include Intervoyages
(☎ 231045) a block south of Place de
l'Indépendance off Rue de Nachtigal,
Camvoyages (☎ 232212) on Ave de l'Indépendance and Cameroun Publi-Expansion
(CPE) (☎ 233921) in Immeuble les Galeries.
American Express is represented only in
Douala.

Bookshops The best bookshop is Librairie
Moderne Hachette (☎ 231688) on Ave
Kennedy. Open to 7.30 pm, Hachette has an
excellent selection of French books and
some in English, as well as *Time*, *Newsweek*
and sometimes maps of Cameroun. For a
good selection of African novels in English,
try Ebibi Book Centre in Immeuble Hajal,
opposite Le Capitole Cinéma on Ave Foch.

For maps, your best bet is the Institut
Géographique Nationale (☎ 223465) on Ave

Monseigneur Vogt opposite the modern BEAC bank. Open weekdays from 7.30 am to noon and 2.30 to 6 pm, it has maps of the entire country, the 10 regions (scale 1:50,000) and various major cities. Unfortunately, supplies sometimes run out.

Film & Photography For film supplies, the best shop is G S Electronics on Ave Kennedy next to the BICIC bank; it's the only place that sells slide film, but watch the expiry dates. Regular Kodocolor print film costs CFA 1500 for 36 frames. Hollywood Photo, a Korean-operated film-developing store with one-hour service, is on Ave Foch, down the hill from the US Embassy.

Supermarkets Yaoundé has a number of large supermarkets including Score on Ave Ahidjo and Prisunic on Ave de l'Indépendance. The best is Tigre Supermarché, 1½ km north of Place Ahidjo on Rue Joseph Essono Bella, which is open Saturday afternoons.

Benedictine Monastery
Musée d'Art Camerounais Built in 1967, the Benedictine monastery has this excellent museum which definitely should not be missed; it's a five-minute walk from the Mont-Fébé Hôtel. Despite its small size, the museum has one of the best collections of Camerounian art in the world and it's all listed in a catalogue which you can use as a guide; explanations are in French and English. Within three rooms are more than 400 invaluable objects of art – masks, bowls, pipes (including some outstanding Bamoun bronze pipes), a royal bed, intricate wooden wall panels, figurines and musical instruments. Most were collected by a Swiss monk, Luitfrid Marfurt, who travelled the country in the 1950s and 1960s collecting various sculptures, mostly Bamoun and Tikar items from the north-west.

It's open Thursdays, Saturdays and Sundays from 3 to 6 pm. If the door is shut, just ring the bell and wait; one of the 10 monks will come eventually. Bus No 5 goes to the base of Mt Fébé; from there you can walk up. You can also get there by shared taxi for CFA 400 (CFA 200 return).

Chapel Even the monastery's chapel is decorated with a beautiful array of Camerounian textiles and crafts. It's the church of choice for many government ministers, and if you come here on a Sunday at 11 am you can join the local elite in attending a sermon of Brother Messi-Malla. (Mass on other days is at 6 pm). As the trailblazing spiritual head of the monastery, this young, overseas-trained monk is playing a key role in the country's struggle for political change and doesn't mince his words when it comes to espousing the cause of democracy and economic justice for the poor.

Musée National
Built in the late 1940s as the residence for the French high commissioner, the building housing the new National Museum is in the administrative district on Ave Marchand (better known as Ave des Ministères) several hundred metres south of the Hilton Hotel. Scheduled to open in 1993, it's an impressive two-storey building designed by a Camerounian architect and hopefully the art selection will be equally memorable. Hours are from 8 am to noon and 2.30 to 5.30 pm on weekdays and 8 am to 1 pm on Saturdays.

Musée d'Art Nègre
This small museum in Quartier Melen, sometimes called the Musée Aliqune Diop, contains the private African art collection of Father Mveng, who travelled extensively around Africa, collecting as he went. The pieces, which are not exceptional, vary from Bamoun pipes and Baoulé textiles to Zaïrian masks and art objects from as far away as Algeria and Ethiopia. The museum is open daily from 8 am to noon and from 2 to 6 pm. If you don't make it here, you won't be missing much. Finding it is also difficult as no-one seems to know of its existence. Take bus No 2 west to Place Melen, then walk west on Rue Melen for 100 metres, then right at the 'Catholique Universitaire' sign down a dirt path to the museum.

Messe de N'Djong Melen

If you're in Yaoundé on a Sunday morning, don't miss the open-air mass outside the Paroisse de N'Djong Melen in Melen, several km west of the city centre and just north of the university. From the post office or nearby SOTUC bus station take the No 2 bus to the Place de Melen, three km west of Place Ahidjo; the church is there. The mass, which is recited in Ewondo, takes place outdoors every Sunday from 9.30 am to noon and is a fantastic blend of African and Western culture, with African music, drums, dancing and a women's chorus – highly recommended.

Palais de Congrès & Palais Présidentiel

On the road between town and the Hôtel Mont-Fébé is the huge modern Palais des Congrès. Built by the Chinese, it is widely used for conferences. The new Presidential Palace is visible in the distance. The latter is also modern and impressive, with peacocks walking around, but is strictly off-limits as are all the roads around it. Police will nab you if you so much as try to set a foot in that direction.

Activities

Swimming & Tennis The top three hotels (Hilton, Mont-Fébé and Députés) have pools and tennis courts open to outsiders. The pools cost CFA 2500 at the first two and CFA 1000 at the Députés. You get what you pay for at the Députés as the water in the small pool is often green-coloured. The tennis courts cost CFA 2500 a game. Also, if you go by the Tennis Club of Yaoundé at the northern end of the Place de l'Indépendance, you may find someone looking for a game. For CFA 1500, you can swim at the Centre Sportif far out on the southern outskirts of town on the road to Douala (take Blvd de l'OCAM); this huge complex has three pools (one Olympic-sized), a sauna and a restaurant.

Jogging Joggers can join the Hash House Harriers; for the time and location, see the marines at the US Embassy or call the British Embassy. The most popular place for jogging, especially on weekends, is Parcours Vita at the foot of Mt Fébé, on your left before reaching the Mont-Fébé Hôtel. There are 25 exercise stations along the course. Take the No 5 bus to get near there.

Warning: don't jog towards the nearby Presidential Palace. You could get shot. At a minimum, the police will ask for your passport. If you don't have it, you may spend the night in jail.

Golf Just below the Hôtel Mont-Fébé is the Golf Club de Yaoundé and a beautiful 18-hole golf course. Green fees for nonmembers are CFA 6000/10,000 on weekdays/weekends, and decent golf clubs can be rented for CFA 2000. While the course is not tournament quality because of the dark sand 'greens', it is in a stunning setting and is clearly the best course in Central Africa.

Places to Stay – bottom end

The *Foyer International de l'Église Presbytérienne*, often called more simply the Foyer International or the Mission Protestante, is where most travellers on the cheap stay. African-run and cheaper than most European-run missions but ridden with mosquitoes, it charges CFA 2000 per person in a four-bed room and CFA 1000 per person for camping. You can also get good meals there for CFA 1500 to CFA 2000 (CFA 500 for breakfast) or use their kitchen facilities. The African lady in charge is likely to warn you to keep your eyes out for bandits as some travellers have had their vehicles broken into, even with a guard on duty. At night the whole area is extremely dangerous, with armed muggers everywhere, so don't walk outside the compound. If you arrive at night, have the taxi driver drop you at the door. During the day you can take a shared taxi or bus Nos 2 or 4 from the main SOTUC bus terminal to Carrefour Nlongkak (long-GHAK) in Djoungolo, which is three km to the north. The Foyer International is several hundred metres to the east.

If the Foyer is full, try *Hôtel des Nations*, which is about 250 metres to the south on a dirt road, off Rue Joseph Essono Balla.

Top Left :   Sunday market, Mora, northern Cameroun (AN)
Top Right :   Vegetable vendors, Maroua, northern Cameroun (AN)
Bottom :   Sunday market, Mora, northern Cameroun (AN)

Top : Rural scene, eastern Cameroun (AN)
Bottom : Grass bridge near Franceville, Gabon (BM)

Somewhat run-down, it has acceptable rooms with private baths for CFA 3000. There's no restaurant but there is a bar with a pleasant tranquil ambience – a definite plus.

A more up-market place near the Foyer International is *Hôtel Idéal* (☎ 220304) at Carrefour Nlongkak; it charges CFA 5250 for a very clean room with a double bed and hot-water baths but has no bar or restaurant.

A decent, more centrally located place to stay is *Hôtel de la Paix* (☎ 233273) on the southern side of town, half a km south of the post office on Blvd de l'OCAM, just south of the gare routière. It's popular, and with only six rooms there's virtually no chance of getting one unless you come early. The rooms, which cost CFA 3000, have interior showers and clean exterior basins and toilets, but no fans. The Paix has no restaurant but there's plenty of street food nearby.

If the Paix is full, try the nearby *Hôtel Casino* (☎ 222203), 100 metres east of the gare routière down a dirt side street. This multistorey place is moribund and looks terrible from the outside but the rooms, which cost CFA 4000, are large and clean with double beds and private baths.

Another hotel within walking distance of the city centre is *Hôtel Aurore* (☎ 230806) on Rue Sebastien Essomba, one km north of the Rond-Point du Blvd 20 Mai towards Briqueterie. The hotel's atmosphere is sterile and from the outside it appears quite dumpy, but the rooms are fairly clean and reasonably priced (CFA 4180 to CFA 5250), which is probably why it's well patronised.

Another possibility is the tranquil *Mission Catholique* (☎ 230264) in Tsinga (north of Messa), but the brothers there are reportedly unfriendly. *Hôtel Relaxe* is a new place not far away on the Nouvelle Route de Bastos, some four km north-west of the central area near the Palais de Congrès. An excellent buy and spotlessly clean, this small home-like hotel has large rooms with comfortable beds and attached showers and toilets (but no fans) for CFA 4000. The CFA 6000 two-room suites have even nicer tiled baths.

The three-storey *Hôtel de l'Unité* (☎ 222-022), opposite the Place de l'Indépendance, is noted for its everpopular bar. Fairly clean rooms with one/two beds and sagging mattresses cost CFA 5500/6500. The rooms have telephones and private bathrooms but no fans, air-con or hot water. All in all, the hotel is OK but business seems slow. The bar, on the other hand, is one of the most popular in town and always packed after work with Africans and expatriates alike.

Places to Stay – middle

Hôtel les Boukarous (☎ 233030) which is in the centre two blocks north of the US Embassy, is hard to beat for the price. The 20 rooms, which are wood-panelled with balconies, are small and the place is definitely showing its age, but at CFA 7000 a room it's hard to complain. Plus the attractive open-air restaurant is still one of the city's more popular places to dine. There's no air-con, but in Yaoundé many people don't want it. The hotel accepts American Express and Diners Club credit cards.

If you'd prefer to be in the heart of the African quarter, try the 60-room *Hôtel Le Progrès* (☎ 224306) opposite the market in Mokolo, about 2½ km west of the central area and just west of the Messa quarter. The rooms are quite decent and cost CFA 6000/8000 with fan/air-con and adjoining tile baths. The restaurant is fairly expensive, with a set menu for CFA 2750. Business at both the hotel and restaurant seems slow despite the friendly management.

Hôtel Impérial (☎ 223566) on Ave Atangana, half a km south of the post office, is more central with air-con rooms for CFA 8000. Some travellers like the ambience, especially the lively working-class bar, but the hotel is in poor condition and poorly managed.

The *Hôtel Indépendance* (☎ 222924), near the city centre, was once a leading hotel and is still quite presentable. However, it now has a somewhat dreary feeling about it even though the nightclub is quite decent. Rooms with air-con, TV, carpet, balconies and fine tile baths cost CFA 12,000. I much prefer *Hôtel Central* (☎ 222844), which is

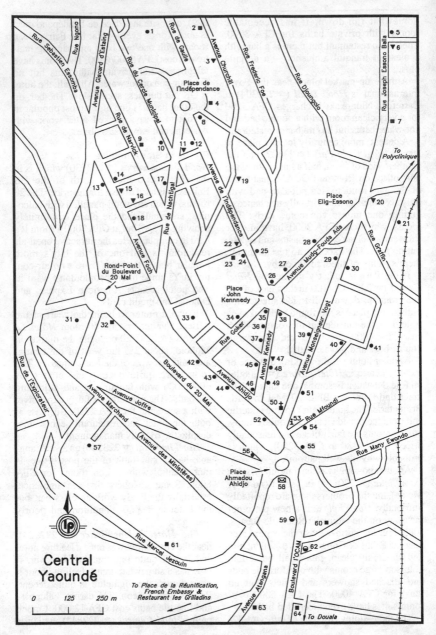

Central Yaoundé

0   125   250 m

To Place de la Réunification,
French Embassy &
Restaurant les Grilladins

■ PLACES TO STAY

2	Hôtel de l'Indépendance
4	Hôtel de l'Unité
7	Hôtel Grand Moulin
9	Hôtel les Boukarous
23	Royal Hôtel
32	Hilton Hotel
60	Hôtel Casino
61	Hôtel Central
63	Hôtel Impérial
64	Hôtel de la Paix

▼ PLACES TO EAT

3	Restaurant la Switza
6	Restaurant la Paillote & Grillade à Go-Go
11	Boulangerie Calfatas
12	Street-Corner Crêpe Maker
15	Restaurant le Bronx
16	Restaurant Central Casa
19	Restaurant la Table du Chef
20	Good Pâtisserie-Boulangerie
22	Restaurant MacDonald
47	Restaurant le Challenge

OTHER

1	Hôtel de Ville
5	Supermarché Tigre
8	Ministry of Information & Culture
10	Intervoyages Travel Agency & Bar Chez Josette
11	American Cultural Centre
12	Prisunic Supermarket, Canadian Embassy & Standard Chartered Bank
13	Cinéma Le Capitole
14	Le Pacha Club
15	Hollywood Photo Shop
17	US Embassy
18	Cameroun Bank
21	Railway Station
23	Oxygen Nightclub
24	BIAO Branch
25	Le Drug Store & Les Nouvelles Papeterie
26	Centre Artisanal
27	Immigration Office
28	Bank of Africa
29	Institut Géographique National
30	BEAC Bank
31	BEAC Bank
33	Marché Central
34	Antoniades Travel Agency (ATA)
35	Campero Bar
36	Librairie Moderne Hachette
37	Crédit Lyonnais Branch
38	Bar le Poker
39	Cameroun Airlines
40	Nigerian Embassy
41	Marché du Mfoundi
42	Le Catios Nightclub
43	French Cultural Centre
44	BICIC Bank
45	BIAO Bank
46	Pharmacie Française
47	Hollywood Photo Shop
48	German Cultural Centre & Cheap Bar
49	BICIC Branch & GS Electronics
50	Nôtre Dame Cathedral
51	Crédit Lyonnais & SGBC Banks
52	Score Supermarket
53	Secrétariat d'État du Tourisme
54	BCD Bank
55	SNI Building
56	Intelcom Office
57	Musée National
58	Main Post Office
59	Gare Routière du Centre
62	Bus Companies (Buses to Douala)

also near the centre, 300 metres south-west of the post office. Well maintained with a colonial feeling, it's in a tranquil setting surrounded by trees, hence the ambience is much better. Rooms with TV, tile bath and balcony cost CFA 12,000.

The new *Hôtel Grand Moulin* (☎ 206819, 220594) is better value. It's a modern structure on Rue Joseph Essono Balla, 250 metres north of the railway station. A spotlessly clean room with TV, telephone, air-con and tile bath costs CFA 9500/10,850 with one/ two beds.

Places to Stay – top end
Yaoundé's top address is the posh new, Moorish-style *Hilton Hotel* (☎ 235919/20; fax 223210) in the heart of town on Blvd du 20 Mai. Rooms start at a whopping CFA 45,000/59,000 for singles/doubles; on weekends, however, you can get a special rate of CFA 30,000 with *petit déjeuner* (breakfast)

but only if you reserve in advance. Facilities include a pool, tennis court, nightclub and business centre; most major credit cards are accepted. However, business seems slow as few can afford the rates, which is one reason why the long-renowned *Hôtel Mont-Fébé* (☎ 214002, 213550; fax 211500; telex 8263) still gets good business. Perched on a hill on the northern outskirts of town and overlooking a golf course, this former Sofitel is much better value and offers the best views, almost as many amenities (pool, tennis, golf course, TV/video, business centre, nightclub), and a noticeably cooler climate. Rooms with mountain views start at CFA 28,000; those with town views at CFA 32,000; most major credit cards (except MasterCard) are accepted.

The large *Hôtel des Députés* (☎ 231055, 231555; fax 233710; telex 8341), several blocks behind the Hilton, is a good two notches down in quality and price. Despite a run-down appearance, at CFA 16,845 per room it's still such good value that it can sometimes be difficult to find a room. The nicest feature is the ever-popular lake-view bar; there's also a popular disco, small pool, tennis court and nightclub. The hotel accepts all major credit cards except MasterCard.

However, with 42 rooms, the smaller *Royal Hôtel* (☎ 231953; fax 224192; telex 8894), is identically priced and seems to be winning the competition. It's a modern new hotel in the heart of town, just off Ave de l'Indépendance. American Express and Visa are accepted.

Places to Eat

Cheap Eats Many of the cheapest restaurants are African and located in the African quarters, such as Briqueterie and Messa, particularly around the markets where even cheaper street food abounds. Those staying at the Foyer International can eat cheaply (beans, rice, omelettes and coffee) at the food stalls opposite the entrance and along Rue Joseph Essono Balla. If you're in Bastos, try *Café Central* on Route de Bastos opposite the fancy Restaurant le Grill. You can get large beers there for CFA 225 and eat African food on the rustic front patio and watch the

cars go by; the woman who serves food there has only one pot of African food. Not far away on Rue Albert Ateba Ébé you'll find *Le Refuge Snack-Bar*, which is good for beer and cheap snacks.

Restaurants in the central area are generally not nearly so cheap. *Restaurant Le Challenge* on Ave Kennedy, for example, has steak & chips for CFA 1800, which is relatively inexpensive for the area. It's more popular as a place for drinks and slightly up-market compared to some bars in the area. Or try *Restaurant MacDonald* nearby on Ave de l'Indépendance, a block northwest of Place Kennedy; it's fairly inexpensive as well, with sandwiches.

Restaurant le Bronx (formerly Porter 39) is reasonably priced, with simple meals such as hamburgers, and good service. Open all day, it's on Ave Foch, two blocks west of the US Embassy. A stone's throw away on the same street, opposite Cinéma le Capitole and on the 2nd floor, is *Le Marseillais*, where you can get a full meal and drink for less than CFA 2000 and meet other travellers as well. The menu is extensive and includes Chinese food. Not far away at the sidewalk cafe of the *Hôtel de l'Unité* you can get brochettes (meat on skewers) for CFA 300 and reasonably priced sandwiches while you watch all the action.

The city's best bakery, *Boulangérie Calfatas*, is on Rue de Nachtigal, a block south of Place de l'Indépendance. Extremely popular and open to about 7.30 pm, it sells all kinds of breads as well as slices of pizza, expensive pastries and ice cream.

African A fabulous place for African food is the *Restaurant Central Casa* a block west of the US Embassy, between Ave Foch and Rue de Narvick. Open every day except Sunday between about 10 am and 5.30 pm, it's a large open-air place where you can eat cheaply, make new acquaintances quite easily and sometimes even listen to a live band. You get a choice of six or seven African dishes, each for CFA 400 a plate, including *poisson en sauce tomate* (fish in tomato sauce) and possibly even the Yaoundé speciality *ntomba* *nam* with peanut based pâte and meat. Brochettes cost CFA 100 and drinks are also available. Also, check out the dead-end alley opposite the Marché Central; it's great for cheap African food and cold beers.

Chicken Houses There are numerous restaurants in Yaoundé, called 'chicken houses' by some English speakers, which specialise exclusively in charcoal braised chicken and fish, usually with a small bowl of Camerounian red-hot sauce. The food is invariably delicious and the service is invariably slow. Some of these places are legitimate with licences; others operate illegally. Prices at all of them are fairly uniform; chicken usually costs CFA 3500, and fish CFA 2500.

For a legitimate chicken house, I recommend the popular, well-marked *Grillade à Go-Go* on Rue Joseph Essono Balla, 750 metres north of the railway station. Besides grilled chicken, you can also get shrimp. Or try *Les Grilladins* on Rue Joseph Atemengue, 150 metres south of the French Embassy; it serves braised fish and chicken at the usual price.

The unregistered, unmarked chicken houses are harder to find. One you could try to find is the *Three Sisters Chicken House* as the Americans call it. To get there, head north to Carrefour Nlongkak, then west on Route de Bastos until you reach a Moto Georges sign. Turn right at the sign, following the road past the Catholic church, then take the next right (a rough road) for one block; the unmarked house is on that corner.

If you can't find it, as a fall-back you could try one of the legitimate chicken houses in that area, such as *Restaurant le Bec Fin*, which is a very short block west of Carrefour Nlongkak, or *Le Coq Hardi*, which is a more attractive place further out on Route de Bastos, about 400 metres before Blvd Jean Paul II. Le Coq Hardi has braised chicken for CFA 3500 and sole for CFA 2500 to CFA 4000. A very friendly lady runs it and you have the choice of dining inside with air-con or outside under thatched-roof paillotes.

Lebanese The popular restaurant at the

Hôtel les Boukarous, open every day and highly recommended, is primarily a Lebanese restaurant, but serves pizza and a variety of Italian and French selections. The ambience is special – tables set in several *boukarous* (African huts) which encircle a charming tropical garden complete with a fish pond. The food is good, especially the Lebanese bread which must be the best in Central Africa. Prices are moderate – CFA 3500 for most main courses and much less for Lebanese chawarma sandwiches or orders of hummus and taboule.

Asian Yaoundé's Asian restaurants are generally less expensive than the city's French restaurants, and several of the former are near the central area. The closest is *Le Grand Muraille de Chine*, which is next to the German Embassy on Ave de Gaulle and popular with expatriates for lunch. Others prefer the similarly priced, family-style *La Paillote* on Rue Joseph Essono Balla, half a km north-east of the railway station. The Vietnamese and Chinese food is excellent and the service is friendly. *Aux Baguettes d'Or* (☎ 223929), which is south-west, towards the old airport and near a Total station, offers good Vietnamese and Chinese food and service at reasonable prices in a pleasant setting. It's closed Mondays.

A number of Asian restaurants are in the Bastos area, including *Restaurant l'Asiana* (with a good variety of Korean and Vietnamese food), and *Chez Nous* and *Chez Wu*, both on Route de Bastos. Chez Wu, which is slightly further out near the Swiss Embassy, is an expensive Chinese restaurant with good food, a pleasant veranda and an elegant inside dining room with air-con. On Sunday there's a buffet-style brunch.

French Restaurants with French and continental cuisine are usually fairly expensive. One with a good reputation is *La Switza*, which is on Ave Churchill near the Hôtel de l'Indépendance; the pizza here is reportedly quite good. On the same street and closer to the centre, near Ave de l'Indépendance, you'll find *Restaurant La Table du Chef*, a moderately expensive French restaurant. If money is of no concern, try *Le Dauphin* (☎ 221254) north of the old airport; it's one of the city's most expensive restaurants, with excellent service and superlative French cuisine. Finally, for Russian cuisine and pizza baked in an outdoor oven, try *Restaurant Samovar*, on Route de Bastos (Rue Mballa Eloumden). It's closed Mondays and the service is excellent.

Entertainment
Bars In the centre, one of the popular bars is the street-side bar at *Hôtel de l'Unité* facing the Place de l'Indépendance. Packed every night after work until about 8 pm with Africans and expatriates alike, it has a pleasant, tranquil ambience with low lights, shade trees and an occasional breeze. It's also a rendezvous for men and African prostitutes. There are no large beers, only small ones for CFA 300.

There are many bars along Ave Kennedy, including *Bar Le Poker* and *Campero Bar* at the northern end and several others further south including *Le Challenge*. Usually crowded, they attract more Africans than foreigners, also some prostitutes.

The lake-view bar at *Hôtel des Députés* has traditionally been a popular up-market place for drinks; the views are still good but business is now much slower.

Nightclubs *Chez Josette* bar is a popular 'pick-up' bar one block north of the US Embassy. Open every night, it is lively for several hours before everyone heads for the discos. Three flashy ones in the heart of town, all quite popular with Africans and expatriates alike, are *Oxygen* next to Hôtel Royal, *Black & White* a block away on Rue Gocker, and *Le Pacha Club* in Immeuble Hajal Massad on Ave Foch, a block from Le Capitole cinema. Drinks at these places are usually about CFA 3000 on weekdays and CFA 4000 on Saturdays.

For a less expensive place catering to the working person, try *Les Caveaux* near the Gare Routière du Centre, *Super Paquita* east of the gare in Mvog-Ada, or *Sanza* near the

railway station. For small African bars with cheap beers, head for Briqueterie and Messa.

If you like jazz, the place to head for is the *Jazz Club* at the Hilton. Open Tuesdays, Thursdays, Fridays and Saturdays from 9 pm to 12.30 am, it frequently has entertainers from Europe; it's also quite expensive.

Cinemas Le Capitole (☎ 224977), in the city centre on Ave Foch, is Yaoundé's best cinema. Shows are at 9 pm. Cinéma Abbia, two blocks away on Rue de Nachtigal, is another.

Things to Buy
The city's two major markets, the Marché Central in central Yaoundé and the Marché de Mokolo in Mokolo four km to the west, are both worth checking out. The former is an amazing spiral circular building crowded with stalls, with lots of African print material and other textiles on sale and music blasting away. You can find everything from fresh porcupine to Chinese incense. The Mokolo market is better known for its batik and tie-dye materials and embroidered dresses.

A third market, the new Marché du Mfoundi, is for food only. It's several hundred metres south of the railway station and a testament to government ineptitude – the long series of stalls there are usually empty as the vendors prefer to sell their goods on the streets.

Artisan Goods The Centre Artisanal at the northern end of Ave Kennedy has a wide variety of crafts in terms of quality and prices. It has a good selection of jewellery (especially malachite and silver), beads, wooden masks, brass and leather goods and tie-dye material. The Catholic Mission also has a shop. For top-quality but expensive African art, head for the fancy art shops at the Hilton and Mont-Fébé hotels; the Musée d'Art Camerounais may also have a few items for sale.

A word of caution – exporting antiques is forbidden and bribe-hungry customs officials have been known to declare obvious tourist art as antiques. Protect yourself with

Bamiléké mask

receipts from handicraft stores or certifications signed by a museum chief.

Gold & Silver For top-quality but expensive jewellery, especially gold and silver, the best place is Le Fétiche on Ave Kennedy. Especially interesting are the gold rings and pendants, the gold Ashanti doll pendants and the silver bracelets with Abbia stone trim.

Getting There & Away

Air Thanks to Nsimalen airport, the city's new international gateway, it's now possible to fly to Yaoundé without having to pass through Douala. However, as of 1993 the only international direct flights were from Zurich twice weekly on Swissair, and from N'Djamena (Congo) once or twice a week on Unitair.

Cameroun Airlines and Unitair between them have about six flights a day from Yaoundé to Douala, daily flights to Garoua and Maroua (CFA 44,950), five flights a week to N'Gaoundéré (CFA 23,950), two flights weekly to Dschang and Mamfé, and one weekly flight to Bafoussam, Bamenda, Bertoua and Batouri. Cameroun Airlines (☎ 234001) is on Ave Monseigneur Vogt, 350 metres north of Place Ahidjo. Most of the other major airlines have their offices in Douala. To charter a plane, contact Air Affaires Afrique (☎ 231423) at the airport.

Bus Buses for western Cameroun leave from the Gare Routière d'Étoudi on the northern outskirts of town. Shared taxis to the gare leave from Place Ahidjo and cost CFA 200 for the five-km journey; SOTUC bus No 2 also goes there. Bus fares are CFA 2500 to Bafoussam (4½ hours) and CFA 3500 to Bamenda or Foumban (six hours). There are numerous companies, but virtually all departures are between 7 am and 7 pm, especially 7 to 9.30 am and 3 to 5 pm. Erko Voyages, for example, has buses to Bamenda at 7.30 am and 1 pm and to Bafoussam at 8.30 am and 5 pm. Étoile Voyages has buses to Bafoussam and Bamenda at 7.30, 8.30, and 9.30 am and 3.30 pm. Others include Fany Voyages, Binam Voyages, Menoua Bus Lines and Daily Express; the latter two also have buses to Dschang.

Buses for Douala leave from the area around the Gare Routière du Centre on Blvd de l'OCAM, about 150 metres south of Place Ahidjo. Many of the bus companies have their own separate offices along that street. The normal fare for the three-hour trip is CFA 2500 but it pays to shop around as companies sometimes offer fares *en promotion* as low as CFA 1500. Most departures are between 6.30 am and 6.30 pm but several companies, including Le Concorde, have departures as late as 8.30 pm. Express Garanti, for example, has departures about every hour between 6.45 am and 6.30 pm. Four others with similar schedules are Express le Bien, Super Voyage Star, Lydie Voyages and Erko Voyages. The area here is the worst in Yaoundé for thieves, so take every precaution imaginable.

Train The railway station (☎ 234003) is a km north-east of Place Ahidjo, off Ave Monseigneur Vogt. The Gazelle du Nord leaves for N'Gaoundéré every evening, most recently at 6.30 pm, arriving about 12 hours later. The 1st-class fare is CFA 11,600, and 2nd class is CFA 6750 (CFA 3170 2nd-class to Belabo). For a couchette you must pay an extra CFA 1750 above the 1st-class fare. Some trains have two-person cabins; others have four-person ones.

There are at least three trains a day for Douala. Departure hours are constantly changing; most recently they were 8.04 am (the Gazelle from N'Gaoundéré), 1.32 pm (the omnibus) and 7 pm (the express). The Gazelle and express take about four hours to Douala (the omnibus takes longer) and the carriages are quite modern, with a restaurant car. Fares are CFA 3500 in 1st class, CFA 1900 in 2nd class.

Bush Taxi Bush taxis headed for western and eastern Cameroun also leave from the Gare Routière d'Étoudi. Those for Bafoussam leave at all hours, even at midnight. The fare is CFA 3000 to Bafoussam and CFA 4040 to Foumban. Taxis to Douala (CFA 2500), Ebolowa (CFA 1500) and Kribi (CFA 2500) leave from the Gare Routière du Centre.

Car You'll find Hertz (☎ 234002; telex 8263) at the Mont-Fébé Hôtel; Avis (☎ 300285; fax 221010; telex 8346) on the southern side of town on the road to Douala; Jully Auto (☎ 223947; telex 8331) and P Z Motors Europcar (☎ 221147) on Ave Ahidjo; and Neuilly Auto (☎ 221535) on Ave de l'Indépendance. Socatour Travel Agency on Ave de Gaulle also rents cars.

Getting Around
To/From the Airport The airport tax is CFA 5000 for international flights and CFA 500 for domestic flights. There is no SOTUC bus service to the airport. A taxi from the centre to Nsimalen airport (18 km south of town) costs at least CFA 2000 and more from the airport to the city centre.

Local Bus SOTUC buses, which operate between 6 am and 9 pm, cost CFA 50 to CFA 75 depending on the route and are usually very crowded. There are six lines:

No 1 – from the south side of town to the centre, westward on Manga Belle to Cité Verte on the western edge of town
No 2 – from the south-western side of town in Quartier Melen to the city centre, then north to Carrefour Nlongkak and the Gare Routière d'Étoudi on the northern outskirts
No 3 – from Cité Verte east to the centre, passing along Ave Kennedy, and then further east towards the Stade Omnisport
No 4 – from Cité Verte east to the centre, then north to Carrefour Nlongkak
No 5 – from the south-eastern side of town to the centre and north-westward towards the base of Mt Fébé
No 6 – from Bive Massi (south-west) to the central area, passing the US Embassy, then north-east towards the Stade Omnisport

Taxi Taxis are supposed to have the official prices on the window. The standard fare for a shared cab is CFA 125 (CFA 200 for fairly long distances). Prices increase after 9 pm (eg CFA 175 for a shared taxi). A *course* (a taxi to yourself) is CFA 500 (CFA 600 after 9 pm), and more for long distances (CFA 1500 to the Mont-Fébé Hôtel). If you bargain well, you should pay no more than CFA 2000 by the hour and CFA 13,000 by the day. Taxis are fairly plentiful but they don't have meters. They are all yellow.

AROUND YAOUNDÉ
For getting away on weekends, some locals like to take the family to **Luna Park** (☎ 231754), 40 km on the main asphalt highway heading north, two km beyond **Obala** (which is just beyond the turn-off for Bertoua and on Bertoua Rd and known for its colourful Saturday-morning market). Surrounded by forests, this complex has 16 African-style huts (boukarous) for about CFA 7000 each, a restaurant, pool, tennis court, mini-golf course and poorly-kept animals.

If this doesn't appeal, you might instead want to see **Nachtigal Falls** (Les Chutes) on the Sanaga River, 30 km beyond Obala on the road to Bertoua. The best time to visit is during the rainy season.

Douala

Called the 'armpit of Africa' by some, Douala has an image problem. Many short-term visitors will tell you all they can remember is seeing some ordinary architecture and feeling like a wet sponge. Lacking the class of Abidjan, the beauty of Dakar and the soul of Kinshasa, Douala is nevertheless admired for its vitality. With over a million inhabitants, Douala is second in size only to Kinshasa in Central Africa, yet much of the activity is conveniently centred in one area – Akwa.

The old Hôtel Akwa Palace in the heart of town on the main drag, Blvd de la Liberté, is the place to have a drink in the late afternoon and haggle with the local vendors. Only a block behind it is the centre of the nightlife district; a number of the cheap bars there are open during the day as well.

The high crime rate – second only to Kinshasa's – has been a major problem in Douala for years, but a new one is the recession. Several major hotels and many of the car-rental agencies have closed, and the death rate among restaurants must be the highest in Africa – seemingly half of the top ones have gone out of business in the last few years. Only the sex business seems to be doing well; male travellers cannot walk anywhere in the city centre without being hissed at by the prostitutes on virtually every street corner.

Perhaps the best thing about Douala is that there are good places nearby to visit. On weekends, the locals can – and do during the dry season – head for Limbe or Kribi to enjoy the beaches, or for Buea to enjoy the cooler climate, perhaps even to climb Mt Cameroun, one of Central Africa's tallest peaks. Both Limbe and Buea are only an hour away from Douala by bush taxi while Kribi is just two hours away via a new German-financed road.

Orientation

The heart of town is Akwa, the main street of which is Blvd de la Liberté and the north-ernmost point of which is Rond-Point Deïdo (dye-doh) at the Blvd de la Réunification intersection. Some 200 metres north-west of that major roundabout is Wouri Bridge leading over to the industrial zone and on towards Limbe, and one km south-east of it is the turn-off for the new railway station. If you head south-east along Liberté from Deïdo, after two km you'll pass the landmark Hôtel Akwa Palace, then the Blvd Ahidjo intersections, Artisanal Camerouanis and the impressive cathedral, ending in Bonanjo. Many of the city's major commercial establishments and restaurants are in Akwa as well as most of the major nightclubs, particularly in the area just behind the Akwa Palace.

If you turn right (north-west) on Blvd Ahidjo, you'll soon come to the Carrefour de la Marine and the main port beyond it. If, instead, you take a left, after passing the wide Blvd de la République (which heads north-eastward past the modest palace of the King of Douala towards the railway station) you'll come to Place Ahmadou Ahidjo; buses headed for Yaoundé leave from here. Several blocks to the east is the Gare Routière de Yabassi (or Gare Routière SOTUC), the city's principal taxi park. The lively area south of Place Ahidjo, which includes the Congo and Banyangui quarters and the large Marché de Lagos, is one of the best places for cheap food and lodging. The airport is a good seven km to the south-east.

Most government buildings, banks, airlines and travel agencies as well as the city museum, and many hotels and restaurants are located in Bonanjo, the administrative quarter. The heart of this district is the Place du Governement, and if you head south from there along Ave de Gaulle, you'll pass some tall modern bank buildings, the US Consulate and the turn-off for the top-end hotels Novotel and Meridien as well as the second major port area, commonly called the Port de Peschaud, which is the largest company there.

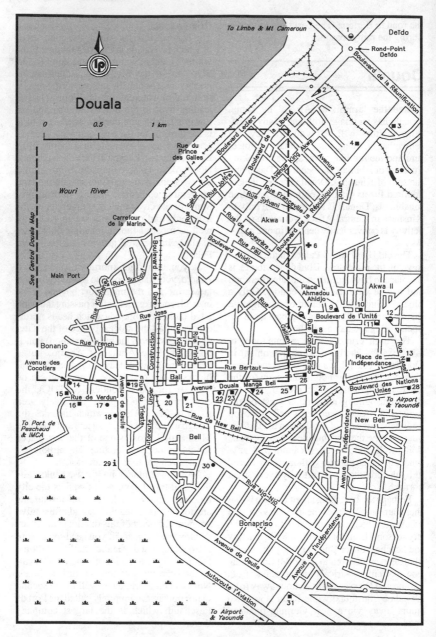

Douala

0   0.5   1 km

Wouri River

To Limbe & Mt Cameroun

Rond-Point
Deïdo

Deïdo

Boulevard de la Réunification

See Central Douala Map

Rue du
Prince
des Galles

Boulevard Leclerc

Boulevard de la Liberté

Avenue King Akwa

Avenue Dr Jamot

Rue Saker

Rue Joffre

Rue Franceville

Rue Sylvani

Akwa I

Rue de Lapeyrère

Rue Pau

Carrefour
de la Marine

Boulevard Ahidjo

Boulevard de la République

Main Port

Rue Kitchener

Rue Surcouf

Boulevard de la Gare

Rue Joss

Place
Ahmadou
Ahidjo

Akwa II

Boulevard de l'Unité

Rue Cdt Prince

Rue Koumassi

Rue Gallieni

Rue Cdt Prince

Bonanjo

Rue French

Rue Bertaut

Place de
l'Indépendance

Rue Nassif

Construction

Ball

Avenue Douala Manga Bell

Boulevard des Nations
Unies

To Airport
& Yaoundé

Avenue des
Cocotiers

Avenue de Gaulle

Autoroute l'Union

Rue de New Bell

New Bell

Rue de Verdun

Bell

To Port de
Peschaud
& IMCA

Rue Njo-Njo

Avenue de l'Indépendance

Bonapriso

Avenue de Gaulle

Autoroute l'Aviation

To Airport
& Yaoundé

■ PLACES TO STAY

3 Hôtel de Wouri
4 Hôtel LH
8 Cameroun Hôtel
10 Hila-Hôtel
13 Hôtel Aristha
15 Meridien Hôtel
16 Sawa Novotel
23 Hôtel du Littoral
25 Restaurant du Centre (Upstairs)
26 Hôtel de Douala
31 Hôtel de l'Air

▼ PLACES TO EAT

21 Good Street Food (Mornings)
24 Street Food Area (Nights)
25 Restaurant du Centre (Upstairs)
31 Restaurant La Coupole

OTHER

1 Gare Routière (Buses to Buea & Limbe)
2 Commissariat de Police
5 New Railway Station
6 Hôpital Laquintinie
7 Buses to Yaoundé
9 Shell Station
11 Shell Station & Buses to Kribi
12 Gare Routière de Yabassi (Minibuses & Bush Taxis to Yaoundé)
14 French Consulate
17 Tennis Club
18 Immigration & Sûreté
19 US Consulate
20 SONEL
21 Lycée Technique
22 Grocery Store
27 Marché de Lagos
28 Marché de Kassalafam
29 Tourist Office
30 Polyclinique de Douala

Information

Tourist Office The Service Provincial du Tourisme (☎ 421422) is on Ave de Gaulle, 1½ km south of the Place du Governement. It has little to offer besides maps of Douala, which cost the same as in the bookshops, and some standard tourist brochures.

Money The best banks for changing money are Crédit Lyonnais opposite the Place du Gouvernement; the BIAO (☎ 428011) and BICIC (☎ 428431), both on Ave de Gaulle two blocks south of the square; SGBC (☎ 427010) on Rue Joss just east of the square; and Standard Chartered Bank (☎ 423612; telex 5858) at 61 Blvd de la Liberté. These banks are open weekdays only and most close by noon; Standard Chartered, however, is also open afternoons from 3.15 to 4.30 pm.

The best bank for changing travellers' cheques is usually Crédit Lyonnais. Its commission on travellers' cheques is CFA 1110 per transaction and its rates are as good as those at Standard Chartered, which charges a hefty CFA 3300 per transaction. Both of these foreign banks offer relatively quick service. The BIAO charges CFA 1300 per transaction but its rates are poor like those at the BICIC, which charges a commission of .05% on travellers' cheques (ie about CFA 1000 for US$500). Most of these banks sell travellers' cheques denominated in French francs but their commissions can be exorbitant, eg CFA 12,580 per transaction at Crédit Lyonnais.

Post & Telecommunications The main PTT (French for 'GPO') faces the Place du Gouvernement in Bonanjo. You can make international phone calls from there. There are also branch offices at the railway station and airport.

Foreign Consulates The following countries have consulates in Douala:

Belgium
   13 Ave de la Marine (☎ 424750)
Equatorial Guinea
   Blvd de la République (☎ 422611)
France
   Rue des Cocotiers, near the Meridien (☎ 426250, 425370)
Germany
   Rue Victoria, behind the BEAC bank on Ave de Gaulle (☎ 423500, 428600)
Italy
   Rue de l'Hôtel de Ville (☎ 423601)

Nigeria
> Blvd de la Liberté, near Nigeria Airways (☎ 427144)

Norway & Sweden
> Rue Alfred Saker, off Blvd Ahidjo (☎ 420288)

UK
> Rue de l'Hôtel de Ville, Bonanjo (☎ 422177)

USA
> 21 Ave de Gaulle (☎ 425331, 420303; fax 427-790)

Cultural Centres The French cultural centre is in Bonanjo on Rue Ivy, a block north of Rue Joss.

Travel Agencies Delmas Voyages (☎ 421184, 426889; fax 428851; telex 5222) on the corner of Rue Kitchener and Rue Surcouf in Bonanjo, is the American Express representative. Open weekdays, also Saturdays from 9 am to noon, it is better for making airline and hotel reservations than for booking tours of Cameroun.

Other agencies in Bonanjo include Camatros Voyages on Rue Joss near Ave de Gaulle; SOAEM Voyages (☎ 420288) a block to the east on the same street; and Transcap Voyages (☎ 429291) half a block to the south on Rue de Trieste. Among other things, these agencies arrange package tours to the north. In Akwa, try the travel agency at the Hôtel Akwa Palace or Chaka Voyages two blocks to the south on the same street.

Bookshops Librairie Aux Frères Réunis, which is on Blvd de la Liberté next to Hôtel Akwa Palace, is the best bookshop in Central Africa. It has maps of Cameroun, Yaoundé and Douala for CFA 2500 and a relatively large selection of books, mostly in French. The city's other major bookshops, both on the same street, are Librairie Aux Messageries four blocks south of the Akwa Palace near the cathedral and Librairie Cocotier, three blocks north of the hotel.

Supermarkets The best and largest supermarkets, with lots of French goods, are Monoprix and Aux Bonnes Courses.

Hôtel Akwa Palace
This famous old hotel, now renovated, is a major attraction. In the morning, you'll see travellers having coffee and croissants on the terrace of the hotel and watching the activity on the city's major street, Blvd de la Liberté. Again, in the late afternoon, activity at the Akwa picks up and lasts well into the evening when the patrons head for the nearby restaurants and, to a much lesser extent, the nightclubs.

Place du Gouvernement
The Place du Gouvernement, in the heart of the Bonanjo district, is a spacious area marked by a curious building that looks like a Chinese pagoda. It was built by the local African ruler, Rudolf Douala Manga Bell, who was executed by the Germans in 1914 for treason (refusing to cede certain land).

Musée de Douala
Just south of the Place du Gouvernement is the Hôtel de Ville (the town hall). The Musée de Douala (open weekdays from 8 am to noon and 2.30 to 5.15 pm, Saturdays from 8 am to 1 pm) is inside on the 2nd floor but unmarked from the outside. Not one of Central Africa's better museums and not well organised, it is at least free and has some interesting old photographs of Douala. The quality of the art, much of which is Bamoun and Bamiléké, is mediocre but still good enough to allow you to distinguish good from ordinary craftwork on the street.

Your introduction will be a disorganised hallway with a wide assortment of objects, including some Bandjoun and Bamoun art, reflecting on the history of the area. Thereafter come four rooms, one focusing on northern Cameroun with lots of military items including helmets and spears, a second focusing on the southern region with numerous carvings and other wooden items, a third with fine displays on Bamoun culture, and the fourth dedicated to the Bamiléké, with a collection of statues and thrones.

Activities
For tennis, try the Tennis Club next to the

Novotel, a private club used by the hotels. For swimming, you have a choice among nine hotel pools. If you are not a guest, expect to pay at least CFA 1000. Try the Meridien – if you are presentable and look like you'll buy food or drink, you have a good chance of getting in free.

The closest beaches are at Limbe and Kribi, one and two hours away. Joggers can join the Hash House Harriers on Saturdays at 5 pm sharp for their weekly run; for the starting point, see the bulletin board at the Foyer des Marins at the end of Rue Gallieni. Sailors could try the marina, which is a km south of the intersection of Ave de Gaulle and Ave de l'Indépendance, however the boats and sailboards there are all privately owned.

Places to Stay – bottom end
Central Area The central area of town is dangerous at any time but particularly at night when it's dark and deserted except for the streets with nightclubs. A popular cheap place is the unmarked, two-storey *Centre Baba Simon* on Blvd de la Liberté, opposite the cathedral. A bed in a fairly clean room costs CFA 3000 and you can wash your clothes there. However, you get what you pay for as conditions are very rudimentary, moreover you may have to wait several days to get a bed as the demand is great.

A better place for the price is the *Temple du Centenaire* in the Église Évangélique du Cameroun on the corner of Rue Pau and Rue Saker, two blocks west of Blvd de la Liberté. It has a Centre d'Accueil with clean rooms starting from CFA 3900.

The nearby *Foyer de la Jeunesse*, sometimes called the Foyer Protestante, no longer rents rooms to travellers but sometimes allows travellers to camp outside. However, camping at this unguarded place would be foolish as attempted theft is almost guaranteed. It's on Blvd Ahidjo, a block west of Blvd de la Liberté.

A great place to stay is the *Procure Générale des Églises Catholiques* on Rue Franceville, 1½ blocks west of the Lufthansa office on Blvd de la Liberté. The French priest welcomes travellers, allowing them to

use the long pool as well as eat there for CFA 2500 a meal (CFA 500 for breakfast); a bed in a dormitory room costs CFA 4500 per person (CFA 8000 per couple).

Marché de Lagos Area The areas with the most bottom-end hotels are Congo, especially along Rue Congo Pariso, and Banyangui, particularly along Ave Douala Manga Bell; the two streets intersect at the Marché de Lagos – roughly two km from both Bonanjo and Akwa. The area is lively day and night with lots of street food but it's also quite dangerous, especially at night. The friendly new *Restaurant du Centre* on Douala Manga Bell, near the Rue Gallieni intersection, is highly recommended. On the 2nd storey of a three-storey building and not well marked, it's primarily a restaurant but has six clean rooms with shared bath for only CFA 2500 a room. A major plus is that the restaurant is one of the city's best for inexpensive Camerounian food.

A cheap alternative is the *Hôtel Coin de Plaisir* (☎ 426970) on Rue Gallieni, half a km north of the Restaurant du Centre and Ave Douala Manga Bell. A room with fan and shared bath costs only CFA 3500, but it's a brothel, noisy at night, and in a particularly unsafe area close to the nightclubs. A much better place is the *Hôtel des Palmiers* on Ave de l'Indépendance in New Bell. Recommended, it's quite clean, with singles/doubles for CFA 4655/5700.

I much prefer des Palmiers to the decrepit landmark *Hôtel de Douala* (☎ 425478) nearby, opposite the Lagos Market. The listed price for a room with fan/air-con is CFA 5000/6000 but they'll usually knock off at least CFA 1000 if you bargain. You get what you pay for however – sagging mattresses, a noisy bar and boisterous late-night crowds outside.

Except for the Douala, the cheapest places are usually full by evening. If you arrive at night and don't want to shop around, there are three recommended hotels. The *Cameroun Hôtel* (☎ 428153) is conveniently located on Rue Congo Pariso, a block south of Place Ahidjo, and has singles/doubles with air-con

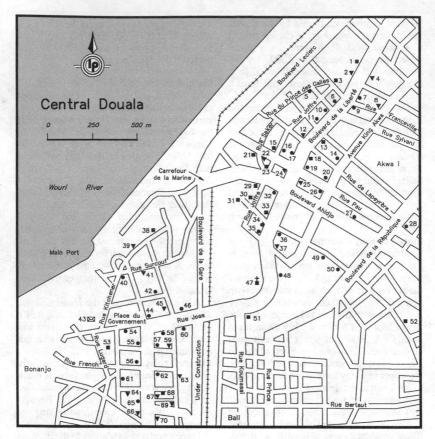

for CFA 5610/6115. The *Hôtel du Littoral* (☎ 422484) is in a slightly safer area about 700 metres to the west of Hôtel Douala at 38 Ave Douala Manga Bell. It's quiet and rooms are almost always available, even late at night. However, at CFA 5900 for an air-con room with private bath it's not a particularly good buy as the maintenance is poor and the air-con is loud. On the plus side, the beds are comfortable enough and there's a bar downstairs and good street food nearby. Finally, the *Hôtel du Wouri* is slightly better and cheaper but it's three km away, out on Blvd de la République near the new railway

station. It charges CFA 5610 for a small, carpeted room with air-con and tile bath; it also has a bar.

Places to Stay – middle

Many travellers have great praise for the friendly *Foyer des Marins* (☎ 422794), which has a wonderfully lively ambience. Centrally located and open to everyone, it has air-con rooms for CFA 7000 to CFA 8000, and a popular pool and restaurant. By noon all the rooms are usually taken and sailors get preference, so you'll have to come early in the morning to have a chance at a

■ PLACES TO STAY

1   Hôtel le Ndé
3   Procure Générale des Églises
    Catholiques
13 Hôtel Parfait Gardens
15 Hôtel Beauséjour
18 Hôtel Akwa Palace
21 Temple du Centenaire
23 Hôtel Kontchupé
29 Foyer de la Jeunesse
30 Hôtel le Lido
31 Foyer des Marins
33 Hôtel Résidence la Falaise
38 Hôtel la Falaise
51 Centre Baba Simon
52 Hôtel Coin de Plaisir
68 Hôtel Ibis

▼ PLACES TO EAT

2   Pizzeria l'Oustaou & Le Bistro
    Snack-Bar
4   Kesst (American Burger)
8   A la Porte Jaune Restaurant
10 Fast Food Mac
11 Snack-Bar le Point
12 Pâtisserie Délices
15 Restaurant le Lyonnais & Cheap
    Street Food
22 Restaurant la Tête d'Art
24 Restaurant le Dragon d'Or
25 Salon de Thé Pélisson
37 Salon de Thé Rencontre
39 Restaurant Le Chalet
41 Restaurant le Grignotage
45 Restaurant la Comédia
48 Cheap Food Stalls
59 Le Nabab Snack-Bar
60 Restaurant Il Canasta
64 Good Street Food (Lunch Time)
66 Restaurant Kohinoor
67 Restaurant le Provençal & Chez
    Therrey Snack-Bar
69 Street Food (Breakfast)
70 Restaurant Chinois

    OTHER

4   The Country Club Bar & Pharmacie le
    Concorde

5   Discotheque le 78
6   Librairie Cocotier
7   Goldfingers Nightclub
9   Lufthansa
10 Standard Chartered Bank & British
    Airways
11 Pharmacie de la Liberté
12 St James Nightclub
14 Cinéma le Concorde
16 First Night Club
17 Aeroflot
18 Avis & Bistro de la Palace
19 Alitalia, Librairie aux Frères Réunis,
    Cameroun Airlines & IVS Auto
    Rental
20 St-Hilaire Nightclub
22 Consulates of Norway & Sweden
24 British Consulate
26 Paris Dancing Nightclub
27 Air Mali
28 Palais du Roi de Douala (Traditional
    Chief's Residence)
32 BP Station & Swiss Air
34 Chez Ali Baba Art Shop & Nigeria
    Airways
35 Librairie Aux Messageries
36 Cinéma Le Wouri
37 Le Pub & Domino Night Club
40 Delmas Voyages
42 French Cultural Centre
43 Post Office
44 Air France/UTA, Air Gabon &
    Camatros Voyages
46 Air Afrique & SOAEM Voyages
47 Cathedral
48 Artisanal Camerounais
49 Macoumba-Macoumba Nightclub
50 Scotch Club
53 Musée de Douala & Hôtel de Ville
54 Crédit Lyonnais Bank
55 Air Zaïre
56 BIAO Bank
57 Cameroun Airlines
58 SGBC Bank
59 Transcap Voyages
60 BCC Bank
61 German Consulate
62 BICIC Bank
65 Le Privilege Nightclub

room. It's at the northern end of Rue Gallieni, several blocks north of the cathedral.

If it's full, you could try *Hôtel le Lido*

(☎ 420445), which is 1½ blocks away on Rue Joffre. It has a good restaurant and bar and caters more to the French; air-con rooms there cost CFA 8500. A cheaper alternative, half a block further north at the intersection of Rue Saker and Blvd Ahidjo, is the old *Hôtel Kontchupé* (☎ 420485). Fairly well maintained, it has air-con rooms with interior/exterior tile baths for CFA 6000/7000 though these prices can drop by as much as CFA 1000.

A new place that I strongly recommend is the modern *Hila-Hôtel* (☎ 421586) on Blvd de l'Unité, between Place Ahidjo and the Gare Routière de Yabassi. Air-con rooms with one/two beds and private tile baths cost CFA 6000/7500. Arriving from Yaoundé by bus, you'll pass it on your right, half a km before Place Ahidjo where the bus companies are located. Spotlessly clean with a chandelier in the lobby, it's doing such good business that getting one of the CFA 6000 rooms is difficult unless you come early. If it's full, you could try *Hôtel LH*, a similar new hotel several km to the north on Blvd de la République.

Hôtel de l'Air (☎ 428159) on Ave de Gaulle, three km south-east of Bonanjo towards the airport, remains good value. Singles/doubles with air-con go for CFA 7214/8422. The bathrooms are fairly clean, the bar is popular, and there's a pizzeria a block away. Another possibility closer to the centre that's definitely worth checking out is the popular *Hôtel le Ndé* (☎ 427034) on Blvd de la Liberté, between the Akwa Palace Hôtel and Rond-Point Deïdo. With air-con rooms for CFA 8425 to CFA 9265, it's good for the price plus there's a pool. The cheaper rooms are hard to get; the more expensive ones have a large bed, TV, telephone, carpets and ice cold air-con.

Hôtel la Falaise (☎ 424646; fax 426891; telex 5625), not to be confused with the top-end Résidence la Falaise, is an older hotel in Bonanjo on a *falaise* (cliff) overlooking the port. Well managed and very presentable, it is highly recommended and matches the best hotels in quality but is medium priced at CFA 12,195 a room with air-con. There is also an attractive clean pool, a good restaurant and views of the port. The seven-storey *Hôtel Beauséjour* (☎ 426332;

telex 5255), on Rue Joffre, has rooms for almost exactly the same price (CFA 12,060). There's a pool and a popular top-floor restaurant, but it's a little run-down and not as good. If you can bargain the price down as some travellers have done, it might be OK.

Places to Stay – top end
The first of Douala's three deluxe hotels is the *Meridien* (☎ 426136, 429046; fax 42-3507; telex 5822), one km from the heart of Bonanjo, the commercial district. It has rooms for CFA 26,270, and facilities including a pool, TV/video, disco, and tennis courts next door.

The *Sawa Novotel* (☎ 424441; fax 423-871; telex 5532), next door to the Meridien, is also top quality and doing good business, with lots of activity. It charges CFA 22,000/26,000 for rooms with city/pool views, and facilities includes a pool, TV/video, sauna, and tennis nextdoor.

The landmark *Akwa Palace* (☎ 428905, 420540; fax 427416; telex 5322) is a Pullman chain hotel and much older with slightly more character. Rooms are CFA 25,200 and facilities include a long pool, shops, and an Avis and travel agency. You'll find a popular street-side terrace for drinks here and lots of activity because of the hotel's location in the heart of town. The Meridien, Novotel and Akwa Palace accept all the major credit cards except MasterCard.

In addition, there are some three-star hotels. The one with the most sparkle and activity and highly recommended is the ever-popular *Ibis* (☎ 425800; fax 423605; telex 5558), which is on a side street off Ave de Gaulle, three blocks from the heart of the Bonanjo district. Rooms cost CFA 16,840. The piano bar here is very lively at night with live music and the guards do a good job of keeping out the prostitutes plus there's a pool.

Two others on the main drag in the centre of town have about as much character as a Wendy's hamburger joint. They are the modern, eight-storey *Résidence la Falaise* (☎/fax 420445; telex 5523), which is several blocks south of the Akwa Palace, well maintained and charges CFA 16,850 per room, and the *Hôtel Parfait Gardens* (☎ 426357; fax 426316; telex 5716) next door to the Akwa Palace, with rooms for CFA 13,475. La Falaise accepts American Express and Diners Club only, while the Parfait Gardens accepts these plus Visa and Carte Blanche.

Places to Eat

Cheap Eats Many of the cheapest places are listed under the African section. Street food, typically African stew, meat or fish with rice, costs from CFA 250 to CFA 350 a plate while beers go for CFA 150, bananas three for CFA 50, and chocolate pâté at CFA 125 for a small cup.

For non-African food, it's hard to beat the prices at *Restaurant la Sanaga* on Rue Gallieni, half a block east of Blvd de la Liberté, next to Cinéma Douala. You can get large plates of rice, beans and spaghetti, for example, for less than CFA 500; you can also splurge on steak & chips and other Western dishes for up to CFA 1500.

Fast Food Mac is an American-style fast-food restaurant with hamburgers and hot dogs for CFA 800, milkshakes for CFA 650, also fried chicken and fries. It's on Blvd de la Liberté two blocks north of the Akwa Palace. *Kesst* (or American Burger), two blocks further north on Liberté, is similar, with fruit juices for CFA 500, a hamburger special with Coke and fries for CFA 1500 and other full meals for up to CFA 1900. *Bar Express*, south on Liberté next to Cinéma Wouri, is similar in all respects.

In Bonanjo, for sandwiches try *Chez Therrey Snack-Bar* on Ave de Gaulle, three blocks south of Rue Joss, or *Le Nabab Snack-Bar* on Rue de Trieste, a block south of Rue Joss.

The city's major pastry shops are all on Blvd de la Liberté. The best is *Pâtisserie Délices*, just north of the Akwa Palace, with pastries starting at CFA 200, *café au lait* (hot-milk coffee) for CFA 450, and good ice cream. Next in line are the *Salon de Thé Pélisson* a block south of the hotel and the *Salon de Thé Rencontre* three blocks further south, before the cathedral.

African My favourite is the new *Restaurant du Centre* on Ave Douala Manga Bell (2nd floor) near the Rue Gallieni intersection and directly opposite a BP station. Sabine, the friendly and beautiful owner, offers three or four choices such as *riz Senegalais* (Senegalese rice), a plantain dish and *riz couscous* northern Cameroun style with *sauce de feuille* (green vegetable sauce) or *sauce gombo* (okra sauce). The food is authentic and delicious and costs CFA 350 a plate (CFA 250 for a large bottle of beer).

A few blocks to the east, past the Marché de Lagos and near the prison on Ave de l'Indépendance, you'll find *Restaurant Pagode d'Or*, which serves rice and a tasty tomato-based sauce without palm oil for CFA 300, also bush meat for CFA 1000.

In Bonanjo, a popular street-side spot for breakfast (Nescafé, bread, omelettes) is on Ave Douala Manga Bell, one block east of Ave de Gaulle. At lunch, those seeking street food all seem to head for a place near the Lycée Technique, three blocks south of the Place du Governement, just before Le Privilege Nightclub on Ave de Gaulle and around the corner on the same block.

In Akwa, every evening outside Cinéma le Wouri you'll find some friendly, English-speaking street vendors selling grilled-beef brochettes and sandwiches. A sandwich with salad and two brochettes costs CFA 250. You'll also find cheap African food served at a small place next to Hôtel Beauséjour on Rue Joffre.

At night, many of the African restaurants serve only braised chicken and fish with the local speciality, *ndolé*, for around CFA 3500 a plate. Two of the most popular, well-known 'chicken houses' are *Restaurant du Wouri* in Quartier Congo, near the Marché de Lagos, and *Le Touristic* (☎ 424088), an outdoor restaurant at the intersection of République and Réunification, 750 metres south-east of Rond-Point Deïdo.

For a fancy African restaurant, you can't beat the famous, long-standing *A la Porte Jaune* (☎ 429854). You can have an entire zoo on your plate – porcupine, crocodile, boa constrictor, ant-eater and antelope – but, eaten with abandon, these increasingly rare animals will surely all be gone one day. The food is quite good but overpriced. It's on Rue Franceville near the Ave King Akwa intersection. *Feu de Bois* (☎ 423778), also in Akwa, is less exotic. At either place a meal could easily cost CFA 12,000.

Pizza Two places specialising in pizza are *Restaurant Le Chalet* on Rue Kitchener in Bonanjo, a block west of the Hôtel la Falaise, and *L'Oustaou* on Blvd de la Liberté, five blocks north of the Akwa Palace. The latter is a small pub-like restaurant with pizza for CFA 2800 to CFA 4500, also *poulet braisser* (chicken casserole) in the evenings for CFA 3500. The menu at Le Chalet, which is closed on Tuesdays, is similar.

Asian *Restaurant Chinois* (☎ 421426) on Ave de Gaulle, six blocks south of Rue Joss in Bonanjo, is one of Douala's best Chinese restaurants. For Vietnamese food, your best bet is the long-standing *Restaurant le Dragon d'Or* on Blvd de la Liberté, half a block south-east of the Akwa Palace. Prices at both places are moderate to expensive.

French Among the many restaurants that have bitten the dust in recent years (mostly French) are *L'Auberge*, *Le Paris*, *La Citane*, *La Marée*, *Croque O Burger*, *Mille et Une Nuits* and *Chez Therese*.

While there are still lots of choices, none of the French ones are cheap. Those less expensive than most include *Hôtel le Lido* (☎ 426206) on Rue Joffre in Akwa, a block off Blvd de la Liberté near Blvd Ahidjo, *Restaurant le Lyonnais* two blocks to the north on the same street next to Hôtel Beauséjour, and *L'Agip* at the Agip station next to the Place du Gouvernement in Bonanjo. The set menu at these places is around CFA 4500; L'Agip also has sandwiches.

If you want to splurge, try *Le Provençal* on Ave de Gaulle in Bonanjo, 3½ blocks south of Rue Joss, or *Restaurant le Grignotage* on Rue Surcouf in Bonanjo, behind the French cultural centre. Also near the cultural centre is *Restaurant la Comédia* while perhaps the best of all is *La Tête d'Art* on Rue Pau in Akwa opposite the Hôtel Beauséjour. All of them are fancy and could easily cost you CFA 15,000 per person. For great views, *Plein Ciel* at the top of Hôtel Beauséjour is unbeatable. The panoramic view of the city is as much an attraction as the good seafood.

Other Cuisines For something a little different – Indian and Japanese cuisine – head for *Restaurant Kohinoor* on Ave de Gaulle, four blocks south of Rue Joss. In addition to French dishes and pizza, *Restaurant la Phoenicia* (☎ 430921) in Bonanjo serves Lebanese fare, while *Il Canasta* on Rue de Trieste, two blocks south of Rue Joss, specialises in Italian cuisine. All of these places are fairly expensive.

Entertainment

Bars For cheap African bars, try Ave King Akwa (east of Blvd de la Liberté), or Rue Gallieni leading from Blvd de la Liberté towards the Marché de Lagos area. Also try north of the market along Rue Congo Pariso towards Place Ahidjo. Large beers cost up to CFA 250 a bottle. **Warning**: all of these streets are fairly dangerous, especially at night.

The drinking places along Blvd de la Liberté are safer but far more expensive. The sidewalk terrace of the Akwa Palace remains the most popular place for a drink but there are also some small pub-like bars, including *Le Bistro Snack Bar*, a few blocks to the north on Liberté, and *Le Pub*, a few blocks in the opposite direction, just past Cinéma Wouri. For the best views in Akwa, however, head for the beautiful pool-side terrace on top of *Hôtel Beauséjour*.

Nightclubs For those travelling on the cheap, the 'bar-dancing' places for ordinary folk are certainly more affordable and more interesting than the nightclubs. The former are concentrated in Akwa, the area around Marché de Lagos and, just beyond, New Bell. Two places among many in Akwa are *La Foi de l'Été* and *Le Mont Cameroun*.

Large rowdy bars like the one at *Hôtel Douala* near Lagos Market are best avoided.

The city's most famous nightclub is *St-Hilaire* on Rue Pau, a block behind (east of) the Akwa Palace. It's also the most expensive; drinks are usually CFA 3000 and on special nights can easily rise to CFA 5000. *Le Night Spot*, a block north on Ave King Akwa, is similar and attracts the same crowd. You can save money by going to *Paris Dancing* across the street from St-Hilaire; it is one of the cheaper dancing halls, with drinks starting at CFA 500.

Another well-known dancing place popular with Africans is *Macoumba-Macoumba*, which is named after the owner and is several blocks to the south on Rue Gallieni, half a block north of the intersection with Blvd de la République. It plays a mixture of African and disco and has an almost entirely African clientele. The *Scotch Club* on the same block is similar and, like the Macoumba, has drink prices in the mid-range. At any of these places, live bands only play on very special occasions; but they're still all good for dancing. While they're perfectly safe inside, even for women, the areas surrounding them are dangerous; so take every precaution imaginable. If you have the money, take a taxi to the door of the nightclub.

Resident expatriates tend to frequent discos with more Western music and which are in slightly less crowded areas. The new 'in' spot is *Le 78* on Rue Sylvani, two blocks north-west of Blvd de la Liberté; it's a modern strobe-lit disco with deafening rap sounds, and a clientele of expats, Africans and lots of prostitutes. Similar discos include *Le Privilege Nightclub* on Ave de Gaulle in Bonanjo, four blocks south of Rue Joss; *Safari* on Rue de la Motte Piquet in Bonanjo; *St James Nightclub* facing the Akwa Palace; and *Domino Night Club* on the same street, a block before the cathedral. Drinks at all these places are CFA 3000 and none of them get crowded before midnight.

Cinemas The two best cinemas, both in Akwa with air-con, are Le Wouri (☎ 421947) on Blvd de la Liberté several blocks north of the cathedral, and Le Concorde on Rue Lapeyrère, the street just north of the Akwa Palace. In Bonanjo, try Le Toula, a block from Hôtel de la Falaise. It's ventilated and cheaper, with two studios and numerous US films.

Things to Buy

Markets There are five markets, the largest and most interesting of which is the Marché de Lagos on Ave Douala Manga Bell, about a km south of Place Ahidjo. It's an amazing place, with a little bit of everything, so don't miss it, even if you aren't interested in buying anything. While you're there, check out the Marché de Kassalafam, only a few blocks to the east.

Artisan Goods An excellent African art shop – good quality, wide selection and reasonable prices – is the long-standing Chez Ali Baba on Rue Gallieni, just off Blvd de la Liberté near the cathedral. Highly recommended, it is open from 8.30 to 11.45 am and from 3.30 to 7 pm every day except Sundays. For even higher quality but very expensive art, try Alain Nyang Ouman a km to the south on the same street, facing Hôtel Coin de Plaisir. Le Fétiche on Rue de Verdun, very near the Novotel, is another. Remember to keep your sales dockets otherwise customs officials may hassle you on leaving, arguing that you're carrying valuable antiques.

The best place for souvenir-quality items and also some top-quality crafts, is the Artisanal Camerounais, an open-air crafts market on Blvd de la Liberté opposite the cathedral. You'll find a decent selection of beads, jewellery and masks, also musical instruments, leather items and ebony. If you bargain hard, you may be able to get lower prices here than at Ali Baba, but you'll be taking a risk as the vendors here are all expert con men and lie about the quality and age of pieces.

Music For cassettes of African music, try the airport or Son et Musique a block south of the Akwa Palace.

Getting There & Away

Air Douala is Cameroun's main international
airport, with more connections to Europe
than any other city in Central Africa. Coming
from the USA you'll have to transfer in
Europe or West Africa and the fare will be
very high, unless you purchase your ticket
through a discount agency. (For details, see
the introductory Getting There & Away
chapter.) In addition, there are plenty of
domestic flights out of Douala, especially to
Yaoundé and cities in the west and north.

To/From Europe You can fly direct from
Douala to Paris every day (Cameroun Air-
lines or Air France), to Brussels on Mondays
(Sabena), to Frankfurt on Mondays
(Lufthansa), to Zurich and Geneva on
Wednesdays (Swissair) and to Rome on
Sundays (Cameroun Airlines). The lowest
one-way fare from Paris is 4620 FF (about
US$850).

To/From Africa Connections with most
neighbouring countries are good – five
flights a week to Lagos in Nigeria (Air
Afrique, Nigeria Airways and Cameroun
Airlines), four to Libreville in Gabon (Air
Gabon and Cameroun Airlines), three to
Brazzaville in the Congo (Air Afrique and
Cameroun Airlines), two to Bangui in the
CAR (Cameroun Airlines and Air Afrique),
two to Kinshasa in Zaïre (Cameroun Airlines) and at least one a week to N'Djamena
in Chad (Cameroun Airlines and Unitair).
Cameroun Airlines also has flights on Tuesdays and Saturdays to Nairobi. They're the
only flights to East Africa and are usually
fully booked; the cheapest one-way ticket is
CFA 176,000 (about US$800).

Cameroun Airlines and Unitair also have,
between them, five flights a week to Malabo
(Equatorial Guinea). Alternatively, you can
also get to Malabo and Bata via Equato
Guineana de Aviation (EGA), which has one
tiny plane. It is represented at Air Affairs
Afrique (AAA) (☎ 422976), which has its
unmarked office just off the autoroute, on
your right about 200 metres before the
airport. AAA/EGA has flights to/from Bata

via Malabo on Tuesdays and Thursdays,
departing Douala at 9 am. The one-way fare
to Malabo/Bata is CFA 27,800/47,800, purchased only through AAA.

Within Cameroun As for domestic flights,
Cameroun Airlines and Unitair have about
six flights a day to Yaoundé and one flight a
day to Garoua and Maroua (CFA 51,150),
also five flights a week to N'Gaoundéré
(CFA 30,050), thrice-weekly flights to
Bafoussam and twice-weekly flights to
Bamenda and Bertoua. To charter a plane,
contact Avia Service (☎ 423892) at the
airport.

Airlines offices in the Akwa area include:

Aeroflot
  Blvd de la Liberté, opposite Hôtel Akwa
  (☎ 427991)
Air Mali
  Blvd Ahidjo, west of Blvd de la République
  (☎ 421700)
Alitalia
  Blvd de la Liberté, next to Hôtel Akwa
  (☎ 423608)
British Airways
  Immeuble Standard Chartered Bank, 61 Blvd de
  la Liberté (☎ 423873)
Lufthansa
  82 Blvd de la Liberté (☎ 426262, 425776)
Nigeria Airways
  17 Blvd de la Liberté (☎ 426234)
Swissair
  Immeuble BP, 33 Blvd de la Liberté (☎ 422929)

The remainder are in Bonanjo:

Air Afrique
  Rue Joss, at the Rue de Trieste intersection
  (☎ 424222)
Air France/UTA
  1 Rue Joss, at the Ave de Gaulle intersection
  (☎ 421555, 428020)
Air Gabon
  3 Rue Joss, at the Ave de Gaulle intersection
  (☎ 424943)
Air Zaïre
  2 Ave de Gaulle, opposite Cameroun Airlines
  (☎ 421941)
Cameroun Airlines
  3 Ave de Gaulle (☎ 424999, 422525)
  Blvd de la liberté, next to Hôtel Akwa
Sabena
  60 Ave de Gaulle (☎ 420515)

Bus The large buses ploughing between Douala and Yaoundé all leave from the area around Place Ahidjo, on fixed schedules mostly between 6.30 am and 6.30 pm, with some, eg Le Concorde, as late as 8.30 pm. Other companies include Express le Bien (☎ 422711), Express Garanti, Super Voyage Star, Lydie Voyages and Erko Voyages. The trip takes about three hours and costs CFA 2500 although there are occasionally specials for as low as CFA 1500.

Minibus & Bush Taxi The main taxi park is the Gare Routière de Yabassi (or Gare Routière SOTUC), which is in Yabassi, 750 metres east of Place Ahidjo at the intersection of Blvd de Japoma and Rue Nassif. Minibuses and bush taxis for Yaoundé and Kribi leave from there; those for western Cameroun leave from a place nearby.

One of the best minibus lines serving Kribi is Transline Voyages, which has fast comfortable minibuses ploughing between Douala and Kribi. Departures in either direction are at 7.30, 9.30, and 11.30 am and 1, 3 and 5.30 pm and the fare is CFA 1700. Its office is just behind the Shell station opposite Gare Routière de Yabassi.

Minibuses for Buea and Limbe leave from a small gare routière in Deïdo on Blvd de la Réunification near Wouri Bridge, two km north of the Hôtel Akwa Palace. At night, this is probably a better place than the main station to look for taxis and minibuses headed for western Cameroun, particularly Bafoussam (even up to midnight).

Standard fares are: CFA 700 to Limbe, CFA 725 to Buea, CFA 1400 to Kumba, CFA 1500 to Kribi, CFA 2500 to Yaoundé, CFA 2500 or CFA 3000 to Bafoussam, CFA 3750 to Foumban and CFA 3600 to CFA 4000 to Bamenda. If you're headed to the Nigerian border via Mamfé, the trip can be done in one long day (about 15 hours); expect to pay about CFA 6500 plus CFA 850 for luggage.

Train The new railway station is off Blvd de la Réunification, just over a km south-east of Rond-Point Deïdo. There are at least three trains a day to Yaoundé and the departure hours are constantly changing; most recently they were 7.30 am (which continues to Belabo), 1.30 pm (the Gazelle du Nord which continues overnight to N'Gaoundéré) and 7 pm. The trains have new cars and now take just four hours to Yaoundé (about 3½ hours according to the schedule) except for the much slower 'omnibus' trains. Fares in 1st/2nd class are CFA 3500/1900 to Yaoundé, CFA 9140/5070 to Belabo and CFA 14,855/8605 to N'Gaoundéré.

If you're looking for kicks and don't mind trains in very bad condition, catch the old train headed north to Kumba (about eight hours) or, in slightly better condition, the one to Nkongsamba.

Car Driving times from Douala are one hour to Buea or Limbe, two hours to Kribi, 2½ hours to Yaoundé and four hours to Bafoussam. The main route to Nigeria is via Kumba and Mamfé, which is being paved to Mamfé. From there to the border drivers can continue to anticipate terrible driving conditions during the rainy season but no major problems during the dry season.

Many of the city's car-rental agencies have failed. Two that remain are Avis (☎ 427056; fax 397774; telex 5374) at the Akwa Palace, and IVS Auto Location (☎ 426409) next door. Their prices are identical: CFA 13,000 per day for the cheapest vehicle, CFA 100 per km, plus 11% tax. For CFA 51,000 extra, you can drop the vehicle off in Yaoundé.

Boat The shipping agents are all in Bonanjo or at the ports. One of the best is Socopao (☎ 426454; telex 5319) at the main port (30 Quai de Dion Bouton); it handles Grimaldi Lines, which has freighters about every two weeks to Europe, stopping at various West African ports. Two other agencies representing freighters, some heading south towards Zaïre, are Camatrans (☎ 444750) at 12 Rue Kitchener, and Cameroun Shipping Lines (☎ 420038, 428103; telex 5615) at 18 Rue Joffre.

IMCA (☎ 423318), which is at the Port de Peschaud (pronounced 'pay-show') and open weekdays from 7.30 am to noon and 2.30 to 6 pm, also Saturday mornings, is the agency for the boat to Malabo, the 20-metre *Doña Elvira*. About once a week, but on no fixed days, it makes one round trip from Malabo via Douala and Bata. There is only one class and the cost is CFA 15,000, whether you get off in Bata or Malabo. It has an interior seating area with a video/TV, also some chairs on deck, but no food or berths. The sailing time on each link is about 24 hours except from Malabo to Douala, which usually takes about 12 hours (overnight). The stopover time in Douala and Bata is rarely more than a day, but depends on the amount of cargo.

Getting Around
To/From the Airport
The airport (☎ 42-2775) is on the south-western outskirts of town, 10 km from the centre; the airport departure tax is CFA 500/5000 on domestic/international flights. It's a fairly modern airport with facilities including a bank, a restaurant/bar, and an Avis agency. Turning right as you leave the airport and walking in the direction of the freight building, you'll find a SOTUC bus stop. Though the No 11 bus to the Marché de Lagos has reportedly been discontinued, this is still a good point to look for cheap shared taxis. If you take one from the airport terminal itself into town, the fare should be about CFA 2000 (CFA 2500 after 10 pm). Bargaining is required. Going to the airport, you can get a taxi for less if you hail one on the street. The cheapest way is to take a shared taxi to Carrefour St-Michel (CFA 125 by shared taxi) and then take another one from there headed past the airport (CFA 125).

City Bus
SOTUC buses operate between 6 am and 9 pm; fares vary between CFA 50 and CFA 75. The major bus routes are as follows:

No 1 – from Bonanjo east along Ave Douala Manga Bell and Blvd des Nations Unies
No 2 – from Carrefour de la Marine east along Blvd Ahidjo to Place Ahidjo and Gare Routière de Yabassi, continuing east on Blvd de l'Unité
No 3 – from the south side of town through New Bell towards Rond-Point Deïdo and across Wouri Bridge
No 4 – from Marché de Lagos to Gare Routière de Yabassi (SOTUC) continuing east on Blvd de l'Unité
No 5 – from Marché de Lagos northward up Ave Dr Jamot and Blvd de la République towards the railway station and Quartier Deïdo
No 6 – up and down Blvd de la Liberté, from Bonanjo to Deïdo
No 7 – from the south side of town through New Bell and up Blvd de la République towards Quartier Deïdo
No 11 – from Marché de Lagos towards the airport via Blvd des Nations Unies

Taxi Fares for a shared cab are CFA 125 (up to CFA 200 for longer distances, ie roughly in excess of four km), while a cab to yourself (a 'course') costs CFA 500 (CFA 600 after 10 pm). By the hour, a taxi should cost no more than CFA 2000, less if you'll be hiring one for a number of hours.

Southern Cameroun

KRIBI
Kribi is Cameroun's best beach resort. The beaches here are white – in contrast to the black, sometimes rocky beaches at Limbe – and there really aren't many foreigners except during the short high season (December to February), when the hotels are full of expatriates, mostly from Douala. Avoid the heavy rain period, from June to mid-October, but the mid-October to November and March to May periods are great times to come here because there's still a good bit of sun and getting a room is easy. The 169-km road from Douala via Edéa is now paved, and finding minibuses is simple; they take only about 2½ hours. The town is fairly small but does have a few amenities, including banks and restaurants, even a disco.

Places to Stay – bottom end
If you want to pitch a tent on or near the beach, you might try asking someone with a house near the beach if you can put your tent

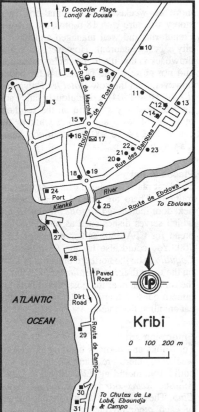

Map of Kribi

■ PLACES TO STAY

3   Hôtel de la Paix
4   Hôtel les Nid'Or
10 Paillote de Cathy
12 Auberge de Kribi
24 Hôtel de Kribi
26 Auberge du Phare
27 Pension Coco-Beach
28 Hôtel Centre d'Accueil
29 Auberge Annette II
30 Hôtel les Polygones d'Alice
31 Chez Pepino

▼ PLACES TO EAT

1   Restaurant la Coquillage
6   Small Restaurants
15 Restaurant la Sizène

OTHER

2   Présidence
5   Agip Station
6   Market, Gare Routière & Pharmacie de Kribi
7   Transline Voyages
8   Le Refuge Night Club
9   Atlantic Relax Bar
11 Liberty Night Club
13 Water Tower (Landmark)
14 Librairie New Bell
16 Hospital
17 Post Office
18 Big Ben Discotheque
19 Texaco Station
20 Le Number One Supermarché
21 SGBC Bank
22 BICIC Bank
23 BP Station
25 Church

in front of their house. Some travellers have done this and been pleasantly surprised at how friendly the people here (the Bassa) can be. However, because of the risk of getting robbed, I recommend doing this out of town, either to the north or south.

There are several cheap hotels in town. The closest to the ocean is the *Hôtel de la Paix*, which is a bit isolated, about 250 metres from the closest beach and a km from the heart of town. It's somewhat dreary-looking but has a big bar and rooms with shared bath for CFA 3395 (CFA 4580 and CFA 5225 for rooms with private bath). If

you'd rather be in the active heart of town, head for *Auberge de Kribi* (☎ 461315), which is near the water tower. Also called Auberge Bello, it has clean rooms with shared bath for CFA 3500; however, Bello, the owner, might accept less. If it's full, try *Auberge Annette I*, which is not far away, or the *Paillote de Cathy*, which is half a km north of the PTT on the same road.

For a hotel on the beach, your best bet is the *Auberge Annette II* (☎ 461057), which is

a good km south of the central area. The
friendly manager charges CFA 7500/10,000
for rooms with fan/air-con but she is likely
to offer you one for CFA 6000 or so during
the off season. Her place has a great African
ambience and good meals for CFA 1500.
Another beach-front possibility is *Chez
Pepino*, which is about half a km further
south. Run-down and poorly managed with
dingy rooms, it's best forgotten unless you
can get the price way down from the quoted
price of CFA 10,000.

The *Hôtel les Nid'Or* (☎ 461435), which
has 20 rooms with fan/air-con for CFA 8000/
11,000, is not particularly cheap. However,
it is definitely worth checking out because I
was offered a room for only CFA 5000
during the off season. It's an attractive, new-
looking place with spotlessly clean rooms
and tile baths, and draws primarily African
clients. You'll have to walk at least half a km
to get to a beach, however, as it's on a sideroad not far from the gare routière.

Places to Stay – top end

Among the top-end hotels, I recommend the
Auberge du Phare (☎ 461106) and the
Pension Coco-Beach (☎ 461584) next door.
Both of these relaxing places cater to expatriates, are within walking distance of the
centre and are right on the beach, with breezy
restaurants overlooking the sea and waves
breaking a stone's throw away. The Coco-
Beach has a slightly more formal ambience,
with air-con rooms for CFA 12,000. The
auberge, however, is a much better buy as it
has rooms with fans for just CFA 6000 (CFA
12,000 with air-con). Main courses at both
hotels' restaurants are mostly between CFA
2000 and CFA 3000, grilled fish invariably
being the best selection.

If these are full, try the relatively new
Hôtel Centre d'Accueil (☎ 461635), 100
metres to the south. Its square bungalows
aren't so attractive but in most other respects
it's fairly similar. Air-con singles/doubles
cost CFA 11,500/13,800.

The *Hôtel de Kribi* (☎ 461475), charges
CFA 11,000 for a room with petit déjeuner
(breakfast) during the week and somewhat

more on weekends. A colonial-era, two-
storey structure with 18 rooms, the Kribi is
French-run and well managed and has the
city's best restaurant. However, its major
drawback is that it's in the centre at the port
and not close to the beach. It's far better,
however, than the new *Hôtel les Polygones
d'Alice* (☎ 461504), a ridiculously fancy and
ugly three-storey structure on the southern
outskirts of town and a long walk to the
centre. At CFA 16,500 for an air-con room,
it's way overpriced.

Places to Eat

The best place for cheap eats is at the gare
routière. There are several cheap eateries
next door including *Gargotte Mongo Ya Jal*,
which serves dishes such as omelettes and
bread for CFA 350, and monkey for CFA
700. You could also try the *Restaurant la
Coquillage* on the northern outskirts of town
on the main drag, or *Restaurant la Sizène* at
the rond-point near the post office; both are
quite modest. Otherwise, the best places to
eat are all at the hotels.

Entertainment

For drinks and perhaps dancing as well on
weekends, there are some cheap bars you
could try, including *Liberty Night Club*,
Atlantic Relax Bar and *Le Refuge Night
Club*. These three are all within 300 metres
of each other on the paved road leading
north-west from the landmark water tower
towards the gare routière. *Big Ben Discotheque*, further south at the Texaco station
roundabout near the bridge, is for more
serious dancing.

Getting There & Away

Virtually all vehicles leave from the gare
routière next to the market and only when
full. Minibuses cost CFA 200 to Londji, CFA
1500 to Douala, CFA 2000 to Ebolowa and
CFA 2500 to Yaoundé. Transline Voyages,
however, offers service to Douala on a
scheduled basis. Located about 200 metres
north of the gare, it charges CFA 1000 to
Edéa and CFA 1700 to Douala, with depar-

tures in either direction at 7.30, 9.30 and 11.30 am and 1, 3 and 5.30 pm.

AROUND KRIBI
North of Kribi
There are also some beautiful white-sand beaches to the north of Kribi, most notably **Costa Blanca** (12 km), **Cocotier Plage** (15 km) and **Londji** (24 km), which is a picturesque fishing village spread around an immense bay, with clean sand and palm trees. You can camp on the beach or rent a hut overlooking the water at all three places for about CFA 1500; thieves are not a major problem but don't leave things lying around. Otherwise take a room at the *Hôtel du Golf de Guinness* in Londji; it has 12 very rustic rooms without water or electricity for about CFA 2000. Somewhat isolated, Londji has virtually no other amenities but it's a great place to lie back and enjoy Africa, eating grilled fish and drinking palm wine with the locals. Each night the men get in their canoes to go out fishing in the bay and further out in the ocean, returning at dawn. It wouldn't take much to convince them to take you along. Try it; it could be an adventure.

South of Kribi
Seven km south of Kribi, just before Grand Batanga, you'll see a sign pointing to the **Chutes de la Lobé**, one of a very small number of waterfalls in the world that empty into the sea. If you hike down to the beach, you'll find a small restaurant which serves some tasty grilled fish but it's not very cheap. This area and further south are particularly good places to stay a few days.

The fishing village of **Eboundja** (20 km) would be a good place to hang out for a few days as the people there are extremely friendly and will let you camp for free on the beach. Moreover, you're far less likely to encounter thieves here than in or just outside Kribi. You could also rent a hut – many of the villagers here (and in other fishing villages on the way to Campo, such as Ebodjé at Km 50) will gladly you rent you one for a song. Indeed, all along this coast, the locals are far friendlier than in many other areas of

the country. As in Londji, they'll prepare you meals of grilled fish and shrimp, offer you some freshly tapped palm wine and take you out on their nightly fishing expeditions if you ask.

If you continue southward to **Campo** (75 km), you can cross the Ntem River by pirogue and venture into Equatorial Guinea. (For details, see the introductory Getting There & Away section in the Equatorial Guinea chapter.) The Réserve de Campo Nyabessan, shown on most maps, exists only on paper, so forget about it.

Getting There & Away
Several minibuses a day leave from the gare routière in Kribi (CFA 200), passing by the northern beaches en route. You should also be able to find at least one minibus or pick-up truck a day (mornings only) headed south along the coast for Eboundja and Campo.

EBOLOWA
Capital of the southern Ntem district, Ebolowa is a town of about 40,000 inhabitants, mostly Boulou, and is of no particular note except that it's the largest town en route from Yaoundé to Gabon and Equatorial Guinea and thus a frequent stopping point. The setting is completely tropical, with cacao trees (the main source of income in this area) scattered amongst the thick rainforests.

The heart of town is a rond-point where seven streets converge; the tiny gare routière for Yaoundé is there, also several petrol stations and Hôtel Anne Rouge. The market is 300 metres to the north-east, just before Lac Municipal, while the Gare Routière d'Ambam is about two km in the opposite direction, on the southern outskirts of town. The immigration office at the Hôtel de Police issues visa extensions if you need them, otherwise there's no need to pass by immigration. If you're headed south, immigration officials posted at the gare for Ambam will check your passport but won't stamp it.

Places to Stay
In town, one of the cheapest places is *Hôtel Cabane Bambou*, which is just beyond the

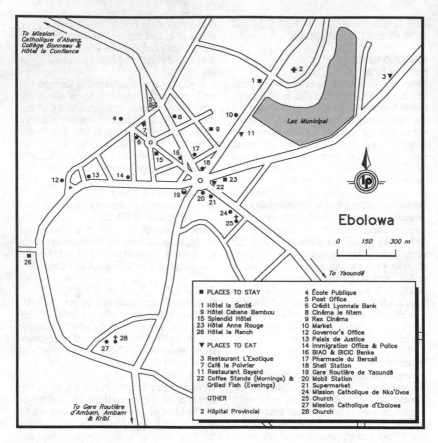

To Mission
Catholique d'Abang,
Collège Bonneau &
Hôtel la Confiance

1 ■
+ 2
3 ▼

4 ●
● 8
10 ●
Lac Municipal

■ 9
▼ 11

17
16 ●
18

15
12 ●
● 13
14 ●
■ 23
22 ▼

19 ●
20 ●
21
24 ●
25

26 ■

Ebolowa

0   150   300 m

To Yaoundé

27 ●
‡ 28

To Gare Routière
d'Ambam, Ambam
& Kribi

■ PLACES TO STAY

1 Hôtel la Santé
9 Hôtel Cabane Bambou
15 Splendid Hôtel
23 Hôtel Anne Rouge
26 Hôtel le Ranch

▼ PLACES TO EAT

3 Restaurant L'Exotique
7 Café le Polvrier
11 Restaurant Bayard
22 Coffee Stands (Mornings) &
   Grilled Fish (Evenings)

OTHER

2 Hôpital Provincial

4 École Publique
5 Post Office
6 Crédit Lyonnais Bank
8 Cinéma le Ntem
9 Rex Cinéma
10 Market
12 Governor's Office
13 Palais de Justice
14 Immigration Office & Police
16 BIAO & BICIC Banks
17 Pharmacie du Bercail
18 Shell Station
19 Gare Routière de Yaoundé
20 Mobil Station
21 Supermarket
24 Mission Catholique de Nko'Ovos
25 Church
27 Mission Catholique d'Ebolowa
28 Church

Rex Cinéma, about 250 metres north of the roundabout. It has clean rooms with exterior/interior bath for CFA 3000/4000, and is a good buy. Or try Hôtel la Santé (☎ 28-3517), which is half a km north-east of the rond-point, past the market and just across the lake. It has equally clean rooms with interior showers for CFA 3500 and nicer rooms for CFA 5000. For convenience, however, Hôtel Anne Rouge (☎ 283438) is unbeatable and, unlike the others, it has a restaurant and a lively bar with TV. A large clean room with mosquito net and private shower costs CFA 4000.

To save money, you could try staying at the Mission Catholique d'Abang or the nearby Collège Bonneau. They're about three km north-west of town on the road leading past the post office. At the turn-off for the mission, you'll see Hôtel la Confiance. It's a grubby little place but a room with a clean bed and interior shower costs only CFA 2500.

The city's top address is Hôtel le Ranch (☎ 283531/2), which is a km south-west of the roundabout, well beyond the governor's office. The hotel's public areas are quite nice but the rooms are cramped. They have carpets and tile baths and cost CFA 7000/9000 (fan/air-con). *Hôtel la Jungle* (☎ 283573) is apparently in the same category.

Places to Eat
The best place for street food is the roundabout. The women there sell coffee and bread in the morning and tasty grilled fish at night. For lunch, try the food stalls on the paved road to the market, such as *Restaurant Bayard* opposite the market.

The city's top restaurant is *L'Exotique*, which is on the same street as the Hôtel Anne Rouge but a km to the east, just beyond the lake. The rustic, tranquil ambience is very pleasant and the menu includes grilled fish or chicken for CFA 2000, both *garni* (accompanied by vegetables and bread or rice), and pork chops garni for CFA 1500. Another possibility is the *Café le Poivrier*, which is a block behind the post office. You can eat on the terrace or inside; it's also a good place just for drinks. Alternatively, there are the restaurants at the *Hôtel Anne Rouge* and, more expensive, *Hôtel le Ranch*.

Getting There & Away
Minibuses for Yaoundé leave throughout the day from the roundabout, cost CFA 1500 and take about 2½ hours. There is also usually at least one minibus a day to Kribi (171 km), which leave from the same gare and costs CFA 1500. Minibuses for Ambam (about four a day) leave from the Gare d'Ambam, mostly between 6 and 9 am; after that, pickup trucks are more common. The 78-km trip through scenic thick rainforests takes up to three hours and costs CFA 1000. If you're headed to Ebebiyin (Equatorial Guinea), the entire trip should take about five or six hours.

AMBAM
Ambam is the last major town before the border crossings to Equatorial Guinea and Gabon. Should you be caught here for the night, you can stay at the cheap *Auberge le Petit Calao*, which is 100 metres from the market. You do not need to get your passport stamped in Ambam as that will be done at the border.

If you're headed to Ebebiyin, you'll have no problem finding taxis to the border. Some 20 minutes south of town you must cross the 50-metre wide Ntem River; a car-carrying ferry runs back and forth every hour. From there it's another 30 minutes to the border where your passport will be stamped. Ebebiyin is two km away; you can walk or take one of the taxis waiting at the border.

If you're headed to Bitam and Oyem (Gabon), you must take the more easterly route from Ambam. As on the other route, finding taxis to the border (27 km) is no problem, and once there you'll have to cross the Ntem River by ferry and catch a taxi to Bitam (43 km), again no problem.

Western Cameroun

LIMBE
On weekends during the dry season, beach lovers in Douala head for Limbe (lem-bay), founded in 1857 by Alfred Saker, a British missionary. The beaches here are of black volcanic sand and are not as scenic as those in the area around Krihi, plus the closest decent beach is six miles away. However, the trip from Douala takes only an hour, even by bush taxi. For those looking for a little local activity in addition to beaches, Limbe can be highly recommended as the town is larger and livelier than Kribi, with more bars and places to eat.

Orientation
The heart of town is the roundabout where the roads to Douala and Idenao intersect. The botanical gardens begin just to the west of the roundabout on Idenao Rd which heads north-west towards the stadium and post office and, much further out, Mile Six Beach. The liveliest section of town, with numerous small bars and cheap restaurants, is to the north, particularly along Church St, which winds for about 1½ km in a somewhat semicircular fashion from the stadium east towards Market St. The less animated administrative district, where all the banks (BIAO, BICIC,

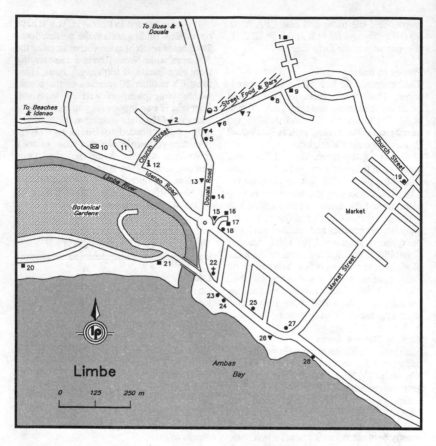

Limbe

To Buea & Douala

To Beaches & Idenao

3 Street Food & Bars

Church Street

Idenao Road

Douala Road

Limbe River

Botanical Gardens

Church Street

Market

Market Street

Ambas Bay

0   125   250 m

SGBC, Crédit Lyonnais), Prescraft and many colonial buildings are located, is along the water, south-east of the roundabout towards the fish market.

Beaches

The beach in the fish-market area is too dirty for swimming and the remaining beaches near town are too rocky, so most people head for **Mile Six Beach** which, like all the beaches here, has black volcanic sand originating from Mt Cameroun, which dominates the area. Mile Six is on the asphalt coastal road leading north-west towards Idenao and

marked; the beach is a 10-minute hike from the sign. Mile Six Beach is not particularly pretty and looks dirty (but isn't) because of the chocolate-coloured sand, plus there's an unattractive oil refinery nearby. However, it's good for meeting other travellers and there's a restaurant open on weekends, also a guard who collects the CFA 200 entrance fee. For entertainment, you can look for monkeys playing in the nearby trees or walk up the beach for two km to Batoké (Km 8), a fishing village where you can check out the fishing scene.

During the week you'll have Mile Six

■ PLACES TO STAY

1 Holiday Inn Resort
9 Mansion Hotel
16 Victoria Guest House
17 Bay Hotel
20 Park Hotel Miramar
21 Atlantic Beach Hotel

▼ PLACES TO EAT

2 Mother's Home Restaurant
4 Pâtisserie de Fako
6 Cameroon Café
7 Vixcam Restaurant
13 Blue Whale Restaurant
15 Black & White Restaurant
26 Mars Restaurant & Snacks

OTHER

3 Total Station & Taxi Stand
4 Victoria Bus Stop Bar
5 AIM Supermarket & Music Store
6 Embassy Bookshop
8 Guinness Club Bar
10 Post Office
11 Centenary Stadium
12 Tourist Office
14 Fako Pharmacy
18 BIAO Bank
19 Friendship Club Bar
22 Church
23 Prescraft
24 BICIC Bank
25 Lively Bar
26 SGBC & Crédit Lyonnais Banks
27 BEAC Bank
28 Fish Market, Fishing Boats & Town Beach

Other Attractions

Limbe has several attractions besides the beach. Near the centre there are some delightful **botanical gardens**. Free and open to the public (there are no walls), the large, well-maintained gardens have some 1500 trees which provide delightful shade and protection from the hot midday sun. The trees were planted about a century ago by the Germans and later maintained by the British who, during the colonial period, made this predominantly anglophone city (called Victoria until 1983) the capital of their section of Cameroun.

Some of the old **colonial buildings** are in the area just east of the gardens, starting with the church. Opposite the church you'll find Prescraft, which is the best place in town to look for handicrafts and local furniture. About half a km further along that paved road you'll come to the **fish market**, where you can chat with the fishers and inspect their boats and gear.

Places to Stay – bottom end

It's possible to get permission to camp in the botanical gardens but you'll be taking a big risk as a heavily populated area is just to the north of the gardens and thieves are likely to spot you. Sleeping on the beach poses the same risk. If you do camp, find someone reliable to guard your stuff.

One of the cheapest hotels is the unmarked, two-storey *Mansion Hotel* on Church St, 300 metres east of the Douala Rd intersection. The rooms and shared baths are very grimy and dark but the sheets are clean enough and the rooms have fans. For CFA 1500 a room, it's hard to complain. Rooms upstairs cost an extra CFA 300, but they are quieter and the showers and toilets work better. *City Hotel*, behind the taxi stand, is next in line and slightly better but it's also more expensive – CFA 2500 for a double with fan and private bath.

Just east of the roundabout and up a small hill you'll find the long-standing *Victoria Guest House* (☎ 322446) and, next door, the *Bay Hotel* (☎ 332332/689). Singles/doubles at the Victoria cost CFA 4500/5000 (CFA

Beach to yourself, however on weekends it can get crowded during the high season (December to February). Getting ripped off is a distinct possibility even with the gate attendant. For shared taxis, wait in front of the stadium; those headed for the villages along the coast pass by there and charge CFA 200 to Mile Six. Otherwise, you'll have to charter a taxi and pay much more. Those looking for a more secluded beach should head further out to Mile Eight, Mile 13 or Mile 20; none of them are marked.

5500 with air-con). The rooms are fairly large with overhead fans and there's a restaurant and bar, but there are no ocean views and the bathrooms are inferior to the nice tile ones at the Bay Hotel. The Bay is a slightly better hotel with views of the ocean and the prices reflect this – singles/doubles with aircon for CFA 5775/7500, and CFA 4665 (singles only) without. Meals are taken at the Black & White Restaurant (see Places to Eat).

A new place worth checking out is the attractive, two-storey *Holiday Inn Resort* (☎ 332290). The spotlessly clean rooms have new tile bathrooms and are unbeatable for the price – CFA 4500/5500 for singles/doubles with overhead fans (CFA 6500 with air-con). The location, two blocks north of lively Church St, is a drawback for those wanting beach views, but for those who like being near the action, it's an asset.

Places to Stay – top end
The picturesque old *Atlantic Beach Hotel* (☎ 332333; telex 5845) overlooks the ocean and is conveniently close to the centre, a 500-metre walk from the roundabout. It's the only really good hotel in town. You have four categories of rooms to choose from, all with air-con: bungalows with single rooms (CFA 8990), chalets (CFA 11,990) and rooms with garden/sea views (CFA 13,990/16,990). Breakfast costs CFA 1500 extra. The saltwater pool is pictured in all the travel brochures – the ocean waves practically spill into it. What the pictures don't show is the rocky, unusable beach and the tennis court overgrown with weeds; still, it's a pleasant place with a wonderful restaurant, the city's best by far.

The *Park Hotel Miramar* is half a km west of the Atlantic Beach Hotel and has the same telephone and telex because both hotels have the same owners. Highly recommended, it overlooks the ocean and offers the best value of any hotel in town – a sparse but clean bungalow with one/two beds costs CFA 4665/6105 (CFA 7770 with air-con) including breakfast. The pool here is just as good as the one at the Atlantic Beach; guests may use either. You can get sandwiches (CFA

650) and drinks here, but full meals usually only on weekends. **Warning:** the road connecting the two hotels looks tranquil but is actually quite dangerous at night as numerous travellers walking that route at night have been mugged!

Places to Eat
The best place for cheap food is along Church St. It's very lively with all manner of street food, small bars everywhere and music blasting away. Heading from east to west along that street, you'll come to *Guinness Club Bar*, which is the first notable place and about 300 metres east of the Douala Rd intersection. It's a very popular outdoor bar and a good place to try some grilled brochettes (known locally as *suya*)) plain or covered with peanut sauce.

About halfway between the Guinness and the intersection is *Vixcam Restaurant*, which is my favourite place for Camerounian food. The home-like African ambience is unbeatable – like eating in someone's house. You can eat inside or on the porch, and the place is very clean. There are about 15 dishes to choose from, all CFA 300 a plate, including fish and sauce, meat and rice, meat and gari, fufu and water. It's also a good place to come just for a beer. About 100 metres away, closer to the intersection, you'll find *Cameroon Café*, which is a good place for breakfast and also full meals including rice and beans, and salads. Continuing west on Church St, about 100 metres past the intersection, you'll come to *Mother's Home Restaurant*, which has fewer but slightly different dishes than the Vixcam (corn fufu is one); otherwise, it's virtually identical, including the option of eating inside or on a porch.

For bread and snacks, try *Pâtisserie de Fako* on Douala Rd, just south of Church St. It's nothing special, with cheap, mediocre pastries and bread, but it also has yoghurt, milk and bottled water. The tiny *AIM Supermarket* is next door.

Two mid-range restaurants that are quite popular with travellers are *The Blue Whale Restaurant*, which is further south on Douala Rd, and *Black & White Restaurant-Night-*

club nearby at the roundabout. The Blue Whale offers about five excellent African selections, including fish and sauce and ndolé (chicken) with plantain, all for CFA 1000, plus large beers for CFA 300. The Black & White is more expensive and has a Western menu (some with three courses) with most dishes for CFA 2500. It's also breezy and a nice place for a drink, but there are no ocean views; a small Guinness costs CFA 250.

The city's best restaurant is at the *Atlantic Beach Hotel*, which has an attractive dining room and bar overlooking the sea. The fixed menu costs CFA 4950 plus drinks. For drinks overlooking the ocean, try *Mars Restaurant & Snacks*, near Crédit Lyonnais and about 100 metres west of the fish market. The food and drinks aren't cheap (CFA 2000 for chicken & chips) but the relaxing ambience is nice.

Getting There & Away

The taxi park is at the lively intersection of Church St and Douala Rd. Bush taxis and minibuses cost CFA 450 to Buea (45 km), CFA 700 to Douala (74 km) and CFA 1000 to Idenao (48 km). Idenao is where you'll find boats headed every day to Oron (Nigeria); for details, see the introductory Getting There & Away section.

BUEA & MT CAMEROUN

There are two reasons to head for Buea, an hour from Douala: to enjoy the refreshingly cool climate at an altitude of 1000 metres, or to climb Mt Cameroun. At 4095 metres (13,428 feet), it is easily the highest mountain in Central and West Africa outside the Ruwenzori mountains on the Zaïre-Rwanda-Uganda border. Mt Cameroun is also one of the easiest to climb and not dangerous – its last, fairly minor eruption was in 1982. The vertical ascent is approximately 3000 metres, a 27-km round trip in all. On the mountain, you'll pass through dense tropical forests which turn into subalpine meadows at

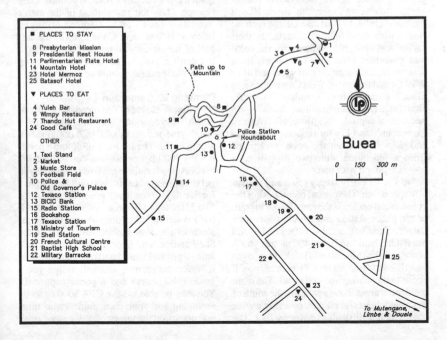

PLACES TO STAY
8 Presbyterian Mission
9 Presidential Rest House
11 Parliamentarian Flats Hotel
14 Mountain Hotel
23 Hotel Mermoz
25 Batasof Hotel

PLACES TO EAT
4 Yuleh Bar
6 Wimpy Restaurant
7 Thando Hut Restaurant
24 Good Café

OTHER
1 Taxi Stand
2 Market
3 Music Store
5 Football Field
10 Police &
   Old Governor's Palace
12 Texaco Station
13 BICIC Bank
15 Radio Station
16 Bookshop
17 Texaco Station
18 Ministry of Tourism
19 Shell Station
20 French Cultural Centre
21 Baptist High School
22 Military Barracks

Path up to Mountain

Police Station Roundabout

Buea

0   150   300 m

To Mutengene, Limbe & Douala

around 2000 metres. Getting good views of or from the rocky peak is difficult as it is shrouded in clouds most of the time, particularly during the rainy season.

Most people come just for the cooler climate, the best time being the dry season, from late November to February, when there's sunshine, it becomes cloudy, with a 50-50 chance of rain. In May the rains begin and Buea becomes a miserable, cold place. A climb at that time of the year wouldn't be pleasant. On the western slopes, it rains practically every day and the area records one of the world's highest rainfalls. Regardless of when you come, don't miss the wonderful old Mountain Hotel which is, for most non-climbers, the city's major attraction. Far from luxurious, it has a rustic English charm but is run by French people. Even if you can't afford to stay there, it's a great place for a drink.

The town has an interesting history, which is easily inferred from the German governor's palace perched above the central roundabout, towering over the town like a medieval castle. In 1901, the Germans chose Buea, with its delightful climate, as their capital and built this residence for the colonial governor, Jesco von Puttkamer. Buea was the capital for only eight years and after WW I it and the rest of West Cameroun were placed under British mandate. In 1961, shortly after independence, Buea again became a capital, this time of 'Western Cameroun', and briefly prospered, but this ended in 1972 when the country changed from a federation with two capitals to a united republic with one.

Now it's a fairly sleepy town and unusually spread out. The central point, but not the commercial centre, is the roundabout in front of the police station and the old governor's palace. Turn left (south-west), just beyond the BICIC bank, and after 400 metres you'll come to the Mountain Hotel; turn right (north-east) and after 800 metres you'll come to the market and taxi stand. The main residential areas, however, are to the south of the roundabout and market, covering a wide area which is difficult to cover by foot. The cheapest hotels, the military base, schools and many stores are in this area, not around the market.

Mt Cameroun Race

Since 1973, Guinness has sponsored an annual mad race (27 km) up and down the mountain. The winning time is usually around three hours and 45 minutes, the descent being made in about 70 minutes – truly amazing when you consider that it's so steep that the runners have to carry poles! And temperatures can vary from 25°C at the start of the race to 0°C at the summit. If you stay up the night before the race, you'll see the local people making sacrifices to appease the mountain spirits.

To enter the race, contact the manager of Guinness Cameroun in Douala, BP 1213 (☎ 422841/906; telex 5327). BP stands for *boite postale* or post office box. The race takes place on the last Sunday in January. Usually about 350 runners enter, including quite a few from other African countries and Europe. Over the years, most of the men's races have been won by Camerounians and Britons. If you're in Cameroun in the last half of January, by all means go and watch, but don't expect to find a hotel room as up to 50,000 spectators show up every year.

Climbing Mt Cameroun

Permits & Guides You need a permit to climb. If you don't get one and you're caught, the penalty is a CFA 20,000 fine or a month in jail. The fee for a guide and a porter is CFA 7000 per person per day (CFA 5000 per person when there are five people). If you get to the second cabin, you will have to pay for two days, even if you return the same day. The Ministry of Tourism office (☎ 322543/656) is on the main drag about 700 metres south of the roundabout, just north of the Shell station, and is open weekdays from 7 am to 2 pm and Saturdays from 7 am to noon. It issues the permits and will assign you a guide (obligatory) and a porter (optional). You may be able to save CFA 3000 or so by arranging for your own guide (who must register you at the tourist office in any event);

Top Left :   Pygmies around the camp fire, the CAR (BH)
Top Right :   Pygmy camp scene, the CAR (BH)
Bottom Left :   Old Pygmy man, the CAR (BH)
Bottom Right :   Balancing pots, the CAR (KW)

Top : Palais Royal, Foumban, Cameroun (AN)
Bottom Left : Crab sorcerer, Rumsiki, Cameroun (AN)
Bottom Right : Tailor, the CAR (KW)

the friendly owner of the Thando Hut restaurant at the market is a good person to ask about this possibility.

The Route Those in great shape can start off from Buea at 5 am and be back by nightfall, around 6 pm. It is several km from Buea to the entrance up the hill, called Upper Farm (or Prison Farm) and the route is fairly obscure. From the farm the route is very clear. Don't plan on more than 30 minutes total in rest stops. If you're very fit and are going to try doing it in one day, chances are you won't get back by nightfall if you don't begin your descent by 1 pm.

Most people should count on taking two days for the climb and descent. Regardless, you are sure to find the descent far harder on your legs and knees than the ascent – that's guaranteed! So once you're at the top, don't be deceived into thinking the descent will be a breeze. Unless you stay overnight in one of the cabins and arrive at the top around 6 or 7 am, chances are you'll be enveloped in a cloud, with a visibility of 30 metres.

You'll pass three cabins on the way up, all unlocked. The first is in the forest at 1875 metres (about a 2½-hour walk), the second in the alpine meadows at 2860 metres (another 2½-hour walk), and the third at 3740 metres (another 1½ hours). From there to the top is another hour. Be sure you get to the top (Fako Point) and not Bottle Top, which is 54 metres lower (4041 metres).

Most climbers stay overnight at the middle cabin because the weather is so cold at the top cabin. The advantage of staying at the third cabin is that getting to the top at the crack of dawn is no problem and the chances of getting a good view are a thousand times better. The cabins are a far cry from those on Kilimanjaro; all you'll find is a hard wooden platform to sleep on.

Equipment It's much colder than you would expect up there. From the second cabin on, be prepared for below-freezing temperatures. On the upper slopes, frost and snow are not uncommon. Rain gear and a change of clothes are essential, especially from February to October. Unless you are certain you can get to the top and back in one day, a sleeping bag is an absolute must.

Footwear is an important consideration too. If you have weak ankles, or choose to climb in the rainy season (May to October), it would be a good idea to use hiking boots. The path is very steep, and there are numerous loose rocks just waiting to be slipped on. In the dry season you might decide that the safety factor is no longer such a major concern so you could go for the comfort of a good pair of running shoes.

There is water stored at all the cabins, but unless it is boiled or treated, it's not drinkable.

Some climbers recommend bringing along rehydrating solution so as to replenish the sugar and mineral salts lost while sweating. The recipe is one litre of boiled water, 10 pinches of sugar, three pinches of salt and the juice of one lemon.

Places to Stay
For the price (CFA 2500 per person), the *Presbyterian Mission* is highly recommended. Only 200 metres north-east of the roundabout, just north of the main road, it's a clean place and the English-speaking African staff is very friendly.

For a typical, cheap African hotel, head for *Hotel Mermoz* (☎ 328228), which is about 1½ km south of the roundabout (specifically, 800 metres south of the roundabout via the main road to the Shell station, then south-west for one long block, then south for about 400 metres, well past the military barracks). Newly enlarged with a 2nd floor, it charges CFA 4000 for doubles which have, on occasion, been bargained down to CFA 3000. The rooms are moderately clean and have private baths but the noise can sometimes be intolerable as this is also a nightclub. If it's full, try the similarly priced *Batasof Hotel*. About one km south-east of the Shell station along the main drag you'll see a sign pointing east to the hotel; it's not far from there.

For slightly more, you can get a much better room at the *Parliamentarian Flats* (☎ 324226). It's a large three-storey hotel which has 30 clean rooms with hot-water baths for CFA 5000. There's also a bar and an upstairs restaurant overlooking the mountains. This old place has lost some of its charm but it's tranquil and a good buy, plus it's only 250 metres west of the roundabout.

Almost all travellers with a few shekels to spare stay at the delightful, highly recommended *Mountain Hotel* (☎ 322235), which is like an old resort lodge, with a spacious restaurant, bar, ping-pong table, a pool, and well-maintained gardens. Some 150 metres past the Parliamentarian Flats, it has 50 rooms with one/two beds and hot-water bath for CFA 11,300/12,350. During the rainy season, when business is slow, you should be able to negotiate the price down by 30% or so. There's no air-con and with good reason – this place is mountain cool. For CFA 1500, nonguests can use the chilly pool.

Places to Eat
There are five or so hole-in-the-wall restaurants around the taxi stand, but the best place by far is the *Thando Hut* a block away at the market. It's a rustic place with cheap beer and food, and good vibes. Big beers cost CFA 250 and the menu is very simple (omelette and chips for CFA 400, chicken and rice, etc). The restaurant used to have poetry readings and plays on Sunday afternoons at 4.30 pm; check it out – as this might start up again.

A good alternative, with seating indoors and outdoors, is *Wimpy*, a small, neat place about 250 metres west towards the roundabout. It has omelette and chips for CFA 500, full breakfasts with eggs for CFA 400, Nescafé for CFA 150, sandwiches and beer. The popular and more rustic *Yuleh Bar* across the street is slightly cheaper, with large Nigerian beers for CFA 250 and sometimes inexpensive African food as well. If you're staying at the Hotel Mermoz, which has no restaurant, you can get a huge plate of fish and rice for CFA 400 at the café just opposite the hotel.

The restaurant at the *Mountain Hotel* is the city's finest; the menu is CFA 4000. To economise, try the *Parliamentarian Flats*

just up the street; it has fairly decent, Western-style meals for about CFA 2000.

Getting There & Away
The taxi stand is just beyond the market. A minibus costs CFA 725 to Douala and CFA 450 to Limbe. You also have the option of taking a shared taxi to Mutengane (19 km; CFA 200), which is the turn-off point for Buea on the Douala to Limbe road, and catching another from there to Douala, Limbe or Kumba.

KUMBA
Kumba is roughly midway on the all-important Douala to Mamfé road, connecting Douala and Nigeria. The modern covered market here is wild, with all kinds of smuggled goods from Nigeria, also some goods from the world over – but no Camerounian artisan pieces. There are also some lovely houses around town, many with gardens, trimmed lawns, hedges and flowers.

Otherwise, this anglophone town of 60,000 inhabitants is not so interesting; it is also somewhat confusing as it is very spread out, requiring lots of walking if you don't take taxis. Compounding this problem is that there is no single core area of town. The main commercial area is the market and taxi stand next door; several banks and the Concorde Hotel are just to the east. Another key area is the much quieter administrative quarter on the north-western side of town; both the gendarmerie nationale and the prison are there.

Lake Barombi Mbo
Just outside of town to the west is the city's star attraction for travellers – Lake Barombi Mbo, a large volcanic crater lake which is quite beautiful, with crystal clear water that's ideal for swimming.

To get to the lake, you can walk the entire distance from Kumba (five km), or take a taxi (CFA 125 in a shared taxi) to just beyond the administrative district to the beginning of the footpath; from there it's a 25-minute walk westward. When you get there, you are sure to find people who'll offer to take you in their canoes to **Barombi**, a fishing village

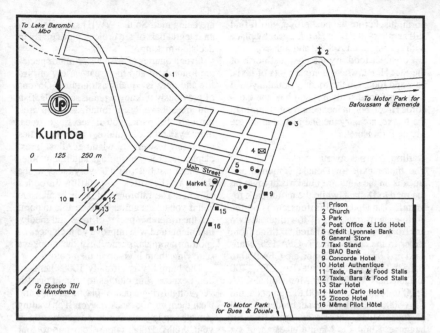

To Lake Barombi
Mbo

Kumba

0   125   250 m

To Motor Park for
Bafoussam & Bamenda

Main Street

Market

To Ekondo Titi
& Mundemba

To Motor Park
for Buea & Douala

1 Prison
2 Church
3 Park
4 Post Office & Lido Hotel
5 Crédit Lyonnais Bank
6 General Store
7 Taxi Stand
8 BIAO Bank
9 Concorde Hotel
10 Hotel Authentique
11 Taxis, Bars & Food Stalls
12 Taxis, Bars & Food Stalls
13 Star Hotel
14 Monte Carlo Hotel
15 Zicoco Hotel
16 Même Pilot Hôtel

which was once a famous pottery centre. A female chief rules over the village and you may be expected to bring her a small gift, such as some of the local palm wine. For swimming, you'll do better going back to the Kumba side of the lake where there have never been problems with bilharzia. Black flies, on the other hand, can be a major nuisance, so bring your repellent.

Places to Stay & Eat

At least three of the bottom-end hotels are on the lively south-western side of town. One of the cheapest is the *Monte Carlo Hotel*, which has rooms for CFA 3000 and CFA 4000, and a bar. It's down a sideroad and has a nice setting in a peaceful garden. However, as this place is also a brothel, with many rooms rented on an hourly basis, noise is a big problem, and is compounded by the paper-thin walls. If you can't take the noise, try the nearby *Star Hôtel*, which has six clean rooms with fans (CFA 6000), a bar and restaurant,

and is one of the city's better hotels. It's a one-man show, but the owner will get you anything. A slightly better place for the money is the nearby *Hôtel l'Authentique* (☎ 354420) which has 10 rooms starting at CFA 5000, hot-water baths, and friendly management.

You'll find several more in the area around the market and taxi stand. Two that are just south of the taxi stand are the *Même Pilot Hôtel* and the *Zicoco Hotel*; a third, the *Queens Hotel*, is behind the market. The Zicoco is the cheapest, with rooms for CFA 2500, but the Même Pilot, which is nearby on the same street, is better, with a friendly staff and clean doubles with fans for CFA 3500, plus there's a good cheap restaurant next door. Rooms with fan at the Queens cost the same.

One of the better ones in this area is the *Concorde Hotel*, which is to the east beyond the BIAO bank; it's relatively expensive at CFA 6000 for a room. Several blocks to the north, just before the post office, you'll find still another – the *Lido Hotel*, a grubby place with rooms for CFA 3000 and a disco.

For street food, try the area just north of the Star Hotel, where there are lots of taxis, bars and food. On the road to Douala, you'll find some food stalls just south of the Concorde Hotel. For an inexpensive restaurant in the market area, try the one just south of the Même Pilot Hotel.

Getting There & Away

The motor park for Douala, Yaoundé and Buea is on the southern outskirts of town on the road to Douala, while the motor park for Mamfé, Bamenda and Bafoussam is on the north-eastern outskirts of town, about two km from the centre. A shared taxi ride from either to the central area is CFA 125. Standard taxi fares from Kumba are CFA 900 to Buea, CFA 1300 to Ekondo Titi, CFA 1400 to Douala, CFA 2500 to Mundemba, CFA 3500 to Mamfé, CFA 4000 to Bamenda and CFA 5000 to Ekok (Nigerian border). On all of these rides, there's an extra fee for baggage. Kumba to Mamfé takes about six hours by bush taxi; the driving time should be less once the road is completely paved.

You can also get to Ikang in Nigeria via a boat from Ekondo Titi (55 km to the west); a minibus takes about 2½ hours. For a lark, you could also take the daily train to/from Douala; it's old and decrepit and takes about eight hours.

KORUP NATIONAL PARK & MUNDEMBA

Cameroun's newest park, Korup National Park, is in an isolated location in the far western corner of the country along the Nigerian border near Mundemba. It achieved status as a park in 1986 at the initiative of the Worldwide Fund for Nature (WWF). An incredible rainforest, it is thought to be the oldest and most biologically diverse in Africa, if not the world. The approach here is total integration with the local community because the park's success depends to a large extent on how well the locals perceive that their needs and concerns

are being met. So the WWF has made them an integral part of the project, particularly in decision-making.

Over a quarter of Africa's primate species are found here and the great variety of bird life and trees is equally astounding. Dozens of previously unknown plants, animals, fish and trees have been found. As you trek through the park, you'll see huge trees, monkeys and birds galore, many butterflies and a few flowers. Lowland gorillas, forest elephants, crocs, bush dogs and many other animals exist but you'd be very lucky to see them as the thick vegetation impedes viewing. The rainforest alone is impressive and if you take a guide, he'll be able to point out the different species of trees and medicinal plants and will improve your chances of spotting animals, particularly the monkeys scurrying about high up in the treetops.

The humidity is virtually 100% here, so don't expect your clothes to remain dry for very long. Bring a pair of plastic sandals and wear them without socks as you'll be wading in water up to your ankles, sometimes up to your thighs. Hikes range from one to four days depending on the trail taken. Also bring high-speed film (1000 ASA or higher) as the forest is dark.

Park Fees

There are various fees, including the park entrance fee (CFA 2500), camera fee (CFA 30,000), guide (CFA 3000 per day plus tip) and transport by Land Rover from Mun-

demba to the park entrance (CFA 2000) where there's an impressive hanging footbridge. Tents, beds and mosquito nets are included in the entrance fee. Hopefully the ridiculously high camera fees will be reduced; if not, travellers are bound to hide them. All these fees are payable at the WWF office in Mundemba, not at the park itself.

Places to Stay & Eat
The camp site has pit toilets, drinking water, bathing spots and free firewood; there are also shelters for camping and two others for cooking and drying clothes. If you prefer not to eat cooked plantains three times a day, go with your guide to buy food in Mundemba.

If you prefer not to camp, you can sleep in Mundemba. One of the cheapest lodgings is the *Iyas Hotel*, which is a 10-minute walk from the centre. Clean doubles with fan and private bath cost CFA 5000. The restaurant doesn't have an extensive menu but the

African and continental meals for CFA 1500 are delicious. There are also more expensive hotels with rooms up to CFA 10,000.

Getting There & Away
Mundemba is about 100 km north-west of Kumba via Ekondo Titi. The road is in bad condition and barely all-weather but bush taxis regularly make the trip, which takes about five hours; the cost is around CFA 2500.

MAMFÉ
Mamfé is the last major town in Cameroun you'll pass through if you're headed overland from Yaoundé or Douala to Nigeria; the border at Ekok is 59 km to the west of Mamfé. The people here speak English. You won't find a bank at Ekok, so look around for some Nigerian money. The maximum amount you can legally import is 50 naira. If you have West African francs or travellers'

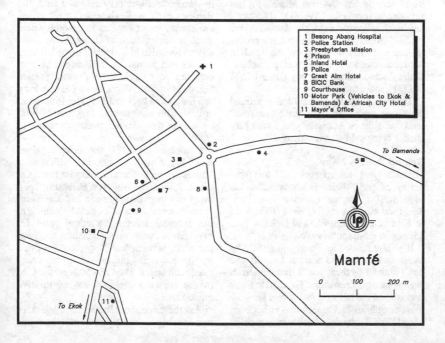

1 Besong Abang Hospital
2 Police Station
3 Presbyterian Mission
4 Prison
5 Inland Hotel
6 Police
7 Great Aim Hotel
8 BICIC Bank
9 Courthouse
10 Motor Park (Vehicles to Ekok & Bamenda) & African City Hotel
11 Mayor's Office

To Bamenda

Mamfé

0   100   200 m

To Ekok

cheques denominated in French francs, you
can change them for Central African francs
at the BICIC bank. People on the street here
and in Ekok, on the other hand, aren't willing
to do this but some will buy any excess naira
that you may have.

The city's main intersection is the centre
of town. The road east from there heads for
Bamenda; that to the west heads for Ekok.
North of the intersection you'll find the
hospital, while the BICIC bank is only a
short distance to the south of the intersection.

Places to Stay & Eat
For CFA 3000, you can get a clean room with
shower at either the *Great Aim Hôtel* or the
African City Hotel which is better. The latter
is an unmarked hotel at the main motor park
while the former, which also has a bar and
restaurant, is several blocks north on the
main drag, well before the main intersection.
For a mid-range hotel, try the *Little Paradise
Hotel* near the Presbyterian Mission; it has
very decent rooms for CFA 6000. The city's
top hotel and restaurant, the *Inland Hôtel*
(☎ 341128), has no competitors. It's on the
eastern outskirts of town on the road to
Bamenda, overlooking the hills and valleys
in the distance. Expect to pay at least CFA
10,000 a room there.

The best place for cheap food is around
the motor park; there are numerous small
food stalls there. At night, you'll find brochettes being sold all over town.

Getting There & Away
Minibuses and pick-up trucks all leave from
the motor park, which is about half a km
south-west of the main intersection. Standard fares are CFA 1500 to Ekok, CFA 3500
to Kumba and CFA 4900 to Douala, plus
15% or so more for luggage.

If you're headed to Ekok, you should be
aware that the borders close at 7 pm. If you
don't make it by then, you'll find numerous
cheap places to sleep there. The road to Ekok
is quite bad but the worst stretch of all – the
most dangerous in Cameroun – is between
Mamfé and Bamenda, which is why pick-up

truck drivers demand as much as CFA 6000
to do the trip, especially when conditions are
bad. The potholes are so large and the cliffs
so perilous on that route that during the rainy
season the trip to Bamenda can be virtually
life-threatening.

FOUMBAN
Some 70 km north-east of Bafoussam,
Foumban, a predominantly Muslim town, is
over 1000 metres above sea level and is one
of Cameroun's major tourist attractions – the
best place in Central Africa for reasonably
priced African art. If traditional African
culture is your bag, you'd be crazy to miss
the Royal Palace of the Bamoun tribe.
Foumban is a little touristy but not to an
unpleasant degree, so don't let that deter you
from coming here.

Palais Royal
Unlike the Bamiléké (around Bafoussam)
who are grouped by allegiance to the chief
in whose chiefdom they cultivate land, the
Bamoun all show allegiance to a single chief,
the sultan. In an area of the world where
some countries, such as Gabon, have virtually no recorded history prior to the colonial
era, it's exceptional that the Bamoun have an
ongoing 'dynasty' – the present sultan,
Seidou Njimoluh Njoya, being the 18th king
in a line dating back to 1394. The 16th sultan
and the most famous, Ibrahim Njoya,
envious of the German governor's palace in
Buea, built his own.

Completed in 1917, this unique palace
looks like a medieval chateau, with a vast,
impressive hall of arms on the 1st floor. On
the 2nd floor, the **Sultan's Museum**, open
every day from 8 am to noon and 3 to 6 pm,
contains a multitude of objects belonging to
the previous sultans, including colourful
royal gowns, arms, musical instruments, war
garments, statues, jewellery, books written
by Njoya, dancing masks, and thrones decorated with beads. The CFA 500 entrance fee
to the museum includes an informative
guided tour.

Ask the guide about Ibrahim Njoya's other
remarkable accomplishments, because

building the palace was only one of them. A brilliant man who was eventually deposed by the French and died in exile, he is responsible for creating the Bamoun alphabet, which is almost unique in Central and West Africa (Vai is the only other alphabet), and then founding schools throughout his kingdom to teach it. Shumom script, as it is called, is still taught today. He also started his own religion, a combination of Christianity, Islam and animism. And it is due in no small part to his book, *Histoires et Coutumes Bamoun*, based on oral tradition as related to him, that we know so much today about their history.

Outside the palace you'll find a number of small shops where wooden masks are sold. In the square just to the east are the sultan's house, the mosque and, between the two, a traditional wooden building housing the sultan's ancient throne and a huge war drum; a donation is required to see the drum and throne.

Musée des Arts et des Traditions Bamoun

This museum, at the end of the Rue des Artisans, is open the same hours but closed Monday and Friday. Free and worth visiting, it houses the extensive private collection of Mosé Yéyap, a wealthy Bamoun during Ibrahim Njoya's time who collected art and historical artefacts. The museum has five rooms, each with a different theme – Bamoun history, military artefacts, musical instruments, cooking utensils and relics from the Bamoun noble families. After passing through the carved doorway, you'll see, among other things, an important collection of pipes, clay statues, masks, gongs offered by the sultan to the nobles for their valiant war efforts, military armaments, and an ornately carved xylophone still used by the Sultan's court orchestra.

Rue des Artisans

Leading towards this second museum, the

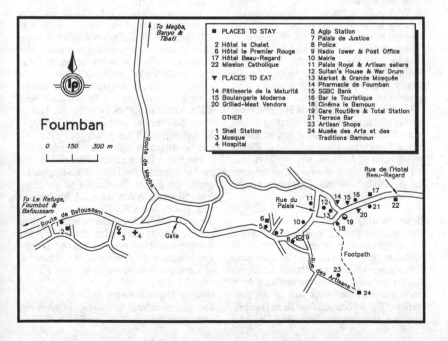

PLACES TO STAY
2 Hôtel le Chalet
6 Hôtel le Premier Rouge
17 Hôtel Beau-Regard
22 Mission Catholique

PLACES TO EAT
14 Pâtisserie de la Maturité
15 Boulangerie Moderne
20 Grilled-Meat Vendors

OTHER
1 Shell Station
3 Mosque
4 Hospital
5 Agip Station
7 Palais de Justice
8 Police
9 Radio Tower & Post Office
10 Mairie
11 Palais Royal & Artisan sellers
12 Sultan's House & War Drum
13 Market & Grande Mosquée
14 Pharmacie de Foumban
15 SGBC Bank
16 Bar le Touristique
18 Cinéma le Bamoun
19 Gare Routière & Total Station
21 Terrace Bar
23 Artisan Shops
24 Musée des Arts et des Traditions Bamoun

Foumban

0   150   300 m

To Magba, Banyo & Tibati
To Le Refuge, Foumbot & Bafoussam
Route de Magba
Route de Bafoussam
Rue de l'Hotel Beau-Regard
Rue du Palais
Rue des Artisans
Gate
Footpath

Rue des Artisans has a dozen or more artisan workshops of sculptors, basket makers, weavers and embroiderers along the way. Most of the wooden carvings are new but the artisans here do much better work than elsewhere, which is why this is the best place in Central Africa to purchase new pieces. Some of the shops carry older, more expensive masks as well. While this is Bamoun territory, you'll also see many examples of Bamiléké art, the style being extraordinarily free and expressive with a lack of finish to the surface. The smiling buffalo masks and amusing dance masks with large shell-like protrusions above the eyes are common examples. It is not difficult to spend a full day wandering around here. The vendors here usually bargain more than those outside the Royal Palace and if you try out a few phrases of Bamoun, they may lower the price more than usual, thinking you live here and know the prices.

Other Attractions

On Fridays the Sultan makes an appearance. It's only in his presence that the traditional Bamoun dance, Mbansié, is performed.

Market days are Wednesdays and Saturdays in Foumban and Sunday morning in Foumbot, a small village known for its pottery. You'll pass through it on the road from Bafoussam.

The best time of all to be in Foumban is at the end of Ramadan – the celebration here is one of the most elaborate anywhere in Africa. Horse races, processions and dances are all a part of the show. Seventy days later at Tabaski, the celebration is again elaborate and marked by a parade of *marabouts* (wise men and fortune-tellers).

Places to Stay & Eat

Most travellers return to Bafoussam where the accommodation is generally better. In Foumban, the best-value place is the *Mission Catholique*, which is in pleasant surroundings on the main drag on the eastern side of town, a five-minute walk east of the gare routière. The accommodation there is excellent and the people, including the two Belgian nuns who run this place, are very friendly. A 'donation' of CFA 1000 is expected.

If it's full, try the 24-room *Hôtel Beau-Regard* (☎ 482182), which is between the mission and the gare routière. It has rooms with comfortable beds and reasonably clean shared baths for CFA 4180, and slightly nicer rooms with decent, private tiled baths for CFA 5225. There are also two apartments for CFA 8500, none with air-con. The Beau-Regard serves the best meals in the central area – full meals from CFA 1500, also sandwiches and omelettes for CFA 600. The two-storey *Hôtel le Premier Rouge* (☎ 482352) is a 10-minute walk to the centre and slightly better value. Entering town from the west, you'll see the hotel's sign at the Agip station and Palais de Justice; it's 100 metres down a dirt path to your left. The cheapest rooms (CFA 4000) consist of a small sitting room and a tiny bedroom with an attached tile bath. There's a TV in the lobby and you can order food there as well.

The city's top hotel is *Le Chalet*, which is on the western outskirts of town on the road to Bafoussam, about 200 metres south of the Shell station via a winding dirt road. The rooms are fairly large, with decent tile baths and cost CFA 6000. Business looks slow, so you may be able to negotiate. The ambience is very tranquil and the French food here (CFA 3000 for the set menu) is the best in town. Still further west and out of town, is *Le Refuge*, which has rooms for CFA 3500, a restaurant and a nightclub on weekends.

For drinks in the centre of town, head for the bar opposite the Hôtel Beau-Regard or, better, the *Bar le Touristique* on the main drag, 50 metres before the hotel. Big beers at both places cost CFA 250. And just across the street you'll find vendors selling grilled meats. For bread and pastries, try the *Boulangerie Moderne* next door to the Touristique or the *Pâtisserie de la Maturité*, opposite the market, which is not as good.

Getting There & Away

The gare routière is in the heart of town just east of the market. You can find bush taxis headed east to Banyo (CFA 2600 plus baggage), north to Jakiri and Kumbo on Ring Rd, and west to Bafoussam. Minibuses charge about CFA 1200 plus baggage to Jakiri and about CFA 1500 plus baggage to Kumbo. From Jakiri it's another CFA 1600 to Bamenda. Getting from Foumban to N'Gaoundéré can take easily two days, with an overnight stay in Banyo or, if you leave early and make connections, in Tibati. You'll also find large buses headed for Yaoundé (CFA 3500) via Bafoussam (CFA 1000); bush taxis charge up to CFA 500 more.

BAFOUSSAM

Bafoussam is north-west of Yaoundé (286 km) and north of Douala (266 km), with good paved road connections. It's a rapidly expanding commercial town with lots of activity but it lacks the interest of Bamenda and Foumban. This area does, however, have an outstanding tourist attraction – the most beautiful chefferie (chief's compound) in Cameroun if not all of Africa. It's just outside of town in Bandjoun, a 20-minute taxi ride from Bafoussam.

The Bafoussam region is the country's major coffee and cocoa area. Cameroun is not the largest producer of coffee in Central and West Africa (the Côte d'Ivoire is), but its coffee is top quality because farmers can grow the higher priced arabica variety here, which thrives only in cooler climates (the cheaper robusta coffee is grown in the lowlands). You'll have to go to Douala airport, however, to find the export-quality variety.

Bafoussam has a population of about 150,000, virtually all Bamiléké. They are noted for their woodcarvings, and vendors sometimes line their wares on the street in front of Hôtel le Président. An interesting way to see the surrounding hills would be to hook up with the Hash House Harriers and follow their rabbit-like jogging course on Saturdays from around 3 pm, but they don't run on a regular basis.

Orientation

The main drag, Ave Wanko (or Ave de la République), runs roughly north-south, with the northern end (Route de Bamenda) heading for the airport and Bamenda, and the southern end (Ave Pachong Adolphe) heading for Bandjoun, Yaoundé and Douala. The central point on this road – and the heart of town – is Place Ouandé Ernest. If you head east from there on Ave Kamga Joseph (Rue du Marché), you'll pass the market and the gare routière on your left and after three blocks arrive at another roundabout, Place Félix Roland Moumie. The road to Foumban continues eastward from there. Many of the cheap bars and restaurants are in the area around Place Moumie.

If you head south-west from Place Ouandé Ernest and back along Ave Wanko, you'll enter the administrative district and pass many of the city's major landmarks including UCCAO (the coffee cooperative), the Préfecture, Palais de Justice, Hôtel de Ville and, at the Place de l'Indépendance, the post office and modern BEAC bank, with the radio tower perched on a hill just to the south. The provincial tourist office (☎ 441189) and an adjoining tiny museum are also in this area, next to the gendarmerie nationale.

Places to Stay – bottom end

The *Foyer Culturel Évangélique* is in the heart of town near the gare routière, 100 metres north-east up a side street from Place Moumie. The caretaker asks CFA 3000 per person or CFA 4000 per couple, but at those prices no-one would stay as it's a dump with two dormitory rooms with mattresses but no sheets. The bath is filthy but does have a shower. If you can find him, chances are he'll bargain or let you camp on the compound, which has a big wall around it. If not, try *Hôtel Fédéral* (☎ 441309), which is 100 metres east of Place Moumie. At CFA 3100 for a room and one free breakfast, it's a great buy and highly recommended. Quiet, friendly and very popular, it has big beds, clean shared bathrooms and a very decent restaurant.

The best alternative to the Fédéral is *Hôtel Kallao*, where a tiny, clean room with private bath costs CFA 3850 (CFA 4950 for the larger rooms); a reduction is possible as busi-

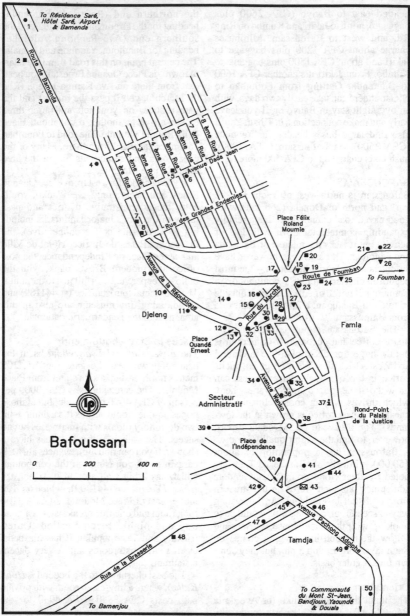

Bafoussam

■ PLACES TO STAY

2 Hôtel de l'Unité
5 Hôtel Kallao
7 Hôtel le Continental
8 L'Auberge & Nightclub
20 Foyer Culturel Évangélique
24 Hôtel Fédéral
35 Hôtel le Président
44 Hôtel de la Mifi
48 Uni Hôtel

▼ PLACES TO EAT

13 Restaurant la Tour
16 Café UCCAO
18 Restaurant le Relais Africain
19 Pâtisserie la Paix
25 Djemoun Coffee Shop
26 No-Name African Restaurant
27 Restaurant la Fofani
45 Restaurant le Cercle Bleu

OTHER

1 Shell Station
3 Bar Dancing Paris-Night
4 Les Grands Chics Mini-Marché
6 Café des Amis
9 Cinéma l'Empire
10 Supermarché les Galaries de l'Ouest

11 Agip Station
12 BIAO Bank
13 Bush Taxis to Yaoundé
14 Market
15 Gare Routière
17 Crédit Lyonnais Bank
21 Club de l'Amitié (Bar)
22 SNEC
23 Shell Station & Bush Taxis to Foumban
28 Menoua Bus Lines
29 Erko Voyages & Binam Voyages
30 Timmy's Bar & Sans Soucis Night Club
31 Étoile Voyages
32 Évasion Nightclub & CCEI Building
33 Fany Voyages
34 UCCAO (Coffee Company)
36 BICIC Bank
37 Service Provincial du Tourisme
38 Palais de Justice
39 Préfecture
40 Hôtel de Ville
41 Résidence du Gouverneur
42 BEAC Bank
43 Post Office
46 Pharmacie de Secours
47 Radio Tower
49 BP Station
50 Mobil Station

ness is clearly slow. A good half a km north of the central area, it's a two-storey structure at the corner of Ave Dada Jean and Rue 5, one block north and five short blocks east of L'Auberge, a lively well known bar on Ave de la République. L'Auberge has a few rooms for CFA 2500/3500 (exterior/interior baths) but it's grubby and very noisy.

Alternatively, try Hôtel de la Mifi, a two-storey building south of the central area and 100 metres east of the post office; it charges CFA 4450/5252 for unadorned singles/doubles. If you don't mind being on the outskirts of town, try the Communauté du Mont St-Jean on the road to Douala; it reportedly has comfortable rooms with hot showers and you can eat there.

Places to Stay – middle
My pick of the mid-range hotels is Hôtel le

Continental (☎ 441458), a well-maintained hotel on the Ave de la République, half a km north of Place Ouandé Ernest. Large attractive rooms with nice tile baths and one/two beds cost CFA 6950/7500, plus there's a decent restaurant. You can save money, however, by staying at the newer Uni Hôtel (☎ 442667), which is slightly further out, a km south-west of the centre on Rue de la Brasserie. Spotless rooms with fine tile baths cost CFA 6175, and there's a decent restaurant with breakfast for CFA 1000 and a set lunch menu for CFA 3150.

The three-storey Hôtel de l'Unité (☎ 441-516) is north of the centre, on the Route de Bamenda, and doing very poor business these days. Singles/doubles cost CFA 7700/8300 but you'll probably be offered a reduction before you ask. It also has a restaurant.

Places to Stay – top end

The only top-end hotel in the centre of town is the old 54-room *Hôtel le Président* (☎ 44-1136), which is about 300 metres south-east of Place Ouandé Ernest. It used to be Bafoussam's top hotel, but business is now fairly slow. It has air-con singles/doubles for CFA 8425/9265 and meals for CFA 3000.

On the northern outskirts of town on the Route de Bamenda you'll find the city's top hotels. The Palace Garden Hôtel has closed, leaving *Résidence Saré* (☎ 442599) as the city's best. It's an attractive place with small round cabins, tall hedges, colourful wall paintings and air-con bungalows for CFA 10,000/11,145 (singles/doubles). Just 150 metres further north is the Saré's sister hotel, *Hôtel Saré le Kamkop* (☎ 441802), which has rooms for CFA 6600 and bungalows for CFA 10,000. It's not quite as attractive and has no restaurant (guests use the restaurant at the former hotel) but the bungalows are nicer, with comfortable sitting rooms and mini-bars. However, without your own transport, you'll find the location a drawback.

Places to Eat

For a cheap breakfast, you can't beat the tiny *Café UCCAO* stand at the gare routière – coffee costs CFA 50. A fantastic place for African food is an unmarked, no-name place on the Route de Foumban, about 300 metres east of Hôtel Fédéral, opposite the three-storey SNEC building. Open only for lunch and always packed, it usually has only two choices, such as corn couscous and sauce feuille avec viande (green vegetable sauce with meat) for CFA 450 a plate (enough for two people), plus large beers for CFA 225. For something less exotic, try the *Djemoun* coffee shop or *Restaurant le Relais Africain*, which are both on the same street closer to the centre. The Relais' menu includes omelettes (CFA 250), spaghetti (CFA 400), fries (CFA 600) and riz garni (rice with vegetables and bread) for CFA 750. *Pâtisserie la Paix* next door is one of the best bakeries and *Restaurant la Fofani*, 100 metres to the south of Place Moumie, is also inexpensive.

For reasonably priced Western dishes such as steak & chips, head for *Hôtel le Continental* or *Restaurant la Tour*, which is on the main drag at Place Ouandé Ernest and open very late, with dining inside and on a terrace. Full meals at either place cost around CFA 2000. The restaurant at *Hotel Fédéral* is also excellent for the price – sandwiches for CFA 700 and full meals such as chicken or steak with rice and potatoes for CFA 1800.

For groceries, try the *Supermarché les Galaries de l'Ouest* on the same street, 250 metres to the north, or *Les Grands Chics Mini-Marché* half a km or so further north. The city's top restaurants are *Le Cercle Bleu*, on Ave Pachong Adolphe, and those at the top-end hotels.

Entertainment

For drinks, try the cheap bars along the Route de Foumban such as the *Club de l'Amitié*. The nightclubs don't get going until around 11 pm. The top one in town is *Évasion*, which is in the CCEI building, a block south of Place Ouandé Ernest. For variety, try the long-standing *La Paillote* nearby on Rue du Marché.

Bar-dancings cater more to the working class and start a little earlier; they include the *Sans Soucis Night Club* on the same block as Évasion, *L'Auberge* on the main drag, half a km north of Place Ouandé Ernest, and *Bar-Dancing Paris-Night* about a km further north on the same street, before Hôtel de l'Unité. L'Auberge is particularly lively but it's also fairly rowdy.

Getting There & Away

Unitair has flights to/from Yaoundé on Fridays, and to/from Douala on Mondays, Thursdays and Saturdays. The gare routière in the heart of town next to the market is where most minibuses and bush taxis leave from. You can also find them at the nearby Shell station at Place Moumie (to Foumban), at Place Ouandé Ernest (to Yaoundé) and near the Catholic church on Bamenda Rd (to Bamenda). A Toyota bush taxi costs CFA 850 to Bamenda, between CFA 2500 and CFA 3000 to Douala, and CFA 3000 to Yaoundé.

You could also rent a car from Avis (☎ 441388; telex 7039), which is on the eastern outskirts of town on Foumban Rd.

The most comfortable way to travel is on the large buses; they plough between Yaoundé and Bafoussam but not between Douala and Bafoussam. The bus offices are all in the area just south of the gare routière, including Fany Voyages, Erko Voyages, Étoile Voyages, Binam Voyages, Daily Express and Menoua Bus Lines. They all charge CFA 2500 to Yaoundé. Erko and Binam have the most departures, with about one every hour between 7.30 am and 6 pm. Menoua and Daily Express continue to Dschang (CFA 1000); most of the others continue to Bamenda (CFA 1000).

AROUND BAFOUSSAM
Chefferie de Bandjoun
Don't miss the chefferie in Bandjoun, which is 20 km south of Bafoussam and in all the tourist brochures; it's well maintained and is the best example of traditional Bamiléké architecture, which is quite unique. Bamiléké buildings are traditionally square and easily recognised by their tall conical roofs made of straw. (Today, many of the roofs are of shiny aluminium but the main buildings at Bandjoun are of straw.) The outside walls are often of bamboo, sometimes with fancy carvings. The Bandjoun buildings are superb examples – huge huts of bamboo with straw roofs supported by tall carved pillars, like totem poles, with elaborate, carved doorways and walls with geometrical designs. The overall sight is quite impressive because the buildings are so much larger than normal African huts, and the sheer number of buildings gives the place a certain grandeur.

The main building was constructed in 1962 (the previous one burned down in 1958) and is essentially a huge meeting room, used every six months. Most of the other buildings are either granaries or houses for the chief's family members, and quite a family the chief has – 10 wives and 17 children, which is nothing compared to that of the previous chief, who had far more wives and almost 250 children! The many houses

Bamiléké wooden mask

of his brothers' and fathers' wives are easily distinguished by their aluminium roofs. The only thing spoiling the traditional picture is the chief's house – a modern building that seems entirely out of place.

Next to the chefferie is an interesting museum which contains the chief's principal treasures including the chief's thrones, one of which is completely covered with cowrie shells. Other items include stools, traditional dance costumes, huge dance hats for the chief (one has a diameter of two metres and weighs 65 kg! – there's a photo of the chief wearing it) and musical instruments. The entrance fee is CFA 500 (CFA 1500 if you want to take photos inside).

If you take a minibus from Bafoussam (CFA 250), you will be dropped in town, almost three km away. A shared taxi direct from Bafoussam to the chefferie costs CFA 400. There's a new hotel in Bandjoun (Hôtel de Bandjoun) but it's overpriced at CFA 10,000 a room.

Lac de Baleng
Lac de Baleng is a small, picturesque crater lake just north of Bafoussam; it's a good place for a picnic and may be free of bilharzia and safe for swimming. If you run into any expatriates living in Bafoussam, they may be able to confirm whether the lake is safe for swimming or not. To get there, take the

Route de Bamenda until just before the Mairie Rurale outside town, where you'll see a sign on your right pointing to the lake. This all-weather dirt road will lead you to the lake's crater, six km to the east.

Lac de Bamendjing

Bamendjing, which is at the southern tip of Lake Bamendjing (the huge lake well north of Bafoussam), can be recommended if you're looking for peace and quiet. There's a tourist complex here (built for deer and duck hunters) with clean bungalows for CFA 2500 as well as a restaurant and bar. To get here, head north from Bafoussam on Bamenda Rd to Mbouda (30 km), then east for another 30 km to Bamendjing (400 CFA by bush taxi).

Bafang

Some 60 south-west of Bafoussam on the road to Douala, Bafang is in the heart of Bamiléké country and on the longer, paved route to Dschang. Stop to see the impressive **Chutes de la Mouenkeu**, some waterfalls which are only a km south-west of town on the Douala highway. They're only 50 metres off the road but there's no sign, so you'll have to ask. The view is from the top and there's no way down, making bathing impossible. If you head for the more famous **Ekom Waterfalls** 30 km away towards Nkongsamba, beware: you may be required to pay CFA 1000 to the village chief and another CFA 2000 for a guide.

If you're caught in Bafang for the night, try the *Auberge du Haut Nkam*, which has doubles for CFA 2500. Next in line is the *Hôtel Samaritan*, which has doubles for CFA 4500, then the *Grand Hôtel le Paradis* (☎ 486362), with rooms for about CFA 6000. The city's top address is the *Hôtel de la Falaise* (☎ 486311/2), which is at the entrance to town coming from Douala and way over-priced at CFA 15,000 for an air-con room.

Mélong & Bangem

If you're in Mélong (38 km west of Bafang) en route to Douala or Bafoussam and you're hot for adventure and trekking, you could check out the twin crater lakes of **Mt Manenguba** outside Bangem (market day is Saturday), which is 38 km further west. There are two small lakes inside the impressive crater, one with blue water and one with green water (due to algae), called Man Lake and Woman Lake by the locals. The mountain begins about five km south of town; you can drive there or walk. From the base to the crater it's about a six-km hike. Boys in town will offer to act as your guide. The grassy plains below the lakes are inhabited by Fulani herders who graze their cattle and horses there. In sum, the area is very picturesque.

You can camp at the lakes or possibly get a room at the *Mission Catholique* in Bangem. For accommodation in Mélong, try *Hôtel la Rochelle*, which has rooms for CFA 2000 or the German-run *Malina Coca*, which has nicer rooms for CFA 4000 and CFA 5000. A bush taxi from Mélong to Bangem costs about CFA 500.

DSCHANG

The cool climate at 1400 metres and a first-class hotel with horse riding are the main attractions of Dschang, a small town 60 km west of Bafoussam (330 km north of Douala). Average temperatures are 16 to 21°C although in April, the hottest month, noon temperatures often reach 31°C. There's nothing else noteworthy in town other than the artisanat (craft centre) near the university and the colourful central market, which is one of the largest in this area and very picturesque, with traditional Bamiléké architecture. The market has a large array of woodcarvings including masks, sculptures, plaques and furniture; prices are marked and relatively high, and there's little bargaining.

Places to Stay & Eat

Virtually all tourists and expatriates stay at the 50-room *Centre Climatique de Dschang* (☎ 451058; telex 7016), which is just outside of town. Guests sleep in bungalows in a garden setting. The facilities include tennis, a pool and horse riding; singles/doubles start at CFA 13,000/16,000. Even the bottom-end hotels in town aren't so cheap. Try *Hôtel Constellation* (☎ 451061); it has clean rooms facing a courtyard, and there's a lively bar next door. Two alternatives are the *Menoua Palace* and the *Auberge de la Menoua*.

Getting There & Away

Menoua Bus Lines and Daily Express offer a service every day to/from Yaoundé via Bafoussam; the fare is CFA 3500 and the trip take about six hours. Alternatively, take a bush taxi to/from Bafoussam.

BAMENDA

Bamenda (population 65,000), with an altitude well over 1000 metres, is popular with travellers primarily because of the cooler climate and the nearby hill country which offers some of the best hiking and camping opportunities in Central Africa. The city itself is not attractive but the hilly location is superb, especially during the rainy season when everything is green (unlike during the dry harmattan season when the countryside is brown and the skies are grey). It's in the heart of anglophone Cameroun, well north of Yaoundé (366 km) and Douala (350 km) by asphalt road and six or seven hours by bus from either. An added plus of a trip to Bamenda is that you'll find lots of handicrafts. The baskets are outstanding and you'll also find beads, woodcarvings and bronze statues.

Warning If you hear of recent violence in Bamenda, it is probably best to avoid the area. During the '90s it has been the centre of opposition against President Biya and the scene of many violent political demonstrations, resulting in numerous deaths and alleged tortures. The famous 'ghost town' campaign, which temporarily shut down all businesses and transportation, has ended but it could be resurrected at any moment.

Orientation

The city's street pattern is somewhat confusing because of the hilly location. Vehicles from Bafoussam arrive via the hilltop plateau called Upper Station. Numerous government buildings and the city's most scenic hotel, the Skyline Hotel, are located there. Then the main street winds down the cliff on the eastern side of town, past the Handicraft Cooperative and the popular Baptist Mission, which is near the motor park, to Commercial Ave (the heart of town). The market, all banks (BIAO, Crédit Lyonnais, BICIC, SGBC) and most businesses line that wide north-south avenue; the post office and many other establishments are strung along the ring road around the centre, including three of the city's better hotels.

Information

To change money, try Crédit Lyonnais; BICIC takes up to three hours and charges a CFA 1110 commission.

The best stores for handicrafts are the Prescraft Artisan Shop (open weekdays 8 am to 12.30 pm and 2.30 to 5 pm, Saturdays 8 am to 1 pm) on Commercial Ave; the Handicraft Cooperative (open 7.30 am to 5 pm every day except Sunday) on the road to Upper Station, and Bamenda Handicraft Centre not far from the Presbyterian Church Centre. Prices are fixed at all three places.

Places to Stay – bottom end

One of the most popular places in town for travellers on the cheap is the friendly *Baptist Mission*, which welcomes travellers wholeheartedly and charges CFA 3000 per person for a clean room with hot shower. Breakfast is free and dinner costs CFA 1500, a super deal. It's two km east of the central area but finding taxis to the centre is no problem because of the nearby motor park.

The *Presbyterian Church Centre*, however, is closer to town and cheaper, with rooms for CFA 2500 and camping for CFA 1000. It also has lockers where you can leave your gear, and meals are prepared if there are enough people. A km north of the Commercial Ave roundabout and well marked, it's on a grassy hill with scenic views.

The cheapest hotel appears to be *Donga Palace Hotel* on the ring road, about 200 metres east of the southern end of Commercial Ave. Highly recommended for the price,

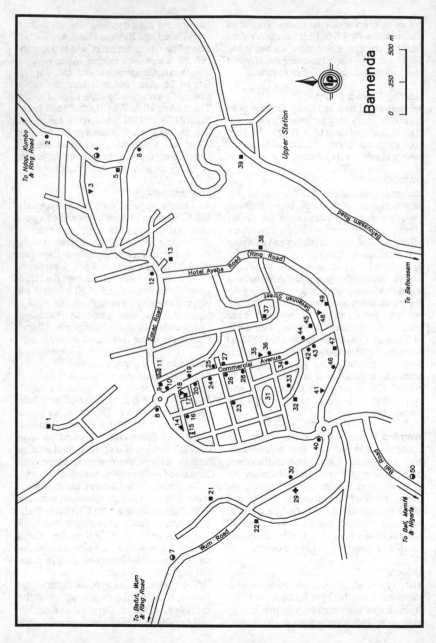

Bamenda

■ PLACES TO STAY

1	Presbyterian Church Centre
5	Baptist Mission
13	Mondial Hotel
17	International Hotel
21	Hotel le Bien
22	Unity Hotel
32	Ideal Park Hotel
37	New City Hotel
38	Ayaba Hotel
39	Skyline Hotel
45	Savannah Hotel
47	Holiday Hotel
49	Donga Palace Hotel

▼ PLACES TO EAT

3	Bakery
14	Classy Burger
15	Bamenda Modern Bakery
18	Rond Point Cafeteria & Snack Concord
35	Boulangerie du Progrès
41	Dallas Restaurant
48	Ambience Restaurant

OTHER

2	Cinema
4	Nkwen Motor Park (Minibuses & Taxis to Bafoussam, Yaoundé and Douala)
6	Handicraft Cooperative
7	Ntarkison Motor Park (Vehicles to Bafut and Wum)
8	Mobil Station
9	Cameroun Airlines
10	Exim Vinson Supermarket
11	Post Office
12	Small Handicraft Shop
15	Office of Tourism
16	Relax Club Bar
18	Roxi Cinema
19	Victory Photo
20	Texaco Station
23	Canne á Sucre Nightclub
24	BIAO Bank
25	Crédit Lyonnais Bank
26	BICIC Bank
27	Total Station
28	Prescraft Artisan Shop
29	Hospital
30	Police
31	Stadium
33	Congress House
34	Market
36	Goldfinger Bookshop
37	Nightclub
40	BP Station
42	New Life Supermarket
43	Mezam Pharmacy
44	SGBC Bank
46	Popular Terrace Bar
50	Bali Motor Park (Vehicles to Bali and Mamfé)

it has a big comfortable bar with TV, and rooms for CFA 2000 and CFA 3000. The cheapest rooms are clean, quite large and have decent beds and shared baths; the CFA 3000 rooms have tiled floors and private baths. Next in line is the somewhat noisy *Savannah Hotel* on Savannah St, 100 metres or so east of Commercial Ave. Its rooms start at CFA 2750, which is not bad for a small room with shared bath. For CFA 3750, you can get a very clean double with private bath (CFA 4750 with hot water).

Ideal Park Hotel (☎ 361166), which is a block behind the market facing the Congress House building, is a better buy than the Savannah. It has carpeted rooms for CFA 3000 with big beds and clean shared toilets; there's also a somewhat fancy restaurant

with full meals for CFA 2500. I prefer it to the *New City Hotel*, which is several blocks east of Commercial Ave, off Savannah St. It has rooms from CFA 3300 to CFA 5000 but it can be noisy because of the lively nightclub. Dishes on offer at the restaurant include pepper soup and chicken ndolé.

For slightly better rooms, try the *International Hotel* (☎ 362527), a five-storey structure near the northern end of Commercial Ave, a block to the west. It has rooms for CFA 5000 and CFA 6000; the cheaper rooms come with carpet, telephones and large attached tile baths.

Another possibility is the two-storey, 25-room *Hotel Le Bien* (☎ 361206). Most rooms here cost CFA 5000 to CFA 5500 (a few are cheaper) and are comfortable and large with tile baths and there's a decent restaurant but business seems slow, possibly because of the hotel's somewhat isolated location on the western outskirts of town. The *Holiday Hotel* (☎ 361382), which has large, fairly bare rooms for CFA 5000 to CFA 6175, is similar and more conveniently located on the southern end of the ring road.

Places to Stay – top end

The city has two first-class hotels – the old *Sky Line Hotel* (☎ 361289; fax 363284; telex 5892) in Upper Station overlooking town, and the modern *Ayaba Hotel* (☎ 361321/56; telex 5387) closer to the centre on the ring road. The well-maintained Skyline has air-con rooms with mini-bars for CFA 14,000 and a long pool which nonguests can use for CFA 600. Credit cards are not accepted. The Ayaba is newer with a pool, tennis court and nightclub but it's showing signs of age and business is slow. Air-con rooms there cost CFA 15,000; American Express and Diners Club cards are accepted.

A good notch down is the large *Mondial Hotel* (☎ 361832; fax 362884; telex 5088), which is further north on the ring road at a major junction (Zonac Rd). Rooms with TV and one/two beds but no air-con cost CFA 7500/9000, and there are reportedly cheaper rooms in the basement for CFA 5000. Business seems slow, but the hotel's nightclub is still very active.

Places to Eat

Good places for street food are along Commercial Ave and also along Zonac Rd starting north of the post office.

For African food, head for the *Ambience Restaurant* on Savannah St, opposite the Savannah Hotel. For about CFA 250, you can get a big plate of corn couscous, rice, beans, gari, corn fufu, etc at lunch time. At night, the selection, which includes beans and chips, is very limited.

Towards the northern end of Commercial Ave on the same block as the International Hotel you'll find the tiny *Rond-Point Cafeteria*; it's quite cheap, with spaghetti for CFA 100 and meat and rice for CFA 200. *Snack*

Concord next door is more up-market, with omelettes for CFA 500, steak for CFA 700, and chicken & chips for CFA 1200. Two blocks further west off Commercial Ave is *Classy Burger*; the speciality is burgers (CFA 500) but there are other selections as well. And just around the corner from there on the ring road you'll find *Bamenda Modern Bakery*, which is one of the better bakeries. *Boulangerie du Progrès* on Commercial Ave near the centre is another. There are also several supermarkets on Commercial Ave including *Exim Vinson Supermarket* at the northern end and a larger one, *New Life Supermarket*, towards the southern end.

One of the most popular up-market places is *Dallas Restaurant* on the ring road, west of Commercial Ave (southern end). You can sit on the front veranda and eat roasted fish (CFA 2000 to CFA 4000) or chicken (CFA 4000). For a classier environment, you can't beat the restaurant and garden setting at the *Skyline Hotel* in Upper Station.

For a drink, look along the ring road on the southern end, west of Commercial Ave. There are one or two lively cheap bars facing the street as well as the more expensive terrace of the Dallas Restaurant (large beers for CFA 350). *Relax Club Bar* at the back of the International Hotel is another.

Entertainment

A number of the city's nightclubs have folded. One of the liveliest nightclubs, and cheaper than many (CFA 1000 drinks), is the ever-popular *Canne à Sucre*, which is a block north of the stadium. The nightclub at the *New City Hotel* attracts the same crowd. Of the expensive discos, the top one is the *N'Jong Club* at the Ayaba Hotel followed by the *Mondial Club* at the Mondial Hotel; drinks at these places, which are open only on weekends, are about CFA 2000.

Getting There & Away

Unitair and Cameroun Airlines (☎ 361162), at the northern junction of Commercial Ave and the ring road have flights on Tuesdays to Douala and Yaoundé, and again on Saturdays to Douala.

Vehicles headed east to Bafoussam, Douala and Yaoundé leave from Nkwen motor park on the eastern side of town, two km from the centre. Those headed west for Bali, Mamfé and Nigeria leave from the Bali motor park on the south-western edge of town on Bali Rd while those north for Wum leave from Ntarkison Motor Park on the north-western edge of town on Wum Rd.

Standard fares for minibuses and Peugeot 504 bush taxis are around CFA 300 to Bafut, CFA 600 to Ndop, CFA 850 to Bafoussam, CFA 1600 to Jakiri, CFA 2000 to Kumbo, CFA 2800 to Foumban via Jakiri, CFA 3600 to Douala, CFA 3500 to Yaoundé and from CFA 3000 to CFA 6000 to Mamfé (depending on road conditions); baggage costs a little extra. Large, more comfortable buses, such Amumba Express and Savannah Express, leave from near Nkwen Motor Park and cost CFA 1000 to Bafoussam and CFA 3500 to Yaoundé.

AROUND BAMENDA
Bali
Some 20 km south-west of Bamenda on the road to Mamfé is Bali. The main attractions here are the fon's palace, the large Wednesday market and an artisan centre, which has a slightly different selection from the ones in Bamenda but similar prices.

RING ROAD
Ring Rd is a 367-km circular route commencing at Bamenda and passing, clockwise, through Bafut (Km 16), Befang (Km 63), Wum (Km 80), Nkambe (Km 188), Ndu (Km 229), Kumbo (Km 258), Jakiri (Km 281) and Ndop (Km 325), ending at Bamenda (Km 367). This region and the Mandara mountains in the north are Cameroun's most popular trekking areas. Most of the hiking is done in the dry season, from October to April. The spectacular mountain scenery is a major attraction and the best months for viewing it are October, and mid-March to April because the mountains are luscious green then and, more important, the hazy skies from November until the first rains in

early March (due to the harmattan winds from the Sahara) ruin the views.

The ideal way to travel is by mountain bike but you can only bike during the dry season (the roads are impossibly muddy during the rainy season) and you'd have to bring one with you as they can't be rented. Driving is also a great way to make the tour as it allows you to stop wherever you like, including camping in the bush. However, Ring Rd is barely all-weather, so driving on it during the rainy season is best forgotten unless you have a 4WD. Minibuses pass year-round but there are fewer and fewer the further you get from Bamenda, making travel slow. Taking minibuses also limits your ability to camp, so you'll spend most of your sleeping hours in the few very basic hotels en route.

In any of the towns en route, consider attending a local church service on a Sunday for an interesting cultural experience. These can be surprisingly lively and very African, with lots of music.

Bafut
This Tikar community has a good market and a very interesting fon's palace which is well worth the CFA 1000 entry fee (photographs permitted). The large palace compound is somewhat unusual in that it contains buildings dating from around the turn of the century – very old by Central African standards. Unfortunately, the most sacred shrine, the pyramidal thatched-roof Achum, is off-limits to the public. You can also see the house where the famous naturalist Gerald Durrell wrote *The Bafut Beagles*, an amusing account of his animal-collecting expedition here during the late colonial period. The best time to be here is 20 December when Bafut has a major festival; it's quite colourful.

For a place to stay in Bafut, ask the people at the palace; they can arrange a place for you to sleep. Expect to pay about CFA 3000. Minibuses/bush taxis from Bamenda cost CFA 300/400.

Befang
To your left several km before Befang, which

Tikar wooden statue

is along the Mentchum River, are some beautiful hidden waterfalls. You may have to ask someone passing by to point them out to you. You might camp near there along the river or at the crater lake near town.

Wum

Wum is a much larger town with a tourist office (friendly people but not very useful), many bars and three cheap hotels, with rooms for CFA 3000 to CFA 5000. The best one is the new *Gay Lodge* as you enter town from Befang; the others, *Lake Nyos City Hotel* and *Happy Day Lodge*, are closer to the centre but the latter is often noisy until late at night. Food will be prepared if you ask in advance, or try a chophouse in town, such as the *Peace, Unity & Hygenic Restaurant*. Cheese is made in Wum, so ask for it. At **Lake Wum** nearby (three km), you can swim and camp.

Lake Nyos & Kimbi River Game Reserve

About halfway between Wu and Nkambe you'll pass Lake Nyos on your right. Now a restricted zone, it was the scene of the horrific gas eruption of 1986 which resulted in some 2000 deaths. (See the introductory History section for details.) At about Km 77 you'll enter the well-posted Kimbi River Game Reserve; it has pitifully few animals, mostly antelope and buffalo, and you'll need a vehicle to see them. If you need a place to stay, ask about their cheap visitors' hut.

Nkambe & Ndu

Nkambe is one of the larger towns on Ring Rd, with numerous bars and chophouses, and nearby Ndu at 2000 metres has a refreshing climate. Yet, despite the interesting terrain and scenic steep hills in the area, the winding, often dusty roads are simply too wearisome for many people, and few travellers make it this far.

Kumbo

The Nso town of Kumbo, on the other hand, is a popular destination and doesn't lack for amenities. There are lots of hotels, a large market and even paved streets! At 2000 metres, the climate is wonderful and if you're here during Nso Cultural Week in November, you'll get to see some wild-horse races, the main event.

One of the best and cheapest places to stay is the *Baptist Mission Rest House*, which has a few rooms to rent. For CFA 2000, you can get a decent single at the *Central Inn*, which has a gorgeous view and is located in the heart of town near the market and motor park. If it's full, try the *Travellers Lodge* near the cathedral. Other places, mostly in the CFA 3000 to CFA 5000 range, include the old *Merryland Hotel*, *Kilo's Rest House* and, slightly more up-market, *Tobin's Tourist Home Hotel* and the *Bonni Hotel*. Some of them will serve food if you order in advance.

A minibus from Bamenda costs CFA 2000 plus around CFA 500 for luggage. Kumbo to Foumban costs CFA 1700 including luggage and the road is in much better condition, with good views; the trip takes about six hours.

Oko

If you're interested in mountain climbing, instead of heading immediately south to Jakiri, you could take a detour north-west to Oko (32 km) to climb **Mt Oko** (3000 metres), which has a crater lake on top; the road to Oko branches off several km south of Kumbo. You can also visit Lake Oko, which is a few km south-west of town, but you'll need to get permission at the fon's palace to go there as it's a sacred lake. If you want to swim, ask permission as it's usually not allowed.

Jakiri

Jakiri is at the junction of the road to Foumban and has little to offer other than pleasant scenery. The only hotels appear to be *Hunters' Lodge* and the small *Auberge Trans Afrique*; they charge about CFA 2000/3000 for singles/doubles. Minibuses cost CFA 1200 to Foumban (100 km), CFA 1000 to Ndop and CFA 1600 to Bamenda; baggage costs extra.

Ndop

The last significant town on Ring Rd is Ndop, which is near the northern shore of Lake Bamendjing. Between here and Bambili (22 km) you'll pass through some of the most spectacular scenery on Ring Rd; it's worth walking to really appreciate it. Coming from Bamenda, you could take an early morning minibus to Bambili (CFA 300) and then hike the remaining distance (about five hours) to Ndop; it's an easy walk, more so in that direction than the reverse. You'll pass through a small village en route; the adventurous could try staying there (there are two missions on either side of town) and trekking further afield. For a bed or a meal in Ndop, try *Festival Hotel*; it charges CFA 3000 for a double. A minibus to Bamenda costs CFA 600.

Eastern Cameroun

BERTOUA

About 345 km east of Yaoundé, Bertoua is rarely visited by tourists and for good reason – it's not a very interesting town. If you'd like to see a little of the real African jungle and possibly Pygmies as well, Bertoua would be a good place to head for because it's the launching place for expeditions into the rainforest.

If you're interested in seeing Pygmies, you'll have to travel to either Yokadouma (about 250 km to the south-east) or Lomié (240 km to the south via Abong-Mbang). Both towns have cheap lodgings.

Places to Stay & Eat

The cheapest places are mostly in the centre near the gare routières, which are all good places for street food. Most travellers on the cheap stay at *Hôtel Jenyf* facing the motor park for Batouri, *Auberge BP* (☎ 241003) a block to the west, or *Hôtel Central*, which is south-west of the Auberge. The cheapest is the Central, which has rooms for CFA 1500 (CFA 2000 with interior bath). A room with detached bath costs CFA 2800 at the Jenyf (CFA 3200 with private bath and CFA 4000 with balcony) and CFA 2500 at the Auberge BP (CFA 3200 with interior bath).

For something slightly better, try the small *Hôtel Relais Goldman* or *Hôtel de l'Est* (☎ 241128), which has a restaurant and rooms for about CFA 5000. The city's top hotel is the *Mansa Novotel* (☎ 241333/251; telex 8520), which has air-con singles/doubles for about CFA 14,500/16,500. Facilities include a pool and tennis courts.

Getting There & Away

Unitair and Cameroun Airlines (☎ 241278) have flights to/from Douala on Mondays and Wednesdays; the latter flight stops in Yaoundé (CFA 16,000). The train from Yaoundé costs CFA 3170 2nd-class to Belabo, from where you can get frequent bush taxis to Bertoua (80 km). If you want to stay in Belabo there's a hotel near the gare routière, the *Auberge du Port*, with rooms for CFA 2500 and another, *Auberge Maria*, between the station and town with rooms for CFA 2000, but you'll get better value at the hotels in Bertoua.

Bertoua has at least three gare routières, all in the heart of town near one another and each with a different destination. Bush taxis with luggage fee cost CFA 1050 to Batouri, CFA 1100 to Belabo and CFA 2800 to Garoua-Boulaï (bad road).

BATOURI

Batouri (90 km east of Bertoua) is on the less travelled southern route to the Central African Republic. The main drag runs east-west through town, with the gare routière in the centre.

Places to Stay

Adjoining the motor park on the southern side is a clean and friendly, well-marked *Auberge* with singles/doubles for CFA 1500/ 2000. The best place is *Le Club des Planteurs de Tabac*, a private club which will rent you a room if you look presentable.

Getting There & Away

Bush taxis for the border town of Kenzou (107 km) leave at the crack of dawn (around 5.30 am); if you miss the dawn departure, you may have to wait until the next day for another. The fare is CFA 1300 (including luggage) to Kenzou and another CFA 1500 on to Berbérati. The border crossing is very simple and quick but on the CAR side you must pay a CFA 1000 'tourist tax'. Surprisingly, once you enter the CAR you'll find the dirt roads in much better condition than the Bertoua to Kenzou stretch, which is quite bad.

GAROUA-BOULAÏ

This is the principal town on the Central African Republic border; the BIAO bank will exchange French francs for CFA. There are two gare routières: one at the border and another, the Gare Sud (minibuses for Bertoua), further south. The best place to stay is the *Mission Catholique*, which is about 200 metres from the border and next to the first bus station. The friendly Polish sister charges CFA 4000 for a room and usually accepts any contribution for a dormitory bed.

There are also some hotels including the run-down *Auberge Centrale* at the Gare Sud,

with rooms for CFA 1500 to CFA 3000 and bucket showers, and the similarly priced, neater *Auberge de la Frontière*, which is on the main drag on the road headed north, one km or so from the border. There's also an *Auberge* at the main gare routière with rooms for CFA 2000; the beds are clean and comfortable.

MEIGANGA

Halfway between Garoua-Boulaï and N'Gaoundéré, Meiganga is at least a pleasant stop for a drink. For cheap beers, try the rustic *Nawe Bar* in the heart of town opposite the Marché Central.

If you're caught here for the night, try *Hôtel Lina* near the Ancien Gare Routière; it may be as cheap as you'll find plus the old gare is one of the best places to find cheap food. The city's most expensive hotel is the *Hôtel de la Jeunesse*, which charges CFA 5000 for its rooms, but *Hôtel Safari* is just as comfortable and charges only CFA 3000. The latter is half a km or so south of the central area, past the commissariat and over the bridge.

For an interesting side trip into the luscious green hills to the east, you could take a bush taxi to **Djohong**, which is 90 km to the north-east. The taxis leave early in the morning on Tuesdays and Thursdays from the gare routière, returning to Meiganga on the same days plus Friday. The *Mission Catholique* in Djohong has a few rooms available to travellers at a moderate price. There's also a restaurant and street food. During the rainy season when the air is clear, the views from Djohong are lovely. Before taking photos, ask the Sous-Préfet (an important government official) for permission, otherwise problems could result.

N'GAOUNDAL, TIBATI & BANYO

These three towns west of Meiganga are the major overnight stops on the N'Gaoundéré to Foumban route.

Places to Stay

In N'Gaoundal you can stay at a simple

no-name place across the tracks from the railway station; all rooms cost CFA 1500.

The best place to stay in Tibati is the *Mission Catholique*; if it's not available, try the *Campement de Papa Kala*, which charges CFA 3000 or less for a clean room with bucket showers, or the *case de passage* on the outskirts of town. In Banyo, head for *Hôtel Posada* in the centre near the BP station; it has clean rooms with private bath for CFA 2500 and is excellent value if the water is running.

Getting There & Away

From N'Gaoundéré bush taxis cost CFA 1415 to N'Gaoundal (the train costs the same 2nd class), CFA 1150 more to Tibati, another CFA 1150 to Banyo, and CFA 2600 from there to Foumban; baggage costs extra. Most departures are around 6 am; if you arrive late, you may have a long wait for the next one. Minibuses from Tibati to Banyo and Banyo to Foumban take about three to five hours and five to eight hours, respectively. The latter stretch is one of the most treacherous in the country, particularly during the rainy season when accidents are frequent despite the slower travel. Going in either direction, you can often catch an onward minibus in Banyo the same day.

Northern Cameroun

N'GAOUNDÉRÉ

Roughly halfway between Yaoundé and the Chadian border, N'Gaoundéré (population 100,000) is the northern end of the Trans-Cameroun Railroad. Since 1974, when the railway line was extended here, the city's population has skyrocketed from about 20,000 to 100,000.

At an altitude of 1100 metres, N'Gaoundéré has a relatively pleasant climate, a peaceful ambience and a major attraction – the Palais du Lamido, which is certainly one of Cameroun's finest examples of a traditional chief's compound. If you're here on a Friday, you'll have the added treat of seeing

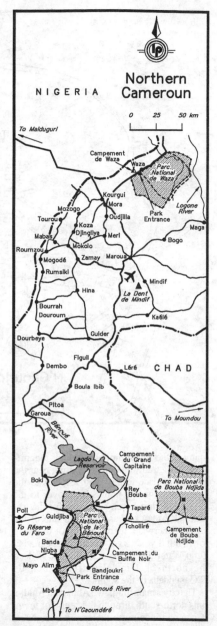

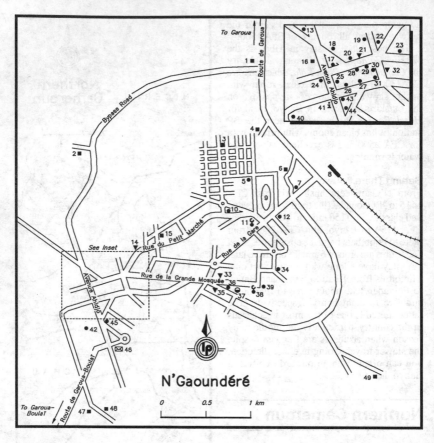

N'Gaoundéré

0   0.5   1 km

many of the Muslim nobles in their magnificent, long traditional dress waiting near the lamido's palace to pay their respects to the chief. At noon the nobles head over to the large modern mosque next door for the traditional Friday prayer, the main one of the week. Otherwise, there's not a lot to see in town, but if you've got wheels, you can visit Tello Waterfalls to the east, Bénoué Park to the north or the delightful Ranch de N'Gaoundaba to the south.

The city's main drag, Ave Ahmadou Ahidjo, runs north-south through the centre of town. If you continue north thereon, it becomes a bypass road, linking up with the road to Garoua about four km north-east of the centre. Most of the city's businesses are in the area east of this main street, continuing past the Cinéma du Nord intersection and along the Rue de la Grande Mosquée eastward towards the gare routière and the adjoining Grand Marché, which is surrounded by a wall; the mosque and the lamido's palace are just beyond. From the motor park you can take another road headed north-east towards the stadium and, half a km beyond, the railway station, where you'll pick up the main highway north to Garoua.

■ PLACES TO STAY		16	Commissariat & Mission Catholique
1	Hôtel du Rail	17	Public Telephone
2	Cacia-Auberge	18	Cameroun Airlines & Pharmacie
3	Auberge de la Colombe		Adama
4	Hôtel Madagascar	20	Boulangerie
5	Presbyterian Mission	22	Cinéma du Nord
6	Auberge Centrale	23	Boulangerie Sagba
15	Auberge le Chateau d'Adamaoua	24	007 Night-Club
19	Hôtel le Relais	25	Vina Tours
47	Hôtel Transcam	26	BICIC Bank & Djabbana Tours
49	Collège Protestant	27	BIAO Bank
		28	Le Prestige Night Club
▼ PLACES TO EAT		29	Dabaji Frères Supermarché & Vina Photos
14	Good Street Food	30	Pharmacie Espérance
21	Restaurant la Girafe	31	Cinéma Adamaoua
32	Pâtisserie Sagba & Café Sagba	34	Traditional House
33	Restaurant Adamaoua	36	Texaco Station
35	Restaurant le Plateau	37	Gare Routière & Grand Marché
43	Café Taxi	38	Grande Mosquée
		39	Palais du Lamido
OTHER		40	School
		41	Tourist Office & l'Artisanat de l'Adamaoua
7	Mobil Station	42	Parade Grounds
8	Railway Station	43	Librairie Sicimex
9	Stadium	44	Crédit Lyonnais Bank & Telecommunications
10	Petit Marché	45	Hôtel de Ville
11	Petite Mosquée	46	Post Office
12	Mascam	48	Le Boukarou Nightclub
13	Agip Station		

Information

Tourist Office The tourist office is in the heart of town on Ave Ahidjo, just north of the parade grounds. The people there are very friendly and can be useful in suggesting places to stay and eat and providing information on surrounding areas.

Money To change money, first try Crédit Lyonnais on Ave Ahidjo next to telecommunications; its service is relatively quick and its combined rates and commissions are usually the best. The understaffed BIAO bank also changes travellers' cheques but the BICIC bank here takes only French franc travellers' cheques. Banks here are open only weekdays, usually from 7.30 to 11.30 am.

Other The best agency for guided tours is

Dhabbama Tours (☎ 251148, 251672; fax 251777), which has English-speaking guides.

The Norwegian Mission hospital is the best place for medical help. Two of the better pharmacies are Pharmacie Adama next to Cameroun Airlines and Pharmacie Espérance between the two cinemas.

Just behind the tourist office is a small handicraft shop, l'Artisanat de l'Adamaoua, which is worth checking out.

Palais du Lamido

Don't miss the lamido's palace. The walled compound consists of several traditional houses, known as *sarés*, all with traditional banco (mud constructed) walls and enormous straw roofs; as you enter the main building you'll see some traditional, colourful designs painted on the walls. The CFA 2000 entrance fee, which is collected in a room just left of the entrance, includes the right to take photographs. This is a great opportunity to photograph men in their traditional dress; Friday is the best day for this but Saturdays and Sundays are also good. The men expect travellers to take their photos and several of them may even voluntarily pose for you, expecting no money in return.

Places to Stay – bottom end

The Mission Catholique no longer rents out rooms to travellers, but the nearby *College Catholique Mazenod* (known by the locals simply as Mazenod) definitely does. It consists of a single building with numerous attractive rooms, all with spotlessly clean shared toilets and showers. The French lady in charge asks only CFA 1500 a room.

If it's full, try the *Collège Protestante* on the south-eastern outskirts of town, a good two km south-east of the gare routière. It has dormitory beds that it rents out for CFA 1500. To inquire, you must go during the day when the main offices are fully staffed as finding the right person is not always easy.

A hotel near the centre of town with rock-bottom prices and quality is the *Auberge le Chateau de l'Adamaoua*, with rooms for CFA 3000. The rooms have interior showers and communal toilets that are passably clean, at least when there's been a recent paint job. You can also eat at the Auberge fairly cheaply. However, it can get quite noisy at night plus it has a bad reputation for thefts, so take precautions. To get there, from Cinéma du Nord head north-east on Rue du Petit Marché for about 300 metres, then left (north) for one block on a dirt side street.

Auberge de la Colombe has better rooms with private bath for CFA 3000 to CFA 3500 but it's basically a brothel with a lively bar and amusing colourful paintings on the walls. You can also eat there. It's about four short blocks north and four short blocks west of the Presbyterian Mission and opposite the municipal stadium.

If you're arriving by train, two of the closest places are the *Auberge Centrale* (☎ 251936) and *Hôtel Madagascar*. Coming out of the railway station, turn right and head north on the main paved road (Route de Garoua). The Centrale is about 300 metres north on that road, then 200 metres on a dirt road to your left, well before the stadium. The Madagascar is about half a km further along the same paved highway north and a short block to the left. The small, somewhat remote Madagascar charges CFA 3500 for a small room with interior bath and serves food but it's not particularly good value. Many travellers seem to like the Centrale, which has rooms with one/two beds for CFA 4000/5000. The beds are large with attractive blankets and the private baths have hot water and Western-style facilities. There's a walled courtyard where visitors can park their vehicles and the restaurant serves good, cheap food such as couscous for CFA 350, and macaroni for CFA 350.

Places to Stay – middle

Hôtel le Relais (☎ 251138; telex 7650) is a popular, mid-range hotel in the centre, half a block behind Cinéma du Nord. A respectable hotel but somewhat infested with bugs, it has large air-con rooms and good hot-water showers for CFA 6960. You can also eat breakfast here and watch TV at the spacious bar. If you have your own vehicle, check out *Cacia-Auberge*, a small shady hotel on the northern bypass road, two km from the centre towards Hôtel du Rail. Rooms are large and clean with Western-style baths, and are a good buy at CFA 5250.

Places to Stay – top end

The top hotel is *Hôtel Transcam* (☎ 251041/172; telex 7641), which is on the southern outskirts of town, 1½ km from the centre. It has 50 rooms and bungalows with air-con and TV/video for CFA 12,500. There's also a tennis court and the city's top nightclub.

On the northern outskirts of town on the road to Garoua, 1½ km north of the railway station, you'll find the *Hôtel du Rail* (☎ 251013), which is a good notch down from the Transcam. It's a modern hotel surrounded by trees, with a moderately attractive, less expensive restaurant and a large parking area. Large air-con rooms with one/two beds cost CFA 7000/7600.

Places to Eat

Good places for street food are the gare routière and the central area between Cinéma du Nord and Cinéma Adamaoua. Between the two cinemas are *Pâtisserie Sagba* and the adjoining *Café Sagba* which sell pastries for CFA 150 to CFA 250 and café au lait for CFA 200.

For cheap full meals in the central area, it's hard to beat the tiny, six-table *Café Taxi*, which is 50 metres east of Ave Ahidjo facing the BICIC bank. The menu includes café au lait (CFA 75), omelettes garni (CFA 175), salade (CFA 250), *avocat garni* (avocado with rice and salad, CFA 300) and ndolé chicken (CFA 300). Or try *Club Bamboula*, which is just west of Cinéma du Nord; it has omelettes and salads for CFA 400 and steak garni for CFA 1200 and is also a good place for cheap drinks. Further west on the same street towards Ave Ahidjo you'll find the newly relocated *Restaurant la Girafe*, which for years has been a popular beer and food stop for the 'Nairobi or Bust' type of expedition trucks. Most dishes, such as beef brochettes and fish, are grilled and cost around CFA 1500 with rice or fried plantains. This is also the best area for supermarkets; one of the largest is *Dabaji Frères* across the street.

At the gare routière, one of the most popular places for food and drink is *Restaurant Adamaoua*, which is just north of the Texaco station. It has a big menu including complete breakfasts for CFA 250, riz macaroni (rice with macaroni) for CFA 300, omelette garni (CFA 400) and roast chicken (CFA 550). Just south of the Texaco station you'll find *Restaurant le Plateau*, which has virtually identical food and prices, as does the hotel *Auberge le Chateau d'Adamaoua*.

The city's top restaurant is the *Hôtel Transcam*; the set menu is about CFA 3500 and the food is average; you can eat better and more cheaply at the outside *Grill-Room Pizzeria*; it serves pizza and grilled chicken for CFA 2000, *entrecôte* (steak) for CFA

2500 and beef and fish brochettes for CFA 1800 to CFA 2500. Or try the attractive *Hôtel du Rail*; the set menu there is only CFA 2000.

Entertainment

For a good nightclub in the centre, try the popular *007 Night-Club* on Ave Ahidjo or *Le Prestige Night Club* a block to the east towards Cinéma du Nord. The city's top disco is *Le Boukarou* opposite the Hôtel Transcam, but drinks are relatively expensive.

Getting There & Away

Unitair and Cameroun Airlines (☎ 251295) have five flights a week to Yaoundé and Douala, and a number of the flights between Yaoundé and Maroua stop in N'Gaoundéré as well. One-way fares are CFA 23,650 to Maroua and CFA 23,950 to Yaoundé.

The railway station (☎ 251377) is about 2½ km east of the town centre. The Yaoundé train departs early in the evening but the exact hour is constantly changing; most recently it was departing at 7 pm. The train takes 12 hours to Yaoundé and continues on to Douala. Fares to Yaoundé are CFA 11,600 in 1st class (CFA 1750 more for a couchette) and CFA 6750 in 2nd class. The 2nd-class fare to Belabo is CFA 3535.

Minibuses and bush taxis leave from the gare routière. Standard fares are CFA 2800 to Garoua-Boulaï, around CFA 3000 to Garoua (four to six hours) and CFA 5500 to Maroua. You can also find vehicles headed for Tibati (and from there to Banyo and Foumban) and to Tcholliré just east of Bénoué National Park. Those for N'Gaoundal leave at 7.10 am, 1 and 6.20 pm and take two hours; the fare is CFA 1415.

Getting Around

Bicycle & Moped A great way to see the area surrounding N'Gaoundéré is by bicycle or moped (Mobylette). To rent one, ask at the gare routière, along the Rue du Petit Marché or, better still, at the stands opposite either cinema. It's fairly easy to find men willing to rent you a Mobylette and you don't need a licence. Expect to pay about CFA 500 a day for a bicycle, and CFA 500 an hour or CFA 3500 a day for a Mobylette.

Car Vina Tours (☎ 252525), which is on Ave Ahidjo just north of the tourist office, charges CFA 13,000 a day for a Mazda but you must also pay for daily insurance (CFA 8250), a driver (CFA 3000) plus CFA 100 per km and CFA 11.5% tax. You may be offered a 10% discount if you ask. For a guarantee, you must provide a credit card or the equivalent of CFA 200,000 in cash or travellers' cheques. Auto Location de l'Adamaoua (☎ 252030) in Quartier Sabongari, en route to the railway station, has virtually identical rates and accepts both American Express and Diners Club cards.

AROUND N'GAOUNDÉRÉ

Some 35 km south of N'Gaoundéré is *Le Ranch de N'Gaoundaba*, a marvellous hotel on the side of a crater lake 1360 metres above sea level. Only open from November to May and popular with Jet Tours, it's almost like being on a ranch in the western USA. It's best for walking and bird-watching; during the winter months you can see thousands of herons settling into their tree roosts at night and flying away early in the morning. You can also swim (free of bilharzia), play tennis (clay courts), take a boat ride, fish, ride horses (in a ring), or hunt. The price of a cabin is about CFA 15,000 per person including meals, which are quite good. To get there, head south on the Meiganga highway to Dibi (30 km), then west for several km.

Some nine km south-east of town is a small crater lake, **Lac Tison**, which is reportedly like a bilharzia soup. To get there, head south on the Meiganga highway for six km to a sign post for the lake, then east for three km.

Alternatively, you could head east from N'Gaoundéré on the dirt road to Mbalang Djalingo village (22 km); two km south of which is another crater lake, **Lac de Mbalang**, which is also not safe for swimming. Continuing east from Mbalang Djalingo towards Tourningal and Bélel, after 28 km past Mbalang Djalingo you can take another

dirt track south for two km to the **Chutes du Tello**, which is a beautiful waterfall and more interesting than either lake. It's possible to make the round trip by Mobylette to Tello Falls in one day but it's hard work. For more information about these falls and lakes, see the tourist office in N'Gaoundéré.

BÉNOUÉ & BOUBA NDJIDA NATIONAL PARKS

Midway between N'Gaoundéré and Garoua are two of the country's best game parks, topped only by Waza park to the north – the Parc National de la Bénoué, on both banks of the Bénoué River, and the Parc National de Bouba Ndjida to the east thereof. Because of its comparative ease of access, Bénoué receives far more visitors than Bouba Ndjida but the latter has a slightly more interesting landscape.

Neither park is teeming with animals but there is good variety at both including various species of antelope (kob, topi, waterbuck, hartebeest and, above all, the prized giant eland), buffalo, baboon, crocodile, lion, monkey, giraffe, wart hog, hippo and, in Bouba Ndjida only, rhino. In Bénoué, there's a great spot on the river for viewing the many hippos. There are also some brightly coloured birds, rollers being the most exquisite; some of the birds can be seen riding on the backs of kobs. The elephant and lion populations, on the other hand, are quite small at Bénoué compared to those at Waza and Bouba Ndjida; you're unlikely to see them at Bénoué or, because of the thick brush, at Bouba Ndjida.

Bénoué is open year-round while Bouba Ndjida is open only from December to May. The best wildlife-viewing time is January to May, especially early in the morning and late in the afternoon. Bénoué park has two entrances from the main north-south highway, at Mayo Alim and Banda, both of which lead to Campement du Buffle Noir. The entrance to Bouba Ndjida is at Tchollire, for which there is a direct daily minibus service from N'Gaoundéré. At both parks, the entrance fee is CFA 2500 and you must also pay CFA 1500 for a guide (compulsory).

For an interesting side trip, head north from Tcholliré to **Rey Bouba** (35 km); market day is Friday. The main attraction is the lamido's palace, but you won't get to see inside unless the lamido (chief), who wears a veil in public, consents to a reception.

Hunting

The major hunting zones in Cameroun are around the savannah grassland national parks of the Bénoué, Faro (to the far west of Bénoué) and Waza. The season is 15 December to 1 June. How anyone could have the heart to kill a lion or elephant in today's Africa is beyond me, but it is permitted. Other trophies include kob, hippo, crocodile, Derby eland, and antelope. Only the rhino, giraffe and leopard are protected. The permit fee for large game is about CFA 85,000, good for six months. Killing an elephant or a giant eland will cost you CFA 150,000 extra, while kobs are a bargain slaughter at CFA 15,000.

Places to Stay & Eat

You have four choices – two in Bénoué, one in Bouba Ndjida, and one between the two. Most tourists stay at the 20-room *Le Campement du Buffle Noir* in Bénoué, 40 km or so east of the highway and near an impressive waterfall. Rooms in a boukarou (bungalow) cost about CFA 8000. There is even a good restaurant where *pâté de phacochère* (wild boar) is the *pièce de résistance*; baboons playing on the nearby rocks are the main source of entertainment. Reserve by calling the Service Provincial du Tourisme (☎ 27-1020/364) in Garoua.

If you want to get away from everybody, stay at the *Le Campement du Grand Capitaine* 110 km to the north on the Guidjiba to Tcholliré road. Most hunters stay here, and on weekends a party may join you. It has eight rooms in four boukarous (CFA 5000 a room), but no restaurant. Reservations can also be made at the Service Provincial du Tourisme. The view dominating the Bénoué River is spectacular. Much further to the east in Bouba Ndjida on the Mayo Lidi River, you can stay at *Le Campement de Bouba Ndjida*, which has a restaurant and 16 rooms in eight boukarous at about CFA 8000 a room. Finally, those on the cheap can stay in Tcholliré at the cheap *Campement de Djiré*, or camp at designated spots in Bénoué or much further north at Lagdo Reservoir, near Boki.

GAROUA

Midway between N'Gaoundéré and Maroua in the far north, Garoua offers nothing of great interest to see but it's an active, prosperous town and the administrative capital of the northern region. It was Ahidjo's home town, which explains in part why this modest-sized city (under 150,000 inhabitants) has modern (but uninteresting) buildings everywhere, an international airport with an international-class hotel, plus direct flights once a week to Paris. Located on the Bénoué River, it also has a port and quite a few factories. For travellers, Garoua is significant in part because it's the starting point for the alternate, more direct route north along the Nigerian border to Rumsiki and the Mandara mountains; scenic hills which begin just north of town.

Orientation

The main drag starts on the southern side of town at the bridge over the Bénoué River and goes northward through town, becoming the Route de Maroua. The main gare routière is on that road, on the city's northern outskirts. The heart of town is the triangular Stationnement on the main drag, one km north of the bridge and easily identified by the Texaco and Mobil stations there. The Petit Gare Routière is 150 metres to the north and the market area begins one block to the west. Another principal street, the Rue Centrale (or Rue des Banques), is two blocks west of, and parallel to, the main drag; along it you'll find most banks (Crédit Lyonnais, SCB, BIAO, BICIC), the commissariat, Mairie (town hall) and, at the northern end, the post office. From there it branches north-westward, heading for the wide Route Peripherique (or Rue de SODECOTON) on the western side of town and, beyond it, the airport. If, instead, you head south-westward from the

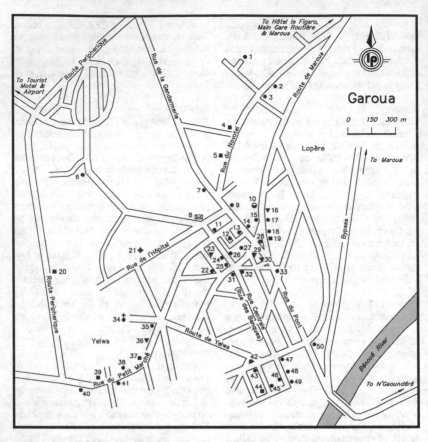

To Hôtel le Figaro,
Main Gare Routière
& Maroua

Garoua

0   150   300 m

To Maroua

Lopère

To Tourist
Motel &
Airport

To N'Gaoundéré

Bénoué River

Yelwa

central area for a km or so, you'll come to the Yelwa district and the Petit Marché, an area noted for cheap bars and street food; it also has several hotels.

Places to Stay – bottom end

The Catholic church's *La Procure*, which is on the northern side of town half a km beyond the Novotel, and the *Mission Protestante*, which is in Yelwa just before the Route Peripherique, no longer take travellers; they say the government prohibits them from renting rooms to people outside their organisations. The best place by far for the

price in the centre of town is the 26-room *Auberge le Salam* (☎ 272216) on the main drag facing the Stationnement. Under new management and highly recommended, it charges CFA 3000 for a small, spotlessly clean room with overhead fan, secure locks and very clean shared baths with excellent showers and flush toilets. A good cheap restaurant is attached to this place. If it's full, inquire about a similarly priced hotel with the identical name in the market area; it may still exist.

Next in line price-wise is the *Hôtel Pacifique* (☎ 271503), which is several km west of the central area on the Route Peripherique.

■ PLACES TO STAY

4 Novotel la Bénoué
5 Le Relais St-Hubert
19 Auberge le Salam
20 Hôtel Pacifique
37 Auberge de la Cité
39 Hôtel le Saré
44 Auberge Hialla Village

▼ PLACES TO EAT

16 Super Restaurant
23 Restaurants Tempête du Sahel & Le Berry
29 Restaurant du Nord
30 No-Name African Restaurant
36 Le Coin de la Pizza

OTHER

1 Stadium
2 La Procure
3 Lycée Classique
6 Radio Station
7 Camp de Gendarmerie
8 Post Office
9 BEAC Bank
10 Petit Gare Routière
11 Mairie

12 Librairie Nouvelle Moderne
13 Photo Mecca
14 Market Area
15 Shell Station
17 Pharmacie du Grand-Marché
18 Alimentation Siddi Mohamed
21 Hospital
22 Cinéma le Ribadou
24 Crédit Lyonnais Bank
25 SCB Bank
26 BICIC & BIAO Banks
27 Grand Marché
28 Le Stationnement, Mobil Station & Total Station
31 Public Telephone
32 Librairie
33 Truck Park
34 Catholic Church
35 Pharmacie du Nord & Mobil Station
38 Petit Marché
40 Mission Protestante
41 Bar El Posso
42 Boulangerie du Centre
43 Maison du Centre
45 Cinéma Étoile
46 Cameroun Airlines
47 Pharmacie Nouvelle
48 Commissariat de Police
49 Supermarché Tigre
50 Brasserie

Unfriendly to travellers and poorly run, it caters more to those seeking rooms by the hour. Grubby rooms with fans and interior baths cost CFA 3500/4000 (one/two people). On the southern side of town, a block behind (west of) Cinéma Étoile, you'll find the *Auberge Hialla Village* (☎ 272407). Though it's primarily a restaurant, it also has several rooms. However, at CFA 5000/6000 for a room with one/two beds and no windows, this place is poor value.

Places to Stay – middle
In Yelwa you'll find two hotels of comparable quality on the Rue du Petit Marché. The first, which is just below the hill at the main, six-street intersection in Yelwa, is the unattractive, three-storey *Auberge de la Cité*. It has 10 rooms with air-con for CFA 6000, carpeted hallways and a decent restaurant with breakfasts for CFA 700 and full meals

such as ndolé au poulet and fish brochettes for CFA 1500. Several blocks further west is the *Hôtel le Saré* (☎ 272211), which has a popular open-air bar and small air-con rooms with tiny tile baths for CFA 6500.

If you have wheels, you'll probably prefer the similarly priced *Hôtel le Figaro*, which is a new hotel somewhat remotely located in the industrial zone, before the French cultural centre. It has decent air-con rooms and an excellent open-air restaurant specialising in grilled dishes. There's a large parking area and the rooms (CFA 6000) are huge with air-con and large tile baths. However, the place is virtually deserted and there's no restaurant or bar, but you can get food and drink if you ask. If you're still interested, head north on the Maroua Rd and take the first left (west) after the Saudia Arabian mosque; the hotel is a short way down the dirt road.

Places to Stay – top end

The city's top hotel is the swanky *Tourist Motel* out at the airport on the western outskirts of town; meals, which are excellent, are served around the pool, which is very clean. Most 1st-class travellers, however, still stay at the less expensive and more conveniently located *Novotel la Bénoué* (☎ 271553; telex 7625), which is only 1¼ km north of the central area. It has modern rooms for CFA 12,500 and a tropical setting with a pool, tennis and nightclub, and the staff will make reservations for you at the Campement at Waza Park if you ask. All major credit cards are accepted.

Le Relais St-Hubert (☎ 271321) is on the same street, 200 metres closer to the centre, with a nice yard in front. It is being entirely renovated and should cost about the same as the Novotel when finished.

Places to Eat

You can get excellent African food at a no-name, hole-in-the-wall restaurant about 20 metres west of the southern point of the Stationnement triangle. Sauce (typically meat with sauce gombo or sauce feuille) with a big plate of pâte de riz and *bouiller* (rice, curdled milk and sugar) costs CFA 400 and is usually enough for two. There's only one table as most of the clients (mostly single men and African travellers) eat on mats on the floor. Spoons are available if you don't want to eat with your hands. Places this good are hard to find, so don't pass it up.

For something less exotic, I recommend the nearby *Restaurant le Salam*, which is attached to the Auberge le Salam and is very popular with overland travellers. Virtually all dishes are in the CFA 250 to CFA 700 range including *sauce-pain* (bread and sauce; CFA 250), macaroni (CFA 300), riz légume (CFA 350) and omelette garni (CFA 500). It's clean with an overhead fan; alcohol is not served.

A block further north on the main drag is *Super Restaurant*, which is very similar and has a TV. The food includes riz sauce (rice with sauce) for CFA 250, *pomme sauce* (potatoes with sauce) for CFA 350, *poulet roti* (roasted chicken) for CFA 600 and *riz filet* (rice with beef) for CFA 700. *Restaurant du Nord*, which is just south of the main market, and *Restaurant Tempête du Sahel*, which is two blocks further west and north of Cinéma le Ribadou, are virtually identical. The Nord has excellent fruit drinks for CFA 250 and good food.

One of the best restaurants in town, but fairly expensive, is the French open-air *Restaurant le Berry*. It's next door to the Tempête du Sahel and has a tranquil, shady setting. A meal at the Berry will cost at least CFA 5000. Another restaurant with a tranquil outdoor setting but simpler cuisine is the *Auberge Hialla Village* on the southern side of town; grilled dishes are the speciality. *Le Coin de la Pizza* on the main drag in Yelwa, just before Auberge de la Cité, is very ordinary. The pizza at the Novotel's *Pizzeria Bénoué* is much better but it's also more expensive. The fixed-priced French menu at the Novotel's main restaurant is CFA 4385.

For groceries and baked goods, you can't beat *Supermarché Tigre* on the southern side of town near the end of Rue Centrale, and *Boulangerie du Centre*, which is nearby, a block west of Rue Centrale. You'll also find groceries including fresh milk in the centre of town at tiny shops such as *Alimentation Siddi Mohamed* opposite the Stationnement.

Entertainment

The best place for cheap beers is in Yelwa, especially along the Rue du Petit Marché. One of the more lively ones there is *Bar El Passo* opposite the Petit Marché. For a nightclub, try *Carnival Disco* or the one attached to *Le Berry* restaurant, half a block north of Cinéma le Ribadou. That theatre is the best in town, with many good films from the West.

Getting There & Away

Air The international airport (☎ 271481) is on the western outskirts of town and once a week there are flights to/from Paris. Unitair and Cameroun Airlines (☎ 271055), at the southern end of Rue Centrale near the port, have flights every day to/from Yaoundé and

Douala. The one-way fare to Yaoundé is about CFA 35,000.

Minibus & Bush Taxi The main gare routière on the northern outskirts of town, four km from the centre, is where you'll find minibuses and a few bush taxis. Most of the latter, however, are stationed at the Petit Gare Routière, just north of the Stationnement. Standard fares are CFA 3000 to N'Gaoundéré and CFA 2500 to CFA 3000 to Maroua. The bush taxis are much faster than the minibuses, for example four hours to N'Gaoundéré by bush taxi compared to about six hours by minibus.

Car To rent a car, contact Avis (☎ 271298; telex 7619), Esgreg Voyages (☎ 271122) or Jean Despotakis (☎ 271211).

AROUND GAROUA
Pitoa
Some 17 km north of Garoua on the highway to Maroua, Pitoa is a good place to head on Sundays, market day. The nomadic Fulani and mountain-dwelling Kirdi tribes predominate, making it very colourful. For food, try *Restaurant Tinguelin*, which specialises in grilled dishes and is not expensive.

Boula Ibib
Boula Ibib, 54 km further north on the same road, is noted for its colourful Saturday market. The great variety of ethnic groups is one of the attractions, especially the nomadic Woddabé (or Bororo) herders, who are easily recognised by their unusually lean bodies, thin noses and refined features.

MAROUA
Cameroun's northernmost major city, Maroua, is popular with travellers and is the starting point for trips to Waza National Park, Rumsiki, Mora, Mokolo and the Mandara mountains. The city's size (population 150,000) allows it to have most of the amenities of a big city but there are shade trees everywhere and the pace of life is agreeably slow. Most important, the people here are some of the friendliest in the country, which

is a major reason why it's a Mecca for travellers.

Since the early '90s, Maroua has acquired another distinction – it no longer has a serious mosquito problem. This is because French researchers have been trialling a natural bacterium whose spores harbour a toxin that is lethal to mosquito larvae but harmless to animals and humans. The type of mosquito in Maroua lays its eggs mostly in sewers, so the researchers have been spraying a 'biopesticide' containing this toxin twice yearly into the sewers. As a result, mosquito numbers have fallen by as much as 90%. Unfortunately, malaria-carrying mosquitoes are not affected, so malaria pills must still be taken.

Orientation
Maroua is fairly spread out, the heart being the Grand Marché. All around it you'll find small shops and cheap places to eat. Most major establishments such as banks, Cameroun Airlines, and the supermarket are a block or two to the east, while the gare routière is much further out, 1½ km to the south-east.

The main street, Ave de Kakataré (or Ave du Marché), heads west from the Rond-Point du Marché for 1½ km to the administrative quarter (with the post office, tourist office, Town Hall and hospital), then south-west over the Kaliao River (usually dry) to the landmark Relais de la Porte-Mayo, the city's most popular hotel and restaurant. From that intersection you can head west on Rue de Camp Sic to the Garoua Rd or south to Campement Bossou, a favourite bottom-end hotel in Quartier Domayo. That area has the highest concentration of cheap hotels; it's also good for street food. In Domayo you can take either of two paved east-west avenues, Blvd de Renouveau or, several blocks further

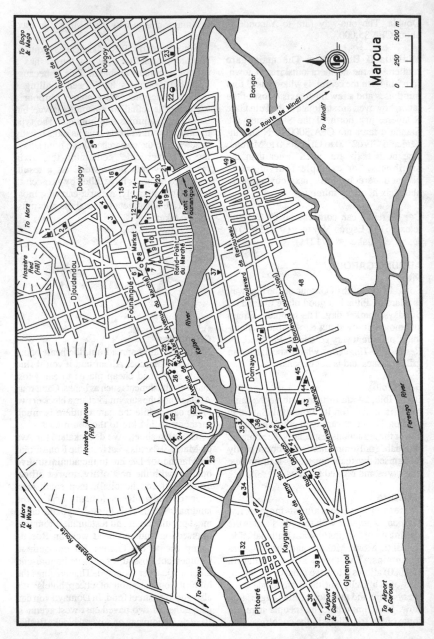

Maroua

■ PLACES TO STAY

1	Hôtel Maroua-Palace
14	Mission Protestante
19	Auberge le Voyager
21	Mission Catholique de Founangué
23	Auberge le Diamaré
29	Mizao Novotel
32	Hôtel Protocole
33	Hôtel Frères-Unis
36	Relais de la Porte-Mayo
39	Motel le Saré
40	Campement Coccinelle
43	Campement Bossou
44	Auberge des Nations
45	Relais Ferngo
46	Auberge le Diamaré
47	Auberge Maljiguilao

▼ PLACES TO EAT

6	Restaurant Chez Hanza
9	Restaurant Provincial & Alimentation Abba Ibrahim
10	Boulangerie Délice
16	Caféteria le Kassaryel (Chez Moussa)
19	Restaurant 007
28	Alimentation le Progrès
37	La Blaise d'Or (Chez Justine)
41	Le Refuge
42	Grilled-Fish Vendor
49	Restaurant Kohi

OTHER

2	Clinique Kaliao
3	Cinéma le Diamaré
4	BICIC Bank
5	Lycée de Maroua
6	Public Telephone
7	Pharmacie de l'Extrême Nord & Bar du Rond-Point
8	Musée du Diamaré, Centre Artisanal & Leather Sellers
9	Public Telephone
11	Bar-Dancing Chez Bossou
12	BIAO Bank
13	SGBC Bank
15	Large Supermarket
16	Cameroun Airlines
17	Boulangerie de la Gare
18	Bar la Paillote
20	Mobil Station
22	Gare Routière
24	Hospital
25	Mairie
26	Grande Mosquée
27	Lamido's House
30	Commissariat de Police
31	Post Office & Telecommunications
34	Kaliao Tennis Club
35	Tourist Office & Socatour
38	USAID
48	Stadium
50	Tannerie Artisanale

south, Blvd de Diarenga (or Blvd Loumo-Kopi), and head east for several km, then north over Pont de Founangué and back to the market. Coming from Garoua or Kousseri, you can easily miss the entire city if, by mistake, you take the bypass road around the city's western side.

Information
Tourist Office The tourist office is close to the Porte-Mayo and before you cross over the Kaliao River on the way to the post office. It should have useful information on trips to Rumsiki, the Mandara mountains, Mora, etc.

Money Banks in town include the BIAO, SGBC, BICIC and SCB, all of which are just east of the market.

Travel Agencies All-inclusive tours of Waza, Rumsiki, the Mandara mountains, etc can be arranged through the Novotel, Socatour at the tourist office or Caravane Cameroun at Hôtel Maroua-Palace. However, for treking in the Mandara mountains, you'll do better contacting Jean-Remy Zra Feu Teri at the Porte-Mayo's gift shop. Pleasant and not pushy, this astute young Camerounian has written a pamphlet on the culture of Rumsiki and is in the business of guiding people on trips to Rumsiki and the Mandara mountains, with a variety of possible itineraries, some quite adventurous.

Market
The market is the city's top attraction. It's open every day, but Monday market day is best as it attracts lots of Kirdi people who

come to sell their goods. This market is the best place in Cameroun to buy leather goods including wallets, purses, sandals, belts, etc. Most leather vendors congregate on the market's western side. Silver jewellery, jade, ceramic beads, embroidered tablecloths, tie-dye clothing and baskets are also hot items. Instead of buying ready-made jewellery, you can also have it made to order by a local jeweller. If you buy indigo material, dip it in vinegar to keep the dye from running. Or pick up some perfume. Maroua might seem like a strange place for a perfume factory, but in the areas bordering the desert, perfume is a highly prized luxury item, especially among Muslim men. Also be on the lookout for one of the 'street pharmacists' who will invariably have a magical herbal potion for whatever ails you.

Musée du Diamaré
This prominent red building at the western end of the market contains the city's museum, which consists of one large room presenting a disorganised jumble of treasures from the 10th century onward. These include articles from the ancient Sao civilisation, numerous musical instruments especially drums, a Fulani chief's gown and other ritual regalia, agricultural implements, weapons, tools, pottery, old pipes and bracelets. It's open Monday to Saturday from 8 am to noon and 3 to 5.30 pm. The entrance fee is CFA 200 (beware: they sometimes ask as much as CFA 1000) and includes a guided tour. For a view from the top, you'll have to pay extra; the asking price is CFA 1000, which is a complete rip-off.

Crafts
The Centre Artisanal next door to the museum gives a complete picture of local crafts, which are reasonably priced if you bargain hard. Leather items predominate, but there's also a good selection of jewellery and other items including a small selection of womens' *caches-sexes*, which are always fascinating and make interesting souvenirs as do the *grisgris* (charms worn around the neck). Outside the centre and museum you'll find a large area filled with vendors of leather goods including sandals (the quality is often poor), belts, bags, purses and wallets; strong bargaining is always required.

In addition, at the Cooperative de Tissage next to Motel Le Saré you'll find a house where women are sewing shirts, embroidered tablecloths, dresses, etc which are for sale at fixed prices.

Tannery
The best selection of leather goods (cowhide, snake and crocodile) is on the southern outskirts of town in Bongor (Le Quartier des Tanneurs), especially at the Tannerie Artisanale on the road to Mindif. Most items are of cowhide, but if you see any goods made from the skins of crocodiles or snakes avoid them, as those animals are becoming increasingly rare.

Activities
For swimming or tennis, head for the Novotel; nonguests are charged CFA 1000 to use either facility. It costs CFA 15,000 for a yearly pass to the pool.

Places to Stay – bottom end
For the money you can't beat the *Mission Protestante*, which is conveniently located a block east of the market, past the SGBC bank. The newly renovated rooms are set out like dorms, with comfortable new beds for CFA 1500 per person. There's electricity, and the new toilets and showers are spotlessly clean. Couples can save money by staying at the tranquil, tree-shaded *Campement Bossou*; a two-bed boukarou with clean sheets, fan, interior shower and shared toilets, costs CFA 2500. There's no restaurant but there are good places to eat nearby. It's on the southwestern side of town, roughly 3½ blocks south of the landmark Relais de la Porte-Mayo.

If these places are full, try *Hôtel Frères-Unis*, which is on the same side of town but further west in the Pitoaré quarter, two blocks from the better-known Hôtel Protocole and 3½ km from the centre. A clean room with a big bed, fan, shared bath and

African-style toilet costs CFA 2500 (CFA 3500 with two beds and private bath). Next in line is the *Auberge Mailjiguilao*, which is a few blocks east of the Bossou. It charges CFA 3250 for a ventilated room with interior baths and African-style toilets.

Auberge le Diamaré (☎ 292668), which is a block east of the gare routière, is a notch above these with a nice ambience. A clean room with fan costs CFA 3500 (CFA 5500 with air-con). There's a pleasant patio outside where you can have drinks, and a restaurant as well. Unlike the Bossou, the Diamaré's clients are virtually all Africans rather than foreigners.

Closer to the centre, just north of the Pont de Founangué you'll find the two-storey *Auberge le Voyager*, which has spotlessly clean rooms and sheets, fans and secure locks for CFA 3500/4000 (shared/private bath), CFA 5000 with air-con. The ambience rates a zero and the Western-style toilets are somewhat dirty but it's only two blocks from the market, and the friendly lady who runs this place will wash your clothes if you ask.

Campement Coccinelle (☎ 291970) is overpriced at CFA 5500 for a fairly dumpy air-con room with a tiny bath and no basin. Two other places in the same category are the *Relais Ferngo* and the *Auberge des Nations* across the street. The former has air-con rooms for CFA 6000, a restaurant and a morbid ambience, while the latter is even more overpriced at CFA 7000 for an air-con room. All three places are near the Bossou.

Places to Stay – middle

The vibrant, ever-popular *Relais de la Porte-Mayo* (☎ 293356) is the best mid-range hotel, with the city's most popular restaurant. It's also the favourite drinking spot of most expatriates and travellers. Air-con bungalows (boukarous) for one/two people cost CFA 6600/7800 (CFA 8900 with two beds). Next to the restaurant is a gift shop (open late) with the best postcards in town, souvenirs and maps of the area, also African art dealers. The hotel is two km south-west of the central market, just south of the Kaliao River.

The *Relais de Kaliao* has closed, leaving the new *Hôtel Protocole* (☎ 291439) as the best alternative. The air-con rooms (CFA 6960/8960 for one/two people) are spotless with nice tile baths. The ambience is pleasantly tranquil but the hotel is quite a long way from the centre in Quartier Pitoaré and not doing good business.

Places to Stay – top end

The two best hotels are the modern nondescript *Mizao Novotel* (☎ 291300; fax 291304; telex 7639), which is 2½ km west of the city centre in a somewhat remote location, and the *Motel Le Saré* (☎ 291194), which is three km from the centre towards Garoua. The 60-room Novotel is newer and has more amenities (pool, tennis, nightclub, art vendors, car rental, cable TV in the lobby), but business is slow and room prices have dropped to CFA 12,500. American Express, Visa and Carte Blanche are accepted. The club-like Saré, which is maintaining its high standards and also has a pool, is special, with an African feel to it. Meeting the delightful French owners is enough reason to stay there, but they also have the best restaurant in town. Singles/doubles are CFA 13,045/15,640 (CFA 1320 for breakfast); American Express is the only credit card accepted.

The newest addition is *Hôtel Maroua-Palace* (☎ 291224/84; fax 291525; telex 7736), which is about a km north of the market. Opened in 1991, this sterile, 53-room high-rise has rooms with one/two beds and cable TV for CFA 12,350/14,000, a restaurant (CFA 3500 for the set menu), a travel agency (Caravane Cameroun) and a pool which nonguests can use for CFA 1000. American Express and Visa are accepted.

Places to Eat

Cheap Eats During the day, the gare routière is the best place to find true African cuisine (ie sauces with some kind of glob-like pâte).

In the market area, you'll find a number of cheap restaurants, mostly Senegalese ones serving dishes such as omelettes, fries and meat with rice. In this category is *Caféteria le Kassaryel*, better known as Chez Moussa, which is very popular with the locals. It's spotlessly clean, with a colour TV and inexpensive cuisine such as fries (CFA 300), *pain sauce viande* (CFA 350), *pain sauce poisson* (CFA 400), and omelette garni (CFA 450). Well known and highly recommended, it serves some dynamite fruit drinks as well. It's next to Cameroun Airlines, a long block east of the market.

The food at *Chez Hanza* is similar but the place is much grubbier, and prices, mostly in the CFA 350 to CFA 900 range, are higher, with omelette garni for CFA 600 and *poulet sauce riz* (chicken with rice and sauce) for CFA 700. On the street just outside you can buy whole roasted chickens for CFA 1500. It's in the heart of town, 30 metres west of the Rond-Point du Marché. *Restaurant Capital*, which is further west on the same street and has a peace symbol sticker on the window, is similar and cleaner as are *Restaurant Sportif* around the corner and the better *Restaurant Provincial* facing the southern side of the market. The Provincial is a good place for breakfast; the speciality is omelettes.

Some 40 metres to the east of the Provincial on the same street is *Boulangerie Délice*, which is one of the better bakeries; *Boulangerie Moderne* is a block north, facing the market's northern side. There are also lots of small grocery stores surrounding the market such as *Alimentation Abba Ibrahim* between the Délice and the Provincial. The largest supermarket, however, is just opposite Cameroun Airlines and Chez Moussa and it's the best place to stock up on supplies.

You'll also find several cheap places to eat in Quartier Domayo, near Campement Bossou and the Porte-Mayo. Between these two hotels, for example, is *Restaurant Mandela*, which serves good food (including breakfast) at reasonable prices. This area is also good for street food, particularly at night. My favourite vendor is a woman who sells delicious grilled brochettes (CFA 100) and fish (CFA 500) at a corner two blocks south and one block west of the Porte-Mayo.

Grillades There are several outdoor restaurants specialising in grilled fish, chicken and/or beef brochettes. The brochettes and fish are cheaper per person than chicken but the fish are often quite large so that you need to be in a group in order for the price to be reasonable. All of these places are similar, usually with a thatched-roof paillote or two and/or metal tables under the stars, and service is slow (often over an hour's wait). The food, however, is delicious. My favourite is *La Blaise d'Or* (or Chez Justine) in Domayo, a block or two north of Blvd de Renouveau and not far from the river. There are signs to it on both that road and Blvd de Diarenga. Grilled chicken costs CFA 3000 (for two people) and grilled fish costs CFA 5000 to CFA 6000 (for five to seven people). Expect to pay about CFA 1100 per person for fish, brochettes, rice or frites and drinks if you come in a group.

A km to the east and two blocks south of the Pont de Founangué you'll easily find *Restaurant Kohi* which, unlike Chez Justine, is more active during the day. You can eat fairly decently for CFA 1000 to CFA 1500. *Le Refuge*, which is about 600 metres southwest of the Porte-Mayo as the crow flies, just south of the Rue de Garnison, is similar, with fish for CFA 1000 and chicken for CFA 2600.

In the centre, try *Restaurant 007*, which is just north of the Pont de Founangué. It has *poulet à la braise* (or poulet braisser) for CFA 2500 among other dishes and is clean but, unlike the others, it's indoors and more like a restaurant. Still another in this category that has been recommended is the *Welcome Bar*, where you can get a large grilled fish for CFA 1500 plus frites.

Other Restaurants For foreigners, the city's most popular place to eat is the long-standing *Relais de la Porte-Mayo*; you eat outside under attractive huts and on Saturday nights it's always packed. The menu includes pizza for CFA 2400 to CFA 2800, Camerounian specialities – *mouton sauce gombo* (mutton with okra sauce), *poulet ndolé avec crevettes* (chicken in green leaf ndolé sauce with shrimp), *foléré* – for CFA 2900 to CFA 3200,

Vietnamese dishes for CFA 1900 to CFA 3400, and French selections. Unfortunately, the souvenir sellers and their wares are everywhere underfoot and get to be a real nuisance (and their prices are invariably high).

Many travellers prefer the Porte-Mayo to the restaurant at the *Motel Le Saré*, which by reputation is still the city's best; regardless, the Sare's setting is truly memorable. The owners have placed lights inside huge African clay pots and arranged them in the garden, which makes a delightful, peaceful backdrop at night as you dine. The fixed-priced French menu is CFA 4395. *Restaurant Jardin Djarengol*, which is still further south-west from the central area, serves equally expensive French food and is also quite good.

Entertainment
Bars The most popular bar for expatriates is the *Relais de la Porte-Mayo*; Peace Corps volunteers like it too. You'll find cheaper bars further south in the area around Campement Bossou and in the centre, such as *La Paillote* just north of the Pont de Founangué.

Nightclubs One of the liveliest dancing places catering to Africans is *Bar-Dancing Chez Bossou*, which is half a block south of the south-eastern corner of the market, near the BIAO bank. It's open-air and cheap, with a large dance floor, and local bands occasionally perform there. For a modern strobe-lit disco, head for *Dack* near the market or the nightclub at the *Novotel*; these are the city's most exclusive.

Getting There & Away
Air Unitair and Cameroun Airlines (☎ 291050) have daily flights to Yaoundé and Douala, some of which stop in N'Gaoundéré. One-way fares are CFA 23,650 to N'Gaoundéré, CFA 44,950 to Yaoundé and CFA 51,150 to Douala. The airport (☎ 291021) is 20 km south of town on the road to Garoua.

Minibus & Bush Taxi Bush taxis and mini-buses leave from the gare routière on the eastern side of town, 750 metres east of the Pont de Founangué. Standard fares are CFA 600 to Mora, CFA 800 to Mokolo, CFA 2600 to Kousseri, CFA 2500 to CFA 3000 to Garoua, and CFA 5500 to CFA 6000 to N'Gaoundéré. Hitching works very well from Maroua to Mokolo. Take a cab to the police post at the southern entrance to town; the police officers there can be quite helpful finding you a free lift.

Getting Around
Taxi Motorcycle-taxis are quite popular and easy to find; the going rate is CFA 100. Shared taxis are usually slightly more expensive. You can also negotiate a taxi for about CFA 12,000 per day, CFA 15,000 to either Mora or Mokolo and return, and CFA 20,000 to Mora, Mokolo and return; these prices include petrol.

Car The Novotel no longer has a car-rental agency but for its guests will arrange car rentals with private entrepreneurs; prices are always negotiable.

Bicycle & Moped Bicycles and Mobylettes are available in the market area for CFA 500 and CFA 3500 per day, respectively.

AROUND MAROUA
La Dent de Mindif
Serious rock-climbers may be interested to learn that the most challenging climb in Central and West Africa is almost certainly La Dent de Mindif (Mindif's Tooth), which is just west of Mindif (25 km south-east of Maroua on the road to Lara). The Japanese considered it to be such a challenge that some years ago they sent out a special team of climbers to make the ascent, all for the TV audiences back home. They were successful. More recently, Mindif village was the scene of action in the French film *Chocolat*. For a cheap place to stay, inquire about *Auberge Maya Boula*.

Maga
On weekends during the winter, particularly December to February, French expatriates

and other foreigners often head for Maga, 80 km north-east on the **Logone River**, which separates Cameroun from Chad. The attractions are the fresh water, the white-sand beaches and the thousands of migrating birds along the river. They all stay at the *Centre d'Accueil Semry II*, which has decent bungalows, a pool, tennis court and restaurant; *Chez Bossou* is cheaper.

MOKOLO

Some 80 km west of Maroua, Mokolo is capital of the Mafa (or Matakam) people. Just before you reach Mokolo you'll begin to see their tiny settlements, which are easily distinguished by the tall, pointed, thatched roofs of their round banco houses. Mokolo itself is not particularly attractive or interesting but the surrounding area certainly is. The one exception is on Wednesdays, market day, when the town comes alive. If you're lucky, you might get to see a Mafa funeral then; it's

a celebration lasting several days with dancing, singing and drinking of millet beer *(la bière du mil)*. Even the cadaver 'participates' by being exposed so that everyone can render homage.

Places to Stay & Eat

Try the *Mission Catholique*, which is up the hill on the western outskirts of town; it was once prohibited from renting rooms to travellers but now the friendly priest is reportedly renting them out again for CFA 1500 a room. That may be because the Bar l'Escale, which is closer to the centre on the main drag, reportedly no longer rents out its rooms (there are four spartan, windowless ones which it used to rent out for CFA 5000). If you're desperate, ask the friendly owner of the nearby Rex Photo on the same street; he has been known to arrange accommodation in private homes for travellers.

Your only other alternative is the 24-room

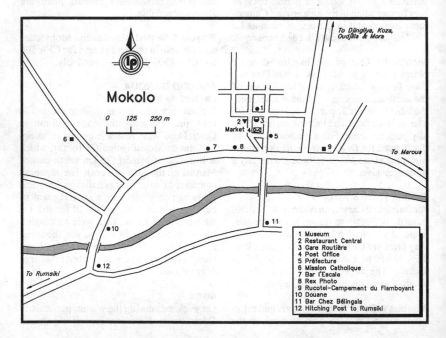

1 Museum
2 Restaurant Central
3 Gare Routière
4 Post Office
5 Préfecture
6 Mission Catholique
7 Bar l'Escale
8 Rex Photo
9 Rucotel-Campement du Flamboyant
10 Douane
11 Bar Chez Bélingais
12 Hitching Post to Rumsiki

Rucotel (or Campement du Flamboyant) (☎ 295116), which is also on the main drag but on the eastern side of town. It's pleasant and by far the nicest place to stay, with air-con bungalows for CFA 9750/12,000 a single/double. Breakfast costs CFA 900 and the fixed-price menu is CFA 4000.

For drinks, try *Bar Chez Bélingais*, which is south of the main road near the CARE office, or *Ombre de Plaisir*, which is a few blocks north of the main drag, beyond the market. For cheap eats, *Restaurant Central* at the market may be your only choice.

Getting There & Away
Minibuses cost CFA 800 from Maroua to Mokolo and leave very early from the gare routière in Maroua; 6.30 am departures are normal. If you miss the first one, you'll have a long wait for another. Bush taxis between Mokolo and Rumsiki (48 km) are erratic and cost about the same. The only day you can be sure there'll be one is Sunday – market day in Rumsiki. In Mokolo ask at the gare routière next to the market and at the intersection (Grand Carrefour) on the western side of town.

If you're heading to Mora, the only days you can be sure of finding transport via Djingliya and Koza, the scenic direct route, are Wednesdays (market day) and Sundays (market day in Mora).

Traffic on the roads to Rumsiki and Mora is light and tough for hitchhiking, which is most feasible on market days and during the tourist season (December to May). So you might consider renting peoples' private Mobylettes in Mokolo or, for shorter trips, their bicycles (which are much cheaper).

AROUND MOKOLO
If you're headed for the Mandara mountains outside Mokolo or the Kapsiki mountains around Rumsiki, bring your camera. This is one of the most fascinating areas in all of Cameroun and also one of the most photographed. You'll find photos of it in many of the tourist brochures. The attractions are the picturesque villages of the Mafa, the Podoko, the Mofou and the Kapsiki. These peoples are collectively called 'Kirdi', meaning pagans, by the Muslim Fulani (or Foulbé) of northern Cameroun who many years ago drove them into their hilltop refuges from the plains below. Their villages are perched on the side of rocky hills and resemble those of the Dogon in Mali. Each round house looks like a tiny fortress.

Djingliya & Koza
From Mokolo there are several major routes; on all of them, bring lots of water or purification tablets. The most well-travelled route is the 67-km dirt road north from Mokolo to Mora, passing through Djingliya (15 km), Koza (five km), Mozogo (the halfway point)

Kirdi Jewellery
Like the Dogon, the Kirdi are known to be hard workers and content to live with few possessions. Jewellery seems to be womens' only luxury, so keep an eye out for it as you travel around. Their lips, noses and ears, for example, are pierced at an early age so that they can later wear ornaments of various types, including ones to show their tribal identity. A dancer might be seen wearing aluminium bracelets and calabash leg rattles filled with seeds or a beaded skullcap with a mongoose fur pompom and a necklace of leopards' teeth. In some areas you may see women wearing polished calabash hats or carrying colourful beaded bags.

Traditionally, women's most noted ornament was a cache-sexe, called *pikuran* by the Kirdi, which is a form of jewellery covering the pubic area and worn in the place of clothing. The different styles denote differences in age, status (married, single, widowed, etc) and tribal origin. They are often quite decorative, which is intended to draw men's eyes to the pubic area, possibly also to ward off evil. As the Cameroun government has outlawed their use in public, you're unlikely to see Kirdi women wearing them except, possibly, in some very remote areas and then only by the older women. You'll definitely see them for sale, however, at artisan shops and some markets. ■

and Kourgui (five km west of Mora). This route passes through the heart of Mafa country.

Djingliya is noted for its Centre Artisanal, a well-run cooperative started years ago by a Dutch volunteer. Items on display include baskets, hand-woven cotton shirts, authentic knives, and ceramic plates and mugs. Prices are fixed and quite reasonable. Ask to see the *forgeron* (blacksmith) who has an interesting old forging stone still used to make tools. There's also a *Chambres de Passage* with rooms for CFA 3000, which is good value.

Koza is noted for its picturesque views, with traditional Mafa houses scattered over the landscape, each looking like a small fortress. The banco houses are round with tall pointed roofs of millet straw and are unusually small, with diameters of less than 2½ metres. The best day to come here is on Sunday, market day. You can also travel from Mokolo to Mora on the more eastwardly route via Méri and Oudjilla, bypassing Koza and Djingliya. The road is in worse condition and less frequently travelled, but the views are also good.

Mabas & Tourou

A second major route, which is circular, leads west from Mokolo to Mabas (20 km) at the Nigerian border, then north along the border to Tourou (15 km), then east to Koza (30 km) and south to Mokolo (20 km). Mabas is a picturesque traditional village overlooking the Nigerian plains to the west. Tourou is also picturesque but fairly quiet except on Thursdays (market day) when the village comes alive. Most distinctive are the women's hats, which are round, reddish coloured half-gourds decorated with geometrical designs. You'll also see lots of Goudour people from the nearby Nigerian plains.

Ziver

A third route is to Ziver, another Mafa village. To get there from Mokolo, you can drive or walk to Nogoumaz (11 km), where you should pick up a guide (easy) to take you to Ziver, over an hour's walk away. It's a heavily eroded, barren area with lots of rocks; the great surprise is that it all ends in a green, water-soaked plateau. Greet the village chief, then take in the spectacular views nearby of the Kapsiki mountains and Mokolo dam.

RUMSIKI

The attraction of Rumsiki, which borders Nigeria, is the volcanic, moon-like landscape including the nearby Pic de Rumsiki, which is probably the most photographed site in Cameroun. The area is overly touristy, but I still recommend coming here because the views are unforgettable.

If you come here between December and May, you'll be disappointed because of the hazy skies from the harmattan. Be prepared to be met by a host of boys each insisting on acting as your guide; nothing you do is likely to get rid of them. Resisting will only make your visit very frustrating because you'll spend half your time trying to get rid of them. So I recommend taking one. You'll be escorted to the weavers, the potters, the blacksmith, the local bar, and finally to the *sorcier aux crabes* who will tell your fortune. He uses crabs in a clay pot to assist him in his divination. For each question you ask him, you must pay about CFA 500. The artisanat, where you'll find gourds, harps and tools, is open all day except during the long noon break, but there's nothing really earth-shattering.

Places to Stay & Eat

Travellers on the cheap usually stay with the locals; boys acting as guides can arrange this. Prices are negotiable but CFA 3000 is typical. The comfortable and well-maintained *Campement de Rumsiki* (no telephone) has a generator, bar and a surprisingly good restaurant (CFA 4000 meals); it charges CFA 12,000 to CFA 16,000 for one of its 26 air-con boukarous which have beautiful mountain views. A word of warning: if you have a reservation and don't arrive until the afternoon, you may find that your room has been given away.

AROUND RUMSIKI

The Kapsiki range around Rumsiki is one of Cameroun's best hiking areas. Rumsiki Peak is a technical climb requiring ropes. What you'll see in addition to the unusual landscape are the villages of the Kapsiki, who are one of the major Kirdi subgroups. You'll need a guide, and they aren't cheap, costing anywhere from CFA 4000 to CFA 10,000 for an all-day excursion.

The possibilities include a three-hour hiking excursion down to **Sina**, the first Nigerian village, with typical Kapsiki housing; an all-day excursion to **Mala** (with good views of the mountains) via Mde and back via Sina; a longer and more tiring two-day, round-trip excursion via Sina and Mala up to the relatively large hilltop village of **Kill**; and week-long excursions to Kapsiki villages such as **Sir, Roulta, Gouala, Kila** and **Lira**. Be prepared for a lot of millet beer on the way and have some Nigerian money on you. As can be seen from the housing construction, all of these villages are very traditional.

MORA

Capital of the Wandala (or Mandara) people, Mora is 60 km north of Maroua on the main highway north and has one of the most famous markets in Cameroun – don't miss it. There are two entrance routes into town from the paved north-south highway. The southern one begins just north of the police checkpoint while the northern one starts about 600 metres further north at the Sous-Préfecture. They converge just before the market, which is the heart of town.

Market

Mora's market is not to be missed. In one small area you'll get to see the entire gamut of people from this area, most in their best dress, including the Islamic plains people (Mandara, Bornouans of Nigeria, Fulani (or Fula) and Choa Arabs) and the animist Kirdi mountain people, particularly the Podoko (POH-doh-koh). It's quite a spectacle, with lots for sale including painted gourds, various leather goods, jewellery, grisgris (necklace charms), millet, onions and other vegetables, and a separate section for trading animals, particularly donkeys. As at Rumsiki, young boys will rush up to you offering their services as guides, but they usually don't pester excessively.

Places to Stay & Eat

The best-value places to stay are the friendly *Mission Catholique* (donation) and the *Auberge Mora Massif*, which has spotlessly clean rooms with fans, clean bedding and interior bucket baths for CFA 2000. You can also get cold drinks and food at the Auberge including beef brochettes, smoked fish and fries. It's off the southern entrance road into town, half a km west of the main highway and half a block south.

If they're full, try *Auberge le Podoko*, which is on the main north-south highway, 200 metres north of the police checkpoint. Inferior to the Mora Massif, it has four bungalows with fans, interior bucket showers and Western-style toilets, and one/two beds for CFA 2500/4000. There's a bar but no food is served.

The top hotel in town is the *Campement du Wandala*, which has bungalows with fans for CFA 4000 (CFA 5000 with air-con but none are working) and a restaurant with a large dining area, tablecloths and fairly expensive meals such as *poulet frites* (chicken & chips) for CFA 3500. It's on the northern entrance road into town, 100 metres before the hospital.

Some six km south of town at Sava is the *Campement du Safari*, which is the best hotel in the area but open only from December to May. It has 12 air-con bungalows for about CFA 8000 and various thatched-roof paillotes for about CFA 4000/6000 a single/double plus a bar and restaurant with meals for CFA 4000. You can also camp there.

For a cold soda (soft drink) or beer in the market area, head for the rustic *Bana Bar* (or Chez Petit Papa) at the junction just east of the market. There's also a guy who sells coffee on the main drag just west of the market. Further west you'll find *Chez Coco*, which is a good place for cold drinks. The Coco and *Restaurant Wandala Club* near the

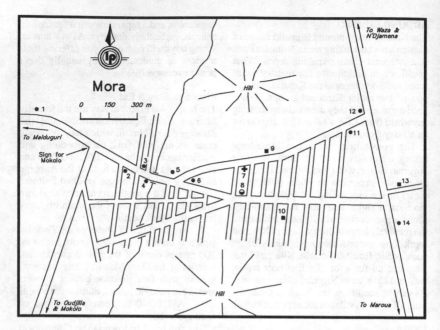

Mora

To Waza &
N'Djamena

To Maiduguri

Sign for
Mokolo

To Oudjilla
& Mokolo

To Maroua

Hill

Hill

0   150   300 m

1	Field
2	Chez Coco
3	Hot Coffee Stand
4	Store with Cold Drinks
5	Market
6	Bana Bar
7	Hospital
8	Gare Routière
9	Campement du Wandala
10	Auberge Mora Massif
11	Gendarmerie
12	Sous-Préfecture
13	Auberge le Podoko
14	Police Checkpoint

market are about the only places serving food (such as dried fish and fries) other than the hotels.

Getting There & Away

A minibus or bush taxi from Maroua costs CFA 600; bush taxis usually cost slightly more. The gare routière is about 400 metres east of the market on the southern entrance road into town. If you head about half a km west of the market on the main drag, you'll come to the well-marked turn-off for Mokolo via Oudjilla and Méri. If, instead, you continue about five km westard, you'll come to Kourgui, the turn-off for the busier road to Mokolo via Koza.

AROUND MORA
Oudjilla

After the morning market in Mokolo you could drive or climb the 11-km dirt road south to Oudjilla (ou-JEE-lah), a Podoko village which is every bit as touristy as Rumsiki but still definitely worth visiting. The 20-minute drive alone is worth the trip as the rocky hilly scenery with conical-roofed mud houses scattered everywhere is superb. The main attraction here is the compound (saré) of the famous village chief and his 47 wives; he's over 60 years old and has

109 children, all of whom he knows despite rumours to the contrary. Inside the compound, each wife has her own closet-sized sleeping chamber made of clay with a five-metre-high pointed roof (the bed is a hard board), and similar structures for cooking and storing grain. At the end of the tour, your guide may offer to have the wives give a dance performance; the cost is negotiable and won't be cheap, especially during the non-tourist season when the women are less prepared.

There are six compounds in all but you'll be shown only a few of them. The asking price for a tour is CFA 3000 a person but if you take the tour first and negotiate afterwards, you can pay what it's worth, about CFA 1000. Sleeping in the village or pitching a tent is no problem. There's also a new snack-bar for drinks and food.

WAZA NATIONAL PARK

Waza is one of the finest game parks in Central Africa in terms of wildlife but from a scenic standpoint, it's one of the most uninteresting – flat terrain and mostly scrub. Elephants are the major attraction. What's unusual is that they tend to congregate in huge numbers around the main watering hole; nowhere in Kenya or Tanzania, for example, are you as likely to see so many in one viewing. Most visitors spot lions as well as giraffes, antelope, kob and monkeys. Other animals include hippos, warthogs, hartebeest, sable roan, waterbuck, baboons and various species of birds including ostriches, rollers, hornbills, bustards, crested cranes, herons, and storks.

Hornbill

Unlike most parks in Africa, the best time for wildlife viewing is not in the wee hours of the morning or in the late afternoon but in the hottest part of the day when the animals head for the water holes to cool off. For the same reason, the best viewing time is the hottest part of the year, from March to May, when the sun literally rounds them up. It's not unusual to see as many as 300 elephants and a few timid giraffes at **Mare aux Éléphants**, the main water hole. The more comfortable viewing time is from November to February but the grasses are thicker then, obscuring the animals.

The park is open from 15 November to 15 June and entrance costs CFA 2500 (CFA 1500 for non-residents). You'll need a vehicle (CFA 25,000 per day rented from the park), and guides (obligatory) who cost CFA 2000 plus tips. A tour will take a minimum of three hours because the straight driving time to the major water hole is 45 minutes. If you don't have a vehicle and can't afford to rent one at the park, flag down vehicles as they pass the park entrance or, better, make friends with guests at the Campement de Waza.

Places to Stay & Eat

Sleeping in the park is forbidden, but you can camp at the park entrance or stay at *Chez Suzanne*, a bar-restaurant on the northern outskirts of the tiny village of Waza, which is just north of the park entrance. It has several stark rooms for CFA 3000. Or ask the owner of the bar-restaurant in the village centre; she may be able to find you a cheaper room.

If money is not a problem, stay at the pleasant Novotel *Campement de Waza* (Maroua (☎ 291007) near the park entrance on a hill overlooking the park. Rooms and bungalows cost CFA 14,500 to CFA 20,000 and have electricity, running water and very noisy air-con which is constantly turning off and starting up again. You'll find a clean pool, which nonguests can use for CFA 800, and a restaurant, which charges CFA 4350 for the fixed-price menu (wild guinea fowl, etc) and CFA 1000 for a sandwich. You can make a reservation through a travel agency or through Novotels in Maroua, Garoua or Douala. Even if you don't stay here, consider coming for a drink – the views of the park from the bar are spectacular.

Getting There & Away

Waza is 122 km north of Maroua on the paved road to Chad; the entrance is just off the highway. It's fairly simple to find a bush taxi headed for Kousseri early in the morning at the gare routière in Maroua. You can drive and return the same day from Maroua, or stay overnight.

KOUSSERI

This northern border town, across the Chari River from N'Djamena, is not particularly interesting, but travellers must sometimes stay here overnight as the bridge at the border closes at 5.30 pm sharp, with no exceptions allowed. Whatever you do, don't pull out your camera near the bridge as you'll be nabbed immediately by police and talking your way out of having your film and/or camera confiscated, or possibly even spending the night in jail, will be difficult.

You may also run into problems with Camerounian police if you head north-west towards **Makari** (95 km) for a view of nearby Lake Chad; it's a sensitive area, and some travellers have been turned back by police there. A better excursion might be to the **Parc National de Kalamaloué**, a 'mini' Waza park near Maltam, which is 26 km west of Kousseri on the Maroua highway. The park officials there are very hospitable and the viewing fee is a pittance compared to Waza's. You won't see many animals but you're virtually guaranteed to see elephants, and also hippos and crocs in the nearby Chari River.

Places to Stay & Eat

One advantage of visiting Kalamaloué is that it has a small hut where you can sleep very cheaply. In town, accommodation is relatively expensive. One of the cheaper places near the centre is *Hôtel Moderne* (☎ 29-4091), which charges CFA 5380 for a modest room with two beds. It also has a much nicer carpeted room with a single big bed and air-con for CFA 6480.

The city's top hotel is *Le Relais du Logone* (☎ 294157), which is half a km away, overlooking the Logone River. It charges CFA 5865/6985 for a room with one/two beds and fan (CFA 8460 with air-con). It also has the town's best restaurant. For street food, look along the main drag and around the gare routière; there's plenty.

Getting There & Away

Bush taxis cost CFA 2600 to Maroua and take about four hours. If you're headed to Chad, you can take a motorcycle-taxi to the border for CFA 100 and another from across the bridge to N'Djamena for CFA 100. There are also bush taxis headed for the Nigerian border (CFA 2000).

Central African Republic

Hunting safaris are big business in the Central African Republic (the CAR). Ever since the French arrived almost a century ago, the chance to stalk and shoot large game here has been a major attraction. The entire eastern half of the country is sparsely populated, and much of it is savannah, making it perfect for game. Those with big bucks think nothing of paying up to US$30,000 for a two-week safari and the opportunity to kill giant eland, lion, leopard, bongo (spiral-horned antelope) and, until recently, elephant. Fortunately, others are content just to see the animals, not kill them.

Most travellers don't even get near the parks and game reserves because they are so remote and neglected. However, with increased assistance from wildlife preservation groups, this is beginning to change. Most promising in recent years has been the establishment of the new Dzanga-Ndoki National Park, in the far south-western corner of the country. It is probably the most pristine park in all of Africa as the dense rainforests there have helped to deter farming and poaching. There are still no facilities for visitors, who are nevertheless most welcome, if they're willing to rough it. A week or two in this area, searching for forest elephants, lowland gorillas, the prized bongo and other animals with the assistance of Pygmy guides, would be a truly unforgettable experience.

The southern part of the country is the area most travellers see because that's where Bangui, the capital, is located. The boundary with Zaïre is formed largely by the winding Oubangui (ou-BHAN-gee) River, which is bordered by lush vegetation. This is the land of Pygmies, muddy roads, and riverboats on their long journey to the Congo. And it's probably the butterfly capital of the world; collages made of butterfly wings are the most popular souvenirs of the CAR.

Bangui sits on one side of the Oubangui River, overlooking Zaïre on the other. Coming from Paris, you may not think much of Bangui, but if you've been travelling for several weeks on muddy roads northward through Zaïre or southward through Chad, it can seem like paradise. Petty thieves and greedy police, however, often ruin the experience there. Elsewhere, Central Africans are usually open, friendly and generous. After bouncing for hours on top of a truck, you may be invited home by a fellow traveller for a meal of *gozo* (manioc paste) and *ngunza* (manioc leaf salad) and offered the only bed. In short, if it's the 'real' Africa you're looking for, then rural CAR, not tourist-oriented countries such as Kenya, may be it.

Facts about the Country

HISTORY
History has not been kind to the CAR. No country in Africa suffered more from slavery and colonial exploitation. The CAR also had

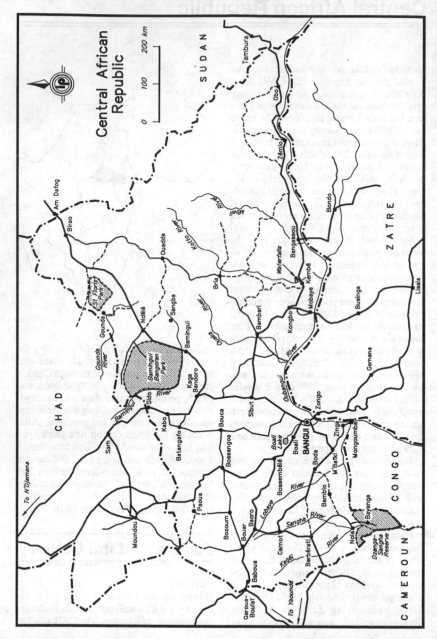

the dubious honour of having a modern day leader – Jean-Bédel Bokassa – whose atrocities rivalled even those of Uganda's Idi Amin.

Archaeological remains indicate that a civilisation existed before Egypt's heyday. The earliest inhabitants from among the present population, however, were Pygmies, who hunted and gathered in the forests. Over 1000 years ago, people migrated west from Sudan and east from Cameroun into the area.

By 1600 the population had attracted slave traders. Unlike West Africa, where most of the slave traders came along the coast, the CAR suffered badly from coastal raids as well as from the Arab empires in Chad and Sudan which needed slaves for themselves and for trade.

The Arabs' armed cavalries periodically swooped down from the north on small settlements, depopulating whole villages at a time. Since no political structure unified the villages, they were easy prey. Even in the late 19th century after slavery had been abolished in much of the world, the Arab empires in Chad continued raiding the area, and many of the captives ended up at slave markets in Cairo.

Colonial Period

In the late 19th century when Africa was carved up, France got most of Central Africa. Some time after colonisation, Chad and the area of the CAR were split up, the latter becoming Oubangui-Chari.

Without the expertise to exploit the area, the French government parcelled it into 17 concessions and handed them over to European companies, in exchange for around 15% of the profits and a fixed annual payment. In need of labour, these companies simply conscripted the local population. Those who refused or deserted were killed or tortured; thousands died.

At the beginning of the 20th century, the French public was outraged by reports of the inhuman conditions in the territory. Savorgnan de Brazza, the famous French explorer who made some of the first explorations in Central Africa, went on an inquisitory mission, but died on the way back. The colonial administration thereafter made vague efforts to curb the tyrannical excesses, but the brutality continued.

Despite famine, sleeping sickness and severe epidemics of smallpox, the population resisted the French well into the 1920s. By 1930, coffee and cotton were on their way to becoming major crops. The forced labour provoked a series of unsuccessful rebellions during the 1930s. Meanwhile, Oubangui-Chari had become a favourite big-game hunting ground for French army officers and administrators. During WW II, cotton production and diamond exports reached record levels.

Independence

In 1949 the charismatic leader Barthelemy Boganda, whose name adorns the main street in Bangui, founded the first political party calling for independence. From the small but politically powerful Lobaye clan, he fought for independence for the next 10 years in the national assembly in Paris alongside Houphouët-Boigny of the Côte d'Ivoire. So when the country became a self-governing republic in 1958, he was a certainty for the presidency. But a year later, while returning from Berbérati, Boganda was killed in a plane crash.

His successor, David Dacko, also a Lobaye, became a highly repressive ruler and attempted no serious economic reforms; he acted like a French puppet, caring only about cultivating French interests. With the government at the point of bankruptcy in 1965, the army's commander-in-chief, Jean-Bédel Bokassa, yet another Lobaye, led a successful coup against his cousin.

Bokassa was cut from the same fabric as Idi Amin. In 1971 he celebrated Mother's Day by releasing all women from prison, and executed all men who were accused of murdering their mothers. The next year he decreed that thieves would have an ear cut off for the first two offences, and a hand for the third. That seemed to have no effect, so he personally supervised the beating of imprisoned thieves; three died and 43 were maimed.

When burglars broke into his house he went to the prison and beat a number of randomly selected inmates to death, gouged out their eyes, and put their bodies on public display. On occasion, when foreign correspondents wrote stories he didn't like, he imprisoned them or assaulted them himself. On another occasion he had a hotel manager repatriated when a minister mistakenly complained of being served partially eaten cheese.

At an Independence Day dinner party Bokassa gave a polished diamond to each of the wives of 13 ambassadors. When Gaddafi visited him in 1976, Bokassa announced that he was adopting the Islamic faith and the name Salah Eddine Ahmed. But after pocketing Gaddafi's US$2 million gift and seeing him off to the airport, he reverted to being Bokassa the Christian.

Two stories made world news. After amassing a fortune through his interference in the diamond business and squandering foreign aid on prestige projects, Bokassa decided to become an Emperor, like Napoleon, his idol. He hired a French firm to design a coronation robe with two million pearls and crystal beads for US$145,000, imported white horses from Belgium to pull his coach, and spent US$2 million on his crown.

On coronation day in 1977, several thousand guests – but not a single head of state – attended. He entered Bokassa stadium wearing a golden wreath on his head, ascended the golden throne, placed the crown on his head and took an oath – à la Napoleon. The Central African Republic became the Central African empire. The cost of this comic opera totalled over US$20 million, and despite the derision the event provoked in the international press, the French picked up most of the tab.

The second newsworthy story (which ultimately toppled Bokassa) was an order in early 1979 that all schoolchildren purchase special imperial uniforms made of cloth from his wife's factory. Pupils took to the streets and were quickly joined by teachers, public employees and the unemployed. Riots resulted, which he put down by calling in Zaïrian troops, at a cost of 50 to 400 deaths. Several hundred teenagers were arrested and at least 100 of them were later taken from their cells and beaten or tortured to death, with Bokassa's active participation, according to many reports.

The news hit the international press. France's Giscard d'Éstaing, who had reputedly accepted hundreds of diamonds as gifts from Bokassa when he was on hunting trips in the CAR, suspended military aid and began plotting a coup. When Bokassa went to Libya seeking aid, the French seized the occasion to fly former president Dacko back to the 'empire' along with 700 French paratroopers, to stage a coup.

Dacko wasn't popular, however, and stayed in power only until 1981, when the head of the army, General André Kolingba, took over. A Yakoma from Mobaye, he remains president.

Meanwhile, the Côte d'Ivoire had granted Bokassa refuge. But in 1983, he was thrown out when he bombarded Bangui with telegrams saying that he was returning. France reluctantly gave him a chateau outside Paris. One of his wives and 15 children joined him.

Three years later, fed up with being confined to a desolate chateau, and believing that Kolingba wouldn't dare kill him, Bokassa shocked the world by returning voluntarily from exile to be tried for treason, murder and cannibalism. After a six-month trial in 1987 he was convicted on all counts and sentenced to death, but Kolingba commuted this to life imprisonment and hard labour.

GEOGRAPHY

Landlocked in the middle of Africa, the CAR is very poor despite its vast mineral resources and adequate rainfall. Bangui, with about 600,000 inhabitants, is the only large city. Bambari and Berbérati have about 60,000 people each.

The country is about the size of France and mostly rolling or flat plateau at 600 to 700 metres, falling to half that altitude near the Oubangui River. There is some variety, however. You'll find dense tropical rainforests in the south, particularly in the south-eastern and south-western corners. Fortunately, deforestation is proceeding fairly slowly – a quarter of the rate in neighboring Cameroun and an eighth of the rate in Kenya and Brazil. The vegetation gradually thins out northward, becoming dry scrub in the sparsely populated Sahelian north-east corner. The Bongo massif near the Sudan border rises to 1330 metres (Mt Toussoro), and the Yadé massif near the Cameroun border rises to 1420 metres (Mt Ngaoui).

There is very little land (2%) under cultivation, because of the low population density, and the tsetse fly ensures that the number of cattle in the country is kept to a minimum.

The CAR has a number of national parks and reserves – at least on paper – mostly dating from the early 20th century, when areas suitable for hunting were carved out by the French. Today, the European Development Fund is helping the government to remark the boundaries more logically in terms of what's worth protecting, including eliminating those areas that can't be protected. The only three areas that are parks other than on paper are, in the north-east, the large Bamingui-Bangoran National Park and the much smaller St Floris National Park further east and, in the south-west corner, the newly created Dzanga-Ndoki Park and the surrounding Dzanga-Sangha Reserve, which acts as a buffer zone. The fauna in these parks is exceptional and includes, most notably, forest elephants, western gorillas, monkeys of various species, the prized bongo, chimpanzees and other animals native to the rainforest. North-eastern CAR, including the park areas, has been ravished by well-armed poachers, many of whom infiltrate from Sudan. During the 1980s, an estimated 80% of the country's elephants in that area were wiped out. Fortunately, St Floris has enough animals, including the big four (lion, leopard, elephant and rhino), monkeys, hippos and various types of antelope, to continue to attract even more visitors than the other parks, while Dzanga-Sangha and Dzanga-Ndoki have more elephants. They are difficult to see, however, because of the thick vegetation.

In the south, the Oubangui River forms the southern boundary with Zaïre and connects Bangui with Bangassou to the east and Brazzaville (Congo) and Kinshasa (Zaïre) some 1200 km to the south-west.

CLIMATE
The rainy season lasts six months (May to October) in the south, diminishing progressively to four months (June to September) in the north. Although temperatures can reach 40°C in the north between mid-February and mid-May, in most of the country mugginess, rather than heat, is the main problem.

GOVERNMENT
When Kolingba came to power, he created a one-party state under the leadership of the Rassemblement Démocratique Centrafricain (RDC) while promising a gradual return to civilian rule. By 1990, progress towards democratisation was virtually nil, other than the establishment of a national assembly. As a result, there were massive pro-democracy street demonstrations later that year, led by the Comité de Coordination pour la Convocation d'une Conference Nationale (CCCCN), resulting in many injuries. At the same time France, the country's major foreign donor and protector with military bases in Bangui and Bouar, made it clear that unless Kolingba took serious steps in moving the country towards full pluralism, further economic assistance would not be forthcoming.

Pushed up against the wall, Kolingba had no choice but to state in public that he favoured immediate moves towards both a multiparty system and a national conference. He was hardly enthusiastic, however, as similar conferences in West Africa (eg in Benin and Niger) had ended up toppling their respective governments. In early 1992, Kolingba granted amnesty to virtually all political prisoners, appointed a French national in charge of the High Court of

Justice so as to assuage criticism of his human rights record, and amended the constitution to make provision for a prime minister: Edouard Frank, a non-political technocrat, was appointed.

In mid-1992 Kolingba finally lifted the ban on political parties and announced that presidential and general elections would be held in October. When October came, 13 parties had been registered but then Kolingba reneged, delaying elections for half a year and, later, to October 1993. If those elections don't materialise, significant aid from France won't materialise either. Regardless, no one believes that Kolingba will permit a national conference and with good reason – the recent one in the Congo toppled that government and one in the CAR would almost certainly do the same. Meanwhile, Kolingba is holding on to power for dear life as his mandate has expired, forcing him to rule by decree while facing increased opposition from all sides.

ECONOMY

The CAR's per capita GNP (US$380) and literacy rate (38%) place it in the middle third of African countries, but its life expectancy and infant/child mortality rates, and access to safe drinking water, place it well in the bottom third. On the UN's human development index, only Chad ranks lower in Central Africa. Unlike countries in the Sahel (the semi-arid area just south of the Sahara, stretching from Mauritania to Chad), the CAR receives easily enough rainfall to feed its small population, but caloric intake is still low (87% of requirements) – just above that of Bangladesh, which is less than a third the size of the CAR, with 40 times the population.

Economically, the country is kept afloat by diamonds. They account for about 25% of the country's foreign exchange earnings, and would account for much more were it not for the enormous amount of smuggling – in the order of half the total production. The diamond export tax greatly encourages smuggling, so not only does the government lose revenue but production remains fairly static. In mid-1992, revenues were so low that civil servants hadn't been paid in months; Kolingba was forced to head for Paris to plead for money. A year later, when government workers again hadn't been paid for several months, troops ringed the presidential palace and the radio station, demanding their wages.

Timber, coffee and cotton, in that order, are the other three major export earners, but none of them seem likely to take the economy out of the doldrums. Cotton and coffee prices are down and the CAR's landlocked position has kept log exports from rising (perhaps fortunately, from an environmental viewpoint).

POPULATION & PEOPLE

With a population of only three million, the CAR is one of the most thinly populated countries in Africa. The slave trade apparently contributed to this. Most people live in the western part of the country, while large areas in the east are virtually uninhabited.

The 80 or so ethnic groups in the CAR live together with little tribal rivalry, quite unlike most of the rest of Africa. One of the principal reasons is the existence of a common language, Sango, which virtually everybody can speak – an equally rare phenomenon, for Africa.

The Banda are found more in the centre and the east, the Baya more in the west; together they constitute roughly 60% of the population. The Mandja, in the centre of the country, follow them in importance.

Many of the people with whom you'll come into contact along the Oubangui River will be from the Oubangui tribe, whose members occupy many of the higher posts in the civil service. Bokassa's powerful tribe, the Lobaye (around M'Baïki), and Kolingba's tribe, the Yakoma, and the Kembé (the latter two are in the south-central area) are all closely related.

In the northern areas, most of the Africans you'll see will probably be Sara, the same group that dominates southern Chad. These people are somewhat taller and bigger than other Africans here. Most of the country's small Islamic population (9% of the total) is also in the north. Country-wide, about one quarter of the people profess to be Catholics, while the remainder practise traditional African religions.

The Pygmies were among the original inhabitants of the area, but now they number only a few thousand, and are found almost entirely in the area south of M'Baïki and in the rainforests in the far south-western corner of the country. Their way of life is not only fascinating but considerably different from that of most Africans.

Pygmy clans are small, with no hierarchy and no division of labour – no chiefs, for instance. All the men have the same job – hunting – and therefore must have the same aptitudes. If a man can't hunt well, his wife may get up and leave. Also, a man must always pick a wife outside the clan. Unlike many other African cultures, monogamy is the rule, not because polygamy is frowned upon, but because hunting for more than one wife and children would be more than one man could bear.

Sharing is also the rule – this means clothes, hunting instruments, cooking utensils, and what they catch. Tribunals, prisons and most forms of coercion don't exist. The only form of punishment is exclusion. In serious cases the culprit may be banned from the clan, but even that is usually temporary.

Pygmies are by no means unaffected by 'civilisation'. Today, many clans have become sedentary, establishing more-or-less permanent camps near Bantou villages and clearing land in return for manioc, bananas and manufactured items.

MUSIC

If you're lucky enough to make contact with some Pygmies, the chances are that you might get to hear some of their music as, traditionally, all of their daily occupations (cooking, hunting, gathering berries, bartering with the locals, etc) are accompanied by music. Whereas in virtually all of Black Africa traditional music is reserved for the men and, most often, for specific castes, frequently semi-professional groups, among the Pygmies everyone is a musician, men and women, young and old alike. They all participate in singing, clapping, stamping and other rhythmical actions.

At first it may seem rather simple, with a fairly uncomplicated rhythmical pattern provided by the clapping of hands and striking of sticks against one another. In fact, it's quite sophisticated in rhythm and form, with lots of improvisation as they perform, especially with the drums which accompany their music most of the time and invariably when they are on the eve of a hunting expedition.

Among other central African groups, the modern African pop music is what's most favoured, especially that from Zaïre, but if you stay long enough in a village you're sure to hear some of the traditional music as well. If you do, check out the instruments as they are quite interesting. The museum in Bangui has a reasonably good collection. One that's commonly used in the CAR, chiefly to accompany singers, is the *ngombi*, a bow harp with 10 strings, which is on the high side for bow harps. (In Gabon, for example, one-string bow harps are typical.)

Another instrument used primarily to accompany singers, particularly during epic narrations, is the *mvet* or harp-zither. It's a plucked-string instrument like a lute or guitar but without a neck. The strings are stretched along a raffia-palm stalk and the sound is amplified by a sound-box consisting of one or more gourds. The men who play the mvet are almost invariably from a special caste whose task it is to recite and keep alive the stories, epic legends and heroic deeds of the community.

For dancing, one of the most commonly employed instruments is the log-xylophone. It commonly consists of two long banana-tree trunks laid on the ground to support 15 or so logs which are struck with sticks in either hand – the forerunner to the marimba in Latin America! The long keyboard is usually played by one or two men and is accompanied in dance performances by drums, whistles and other rhythmical instruments. Or it might be used for a duet with a *sanza*, which is probably the smallest keyboard instrument in Africa (usually 15 to 25 cm long and five cm high) and sometimes known as the thumb piano. It's a small soundbox of wood or bamboo with a number of keys made of strips of bamboo, and played with the thumbs. Sanzas also make great souvenirs. None of these instruments are unique to the CAR, but elsewhere in Africa they take different forms and shapes.

LANGUAGE

French is the official language. Sango is the national language and is used considerably in government and on the radio. Originally a trading language along the Oubangui River, Sango is related to Lingala, one of Zaïre's principal languages.

Some useful expressions in Sango include the following:

Good morning
  m-BEE bar-ah-moh
Good evening
  m-BEE bar-ah-moh
How are you?
  TOHN-gah-NAH-nee-aye?
I'm fine
  YAH-pay
Thank you
  seen-GAY-lah MEEN-gee
Goodbye
  bee-GUAY-ah-way

Facts for the Visitor

VISAS & EMBASSIES
Central African Republic

Only nationals of France, Germany, Israel and Switzerland do not need visas. Note also that exit visas are no longer required by any visitors to the CAR.

In Washington, the CAR Embassy (☎ (202) 483-7800) requires two photos and charges US$30 for a visa valid for two to three months from the date of issue and good for a 45-day stay.

Central African Republic visas issued in Africa are usually more expensive (around

CFA 10,000). In Africa, there are CAR embassies in all neighbouring countries except Sudan; for people of most nationalities they all issue visas quickly, usually within 24 hours.

There is no CAR embassy in the UK and only a few in Europe, but that is generally not a problem because in most of Africa (maybe some European countries as well), wherever there's no CAR embassy, the French embassy usually has authority to issue CAR visas.

In Rwanda, for example, the French Embassy issues visas within several days and charges the equivalent of US$12.50 for a visa valid for 90 days. In Khartoum, the CAR Embassy is now closed, so the French Embassy issues visas for 60 Sudanese pounds and takes two or three days.

In many countries, however, visas issued by French embassies are valid only for two days and must be extended as soon as you arrive in Bangui. Travellers have reported that even in cases where they travelled for a week in the country before arriving in Bangui, they weren't hassled by police on the way.

The immigration office in Bangui is responsible for granting visa extensions. They cost CFA 2500 (30 days) and CFA 5000 (90 days) and are often delivered the same day if you come early. You'll have to buy tax stamps in advance from the Ministry of Finance nearby. (One-month visa extensions beyond this cost CFA 2500 and are also fairly easily obtained, sometimes on the same day, but immigration may ask you to give them a letter in French explaining why you want to stay longer.)

For certain nationalities, including Australians, New Zealanders and the Irish (but no longer Britons), getting visas for the CAR is a major hassle because the embassy must first contact Bangui for permission to issue the visa, a process that can take up to a week or more. Also, people of those nationalities may find that French embassies have no authority to issue them visas.

If you're coming from Zaïre to Bangui via Zongo and don't have a visa, it is reportedly possible to get one by going directly to immigration. First, however, buy tax stamps at the Ministry of Finance and then bring the stamps, CFA 5000 and two photos with you to immigration. If you get there before 11.30 am, you may receive the visa the same day.

The CAR has diplomatic representation in Abidjan, Algiers, Berne, Bonn, Brazzaville, Brussels, Cairo, Kinshasa, Lagos, Libreville, N'Djamena, Ottawa, Paris, Rabat, Rome, Tokyo, Washington and Yaoundé.

Other Countries

Visas to East African countries are not available in the CAR. The French Consulate issues visas to Burkina Faso, Côte d'Ivoire, Gabon and Togo. Visas good for trips of one to five days cost CFA 3000 and those good for trips of up to 90 days cost CFA 10,000. The Consulate is open on weekdays from 7.30 am to 1 pm and on Saturdays from 7.30 am to noon and gives 24-hour service except for Gabonese visas, which require two weeks to issue, because a cable (for which you may have to pay) must first be sent to Gabon. Bring two photos.

For a list of foreign embassies in the CAR capital, see the Bangui Information section.

Cameroun The Camerounian Embassy requires one photo and issues visas in 24 hours. Single-entry visas vary in cost from CFA 5000 (10 days) and CFA 7000 (15 days) to CFA 12,000 (one month). The three-month visa for CFA 20,000, however, is good for multiple entries. The embassy is open weekdays from 9 am to 1.30 pm.

Chad Single-entry visas cost CFA 5000 and are good for three-month stays. The Embassy gives same-day service if you come early. It's open Monday to Saturday from 8 am to 1 pm (to noon on Fridays).

Congo The Congolese Embassy, which is open weekdays from 7 am to 1 pm and Saturday from 7.30 am to 12.30 pm, requires two photos and CFA 5000 and issues visas in 72 hours. They are good for maximum two-week stays.

Nigeria Visas to Nigeria are good for three months and vary in cost from free for Americans to CFA 9340 for Britons. The embassy is open weekdays from 8 am to 3 pm and gives 24-hour service. Bring two photos.

Sudan If you will be flying to Khartoum, the Embassy gives same-day service if you come early. They require two photos, CFA 15,000 and proof of an airline ticket. The Embassy is open Monday to Saturday from 7.45 am to 2 pm (noon on Fridays). However, if you want to travel overland to Sudan, Bangui is not a good place to get a visa because the request must be sent to Khartoum, a process that takes up to two months, and there's no guarantee the wait will be fruitful. Moreover, overland visas are issued only during the period from 15 October to 15 April and four photos are required.

Zaïre The Zaïrian Embassy (open weekdays from 7.30 am to 1.30 pm and Saturdays from 7.30 am to 12.30 pm) requires two photos and gives same-day service. As everywhere in Africa, prices vary from CFA 18,000 for a one-month single-entry visa (CFA 33,000 for multiple-entry) to CFA 53,000 for a three-month single-entry visa (CFA 60,000 for multiple-entry).

DOCUMENTS

You'll need a passport with a CAR visa and an International Health Certificate with proof of having received a yellow fever vaccination within the past 10 years. If there's been a cholera outbreak you'll also need evidence of having received a cholera shot.

You should carry your passport or at least a photocopy of it, as police occasionally ask to see travellers' papers. Arriving at Bangui by road from other points in the CAR, you will have to pass through immigration at Km 12, just north of the city. Officials there will give you a piece of paper and will demand it when you leave, so be sure to keep it well guarded.

CUSTOMS

There is no restriction on the importation of local currency but declare any large sums you may bring in because the export of foreign currency must not exceed the amount declared on arrival. Theoretically, you may not export more than CFA 25,000 but in practice customs officials don't seem to care and rarely ask. At the Mobaye ferry crossing, you'll be searched very thoroughly on the Zaïre side; customs officials there are looking more for illegal drugs than hidden Zaïre currency.

MONEY

US$1 = CFA 280
UK£1 = CFA 425

The unit of currency is the Central African CFA. The only banks that change money are the Banque Internationale pour l'Afrique Occidentale (BIAO) and the Union Bancaire en Afrique Centrale (UBAC). The BIAO gives unusually quick service but charges a CFA 2500 commission on each travellers' cheque regardless of the amount, while the latter is somewhat slower but charges only a 1% commission on all travellers' cheques. Even if the BIAO's exchange rate is better, that is unlikely to overcome the big difference in commissions. If you have cash, you can avoid these commissions but you'll find the exchange rates much lower than for travellers' cheques. Outside Bangui there are no banks that change money, except in Berbérati. If you're in Bouar and need money, try the pharmacy in the centre; they reportedly accept cash and possibly travellers' cheques.

Some travellers crossing the river to Zongo (Zaïre) buy their zaïres in Bangui, believing that the black-market rate in Bangui is better. While on occasion this may be true, the problem is that the rule against importing more than the equivalent of about US$5 in zaïres is strongly enforced. The border officials there usually conduct very thorough searches and zaïres are difficult to hide because they are so bulky. If they find any, they'll confiscate all of them. So I strongly recommend you wait until you arrive in Zaïre. There's a bank in Zongo for changing money but most travellers prefer the black market.

BUSINESS HOURS & HOLIDAYS

Business hours are weekdays from 7.30 am to noon and from 2.30 to 5 pm, and Saturdays from 7.30 am to noon. Government offices are open on weekdays from 6.30 am to 1.30 pm, and on Saturdays from 7 am to noon. Banking hours are weekdays from 7 to 11.30 am.

Public Holidays

The biggest holiday is National Day, which is celebrated with dancing, boat and horse races, theatre and wrestling. In the north, Muslims celebrate the end of Ramadan and Tabaski.

1 January (New Year's Day)
29 March (President Boganda's remembrance day)
Easter Monday
1 May
Ascension Thursday
Pentecost Monday
30 June (National Day of Prayer)
13 August (Independence)
15 August
1 September (Kolingba's government anniversary)
1 November
1 December (National Day)
25 December (Christmas Day)

POST & TELECOMMUNICATIONS

The mail service is reportedly very slow so, if possible, post your mail outside the country. The poste restante in Bangui is efficient and charges CFA 125 per letter and CFA 300 per parcel but keeps letters only for a very limited period.

You can now direct dial to Bangui (the telephone code for the CAR is 236). You can make telephones calls, and send faxes and telexes, from the post office or from one of the city's top two hotels, although the latter option is more expensive. For long-distance calls, you can also use the phone at the ever-popular Centre d'Accueil Touristique in Bangui. Rates there for three-minute calls are CFA 5125 to Europe, CFA 7885 to the US and CFA 6745 to Australia. If you want to talk for only three minutes, tell the operator to cut you off then, otherwise you risk going over the limit by several seconds and being charged for four minutes.

TIME

Time in the CAR is GMT plus one hour, so when it's noon in Bangui, it's 11 am in London and 6 am in New York.

PHOTOGRAPHY

Photo permits are apparently not required; in any case no-one gets them. Nevertheless, you should be very cautious of what you photograph, as the police are always suspicious. Don't take photos when they are around and never take photos of military installations, ferry crossings, bridges, radio stations, the port, government buildings, the presidential palace, etc. In Mobaye, for example, the police will confiscate your camera if they see you taking a photo, even if you've previously asked them for permission, and it'll cost you money, typically UK£30, to get it back! There are several shops in Bangui where you can buy film, but check the date on the roll of film before you purchase it.

HEALTH

A yellow fever vaccination is required, as is a cholera shot if you've visited an infected area within the previous six days. Chloroquine-resistant malaria is a major problem, so don't fail to take your anti-malaria tablets. Swimming is not safe anywhere because of bilharzia (schistosomiasis). AIDS is also a very serious problem. A large number of adults in Bangui, particularly prostitutes, are believed to be infected.

DANGERS & ANNOYANCES

Bangui is one of the most dangerous cities in Central Africa in terms of petty thievery and muggings; the worst area by far is around the 'Km 5' intersection, which is the most active area of the city. This spot is the transportation hub as well as the best area for cheap food and

lively nightclubs and is thus very crowded – perfect for thugs. At night, city lighting here and elsewhere is very poor and aggravates the problem, so definitely avoid walking around the city then, regardless of the area.

Some of the overland companies out of London have had so many clients, even in large groups, threatened and robbed at knifepoint or mugged in broad daylight in Bangui, particularly around Km 5, that they now refuse to stay overnight there. They stop briefly during the day for supplies, then move on. All of this is closely associated with one of the country's major social problems – alcoholism. If you start drinking with the locals, bear in mind that they'll be able to drink you under the table.

If you'll be travelling overland through the CAR, expect the worst from the police along the way, particularly if you're driving. Those who have travelled from Algeria to Kenya say the CAR police are the worst. At the Cameroun border, customs officials conduct interminable baggage and body searches if you don't offer CFA 1000, and they almost certainly will demand an 'inspection fee' if you have a car – another CFA 1000 minimum. Also, at virtually every stop along the way police will demand money (CFA 1000 will usually suffice) and if there is the slightest problem with your vehicle, such as a blinker not working, they will be sure to levy you a stiff fine, typically CFA 8000. No-one is exempt from this extortion, not even the local clergy.

During late 1991 and 1992, bandits caused disturbances in the north central area of the CAR; one foreigner was killed there, and travel warnings were issued as a result. Check with the police or your embassy to see whether these problems still exist when you get there.

Getting There & Away

AIR

From Europe the only direct flights are from Paris on Air France/UTA and Air Afrique; between them they have two or three flights a week depending on the season. Le Point Mulhouse, which used to have the cheapest fares from France, no longer exists. Regular fares are sky-high – about £1000 for a 30-day excursion ticket from London. London's bucket shop prices, on the other hand, are quite reasonable, the cheapest being Aeroflot's flight via Moscow for about £500.

From New York you can take Air Afrique all the way to Bangui, changing in Abidjan; or Air France/UTA, changing in Paris. The return economy fare is around US$2700 each way; the 45-day excursion fare is around US$2080 (US$100 more in the high season).

There are some direct air connections with other Central and West African countries but none to the other parts of Africa. Air France/UTA and Air Afrique provide twice-weekly connections with Brazzaville and N'Djamena, while Air Gabon has a Wednesday flight to/from Libreville. The only flight to/from West Africa is one on Air Afrique, with stops in Douala, Lagos, Lomé, Abidjan and Dakar.

LAND
Minibus & Bush Taxi
To/From Cameroun Coming from Cameroun, you may find a minibus or bush taxi (shared car taxi) direct to Bangui but more likely you'll have to take one to Bouar and switch there, in which case the trip will probably take two days, with a night in Bouar. A truck or minibus usually takes half a day (four hours) from the border to Bouar and one full day (12 to 14 hours) from Bouar to Bangui, often arriving late at night (two days if the road is blocked after rain).

Hitchhiking is also possible on this well-travelled route from Bangui to the Cameroun border, although truck drivers frequently ask as much as a minibus (CFA 4500 for Bangui to Bouar, CFA 1800 for Bouar to the border). One particularly friendly Camerounian man who plies this route every day in a Toyota pick-up is Agbor Solomon, who oversees the passage and repair of all the huge Union des Transporteurs Camerounais (UTC) trucks from Cameroun. What you pay him is up to you.

To/From Chad There's at least one minibus a day in either direction between Bangui and Sido, the border town on the route to Sarh. The trip, which costs CFA 6500 (although the driver may ask for more), takes about 15 hours during the dry season and more when the roads are very muddy, especially north of Kaga Bandoro. Between Sido and Sarh there's one minibus a day (CFA 2000) in either direction. There's no fixed schedule but they usually leave Sido in the morning and Sarh around noon.

If you travel to Chad via Bossangoa, the trip will take longer as there are no bush taxis direct to the border. There are minibuses every day in either direction between Bangui and Bossangoa. From there further northwest to Paoua is a bit more difficult, and from Paoua to the border is the most difficult of all, as very few vehicles cross the border there. From the border the main route is north-west to Moundou (Chad), not north to Doba as the Michelin map seems to indicate.

To/From Zaïre The principal river crossings to Zaïre are at Bangui, Mobaye and Bangassou. I don't recommend crossing at Zongo, as many travellers have had problems with bandits in Zongo and the road from there to Kisangani is the worst of the three routes. If you're looking for free rides, cross at Mobaye as the ferry there is usually working, making it the most popular crossing point for those with vehicles (CFA 25,000 per vehicle). The ferry is usually not working at Bangassou, but this is not critical if you don't have a vehicle since, as at all crossing points, you can always take a canoe. Canoe prices vary considerably, from as low as CFA 150 a person if you take a regular one full of passengers, to 20 times that amount or more if you charter one. There are several minibuses each day in either direction between Bangui and Bambari (CFA 4000) and between Bambari and Bangassou (CFA 3500). They depart very early in the morning and take about nine hours for each segment during the dry season and more during the rainy season. If you're headed for Mobaye, you can get off in Kongbo and hitch the remaining 66 km without too much difficulty. Alternatively, take the minibus connecting Bambari and Mobaye.

To/From Congo Almost nobody goes overland to the Congo. If you do, you should count on taking at least two weeks to get from Bangui to Ouesso, or more if you stop en route. The easiest part is taking one of the daily minibuses from Bangui to Berbérati. From there you have two choices. The most interesting would be to take another bus south to Nola and then take a series of motorised canoes downstream on the Sangha river, eventually arriving in Ouesso. One major advantage of this route is that it affords you the opportunity of stopping at Dzanga-Sangha Reserve, near Bayanga. The other alternative, which is more viable during the dry season, is to head west from Berbérati on the well-travelled route towards Batouri (in Cameroun), then south via Yokadouma to Ouesso, a 550-km trip on a road that has vehicles only very rarely. It is also extremely muddy for half the year (June to October), making passage next to impossible then.

To/From Sudan A major obstacle to travelling overland to Sudan is getting permission from Khartoum, which can take up to two months. There are two equally bad routes to Sudan: one east from Bangui to Juba via Bangassou (2107 km), and a slightly longer route north-east from Bangui to El Obeid via Birao in the north-eastern corner of the CAR. Both trips can easily take a month or more and are best done in the dry season, because from May the roads can become hellishly muddy, tripling travel times. There's extremely little traffic on either route. Travellers on the latter route have reported people having to wait up to two weeks in Birao for a truck and taking 22 days to travel from there to Sibut during the rainy season.

Car
To/From Cameroun The road from Yaoundé to Bangui via Bouar is fairly rough, particularly on the Cameroun side. The 596-km Bangui-Cameroun border stretch is asphalt

for only about a quarter of the way and the 610-km portion in Cameroun is paved for only 100 km. If you drive fast you can make the trip in two long days during the dry season; otherwise three days is more typical.

To/From Chad From N'Djamena, the driving time in a fast vehicle is two long days. The easiest route is through Cameroun and Bouar (the CAR) as 700 km of the 1634-km trip is asphalted, but with the improved roads in Chad the driving time on the shorter route through Sarh (1300 km) is probably less. Only about 350 km are paved but the road is in excellent condition all the way, except for the section between Kaga Bandoro and the border, which is virtually unmaintained and has lots of deep ruts.

To/From Zaïre Those travelling south to Zaïre should be prepared for the worst road conditions in Africa, with lots and lots of mud. Once in a great while, someone tries to take a vehicle to Brazzaville/Kinshasa. About the only way to do this is by riverboat, which operates from July to December (see the River section later in this chapter). The cost of the vehicle alone will be at least CFA 60,000, possibly much more.

If you're headed for eastern Zaïre, you can cross over at Bangui, Mobaye or Bangassou. The ferry at Bangassou is very unreliable and frequently not working, so virtually everybody now crosses over at Bangui or Mobaye. If you're travelling north to south, check for the latest information at the Centre d'Accueil Touristique in Bangui as ferry conditions can change very quickly. Mobaye is usually the better choice because the route from there to Kisangani is much better than that from Zongo to Kisangani and because you will avoid the many thieves in Zongo and the hassles of dealing with the notorious customs officials there. There's an excellent, well-known camp site 13 km north-west of Mobaye and the ferry there has a larger load capacity and is much more reliable than the one at Bangui. The ferry's fees are CFA 25,000 for vehicles, CFA 3500 for motorcycles and CFA 200 for passengers.

The road east from Bangui to Mobaye (454 km) and to Bangassou (747 km) is all dirt after Sibut. It's in excellent condition during the dry season, from November to May, but during the rainy season it can get quite muddy in sections, increasing driving times considerably. You should have no problem finding petrol in Sibut, Bambari or Bangassou. The latter two, not Bangui, are where you go through exit formalities. If the ferry in Bangassou is operative, the two 12-volt batteries will probably need a charge from your battery, and the operator will probably want up to five litres of diesel fuel plus a tip. If you cross the river by pirogue, apparently you can run up a bill of CFA 10,000 or so.

If you cross over at Bangui, you should be aware that Zongo is notorious for thieves. Customs services are now available on weekends. The *bac* (ferry) operates on weekdays from 7 am to 4 pm and on Saturdays from 7 am to noon, but canoes go at all hours. Rules and procedures change every so often, so make inquiries at the port captain's office near the river.

RIVER

Of the some 170,000 visitors to the CAR each year, about 80% come by boat. Almost all of these are Africans, not tourists, but it illustrates the importance of river transportation, most notably the two Congolese riverboats, *La Ville de Brazza* and *La Ville de Impfondo*.

To/From Congo

About every two weeks starting in early July, one of the two riverboats departs Bangui for the 1200-km journey to Brazzaville (Congo). The boat stops at Zinga, the border town of Mongoumba, and 13 Congolese villages; be sure your passport is stamped in Mongoumba and Bétou (Congo). The trip normally takes about 10 days going downriver to Brazzaville, and 14 days returning.

This trip provides an excellent opportunity to meet Africans. Various barges are attached to the riverboats, with people and cargo stuffed to the hilt on each, so it's like a floating village. People travelling deck class tend to form cliques, cooking together, joking and protecting one another from theft. As you approach a village, the locals will approach the floating barges in their canoes, offering all kinds of foodstuffs. If you have cooking gear, you can prepare your own food. Alternatively, you shouldn't have a problem finding someone on board who wants to earn some extra change by selling you some of the food they've prepared.

'Hors' class (super deluxe) on the riverboat consists of a cabin with one double bed, interior bathroom and air-con. The price including all meals is CFA 138,000 per person. First class, which has two single beds and no air-con, costs CFA 110,000 per person including meals. Tourist class consists of four beds to a room and exterior shared bath; the price per person without meals is CFA 26,600. The two remaining classes are intermediare (CFA 12,400) which entitles you to a seat, and deck class (CFA 9900), which is by far the most popular way to travel.

The first riverboat of the year from Brazzaville usually arrives in Bangui in early July and the last one usually arrives in mid-December. They stay for a day or two, then return to Brazzaville. The estimated date of departure isn't fixed until about two weeks in advance, when L'Agence Transcongolaise des Communications (ATC) in Brazzaville notifies its office in Bangui that the boat has left.

Instead of taking the riverboat, it's possible to catch a barge headed for Impfondo (Congo) and on to Brazzaville. The port in Bangui is extremely confusing and it's easy to miss boats, but Zinga (100 km south of Bangui) is smaller and all boats have to stop there for customs. So meeting boats and people is much easier in Zinga, which you can easily reach by minibus. Between February and May you'll find only pirogues on the river as the river is very low then, but during the rest of the year there are lots of petroleum barges.

One group of four travellers reported paying only CFA 2500 a person for a four-day trip on a barge from Zinga to Impfondo. The trip was quiet and peaceful – quite unlike the noisy, crowded riverboat. They reported basking in the sun, watching birds and hippos, and swimming in the river every evening when the barge stopped. You must take all of your sleeping gear and food although you can sometimes purchase fish.

Getting Around

AIR

The only city with regular air links to Bangui is Berbérati; flights to/from Bangui are on Tuesdays and Saturdays. CentreAvia (☎ 611193) and TAC (☎ 612020), located at the aeroclub next to the airport in Bangui, each has a five-passenger plane for charter. Prices are high – for example, CFA 350,000 to charter the entire plane for a one-way flight (or same-day round-trip flight) from Bangui to St Floris Park. If they take you out one day and bring you back another, the price is double.

BUS & TRUCK

Road conditions are poor throughout the country. The only sealed roads lead from Bangui: 107 km south-west to M'Baïki, 157 km north-west to Bossembélé and 188 km north-east to Sibut. The remaining dirt roads to major towns and the Cameroun and Chad borders (north of Kaga Bandoro and Bossangoa excepted) are mostly in good condition during the dry season. But when the rains begin in May, it's a different story – the dirt roads gradually become, at best, very muddy and slippery and, at worst, a mess. Portions of the Bangui to Cameroun border road can be closed for many hours, sometimes days, during and after heavy rainstorms. This is done so that the numerous large trucks to/from Cameroun don't tear up the road, but for travellers it can mean spending the day and/or night crowded with other passengers in a truck or van, waiting for the road block to be lifted.

Minibus

Private 24-seater minibuses connect Bangui with all the major towns. They aren't uncomfortable per se but overcrowding makes them that way. During the dry season, on long trips on major roads they often make good time, averaging up to 70 km/h, but on shorter trips, such as Bangui to Bossembélé, they may average no more than 30 km an hour, stopping every few km to pick up passengers and let others off. During the rainy season, they are even slower, particularly on difficult stretches. On long trips, such as Bangui to Bouar, it is normal for the buses to leave very early, usually around 6 am.

Truck

Trucks are called *occasions* in the CAR and are a popular way to travel, as the number of minibuses is inadequate to handle all the passenger traffic. Their prices, however, are often no lower.

CANOE

For fun, you could go upriver from Bangui, buy a pirogue and then paddle down to Bangui. The trip would take about 12 days from Bangassou, for example, and proportionally less from Mobaye. You would have to take all of your food and be prepared to sleep on sandbanks along the way. You are sure to see lots of hippos and the occasional crocodile along the way. Or you could buy a pirogue in Bangui and paddle down to Zinga, a three to seven-day trip (see Zinga, in the Around Bangui section, for a description of that trip). One Peace Corps volunteer took a pirogue from Bangui all the way down to where the Oubangui meets the Zaïre River and then caught the steamer to Kisangani. You can buy the pirogue and paddle yourself, or rent the pirogue and have the owner do the paddling.

Bangui

Bangui is in the heart of the tropics, on the Oubangui River and bordering Zaïre. The rainfall here is much heavier and the vegeta-

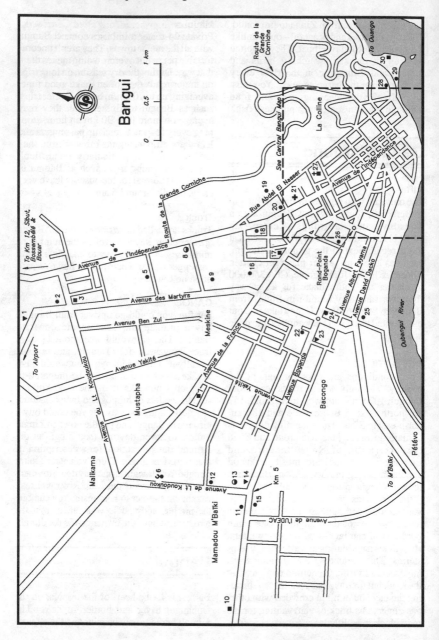

Bangui

■ PLACES TO STAY

3   Maison de Jeunesse du Centre
    Protestant
7   Iroko Hôtel
10 Centre d'Accueil Touristique
17 National Hôtel
30 Sofitel Bangui

▼ PLACES TO EAT

1   Restaurant Mirandela
14 Restaurant de l'Amitié
15 Breakfast Stands
23 Restaurant au Diapason Nganda à la
    Bantu

    OTHER

2   Nigerian Embassy
4   Assemblé Nationale
5   Commissariat Central
6   Mosque
8   Gare Routière ONAF
9   University
11 Marché Mamadou M'Baïki
12 Bar ABC Nightclub
13 Gare Routière Km 5
14 Le Punch Coco Nightclub
16 Stadium
18 Sudan Embassy
19 Zaïre Embassy
20 Institut Pasteur
21 Hospital
22 Worldwide Fund for Nature Office
24 Bar l'Oasis
25 Mission St-Charles
26 French Cultural Centre
27 Cathedral
28 French Embassy
29 Ferry for Zongo, Commissariat du
    Port & Pirogues

tion much thicker than in the north. The city was founded by the French in 1889, and named after the rapids nearby. Travellers rarely have many good things to say about Bangui. However, with the river on one side, hills covered with lush vegetation on the other, and broad avenues shaded by large mango and flowering *flamboyant* trees, the city has its charm, particularly the administrative district near the river. From the Sofitel

Bangui or anywhere along Blvd Général de Gaulle you are a stone's throw from the river, and for CFA 1000 or so you can hire a canoe to take you on a short trip (see Activities).

As you move away from the river you'll begin approaching the African quarter, the heart of which is the unmarked Km 5 intersection (known as 'K-Cinq'), which is five km from the centre and has the largest market, lots of bars, various dancing places and public transport headed in all directions. This is the city's liveliest area, a potentially fun place to roam around, but it is also the most dangerous. Muggers, sometimes drunk, are on the streets here day and night, always ready to give you – and the city's reputation – a black eye.

Orientation
The heart of town is the Place de la République, which has a huge white triumphal arch, an absurd monument to Bokassa's coronation and empire. Two blocks south-east near the port is the Marché Central (Central Market), while two blocks north-east of the plaza is the presidential palace. Immigration, police, banks and the post office are all nearby.

Three major avenues start at the plaza, extending northward and westward. The most northerly is Ave de l'Indépendance, which extends out past the Centre Artisanal and the new *assemblé nationale* (national assembly) in the direction of the golf club at Km 11 and the immigration checkpoint intersection at Km 12 ('K-Douze'). (The police there are likely to ask for money and gifts for stamping your passport; don't oblige.) There the road splits, one fork heading north-east to Sibut and the other heading north-west to Bossembélé. Next is Ave Boganda, which is the city's major commercial street, particularly between the triumphal arch and Rond-Point Boganda (Boganda's statue overlooks it), extending westward out to Km 5 (or Pk 5) at the intersection with the wide Ave du Lt Koudoukou and, 1½ km beyond, the ever-popular camping ground, the Centre d'Accueil Touristique. The last major street originating at the Place de la République is Ave David Dacko, which passes Hôtel

Minerva and the US Embassy, eventually becoming the main road south-west to M'Baïki.

Information

Money The BIAO (☎ 611768), which faces the Place de la République, changes money and travellers' cheques very fast but commissions are lower at the UBAC (☎ 612990), which is nearby in the direction of the post office.

Foreign Embassies Some of the major embassies include:

Cameroun
 Ave de la France, near the museum (☎ 611687)
Chad
 Ave Col Conus, near Place de la République (☎ 614677)
Congo
 Ave Boganda, facing Restaurant Baalbeck (☎ 611877)
France
 Blvd du Général de Gaulle, near the Sofitel Bangui (☎ 613000)
Germany
 BP 901 (☎ 610746)
Nigeria
 Ave des Martyrs, near the Ave Koudoukou intersection (☎ 610744)
Sudan
 Ave de l'Indépendance, one km beyond the cathedral on your left
USA
 Ave David Dacko (☎ 610200; fax 614494; telex 5287)
Zaïre
 Rue Abdel El Nasser, behind Institut Pasteur (☎ 613344)

There is also an Egyptian embassy in Bangui, as well as honorary consulates for: Belgium (c/o Mocaf on Ave du 1er Janvier, ☎ 614041), the Netherlands (c/o Ponteco on Ave du 1er Janvier, ☎ 614822) and the UK (c/o Diamond Distributors on Ave Boganda).

Travel & Safari Agencies Manovo Safaris (☎ 616677, 613732), a tiny, inconspicuous place on Ave Boganda, directly behind Restaurant New Montana (in the same building), is French-run and handles all-inclusive tours

to St Floris park. Manovo has a lodge in the park, the Campement de Gounda, where all its clients stay; the all-inclusive daily price per person varies between CFA 26,000 and CFA 43,000, depending on the type of accommodation and the number of people. The biggest cost is getting there. Manovo Safaris can make arrangements with TAC or CentreAvia for chartering a plane. It's open from 10 am to noon and from 4 to 6 pm except on Saturday afternoons and Sundays, when it's closed. For more information, see the St Floris and Bamingui-Bangoran Parks section later in this chapter.

For trips to Dzanga-Ndoki Park, see Jean-Jacques, the owner of the Pharmacie du Port (☎ 611295), on the left at the entrance to the port. His wife Martine, under the name Aouk-Sangha Safaris, runs hunting trips to the adjoining buffer reserve between May and July for very wealthy foreigners (mostly Americans) who come here and pay CFA 7,000,000 (!) to hunt and kill a bongo, the prize game of the area. In the off-season (August to April) Martine may start much less expensive tourist trips with Pygmy guides to the area for groups of five to 10 people. In any case, she could be extremely useful in helping you arrange a trip to the area.

The only agency known to conduct trips (large groups only) to the Pygmy areas (mostly south of M'Baïki) is the government tour operator, Ocatour (☎ 614566), which is in the heart of town a block west of Ave Boganda, near the well-known Sunset (formerly Blow Up) nightclub.

Bookshops The best bookshop, which isn't saying much, is Librairie Centrale (sign says 'Librairie Larousse') on Ave Boganda, 2½ blocks west of the Place de la République, before the Dias Frères supermarket on the other side of the road. Another is Librairie Avenir on the same street closer to the Place de la République. You'll find better postcards, and books on the CAR, *Time*, *Newsweek* and international newspapers and magazines in French, at the small bookshops at the Novotel and Sofitel hotels. The latter is better and is open Monday to Saturday from 8.30 am to 2 pm and from 3 to 9 pm, and on Sundays from 9 am to 12.30 pm.

On weekdays from 8 am to 1 pm, the air-con Martin Luther King library next to the US Embassy is a good place to cool off, read US newspapers and magazines, and see the latest ABC news, which is on video and available free on request at any time. And on Fridays at 4 pm you can catch a free US movie.

Supermarkets Supermarket prices are often 50% higher than in Cameroun. Of the major modern supermarkets, the cheapest is Eco-Cash, which is very near the central market. The selection, however, is limited mostly to canned and dry goods. Bamag (formerly Score), on Ave Boganda at Rond-Point Boganda, is the largest supermarket with the widest selection and highest prices (CFA 395 for a litre of Supermont mineral water from Cameroun). There's a good bakery in the two-storey mall next door. Another good, large, but not so spotless, supermarket on the same street is Dias Frères, near Librairie Centrale. All three supermarkets close around 6.30 pm.

Pharmacies Two of the best-stocked pharmacies are the excellent French-run Pharmacie du Port, which is two blocks east of Place de la République at the entrance to the port, and Pharmacie Centrale, across from the Novotel Bangui.

Useful Organisations The Peace Corps (☎ 611956, 615972), whose volunteers are always a good source of information about a wide range of topics, is in the centre of town on Ave de la France, half a block beyond the museum.

For information on parks in the north-east, particularly St Floris Park and Bamingui-Bangoran Park, contact the European Development Fund (☎ 610113, 613053) which is two blocks further out on Ave de la France at the corner of Rue d'Uzès.

Similarly, for information on Dzanga-Ndoki National Park and surrounding

Dzanga-Sangha Reserve, see the friendly people at the Worldwide Fund for Nature office (☎ 614299). To get there from the centre of town, head out along Ave Boganda to the second rond-point, then continue one block (100 metres) further past an eight-storey apartment building and take a right down a small dirt road. It's the second house on your left and poorly marked.

Musée de Boganda

The Musée de Boganda (Boganda Museum) is definitely worth a visit. The great variety of musical instruments is particularly interesting, as is the display of Pygmy utensils. There are some ancient artefacts as well, including old coins. Paradoxically, even though the country is noted for its rainforests, wood carvings are fairly rare. It's in an old two-storey building that was once the presidential palace, on Ave de la France (one of the diagonal side-streets off Ave Boganda) at the intersection with Rue de l'Industrie. The entrance fee is CFA 300 and it's open every day, except Sundays, from 7.30 am to 1.30 pm and from 3 to 5.30 pm.

Bokassa's Residence

Bokassa's former palace is nine km from the centre on the south-western outskirts of town in Kolongo, on the route to M'Baïki. It was plundered and stripped of all items of value after he departed but it's still an interesting place to see. For a few hundred CFA, a guide will happily show you the lion cages and other gruesome reminders of his reign.

Canoeing

A canoe trip on the Oubangui River can be interesting. The best area to find them is on either side of the Commissariat du Port on Blvd Général de Gaulle. The asking price for an hour's trip is CFA 2000 but you should be able to get one for half that. A popular destination is the Ile des Serpents; don't expect to see any hippos en route, because there aren't any near Bangui.

Other Activities

There are small pools at the top two hotels,

but nonguests can use them only on a monthly membership basis, which is expensive (CFA 12,000 at the Sofitel and CFA 15,000 at the Novotel). For tennis, try your luck at the local tennis club about four blocks from the Place de la République. There's also a nine-hole golf course with 'greens' of hard sand at the Golf Club du Bangui on the northern outskirts of Bangui, one km before the Km 12 junction on your left.

Places to Stay – bottom end

The long-standing *Centre d'Accueil Touristique* (☎ 611772) continues to be the place where virtually all overland travellers stay. It's relatively cheap and clean, has a nice ambience and is only 1½ km beyond the lively Km 5 intersection, on the extension of Ave Boganda. You can catch a minibus from Km 12 to Km 5 for CFA 75 and walk from there. A taxi from the camp site to the centre of town costs CFA 1000, so either stuff lots of people inside or walk to Km 5 and take a shared cab (CFA 100 per person).

Camping costs CFA 650 a person plus CFA 100 per tent; vehicles are free. Many campers have been robbed here so take precautions. The new, high, metal fence and

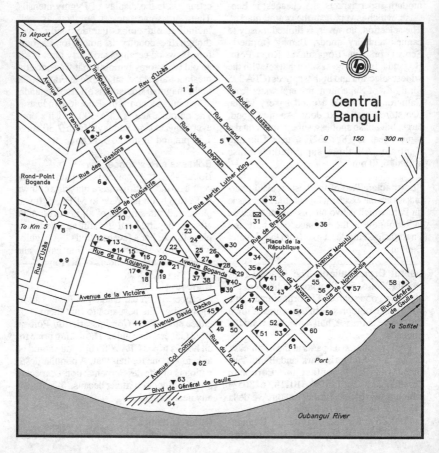

■ PLACES TO STAY

39 Hôtel Minerva
49 Novotel Bangui

▼ PLACES TO EAT

5   Restaurant le Perroquet
8   Restaurant le Bistro
12 Pizzeria les 4 Saisons
13 Boulangérie Indépendance
16 Restaurant Mac Donald
22 Restaurant Saigon
25 Restaurant Baalbeck
28 Pâtisserie la Marquise
38 Salon de Thé de la Paix
40 Restaurant New Montana
41 Restaurant Keur Teranga
49 Pâtisserie Socotra
51 Restaurant le Baachus
57 Restaurant le Petit Pimente
63 Restaurant Ewaton
64 Cheap Restaurants

OTHER

1   Cathedral
2   European Development Fund & UN
    Office
3   Mission Evangélique
4   Centre Artisanal
6   Peace Corps
7   Bamag Supermarket & Petroca
    Station
9   Public Gardens
10 Musée de Boganda
11 Cameroun Embassy
14 Ocatour
15 Sunset Nightclub
17 Cinéma Club

18 Apic Photo Service
19 Prestige Nightclub
20 Tsiros Auto Rental
21 Dias Frères Supermarket
22 Librairie Centrale
23 Le Sango Nightclub
24 Renault Dealer/Garage
25 Air France/UTA
26 Super Continental Supermarché
27 Grocery Store
29 BCAD Bank
30 Camico
31 Post Office
32 BEAC Bank
33 UNICEF Office
34 UBAC Bank
35 Air Gabon Office
36 Presidential Palace
37 Congo Embassy
40 Manovo Safaris
42 BIAO Bank
43 Air Afrique Office
44 US Embassy & Martin Luther King
    Library
45 Pharmacie Centrale
46 Chad Embassy
47 Cinéma Oubangui & Bar le Palace
48 SCKN Department Store
50 Radio Station
52 CFAO General Store
53 Petrol Station
54 Marché Central & Eco-Cash
    Supermarket
55 Police
56 Immigration Office
58 Mango Beach Bar
59 Perroni Art Shop
60 Pharmacie du Port
61 Taxi Stand for Ouango & ATC
62 Radio Station

guard dog are helping to correct this problem. There are also about 10 rooms for rent. The cheapest cost CFA 2100/2700 for singles/doubles (dirty mattresses with clean sheets, a tiny window and grubby toilets and showers). If you use one of these rooms, take special precautions because the locks on the doors are of poor quality, and numerous travellers have reported being ripped off. For CFA 3600, you can get a large, clean room with a new, secure lock, big bed, fan, mosquito net plus a clean private bath with a

good shower, flush toilet, basin and clothesline.

The Centre provides same-day laundry service (CFA 100 for all items except jeans) and international telephone connections (CFA 5125 for three minutes to the UK).

If you come across James Bewi, a woodcarving seller, he will undoubtedly offer his services to help you change money on weekends, get visas, etc. Take him up as he is reliable and used quite frequently by overland trucks.

If the Centre is full, try the *Maison de Jeunesse du Centre Protestant*, which is near the eastern end of Ave du Lt Koudoukou, just east of Ave des Martyrs. It has cheap, decent dormitory-style accommodation and is convenient for catching shared taxis in town and minibuses headed out of Bangui. Forget the *Mission Catholique de Nôtre Dame* in the centre of town next to the cathedral – it no longer accepts travellers.

Places to Stay – middle

The city has several decent mid-range hotels which are all overpriced. The 23-room, colonial-era *Hôtel Minerva* (☎ 610233, telex 5240) is fairly well maintained and charges CFA 15,000/18,000 for its air-con singles/doubles. There's no restaurant but it has a bar that's popular with French expatriates. It's in the heart of town, a block off Place de la République. The *National Hôtel* (☎ 612971) out on Ave de la France, two km from the heart of town, has been renovated and is much improved. Its best feature is the shaded terrace in front, which is a popular place with Africans for drinks. However, at CFA 18,115/20,645 for air-con singles/doubles, it's hard to recommend. The *Iroko Hôtel* further out on Ave de la France, before Ave du Lt Koudoukou, is cheaper and worth checking if price is your only concern. None of these places accept credit cards.

Places to Stay – top end

The *Sofitel Bangui* (☎ 613038/48; fax 611-239; telex 5340) is the nicest hotel because of its setting on the banks of the Oubangui River, 1½ km from the centre with all 60 rooms facing the river, but it's somewhat run-down and way overpriced at CFA 39,000 a room. The amenities include a tiny pool, beauty salon, bookshop and casino. The *Novotel Bangui* (☎ 610279; fax 614790; telex 5297) is more centrally located, with good restaurants and commercial establishments nearby, and it's also a better buy at CFA 27,500/29,000 for singles/doubles. The pool, however, isn't very clean and the bookshop is tiny. Both places accept American Express and Visa cards.

Places to Eat

Cheap Eats The best area for street food and African stalls is around the Km 5 intersection. In the mornings and evenings, you'll find lots of stalls where coffee with sweetened milk, delicious French bread and lots of butter is served for CFA 150 or so.

For a restaurant, try *Restaurant de l'Amitié* just east of Km 5. It serves great chicken and beef steak; a full meal costs under CFA 1000. Another place nearby is *Africa No 1*, which has music and serves cheap sauces, baked bananas, spaghetti, salad and rice with meat.

I highly recommend a strip of cheap restaurants in the town centre, just south-west of the port. From the Place de la République, head south-west on Ave Col Conus past the Novotel Bangui to the end. Starting there you'll find a 100-metre strip along the river towards the port with about 35 very rustic stalls, each selling primarily grilled capitaine fish but also other dishes such as beef brochettes. The fish with sauce dishes tend to be far better than the grilled fish dishes unless the latter are hot off the grill (most aren't). One of the better stalls is *Restaurant Ewaton*. The fish with sauce is delicious (hot sauce to the side) but you can also get liver with sauce. A plate (CFA 500) is plenty for two people, so if you're alone ask for a half plate. Big beers are the standard CFA 250 a bottle. Peak time is noon but you can get food here until about 4 pm at the latest.

At the Centre d'Accueil Touristique's *Restaurant Kirite* you can relax and eat under the stars or under a huge, open-air paillote. The service is painfully slow, even for the simplest dishes, so order an hour or two in advance of when you want to eat, even for a sandwich. Prices are reasonable – CFA 275 for a large Mocaf beer, CFA 350 for a large salad and CFA 500 for steak, beef brochettes or omelette. Boa is also sometimes on the menu but costs much more. Otherwise, take a 20-minute walk to the cheap food stalls at Km 5. **Warning:** at night this is very risky, even with a group of people.

A decent but cheap restaurant is the very popular, French-run *Restaurant le Bistro*, facing Rond-Point Boganda. Inexpensive by

Bangui standards, it is one of the town's most popular restaurants, and most interesting at lunchtime because the outdoor patio is adjacent to a menagerie of turkeys, crocodiles and monkeys. The menu ranges from prodigious hamburgers and French fries to frog legs and crocodile tails. It's closed on Mondays.

Two blocks down Ave Boganda you'll come to the modern *Restaurant Mac Donald* (the sign says 'American Hamburger'), Bangui's answer to the real McDonald's. A hamburger, fries and a Coke will cost you about CFA 2000.

For snacks including coffee, pastries, sandwiches and ice cream, you have several pastry shops to choose from, none particularly cheap for what you get. The most popular for years has been the *Salon de Thé de la Paix* further down Ave Boganda near the centre; it's also a meeting place and its prices are typical – CFA 400 for café au lait and CFA 250 to CFA 350 for most pastries. Two newer ones are the *Pâtisserie la Marquise* across the street and a block down and, better, *Pâtisserie Socotra* next to the Novotel Bangui.

For bread, try the *Boulangérie Indépendance* on Ave Boganda or, better and only slightly more expensive, the bakery in the small shopping centre next to Bamag supermarket. You can also get great milkshakes on the ground floor of the shopping centre, just inside the main doors and to the left.

African The famous Maman Mado African bush-meat restaurant at the Centre Artisanal is closed but there are still places where you can get good African food. One of the best is *Restaurant Keur Teranga*, a relaxing, unpretentious restaurant 30 metres north-east of the Place de la République. It offers Senegalese specialities such as poulet yassa and mafé. A meal here will cost you at least CFA 3000 to CFA 4000 but it's worth it if you can afford it.

For less expensive Central African food, you can't beat the riverside stalls mentioned earlier in the Cheap Eats section. For a restaurant, one possibility is *Restaurant le Petit Piment*, which is several blocks east in the direction of the Sofitel Bangui. Another one, recommended by taxi drivers and worth trying is the inexpensive *Restaurant au Diapason Nganda à la Bantu*, which is on Ave Boganda, halfway between the centre and Km 5 on your left and open only for lunch. Some Central African specialities to look for are crocodile, *gazelle* (antelope), *singe* (monkey), *phacochère* (wart hog) and fried *gozo* (manioc).

For a restaurant with great, breezy, African ambience, head for the friendly, ever-popular *Restaurant Mirandela* (☎ 614045) out on Ave des Martyrs, between the Nigerian Embassy and the airport. Grilled food is the only offering, and includes beef brochettes (CFA 600), French fries (CFA 700), chicken (CFA 975) and capitaine brochettes (CFA 1500). It's open every day from 11 am to 11 pm.

Pizza One of the more popular, informal restaurants in Bangui is the French-run *Pizzeria les 4 Saisons*, which is in the town centre on Rue de l'Industrie, a block south of Ave Boganda. The speciality is pizza but there are other selections including sandwiches and good desserts. Like the Mirandela, dining is open air under thatched-roof paillotes, and prices are in the CFA 3000 to CFA 4000 range.

Lebanese By Bangui standards, the *Restaurant Baalbek* on Ave Boganda, two blocks up from the Place de la République, is moderately priced. Lebanese cuisine is the speciality and multi-plate mezzas (Lebanese smorgasbords) are among the offerings. The service is quick and the portions are generous. Lebanese food is also the speciality at *Restaurant le Perroquet* on Rue Joseph Degrain, between the presidential palace and the cathedral. Open for dinner only, it has good brochettes and wine by the carafe, but the service can be a little on the slow side.

Vietnamese The popular *Restaurant Saigon* (☎ 611737) on Ave Boganda, near Restaurant Baalbek, has a family-style setting and offers good Vietnamese food, particularly the Vietnamese version of Mongolian hotpot.

French Of the two major French restaurants, both of which are expensive, the best value for money is *Restaurant New Montana*, which is also on Ave Boganda. It has a pleasant bistro atmosphere, the food is good (particularly the homemade terrines and fish dishes), and Freddie, the owner, is very friendly. If price is of no concern, you may prefer *Restaurant le Bacchus*, around the corner from the Novotel Bangui. The mousses and terrines are homemade, and there's a special of the day. It is open only for dinner and is closed on Sundays.

Entertainment

Bars For drinks, the Sofitel Bangui has an unbeatable location on the bank of the river, but is ridiculously overpriced at CFA 600 for a Coke and CFA 700 for a small beer. That's why expatriates prefer bars such as the publike one at Hôtel Minerva. Even this bar, however, is nothing special. For a cheap beer in the town centre, try: *Bar le Palace*, a derelict African hangout facing the Place de la République; *Mango Beach Bar*, facing the Commissariat du Port; or, far better, the long row of riverside African stalls mentioned in the earlier Cheap Eats section.

The liveliest bars are all in the African quarter, especially around Km 5. None are suitable for women; even for men in groups they are risky places, as many of the local men become belligerent when drunk. The local brews, Mocaf and Castel (considered superior), cost only CFA 250 for a one-litre bottle (eg a Castelgrande) at these places – a real bargain by CAR standards. There is also a local wine, Castelvin, which is incredibly bad. If you ask around, you might even find some *ngbako*, a very potent home-distilled vodka made from manioc.

Because of the security problem around Km 5, a better area for cheap drinks is Meskine, which occupies several blocks just behind the university. It consists of cheap dancing bars and grilled meat stands where an enjoyable evening can be spent talking with students at minimal cost – and safely. There is a Meskine taxi route that originates from the Place de la République.

Nightclubs The best places in Bangui for dancing are the nightclubs around Km 5; they play African music and are terrific, the only problem being that the area is definitely not safe at night. The safest way to get to them is to take a taxi right to the door of the nightclub; that way the risk is minimal. And when coming out, you'll usually find one there waiting.

Two nightclubs in particular are outstanding. One is le *Punch Coco Nightclub*, 100 metres south-east of Km 5 on Ave Boganda. It's very popular for dancing and rarely has a cover charge, although it regularly has live music. Drinks are cheap (about CFA 300 a bottle) and the dance floor is invariably crowded, particularly on Thursdays and Sundays, the big nights when there is often live music.

The other is *Bar ABC*, owned by Musiki, still the country's most popular singer. He usually plays on Thursday, Saturday and Sunday nights. There's a cover charge (CFA 1000) only on the nights when he plays and the drinks here are cheap. It's half a km north of Km 5 on Ave du Lt Koudoukou. Unlike the fancy downtown discos which start late (around 11 pm), the dancing at these two places starts as early as 8 pm and gets livelier later in the evening.

The modern discos are all in the centre of town and appeal mainly to expatriates and French soldiers. Drinks are expensive (around CFA 2000), and on weekends there may be a cover charge. The top clubs are close to one another, on poorly lit streets which are nevertheless safer than those in the Km 5 area. *Le Sango Nightclub*, at the corner of Ave de l'Indépendance and Ave Martin Luther King, has a good sound system and dim lights, and is one of the top nightclubs, with mostly European and US hits but also some African music. Two of the city's other top discos are only three blocks away to the south, a block beyond Ave Boganda. One is *Prestige Nightclub* (formerly Le Peuch del

Sol) on Martin Luther King; the other is *Sunset Nightclub* (formerly Blow Up), less than 100 metres away, facing Cinéma Club. All three places are similar but the latter has a more open feel. Afterwards, you could try the casino at the Sofitel Bangui, which opens every night at 10 pm.

Cinemas The best movie theatre by far is Cinéma Club, in the centre of town on Rue de la Kouanga, a block behind (west of) Restaurant Mac Donald on Ave Boganda. Cinéma Oubangui, facing the Place de la République, has karate films and others of similar quality at 6 and 9 pm.

Things to Buy
Market Goods Both of the city's main markets are primarily for food and cheap clothing. The Marché Central, in the centre of town, is very active in the morning and closed in the afternoon, while Marché Mamadou M'Baïki, just west of Km 5, is even bigger and has lower prices.

Artisan Goods For souvenir-quality African art, head for the Centre Artisanal on Ave de l'Indépendance, one km from the Place de la République and near the Mission Catholique. Among the numerous stalls here, you'll find butterfly-wing art, ebony, leather goods, batiks, appliqué, porcupine-quill bracelets, African clothing, malachite, grass dolls, woodcarvings and masks. It's open every day until 6 pm.

Many of the goods come from neighbouring countries, but the designs made with butterfly wings, and the small rugs with a yellow background and angular patterns, are from the CAR.

The only store specialising in high-quality African art is Perroni Art Shop, which has everything from butterfly-wing art to carved tables, all way overpriced. From the Place de la République, it's two blocks towards the port and one block to your left.

Music Finding records is difficult, and the quality of locally made cassettes is low. The best thing is to buy good quality empty cas-

settes, which are available from the Novotel Bangui's tiny bookshop, and look for one of the small shops that will record your choice of their records. Musiki is still the leading star and his nightclub, Bar ABC, is the best place during the day to buy cassettes of African music. The groups Canon Star, Super Commando Jazz and Makembé are also popular.

Getting There & Away
Air Air Afrique (☎ 614700, 614660) is the major international airline carrier serving Bangui, with north-south connections to Paris, N'Djamena and Brazzaville, and east-west connections to Douala and various West African coastal cities. It's in the centre of town on Ave Mobutu, a block from the Marché Central. Air France/UTA also has flights to/from Paris; its office is on Ave Boganda. Air Gabon (☎ 612710), just off Place de la République, has flights to/from Libreville on Wednesdays. It's also reportedly possible to fly to Berbérati on Tuesdays and Saturdays.

Minibus & Bush Taxi A major oddity of the city's public transport system is that the modern two-storey Gare Routière ONAF on Ave de l'Indépendance just beyond the university is not the real gare routière – Km 5 is. The major departure area for minibuses headed in all directions is along Ave du Lt Koudoukou, just north of Km 5. Ask anyone in that area and they'll point you in the right direction. Those for most towns start filling up around 6 am, then cruise up and down Koudoukou and sometimes over to the gare routière, looking for passengers, then back to Km 5. This process can easily take two hours. Once full, they head for the gare routière, where they stop briefly to pay a fee for a *laissez-passer* and then head off. If you go to the gare routière, even at peak hour (6 to 8 am), you'll see what a joke it is – it will be virtually empty, while most of the other vehicles, which pass through only briefly, are already full.

By 8 am most vehicles will have departed from Km 5, but up until 9 am you may still have a slim chance if you take a taxi to the immigration post at Km 12, where vehicles often have to wait 30 minutes or more while passengers complete formalities; drivers are often willing to squeeze one final passenger on board before departing. Km 12 is also the best place by far for hitching rides; with lots of luck Bangui to Bouar can be done in one day (but I wouldn't wager on it). Hitching rides in other directions usually takes longer, as the traffic is extremely light.

Some typical minibus fares are CFA 1200 to M'Baïki, CFA 1500 to Sibut, CFA 1800 to Bossembélé, CFA 4000 to Bambari, CFA 4500 to Bouar, CFA 6000 to Berbérati and CFA 7500 to Bangassou – all slightly less than the official prices posted at the gare routière.

Riverboat to Congo Between approximately mid-July and late December there is one Congolese riverboat (either *La Ville de Brazza* or *La Ville de Impfondo*) about every two weeks to Brazzaville, stopping at Zinga and some 13 Congolese villages en route. Prices per person to Brazzaville are: deck class (CFA 9900), intermediare (CFA 12,400), tourist class (CFA 26,600), 1st class (CFA 110,000 with meals) and hors class (CFA 138,000 with meals). The trip takes about 10 days downriver to Brazzaville and 14 days return. The exact departure date is not estimated until about two weeks before departure, when the boat sets off from Brazzaville. ATC at the port has information. It's open on weekdays from 6.30 am to 1.30 pm and on Saturdays from 7 am to noon.

Instead of taking a journey all the way to Brazzaville, you could take a boat south just to Zinga (a one-day, 100-km trip), and then catch a minibus back to Bangui. This trip can be done year-round as there are many smaller boats that ply fairly regularly between the two cities.

Ferry to Zongo The ferry to Zongo costs CFA 150 a person and operates every day between 7 am and 4 pm. It leaves from near the Commissariat du Port (same hours) on Blvd Général de Gaulle, where you must pass through customs. You can also take a pirogue from here; the cost is about CFA 1000 for the canoe.

Getting Around
To/From the Airport The airport departure tax is CFA 2000 for destinations in West and Central Africa, and CFA 3500 for destinations elsewhere. Bangui airport has a restaurant, a bar and a post office. A taxi from the town centre to the airport (eight km) costs CFA 1000 (CFA 1600 after 9 pm), but only the most persistent will get one for less than CFA 2000 at the airport. With luck, you may find a much cheaper shared taxi into town. Otherwise, walk the three km to Ave du Lt Koudoukou and hail a shared taxi or minibus there.

Minibus & Taxi Taxis do not have meters and are plentiful all over town until around 8 pm. Shared taxis have fixed routes and charge CFA 100 for most trips, including from the town centre to Km 5. However, if you ask to be dropped off two km further out at the Centre d'Accueil Touristique you'll be charged the rate for a *course* (a taxi to yourself), which is CFA 1000 to the Centre but CFA 800 to most other destinations (CFA 600 from the centre to the university). After 9 pm the rates go up (eg CFA 1500 for a course) and taxis become virtually impossible to find except at the Sofitel Bangui and the Novotel Bangui, outside major restaurants and nightclubs and at Km 5. To hire a taxi by the hour or the day, you should pay about CFA 2500 and CFA 20,000, respectively, if you bargain very hard.

Minibuses are even cheaper – CFA 75 for most rides (eg Km 5 to Km 12).

Car Tsiros Auto Rental (☎ 614446), in the centre of town just past Dias Frères supermarket on Ave Boganda and around the corner, is the city's major car rental agency and quite reliable. The cheapest car, such as a Renault 12, costs CFA 21,775 per day plus CFA 235 per km (50 km free). You can drive it yourself but only in town. A 4WD vehicle for out-of-town driving costs CFA 65,000 per day plus CFA 150 per km (100 km free). There are no hidden charges as these prices include all taxes, insurance and, for out-of-town trips, a driver. Christelle Location (☎ 613536) is another that you might try.

AROUND BANGUI
Les Chutes de Boali
Les Chutes de Boali (Boali Waterfalls), 99 km north-west of Bangui, are worth an excursion in the rainy season if the water is flowing. The water flow on the Mbali River is now controlled by a huge new Chinese-built dam just north of Boali village, so the only time you'll see any water at the waterfalls south of the dam is during the rainy season. Go on a Sunday as the dam control people usually allow the water to flow then for the tourists. The falls are splendid then.

Boali is 94 km north-west of Bangui on the road to Bossembélé – CFA 1200 by bush taxi. The turn-off for the falls to the right (east) is just south of the village with a sign 'Chutes de Boali – 5 km'. At the falls you might encounter some menacing people who may even demand up to CFA 2000 for use of the picnic tables, which are free.

Places to Stay & Eat The *Hôtel des Chutes de Boali* has a restaurant and charges CFA 3500 for its rooms but some travellers, seeing the hotel virtually empty, have negotiated the price downward to half that amount. The hotel will usually let you camp there (CFA 500 a person) and use the shared showers, but be careful when camping as some travellers have been robbed there. In town, the thatched-roof *Paillote Lisimoba*, on the main drag in the centre of town, serves cheap, cool drinks, and possibly meals as well. There's also a market in town where you can buy food if you intend to camp at the falls.

M'Baïki & Pygmy Territory
Another possibility is M'Baïki, 107 km south-west of Bangui. M'Baïki is a major coffee and timber-growing area and the home of the Lobaye and some Pygmies. While the latter average about 120 cm (four feet) in height, some are much smaller. There are no organised tours to see them but in M'Baïki you should have no problem finding someone who wouldn't mind earning a little money by leading the way. A few of their camps are located a little south of M'Baïki and some are now permanent, making viewing easier. One in particular is accustomed to visitors, as the inhabitants make a fair living by allowing themselves to be photographed by the occasional tourist. The more traditional Pygmies do not have permanent settlements because they are hunters in the rainforests and are constantly moving whenever game gets scarce.

About 10 km north-east of M'Baïki on the road to Bangui is the village of the *ébonistes*, where you can watch men carving ebony, and buy good pieces at fair prices if you bargain hard. There is also a good **waterfall** near M'Baïki and if you ask around, you should be able to find a young boy to guide you there.

If you're in M'Baïki during July or August, you are likely to see Peace Corps volunteers in town, as the training camp is here and those months are the major time of year for training *stagiaires* (new arrivals). They're often visible on the streets on weekend afternoons.

Places to Stay & Eat During Peace Corps training season, if you meet and strike up a conversation with one of the stagiaires, you may find yourself invited back to their training site, l'Institut Superieur (known as 'Koukou' by the locals), for dinner and a flop in someone's dormitory room, which is technically not permitted but often overlooked. Otherwise, there's a basic hotel in town that has rooms with beds but no showers.

Try the market area for food and at night head for Tanti Helene for the best dancing in town. This place is all atmosphere, with a tree growing up through the dance floor. If you're a man and an African man asks you to dance, he's not gay but simply being friendly.

Getting There & Away Peugeot 404 bush taxis for M'Baïki (CFA 1200) leave from Bangui at the Km 5 market at the beginning of Ave de l'UDEAC.

Zinga

About 100 km due south of Bangui, Zinga is a beautiful and friendly town on the Oubangui River, with houses made from wooden planks, which is rare for this part of Africa. All boats up and downriver stop here to go through customs formalities, so it's a good place to catch boats.

Canoeing You could buy a canoe in Bangui and float down here in three days to a week, then return to Bangui by minibus, or continue on down to the Congo in a larger boat. The following is an account, by Penny & Rachel of England, of their trip from Bangui to Libenge, which is across the river from Zinga on the Zaïre side and slightly further south.

After weeks of being beaten about atop trucks in Sudan and the CAR, we wanted a break. So in Bangui, we haggled for four hours one morning for a dugout canoe and agreed on CFA 7500 for the canoe and an old cooking pot, plus CFA 500 for paddles, then we set off down the Oubangui River for Libenge. This journey was one of the highlights of our trip.

It took almost a week to reach Libenge (the last CAR-to-Zaïre crossing point south). This was travelling too fast – you should travel more slowly as there are plenty of side trips to be made. Along the way there are many small villages on the riverbanks where you can stop and buy food, and many islands to camp on in the middle of the river. Some fruit and bread is

available in the villages, and we found the river water safe to drink and swim in.

We had no canoeing experience, but found it easy to learn and out there on the river it's a different world. It's extremely peaceful, but it gets hellishly hot after 11 am, so we stopped every day around this time, set up camp on an isolated island and swam and rested. It was almost impossible to camp on the river banks, as the rainforest came right up to the bank. Next morning, we would wake in darkness, pack up and move on just as it was growing light, so as to travel as far as possible while it was still coolish. This was a truly fantastic part of the day – we would float downriver through the steam as it rose from the water and the rainforest.

The river is very warm, so you can't really cool off, but it's very refreshing. Drink gallons of water – we lost enormous amounts of sweat and nearly dehydrated one day. A powerful sun block helps a great deal too, as there is no shade on the river.

A tent is a necessity here as you are in the middle of the rainforest. If you can't shelter from the mosquitoes, we've no idea how you would sleep. You need to put your sleeping bag and other possessions in a plastic bag to keep them dry.

The fourth island after Bangui has rapids on the western side of it. Take these rapids through the narrow channel of water closest to the island – it's away from the rocks – not too fast, and the current carries you nicely by without the need to row. The canoes float in very shallow water, but try to steer well clear of sand banks.

The East

SIBUT

Some 188 km north-east of Bangui and a major centre of the Mandjia group, Sibut is where the paved road ends and the road splits eastward towards Bambari and Bangassou and northward towards Kaga Bandoro and Sarh (Chad). It is thus a major crossroads and a fairly active little town. The town is basically a fork in the road, with most of the action on the fork leading north, particularly the first 200 metres. That's where you'll find the market, gare routière and most places to sleep, eat and drink. If you stop here for the night, don't worry. There's a lively bar, good accommodation and food available.

Places to Stay

The *Mission Catholique* has no rooms but

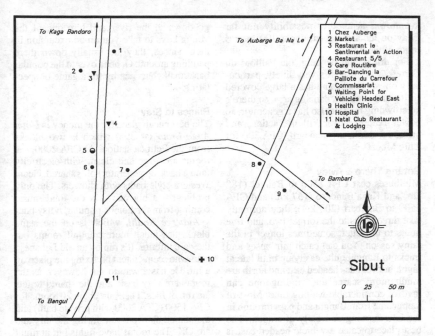

To Kaga Bandoro

To Auberge Ba Na Le

1 Chez Auberge
2 Market
3 Restaurant le Sentimental en Action
4 Restaurant 5/5
5 Gare Routière
6 Bar-Dancing la Paillote du Carrefour
7 Commissariat
8 Waiting Point for Vehicles Headed East
9 Health Clinic
10 Hospital
11 Natal Club Restaurant & Lodging

To Bambari

To Bangui

Sibut

0   25   50 m

you can camp here for free and use their shelters, showers and laundry facilities. There are also Peace Corps volunteers in town who might be willing to put you up. The best hotel is the eight-room *case de passage* at the *Bar-Dancing la Paillote du Carrefour*, which is just south of the gare routière. The rooms here cost CFA 1200 and CFA 1600. The latter are newer, with freshly painted walls, electricity, a small window, a large foam mattress bed with sheets, a clean shared shower and African-style toilet. The friendly guard will bring an emergency paraffin lamp and water to your room.

If money is your only concern, try the four-room *Chez Auberge* across and down the street from the market. It's dumpy, with bare rooms for CFA 1000.

If these two places are full, there are two more possibilities. One is the *Natal Club Restaurant & Lodging*, which is about 100 metres south of the fork, and the other is *Auberge Ba Na Le*. You get to the latter by taking the right fork for about 200 metres, then the first left (north), and that dirt track for several hundred metres. Look for the sign.

Places to Eat

The best place for street food is on the main drag between the Paillote du Carrefour and the gare routière; the selection, however, is limited mainly to grilled meats, coffee, hot chocolate and bread. You'll do a lot better eating at the wonderful, highly recommended, *Restaurant le Sentimental en Action*, which is on the main north-south road next to the market. The owner is very friendly and each day a different menu is posted outside. There are about five selections; typical ones include beef with vegetables, fish with sauce, and monkey. A filling, delicious plate costs CFA 250. Or try *Restaurant 5/5* (Chez Tantine Collete) across the street and 50 metres south, before the gare routière; Collete's food and prices are similar. The *Natal Club*

Restaurant is another possibility not far away on the same road, about 100 metres south of the fork.

For drinks and dancing, the Paillote du Carrefour is great. It's very lively, particularly on weekends, and has a large covered sitting and strobe-lit dancing area, so there's no crowding here. It also has a generator, so power failures never kill the action, and prices for drinks are standard (CFA 300 for a big Mocaf).

Getting There & Away

Minibuses cost CFA 1500 to Bangui (188 km) and Kaga Bandoro (157 km) and CFA 2500 to Bambari (200 km); they normally take three hours to the former two, and five hours to the latter, sometimes longer in the rainy season. You can catch minibuses and trucks to Bangui quite easily up until late at night, but vehicles headed east and north are much more scarce and finding one can involve considerable waiting time. Most of them come from Bangui and pass through in the late morning and early afternoon. The best place to catch a vehicle headed east is not at the gare routière but on the Bambari road, about 200 metres east of the main fork, just before the health clinic.

BAMBARI

With some 50,000 inhabitants, Bambari is the country's third-largest city and a major commercial centre. There are a surprising number of Lebanese-owned enterprises, as you'll soon find out if you're looking for dry goods; the four major stores in the centre are all owned by them, as are a major hotel and restaurant. If you are desperate to change money, these would be the places to ask at.

Coming from Sibut, you'll pass the Mission Catholique on your right on the outskirts of town, and eventually cross over the Ouaka River bridge into the commercial area, the heart of which is the tiny gare routière at the Petroca petrol station. The general stores, including Molato-Bang and Sandy, as well as the main market, most hotels, restaurants and bars are all within a block or two. For entertainment you could go down to the river and hire one of the young boys to take you on an excursion in their canoes; they are usually down there paddling around. Or head over to the popular basketball court nearby for a game or spectating.

Places to Stay

The best cheap place for the money is *Hôtel Ango-Broto* (☎ 396) which is two blocks from the Petroca station. At CFA 2000, the rooms are large and clean, with electricity (and a back-up generator) plus shared, clean, Western-style baths with showers. The only problem – a big one – is the loud music coming from the hotel's popular, noisy bar.

Auberge Khalil, which is on the same block, has much more tranquil rooms but they are inferior. It's run by an old Lebanese man who seems intent on fixing the place up a bit. He has a way to go, however, as the rooms are very basic and the shared toilets are full of flies. There are about 20 rooms for CFA 1500 (CFA 2000 with private bath) and the shared showers run during the day and are OK. The rooms have lights but at night there's usually no electricity, so paraffin lamps are needed then. There is, however, a generator for the popular restaurant next door.

If you're desperate for a room, try the *Auberge JJ*, which is about 100 metres before the bridge on your left as you're heading for Bangui. It has a bar and charges CFA 1500 for a tiny room with a marginally clean shared bath.

The best hotel is the *Motel d l'Étoile de l'Ouka*, which is in the heart of town, a stone's throw north of the Petroca station. It has an attractive thatched-roof paillote bar in a tranquil garden setting and rooms for CFA 3500 to CFA 8000, with several for CFA 1750. The CFA 3500 rooms are bare and don't have fans but the shared Western-style baths are reasonably clean. The CFA 6000 rooms have fans, mosquito nets and clean shared baths; those for CFA 8000 are the same but with private baths.

For camping, try the *Mission Catholique*, which is three km west of the central area on

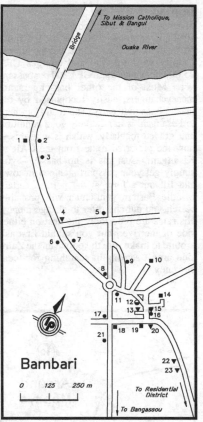

Bambari

0   125   250 m

To Mission Catholique,
Sibut & Bangui

Bridge

Ouaka River

To Residential
District

To Bangassou

■ PLACES TO STAY

1   Auberge JJ
14   Motel de l Étoile de l'Ouaka
18   Hôtel Ango-Broto
19   Auberge Khalil

▼ PLACES TO EAT

4   Boulangerie Jamal
12   Street Food
13   Halles des Bambari
15   Restaurant Bar de l'Étoile de l'Ouaka
20   Pâtisserie-Restaurant Khalil &
     Boulangerie de Khalil
22   Grilled-Meat Vendors
23   Petit Marché

     OTHER

2   Petroca Petrol Station
3   Basketball Court & Football Field
5   Commissariat
6   Market
7   Garage
8   Molato-Bang General Store
9   Bar le Paillote
10   Hôtel de Ville
11   Surété (Security Police)
12   Gare Routière & Petroca Petrol
     Station
16   Sandy General Store
17   BCAD Bank
18   Nightclub
21   Pharmacy de l'Ouaka
23   Bar La Paillote de Souvenir

the Bangui road. They give campers access to the showers and have been known to change travellers' cheques (US dollar ones only)! If you're here around May or June, when mangoes are in season, you can eat some of the delicious mangoes from the huge mango trees. The Peace Corps volunteers also might be willing to put you up.

Places to Eat

The best places to eat are all within a block of the central Petroca station. Next to the station, on the street, you'll find men selling grilled meat and women selling *bouiller* (bou-EE), which is a delicious white porridge of rice, peanut butter and sugar and easy to find all day long in the market but not always at night. It costs only CFA 50 a plate. Next to them is the *Halles des Bambari*, which is really an alley (dark at night) lined with bars, many of which sell typical African food with sauces, for CFA 250 to CFA 600.

If you're tired of African food, try *Pâtisserie-Restaurant Khalil*, a popular Lebanese restaurant adjoining Auberge Khalil. The menu includes brochettes (CFA 400), steak (CFA 800), steak kafta (CFA 1000), fish (CFA 1200) and roasted chicken (CFA 1900) plus some wonderful home-made yoghurt and pastries for CFA 100 and up. For bread, there's *Boulangerie de Khalil* next door.

Restaurant de l'Étoile, a block away, has similar food and prices (roast chicken for CFA 1500, steak garni for CFA 800, omelette for CFA 350). Try the home-made yoghurt for CFA 50 to CFA 200 – it's great and a meal in itself.

Entertainment
At night, head for the adjoining *Bar de l'Étoile de la Ouaka*. It's one of the best nightclubs in the CAR, mainly because a great Zaïrian band of the same name plays here regularly. And, unlike Bangui, safety is not a major problem, possibly even for unescorted women. On Tuesday, Thursday, Saturday and Sunday nights starting around 8 pm you'll find them here – don't miss them. There's a large open-air patio in the centre which is usually packed by 9.30 pm with people dancing to their lively Zaïrian sounds. Entrance is free but you should buy a drink; a small beer or Coke costs only CFA 300. When the band's not playing, the same drinks cost CFA 250 (CFA 300 for a big beer).

For variety you could try the noisy bar with loud music at Hôtel Ango-Broto, but I don't recommend it. If you're looking for a more tranquil setting for a drink, try the thatched-roof *Bar la Paillote* nearby; you can also get food here but you must order in advance.

Getting There & Away
Minibuses cost CFA 2500 to Sibut, CFA 3000 to Mobaye, CFA 3500 to Bangassou and CFA 4000 to Bangui. All of them start filling up around 5.30 am and leave around 6 am from the Petroca station in the centre, so get there early. The trip to Sibut takes about five hours, and to Bangui nine hours during the dry season, and longer during the peak of the rainy season. You can make arrangements the previous night with the driver to have a good seat; he'll also wake you up. You could also catch a truck but the driver will ask just as much.

MOBAYE
The dam/bridge under construction here is still not complete because of a dispute between the CAR and Zaïre, but the ferry is usually working fine and charges CFA 25,000 per vehicle and CFA 200 per passenger. Most of the other passengers are moneychangers, easily recognised by the plastic bags they carry. The road from here to Kisangani is in relatively good condition and graded regularly, which is why this is now the preferred route from the CAR to Kisangani. Customs is no hassle – you simply get your passport stamped in town and fill out a form at the port. A certain Middle Eastern gentleman will probably search you out and offer to change money. His rates are reportedly the best on either side of the river, but you should first ask around to make sure the police on the Zaïre side aren't serious in searching for local currency.

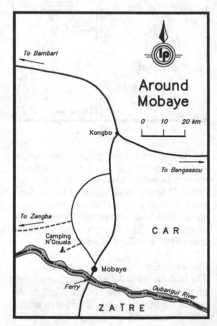

Around Mobaye

Places to Stay

Virtually everyone with a vehicle stops for the night at *Camping N'Gouala*, which is an excellent camping ground run by Jacques Vigner. It's 13 km north-west of Mobaye. From Mobaye, instead of taking the main road north to Kongbo (66 km), take the more westwardly route heading north-west. The camp site is 10 km up that road, then left (west) for three km. Look for the sign.

This alternative route is a good dirt road, not on the Michelin map. It intersects with the main road 17 km south of Kongbo.

KEMBÉ

Some 70 km east of Kongbo, the turn-off for Mobaye, on the Bangassou road, Kembé is a frequent overnight point for those on their way to/from Bangassou. Five km east of town (50 metres beyond the bridge) there are some wonderful falls but watch out for thieves there. Camping there is not allowed but there is a camp site at the hotel beyond the falls which costs about CFA 600 per night. There are toilets and, if the generator is working, hot showers.

BANGASSOU

With about 40,000 inhabitants, Bangassou (ban-gas-SOU) is one of the larger towns in the CAR. Until the mid-1980s it was the major crossing point into Zaïre for travellers with their own vehicles, but with the route through Mobaye now better and more popular, this town rarely sees travellers and is shrinking. Even when the ferry is working, the ferry operator is difficult to find, so

expect to spend at least one night there. Those without vehicles can, of course, always take a pirogue. Check out the market, as you can find all kinds of bush meat there, including monkey, anteater, bush pig, wart hog, buffalo, gazelle, and even elephant meat on occasion. Leopards, lions and elephants are still occasionally seen very close to town.

Places to Stay

The *Tourist Hôtel* has rooms, but you can also camp there for a small fee or at the *Mission Protestante* for nothing. Wherever you camp, beware of thieves. Alternatively, ask some of the local kids to lead you to the houses of the Peace Corps volunteers; they may offer you a mattress to sleep on.

Getting There & Away

There are minibuses every day in either direction between Bangui and Bangassou. The cost is CFA 7500 (CFA 3500 to Bambari) and the trip usually takes two days, with the night spent in Bambari.

The North

KAGA BANDORO

Most travellers to/from Chad pass through Kaga Bandoro without staying the night, but you might stay if you're headed to the parks in the north-east. In the evenings the market-gare routière area is lit up by oil lamps. You can get cheap munchies there and sit and natter with the local Banda people while sampling their delicious local booze, *hydromiel* (a sort of honey beer). During the day you can climb the Kaga hill about three km from town, for good views of the surrounding area.

Places to Stay & Eat

Facing the gare routière is a fairly decent 10-room *case de passage* with very basic rooms for CFA 1000. Your only other alternative may be to look up the Peace Corps volunteers or the French volunteers; they may offer you a place to sleep.

In the centre of town, just in front of the *case de passage*, a great place to eat is *Restaurant 24h/24h en Afrique*, which is run by a Sudanese bloke and open late. While lively music blasts away, he'll prepare you a tasty soupe de boeuf for CFA 250 (or a half plate for CFA 125) or sauce de poulet or poisson for CFA 500. There's also Nescafé for CFA 75 and cold drinks. Grilled-meat vendors are right outside and all around the gare routière area, which is very lively at night. For beer, the closest and best place may be the attractive Bar la Paillote, which is 150 metres north on the main drag.

Getting There & Away
The minibuses plying the Bangui-Chad border route usually pass through town in either direction sometime between mid-afternoon and early evening. For either destination you can expect to pay about CFA 3000 if you're lucky and there's room. The road between here and Sibut is graded regularly, allowing minibuses to do that section in about three hours or less during the dry season. The road north to Kabo and Sido, however, is in bad condition and full of gullies. Driving times on it are considerably slower, particularly during the rainy season (starting in June).

If you are headed east to the parks, you may have to wait several days for transportation as the road is very lightly travelled even in the dry season.

KABO
Kabo is roughly equidistant between Kaga Bandoro and Sido, the Chad border town en route to Sarh. The road connecting these three towns is in bad condition, with lots of holes and deep ruts, slowing driving considerably. Travellers rarely stay the night in Kabo but they all stay here a few hours because they must pass through immigration, the gendarmerie and the commissariat, a procedure that can easily take up to three hours. It's mind-boggling because officials at each of these separate checkpoints write down, very slowly, identical information; if

one of them is drunk, this painful process can take even longer.

Fortunately, you can get delicious, cheap, African food while you wait. There's a woman on the front side of the market (200 metres from the southernmost control point, the commissariat's) in a very rustic surrounding who serves local food, including beef with a tasty sauce. Even better is her fabulous sauce *feuille* of deep green manioc leaves with fish or meat and lots of tasty local spices. The cost is CFA 250; your pick of bread or sticky manioc is about CFA 70 extra.

SIDO
Sido is the tiny border village on the route to Sarh (Chad). The town extends across the border into Chad. The latest you can cross the border is about 6 pm. It reopens around 6 am.

Places to Stay & Eat
The only lodging is an unmarked nine-room *Auberge* about 100 metres from the border station. The rooms, which cost CFA 1000, are very basic and don't have windows or a place to bathe.

There's no restaurant in town but at the tiny market nearby you'll find some food including unbearably salty fish and, better, African sauce and mangoes when in season. Be sure to try the bouiller (sweet rice porridge).

Getting There & Away
Minibuses for Sarh leave from the other side of the border every morning after 7 am, so there's enough time in the morning to pass through border formalities and still catch the bus. The cost to Sarh is CFA 2000; the trip can take up to five hours because of the many police stops en route.

There's also a minibus every day to Bangui. The departure point is in front of the Auberge. It usually leaves around 8 am or so and arrives in Bangui around midnight, often later. The cost is CFA 6500 (CFA 500 more for a front window seat) but the driver may initially ask for more.

ST FLORIS & BAMINGUI-BANGORAN PARKS

Maps of the CAR still show a number of national parks and reserves in the north-east which were carved out during colonial times for hunting purposes, but today there are only two de facto parks – St Floris and Bamingui-Bangoran.

In terms of topography and vegetation these parks are not remarkable; in both the land is fairly flat and the vegetation is primarily woodland savannah with lots of plains, facilitating viewing. However, these parks have a rich variety of wildlife typical of many different zones. Both, for example, harbour the 'big four' (elephants, lions, leopards and rhinos) as well as giraffes, buffalo, hippos, monkeys, baboons, cheetahs, crocodiles, wart hogs, bee-eaters, bushbabies, pelicans (seasonal) and a wide variety of buck including roan antelope, topi waterbuck, hartebeest, kob, oribi, duiker, reedbuck, bushbuck and the prize of trophy seekers – the giant Lord Derby eland.

The animal densities in these parks are not high, however, because during the last 20 years poachers have killed a staggering number of animals in the area. In all of Africa, for example, the number of rhino has gone from approximately 60,000 in 1970 to fewer than 4000 in 1990. The slaughter in the CAR has been as bad as anywhere else. Years ago, between these two parks and surrounding buffer zones there used to be about 80,000 elephants. Today there are only about 3000. The rhino, crocodile, leopard and giraffe populations have also been hit hard. The poachers are primarily armed gangs, many from neighbouring Sudan, but it's not unusual to hear of local businessmen and even public officials being involved.

Fortunately, something is finally being done about the problem. Since 1988, the European Community(EC) has been actively involved in rehabilitating these two parks. Their initial efforts have been aimed primarily at controlling the poaching and they have been quite successful – the animal populations in the two parks have now stabilised.

More recently, the European Develop-

ment Fund (EDF) has concentrated efforts into redefining the park boundaries and developing a handbook on the parks, and copies may be available from the EDF offices in Bangui. It's not a tourist guide but, rather, a guide to the parks' animals – their distribution in the park and relationship to one another, among other things. If you have any questions about these parks or the animals, talk to the EDF people because they are now the country's most knowledgeable people about the area.

Of the two parks, St Floris has always been more controlled, and as a result it has a much higher animal population density. For this reason, virtually all the few visitors who come here head for St Floris. It's open from the beginning of December to mid-May. It's also the only park equipped to receive visitors. Bamingui-Bangoran Park is open during the same period, and is accessed from Bamingui in the south. Tracks lead into the park from there. Entrance to both parks is free.

According to EDF officials, starting in 1994 a new area called the Zone Banal centred around Sangba, about 80 km east of Bamingui and 100 km south of N'Délé, will be opened to visitors. It's an area with lots of potential as the number of animals here is relatively high. Unlike the other two parks, it's a heavily forested area with interesting cliffs, so the only way to see the animals will be on foot, and lots of stalking will be

required. It will have camping grounds with thatched-roof huts. Accommodation will be cheap, basic and run by the villagers, who will also act as guides for treks into the forest. You can talk to the EDF people about it when you're in Bangui; they are very friendly and are glad to answer questions.

Places to Stay

Manovo Safaris (headquarters in Bangui) maintains a small lodge, the *Campement de Gounda*, at the western corner of St Floris Park. It has six bungalows with two rooms each; the rooms are very decent, with three beds, fans and private baths. The cost per person including three meals a day is CFA 24,000 if there are at least three people in the group and CFA 28,000/36,000 if there are only two or one. You can save money by sleeping in one of their tents, which are not so rustic as they have comfortable beds, fans and shared baths.

Manovo Safaris maintains vehicles at the Campement so that visitors arriving by plane will have transport within the park; the cost is CFA 7000 per person per day, which includes two viewing trips a day. If you bring your own vehicle, the only assessment is a fee of CFA 2500 per day per vehicle for the park ranger who accompanies all vehicles.

For Bamingui-Bangoran Park, you'll find a very rustic campement at Bamingui. Bamingui is also the turn-off point for Sangba to the east, where the campement serving the Zone Banal will be located. If you're caught for the night in N'Délé, there's a friendly Mission Catholique there (see the N'Délé section).

Getting There & Away

The great majority of visitors who come to St Floris come by chartered plane (either TAC or CentreAvia, which are at the aeroclub next to the airport in Bangui). Most people fly up on Friday morning and return on Sunday afternoon. The return fare per person is CFA 140,000 if the five-seater plane is filled, and more if it is not. Manovo Safaris will handle the reservations. The airstrip is at the Campement.

Driving the 800 km from Bangui to St Floris normally takes 1½ days. Kaga Bandoro is the last town where you are guaranteed to find petrol, so you'll need to bring jerrycans of petrol for the trip. The turn-off for the Campement is about 70 km east of N'Délé. After the turn-off, you will pass along the Gounda River and the surrounding plains. It's a good viewing area and the river is full of hippos.

If you're hitchhiking, getting to the parks will be very difficult, as the route east of Kaga Bandoro is very lightly travelled. Your best bet is to head for the campement at Sangba, as no vehicle will be required once you get there. It's also roughly 200 km closer than St Floris.

N'DÉLÉ

Coming from Sudan, you will think that N'Délé, at the eastern end of Bamingui-Bangoran Park, is the height of civilisation. The market is typical of the major ones elsewhere in country, with café au lait, bread and butter, fruit, bouiller etc, and there are even bars with cold beer – almost unbelievable if you've been in dry Sudan for several months.

Places to Stay

At the *Mission Catholique*, where you can get a room and a shower, the people seem genuinely pleased to have guests.

BIRAO

In the far north-eastern corner of the country on the major road to Sudan, Birao is truly remote. If you're coming from Sudan, buy food and supplies before crossing the border as prices are generally lower there than in Birao.

Places to Stay & Eat

The *Mission Catholique* puts up travellers but for free you can camp fairly safely next to the customs office. You'll find numerous wells where you can get water, and a small market with very limited supplies and coffee vendors who can rustle you up a very basic meal.

Getting There & Away

If you're hitchhiking, good luck – some travellers have been known to wait up to two weeks before finding a truck going their way. Travelling by truck is always extremely slow but it's exceedingly so once the rains begin in May. One group of travellers reported that it took them 22 days to travel from Birao to Sibut in late May because of the horrendous condition of the roads!

The West & South-West

BOSSEMBÉLÉ

Bossembélé is a very small town 157 km north-west of Bangui. Nevertheless, it's the second-largest town on the road to Cameroun and a major crossroad, with an occasional vehicle headed north toward Bossangoa and Moundou (Chad).

People driving through Bossembélé frequently remember only the nasty police at the control point on the eastern outskirts of town, who are notorious for stopping motorists and levying ridiculously high fines (typically CFA 8000) for the slightest thing wrong with the vehicle.

Places to Stay & Eat

For a cheap room, try the unmarked, cement-covered *case de passage* on the main drag, 150 metres west of the market and past the cinema-bar. Run by a friendly old man, it has four small rooms for CFA 1100; each has a single bed with two clean sheets, a window, paraffin lamps, a shared bucket shower and African-style toilets.

If it's full, try the *Auberge de 7 Jours*, which is 100 metres further west and down a side street. The owner is very friendly and the rooms, of which there are 12 (each named after a month of the year), cost CFA 1000 and are windowless but very clean, with paraffin lamps and shared bucket baths. There's also another similarly priced *case de passage* in the heart of town between the market and the gare routière, but it's grubby-looking, the owner is difficult to find, and the noise level could be high, as Wililoko 'Transit' Bar is next door. Lastly, you might look up some of the Peace Corps volunteers here.

For food, the choices are very limited. *Restaurant Oasis*, which is on the main drag near the Auberge, is usually open at lunchtime. Otherwise, the only place to get food is at one of the stalls at the gare routière, most notably *Chez Tantine Eugenie*, who likewise is open only for lunch. Eugenie serves a variety of good cheap African sauces; directly behind this place is an open-air bar where you can get cheap drinks. At night, grilled meat is all you're likely to find in this area. The best place for a drink is not here but at the peaceful, shady bar adjoining the cinema; beers there cost CFA 200 (small) and CFA 350 (large).

Entertainment

The market, which sells mostly foodstuffs, is busy in the morning but dead by the early afternoon. For thrills, during the late afternoon the locals take in the flics at the local cinema, which is also a bar, while at night they head to *Bar-Dancing Benikon* across from the market, for drinking and dancing. For such a small town, it's a surprisingly big place with a huge dance floor and large speakers. It's a fun place, especially on weekends. For variety, there's also *Bar-Dancing Wililoko 'Transit'* a stone's throw away.

Getting There & Away

Minibuses for Bangui leave from the gare routière early in the morning and cost CFA 1800 (CFA 800 if you want to be dropped off in Boali). The journey can take up to five hours as the buses are constantly stopping en route. Those from Bangui leave around 9 am or later and you can sometimes catch one as late as 11 am at Km 12.

The best place to catch a minibus to Bossangoa (148 km to the north) is at the Petroca petrol station at the eastern entrance to town; those from Bangui usually pass through between 10 am and 1 pm. They also stop on the main drag, just east of the market. The cost is CFA 1800.

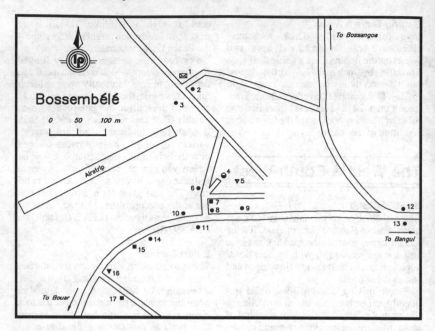

Bossembélé

0   50   100 m

To Bossangoa

To Bangui

To Bouar

1	Post Office
2	Gendarmerie
3	School
4	Gare Routière
5	Chez Tantine Eugenie & Open-Air Bar
6	Commissariat
7	Case de Passage
8	Bar-Dancing Wililoko 'Transit'
9	Black-Market Petrol
10	Bar-Dancing Benikon
11	Market
12	Petroca Petrol Station
13	Police Checkpoint
14	Cinema & Open-Air Bar
15	Case de Passage
16	Restaurant Oasis
17	Auberge de 7 Jours

If you're headed to Bouar (280 km), you can wait anywhere along the main drag but preferably just east of the market. Minibuses from Bangui usually pass by in the late morning. The cost is about CFA 2700. Truck drivers will demand at least as much but they pass by at all hours of the day and night. The road west of town towards Bouar is slowly being repaired and some day soon may be in good condition.

Around Bossembélé

Lambi Chutes These waterfalls are more spectacular than those at Boali, rainy season or dry, and could provide some entertainment or adventure. However you need your own vehicle to get there. Going south to Bangui, after 20 km you reach a dirt road crossroad, which has a stop sign. Turn right and go 33 to 35 km and look for a marked sideroad on the left. If you come to a bridge over the river you have gone too far.

BOUAR

With some 35,000 inhabitants, Bouar is the largest town on the Bangui-Cameroun border route and a frequent overnight point. The town is in a pleasant location on a rolling plateau at an altitude of 950 metres, with many expansive views from the higher points. If you walk up the Rue du Commissariat for half a km or so from the city's main intersection, for example, you'll get some nice views of the surrounding countryside. Bouar also has a busy market near that intersection but no bank. To change money, try the pharmacy at the intersection; it has done so in the past. If you have no luck at the pharmacy, inquire about Maison Murt; some travellers have reported changing money there.

Bouar is perhaps most famous for the large French military base, Camp Laclerc, on the eastern outskirts of town. You may not see any soldiers in town but if you go any night of the week to Bar de l'Amitié, near the base, you'll find some there. Due to their large numbers and the fact that this is a popular route for overland travellers, theft has become a serious problem; rip-offs from campers around Bouar are common.

Places to Stay

The cheapest place is the friendly *Auberge Central 'Maman Pauline'* (Chez Pauline) in the town centre just behind the gare routière. Pauline charges CFA 1500 for one of her 14 medium-size rooms. They have no windows but they do have electricity, beds with two clean sheets and moderately clean shared bucket baths. It's also relatively safe for guarding luggage as Pauline or members of her family are always there.

Those with vehicles are likely to prefer *Auberge le Maigaro*, which is the best hotel in town. It has about 20 rooms ranging in price from CFA 1500 to CFA 3000 – all quite clean and well-lit but without fans. The cheapest rooms are similar in quality to Pauline's. Those for CFA 2500 have very clean sheets, private showers and shared toilets, while the CFA 3000 rooms have an extra, tiny room that is virtually unusable. There's also a central courtyard where you can park your vehicle, but no restaurant. From the main intersection, it's 300 metres north-east along an unlit road towards the hospital.

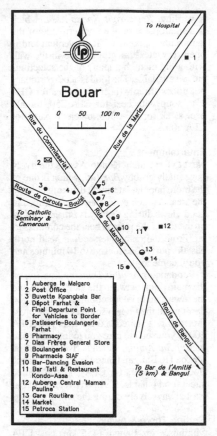

If you want to camp, you might check the large *Catholic Seminary*, which is about six km west of town off the road to the Cameroun border. You'll see it in the distance from the main road.

Places to Eat

The principal area for street food is between the main intersection and the nearby gare routière. Coffee, bread and butter, fried fish, sandwiches and beef brochettes are some of the offerings. You'll also find several bakeries in the area selling French baguettes.

Finding a restaurant isn't so easy or

rewarding. *Restaurant Kondo-Assa*, which is a small place on the northern side of the gare routière, is the most convenient and is open very late. It's a grubby hole-in-the-wall with a big menu but many of the selections are not available. The food is at best ordinary but prices are low (beef brochettes for CFA 150, soup with beef for CFA 250, tomato beef steak for CFA 300, omelette garni for CFA 500).

Entertainment

Next to Restaurant Kondo-Assa is the lively but equally grubby *Bar Tati*, which is one of the more popular late-night drinking holes in the area. A much better place for a drink and good views during the day is *Bar la Paillote* on the top of the plateau near the commissariat. From the main intersection, head north past the post office for five to 10 minutes and you'll come to it.

For dancing, try *Bar-Dancing Évasion* on the main drag, between the gare routière and the town's main intersection. Or better, if you don't mind the French soldiers and the prostitutes, hire a shared taxi for CFA 100 (CFA 200 to yourself) to take you to the rustic and breezy *Bar Amitié*, which is five km east on the road to Bangui. It has a good-sized dance floor, small beers for CFA 200 and grilled street food outside. It's open every night but isn't always lively during the week.

Getting There & Away

Minibuses for Bangui (455 km) cost CFA 4500 and all leave from the gare routière, taking 14 hours or so if the road isn't temporarily blocked due to a heavy rain.

Minibuses for the Cameroun border (159 km) leave from the main intersection in town, cost CFA 1800 and take four to six hours, with time-consuming police checks along the way. All of these vehicles start filling up around 5 am and leave when full (around 6 am), so get there early. Try to meet the vehicle owner the night before as he'll pick you up at your hotel if you ask.

If you are heading from the border to Bangui, most of the minibuses for Bouar will leave around 9 am. Anticipate staying in Bouar as it's extremely rare to find vehicles at the border which go direct to Bangui without stopping the night in Bouar.

If you're heading for Cameroun and want to catch the night train to Yaoundé, from the border take the route north-west to N'Gaoundal (240 km on mostly paved road) instead of the longer, rougher trip south to Bélabo. Since your minibus should arrive at the border at around 11 am or so, you should have time to catch the train that night from N'Gaoundal (about 9 pm) but not from Bélabo.

AROUND BOUAR

Les Mégalithes One of the more interesting attractions of the Bouar area are *les mégalithes* (the megaliths), some of which are on the outskirts of town and weren't excavated until the mid-1960s. There are 70-odd groups of these curious, standing granite stones in varying arrangements in the Bouar area. Those of Beforo, Gam and Tia are to the north and east of Bouar. The megaliths, some of them weighing as much as three or four tons, appear to be evidence of an ancient culture that existed long before any of the present Africans arrived. Many of the locals know nothing about the megaliths but if you ask around long enough, you'll find someone familiar with them who'll offer to act as your guide.

CARNOT

Some 98 km north of Berbérati and 432 km west of Bangui via M'Baïki, Carnot has at least three hotels, all on the main drag and mostly costing CFA 1500/2500 for singles/doubles. One is at the gare routière in the centre and the others are about 200 metres in opposite directions on the main drag. The gare routière is the best place for finding street food and rides.

BERBÉRATI

The country's second-largest city, with some 60,000 inhabitants, Berbérati is on the alternative, less-travelled route to Cameroun via Batouri (in Cameroun), 213 km to the west, as well as to Dzanga-Ndoki Park, some 250 km to the south. The city is not of great interest to travellers but it does have a good hospital supported by UNICEF. If you need to change money, try the supermarket, as the bank here charges a fixed commission of CFA 2320 per transaction.

Places to Stay & Eat

Those with tents can camp for free on the grass in front of the airport. The best place to stay is the *Mission Catholique*; the French priests there welcome travellers. The foreign-run *Lutheran Mission* is another possibility. The cheapest place may be *Chez Alice*, which is near, and to the north-west of, the main intersection; Alice has singles/doubles for CFA 2000/3000 with bucket showers in the rooms. You'll find other hotels at the gare routière – which is also near the intersection, in the direction of Carnot – as well as street food (coffee, bread and omelette for CFA 400; in restaurants, the same will cost you CFA 700).

Getting There & Away

There are flights to/from Bangui on Tuesdays and Saturdays, and minibuses every day in either direction via Carnot; the cost for the latter is CFA 6000 and they leave from the gare routière in the town centre. The people at the petrol station are very friendly and full of information on transport to/from Berbérati.

DZANGA-SANGHA RESERVE

Dzanga-Sangha Reserve, which includes Dzanga-Nkodi National Park, is in the far south-western corner of the CAR and is the newest addition to the country's park system. It is also potentially the most interesting as it contains the country's last remaining undisturbed virgin rainforests, and some of the highest densities of lowland gorillas (estimated 2000) and forest elephants (estimated 3000) recorded in Africa.

It is also home to the bongo, one of the most prized bucks in the world; a few hunters spend a small fortune every year to come here to shoot one of these extremely shy, striped antelopes. Fortunately, bongo populations have stabilised. Other animals in the area include crowned eagles, waterbuck, buffalos, wart hogs, duiker, chimpanzees and various kinds of monkey, including the white-bearded De Brazza's monkey. Some 42 species are described in detail in the *Guide des Mammifères à Bayanga*, available from the Worldwide Fund for Nature (WWF) office in Bangui or at the reserve's Welcome Centre.

Until 1986, anyone could walk into this expanse of wild land and shoot anything they wanted. Armed men seeking elephant meat and ivory would regularly ride up the Sangha River from the Congo in motorised dugout canoes or come overland by foot from Cameroun. Trails of smoke could often be seen from a distance from the fires of successful hunters, who would smoke the elephant meat before returning home with it.

Fortunately, this is now illegal and dealers in wildlife products have been arrested. Not only are poaching levels way down but animals are actually moving into the park from unprotected areas. This has been accomplished through the efforts of the WWF (1250 24 St, NW, Washington, DC 20037) which has been successful in getting the government to declare the area a national park, and reserve and hire some well-trained park rangers, who maintain anti-poaching patrols. They have been working not just to protect the rich and varied wildlife but also to find new ways for the local villagers and Pygmies to support themselves and their families without destroying their environment. The park entrance fee of CFA 3000 helps in this effort.

The entire protected area (4359 sq km) is known as Dzanga-Sangha Reserve, and within it are two national parks, Dzanga Park, which is a 12-km walk east of Bayanga, and the less accessible Ndoki Park, which begins about eight km south of Lidjombo and constitutes the southern tip of the zone. Almost three-quarters of the reserve, however, consists of three hunting zones plus buffer areas where rural development activities are being undertaken, including the towns of Bayanga and Lidjombo. There are three research camp sites in or bordering Dzanga Park and one to

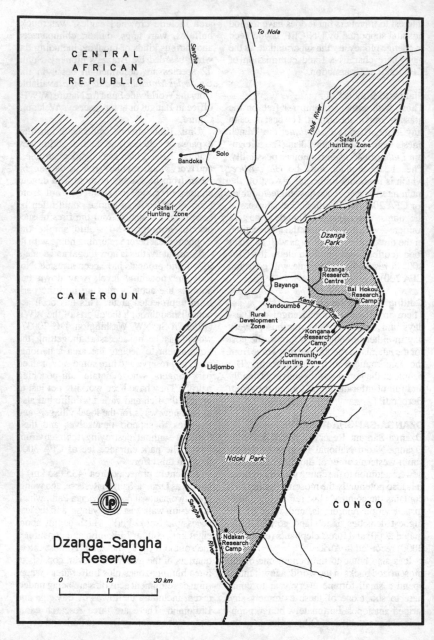

Dzanga–Sangha
Reserve

0   15   30 km

the south along the Sangha River in Ndoki Park.

Gorilla research – particularly on their eating habits – has been the principal initial focus at Dzanga-Sangha. Far less is known about the western lowland gorilla than about the well-studied mountain gorilla in Zaïre and Rwanda. Unlike the latter, which are mostly terrestrial animals, the smaller lowland gorillas spend much more time in the trees and are thus more difficult to observe. Because of this, the density of the terrain and their fear of poachers, none of the gorilla families has yet become habituated to humans and, consequently, seeing these very timid animals is difficult. Much of this research is centred around Bai Hokou camp – hence this area is off limits to visitors.

Activities

The reserve has a Welcome Centre in Bayanga which is open every day from 8 to 11 am and from 2 to 6 pm. This is where you pay the CFA 3000 park entrance fee. It is staffed by the reserve's local guides who can make arrangements for your trek, including putting you in contact with the Peace Corps volunteer whose job is to promote tourism in the area and who has developed specific activities for visitors. The park has no vehicles for transporting visitors and there are no taxis in Bayanga, so all viewing must be done on foot.

The park-reserve is in a major Pygmy area and the volunteer can arrange for one of the local inhabitants, the BaAka, to be your guide and may even accompany you on a trip. Tracking gorillas and forest elephants is the most popular activity. From November to April you don't have to contend much with rain but any time of the year is good for viewing. The vegetation is thick, so it takes a lot of stalking to see the animals and even then you are unlikely to see large numbers of elephants, except possibly at the salt licks. With the gorillas it's even more hit or miss, so you should plan on taking a trek of at least four days or so. A major part of the fun is simply learning how the BaAka Pygmy guide lives in the forest and stalks the animals.

Other activities which can be arranged through the Welcome Centre include pirogue rides on the Sangha River, forage walking through the forest with several BaAka Pygmy women, tapping palm trees with the village men to make palm wine, viewing animals and birds at various salt licks, and hunting small animals with the Pygmies in the hunting zones.

Places to Stay

The American park director, Richard Carroll, and several staff members and Peace Corps volunteers all live in Bayanga. Most visitors stay in one of the four villas at the old saw mill in town; they were owned by the former logging concession here and are now run by the park. The houses, which rent for CFA 8000 a night, have three big bedrooms with beds but no electricity or running water and are thus comparable to camping indoors (so bring lamps, petrol, stoves, etc). You can reserve one through the WWF office in Bangui (they will then radio Bayanga) or directly through the Chef de PCA when you arrive in Bayanga. In any case, do not head out for Bayanga without contacting the Bangui office as otherwise the park staff will be totally unprepared to receive you!

There are three alternative lodgings in Bayanga. One is the *Auberge 'Mon Pays'* which faces the bar of the same name. It has rooms with mattresses, sheets, mosquito nets and running water in the showers out the back. Secondly, Mr Gunja, a businessman in town, has a house for rent on a nightly basis; it has a cabinet and an area for showering.

Finally, you can stay for free in one of the reserve's camps. Kenié camp is in town and has an open paillote to sleep under and a place for taking bucket showers. There are three similar camps (Kongana, Libwe and Ounga) in the forests well outside Bayanga; these are used when visitors go on treks deep into the forest. (Some of the research centre camps are off-limits to visitors.)

The park is unequipped for receiving visitors, so when camping you must bring everything you'll need – stove, kerosene, mosquito net, sheets, food, water, swimsuit (most people bathe in the river) and blanket (it's chillier here than in Bangui). Except for water, all of these items including food are either very difficult to find or not available in Bayanga. So stock up in Bangui or Berbérati before you get here.

Getting There & Away

Dzanga-Sangha receives very few visitors and the few who do come almost invariably have a vehicle. It's possible to rent one in Bangui but this would be outrageously expensive. Even more expensive would be arranging this through Aouk-Sangha Safaris in Bangui. During the dry season, the route from Bangui to Bayanga is via M'Baïki, Boda, Bambio and Nola, a distance of about 525 km. The straight driving time then in a 4WD vehicle is 10 to 12 hours. During the rainy season you have to go on the better but longer all-weather road west to Carnot and Berbérati; you can stay overnight in Berbérati at the Mission Catholique, then continue south for about 240 km to Bayanga.

If you're without wheels, getting there will be a major hassle. The easy part is taking one of the daily minibuses from Bangui to Berbérati. Finding a vehicle headed from there to Nola (135 km) shouldn't be so difficult but from Nola to Bayanga (105 km) would be extremely difficult. You might find a boat in Nola headed in that direction.

Chad

Chad's 25-year war, which started in 1965 as a civil war and later became more of a Chadian-Libyan affair, has now ended, with the country's total expulsion of Libyan troops from the north, a region they controlled for years. In 1987, newspapers worldwide recounted the stunning victory when Libya's well-equipped troops were totally overwhelmed by rifle-armed Chadian troops charging in Toyota pick-up trucks. Today, while forces of the ousted President Hissène Habré occasionally attack government posts, causing short-term travel warnings for certain areas, travellers now have, in general, little to worry about in terms of security and are beginning to trickle back into the country. Of the 10 largest cities in Central Africa, the capital city, N'Djamena, is the safest.

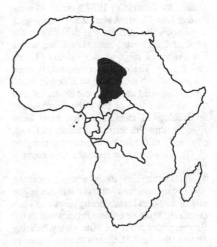

During the war, the country's infrastructure was in a shambles. You could walk down the main streets of N'Djamena and see empty buildings riddled with machine-gun bullets and soldiers everywhere, many of them wounded. It is amazing how much has changed since then. In N'Djamena, most of the bullet-pocked buildings have been repaired and many new establishments are thriving. Because of the country's mammoth road improvement programme, all externally financed, the trip overland from N'Djamena to Sarh, which used to take 24 hours, now takes just eight hours in a fast, private vehicle. And for the first time ever, there are now buses on this route, some air-conditioned.

Chad is lively again, at least in the southern half, and the people you'll meet here (and in São Tomé) are likely to be the friendliest in Central Africa. On a Sunday in N'Djamena you almost certainly will have a choice of *pari-matches* – a unique Chadian institution in which a group of women, hoping to make money from the drinks, rent an entire bar for the day and send invitations to all their friends (but anybody can come). For African music, lively dancing and a guaranteed good

time, these affairs are unbeatable in all of Central Africa. You'll find them in Sarh and Moundou as well.

The far north is still not open to travellers. Some foreign-aid technicians, however, travel to the area quite frequently; organising a ride with them is about the only way to get there. The area includes one of Chad's most interesting sites, the Tibesti region, the most mountainous area in the entire Sahara, with spectacular scenery, lunar-like craters, volcanic massifs, gorges, ancient cave paintings and small desert lakes. Even if the Tibesti area remains off-limits, N'Djamena, southern Chad and the Lac Chad area, particularly in conjunction with a side trip to Waza Game Park in northern Cameroun, are sufficiently interesting to make a short visit here quite worthwhile.

Facts about the Country

HISTORY

During the drought of 1984, you could walk across Lac Chad. About 2500 years ago, however, when Pericles was debating on the floor of the Greek senate, Lac Chad was a sea almost as large as present-day Greece and former Yugoslavia combined. It even connected with the Nile. The area was much wetter and wild animals were abundant. For this reason, some of the richest prehistoric archaeological sites in Africa have been found within the territorial limits of Chad, especially in the far north around the region of Tibesti, where hunters made rock engravings.

At about the time the lake began receding 2500 years ago, some of these hunters began raising cattle and establishing permanent settlements. A people collectively known as the Sao migrated from the Nile valley, settling around the lake. Legends depict them as giants capable of feats of superhuman strength and endurance. Their settlements eventually grew into walled cities of brick.

The Sao's forte was pottery; so if anyone tries to sell you some *ancien* pottery, at least you'll know how old it might be. Chances are, however, that it was made the day before. The Sao also developed the method by which all African bronze art is made today – the sophisticated 'lost wax' technique of metal casting.

Arab Kingdoms

Sometime before the 9th century, people living along the Nile valley, possibly those involved in the salt trade between Lake Chad and the Nile valley, began moving into the area, intermarrying with the Sao who eventually disappeared. In the 9th century, one who established himself as king founded the state of Kanem, which was to last for 1000 years. Chad was the intersection for two major African caravan routes, one north to the Mediterranean coast and the other east towards the regions of the lower Nile. The trade in salt, copper, cotton, gold and slaves brought about increasing contact with the Muslim world, and by 1200 AD, Islam was the dominant religion.

The kingdom expanded and became known as Kanem-Bornu. Its economy was solidly anchored in the slave trade. By the 17th century, it was an empire, with a sizeable army noted for its cavalry of men and armoured horses. The great king, Alooma, even had a small force of musketeers trained in Turkey and outfitted with iron helmets. So great was his reputation that the sultan of Turkey sent an ambassadorial party of about 200 across the desert to his court. The empire didn't last long, however, and by 1812, the Fulani people had sacked the capital.

Two other slave-trading Arab kingdoms flourished during this period – the Baguirmi and the Ouadaï which appeared in the 16th and 17th centuries. During the 19th century, the city of Abéché, which was controlled by the Ouadaï, was a major commercial centre as it was on one of the principal routes to Mecca. The Ouadaï became very rich and had one of the most militarily powerful kingdoms in Africa. A sultan ruled and their cavalries of fierce, rifle-armed warriors were truly legendary. Like the Kanem-Bornu empire, the Ouadaï and the Baguirmi controlled the trans-Saharan caravan trails and raided the southern populations for slaves.

The Black people in southern Chad had decentralised political systems and were easy prey to these well-organised Arab kingdoms which could rely on cavalries to round up the slaves. Slaves became so prevalent among the Arabs that even in poorer regions, such as the reed islands of Lac Chad where many poor Buduma fishers lived, the average person owned two or three slaves.

Slave Raids

Nowhere in Africa was the slave trade stronger than in Chad and it lasted longer too, until the beginning of the 20th century. For the Baguirmi and Ouadaï, slavery was the main export. A young man sold for the equivalent of a good horse; a young woman or eunuch fetched three times that amount.

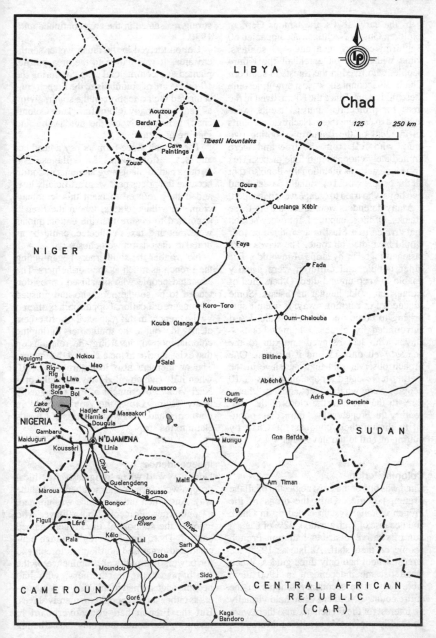

In the early 1870s, the famous German explorer, Gustav Nachtigal, accompanied 60 Baguirmi cavalry men and 400 soldiers, some with guns, on a raid of the Kimre people, who lived in the forests in southern Chad. His account shows just how gruesome these raids were. Since the Kimre lived in the trees for protection, unusual tactics were required to capture them. Nachtigal recounts an incident of the Baguirmi shooting two men, who fell from the tree and were immediately chopped into little pieces. This grotesque act was intentionally done so that all the people would eventually descend and two boys who tried to escape were beheaded.

Many defenders were killed during these attacks. Of those captured, for every person that arrived in a Muslim area, three or four would have died en route. The slaves were fastened together by strips of raw hide. The older people and children were usually unable to keep up and died. Others died of exhaustion, cold, hunger or disease. Some succeeded in running away. It wasn't surprising to come upon a well in the desert surrounded by bleached human bones – slaves who had escaped and run to the nearest well only to find it blocked. One French observer said that one slave in the market represented a population loss of 10 people. Somewhat understandably, therefore, in the south at the close of the 19th century the French gained immediate popularity during their conquest of Chad by putting an end to the slave raids.

Colonial Period

Chad was one of the most neglected of all the French colonies. Only the dregs of the French colonial system ended up in Chad, and because of high attrition, 42% of Chad's administrative districts had non-French people on their staff. As late as 1933, the largest school had only three grades. When Chad became independent in 1960 there were only three secondary schools in the entire country. Northern Chad held virtually no interest for the French because there were no readily exploitable resources. Moreover,

strong resistance in the area continued until 1930.

Cotton thrived in the much wetter southern area. It was native to the area but not planted as a commercial crop. So during the 60-odd years of colonialism, the French concentrated their attention on the south, giving a French company (Cotonfran, later Cotontchad) a monopoly on the purchasing and ginning of cotton.

The French made farmers pay a head tax and set cotton quotas for villages. The farmers had to plant large amounts of cotton because the prices paid were artificially low, and if they refused to plant this 'colonial' crop, the village chiefs, whom the French appointed to ensure that the cotton quotas were met and taxes collected, could be as brutal as they damn well chose.

No wonder the southerners began hating the French as much as the northerners. The educated people who organised opposition tended to be southerners who had grasped the meagre educational opportunities offered by the French. In this respect, the northerners clearly lost out to the southerners during the colonial period, inverting the relationship that existed prior to the arrival of the French. The northerners also lost during WW II, when Italy (which ruled Libya) and the pro-Nazi Vichy government of France signed a treaty giving Libya the Aouzou Strip in northern Chad. This was the basis of Libya's claim to the strip.

Independence

During WW II when 'progressive' political groups were formed, the southerners led the way. And when independence was granted, a southerner, François Tombalbaye, who enjoyed the support of the French, gained control. There simply weren't enough educated and organised northerners to contend for power. The political prominence of the south jarred the northerners, who had become accustomed to thinking of southerners as either subject peoples or merely slaves. But the French had gone overboard in favouring the south, not only exacerbating ethnic animosities and regionalism but also upsetting the political apple cart.

Chad was in bad shape at independence in 1960, and the economy began deteriorating almost immediately. Nevertheless, the country was self-sufficient in food grains such as sorghum and millet until the onset of cyclical droughts in 1967. Independence solved little; indeed, it set in motion a civil war that turned into a 20-year war with Libya.

The immediate advantages of independence went to the south. Administrators, civil servants and senior army officers had to read and write, so the bulk of those recruited were the better educated southerners. The northerners began to view the new government, dominated by southern civil servants, as representing the interests of the southern Sara tribe.

Within two years President Tombalbaye declared all opposition political parties illegal and began killing off his political rivals. Revolts erupted, which he met with force and mass killings.

In 1966, Frolinat (the Chad National Liberation Front), the guerrilla movement opposing the dominance of the southern elites, was formed in exile. There was a ground swell of support in the north for the rebels in the field and the movement spread quickly. By 1968 the situation became very serious and the government was saved only by calling in French troops.

Libyan Intervention

In 1971 Libya began supplying the guerrillas with arms. In the same year the government attempted a policy of national reconciliation by releasing some political prisoners and appointing Muslim ministers but it didn't work. The Libyan leader, Colonel Gaddafi, took advantage of the situation by secretly offering to withdraw his support of Frolinat in return for CFA 23,000 million in aid and Tombalbaye's recognition of Libya's right to occupy the northern border strip of Aouzou (about half the size of the UK).

In desperation, Tombalbaye agreed but then he virtually went crazy. He got hooked on Haitian voodoo practices and went on a campaign of cultural revolution, requiring people to replace their Christian names with African ones, and forcing all civil servants and ranking military officers to undergo the *yondo* initiation rites of Tombalbaye's own tribe. The army summarily executed anyone refusing to undergo the ritual.

This was too much. The man who once boasted that he had survived more plots against his life than any other African leader finally saw his luck run out. In 1975, he was assassinated in an army coup and replaced by another southerner, General Félix Malloum.

In 1976 Gaddafi was again sending arms and supplies to Frolinat. But the Arab northerners were more loyal to the rebel leaders from their own areas than to Frolinat, and as a result, the organisation was constantly plagued by internal dissent.

Three or four splinter groups formed, largely along tribal lines. Hissène Habré (pronounced ah-BRAY), was the leader of one of these groups, the tiny Garone tribe in northern Chad near Faya; Goukouni Oueddei was the leader of another group. In 1976, the Frolinat leadership threw Habré out because of his opposition to Libya's occupation of the Aouzou Strip. So he took his 500-man army and continued fighting separately.

Libya responded by increasing its aid to the Frolinat, which in turn inflicted some crushing defeats on the government army and marched within 250 km of N'Djamena. French troops came to the rescue once again. Frolinat's defeat wrecked the chances of a conference on national unity held subsequently in Tripoli. The French seized the opportunity to sponsor a new political solution: a coalition government with Habré as the president and Malloum remaining head of state.

A power struggle between Habré and Malloum was inevitable. Both Habré's and the government's armies were in N'Djamena and, in early 1979, fighting broke out between the two. France declared itself neutral but in fact supported Habré. Thousands of people in N'Djamena were killed and the city was badly damaged. A truce was arranged, and both Habré and Malloum were forced to resign.

But a year later fighting broke out again among the five remaining armies, the most powerful of which were Habré's forces and those of the new president, Goukouni Oueddei, a northern Toubou like Habré. A second, more destructive 'Battle of N'Djamena' was waged, with many people fleeing the city. Libya sent 2000 Libyan-trained Chadian troops to N'Djamena to support Goukouni. After their withdrawal in late 1981, the compromise transitional government led by Goukouni proved unable to govern. In June 1982 Habré's better trained and disciplined troops marched victorious into N'Djamena.

Gaddafi backed Goukouni Oueddei, who returned to the north to lead the Frolinat forces, but Gaddafi put him under house arrest in Libya when he tried to switch sides in 1985. By then the war was no longer a civil war. Forced to conscript 12 and 13-year olds, most of the other rebels eventually changed sides and began fighting the Libyans. In 1987, Chad, with considerable military assistance from France and economic assistance from the USA, drove the Libyans back into the Tibesti Mountains, their last stronghold. Two years later Gaddafi signed a peace agreement relinquishing all claims to the mineral-rich Aouzou Strip; his troops then abandoned the country. Several months later, a UTA flight from N'Djamena with the US Ambassador's wife on board among others was blown up, possibly by Libyan terrorists.

Habré was less successful in governing than in fighting. Even before his major diplomatic victory in the Aouzou Strip, there were signs of treachery within the presidential palace. Habré's inner circle of advisers, disillusioned with his programme of reconciliation with former opponents, abandoned him and plotted his overthrow. In late 1990 Habré was run out of office by Idris Deby (DAY-bee), one of Habré's key military advisers and a member of the same powerful Toubou clan.

The day before leaving the country, the volatile Habré went on a senseless killing spree, ordering the execution of some 300 political prisoners, among others. But Habré, now in exile in Dakar (Senegal), is by no means out of the picture. In early 1992, roughly 500 of his armed supporters entered the country near Lake Chad and captured two towns, causing organisers of the Paris to Cape Town auto rally to cancel the Chadian leg of the race. Government troops supported by French paratroopers eventually drove the attackers away. Meanwhile, the pragmatic president Deby is holding the fragile government together reasonably well.

GEOGRAPHY

Chad is the fifth largest country in Africa, landlocked and with less than six million people. The only major city is N'Djamena with about 650,000 inhabitants and about 300 metres above sea level; the southern towns of Sarh and Moundou follow with roughly 80,000 and 70,000 inhabitants, respectively. Lac Chad is only a two-hour drive north-west of N'Djamena and borders Niger, Nigeria and Cameroun. In recent years the water level has dropped significantly, reducing its size to about half that shown on most maps. The border areas, once under water during the flood season, are now marshy, complicating the chances of finding a *pirogue* (canoe).

The country is divided into three climatic zones. When you're in N'Djamena and suffering in 40°C temperatures, it's hard to imagine that in the northern Saharan region of Chad, north of the 16th parallel and in the heart of the desert, there are real mountains, not just hills, and that temperatures frequently fall below minus 8°C. Two peaks rise well over 3000 metres (Emi Koussi is 3415 metres), by far the highest points in the Sahara. This is the Tibesti region. When Lac Chad was at its largest several thousand years ago, these mountains formed the northern edge, which is why the area is loaded with archaeological artefacts.

In the central region of Chad, including N'Djamena and Lac Chad, you'll see a mixture of scrub and sand; this is part of the Sahel, where rainfall is very light.

In the more tropical southern third of the country the Chari and Logone rivers, which originate in the Central African Republic (the CAR), cut through the area as they flow northward to N'Djamena where they join before emptying into Lac Chad, which lacks an outlet. Between August and December, the Chari usually overflows in the south, inundating huge areas of land. The irrigation potential of this fertile area, which feeds the entire country, is most obvious at this time as it is very green and wet. It's also the only area of Chad with any significant fauna, mainly birds and antelope.

The Chari is usually navigable, but if you're in Chad at the end of the dry season in May, don't be surprised if it has largely dried up around N'Djamena.

CLIMATE

Chad is hot, particularly from March through to May. Daytime temperatures of 45°C (115°F) and higher are usual during this period. However, from December to mid-February, day temperatures are ideal and the evenings quite chilly, with temperatures lowering to 6°C or so. The skies during this period are hazy owing to the harmattan.

In the south the rainy season is from June to September. The rainfall is much heavier than most travellers expect. In N'Djamena, on the other hand, the rainy season lasts only about three months, from late June to early September, August being the wettest month. It takes very little rain, however, for the sandy tracks north of N'Djamena to become muddy and impassable. (The main roads to the south are all-weather.)

GOVERNMENT

Despite broad international support, even from Libya, Deby has a weak internal power base and has had to spend most of his time attempting to consolidate power. The political division between the northerners and the southerners is as deep as ever, and to unite them to any degree Deby has had no alternative but to move in the direction of a multiparty system, especially since much of the government's budget is being underwritten by the French who insist on this as a condition of support.

Jean Bawoyeu Alingué, a southerner, was named prime minister in 1991 and given the task of creating a new constitution, to be submitted to referendum. Since then, however, Deby has had more major concerns than preparing the country for civilian rule. One headache has been how to reward the Zaghawa tribesmen of Sudan, whom he recruited while in Sudan plotting Habré's overthrow. Integrating them into the armed forces is out of the question, leaving resettlement as the only option although there is no money to finance this.

Deby has also faced a power struggle with Maldoum Bada Abbas, the minister of the interior, a northerner and the country's de facto second in command, and ended up by arresting him on reportedly trumped-up charges of treason. With these problems and the security difficulties caused by dissidents loyal to Habré, Deby has been very slow to follow up on his commitment to pluralism, and in 1993 most efforts in this regard were moving at a snail's pace.

ECONOMY

On the economic front, there are signs of hope. During the 1980s Chad was invariably ranked as the world's poorest country, but since then conditions have improved and the country no longer has that distinction. Foreign donors are pumping money into the country's road network, mostly the southern half, and the road system in this area has greatly improved. Still, Chad's case would seem to contradict the classical theory of world trade and comparative advantage, which says that everybody is better off when countries specialise in those goods which they can produce more cheaply than anybody else – Chad has a comparative advantage in nothing.

However, Chad does have three potential sources of revenue – oil, minerals and a giant neighbour, Nigeria, that can't feed itself. A three-company consortium has discovered major oil reserves near Sarh. A major stumbling block is the high cost of building a pipeline through Cameroun to the coast. If funds can be found and arrangements for a pipeline can be worked out with the Camerounian government – another big 'if' – oil will undoubtedly become the country's major foreign exchange earner. In addition, far west of Sarh near Léré and the Camerounian border are major deposits of gold, another potential source of hard currency for the country. Finally, the southern area of Chad is fertile and highly productive, with major irrigation possibilities. The vastly improved road system in this area has significantly increased the possibility of exporting basic food crops to Nigeria, which is the continent's number one food importer, with 20 times the population of Chad.

All of these potential money earners, however, are purely speculative at the moment. Cotton is still king in Chad and it is cotton which puts hard cash into the hands of southern farmers and foreign exchange in the government coffers. Chad is the second-largest producer of cotton in Africa after Egypt and cotton accounts for about 70% of all export earnings. But when cotton prices fall, Chadian farmers cannot just give it up and plant something else. It takes years in Africa to introduce a new cash crop, and in the case of Chad, transportation costs are high because the country is landlocked, greatly limiting alternatives. So when the world cotton prices fall, as occurred during the late 1980s, farmers have no alternative but to continue planting. The cotton processing company, Cotontchad, often loses in the process but since the end of the war, whenever there's a bumper crop as in 1991, it usually turns a small profit. However, monocrop cotton farming will never be the country's saviour – only oil, gold and/or diversified food crops for the Nigerian market seem to have that potential.

POPULATION & PEOPLE
Toubou
It is common to hear that the people of Chad are divided between the Arabs in the north and Black, sedentary Africans in the south. This is an over-simplification. In the northern third of the country, the heart of the Sahara, the people are not Arabs but mostly indigenous Saharan people of the Tuareg-Berber people known as the Toubou, numbering about 150,000.

Toubou refer to themselves as Téda or Daza depending on whether they speak Tédaga or Dazaga, two dialects of a distinct Saharan language. Like the Arabs, they are Muslims but there are differences. Unlike the Arabs, they do not consider themselves to be descendants of one mythical founder; rather, they consider themselves to be from a certain locality. Toubou, for example, means 'man from Tibesti'. They are herders and nomads, although some are only semi-nomads, returning to their permanent villages during the rainy season from early July to September.

They are fiercely independent and very much bound to clans, each clan having access to specific wells, pastures and oases. Small in number, largely uneducated but fierce warriors, the Toubou have controlled the country since 1982. President Deby is from one of these small clans, the Zagawa Goran; his two predecessors were from others.

Another group of people who historically have resisted Islam and whose leaders now give political support to the Toubou are the Hadjeraï, 'men of the rocks', who reside in the Guére plateau several hundred km east of N'Djamena.

Arabs
The Arabs are concentrated in the middle third of the country, the region of the former Kanem-Bornu, Baguirmi and Ouadaï kingdoms. The northern limit is a wavering line between the 14th and 16th parallels (14° latitude) north of the equator which is too dry for millet even in the best of years. The southern limit is the 10th parallel (10° latitude) south of the equator, where the nomads generally don't wander. Arabs constitute about a third of Chad's population and are mostly semi-nomads who range their herds

over the Sahel, leaving the area above the 16th parallel (16° latitude) to the Toubou. Those to the south are more often cattle herders. But not everybody in this area is Arabic; there are many non-Arabic sedentary farmers.

The broad classification 'Arab' disguises a lot of subgroups that could be classified as separate ethnic groups. Two groups in the Abéché area are the Ouadïens, descendants of the Ouadaï kingdom, and the Maba, who speak the Bora-Mabang language. What is unique about the Maba is their pre-Islamic institution of age-grades, a device for handing power over to each successive generation as it reaches maturity. There are four such groups for each sex, cutting across kin and caste divisions. People born within a certain time period move together from one grade to another, bound together by strong bonds of friendship and obligations for mutual aid.

Sara

In the far south below the 10th parallel (10° south of equator) including the area of Sarh, the population becomes more dense and almost entirely agricultural. Most are Black Africans and non-Muslim. A few (about 5% of the country's total population) are Catholics; the remainder practise traditional African religions.

The largest group is the Sara people, who account for about 30% of the population. Over the past four or five centuries, they have been subjected to some of the most inhuman treatment of any Africans on the continent, first by the Arab slave traders and then by the French who likewise decimated Sara villages when they forcibly sent their men away to work on the Congo-Ocean railroad in the Congo. Later the French forced them to convert to mono-crop cotton farming to pay off taxes, which were collected in a way that undermined the power of the traditional village chiefs, leading to a major breakdown of the social order.

You may have seen pictures of Africans with artificially elongated lips. The Sara women used to do this to make themselves unattractive to the slave raiders. With such fierce survival skills, as evidenced also by their grasping of the meagre educational opportunities offered to them by the French, the Sara have not only survived intact but now occupy most of the civil service positions and many mid-level military positions.

MUSIC

In N'Djamena, which is the Mecca for virtually all travellers to Chad, those interested in hearing the very danceable African pop music head for the lively, beer-flowing districts where the southerners live. However, for hearing traditional African music you should go to the areas of town where the Muslims predominate. These districts are quieter at night, without bars on every corner, and initially don't seem to have much going on. But the Arab sections of town are where you're most likely to hear traditional African music, and maybe even see a group performing.

The men who play such music – extending all across West Africa to Lake Chad and the Muslim areas of Chad – come from a special caste known as *griots*, who are professional musicians and troubadors, the counterpart of the medieval European minstrels. They are the living archives of the people's traditions and their songs and epic narrations, handed down from generation to generation, are a feature of special occasions such as weddings.

They use an assortment of instruments to accompany their singing, one of the most notable being the bow-harp. There are several varieties in Chad, the most common being the five-stringed *kinde*, which is placed laterally with the strings to the ground. The flute is another commonly used instrument, although it is the Fulani shepherds who are most renowned for their beautiful flute music, usually from instruments which are simply lengths of reed.

Trumpets are also popular and are invariably made from what's available locally, such as goat horns. One, called the *hu-hu*, is made from calabashes. It consists of a long tube attached to a bell and, unusually, doubles up as a loudpeaker. Another, called the *kakaki*, is made of tin and is remarkably long, measuring up to almost three metres. It only has two notes but its majestical tone augments orchestras quite nicely.

There's a lot more to traditional music than merely the sounds themselves, which are not easy for foreigners to appreciate initially. The musicians and their instruments are fascinating. So even if the music seems weird at first, especially if your introduction to it is via the radio, do try to hear a live performance (in N'Djamena, by wandering during the day on the weekends or holidays through the streets of the Muslim sections), as that is the best way by far to kindle an interest in traditional music.

LANGUAGE

French is the official language. The principal African languages are Sara (pronounced SAH-rah), spoken primarily in the south, and Turku, a less 'pure' Arabic frequently referred to as Chadian Arabic, spoken in N'Djamena and northern Chad.

Greetings & Civilities in Chadian Arabic
Good morning
  Mah-lam-ah-LEK
Good evening
  Mah-sah-el-HAIR
How are you?
  AH-fee-ah?
Thank you
  SHOE-kran
Goodbye
  Mah-sah-LAM

Greetings & Civilities in Sara
How are you?
  Dah-bahn-YOH-ah?
Fine
  Um-DEE-car-ree
Thank you
  An-GAIN (nasal)
Goodbye
  Mah-MOH-ee

Facts for the Visitor

VISAS & EMBASSIES
Chadian Visas
Only German and French citizens do not need visas. Visas are usually for three months and can be renewed without difficulty. The Chadian Embassy in Washington, USA (☎ (202) 462-4009) issues visas valid for two months from the date of issue and good for maximum stays of one month. These visas cost US$12.50. In addition to three photos, they may ask to see a copy of your International Health Certificate.

There are Chadian embassies in neighbouring Cameroun, Central African Republic (the CAR) and Nigeria; they issue visas quickly and without hassle. You can obtain a Chadian visa in every country in West and Central Africa (except the Gambia and São Tomé). Even if there isn't a Chadian embassy in particular countries such as Niger, there will be a French embassy which has the authority to issue visas to Chad. In Niamey (Niger), for example, the French Embassy charges CFA 3500 for a Chadian visa for a seven-day stay and issues them in 24 hours. For the same reason you can get visas to Chad in most African countries with the exception of Rwanda, including Algeria, Ethiopia and Kenya. It usually takes only 24 hours for visas to be issued at French embassies. It is also possible to get a Chadian visa in Kousseri (Cameroun) across the river from N'Djamena.

Immigration officials in Chad are far more friendly than those elsewhere in Central Africa (with the exception of São Tomé). If you are arriving by plane and are coming from an area where you could not obtain a visa (eg Asia and Australia), don't sweat. After explaining the situation at the airport, you'll be told to go to the Sûreté (immigration) where they'll issue you a visa. Even in cases where the traveller could have obtained a visa but had a plausible excuse for not getting one, the Sûreté has been known to issue visas.

Regardless, even those with visas must register at the Sûreté within 72 hours upon arriving at N'Djamena, whether by land or air. You'll need two photos; the process takes only about 10 minutes. If you've been to Chad recently, let officials at the airport know this; they may waive the reporting requirement. Visa extensions, which are fairly easy to obtain, and *permit de sortir* (exit visas) which are only required for those travelling overland to Niger or Sudan, are issued at the same place.

Other African Visas

The French Consulate, open weekdays, 7 am to noon for visa inquiries, issues visas valid for one-month stays to Burkina Faso, Côte d'Ivoire and Togo (but not to Gabon or Mauritania). You'll need CFA 10,000 and three photos; the process takes 24 hours. You can also get Algerian and Egyptian visas fairly easily at their respective embassies in N'Djamena.

Cameroun A single-entry Cameroun visa costs CFA 7000 for a 10-day stay and CFA 10,000 for a one-month stay, while a three-month multiple-entry visa costs CFA 15,000. The embassy is open on weekdays, 7.30 am to 3 pm (although it is only open until 12.30 pm on Fridays), two photos are required and it takes 48 hours to issue visas. The Kousseri border station no longer issues visas.

If you plan to pass through Cameroun just to get to Nigeria, ask at the embassy whether they issue cheap transit visas as is the case if you are coming in the opposite direction from Maiduguri (Nigeria) to N'Djamena. You can get them at the Cameroun/Nigeria border for CFA 1500. (Initially, the Cameroun officials at this border may demand as much as CFA 15,000 for a regular visa but with much persistence you should be able to get a transit visa.)

The CAR The CAR Embassy, open weekdays 7 am to 1.30 pm, requires two photos and CFA 10,000 (CFA 15,000 for multiple-entry), and takes 24 hours to issue visas, which are valid for three months from the date of issue and permit stays of up to one month. As at all the CAR embassies, in the case of citizens from Australia, New Zealand and Ireland, the embassy must first send a telex to Bangui seeking approval. This process can take up to a week.

Niger If you're travelling to Niger, you cannot get a Niger visa in N'Djamena or anywhere in Central Africa, but you can easily obtain one in Kano (Nigeria) at the Niger Consulate as well as in Lagos, Cotonou and Addis Ababa.

Nigeria The Nigerian Embassy, which is open weekdays, 7 am to 2 pm, requires one photo and 48 hours to process visas. Costs vary considerably, from CFA 1000 for Americans to CFA 10,352 for Britons.

Sudan The Sudanese Embassy is open 8 am to 2 pm, Monday to Saturday except Fridays when it closes around noon. It costs CFA 15,000, two photos are required and visas are issued in 24 hours. However, if you want to travel overland, the process takes up to two months as the embassy must first get permission from Khartoum. Instead, you should consider making an application before arriving in N'Djamena. (Sudan has embassies in Abidjan, Bangui, Kinshasa, Lagos and Nairobi among others.)

Zaïre The Zaïrian Embassy, which is open weekdays, 7.30 am to 2.30 pm, requires two photos. As at all Zaïrian embassies, charges for single/multiple-entry visas are very high – from CFA 23,500/38,000 (one-month stays) to CFA 62,500/71,000 (three-month stays).

Chadian Embassies

Chad has embassies in Algiers, Bangui, Bonn, Brazzaville, Brussels, Cairo, Cotonou, Jeddah, Khartoum, Kinshasa, Lagos, Libreville, Paris, Tripoli, Washington and Yaoundé.

Foreign Embassies in Chad
See the N'Djamena Information section for details of foreign embassies in the capital.

DOCUMENTS

All travellers must have a valid passport and an International Health Certificate. Those driving must also have a *carnet de passage en douane*, insurance and a driver's licence.

To travel north to Abéché, Fada or Faya, you need an *autorisation de circuler*, sometimes referred to as a *laissez-passer*. These are issued by the Ministry of the Interior but first go to the Direction du Tourisme between Hôtel du Chari and the Novotel la Tchadienne and tell them your itinerary and licence number. If you're travelling by truck, just ask for *un camion particulier*. The ministry will then give you a letter which you take to the Ministry of the Interior to be signed. The chances of finding the appropriate officials there are much better between 7 and 8 am. The process is simple and can be done in a day if you're lucky, despite what you may hear to the contrary. Nevertheless, start the process early, even before you find a truck, because it could take longer.

Many have travelled on pick-up trucks to Abéché without such a permit and encountered no problems – police rarely ask to see it. But who knows; you may be the unlucky one. For points north of Abéché, the same is not true. The police will ask; moreover, the Ministry of the Interior is unlikely to issue you a permit, particularly if your mission is tourism. So about the only way to see Fada or Faya is to tag along with an expatriate who is going to these places on 'mission'. Nevertheless, conditions are improving every day in Chad and these requirements could be dropped or eased, so do inquire.

A permit to travel south towards Moundou, Sarh and the CAR has not been required since the early 1980s. If, nevertheless, you double-check and someone at the Ministry of the Interior, as happened to me, says you need one, be very sceptical as they are likely to be misinformed or overly cautious. Regardless, they are likely to issue you a permit on the spot. Otherwise, ask a knowledgeable expatriate. CARE (Cooperative for American Relief Everywhere, Inc) is across the street from the Ministry of the Interior.

CUSTOMS

There are no restrictions on the import of local currency. Export of local currency is theoretically restricted but the rule is generally not enforced. Customs officials in general are not strict and at some border posts (eg N'Djamena/Kousseri) often don't bother to search travellers' bags.

MONEY

US$ =   CFA 280
UK£1 =   CFA 425

The unit of currency is the CFA. Bottom-end and middle-range hotels in Chad are significantly more expensive than in neighbouring Cameroun, Nigeria and Niger but are roughly comparable to those in the CAR. Foods prices are high as well.

If you come with West African CFA bills, do not expect many places to accept them; however, the banks and major hotels do. There's a bank at the airport but it is frequently closed. If this is the case and you are carrying French francs or West African CFA, ask the Air Afrique representatives at the airport to change your money; they are usually glad to do so. Credit cards are not accepted anywhere except at the two top hotels in N'Djamena.

Banks for changing money include the Banque Internationale pour l'Afrique au Tchad (BIAT) and the Banque de Développement du Tchad (BDT). In N'Djamena, the BIAT bank accepts Barclays, American Express and Visa travellers' cheques and charges a CFA 750 commission per cheque regardless of the amount. Changing money at this bank can take up to an hour because of the crowded, disorderly lines and slow procedures.

BUSINESS HOURS & HOLIDAYS

Business hours are from 8 am to 1 pm and 4 to 6.30 pm (approximately) on weekdays, and from 8 am to 1 pm, Saturdays. Banking hours are from 7 to 11 am, Monday to Saturday. Government offices are open from 7 am to 2 pm, Monday to Thursday and from 7 am to noon, Fridays and Saturdays.

Public Holidays
1 January (New Year's Day)
End of Ramadan
April (Easter Monday)
1 May
25 May (African Liberation Day)
Tabaski
11 August (Independence)
1 November
Mohammed's Birthday
28 November
25 December (Christmas)

POST & TELECOMMUNICATIONS
Postal service is reliable. International telephone connections, which are by satellite, are usually but not always good. To make a call or send a fax or telex, go to Telecommunications at the post office in N'Djamena or next to the museum in Sarh. Costs are high; expect to pay CFA 9000 for a three-minute call to the USA. You can now direct dial from N'Djamena to Sarh, Moundou and Abéché.

TIME
Time in Chad is GMT plus one hour. When it's noon in Chad, it's 11 am in London, 6 am in New York and 9 pm in Sydney. Add one hour during daylight-saving periods.

PHOTOGRAPHY
Theoretically you need a photo permit, but because the process is so time-consuming, most people don't bother and just use discretion. The process takes anywhere from two days to a week depending on whether the people who issue them are at their desks. The best time to catch them is 7 to 8 am. Take two photos and your passport to the Ministry of Information next to the museum to fill out forms, then get the forms stamped at the sûreté a block away. Take them to the Treasury (Trésor) opposite the museum to pay CFA 10,000, and then back to the Ministry of Information for the minister's signature and the permit.

Even with a permit, never take a photograph of a soldier, bridges, airport, radio station or any government building.

Photo Victoire, in N'Djamena (in the centre of town, next to Librairie Al Akhbaar) is the best place for photo supplies and developing film.

HEALTH
A vaccination against yellow fever is mandatory as is one for cholera if you're travelling within six days from an infected area.

Emergency
For emergencies, there is the Hôpital Central (emergency ☎ 513593) in N'Djamena.

DANGERS & ANNOYANCES
Security is no longer a major problem although forces loyal to the former president, Habré, do occasionally cause short-term disturbances. In early 1992, for instance, they temporarily overtook two towns near Lac Chad. In N'Djamena, between the French Embassy and the Novotel la Tchadienne there are several side streets near the river which you should avoid, particularly at night as the area is guarded with soldiers. Most importantly, avoid walking on the footpath outside the President's Palace (La Présidence).

In terms of pickpockets and petty street crime, N'Djamena is one of the safest cities in Africa but travellers still need to be on their guard. The major problem area is along Ave Charles de Gaulle in the central area between Cinéma Vog and the cathedral. The area in front of Alimentation la Concorde is the most notorious hang-out for young male pickpockets. It's not always just money and valuables that they are after.

If you rent a motorcycle, don't fall into the same trap that I did. When I walked away from it, in broad daylight, some pickpocketers successfully blocked my view while another one ripped parts off the bike. They crowded around me when I returned, to explain how the thief had escaped, and the next thing I knew was that my watch and sunglasses had walked away too.

Getting There & Away

AIR

Between Air France/UTA and Air Afrique, you can fly two to four times a week to/from Paris depending on the season (high season is around December, June and September), two or three times weekly to/from Brazzaville (the Congo) and twice weekly to/from Bangui (the CAR). There are no other direct connections to the north or south of Chad. The few remaining flights are all east-west or west-east. There are no direct flights into Chad from Algeria, Egypt, Zaïre or Kenya. There are now two flights a week to Cameroun, on Tuesdays and Fridays, on Unitair/Cameroun Airlines.

Flying east to west, Ethiopian Airlines provides an excellent twice weekly service from India (Bombay) to N'Djamena with a change of planes in Ethiopia (Addis Ababa). One of these flights originates in Thailand (Bangkok).

From Australia, the quickest route to Chad is via Bangkok, connecting with the Ethiopian Airlines flight. Once a week you can also take Air Afrique to/from Saudi Arabia (Jeddah) and Sudan Airways to/from Sudan (Khartoum); the latter flight is extremely unreliable (frequent cancellations or delays of several days) and probably rates as the worst airline in Africa.

As for direct connections to West Africa, between Ethiopian Airlines and Air Afrique you can fly three times a week to/from Mali (Bamako) and once weekly to/from Senegal (Dakar), Côte d'Ivoire (Abidjan), Niger (Niamey), Burkina Faso (Ouagadougou) and Mauritania (Nouakchott).

LAND

Bush Taxi & Minivan

To/From Cameroun and Nigeria From Maroua (Cameroun), the major border town

for crossing into Chad is Kousseri. N'Djamena is just across the river. There are frequent minivans and bush taxis ploughing the Maroua-Kousseri route (CFA 3000); some also plough between Kousseri and Maiduguri (Nigeria) via Gambaru (CFA 2000 from Kousseri to Gambaru, plus the equivalent of US$200 from Gambaru to Maiduguri). Both trips take about four hours. Cheap motorcycle-taxis (*taxis-motocyclettes* in French) take travellers back and forth between Kousseri and the border station for CFA 100, and numerous shared taxis and minivans take them from there across the bridge to N'Djamena for another CFA 100. In N'Djamena, these taxis wait just north of the bridge at the roundabout at the end of Ave Mobutu. The border station closes at 5.30 pm sharp.

To/From the CAR The most well-travelled route from southern Chad into the CAR is via Sarh and the border town of Sido. Travelling south from Sarh you should get your passport stamped beforehand at the commissariat in Sarh, otherwise the police just outside Sarh may send you back. There is one minivan a day from Sarh to the border town of Sido, which usually leaves Sarh around noon and returns the next day. The 150-km trip is slow, taking about five hours because of several police checks. The police are friendly but check baggage thoroughly. If you're travelling from Sarh to Bangui, you'll find a minivan just across the border, usually leaving around 8 am. The trip from Sido to Bangui takes all day and a part of the night. The alternative Bangui to Doba route has fewer vehicles. Between Doba and Bossangoa your only choice is a truck.

Travelling north from Sarh or Moundou to N'Djamena (or vice versa), get your passport stamped in Guelengdeng.

Bus & Truck

To/From Niger Travelling from N'Djamena to Niamey via Mao (Chad), Nguigmi (Niger) and Zinder (Niger) is only for the adventurous and takes at least a week, sometimes two. There is a bus service from Mao Parc in

N'Djamena to Mao but not every day. Otherwise, look for a Toyota pick-up truck; some plough that route. Every two or three days there are Toyota pick-up trucks which carry people from Mao to Nokou (CFA 2500) and from Nokou to Nguigmi (CFA 7500). The slow, sandy stretch from Nokou to Nguigmi is supposed to take 1½ days but one group of travellers reported that it took three days. Although the driver carries a supply of water, you should carry your own food and water.

Between Nguigmi and Zinder (Niger) there's one bus a week, leaving Zinder on Thursdays and Nguigmi on Fridays. If you miss it, look for a ride to Diffa (150 km) as there is at least one minibus (CFA 3000) a day between Diffa and Zinder. Get your passport stamped in all four of these towns between N'Djamena and Zinder.

To/From Sudan Occasionally one hears of someone travelling overland from Chad to Sudan or vice versa. On my last trip to Chad I met an Australian guy who was riding his bike across Central Africa and planned to ride from N'Djamena to Khartoum if he could get permission from the Sudanese government – a very time-consuming and uncertain process. (See the Visas & Embassies section.) The only vehicles you are likely to see on this route are trucks and they are very scarce east of Abéché. Anticipate very long waiting periods if you hitchhike.

Car

Petrol costs CFA 295 a litre at petrol stations. Most people prefer the cheaper black-market petrol from Nigeria. In N'Djamena it's sold openly all along the streets in glass jars for CFA 175 a litre. In the south, the cost is higher – CFA 225 a litre.

To/From Cameroun Driving time from Maroua to N'Djamena is three to four hours; from Yaoundé, count on three days. A new bridge over the Chari River connects N'Djamena and Kousseri. The border post, which is south of the bridge, is open every day at 6 am and closes at 5.30 pm on the dot.

Even an ambassador won't get across after this time.

To/From Niger It's a cinch getting from Niger to N'Djamena via Kano and Maiduguri (Nigeria); the road is paved all the way. However, the adventurous should consider the direct route through eastern Niger, from Zinder (Niger) to N'Djamena passing north of Lac Chad. During the day the Zinder-N'Djamena trip takes about four days if you're lucky and don't have problems on the difficult Chad section. The road is paved from Zinder to the border (Nguigmi); you must get your passport stamped not only at the border but also at Diffa. You're supposed to pick up a guide at the border, but some people have reported getting away without one. Giving a military guy a lift is one way to get rid of the guide, and your trip will be smooth sailing.

Continuing into Chad, there are two routes, both passing north of the lake and both very sandy and more difficult than the route from Agadez to Tamanrasset (Niger to Algeria). The main route is via Nokou and Mao and a shorter route (usually preferred) just north of Lac Chad is via Liwa, Baga Sola, Bol and Massakori. Either road can become very muddy between July and September and virtually impassable. At other times be prepared for lots of soft sand.

Stop in Bol (or Mao and Nokou on the other route) to get your passport stamped. Don't be surprised if the police in Bol, who have been known to hassle travellers, ask for a bribe, such as a small tip for 'supplementary hours'. One traveller reported that they demanded CFA 1000 for a new visa, saying her visa issued in Paris was invalid. She and those in her group resisted and, after six hours in the hot sun, won out.

As for petrol, try to bring all you'll need because you can't be guaranteed of finding any en route. Remember too that on the sandy sections in Chad, consumption will be double normal rates. Between Zinder and N'Djamena you may find petrol in Diffa, Mao and Massakori but it'll cost you far more than in N'Djamena.

To/From the CAR & Cameroun The road from N'Djamena to the CAR border via Sarh is now so good that the N'Djamena to Sarh and Bangui route is now at least as fast as the route to Bangui through Cameroun. This is true even though only about a fourth of the former route is paved. Either way, the trip can be done in two very long days. The route through Cameroun has three advantages: many more km of asphalt, more mechanics along the way, plus the opportunity of seeing a little of northern Cameroun, a very interesting area.

If you take the route through southern Chad, get your passport stamped in Guelengdeng and in Sarh. The only bad stretch of road is in the CAR, the 243-km section from the border to Kaga Bandoro. This section has many gullies, making driving slow, particularly during the rainy season.

A third alternative, also via Sarh but 307 km longer, is to go south from N'Djamena into Cameroun to Maroua and Figuil, then east into Chad to Léré, Moundou and Sarh. The advantage of this route is that you pass through northern Cameroun as well as southern Chad. The Figuil to Moundou and Sarh portion of this route is in excellent condition so you can drive from Maroua to Sarh in one long day. Alternatively, you could drive south from Moundou to Bangui; the road is comparable to the Sarh to Bangui stretch.

To/From Sudan It is possible to enter Chad from Sudan, passing through Adré and Abéché although it is almost unheard of to take this route; take all your petrol if you do. From Chad to Sudan, you won't be allowed to enter Sudan unless your visa authorises overland passage; it can take several months to obtain permission. (See the Visas & Embassies section.)

Getting Around

AIR
Air Tchad has an old prop Faukker plane which flies from N'Djamena to Moundou and Sarh on Tuesdays and Saturdays at 6.30 am and to Abéché on Fridays at 6.30 am, returning the same days. One-way fares are high: Moundou (CFA 37,250), Sarh (CFA 40,325) and Abéché (CFA 43,000). Only cash is accepted. Flight schedules are more theoretical than real as flights are frequently cancelled, particularly when the plane is sent to the Netherlands for repairs (a military cargo plane is often used then) and during the cloudy harmattan season (December to March). During the harmattan, pilots of small planes headed to Abéché sometimes have to ask the passengers to help look for landmarks; on occasions they end up in the wrong town! Every so often you hear of a plane barely missing camels on the runway in Abéché!

BUS
There is now a bus service between N'Djamena and the south. In 1992, there were three buses a week to Sarh and an occasional one as well to Moundou but they were still not running during the rainy season (June to September). The only other bus is one that connects N'Djamena with Mao, north of Lac Chad. The ones to the south are large, relatively comfortable buses and not crowded.

The Tchad Tour bus is air-conditioned and costs CFA 6000 (CFA 10,000 round trip) – CFA 500 more than the other two and well worth the difference. Its schedules aren't fixed because it only leaves when full. However the Tchad Tour bus usually leaves N'Djamena Wednesday afternoons around 3 pm, arriving in Sarh around 6 am the next day. If you arrive before then, you can sleep on the bus until 6 am or so. The other two buses usually leave N'Djamena sometime between Mondays and Thursdays and usually in the afternoon.

TRUCK
There are large trucks leaving regularly in either direction between N'Djamena and Abéché. The trip usually takes three to four days, longer in the rainy season, and costs CFA 15,000. There are also trucks going regularly between Abéché and Fada, but

you'll need an *autorisation de circuler* to get there.

Trucks, large and small, are the main mode of transportation between Moundou and N'Djamena but on the N'Djamena-Sarh route the large buses are more popular. Between Sarh, Moundou and Léré, Toyota pick-up trucks are the principal mode of public transportation.

CAR

The principal roads south of N'Djamena are now all-weather and in excellent condition during the dry season and fair to good condition during the rainy season. The nonstop driving time between N'Djamena and Sarh (562 km) or Moundou is about eight hours; between Sarh and Moundou (290 km) and between Moundou and Léré it is about half this time. During the rainy season, driving times are somewhat longer.

The driving times between N'Djamena and Abéché (762 km), N'Djamena and Faya (948 km), and N'Djamena and Fada via Moussoro are all usually two days. The overnight stop on the Abéché trip is usually in Ati while on the Faya and Fada trips it is usually in Moussoro, which is only a seven-hour drive north of N'Djamena. The second leg of the Fada and Faya trips is much longer but can still be done in one day if you leave at or before the crack of dawn.

N'Djamena

When President François Tombalbaye scrapped all the French names in 1973, Fort-Lamy became N'Djamena (pronounced n-jah-MAY-nah). In the days before the civil war, the city had a reputation for being one of the most pleasant cities in the Sahel (which stretches westward all the way to Senegal). After years of civil war, it is now slowly regaining this reputation. Certainly the people you'll meet are among the friendliest in Central Africa.

N'Djamena, with about 650,000 inhabitants and growing fast, now boasts two 1st-class hotels, numerous good restaurants, about six nightclubs, various supermarkets, a thriving Grand Marché, an interesting selection of artisan goods, and African bars galore, occasionally with live music. What more could you want? 'Cheaper accommodation and food that isn't quite so expensive,' you'll probably say. Well, no place is perfect.

It won't take much exploring to note the difference between the Arab section of town and the area of town where the southerners live. The southerners drink beer while the Arabs generally do not, which is one reason why the Arab section of town is fairly dead at night. The section where the southerners live, and where most of the bars are located, is very lively. In the bars you'll find the famous Gala beer, but on the streets and in people's houses you may also find the local millet beer, *bili-bili*, as well as some non-alcoholic sour milk based drinks. The southerners' section of town is also where you'll find the Sunday gala pari-matches, although the government occasionally threatens to put a stop to them.

Orientation

The city is divided into two sections, the European or administrative quarter and the African quarter. The former is spread out with wide streets lined with trees, and is where most of the major businesses, hotels and government buildings are located. It's also where all the fighting took place back in the late '70s; numerous buildings are still full of bullet holes. The African section was largely unscathed; it's much larger, more crowded and livelier.

The centre of the administrative section is the Place de l'Étoile and the main commercial street is Ave Charles de Gaulle, one of the few streets exempted when they changed all the names in the early '70s. Ave Félix Éboué, which becomes Ave Mobutu east of Ave Bokassa, passes alongside the Chari River. Ave Félix Éboué and Ave Charles de Gaulle are the city's two main arteries and they both run roughly parallel to each other, west to east, for about six km.

Ave Charles de Gaulle starts at the Rond-

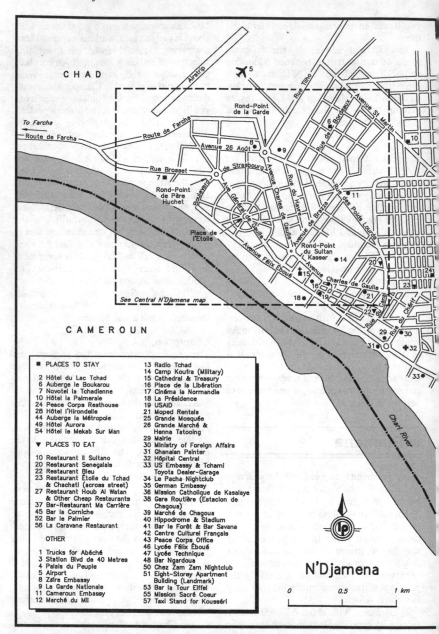

PLACES TO STAY

2 Hôtel du Lac Tchad
6 Auberge le Boukarou
7 Novotel la Tchadienne
10 Hôtel la Palmeraie
24 Peace Corps Resthouse
28 Hôtel l'Hirondelle
44 Auberge la Métropole
49 Hôtel Aurora
54 Hôtel le Mekab Sur Man

PLACES TO EAT

10 Restaurant Il Sultano
20 Restaurant Senegalais
22 Restaurant Bleu
23 Restaurant Étoile du Tchad
   & Chachati (across street)
27 Restaurant Houb Al Watan
   & Other Cheap Restaurants
37 Bar-Restaurant Ma Carrière
45 Bar la Corniche
52 Bar le Palmier
56 La Caravane Restaurant

OTHER

1 Trucks for Abéché
3 Station Blvd de 40 Metres
4 Palais du Peuple
5 Airport
8 Zaïre Embassy
9 La Garde Nationale
11 Cameroun Embassy
12 Marché du Mil

13 Radio Tchad
14 Camp Koufra (Military)
15 Cathedral & Treasury
16 Place de la Libération
17 Cinéma la Normandie
18 La Présidence
19 USAID
21 Moped Rentals
25 Grande Mosquée
26 Grande Marché &
   Henna Tatooing
29 Mairie
30 Ministry of Foreign Affairs
31 Ghanalan Painter
32 Hôpital Central
33 US Embassy & Tchami
   Toyota Dealer-Garage
34 Le Pacha Nightclub
35 German Embassy
36 Mission Catholique de Kasalaye
38 Gare Routière (Estacion de
   Chagoua)
39 Marché de Chagoua
40 Hippodrome & Stadium
41 Bar le Forêt & Bar Savana
42 Centre Culturel Français
43 Peace Corps Office
46 Lycée Félix Éboué
47 Lycée Technique
48 Bar Ngardoua
50 Chez Zam Zam Nightclub
51 Eight-Storey Apartment
   Building (Landmark)
53 Bar la Tour Eiffel
55 Mission Sacré Coeur
57 Taxi Stand for Kousséri

N'Djamena

0   0.5   1 km

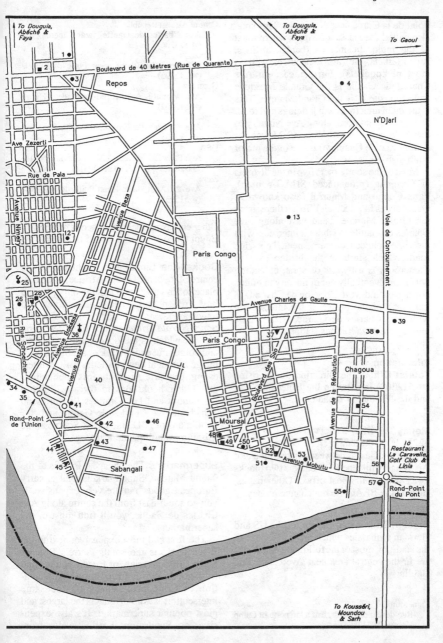

To Douguia, Abéché & Faya

To Douguia, Abéché & Faya

To Gaoul

Boulevard de 40 Metres (Rue de Quarante)

Repos

N'Djari

Ave Zezerti

Rue de Pala

Avenue Ninery

Avenue Béza

Paris Congo

● 13

Paris Congo

● 4

Avenue Charles de Gaulle

● 39

38 ●

Rue Schoecher

Rue Bokassa

Avenue Béza

40

Paris Congo

37

Chagoua

Rond-Point de l'Union

Boulevard des Sao

Avenue de la Révolution

54

Moursal

Sabangali

Avenue Mobutu

To Kousséri, Moundou & Sarh

16 Restaurant La Caravelle, Golf Club & Linia

Rond-Point du Pont

Voie de Contournement

Point de la Garde near the airport. This area, also called the Nassara Strip, is where most of the major businesses (banks, airlines, supermarkets, etc) are located (as well as most pickpockets). Further east on Ave Charles de Gaulle is the Grande Mosquée and, opposite it, is the Grand Marché. This is the main area for cheap lodgings and food. From this point north along Ave Nimeiry to the wide east-west Blvd de 40 Metres (or simply Rue de Quarante) is one of the major Arab districts.

Most of the southerners live in the districts of Chagoua (pronounced SHAG-gou-ah), Paris Congo and Moursal (also known as Quartier des Intellectuels). To get there, from the Grand Marché, head east along Ave Charles de Gaulle to where it intersects with the wide Voie de Contournement. This wide road, which starts at the bridge over to Cameroun, is a bypass of sorts, extending north and eventually out of the city to points north, east and west. Estacion de Chagoua, a km north of the bridge at the intersection with Ave Charles de Gaulle, is the city's major *gare routière* (bus station).

Information

Tourist Office The Direction du Tourisme (☎ 512303) is between the Hôtel du Chari and the Novotel la Tchadienne.

Money The BIAT bank (☎ 514314/21; telex 5228) is in the commercial centre on Ave Charles de Gaulle between Air Afrique and Air Tchad while the BDT bank is two blocks away next to the post office. Other banks, such as the BEAC, do not change money.

Foreign Embassies Except for the US and German embassies which are fairly close to the stadium, most of the following embassies are in the central area near Ave Charles de Gaulle:

Cameroun
    Rue des Poids Lourds, half a km north of Camp Koufra (☎ 512894)

Central African Republic
    Ave Charles de Gaulle, near Cinéma Vog (☎ 513206)
France
    Off Ave Félix Éboué, near Place de l'Étoile (☎ 513793)
Germany
    Ave Mobutu, near Rond-Point de l'Union (☎ 516202)
Nigeria
    Ave Charles de Gaulle, near Cinéma Vog (☎ 512498)
USA
    Ave Félix Éboué, near Hôpital Central (☎ 516-211/18; fax 513372; telex 5203)
Zaïre
    Ave 26 Août, near Rond-Point de la Garde (☎ 515935)

Other embassies include: Algeria (☎ 513815), Egypt (☎ 513660) and Sudan (☎ 513497).

Bookshops Librairie Al Akhbaar, in the centre of town next to Air Afrique, is the best place to find postcards and the only place to buy French and African magazines and newspapers, and sometimes the *International Herald Tribune*. Look for *N'Djamena Hebdo*, which is the opposition newspaper and comes out every week or so. *Info Tchad*, the government news bulletin, isn't so interesting. Librairie Al Akhbaar is open until 7 pm. Other bookshops to try are Librairie Absounout and Les Grandes Librairies du Tchad on Ave Charles de Gaulle and, for good maps of N'Djamena, La Source at the Mission Catholique de Kabalaye.

Supermarkets The cheapest food is at the Grand Marché. Supermarkets tend to carry European goods and are very expensive. If you go south-east from the centre along Ave Charles de Gaulle, you'll find most of the supermarkets.

The first and most expensive, next to the BIAT bank, is the small Pierre's Butcher Shop. It has a variety of frozen, canned and fresh goods, mostly from Europe. Alimentation la Concorde, nearby on the same intersection as Air Afrique, is the largest and most popular supermarket. It's also expensive, eg Supermont bottled water from

Cameroun sells for CFA 550 (CFA 880 from France), a gouda cheese roundel for CFA 1350 and a small box of Nigerian cornflakes for CFA 2300! It's open to 7 pm every day except Sunday when it's open 8 am to noon.

A block further south is Alimentation Générale, which sells mostly cheaper canned goods but it also sells some dairy products. The long-standing Dom Supermarket, across the street, is closed as the owner was killed by Habré's forces during Habré's last-minute shooting spree before fleeing N'Djamena.

Alimentation du Centre, about 750 metres further south, carries much the same stock. Alimentation de la Paix, next door, is noted for its good drip coffee from Cameroun. For cheap soft drinks as well as beer and other alcohol, try Chachati which is further down Ave Charles de Gaulle and opposite Restaurant Étoile du Tchad.

Musée National

One 'must see' is the National Museum which reopened in 1986. Even though some 3000 objects were stolen when N'Djamena was partially sacked in the early '80s, the collection is still big enough to fill six rooms. It's on Ave Félix Éboué, a block south of the cathedral, and open 8 am to noon except Sunday. The entrance fee is CFA 1000 and there are no student discounts.

Grand Marché

The Grand Marché, which is spread out over a wide area south of the Grande Mosquée, has a great atmosphere and is a fascinating place to wander around. The people are friendly and the vendors are not pushy. Look for the women in the business of painting designs on other women's arms. They use henna so the designs, which can be quite intriguing, last only about two months. Try it; the cost is only about CFA 1000 per design.

Activities

Some of the big hotels allow nonguests to use their pools for a fee. Nonguests can use the long pool at the Novotel la Tchadienne

for CFA 1200. The price for swimming in the pool at Hôtel du Chari is comparable.

For tennis, try the two courts at the Novotel la Tchadienne. The German and US embassies each have courts as does the International Club (Base Kosei), but you need to be invited by a member to play.

The Americans play softball on Saturdays at 4 pm in Sabangali, at the end of the dirt road which leads south-east from the Rond-Point de l'Union, near the Auberge la Métropole. They need players so visitors are welcome.

The horse races held on Saturday and Sunday afternoons (starting around 3 or 4 pm) at the hippodrome which is one km east of the US Embassy can be fun. Also, east of town on the road to Linia, about four km beyond the Rond-Point du Pont, is a place that hires horses for riding and, across the road, a golf course with sand greens.

Places to Stay – bottom end

For those on the cheap, if you're really lucky you might get offered one of the dormitory beds at the *Peace Corps Resthouse*, which is definitely not open to the public. It's entirely up to the volunteers as to whether they'll take you and what they charge (CFA 250) and there may not be room, so don't count on this possibility. Moreover, if they get lots of travellers passing by or if the privilege is abused, you can be sure they'll begin refusing all travellers. It's half a block west of the Grande Mosquée and one block north of Ave Charles de Gaulle. The place is unmarked, has a green door with the number 417.

Most travellers on the cheap stay at the nearby *Hôtel l'Hirondelle* (☎ 515470), which charges CFA 5500/8500 for a room with one/two beds. The rooms are small and clean with ceiling fans. It has a restaurant and the Bristo Nightclub is next door. From the Grande Mosquée, go two blocks east on Ave Charles de Gaulle, then half a block south.

Other travellers prefer the nearby *Mission Catholique de Kabalaye*, which is half a km away to the south-east, just east of Ave Bokassa in the Kabalaye area. The facilities

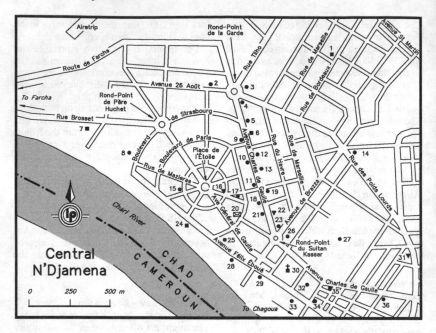

Central N'Djamena

are spotless, with good showers, washing facilities and a dining room with cold drinks always available, but at CFA 6000 a person (plus CFA 2000 for a very filling meal) it's hardly cheap. Ask at the Centre d'Accueil which is next to the church. The mission bookshop and artisan shop are nearby.

Another possibility in the central area is the shady *Auberge le Boukarou* (☎ 512329) on Rue de Bordeaux, about a km east of the airport and a km north of Ave Charles de Gaulle. It's a bordello but presentable, and the four rooms are reasonably priced (CFA 3000/6000, hour/night), clean and spacious, with fans and interior showers and basins. The bar is active with prostitutes and foreigners but the ambience is subdued, so noise may not be a major problem.

Still another possibility is the little-known, two-storey *Hôtel le Mekab Sur Man* (☎ 514036) in the Chagoua area, about a km north of the bridge and a block or two east of the Voie de Contournement. Look for the

signs on Voie de Contournement and Ave Mobutu. It appears to be the cheapest hotel of all, particularly for couples – CFA 5000 per room; highly recommended. The rooms are tiny but clean and have big beds, overhead fans and attached bathrooms with showers and running water. You can eat here and drinks are available as well; a Coke costs CFA 250. At night you'll be within walking distance of numerous lively bars.

Those with vehicles looking for a camping spot should inquire at the Novotel la Tchadienne, which used to accept campers, the nearby Direction du Tourisme, or in the Chagoua area.

Places to Stay – middle

The hotels in this category have air-con but are all fairly poor value. My choice is *Auberge la Métropole* (☎ 516292), a hotel with a rustic but pleasant ambience. It has five small clean rooms out the back for CFA

■ PLACES TO STAY

1 Auberge le Boukarou
4 Caféteria Black & White
6 Hôtel le Central
7 Novotel la Tchadienne
24 Hôtel du Chari

▼ PLACES TO EAT

4 Restaurant le Chinois
10 Pâtisserie l'Armadine
16 Restaurant l'Oustaou
22 Restaurant le N'Djamena
31 Restaurant Senegalais

OTHER

2 Zaïre Embassy
3 La Garde Nationale
4 Cinéma Vog
5 Nigerian Embassy & CAR Embassy
6 Le Feeling Nightclub, Air France/UTA
   & La Terrace
8 Off-Limits Area
9 Palace Nightclub
10 Ethiopian Airlines

11 Alimentation la Concorde & Artisan
    Vendors
12 Air Tchad & Air Sudan
13 BIAT Bank & Pierre's Butcher Shop
14 Cameroun Embassy
15 French Consulate
17 BDT Bank
18 Librairie Al Akhbaar & Alimentation
    Générale
19 Air Afrique
20 Post Office
21 Photo Victoire
23 Total Station
25 CARE
26 BEAC Bank
27 Camp Koufra (Military)
28 Immigration, Sûreté & Ministry of
    Interior
29 National Museum & Ministry of
    Information
30 Cathedral & Treasury
32 Place de la Libération
33 La Présidence
34 USAID
35 Cinéma la Normandie
36 Moped Rentals

12,500, each with a large bcd, telephone, private shower and air-con. The biggest plus is the open-air bar on the rooftop, where the American softball players meet on Saturdays at dusk for beers after the games. It's in Sabangali, south of the stadium. From the Rond-Point de l'Union, head south-east on a dirt road along the river for several blocks, then right towards the river for 50 metres.

Alternatively, you could head east from the Rond-Point for two km along Ave Mobutu to *Hôtel Aurora* (☎ 514051), which has more of a reputation for its nightclub than its rooms or restaurant. The rooms have carpets, air-con and attached bathrooms but are tiny and overpriced at CFA 15,000. Worse still is the similarly priced *Hôtel du Lac Tchad* (☎ 515530) on Blvd de 40 Metres, a block or two west of Station Blvd de 40 Metres autopark. The rooms are clean with interior bathrooms and air-con but there's no restaurant and the ambience is dreary.

Places to Stay – top end
The city's most expensive hotel is *Novotel la Tchadienne* (☎ 514312; fax 514397; telex 5308), which charges CFA 32,500/35,000 including tax for singles/doubles with video TVs. This hotel accepts all major credit cards. Since Novotel took over in 1987 this long-standing hotel has been completely renovated. Overlooking the Chari River and a km west of the centre of town, it has a long pool and an adjoining terrace restaurant which is usually packed at noon, a car-rental service, airport bus, tennis courts and a business centre.

Some 1st-class travellers now prefer the attractive, newly renovated *Hôtel du Chari* (☎ 515350; fax 512261; telex 5358), which is within easy walking distance of the centre of town and has a new, unusually shaped pool and offers the best view of all of the Chari River. Singles/doubles cost CFA 30,500/32,500 each (including tax) and all major credit cards are accepted. Except for tennis courts, it has the same amenities as the Novotel la Tchadienne, including a comfortable bar and expensive and popular disco.

Many travellers prefer the cheaper *Hôtel le Central* (☎ 512690), which is centrally located in the Nassara Strip on Ave Charles de Gaulle and has one of the best restaurants in town and a popular bar. The 10 rooms cost CFA 23,500 each and include laundry service; some are equipped with minibars and coffee-makers but none have video TVs. A popular nightclub, Le Feeling, is next door.

The new *Hôtel la Palmeraie* (☎ 515569/83) is not in the same league as the Central. On Ave Zezerti, about 12 blocks north of the Grande Mosquée, the Palmeraie is less centrally located and declining rapidly (the pool is dry) plus the ambience is dreadfully sterile. The 16 carpeted rooms, which come with a small video TV and minibar, are overpriced at CFA 20,450/25,500 including tax for one/two beds.

Places to Eat

Cheap Eats The Grand Marché area is one of the best places for cheap food. In the evenings, for example, you'll find good street food on the corner of the Grande Mosquée and Ave Charles de Gaulle, most notably the CFA 150 sandwiches with ground beef, fries and sauce. During the day, you can get wonderful mixed fruit drinks at *Restaurant Number One* opposite the Grande Mosquée. You can't beat the CFA 250 price or the atmosphere – very authentic down to the Saddam Hussein poster over the juice machine. These pint glasses of blended fruit, ice and milk are meals in themselves.

In the Grand Marché there are a number of restaurants serving meals for CFA 250 to CFA 500, particularly on the north-south street, a block west of Hôtel l'Hirondelle. *Restaurant Houb Al Watan* serves kebabs for CFA 250, fish for CFA 400 and chicken for CFA 500, among other things. A restaurant that is recommended is *Restaurant l'Oasis*, which is about four blocks south of the Grande Mosquée and Ave Charles de Gaulle. You can also get meals at the *Hôtel l'Hiron-*

delle restaurant, but they're not as cheap (eg CFA 1500 for fish), with the exception of petit déjeuner and soft drinks for CFA 250. For a splurge, it's hard to beat the delicious filling meals at the *Mission Catholique de Kabalaye*. They cost CFA 2000 and are excellent value.

In the Chagoua area, the best place to look for cheap food is along the Voie de Contournement. One hole-in-the-wall is *La Caravane*, a block north of the Rond-Point du Pont.

In the Nassara Strip on Ave Charles de Gaulle there are no cheap places to eat. The least expensive is the *Caféteria Black & White* next to Cinéma Vog. It has soft drinks for CFA 250, decent hamburgers for CFA 1600 to 2000, pizza for CFA 3000 to 4000, among other things.

African In addition to the cheap eats, you can get good African food at several slightly more up-market restaurants. One of the best in the centre is the *Restaurant Senegalais* on Rue du Canal St Martin, about two blocks north of Ave Charles de Gaulle. The owner serves authentic Senegalese meals for CFA 500. The door is green and there's no sign. If you can't find it, try the better-known, equally cheap *Restaurant Bleu* on the same street, two blocks south of Ave Charles de Gaulle. There are several such restaurants in the same general area; the *Assalaam* (or the Cosmos) and the *Choix de Jeunes*. At all of these restaurants you can get a variety of wonderful fruit juices, meat and chicken dishes with sauce, rice and omelettes.

Proceeding south-east to the Sabangali area you'll find the *Auberge la Métropole*, which is an excellent choice and high on African ambience, and you can choose to eat under the stars or inside. It serves superb capitaine fish for CFA 2250, grilled chicken for CFA 1750 (an extra CFA 750 for rice, vegetables and bread) and Gala beers for CFA 500. Several blocks further east is *Bar la Corniche*, a cheaper, outdoor restaurant with a large courtyard, good brochettes and quick service. It's popular with Chadians and expatriates alike. Much further east along

Ave Mobutu, one km before the bridge, is the *Bar le Palmier*, which reputedly serves good Malagasy food.

For wonderful African atmosphere and good food, some of which is Chadian, I recommend the *Restaurant Étoile du Tchad* on Ave Charles de Gaulle, about four blocks west of the Grand Marché. It's open every day, evenings only. The rooftop setting and reasonable prices have made it a favourite for many years. It's best known for its fabulous, freshly made fruit juices for CFA 250. The brochettes – especially the peanut sauce ones – are also highly recommended. Chicken, a few other meat dishes with several vegetables are offered, as well as steak and fries. A meal with drinks costs about CFA 3000.

For a truly unusual dining event, I highly recommend *Restaurant la Caravelle* – an old French Caravelle that has been converted into a restaurant with a disc jockey in the cockpit. You can have drinks outside in the spacious surrounding garden under sun umbrellas, then eat inside the airplane. Fish, brochettes and other simple fare are on the menu and prices are reasonable by N'Djamena standards. It's on the eastern edge of town, one km east of the Rond-Point du Pont on the road to Linia.

French Five of the city's main French restaurants are on or near the Nassara Strip on Ave Charles de Gaulle. All are fairly expensive and similarly priced. N'Djamena's two best French restaurants, both comparable in price to the city's other major restaurants, are *Restaurant l'Oustaou* (☎ 513614), two blocks south of Alimentation la Concorde, and *Restaurant le N'Djamena* (☎ 513922), two blocks south-east of La Concorde on Ave Charles de Gaulle above the former Dom supermarket (entrance via the courtyard of the building). The French owner of l'Oustaou closed his renowned restaurant in Bangui and returned here when the war ended. He takes the orders himself, oversees the service and food production and makes a big production of his meals, serving lots of flambée dishes. Le N'Djamena is run by a French couple. Prices and the quality of the

food are similar, but portions are small. The menu is interesting and the atmosphere is elegant. Both places are closed on Sundays.

Also on Ave Charles de Gaulle, two blocks in the opposite direction of La Concorde, are three more restaurants, all on the same block. The best of these is the ever-popular *Le Central* (☎ 512690), which is also a small hotel (Hôtel le Central). The vigorous Belgian who runs it offers French cuisine (plus pizza which is one of the specialities), good service and dining inside (with air-con) or outside on the terrace. Most dishes cost CFA 3700 to CFA 4700. It's closed on Wednesdays. Several doors down towards La Concorde is *La Terrace* (☎ 512808), a pleasant French-owned restaurant with great ice cream, a popular bar and a choice of outside or inside dining. It's closed on Tuesdays.

Pizza For the best pizza in town, head for *Restaurant Il Sultano* (☎ 515583) at Hôtel la Palmeraie on Ave Zezerti, a good km north of the Grande Mosquée. It's an attractive, popular restaurant with Franco-Italian cuisine and recommended. Also try the poolside terrace restaurant at the *Novotel la Tchadienne*; it has a booming business at lunch time because the prices are reasonable. Pizza, for example, costs CFA 3000 to CFA 4000. The indoor restaurants in this hotel and at the *Hôtel du Chari* are fancier and more expensive.

Pastry Shops For pastry and coffee, head for *Pâtisserie l'Amandine* in the Nassara Strip on Ave Charles de Gaulle, just north of Alimentation la Concorde. It's expensive; most sweets cost about CFA 350. Nevertheless, both Chadians and expatriates patronise it heavily, particularly for breakfast on weekends. It's open 6.30 am to 1 pm every day and 4 to 6.30 pm except on Sundays when it closes in the afternoons.

Entertainment
Bars Chad has one of the best brews of beer in all of Central and West Africa, Gala. Brewed in Moundou, you'll find it every-

where. Not once in over twenty years of war has the brewery shut down for any significant time. It seems that the Chadians have their priorities in the right order. A big bottle sells for CFA 375 (CFA 150 for a Fanta) at cheap bars and CFA 500 at inexpensive restaurants. CFA 800 is typical at fancy restaurants.

Most of the African bars are in the area east of the stadium. Unless you like seeing or getting into fights, avoid *Bar le Forêt* and *Bar Savana* next door. They're next to the stadium on Ave Mobutu. The best places are further east in Moursal, Paris Congo and Chagoua. Most of the bars are in these areas and become pari-matches on Sundays, starting in the afternoon or early evening. If you proceed east on Ave Mobutu, you will find three of the bars which do this. They are *Bar Ngardoua*, just behind Hôtel Aurora on Ave Mobutu; *Chez Zam Zam Nightclub*; and *Bar le Palmier*, about one km before the Rond-Point du Pont. In case you're bar-hopping, a fourth one to go to is *Bar Motema*. During other times, these bars are great places for drinks and meeting Africans. Big Gala beers cost CFA 375 and outside on the streets you will most likely find brochettes for CFA 100.

These are the bars to go to if you want to dance to African music. The people at these open-air affairs are usually very friendly, so finding a dancing partner is rarely a problem. You may see people with written invitations but everyone is welcome. If you are extremely lucky, you might get to hear a Chadian group such as *African Melody* or *L'International Challal*. If the bar isn't having a pari-match, there may be more drinking than dancing.

Nightclubs *Bar-Restaurant Ma Carrière* (☎ 515035), in Paris Congo, two blocks south of Ave Charles de Gaulle, doesn't have pari-matches, but it's one of the most popular places in town for dancing to recorded African sounds. Going east on either Ave Charles de Gaulle or Ave Mobutu, you'll see a small sign pointing towards it when you come to Blvd des Sao, which connects the two. It's down this boulevard. It's attractive

and of a slightly higher class than the typical pari-match bar but only marginally more expensive, eg CFA 300 for a Coke and CFA 600 for a beer. You can also get brochettes for CFA 400 a stick. There is ample seating in a semi-open area, with a large dancing floor in the middle. The clientele is almost all Chadian.

The discos, which are all expensive and inside with air-con, cater to expatriates and wealthy Chadians, prostitutes and French soldiers. Two of the top nightclubs are in the Nassara Strip on Ave Charles de Gaulle. The first, next door to Hôtel le Central, is *Le Feeling Nightclub*, roughly 300 metres down from the Rond-Point de la Garde. A block further down and across the street is *Le Palace* (formerly Booby).

Three other major nightclubs are on Ave Félix Éboué-Mobutu. From west to east they are the *Hôtel du Chari* disco, *Le Pacha Nightclub* just east of the US Embassy and, further east on Ave Mobutu, a good km before the bridge, the *Hôtel Aurora* nightclub. Many of these places are closed on Sunday or Monday nights. They are expensive, charging as much as CFA 5000 for entrance (and one free drink on weekends), and some of them, such as Le Feeling, are often full of prostitutes and French soldiers.

Cinema Cinéma Vog is a very decent outdoor theatre with a good selection of films. Show time is usually 6.30 pm (CFA 500) and 9 pm (CFA 800). It's at the northern end of the Nassara Strip, facing Rond-Point de la Garde. In addition, the US Embassy has films throughout the week; the cost is CFA 500 and there's even popcorn for sale.

Things to Buy

Artisan Goods The Chadian wool rugs are beautiful but heavy. More practical items for travellers include beads, leather sandals, jewellery and boxes. Street vendors sell these items in the Nassara Strip on Ave Charles de Gaulle, particularly outside the two major supermarkets, Alimentation la Concorde and Alimentation Générale. You can find some of these items at the Grand

Marché. There are also magnificent saris sold in five-metre segments in the CFA 5500 to CFA 13,000 range.

One of the main artisan centres in town is at the well-known Mission Catholique de Kabalaye, roughly 750 metres east of the Grand Marché and just east of Ave Bokassa. The centre is behind the mission's bookshop, La Source. It sells some unusual embroidery with patterns from the Tibesti rock drawings in northern Chad. The tablecloths and napkins are especially popular. The work is all done by a women's group. Officially the shop is only open from 4 to 6 pm, Monday to Saturday. However, the women work here every morning except on Sundays and they'll be glad to show you their wares.

There are two government-sponsored artisan centres, one next to the Novotel la Tchadienne which has items from various African countries and another near the French school which has mainly Chadian items. The former is generally unpleasant as the vendors are pushy and there are young pickpockets in the area.

Jewellery Gold and silver are generally sold by the gram. The three best jewellery stores are La Paix, Gerbe d'Or and Les Étoiles Brillante, all in the central area. You can also find women across the street from the Grande Mosquée selling gold and silver, sometimes at slightly lower prices than the stores. For beads and malachite, try the vendors outside the supermarkets in the Nassara Strip.

Fabrics For locally printed cotton cloth, try the market and the STT outlet store on Ave Charles de Gaulle, two blocks east of the cathedral on the opposite side of the street. The STT cloth is usually sold in five-metre lengths but you can sometimes get them to cut it. Both places also have imported tie-dyed cloth and batiks.

Portraits There's an enterprising young Ghanaian in N'Djamena who paints some very amusing pictures, mostly portraits of world leaders but will also paint your portrait or a portrait from photos. You can see his pictures lined up along Ave Félix Éboué, opposite the Mairie (town hall).

Getting There & Away
Air Two to four times a week, depending on the time of year, there are round-trip flights from Paris to Brazzaville on Air France/UTA and Air Afrique, stopping in N'Djamena. Twice a week there are flights in both directions between N'Djamena and Dakar (Senegal), stopping in either Niamey (Niger) or Bamakao (Mali). Ethiopian Airlines serves this route. The latter also provides two-weekly connections from N'Djamena to Addis Ababa, with connections to Bombay, Bangkok and Nairobi. Travellers have reported that Sudan Airways' flights are frequently cancelled or delayed for days.

Air Afrique (☎ 514020), Air France/UTA (☎ 514981), Ethiopian Airlines (☎ 513027), Sudan Airways (☎ 515148, 513497) and Air Tchad (☎ 514564) all have their offices in the Nassara Strip on Ave Charles de Gaulle.

Bus Buses for Sarh leave from the Station de Chagoua at the intersection of Ave Charles de Gaulle and the Voie de Contournement. There are three a week; the best service is offered by Tchad Tour Buses, which have air-con and leave Wednesday afternoons, arriving in Sarh early the next morning. The cost is CFA 6000. The other two buses charge CFA 5500. Occasionally, there are buses going to Moundou and in the future there may be regular schedules (inquire at the station). Buses also plough the N'Djamena to Mao route; the trip normally takes about seven hours. Inquire at the Station de Blvd de 40 Metres; they leave from a point north of here.

Taxi If you're heading for Cameroun you will find shared taxis waiting at the Rond-Point du Pont which will go across the international bridge to the border station (CFA 100). From here, a motorcycle-taxi (CFA 100) will take you on to Kousseri. In Kousseri, you'll find bush taxis heading for

Maroua (CFA 3000) and Maiduguri (Nigeria) via Gamboru (CFA 2000).

Truck You'll find trucks headed for Abéché in an area a block or two north of Blvd de 40 Metres, opposite the gare routière of the same name. Drivers usually ask for CFA 15,000 and the trip usually takes three or four days, sometimes more. Trucks to Moundou and Sarh leave from the Station de Chagoua on the Voie de Contournement. The trip can take anywhere from 12 to 24 hours.

Car The nonstop driving time to Sarh or Moundou in a good vehicle is eight hours and the road is paved for the first third of the way. If you're going to Cameroun or Nigeria, the drive to Maroua or Maiduguri should take about four hours. The road is paved all the way on both routes.

Getting Around
To/From the Airport The airport departure tax is CFA 5000 for international flights and CFA 500 for domestic flights but the price is included in the ticket if you buy one locally. The airport (☎ 515526 for information) has a bank but it's often closed. Taxi drivers demand CFA 3000 for even the shortest trip to town. With considerable bargaining they'll usually accept CFA 2000, but only if they believe that you reside in the town will you ever get the local rate of CFA 1000 to anywhere in the central area. Returning to the airport you shouldn't pay more than a third of this. Those on the cheap should walk; the Rond-Point de la Garde, where Ave Charles de Gaulle begins, is only about one km away.

Car Petrol costs CFA 295 a litre at petrol stations, but the cheaper black-market petrol from Nigeria (CFA 175 a litre) is quite reliable and preferred by most drivers. You'll see it and diesel fuel (gas oil), as well as oil, being sold in bottles all over town, particularly along Ave Charles de Gaulle and Blvd de 40 Metres.

If you are interested in renting a car, there are branches of Diagnose Location des Voitures 515098) at both the Novotel la Tchadienne and Hôtel du Chari. Rates are very high. Other agencies include COOP Taxi (☎ 514316), Habiba (☎ 514372) and SONER (☎ 513198). Renting a taxi by the day is usually cheaper with less hassle.

Taxi Fares in N'Djamena are CFA 100 for a 'seat' in a shared cab and CFA 500 for a taxi to yourself. During the day, shared yellow taxis and beat-up minibuses plough up and down the main streets, particularly Ave Charles de Gaulle, so getting to areas outside the central area, such as Chagoua, is fairly easy and cheap. At night your only hope of finding a taxi may be outside the top hotels.

Motorcycle Motorcycles are a fun way to get around N'Djamena and they're also great for short side trips out of town, to places such as Gaoui. The going rate for a small motorcycle is CFA 750 per hour and CFA 5000 per day. They are economical, something to note if you plan on going out of town on one. No deposit is required but you must bring your passport for identification and pay everything up front. To find the place which hires motorcycles, from the cathedral head east on Ave Charles de Gaulle for half a km (about 10 short blocks). Look out for about 20 motorcycles parked under trees on your right, a block before the paved Rue du Canal St Martin. The mirrors and back seat are easily stolen (mine were), so I strongly recommend you ask the owner to remove them. If they are stolen, you'll have to bargain hard to get the price down to CFA 1000 per mirror and CFA 5000 for the seat. The thieves probably resell them to the owner for less.

AROUND N'DJAMENA
Gaoui
The best short excursion out of N'Djamena is Gaoui (pronounced GOW-wee). This picturesque hillside village, reminiscent of Djenné in Mali, is said to be the capital and oldest surviving town of the Sao people, who have now completely disappeared. Today, Gaoui is one of the country's major pottery centres, and you'll see pottery being made all

over town. The pottery is no cheaper here than in N'Djamena, and sometimes it is even more expensive. If you want to buy some, be sure the pottery has been kiln-fired, otherwise it will crack easily. The attractive ones with sooty black bottoms generally have not been fired.

What's even more interesting is the village architecture. The traditional houses, all made of banco, are painted with interesting designs, often of animals. The town has recently tried to revive this old art form, hoping to attract travellers and money. The most stunning example is the new museum in the centre of town; the drawings inside and outside it are among the best. The entrance fee to this multi-room structure is CFA 500 and they'll let you in at any hour of the day as the proud villagers want to show it off. If you ask, the young guides will then take you all over the village, showing you the various traditional houses, many with freshly painted designs. Photographs are actually encouraged and they usually don't ask for a fee.

Getting There & Away
Gaoui is 10 km north-east of the Palais du Peuple (a huge Chinese-built cultural centre) at the intersection of the Blvd du 40 Metres and the Voie de Contournement. It's difficult to find or stay on the route as the tracks, starting at the Palais and passing through the outskirts of town, seem to go in all directions. So on the way be sure to ask passers-by for directions. A compass might help. If you come by rented motorcycle, consider carrying extra petrol as you could easily get lost. You can probably count on finding someone in the village who'll sell you some petrol; just don't expect to pay the N'Djamena price.

LINIA MARKET
The major attraction of Linia (LEE-nee-ah), 30 km east of N'Djamena, is the colourful Sunday morning market. It's primarily an Arab market and very picturesque. Resist the temptation to take pictures, however, as you can get into serious trouble if you're caught. The people just don't like it.

A little bit of everything is sold here, but the huge number of donkeys definitely stand out. People bring them here from all over the country to sell. You'll also see clothing, colourful prints, toiletries, etc for sale as well as all kinds of weird food and local spices. Sampling the food and trying to figure out what the spices are could take all day. The markets wind down around 1 pm however, so be sure to get here well before then. The adventurous should try some of the curdled milk sold by the Arab women or, more prevalent, the red *carcajé* (car-CAH-hay) drink made from carcajé leaves. Or play it safe with a cold soft drink; there's one place opposite the market that sells them.

Getting There & Away
The dirt road to Linia starts at the Rond-Point du Pont and heads eastward, beyond the golf course. By car the 30-km trip takes about 45 minutes from the Rond-Point du Pont. Those without wheels should have no problem finding a pick-up truck going in that direction from the Rond-Point du Pont. The drivers pack the passengers in like sardines, however. The cost is CFA 500. Hitching a ride shouldn't be too difficult either but you may have to pay unless you ride with an expatriate. Similarly, starting around noon it's easy to find pick-up trucks returning to N'Djamena. Or hitch a ride back with one of the expatriates; it's easier doing this returning than going as you can meet them in the market.

LAKE CHAD & DOUGUIA
Don't be fooled by the maps, most of which show Lac Chad as it was in the early 1960s – about the size of Belgium. Nowadays it is about half this size. In 1908 it dried up completely and again in 1984. The size of the lake varies considerably during the year, and the water level is at its highest from August to December. The average depth is about a metre and a half, which is why about 90% of the water flowing into it from the Chari River evaporates within a week or so.

The best time to see the lake is when it is high, as thereafter, the lake recedes and the border area becomes very muddy and covered with recessional agriculture, making viewing difficult. The lake is full of papyrus and reed beds and floating islands of vegetation, further complicating viewing. If you are lucky and get far out enough into the lake, you can see the Buduma people fishing from their dugout canoes dotted across the lake. You might also see some hippos and crocodiles.

The entrance to the lake is from **Hadide**, about 30 km along the Chari River beyond Dougia, which is between N'Djamena and the lake. From Hadide, a motorised boat costs about CFA 5000 plus the guide's fee. Taking a non-motorised boat is cheaper but much more time-consuming as the lake (or at least areas of it where you can view the lake's vastness) is still some distance away. You're sure to see hippos en route. They are far more dangerous than they look, so don't get too close.

Most expatriates heading this way aren't going to the lake but to Dougia, a small village which was once a large farm. The old hotel here, which a Frenchman completely renovated in the early 1990s, is the attraction. It's a restful, shady place by the Chari River with a refreshing pool in good order and lots of thatched paillotes and picnic tables along the river.

Hadjer el Hamis

If you're up for some climbing, there are several rock formations, known as Hadjer el Hamis, which jut out of the flat sand several km beyond **Karal**, about 20 km north of Dougia and 20 km east of Hadide. One rock is 150 to 200 metres high and looks like an elephant, hence the nickname Elephant Rock. Unfortunately, the government is slowly destroying it for gravel for the country's new roads. It's fairly simple to find a local who'll act as a guide. But take heed: one small section of the climb is so difficult and dangerous that if you slip and fall, it's *adios amigos*.

Places to Stay

In Dougia, the newly renovated *Hôtel Dougia* has 15 air-con bungalow rooms that are clean and quite comfortable. They cost CFA 12,500 per room – about double that when you include three meals a day plus drinks. Technicians from the company, Cotontchad, and other expatriates descend on the place on the weekends so reservations are definitely required at this time. Hôtel du Chari in N'Djamena handles reservations.

Karal is a tiny village with no lodgings, so you'll have to ask someone to let you roll out a mat in their compound and sleep under the stars, possibly to the sound of drums.

Getting There & Away

The 75-km road from N'Djamena to Dougia is now paved all the way and takes one hour by car, plus another hour on to Hadide or less to Hadjer el Hamis. If you're without a vehicle, getting to the lake area takes some effort. There's no regular transport, so you'll have to hitchhike, which can be quite difficult beyond Dougia due to the lack of traffic. During the week you may be able to jump on one of the trucks heading for Hadjer el Hamis to pick up gravel. On weekends you may find expatriates going to Dougia but probably not from Dougia to the lake, as vehicle traffic generally disappears. To get to the lake, take the dirt road from Dougia north-west to Hadide, 30 km or so beyond Dougia. Karal and Hadjer el Hamis are about 20 km further, to the east, but are more easily reached direct from Dougia.

The South

SARH

Historically, Sarh was a risky area to live in. Before the 20th century the area was constantly raided by Arabs from the north looking for slaves. In the early 20th century the village was named Sarh which means 'encampment', and referred to the forced labour camps into which the French brutally interned the Sara people during construction of the railroad in the Congo. Today, Sarh is the capital of the southern region, the cotton centre of Chad, the country's second most

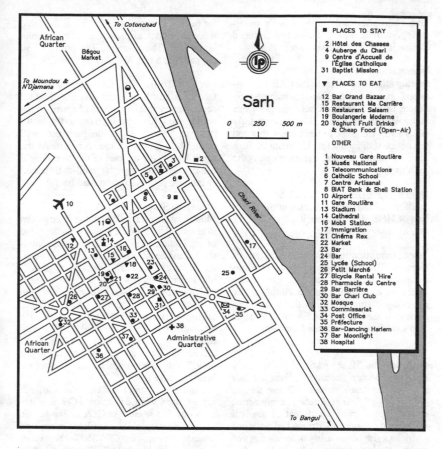

Sarh

PLACES TO STAY
2 Hôtel des Chasses
4 Auberge du Chari
9 Centre d'Accueil de l'Église Catholique
31 Baptist Mission

PLACES TO EAT
12 Bar Grand Bazaar
15 Restaurant Ma Carrière
18 Restaurant Salaam
19 Boulangerie Moderne
20 Yoghurt Fruit Drinks & Cheap Food (Open-Air)

OTHER
1 Nouveau Gare Routière
3 Musée National
5 Telecommunications
6 Catholic School
7 Centre Artisanal
8 BIAT Bank & Shell Station
10 Airport
11 Gare Routière
13 Stadium
14 Cathedral
16 Mobil Station
17 Immigration
21 Cinéma Rex
22 Market
23 Bar
24 Bar
25 Lycée (School)
26 Petit Marché
27 Bicycle Rental 'Hire'
28 Pharmacie du Centre
29 Bar Barrière
30 Bar Chari Club
32 Mosque
33 Commissariat
34 Post Office
35 Préfecture
36 Bar-Dancing Harlem
37 Bar Moonlight
38 Hospital

important transport junction and it is the second largest city, with at least 80,000 inhabitants.

At first sight, Sarh, with its broad, tree-lined streets, may seem like a sleepy, dull agricultural town. But after a day or two, you'll find that it's actually a fairly active town, with lively dancing bars and a number of small restaurants plus a decent French one – all good places to eat and drink, meet people and try out your Sara, the local language. Air Tchad has two-weekly services but you can also take an overnight air-con bus from N'Djamena.

In town, you can rent a bicycle for the day to take a tour and see the central market in the town centre and the museum. Then ride or walk along the banks of the Chari River, and see the ruins of old colonial houses that recall the city's past grandeur. On Sundays you may even see some exotic, nomadic Woddabé herders cross the river on their way to the central market. They'll stare at you as much as you stare at them. The city's top hotel is on the banks of the river and has a pool. If you have wheels, you can take a guided tour of the Cotontchad textile factory or the sugar factory, both out of town, then take a dip afterwards in the latter's swimming pool. In short, Sarh has a lot to recommend it, plus it is generally hassle-free.

Information

Immigration Travellers to the CAR are supposed to get their passports stamped by Sûreté in Sarh (situated between the *lycée* (school) and the river). The process only takes a few minutes. I didn't know this and the police stationed a few km south of Sarh gave me major hassles; the others en route didn't ask.

Banks The BIAT has a branch here, half a km north of the central market in the direction of Hôtel des Chasses. It's open 7 to 11 am, Monday to Saturday.

Telecommunications Across the street from the BIAT is a modern new telecommunications centre where you can make overseas calls quite easily although the reception is sometimes not the best. Three minutes to the USA costs CFA 9000! You can also send faxes and telexes from here.

Things to See

Museum The Musée National is extremely good and shouldn't be missed. There are four small rooms, each with a different theme. One room is full of kitchen implements, another has a wide assortment of musical instruments, especially drums and balafons (African xylophones using differing sizes of gourds instead of wooden bars). The other two rooms have an assortment of interesting objects including some very impressive N'Gambaye straw initiation masks, as well as 19th-century traditional clothing, old photos, spears, coins, etc. It's a km from the central market, a block before Hôtel des Chasses and open from 7 am to 2 pm, Monday to Saturday. There is no entrance fee and the guide is free but contributions are most appreciated.

Centre Artisanal Five short blocks up the same street is a one-room dusty artisan centre. It's worth a look if you're searching

for quality African art. Check out the huge wooden model airplanes as they're quite impressive. The hours are 7.30 am to 12.30 pm and 4 to 6 pm, Monday to Saturday.

Factory Tours The Cotontchad textile factory is north of town and the Sonasut sugar factory is 25 km south of town, on the road to the CAR. If you go out to the factories, the French expatriate managers will most likely arrange a tour for you. At the sugar factory, at the end of the tour they'll usually let you use the well-maintained swimming pool across the road for free.

Places to Stay

Most travellers stay in one of the three places in town and they are all within a block or two of each other, a km north-east of the central market and near the river. The cheapest hotel, the *Auberge du Chari*, is run by a friendly old Frenchman. Each of the five rooms, which cost CFA 5000, has one big bed with a foam rubber mattress and a fan. Before taking a room, travellers (particularly women) should check the single shared bathroom. The toilet, shower and basin, all incredibly filthy, are in one area without a door. There's a late-night bar and you can get breakfast here too.

Across the street next to the Catholic school, the Catholic mission's *Centre d'Accueil de l'Eglise* charges CFA 5000 a person for a spotlessly clean ventilated room and shared bathroom plus CFA 350 for breakfast. If you advise the friendly French priest in advance, he'll include lunch or dinner. The meals cost CFA 2000 and are delicious and filling. If it's full, check the *Baptist Mission*, two blocks south of the central market, towards the hospital, or try meeting the friendly Peace Corps volunteers. They don't have a *case de passage* (resthouse) but you might get an invitation to stay in one of their houses. Some of them are teachers and their houses are a stone's throw from the lycée, a 10-minute walk from the central market.

Sarh's top hotel, the *Hôtel des Chasses* (☎ 681354) near the Auberge, has nice air-con rooms with balconies overlooking the river. The rooms with one/two beds and attached bathrooms cost CFA 12,900/16,400 – a steal by N'Djamena standards. Well maintained by the French owners, it's a colonial-era hotel with a very attractive breezy dining area and bar on the 2nd floor – perfect for viewing the river. You should count on paying CFA 3000 and up for a meal, but for French food there's no competition. Even if you don't stay here, it's a good place to come for a drink, swim in the small pool and view the river.

Places to Eat

Cheap Eats At night, the area in front of Cinéma Rex is always very lively, with lots of tables spread out over a huge cement courtyard and people eating and drinking – the best place in town for people-watching but beware of rogues as they like it here too. There are numerous small restaurants surrounding the courtyard which service this area, selling roasted and other cheap food, mostly meat, sauce and bread, but no beer. At least one of these places, on the main drag, offers yoghurt and milk-fruit shakes in pint glasses for CFA 250-300. They are yummy and highly recommended but there's no guarantee that your stomach will agree.

For above average street food, head for the ever popular *Restaurant Salaam* nearby, in the heart of the market area. For CFA 300 you can get a variety of African/Arab dishes, including salads, kissar and chicken, meat and liver dishes but no beer. It's a lively place and a good place to try out your Arabic and, on occasion, meet Peace Corps volunteers.

A few blocks to the north on the main drag, just before the airport, is *Bar Grand Bazaar*. Between 6 and 8 pm, a woman sets up a stand in front and serves delicious grilled carp and salad to order for CFA 500 – highly recommended. The bar itself, where you'll find loud music and jovial hard-drinking Sara people is open until much later.

Up-Market Restaurants There are only two up-market restaurants in town; the cheapest with the cleanest bathrooms in southern Chad is *Restaurant Ma Carrière*, which is half a block south of the central market. The owner prepares a good combination of African and Western-style meals at reasonable prices – beef brochettes (CFA 1500), capitaine fish (CFA 1500-2000), fried chicken (CFA 2000), etc, all with lots of side dishes. It's a friendly place with a pleasant atmosphere and a good place to come for a quiet relaxing meal, lunch or dinner.

Sarh's top place for food and atmosphere is, not surprisingly, *Hôtel des Chasses*. It's run by a French couple who serve French meals in a lovely 2nd-floor setting overlooking the nearby Chari River. Prices are fairly reasonable as most dishes are in the CFA 1500 to CFA 2500 range. Even if you don't eat here, it's a great place to come for a drink as the beers (CFA 500) are always ice cold and, on occasion, a monkey may jump on to your table and steal your peanuts.

ENTERTAINMENT
Bars

At the eastern end of the central market are two lively bars with standard Chadian bar prices – CFA 175 for soft drinks and CFA 300 for Gala beers. The better one is *Bar Chari Club*; the other one almost next door is *Bar Barrière*. The former is a popular hang-out at lunch time for local bureaucrats. It's quiet, less crowded and more relaxing than many other bars in town, plus the drinks are ice cold and there's good music, mostly reggae which is a favourite of the Nigerian owner.

For dancing, there are two very lively bars in the African quarter on the south side of town which I recommend. *Bar-Dancing Harlem*, in the heart of the African quarter, is always packed after 9 pm and the dancing goes until the wee hours of the morning. The music is loud but fortunately the sound system is reasonably good. Many of the young men outside the door are hoodlums, so be careful.

Bar Moonlight is several blocks east on the main drag, a block from the commissariat. Look for the blue light in front. The Camerounian and Zaïrian music blasts away until midnight and, like the Harlem, the bar is usually packed. Drinks here are almost always cold and next door you can get grilled meat.

Getting There & Away

To/From N'Djamena Air Tchad has two flights a week, on Tuesdays and Thursdays in the late morning. The airport is only one km north of the central market. The air fare is CFA 40,325 – seven times higher than the bus fare, which is CFA 5500 (CFA 6000 with air-con).

There are three big buses a week for N'Djamena except during the rainy season, June to September. They begin filling up as soon as they arrive from N'Djamena and they leave only when full, so even though you may find a schedule of arrivals and departures at the gare routière, schedules are still fairly erratic. Don't be surprised if you have to wait all day for one to fill up. The trip takes about 15 hours. The best bus with air-con, Tchad Tour, usually arrives in Sarh early Thursday mornings. You can usually see the buses waiting at the gare routière near the cathedral but check the Nouveau Gare Routière on the north side of town, two km from the centre, because you might find one there.

To/From the CAR The road to the CAR border is in excellent condition. To avoid hassles en route, be sure to get your passport stamped by sûreté in Sarh. There are buses every day in either direction between Sarh and the CAR border. The cost is CFA 2000 and it leaves from the gare routière near the cathedral. The bus usually takes until around noon to fill up and about five hours to make the trip to Sido at the border, usually arriving before the border closes at 6 pm sharp, and returning to Sarh the next morning.

To/From Moundou For vehicles to Moundou, inquire at both the gare routières. Alternatively, you could wait at the police checkpoint on the outskirts of town and try to hitchhike. The road west to Moundou is, for the first few km, the same as the one north to N'Djamena. The police checkpost on the outskirts of town is the best place for hitch-hiking to either place. There's at least one pick-up truck a day to Moundou, usually leaving around 9 am. The cost is CFA 3000 (more for a cabin seat) and the trip takes about 12 hours, stopping for at least an hour in both Koumra and Doba.

Getting Around

Car There are several petrol stations in town, including a Shell station next to the BIAT bank. Petrol at this station costs CFA 295 while petrol on the black market from Nigeria sells for CFA 225 a litre, CFA 50 more than in N'Djamena.

Bicycle The best way to get around town is by rented bicycle. They cost CFA 500 per day at the 'Hire' bike-rental place in the African quarter on the road connecting the central market and the Petit Marché, roughly halfway between the two.

ZAKOUMA NATIONAL PARK

No game park in Africa has been more ravished by poachers than Zakouma, some 400 km by road north-east of Sarh via Am Timan, on the road to Abéché. It was once noted for its vast herds of elephants, buffalo, rhinos, giraffes and many species of antelope. Hunting in this area and around Sarh was Chad's prime tourist attraction and Sarh was the base for these hunting trips. Starting in the early 1970s, poaching became uncontrolled and the wildlife was virtually extinguished. The government reportedly has plans to begin protecting the park and reopen it to tourists, but for sure there won't be many animals to see for a long time to come. If you're interested, ask the people at the Direction du Tourism in N'Djamena.

SIDO

The town of Sido, 150 km south of Sarh, borders the CAR and part of the town is in the CAR. The Chadian side, however, seems livelier. For information on travel between the CAR and Sarh, see the Sarh section. The border closes at 6 pm and if you arrive here before then, you'll have the option of sleeping the night on either side of the border.

There's a *case de passage* on either side but the one on the CAR side of Sido seems better; the cost is CFA 1000 per room. Whichever country you stay in, there'll be plenty of time in the morning to cross the border and catch the minibus for Sarh or Bangui because the border opens early, around 6 am, and the minibuses usually don't fill up until an hour or so after that.

KOUMRA

Koumra is a small town on the Sarh to Moundou road, 100 km west of Sarh. If you

Giraffe

stop here, head for *Chez Madame Asseme*, which is in the centre on the street behind the large *Bar Mandoul* and unmarked. The bar/ restaurant is the best place in town to have a cold drink and get food. You can cool off out the back under the shady trees with your feet in the sand. Madame Asseme makes a dynamite beef *soupe* (stew), so ask for it.

Coming from Sarh, just after passing the police barrier on the eastern outskirts of town, you'll see the 10-room *L'Auberge*, which looks fairly decent and cheap. It may be the only place you'll find to sleep unless, perhaps, you can convince one of the Peace Corps volunteers who live here to put you up. You'll also find them in Doba, the other major stop on this route.

MOUNDOU

Pleasantly located on the banks of the Logone River, Moundou is Chad's third largest city, with a population of roughly 70,000 inhabitants. The population seems less as the buildings and houses are fairly spread out. The N'Gambaye people, who speak a dialect similar to the Sara people, are very friendly, making this one of the more pleasant towns in Chad.

Crossing the bridge over the Logone, you'll immediately notice the huge Gala brewery along the river. Despite all the hardships that the 20-year civil war produced, Chadians were fortunate that the brewery never once stopped operations. By Chadian standards, this is a factory town as there are also cotton, oil and tobacco factories here.

Logistically, the city is easy to understand as the main street, the only one paved, stretches from the bridge north-eastwardly to the opposite end of town (and eventually to the airport), following the river. Many of the principal commercial establishments are lined along this street. The heart of town is at the intersection where the Restaurant de la Paix is. The city's only taxi stand is across the street from the restaurant. CFA 100 is the going rate for a shared taxi for most destinations in town but the drivers often demand more from foreigners. The town is small enough to walk anywhere but not without a little sweat as temperatures can get very high here.

Places to Stay

Finding an inexpensive place to stay in Moundou is a major problem as none of the hotels are cheap. Your best bet is to meet one of the Peace Corps volunteers here. Some of them are teachers and live very near the lycée. They almost never see travellers, so don't hesitate to look them up as they might end up inviting you to stay at their *case de passage*, especially if you've bought them a few beers. The lycée is on the south-western

side of town between Bar le Gran Village and the brewery and is minimally equipped with several bunk beds and mattresses.

The cheapest hotel you are likely to find is *Hôtel la Crosière* (☎ 343), which is on the main drag on the outskirts of town, two km from the centre in the direction of the airport. It has a restaurant and charges CFA 6500 for one of four rooms out the back. Each comes with a large bed, air-con and a clean, attached bathroom with shower.

It's a better deal than the *Auberge du Logone*, which charges CFA 8500 for its rooms and is better known as a bar than a

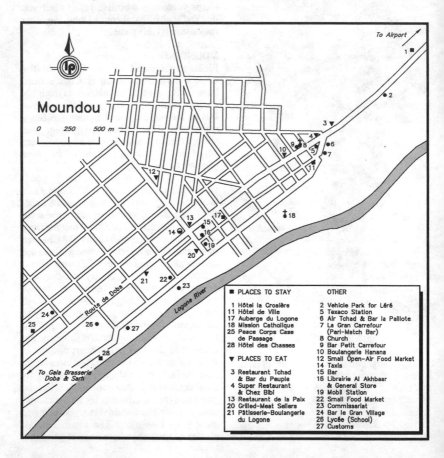

■ PLACES TO STAY

1 Hôtel la Crosière
11 Hôtel de Ville
17 Auberge du Logone
18 Mission Catholique
25 Peace Corps Case de Passage
28 Hôtel des Chasses

▼ PLACES TO EAT

3 Restaurant Tchad & Bar du Peuple
4 Super Restaurant & Chez Bibi
13 Restaurant de la Paix
20 Grilled-Meat Sellers
21 Pâtisserie-Boulangerie du Logone

OTHER

2 Vehicle Park for Léré
5 Texaco Station
6 Air Tchad & Bar la Paillote
7 La Gran Carrefour (Pari-Match Bar)
8 Church
9 Bar Petit Carrefour
10 Boulangerie Hanana
12 Small Open-Air Food Market
14 Taxis
15 Bar
16 Librairie Al Akhbaar & General Store
19 Mobil Station
22 Small Food Market
23 Commissariat
24 Bar le Gran Village
26 Lycée (School)
27 Customs

hotel. There are four air-con rooms, each with two large beds, and clean bathrooms down the hall. The rooms are just off the interior patio, which has several large speakers and is for late night dancing, so noise could definitely be a problem here. It's several blocks from the main intersection in town, on the same street as the well-known Librairie Al Akhbaar (which has a good selection of French magazines), and two blocks up.

Moundou's best hotel is *Hôtel des Chasses*, which overlooks the Logone River on the brewery side of town, 1½ km from the centre. This old hotel has clearly lost much of its original splendour as the pool is dry, the yard is bare and the place hasn't been painted in years. The rooms cost CFA 8000/12,000 for one/two people. They are large and clean with air-con, views of the river and attached bathrooms with working showers. The spacious restaurant is somewhat rustic but the best in town, with meals mostly in the CFA 1000 to CFA 2000 range. For drinks the hotel has a big bar and, better, a small thatched paillote in a tranquil setting overlooking the river where you can have a big Gala beer for CFA 350 or a soft drink for CFA 250.

Places to Eat
For a cheap place to eat, head for the new, highly recommended *Super Restaurant*, a tiny rustic place on the main drag, 1¼ km north-east from the central intersection. The owner, Jean M'Baigoubé, is very friendly and loves to talk with foreigners. His prices are very reasonable and he'll try to fix you what you like. The menu includes spaghetti (CFA 175), omelettes (CFA 250 to CFA 325), fried chicken with macaroni (CFA 350), carp (CFA 500), soft drinks (CFA 170), beers (CFA 300), among other things.

An equally cheap, more convenient place is *Restaurant de la Paix*, at the city's main intersection. This place and the virtually identical restaurant adjoining it are mobbed at meal times, and meals, mostly in the CFA 250 to CFA 300 range, go down fast. You can also just sit here and have tea for CFA 25 and watch the crowds, then have one of the delicious grilled chickens sold on the street just outside the restaurant. The vendors ask CFA 1000 for a whole chicken but the real price is CFA 850. The Paix doesn't sell beer but a block north-east on the main drag you'll find a bar or two that does.

There's also plenty of street food in Moundou. Vendors selling grilled meat with hot spicy sauce are lined up along the short street from the main intersection towards the river. A small market with vegetables is further along, around the corner. North-east from this intersection, up the main drag, is another good area to look for street food. Several hundred metres in the opposite direction from the intersection is *Pâtisserie-Boulangerie du Logone*, which has the best bread in town as well as some canned items. A baguette costs CFA 60.

For a meal at a more up-market place, your choices are very limited. One is *Hôtel la Crosière*, two km from the centre towards the airport. Main dishes, including carp, chicken and beef brochettes, are in the CFA 800 to CFA 1600 range and cost about CFA 800 more if *garni*, ie accompanied by rice, vegetables, salad and bread.

The city's other major restaurant, at *Hôtel des Chasses* on the opposite side of town, has a more pleasant riverbank setting with similar dishes in the CFA 800 to CFA 1600 range. It also has delicious grilled capitaine fish for CFA 2000 and couscous (ordered in advance) for CFA 3000 as well as sandwiches for CFA 500.

Entertainment
Bars A good place for bars is the area around Super Restaurant. *Bar la Paillote*, for example, is at this intersection, across the street near Air Tchad, and *Le Gran Carrefour* bar is nearby. Like several other bars in town, the latter is, on occasion, a pari-match, so inquire what's on. Closer to the centre of town, the most notorious bar is the *Auberge du Logone*. There's lots of drinking on the street-side patio at all hours and on weekends the interior open-air dancing area can be packed. Look at the walls around this patio;

they are lined with some wonderful old posters of Chad.

As the Auberge can get a little rough at times, you may prefer the friendlier, lively *Bar le Gran Village*; it's best at night. From the central intersection, head south-west along the main drag for about a km, then to your right for about 100 metres. It's not obvious, so you'll have to ask for directions. Gala beers at all these places sell for about CFA 300.

Getting There & Away

Vehicle traffic in and out of Moundou is very light. One or two vehicles per hour on any route seem to be the norm. So be prepared to wait awhile. If you're headed for N'Djamena, inquire about the large bus. There is occasionally one and, in the future, the service might become regular. Otherwise, your only choice is hitching a ride on a large truck. Even though the road to N'Djamena is in excellent condition, trucks are slow and can easily take up to 24 hours.

The main route west to Cameroun is via Pala and Léré. Pick-up trucks in that direction leave in the morning from a point on the main drag several hundred metres beyond Super Restaurant. The fare to Léré is CFA 3000 and the trip takes all day in the dry season when the road is in good condition. During the rainy season the road can become very muddy, sometimes doubling the driving time. From Léré it's usually a half-day trip to Maroua or Garoua (Cameroun). If you want to re-enter Chad at N'Djamena, you can probably do so on the same single-entry visa provided your passport is full of stamps as the Chadian border officials are usually very lax.

There are also several pick-up trucks ploughing the Moundou-Sarh route daily; the route is in excellent condition. To catch one, head for the police barrier across the bridge, about five km south of the central intersection (CFA 200 by shared taxi). At the barrier the police will help you find a ride. The best time to catch vehicles is 7 to 10 am. The fare to Sarh is CFA 3000 (up to 50%)

more if you take a cabin seat) and the trip usually takes 12 hours.

The East

ABÉCHÉ

Abéché was the capital of the powerful Ouadaï kingdom, and when the French arrived, it was by far Chad's largest urban centre with 28,000 inhabitants. By 1919 the population had fallen to 6000 people because of major epidemics. Today it's Chad's fourth largest city, with over 40,000 inhabitants. The centre of town is the Place de l'Indépendance and the market is several hundred metres to the north. Many travellers find it an interesting town – oriental in appearance with its mosques and minarets, narrow and winding cobbled streets, old markets (souks), nomadic traffic and run-down structures, including the sultan's palace. If you're interested in camel-hair blankets, this may still be a good place to buy them.

Places to Stay & Eat

Abéché has at least one hotel and a restaurant, so the chances are good that you won't have a problem finding a place to sleep and eat though it may not be cheap. There is also a government *case de passage* but independent travellers may encounter difficulty getting access to it. There are no Peace Corps volunteers stationed here, so staying with them is not an option. You may, however, find friendly expatriates with other organisations who could put you up for the night.

Getting There & Away

The easiest way to get to Abéché from N'Djamena is on the Friday morning Air Tchad flight. Unfortunately, the flight is often cancelled. The one-way fare is CFA 43,000. The cheapest way is to hitch a ride on top of one of the huge trucks that plough the N'Djamena to Abéché route. There's usually at least one leaving almost every day from N'Djamena. It'll be loaded to the gills with goods and, if it's one of the larger ones,

could have up to 100 people on top with their luggage. One traveller said: 'Arab headgear and lots of patience is recommended'. They take a minimum of three days, sometimes more.

If you drive, the chances are excellent that the friendly police won't ask to see your *autorisation de circuler* but I wouldn't take the risk. During the dry season the road is in good condition and the straight driving time from N'Djamena (762 km) is roughly 18 hours, with an overnight stop in Ati. However, during the rainy season, July to September, the route can become exceedingly difficult. Expect to pay a fortune if you have to get yourself dug out of the mud.

AROUND ABÉCHÉ

Ouara, a few km away from Abéché, may be worth checking out. It has a huge six-metre thick wall surrounding the remains of a palace, mosque and sultan's tomb. **Adré** is 166 km east and on the border with Sudan;

every now and then someone makes the trip overland to Sudan via this route.

The North

FADA

The small oasis town of Fada, with about 5000 inhabitants, is the administrative capital of Ennedi, one of the three northern regions. It's a beautiful area with interesting weird rock formations and numerous grottos containing cave paintings, most dating prior to 3000 BC. The most famous geological formation in the area is the Guelta d'Archei, 80 km away.

Places to Stay & Eat

There's an official *case de passage* here and it's in good condition as the French have spent money fixing it up. The bathrooms even have running water. There are no restaurants in town but getting food is not a problem as people are friendly and will invite you into their homes.

Getting There & Away

Fada is 405 km from Faya, 526 km from Abéché and roughly 1100 km from N'Djamena (1288 km via Abéché). There are trucks going regularly between Abéché and Fada and hitching a ride on one is fairly easy, but you'll need an *autorisation de circuler* as for all destinations in the north. The Abéché-Fada road is in excellent condition, so the driving is fast. Along the way you'll see Libyan tanks rusting away in the desert sun.

From N'Djamena, the shortest and fastest route is not via Abéché but north on the Faya road to Kouba Olanga, then north-east to Fada via Oum-Chalouba. You can get petrol in Kouba, but it's generally rationed and reserved for vehicles of the government and foreign-aid projects. East of Kouba is the real desert, an area full of impressive sand dunes. You must pick up a guide in Kouba as the route eastwards is not marked and you'll definitely get lost without one. The trip from N'Djamena to Fada can be made in as little as two long days in a 4WD vehicle. Hitching is possible as trucks plough this route; they usually take three to five days.

As you're approaching Fada, you'll pass a forest growing out of a wadi.

MOUSSORO

Around Moussoro, which is a six-hour, 283-km drive north of N'Djamena, you'll notice that the route becomes surprisingly green, with lots of vegetation. That's because Moussoro and the route north are in a dried upriver bed. Most people driving from N'Djamena stop in Moussoro for the night. It's amazingly active for such a small town. You won't find a *case de passage* there but if you see the Sous-Préfet (a government official) he'll find you a place to stay, probably in his own large colonial house.

FAYA

Faya, in the north-central Borkou region, is the administrative capital of the north and has approximately 15,000 inhabitants. It is not only by far the largest town in the rocky northern third of the country but it's also one of the larger oasis towns in the world. During the colonial era Faya was renamed Largeau after a French military commander. Following independence it became known as Faya-Largeau to avoid confusion but now the original name, Faya, is generally used.

Amazingly, here in the middle of the desert, some 2000 km from the nearest coast, where a decade can pass without a drop of rain falling, agriculture is the mainstay of the economy. That's because subterranean water is plentiful here, barely a few metres under the surface. North of town are three small lakes with different coloured waters, all called Ounianga but with different suffixes. In and around town you'll see millet, wheat, dates and figs growing. The figs here are particularly delicious and if you're here in October or November you can observe the huge date harvest. Trade is important too, as a good portion of the inhabitants are Fezzani merchants who act as intermediaries for the trade with Libya.

Places to Stay & Eat

Faya has a official guesthouse where government officials and foreign visitors are lodged. Food is relatively plentiful here and you should be able to make arrangements at the guesthouse to be fed. Regardless, people are very friendly and will probably invite you to their homes to eat.

Getting There & Away

Faya is 948 km north of N'Djamena. The road is in good condition and most people in 4WD vehicles make the trip in two days. There's petrol in Faya but it is rationed. Hitching is possible as trucks cover this route, usually taking three to five days, but you'll need an *autorisation de circuler*.

TIBESTI MOUNTAINS

The Tibesti Mountains, in the north-western corner of Chad, form the highest mountain range in the Sahara. Some of the volcanoes are still active, eg Mt Tousside (3315 metres), which still emits smoke. The therapeutic springs of Soboroum have geysers and hot sulphuric water. This is also one of the hottest areas in the desert, and 50°C temperatures are typical. Yet the Toubou, one of Africa's oldest tribes, have lived here for thousands of years. As early as 500 BC, merchants from Carthage used to travel here to trade with them and other local people. Always armed with knives and not very religious, the Toubou are constantly occupied with survival and, as a result, are probably the most suspicious, individualistic people in Africa. Without a Toubou guide, you might be risking your life.

Warning
The Tibesti Mountains are still off-limits to travellers.

Cave Paintings
The most special feature about the Tibesti region is the *paintres rupestres* (cave paintings), some of the oldest in Africa. Many of the rock paintings and engravings date from 5000 to 2000 BC and depict simple hunting scenes, providing evidence of the region's former tropical climate and abundance of water. The best place for seeing these paintings is the far north-western corner of the country around the oasis town of Zouar (administrative capital of the Tibesti region) and between Zouar and Bardaï further north, near Libya. The area is still off-limits to travellers but expatriates with projects in the north are increasingly finding the opportunity to visit these sites while on mission there, and most are impressed with what they see.

The Congo

Everybody usually finds something to like about the Congo – it is safe (outside Brazzaville), the locals are friendly (especially in the rural areas), there are clean beaches and good ocean fishing, you can go dancing to the music of some of Africa's most popular recording stars, or look for carved wooden statues. Getting around is half the adventure – you can cruise down the Congo on a riverboat, travel by train to the coast, trek through the rainforests, or fly.

The Congo is like a small version of neighbouring Zaïre (the old Belgian Congo), only more relaxed with friendlier police and far fewer logistical obstacles. To get to the beach or go fishing, you can hop on one of two daily aeroplanes from the capital city of Brazzaville to the port of Pointe-Noire on the south coast, or take a comfortable overnight train. If you want to enjoy the sights and nightlife of Brazzaville, you have less to worry about than in next-door Kinshasa (Zaïre), where crime is the major topic of conversation.

Travelling in the interior, you'll find the road system in the central plateau area as far north as Makoua quite good in contrast to that of Zaïre, which is the worst in Africa. If you're an adventure lover, you are likely to find an overland trip from Brazzaville to Gabon or north-eastern Congo almost as interesting as a trip from Kinshasa to eastern Zaïre, though not anywhere near as time consuming. And with the country's recent changeover to a democracy and a new government, the people have become amazingly open with foreigners and are willing to express their opinions as never before. Finally, there's a new wildlife reserve being mapped out just north of Ouesso (north-eastern Congo); it offers an incredible adventure to those with the time and money to get there.

Facts about the Country

HISTORY

The Congo was the first former French colony to go Marxist, in ideology if not in practice. Perhaps France was just being repaid for forcing onto the Congo one of the most infamous projects of the colonial era: the building of the Congo-Ocean Railway, which resulted in the deaths of untold thousands of Africans.

Pygmies were the first to inhabit the area. Bantu groups, including the Téké and the Kongo, followed them and established powerful kingdoms. Some of these kingdoms were in the practice of capturing men from other areas. This played into the hands of the Portuguese, who arrived here in the late 15th century. They offered these kingdoms European goods in exchange for slaves. As a result, a number of small independent kingdoms arose on the coast, each of which milked the interior for slaves. When the Por-

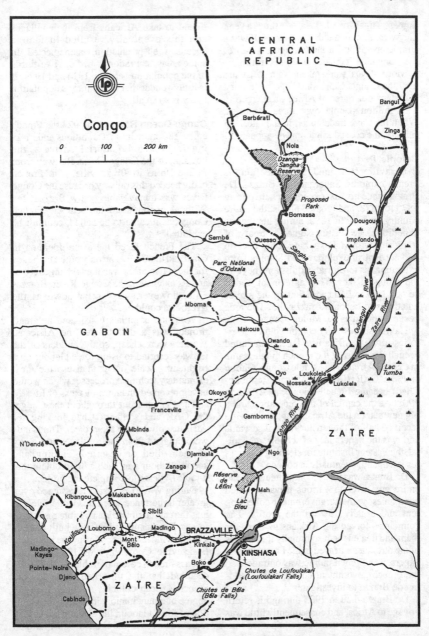

Congo

0   100   200 km

CENTRAL
AFRICAN
REPUBLIC

Bangui

Zinga

Berbérati

Nola

Dzanga
Sangha
Reserve

*Proposed
Park*

Bomassa

Dougou

Impfondo

Sembé

Ouesso

Sangha River

Oubangui River

Zaïre River

Parc National
d'Odzala

Mboma

Makoua

Owando

Oyo

Loukolela

Mossaka

Lukolela

Lac
Tumba

GABON

Okoyo

Franceville

Gamboma

Congo River

ZAÏRE

Mbinda

Djambala

Ngo

N'Dendé

Doussala

Zanaga

Réserve
de
Léfini

Mah

Kibangou

Makabana

Sibiti

Lac
Bleu

Kouilou

Louboma

Madingo

BRAZZAVILLE

Mont
Bélo

Kinkala

KINSHASA

Madingo-
Kayes

Boko

*Chutes de Loufoulakari
(Loufoulakari Falls)*

Pointe-Noire

Djeno

ZAÏRE

Cabinda

*Chutes de Béla
(Béla Falls)*

tuguese ships arrived, five or six times a year, they were merely handed the slaves. It was a simple operation for the Portuguese, but for the Congolese it created internal turmoil.

More slaves were taken from what are now the Congo, Zaïre and Angola than just about any other area of Africa – a staggering 13.5 million people over three centuries. When the slave trade ended in the late 19th century, the coastal kingdoms disappeared.

Colonial Period

Brazzaville is named after the famous French explorer, Savorgnan de Brazza. De Brazza made his first expedition here during 1875 to 1878, and crossed almost the entire country on foot. In 1880, during his second expedition, he hastily signed a treaty of friendship with Makoko, king of the Téké, to prevent British explorer H M Stanley from extending his territorial acquisitions beyond the Congo River. This agreement ceded certain land to France, including the site of what was to become Brazzaville. The area became known as the Middle Congo.

Having successfully combined their territories in West Africa in a federation called French West Africa, the French did the same in Central Africa. The Middle Congo, Gabon and the CAR (Central African Republic-Chad) became French Equatorial Africa in 1908. As the capital of this federation and a big new star on the African map, Brazzaville received half of the territory's civil servants and was the beneficiary of schools, a hospital, the Pasteur Institute for sleeping sickness research, and, eventually, a college.

De Brazza was instrumental in turning the entire area over to various private French companies, with the government collecting rent and usually 15% of the profits. The companies forced the Africans to work for them and treated them so brutally that stories of the atrocities surfaced in the French newspapers. The French public was outraged, so the French government countered by sending de Brazza to investigate.

De Brazza died in 1905 during his return voyage to Africa, and consequently little was done to curb the abuses. The companies continued to take Africans from their villages and this eventually resulted in famine because food production was neglected. In some areas, starvation wiped out two-thirds of the population between 1914 and 1924. It is little wonder that the country's population today is so small.

Congo-Ocean Railway In 1924 the French embarked on their most ambitious undertaking in French Equatorial Africa – the building of the Congo-Ocean Railway from Pointe-Noire to Brazzaville. The French badly needed this railway because the Congo River was unnavigable below Brazzaville. Without an outlet to the sea, the French Congo, as it came to be called, couldn't be exploited.

The French faced the same dilemma in Chad and the CAR. The only outlet to the sea for these two areas was the Oubangui River and its extension, the Congo River. Brazzaville, however, was as far down as the riverboats could go.

What the colonials considered a 'great' project was a disaster for the Africans. Workers were cheap, so the builders of the railway resorted to using forced labour on a frightening scale rather than use the most elementary technical processes which would have prevented an enormous loss of life.

The French went throughout the Congo, the CAR and southern Chad looking for Africans to work on the project. Thousands were dragged from their villages and many of them died or deserted. Finding and keeping labour was such a big problem that it took 14 years to complete the project.

During WW II Brazzaville assumed even greater importance when de Gaulle selected it as the capital of La France Libre resistance forces. The beautiful house he built there is a Brazzaville landmark. During the historical Brazzaville Conference of 1944, held to discuss French colonial problems, de Gaulle declared that the time had come for the French African colonies to enjoy a certain degree of emancipation, including the abolition of forced labour, the election of African representatives to the French Constitutional

Assembly and the formation of their own elected parliaments.

Thereafter, African political leadership developed and progressive political parties emerged, hand in hand with considerable strides in education.

Independence

Because the French had exploited the Congolese so brutally, particularly during the construction of the railway, it is hardly surprising that these new leaders were attracted to communist ideology. The French saw this as a threat to their continued control, so they set about grooming moderate politicians to assume control at independence, which finally came in 1960. Fulbert Youlou became president and quickly established markedly pro-Western policies.

The student and union leaders, however, had other ideas. When the unpopular Youlou drafted a scheme to merge the opposition parties and force the trade unions to toe the line, massive demonstrations took place in Brazzaville. He retaliated by imprisoning some of the labour leaders.

Thus began 'The Three Glorious Days' in mid-August 1963, now the country's major holiday. The trade unionists declared a general strike, freed their arrested members, and forced Youlou to resign. The more radical elements seized power and appointed Alphonse Massemba-Débat as president of the National Assembly during the Youlou period, and Pascal Lissouba, an agricultural technocrat, as prime minister. Thereafter, they formed the National Revolutionary Movement (MNR) as the sole party, which declared itself Marxist-Leninist.

For an outsider, the period from 1963 to 1979 can seem a little confusing. It was a period of constant struggle between the army and the political party (MNR), with the militancy of the people and the trade unionists always a factor. Lissouba was replaced after three years by a pro-communist minister, Ambrose Noumazalay, but Massemba-Débat held on to power for five years, during which time the MNR held the centre of power. The youth wing of the MNR developed a paramilitary force with enough power to threaten the army.

By 1968 they reached a stalemate, which was resolved by a political compromise replacing Massemba-Débat with a leftist army officer, Marien Nguouabi, and merging the party's civil defence group into the military. Proceeding to turn the country into a sort of African Albania, Nguouabi abolished the National Assembly and the MNR and replaced the latter with the new Congolese Workers' Party (PCT), which continued the Marxist rhetoric. Even the country's flag, red with a crossed hammer and hoe, resembled that of the Soviets.

The French supported Nguouabi until he backed away from supporting the West's attempt to keep oil-rich Cabinda (an exclave of Angola) out of Angolan hands. This led to his assassination and replacement by Brigadier Joachim Yhombi-Opango who, they thought, as head of the army would reassert the army's control over the party. He did, but when he went so far as to try destroying the PCT by annulling its congress, the trade unionists took to the streets in protest.

The PCT's central committee then met to make preparations for the party congress. By the time of the congress in 1979, the Congolese radio was accusing Yhombi of having embezzled over US$50 million, including some US$15 million donated by Algeria for a water project in the country's most impoverished area, the Batéké plateau. One of the many rumours at the time was that he had purchased a gold bed from abroad. The congress demanded Yhombi's arrest, expelled him from the party and confiscated his goods. Colonel Denis Sassou-Nguesso, a M'Bochi, took over the presidency.

The 1980s

Starting in 1979, it was the party, not the army, which called the shots. Trade union militants were once again very influential and demanded enactment of radical, anti-colonial measures. The French lost out. With Yhombi gone, they no longer had close ties with the government.

Previously the French oil companies considered it was in their interest to claim that the oil reserves were lower than forecast. But with the new radicalisation accompanying the rise of Sassou-Nguesso, they wanted to be the bearers of good news. The new director of the French oil company ELF Congo changed the company's tune, saying that their forecasts for petroleum production in certain fields were 100% higher than their previous estimates and that they would step up exploration. Production in crude oil thereafter rose significantly, from 1.2 million tonnes in 1979 to 6.3 million tonnes in 1985.

While the party spouted Marxist rhetoric, the country began moving away from a pro-Soviet position to one of political neutrality. On the one hand, the government rolled out the red carpet for the French during Brazzaville's 100th anniversary celebrations and gave the Soviets second billing. Then the Congolese turned around and signed a treaty of friendship with the USSR, something few other African countries had done. This delicate balancing act continued until the end of the decade when the Berlin wall came down; at this time the government's strong ties with the USSR collapsed as well.

Even before then, pragmatism, not socialism, ruled. President Sassou-Nguesso went on a campaign to encourage Western investment and to return unprofitable state-run firms to the private sector, much to the applause of the West. The government even sent groups of Congolese on state department tours of the USA and invited American marketing professors to give management seminars in Brazzaville.

GEOGRAPHY

The country has three distinct zones: the north, the central area and the south coast. The northern area is flat, very wet and covered with rainforests, which are virtually inaccessible for lack of roads. This area contains most of the country's vast forest reserves, which represent about 10% of Africa's total and are the second largest in Africa after Zaïre, covering over 60% of the country. Forest exploitation in the area is increasing at an alarming rate. According to

one study, however, if colonisation for agriculture can be avoided, sustainable harvesting promoted and deforestation kept at existing levels, there is reason to be cautiously optimistic.

The area just north of Ouesso is most noteworthy. It is in the same biosphere as the contiguous Sangha Reserve in south-western CAR and has the highest density of elephants in the country. Like that reserve, it is also full of lowland gorillas, bongo, various kinds of monkeys and many other animals native to the rainforests. While two other areas in the Congo are listed as 'parks' or 'reserves', this area, which is still being mapped out for the establishment of a potential park, is the only one being afforded any protection whatsoever. That's because since the late 1980s, Wildlife Conservation International (WCI) has been working to protect the area. Because of WCI, it is now possible to visit the area, usually on week-long treks through the rainforest with Pygmy guides.

The central area, by contrast, is a succession of rolling green plateaus, with panoramic views, interrupted by valleys cut with deep gorges by rivers flowing towards the Congo River. The most spectacular area is the Réserve de Léfini, which is some four hours north of Brazzaville along the major north-south route. The treeless rolling hills in this area are simply breathtaking – don't miss it!

The central plateau is also the Congo's breadbasket, particularly the 320-km-wide Niari Valley north-west of Brazzaville. It is largely savanna, making agricultural development easier. Roads in the plateaus are relatively good, and the altitude, varying between 500 and 800 metres, makes the climate more bearable.

The coastal plain is flat and drier and is the coolest area in the country. Sizeable offshore petroleum reserves have helped make the port of Pointe-Noire the country's second-largest city. Building roads through the thick vegetation is very costly so the road system is bad, especially between Pointe-Noire and Loubomo on the road to Brazzaville. Consequently, the railway plays a critical role, perhaps more so in the Congo than in any other country in Africa. It's also why three out of four Congolese reside near the 515-km stretch of track.

The Congo River, with the second-highest water flow in the world, also plays a critical role. At Brazzaville, it forms a lake-like expanse called Stanley Pool, which measures 33 by 23 km and separates the city from Kinshasa. It then turns into rapids for most of the remaining journey to the sea. Steamers plough the river northward from Brazzaville towards Ouesso via the Sangha River tributary and towards Bangui via the wider Oubangui River tributary, providing a critical link to the remote northern region.

CLIMATE

The Congo lies on the equator in the thick of the African rainforests. Excessive humidity, not heat, is the main concern. The best time to see the Congo is from June to September, when there's little or no rain, or around late December or January when the rains sometimes let up slightly. The worst times are November and February to April, when there are downpours almost every day.

GOVERNMENT

Since 1990, the Congo has undergone profound political changes. The entry of the US Peace Corps on the scene was one clear sign; another was the rupture in early 1991 of the longstanding alliance between the unions and the PCT. The economy stagnated from the government's oppressive foreign debt (which was 150% of GNP in 1989) and the events in Eastern Europe and elsewhere in Africa opened up the eyes of the Congolese. The government's popularity slumped to such an extent that Sassou-Nguesso was forced to call a national convention to establish a new political order. Glued to their TVs, the fascinated public saw delegate after delegate arise to publicly condemn the PCT and accuse its leaders of corruption; the humiliated president could do nothing.

In a great symbolic break with the past, the conference then adopted a multiparty democratic system, changed the country's name back to the Republic of Congo and resur-

rected the old red-and-orange flag. Later in 1991, Sassou-Nguesso was forced to hand over his principal authorities to André Milongo, who held the new post of prime minister, with Sassou-Nguesso nominally retaining his post as president.

In early 1992, Milongo made the tactical mistake of angering the army by dismissing the defence minister and reshuffling its leadership. Shortly thereafter, rebellious soldiers removed him from office and ordered the interim legislature to name a replacement. The transition government was restructured and the campaign for a new president was inaugurated.

The various parties in opposition to the PCT held huge rallies all over the country but they were in such disarray, with 18 candidates in the running, that it appeared Sassou-Nguesso would be re-elected. Sassou-Nguesso was no fool. Having sensed a change in the wind, he had become an avowed advocate of capitalism. Similarly, the PCT tried to dissociate itself from its past hardline tactics and corruption by advertising itself as 'le nouveau PCT' (the new PCT) and 'le PCT rénové' (the reformed PCT). Its major pitch was that the country needed a government of consensus, like that of a typical African village council, and in contrast to combative Western-style politics where the winner takes all.

The sceptical public didn't buy the party's new line and when the votes were counted in the country's first fair elections in 30 years, Pascal Lissouba won and was sworn into office in late 1992. André Milongo again became prime minister. Trying to diffuse the opposition, Lissouba proposed an amnesty to high officials of previous regimes for any wrongdoing. One of the fruits of the country's new democratic order has been an increased openness to Westerners, including Americans who in the past have been virtually shunned. Another has been the abolition of the dreaded Securété and the many police checkpoints in the countryside.

In mid-1993 elections were held for the National Assembly. A coalition of some 60 parties backing Lissouba won a bare majority and Milongo was returned as prime minister. Opposition leader Bernard Kolelas contested the results and appealed for a 'military solution' which sparked off widespread rioting and looting. This resulted in the death of the Libyan ambassador when he failed to stop at a police checkpoint. Clearly the road to democracy won't be easy.

ECONOMY

With per capita incomes of US$1100, Congo-Brazzaville (as the country is frequently called to avoid confusion with Zaïre) is a wealthy country by African standards but is declining in relative terms – it has moved from third to fifth position in Black Africa, behind Gabon, South Africa, Botswana and Swaziland. On the bright side, petroleum production has increased significantly in recent years because of new offshore discoveries by ELF. Food production, on the other hand, remains a major problem. The country cannot feed itself, and the problem is only worsening as people continue to move into Brazzaville and Pointe-Noire.

The revenue earned from all the wood that the Congo exports from its extensive rainforests barely covers the country's food import bill. The government has given higher priority to improving transportation, building dams and paper mills, and creating rubber plantations and forestry complexes.

Don't be surprised by your restaurant bill as the cost of living is the second-highest in Black Africa (Gabon has the highest). This is especially true of Brazzaville, the world's third most expensive city by 1993 figures (Tokyo and Libreville are the top two).

POPULATION & PEOPLE

The Congo has a population of 2.2 million as compared with 100 million in Japan, which is roughly the same size. The major ethnic groups are the Kongo (or Bakongo) (45%) followed by the Sangha, the Téké (or Batéké), the Vili and the M'Bochi. The Kongo are also a major ethnic group in Zaïre and Angola, and were part of the Kongo kingdom centred in Angola which was flourishing when the Portuguese explorers

Téké headrest

arrived in the 15th century and reached its height a century later. You'll find the Kongo living more around Brazzaville, the Vili more along the coast, the Sangha along the Oubangui and Sangha rivers, and the Téké just to the north of Brazzaville.

In terms of religion, about half the people are Catholics or Protestants and 2% are Muslims. The remainder practise traditional African religions.

ARTS & CULTURE

The art of the Congo is among the most prized in Africa and, unlike in neighbouring Gabon, the peoples' artistic talents have by no means been lost. Kongo and Téké are the two major art styles. *Fétiches* (fetishes), objects believed to be inhabited by a spirit, play an extraordinary role in both. In Kongo art, carved human figures are more realistic than in Téké art and are usually depicted with the mouth open. If the figure is in a natural pose, it's probably an ancestral effigy, not a charm. The charms can be quite large and the figures are more stiffly posed than the ancestral figures.

If you're buying a fetish, find out whether it embodies good or evil spirits. The power of each depends on magical substances being inserted into cavities in the abdomen or head.

Both types are often covered with clay. Those that are inhabited by malevolent spirits are embedded with nails or sharp iron pieces, which are driven into the figures to activate them in retaliation against people who have committed a serious offence. Those that are inhabited by benevolent spirits usually have more peaceful expressions and are activated by rubbing the nose or forehead while offering a prayer.

You may also see the Téké *buti* (male charm figures), which have rigid postures and are supposed to have a magical substance stuffed into their abdominal cavities. Their faces are usually lined and bearded, the feet bent, and the arms concealed by clay or some type of wrapping that secures the magical substance. They represent a specific ancestor, and, depending on the nature of the *bonga* (magical substance), they can counteract sorcery, cure diseases, ensure success in hunting, and so on.

Without the magical substance, they are known as *tege* and are powerless. If yours is wrapped in clay, pack it carefully. Mine was broken in transport.

LANGUAGE

French is the official language and Lingala is the main African language spoken in the north and around Brazzaville. Munukutuba, an offshoot of Kikongo, the native language of the Kongo people, is the main African language in the south around Pointe-Noire.

Greetings & Civilities in Lingala

Good morning
   M-BOH-tay
Good evening
   M-BOH-tay
How are you?
   San-goh-BOH-nee?
I'm fine.
   NAH-zah-lee, MAH-lah-mou.
Thank you
   MAY-lay-zee
Goodbye
   CAN-day, MAH-lah-mou

Greetings & Civilities in Munukutuba

Good morning/evening
   M-BOH-teng-gay
Response
   M-BOH-teng-gay
How are you?
   Wah-fah-SONG?
I'm fine.
   Mou-KAY m-BOH-tay.
Thank you
   Mah-TONE-doh
Goodbye
   Bee-KAH-nah m-BOH-tay

Facts for the Visitor

VISAS & EMBASSIES
Congolese Embassies

The Congo has embassies in Bangui (the CAR), Conakry (Guinea), Kinshasa (Zaïre), Libreville (Gabon), Luanda (Angola), Yaoundé (Cameroun), Bonn, Brussels, Paris, Rome and Washington.

Congolese Visas

Only French citizens are not legally required to have visas, but even they are strongly advised to get them because there have been many instances where French visitors without visas were refused entry. Written proof of exemption, even a notice on the wall at customs confirming it, won't help. In addition, German nationals are apparently routinely admitted at Brazzaville airport without visas for stays of up to 15 days. However, this is not official policy and the Congolese Embassy in Germany advises Germans to get visas.

In Washington, the Congolese Embassy (☎ (202)726-5500/1) charges US$15/20 for single/double-entry visas valid for two months from the date of intended entry. It requires three photos and proof of an onward airline ticket. In London, there is no Congolese embassy, so you'll have to try the French Embassy or the Congolese Embassy in Brussels, Bonn, Paris or Rome.

If you'll be travelling overland, you can

wait until you arrive in Africa as visas are easy to obtain in neighbouring Gabon, Cameroun and Zaïre. However, they are much more expensive than in Europe or North America (eg CFA 25,000 in Cameroun) and those issued in Gabon are only valid for 15 days from the date of entry. The Congolese Embassy there gives same-day service if you bring CFA 20,000 and one photo. In Kinshasa the Congolese Embassy issues visas in 48 hours and requires CFA 10,000, two photos and a *note verbale* from your embassy (ie a letter of introduction requesting that you be issued a visa); the visas are valid for at least one month or longer if you ask. Immigration is very close to the US Embassy in Brazzaville and is responsible for issuing visa extensions. In the past, obtaining them was next to impossible; however, with the new, more open government, they may be loosening up a bit.

A visa is not required if you are merely in transit at Brazzaville to catch another flight and have a ticket with a confirmed seat on the next flight to your destination. In that case, you will be allowed to leave the airport. If you will be coming to Brazzaville via the ferry from Kinshasa, you no longer need a *laissez-passer* in addition to a visa. Similarly, exit visas are no longer required.

Other African Visas

The French Consulate issues visas to Burkina Faso, the Côte d'Ivoire and Togo. The visa section, which is open to the public on weekdays from 8 to 10.30 am, requires CFA 10,000 and two photos and gives 24-hour service.

Angola The embassy is open to the public Monday to Thursday from 9 to 11.30 am, receives visa applications on Mondays and Wednesdays and returns them the next day. It charges CFA 12,000/24,000 for visas valid for stays of 15/30 days; you must also pay CFA 5000 for the telex they send to immigration in Luanda requesting permission, and this process can easily take seven days or more. If you're not going on business, the application will probably be rejected.

Cameroun Single-entry visas good for one/two/three-month stays cost CFA 7000/12,000/16,000 (about double for multiple-entry visas of the same duration). The Camerounian Embassy, which is open weekdays from 7 am to 2 pm, issues visas in 48 hours and requires two photos. If you are not a resident of the Congo, you will need a note verbale from your embassy.

The CAR Brazzaville is not a good place to get a visa to the CAR because the embassy, which is open Monday to Saturday from 8 am to 1 pm (to noon on Friday), must first send a telex to Bangui, a process that takes five to 10 days. This requirement applies to all nationalities. You must bring two photos and CFA 10,000/24,000 for multiple-entry visas valid for one/three-month stays.

Chad With CFA 5000 and two photos in hand, you can get visas to Chad the same day from the Chadian Embassy, which is open Monday to Saturday from 9.30 to 2 pm (to noon on Fridays).

Gabon Brazzaville is not a good place to get visas to Gabon either because, as with the CAR, the embassy (open weekdays from 8 am to 2 pm), must first telex Libreville, a process which takes one to two weeks. If you can wait, bring CFA 10,000, an additional CFA 2500 for the telex and two photos; visas are valid for three months.

Nigeria Nigerian visas cost anywhere from CFA 850 for Americans to approximately CFA 10,000 for Britons. Visas are issued in 24 hours by the Nigerian Embassy (open from 7.30 am to 3.30 pm Monday to Friday) and are good for stays of one or two months, depending on what you request. You must bring two photos and, if you are not a resident of the Congo, a note verbale from your embassy.

Zaïre The Zaïrian Embassy generally issues visas only to residents of the Congo. If you have been travelling for a long time and obviously couldn't have obtained a visa in your home country and you also have a note verbale from your embassy, officials there say that they may be willing to consider issuing you a visa but I definitely do not recommend taking the chance, as it's easy to get Zaïrian visas from any other country in Africa. The embassy, which is open weekdays from 8.30 to 11 am, requires two photos and lots of money (CFA 23,500 for a one-month single-entry visa to CFA 71,000 for a three-month multiple-entry visa). It issues visas on the same day to residents of the Congo.

DOCUMENTS

You will need a passport with a Congolese visa and an International Health Certificate with proof of having received a yellow fever vaccination within the past 10 years and, sometimes (when there's a cholera outbreak), a cholera shot. You should carry your passport at all times or at least a photocopy of it, as police occasionally ask travellers to see their papers.

CUSTOMS

Importing foreign currency is not a problem but if you'll be exporting large amounts of cash, declare it on arrival, otherwise customs officials may give you problems on departure. The importation of CFA is not restricted but you may not export more than CFA 25,000 and, unlike in many African countries, this rule is strictly enforced by customs officials, whether you are leaving by air or land. Anticipate a thorough search when leaving the country.

MONEY

US$1 = CFA 280
UK£1 = CFA 425

The unit of currency is the Central African CFA. Only the hotels will accept the West African CFA. You can exchange them with Air Afrique in central Brazzaville or at the airport; they usually do this as a matter of course. The Hôtel M'Bamou Palace will sometimes change CFA even if you're not a guest. This is a lot easier than going to the Banque Centrale (the only bank that can exchange West African CFA for Central African CFA).

When exchanging money it is essential to compare rates as they can vary considerably. In one comparison, when the US dollar was slightly weaker, the Banque Internationale du Congo (BIDC) was offering CFA 245 for US$1 cash or travellers' cheques without charging any commission, whereas the Union Congolaise de Banques (UCB) in Brazzaville was offering CFA 259 for travellers' cheques (CFA 254 in Pointe-Noire), with a commission of 0.5% and a transaction fee of CFA 1500, and CFA 251 for cash (CFA 245 in Pointe-Noire). In general, rates at the UCB seem most favourable, especially for large transactions; it also accepts Barclays', Thomas Cook and American Express travellers' cheques.

There are three banks where you can change money: the Banque Commerciale Congolaise (BCC), the UCB and the BIDC.

BUSINESS HOURS & HOLIDAYS

Business hours are from 6.30 am to 1 pm and 3 to 5 pm on weekdays and from 6.30 am to 1 pm on Saturdays. Government offices are open on weekdays from 7 am to 2 pm and on Saturdays from 7 am to noon. Banks are open on weekdays and Saturdays from 7 to 11 am.

Public Holidays

1 January (New Year's Day)
1 May
31 July
13-15 August (the Three Glorious Days. This anniversary of the 1963 revolution, which coincides with independence, is by far the biggest celebration in the country.)
1 November
25 December (Christmas Day)
31 December

POST & TELECOMMUNICATIONS

The post is fairly reliable and making international calls from the post office is not a major problem. You can send a telex at the post office (the PTT) or, at much more expensive rates, at the Méridien and M'Bamou Palace hotels in Brazzaville.

TIME

Time in the Congo is GMT plus one hour.

PHOTOGRAPHY

Photo permits are no longer required, but you must still exercise extreme caution in taking photos. Some police may not be aware of the new, more relaxed rules, and many locals do not like having their photos taken by strangers. As usual, photographs of the airport, government buildings, the harbour, ferries, dams, radio stations, etc are strictly forbidden.

HEALTH

Yellow fever and cholera vaccinations are required. The Congo is one of the 11 African countries that have been worst hit by AIDS. Among prostitutes the disease is rampant.

In Brazzaville, the best place for medical treatment is the Association Médicale des Français au Congo (open weekdays from 8 am to noon and 3 to 5 pm). The best hospital is the CHU, the Centre Hospitalier et Universitaire de Brazzaville (☎ 832365/7/8).

Two general practitioners in Brazzaville are Dr Gérard Grimaud (☎ 832594) and Dr Jean-Marie Zimmerman (☎ 832365, 83-4536). Two of the best pharmacies in Brazzaville are Pharmacie Bikoumou (☎ 82-0847) near CHU and Picolet (☎ 821758) on Route du Djoué in Bacongo, next to Marché Total.

In Pointe-Noire there is the general Hôpital A Sicé (☎ 942198/9). A better choice would be the Polyclinique Bethesda (open 24 hours a day) opposite the Mbou-Mvou-mvou Novotel or the Centre Polyclinique Mahouata (☎ 971297). Dr Gérard Guenin (☎ 941751) has his office on Ave de Gaulle.

DANGERS & ANNOYANCES

Security is a major problem in Brazzaville, but nowhere near as bad as it is in next-door Kinshasa, and in terms of theft, Brazzaville seems safer than Douala or Yaoundé (Cameroun) or Bangui (the CAR). The central town area is very dark at night. Normal precautions for a big city are required, particularly in the Marché Total area. Travelling upcountry presents no significant problems.

Until recently, there were numerous police checks on the main roads, delaying travel significantly, and travellers had to be particularly careful in towns because of the presence of plain-clothes police officers. This is generally no longer the case. Nevertheless, traditions die hard and if you are travelling overland from Gabon, you may find that the police from the border south to Loubomo (Dolisie), unlike those on the Brazzaville to Owendo road, still stop travellers and search them. In the past, if you missed one of the police posts you could expect a big hassle at the next one on the way.

FOOD

The food in the Congo is very similar to that of Zaïre. My favourite dish is saka saka (or *feuille de manioc*), which is a delicious stew based in manioc leaves. There are also numerous bush-meat specialities such as *singe fumé* (smoked monkey), *antilope fumé* (smoked antelope), *porc-pic* (porcupine), *boa* (snake) and grilled crocodile.

Bouillons (stews) are also popular, and include *bouillon de poisson* (fish stew), *bouillon de singe* (monkey stew), *poisson salé* (spicy fish) and *ragoût de mouton* (lamb stew), usually accompanied by a starchy glob such as *pâte d'arachide* (peanut paste) or *pâte de manioc* (manioc paste).

The local beers are Primus (a Zaïrian beer) and Kronenbourg, which are comparable in price except in Pointe-Noire, where Kronenbourg is cheaper because of the brewery there. Kronenbourg comes in two different grades, the highest being the '1664' label, which is more often called a 'cravété'. The lower grade beer is called a 'Kronen-bourg ordinaire'.

Getting There & Away

AIR
There are direct flights daily from Paris on Air France/UTA and Air Afrique, twice a week from Brussels on Sabena and from Geneva and Zürich on Swissair, and once a week from Lisbon and Moscow on TAP (Air Portugal) and Aeroflot respectively.

From New York, a 45-day excursion ticket via Paris will cost you about US$2100, but you can get much better deals from one of the budget agencies mentioned in the introductory Getting There & Away chapter. You also have the option of flying to neighbouring Kinshasa and hopping on the ferry to Brazzaville, but the security situation in Kinshasa is so bad that few people choose to travel that way.

The only connections with East Africa are provided by Ethiopian Airlines, which has a weekend flight to/from Addis Ababa via Nairobi. Cameroun Airlines, Air Gabon and Air Afrique provide connections with Libreville (four times a week) and Douala (three times a week) as well as various West African cities, including Dakar (Senegal) and Abidjan (Côte d'Ivoire). Three times a week you can fly to/from N'Djamena or Bangui on Air Afrique and Air France/UTA.

LAND
To/From Gabon
Via N'Dendé The major route connecting Libreville and Brazzaville is by road via Lambaréné, N'Dendé and Loubomo; only the stretch between Brazzaville and Loubomo is normally taken by train. Altogether, the Brazzaville to Libreville trip should take a minimum of six days. Every day there are trucks going north from Loubomo to Kibangou, a picturesque 100-km road. The fare is CFA 1500 and the trip takes three hours. Between Kibangou and N'Dendé (185 km) in Gabon, you'll find only occasional trucks. About twice a week there are beer trucks, for example, which run between the two; just be prepared for a very long beer stop and a fiesta at each village on the way. Drinking is what life is all about in this area of Africa. The N'Dendé to Libreville trip usually takes two days by a series of trucks and/or minibuses and costs about CFA 18,000.

Via Mbinda The alternative Libreville to Brazzaville route takes about four days and is mostly by train. It is less complicated but slightly more expensive. You take the 12-hour Transgabonais to Franceville (CFA 22,100 for 2nd class), a series of two or three minibuses or trucks for the 145-km trip from there to the border via Moanda (about CFA 4000), then the daily train from Mbinda to Loubomo (CFA 8975/4574 for 1st/2nd class), which connects with one of the thrice-daily trains from Pointe-Noire to Brazzaville (from CFA 4195 for 2nd class on the cheaper express to CFA 10,360 for 1st class on the more expensive Train Bleu). Mbinda to Brazzaville takes two days, departing from Mbinda at 5 am with a night in Loubomo, but Brazzaville to Mbinda can be done in one long day if you take the 6.30 am Soleil to Mont Bélo (20 km east of Loubomo) where a connecting train will be waiting. It is supposed to reach Mbinda the same day at 11.22 pm but an early morning arrival the next day is more likely. In 1992 the Mbinda to Loubomo train wasn't running because of a strike, so first you will need to verify that the train is operating.

Car
Driving from Libreville is possible throughout the year. The preferred route is via Lambaréné, N'Dendé and Loubomo, not via Franceville. The distance is 1175 km, almost all on improved dirt road. While roads on the Gabon side are well maintained even during the rainy season, in the Congo the roads can become nearly impassable during the long rainy season (October to May), especially from February to April. Four days' driving from Libreville to Brazzaville is normal. There are petrol stations in Loubomo, N'Dendé, Mouila and Lambaréné but you

can buy black-market petrol just about anywhere.

If you're going to the CAR, your only realistic option may be to put your vehicle on a steamer from Brazzaville; however, it only operates between July and December and the cost is fairly high. It is possible, however, to drive overland to the CAR via Ouesso, Yokadouma (Cameroun) and Berbérati (the CAR) during the dry season in the north (June to September) with a 4WD. The road between Makoua and Berbérati is in very bad condition, so expect the worst.

If you're going to eastern Zaïre, getting there overland can be very expensive as your only realistic option may be to cross over to Kinshasa and put your vehicle on a Zaïrian steamer to Kisangani, which can cost well over US$1000.

SEA & RIVER
Freighter
There are freighters plying between Europe and Zaïre, some of which stop in Pointe-Noire. For information on passenger services, you'll have to go to Pointe-Noire (see Socopao at the port) because the major shipping company in Brazzaville, Delmas Congo, handles only freight. Shipping either a car or a motorcycle to Europe with Delmas costs CFA 450,000 as containers must be used for both. Count on driving the vehicle from Brazzaville to Pointe-Noire because shipping it on the train (about CFA 625,000) is out of the question.

Ferry
Between Brazzaville and Kinshasa, there are ferries every hour on the hour in both directions starting at 8 am (9 am on Sunday), the last one leaving at 3 pm (noon on Sunday), with no ferry at 1 pm. The trip itself takes only 20 minutes, but you should get there about 45 minutes in advance to allow sufficient time to clear customs. There are two ferries, one Congolese and one Zaïrian (the old *Matadi*), and they cost the same – CFA 6500 (or the equivalent in zaïres). The first ones in the morning are the most crowded and should be avoided if possible because of the increased risk of being robbed. In early 1993, over 100 people drowned when hundreds of Zaïrians, who were being deported, rushed to board the *Matadi*, causing the plank to collapse.

Riverboat
You can take a riverboat to Bangui (the CAR), and also to Ouesso in north-eastern Congo. The boats move at a snail's pace, but if you have the time, you will find this an excellent way to see Africa and meet Africans. There are two boats to Bangui, each with three classes and offering about the same quality: *La Ville de Brazza* and *La Ville de Impfondo*, both operated by the Agence Transcongolaise des Communications (ATC).

Most important, these steamers run only when the river is high, which is between early July and the end of December. They also operate in June and January but during those months they can't make it all the way to Bangui. During the high-river season, one steamer leaves Brazzaville about every two weeks; the exact departure date is not determined until about two weeks before departure. The trip upriver to Bangui normally takes about 14 days (nine days returning), stopping at Ngabé, Mpouya, Makotipoko, Mossaka, Loukolela, Liranga, Djundu, Ballois, Mobenzélé, Bolembé, Impfondo, Dougou, Bétou, Mongoumba (the CAR), Zinga (the CAR) and Bangui.

The cost per person all the way to Bangui is CFA 110,000 for a 1st-class cabin with a double-bed, air-con, bathroom and all meals, CFA 26,600 for tourist class with four beds per cabin and no meals, CFA 12,400 for 2nd class with seats and CFA 9900 for the deck. If you ship a vehicle, expect to pay at least CFA 60,000 for the vehicle plus at least the deck-class fare for each passenger even if everybody sleeps in the car.

If the steamers aren't operating, you could also take a barge, such as the *M'Bamou* which operates between the two capitals, pulled by a tug. The barges take at least twice as long but they are often far less crowded and there are departures about every week.

The fare is also low at around CFA 9000. For a description of what to expect on these trips by steamer or barge, consult the introductory Getting Around section of the Zaïre chapter as the Congo steamers and barges are very similar in most respects to those in Zaïre. For more details, see the Getting There & Away section under Brazzaville.

Getting Around

AIR

One of Lina Congo's jets crashed in 1991, leaving the company with only two jets; as a result domestic services have been significantly curtailed, but full services may eventually return. There are usually two flights a day from Brazzaville to Pointe-Noire (CFA 22,000 one way), stopping en route at Loubomo twice a week, and two a week to Ouesso. You can also take Aéro Service, which is a small private airline with once-a-week service from Brazzaville northwest to Zanaga (CFA 16,500) and north to Owando (CFA 31,500) and Impfondo (CFA 52,000).

MINIBUS

There are minibuses and taxi pick-ups linking Brazzaville with Loubomo, Owando (nine hours) and Djambala (nine hours) but not with Pointe-Noire. On other routes, you'll have to catch a truck. Between Brazzaville and Loubomo, the road is also bad, so almost all travellers catch one of the thrice-daily trains.

TRAIN

There are three trains a day in each direction between Brazzaville and Pointe-Noire. From both Brazzaville and Pointe-Noire there are daily departures at 6.15 am (le Soleil, which is an old train), 10.30 am (Train Bleu) and 6.30 pm (express). According to the schedule, they should arrive at 7.36 pm, 8.34 pm and 6.08 am, respectively. Don't be surprised, however, if the old Soleil arrives five or more hours late. The express is the night train and the only one with a sleeper. The Train Bleu, which is the fastest and runs during the day, is normally only about an hour late unless there is a major problem like a derailment, which is not unusual. In this case it can take 20 hours or so. It is very comfortable and one of the best trains in Central Africa. There are four berths to a cabin, and they are available daily in both directions. The bar-restaurant, however, is 2nd-class quality and packed – this is all right for a drink, but you would do better to bring your own food.

Prices on the Train Bleu from Brazzaville to Pointe-Noire are CFA 14,400 for 1st class, and CFA 8385 for 2nd class. Students with international student identity cards can get discounts of 50% on the Soleil but you must get a permit from an office at the university in Brazzaville, near the French cultural centre. First/2nd class on the Soleil and express is CFA 12,270/6035 (CFA 15,550 for a sleeper on the express). First and 2nd class seats on the express are virtually the same, but 1st class is preferable because it's not overcrowded. To avoid having to stand for much of the trip, buy your tickets and reserve your seats in advance, which costs CFA 300 extra, because when the gates open there's a mad rush for seats.

There is also a train running north-south between Mbinda and Loubomo (see the preceding Getting There & Away section).

CAR

Diesel fuel and petrol cost CFA 190 and CFA 295 per litre respectively. Road conditions vary considerably in the Congo depending primarily on whether you're travelling in the plateau area (not too bad) or in the lowlands (terrible), but almost anywhere you go from Brazzaville you'll need a high-clearance vehicle, preferably a 4WD. The Brazzaville to Owando road, for example, is paved north to Owando but from about 50 km north of Brazzaville to the turn-off for Djambala the paving virtually disappears and is in terrible condition, with huge potholes. Similarly, the route connecting Brazzaville and Pointe-Noire is passable between Loubomo and

Brazzaville but terrible between Loubomo and Pointe-Noire. Brazzaville to Pointe-Noire takes two days and it is advisable to bring an axe, because between Loubomo and Pointe-Noire it is not unusual to find the road blocked by fallen trees! Putting your vehicle on the train is ridiculously expensive (over CFA 600,000!).

On the other hand, the main road north from Brazzaville is fairly decent as far north as Makoua (71 km north of Owando), including the 125-km turn-off for Djambala. About three-quarters of the Brazzaville to Owando road is paved; the section which isn't sealed (from about 50 km north of Brazzaville to the turn-off east for Djambala) is in horrendous condition with huge pot-holes and is passable only with fairly high-clearance vehicles though not necessarily a 4WD. You can drive from Brazzaville to Owando in about nine hours.

Car Rental

Eurocar, Hertz and Avis are all represented in Brazzaville and Pointe-Noire but their rates are very high, eg CFA 16,000 a day for a Toyota Starlet, plus CFA 160 per km (40 km free), CFA 4000 a day insurance plus 22.7% tax. This works out to about US$207 for a day's drive of 200 km. For the office addresses, see the Brazzaville and Pointe-Noire Getting Around sections.

RIVERBOAT

In addition to the steamers which travel up and down the Congo and Oubangui rivers between Brazzaville and Bangui, stopping at various Congolese towns along the way, ATC operates two steamers between Brazza-ville and Ouesso via the Congo and Sangha rivers: *La Ville de Ouesso* and *La Ville de Mossaka*. From late June to early January they connect Brazzaville and Ouesso at least once a month with no fixed schedule. The 1000-km trip takes about 10 days up and six days back, stopping at about 20 villages along the way. The cost per person is about CFA 70,000 for 1st class, CFA 45,000 for 2nd class, and CFA 9000 for deck class. Accommodation is similar to that on the

boats to Bangui. Barges pulled by tugs also operate along this route, approximately once every two weeks between June and January and less frequently during other months.

Brazzaville

Brazzaville provides quite a contrast to its twin city, Kinshasa, which you can see just across the mighty Congo River. Whereas Kinshasa has over four million people, sky-scrapers and a multitude of restaurants and nightspots, Brazzaville, with 700,000 people, looks like an innocent, overgrown town nestled in greenery, with streets bordered by elegant mango and *flamboyant* trees which blossom in November, the city's real springtime.

Most foreigners prefer Brazzaville because it doesn't have the crime rate that has made Kinshasa so infamous and given everybody there the jitters. To the residents of Kinshasa, Brazzaville is a breath of fresh air. The river, however, enhances the city's atmosphere only slightly as there are few good views of it from the city centre. More impressive than the river are some of the city's modern new buildings and skyscrap-ers, such as the ELF Tower, and the markets.

Orientation

Of the eight sections of town, the five major ones are the Plateau, Plateau des 15 Ans, Poto-Poto, Bacongo and Moungali. The Plateau is where the administrative buildings were constructed when the French started building Brazzaville at the turn of the century and this is where you'll find the major shops, hotels and businesses.

One of the main streets is Ave Amilcar Cabral/Ave Éboué, which runs along the river. The 30-storey ELF Tower (Tour Nabemba), the tallest building in Central Africa, is on this street. Further west on the same street are the landmark Hôtel M'Bamou Palace, Score supermarket, the US Embassy and immigration. Another major thorough-fare, one block up, is Ave Lumumba, which becomes Ave Conus at the square named Place de la Poste, the heart of town. The post office is in this square and the railway station is 500 metres to the east on Ave Conus. If, instead, you head west on Ave Lumumba for two km past the National Museum, you'll come to the Rond-Point du Centre Culturel Français (French cultural centre roundabout). From there you can head further west on Ave du Djoué towards the lively Bacongo area (also known as the Cité), the centre of which is Marché Total, one of the city's largest markets. Or, instead, head north on Ave de Maya-Maya to the Rond-Point de la Patte d'Oie (pat dou-AH), where you'll find the imposing modern Palais de Congrès and, one km further, Maya-Maya Airport. Otherwise forget street names – nobody knows them because every block or so they change.

Business activity is spread out in the various sections of town, each with its own market. The one in Poto-Poto is perhaps a little more colourful and the one on the Plateau is better for crafts. Streets get very dark at night and you won't see many people walking in the Plateau area after sunset. The Plateau is where you'll find most of the better restaurants and posh nightclubs. For cheap hotels, head for Bacongo. For nightlife, head for Poto-Poto and Moungali. The latter pale in comparison to Kinshasa's lively Cité area, but they're far safer and if you head north on Ave de la Paix towards the Rond-Point de Moungali, you'll find several lively bars and nightclubs along, or just off, it.

Information
Tourist Office
There is no tourist office, but you may be able to get some information from the Direction Générale du Tourisme et des Loisirs (☎ 830953). The Peace Corps (☎ 836771), a block south of the Méridien Hôtel, is another potential source of useful information. The Direction de l'Immigration (☎ 832534) is responsible for issuing visa extensions; it's in the city centre about 100 metres west of the US Embassy.

Money
Among the UCB (☎ 831068; telex 5206), BCC (☎ 830880; telex 5237) and

BIDC (☎ 830308; telex 5339) commercial banks, you are likely to find that the UCB, which is in the city centre on Ave Amilcar Cabral facing the US Embassy, gives the best rates.

Post & Telecommunications The post office is in the heart of town at the Place de la Poste opposite the French Embassy and there are coin-operated public telephones outside for making local calls. Poor-quality postcards are sold just outside for CFA 100; postage to Europe or North America is an outrageous CFA 250 per letter or postcard.

Foreign Embassies The following embassies are in the heart of town:

Belgium
  Ave Lumumba, west of the Place de la Poste (☎ 832963)
Cameroun
  Rue Général Bayardelle, a block west of Méridien Hôtel(☎ 833404)
France
  Ave Alfassa, at the Place de la Poste (☎ 831086)
Germany
  Place de la Mairie, at the western end of Ave Amilcar Cabral, near the US Embassy (☎ 832-990)
Guinea
  Ave Maréchal Foch (☎ 832466)
Italy
  3 Blvd du Maréchal Lyautey, near the Nigerian Embassy (☎ 832482)
Nigeria
  11 Blvd du Maréchal Lyautey, opposite CHU University Hospital (☎ 831316)
USA
  Ave Amilcar Cabral, two blocks west of Hôtel M'Bamou Palace (☎ 832070; fax 836338; telex 5367)
Zaïre
  130 Ave de l'Indépendance, a block east of the main post office (☎ 832938)

There are four embassies just west of the Rond-Point du Centre Culturel Français, west of the Plateau area, including:

Angola
  Rue Fourneau (☎ 836565)
The CAR
  Rue Fourneau (☎ 834014)

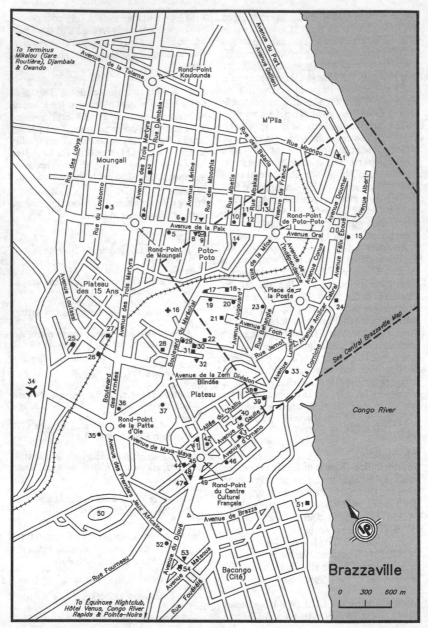

To Terminus
Mikalou (Gare
Routière), Djambala
& Owando

Rond-Point
Koulounda

M'Pila

Avenue de la Taleme

Avenue Gallieni

Avenue du Port

Rue des Bateris

Rue Mbongo

Rue des Lobys

Moungali

Avenue des Trois Martyrs

Rue Djambala

Avenue Lénine

Rue des Mbochis

Rue Mbetis

Rue Mbkas

Avenue de France

Avenue Doumer

Avenue Albert

41

Rue du Loubomo

3

4

2

6

7

11 13

10 12

Avenue de la Paix

5

8 9

Poto-Poto

14

Rond-Point
de Poto-Poto

Avenue Oral

Ebdu

Avenue Félix

15

Rond-Point
de Moungali

Rue de la Mion

Avenue de
l'Indépendance

Avenue Corua

Plateau
des 15 Ans

Avenue des Trois Martyrs

17 18

16

19 20

21

Place de
la Poste

23

24

Avenue Loutassi

Boulevard du Maréchal

27

28

29
31 30

22

Avenue Augouard

Rue Triangle

Avenue Ben Foch

Rue Jamot

Rue Lumumba

Avenue Amilcar Cabral

See Central Brazzaville Map

25

26

Boulevard des Armées

32

Avenue de la Zem Division
Blindée

33

La Corniche

Congo River

34

36

37

Plateau

Allée du Challu

38

39

40

Rond-Point
de la Patte
d'Oie

35

Avenue de Maya-Maya

42

Avenue de Gaulle

43

Avenue d'Omano

44
45
48
47

49

46

Rond-Point
du Centre
Culturel
Français

Avenue des Premiers Jeux Africains

51

50

Avenue de Brazza

Rue Fourneau

52

Avenue du Dioué

53
54

Rue Matsoua

Bacongo
(Cité)

Rue Foukkés

Brazzaville

0   300   600 m

To Équinoxe Nightclub,
Hôtel Venus, Congo River
Rapids & Pointe-Noire

■	**PLACES TO STAY**	12	Four-Storey Express Marketing Building (Landmark)
2	Hôtel Kalbas	13	Marché de Poto-Poto
18	Méridien Hôtel	15	Tour Nabemba (EFL Tower)
21	Église Sacré Sœur (The Cathedral)	16	CHU (University Hospital)
22	Olympic Hôtel	17	Italian Embassy
24	Hôtel M'Bamou Palace	19	Peace Corps Office
25	Hôtel Nsono	20	Camerounian Embassy
26	Hôtel Majoca	23	Radio Congo
27	Église Kimbanguiste	29	Nigerian Embassy
28	Hôtel Bikoumou	33	Musée Marien Nguouabi
30	Hôtel les Bougainvillées	34	Airport
31	Hôtel Bassandza	35	Tennis Club
51	Hôtel du Marché	36	Palais du Congrès
		37	Zoo
▼	**PLACES TO EAT**	38	Marché du Plateau
		39	Librairie du Plateau
1	Restaurant la Congolaise	40	Wildlife Conservation International (WCI)
7	Pâtisserie Sélé	41	Palais de Justice
8	No-Name Cheap Restaurant	42	Ministère de Plan
14	Restaurant Soir au Village	43	BDEAC Bank
32	Pizzeria le Banatha	44	Chadian Embassy
53	Restaurant le Petit K	45	French Cultural Centre
		46	Commissariat Central
	OTHER	47	Angolan Embassy
		48	Gabonese Embassy
3	Malibu Night-Club	49	CAR Embassy
4	École de Peinure de Poto-Poto	50	Stade Omnisport
5	Bar Nganda Lidame	51	Case de Gaulle
6	Marché de Moungali	52	Institut Géographique
9	Branch Post Office	53	Gare Routière
10	Pharmacle de Nuit	54	Marché Total
11	Club le Visa		

Chad
22 Rue des Écoles, one block behind the French cultural centre (☎ 832222)
Gabon
Rue Fourneau (☎ 830590, 832619)

Many countries, such as the Netherlands, the UK and Japan, use their embassies in Kinshasa as the official chanceries for the Congo. Honorary consulates include Denmark, Greece (☎ 830098), Netherlands (☎ 833426), Portugal (☎ 832821), Sweden (☎ 833248) and Switzerland (☎ 832788). Angola, Belgium, Benin and France have consulates in Pointe-Noire.

Cultural Centres The American cultural centre is in the heart of town on Ave Amilcar Cabral opposite the US Embassy. In addition to occasional cultural events, including American films, it has a refreshing air-con library where you can read English-language books and newspapers. The French cultural centre has similar facilities and is located at the *rond-point* (roundabout) at the southern end of Ave de Maya-Maya, which extends north to the airport.

Travel Agencies The best travel agency is Delmas Congo (☎ 830293; fax 832205; telex 5404) in the centre on Ave Félix Éboué, a block west of Tour Nabemba. It's the agent for American Express and can also organise trips and excursions outside Brazzaville.

Bookshops The best bookshop is Librairie

Raoul (☎ 830023) on Ave Félix Éboué in
Immeuble ELF Congo just east of Tour
Nabemba. It's quite good, with lots of maps,
colourful books on the Congo, newspapers,
etc. It's far better than Librairie ONLP in the
centre on Ave Maréchal Foch, half a block
north of immigration, or the tiny magazine
store at the Hôtel M'Bamou Palace.

For maps of Brazzaville and the Congo,
go to the Institut Géographique (☎ 830780)
in the southern section of the city on Ave du
Djoué in Bacongo, just before Marché Total
on the opposite side of the road. Open
Monday to Saturday from 7 am to 1 pm, it
has excellent large maps of Brazzaville and
the Congo for CFA 2500 as well as some old
maps from the 1960s.

For photo supplies, try Photo Zoom,
which is in the centre between Restaurant le
Central and the Zaïrian Embassy.

Supermarkets The best and largest supermarket by far is Score, which is in the centre
on Ave Amilcar Cabral, one block east of the
US Embassy. Presto is another.

Wildlife Conservation International
Wildlife Conservation International (WCI)
(☎ 832291) has all the information on the
fabulous wildlife reserve (gorillas, elephants, bongo, etc) north of Ouesso which is
being discussed and tentatively mapped out.
Matt Hatchwell and Mike Fay, two Americans who run the operation from the
Brazzaville end, are very friendly and will
help you make plans for visiting the area,
which is a major expedition and requires you
to bring everything. For details, see the
Bomassa section.

To get to the WCI office from the Rond-
Point du Centre Culturel Français, head east
one block just past the Palais de Justice (Law
Courts), then right on Allée du Choillu for
three blocks (400 metres), right again for 70
metres and then take the first left. WCI is the
second house on your right and very poorly
marked; look for a small WCI sign over the
doorway of the white building at the back.

Musée Marien Nguouabi
The National Museum, named after the
country's third president, has an interesting
collection of Congolese art, particularly
masks, and it is well worth checking. It's on
the wide Ave Lumumba, one km west of the
Place de la Poste and is open daily from 8 am
to 1 pm.

Basilique St-Anne
St Anne's Basilica, near the centre at the
Rond-Point de Poto-Poto, is one of the city's
most prominent landmarks. Built in 1949, it
is 85 metres long with a high ceiling and has
an unremarkable brick interior. The exterior,
however, is fascinating, especially the huge
roof, which is made of stunning bright-green
tiles from France. It was the crowning
achievement of the French architect Eyrelle,
who built three other beautiful buildings in
the city, including a house for Charles de
Gaulle. Mass, which is held at 6 am and 6 pm
on Sundays, is the best time to go because
you can hear the music then. It's also a good
way to meet people, as they always seem
particularly friendly there.

École de Peinture de Poto-Poto
One of Brazzaville's major places of interest
is the École de Peinture de Poto-Poto, a
well-known art school which dates from
1951 and got a fast start, with expositions
shortly thereafter in Paris and at New York's
Museum of Modern Art. What captured
people's attention was the combination of
African themes, angular compositions and
bright colours. The school now has about 30
students and several professors, all of whom
are very friendly and work almost exclusively in oils and acrylics. Works of the
professors, particularly those of Sylvestre
Mangouandza, who has had personal shows
in Geneva and elsewhere, are shown in the
gallery. Most of the paintings are fairly
abstract and in the CFA 10,000 to CFA
50,000 price range. This small school is
hidden in a banana grove at the south-eastern
corner of the Rond-Point Moungali on Ave
de la Paix, several km from the centre. The
gallery is open weekdays and Saturdays

from around 7.30 am to 5.30 pm and photographs are permitted.

Zoo
The zoo is in the Plateau area just west of Blvd du Maréchal, between the CHU University Hospital and the Rond-Point de la Patte d'Oie. The zoo is not particularly interesting but the gorillas are fascinating. An Englishman is financing a programme which is attempting to rehabilitate orphaned lowland gorillas to the wild. The gorillas are babies that were previously confiscated by poachers (who kill the parents and use parts of their bodies as fetishes) and sold as pets, often to expatriates who later turned them over to the zoo, perhaps in remorse. While some of the gorillas may be temporarily in the forests, there are always at least one or two at the zoo. You can also see bongo there, one of the prize trophies of big-game hunters.

Poto-Poto
The most colourful borough is Poto-Poto. Sunday afternoon is a good, relatively safe time to visit and if you're lucky, you might see some traditional dancing in the streets or a marriage ceremony, in which case you'll almost certainly be treated as a guest and asked to participate.

Congo River Rapids
The famous, huge white-water rapids of the Congo River, Les Cataractes du Congo or Les Rapides du Djoué, arc nine km west of the centre, well past Bacongo on the outskirts of town where the Djoué River runs into the Congo. They are a 'must see', especially when the river is at its highest from July to December. To get here, take a bus from Marché Total to Pont Djoué; it's a 20-minute ride.

You can see the rapids while having a drink or eating at Les Rapides restaurant and contemplating the fact that 13% of the world's untapped hydroelectric energy is flowing in front of you. The rapids are impressive only when seen up close, so hire a *pirogue* (canoe) to take you to the nearby sand bar.

Activities
The top four hotels all have pools and tennis courts. For CFA 1000 (CFA 1500 on weekends), nonguests can use these facilities, including the pools at the M'Bamou Palace and Méridien hotels which are good for doing laps. The best place for tennis, however, is Le Tennis Club de Brazzaville on the western side of the Rond-Point de la Patte d'Oie. It has 10 well-maintained clay courts and nonresidents can become temporary members for about CFA 27,000 for two weeks, or about CFA 38,000 for a month.

Golfers can try out the nine-hole golf course 12 km west of town near the World Health Organisation. The location overlooking the river is ideal, with lush green fairways, 'greens' of hard sand and golf clubs for rent. For information, call the Club de Golf (☎ 833860) or ask at the M'Bamou Palace or Méridien hotels.

Places to Stay – bottom end
The best places for the money are the Catholic missions. One is at the *Église Sacré Sœur*, better known as The Cathedral, which is near the centre, 800 metres north-west of the post office and behind the Méridien. The guesthouse is located directly behind the cathedral. Travellers are welcome here. The rooms (mostly single) are very clean and go for CFA 3000 per person; the one room for couples costs CFA 6000. Peace Corps volunteers usually stay here when there's no room in their *case de passage* (resthouse), which is above the nearby Peace Corps office. Another is the *Église Kimbanguiste* in the Plateau des 15 Ans, two km east of the airport and near the well-known Hôtel Majoca. It charges CFA 5000 for a clean room with two single beds. The people here are very friendly and welcome travellers wholeheartedly. You might also inquire about the *Mission Catholique Nôtre Dame de Fatima* in the M'Pila district one to two km north of

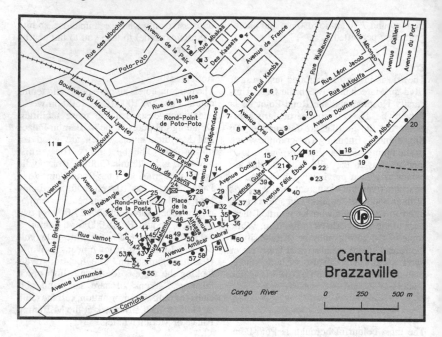

Central
Brazzaville

Congo   River

0   250   500 m

the railway station. It reportedly has rooms for CFA 2000 and if this is so, it is clearly the cheapest place to stay.

If these places are full and money is your only concern, try *Hôtel Exa*, which usually has space. It has 19 clean rooms with double beds and showers for about CFA 3500 a room, and also serves food and relatively cheap drinks in a tranquil setting. It's on the western edge of the city on a dirt road in the Kinsoundi section of the Quartier Makélékélé, eight km from the centre, next to the Kinsoundi textile mill.

Among the cheap, less remote hotels, there are at least three with rooms for CFA 5000. My choice is *Hôtel Kalbas* (☎ 834742) at 119 Rue Djambala, which is two blocks south and 4½ blocks east of the Rond-Point de Moungali. It has fairly clean rooms with fans and private bathrooms for CFA 5000 (CFA 8000 with air-con). The numerous paintings on the walls give the place a somewhat comical ambience.

On the opposite side of town in Bacongo there's the popular, long-standing *Hôtel du Marché*, which overlooks the market of the same name and charges CFA 5000/7000 for one of its 14 small rooms with fans/air-con and private bathrooms. The area is very lively during the day but at night it's dead, as well as being dark and relatively dangerous.

About 1½ km further west on Ave du Djoué, facing Marché Bifuiti, you'll find *Hôtel Venus*, which has clean rooms with fans and private bathrooms. At CFA 5000 a room, it's better value and recommended despite the somewhat remote location (five km from the centre), as it is on a major avenue with easy access to transportation.

In the centre, a hotel that I highly recommend is the popular *Petit Logis*, which charges CFA 8000 for one of its 41 large quiet rooms with air-con, comfortable chairs, dirty carpeting and private, cold-water bathrooms. Even late at night it is often

■ PLACES TO STAY

3 Hôtel Domingo
6 Hôtel Moliba
11 Église Sacré Sœur (The Cathedral)
16 Ntsono Hôtel
17 Siringo Hôtel
18 Hôtel Cosmos
32 Hôtel Jumbo
33 Hôtel Parc II
38 Hôtel Petit Logis
45 Hôtel la Pergola
60 Hôtel M'Bamou Palace

▼ PLACES TO EAT

1 Grilled Meat (Traoré Dahouda)
8 Chez Rachel Restaurant
14 Restaurant Chez Tantine Sylvia & Other Cheap Restaurants
15 Restaurant la Couscousserie
17 Salon de Thé Black & White
25 Restaurant le Pichet
27 No-Name Snackbar
28 Jo Burger & Restaurant Arc-en-Ciel
30 Restaurant la Coupole
32 Café de Paris
34 Street Food (Cheap Sandwiches)
36 Restaurant le Pékin & La Cave Snack-Bar
37 Restaurant le Central & Le Pizzeria du Centre
44 Restaurant l'Arbalette
50 Restaurant le Soleil
53 Restaurant le Foch
54 Restaurant les Ambassadeurs

OTHER

2 Four-Storey Express Marketing Building (Landmark)

4 Marché de Poto-Poto
5 Le Millionaire Nightclub
7 Basilique St-Anne
9 Taxi Stand for Rond-Point de Moungali
10 Railway Station
12 Radio Congo
13 Zaïrian Embassy
19 Ferry Port (for Kinshasa)
20 ATC Ticket Office & Dock for Boats to Bangui
21 Pharmacie Mavré R
22 Librairie Raoul
23 Tour Nabemba (ELF Tower)
24 Post Office
26 Cinéma Vog
28 Ethiopian Airlines & Cameroun Airlines
29 Aeroflot
31 French Embassy
32 Photo Zoom & Pharmacie Goutal
34 Lemai-Congo (Eurocar)
35 Bar la Rénouvation
39 Delmas Congo Travel Agency
40 ATC Office (Riverboat & Information for Bangui & Ouesso)
41 Pharmacie du Congo
42 Swissair
43 Librairie ONLP
46 BDC Bank
47 Sabena
48 UCB Bank & American Cultural Centre
49 Lina Congo
50 Air Afrique
51 Air France/UTA
52 Lycée Lumumba
54 German Embassy
55 Immigration Office
56 US Embassy
57 Aéro Service
58 Score Supermarket
59 BIDC Bank

possible to get a room. If it's full, try the *Siringo Hôtel*, which is on the 1st floor of a building 1½ blocks to the east, opposite Tour Nabemba. It has only about five rooms and is kind of grubby, but the rooms are slightly cheaper (CFA 7500) and have air-con and moderately clean shared bathrooms.

Alternatively, try *Dongui Hôtel* (☎ 834-388), which features a very lively bar. It is several km from the centre on an active street with lots of food stalls. Rooms here which

cost CFA 7500 and have private bathrooms are difficult to get. Two more expensive but more centrally located options are *Hôtel Moliba* (☎ 835781), which is better known as a nightclub and has air-con rooms for CFA 10,000, as does the multistorey *Hôtel Domingo*. The former is three blocks north-west of Tour Nabemba, off Ave de la Paix, and the latter is on Ave de la Paix, several blocks further north-west, opposite the well-known Le Millionaire Nightclub.

Places to Stay – middle

Among the mid-range hotels, a very good choice is the *Hôtel les Bougainvillées* (☎ 834463; fax 830428), which is run by a friendly Russian woman and is well managed, with a primarily European clientele. A large room with air-con, huge wardrobe and fine bathroom costs CFA 13,500. It has a tranquil ambience and the French food served at the hotel's popular restaurant is quite tasty. The hotel is two km west of the post office, near the CHU hospital.

If it's full, try *Hôtel Parc II* (☎ 815195), which is in the heart of town opposite the M'Bamou Palace. The rooms, which cost CFA 13,000 or more, are tiny but have TVs with videos, refrigerators and clean, tiled bathrooms. The nicest feature is the French-run restaurant, which is pleasant and relaxing, moderately priced and popular with the French. The rooms are better but the ambience is sterile at *Hôtel la Pergola* (☎ 831962), nearby and centrally located on Ave Malamine, near Sabena and east of Pharmacie du Congo. Prices for one of its 10 air-con rooms are similar to those of Hôtel Parc II.

Hôtel Jumbo is also in the centre, a block to the north-east opposite Aeroflot, but it's not recommended unless price is an overriding consideration; the 14 rooms cost CFA 11,500 and have air-con and wood-panelled walls.

A better alternative in the centre is the six-storey *Ntsono Hôtel* (☎ 830971), which is a block east of Tour Nabemba. Well maintained and presentable, it charges CFA 12,000 to CFA 16,000 for one of its 54 rooms including breakfast. The cheaper rooms are hard to get and the more expensive ones have a TV and refrigerator.

Another mid-range place that I recommend is the two-storey *Hôtel Nsono* (☎ 820082), which attracts well-heeled Africans. Somewhat remotely located in the Plateau des 15 Ans area near the airport, two blocks west of Ave Loutassi on a dirt back alley, it charges CFA 14,000 to CFA 16,000 for its air-con rooms and is well patronised by Africans in the know. It's a lot better than

the nearby *Hôtel Majoca* (☎ 826692), which has slightly tarnished air-con rooms between CFA 13,260 and CFA 18,870; the cheapest rooms are difficult to get and the more expensive ones often have a 15% reduction offer. All the rooms are beginning to show their age, and there's no restaurant but breakfast is served.

Two places to be tried only in desperation are *Hôtel Bassandza* and *Hôtel Bikoumou* (☎ 822911), which are both near Les Bougainvillées. The former, which has only 10 rooms, will often immediately reduce the CFA 15,000 room price to CFA 12,000 or lower for lack of clients (mostly local men with their girlfriends). The Bikoumou, which charges CFA 11,500 for its tiny air-con rooms and has a decent adjoining restaurant, looks like a grubby college dormitory.

Places to Stay – top end

The best top-end hotel by far for the money is the *Hôtel Cosmos*, a Pullman-chain hotel which costs at least a third less than the city's other top hotels. Modern and well maintained, it's conveniently located near the centre of town, 100 metres from the river, and has all the amenities of the other posh hotels, including a pool.

Among the three hotels vying for top honours, the best buy is the *Méridien*, which has slightly lower prices and a more informal atmosphere and tropical setting. It's near the centre, one km north-west of the Place de la Poste. For years the city's top hotel has been the landmark PLM *M'Bamou Palace*, in the very heart of town next to the river, but it's now getting stiff competition from the newly renovated *Olympic Hôtel*, which is not far from the Méridien and is slightly smaller than the others. It is very elegant, with sumptuous rooms and an active bar that's quite inviting.

Hôtel Cosmos (☎ 834846; fax 835159; telex 5342), CFA 19,200 a room, pool, tennis, Eurocar, magazine stand, shops, nightclub; accepts AE, D, V, MC credit cards

Hôtel M'Bamou Palace (☎ 831040, 832010; fax 831527; telex 5366), CFA 35,000 per room, pool, tennis, magazine stand, nightclub, TV/video; accepts AE, D, V, MC credit cards

Méridien Hôtel (☎ 830910/2; fax 833905; telex 5223), CFA 28,000-30,000/30,000-32,000 for singles/doubles, tennis, short pool, Hertz agent, nightclub; accepts AE, D, V, MC credit cards

Olympic Hôtel (☎ 832502/3; fax 833709; telex 5277), CFA 32,890 per room, pool, magazine stand; accepts AE, V, MC credit cards

Credit Cards: AE – American Express, D – Diners Club, V – Visa, MC – MasterCard

Places to Eat

Cheap Eats Some of the cheaper places to eat are listed under the African food section. For food stalls, two good places to look during the day are Marché Total and Marché de Poto-Poto, particularly along Rue Mbakas in Poto-Poto where you'll find grilled-meat stands, all with beef brochettes (kebabs) for CFA 100. The meat can be so tough as to be unchewable, so inspect it first. Further north-west along Ave de la Paix, one block beyond the branch post office and on the same side, you'll find a cheap, no-name food shed with rock-bottom prices; this hole-in-the-wall closes around 3 pm.

Just east of the central post office is a tiny no-name café where you can get large Primus beers for CFA 350, coffee and bread for CFA 400 and omelettes for CFA 800. There's also *Chez Rachel Restaurant* near the southern end of Ave de la Paix, some 150 metres south of Basilique St-Anne. It's a small place with a terrace facing a busy street. Dishes are moderately priced – grilled fish, for example, costs CFA 1000. Rachel's grilled chicken is also very popular.

For a modern, American-style hamburger place, head for *Jo Burger*, which is 100 metres east of the post office and on the same street. It is clean and popular with the younger set, offering hamburgers and sandwiches in the CFA 1000 to CFA 1800 range and dining inside or on the terrace. For pastries and coffee, try the *Salon de Thé Black & White* in the centre facing Tour Nabemba.

The landmark *Restaurant le Central*, one block north of the M'Bamou Palace, has a streetside terrace and is the city's most popular watering hole for expatriates. It's modest-looking but not particularly cheap, with beers for CFA 700, sandwiches for CFA 800, brochettes for CFA 1500-2000, and more expensive full meals including a plat du jour (daily special) for CFA 2500. On the same street half a block to the west next to Hôtel Jumbo, you'll find *Café de Paris*, which serves beef brochettes for CFA 1500 and chips for CFA 800.

African For cheap African bush meat and breakfast food, you can't beat *Chez Tantine Sylvia* and some 15 other food stalls just east of the Zaïrian Embassy. To get there from the post office, head east on Ave Conus for about 250 metres and, some 50 metres past the intersection with Ave de l'Indépendance, you'll see a row of food stalls along a dirt path to your left. Tantine Sylvia, who is very friendly and first in line, serves monkey and antelope for CFA 800, boiled sea fish and steak *garni* (ie with rice and bread) for CFA 600 and coffee, butter and bread for CFA 175. Others along the alley serve grilled meat for CFA 500, fresh grilled fish for CFA 700 and porcupine for CFA 800, among other things. All of these places open early and close around 3 pm.

A more up-market place that's highly recommended is *Restaurant le Petit K*, which is in Bacongo facing the eastern side of the Marché Total Gare Routière, one block south of Ave du Djoué. Marie, the owner, serves saka saka (manioc-leaf stew), bouillon de mouton (lamb stew), steak, fresh grilled fish, and poisson salé all for CFA 1000. It's fairly rustic but there are tablecloths and you have the choice of eating inside or on the terrace until 11 pm when it closes.

The best place for Camerounian food is *Restaurant Soir au Village* (☎ 823609) at 14 Rue Mbetis in Poto-Poto. To get there from the Rond-Point de Poto-Poto, head north-west for about 10 short blocks (300 metres) on Ave de la Paix to Rue Mbetis, where you'll find a sign pointing to the restaurant, which is one block to the left (south-west). Open daily except Mondays for lunch and dinner, Elaine the chef serves chicken ndolé and other Camerounian specialities for around CFA 2500 as well as grilled meats.

The best known African restaurant is the famous *Restaurant la Congolaise*, which is the frequent site of musical concerts. It's the place to head for if you want a filling decent meal (African or continental) at relatively moderate prices – CFA 2000 for a huge meal and CFA 300 for a large cold beer. Open Monday to Saturday from 7.30 am to 5.30 pm, this large open-air place offers indoor and outdoor dining and is about 700 metres north-east of the railway station in the direction of the brewery.

You can also get Moroccan food at *Restaurant la Couscousserie*, which is on Ave Conus, 2½ blocks south-west of the railway station on the same street. Closed on Sundays, this French-run place with Moroccan décor and air-con offers Moroccan tagines (stews) and couscous (dishes start from CFA 3500), as well as a few French selections.

Italian The place with the best pizza is the popular *Pizzeria le Banatha* (☎ 837010), which is west of the cathedral, a block southwest of (behind) Hôtel les Bougainvillées on a dirt road. Open in the evening from Tuesday to Sunday and highly recommended if price is of no concern, it's an attractive place run by a French man named Jean-Claude, who serves excellent pizza for CFA 5000 to CFA 7000. On Tuesday couscous is the speciality while on Friday it's paella. For cheaper pizzas in the centre, try *Le Pizzeria du Centre*, which is a block north of the M'Bamou Palace and next to Restaurant le Central. You can get pizzas here from CFA 3200, pasta dishes for CFA 2200 and large/small beers for CFA 700/400.

Chinese *Restaurant le Pékin* (☎ 834705), a block east of the M'Bamou Palace on the same street, is fairly popular. Open daily, it offers an extensive Chinese menu, an attractive oriental setting and good service. Most main courses are in the CFA 3200 to CFA 4300 range. Another possibility is *Le Bambou* (☎ 833290), four km from the centre of

town near Cimetière de Ngouaka. It's reportedly one of the city's finer restaurants and is open daily except Tuesday.

Lebanese *Restaurant Arc-en-Ciel* (☎ 834-062), on the 9th floor of a building that is 100 metres east of the post office, next to Jo Burger, offers good Lebanese and French cuisine and a panoramic view. Prices are high, though, and it's closed on Sundays.

French A popular place in the centre is *Restaurant le Foch* (☎ 833951), an outdoor café on the corner of Lumumba and Maréchal Foch Aves. The popular plat du jour here is CFA 3900, but you can order cheaper brochettes for CFA 1800 to CFA 2500 and chips for CFA 1000. On weekend evenings when this place is often full, there's usually a two-person band playing.

Chez Colette (☎ 831413), on Ave Doumer, four blocks north-east of the railway station, is popular with the French, especially for Sunday lunch. Don't let the unpretentious terrace setting fool you. The menu is excellent with prices to match: no main course is less than CFA 4000.

Restaurant le Soleil (☎ 834572), 1½ blocks east of the M'Bamou Palace on the same street, is a good French bistro with air-con and a limited selection. Most main courses are in the CFA 2700 to CFA 3700 range. It's open daily, and you can dine inside (with air-con) or outside.

In the centre across the street from Jo Burger you'll find *Restaurant la Coupole*, which offers primarily grilled dishes, such as braised chicken, starting from CFA 4000, plus a pleasant terrace setting and live entertainment at night on weekends similar to that at Le Foch. It's closed on Sundays.

If food rather than price is your main concern, head for *Restaurant l'Arbalette* (formerly La Pizzeria); it's very attractive, extremely popular and serves some of the best French cuisine in town. The setting, both inside with air-con and on the terrace, is one of the nicest in town. It's in the centre on Ave Malamine near the US Embassy. An equally expensive alternative is *Restaurant les Ambassadeurs* (☎ 832670), which is at the intersection of Lumumba and Maréchal Foch Aves.

Entertainment

Bars For a rustic African bar, look around Marché Total and Marché de Poto-Poto during the day. There are also several bars along Ave de la Paix, such as *Bar Nganda Lidame*, which is over a km north of the Rond-Point de Poto-Poto, and further north around the Rond-Point de Moungali, such as *La Source Mary Luiz* and *Elysée Bar*.

In the city centre, getting the local brew is difficult because most bars offer only foreign beer, usually CFA 800 for a small can. One exception is the tiny, no-name café just east of the post office, where a big Primus costs CFA 350. *Restaurant le Central* also offers the local brew, but at CFA 700 for a Primus it is hardly cheap. It is, however, the city's most popular watering hole and stays open late; *Le Rénovation* across the street is similar. The bar at the *Hôtel Petit Logis* two blocks to the east caters to those looking for a more derelict ambience; it closes around 10 pm. The fancy bar at the *Hôtel M'Bamou Palace* is usually dead, whereas the posh one at the *Olympic Hôtel* is both inviting and popular.

Nightclubs Finding places with live music is becoming increasingly difficult in Brazzaville. For concerts, which often feature visiting bands from Zaïre, check the local newspaper. The most likely places for these concerts are the Palais du Congrès and Restaurant la Congolaise.

The Bacongo (Cité) is no longer the nightclub centre. Two good places there, *Palace Libération* and *Le Pacha*, for example, have both closed or moved. A good one that remains is *Équinoxe Nightclub*. To get there from Marché Total, continue about one km west on Ave du Djoué until you see the club's sign pointing left (south) for one block. Like many of the other nightclubs, it has strobe lights, charges CFA 1000 for drinks but has no cover charge, and is closed on Mondays.

The best nightclub areas are now Poto-Poto and Moungali. One of the best known and liveliest is *Le Millionaire Nightclub* on Ave de la Paix, 150 metres north-west of the Rond-Point de Poto-Poto. Open nightly, it's one of the fancier African nightclubs and apparently the only one with a cover charge (CFA 1000 on weekdays and CFA 2000 on weekends). Drinks cost CFA 1000 (standard price). The music is mostly American, also some African. Not far away is *Club le Visa*. It's about seven short blocks further north-west along Ave de la Paix and 100 metres to your right down a dirt road; look for the club's sign on the right-hand side of that avenue. Similar to the others, this place is very lively on weekends and has strobe lights, drinks for CFA 1000 and mostly African music.

Much further north-west along Ave de la Paix, nine short blocks (250 metres) beyond the Rond-Point de Moungali and to your right for one block, is the *Malibu Night-Club*; look for the nightclub's sign on the main avenue. It's similar in all respects to the others and plays mostly African music.

Expatriates tend to prefer the expensive modern discos near the centre, which they feel are less risky at night than those in other sections of town. The liveliest is *5 x 5*. Other choices include those at the major hotels, particularly *Le Kébé-Kébé* at the M'Bamou Palace, *Le Ram Dam* at the Méridien, and *Lekembe* at the Cosmos, as well as *Le Colibri* on Ave Maréchal Foch near Ave Lumumba. All have cover charges of about CFA 3500 and, for the most part, are closed on Mondays.

Cinemas Le Vog (☎ 832885), a block southwest of the post office on the same street, is an excellent modern theatre and shows most of the latest movies. Films are shown daily at 6.30 and 9 pm and tickets cost CFA 1000.

Things to Buy

Artisan Goods Each of the four major sections of town has its own market. Marché Total in Bacongo is the most active food and clothing market because it's also a transportation hub, but the Marché du Plateau is the

Bakongo wooden statue

place to head if you're looking for souvenirs, particularly masks and other wooden carvings, fetishes (not always on display), drums, straw products, ivory, malachite and paintings. Even though many of the items are souvenir quality, I highly recommend this place as some of the masks and fetishes are authentic and superbly made.

Music One of the better music stores is that of Pierre Moutouari on Ave Matsone in Bacongo, several blocks south of Marché Total, but there are also some in Moungali and Poto-Poto, including along Ave de la Paix. Popular Congolese singers include Pierre Moutouari (Somsa band), Locko Massengo (Rumbayas International band), Youlou Mabiala (Kamikaze band), Pamelo Mounk'a (Les Grands As band) and Jacques Loubelo.

Getting There & Away

Air For details on flights from Europe, see the introductory Getting There & Away section. Ethiopian Airlines offers services on the weekend between Brazzaville and Addis Ababa via Nairobi, while between Air France/UTA and Air Afrique there are three flights a week to/from Bangui and N'Djamena. You can also fly thrice weekly to/from Douala on Air Afrique or Cameroun Airlines and four times weekly to/from Libreville on both these airlines and Air Gabon.

As for interior flights, Lina Congo offers flights to Pointe-Noire (CFA 22,000) two or three times daily, Ouesso (CFA 28,000) on Monday, Thursday and Saturday, Owando on Thursday and Saturday, Makoua on Saturday, Loubomo and Nkayi on Monday and Friday, Zanaga on Wednesday and Friday, and Makabana and Impfondo on Saturday. It also has occasional flights to Souanké, Kellé, Lékana and Boundji. You can also fly Aéro Service to Impfondo (CFA 52,000) on Wednesday, Owando (CFA 31,500) and Makoua (CFA 35,500) on Friday, and Zanaga (CFA 16,500) on Saturday.

Minibus There are about three 30-seat minibuses a day going north to Owando and the fare is CFA 9000. They leave from Terminus Mikalou, which is on the northern outskirts of town about 10 km from the centre on Route Nationale No 2. To get there from the centre, head out on Ave de la Tsieme and continue past the only bridge; buses will be loading up in a small area to your left. You should arrive there by 6 am as they are all usually full by 6.30 am and off by 7 am. The trip takes about nine hours during the dry season and longer during the rainy season.

Terminus Mikalou is also where you catch pick-up trucks north to Djambala. Crammed with passengers and not comfortable like the minibuses, they likewise leave around 7 am, take about nine hours and cost about the same. There are no police stops along the way.

Almost everybody travelling south overland towards Loubomo and Pointe-Noire takes the train but you can also take a truck.

Train There are three departures daily for Loubomo and Pointe-Noire: the Soleil at 6.15 am, the Train Bleu at 10.30 am and the express at 6.30 pm. According to the schedule they are supposed to reach Pointe-Noire at 7.36 pm, 8.34 pm and 6.08 am respectively, but in practice they are usually one to five hours late, especially the slow Soleil which often arrives around midnight. First and 2nd-class fares to Pointe-Noire are CFA 14,400/8385 (CFA 10,360/6325 to Loubomo) on the Train Bleu and CFA 12,270/6035 (CFA 8230/4195 to Loubomo) on the other two (CFA 15,550 for a sleeper on the overnight express). The railway station (☎ 831482) is in the centre of town, two blocks north of Tour Nabemba.

Car One of the main car-rental agencies is Lemai-Congo (☎ 832148; telex 5442), which faces the Hôtel M'Bamou Palace and is the Eurocar representative. You'll also find Eurocar at Hôtel Cosmos (☎ 834846), Avis (☎ 831581, 833643; telex 5366) at the M'Bamou Palace, and Hertz (☎ 830898) at the Méridien (☎ 830910/2; fax 833905) among other places. All of these companies also have booths at the airport as do two local agencies, Auto-Location (☎ 831611) and Leader. AG Rent-A-Car (☎ 831156) and Sotrafor (☎ 830898) are two others.

Boat There are ferries to Kinshasa every hour on the dot starting at 8 am (9 am on Sundays), with the last departure at 3 pm (noon on Sundays). The fare is CFA 6500. The ferry port is just south of Hôtel Cosmos. Procedures are somewhat cumbersome, so get there about 45 minutes before departure and don't forget the CFA 25,000 exportation limit.

For information on the riverboats to Bangui and Ouesso, go to the ATC office (☎ 830441) in the centre on Ave Éboué, a block west of the landmark Tour Nabemba. It is open Monday to Saturday from 6.20 am to 1 pm and the people there are very helpful. The ATC office at the port sells the tickets but has no information. The boats operate from late June to December, with a few earlier and later departures that don't make it all the way to either city because the river is too low. During the season, there is about one departure every two weeks to Bangui and every month to Ouesso. The trip takes about 14 days upriver to Bangui and nine days back and costs between CFA 9900 for deck class to CFA 110,000 for 1st class with meals (CFA 138,000, 'dehors class', ie super deluxe).

Barges to Ouesso (about one every two weeks) and Bangui operate during the same months and charge about the equivalent of deck class on the riverboats. To make contact with them, inquire at the port, which is just below Hôtel Cosmos. For more details, see Riverboat under the introductory Getting Around section.

Getting Around

To/From the Airport At Maya-Maya Airport (information ☎ 830070), there's still no departure tax. You'll find a bar, Eurocar and Hertz agents, but no bank or restaurant. If you have West African CFA, don't hesitate to ask Air Afrique officials at the airport to exchange them for Central African CFA; they will usually do so gladly and it will save you a lot of hassles. Departure procedures are very slow, so arrive early.

The taxi fare to the airport (five km from the post office) should be CFA 1000, but coming from the airport expect to pay CFA 1500 or CFA 2000 after 8 pm, and be prepared to bargain. There are no buses that pass by the airport; from the airport, you'll have to walk one km south on the main thoroughfare (Ave de Maya-Maya) to the Rond-Point de la Patte d'Oie where you can get the large No 1 bus and numerous minibuses.

All the major airlines are in town in a three-block area:

Aeroflot
  Ave Fondère at Ave du Camp, facing Restaurant le Central (☎ 831665)
Aéro Service
  Ave Amilcar Cabral, just west of Score (☎ 833766)
Air Afrique
  Ave Amilcar Cabral, facing Score (☎ 830173/4)

Air France/UTA
Ave Amilcar Cabral, opposite Score supermarket
(☎ 833426)
Cameroun Airlines
Ave Conus, half a block west of the post office
(☎ 834443)
Ethiopian Airlines
Ave Conus, next door to Cameroun Airlines
(☎ 834857)
Lina Congo
Ave Amilcar Cabral, facing the US Embassy
(☎ 833065, 834143)
Swissair
Ave Maréchal Foch, half a block north of
immigration (☎ 830228)

Bus Large STB buses operate along Brazzaville's main streets between 5.30 am and 9 pm; a ticket costs CFA 60 for local stops and CFA 100 for express buses.

Taxi Fares are CFA 100 for a shared taxi, and CFA 500 to CFA 800 for a *course* (a taxi to yourself), depending on the distance, plus CFA 100 more for each additional passenger. Meters are not used and rates increase by CFA 200 at 9 pm. You can get a taxi by the hour for CFA 2500 (at least CFA 3000, however, for just one hour) and a taxi for the day for CFA 15,000 to CFA 20,000, but you'll have to bargain. They are plentiful, but not always easy to find at night. All taxis are green and white. If you're going to Poto-Poto, Moungali or beyond, you'll find shared cabs filling up at the southern end of Ave de la Paix near the railway station.

AROUND BRAZZAVILLE
Chutes de Loufoulakari
One of the best day trips from Brazzaville is to the impressive Chutes de Loufoulakari (Loufoulakari Falls), which are pictured in many tourist brochures. They are 80 km south-west of Brazzaville at the confluence of the Loufoulakari and the Congo rivers, about halfway between Brazzaville and Boko as the crow flies. By car, the round trip can be made in a day, but you will need a 4WD as the road is in very bad condition. Indeed, the road's poor condition caused the closure of the *Auberge de Loufoulakari*, which overlooks the falls.

Getting There & Away To get there by car from Brazzaville, take the road to Pointe-Noire for about 20 km to Gangalingolo. There you'll find a dirt road which branches off to the right (south) and follows the Congo River south-westward first to Linzolo village, then to the town of Mbandza-Ndounga and, about 15 km further, to the falls (and on to Boko). The 60-km stretch from Gangalingolo is almost impassable at times between February and April, the heavy rainy season.

It's also possible to get to the falls by public transport from Brazzaville along the river. You must go to Marché Total in Bacongo around 5 am and look for a minibus to Boko via Mbandza-Ndounga. Shortly after passing Mbandza-Ndounga, the minibus stops at a crossroad about seven km from the falls. The road between there and the falls is well marked. To return, you must walk back to the crossroad and hitchhike. Here, as throughout the Congo, hitchhiking is safe but most Africans will expect payment, usually the same as the bus fare, which is why few people attempt it.

Chutes de Béla
Chutes de Béla (Bela Falls), which are further south-west at the confluence of the Louvoumbi and Congo rivers, are over 70 metres high but not as high as Loufoulakari Falls; however, they are wider and quite impressive. A trip here, which invariably involves camping at the waterfalls, can be a fun adventure, but you must have your own vehicle unless you are prepared to walk the last 26 km, and you must bring everything with you, including food and camping gear.

Getting There & Away For public transport from Brazzaville to Boko, see the earlier Getting There & Away section. From Boko you will have to walk the remaining 26 km, as virtually no vehicles pass this way. By car, take the road to Pointe-Noire for 85 km to Kinkala, then head south for 61 km to Boko; the falls are 26 km further, to the south-west – a total distance of 172 km. The road is, relatively speaking, not so bad to Boko but from there the road is terrible and generally accessible only during the dry season.

Lac Bleu

Another interesting excursion from Brazzaville is a trip to Lac Bleu (Blue Lake), which is some 139 km north-east of Brazzaville via the road to Owando. It's in an area of rolling green hills bordering the Réserve de Léfini, which is one of the most beautiful areas in the Congo, so you probably won't be disappointed. You can stay at a lodge in nearby Mah which is ideally located on top of a cliff just beyond the village, overlooking a grassy plain and forests. Run by a French man, the lodge has dormitory-style beds and costs about CFA 5000 a person. Lac Bleu is in the valley below the cliff, about a five-km walk away. The route is all downhill and easy. During the walk you'll come to a fork: the right path on the right leads to the lake and the left leads to a river, which is the best camping spot if you don't stay at the lodge. In Mah, you should be able to find someone to take you out on the lake in a boat. Don't go swimming however, as the lake reportedly has bilharzia.

Getting There & Away From Brazzaville, take the road north towards Owando. After passing Odziba (98 km), which is basically an intersection where a sideroad forks to the east towards Ngabé, continue north towards Owando for another 29 km to the unmarked turn-off for Mah. If you're coming by public transport (vehicles to both Owando and Djambala pass by here), ask the driver to drop you off there. You'll then have to walk the seven km west to Mah.

The West

POINTE-NOIRE

The petroleum industry is what draws most people to this port city of 250,000 people. There are direct flights from other African countries, which attests to its importance. For expatriates from Brazzaville, the main attraction is the beautiful, safe beach, which is only a 15-minute walk from the city's main drag, Ave de Gaulle, and the railway station, the city's architectural jewel. Windsurfing enthusiasts will find sailboards for rent, and those who enjoy fishing won't be disappointed either, provided they can afford the stiff price of deep-sea fishing here – the lagoons along the coast abound in swordfish, barracuda, tarpon, tuna and skate. If you're looking for action and a festive time, try to arrive during the first week in April, when the Trans-Congo car rally ends here, with an onslaught of vehicles.

The city is less expensive than Brazzaville and the crime rate is lower as well. The atmosphere is far more relaxed, particularly in the Cité, where you'll find some famous Congolese restaurants, such as the rustic Chez Gaspard, which even wealthy expatriates frequent. There are also some good places for dancing. If you like the sound of a small city that's easy to get around, with friendly people, a laid-back ambience and an African quarter that's noticeably safer than those in most large Central African cities, chances are you will enjoy Pointe-Noire as much as I do. Having a great beach is just icing on the cake.

Orientation

The city is divided between the modern section near the water and the African section to the east called the Cité, with the airport area to the south. Ave de Gaulle is the main drag in the modern section, stretching for three km eastward from the railway station through the centre of town past the landmark Novotel hotel (km 1) and the Rond-Point Kasaï (km 2) to the Rond-Point Lumumba where the Cité begins.

Seven streets branch out from the Rond-Point Lumumba in a 90° wedge, with the market in the centre. Instead of calling them by their proper names, which few people know, the locals call these streets by the days of the week, starting with Lundi (Monday) on your right heading east and proceeding northward to Dimanche (Sunday) heading north. The latter and Ave Jeudi (Thursday),

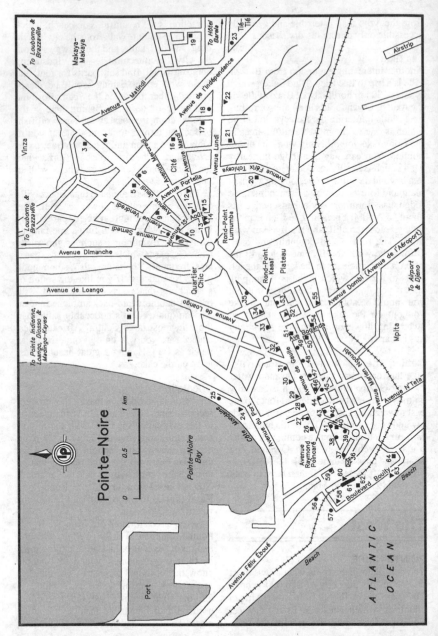

■ PLACES TO STAY

1 Hôtel le Ndey (No 1-Cheapest)
2 Hôtel le Ndey (No 2) & Lycée Augagneur
3 Motel Kingoy
5 Hôtel Pontegrene
9 Hôtel Okoumé
16 Hôtel Paul Bambi
17 Hôtel ABC Palace
19 Auberge Centre Cité
20 Hôtel Mario Adolphe (or Hôtel Bakadila)
21 Motel Mapila
26 Hôtel de Ville
40 Victory-Palace Hôtel
46 Mbou-Mvoumvou Novotel
51 Hôtel Migitel
54 Le Guest-House
62 Hôtel Palm Beach
64 Hôtel Azur Zamba

▼ PLACES TO EAT

8 Restaurant le Sabar
11 Coupé-coupé
12 Restaurant Chez Gaspard & Restaurant Bibaka
13 Coupé-coupé
14 Restaurant Marie Diallo
15 Coupé-coupé
22 Restaurant BTB
24 Vegas Pub & Restaurant la Baraka
29 Restaurant le Biniou
30 Restaurant Mikado
32 Restaurant l'Imprévu
34 Bar-Restaurant le Retro
44 Restaurant Ali Baba
47 Hamburger Place
52 Restaurant Amitié
55 Restaurant Chez Wou

58 Le Sea Club Restaurant
60 Good Street Food
63 Restaurant la Plage Sportif
64 Restaurant la Langouste

OTHER

4 Le Jumbo Nightclub
6 Cinéma Roy
7 Bar la Capricorne
10 Le Crépuscule Nightclub
18 Le Bimoko Nightclub
23 Marché de Tié-Tié
25 Cercle Naval (Sailing Club)
27 Church
28 Benin Consulate
29 Air Afrique
31 Pharmacy
33 Le Balafon Disco
35 Centre Culturel Français
36 Post Office & Artisanat
37 BCC Bank
38 Cinéma Club 7
39 French Consulate
41 Score Supermarket
42 Lina Congo Airlines
43 Librairie Maison de la Presse
45 Polyclinique Bethesda
46 Public Telephone & UTC Travel Agency
47 UCB Bank
48 Librairie le Paillet
49 Photo 2000
50 Mission Catholique (La Procure/Le Vichy)
53 Air Gabon
56 Supermarché Tigre
57 Boule Playing Area
59 Immigration
61 Railway Station

the real name of which is Ave des Maloangos, eventually unite heading out of town towards Loubomo. Most of the city's cheap hotels and restaurants are in this wedged area. Cutting across these finger-like streets further east is Ave de l'Indépendance, a wide avenue that is the most congested in the city. It runs north-west to south-east for six km, past the picturesque Marché de Tié-Tié all the way to the city's other train stop, which is scarcely ever used by foreigners.

Information
Tourist Office The Direction Régionale du Tourisme et des Affaires Culturelles (☎ 941013) organises trips to the museum in Loango, 25 km north of town.

Money Two of the city's principal banks, both open Monday to Saturday from 6.30 am to 1 pm, are on Ave de Gaulle. These are the BCC (☎ 941424), which is 1½ blocks east of the railway station, and the UCB, which is further east, a block past the Novotel. The latter offers unusually quick service and accepts Barclays', Thomas Cook and American Express travellers' cheques, and possibly others as well. The rate is significantly better for travellers' cheques than it is for cash and no commission is charged.

Consulates Angola (☎ 942075), Belgium (☎ 941192), France (☎ 940962) and Benin (☎ 944480) all have consulates here. Open weekdays from 9 am to 1 pm and 4 to 6.30 pm, the Benin Consulate is on Ave de Gaulle, just before the Novotel, and the French Consulate is a block south of that avenue on Ave Raymond Poincaré, behind Cinéma Club 7.

Travel Agencies The best travel agency is Universal Travel Congo (☎ 944882; telex 8915), next to the Novotel. UTC's bread and butter is making airline reservations but they can also organise tours if you ask.

Bookshops The city's two best bookshops, both quite decent and on Ave de Gaulle, are Librairie Maison de la Presse, two blocks west of the Novotel, and Librairie le Paillet, 1½ blocks to the east of the Novotel. They carry *Time*, *Newsweek*, the *International Herald Tribune* and numerous French newspapers and magazines as well as lots of good books in French, some of which are about the Congo, but no maps.

Supermarkets The city has two large modern supermarkets: CFAO Supermarché Tigre, just to the north of the railway station, and Score, on Ave de Gaulle, three blocks east of the railway station.

Activities
The most popular pastime is sunbathing and swimming in the ocean – the waves here are quite large. Nonguests can use the pool at the Novotel for CFA 1000 and play tennis there for CFA 1500 to CFA 2000 per 45-minute session. Sailboards and small sailboats are available for rent at the Cercle Naval (Sailing Club) for CFA 1500 an hour and CFA 10,000 for half a day. It's off Ave du Port, a km north

of the Novotel facing the protected Pointe-Noire Bay, and open weekdays from 3 to 7 pm and all day at weekends.

For fishing, call ☎ 942705 or inquire at Hôtel Azur Zamba for charter boats. February to April is the season for tarpon, November to April for barracuda and carp, and May to September for sea bream, tuna and other fish. **Djeno**, which is south of town on the road to Cabinda, is well known for surf casting; a world-record tarpon catch was made here.

For even more excitement – motorised hang-gliding – call José (☎ 941105) weekdays from 1 to 2.30 pm, Saturday afternoon or all day Sunday; he'll take you up for some great views.

Places to Stay – bottom end
Some hotel receptionists in Pointe-Noire have the nasty habit of quoting foreigners room prices that are higher than the real rates, so if a quoted price seems out of line, you may have to bargain. All of the cheap places to stay are in the Cité except the *Mission Catholique* (☎ 941636), better known as La Procure or Le Vichy. It is in the modern commercial centre, a block south of the well-known Hôtel Migitel, and has about 10 spotlessly clean rooms ranging in price from CFA 3000 to CFA 5000.

In the Cité, a super place for the price is *Motel Kingoy* (☎ 941846), out on Ave Jeudi (which heads out of town towards Loubomo), roughly two km north-east of the Rond-Point Lumumba. Rooms with fans/aircon and private showers cost only CFA 1500/2000, which is incredibly cheap for the good quality. The rooms and toilets are quite clean and there's a bar with TV and friendly people. An added plus is that it's near one of the best African nightclubs in town, Le Jumbo.

Motel Mapila (☎ 944009) is very similar in quality and charges CFA 5000 for a room with air-con and private bathroom. To get there from the Rond-Point Lumumba, head east on Ave Lundi and about 200 metres past the paved Ave Félix Tchicaya, turn right for 100 metres or so down a dirt road. *Hôtel ABC*

Palace is nearby and similar in quality but at CFA 7000 for a room (the price I was quoted) it's overpriced. However, the real price may be less. It's about 200 metres further east on Ave Lundi and 100 metres or so to your left.

Hôtel Paul Bambi (☎ 943448) is nearby and further to the north on the wide Ave de l'Indépendance, just north of the intersection with Ave Mardi. It's better for the price and recommended. The rooms are small and cost CFA 6000 but they have air-con, TVs and clean attached bathrooms. There's also a bar with TV but no restaurant.

If you'd rather be within walking distance of a beach (one that's infrequently used), try *Hôtel le Ndey (No 1)* (☎ 940517). There are two hotels of this name close to one another. This one is *vers la plage* (near the beach), about 300 metres from Pointe-Noire Bay, off Ave de Loango. The location is a bit remote but it's very breezy here and there's lots of greenery. There are eight rooms with fans and private bathrooms costing from CFA 5000 to CFA 6000. The hotel is near the Lycée Auganeur (formerly Lycée Karl Marx) and the main clients are youngsters with their dates, staying at hourly rates.

If you're here during an unusually crowded period and you're getting desperate, try *Auberge Centre Cité* or *Hôtel le Barela*. Both these places are somewhat remotely located. The former is in the Tié-Tié district and the latter is nearby in Makaya-Makaya, several blocks east of Ave Matindi. The Barela has rooms for CFA 6000/8000 (fans/air-con) and a lively bar with TV. The Centre Cité seems overpriced at CFA 8000 for a room with tiled floor, fan and private bathroom, but they may let you stay there for up to 12 hours at half the price. *Mantala Auberge* is still another to inquire about in this price range if all of these places are full.

Places to Stay – middle

The best mid-range hotel, and the only one in the central area, is the 24-room *Hôtel Migitel* (☎ 940918; fax 940258) on Ave de Gaulle, but at CFA 14,050 and CFA 17,900 for air-con rooms and CFA 1800 for breakfast, it's also the most expensive. The clients here are all expatriates, many of whom hang around the air-con bar. It's much better value than *Hôtel le Pontegrene* (☎ 941357), a relatively new two-storey hotel at 64 Ave Jeudi, near Ave de l'Indépendance. It's overpriced at CFA 14,000 to CFA 17,500 for a room.

Price-wise, the small eight-room *Hôtel Okoumé* (☎ 941149), which is just off Ave Jeudi near Ave de l'Indépendance, is not so bad. It charges CFA 9000 for a room with a fan and a spotless private tiled bathroom. The two-storey *Hôtel Mario Adolphe* (☎ 94 1139), also called Hôtel Bakadila, on Ave Félix Tchicaya, several hundred metres south of Ave Lundi, has 17 rooms with fans/air-con for CFA 8000/10,000, a cafeteria and a nightclub. It's overpriced and recommended only if the price is reduced, which it sometimes is.

Two other possibilities – both inconveniently located and, therefore, difficult to recommend – are the three-storey *Hôtel Ibangui* (☎ 941204) out in the Tié-Tié district and the second *Hôtel le Ndey (No 2)* (☎ 943772), which is near the first hotel of that name but closer to Lycée Auganeur. The Ibangui charges CFA 11,500 for a neat room with air-con and private, tiled bathroom and has a nightclub, while the Ndey has an attractive outdoor restaurant and charges CFA 13,000 for its large clean air-con rooms and less by the hour.

Places to Stay – top end

There are only two hotels on the beach, the least expensive of which is the modern *Hôtel Palm Beach* (formerly the Motel de la Côte Sauvage). It is directly behind the railway station and has virtually all of the amenities of the city's top hotels. The ambience, however, is sterile and maintenance is not the best. The best beach hotel is *Hôtel Azur Zamba*, 400 metres down the beach. A PLM-chain hotel run by a Congolese woman and her French husband, it has a relaxed atmosphere and one of the best restaurants in town. The hotel with the most amenities (pool, tennis, etc) is the 209-room *Mbou-Mvoumvou Novotel*, which is in the heart of

town on Ave de Gaulle. It's quite active but
at 1½ km from the beach, it appeals more to
business people.

There are two top-end hotels with rooms
for under CFA 20,000. *Le Guest-House*, near
the central area at 13 Ave Boganda, two
blocks south of Ave de Gaulle, has modern
apartment-like rooms with TV, video and
telephone. This small, well-managed place is
a great choice for longer stays, which is why
it's so popular with petroleum technicians.
The *Victory-Palace Hôtel* is another possibility if you want to save money. An old-style
hotel and somewhat run-down, it's a block
south of Ave de Gaulle and closer to the
beach. Its 60 rooms are carpeted and have
TVs and refrigerators. Two other old hotels,
the *Atlantic-Palace* and *Beauséjour*, are now
closed.

Hôtel Azur Zamba (☎ 942771; fax 942751; telex
8297), CFA 26,000 per room, beach, pool, tennis;
accepts AE, D credit cards
Hôtel Palm Beach (☎ 944517; telex 8355), CFA
21,347 a room, beach, pool, mini-refrigerators,
TV, video; accepts AE, D credit cards
Hôtel Victory-Palace (☎ 940703/4; telex 8267), CFA
17,000 and CFA 21,000 per room, Hertz car
rental; accepts AE, D credit cards
Le Guest-House (☎ 940187), CFA 19,000 a room, TV,
video
Mbou-Mvoumvou Novotel (☎ 941200; fax 941464;
telex 8240), CFA 23,000/26,000 for singles/
doubles, pool, tennis, Hertz car rental, travel
agency; accepts AE, D, V credit cards

Credit Cards: AE – American Express, D – Diners, V
– Visa

Places to Eat
Cheap Eats Most of the cheapest places to
eat are African restaurants in the Cité area,
listed under the African food section. The
Cité is also the best area for food stalls.
You'll find men grilling beef on the streets
along and just off Ave Mardi, starting from
the Rond-Point Lumumba for about 300
metres eastward.

For inexpensive food in the modern commercial district, it's hard to beat the no-name,
open-air place some 25 metres north of the
railway station. Open from about 7 am to
noon, it serves big portions of African food,
such as saka saka, *courge* (marrow), coco au
poisson fumé (fish in coconut sauce) and
poisson salé, for CFA 500, including a big
plate of manioc.

Further east along Ave de Gaulle there are
several places that aren't so expensive. Just
beyond the UCB bank, for example, you'll
find a hamburger place with hamburgers and
sandwiches in the CFA 600 to CFA 1600
range and cheap coffee. The *Restaurant
Mikado* is across the street; it's a tiny café
offering braised chicken and fish and other
grilled dishes, mostly for CFA 1500, and
large beers for CFA 700. The bar at the
Migitel, which is several blocks further east,
is popular with expatriates for light food,
such as ham sandwiches for CFA 1200, but
beers are expensive (CFA 1000 for a large
Kronenbourg).

You'll also find an outdoor café very close
to the Chinese restaurant on Ave de Gaulle
that's a favourite during the day with expatriates for coffee, pastries and snacks.
However, the most popular meeting place for
expatriates, day and night, is the *Vegas Pub
& Restaurant* on Ave du Port near the Cercle
Naval. Prices range from CFA 1000 for
croque messieurs (toasted ham and cheese
sandwiches) to CFA 1800 for Lebanese
chawarma sandwiches. Some people,
however, come just for beer and billiards –
there are two tables.

African The best African restaurant, *Chez
Gaspard*, is one of the city's long-standing
institutions and famous even in Brazzaville,
including among expatriates who normally
don't frequent African restaurants. To get
there from the Rond-Point Lumumba, head
east on Ave Mardi, turn left at the third
intersection (Ave Portella) and it's about 40
metres from there. It's open daily from late
morning to late evening. Most of the dishes
are between CFA 700 and CFA 1000, including ragoût de mouton, saka saka, coco au
poisson fumé, bouillon de singe fumé,
gazelle fumé, pâte d'arachide and poisson
salé, as well as more expensive European
dishes, such as steak and sole, both for CFA

2000. At night the menu changes to grilled dishes, mostly for CFA 800, such as grilled chicken and carp.

Nearby, on the same street, you'll find *Restaurant Bibaka*. Grilled meats are the speciality here and late at night it becomes a nightclub. A place very much like Chez Gaspard is *Restaurant Marie Diallo*. The food and prices are similar, and at night grilled dishes are served under the stars as at Gaspard. It's nearby on Ave Mardi, about halfway between the Rond-Point Lumumba and Chez Gaspard. Another place like Chez Gaspard is *Restaurant BTB*, which is on Ave Lundi, about 200 before (west of) Ave de l'Indépendance.

Restaurant Amitié (Chez Aby) specialises in food from Senegal and the Côte d'Ivoire, including Senegalese fish, poulet yassa, Senegalese fish thiéboudienne (the national dish of Senegal), and Ivoirian chicken kedjenou, as well as various Congolese bouillons. Most dishes are in the CFA 1000 to CFA 1800 range. The restaurant is in the modern section, one block south of the Rond-Point Kasaï and 1½ blocks west.

Surprisingly, you can also get Ethiopian food. *Restaurant le Sabar*, on Ave 15 Août between Vendredi and Samedi Aves, offers 13 Ethiopian specialities, from CFA 2000 to CFA 3500, as well as some bush meat dishes, including crocodile and boa, all for CFA 2000. Braised meats and fish are also on the menu, starting from CFA 1000. Open in the evenings only, it has good music and a good atmosphere and is highly recommended.

French The city's French restaurants are generally quite expensive. The most reasonably priced are *Restaurant le Chaudron* at the Hôtel Migitel on Ave de Gaulle (eg cassoulet for CFA 2000, and Vietnamese selections), *Restaurant l'Imprévu* (formerly Pizzeria) across the street and, most reasonably priced, *Restaurant Ali Baba* (☎ 942467), just west of the Novotel. The latter also serves Lebanese dishes (CFA 2000 to CFA 2500) and has air-con and an attractive décor.

The French restaurant with the nicest setting is *Restaurant la Baraka*, which is on Ave du Port near the Cercle Naval (Sailing Club). Overlooking the port and Pointe-Noire Bay, it has an attractive breezy ambience, a four-course set menu for CFA 4900 and à la carte dishes starting from CFA 3000. The city's two best French restaurants by reputation – *Restaurant Le Biniou* (☎ 942227; closed on Sundays), opposite the Novotel on Ave de Gaulle, and *Chez Paulette* (☎ 941688), between the railway station and the Cercle Naval – are quite expensive. The latter, which is open daily, has a special four-course menu plus à la carte selections, including some seafood.

Other Restaurants There are four good restaurants along Blvd Bouity, the sandy beach road west of the railway station. All are expensive except for the very informal *Restaurant la Plage Sportif*, which is at the southern end of the road, directly on the beach opposite *Hôtel Azur Zamba*. Among the city's hotels, the Azur Zamba has the reputation for serving the best food. Next door is *Restaurant la Langouste* (☎ 943750), which specialises in seafood as does *Le Sea Club* (☎ 941211; closed on Sundays), an open-air restaurant at the northern end of the same street.

Restaurant Chez Wou, at the northern end of the airport road where it intersects with Ave Marien Nguouabi, and *Restaurant le Mékong* on Ave de Gaulle are the places to go for Chinese food.

Entertainment

Bars For cheap brew in the central area, try the open-air place just north of the railway station. You can get large cold beers there for CFA 350. There are lots of cheap bars in the Cité with similar prices. *Bar Parafifi* on Ave du 15 Août near Ave Samedi is one of the livelier ones but it's also well known for thieves and probably best avoided at night. For a more tranquil setting, try one of the African restaurants, such as *Chez Gaspard*, where the beers are just as cheap.

Vegas Pub on Ave du Port near the sailing club is one of the most popular watering holes for expatriates. The bar at the *Hôtel Migitel* on Ave de Gaulle is another possibility but the beers there are expensive at CFA 1000 for a large beer.

Nightclubs Pointe-Noire has a good number of *boîtes* (nightclubs), many of which are closed on Mondays. Reputed to be the best for disco music and African sounds is *La Pagode* (formerly Jhimisy), in the centre of town off Ave de Gaulle. It's popular with both Africans and expatriates. *Le Balafon* is similar and also has an excellent reputation for good music and dancing.

Most nightclubs in the Cité are cheaper and cater just to locals. One club that I like is *Le Jumbo Nightclub*, which is a bit far out on Ave Jeudi, half a km north-east beyond Ave de l'Indépendance. It's at the top of the hill on your right and unmarked, 100 metres before Motel Kingoy. Big beers cost CFA 1000 and there's no cover charge. The dance floor is strobe-lit, the music is African and the people are friendly.

One much closer to the Rond-Point Lumumba is *Le Crépuscule*, roughly 50 metres north of the roundabout on Ave Vendredi. Popular with lovers and open both day and night, it has air-con, big beers for CFA 600 and a very dark dance floor. Another possibility is *Le Saphir* at Hôtel Ibangui out in the Tié-Tié district; it's reportedly not so bad for dancing on weekends.

Cinema The city's top movie theatre is Cinéma Club 7 on Ave de Gaulle near Score supermarket. The largest in the Cité is Cinéma Roy on the corner of Aves Jeudi and de l'Indépendance.

Things to Buy

There's an artisanat opposite the railway station where vendors sell wooden carvings, batik and other local crafts, mostly of souvenir quality.

Getting There & Away

Air Lina Congo (☎ 940806/7) has two or three flights a day to/from Brazzaville (CFA 22,000), stopping en route at Loubomo on Mondays and Saturdays. The airport is five km south of the central area. Air Gabon (☎ 941592), which has an office just west of the Rond-Point Kasaï, provides a service to/from Libreville (CFA 72,500) on Wednesday, Friday and Saturday. Air Afrique (☎ 940931) is represented here but has no flights.

Train Because of the terrible road conditions between Loubomo and Pointe-Noire, it's almost impossible to find trucks going between the two cities and only occasionally will you find 4WD vehicles. As a result, most travellers arrive here from Brazzaville by train. The main railway station (☎ 941532) is at the western end of Ave de Gaulle. The Train Bleu costs CFA 14,400/8385 1st/2nd class to Brazzaville and CFA 4150/2060 to Loubomo. Fares on the slower express and Soleil are CFA 12,380/6255 1st/2nd class to Brazzaville (CFA 15,550 for a sleeper on the express) and, like the Train Bleu, CFA 4150/2060 to Loubomo. You can pay CFA 300 extra to reserve a seat, otherwise you risk standing much of the way. Their departure times are the same as from Brazzaville: 6.15 am Soleil, 10.30 am Train Bleu and 6.30 pm express; the scheduled arrival times are 7.36 pm, 8.34 pm and 6.08 am, respectively.

Getting Around

Bus The blue-and-yellow striped public buses, which run up and down Ave de Gaulle and Ave de l'Indépendance, charge CFA 125. There used to be 10 lines but they are now down to three and could go out of business altogether.

Taxi Shared taxis cost CFA 100 to CFA 200 per ride, depending on the distance, and about CFA 2500 by the hour.

Car Eurocar is represented by Taxi Frégate (☎ 940359; fax 944062; telex 8263), which has a booth at the airport and an office at the Marché du Plateau. Most major credit cards are accepted. Hertz (☎ 941513/40; telex 8236) and Taxis-Baya are both represented at the Mbou-Mvoumvou Novotel. Others include Panda Location/Georges Bouyou (☎ 941777) at the petrol station facing Immeuble ATC and Taxi-Service (☎ 940-495), which is also a driving school. Fares are high – Taxi-Baya, for example, charges CFA 25,500 a day, including insurance, plus CFA 220 per km (40 km free) and 22% tax, with a CFA 200,000 deposit. This is about double what you would pay renting a taxi by the day.

AROUND POINTE-NOIRE
Pointe Indienne
If you want a more secluded beach than the one in Pointe-Noire, head for Pointe Indienne, which is 15 km north of the city by paved road. It's a beautiful beach with a few round, thatched-roof cabanas for shade. Lots of tourist brochures include photos of this spot. The hotel here is closed but it is possible to camp. You can get here by hitching but it is easier to take a private taxi or public transport to Madingo-Kayes.

Loango
There's no museum in Pointe-Noire, but if you head 10 km beyond Pointe Indienne to Loango, you'll find a good new museum called Le Musée Ma Loango, which is in a colonial-era house and well worth a visit. Four km further north you can visit the mausoleum of the Loango kings in **Diosso**, the capital of the former kingdom of Loango. Those without wheels should inquire at the tourist office (Direction Régionale du Tourisme et des Affaires Culturelles) in Pointe-Noire or see the UTC travel agency. The tourist office sponsors tours to the museum on Tuesday, Thursday, Saturday and Sunday in the morning and afternoon when there is sufficient demand.

Madingo-Kayes
If you continue north another 33 km along the coastal road, you'll come to where the Kouilou River empties into the sea and, just beyond, Madingo-Kayes (62 km), where the paved road ends. This is one of the best areas in the country from which to view the rainforests, so a trip can be well worthwhile,

especially if you have a vehicle to get around. The rainforests begin a short way inland, beyond the city.

LOUBOMO (DOLISIE)
Loubomo, the major town on the railway between Brazzaville and Pointe-Noire, theoretically reverted back to its original French name of Dolisie (in memory of Albert Dolisie, de Brazza's righthand man who later became governer of the Middle Congo) in 1991 when the country began opening up politically, shaking off its semi-Marxist past. When you arrive here by train that's what the station sign will show. However, Loubomo is still the name commonly used. It's the country's third-largest city and is at the western edge of the plateau area, with thick rainforests separating it from Pointe-Noire. Loubomo is where you get off the train if you're going overland to Gabon. You do not have to get your passport stamped here unless you're going to Gabon, but I'd recommend doing it anyway just to avoid potential hassles from police.

The heart of the modern commercial district is Place Marien Nguouabi. Very near there you'll find the top-end hotels, some stores, such as the Serrano general store, and two banks, UCB and CCB. They will change French franc travellers' cheques but not those denominated in other currencies. The Mission Catholique is just a block north of the square and the new hospital is roughly a km beyond. The liveliest section is the Cité, which is south of the railway station (across the tracks) and has inexpensive restaurants, bars and nightclubs. Most of the action is within two or three blocks in any direction of the main roundabout, which is a short walk south of the railway station.

Places to Stay – bottom end
If price is your only concern, try *Bar Faisceau*, which is on the eastern side of town just beyond the railway tracks, a good 15 to 20-minute walk from the railway station. Most of the clients are men with prostitutes. The 10 rooms here cost CFA 3000 but they have no ventilation and the

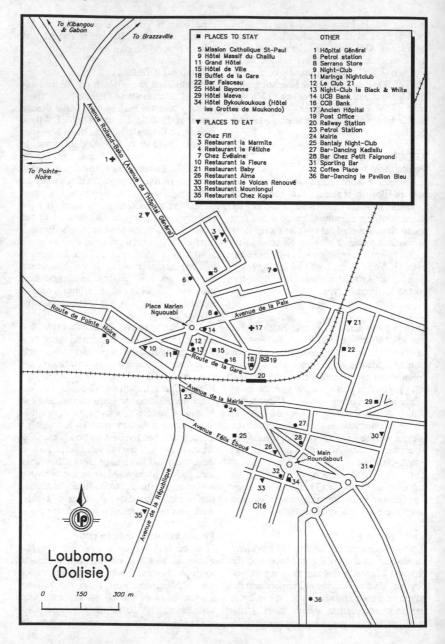

To Kibangou & Gabon

To Brazzaville

To Pointe-Noire

■ PLACES TO STAY

5 Mission Catholique St-Paul
9 Hôtel Massif du Chaillu
11 Grand Hôtel
15 Hôtel de Ville
18 Buffet de la Gare
22 Bar Faisceau
25 Hôtel Bayonne
29 Hôtel Maeva
34 Hôtel Bykoukoukous (Hôtel les Grottes de Moukondo)

▼ PLACES TO EAT

2 Chez Fifi
3 Restaurant la Marmite
4 Restaurant le Fétiche
7 Chez Évélaine
10 Restaurant la Fleure
21 Restaurant Baby
26 Restaurant Aima
30 Restaurant le Volcan Renouvé
33 Restaurant Mounlongui
35 Restaurant Chez Kopa

OTHER

1 Hôpital Général
6 Petrol station
8 Serrano Store
9 Night-Club
11 Maringa Nightclub
12 Le Club 21
13 Night-Club le Black & White
14 UCB Bank
16 CCB Bank
17 Ancien Hôpital
19 Post Office
20 Railway Station
23 Petrol Station
24 Mairie
25 Bantaly Night-Club
27 Bar-Dancing Kadisilu
28 Bar Chez Petit Faignond
31 Sporting Bar
32 Coffee Place
36 Bar-Dancing le Pavillon Bleu

Avenue Roland-Bako (Avenue de l'Hôpital Général)

Route de Pointe Noire

Place Marien Nguouabi

Avenue de la Paix

Route de la Gare

Avenue de la Mairie

Avenue Félix Éboué

Main Roundabout

Avenue de la République

Cité

Loubomo
(Dolisie)

0   150   300 m

toilets are barely tolerable. There is, however, a nice shady area at the back that's pleasant for drinks. A much better place for the price is the friendly *Mission Catholique St-Paul*, which has clean rooms for CFA 4000, including two rooms for couples. It's half a km north of the railway station and only a block north of Place Marien Nguouabi.

Alternatively, try the popular *Buffet de la Gare*, which conveniently faces the railway station. It charges CFA 5800 for quiet rooms with secure locks, showers and shared toilets, and has a decent cheap restaurant. The beds are reasonably comfortable with two sheets and the lighting and showers are good, but there are no fans and the African-style squat toilets aren't the cleanest. If you're arriving on the night train, head here immediately to beat the other travellers, otherwise you may find it full. *Hôtel Maeva* is very similar in most respects, with rooms for CFA 5800 and a restaurant. It's on the far eastern side of town just off Ave de la Mairie, about 800 metres from the railway station. *Hôtel les Grottes de Moukondo* (☎ 910172, better known by its old name of Hôtel Bykoukoukous), is similarly priced and in the heart of the Cité and market area, half a km south of the railway station.

Places to Stay – top end

The city's top hotel is the *Grand Hôtel* (☎ 910102/3), in the heart of town on Rue de la Gare, a block south of Place Marien Nguouabi. There are three classes of rooms, all with air-con and some with uneven floors and sagging mattresses: CFA 13,500, CFA 20,000 and CFA 26,000. The least expensive are much more difficult to get than the other two. It's an old-style, two-storey hotel with 39 rooms, a pool and a nightclub and is fairly well maintained, but it still seems overpriced. The artwork in the lobby was done by a French woman whose portrait is hanging in the hotel.

Three blocks to the west on the road to Pointe-Noire is *Hôtel Massif du Chaillu* (formerly the Hôtel Niari). Although not so well managed, it's fairly neat and bright with air-con rooms for CFA 12,000 with private hot-water bathrooms and a pleasant bar. Another alternative is the *Hôtel Bayonne* (☎ 910044), which has 24 small, air-con rooms with comfortable chairs. It also has a bar, restaurant and nightclub. The listed price for a room is CFA 14,000, but they will often agree to a reduction if you insist. It's in the Cité on a paved street (Ave Félix Éboué), 200 metres east of Ave de la République.

Places to Eat

Cheap Eats The Cité is a good place for cheap eats. One of these is *Restaurant Mouniongui*, a hole-in-the-wall with rock-bottom prices in the heart of the Cité. It's a block south of the main roundabout, on the same dirt street as Hôtel Bykoukoukous and one block west. There are only one or two selections, such as sibissi (a bush meat), and the meals are nothing special but they are cheap. It closes in the early afternoon. For coffee, there's a tiny, cheap place between the restaurant and the hotel. *Restaurant Aima* is a short block to the north at the main roundabout on Ave Félix Éboué. Also worth trying is *Restaurant le Volcan Renouvé*, which is about 300 metres further east, past another roundabout and one block north of the *Sporting Bar*.

The *Buffet de la Gare* facing the railway station is decent and cheap, with Primus beers for CFA 325, omelettes for CFA 400 and poisson salé for CFA 600. This is all they had when I was there despite the long menu. If you're staying at Bar Faisceau, you could try *Restaurant Baby*, which is on the same street and 100 metres further north.

African Loubomo is a fantastic place for sampling Congolese food because the choices here are surprisingly large. My favourite is *Chez Évélaine*, where you can get singe fumé, sanglier (wart hog), poisson fumé, silure fumé or salé (smoked or spicy freshwater fish) among other things, all for CFA 600 to CFA 700, plus beers for CFA 350. Open from 8 am to 8 pm, it's unbeatable for price and quality. To get there from Place Marien Nguouabi, head east on Ave de la

Paix for about half a km and turn left (north) for 150 metres down a dirt road; there's no sign.

Restaurant la Marmite (or Chez Ma N'Goudi) is similar, with a smaller menu and higher prices because the dishes are larger. Antelope, poisson salé, ngoki and boa all cost CFA 1000. It's on the dirt road behind the Mission Catholique and 150 metres north. *Restaurant le Fétiche* is also similar and directly behind the Marmite, one street further east. It's open from noon to around 10 pm and prices are slightly higher.

Another place on the northern side of town is *Chez Fifi*, which is on the same paved street (Ave Rolland-Bako) as the Mission Catholique and 350 metres further north and well before the new hospital. Attractive with a large thatched roof, it's clearly more up-market and a good place to go to in the evenings when they serve both Congolese food and braised meats. On the south side of town along the paved Ave de la République, about 600 metres south of the railway tracks, you'll find *Restaurant Chez Kopa* (or Au Circuit Kam), which is also quite good and recommended. It has a good rustic ambience and typical Congolese dishes (eg sanglier and bouillon for CFA 1200) and grilled meats at night.

Other Restaurants The most up-market restaurants, with primarily continental food, are all at the hotels, the best being that at the *Grand Hôtel* followed by the *Hôtel Massif du Chaillu*, three blocks to the west. Between them is the *Restaurant la Fleure*, which seems better for a drink than a meal.

Nightclubs
Loubomo has several places that are good for both drinking and dancing to African music, and all are in the Cité. Two north of the main roundabout are *Bar Chez Petit Faignond* and *Bar-Dancing Kadisilu*, north of the round-about. A third is *Bar-Dancing le Pavillon Bleu*, which is half a km south of the round-about on a wide north-south avenue. You might also try the *Bantaly Night-Club* at

Hôtel Bayonne, which is roughly 300 metres west of the roundabout on Ave Félix Éboué.

Expatriates and wealthy Congolese prefer the more modern discos, most of which are in the centre of town, a stone's throw south of Place Marien Nguouabi. The best by reputation is *Le Club 21*. Two others which are similar and virtually next door are *Nightclub Le Black & White* and *Maringa Night-Club* at the Grand Hôtel. These places don't get going before 11 pm and prostitutes frequent them all. The ambience is disco-like but the music is primarily Congolese and Zaïrian.

Getting There & Away
To/From Brazzaville & Pointe-Noire The easiest way to get here is with Lina Congo (☎ 910169), which has flights to/from Brazzaville and Pointe-Noire on Mondays and Saturdays. Most people, however, come by rail; three trains pass by here daily in either direction. The Train Bleu, which is the best, costs CFA 10,360/6325 1st/2nd class to Brazzaville (eight hours) and CFA 4150/2060 to Pointe-Noire (three hours). According to the schedule it should pass through Loubomo at about 1.30 pm on its way to Brazzaville and about 5 pm on its way to Pointe-Noire, but late arrivals are common. Fares on the slower express and Soleil are the same to Pointe-Noire and CFA 8230/4095 1st/2nd class to Brazzaville.

If you are travelling by car between Brazzaville and Pointe-Noire, you absolutely must have a high-clearance 4WD as the road from Loubomo to Pointe-Noire is terrible. Finding a truck going there or to Brazzaville is fairly difficult, which is another reason why almost everyone without a vehicle takes the train.

To/From Gabon There is a train daily in either direction between Loubomo and Mbinda, leaving Loubomo in the late morning and Mbinda (on the Gabon border) at 5 am. The train from Loubomo waits in Mont Bélo (on the Brazzaville-Pointe-Noire line) until the arrival of the Soleil from Brazzaville (which departs at 6.30 am and, according to the schedule, arrives in Mont

Bélo at 2.30 pm). This means you can leave Brazzaville at 6.30 am and, without stopping in Loubomo, theoretically arrive in Mbinda on the same day (at 11.22 pm according to the schedule, but 3 am or so is more likely). However, coming south from Mbinda you will arrive in Mont Bélo after the Soleil from Pointe-Noire has passed, so you will have to continue on to Loubomo to catch a train the following day to Brazzaville or Pointe-Noire.

The Loubomo to Mbinda train takes about 12 hours and the fare is CFA 8975/4575 1st/2nd class. There are usually lots of empty seats and vendors sell sandwiches along the way. It's by far the easiest way of getting to Gabon.

Alternatively, you can take a truck. The most travelled route is further west via Nyanga and N'Dendé (Gabon), not via Mbinda. There are trucks almost every day direct to Nyanga at the border, and they usually charge about CFA 6000 for the all-day trip with a stop in Kibangou for lunch. If you can't find a direct truck, you'll have to take several trucks, starting with one to Makabana or Kibangou. They fill up in front of the railway station, cost CFA 1500 and take at least three hours to reach either town.

NYANGA
If you're travelling between Loubomo and Lambaréné (Gabon), you'll probably stay overnight in the Congolese border town of Nyanga. It has no electricity or running water but you can find a bed. Look for some simple rooms next to the market (CFA 1000). There's also a small hotel with rooms for CFA 1500. For food, try the market or general store next to it; the latter also has bottled water.

MBINDA
Mbinda is the Congolese border town on the route from Loubomo to Franceville (Gabon). Many travellers come this way because of the train connections between here and Brazzaville.

Places to Stay
The only lodging in town is the *Comilog* hostel, which charges CFA 7000 for a room. However, the administrator leaves in the early evening and if you arrive after he has left, your only choice may be sleeping on the floor of the railway station.

Getting There & Away
A pick-up truck from here north to the border costs between CFA 500 and CFA 1000, and from there you will find trucks headed to Franceville (CFA 3000). You can also get bush taxis to Franceville and Moanda.

The train south for Loubomo leaves daily at 5 am, arriving in Loubomo about 12 hours later; the 1st/2nd-class fare is CFA 8975/4575. It normally arrives in Mont Bélo too late to catch the Soleil from Pointe-Noire (the other trains don't stop here), so you'll have to continue on to Loubomo. However, coming from Brazzaville, you can take the 6.30 am Soleil and get off in Mont Bélo, where the train from Loubomo will be waiting to take you on to Mbinda, usually arriving there the next day around 3 am or so (11.22 pm on the same day according to the schedule). The 1st/2nd-class fare from Brazzaville to Mbinda is CFA 15,665/7,950.

Alternatively, you could take minibuses and trucks but the trip takes at least two days and the cost is much higher, eg CFA 3000 for a minibus from Loubomo to Sibiti and CFA 8000 for a truck from there to Mbinda.

SIBITI
Sibiti has only one hotel, which charges CFA 8500 for a room, plus a place with dormitory rooms for CFA 2000. One possible alternative is to look up the local Peace Corps volunteers and see if they'll put you up for the night. You can get here by minibus or truck from Loubomo for CFA 3000 and from Mbinda by truck for CFA 8000.

KINKALA & MATOUMBOU
These two towns, both on the main railway line, are only a two-hour drive west of Brazzaville on the road towards Pointe-Noire; the road is in terrible condition. By

bus the trip to Kinkala costs CFA 600 from Brazzaville, with numerous departures throughout the day from Marché Total. Kinkala's best hotel is the three-storey *Hôtel de Makoumbou* (☎ 852053) with 15 rooms. The *Hôtel de Kinkala* is another. In nearby Matoumbou, the *Hôtel de Matoumbou* (☎ 852057) has 12 air-con rooms and a restaurant.

The Centre & the North

DJAMBALA

Some 382 km north of Brazzaville via the Owando road, Djambala is in the centre of the Congo's plateau area and can be reached in one long day by passenger-carrying pick-up trucks or private vehicle. The pick-up trucks, which leave Brazzaville from the same place as the minibuses for Owando, are very uncomfortable because they are invariably crammed with passengers. They charge about CFA 8000 and take about nine hours during the dry season or longer during the rainy season. The route is all-weather but very little of it is paved and much of it is in very bad condition, requiring a high clearance vehicle if not a 4WD. Hotels include *Hôtel de Djambala* and the nine-room *Auberge des Jeunes* on the road to Camp Matsouaniste.

OYO

On the road to Owando, Oyo is perhaps best known for being near the village of former president Sassou-Nguesso which is 10 km to the west. He owns most of the cattle you'll see in this area. If you're caught here for the night, two hotels to try are the *J B Motel* and *Hôtel Bel-Air d'Oyo*; you'll see signs to both on the main north-south drag through town. For cheap eats, try *Restaurant Petit Coin* on the main road.

OWANDO

Owando is one of the largest towns in the north but is still quite small. The people here are among the friendliest that I have met in all of Central Africa, so you may find it quite pleasant, as I did. The heart of town is the market, around which you'll find several bars and restaurants and numerous small shops where you can stock up on tinned goods. These general stores are run mostly by West Africans, particularly Mauritanians, who have lived here for years. For a little tranquillity, go down to the nearby Kouyou River.

Places to Stay & Eat

For a nice clean room, go to the *Mission Catholique*, a five-minute walk north of the market. The friendly Congolese priest charges CFA 6000 for a room with fan, single bed, basin and shared bathroom. You can save money, however, by staying at the *Mini-Hôtel du Marché*, which is behind the market, overlooking its south-eastern corner. The rooms here are tiny and basic but the rates (CFA 3000 a room) are lower.

The city's top address is *Hôtel le Kouyou*, which is on the main north-south drag just before the river. It charges CFA 7900/9000 for rooms with fans/air-con and is a fairly decent hotel, with a shady terrace at the front for drinks. Large beers cost CFA 460 and most meals, such as grilled fish, cost CFA 1000. There's little else in the way of food other than some food vendors in front of the market and a cheap restaurant at the back of the market, which is open only until around 1 pm or so.

At night, there's a woman who makes fantastic waffles hot off the griddle for CFA 25. She is stationed on the main drag running past the market, half a block past *Ébina Bar* (☎ 971090), which faces the market. Rustic and open-air, this bar is the best place in town for drinks. At the front there are some tables and chairs surrounded by a hedge – a tranquil setting for a drink day or night. It's also a great dancing place and at the back it's always packed on weekends, with music blasting away and large beers for CFA 375 to CFA 450 and Cokes for 250. The open-air *Garden-Eden Nightclub*, two blocks to the west on the same street, is also quite lively and better than *Bar les Retrouvailles* behind

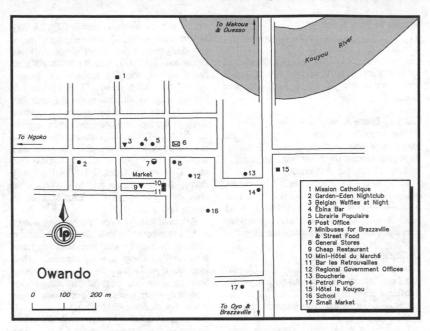

To Makoua & Ouesso

Kouyou River

To Ngoko

Owando

0   100   200 m

To Oyo & Brazzaville

1 Mission Catholique
2 Garden–Eden Nightclub
3 Belgian Waffles at Night
4 Ébina Bar
5 Librairie Populaire
6 Post Office
7 Minibuses for Brazzaville
   & Street Food
8 General Stores
9 Cheap Restaurant
10 Mini-Hôtel du Marché
11 Bar les Retrouvailles
12 Regional Government Offices
13 Boucherie
14 Petrol Pump
15 Hôtel le Kouyou
16 School
17 Small Market

the market, which is most notable for some colourful paintings on the walls.

Getting There & Away

Lina Congo (☎ 971324) has flights to/from Brazzaville on Thursdays and Saturdays, and Aéro Service has flights on Fridays. The latter was charging CFA 31,500 one way while Lina Congo wasn't flying, but they may fall as Lina Congo's fares are lower.

Owando is a long day's ride north of Brazzaville (522 km), and there are three or four minibuses travelling daily in either direction. In Owando buses leave from the market around 3 am but sometimes as early as midnight. Regardless of departure times they arrive in Brazzaville around noon the following day. If you make arrangements the night before, the drivers will pick you up at your hotel. In Brazzaville, buses leave from Terminus Mikalou; they are usually all full by 6.30 am and leave by 7 am, arriving in Owando around 4 pm (later during the rainy season). The fare is CFA 9000 and, amazingly, there are no police checks along the way.

From Brazzaville, the road is paved for about the first 20 km, and then again from 20 km south of Ngo all the way to Owando, where the paved road ends. The middle section is full of huge potholes, requiring a high clearance vehicle but not 4WD except, perhaps, during the worst parts of the rainy season. The scenery in that section is fabulous.

MAKOUA

Makoua marks the end of the plateau area and the beginning of the great rainforests. North of here the roads are in terrible condition and are generally passable only during the dry season. If you're going to Ouesso, you might end up staying here for several days as very few trucks attempt the very difficult 247-km stretch to that northern outpost.

Places to Stay & Eat

The best place to stay is *Hôtel Okouango*, which charges about CFA 5500 a room. The only other hotel is *Hôtel Fonga*, which has similar prices. The town has several small restaurants, one of which is *Restaurant Gassaki*.

Getting There & Away

See the preceding section on Owando for the logistics of getting to that town. On Saturdays you can also fly direct from Brazzaville on Lina Congo via Owando.

Makoua is some 71 km north of Owando, but getting there by car or hitching a ride from Owando is not so difficult as the road is all-weather and there are quite a few vehicles that pass along this route each day.

OUESSO

Some 840 km north of Brazzaville, Ouesso is a fairly dreary town in the middle of the rainforest along the Sangha River, but it's the gateway to one of the most interesting areas in the country.

If you arrive by plane, there's a good chance that a young man will meet you there and offer to be your guide to see the Pygmies nearby. He's a good guy and his tour is not so bad; you may get to eat monkey with the Pygmies and see a dance performance as well. He does not take visitors as far north as Bomassa, which is the best place to start expeditions into the rainforest. However, if you inquire in Ouesso at the tourist office down by the river, you may encounter Gérard, a French man who has been known to take people to Bomassa and the rainforest area. At the very least, he's a good source of information.

Places to Stay

The best place to stay is the *Mission Évangélique*, but the *Mission Catholique* also accepts travellers. The hotel down by the river has closed.

Getting There & Away

Lina Congo (☎ 983022) has flights to/from Brazzaville on Monday, Thursday and Sat-urday, and the one-way fare is CFA 28,500. If you come overland, you can catch one of the daily minibuses from Brazzaville to Owando (CFA 9000), which takes about nine hours during the dry season and longer during the rainy season. The 71-km trip further north to Makoua is not difficult, but the 247-km road from there to Ouesso through the lowland rainforest is in terrible condition and impassable during much of the rainy season. Very few trucks pass this way and sometimes there aren't any for days on end. Driving to Ouesso is feasible only during the dry season and in a 4WD. You should be able to make it from Makoua in one to two days.

Alternatively, you could try taking one of ATC's steamers (*La Ville de Ouesso* and *La Ville de Mossaka*) or a private barge from Brazzaville. There are no schedules, but from June to January there is usually one leaving from the port in Brazzaville or returning from Ouesso about every other week. By steamer, the trip takes about 10 days upriver to Ouesso and six days downriver to Brazzaville; the barges are slower. Deck class on either costs about CFA 9000.

BOMASSA

Some 100 km north of Ouesso by the Sangha River, Bomassa is the border village with the CAR and is where Wildlife Conservation International (WCI) is in the long process of delineating the boundaries of a potential wildlife park for this area. The virgin rainforests to the east of Bomassa are about as unspoiled as any you'll find in Africa, which is why environmentalists are so interested in the area. It's also contiguous with the CAR's new Sangha Reserve that the Worldwide Fund for Nature is supporting. If you make a trip here, be prepared for some tough trekking. The WCI camp site is 1½ km from the village. They won't be able to receive you, however, unless you've made arrangements beforehand with their Brazzville office for a trip here.

Without WCI's services, an expedition in this area is next to impossible, as you'll need them to set up the trip from Bomassa. You must bring everything you'll need from Ouesso, including food, as there's none for sale in Bomassa. WCI will make arrangements for Pygmies to act as guides, but you must bring food for them also. They'll first lead you on a two-day walk eastward through a logged area to get to the virgin rainforests. Then the real fun – animal stalking – begins. There are lots of monkeys; seven species have been reported but black-and-white colobus monkeys predominate. Other animals that you will almost surely see are buffalos, bongo, duiker, chimps and gorillas; the latter two are guaranteed to serenade you at night with their grunting. There are also lots of forest elephants but seeing them moving about is a little more difficult because of the thick vegetation.

Buffalo

Getting There & Away

Getting from Ouesso to Bomassa is no mean feat. You must take a motorised pirogue up the Sangha River to Babali, where the Société Nationale de Bois de Sangha (SNBS) has a logging camp, and 30 km further north on to Bomassa. The 100-km trip to Bomassa takes all day by motorised boat. Finding one going to the SNBS camp is fairly easy but from there to Bomassa is another story. As noted in the Ouesso section, see Gérard as he may be able to help you arrange transport all the way from Ouesso to Bomassa if WCI hasn't made these arrangements.

IMPFONDO

If you'll be travelling by riverboat or barge

from Bangui to Brazzaville or vice versa, you'll stop at Impfondo, the largest Congolese city on the Oubangui River, along the way. If you're going to Brazzaville or Bangui and there's no riverboat scheduled to pass, with luck you should be able to find a petroleum barge, even between February and May when the riverboats don't operate. As for barge fares, from here to the border town of Zinga, for example, should cost about CFA 2500 per person. The trip there by barge usually takes four or five days.

Lina Congo has a flight here from Brazzaville every Saturday and Aéro Service has one on Wednesday; the latter charges CFA 52,000 one way. There's one hotel in town, which is quite expensive. If you prefer to camp, see Pastor Thomas, an energetic American Baptist missionary who may be too busy to chat but will probably allow you to pitch a tent in his magnificent garden.

Equatorial Guinea

Tarzan would have loved Equatorial Guinea, and so will you if you're the type who likes to go off the beaten track. Away from the main towns of Malabo and Bata, Equatorial Guinea is a land of tropical forests, with cloud-covered volcanoes providing a backdrop to almost every view on Bioko Island. The vegetation is so thick at times on both the island and the mainland that paths can simply disappear beneath your feet. Without surfaced roads, the only way to move about in some parts would be to swing from the vines.

On the other hand, on arrival in Malabo, the capital city on Bioko Island, or Bata on the mainland, you may wonder why you came, especially if you enter from Cameroun or Gabon. Poverty is widespread in these towns, and the economy is so stagnant that the only thing available to cheer up the locals is the bars, which seem to be on every corner. Children often have no toys, or make do with cardboard boxes pulled around with string, or dancing to the banging of tin cans. Most noticeably, there's no music blasting away on the streets, inside bars or in the bush taxis – people can't afford cassette players.

In spite of its poverty, the undeveloped, backwater nature of Equatorial Guinea is very much part of its charm and possibly an asset in attracting visitors looking for something different.

There are areas throughout the country where very few people live – perfect if you're looking for remote hamlets where few foreigners have trodden, or isolated beaches with scenic surroundings. Spaniards are hardly new to the locals but independent travellers passing through are so rare that they may initially be treated with suspicion. Often, however, the locals end up becoming fast friends with them. The recent arrival of Peace Corps volunteers in Rio Muni may open the place up to visitors even more.

In any case, Equatorial Guinea is unlikely to disappoint the adventurous traveller, espe-

cially if you like socialising with the locals. Even if you don't speak Spanish, don't worry – many of the locals don't speak it either.

Facts about the Country

HISTORY
Equatorial Guinea is a small country that gets little press, except when there's a major scandal. The first such scandal was in the late 1920s, when working conditions on the cocoa plantations were so akin to slavery that the League of Nations sent a special mission there to study the situation.

The second scandal wasn't so much a single event as a decade (the 1970s) during which the country was saddled with Macias Nguema (n- GUAY-mah), a ruler of the same calibre as Idi Amin and Jean-Bédel Bokassa.

Contact with Europeans dates from 1470, with the Portuguese discovery of the tiny

island of Annobón near the island of Bioko. During the 19th century, Britain used Bioko (until recently called Fernando Pó) as a maritime base. In the second half of the century, the Spanish returned and established cocoa plantations.

The mainland province, Rio Muni, is much larger in area and population, but was largely ignored by the European powers until 1900, when it was united with Bioko as a single colony under Spanish rule. Much of it remained unexplored for another quarter of a century. Most of the Spanish lived on Bioko, which is why Malabo (MAH-lah-boh), not Bata (on the mainland), is the capital today.

Cocoa is Bioko's *raison d'être*. About 90% of it is grown on the island's fertile volcanic soil. For several decades until the 1920s, Bioko was the largest producer of cocoa in the world. While Africans cultivated many small plots, the Spanish landlords, many living in Spain, owned big plantations and controlled most acreage and production.

Since the local labour pool was small, labourers had to be brought from elsewhere in Africa, primarily from Liberia, Nigeria and Ghana. Returning Ghanaians started planting cocoa on their own, and Ghana soon became the world's leading producer.

Labourers from Liberia worked under slave-like conditions, recruited apparently under false pretenses and receiving no pay until they returned to Liberia. The matter came to the attention of the League of Nations in the late 1920s, and an international scandal resulted.

Independence

Spain did little to develop the country, preferring to leave it in the hands of the few large landowners. But after WW II, the Spanish government took a much more active role, subsidising cocoa and coffee exports to encourage production, building roads to open up the hinterland of Rio Muni, and improving the educational system. Nevertheless, the Africans were treated as legal minors until 1959, when they were finally granted full citizenship.

By then, however, a nationalist movement, led by the Fang tribe in Rio Muni, was already well under way, intent on reversing the favouritism given by the Spanish to Fernando Pó and the controlling Bubi tribe there. Pressure mounted and, by 1968, Spain was forced to grant independence. A Fang nationalist from the mainland, Macias Nguema, won the election, relegating the comparatively rich Bubi and the other communities of Fernando Pó, renamed Bioko, to the status of political minorities.

Relations with Spain went from bad to worse. Nguema ordered all but one Spanish flag to be pulled down, and encouraged his supporters to intimidate the 7000 Spaniards still living there. Anti-White incidents in Mbini were followed by an exodus of Spanish residents and the near-collapse of the economy. Nguema even made fishing illegal and ordered every fishing boat that could be found destroyed, thus closing off the country from the outside world.

The Reign of Terror

This was just the beginning of an 11-year reign of terror rarely publicised in the inter-

national press, making Nguema, the self-styled 'Unique Miracle', possibly the worst modern-day dictator in Africa. Nguema's brutality and devastation of the country's economy surpassed even the efforts of Idi Amin in Uganda, and the Central African Republic's Bokassa.

Using an alleged coup attempt in early 1969 as an excuse, Nguema, obviously unsure of his power and fearful of all other leaders, had his foreign minister and ambassador to the UN executed. The minister was the first of a long line of political rivals who were killed or tortured to death for alleged conspiracies. Every few months, another 'plot' would be 'exposed' and more deaths would result.

Even the church did not escape Nguema's wrath. He accused priests of participating in the conspiracies, then closed down their schools and expelled the Spanish teachers. Thereafter, children were taught only political dogma. He eventually closed down the churches and expelled all the missionaries. Being a journalist became a capital crime.

At the peak of Nguema's lunacy, an estimated one-third of the population (ie over 100,000 people) had fled the country; of those remaining, over 10% were jailed as political prisoners in forced labour camps. Rumour has it that Nguema celebrated one Christmas holiday by having a group of prisoners executed in a stadium while a band played music.

About 50,000 people are thought to have been killed during the 11 years of Nguema's rule. In that time, the country lost half its population, and almost every politician prominent at the time of independence was killed or imprisoned. The listing of the country's cabinet of ministers in *Africa South of the Sahara 1975* (Europa Publications, London) is accompanied by the statement: 'It has been reported in the press that some of the Ministers may be dead.' In truth, at least seven of Nguema's former ministers had been executed along with, according to the weekly magazine, *West Africa*, nearly every former minister and senior civil servant in office just prior to his election.

The paranoid, megalomaniac dictator virtually destroyed the country's economy. Cocoa and coffee production fell by 80%, and most farmers either left the country or were reduced to subsistence farming. Per capita incomes fell from one of the highest in Africa at independence in 1968 (US$320) to a level of those in the Sahel, the poorest area of Africa (about US$175) in the early 1980s. To combat the labour shortage on the cocoa farms, he re-introduced a form of slavery – forced labour like that used by the Spanish during the colonial period – justifying it by calling it a step towards socialism. Yet production continued to fall.

You could probably spend your entire time in Equatorial Guinea just listening to Nguema stories. Fortunately, it's all over – unlike Amin and Bokassa, who escaped, Nguema got his just deserts in 1979 following a successful coup led by Théodore Obiang Nguema Mbasogo, a nephew, whose brother had become one of Nguema's random victims. By the time of his capture in his native village of Mongomo, Nguema had squandered the entire national treasury, an estimated US$105 million. After a four-day, open trial, he was executed.

The 1980s

When Obiang first came to power, the future looked bright. He released most of the political prisoners, lifted restrictions on the Catholic Church, and resumed official relations with Spain and other countries. Pope John Paul II passed by on his 1982 African tour, and Guineans voted to approve a new constitution, one of the most liberal in Africa.

On the economic front, the best news was the replacement of the worthless non-convertible ekuélé with the CFA franc, giving the country a valuable hard currency. Within only a year the change was remarkable. Many stores reopened and the markets became jammed with both local and imported foods, clothing, medicines, etc. The streets began to look and sound more like those of a living African country than a museum piece.

Still, the economy continued to stagnate, causing the political situation to remain uncertain. Obiang faced three unsuccessful coup attempts. As in many African countries, coups in Equatorial Guinea don't require a huge force. The one in 1986 involved only 30 civilians and military officers. These were all low-key, virtually in-house coup attempts. To defuse opposition, Obiang held himself up for re-election in 1989 but reporters weren't allowed to witness the polls. However, since there was only one party then, the Partido Democrático de Guinea Ecuatorial (the PDGE) and he was the only candidate, the outcome was never in doubt.

GEOGRAPHY

The country is made up of two provinces – cloud-covered Bioko Island (and a number of other tiny islands) 40 km off the coast of Cameroun, and Rio Muni, the much larger mainland section wedged between Cameroun and Gabon.

Bioko, formerly called Fernando Pó, is a mountainous, rainforested island, with three extinct volcanoes covering most of the island, and cocoa trees seemingly everywhere except in the south, where pure rainforest takes over. The soil is good on Bioko. Farmers constantly chop away at the vines to keep the rainforest from engulfing the plantations. Black-sand beaches surround most of the island. The road system is good by African standards, with sealed roads encircling the island.

Rio Muni is less interesting geographically, being thickly forested and rather flat along the coast, turning into plateau towards the east. It's also the only area where you can see many animals. Dead monkeys are sold all along the roads. Other animals include wart hogs, antelope, crocodiles, boar, snakes (all of these are eaten), also forest elephants, gorillas, chimpanzees and hippos.

CLIMATE

Like Gabon and southern Cameroun, Equatorial Guinea is a rainy area. On Bioko Island, the rainy season is from July to early January and heaviest from July to October, especially July and August. Rainfall on the mainland is somewhat lighter, with most of the rain falling in April and May, and from October to December.

GOVERNMENT

At the end of 1991, Obiang finally permitted a referendum on the conversion to a multi-party system. The result was 146,000 in favour and 1800 against. Since then several new parties have been legalised but Obiang is still firmly in power, with no parliament or other popularly elected body to contest his will.

ECONOMY

History has been so unkind to Equatorial Guinea during the last 25 years or so that it's no wonder that between 1960 and 1990 the country had the lowest population growth rate in Africa – 1.1% annually. With their worst years – hopefully – behind them, the people are tranquil and the population is again on the increase (2.6% annually).

With the expulsion of the Spanish land-lords in 1970, labourers abandoned most of the cocoa plantations, and workers on con-tract (mostly Nigerians) left the country. As a result, cocoa production dropped drasti-cally. During the 1980s, the government appealed to the former Spanish landowners to return, but few took up the invitation, because of the government's reputation for corruption and high-handedness, its uncer-tain future and its scarce labour pool.

A few cocoa plantations were converted to banana plantations but others have been replanted, with foreign technical assistance, primarily from Spain. With this help and World Bank financing, cocoa production is now on the rise, although it's still only at a quarter of its pre-independence level.

During the 1970s, coffee suffered the same fate as cocoa. Grown primarily in Rio Muni by the Fang in the north near the Cameroun border, it is now the third major export crop, having fallen behind lumber. The quality, never very high, deteriorated

after independence and hasn't improved. Production has rebounded somewhat but remains below pre-independence levels. Its chances for revival are less than those of cocoa.

The sleepy look of the country today is a reflection of its generally stagnant economic condition. Large fiscal and balance-of-pay-ments deficits, low foreign exchange reserves, a depressed level of economic activity, and inflationary pressures still plague the country.

However, there are modest signs of improvement, most notably in the cocoa sector. Despite depressed world cocoa prices, it's still the main industry.

Because most of the country's cocoa is grown on Bioko, the island is more important economically than the mainland, which relies mainly on timber and coffee exports for earning foreign exchange. But Bata, the largest town in Rio Muni, has more people than Malabo – some 40,000 inhabitants. Still, only a quarter of the population live in urban areas; the rest are farmers. Virtually everyone is very poor, with average per capita incomes hovering around US$330, well below the sub-Sahara average of US$475.

Overall, Equatorial Guinea is on a par with the CAR on the UN's human development index – only Chad in Central Africa is lower. Whether the present regime can, with exter-nal assistance, lift the country out of its present economic quagmire is still unknown, but many economic factors, such as the world market for cocoa and coffee, are simply beyond its control. Petroleum is clearly one answer. A Spanish company recently discovered some offshore oil and gas reserves, and by the mid-1990s Equato-rial Guinea will be producing enough to meet its domestic requirements. Exporting food crops to its prosperous neighbours, Gabon and Nigeria, may be another answer. The easy way out of the country's economic malaise, however, may be to rely on France, which has a huge new embassy and has replaced Spain as the country's largest aid donor.

POPULATION & PEOPLE

The total population is about 390,000, split about three-to-one between Rio Muni and Bioko.

The Fang dominate the mainland, representing about 80% of the people there. The remainder are mostly Kombé, Balengue, Bujeba and Ndowé. Before Macias Nguema's time, there were also 30,000 to 40,000 Nigerian migrant workers on Bioko who constituted an absolute majority of the population there; the Nigerians were all repatriated in 1976 and few have returned. The original inhabitants of Bioko, the Bubi, number about 15,000, but they are now outnumbered on the island by the Fang, some 20,000 of whom were brought over by force from Rio Muni during the 1970s to work on the cocoa plantations. Others flocked to the island to join the civil and military services. As for Europeans, before independence there were about 7000, mostly Spaniards. During the 1970s, the number dropped to about 200 or so; only a few have returned. In terms of religion, the people are evenly divided between Catholics and those who practise traditional African religions.

ARTS & CULTURE

Travellers searching for black magic may be in for a real treat in Rio Muni. The Fang have held strong to their traditions. Sorcerers, for example, play a particularly strong role in community life. One of the more fascinating celebrations is the *abira*, a classic ceremony which helps cleanse the community of evil spirits. Then there is the *balélé*, an incredibly intense and vibrant dance; passion and sexuality embrace the dancers, causing them to go into all sorts of violent contortions. This dance is executed by the *onxila*, a well-known dance group wearing costumes of grass skirts, metal and grass bracelets for the arms and legs, leopard and monkey-skin belts, topped off with feather headdresses which are shaken wildly.

Along the coast of Rio Muni you are more likely to see the *ibanga*, an extremely suggestive but less frenetic dance than the balélé. If at night you see dancers covered in white powder, that's probably it. On Bioko, the Bubi also dance a form of the balélé, particularly on holidays and at Christmas time. So be on the lookout for these dances; they are likely be the best souvenir of your trip.

The dancing, of course, is not without music, typically from an orchestra of three or four men with drums, xylophones (a string of logs struck with wooden sticks), *sanzas* (small thumb pianos with keys of bamboo), bow harps and, possibly, zithers (instruments with plucked strings but, unlike guitars, no necks).

For other aspects of Fang culture, see the Arts & Culture section in the chapter on Gabon, where the Fang also predominate.

LANGUAGE

Equatorial Guinea is the only country in Africa where the official language is Spanish. Many people don't speak it; even children presumably in school speak it only with great difficulty. To increase the country's ties with the CFA franc zone, the government is strongly pushing the instruction and use of French. Fang is the main African language; on Bioko Island, Bubi is also widely spoken.

Greetings & Civilities in Fang

Good morning/evening
  um-BOH-loh
(to several people)
  um-BOH-lah-nee
Response
  ahm-BOH-loh
(to several people)
  ahm-BOH-lah-nee
How are you?
  yoh-num-VUOY?
I'm fine
  men-num-VUOY
Thank you
  AH-kee-bah
Goodbye
  ma-khan

Facts for the Visitor

VISAS & EMBASSIES
Equatorial Guinea
Visas are required of everyone. There are Equatorial Guinea embassies in Addis Ababa, Lagos, Libreville, Madrid, Paris, Rabat, Yaoundé and New York. There are also consulates in Calabar (Nigeria), Douala and Las Palmas (Canary Islands).

In New York, the Equatorial Guinean Embassy (☎ (914) 667-4330), 57 Magnolia Ave, Mt Vernon, NY 10553, requires US$25, two photos and a signed letter from the applicant stating that he/she has at least US$200 to cover expenses while in the country. Visas, which are usually issued in 24 hours and permit stays up to 30 days, are valid for only 60 days from date of issue. In Europe, Equatorial Guinea has embassies only in Madrid and Paris; their procedures, requirements and prices (FF150 in Paris) are virtually identical and they do not ask to see an onward airline ticket.

In Africa, two of the easiest places to get an Equatorial Guinea visa are in neighbouring Cameroun and Gabon. The Equatorial Embassy in Yaoundé and the consulate in Douala both give same-day, hassle-free service. Those issued in Douala, for example, are valid for two months and good for 15-day stays; bring three photos and CFA 10,000 and the consulate will issue you one on the spot.

In Gabon, the Equatorial Guinean Embassy in Libreville, which gives same-day service, requires CFA 10,000 and two photos for visas valid for 60 days and good for stays of 30 days. In Nigeria, the Embassy in Lagos charges the equivalent of about US$25 in Naira for a visa valid for two months and good for stays of 15 days. If you get to the embassy early, the visa is likely to be issued while you wait. You'll need two photos and 'sufficient funds' – whatever that is.

Visa extensions are usually issued as a matter of course in Malabo, Bata and Ebebiyin. Bring CFA 4500 and several photos to the police station (near the hospital in Bata) and you'll be issued a 15-day extension, usually within 24 hours. Exit visas from the police are not required unless you have overstayed your visa.

Other Countries
The Nigerian Embassy in Malabo issues visas to that country without hassle, with charges varying between almost nothing for Americans to about CFA 10,000 for Britons. For visas to the Côte d'Ivoire, Togo, Burkina Faso, Chad and the CAR, inquire at the French Embassy.

See the Malabo Information section for a list of foreign embassies in the capital.

Cameroun You can get visas to Cameroun relatively easily in both Malabo and Bata and you do not have to show proof of an onward airline ticket. The Cameroun Consulate in Bata issues only transit visas, valid for seven days.

Gabon The Gabon Embassy in Malabo and the consulate in Bata both issue visas to Gabon, usually quickly and without any major hassles, and they do not require that you have an onward airline ticket.

DOCUMENTS
Everybody needs a passport and an International Health Certificate. If you arrive by plane, have one photo ready to give to officials at the airport. If you arrive by car, you'll need a *carnet de passage en douane*.

CUSTOMS
There's no limit on the amount of foreign currency and CFA that may be brought into the country, but there may be a limit on both for exporting. In any case, airport officials will definitely ask you upon leaving how much you're carrying and will search you. So if you must take fairly large sums of cash out of the country when leaving, you should definitely declare it upon entering.

MONEY

US$1 = CFA 280
UK£1 = CFA 425

The unit of currency is the Central African CFA – hence there is no black market and currency declaration forms aren't used. Prices of imported goods are noticeably more expensive here than in Cameroun (CFA 300 for a soft drink compared to CFA 175 in Cameroun).

There are several banks but the only one for changing money is the Banque Internationale pour l'Afrique Occidentale (BIAO), which has branches in Malabo and Bata. Travellers' cheques in French francs are readily accepted but the bank, particularly the one in Bata, is more reluctant to change those denominated in other currencies. However, if you are persistent, the director will usually approve changing them. The bank's commission is 5%. Note: unlike most banks in Central Africa, it may require that you show the purchase receipt, so don't discard it! Unusual in Africa, the BIAO will reconvert your CFA into US dollars, French francs or pesetas without problem, providing it has enough on hand.

BUSINESS HOURS & HOLIDAYS

Business hours are weekdays from 8 am to 1 pm and from 4 to 7 pm, and Saturdays from 9 am to 2 pm. Government offices are open on weekdays from 8.30 am to 3 pm, and on Saturdays from 8.30 am to noon.

Banking hours are weekdays from 8 to 11.30 am and from 1.30 to 2.30 pm.

Public Holidays

1 January
Good Friday
1 May
25 May
Corpus Christi
5 June (President's birthday)
3 August
15 August (Constitution Day)
12 October (Independence Day)
10 December (Human Rights Day)
25 December

POST & TELECOMMUNICATIONS

The poste restante, called *lista de correos* in Spanish, is fairly reliable – more so in Malabo than in Bata. The mail takes a long time to arrive, as incoming mail goes first to Spain, then to Malabo and finally to Bata by boat. Mailing letters out, on the other hand, is no problem, particularly from Malabo, as it all goes out on the Iberia flight to Madrid.

Calling outside the country is now quick and easy and much less expensive than in other Central African countries – CFA 4550 for three minutes to anywhere in Europe and CFA 5940 for three minutes to the USA or Canada. For telephone calls or telexes in Malabo or Bata, go to the GETESA telecommunications centre in those towns. They are open every day from 6 am to 8 pm and use the card system. The telephone code for Equatorial Guinea is 251; the area code for Malabo is 9, for Bata 8.

TIME

Time in Equatorial Guinea is GMT plus one hour, so when it's noon in Equatorial Guinea, it's 11 am in London and 6 am in New York.

PHOTOGRAPHY

Photo permits are issued by the Ministry of Information and Tourism in Malabo (near the cathedral) and cost CFA 3000 (CFA 8000 for a video). One traveller reported that the process took only two hours but others say the process of getting one is so tortuously long that no-one ever bothers except the embassies, some of which apparently have permits covering their employees. My advice is simply to avoid taking pictures in the cities. If you want to try, look for a police officer nearby and ask permission. Otherwise, if you try to take photos and the police see you, they will stop you, take you to their headquarters for interrogation and, at the very least, confiscate your film, and probably your camera as well.

Taking photos in rural areas, on the other hand, is rarely a problem, but ask permission of your subject first, because most people definitely do not like having their photos taken by strangers. Shooting first and asking later could cause problems.

There is at least one photo shop in Malabo and Bata, where you can purchase film.

HEALTH

A yellow fever certificate is required and so is a cholera shot if you are arriving from an infected area. One guy who didn't have his cholera vaccination had to pay CFA 2000 in exchange for a stamp in his health certificate – but, of course, he didn't get a shot. Malaria is also a problem, so taking anti-malarial tablets is essential. For a good doctor, ask US or French embassy officials who they use. Dr Khalil (☎ 2901) does lab analyses.

DANGERS & ANNOYANCES

You have little to worry about despite the high alcohol consumption and poor state of the economy – the paucity of visitors has discouraged the pickpocketing profession. Violent crime is virtually nonexistent, even in Malabo and Bata. Nevertheless, travellers should take care.

Getting There & Away

AIR

From Europe, there is now only one direct flight a week (on Friday evenings) to Malabo, on Air Iberia from Madrid via the Canary Islands. The return cost is approximately US$1000. You can also fly to Douala (Cameroun), connecting with one of the five weekly flights to Malabo, one with Cameroun Airlines (US$112 one way) and four with Equato Guineana de Aviation (EGA), a very small, local airline. There are direct flights to Douala from Brussels, Frankfurt, London, Marseilles, Paris and Rome but not Moscow (Aeroflot has discontinued service).

From the USA, your fastest and cheapest route to Malabo is via Madrid, connecting with the Iberia flight to Malabo on Fridays. If you fly to Douala, you'll have to spend at least a night there. In addition to flights on various airlines to Douala via Europe, both Nigeria Airways and, better, Air Afrique, offer a twice-weekly service to Douala via West Africa, changing in Lagos (Nigeria Airways) and Dakar or Abidjan (Air Afrique).

EGA has flights from Libreville (Gabon) to Malabo via Bata on Tuesdays and Fridays, and from Lagos (Nigeria) on Thursdays. Cameroun Airlines also offers one flight a week from Lagos to Malabo. Theoretically, Concord Airlines, a small Nigerian airline, also flies from Lagos to Malabo (via Calabar) on Tuesdays and Fridays from the old domestic airport in Lagos. Because of the airline's unreliability, however, I don't recommend taking it, although it's cheap – previously US$65 one way but possibly more now (compared with US$140 one way for Lagos-Malabo via Douala on Cameroun Airlines). However, with Concord you cannot make advance reservations – you must go to the airport two hours before departure and buy your ticket then and there. And beware: flights are often cancelled a few hours before departure!

LAND
Minibus

Most travellers arrive at Rio Muni by minibus from either Cameroun or Gabon. If you're hurting for shekels, you could try hitchhiking, but expect long waits in Equatorial Guinea, as there are very few vehicles and most of them are minibuses. Still, there are so few foreign travellers that drivers sometimes like picking them up just for the novelty. Taking minibuses from Cameroun, you should count on at least one day from Yaoundé (Cameroun) to Ebebiyin (at the Cameroun-Gabon border in the north-east corner of the country) and another on to Bata. The total cost for Yaoundé to Bata is CFA 5000.

Bush Taxi

It's possible to enter Equatorial Guinea from Cameroun via the coast. Although few travellers try this route, it can be adventuresome and fun. At the gare routière in Kribi (Cameroun) you'll find bush taxis headed south to Campo (75 km) at the border, then continue by bush taxi to Ipono where you'll find pirogues for CFA 1000 to take you up the Ntem River to Yengüe, 10 km or so away. Police there will stamp your passport, and you can also find bush taxis to Bata. Alternatively, stop in Campo and ask a fisherperson to take you in a canoe to the other side of the river, a 10-minute ride. After having the Guinean border police stamp your passport there, you'll have to walk about 40 km south to Mary, a small fishing village along the coast, where you can take a taxi (not available every day) to Bata.

The trip from Bata to Libreville can usually be done in one long day, since you should arrive in Acalayong in time to catch one of the last motorised pirogues to Cocobeach. Going from Libreville to Bata, on the other hand, usually takes 1½ to two days because by the time you arrive in Acalayong, all vehicles headed for Bata will usually have left. Broken down into segments and not including waiting time, Bata to Acalayong, with a ferry crossing at Mbini, takes around six hours, and crossing the Estuario del Muni on a motorised canoe to Cocobeach takes from 40 minutes to 1 hour and 20 minutes and costs CFA 4000 (beware: they often try to charge foreigners more). Thereafter, it's another 2½ hours to Libreville. The entire trip from Bata to Libreville costs CFA 12,000 plus CFA 2500 in passport registration fees at the border posts.

Going from Bata to Libreville via Acurenam is apparently not an option, as you reportedly cannot cross the border at that point.

Car

Petrol in Equatorial Guinea costs CFA 350 a litre. Driving to Rio Muni from Cameroun, you should count on half a day from Yaoundé to Ebebiyin (280 km), and five or six hours from there to Bata (230 km). Between Ebolowa (Cameroun) and Bata the road is unpaved except for very short stretches starting about 100 km east of Bata.

You cannot drive directly south from Bata to Libreville because there is no car-carrying ferry at the border between Acalayong and Cocobeach. So most people take the road from Bata east to Mongomo and Oyem (Gabon), then south-west to Libreville. On this route you can take advantage of the mainland's only sealed road, the 120-km stretch from Ncue to Mongomo, which was the former president's home town (of course) and gets hardly any traffic. Driving to Libreville via Acurenam is apparently not an option because there's no bridge at the river crossing.

You could take your vehicle on the ferry to Bioko, but you'd have to be nuts to go through the hassle. The road system on the island is pretty good, with sealed roads circling the island.

SEA

The overnight ferry, the *Trader*, connecting Malabo with Douala and Bata, has been replaced by the *Doña Elvira*, which makes a clockwise trip (Malabo-Douala-Bata-Malabo) once a week on an irregular basis. The Malabo-Douala segment is usually a 12-hour, overnight trip, while the Douala-Bata and Bata-Malabo segments take about 24 hours. The boat's agent in Douala, known simply as IMCA (☎ 423318) is at the Port de Peschaud from where the ferry departs, and the fare from Douala to either city is CFA 15,000. This single-class boat has a large room inside with tables, chairs and a TV/video but no restaurant or cabins.

Freighter

The Barcelonato to Bata route (via Malabo) is served by the Spanish shipping line Compañia Transmediterranea on a monthly basis. It may take passengers but the cost is sure to be high. Every few months there is also a boat connecting Malabo with São Tomé; the trip takes about two days and costs CFA 7000 deck class.

Getting Around

AIR
Equato Guineana de Aviation (EGA), the country's national airline, has six flights a week between Malabo and Bata (CFA 35,000 one way).

BUSH TAXI
On Bioko, there are good bush taxi connections between Malabo and the island's two other major towns, Luba and Riaba; the trip takes about one hour to Luba and 1½ hours to Riaba. Vehicles leave throughout the day. You can also hire them by the hour (about CFA 3000) or day.

On the mainland, about three minibuses a day in either direction travel the coastal road (Bata-Mbini-Acalayong), which takes about six hours. About six a day take the inland route between Bata and Ebebiyin, which takes eight to 10 hours during the dry season. The former is dirt road all the way; the latter has some pavement off and on for about a third of the distance (the part closest to Bata). There are also bush taxis and minibuses along the Bata to Mongomo and Bata to Evinayong routes; those trips take about five or six hours. The mainland's one completely sealed road is from Ncue to Mongomo, the president's home town. The other roads are muddy or dusty according to the season.

CAR
On the mainland, typical driving times from Bata are one hour to Mbini, four or five hours to Acalayong, Evinayong or Mongomo, and five or six hours to Ebebiyin. Forget about car rentals – they don't exist here.

BOAT
Once a week, the *Doña Elvira* plies between Malabo and Bata; the fare is CFA 15,000. The boat is more convenient to take from Malabo to Bata (a 24-hour trip approximately) than vice versa because from Bata it goes via Douala and therefore usually takes at least two days. Every few months there's also a boat from Malabo to Annobón via São Tomé; the trip takes four or five days.

Bioko Island

MALABO
In the mid-1980s, Malabo had a grand total of four restaurants, three hotels, numerous dilapidated buildings, little food in stock and a bar on every corner, or at least a street vendor who'd sell you a shot of liquor, cigarettes, and gum – hardly the makings of an attractive destination for visitors.

The bars and street vendors selling liquor are still there but on other fronts things are looking up a bit. In 1990 the city had a facelift when the president ordered everyone to paint their buildings. The people complied, so now there are freshly painted, pastel-coloured buildings everywhere. The city is now clean and has at least 10 restaurants and six hotels, and food is plentiful in the market. Still, this quaint, sleepy city has a way to go before matching the conditions that existed during the colonial era when the Spanish buildings were well maintained and there were some fine restaurants and hotels.

Malabo's potential for tourism is apparent. With the ocean waves on one side and cloud-capped Pico Malabo on the other, the island's location is appealing even though you have to travel some distance to get to a good beach. Most travellers to Africa never see the real tropics; Bioko is in the heart.

With a population of only about 35,000 people, the entire town, called Santa Isabel during Spanish times, can be covered on foot. You can also take inner-city taxis but they are sometimes difficult to find. You'll probably see a number of Spanish and French men – many are technical advisors. There used to be a number of Russians, North Koreans and Chinese as well, but they have gone home. Checking out the stores and chewing the fat with the locals at the bars is about all there is to do until the evening, when the restaurants, bars and nightclubs wake up.

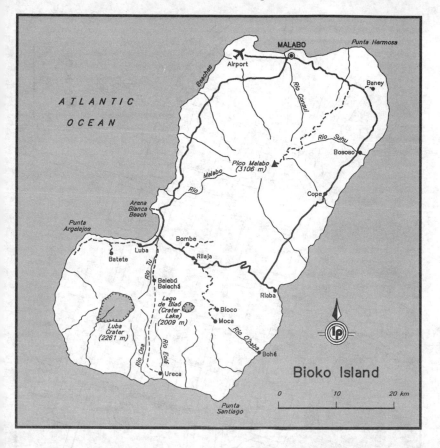

Bioko Island

Information

Money The only bank for changing money is the BIAO (☎ 2367), which is on Calle de Algeria, overlooking the new port.

Foreign Embassies There are three embassies in the central area: the Camerounian Embassy (☎ 2263) on Calle del Rey Boncoro, the Gabonese Embassy (☎ 2420) on Calle de Algeria opposite the BIAO, and the Nigerian Embassy (☎ 2386) on Calle de Nigeria, a block east of the well-known Restaurante Beiruth.

On the western side of town you'll find the large new French Embassy and the Chinese Embassy on the road to the airport, the Spanish Embassy nearby opposite Hotel Ureca, the US Embassy (☎ 2406, 2507, Box 597) not far away on Calle de los Ministros a block north of Carretera del Aeropuerto, and the GTZ (German Technical Assistance Agency) nearby.

Bookshops Libreria MBA Ndemezoo, in the centre of town on Ave de la Libertad near the intersection of Calle del Rey Boncoro

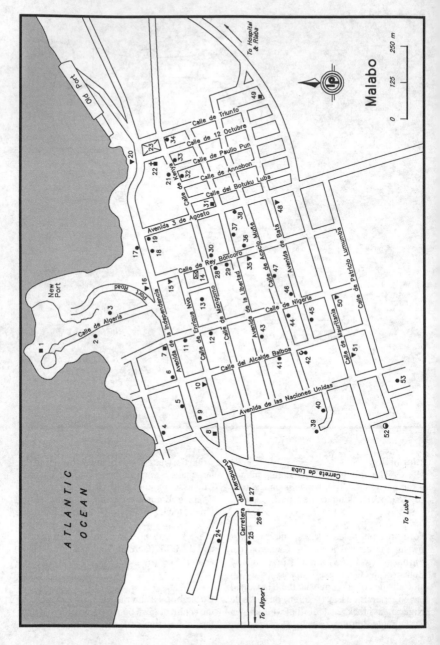

Malabo

■ PLACES TO STAY

1   Hotel Bahia
7   Residencia Ana José
8   Aparthotel Impala
27 Hotel Ureca
31 Hotel Flores
49 Hotel Bambu

▼ PLACES TO EAT

10 Beiruth Restaurante-Discoteca
15 Restaurante Chez Yeni &
    Restaurante Gamba de Oro
16 Restaurante Gue-Gue
20 Restaurante Club Náutico
25 Restaurante Abayak
35 Fried Chicken Place
48 Cafeteria El Cachirulo
50 Restaurante Bodega Don Pedro
51 Restaurante Alexia

    OTHER

2   Gabon Embassy
3   BIAO Bank
4   Discoteca Sueños
5   Supermarket
6   Iberia Airlines Office
9   Nigeria Airways Office
11 Nigerian Embassy
12 Farmacia Claudia & Nora Bakery
13 Town Hall

14 Post Office
17 Bar
18 Spanish Cultural Centre
19 Police
21 Ministry of Information
22 Cathedral
23 Plaza de España
24 US Embassy
25 Chinese & French Embassies
26 Spanish Embassy
28 UN Office
29 Artesana Guineana
30 Telephone, Telex & Telegrams
32 EGA Airlines Office
33 National Shipping Company
34 People's Palace
36 Cameroun Embassy & Cameroun
    Airlines
37 Mini Mercado El Cedro, Bookshop &
    Number Two Club
38 Herbo African Music Shop
39 Clothes Market
40 French Cultural Centre
41 Bantu Nightclub
42 Mosque
43 Discoteca Tahiti
44 Bar Franco Iglesia
45 Fish Market
46 Scala 1 Club
47 La Nina Nightclub
52 Bus/Taxi Stand
53 Mercado Central

and around the corner from the Camerounian Embassy, is a tiny bookshop of sorts, with stationery and a few postcards.

Supermarkets There are now several small supermarkets in town. The best is the new one at the western end of Ave de la Independencia near the Iberia Airlines office. It offers a decent range of imported foods and alcoholic drinks, all highly priced. Closer to the town centre, on Ave de la Libertad, you'll find Mini Mercado El Cedro, which is indeed 'mini,' but you can get bottled water (CFA 500) among other things. Supermercado Africa near the Spanish housing complex *(las caracolas)* also caters for expatriates and has imported food

items at high prices. Food is also sold in several other stores: near the Ajuntamiento (town hall), on Calle de Nigeria and on the same block as El Cedro.

For much cheaper local produce head for the Mercado Central, next to the stadium on Calle de Patricio Lumumba. Unusual for African markets, there's lots of liquor for sale. There's no restaurant area but there is food to nibble.

Travel Agencies There are none. For airline reservations and reconfirmations, go to the airline offices (see the Malabo Getting There & Away section), the best of which is the Iberia Airlines office; most of them normally open around 9 am.

Centro Cultural Hispano-Guineano
As well as the old colonial buildings, check out the Spanish cultural centre at the end of Ave 3 de Agosto near the harbour. It's a striking Spanish-style building in the town centre above the new port. There you'll find maps of the island and mainland, and maybe something interesting going on there or at the French cultural centre off Ave de las Naciones Unidas.

Cathedral
The cathedral is on Calle de 12 Octubre, above the old port. It's gothic in style, with stained-glass rose windows, high ceilings, and an ornate sermon platform – no great loss if you don't get around to it. Sunday mass is at 8 and 10.30 am and at 7 pm. The rest of the time you can spend bar-hopping.

Those into architecture may find the three-storey court building rather interesting. It's several blocks from the cathedral on the same street.

Activities
There's a decent tennis court at the Hotel Ureca. The best courts in town, however, are at the US Embassy and the GTZ nearby. For swimmers, there are no accessible pools, nor are there any good beaches within walking distance. For good beaches, see Around Malabo.

Places to Stay – bottom end
The best budget hotel is *Residencia Ana José*, in the centre of town on Ave de la Independencia; it's clean and cheap, with rooms for CFA 3000 including breakfast. If it's full, try *Hotel Bantu*, which is a run-down place with singles/doubles for CFA 5000/7000, or the similarly priced *Hotel Flores* on Ave 3 de Agosto. A good notch up is the large old *Hotel Ureca* (☎ 3319) on the western outskirts of town; coming from the airport you'll pass it on your right as you enter town. It charges CFA 7000/10,000 for singles/doubles with clean, private baths. There's no restaurant or hot water, and as with all the bottom-end hotels, electricity and water are often cut off during the day. Nevertheless, the rooms are clean and decent, and there's good lighting and a balcony, plus a tennis court in playable condition. It's a 10-minute walk to the nearest restaurant and a 15-minute walk to the town centre.

Places to Stay – top end
Among the top-end hotels, the one with the nicest location by far is *Hotel Bahia* (☎ 3321), which is ideally located, with a pleasant patio overlooking the ocean. It was here that Frederick Forsyth sat and wrote *The Dogs of War*. (The city of Clarence in the book is actually Malabo.) At the end of Calle de Algeria above the new port, it's 100 metres or so beyond the Gabonese Embassy, a short walk from the Spanish cultural centre and a five to 10-minute walk from the city's heart. It has large, clean rooms with fans, and clean private baths for about CFA 13,000, as well as a restaurant.

The city's most expensive hotel is the *Aparthotel Impala* (☎ 2492), an apartment tower at the junction of the Luba and airport roads. The apartments cost about CFA 15,000 and the building is full of long-term expatriates, so getting a room isn't easy. If none are available and you are a US citizen, call the US Embassy to see if it will lend you one of theirs. It usually will if one is available. The rooms are large and clean, with air-con, hot showers, electricity 24 hours a day, a balcony, dining-table and cooking facilities. There's no restaurant, but Beiruth Restaurante is only a block away.

A final possibility is the new *Hotel Bambu* on the eastern side of town, five blocks east of Ave 3 de Agosto. It charges CFA 12,000 for a double with private bath and has a relatively expensive restaurant as well.

Places to Eat
Cheap Eats For a good breakfast or a light meal, head for the long-standing *Cafeteria El Cachirulo*, in the centre of town near the corner of Ave de Bata and Ave 3 de Agosto. It's a very popular place with expatriates and the better-off locals. They serve omelettes and sandwiches for CFA 500 to CFA 1000,

ice-cream, beer, and the best coffee in town, but they're often short of many items.

For good, relatively inexpensive African food, you can't beat *Restaurante Alexia* on Calle Mauritania, a good block north-east of the market, and *Restaurante Chez Yeni* in the town centre on Calle del Rey Boncoro. A filling meal at either place costs about CFA 1000. For bread and pastries, head for *Nora Bakery* on Calle de Nigeria, near the Nigerian Embassy.

At night you can get good cheap food at many of the bars and discos. The food is reasonably safe to eat but random shortages of certain foods can drastically restrict the choices. There are two noteworthy bars – one on Calle del Rey Boncoro facing Cameroun Airlines and one on Ave de la Independencia facing the Spanish cultural centre. Both places serve chicken, beef and fish dishes for around CFA 500 a plate. Even better is the *Bar Gamba d'Oro*, which is near the latter at the northern end of Ave 3 de Agosto. It's run by a garrulous Madagascan women who offers snacks and light meals such as omelettes and is a good source of local information. *Tahiti* nightclub on Ave de la Libertad serves similar fare including hot fried chicken for CFA 500.

Other Restaurants Virtually all the remaining restaurants serve primarily Spanish and continental fare and cater for the Spanish expatriate community. For a meal costing about CFA 3000, you have at least three choices. The first, *Restaurante Bodega Don Pedro* at the corner of Calles Mauritania and Calle de Nigeria, serves Spanish cuisine and seafood and is highly recommended. The long-standing *Restaurante Gue-Gue* (☎ 2331), on Ave de la Independencia near the Spanish cultural centre, has an ordinary setting but the food and service are good and the prices are similar to Bodega's. Open every day from 7 am to 11 pm, it also has a bar that is a popular watering hole for Spanish expatriates. The third, which serves a number of seafood dishes, is *Restaurante Gamba de Oro* in the town centre on Calle del Rey Boncoro.

The city's top three restaurants are on the pricey side. The cheapest is *Restaurante Club Naútico*, which is ideally located on a cliff above the old harbour near the cathedral. It's justifiably popular with the local expatriates. Formerly a restaurant school, it has an awning-covered patio just above the water's edge with an excellent view of the harbour, which is usually accompanied by a breeze. A good three-course Spanish or continental meal will cost you around CFA 7000, and the friendly Lebanese owner speaks English and can help you with the menu if you don't speak Spanish.

There's also the long-standing *Restaurante Beiruth* (☎ 3330) on Calle de Enrique Nvo, a block east of the Aparthotel Impala. It offers a number of main courses including steak, pizza and a Lebanese dish or two. This place is popular because the manager is friendly, the food is decent, and you have a choice of inside or outside dining. However, the service is slow and a meal will cost you CFA 5000 to CFA 10,000. It's open every day from 7 am to 11 pm.

The city's top restaurant is the *Restaurante Abayak* on the western outskirts of town on the road to the airport, a little beyond the landmark Hotel Ureca. A French meal with imported food will set you back CFA 15,000 to CFA 20,000.

Entertainment

Bars Beer is expensive in Equatorial Guinea, but the local sugarcane brew, *malamba*, and the local palm wine are dirt cheap and sold along the roads.

For daytime relaxation in pleasant surroundings, try one of the quaint bars in front of the Ajuntamiento (city hall) on Calle de Nigeria. For tranquillity and great views at sunset, you can't beat the patio at the Hotel Bahia. Expatriates also head for Cafeteria Cachirulo and Gue-Gue, but if you want to mingle with the locals, there are scores of other bars to choose from. Many of them now serve food as well. One of the more popular ones is *Bar Franco Iglesia*, at the corner of Calle de Nigeria and Calle de Acacio Muñe.

Nightclubs One of the top nightclubs, popular with expatriates and locals alike, is *Discoteca Beiruth*, on Calle de Enrique Nvo; it's part of the restaurant of the same name. It's fancy, with disco music and imported beers for CFA 1500. Don't expect much action before midnight. Three good cheaper places are *Discoteca Sueños*, *Discoteca Tahiti* and, a favourite of the locals, *Discoteca Joey*, which is several km from the centre of town on the south-eastern side, towards Riaba.

If you're into nightclub hopping, others that you might try in the central area are: *Bantu* (or *Don Fausta's*) on Ave del Alcalde Balboa near Ave de la Libertad and three blocks from Discoteca Beiruth; the *Scala 1 Club* two blocks away at the intersection of Ave de Bata and Calle de Nigeria; *Number Two Club* on Ave de la Libertad near Ave 3 de Agosto; and *Discoteca La Nina*, near the intersection of Calle de Acacio Muñe and Calle de Rey Boncoro.

Cinemas Cine Jardin is your only choice – Kung Fu film after Kung Fu film. It's on Calle de Mongomo, one block behind the Spanish cultural centre. Show time is 7.30 pm.

Things to Buy

Artisan Goods The country produces very little in the way of artisan goods, although you can find crafts here. They may not be produced locally but the quality is not bad. Two good places to look for vendors are in front of the telecommunications building and outside Hotel Ureca. Since visitors are so rare, they may even track you down at your hotel. There are also two outlets in the town centre – a hole-in-the-wall place on Ave de la Libertad just to the left of Mini Mercado, and Artesana Guineana, half a block away on Calle del Rey Boncoro.

Music For Guinean music, your best bet is Herbo Music, in the centre of town on Ave 3 de Agosto, 50 metres from Cachirulo. Have them make you a cassette from the various records they have for such purposes. Local

Fang wooden statue

stars include Maele, Baltasar Nsue and guitarist Toto Guillaume.

Getting There & Away

Air Iberia Airlines' (office on Ave de la Independencia) weekly flight to Malabo via the Canary Islands leaves Madrid on Fridays, arrives in Malabo usually several hours late, and returns the following day. Cameroun Airlines (office on Calle de Rey Boncoro) has a flight on Sundays from Douala to Malabo and back; the one-way fare is CFA 31,100. Chronic overbooking on the flight to Douala is common, so reconfirm your seat early. Some travellers report that bribes are needed to secure seating on this flight.

EGA (☎ 2325), with an office on Calle de Kenya near the cathedral, has four return flights a week from Douala to Malabo, and flights every day except Sunday between

Malabo and Bata. The one-way fare from Douala to Malabo is CFA 27,800, and to Bata is CFA 47,800. EGA's agent in Douala is Air Affairs Afrique (AAA) (☎ 422976) very near the airport.

In addition, EGA offers twice-weekly connections between Libreville (Gabon) and Malabo via Bata; the one-way fare is CFA 54,000. In Libreville, tickets can be purchased only from Air Gabon at the airport, which is EGA's agent there. You can also get to Malabo from Lagos on EGA on Thursdays and, less reliable, on Concord Airlines which has an office at the airport, on Tuesdays and Fridays via Calabar. The fare on the latter used to be US$65 (payable in naira) but air fares in Nigeria have been rising, so expect to pay more.

Sea The single-class *Doña Elvira* makes the Malabo-Douala-Bata-Malabo trip once a week on an irregular schedule. The trip from Malabo to Douala takes all night; Bata to Malabo takes about 24 hours. The fare from Malabo to either Douala or Bata is CFA 15,000. For information, inquire at the new port.

Every few months, there's a boat headed to São Tomé and Annobón. The trip takes two days to São Tomé and two or three days more to Annobón; deck class costs CFA 7000 to São Tomé and CFA 11,000 (CFA 20,000 for a cabin) to Annobón. Inquire at the port about the schedule, which is irregular.

Getting Around
To/From the Airport Malabo airport is seven km west of the city. The airport departure tax is CFA 5000 for international flights and CFA 425 for domestic flights. Before arriving, make sure your shots are up to date; like many islands in the world, enforcement is strict. Bring an extra photograph; they may ask for one. The luggage search is often thorough.

A taxi from the airport into Malabo costs about CFA 3000; bargaining is definitely required. They are unmarked, so don't think there aren't any. Since there aren't any buses, the only way to reduce the cost is to try

sharing a cab, or hitching, which is fairly easy since the road leads only one way – to town.

Taxi City taxis are fairly numerous now and not too hard to find during the day on the main avenues and at the taxi stand just west of Mercado Central. If you are a business person and you get one at the airport, make arrangements then and there for future pick-ups. A taxi by the hour costs about CFA 3000. Bush taxis going to Luba and Riaba are also stationed at the taxi stand and connections are good. Malabo to Luba takes about one hour and costs CFA 1000; Malabo to Riaba takes about 1½ hours and costs CFA 1500.

AROUND MALABO
Beaches
The closest beach is 15 km away on the road to Luba, and there are others further on, near Luba. If you can't afford a taxi, try hitching a ride on Sundays when a number of expatriates head that way. Don't expect much sun between June and November. (Rio Muni has better beaches; they also get more sun.)

Pico Malabo
Hikers may want to try 3106-metre Pico Malabo, also known as El Pico. You could simply walk up the 30-km road to the top; any other route would be extremely difficult because of the thick rainforest. The problem is getting permission, because the government's radio transmission antenna is at the top of Malabo. Both the Foreign Ministry and the radio station people have the authority to grant permission, but without connections, you are unlikely to get it. The starting point is about 12 km east of Malabo on the hard-surfaced road to Riaba. Look for a dirt road off to your right and a staffed gatehouse next to it.

LUBA
For the best beaches on the island of Bioko, or a view of the interior, head toward Luba, 50 km (an hour's bush-taxi ride) south-west of Malabo. Luba is the island's second-largest town, with about 1000 inhabitants.

It's a rather unattractive logging port with a few bars and shops, and little else to recommend it. The old white hospital at the top of town is the major landmark but has the same general air of neglect as the town itself.

The town's backdrop, on the other hand, is spectacular, especially on those rare days when the clouds clear from the jagged southern mountains. At the base of the volcanoes and bordering the ocean, Luba's surroundings are similar to those of Malabo but more striking because of the town's small size.

Places to Stay & Eat

Hotel Jones, the only hotel in town and in the heart thereof, is where most travellers stay who can afford CFA 7000/11,000 for singles/doubles. It's run by a grouchy old German who speaks German, French, English and Spanish and gives the place character if nothing else. There's a bar that looks something like a hunting lodge, a patio for drinks, a TV, and edible food, including good fish dishes – hardly bad for such a small village. If you can't afford to stay here, then camp in Arena Blanca (see Around Luba) or inquire about the *Catholic Mission*, which is reportedly 12 km or so out of town.

Getting There & Away

Bush taxis run between Malabo and Luba all day. The trip takes an hour and costs CFA 1000. The sealed road is narrow and would be completely engulfed by grasses and vines were it not for the road crews. This is not a trip for the faint-hearted – your driver will probably race blindly around the corners at life-threatening speeds, as mine did. The view of the bay from the road, however, is wonderful.

Bush taxis also run between Luba and Riaba but much less frequently. The road passes over cultivated plateau and near the Moca Valley with its crater lake. There are also occasional taxis from Luba to Belebú Belechá and Moca.

AROUND LUBA
Beaches

The isolated beaches near Luba are lovely and, unlike most beaches on the island, have white sand. The best-known is **Arena Blanca**, which is seven km north of town; look for a badly weathered wooden sign with the beach's name. The beach is 1500 metres down a muddy forest track and is well worth the hike. The friendly local fisherpeople in the huts on the shore and the palm-fringed beach make it an idyllic location.

A number of travellers have spent time here, so you won't be the first if you stay for a few days. You can camp on the beach, but register with the nearest police; otherwise you might cause trouble for the fisherfolk – if the police catch you without a permit, they'll reportedly fine them and refuse to let you pay the fine!

Hiking

If you're interested in hiking, there are two routes you can try, around Moca and to the fishing village of Ureca.

Moca One trek is around Moca, which is an African equivalent of hiking through the Swiss Alps without the snow. Lago de Biaó, a volcanic lake in Caldera Volcánica de Biaó (Biaó Crater) is just north-west of Moca and is one of the most scenic spots in the area. Occasionally it is possible to find bush taxis in Luba headed for the tiny hamlet of Moca, which is about 38 km south-east of Luba by a muddy dirt road. Alternatively, take a bush taxi east towards Riaba and have the driver let you off at the junction for Moca (about 18 km past Riaba) and walk southward from there (20 km). Biaó Crater, 2009 metres high at the rim, will be on your right.

Ureca The other trek starts at Belebú Belechá and ends up in the fishing village of Ureca, which is the only inhabited place on the south shore. In January and February, thousands of sea turtles lay their eggs on the beach there. The trek takes about eight hours from Belebú and passes just east of Luba Crater (el Grand Volcano de Luba). As at Moca, if you don't have a tent, you could probably find somewhere to stay in the village. To start your trek, if you can't find

one of the rare bush taxis in Luba headed for
Belebú, which is about 12 km south-east of
Luba, hire a taxi in Luba and ask the driver
to let you off at the tracks heading up the
steep mountain to Belebú. If you don't have
a permit from the police in Luba or Malabo,
the villagers in Belebú may not let you
through.

Rio Muni (The Mainland)

BATA

Capital of the mainland and slightly larger
than Malabo, Bata lacks Malabo's picturesque volcanic setting, but its streets are
wide and clean by African standards, and to
some people the town has its charm. Compared with the rest of Rio Muni it seems very
lively, with busy markets and lots of bars,
restaurants and hotels.

There's little of interest to see, although
Rio Muni has the best beaches in the country,
and some of the most beautiful are near Bata.
You'll find several isolated ones along the
coast both north and south of Bata. One lined
with coconut trees is only several km north
of town in the direction of the airport.

Orientation

Running north-south from Mercado Mondoasi to Restaurante Club de Tenis is
Carretera Principal. There are a number of
shops on this road and on Calle del Mercado
Central, one block east and parallel to it,
from the landmark telecommunications
antenna to the city's main roundabout just
beyond Mercado Central.

Information

Money The BIAO is on Carretera Principal,
a block north-west of the telecommunications antenna; it usually accepts travellers'
cheques denominated in French francs,
although even then only with great reluc-
tance.

Foreign Consulates Both the Gabon and

Cameroun consulates are on the southern
side of town – the former just south of the
main roundabout and the latter nearby on a
minor dirt road not far from the well-known
Hotel Rondo. The Nigerian Consulate is not
far away, at Hotel Pan-Africano at the southern end of Avenida del Mar. The Spanish
Consulate is at the northern end of the carretera near the port.

Places to Stay – bottom end

One of the cheapest places in town is *Hotel
Mayca*, on the northern side of town off the
road to Ebebiyin, about one km by road from
the telecommunications tower (a CFA 200
private taxi ride from the Mercado Central).
It has electricity and charges CFA 2500 for a
tiny freshly painted room with big foam
mattress, overhead fan and spotlessly clean,
Western-style shared baths. It's in a safe
African quarter and although there's no restaurant, it's only a 10-minute walk to a good
street-food area at night.

For a place in the heart of town, I recommend *Hotel Finistère* at the southern end of
Carretera Principal, opposite Bar Levi. It
charges CFA 3000 for a large, clean room
with comfortable foam mattress, fan and
decent shared bath with bucket showers.
Unlike the Mayca, you can eat cheaply and
well next door.

Both places are better than the *Casa de
Huespédes* in the main market area, which
charges CFA 3000 for an incredibly small
room with a prison-like window. There's
never any electricity in the evening except
when the owner wants to watch TV, so the
fan and light in your room are likely to prove
useless.

A much better place is the unmarked *Hotel
Continental*, in the centre of town on the
second storey of a building on Calle del
Mercado, about 200 metres north of
Mercado Central (central market). The
rooms, which cost CFA 4000, are large and
clean, with comfortable beds and sitting
chairs, and private baths with bucket
showers, washbasin and Western-style
toilets. There's a TV in the lobby and you can
eat here too.

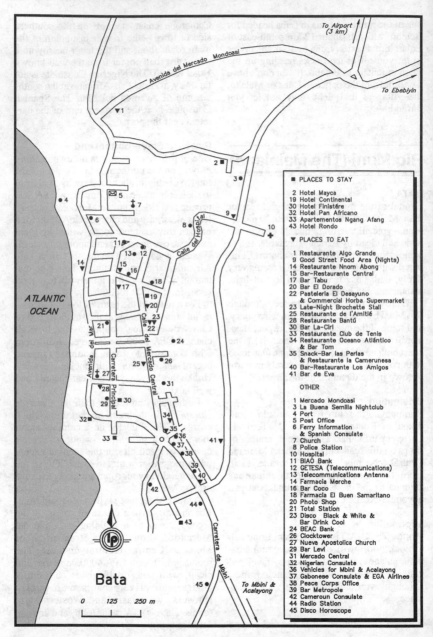

To Airport
(3 km)

To Ebebiyin

Avenida del Mercado Mondoasi

ATLANTIC
OCEAN

Calle del Hospital

Avenida del Mar

Carretera Principal

Calle del Mercado Central

Carretera de Mbini

To Mbini &
Acalayong

Bata

0   125   250 m

■ PLACES TO STAY

2 Hotel Mayca
19 Hotel Continental
30 Hotel Finistére
32 Hotel Pan Africano
33 Apartementos Ngang Afang
43 Hotel Rondo

▼ PLACES TO EAT

1 Restaurante Algo Grande
9 Good Street Food Area (Nights)
14 Restaurante Nnom Abong
15 Bar-Restaurante Central
17 Bar Tabu
20 Bar El Dorado
22 Pastelería El Desayuno
    & Commercial Horba Supermarket
23 Late-Night Brochette Stall
25 Restaurante de l'Amitié
28 Restaurante Bantú
30 Bar La-Ciri
33 Restaurante Club de Tenis
34 Restaurante Oceano Atlántico
    & Bar Tom
35 Snack-Bar las Perlas
    & Restaurante la Camerunesa
40 Bar-Restaurante Los Amigos
41 Bar de Eva

OTHER

1 Mercado Mondoasi
3 La Buena Semilla Nightclub
4 Port
5 Post Office
6 Ferry Information
    & Spanish Consulate
7 Church
8 Police Station
10 Hospital
11 BIAO Bank
12 GETESA (Telecommunications)
13 Telecommunications Antenna
14 Farmacia Merche
16 Bar Coco
18 Farmacia El Buen Samaritano
20 Photo Shop
21 Total Station
23 Disco Black & White &
    Bar Drink Cool
24 BEAC Bank
26 Clocktower
27 Nueva Apostolica Church
29 Bar Levi
31 Mercado Central
32 Nigerian Consulate
36 Vehicles for Mbini & Acalayong
37 Gabonese Consulate & EGA Airlines
38 Peace Corps Office
39 Bar Metropole
42 Cameroun Consulate
44 Radio Station
45 Disco Horoscope

Places to Stay – top end
The city has three top-end hotels, but by far the best value for money is the popular, highly recommended *Hotel Rondo* on the southern side of town, about 500 metres south of Mercado Central on a dirt road behind the radio station. The very friendly woman who runs this place charges CFA 5000 to CFA 6000 for a room but she has been known to reduce the price to CFA 4000 if you barter. The rooms are small and clean, with very soft foam mattresses, pressed sheets, fans, private basins and shared clean showers with reliable running water. The central area has a TV with comfortable seats and a good restaurant with full breakfasts for CFA 1000.

Not far away is Bata's top hotel, the *Apartementos Ngang Afang*, which is next to the Restaurante Club de Tenis at the southern end of Carretera Principal. It charges CFA 10,000 for a double, but one traveller reported that he got three nights for CFA 15,000. The large *Hotel Pan Africano* is two blocks away in an ideal location facing the sea; it charges CFA 12,000 for a room but is virtually deserted and seems on the verge of closing.

Places to Eat
Cheap Eats For street food at night, one of the best places is the intersection just west of the hospital. Also, from around 9 pm, a woman starts grilling beef brochettes (CFA 100) just outside Disco Black & White, about 100 metres or so north of Mercado Central.

During the day the best area for cheap food is around Mercado Central. There are several dirt cheap hole-in-the-walls here; one is the *Restaurante Oceano Atlántico* near where minibuses for Acalayong load up; *Bar Tom*, which is very near, serves brochettes and chicken for around CFA 500, and large cold beers.

Three other cheap restaurants worth trying are *Snack-Bar las Perlas* just south of the market, *Restaurante la Camerunesa* at the roundabout (full African meals cost around CFA 800), and *Bar-Restaurante los Amigos*

100 metres further south, just beyond the Peace Corps office. All three are potentially good spots for meeting Peace Corps volunteers. Two other places where you can get good cheap African food are *Bar de Eva*, which is east of the market on the paved bypass road, and *Restaurante Algo Grande* at Mercado Mondoasi.

My favourite restaurant is *Bar La-Ciri*, which is west of Mercado Central on the Carretera Principal, next door to Hotel Finistère. It serves about three dishes, such as crocodillo and pepe soup, for CFA 500, but for dinner get there early as it closes around 8.30 pm.

Another fairly cheap place in the town centre is *Bar El Dorado* on Calle del Mercado Central, about 150 metres north of the Mercado Central. It has about 10 kinds of bocadillos, all in the CFA 300 to CFA 500 range, plus beef brochettes for CFA 300, fish soup for CFA 500, braised fish or chicken for CFA 1000 and large beers for CFA 400. The *Pasteleria El Desayuno* and one of the better grocery stores, *Commercial Horba*, are virtually next door.

Further south along the same street, opposite the market, you'll come to *Restaurant de l'Amitié*, which is a very decent, middle-class restaurant that's open late. The menu, which is quite long, includes yoghurt for CFA 400, omelettes for CFA 500, steak for CFA 1000, fish and rice for CFA 1300 and chicken with peas for CFA 1500.

Other Restaurants The *Hotel Rondo* is a good place to eat. The menu includes 10 choices, all in the CFA 1000 to CFA 2000 range, including brochettes and fried fish for CFA 1000 and fillet of beef for CFA 1500, plus large beers for a pricey CFA 700.

Two watering holes that cater for expatriates and also serve food are *Bar-Restaurante Central* and *Bar Tabu*, which are open late and almost next door to one another on Carretera Principal. The former has, among other things, hamburgers for CFA 1000, steak for CFA 1500 and langoustines for CFA 3000, while the latter has *pirogis* (pies) for CFA 500 and pizza for CFA 1500. A large beer at both places costs CFA 700. The long-standing Central is a meeting spot with an open-air terrace bar that's good for people-watching, while outside the Tabu is where all the prostitutes and transvestites hang out late at night.

One of the city's top restaurants is the breezy *Restaurante Nnom Abong*, which is a block to the west overlooking the ocean. The menu includes such things as braised fish for CFA 2500, langoustines for CFA 4000, calamari for CFA 3000 and bananas flambé for CFA 500. The food, however, is reportedly not particularly good. Further north, near the port, is *Bar Miramar*. It's worth visiting at sunset for drinks and grafis (small crayfish) as well as for full meals, including spaghetti for CFA 1000 a plate.

The city's top restaurant is *Restaurante Bantù*, which is four long blocks south of the Nnom Abong, opposite the Nueva Apostolica church. The owner is Portuguese and the food is good, and expensive – a typical meal costs from CFA 5000 upwards. Another good, similarly priced restaurant with imported food is the *Restaurante Club de Tenis*, which is two blocks further south, at the end of Carretera Principal.

Entertainment

The city's two top bar-nightclubs, both with European music, are *Disco Black & White* and, next door, *Bar Drink Cool*. The former is also a bar and opens around 9 pm. The latter is open every night and there's no cover charge except on Friday and Saturday nights, when the entrance fee is CFA 1000. Both are good places to meet and dance with the locals and expatriates; as at most nightclubs in town, the dancing doesn't start until around 11 pm.

For a nightclub catering for the working person, you might try *Disco Chochi* or *La Buena Semilla Nightclub*. The latter is not far from Hotel Mayca, about 800 metres from the telecommunications antenna on the road to Ebebiyin, and north of the turn-off for the hospital. If you're at the southern end of town, try *Disco Horoscope*, which is on the main drag heading out of town, well beyond

the radio station. All three places have mainly African music.

Getting There & Away

Air EGA (☎ 2925), which has an office just south of the roundabout and next to the Gabonese Consulate, offers flights to/from Malabo every day except Sunday; the one-way fare is CFA 34,000. Some of those flights connect with onward flights to Douala. EGA also offers a twice-weekly service to/from Libreville; the one-way fare from Libreville to Bata is CFA 39,000.

Minibus Minibuses for Mbini and Acalayong leave from Mercado Central; those for all other destinations leave from Mercado Mondoasi on the northern side of town. They leave early, so get there by around 6 am (7 am at the latest). Minibuses cost CFA 1000 to the ferry crossing at Mbini, CFA 2500 to Ebebiyin, CFA 3000 to Mongomo, CFA 3500 to Evinayong and CFA 4000 to Acalayong. Average trip times are one hour to the ferry crossing at Mbini, six hours to Acalayong, Mongomo and Evinayong, and eight to 10 hours to Ebebiyin.

From Bata to Yaoundé by minibus takes two days, with a night in Ebebiyin. Bata to Libreville can usually be done in one long day as the minibus usually arrives at Acalayong before the departure of the last canoe (CFA 4000) to Cocobeach, where you can catch a taxi (CFA 4000) to Libreville. Going from Libreville to Bata, on the other hand, usually takes 1½ to two days because connections are not as good. All vehicles headed to/from Acalayong now pass through Mbini because the bridge on the more eastward route is broken.

Truck Clusa, a US transport company, sends trucks once a week from Bata to Nsok-Nsomo, Aconibe, Acurenam and Nsoc. They take passengers, charge the same as bush taxis and leave from Mondoasi market.

Car You could drive from Yaoundé to Bata in one very long day if you started at the crack of dawn; otherwise, count on sleeping in Ebebiyin. If you're headed to/from Libreville (Gabon), you cannot take the most direct route via Acalayong because there is no car-carrying ferry connecting Cocobeach and Acalayong. The best road from Bata is east through Mongomo and Oyem, which is sealed between Ncue and Mongomo (120 km).

Ferry Once a week, you can take the *Doña Elvira* to Malabo, continuing on to Douala. Bata to Malabo takes about 24 hours; Malabo to Douala is usually an overnight trip. It's a single-class vessel without a restaurant or sleeping quarters; the fare from Bata to either Douala or Malabo is CFA 15,000. The schedule is irregular so you'll have to inquire at the port about the next arrival/departure.

Getting Around
City taxis in Bata are now plentiful and are fairly easy to find during the day on the main avenues; shared ones cost CFA 100 to CFA 200 for most destinations. There are no car rental agencies so if you want a vehicle, hire a taxi by the day.

MBINI
Some 50 km south of Bata along the coast on the road to Acalayong, Mbini is a pleasant, small town at the mouth of the Rio Benito. It's a good destination if you're looking for deserted beaches.

There are two places to stay in town, including the *Bar Central* and if you ask in advance they can arrange meals for you. Seafood, particularly turtle, is the speciality of the area.

Getting There & Away
Mbini is just south of the Rio Benito, and every hour between 8 am and 5 pm a car-carrying ferry shuttles between it and Bolondo on the other side. The passenger fare for the 300-metre, seven-minute ride is CFA 250. Because the ferry has room for only four cars, there can sometimes be a considerable wait. All vehicles headed for Acalayong take

this ferry because the bridge on the route further east, bypassing Mbini, is broken.

There are several minibuses a day between Bata and Mbini for CFA 1000; the trip from Bata to Bolondo takes one hour. If there isn't space on the ferry for your minibus, simply ride across and walk into town.

THE SOUTHERN BORDER
Acalayong
Acalayong (ah-cah-LYE-ong) is the major southern border town and consists of a few bars, shops and houses, and the police post. As at the border near Ebebiyin, the police demand a 'transaction fee' for stamping your passport – CFA 1500 when entering the country and CFA 500 when exiting. (At Cocobeach the Gabonese officials do likewise – CFA 2000 when you enter.)

The *cayucos* (motorised canoes) for Cocobeach have no fixed schedule and depart when full; the first one usually leaves around 8 am and the last one around 4.30 pm. The trip across the estuary takes 40 minutes (sometimes double that) and the fare is CFA 4000 – the same as a minibus from Acalayong to Bata via Mbini (six hours).

Cogo
Cogo, a small settlement to the east across the inlet from Acalayong, is full of old, partially destroyed colonial buildings and has been described by one traveller as the 'nicest city of Guinea'. The isolation of this town is part of its charm. The best way to get there is by cayuco from Acalayong.

Islas Elobey
From Cogo or Acalayong you can hire a cayuco for CFA 5000 (oars and sails) to CFA 20,000 (motorised) to take you to the islands at the mouth of the river – Isla Elobey Grande and, several km to the north, Isla Elobey Chico. If you take a motorised cayuco, be prepared to be get soaked with spray from the water. Those with oars or sails are much slower but at least you'll be dry.

You could stay there a few hours or days and arrange to be picked up by the same cayuco owner and taken back to Acalayong or on to Cocobeach. The few people who live on Elobey Grande are very friendly. Nobody, on the other hand, lives on Elobey Chico, which is an odd but interesting place that was once the capital of the mainland. All that remains is an old, deserted city covered by the forest.

Isla Corisco

It's also possible to hire a cayuco in Cogo, Acalayong or Cocobeach for around CFA 30,000 to CFA 50,000 to take you to Isla Corisco, which is further out. The people there are reportedly very friendly. You need to bring food but possibly not bedding as the inhabitants will probably offer to let you sleep in their homes. On the eastern side of the island, for example, a woman named Hinestrosa takes guests at her house and charges CFA 10,000 for two with full pension. You can sleep a little more cheaply on the other side of the island at the house of Felisa, the representative for women's affairs.

EVINAYONG

About 180 km south-east of Bata, Evinayong is a pleasant town on the top of a small mountain, with a slightly cooler climate and several waterfalls nearby. The town is not particularly interesting but the area around it is one of the best in Rio Muni for hiking. Even if you're not interested in hiking, it would be a good place to head if you are just looking for a remote town that almost never receives travellers.

Places to Stay & Eat

The town's only hotel is the *Casa de Huéspedes* which charges CFA 2500 to CFA 3000 a room and can arrange meals for you if you ask in advance. There's also a small place to eat near the market.

Getting There & Away

There is at least one minibus a day in either direction between Evinayong and Bata. The fare is CFA 3500 and the trip usually takes six or seven hours.

EBEBIYIN

Ebebiyin (sometimes spelled Ebibeyine), the second-largest town in Rio Muni, is most noteworthy because it's in the far north-east corner of the mainland, where most overland travellers stay before or after crossing the Cameroun border. The town is only about 1½ km from end to end and thus is easy to cover on foot. Drinking seems to be the only form of entertainment, as there's a bar seemingly on every corner. However, you could look for a game of *acomg*, a favourite of Rio Muni inhabitants, and inquire about the Museum of Biyabiyan which is in Biyabiyan, 20 km west of town on the road to Bata. Owned by Felipe Ossa, it has traditional Fang sculptures and works of art.

Places to Stay

The town's electricity and water supply are cut off between 6 and 10 pm, so some of the hotels have installed small generators. Hotel Gloria has closed, leaving the city with three hotels. The cheapest is *Hotel Mbengono*, which is on the western outskirts of town, just off the road to Bata. The rooms cost only CFA 1500, mainly because the hotel has no generator. However, it's still the best buy in town and recommended. The owner is very friendly and at the back of the hotel he has constructed a thatched-roof paillote surrounded by greenery – perfect for drinks, which he serves. You can't eat here but the rooms are quite clean and have paraffin lamps, shared showers and, usually, running water.

Next in price is *Hotel Nsi Ndongo*, which is a block north-east of the market. There's no restaurant here either but there is a small generator that runs the refrigerator and lights up the reception area, which has comfortable sofas for relaxing and drinking. The rooms cost CFA 2000 to CFA 3000 and have double beds with foam mattresses, paraffin lamps and bucket baths out the back with Western-style toilets but no running water.

The city's top address, where all visiting dignitaries stay, is *Hotel Central*, which is in the heart of town a block east of the park. The rooms are very reasonably priced at CFA

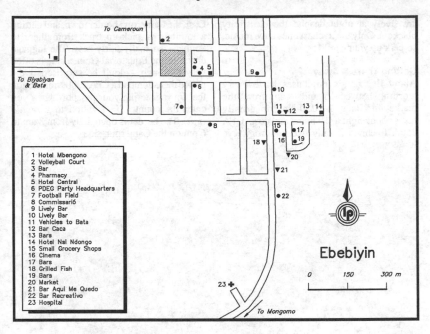

Legend:

1 Hotel Mbengono
2 Volleyball Court
3 Bar
4 Pharmacy
5 Hotel Central
6 PDEG Party Headquarters
7 Football Field
8 Commissarió
9 Lively Bar
10 Lively Bar
11 Vehicles to Bata
12 Bar Caca
13 Bars
14 Hotel Nsi Ndongo
15 Small Grocery Shops
16 Cinema
17 Bars
18 Grilled Fish
19 Bars
20 Market
21 Bar Aqui Me Quedo
22 Bar Recreativo
23 Hospital

Ebebiyin

2500 to CFA 4000 and, most important, there's a generator which lights both the restaurant and the rooms. If you can afford the slightly higher prices, I highly recommend staying here. The CFA 2500 rooms, which are bare except for a bed with ironed sheets, have clean shared baths and (usually) running water; the CFA 4000 rooms are similar but have private baths.

Places to Eat

The *Hotel Central* also has the city's top restaurant, part inside and part outside on a rustic patio, and the friendly old man who runs it is a major part of the attraction. It's the only place that serves food and has electricity at night; consequently it has the coldest drinks by far in town. Prices are very reasonable – CFA 700 for greasy but tasty chicken with rice, bread and banana; large Camerounian beers for CFA 350; and large 'Top' soft drinks for CFA 300. On occasion

it gets frozen seafood from Camcroun, which is not too bad.

Some of the bars also serve food. Two that have been recommended are *Bar Aqui Me Quedo* and *Bar Recreativo*, both of which are on the main street heading south of the market towards the hospital. Eggs, chips, salad and chicken are all on the menu; a very filling meal can cost up to CFA 1000. *Bar Caca* opposite the market usually has one or two bowls of African food, often fish, on top of the bar; the food here is about as cheap as you'll find in a bar.

Street food is cheaper but there's precious little of it. North of the market on the road to the hospital you'll find delicious fish being grilled at night; a sizeable piece with manioc costs CFA 100. This street is also best for finding stores selling tinned goods, such as sardines.

For drinks, in addition to Hotel Central there are some bars – in particular several bars a block or two east of the hotel – which are lively at night despite the electricity blackout. Only the liveliest ones have music, so perk up your ears.

Getting There & Away

About five or six minibuses leave every morning between 5 and 7 am from the market for Bata; the 230-km trip usually takes about eight to 10 hours and costs CFA 2500. Ebebiyin is only two km from Kye Ossi, the Cameroun border town, and getting a minibus or pick-up truck from there to Ambam is usually fairly easy. The luggage check on the Equatorial Guinea side is often very thorough – don't be surprised if the police there demand a CFA 2000 'transaction fee' for registering your passport when you enter the country, in addition to a *regalo* (gift). The border is open daily from 8 am to 6 pm on the Cameroun side.

Gabon

Gabon gets mixed reviews. Some complain it's too expensive. Others say the traditional African culture disappeared with the discovery of oil. If you're seeking the 'real' Africa, however, Gabon is as real as anywhere else. Most of the country is densely forested and teeming with all kinds of wildlife. Consequently travelling on the muddy roads through the interior is almost always interesting if not always sheer fun.

Although some of the rural areas may seem fairly poor, Gabon has oil and minerals. Even with decreased oil revenues, it still ranks number one in Black Africa in per capita income (US$2900). Some of this is obviously trickling down as Gabon now ranks number two in Black Africa in the United Nation's more broadly based 'human development index'. The average Gabonese, unlike many Africans, can afford to buy you a beer and many of them will. For those who have been travelling through Muslim-dominated West Africa where Coca Cola is the number-one drink, not beer, Gabon can be a refreshing change. If you don't like the local beer (Regab), palm wine, or the local corn and *mengrokom* (manioc) squeezings, just try to grin and bear it.

But there's more to Gabon than that. Albert Schweitzer put Gabon on the map when he founded his hospital here in 1913. You can see it, then venture into the heart of the African jungle by taking a canoe trip down the Ogooué River. With this exception, travel in the rural areas is totally unorganised, which is why Gabon is really for those who like to make up their own adventures, travelling to remote areas that few foreigners see and meeting the people.

Gabonese can sometimes be initially suspicious of travellers and view them solely as sources of money, but once you offer them a drink and get to know them they can be as friendly as any other Africans on the continent.

If, on the other hand, you like your crea-

ture comforts, sports, lovely beaches and Western entertainment, Libreville and Port-Gentil have them all. But behind the somewhat artificial glitz of modern buildings and fancy shops there are real African quarters where life is as spontaneous and people are as friendly as in the rural areas. If you hang out in these areas and can find ways to avoid the high prices, these cities aren't such a total waste as some travellers warn.

Facts about the Country

HISTORY

Two things in particular stand out about Gabon's history: firstly, less is known about Gabon prior to the colonial period than any other country in Africa and, secondly, no country in Africa, perhaps the entire world, has gone through such a dramatic transformation in the 20th century – from basic traditional housing in the rainforests to mini-skyscrapers. Before the 20th century, only one settlement, Libreville, warranted being called a town.

Of the present inhabitants, the Pygmies were the first to arrive in the area. The first Bantu people began migrating into Gabon around 1100. Thereafter, other Bantu tribes moved into the area and the Pygmies began assimilating into them. The strongest migration, however, was of the last group, the Fang, who started moving south from Cameroun in the 18th century.

The Fang were among the fiercest tribes in Africa (reputedly practising cannibalism although that has never been proven). During the 19th century they were the pre-eminent ivory-hunters, exchanging ivory for European goods, especially guns. Mary Kingsley, an Englishwoman travelling in these parts in 1894, wrote:

To be short of money in a Fang village is extremely bad, because when a trader has no more goods to sell them, these Fangs are liable to start trade all over again by killing him and taking back their ivory and rubber and keeping it until another trader comes along.

The environment, mostly rainforest, wasn't conducive to the growth of towns, much less empires like those that arose elsewhere in Central and West Africa.

In 1472 the Portuguese arrived, but they virtually ignored 'Gabao' (meaning hooded cloak), their name for the coastal area, concentrating their attention instead on the nearby island of São Tomé. Dutch, French and British ships began arriving sometime thereafter in search of ivory and slaves. The coastal tribes acted as intermediaries and raided settlements in the interior for slaves.

Eventually the coastal tribes no longer produced anything – the slaves did all their work. By ruining fraternal relations between villages, concentrating power in the chiefs of the coastal tribes, and upsetting the balance of power between the coastal and interior tribes, the slave trade destroyed the social fabric.

Colonial Period

By the mid-19th century, the slave trade had come to an end. The French signed treaties with various Mpongwé coastal chiefs, most notably the famous King Kowe Rapontchombo, who lived on Pointe-Dénis. In exchange for cloth, gunpowder, guns, tobacco and hats, King 'Dénis' recognised French sovereignty, with France assuming the status of protector. In 1849, the French captured a slave ship, releasing the passengers at the mouth of the Komo River. The slaves named their settlement Libreville (Free Town). At about the same time, French Catholic and American Protestant missionaries began flocking to the scene, vying for influence.

In the late 19th century, various French explorers, including Savorgnan de Brazza, travelled up the Ogooué River looking for the headwaters of the Congo River; hostilities from the locals forced some of them to turn back. When the European powers carved up Africa, France snatched Gabon. Libreville became the capital of the French Congo, but a few years later it was transferred to Brazzaville. Thereafter, in 1910, Gabon became one of the four territories of French Equatorial Africa.

In 1912, Albert Schweitzer, an Alsatian who had studied theology and later medicine, set off with his wife Hélène for Gabon to do missionary work. Settling in Lambaréné, he eventually set up a hospital and sparked some controversy by allowing patients to bring their families to the hospital to prepare their food, thus relaxing the standards of hygiene somewhat.

During the same period, exploitation of Gabon was left to French private companies which forced the Africans to work for them. Like Africans elsewhere in French Equatorial Africa, the Gabonese revolted against this new form of slavery, but each revolt was eventually put down. These concessionary companies systematically destroyed the forests and other resources and sent the economy into a major slump which lasted until after WW I.

Nowhere in Africa did the French do less

in terms of development – they built few roads and left agriculture basically untouched. The only economic activity of interest was forestry along a narrow coastal strip. As late as independence in 1960, 75% of the country's exports consisted of timber, particularly the semi-hard *okoumé*, a giant forest tree that the Gabonese use for making canoes and the paper companies use for making plywood.

Independence

The mayor of Libreville, Léon M'Ba, whose name adorns a major street in Libreville,

formed the first political party in the mid-1950s and was elected Gabon's first president following independence in 1960. He was a popular man, in part because he used to end his speeches by tossing coins to the crowd.

The new government started off with two strong political parties in existence. A coalition government was formed and the leader of the opposition, Jean Hilaire Aubame, became Foreign Minister. Both were Fangs but M'Ba became increasingly authoritarian and finally in 1964, the military, fronting for Aubame, staged a successful coup. The next day French paratroopers intervened to reinstall M'Ba, saying they were acting pursuant to a bilateral defence agreement with Gabon.

In 1965, Schweitzer, who had received the Nobel Peace Prize for his work in Lambaréné, died, and two years after that M'Ba died. By then Gabon had become a de facto one-party state. M'Ba's diminutive 31-year-old deputy, Albert-Bernard Bongo (he is 1½ metres or five feet tall), a Téké from the Franceville area, was his chosen successor. After taking over, Bongo dissolved all political parties and founded a single new one, the Parti Démocratique Gabonais (PDG). He later converted to Islam and is now El Hadj Omar Bongo.

Manganese (around Moanda) and uranium (around Mounana) exploitation began almost immediately after independence and started the 'Gabonese Miracle'. Oil production began its spectacular growth in 1967. By the end of the decade, the Gross Domestic Product (GDP) had doubled in real terms.

In the 1970s, manganese and uranium production levelled out, but the fourfold increase in oil prices in 1973 and the doubling of oil output sent Gabon into nirvana. Oil prices peaked in 1977, the year Gabon spent a staggering US$1 billion hosting the most extravagant summit in the history of the Organization of African Unity (OAU). David Lamb describes the event in *The Africans*:

Presidents roared through Libreville, the somnolent capital on the Atlantic coast, in Mercedes-Benzes and Cadillacs with sirens wailing, each jammed into the back seat between his bodyguards. (Bongo, like President Mobutu Sese Seko of Zaïre, used Moroccan bodyguards, not wishing to trust his safety to local soldiers; Idi Amin used Palestinians.) The Gabonese honour guard, wearing red velvet capes and holding gold swords, lined the entrance to the conference hall...

There was no laundry service in Libreville that week because the city's women had been recruited to perform traditional dances in honour of the arriving presidents. Nor were there any working prostitutes because Bongo had swept the streets clean with the warning to the nation's ladies of the night: 'Open your hearts during the summit, but not your bodies'...

Some journalists arrived at their assigned hotels and found buildings still under construction; the hotel had no employees, doors, water or electricity, and the guests' US$50-a-night rooms were nothing more than open space in uncarpeted corridors, to be shared with bags of cement.

Thereafter, oil prices went tumbling and Gabon's ambitious US$32-billion development plan (with the exception of the Transgabonais railway) was shelved.

The 1980s

During the 1980s Bongo remained firmly in power. The Moroccan troops and French mercenaries continued acting as palace guards. Every so often he would reshuffle the cabinet so as to distribute the lucrative posts to the small number of political faithful who make up the country's political elite.

Despite some 400 French airborne troops, all was not calm. An opposition party called Morena was actively fighting for a two-party system, but was outlawed and it operated out of Paris. Every now and then members were arrested and, as occurred in 1982, given stiff prison sentences for distributing leaflets or other such horrendous activities.

Between 1985 and 1987, oil revenues dropped drastically and for the first time ever, unemployment became a problem. Bongo responded by expelling illegal immigrants and cutting government spending drastically in line with International Monetary Fund (IMF) recommendations while completing the Transgabonais railway roughly on schedule.

The huge 13-year Transgabonais project was one of the most costly projects to be carried out anywhere in Africa since independence and its successful completion was a feather in Bongo's cap. As a result, Gabon (and Bongo) weathered the storm fairly well and Bongo was re-elected in 1986 for another seven-year term with 99.97% of the vote. For the next three years, however, the country's GDP continued to decline as did Bongo's popularity.

GEOGRAPHY

Gabon is about half the size of France and straddles the equator. The area covered by rainforest is 74%, among the highest in Africa and only 1% of the land is cultivated. (Gabon imports over 50% of its food.) Inland, you'll find a series of plateaus which cover most of the country, with a number of peaks of about 1000 metres. In the east, there are two mountain chains, the Monts de Cristal and the Masif du Chaillu, which rise to the north and south of the Ogooué River, respectively.

The Ogooué, which passes through Franceville and Lambaréné on its way to the sea, cuts the country almost in half. Port-Gentil, the centre of operations for Gabon's on-shore and offshore oil rigs, is on an island at the mouth of the Ogooué and is cut off from the rest of the country; it's accessible only by air and ferry. The river is navigable between Port-Gentil and Ndjolé; big boats and barges plough up and down carrying passengers and cargo.

The estuaries all along the coast are perhaps the most beautiful areas but they are almost inaccessible and so few travellers visit them. The four major ones south of Port-Gentil are, north to south, Fernan Vaz, Iguéla, N'Dogo (where Setté Cama and Gamba are located) and M'Banio. Most are accessible only by air and flying to them is expensive. Only the last of the estuaries, near the Congo border, is connected to the mainland by an all-weather road.

The capital city of Libreville is at the mouth of an estuary in the north. A 12-km ferry ride across that estuary will take you to Pointe-Dénis, one of the best beaches near Libreville.

An asphalt road leads inland from Libreville for about 250 km, but all the remaining are dirt roads except for a 90-km stretch between Mounana and Franceville (via Moanda). Why are there so few paved roads when Gabon is so rich? It's not just because the cost of building roads through the impenetrable tropical forest is enormous. Bongo simply has had other priorities – primarily the enormously expensive Trans-gabonais railway to Franceville, the centre of Gabon's rich manganese and uranium deposits.

Because of the low population growth and the reliance on oil and minerals instead of timber exports, Gabon is doing better than most African countries from an environmental standpoint. The country's vast coastal wetlands and marshes, for example, are still largely intact. Deforestation is the main concern. While the percentage of forests being destroyed each year is among the lowest in Africa (one-eighth that of Cameroun, for example), the total annual loss is not insignificant.

The forests vary from stunted woodland along the coast to humid tropical rainforests everywhere else. The latter include the okumé tree which is unique to central Africa, various hardwoods including ebony, purpleheart and mahoganies interspersed with climbing palm and rubber vine. These rainforests tend to be so thick and inaccessible that viewing the bountiful wildlife (most notably forest elephants, western gorillas, crocodiles, chimpanzees and aardvarks, as well as the extraordinary giant pangolin, the rare sitatunga antelope along the coast and the shy bongo) is quite difficult.

NATIONAL PARKS

Gabon's parks and reserve areas are: Réserve de la Lopé and the adjoining Parc National de l'Okanda in the centre of the country; Réserve de N'Dendé in the south near N'Dendé; and Parc National du Petit Loango, which is a newly created coastal park combining the Petit Loango Game Reserve (300 km south of Libreville) and seven other protected areas along the coast, including the Réserve de Moukalaba. The Parc National du Petit Loango protects critically endangered leatherback sea turtles as well as forest buffalos, elephants, chimps, gorillas, monkeys, antelope, hippos and manatees. Only Loango and Lopé are actively protected and potentially good for viewing wildlife, and of these two only Lopé is readily accessible. The Okanda and N'Dendé reserves are more theoretical than real and are perhaps best forgotten.

In the near future, there may be a park established in the north-east above

Makokou. If you're looking for real adventure in nearly unexplored territory, you can go on a river trip up the Nouna River to an area with some of the largest numbers of elephants in Africa and an absolutely pristine environment (see the Around Makokou section).

CLIMATE
The weather is warm, with typical noon temperatures around 30°C. Excessive mugginess is the main problem. The best time to visit Gabon is during the dry season (June to September). During the rest of the year the rainfall is rather heavy. During the rainy season (January to May) the rain sets in between 4 and 6 pm almost every day. It usually stops by 6 am the next morning, and by 8 am all the clouds have generally evaporated and the sun becomes unbearable by noon.

GOVERNMENT
Bongo's popularity has plunged, particularly since 1990 when Libreville and Port-Gentil witnessed their worst post-independence riots following the mysterious death of Joseph Rendjambe, head of the Parti Gabonais de Progress (PGP). His body was found under suspicious circumstances in a room at the Dowé Novotel with needle marks on his abdomen.

Thereafter rioters rampaged through Libreville, burning buildings belonging to Bongo and his associates, including most notably the Dowé and parts of the ultramodern Hypermarché M'Bolo shopping centre, the charred remains of which are still standing. His death also sparked off a week of riots in Port-Gentil. France responded by sending paratroopers and Bongo responded by arresting PGP President Pierre-Louis Agondjo Okawé.

Bongo has since ended the country's 22 years of one-party rule with legalisation of opposition parties and multiparty elections to the National Assembly, but he is still firmly in control, at least until the next presidential elections in late 1993, which will surely be hotly contested if they in fact occur.

Meanwhile, everywhere in central Libreville you can continue to see the same picture, mounted in a glass cabinet and lit at night, of Bongo in a debonair pose and a pin-striped suit with scenes of bustling commercial activity below.

ECONOMY
On the economic front, the recession appears to be over. One of the driving forces of the recovery has been Rabi-Kounga, a major new onshore oilfield which reached full production in 1990 and has not only significantly increased the country's oil production capacity but has also attracted new oil company exploratory operations and additional loans from foreign banks.

The increased oil production, which provides 65% of total export revenues, means that Gabon can stave off relying on its vast mineral deposits, particularly manganese, iron ore and uranium, which are continuing to suffer from low world prices. The manganese reserves are the largest in the world and will last until around the mid-2100s at the present rate of exploitation. Bongo would like help in financing the third phase of the Transgabonais to Bélinga in the north-east so that the country can mine the rich iron ore deposits there, but low world prices for iron ore have made the expensive project uninteresting to investors. Meanwhile, the country's second major export earner, timber plywood, shows no signs of letting up.

With over half the population involved in the agricultural sector, many people are simply not prospering very much from the country's wealth and progress. Certainly the workers in the cities have relatively high incomes by African standards, but considering that the cost of living is among the highest on the continent, the somewhat inflated salaries are rather deceptive. In reality, while young people have benefited significantly from increased educational opportunities, most of the benefits are reaped by the political elite and a small middle class. It's no accident that despite its tiny population, Gabon is the world's 20th largest consumer of French champagne.

POPULATION & PEOPLE

Although Gabon's population is estimated to be 1.2 million, no-one is sure exactly how many people live here. Major publications on Africa often differ widely in their estimates. The government tends to overestimate the number to make the country appear less wealthy per capita. Regardless, only three countries in Africa have a lower population density. Gabon is unusual as well in that most people have work. Indeed, the government is studying ways to increase the fertility of Gabonese women.

Health care in Gabon is not so good as life expectancy is 52 years, about average for Africa and on a par with Bangladesh.

For years Africans from all corners of the continent have come here looking for work, most of them ending up with jobs in the mining centres, the ports and the construction industry, with the Gabonese preferring prestigious posts in the government and services sector. Because of this job stratification and the fact that most of the foreigners are here illegally, the labour movement is weak, and the government keeps it under close control. Some 50,000 French people are here as well – more than when Gabon was a French colony!

Among the Gabonese, there are 10 large groups, all Bantu people. The Fang (primarily in the north and north-east) are the dominant ethnic group (31%), followed by the Mbédé (25%) in the south-east (this group includes the Téké, the Mbété and all other groups of the south-eastern area), the Eshira (22%) in the south-west and the Myéné along the coast.

EDUCATION

Gabonese are becoming increasingly well educated – 61% of the adult population is literate. In all of Central and West Africa only São Tomé has a higher literacy rate.

RELIGION

About half the population profess to be Christian – the highest percentage of Christians in continental Central and West Africa – but traditional animist religions are still very strong. El Hadj Omar Bongo is of the 1% that is Muslim, but his relations with the Arab world are strained.

ARTS & CULTURE

While Gabon's relative wealth and contact with the West have made life easier for its citizens, they are worse off than other Africans in terms of preserving their cultural identity. All the young men want to leave the villages for Libreville. What they find is an undistinguished modern city run by foreigners.

A hundred years ago the Fang were producing some of the most beautiful woodcarvings in Africa. They are most noted for being masters of form, and if you inspect closely some of their prize statues in museums you may see why. Characteristic features of Fang statues include heart-shaped faces with sunken cheeks, distinctive headdresses and full rounded arms, legs and other body parts, with a smooth fleshy skin needing no decorative enhancement. By their exceptional attention to these body parts, the artists seem to have been expressing a certain sensuous humanism.

Fang masks tend to be more varied. Some embody similar qualities and are almost oriental in quality, with elongated, heart-shaped faces reminiscent of Modigliani. (Picasso and Matisse were also profoundly influenced by Fang masks.) Others – often painted red, black or white, with horns, feathers and nails sticking out – seem to reflect more concern for effect than form. Unfortunately, this exceptional artistic talent has been totally lost. Today the Fang don't even bother to make cheap imitations! You can only see these statues and masks in museums these days.

Understanding Fang sculpture – or any African art – is not easy, but reading and viewing helps. If you observe the form of some typical Fang statues in museums or books, for example, you will soon note that the proportions are totally unnatural. The head and torso are usually overly large and the legs disproportionately small. This was intentional. With reliquary statues, for example, the intent of creating the ancestor figure was to represent age and the august powers of the ancestor while also recognising the infantile qualities of the figure itself. These contradictory qualities in the ancestor figure reflect Fang theology – a belief that the newborn are especially close to the ancestors and are only gradually weaned away by ritual and time to attain human status. It is these contradictions which give the sculpture a greater vitality for the Fang than if it is represented simply as an aged person or an infant.

One aspect of Fang culture that definitely has not been lost is the use of *eboka*, especially among members of the *Bwiti*, a secret society for the men. Eboka is a fatigue suppressant, like coca and kola nuts. The plant reaches a height of about one metre and grows wild, although you may also see it being used in villages as a decorative bush, with its yellowish or pinkish-white flowers and small, orange-type fruit. The root bark is the main source of the alkaloid. It is rasped and eaten directly, ground as a powder and eaten, or soaked in water and drunk.

By tradition, it is used by the Bwiti (who have a temple in Oyem) in all-night rituals in the villages to assist the participants to 'break open their heads' in order to effect contact with their ancestors – a brief encounter with the afterlife and, therefore, a coming to terms with death. You can read accounts of these visions in *African Folklore* (Doubleday, Garden City, New York, 1972), edited by Richard Dorson.

The main reason why they take eboka is to enable them to endure the night-long rite without fatigue, but if taken in large quantities eboka can cause hallucinations. It also causes many people to vomit. In the villages you might encounter people who have taken eboka. However, this doesn't necessarily mean they've been through such an initiation. Eboka is eaten for other reasons, such as for pleasure or to keep awake for whatever purpose.

LANGUAGE

French is the official language. The main African language in the north is Fang; about half the people speak it. Other widely spoken languages include Bapunu (BAH-pou-nou), spoken in the south, Bandgabi (BAND-jah-bee), spoken in the east and in the south around Franceville, and Eshira.

Greetings & Civilities in Fang

Good morning/evening
Um-Boh-loh
(to several people)
Um-BOH-lah-nee
Response
Ahm-BOH-loh
(to several people)
Ahm-BOH-lah-nee
How are you?
Yoh-num-VUOY?
I'm fine.
Men-num-VUOY.
Thank you
AH-kee-bah
Goodbye
Ma-khan

Greetings & Civilities in Bandgabi

Good morning/evening
When-nah-SOH-lah
How are you?
Way-WAY-day?
I'm fine.
May-WAY-day.
Thank you
Mah-LOUM-bee
Goodbye
Nah-BUAY-dee

The local word for people of European descent is *otangani*. Travellers with light skin will hear the word whenever children are around, just as *mzungu* is heard all over East Africa.

Facts for the Visitor

VISAS & EMBASSIES
Gabonese Visas

Only Germans, theoretically, do not need

visas to Gabon. However, immigration officials at Libreville airport and elsewhere are rarely aware of this. So Germans are advised to get visas, particularly those entering over land borders. If you arrive at Libreville airport without a visa and have problems, call the German Embassy there; they can confirm that German travellers don't need visas.

In the days of the oil boom, getting a visa was very difficult, mainly because there weren't enough hotel rooms. Those days have passed, at least if you get your visa in Europe or in the USA. The Gabonese Embassy in Washington (☎ (202) 797-1000) requires US$20 and two photos for a single-entry visa valid up to one month (US$50 for a multiple-entry visa good for four-month stays), while the embassy in London (☎ (071) 937-5285) requires UK£20 for a three-month visa and issues them in three days. Both embassies have dropped two long-standing requirements: proof of a round-trip (return) airline ticket (or a letter from a bank proving sufficient funds to leave the country) and a confirmed hotel reservation (or a *certificat d'hérbergement* from a Gabonese citizen certifying that you'll be provided with lodging). The Gabonese Embassy in Bonn, which charges DM100 for visas, has likewise dropped these requirements but the visa application still has to be referred to Libreville, a process which takes about two weeks.

If at all possible, get a visa outside Africa because Gabonese embassies in many African countries still insist upon sending a cable to Libreville, and they may not get a response for a week or more. The embassies in Brazzaville (the Congo), Yaoundé (Cameroun) and the French Consulate in Bangui (the CAR) for example, require this, and you must pay the telex fee (CFA 2500 and CFA 5000, respectively) and wait one to two weeks for a response.

There are a few countries where getting visas to Gabon is not such a hassle. In Malabo and Bata (Equatorial Guinea), the Gabonese embassy and consulate, respectively, do not have the cable requirement and

issue visas in 24 hours, while in São Tomé the embassy gives same-day service.

At the embassy in Kinshasa you need a letter from your embassy; otherwise getting a visa there is easy but not cheap (CFA 20,000). The only Central African country where you cannot get a visa to Gabon is Chad. Cities in West Africa where travellers have reported no hassles in getting visas to Gabon are Lagos (Nigeria) and Lomé (Togo).

Police at Libreville airport almost never give travellers problems, but at the borders they sometimes do. Officials in Bitam, for example, told a French traveller heading south from Cameroun that the two previously mentioned requirements still applied and turned her away when she was unable to produce a confirmed hotel reservation or lodging certificate. It is quite possible that they were just looking for a bribe, but it is wise to be extremely careful about bribing the officials in Gabon. Travellers have been known to get into serious trouble for offering bribes to officials (naturally the trouble only comes after money has been parted with). The moral is never to travel without all your papers on you.

If you're travelling overland to the Congo, be sure to get an exit stamp at N'Dendé, 40 km from the border.

Other African Visas
You can get visas to Burkina Faso, Chad and Togo from the French Consulate, which is open on weekdays from 7 to 11 am and issues visas in 24 hours.

Benin The Benin Consulate is open Monday to Wednesday from 9 am to noon and 3.30 to 5.30 pm and issues visas in 24 hours. Visas are good for stays of two weeks, require two photos and cost CFA 2000.

Cameroun The Camerounian Embassy requires CFA 6500, two photos and a round-trip or onward airline ticket. In the past the embassy has on occasion refused to issue visas to people not residing in Gabon, but it now states that it issues visas to both residents and nonresidents. However, because of the onward ticket requirement, getting visas here can still be problematic for those travelling overland. The embassy is open on weekdays from 9 to 11.45 am and 3 to 4.30 pm and issues visas in 24 hours if you deposit your passport and visa forms in the morning.

The CAR Visas to the CAR cost CFA 10,000 and are good for one-month stays. The embassy, which is open on weekdays from 8 am to 1.30 pm, requires two photos and often gives same-day service. However, in the case of Australians, New Zealanders, Irish people and a few other nationalities, the embassy must first wire Bangui, a process that can take a week or more.

Congo Visas to the Congo require one photo, cost CFA 20,000 and are valid for 15 days from the day of entry. They are issued the same day by the Congolese Embassy, which is open on weekdays from 8 am to 2 pm.

Côte d'Ivoire The embassy, which is open on weekdays from 8.30 am to 1.30 pm, requires CFA 6000 and two photos and issues visas, permitting visits of up to 90 days, in 24 to 48 hours. The visas are valid for three months from the date of issue. However, people of many nationalities, including Americans, Britons, the French and Germans, don't need visas to Côte d'Ivoire.

Equatorial Guinea Visas to Equatorial Guinea require two photos, cost CFA 10,000, are valid for 60 days from the date of issue and permit visits of up to 30 days during that period. The embassy, which is open on weekdays from 8 am to 3 pm, gives same-day service.

Nigeria The Nigerian Embassy is open on weekdays from 8 am to 3 pm and 90-day visas require two photos and are issued in 48 hours. Prices vary from about CFA 1000 for Americans to about CFA 10,000 for Britons.

São Tomé Visas, permitting visits of up to 15 days, cost CFA 14,495 and are valid for 120 days from the date of issue. In the morning bring your passport, money and two photos to the embassy (open on weekdays from 8 am to noon and 3 to 5 pm) and you'll receive the visa that afternoon.

Zaïre Single-entry visas to Zaïre good for a stay of up to one month cost CFA 20,000 (CFA 32,000 for multiple entry) to CFA 52,000 for a single-entry visa good for a stay up to three months (CFA 60,000 for multiple entry). The embassy is open on weekdays from 9 am to 3 pm and Saturdays from 9 am to noon, and issues visas in 24 to 48 hours. The embassy requires two photos and a *note verbale* from your embassy if you are not a resident of Gabon. A note verbale should read approximately as follows:

Par la présente, nous attestons que Mr ----- est titulaire de passporte No -----. Il doit se rendre au Zaïre pour faire le tourism. Toute assistance que pourrait lui être accordeé serait appréciée.
En foit de quoi nous lui délivrons cette lettre pour servir et valoir ce que de droit.

Gabonese Embassies
Gabon has embassies in Abidjan, Algiers, Bonn, Brazzaville, Brussels, Cairo, Dakar, Geneva, Kinshasa, Lagos, Lomé, London, Madrid, Malabo, Nouakchott, Ottawa, Paris, Rabat, Rome, São Tomé, Tokyo, Washington, Yaoundé. It also has a consulate in Bata (Equatorial Guinea).

Foreign Embassies in Gabon
See Information in the Libreville section for a list of foreign embassies in the capital.

DOCUMENTS
A passport and an International Health Certificate are required by all. If you have a car, you'll need a *carnet de passage en douane*.

CUSTOMS
Importing foreign currency is not a problem but if you'll be exporting large amounts of cash, declare it on arrival, otherwise customs

officials may give you problems on departure. Theoretically, there is a limit of CFA 200,000 on the amount of CFA that you may export, but in practice customs officials at Libreville Airport don't seem to care and most of the time don't even ask how much you're carrying. The same is not true of customs officials at the borders as they often like to hassle travellers. For sure, most officials don't know what the rules are.

MONEY
US$1 = CFA 280
UK£1 = CFA 425

The unit of currency is the Central African CFA. There are at least six banks in Libreville (and almost as many in Port-Gentil) which change travellers' cheques, including Barclays, Citibank, Banque de Paris et des Pays-Bas Gabon, the Banque Internationale pour le Commerce et l'Industrie du Gabon (BICIG), the Union Gabonaise de Banque (UGB), and the Banque Internationale pour le Gabon (BIPG). You'll have to shop around to get the best rate. Virtually all of them offer higher rates for travellers' cheques than for cash (eg CFA 249 versus CFA 243 per US$1 at Barclays) but with cash you escape the high commissions.

Some banks offer good exchange rates but charge high commissions on travellers' cheques. Barclays and BICIG, for example, charge commissions of CFA 7400 and CFA 5760, respectively, per transaction for cashing travellers' cheques, regardless of the amount, so you wouldn't want to change money at them unless you were cashing lots of cheques at one time. In Libreville, taking both commissions and exchange rates into consideration, I found that for US$500 in travellers' cheques I would get CFA 128,500 at the BIPG, CFA 122,240 at the BICIG, CFA 121,650 at the UGB, CFA 121,000 at Citibank, and CFA 117,100 at Barclays. The BIPG, however, no longer accepts American Express travellers' cheques and Barclays gives the quickest service.

There are banks in the largest towns (eg Franceville, Lambaréné, Moanda, etc) but

many of them refuse to change money (or travellers' cheques) that isn't tied to the French franc. The few that will accept such money usually have to wire Libreville first to check the day's exchange rate. So if you're likely to spend an extended period travelling outside Libreville and Port-Gentil, it would be wise to stock up on CFA.

BUSINESS HOURS & HOLIDAYS
Business hours on weekdays are from 8 am to noon and 3 to 6 pm and Saturdays from 8 am to noon. Government offices are open on weekdays from 9.30 am to noon and 3.30 to 5.30 pm.

Banking hours on weekdays are from 7.45 to 11.30 am and 2.45 to 4.30 pm.

Public Holidays
1 January (New Year's Day)
12 March
End of Ramadan
Easter Monday (April)
1 May
Pentecost Monday
Tabaski
16-18 August (Independence; by far the biggest celebration, with festivities more evident in the towns and villages than in Libreville)
1 November
25 December (Christmas)

POST & TELECOMMUNICATIONS
International telephone connections are good. Telex and fax facilities are available at the main post office and the top hotels in Libreville. Telephone rates are very high, eg about CFA 2500 per minute to the USA. However, AT&T now has direct service from Gabon to the USA. So if you have an AT&T card, you can ask the international operator to charge your call to it and the cost will be far less, about CFA 250 a minute to the USA.

Almost all the public telephones in Libreville require a special telephone card, which can be bought for about CFA 4000 from the telephone headquarters in the centre of town east of the Air Afrique office. However, there are a few coin-operated public telephones in

Libreville, including one on Blvd de l'Indépendance one block north of the main post
office and at the airport.

Sending and receiving letters is expensive, eg CFA 225 to receive a letter at the
poste restante and at least CFA 120 to send a
postcard anywhere.

TIME
Time in Gabon is GMT plus one hour, so
when it's noon in Gabon, it's 11 am in
London and 6 am in New York. Add one hour
during the daylight-saving period.

FILM & PHOTOGRAPHY
A photo permit is not required. Nevertheless,
you could easily end up in jail if you are
caught taking a photo of any military installations, the port, airport or government
buildings including the Palais Présidentiel in
Libreville. Even if the building or subject
matter doesn't seem sensitive, the police
may think it is, so if you don't want to risk
having your camera confiscated and being
put in jail, ask first.

Taking photos of people is a major problem in Gabon. Most Gabonese find having
their pictures taken by strangers to be
extremely offensive. Others don't mind but
feel that it is unjust unless the photographer
pays a ridiculously high fee; in their minds,
everyone taking photos is there for a purpose
– to make money by selling their photos to
book publishers and magazines.

Even if you just want to take a picture of
someone's store, many Gabonese would
consider it to be illegal without the owner's
permission (and most owners will demand
payment). The only way to take photos of
people or their possessions is first to make
friends with them, chat a while, then ask. But
don't pay, otherwise you'll only be making
it more difficult for travellers that follow. If
you're taking a photo of a crowd of people,
use a telephoto lens and as a courtesy to those
who don't want to have their pictures taken,
give people time to get out of the picture.

In Libreville, for photo supplies try Studio
Steph opposite the French Consulate or
Photo la 3em Oeil on Ave Col Parant near the

Score supermarket; a roll of Kodachrome
film with 36 frames costs CFA 2500.

HEALTH
A cholera vaccination is required. If you
have been in an infected area six days prior
to your arrival in Gabon or if you'll be spending more than two weeks in the country, a
yellow fever vaccination is required. Sexually transmitted diseases in Gabon are as bad
as or worse than anywhere else in Africa; an
estimated 30% of the women are infected
with one disease or another. AIDS is also a
major problem as is malaria, strains of which
are chloroquine resistant.

Medical Services
There are various hospitals and clinics in
Libreville; for emergencies the Peace Corps
and US Embassy use Hôpital Jeanne Ébori
(☎ 732771, 733177; 24-hour service), which
is better than the Hôpital Général (☎ 761747,
763017) or Hôpital N'Kembo (☎762460,
722130). Most of the better doctors work at
the private clinics; the best by reputation is
the Cabinet de Groupe (☎ 761382), which is
near the centre in Montagne Sainte. Others
include Polyclinique Chambrier nearby on
Rue d'Alsace Lorraine and Polyclinique
Mengué (☎ 745195). For a general practi-
tioner, try Dr Gugliemi (☎ 742659) or Dr
Valerie (☎ 766658).

DANGERS & ANNOYANCES
The relatively low unemployment rate in
Gabon has made Libreville and Port-Gentil
a lot safer than might otherwise be expected
of growing cities with lots of money floating
around.

Immigration from neighbouring countries
has spurred an increase of misdemeanours
and robbery, so security precautions are definitely required. In Libreville, the *gare
routière* (bus station) and Marché du Mont-
Bouët are the worst areas for pickpockets, so
be particularly careful there as well as in the
area around Score supermarket in the centre
and along the often deserted beach north of
the Hôtel Dialogue.

FOOD

Finding real Gabonese food takes a little searching because many of the cheap restaurants do not serve authentic Gabonese fare. Real Gabonese fare is usually a manioc paste (or rice) served with a spicy sauce, the main ingredient being some kind of bush meat, most commonly *antilope* (antelope), *porcpic* (porcupine), *singe* (monkey), *sanglier* (wild boar), or *boa* (snake).

The 'Senegalese' restaurants are found in every major town and city in the country and even though African dishes are often not on the menu, these stalls are still referred to as Senegalese restaurants because most of them are operated by West Africans, often by Senegalese but almost as frequently by Malians, Ivoirians or Togolese. The food (which is definitely not Senegalese but, rather, cheap Western fare) and prices at all of them are very similar, eg CFA 300 for the standard breakfast of coffee with milk and bread with butter; CFA 400 for a beef sandwich; CFA 550 for an omelette (CFA 750 for an *omelette garni*); CFA 800 for rice or spaghetti with beef; CFA 1200 for steak frites; CFA 1500 for chicken with green beans, etc.

Occasionally some of them will also serve African dishes such as *riz gras* or *foufou*, usually for about CFA 800. Alcohol is rarely served since the stall owners are usually Muslims.

On the streets in all the major cities and towns you'll find people selling *coupé-coupé*, the local expression for grilled beef. The best is imported from France and is no more expensive than the local beef, which is sometimes so tough that it can't be chewed; to avoid disappointment, ask before buying.

Getting There & Away

AIR

There are direct flights to Libreville from Brussels, Paris, Rome, Madrid and Geneva on Sabena, Air France/UTA, Air Afrique, Swissair, Air Gabon and Royal Air Maroc. Most travellers consider Air Gabon to be one of the three or four best African airlines serving Central and West Africa.

Various airlines, including Air Afrique, Nigeria Airways, Cameroun Airlines and Air

Itanga

Itangas are an unusual local fruit definitely worth trying at least once. When in season, they're found everywhere. About 10 cm long, egg-shaped and violet-coloured (when ripe), they're immersed in hot water for several minutes, and then eaten with salt and hot pepper. The green meat around the nut has a consistency similar to yam, but a taste all of its own.

Kola Nuts

You'll find kola nuts, the 'African No-Doze', in every market and many small shops. They're terribly bitter, but tolerable when washed down with beer. Most important, they'll keep you up when dancing all night. Splitting one with someone else or receiving a piece as a gift is a sign of friendship and respect.

Iboga

Africans sometimes chew or smoke *iboga* (ee-BOH-gah), a hallucinogenic plant that is used in some adolescent initiation ceremonies. It's a small plant with white flowers and golden yellow fruit that grows wild everywhere but perhaps more so in the south-east where the Mitsogho cultivate it around their homes. They scrape off the bark and chew it, sometimes smoking it in a pipe.

If you chew a little of this nasty tasting bark, it'll give you a buzz like kola nuts or coffee, keeping you awake. Apparently some people make themselves throw up so that they can eat more to keep the all-night buzz going. Some say the Pygmies were the first users, aiding them to beat the *tam-tams* (drums) all day long. But if you take a lot...wow! ■

Gabon, provide good connections with West African coastal cities. From East Africa, there are no direct flights, so you'll have to change flights at Douala, Brazzaville or Kinshasa.

As for connections to/from other Central African countries, you'll find direct flights from every country except Chad. Air Afrique, Cameroun Airlines, Air Gabon and Nigerian Airways service the popular Libreville to Douala and Libreville to Brazzaville routes. Air Zaïre and Nigerian Airways connect Libreville with Kinshasa. You can also fly direct from Libreville to Pointe-Noire (the Congo) two days a week. There's only one flight a week between Libreville and Bangui (the CAR) – a Wednesday flight on Air Gabon – but there are two flights a week (Tuesdays and Saturdays) to Bata and Malabo (Equatorial Guinea) on Equato Guineana de Aviation (EGA), whose agent is Air Gabon, and four flights a week (Monday, Tuesday, Thursday and Friday) to São Tomé on Equatorial International Airlines, an excellent airline whose agent is Mistral Voyages. One-way fares from Libreville are: CFA 39,000 to Bata; CFA 59,850 to São Tomé; and CFA 72,500 to Pointe-Noire.

LAND
Minibus & Bush Taxi
Gabon has a good system of minibuses, although they are the most expensive in Africa (ie, about the same as 2nd-class on the train). Fares from Libreville are: CFA 8000 to Lambaréné; CFA 14,000 to Mouila; and CFA 15,000 to Bitam.

To/From the Congo The major route is via Mouila and N'Dendé. From Libreville to Mouila, it's a long one-day trip by minibus. Do not expect to see much traffic south of N'Dendé. There's reportedly a truck from N'Dendé to Kibangou (the Congo) on Tuesdays and Fridays; anticipate quite a few beer stops along the way.

You can also get to the Congo via Franceville – the trip is more comfortable but also longer and more expensive. The big advantage is that all but about 150 km of the trip is by train provided the train on the Congo side is running again (it wasn't in 1992). After taking the Transgabonais to Franceville, take a series of bush taxis south-west to Moanda, Bakoumba and Mbinda (the Congo), then board the Mbinda to Loubomo train, and at Loubomo transfer trains and proceed to Brazzaville or Pointe-Noire.

To/From Cameroun Travelling by bush taxis and minibuses from Yaoundé to Libreville takes about three days, the longest day being the 529-km stretch from Oyem to Libreville, which takes about 15 hours and costs CFA 17,000.

Warning: Coming from Cameroun, you absolutely must get an entry stamp in Bitam from immigration. The standard fine for infractions is CFA 35,000!

To/From Equatorial Guinea The Libreville to Bata (Equatorial Guinea) route is via the border town of Cocobeach. From Bata the trip to Libreville can be done in one long day as taxis leave from Cocobeach for Libreville (CFA 4000, 2½ hours) until at least 6 pm, but from Libreville to Bata it takes 1½ to two days with a night in Acalayong where there is no accommodation. You'll find large motorised dugout canoes between about 8 am and 4 pm (sometimes later) to take you across the Estuaire du Muni to Acalayong; they leave when full and take 40 minutes, sometimes double that. The fare is CFA 4000 but with foreigners they often try to charge much more. Customs officials charge CFA 2000 (passport registration) at Cocobeach and CFA 1500 on the Equatorial Guinea side (CFA 500 when leaving Equatorial Guinea).

Car
Petrol and diesel cost CFA 300 and CFA 195 a litre, respectively. Despite the country's wealth, Gabon has fewer km of paved roads than just about any country in Africa of comparable size – less than 400 km in the countryside. However, the dirt roads are well maintained, and during the rainy season, the rains usually occur at night. So the roads are

actually not as bad as you might expect. The extreme slipperiness of the dirt roads during and shortly after a rainfall is a major concern as it can make driving dangerous. Even after the roads have dried a bit after rain, drive slowly as getting stuck in the mud is always a possibility. Come prepared for all eventualities (eg carry a strong rope or a cable).

The journey times during the dry season (June to September) are as follows:

Route	Distance	Time Taken
Yaoundé to Libreville (via Oyem)	940 km	two long days
Libreville to Brazzaville	1245 km	three to four days
Libreville to Lambaréné	232 km	three to four hours
Libreville to Franceville	762 km	two days

The Libreville to Lambaréné road is paved for two-thirds of the distance. You cannot drive from Libreville to Port-Gentil.

The major road to the Congo is via Lambaréné, Mouila and N'Dendé. During the dry season, it's possible to make it from Libreville to the Congo border in one very long, gruelling day but 1½ days is more typical. It's not possible to drive along the coast from Libreville to Equatorial Guinea because there are no car-carrying barges at Cocobeach, only canoes. (Ask, as this could have changed.) For now the best route to Equatorial Guinea is via Oyem.

Car Rental Avis, Hertz and Eurocar are all represented, as well as local car-rental companies. For their office addresses, see the Libreville and Port-Gentil Getting Around sections. Rates are ridiculously high. Hertz in Port-Gentil, for example, charges CFA 20,730 per day for its cheapest vehicle plus CFA 185 per km plus CFA 3800 daily insurance plus 14% tax (ie almost US$300 per day assuming you travel 200 km). So do what most business people do – hire a taxi by the day.

SEA

The *Solmar II* leaves Port Môle (the *ancien* (old) port) in Libreville for São Tomé about every five days. The cost is CFA 25,000 and the trip takes 24 hours. The boat stays overnight in Libreville and then heads back to São Tomé the next day around noon. The day of departure from Libreville is only known a day or two in advance. You can find out by calling the São Tomé Embassy in Libreville, which is notified as the boat is leaving São Tomé.

Getting Around

AIR

Air Gabon has regular flights from Libreville to all the major interior towns, including two flights on most days from Libreville to Port-Gentil (CFA 21,500 one way) and one a day to Franceville (CFA 48,100 one way). Air Gabon offers a 30% reduction on weekend trips on its domestic flights to/from anywhere within Gabon but you must depart on a Friday or Saturday and return on a Sunday or Monday. It also offers, reportedly, a 30% student discount on interior flights.

Flying to the coastal regions is much more complicated. Air Gabon has three flights a week from Libreville via Port-Gentil to Gamba (near Setté Cama), two of which also stop in Omboué near Iguéla. The one-way fare from Libreville to Omboué is CFA 20,400. The only other option is to charter a plane with Air Inter Gabon out of Port-Gentil. Prices are sky-high, eg CFA 390,000 for an eight-seater plane from Port-Gentil to Iguéla (CFA 780,000 round trip). The other charter companies are Air Affairs Gabon, Héli-Afric and Air Service.

MINIBUS, BUSH TAXI & TRUCK

Minibuses are much more popular than bush taxis but both are very expensive (eg the Libreville to Lambaréné fare is CFA 8000). They also vary greatly in quality. Everything may be smooth sailing on one trip but on another the vehicle may sputter along and finally conk out for good in the middle of the trip.

Bush taxis in Gabon can sometimes be quite dangerous – during the rainy season the roads can become very slippery.

Moreover, some of the drivers are maniacs and are liable to get drunk if given half a chance. Most drivers are sober but if yours gets drunk, catch the next car.

Minibuses go in all directions, but the number of people travelling is relatively small, so don't expect much choice of vehicles, even from Libreville. From Libreville to Franceville, Moanda or Lastoursville, travelling 2nd-class on the train is as cheap as on a minibus. Travelling by train is a lot faster, but road travel is far more interesting and sometimes more fun although less comfortable.

For other destinations, you can sometimes cut costs slightly by taking trucks; the place to catch them in Libreville is on the outskirts of town at Km 5.

TRAIN

The Transgabonais to Franceville was inaugurated in December 1986. Be appreciative – it cost over US$4 billion and took 12 years to complete. First and 2nd-class fares from Libreville to Franceville cost CFA 27,600 and CFA 22,100, respectively. There's a 30% discount for groups of 10 people or more; it's worth forming a group with other people heading for the same destination. If your ticket seller doesn't know about the special group fares (often the case), ask to see the station manager.

The 1st-class compartments have air-con and a bar but no restaurant or sleeping berths. Neither 1st-class nor 2nd-class seats can be reserved, so even in 1st class you may find yourself standing for long distances if you do not get to the railway station well in advance of departure. The 2nd-class compartments have no air-con, carpeting or bar carriage but otherwise they are very similar, hence the small difference in price. There's far more overcrowding in the 2nd-class compartments, which accounts for all the yelling,

pushing, screaming and fighting to get on the train. The trains, which have well-padded reclining seats with arm rests, are already showing considerable wear but they are still quite comfortable.

Libreville's railway station is in Owendo, about 10 km south of central Libreville. Trains leave Owendo at 9 am (Tuesdays and Saturdays) and 8.15 pm (Wednesdays, Fridays and Sundays). From Franceville they leave for Libreville at 9.10 pm on Tuesdays, 9.30 am on Thursdays, 8.10 pm on Fridays, and 12.30 pm on Saturdays and Sundays. The Libreville to Franceville trip is supposed to take about 10½ hours but trains often arrive several hours late despite their punctual departures. Most stations along the route are way out of town and taxis may charge outrageous prices. Unfortunately there is often no alternative.

BOAT

There are several boats which plough between Libreville and Port-Gentil almost every day, and they all cost between CFA 13,000 and CFA 14,500. The fastest is the *Elsa-Dorothie* (La Vedette) which takes four hours, with five departures a week in either direction. Uro-Gabon also has two small boats which leave every morning in either direction, taking five hours. The boats are quite comfortable and serve drinks and sandwiches but they occasionally break down. Finally, there is the slower *La Léombi* (the *grand bateau*, or large boat) which is better for those with considerable luggage. It takes eight hours, with one round trip every two days.

There are also boats ploughing up and down the Ogooué River between Port-Gentil and Lambaréné (some go on to Ndjolé). The smaller boats leave Port-Gentil on Mondays and Fridays, cost CFA 10,000 and take about 10 hours. The larger *Azingo* (a grand bateau) makes only one round trip a week, leaving Port-Gentil on Mondays and Lambaréné on Thursdays. The *Azingo* is more like a floating village and potentially more fun if you don't mind sleeping overnight on board.

First-class/2nd-class fares are CFA 11,550/
7500 and it takes 1½ days upriver and 24
hours downriver, with stops in lots of villages en route. For details, see the
Port-Gentil Getting There & Away section.

Libreville

At first glimpse, Libreville, which has a population of 350,000, looks like a diminutive
Miami Beach – with big ocean-view hotels,
office buildings, wide highways, fancy
shops, and taxis everywhere. You won't find
any beggars, and there are good beaches
right in town – a rarity for major African
cities. Those who insist on having their creature comforts shouldn't find too much to
complain about. The main problem is that it
all costs so much. According to 1993 figures,
Libreville is the world's second most expensive city, exceeded only by Tokyo.

Those who know Libreville, however,
will tell you that the African quarters are as
lively and vibrant as you'll find anywhere in
Africa. Certainly there is no lack of nightclubs and the African quarters are full of
fairly cheap places to eat and drink, and you
get to mix with the locals. Moreover, they are
convenient to get to and not nearly as dangerous as those of some African capitals.

In short, while Libreville is expensive, it's
no more expensive than N'Djamena, Bangui
or Brazzaville if you know where to go, and
it's safer than Bangui, Brazzaville, Yaoundé
or Douala.

The people can be very friendly; perhaps
you'll end up in an African home as I did.
Just be careful if you decide to drink with
Gabonese. When it comes to drinking beer
or palm wine, what you may view as an
extraordinary day of boozing is likely to be
routine for them.

Orientation
Boulevard de l'Indépendance, often referred
to as the Blvd de la Mer or the Bord de Mer,
runs along the coast from the airport south
through town, eventually becoming the

highway to Owendo 10 km to the south,
which is where you'll find the port and
railway terminal. The heart of the city is the
one-km stretch between the Palais
Présidentiel and the landmark Novotel
Rapontchombo, both on this street, plus the
area inland for one km towards the Complexe Omnisports which includes the Omar
Bongo Stadium. The wide Cours Pasteur
heads inland past the Palais Présidentiel
towards Ave Félix Éboué and Ave Col
Parant, which run diagonally, connecting the
Rapontchombo and Marché du Mont-Bouët,
just north of which is the gare routière on
Blvd Bessieux.

Three of the livelier African sections, all
near the centre around the Complexe
Omnisports, are Nombakélé to the south of
the Complexe Omnisports, Akébéville to the
east, and the Marché du Mont-Bouët area to
the north.

Further north, just off the wide Blvd Omar
Bongo, is the famous Hypermarché M'Bolo
shopping centre, half of which was burned
down during the riots of 1990. North of it is
Quartier Louis, which is a major restaurant
area; you enter it on Blvd Joseph Deemin just
north of the fairgrounds and the old port, Port
Môle. East of Louis is Quartier Derrière
Prison, where you'll find a number of embassies as well as the university and the Peace
Corps. Further east is the Voie Express
(Autoroute), which is a wide bypass around
the city, starting near the airport and forming
a semi-circle around the city.

Information
Tourist Office Gabontour (☎ 746788/90),
the government's travel advisory service,
has a small office at the airport.

Money Most of the major banks for changing money are in the heart of town – Barclays
(☎ 741300; fax 773223), BIPG (☎ 722626)
and Banque de Paris et des Pays-Bas Gabon
(☎ 722507), which are within a block of each
other on Blvd de l'Indépendance, and BICIG
(☎ 722613) and UGB (☎ 721514), which are
on the same block on Ave Col Parant.

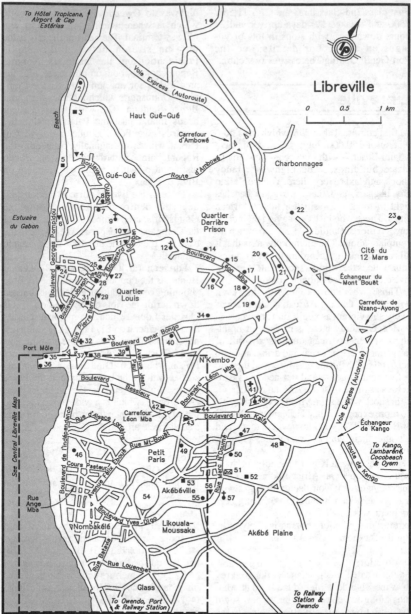

Libreville

To Hôtel Tropicana,
Airport & Cap
Estérias

Voie Express (Autoroute)

0   0.5   1 km

Haut Gué-Gué

Carrefour
d'Ambowé

Beach

Boulevard Gué-Gué

Gué-Gué

Estuaire
du Gabon

Route d'Ambowé

Charbonnages

Quartier
Derrière
Prison

Boulevard Georges Pompidou

Boulevard Joseph Deemin

Boulevard Quaben

Quartier
Louis

Boulevard Léon Mba

Cité du
12 Mars

Échangeur du
Mont Bouët

Carrefour de
Nzang-Ayong

Boulevard Pierre Beto

Rue Pierre Beto

Boulevard Omar Bongo

Port Môle

Avenue Jean Paul II

N'Kembo

Boulevard
Bessieux

Boulevard Léon Mba

Carrefour
Léon Mba

Boulevard Léon Kala

Rue d'Alsace Lorraine

Rue d'Alsace Lorraine

Rue Mt-Bouët

Petit
Paris

Échangeur
de Kango

To Kango,
Lambaréné,
Cocobeach
& Oyem

Route de Kango

Voie Express (Autoroute)

See Central Libreville Map

Boulevard de l'Indépendance

Cours Pasteur

Avenue Félix Éboué

Rue Marc N'Douna

Rue
Ange
Mba

Akébéville

Akébé Plaine

Boulevard Yves-Digo

Nombakélé

Likouala-
Moussaka

Rue Batana

Glass

Rue Louembet

To Owendo, Port
& Railway Station

To Railway
Station &
Owendo

■ PLACES TO STAY

3 Hôtel Okoumé-Palace Inter-
   Continental
5 Hôtel Dialogue
28 Hôtel Louis
31 Hôtel l'Oiseau de Paradis
38 Mission Catholique Sainte-Marie
42 Maison Liebermann
48 Motel Rio
52 Motel Will-Jess
53 Ebéné Hôtel

▼ PLACES TO EAT

4 Restaurant les Terraces d'Estuaire
6 Chez Moustache
10 Restaurant Papa Union (No 1)
11 Restaurant le Baobab
17 Restaurant Pic Nic
26 Restaurant Bon Coin de Glass &
   Restaurant la Pinède
27 Restaurant Africana
29 Restaurant le Paradiso & Gabon Pain
30 Restaurant le Paillote
31 Restaurant l'Oiseau de Paradis
32 Restaurant Papa Union (No 2)
33 Restaurant American Burger
35 Café des Marins & Coupé-Coupé
   Vendor
37 Restaurants Chez Michel de
   Gonfaron & la Bonne Bouffe
44 Cheap Senegalese Restaurants
53 Good Street Food Area
56 Restauant le Palmier
57 Restaurant le Pippermint

OTHER

1 CAR Embassy

2 Belgian Embassy
7 Zaïrian Embassy
8 Congolese Embassy & Citibank
9 Église St-Anne
12 Église Evangélique
13 Benin Consulate
14 Nigerian Consulate
15 École Normale Superieure
16 University
17 Camerounian Embassy
18 Brasserie SOBRAGA
19 TV Station
20 Peace Corps Office
21 Palais de la Justice
22 Palais de Conférences
23 Palais des 12 Mars
24 Maringa Nightclub
25 Marché de Louis
32 Hôpital Jeanne Ébori & Fairgrounds
33 Hypermarché M'Bolo Shopping
   Centre (Grande Pharmacie des
   Forestière)
34 Japanese Embassy
35 Boats for Ekwata Beach & Pointe-
   Dénis
36 Ferry Port for São Tomé (Solmar II)
   & Port-Gentil (Elsa-Dorothie)
39 Banque Centrale
40 Hôtel de Ville
41 Hôpital N'Kembo
43 Gare Routière
45 L'Église St-Michel
46 Palais Présidentiel
47 São Tomé Embassy
49 Marché du Mont-Buët
50 Maison du Parti
51 Branch Post Office
54 Complexe Omnisports (Stadium)
55 Equatorial Guinea Embassy
57 Église d'Akébé

Citibank is inconveniently located four km north of the centre. When comparing rates, don't overlook the BIPG as its rates are often the lowest.

Post & Telecommunications Libreville has four post offices; the main one, Centre Ville, is on Blvd de l'Indépendance and there's a coin-operated phone one block to the north of it. To make long-distance calls, try the communications centre on Ave Félix Éboué, east of Air Afrique.

Foreign Embassies Some of the major embassies and consulates in Libreville's central area and west thereof are:

Côte d'Ivoire
    Immeuble Diamont (Barclays Bank building)
    Blvd de l'Indépendance (☎ 720596)
Equatorial Guinea
    Blvd Yves-Digo, before Église d'Akébé,
    Akébéville (☎ 763015)
France
    Consulate, Rue Ange Mba, near Air Afrique
    (☎ 743420/1)

Germany
BP 299 (☎ 760188) ·
São Tomé
Blvd des Frères de Bruchard, near the Maison du Parti (☎ 721546)
USA
Blvd de l'Indépendance, near the Novotel Rapontchombo (☎ 762003/4; fax 745507; telex 5250)

Those north of the central area include:

Benin
Consulate, Blvd Léon Mba, Quartier Derrière Prison (☎ 737692)
Cameroun
Blvd Léon Mba, Quartier Derrière Prison
The CAR
Ambassador's residence and consulate, north of Voie Express near the airport (☎ 737761)
Congo
Gué-Gué, just off Blvd Ouaban near Citibank (☎ 677078)
Nigeria
Blvd Léon Mba, Quartier Derrière Prison (☎ 732201)
Zaïre
Gué-Gué, just off Blvd Ouaban near Citibank (☎ 738141/2)

Other diplomatic missions and honorary consulates include: Algeria, Belgium (☎ 73-2992), Canada, Egypt, Italy, Japan (☎ 732297, BP 2259), Mauritania, Morocco, Netherlands, Senegal, Spain (Barclays Bank building), Sweden, the UK (☎ 722985, BP 476).

Bookshops The best bookshops are at the top hotels (Méridien, Rapontchombo and Okoumé Palace). In the town centre, the Sogalivre has closed down; Librairie Nouvelle on Ave Col Parant (the same block as Air Afrique) and the Maison de la Presse a block south on the same street are about as good as you'll find. They carry mostly French magazines and newspapers in addition to stationery items, so you won't find many books in English, such as Mary Kingsley's *Travels in West Africa*.

Supermarkets The two best supermarkets are Score (formerly Paris-Gabon), which is in the heart of town on the corner of Rue Lafond and Ave Col Parant, and the M'Bolo supermarket at the Hypermarché M'Bolo shopping centre on the wide Blvd Omar Bongo. The latter has not just food but household items, books, clothing, etc; there are all kinds of stores in the adjoining mall. Another large supermarket in the town centre is Libre Marché on Blvd Yves-Digo.

For a large department store stocked with all kinds of goods, head for CK2, which is in the centre one block south of the intersection of Blvd de l'Indépendance and Cours Pasteur.

Travel Agencies One of the best travel agencies is Eurafrique Voyages (☎ 762787, 766659; fax 761897; telex 5458) in the town centre on Rue Lafond near Score. For airline reservations this agency is the best but like all the travel agencies here it will not accept payment for airline tickets with credit cards.

Eurafrique can also arrange tours. A tour to Lambaréné, for example, should cost about CFA 20,000 a person (seven people minimum). Eurafrique is the agent for American Express, but if you're desperate for cash, don't expect much using your card here because the limit is US$200 (US$500 with a gold card) every 21 days.

Another excellent and friendlier agency is Mistral Voyages (☎ 760421, 761222), which is three blocks away in Immeuble Diamont (Barclays Bank building) at the intersection of Blvd de l'Indépendance and Rue Cureau. Its principal business is handling airlines reservations but it's also the agent for Equatorial International Airlines and offers special weekend package deals on flights to São Tomé which are not available through other agencies. Round-trip air fare plus lodging and meals for three days and three nights at the island's best hotel, for example, costs CFA 160,000 a person (double occupancy), compared to the round-trip air fare alone of CFA 119,700.

Other travel agencies include Ekwata Loisirs (☎ 761338), Inter Tours (☎ 762787) and Opépé Voyages (☎ 762932).

Pharmacies Two of the best pharmacies are

the Grande Pharmacie des Forestière (☎ 722352) at the Hypermarché M'Bolo shopping centre and Pharmacie le Président (☎ 741155), which is in the town centre on Ave Félix Éboué opposite Air Afrique.

Medical Services See Medical Services in the Facts for the Visitor section at the start of this chapter.

Musée des Arts et Traditions
This poorly marked museum, in town on the ocean road next to the modern Elf Gabon building, two blocks north of the Novotel Rapontchombo, is one of the best in Central Africa and definitely worth a visit as the quality of the objects on display is high. In particular, the wooden and grass-covered masks, which are mostly Téké, Fang and Mitsogho pieces, stand out. There's also a wonderful collection of small carved harps, *fétiches* and baskets plus an authentic Mitsogho temple.

Other displays include wooden musical instruments (drums, xylophone, mvet, etc), kitchen implements, blacksmith tools and photos of them at work, as well as Fang headdresses, *caches-sexes* (woven jewellery which covers the pubic region) and pottery. The animated guide, who is really captivating, makes the tour even more worthwhile. There's no entrance fee but the guide expects a tip for his standard 45-minute tour. Opening hours are from 8 am to noon and 3 to 6 pm on weekdays.

Marché du Mont-Bouët
This vibrant market a km from the centre, a few blocks north of the Complexe Omnisports, is worth checking out, as it compares favourably with the best markets in Central Africa.

L'Église St-Michel
St-Michel church, in N'Kembo about a km further inland from Marché du Mont-Bouët, is a landmark because of the unusual wooden columns carved by a blind Gabonese craftsman. There are 31 columns in all, each with a biblical scene carved in an imaginative and vigorous style. Equally interesting is the choir, which is accompanied by drums and balafons. The best time to hear it is at the Sunday 10.30 am mass.

Palais Présidentiel
The president's mansion, a Libreville landmark in the heart of town overlooking the ocean on the corner of Blvd de l'Indépendance and Cours Pasteur, was built in the 1970s at a cost of US$800 million. The marble used was imported from Italy (even though Gabon produces its own), and the Greek columns are unique in this area of the world – another example of Bongo's strong attachment to Western culture. Photographs are not allowed.

You're not allowed inside the palace, but reportedly among the contents are an elevated throne-like marble chair, a long marble-topped desk with push-button controls to make walls recede and doors open, a banquet hall for 3000 people, a bathtub big enough to swim several strokes in, two theatres, and a nightclub.

Organised Tours
For tours of the city, Lambaréné and elsewhere plus return boat rides on weekends to Ekwata Beach, see Ekwata Loisirs (☎ 761-338), which has a branch office at the Hôtel Okoumé Palace; tours are their speciality.

Activities
The cheapest pool is the one at the Complexe Omnisports; it's open every afternoon and costs CFA 500. Most of the major hotels also have pools that are open to the public. Those at the Okoumé Palace and Gamba hotels cost CFA 1000 while those at the Méridien and Rapontchombo hotels cost CFA 2000; all of them are quite popular at lunch time. If you use the pool at the Hôtel Gamba, you can also use the beach there. The Gamba and Tropicana are the only hotels with good beaches. (The Gamba also has sailboards for rent.) The beach just north of Hôtel Dialogue is the most accessible public beach in town but it attracts only a few bathers, mostly on weekends.

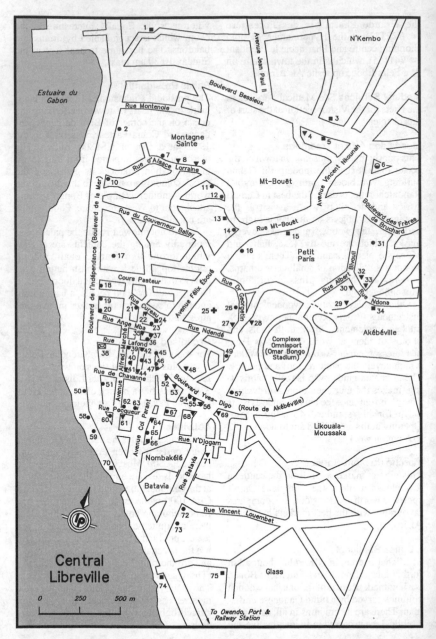

Estuaire du
Gabon

N'Kembo

Montagne
Sainte

Mt-Bouët

Petit
Paris

Akébéville

Likouala-
Moussaka

Complexe
Omnisport
(Omar Bongo
Stadium)

Nombakélé

Batavia

Glass

Central
Libreville

0   250   500 m

To Owendo, Port &
Railway Station

■ PLACES TO STAY

1 Mission Catholique Sainte-
Marie
3 Mission de l'Immaculée
Concepcion (Seminaire St-Jean)
5 Maison Liebermann
13 Hôtel Équateur
15 Hôtel Mont-Bouët
24 Hôtel Mont de Crystal
34 Hôtel Ebéné
66 Hôtel le Castel
70 Novotel Rapontchombo
74 Le Méridien Re-N'Dama
75 Auberge de l'Estuaire

▼ PLACES TO EAT

4 Bar-Restaurant les Loucioles
8 Restaurant Keur Bamba
9 Coupé-Coupé (Grilled Meat)
Vendor
14 Pizzeria
15 Restaurant les Cinq Palmiers,
Royal Hamburger & Cheap
African Restaurant
22 Salon de Thé Kilimanjaro
23 La Brasserie de l'Ocean
27 Restaurant le Grillade
28 Trait d'Union (African)
29 Good Street Food
30 Brochette Seller
32 Restaurant Las Vegas &
Restaurant Africain
33 Street Food
35 Boulangerie le Bon Pain
41 Restaurant le Pescadou
44 Pâtisserie Pélisson
46 Terrace le Petit Gourmand
48 Restaurant le Paris
52 Restaurant le Crepuscule
53 Restaurant Bigmag
56 Two No-Name Senegalese
Restaurants & L'Étoile Senegalese
Restaurant
61 Restaurant le Tarpon
64 Restaurant Chez Nous & Le Moka
d'Or Salon de Thé
68 Grilled Fish/Chicken Vendors
69 Brochette Vendors
71 St Hilaire Restaurant

OTHER

2 BICIG Bank

6 Gare Routière
7 Black Moon Nightclub
10 Air France/UTA
11 Le Palace Nightclub
12 Vertigo & Midnight Express
Nightclubs
13 Polyclinique Chambrier
14 Komo Cinéma, Komo Nightclub &
Pizzeria
16 Sûreté
17 Palais Présidentiel
18 CK2 Department Store & Banque
de Paris et des Pays-Bas
19 Mistral Voyages, Barclays Bank &
Côte d'Ivoire Embassy
20 BIPG Bank & Air Gabon
(International Flights)
21 Sabena
23 Scotch Club & Studio Steph
(Photo Supplies)
25 Hôpital Général
26 New Miami Club
31 Marché du Mont-Bouët
35 Small Supermarket
36 Librairie Nouvelle & Artisanat
37 Air Afrique & French Consulate
38 Post Office (Centre Ville)
39 Eurafrique Voyages
40 Cameroun Airlines & Nigeria
Airways
41 Fisher's (Sport Fishing Store)
42 Score Supermarket
43 Air Zaïre, Mobil Station & Photo la
3em Oeil
45 BICIG Bank & Pharmacie le
Président
46 Librairie Maison de la Press
47 UGB Bank
49 Sporting Club
50 National Museum & Elf Gabon
51 Air Gabon (Domestic Flights)
54 Le Diam's Nightclub
55 Libre Marché Supermarket
57 Shell Station
58 Swiss Air
59 French Embassy
60 US Embassy
62 Le Village des Artisans
63 Art Malgache
65 American Cultural Centre
67 Key Club
68 Cinéma le Gabon
71 St Hilaire Nightclub
72 La Frégate Nightclub
73 Lambada Nightclub

To rent scuba-diving tanks and equipment, see Gaboa (☎ 700746) on Blvd de l'Indépendance in Quartier Glass or Brigade Nautique on the same road next to the fairgrounds. For fishing, especially deep-sea fishing, see Fisher's in the town centre on Ave Alfred-Marché near the US Embassy.

For tennis or squash, try the Hôtel Okoumé Palace; it has two courts of each. Nonguests may play tennis for CFA 1500 a person (CFA 2000 under lights) and squash for CFA 1000. The Méridien and Gamba hotels also have tennis courts. And you can bowl and eat hamburgers at the Sporting Club near the Complexe Omnisports.The Golf Club de l'Estuaire on the road to Owendo has an 18-hole golf course with sand greens.

Places to Stay – bottom end

Libreville is very expensive, but there are several places to stay which are relatively cheap. The most popular is *Maison Liebermann* (☎ 761955), which is 300 metres west of the gare routière at 1390 Blvd Bessieux. Part of the seminary across the street, it has quite a few rooms and the friendly staff welcome travellers enthusiastically. The rooms and baths are spotless and cost CFA 5000/6000 for one/two people. You don't have to walk far to find cheap food, either.

You might also try the *Mission de l'Immaculée Conception* (or Seminaire St-Jean) across the street. In the past travellers have got clean double rooms there with access to hot showers for CFA 2500, but it's not clear whether they continue to rent rooms.

Mission Catholique St-Marie charges about the same as the Liebermann for its rooms but they're harder to get as there are fewer of them. To get there, from Maison Liebermann, walk west along Blvd Bessieux to the end (1¼ km), then turn right for one short block along the ocean road. The two-storey dormitory lodging is next to the church.

There are also other Catholic missions in town but it's not clear if any of them have rooms for rent. Paroisses St-André and Église St-Michel, for example, do not. The *Peace Corps* (☎ 733333), which is four km north-east from the town centre just beyond the Palais de la Justice, can't accept travellers because their rooms are reserved for volunteers. On the other hand, do check the *Imprimerie St Joseph* opposite the Palais Présidentiel; it has rooms for CFA 4000 but the owner is unfriendly and it's often full.

Among the hotels, the best by far is the well-managed *Hôtel Mont-Bouët* (☎ 765-846/7; fax 722008). Relative to other hotels in town, it's an outstanding deal at CFA 7000/11,000 for spotless rooms with fans/air-con, firm mattresses and clean private bathrooms (with good hot showers). It has secure locks, safe luggage storage and is centrally located – only a seven-minute walk from the gare routière down Rue Mont-Bouët towards the centre. It doesn't have a laundry service or a restaurant; there are plenty of good cheap places to eat nearby. If you get here before noon, your chances of getting a ventilated room are good, otherwise you may have to settle for a more expensive air-con room.

Next in line price-wise is the *Ebéné Hôtel* (☎ 744093; formerly La Corbeille), which is a km east on Rue Ndona in Akébéville near the Complexe Omnisports. The rooms, which cost from CFA 8000 to CFA 10,000, are fairly large and have fans but the management is rude and the hotel is a dump compared to the Mont-Bouët. It is, however, in an excellent area for street food. If you stay here, check your room key; they used to be all the same and may still be. The similarly priced *Hôtel Ozouaki* is closed.

Motel Will-Jess (☎ 740862), which is a km further east on the same road as the Ebéné is good value but less conveniently located. It has eight decent air-con rooms with TVs, phones and attached tiled bathrooms for CFA 10,000 to CFA 15,000. It also has the 'Eden' nightclub and an attractive thatched-roof restaurant in the front with African and European specialities. The food may be good but it is not all that cheap.

Places to Stay – middle

Hôtel Tropicana (☎ 731531/2; fax 736574; telex 5558), with clean, air-con singles/doubles for 12,000/15,000, has the ambience of a 1st-class hotel and is the best hotel in this category and hence frequently full; credit cards not accepted. Only one km before the airport (10 km from the town centre), it has an excellent beach but no pool and a very pleasant breezy restaurant. However, at CFA 4500 for the plat du jour, eating here can be quite expensive and there are no cheap alternatives nearby.

Quartier Louis, which is closer to the centre (three km to the north), has two good alternatives. The long-standing *Hôtel Louis* (☎ 732569/97), on Rue Pierro Barro, has 18 air-con rooms with TVs and carpets plus a decent restaurant. The rooms start from CFA 12,500. Unlike the Tropicana, the hotel is in a good, relatively inexpensive restaurant area.

Two blocks away on the same street is the *Hôtel-Restaurant l'Oiseau de Paradis* (☎ 734716), a popular, family-run Chinese restaurant which has some very decent accommodation. The spotless, air-con rooms with Chinese wall decorations and high quality tiled bathrooms, are excellent value at CFA 12,000.

About a km south of the central area, one long block inland from the top-end Méridien hotel, the 10-room *Auberge de l'Estuaire)* (☎ 725337; formerly Hôtel Glass), is a B&B with a French atmosphere. Highly recommended, it's a super buy at CFA 10,000 for an air-con room. The rooms are immaculate and have tiled floors, basins and showers, with shared toilets. You may want to look elsewhere for meals (breakfast costs CFA 1500 and lunch/dinner costs CFA 5000).

There are also two mid-range hotels in the town centre. One is the popular new *Hôtel Equateur* (☎ 740786), a block behind the Komo Cinéma, with only about 12 rooms. It has a homey atmosphere and charges CFA 16,600 for an air-con room.

The other is the older French-run *Hôtel le Castel* (☎ 725019), roughly two blocks north-east of the top-end Novotel Rapon-

tchombo. The air-con rooms which cost CFA 15,000 are not as good value as those at the Estuaire and Equateur. The restaurants at both these places are decent but relatively expensive.

Hôtel Dialogue (☎ 732085; telex 5355) on Blvd de l'Indépendance was once the city's top hotel but now it's closed except for one section which, judging from the hotel's morgue-like ambience, seems likely to close soon. You can get a room for CFA 17,000 but I certainly don't recommend it.

Motel Rio, on busy Blvd Léon Kalfa near the Voie Express (Autoroute) and the inland highway (Route de Kango), has clean but overpriced air-con rooms at CFA 12,500; unless you're arriving by road late at night and are looking for the first hotel you see, avoid it.

Places to Stay – top end

The newest and most popular deluxe hotel is the *Le Méridien Re-N'Dama* (formerly Sheraton). It's about a km south of the central area and on the water, with a pool overlooking the ocean, but the beach is not usable.

The popular *Novotel Rapontchombo*, which is also doing good business but is not so luxurious, is just up the road and even better situated near the centre of town. As at the Méridien, there's a breezy pool overlooking the ocean and a beach that cannot be used. The empty *Dowé Novotel*, which is further north on Blvd de l'Indépendance, is perhaps more inspiring as a charred memorial to the riots of 1990 than it ever was as a hotel.

Hôtel Okoumé Palace Inter-Continental has more facilities than any of these hotels and is probably the most deluxe of all, but the location, five km north of the Rapontchombo in the direction of the airport and a block off the ocean, is not as ideal. Business is slower here, so you may be able to cut a special rate. If you can show them you're connected with any business or organisation in Libreville, for example, the manager is very likely to offer you a corporate discount. Even a business card might do the trick.

The only advantage of the overpriced *Hôtel Mont de Crystal*, a modern 49-room highrise, is that it's right in the centre of town.

If you're looking for a hotel with either a good beach or slightly more reasonable rates, your best bet is the *Hôtel Gamba* facing the airport, about 11 km from the centre. Because it's such good value for money, it is popular and usually full, so you will definitely have to make a reservation.

The prices below do not include the CFA 500 per person tax.

Hôtel Gamba (☎ 732736, 732267; telex 5375), CFA 24,200/28,200 for singles/doubles, pool, bookshop, tennis, sailboards, excellent beach, credit cards AE, D.

Hôtel Mont de Crystal (☎ 762520; fax 746501; telex 5724), CFA 28,200/32,200 for singles/doubles, tiny pool, credit cards AE, D.

Hôtel Okoumé Palace Inter-Continental (☎ 732614; fax 731629; telex 5271), CFA 29,600 to CFA 35,800 per room, pool, tennis, squash, nightclub, Hertz car rental, bookshop, credit cards AE, D, V, CB.

Le Méridien Re-N'Dama (☎ 766161; fax 742924; telex 5432), CFA 32,700 per room, pool, tennis, oceanfront, good bookshop, casino, Avis car rental, credit cards AE, D, V, CB.

Novotel Rapontchombo (☎ 764742; fax 761345; telex 5350), CFA 28,200/32,200 for singles/doubles, pool, casino, oceanfront, Avis car rental, credit cards AE, D, V, CB.

Credit Cards: AE – American Express, D – Diners, V – Visa, CB – Citibank

Places to Eat

Cheap Eats One of the better places for cheap eats is the area around the gare routière and south of the nearby Marché du Mont-Bouët. Across from the gare, for example, you'll find several Senegalese restaurants, including *Restaurant Rio Nunez*, where you can get breakfast for CFA 300 among other things.

Further south past the market towards the Ebéné Hôtel and the Complexe Omnisports is Rue Ndona, which is lined with cheap restaurants and street food places. One is *Restaurant Las Vegas*, which has standard Senegalese restaurant food and is very crowded at lunch time with single men. You may find virtually everyone eating foufou viande. It's not on the menu and costs CFA 300 a plate. *Restaurant Africain* next door is similar in all respects except that its plate of foufou viande is larger and costs CFA 500. Across the street, a brochette lady serves delicious beef brochettes and fries, each for CFA 100. Further down the street near the Ebéné, there are lots of stalls with street food, mostly brochettes, fries, grilled fish and fried plantain. These places are open all day and until late at night.

Another good area for cheap food day and night is around Cinéma le Gabon on Rue Batavia in Nombakélé, south of the Complexe Omnisports. There are three very popular Senegalese restaurants near the cinema intersection including *L'Étoile Senegalese Restaurant*, which has lait couscous for CFA 500, omelette with peas for CFA 700, etc. Across the street you'll find wonderful grilled brochettes for CFA 100 as well as a lady selling grilled fish for CFA 300 to CFA 700 and grilled chicken for CFA 800. A block down Rue Batavia is the famous *St Hilaire Restaurant-Nightclub*, which has an adjoining cafeteria serving cheap food, eg riz viande for CFA 600. *Mama Martine's*, also in Nombakélé, has also been recommended; she apparently serves good Camerounian food for CFA 700 a plate.

If you're staying at Maison Liebermann, try the *Bar-Restaurant les Loucioles* which is slightly up-market compared to the food places at the gare routière. If you're staying at Hôtel Mont-Bouët, I highly recommend the no-name restaurant almost next door. For CFA 400 to CFA 600 a plate, depending on what you select, you can fill up on a huge plate of beans, spaghetti, rice and/or plantain with two or three African sauces to choose from. Very popular with taxi drivers in the mornings, it's open only until around 1 pm.

At Port Môle, you'll find a good French bread stand with croissants, etc as well as *Café des Marins*, a popular Senegalese restaurant at the end of the port. Next to it, there's a coupé-coupé vendor.

Libreville has a good number of restaurants, all popular with travellers on the cheap, where you can get excellent meals for CFA 2000 or so. I recommend all listed herein.

One of the best in the centre is the popular breezy *Restaurant Les Cinq Palmiers* (Chez Ali Baba) on Rue Mont-Bouët, 50 metres south from Hôtel Mont-Bouët; it's closed on Sundays. Senegalese poulet yassa, roasted chicken and steak frites all come with salads and cost CFA 1500; with a big Regab beer the bill will come to CFA 1800.

Almost next door is one of the city's most popular fast-food restaurants, *Royal Hamburger*, which is also closed on Sundays. The hamburger, fries and drink special costs CFA 1300 and the fish and chawarma burgers cost CFA 1200 each. About 150 metres further south along the same street is *Las Palmas*, a popular restaurant similar to the Palmiers with a street-side terrace; it's closed on Sundays.

Quartier Louis has a number of inexpensive restaurants, all of which are on Blvd Ouaban, which becomes Rue Pierre Barro, a one-way street heading downhill towards Blvd de l'Indépendance. The most famous is the *Papa Union*, which is very close to the intersection with Blvd de l'Indépendance. Most dishes cost CFA 1750, including filet de boeuf, steak, chicken and merou fish. All of these dishes come with a French salad and a big serving of frics, green peas or rice. Soft drinks/Regab beer cost CFA 400/500. It's popular with Gabonese and expatriates alike for both lunch and dinner; it has air-con and is open daily.

One km further up the hill is the long-standing *Restaurant Bon Coin de Glass*, which is very similar and slightly cheaper – poulet yassa with a quarter carafe of wine, for example, costs CFA 1800. Beyond it you'll pass several other inexpensive restaurants, including a second *Papa Union*.

For the best American fast food in Central Africa, head for the ultramodern *American Burger* (marked 'American Food') at the Hypermarché M'Bolo shopping centre. It's like a real MacDonald's, with hamburgers for CFA 1000 to CFA 1900 among other

things. *Danny's Burger*, opposite the Complexe Omnisports in the Westwood shopping centre, is open 24 hours and has similar fare plus pancakes and three TVs with American and French videos. Or try the more sedate *Terrace le Petit Gourmand*, a tiny sidewalk café on Ave Col Parant near Score supermarket which serves hamburgers for CFA 900, crêpes for CFA 600 to CFA 1500 and pizzas for CFA 2500 and up.

African For authentic African food at rock-bottom prices, try *Restaurant Las Vegas* and the no-name restaurant next to Hôtel Mont-Bouët – both mentioned under Cheap Eats. For West African cooking or something a little more up-market with tablecloths, etc, I highly recommend *Restaurant Keur Bamba*, a very modest restaurant on Rue d'Alsace Lorraine, several blocks down the hill from Komo Cinéma. The food is 100% Senegalese, with specialities such as poulet yassa (CFA 1500), mafé (CFA 800) and fish thieboudienne (CFA 800), the national dish of Senegal. It's open every day.

For more up-market restaurants with Gabonese fare but still relatively inexpensive by Libreville standards, try one of the following: *L'Odika* (☎ 736920) (bush-meat dishes) in Quartier Louis near Gabon Pain; *Chez Marceline* (brochettes recommended) in Akébéville; and *Barracuda* (☎ 701300) (has grilled food and a great atmosphere; closed on Sundays), on the southern outskirts of town on the Owendo road.

Italian Two of the best Italian restaurants are both in Quartier Louis and reasonably priced by Libreville standards, ie fairly expensive. *Restaurant Le Paradiso*, on Rue Pierre Barro, a block away from Hôtel Louis, has excellent food and the ambience is quite relaxed. *Sol Mio*, which is on the same street further down the hill towards Blvd de l'Indépendance, has pizza among other selections and a nice décor. There's also *La Tomate* (☎ 736477) nearby on Blvd Joseph Deemin leading into Quartier Louis. It serves pizza, fish, etc and has a pleasant ambience.

Asian Two of the better and least expensive Chinese restaurants are on Rue Pierre Barro in Quartier Louis. The closest to Blvd de l'Indépendance is *Le Dragon d'Or* (☎ 732512), which is just north of Hôpital Jeanne Ébori. For about CFA 3500 (CFA 2500 at lunch) you can get a meal here as well as at the family-run *Hôtel- Restaurant l'Oiseau de Paradis* (☎ 734716), which is further up on Rue Pierre Barro before Hôtel Louis. Also listed under mid-range hotels, the latter has an elaborate Chinese décor and an inviting ambience.

Lebanese One of the city's best Lebanese restaurants, *Restaurant la Pinède* (☎ 734-584), on Rue Pierre Barro, is roughly 400 metres north of Hôtel Louis on the left. Its prices are in the same range as those of the Asian restaurants (ie CFA 2800 to CFA 3600 for most dishes), and the menu includes fish brochettes, beef dishes and deluxe chicken chawarma sandwiches among other things. Open daily, it's fairly popular at lunch and offers indoor dining as well as outdoors on a breezy porch.

In the centre, *Restaurant Bigmag*, on Blvd Yves-Digo, 200 metres west of the intersection with Rue Batavia, looks like a snack bar and has slightly lower prices – CFA 2500 for a meal; not recommended.

French The cheapest French restaurant in town is probably *Restaurant Chez Nous*, which is in the centre on Ave Col Parant, a block east of the US Embassy and popular with the embassy crowd at lunch time. Main dishes cost around CFA 2200 and you have the choice of eating inside or out on the front terrace. It's closed on Sundays.

A long-time favourite which is slightly more pricey is *Restaurant Chez Michel de Gonfaron* (☎ 762476), which has delicious French food. The setting is very ordinary, so at least when you pay CFA 5000 to CFA 8000 for a meal you'll have the satisfaction that you're paying mainly for the food and not the décor. It's on Blvd Omar Bongo, 50 metres east of Blvd de l'Indépendance and Port Môle. While you're there check the

menu of *Restaurant la Bonne Bouffe* next door; it's somewhat cheaper.

Restaurant le Paillote (☎ 732660), half a km north along Blvd de l'Indépendance, specialises in grilled seafood and steaks; a standard meal costs between CFA 7000 and CFA 10,000. It's closed on Sundays.

Further north on Blvd de l'Indépendance, two km north of Blvd Omar Bongo, is the popular *Chez Moustache* (☎ 732490). It has great food – the steaks here are particularly good; a steak with a glass of wine costs about CFA 5000. It's a friendly place and the owner Patrick knows a lot about Gabon; it's highly recommended.

If price is of no great concern, there are two places in the centre that have been around for a long time, which suggests they must be doing something right – *Restaurant le Paris* (☎ 763093), which is on Blvd Yves-Digo 300 metres south-east of Air Afrique, and *Restaurant le Crepuscule* (☎ 722593), which is 1½ blocks to the west and a block off Blvd Yves-Digo. Le Paris is like a Paris bistro with a nice atmosphere while Le Crepuscule, which is closed on Sundays, has Belgian specialities, with excellent seafood, shrimp curry, veal and crêpes flambés.

Seafood Unless you don't mind paying CFA 15,000 or so, forget about the seafood speciality restaurants. The most central, *Le Pescadou* (☎ 740733), on Ave Alfred-Marché, is open daily. In addition to fish, it specialises in dishes from the Périgord region of France. *L'Ancre de Bacchus* (☎ 732161), on Blvd de l'Indépendance, is the city's top restaurant. It has a fixed menu for CFA 15,800 plus à la carte; it's closed on Sundays.

Hotel Restaurants If you want to gorge yourself, try one of the buffets at the major hotels. The all-you-can-eat lunch buffet at the *Méridien*, for example, costs CFA 7500, ie half the price of a meal at an expensive restaurant.

Pastry Shops For bakeries, keep an eye out for *Chaud Show*, a chain of small white, green-roofed shops scattered across the city. Open until late at night, they serve some of the best bread in town, including pain complet (whole wheat bread), pain de son (bran bread), pain de seigle (rye bread) as well as French baguettes and croissants. In the centre, try *Boulangerie le Bon Pain* a block west of Air Afrique.

For pastries and croissants plus the best ice cream in town, head for *Le Moka d'Or Salon de Thé* on Ave Col Parant near the US Embassy. Open daily to 7.30 pm except Monday, it charges CFA 250 per ice-cream scoop and is understandably popular. *Pâtisserie Pélisson*, 1½ blocks to the north and just off the same street, is one of Libreville's oldest institutions. Expensive pastries and bread are the main attraction.

Entertainment

Bars For African bars, the best areas are Nombakélé and Akébéville. Just walk around these areas and you'll find quite a few, all very rustic. One of the Peace Corps favourites is *M'Passa* in Nombakélé; their nickname for the bar, 'Attack Bar', suggests going alone may be unwise.

The bars in Libreville that attract foreigners are nothing to write home about. The street-side terrace at *Restaurant Chez Nous* on Ave Col Parant is relaxing and less expensive than *La Brasserie de l'Ocean* opposite Air Afrique. Among the hotels, the bar at the Méridien has a piano player and gets very lively from around 7 pm.

Nightclubs The city's most famous nightclub is *St Hilaire Restaurant-Nightclub* in Nombakélé on Rue Batavia. It's about the only place where you might get to hear live music. The crowd is mostly African with a few foreigners. The cover charge is normally CFA 4000 when there's a band and CFA 2000 when there isn't; this includes a drink. However, they desperately want to attract foreigners and on off nights it's easy to bargain the price down. It's also a restaurant, so some people come here first for a meal (CFA 2500 to CFA 3500 for main courses). For a cheap rustic nightclub catering to the

working person, try the *Key Club* several blocks to the west.

Many of the other nightclubs cater more to foreigners, particularly those along Rue Cureau starting from Komo Cinéma. The *Komo* has a nightclub of the same name with a live disc jockey above the cinema. A block down the hill you'll come to the *Vertigo Nightclub* followed by *Midnight Express Nightclub*, *Le Palace Nightclub* and finally *Black Moon Nightclub*. Vertigo is a typical disco while Midnight Express is more of a jazz club with live jazz entertainment. Le Palace is the most rustic of the group and Black Moon has the most striking décor. *Le Scotch Club* in the centre near Air Afrique is a disco catering to the same crowd, while *Night Fever* near the Complexe Omnisports has a large floor and roller skating and attracts teenagers.

Cinemas Classic French films are shown at the French cultural centre; there are usually three different ones every day, at 4, 6.30 and 9 pm. The 4 pm show on Saturdays is often an African film. For recent films, go to Komo Cinéma which is on Rue Mont-Bouët halfway between Air Afrique and Marché du Mont-Bouët. Since Bowlingstore went up in smoke during the riots of May 1990, Komo has had no competition, certainly not from the Akébé and Le Gabon. Movies, which cost around CFA 1500, change nightly, so consult *L'Union* newspaper. Typical show times are at 6, 9 and 11 pm. There's a fast-food restaurant outside but it's not cheap (eg CFA 3100 to CFA 3900 for pizza).

Things to Buy

Artisan Goods Despite the magnificent wooden carvings from Gabon that you may see in African museums, Gabon is not known today for its artisan work. Carved soapstone is about the only art form which stands out; unfortunately it's fragile and doesn't ship well. Many of the other artisan items for sale here are not from Gabon.

For artisan goods, don't miss Le Village des Artisans in the centre on Ave Alfred-Marché, just north of the US Embassy. It has

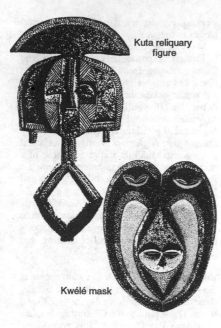

Kuta reliquary
figure

Kwélé mask

a number of stalls with souvenir-quality crafts, including soapstone carvings as well as wooden carvings and other items which may not be from Gabon. Art Malgache, which is on the same block but on Ave Col Parant, is a store with a few items of interest perhaps. In addition, you'll find Senegalese and Hausa traders along Ave Alfred-Marché, particularly behind the post office, as well as at a tiny *artisanat* (artisan stall) opposite the Score supermarket. Hard bargaining is required because starting prices are highly inflated.

Music Around Marché du Mont-Bouët, you can find recordings of modern Gabonese music. The three biggest stars, all men, are still Akendéngue, Hilarion Nguema and Makaya Madingo.

Two of the most popular women vocalists are Ma Philo Batassouagha and the president's former wife, Madame Bongo, a member of the group Kunabeli de Masuku.

In 1985 Bongo made it illegal to record cassettes from records. According to the gossip, he did this to increase sales of his wife's records. Those making a living selling records and cassettes took revenge by surreptitiously taking all of her records off the rack. Madame Bongo later left her husband for a musician.

Getting There & Away
Air Air France/UTA (☎ 766593), Swissair (☎ 743451/2), Sabena (☎ 761315), Air Afrique (☎ 764400), Air Gabon (☎ 762340, domestic; 762358, international) and Royal Air Maroc (☎ 731025) all provide direct connections to/from cities in Europe, including Brussels, Paris, Geneva, Rome and Madrid. Their offices are all in the centre except for Royal Air Maroc which is at the Okoumé Palace. Air Gabon has two offices along Blvd de l'Indépendance; the one a block north of the post office handles international flight bookings and the one two blocks south of it is for domestic flights.

As for connections to other Central African countries, there are direct flights to every country except Chad. Air Afrique, Cameroun Airlines (☎ 721315) and, next door, Nigerian Airways (☎ 764524), which are all in a two-block area, provide regular services to Douala (Cameroun), Brazzaville and Pointe-Noire (the Congo) as does Air Gabon. (These are also the major airlines serving cities along the coast of West Africa.) Air Zaïre (☎ 763885), which is in the same two-block area, and Air Gabon also have flights to Kinshasa (Zaïre) and, on Wednesdays, to Bangui (the CAR), respectively, while Equatorial International Airlines, which is represented by Mistral Voyages (☎ 760421) has round-trip flights four times a week to São Tomé. Fares are high, eg from Libreville to Pointe-Noire is CFA 72,500 (one way) and from Libreville to São Tomé is CFA 59,850 (one way).

The only other Central African country connected to Libreville by air is Equatorial Guinea. EGA, a very small airline, has a flight on Tuesdays and Saturdays to Bata and Malabo. A one-way ticket to Bata/Malabo costs CFA 39,000/54,000 and can be purchased in Libreville only from Air Gabon, its agent.

Mistral Voyages and Eurafrique Voyages in Libreville operate all-inclusive package tours to Lambaréné.

Air Gabon offers a 30% reduction on weekend trips on its domestic flights to/from anywhere within Gabon. You must depart on a Friday or Saturday and return on a Sunday or Monday.

Bush Taxi & Minivan Most minivans leave from the gare routière just north of the Marché du Mont-Bouët but you can also find them further east on Blvd Léon Kalfa near the Voie Express. The great majority leave during the morning before 10 am. Fares are high, eg to Lambaréné (232 km) it's CFA 8000 and to Mouila it's CFA 14,000. If you're going to Cap Estérias, take a taxi-bus (an intercity minivan) to the end of the line just past the airport; from there you'll easily find shared taxis to Cap Estérias all during the day (CFA 500, 30-minute ride).

Train The gare routière for the Transgabonais is just before Owendo, about 10 km south of town. A taxi-bus to the railway station costs CFA 300 compared to at least CFA 1000 for a taxi. The trains leave punctually at 9 am on Tuesdays and Saturdays and at 8.15 pm on Wednesdays, Fridays and Sundays. These schedules could change, so consult the *L'Union* newspaper or call the station (☎ 703539). The Libreville to Franceville trip is supposed to take about 10½ hours but the train often arrives several hours late.

The 1st and 2nd-class fares are CFA 27,600 and CFA 22,100 respectively. First-class tickets do not guarantee you a seat, so there is no advantage in purchasing a ticket beforehand. The train is almost never full when it pulls out of Franceville (it fills up en route) but from the Libreville end it can be very crowded, especially the Wednesday and Friday night trains when the aisles are usually full of standing passengers. On those days you need to get to the station a good

1½ hours early to buy your ticket and secure a seat. Otherwise you may stand for half the trip, even in 1st class. On the other days, if you're travelling 2nd class, it probably makes sense to get to the gare 1½ hours early.

Restaurant service has been discontinued so bring food if you plan to eat during the trip. There's still a bar in the 1st-class section however, and plenty of street food and drinks for sale just outside the gare routière entrance. It's extremely crowded around the ticket booths, so guard your baggage carefully.

Ferry About every five days the *Solmar II* departs for São Tomé. It leaves from Port Môle in Libreville around noon and arrives 24 hours later; the São Tomé Embassy can tell you the exact day of departure. The fare is CFA 25,000. In addition, about once a month the *Onangue* makes the trip from São Tomé to Libreville, Douala and back to São Tomé.

Uro-Gabon has a small boat leaving Libreville for Port-Gentil at 8 am daily from Port Michel-Marine, which is about three km south of the town centre; the trip costs CFA 14,500 and takes five to seven hours. The *Elsa-Dorothie* makes the same trip, leaving Libreville at 8 am on Fridays and at 1.30 pm on Mondays, Tuesdays, Saturdays and Sundays. It departs from Port Môle in the town centre; the fare is CFA 13,000 and the trip takes about four hours. The only people who take the larger *La Léombi* (grand bateau), which leaves every other day in the morning, are usually those carrying lots of goods as it takes eight hours and costs CFA 1000 more. (For more details, see the Getting There & Away section at the start of this chapter and also the Port-Gentil Getting There & Away section.)

Getting Around

To/From the Airport There is no airport departure tax. The airport (information ☎ 736128) is quite modern, with a bank, cafeteria and pay telephone. The normal fare for a taxi from the town centre to the airport

(12 km) is CFA 1000 but from the airport to the centre the standard price is CFA 2000. (However, if you walk from the airport to the main drag and hail a taxi from there to the town centre it'll cost CFA 1000.) Prices double after 9 pm. Cheaper still are the taxi-buses which pass in front of the airport. They're all headed to the gare routière in Mont-Bouët and charge CFA 200.

Bus The Sotravil bus company went bankrupt and in its place there are the private red and white minibuses (taxi-bus) which plough up and down all the major thoroughfares, charging between CFA 100 and CFA 200 for all rides in the city. There's no numbering system, so you'll have to yell out your destination.

Taxi Fares for a shared taxi are CFA 100 for short trips and CFA 200 to CFA 300 for longer ones (say, up to five km). Fares for a taxi to yourself are CFA 500 for a 'demi course' (up to about six km) and CFA 1000 for a 'course' (up to about 12 km, including to Libreville airport and the railway station). In some instances, the driver may insist you pay the demi-course fare even though there are other passengers in the cab, especially if you're going to be dropped off first. Rates double at 9 pm. By the hour and day, the asking price is usually around CFA 3000 and CFA 30,000, respectively, but you should be able to bargain the price down to CFA 2500 and CFA 25,000 provided you remain in the greater city area.

Taxis are plentiful during the day and less so at night. Taxi drivers rarely know the names of streets, so you'll have to give directions such as: 'It's in Quartier Louis, several blocks beyond Port Môle.'

Car Avis is represented in town by Eurafrique Voyages (☎ 766659; fax 761897; telex 5458) and has offices at the Méridien and the Rapontchombo. Hertz (☎ 732011; telex 5271) is at the Okoumé Palace and Eurocar (☎ 745845/6) is at the airport and opposite the fairgrounds. Mondial Location SARL (☎ 742171) is another. Costs are sky-high and rented cars are often restricted to use within or around Libreville.

AROUND LIBREVILLE
Pointe-Dénis & Ekwata Beach
If you're looking for some remote beaches, you have two choices – Pointe-Dénis and Ekwata Beach. They are both on the peninsula on the other side of the estuary, about 12 km away. The beaches are nearly deserted except for an occasional fisher; there are some forests to wander around. If you want to stay overnight, you could camp or stay at some chalets at Pointe-Dénis, which may still be available despite the cessation of regular tourist boat services from Libreville.

Getting There & Away Boats for both beaches leave from Port Môle. Until recently Pointe-Dénis was the most popular destination as there were three round trips a day on weekends, but now the only way to get there is on the *Olivier*, a 12-metre covered canoe that transports Africans back and forth about three times a day. Its schedule is completely erratic. You could be at the port at 9 am and find yourself waiting three hours for a ride. You might also find yourself without a ride back unless you pay a high fee. Round-trip prices are negotiable; to get the best price you should team up with other foreigners, often French soldiers, which is generally possible only on Sundays when you may encounter a few at the port; you could still end up paying CFA 5000 a person for the round trip.

The only way to get to Ekwata Beach is through Ekwata Loisirs travel agency (☎ 761338); reserve a seat on their 26-seater, covered motor boat. It leaves Saturdays and Sundays at 9 am from the tip of the port and returns at 4.45 pm. Usually only foreigners take this excursion.

Cap Estérias
Cap Estérias is 32 km north of Libreville and although the beaches are rocky here, there are some small sandy stretches and usually only a few bathers, even on weekends. It is an ideal place for sailboards as the beach is

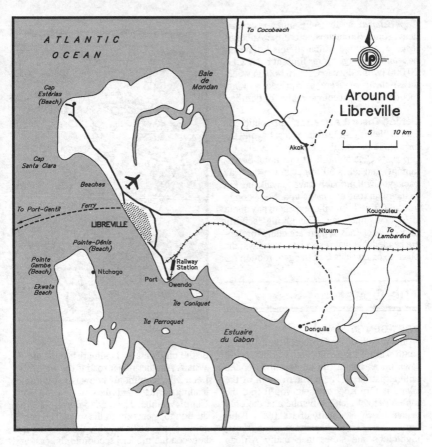

Around Libreville

protected. Most people, however, come only for a meal, usually on Sundays for lunch.

Places to Stay & Eat The best place to stay here is *L'Auberge du Cap* (☎ 745554 Libreville). It is at the tip of the cape and has a nice sandy beach directly in front of it. The new owners (Gerard, a friendly Frenchman and his African wife) have completely renovated this place. The eight rooms are now spotlessly clean with fans; a room with breakfast costs CFA 10,000 (reservations advisable for Saturday nights) but Gerard will reduce it to CFA 8000 or so during the week and much

more if you stay for an extended period. Their breezy bamboo restaurant is the best here and main courses, such as merou fish brochettes and rice, start at CFA 3000. He has plans to rent sailboards, so ask.

Next to the Auberge is *La Balise*, which is the other main restaurant in this area. Also popular and with similar prices, it has some exotic dishes including pithon à la bierre, bar au pastis and feuille de manioc au couteaux. The ocean views, however, are definitely not as good.

Le Relais de Cap Esterias is closed, leaving the modern Lebanese-run *Le Cauris*

Cap Estérias as the only other restaurant here. Some 200 metres before the Auberge, it has a restaurant which attracts little business and two large rooms for rent but at CFA 20,000 (will reduce to CFA 10,000 on weekdays) the rooms are overpriced and not recommended except, possibly, for families.

Getting There & Away The gare routière in Libreville for Cap Estérias is just beyond the airport. Taxis usually fill up quickly and the trip costs CFA 500 (direct to a hotel or restaurant) and takes 30 minutes. On the way back, you will probably have to walk one km to the main road and hail a taxi. For a taxi to yourself from Libreville, expect to pay about CFA 6000 one way. Hitchhiking is fairly easy on weekends as there are many foreigners headed that way, especially Sundays; the place to catch rides is at the gare routière.

The Coast

PORT-GENTIL

At the mouth of the Ogooué River, 140 km south-west of Libreville, Port-Gentil is an oil town on an island (Ile de Mandji) flooded with expatriates. The northern point of the island is Cap Lopez, where you'll find the top-end Hôtel Neng' Abembé and the only decent beach. For a city of 100,000 inhabitants, Port-Gentil has more restaurants, nightclubs and stores than many African cities five times the size; it even has a casino and a decent hospital. The African sections predominate however, and they are full of cheap restaurants, bars and nightclubs which are as lively and interesting as those in Libreville and even safer to visit.

Orientation

The main drag with stores and banks galore is Ave Savorgnan de Brazza, which runs north-south through the modern section, one block from the water. Running parallel to it along the water is Blvd du Gouveneur de Chavannes, where you'll find the Méridien, the old port (petit port or vieux port) and one

of the city's major landmarks, the Café du Wharf. Another major road is the wide Blvd Léon Mba (commonly known as Autoroute) leading north towards the new port and Hôtel Neng' Abembé. The road to the airport, Ave du Bongo, stems off to the west. The north-south Autoroute is roughly the dividing line between the modern section to the east and the popular African quarters (Mosquée, Chic, Balise, Grand Village and Aviation) to the west, the main street in the latter being the Ave du Grand Village which runs past the Marché du Grand Village.

Information

Money Most of the banks are along Ave Savorgnan de Brazza including UGB, BIPG and BICIG, while Citibank (☎ 752955/6) is 1½ blocks to the west. The best bank for changing money is the BIPG, which usually offers not only the best rates but charges no commission on travellers' cheques. Both UGB and Citibank usually give lower rates and charge commissions on travellers' cheques (CFA 2850 per transaction at the UGB and CFA 100 per US$100 changed at Citibank). Most of them are open on weekdays from 7.45 to 11.30 am and from 2.45 to 4.30 pm; Citibank, however, is open on weekdays from 7.30 am to 1.30 pm.

Consulate The French Consulate doesn't represent any African countries, so don't go there expecting to get a visa to, say, the CAR.

Travel Agencies One of the best travel agencies is Gabon Voyages (☎ 751419/21) which is in the centre just south of the Cinéma l'Ogooué. It now has a computer terminal for making airline reservations. Two others worth checking are Eurafrique Voyages (☎ 753833; telex 8234) and SNCDV (☎ 752475).

Supermarkets The Score supermarket, which is by far the best, has one store in the centre just south of the post office, and another on the Autoroute, at the intersection with Ave du Grand Village. They are stocked with a little bit of everything.

Activities

The top-end Méridien and Neng' Abembé hotels have pools which nonguests can use for CFA 1500 or so. You can also use the beach, which is the only decent accessible one near the city.

Club Adonis, which is 2½ blocks south of the stadium, has squash courts (CFA 3000 a game or CFA 20,000 a month). You can also use the sauna and hot tub there for CFA 3500. For ocean swimming, sailing or tennis, head for Club Sogara next door to the Neng' Abembé, five km from town. In addition to a free beach, it has a bar, toilet facilities and tennis courts, and sailors might find people needing extra crew, especially on Sundays.

Places to Stay – bottom end

Port-Gentil has no cheap hotels, so your only hope of finding a relatively cheap place to sleep may be at one of the Catholic missions, of which there are several. None of them are accustomed to renting rooms to travellers as so few travellers pass this way. Your best bet is the *Mission Catholique St-Louis* in the heart of town on Rue Bichet. Or try the *Mission Catholique St-Paul-des-Bois*. Expect to pay about CFA 5000 for a room if they accept you.

The two best hotels in this range are the ever-popular *Hôtel le Printemps* on the Autoroute in a very lively, central area dividing the modern and African quarters, and *Hôtel Matanda* (☎ 751653), which is near the southern end of the Autoroute, 1½ km south of the centre in a much darker, more tranquil area. The Printemps charges CFA 10,500 for an air-con room and is often full. Its best feature is the very popular restaurant, which charges CFA 1500 for most dishes and is open late. The French-run Matanda is quieter with better rooms. It charges CFA 10,000 for an immaculately clean air-con room with tiled bathroom. There's no restaurant but breakfast is served, and the bar has a billiards table and TV.

If these places are full, try *Hôtel Okolongo* (☎ 755135), which is near the intersection of Blvd Léon Mba and Rue du Quartier Chic, or *Motel Abône* (☎ 750059), which is 2½ blocks south of the stadium and 1½ km from the centre. The Okolongo is the only one in this category which has an African ambience and a bar that is frequently packed, but at CFA 11,000 to CFA 12,000 for an air-con room it's overpriced. It's better as a gamey African restaurant – crocodile and porc-pic (porcupine) are both on the menu. The Abône has good sized rooms with carpeting but at CFA 12,000 they're also overpriced.

Places to Stay – middle

Of the mid-range hotels, I highly recommend the *Hôtel-Club Hippique* (Restaurant le Ranch) (☎ 752528). It's particularly popular with people staying for long periods and is often full, so book in advance. It charges CFA 13,500 for an air-con room and CFA 20,000 for a studio with kitchenette, but the studios can often be negotiated downward to CFA 15,000 for longer stays. The French owners are particularly friendly and

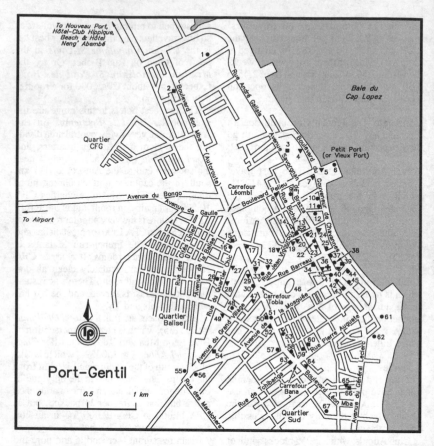

Port-Gentil

the adjoining restaurant has a pleasant relaxed atmosphere and is quite popular. The main drawback is its location – you need a taxi to get around as it's on the northern side of town near the new port, about four km from the centre.

If you're looking for a hotel with an air of exclusivity or one closer to the centre, try *L'Auberge du Forestier* (☎ 752980; telex 8304), which is on Ave Savorgnan de Brazza, one km north of the heart of town. There is no pool or tennis court, but it looks like a Swiss chalet and has one of the city's most attractive restaurants. Its 10 air-con rooms

each have TV/video and cost CFA 20,000. American Express credit cards are accepted.

The *Hôtel Abéla* (☎ 753922; telex 8271) has a dreadful ambience, poor service and seemingly few clients and the rooms, which have air-con and good work tables, cost CFA 18,000. It's fairly convenient for the airport and the new port but it's on the Autoroute two km from the centre and you need a taxi to go anywhere.

Places to Stay – top end
The deluxe *Le Méridien Mandji Hôtel* (☎ 752103; fax 752806; telex 8234) is the

■ PLACES TO STAY

2 Hôtel Abéla
3 L'Auberge du Forestier
15 Hôtel Okolongo
34 Mission Catholique St-Louis
39 Le Méridien Mandji Hôtel
50 Hôtel le Printemps
54 Mission Catholique St-Paul-des-Bois
60 Motel Abône
66 Hôtel Matanda

▼ PLACES TO EAT

4 Restaurant la Bisquine
5 Restaurant Bon Gôut
7 Café du Wharf
8 Restaurant Manadrin 'Kim'
14 Entre-Act Snackbar & Boulangerie-
   Pâtisserie
18 Boulangerie-Pâtisserie
19 Restaurant le Rétro
20 Restaurant l'Escale
23 Bar le Central
24 Snack-Bar la Rumerie
27 Cheap Restaurants & Bars
28 Restaurant Chez Tonton
29 Brochette & Coupé-Coupé Vendors
31 Restaurant le Zaïko
32 Restaurant la Chiminée
35 Bar des Copains
40 Restaurant Jardin d'Asie
42 Restaurant Éridan
47 Restaurant le Kilimanjaro
49 Restaurants Azingo & la Palmeraie
64 Restaurant Tam-Tam
65 Restaurant Tom Pouce

OTHER

1 Lycée Technique
6 Ticket Office for Boats to Libreville
7 Supermarché Supergros

9 Immigration
10 Marché du Port
11 Pharmacie Gabonaise
12 Commissariat
13 Post Office
14 Cinéma l'Ogooué & Casino
16 Le Pacha Nightclub
17 Bar Royal
20 Citibank & Gabon Voyages
21 Score Supermarket
22 Piano Bar & Le Safari Nightclub
23 Air Gabon & Blue Moon Nightclub
24 French Consulate
25 Shell Station
26 La Samba Nightclub
30 Score Supermarket & Le Baobab
   Nightclub
31 Le Kint Nightclub
33 Mission Protestante
36 Hôpital Paul Igamba
37 BICIG Bank & BIPG Bank
38 UGB Bank & Palais de Justice
41 Air France/UTA & Hertz
42 BGD Bank
43 Flash Department Store
44 BEAC Bank
45 Elf Petrol Station
46 Stadium
48 Marché du Grand Village
51 Carrefour le Printemps
52 Le Marseillais Nightclub
53 Mosque
55 Water Tower
56 Las Vegas Nightclub
57 Bar Américain
58 Water Tower & Mission Catholique
   Sainte-Barbe
59 Club Adonis
61 Elf-Gabon
62 Elf-Gabon Club
63 Le Mirage Nightclub
67 Izuwa Nightclub

city's top address and has the advantage of being in the centre on Blvd du Gouverneur de Chavannes overlooking the water; the only problem is that you can't use the beach. It has singles/doubles for CFA 30,500/35,000, a pool and a Hertz agent, and it accepts all major credit cards.

The big advantage of *Hôtel Neng'Abembé* (☎ 750242; telex 8326), a former Novotel, is that it's the only hotel with a usable beach. It

has a pool, an Avis agent and singles/doubles cost CFA 27,700/31,700 (CFA 20,000 weekend special with breakfast; American Express, Diners and Visa cards are accepted), and guests have access to the tennis club next door. However, the location, about five km north from the centre of town, is not ideal.

Places to Eat
Cheap Eats A great place for breakfast and

lunch is the *Restaurant Bon Gôut* just in front of the old port on Blvd du Gouveneur de Chavannes, a favourite of the Senegalese taxi drivers. All of them seem to head here around 9 am for breakfast, typically a huge bowl of coffee with milk (CFA 200) and bread. Other offerings include beef sandwiches for CFA 500, a meat plate for CFA 600, and omelette garni for CFA 900.

Quartier Chic, which is just west of the Autoroute, is a good place for cheap food. In the evenings, for example, you'll find good beef brochettes for CFA 200 and coupé-coupé vendors along the Autoroute, a block north of Score supermarket. Several blocks west, just beyond Marché du Grand Village, is the highly recommended *Restaurant la Palmeraie*, which is a small African place that is open late and has seating indoors and on a terrace. Many of the clients here are foreigners attracted by the good food and a wonderful homely African ambience. The food is limited to grilled beef brochettes (CFA 1000) and grilled fish (CFA 1000 to CFA 2500).

Next door is *Restaurant Azingo*, a popular working person's place which is open late and charges relatively little for its greasy fare, eg steak frites for CFA 1000, omelette garni for CFA 1000, riz poisson for CFA 1100, etc. *Restaurant Chez Tonton*, which faces La Samba Nightclub on Rue du Quartier Chic, has a similar menu and prices but is somewhat grubbier.

A place highly recommended in this category for the low price is *Restaurant la Chiminée*, which is south-west of Score. It's African-owned with a rustic terrace in front and very popular with expatriates looking for an inexpensive meal. The menu includes fries for CFA 700, various types of brochettes for CFA 1200 to CFA 1500, grilled chicken for CFA 1500 and shrimp farci for CFA 2000.

Another popular place is *Hôtel le Printemps*, which is a well-known meeting place on the Autoroute. Most dishes cost around CFA 1500, including quiche, hamburgers and steak haché. At around 8 pm the terrace and inside area are typically full, many

people just having drinks. For good grilled food and an attractive, tranquil ambience I much prefer the popular, open-air *Restaurant Tom Pouce* (☎ 752771), which is about one km to the south-east. The menu includes various brochettes (CFA 600 to CFA 1500), steak (CFA 1600), grilled chicken (CFA 1500), fries (CFA 500) and wine (a quarter carafe for CFA 900).

In the centre of town, try the breezy, long-standing *Café du Wharf* opposite the old port. In addition to the expensive menu du jour, you can get brochettes (beef, shrimp or fish) for CFA 1500, other dishes up to CFA 2000 and fries for CFA 800.

African For African food, if you can afford to pay CFA 2500 per dish, I recommend *Restaurant Tam-Tam*. It's a fairly rustic place near the southern end of the Autoroute, with an unusually wide selection of Senegalese specialities including riz senegalais, poulet yassa, thiou (fish), all CFA 2500, as well as small brochettes for CFA 500 to CFA 700, couscous royal for CFA 4000, and a different speciality of the day.

For Gabonese bush meat, head for *Restaurant le Kilimanjaro* in Quartier Chic, 100 metres south-west of Score supermarket. It's a tiny rustic place with only about four offerings, all CFA 2000 to CFA 3000, including crocodile, boa and bush rat. You can also get bush meat at *Hôtel Okolongo*, which is north on Rue du Quartier Chic. Crocodile and porc-pic are both on the menu.

French The *Bar des Copains* in the town centre near the hospital has a fixed menu for CFA 5000 including wine and is popular with the French. The two best and most expensive French restaurants by reputation are the long-standing *L'Auberge du Forestier* (☎ 752980) on Ave Savorgnan de Brazza and *Restaurant la Bisquine* on the same block facing Blvd du Gouveneur de Chavannes and the water.

Asian For Vietnamese food, the best place is *Restaurant Jardin d'Asie*. It's fairly fancy with a big menu (most dishes around CFA

3500) and attracts clients from the Méridien hotel next door; it's closed on Sundays. As an alternative, try *Restaurant Manadrin 'Kim'* (☎ 755370), which is near the centre on Blvd Pelieu, three blocks west of the petit port. It has Vietnamese, Chinese and Thai specialities, with a choice of inside or outside dining.

Pizza & Hamburgers *Le Rétro*, in the centre on Rue Jean Vigouroux, two blocks north of Score, has a formal atmosphere and serves pizza and wonderful chocolate crêpes among other things but is fairly expensive, eg CFA 2800 to CFA 4000 for pizza and around CFA 4000 for most French selections; it's open daily. *Restaurant le Zaïko* (☎ 750870) on the Autoroute is slightly cheaper, with pizzas in the CFA 2000 to CFA 3200 range and also Italian noodle dishes starting from CFA 2800. You can also play billiards here while you wait.

Snack-Bar la Rumerie, opposite Score on Ave Savorgnan de Brazza, is a trendy ice-cream parlour serving fancy ice-cream concoctions starting at CFA 1000 for plain ice cream, chocolate crêpes for CFA 1000, hot dogs for CFA 1000, among other things. It's open until 11.30 pm daily except Sundays. Across the street at the modern, informal *Bar le Central* you can get food as well as drinks, but it's fairly expensive, eg CFA 2500 for omelette champignons and CFA 3500 for steak. The *Entre-Act* snack-bar at the nearby cinema is not much cheaper, eg CFA 2500 for a hamburger with fries.

Entertainment

Bars One of the most popular bars during the day is the old landmark *Café du Wharf* in the town centre opposite the old port, but drinks here are not cheap. In the evenings, the sidewalk café-bar at *Hôtel le Printemps* on the Autoroute is often full and the drinks are cheaper. For African bars with rock-bottom prices (CFA 200 for a big Regab beer), head for Rue du Quartier Chic; there are lots of lively late-night bars along that road.

Among the more up-market bars, *Bar des Copains*, which is in the centre behind the

hospital, stands out as being a favourite of the French cooperants. The younger crowd, however, tend to prefer the relatively expensive bars nearby along Ave Savorgnan de Brazza, particularly the *Piano Bar*, where many prostitutes hang out, waiting for the nightclubs next door to open, and the similar *Bar le Central* a stone's throw away.

Nightclubs The major nightclubs catering to foreigners are the *Blue Moon* and *Le Safari*, both in the heart of town on Ave Savorgnan de Brazza, plus four on the Autoroute, north to south: *Le Kint* (formerly African Queen), *Le Marseillais*, *Le Baobab* and *Le Mirage*. Most of them are open every night starting around 10.30 and levy a cover charge (typically CFA 2500 which includes a drink) only on weekends. They are all strobe-lit discos and usually full of prostitutes.

Far more interesting are the African nightclubs, two of which are on Rue du Quartier Chic – *La Samba* and *Le Pacha* (formerly Port Gentillais), just off the Autoroute. Two more, not so conveniently located, are *Izuwa Nightclub*, which is near the southern end of the Autoroute and a block west thereof and, my favourite, *Las Vegas* (formerly Number One) at the western end of Ave du Grand Village. Some of them such as Izuwa are open only on weekends, when there's dancing and a cover charge of CFA 1500 which includes a drink. Most don't really liven up until around 1 am.

Cinema The modern Cinéma l'Ogooué, one block behind the Score supermarket, shows the latest flicks from abroad. A ticket costs CFA 1500 and the hours are usually 6.30 and 9 pm (plus a late-night show on weekends), with a different film at each hour. You can also eat there but the meals are expensive, and behind the cinema is a casino.

Getting There & Away

Air Air Gabon (☎ 752572) has at least two flights a day to/from Libreville; the round trip costs CFA 43,000 (CFA 31,000 on weekends or with a student discount). The plane stops in Gamba thrice weekly (along the coast just south of Setté Cama) en route to Libreville; the fare to Gamba is CFA 28,000. Air France/UTA (☎ 753820) also has an office here, a block from the Méridien.

To charter a plane, contact Air Inter-Gabon (☎ 752112, 753144; fax 752108; telex 8204), which is a French-run company at the airport. The one-way fare (or same-day return) on an eight-seater plane to Iguéla (one of the coastal villages), for example, is CFA 390,000.

Ferry There are several boats which make trips from Libreville to Port-Gentil almost daily in either direction. The *Elsa-Dorothie* (La Vedette) leaves the old port or petit port, Port-Gentil (CFA 13,000) at 8 am on Mondays, Tuesdays, Thursdays, Saturdays and Sundays, and from Port Môle, Libreville at 8 am on Fridays and at 1.30 pm on Mondays, Tuesdays, Saturdays and Sundays. The trip takes four hours.

Uro-Gabon also has two small boats serving this route; they cost CFA 14,500 and leave in either direction (from the petit port in Port- Gentil and from Port Michel-Marine in Libreville) at 8 am, arriving at 1 pm. In addition, every other day *La Léombi* (grand bateau) leaves in the morning from the main port (Nouveau Port) for Libreville, returning the following day. The trip takes eight hours and costs CFA 14,000. It's used primarily by those with lots of baggage.

Riverboat To add a little interest to your trip, you could float down the Ogooué River from Ndjolé or Lambaréné to Port-Gentil (or vice versa). The Ogooué is navigable by barge for 315 km up to Ndjolé where the first rapids begin and the journey by boat is fascinating.

The smaller boats, of which there are three, leave from the old port in Port-Gentil for Lambaréné on Mondays and Fridays at 6 am, arriving around 4 pm the same day. From Lambaréné they leave on Sunday and Thursday mornings. The fare is CFA 10,000. There is also a high-speed boat with daily departures which costs CFA 15,000 and does the trip in about six hours; sit in the back to avoid

the loud sounds from the kick-boxing videos.

The larger *Azingo* (a grand bateau) makes only one round trip a week, leaving Port-Gentil from the petit port on Mondays usually around 11 am or so depending on the tide, and Lambaréné on Thursday mornings. (A small barge leaves Ndjolé on Wednesday mornings and connects with the Azingo on Thursdays.) It is more like a makeshift floating village and potentially more if you can tolerate the many mosquitoes and don't mind sleeping overnight on board. Music blasts from giant ghetto blasters and children scream and play all day and night. Every bit of space on the lower deck (2nd-class) is filled with mattresses, straw mats and families' cooking facilities. The beer flows freely, facilitating conversation with the curious locals.

The 1st-class/2nd-class fare is CFA 11,550/7500 and the trip takes about 30 hours upriver and 24 hours downriver, with stops in lots of villages en route. The Azingo has no beds or restaurant, but you can buy drinks. If you don't take enough food, don't worry. The people on board are very friendly and there's a good chance of someone offering to share their meal with you.

You can take a similar overnight barge from Port-Gentil southward to the lagoon of Fernan Vaz, stopping at Omboué, Ste-Anne and Ndougou. It leaves on Tuesdays and Saturdays; ask at the petit port for details.

Getting Around
To/From the Airport
The asking price for a taxi from the airport to the centre is CFA 2000 but you shouldn't pay more than CFA 1000 (CFA 500 from the centre to the airport) for the short five-km trip.

Taxi The city has no buses but taxis are plentiful during the day and are not expensive, ie CFA 100 for a short trip in a shared taxi and CFA 2500 by the hour if you bargain hard.

Car There are numerous car-rental companies, including Hertz (☎ 752231) which has offices at the Méridien and a block west thereof, Avis (☎ 750242) at the Neng' Abembé, and a local company EGCA (☎ 753028). All have booths at the airport. Rates are very high (see Car Rental in the introductory Getting There & Away section).

IGUÉLA & SETTÉ CAMA

Two areas renowned for fishing are Iguéla and Setté Cama. They are isolated spots south of Port-Gentil bordering two large *lagunes* (estuaries), 180 km and 280 km, respectively, south of Port-Gentil. Tarpon is the speciality; they are furious fighters and can weigh up to 70 kg. December to February is the fishing season. Perch, barracuda, ray, bass and sailfish are also plentiful.

Iguéla is also a good place for viewing wildlife as the nearby **Réserve d'Iguéla** has about 600 protected forest elephants as well as buffalo, wart hog, crocodile, monkeys, lowland gorillas and numerous species of birds. The best time to go there is between April and October when the weather is drier and travelling around the reserve is easier.

Heron

Organised Tours

Mistral Voyages in Libreville offers special all-inclusive excursions to the Iguéla area including lodging and meals at the Campement (see Places to Stay & Eat below) and photo-safari and fishing trips through the reserve by canoe and 4WD vehicles. The total cost per person including air fare from Libreville ranges from CFA 120,000 for a weekend excursion to CFA 275,000 for an all-week excursion.

Places to Stay & Eat

The only accommodation in this area is the *Centre Touristique de Setté Cama* (BP 240, Port-Gentil) in Setté Cama, the *Centre Saint-Aubert* (BP 1851, Libreville) in Iguéla, and a *Campement* at Yé-Tsanou village near Omboué, just north of Iguéla. The Campement consists of 12 comfortable bungalows equipped with private bathrooms and fans plus a restaurant.

Getting There & Away

Air Gabon has flights on Monday, Wednesday and Saturday mornings from Port-Gentil to Gamba, continuing on to Libreville. The cost to Gamba is CFA 28,000. From Gamba it's a short drive north to Setté Cama. The Monday and Saturday flights also stop in Omboué; during dry spells you can sometimes get to Omboué and Iguéla by road from the mainland.

COCOBEACH

Some 120 km north of Libreville via Ntoum (on the road to Lambaréné), Cocobeach is where you catch a motorised canoe across the Estuaire du Muni to Equatorial Guinea. If you plan to cross the border on a Sunday, you may find difficulty getting your passport stamped by the police.

Places to Stay & Eat

The *Hôtel Restaurant* is near the port and

way overpriced at CFA 10,000 for a double. *Hôtel Chez Tante Mapo*, which is a 15-minute walk away, is much more reasonably priced at CFA 3000 for a very basic double. You can also get food there, eg meat, rice and a beer for CFA 1600.

Getting There & Away
Coming from Equatorial Guinea, you'll find the bush taxis (*taxis-brousses* in French) very near the port area and if the drivers are pressed to leave, they may facilitate your passage through police and customs. The police charge CFA 2000 for registering your passport and the taxi drivers charge CFA 4000 for the 2½-hour trip to Libreville, with departures up to around 6 pm.

Pirogues (motorised canoes) to Acala-yong, Equatorial Guinea normally take 40 minutes but sometimes double that. They leave when full, usually starting around 8 am, with the last departure around 4 pm, sometimes later. The fare is CFA 4000 (with foreigners they often try to charge more) and they don't carry vehicles. Every morning, there are minibuses departing from Aca-layong, which has no hotels, for Bata, a six-hour journey.

The Western Interior

NDJOLÉ
Some 221 km east of Libreville by mostly paved road, Ndjolé (n-doh-LAY) is strategi-cally located between the country's two major crossroads – one 60 km to the west where the highway splits north-west for Libreville and south for Lambaréné and one 37 km to the west where the highway splits north for Oyem and east and south-east for Booué and Franceville. In addition, the Transgabonais passes by north of town while the Ogooué River flows through the town centre. A small barge leaves for Lambaréné weekly and from there connections with larger boats going to Port-Gentil can be made. Consequently, this town is a hub and fairly active for its small size, with quite a

few travellers passing through, some staying for the night.

Places to Stay
The new *Hôtel la Vallée*, 150 metres east of the central market near the river, is good value. There are some 10 very clean rooms with shared bathrooms that have working showers, basins and Western-style toilets; rooms cost CFA 4000. Adjoining it is the Bar-Restaurant Show-Show. You could also ask the African priest at the *Mission Catholique* across the street whether he has a room to let.

Moving up-market, you could try the somewhat sterile *La Papaye Chambre de Passage* (☎ 793035), a long cement building next to the market. It has a bar and about eight rooms with fans and exterior bath-rooms; rooms cost CFA 7000. *L'Escale*, which was another up-market place, has closed.

The city's best hotel by far is the French-run *Auberge St-Jean* (☎ 793106), which is an attractive two-storey structure overlook-ing the river some 300 metres south-west of the central market near the port and Mobil depot. The hotel, which has been operating since the late 1980s, has air-con rooms from CFA 12,000 to CFA 15,000 and the town's top restaurant. There's also a section of the hotel closer to the centre with ventilated doubles for CFA 9000.

Places to Eat
One of the town's best places for cheap food and recorded music is *Bar-Restaurant Show-Show*. Most dishes cost around CFA 800 including riz gras, riz poisson, spaghetti viande and foufou viande. You can also get sandwiches for CFA 500 and the standard breakfast (coffee, bread and butter) for CFA 350. For drinks, a more interesting place might be the open-air bar across the street which has two thatched-roof paillotes.

Across the bridge towards the market are the *Restaurant Maman Foufou* and coupé-coupé vendors, and opposite the market are other cheap places to eat and drink including *Restaurant Africain* and *Bar le Travail Avant*

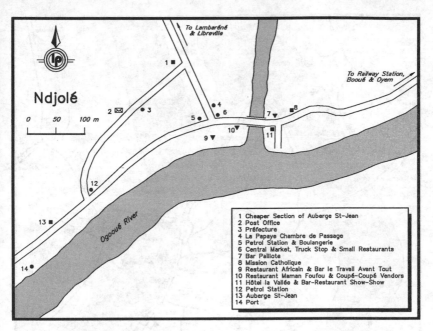

Ndjolé

0   50   100 m

Ogooué River

To Lambaréné
& Libreville

To Railway Station,
Booué & Oyem

1 Cheaper Section of Auberge St-Jean
2 Post Office
3 Préfecture
4 La Papaye Chambre de Passage
5 Petrol Station & Boulangerie
6 Central Market, Truck Stop & Small Restaurants
7 Bar Paillote
8 Mission Catholique
9 Restaurant Africain & Bar le Travail Avant Tout
10 Restaurant Maman Foufou & Coupé-Coupé Vendors
11 Hôtel la Vallée & Bar-Restaurant Show-Show
12 Petrol Station
13 Auberge St-Jean
14 Port

Tout. You'll also find several small bars in the market itself, but they are not as good as those mentioned earlier.

For French food, head for the French-run restaurant at *Auberge St-Jean.*

Getting There & Away
Minibus & Bush Taxi Minibuses and bush taxis cost CFA 5000 to Lambaréné (three hours), CFA 7000 to Libreville and CFA 10,000 to Oyem (CFA 9000 by pick-up truck). They all leave from the central market, mostly in the morning. If you're headed for Booué, the quickest way may be by train as there are very few vehicles headed in that direction.

Train The railway station is 11 km north of town (CFA 300 by taxi). First-class/2nd-class fares are CFA 7700/6200 to Libreville, CFA 12,850/10,250 to Lastoursville, and CFA 19,900/15,900 to Franceville.

Boat In addition, on Wednesday mornings (possibly other days as well) you can take a small barge to Lambaréné (CFA 3500 to CFA 5000) and connect there with the *Azingo* leaving on Thursday mornings for Port-Gentil. The trip takes about seven hours and the port is just beyond the Auberge. You can stock up on food and drinks at the central market. Have your camera ready – this is a very scenic trip. For information about this and oil barges running between here and Port-Gentil, ask at the Auberge or around the docks.

LAMBARÉNÉ
Lambaréné, Gabon's third-largest city, is some 300 km up the Ogooué River from Port-Gentil. It has about 30,000 inhabitants. Albert Schweitzer put this town on the map, and his hospital is still the major draw card.

Supported by missionary groups in Europe, Schweitzer and his wife came here in 1913 and built the first hospital about three

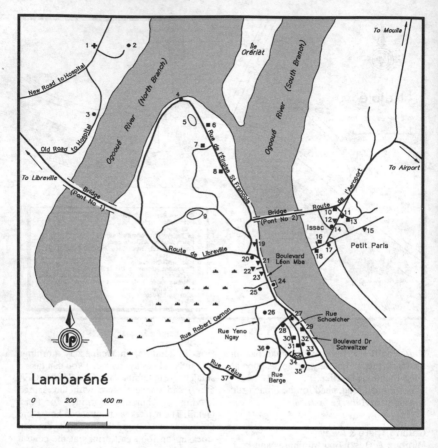

Lambaréné

0   200   400 m

km upstream from the present one, which dates from 1926. He died at the latter in 1965; you can see his grave. The idea was to build a hospital that would attract suspicious locals by providing the most familiar surroundings. The patients were fed by their families, who camped out at the hospital. This lowered hygienic standards somewhat, causing considerable controversy among Schweitzer's peers in Europe.

Since the mid-1970s the hospital, which is run by a Swiss foundation, has received most of its funding from the Gabonese government, and with the new annexe built in 1981

the hospital looks more like it was prefabricated in Switzerland – with nothing but the most up-to-date equipment. At a time when everybody else in Africa seems to be turning away from modern hospitals and copying the Chinese barefoot-doctor approach, this once innovative hospital now seems strangely out of step.

Schweitzer was obviously a gutsy guy, certainly deserving of the many accolades that he received. But he was no saint. John Gunther visited Schweitzer here and wrote about him in *Inside Africa*; he had problems reconciling Schweitzer's lofty greatness

■ PLACES TO STAY

6   Hôtel Ogooué Palace
7   Mission Catholique St François-
    Xavier
8   Mission de l'Immaculée
    Concepcion (École Catholique des
    Soeurs)
10 Hôtel Lépopa
13 La Petite Auberge
16 Motel du Peuple
18 Case de Passage à Isaac
29 Hôtel Angleterre & Hôtel Évaro
    Reservation Office
30 Hôtel Schweitzer
31 Case de Passage

▼ PLACES TO EAT

12 Restaurant Imanenzal
15 Restaurant Chez Tante Marie
19 Restaurant Touba & Restaurant
    Welcome
21 Café des Grands Lacs
22 Restaurant le Chai de TT
23 Excellent Coupé-Coupé Vendor
30 Hôtel Schweitzer

    OTHER

1   Albert Schweitzer Hospital
2   Albert Schweitzer Museum
3   La Pagaïe Nightclub
4   Pirogues for Hospital
5   Football Field
9   Stadium
10 Bar-Dancing le Capitole, Bar
    Kafaïte & Lifts to Monila &
    N'Dendé
11 Alimentation aux Bonnes Courses
14 Minibuses to Mouila & Lambaréné
17 Marché No 2
20 Mobil Station
21 Halle des Grands Lacs
24 Pirogues to Port & Minibuses to
    Libreville
25 Marché No 1
26 École Protestante
27 Mairie
28 Air Gabon
29 Gaboprix General Store
32 Commissariat
33 Place de l'Indépendance
34 Post Office
35 Gendarmerie
36 Résidence du Gouverneur
37 Lycée d'État

with the tyrannical and bigoted qualities he apparently possessed.

Orientation

The city is on a large island in the Ogooué River, with a bridge (Pont No 1) on the western side leading towards Ndjolé and Lambaréné and a bridge on the eastern side (Pont No 2) leading south towards the airport and Mouila. Coming from Libreville you'll find the hospital on your left before crossing the first bridge. From the new entrance on this highway it's about half a km down a dirt road. Coming from the airport or Mouila, before crossing the bridge you'll pass just north of the Issac and Petit Paris quarters, where you'll find the port, Marché No 2 and the cheapest places in town to stay and eat.

The heart of town is the island, particularly Marché No 1 on Blvd Léon Mba. North of the market are the Hôtel Ogooué Palace (formerly the Sofitel), two Catholic missions and the city's best supermarket, Halle des Grands Lacs, which has tinned goods, bread, etc. South of it are most of the major offices including Air Gabon, several hotels, post office, commissariat, *lycée* (school), bank (changes only French franc-denominated travellers' cheques), etc.

Hospital Museum

The original hospital stands alongside the new one; part of it has been converted into a museum. The museum hours are 9 am to noon and 2.30 to 5 pm, except on Sundays when it's open from 11.30 am to 5 pm. There's no entrance fee but contributions are appreciated. If you're real lucky, your tour guide might be Schweitzer's godson, Albert Frey, an old Alsatian protestant preacher. His English is shaky but his enthusiasm makes up for it. The museum has a reasonably good gift shop where you can buy postcards, T-shirts and local crafts made largely by people from the leper colony. It also has the original old pharmacy and Schweitzer's house, and on the grounds of the museum you can see the graves of both Schweitzer and his wife.

Canoe Trips

After the hospital, the most popular tour is one by pirogue to some of the nearby lakes and tributaries. This would be a good choice if you're looking for tranquillity, good fishing, rainforests, or the chance perhaps to see a few animals, especially during the dry season from June to September and from mid-December to the end of January. Pirogue owners aren't accustomed to charging by the hour, rather they think in terms of the entire trip, eg CFA 15,000 per boat for a half-day tour. However, it is also possible to hire them by the hour. CFA 3000 per hour for the boat is usual if you bargain hard.

For shorter trips, the most popular tour is one to the nearby **Petits Lacs**. The tour takes half a day and the fare for the entire canoe is about CFA 15,000. The vegetation is lush and interesting but, unlike the trip to the Grands Lacs, you are unlikely to see many animals. See the Around Lambaréné section for details on the Grand Lacs.

Places to Stay – bottom end

The hospital no longer puts up travellers. Unusual for Gabon, there are lots of cheap hotels, most of which are across the river in Isaac and Petit Paris, about one km by road from the centre. The largest and best known is *Hôtel Lépopa*, 200 metres beyond the bridge (Pont No 2) on your right, next to Bar-Dancing le Capitole. It has about 15 rooms. Prices range from CFA 2500 to CFA 5000 per room; the cheapest ones are smelly with single beds while the CFA 5000 rooms are cleaner with fans. Both share the same bathrooms which have showers.

La Petite Auberge, which I prefer, is two blocks to the south-east and is run by a friendly English-speaking man from Benin. The rooms, which are slightly grubby, have mosquito nets and fans and cost CFA 2000. The bucket showers are inferior, but otherwise this place is not so bad. It's definitely better than either *Motel du Peuple* or the *Case de Passage à Issac*, both at the port itself. The tiny rooms at the former have mosquito nets and very grubby shared bucket showers; they cost CFA 2500 and are

essentially wooden crates attached to a noisy bar. Rooms at the latter cost CFA 2000 and are noisier still.

On the island itself there are two cheap places worth checking. *Hôtel Angleterre*, which is 100 metres south of the Mairie (town hall) facing the river, has three classes of rooms from CFA 2500 to CFA 5000. The cheapest are in a shabby building with poor ventilation while the most expensive rooms, which are recommended, are on the 2nd floor of an old two-storey house next door, overlooking the river. They have comfortable beds, mosquito nets, fans and exterior bathrooms with showers. A block inland on Rue Schoelcher, opposite the commissariat, is an unmarked pink-coloured *case de passage* with rooms for CFA 2500. The beds are clean enough but the bucket showers are filthy.

If these places exceed your budget, inquire about the *Collective Rurale de Lambaréné*, which is likely to be cheaper than all of these places if it is still open.

Places to Stay – middle

The best places to stay in this category are the two Catholic missions on the northern side of the island, along the same street as the Hôtel Ogooué Palace. Heading north from the centre for half a km, the first you'll come to is the *Mission de l'Immaculée Conception* (or École Catholique des Soeurs). The French sisters here are very friendly and charge CFA 4500 per person for a spotlessly clean, four-bed dormitory room (you'll probably have the place to yourself) with adjoining cold showers and hot showers around the back. Travellers may also use the laundry room. Some 150 metres further up the road, 70 metres before the Hôtel Ogooué Palace, is the *Mission Catholique St François-Xavier*, which has an attractive two-storey brick lodge. The French priests here charge CFA 3500 per person for a bed in a dormitory room and CFA 4500 per person for one in a clean private room. Both places are open to men and women.

Places to Stay – top end

For years the city's top hotel has been the

modern *Hôtel Ogooué Palace*, which has a pool and lighted tennis courts. Run by Sofitel, it went bankrupt in the early 1990s and was purchased by one of Bongo's sons – it's likely to reopen. If so, expect to pay about CFA 25,000/28,000 for singles/ doubles, which is what Sofitel used to charge. The location on the outskirts of town near the river is not ideal as there is no view of the river or the hospital on the other side, and it's a 15-minute walk into town.

The newly renovated *Hôtel Schweitzer* (formerly Relais Mulebi) (☎ 781055), which is on the top of a hill in the heart of town 100 metres south of Air Gabon, is better value. Under new French management and attractively redecorated, it has very decent singles/doubles with air-con for CFA 10,500/ 11,000, a breezy restaurant and bar with good views of the river plus a billiards table for entertainment.

Places to Eat

There's a great coupé-coupé place along the main drag, Blvd Léon Mba, just north of the Marché No 1. The vendor is friendly and the coupé-coupé is tender (minimum purchase is CFA 300). Some 50 metres further north on the same street, next to the Halle des Grands Lacs supermarket, is the *Café des Grands Lacs*, which is a typical Senegalese restaurant, with prices in the CFA 600 to CFA 1200 range for meat sandwiches, steak spaghetti, etc. At lunch time it's difficult to get a seat as there are only about 10 stools surrounding an open-air counter.

Further north, before the bridge, *Restaurant Touba* is a typical Senegalese restaurant recommended by the nuns. Almost next door is *Restaurant Welcome* where you can eat bush meat (crocodile, etc). Meals at both places cost about CFA 1500.

A better place for cheap eats is across the river in the Issac and Petit Paris quarters. Some of the places in this area occasionally offer bush meat, such as crocodile, wild boar, turtle and antelope. One of the better places is *Restaurant Imanenzal* near Marché No 2. It's a typical Senegalese restaurant with standard fare such as riz sauce, omelette pain etc,

and prices range from CFA 600 to CFA 1200. About 100 metres further up the same road is Alimentation aux Bonnes Courses, the only grocery store in this area, which is saying very little.

The best place to eat in this area – if you want to try bush meat – is *Restaurant Chez Tante Marie* near Marché No 2. Monkey, wild boar, gazelle and crocodile are all on the menu as well as more mundane Senegalese fare (meat and rice, omelettes, etc). An added plus is Marie, a friendly lady who loves to chat.

The best restaurant in town is the air-con *Restaurant le Chai de TT* (formerly Okolongo) (☎ 781188), which is in the centre just north of Marché No 1. Owned by Tété, a friendly French woman, it's very popular with local expatriates. It has a small menu with limited choices; main courses cost CFA 3500 and an entrée and dessert will double the price of a meal. The menu is French but includes some bush meat such as antelope. Another good place to eat is *Hôtel Schweitzer*, which has similarly priced French meals, a breezy ambience, attractive décor and good views of the river.

Entertainment

The city's top nightclub, *La Pagaïe Nightclub*, is across the river on the old road to the hospital. Most of the activity occurs on weekends when there's a cover charge (CFA 500 on Fridays and CFA 2000 on Saturdays). If you're on the eastern side of town, try *Bar-Dancing le Capitole*, which is next to Hôtel Lépopa on the paved road heading east towards the airport.

Getting There & Away

Air There are flights on Mondays and Saturdays from Libreville to Lambaréné and return; the one-way cost is CFA 19,600.

Minibus Most travellers arrive/leave by way of minibus; they cost CFA 5000 to/from Ndjolé (where you connect with the train), CFA 3000 to/from Fougamou, CFA 6000 to/from Mouila and CFA 8000 to/from Libreville. If you take a pick-up truck, it's

possible to get to N'Dendé for as little as
CFA 8000. The gare routière is the Pizo
petrol station at the Marché No 1 on Blvd
Léon Mba and rides both north and south are
fairly easy to find here. A better place for
finding trucks headed to Mouila and
N'Dendé, however, is at the intersection
where Hôtel Lépopa is located.

Boat There are three small boats that leave
on Sunday and Thursday mornings around 8
am for Port-Gentil via the Ogooué River; the
fare is CFA 10,000 and the trip takes around
10 hours. There is also a high-speed boat
which leaves daily, costs CFA 15,000 and
does the trip in about six hours. The much
larger *Azingo* leaves Lambaréné on Thursday mornings and arrives at Port-Gentil
approximately 24 hours later. Boats depart
from the small port on the eastern side of the
south branch of the Ogooué River. For more
details, see the Port-Gentil Getting There &
Away section.

Getting Around
To/From the Airport You might find a taxi
(if you're lucky) at the airport into town
otherwise you'll have to hitch a ride or walk.
The Ogooué Palace's *navette* (bus) to the
airport no longer operates.

Taxi Shared taxis cost CFA 100 for most
short trips in town, including one to the
entrance of the hospital on the main highway.
They are difficult to find, the best place on
the island being in front of the market on the

Autoroute. A taxi to yourself costs around
CFA 500 for most destinations, including
from the centre to the hospital. If you can't
find a taxi, you can always walk to the hospital, which takes 45 minutes or so.

Canoe You can get a pirogue near the Hôtel
Ogooué Palace to take you across to the
hospital for CFA 500.

AROUND LAMBARÉNÉ
Grands Lacs
These lakes – Evaro, Ezanga and Onangué –
are some 30 to 40 km downriver, and it takes
1½ to two hours by motorised pirogue to get
to them. It's an all-day trip as you will want
to eat and paddle around the lakes once
you're there. A pirogue (seats 10 people or
so) should cost about CFA 25,000 (ask
around the port or the Hôtel Ogooué Palace);
for CFA 30,000 you can also hire the four-
person boat owned by the people who run the
hotel at Lac Evaro (the office next to
Gabonprix and Hôtel Angleterre). The trip is
scenic and fascinating, with the rainforest
vegetation closing in on you on both sides of
the river. Along the way you will almost
certainly see hippo, probably pelicans and
monkeys, and possibly crocodiles.

Lac Evaro Of the Grands Lacs, the most
visited is Lac Evaro, which is some 30 km
south-west of Libreville, 1½ hours by
motorised pirogue. The main reason is that
there's a place to stay, *Le Relais Touristique
d'Evaro* (Hôtel du Lac Evaro), which is on
an otherwise uninhabited island in the centre
of the lake. It's run by a French man, Mr
Legrand, his nephew and the nephew's
Mauritian wife, who is a great cook. There
are four simple but very decent bungalows
with four or five rooms each and a generator.
A room with fan, mosquito nets and private
bathroom costs CFA 10,000 and the meals at
the restaurant are excellent, with bush meat
available as well as Gabonese specialities
such as feuilles de manioc and chicken
nyemboué.
  Most people take the two-day weekend
special, which costs CFA 35,000 per person,

Pelican

including transportation from Lambaréné, one night's lodging, all meals and excursions on Lac Evaro. If you pay for these items separately, you'll pay CFA 10,000 for a room at the hotel and up to CFA 45,000 for round-trip transportation by pirogue from Libreville. If you take the weekend special, Legrand will pick you up in Lambaréné and point out animals and trees along the way that you would otherwise miss, possibly stopping at one of the tiny settlements along the way (Bordeaux and Junkville are two) to harvest a few lemons or mangoes.

There's lots to do here, including swimming in the lake or the hotel's 14-metre pool, sailboarding, water skiing, ping-pong, fishing and nature excursions on the lake by canoe or paddle-boat and through the rainforest. Mr Legrand will also take you to local fishing villages and, most interesting, if the night is bright he will show you where hippos go grazing in the plains. You can make reservations in Lambaréné; the hotel's office (☎ 781075) is about 100 metres south of the Mairie, next to Gaboprix.

MOUILA

Mouila is the major town between Lambaréné and the Congo border. On Sundays, you're likely to find a number of people picnicking, bathing (despite bilharzia!) and fishing at Lac Bleu five km away. There's a road, but taking a pirogue ride from the town centre *débarcadère* (docks) to the lake would be far more interesting.

Places to Stay & Eat

For an inexpensive room, try the *Mission Catholique*, the American-run *Mission Protestante*, or the *Mess Militaire*, which is open to travellers and has seven rooms with air-con and a bar-restaurant. The city's top hotel-restaurant is the modern, 20-room *Hôtel du Lac Bleu* (☎ 861096; 733156, Libreville). Part of the Relais Mulebi chain, it overlooks the Ngounié River and has singles/doubles for about CFA 10,000/ 12,000. Two nightclubs to inquire about are *O Imogu* and *O Wetsiga*.

Getting There & Away

Minibuses leave every morning south for N'Dendé (CFA 3000) and north for Lambaréné (CFA 6000) and on to Libreville (CFA 14,000). They take about three hours to N'Dendé, six hours to Lambaréné and all day to Libreville, but sometimes more during the rainy season. On Mondays, Thursdays and Saturdays you can take an Air Gabon flight to/from Libreville for CFA 27,200 (one way).

N'DENDÉ

N'Dendé (n-den-DAY) is notable only because it's on one of the two major routes (the most westerly one) to the Congo and the last major town travellers pass through before reaching the border. The centre of town is the intersection where Nounes supermarket is located. Don't forget to get your exit stamp at immigration, which is on the south-western side of town beyond the market.

Places to Stay & Eat

There are two cheap places to stay. One is the *Mission Catholique*, which is a little way north-east (as the crow flies) of the intersection. It charges CFA 3000 for a double for the first night and CFA 2000 per night thereafter; there are showers but no fans. If there's no one at the mission, you'll have to go to the Sisters' residence about two km away on the edge of town on the road to the Congo, to get the key.

The other place is a similarly priced *case de passage* west of the main intersection, just beyond the *Relais St-Hubert*. The latter is the best hotel in town, with ventilated doubles and private baths for CFA 7500. For food it's way over-priced, with Cokes for CFA 500, large Regab beers for CFA 1000 and continental breakfasts for CFA 1200. Still, the St-Hubert is a good place to come at night for a relaxing drink on the veranda, a game of ping-pong and/or meeting expatriates.

For cheap eats and drinks, try the bar well south of the main intersection. It offers excellent beef brochettes for CFA 100 and grilled fish for CFA 500, but for a full meal

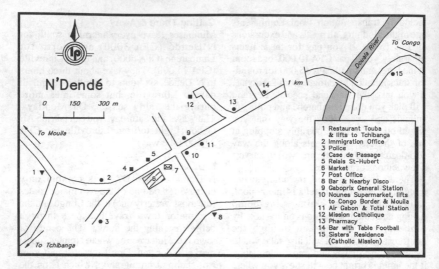

N'Dendé

To Congo
To Mouila
To Tchibanga

Douala River

0   150   300 m

1 km

1 Restaurant Touba
  & lifts to Tchibanga
2 Immigration Office
3 Police
4 Case de Passage
5 Relais St–Hubert
6 Market
7 Post Office
8 Bar & Nearby Disco
9 Gaboprix General Station
10 Nounes Supermarket, lifts
   to Congo Border & Mouila
11 Air Gabon & Total Station
12 Mission Catholique
13 Pharmacy
14 Bar with Table Football
15 Sisters' Residence
   (Catholic Mission)

you must order in advance. (There's also a good disco which a Belgian teacher living nearby helped build.) Otherwise, your only choices may be *Restaurant Touba* on the outskirts of town on the road to Mouila, just beyond the turn-off for Tchibanga (mediocre food and not very pleasant), the central market near the main intersection or, for tinned goods, Nounes supermarket at the intersection.

Getting There & Away
Most transportation in this area is by pick-up truck or minibus. Expect to pay about CFA 3000 to the Congolese border or Mouila (three or four hours to either) and CFA 2000 or CFA 3000 to Tchibanga, 207 km to the south-west. The main intersection is generally the best place to look for lifts. For Tchibanga, however, you may do better waiting opposite the Restaurant Touba. The road to Tchibanga is in terrible condition, with lots of potholes, so be prepared for a bone-shattering trip of about 2½ hours. Fortunately, the landscape en route is fascinating.

TCHIBANGA
A prosperous town with paved streets, 207

km to the south-east of N'Dendé near the coast, Tchibanga is in a valley which suddenly spreads out in front of you as you're descending from the hills en route from N'Dendé. This is a savanna area surrounded by forests and the starting point for the rare traveller bent on a trip or hunting safari to the **Réserve de Moukalaba** to the north-west and to the **Réserve de N'Dendé** to the east. While excursions to these reserves are rare, you may be able to arrange something through Hôtel de la Nyanga, the city's best hotel and named after the river which passes along the outskirts of town and is best viewed from the bridge.

Places to Stay & Eat
If you can't get a room at the *Mission Catholique*, try *Hôtel Dissiégoussou*, which has air-con rooms and a restaurant. The city's top hotel, the three-storey, 35-room *Hôtel de la Nyanga* (☎ 8006; 733156 in Libreville), is part of the Relais Mulebi chain and charges about CFA 10,000/12,000 for air-con singles/doubles.

Getting There & Away
You can fly here on Mondays, Tuesdays and

Fridays from Libreville on Air Gabon for CFA 29,500 (one way). There are minibuses every day ploughing the route between Tchibanga, N'Dendé and Mouila.

The North & East

BITAM

A very active town with a large market, Bitam is 36 km south of the Cameroun border in the heart of Fang country. It is the first town you pass through after crossing the border. Border officials here have been known to give travellers a hard time; they may be looking for drinking money.

Surprisingly, you'll find a *quartier* (an area) of Hausa traders from northern Nigeria. You'll find these traders around the market and the Place de l'Indépendance. Whatever you do, if you're coming from Cameroun you must get an entry stamp put into your passport in Bitam by immigration. Travellers failing to do this have been fined CFA 35,000!

Places to Stay & Eat

The cheapest place to stay appears to be *Hôtel Beau Séjour*, which has adequate rooms for CFA 3000. *Hôtel des Voyageurs* is nicer, with 25 rooms starting at CFA 6000. Both places are recommended by Peace Corps volunteers. Other possibilities include the five-roomed *Hôtel Rachelle* with bar, the 14-roomed *Hôtel du Peuple* and the *Mission Catholique*.

Two inexpensive Senegalese restaurants which have been recommended are one opposite the Beau Séjour and one behind the Akiba store. As in most towns throughout Gabon, coupé-coupé (CFA 200 to CFA 300) cut to your order and brochettes (CFA 100) are available on the streets.

Getting There & Away

Minibuses and bush taxis leave from the gare routière near the market. There are lots of them ploughing the Bitam to Oyem road (75 km, one hour) and they are generally in good condition. Fares are CFA 2000 to Oyem and CFA 15,000 to Libreville. If you're headed north for Cameroun, you may need to get an exit permit stamped in your passport here, so check.

OYEM

Some 400 km north-east of Libreville on the road to Cameroun, Oyem is cocoa country and a Fang area. It's the largest city in the north with many amenities including a 1st-class hotel, several banks, supermarkets, stores and lots of places to eat and drink. As in Bitam to the north, you'll find numerous Muslim Hausa traders in the city's two markets and no less than three mosques scattered over town catering for them.

If you're here on a Sunday, you might head for the huge cathedral in Angon, a suburb north of Oyem, for an interesting mass with wonderful singing to African musical instruments. The bus leaves from opposite the Air Gabon office (CFA 100); otherwise take a shared taxi (CFA 200).

For some real exercise you could try climbing Mont Nkoum 32 km away; coming from Bitam, you'll recognise it by the giant metal cross which was planted on top of it by some protestant ministers.

Orientation

Most of the major stores and offices are along the main drag, which extends north-south in an undulating fashion. The heart of town is the intersection at the Shell station and the nearby gare routière and the Place de l'Indépendance. Cinéma le Woleu, the post office and most stores, banks and hotels are in this area, while most government offices, including the Hôtel de Ville and *gendarmerie* (police), are about a km to the north along the main drag. The main market, Marché d'Adjougou, is south-west of the Shell station intersection, just off the main drag, while the new market, Marché d'Akoakam, is on the north-western outskirts of town. One of the best places to buy groceries is the Supermarché Maxi-Centre, which is a short distance south of the Shell station.

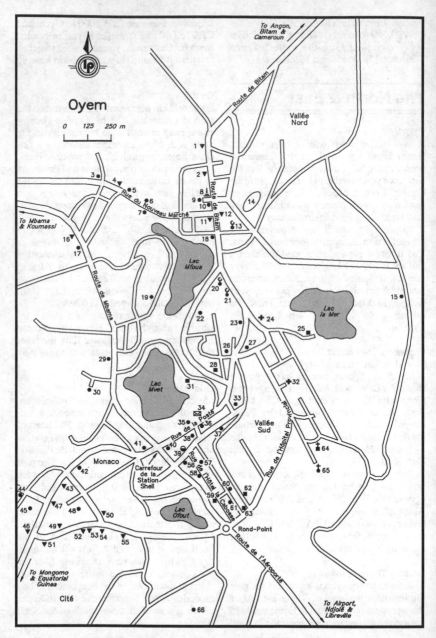

Oyem

0   125   250 m

To Angon,
Bitam &
Cameroun

Route de Bitam

Vallée
Nord

1 ▼
2 ▼
3 ●
4 ▼
5 ●
Rue du Nouveau Marché
6 ●
7 ●
8 ↓
9 ●
10 ●
Route de Bitam
11 ▼
12 ▼
13 ●
14
18 ▼

To Mbama
& Koumassi

16 ▼
17 ●

Route de Mbama

Lac
Mfoua

19 ●
20 ●
21 ●
22 ●
23 ●
24 ✝
25 ●

Lac
la Mer

15 ●

26 ●
27 ●
28 ■
29 ●
30 ●

Lac
Mvet

31 ■

32 ✝

33 ●
34 ✉
La Poste
35 ●
36 ■
37 ●

Vallée
Sud

Rue de l'Hôpital Provincial

41 ●

40 ●
38 ●
39 ●

Monaco

42 ●

Carrefour
de la
Station
Shell

Rue de l'Hôtel la Cabosse

56 ●
58 ●
57 ●
59 ●
60 ●
61 ●
62 ■
63 ●

64 ✝
65 ✝

44 ▼
43 ▼
45 ●
47 ▼
48 ●
50 ▼
46 ●
49 ▼
52 ▼
53 ▼
54 ▼
55 ▼
51 ▼

Lac
Ofout

Rond-Point

Route de l'Aéroport

To Mongomo
& Equatorial
Guinea

Cité

66 ●

To Airport,
Ndjolé &
Libreville

■ PLACES TO STAY		10	BP Station
		13	Old Mosque
25	Mission Catholique	14	Municipal Stadium
28	Hôtel de Ville	15	Wood Sculptor
31	Hôtel Relais du Mvet	18	Boulangerie
59	Hôtel la Cabosse	19	Gendarmerie
62	No-Name Hotel-Nightclub	20	Grande Mosquée
63	Mission Protestante	21	New Mosque
		22	Governor's Residence
▼ PLACES TO EAT		23	BEAC Bank
		24	Hospital
1	Le Bambou Restaurant Nightclub	26	Courts
2	Coupé-Coupé Vendor & Senegalese	27	Gendarmerie
	Restaurant	29	Amadou Baro's Boutique
4	Restaurant le Manguier	30	Lycée d'État
9	Senegalese Restaurant	31	Préfecture
11	Restaurant Alimentation	32	Hôpital Provincial
12	Restaurant Moderne	33	Commissariat
16	Bar-Restaurant Aquarium	34	Post Office
17	Coupé-Coupé Vendor	35	BICIG Bank
43	Senegalese Restaurant Hibiscus	36	UGB Bank
46	Bar Matita ô Bloqué, Restaurant les	37	Pharmacy
	Voyageurs & Bar Safari Ambiance	38	Place de l'Indépendance
47	Restaurant Grand Canari	39	Gare Routière
49	Bar Confiance & Bar la Source	40	Shell Station
50	Restaurant Moderne d'Adjougou	41	Cinéma le Woleu & Le Balafon
51	Bar-Restaurant Dicky		Nightclub
52	Bar Beau Séjour	42	Bookshop
53	Coupé-Coupé Vendors	44	Bar Coleçon
54	Bar le Futbol Canon 120	45	School
55	Bar Énergie	48	Main Market
61	Biliba Restaurant-Nightclub	56	Mobil Station
		57	Supermarché Maxi-Centre
OTHER		58	Boulangerie, Ruptier's General Store
			& Air Gabon
3	Marché d'Akoakam (Nouveau Marché)	60	Auto Garage Shop
5	School	64	St-Charles Cathedral
6	Catholic School	65	École Catholique St-Basile
7	Bar Baracuda	66	École Protestante
8	Bwiti Temple		

Places to Stay

For cheap accommodation, try the *Mission Catholique* on the eastern side of town, 400 metres east of the main drag near Lac la Mer, the *Mission Protestante*, which is 500 metres south of the gare routière, or the Peace Corps *case de passage* where some travellers have stayed.

Among the hotels, the seven-room *Hôtel la Cabosse* (☎ 986088), 300 metres south of the gare, charges CFA 5800/6800 for singles/doubles and operates both a restaurant and a nightclub, the *Nthe*. If it's full, try the *no-name hotel-nightclub* two blocks to the east; it has air-con rooms for CFA 10,000 and a restaurant. The city's top hotel and restaurant is the modern, six-storey *Hôtel Relais du Mvet* (☎ 986226; 733156 in Libreville) in the heart of town, off the main drag overlooking Lac Mvet. It's part of the Relais Mulebi chain with 70 air-con rooms starting from CFA 17,400.

Places to Eat

The highest concentration of bars and cheap restaurants, many of them with Senegalese fare, is on the south-western side of town around the main market area; main meals are in the CFA 500 to CFA 1500 range. At the market itself you can buy bean sandwiches for CFA 200 and nearby, at *Bar Cheers* the owner, Martine, makes the best brochettes in town for CFA 100. Or have an excellent meat sandwich at *Mini-Pipermint* for the bargain price of CFA 350.

Two of the best Senegalese restaurants in town are *Chez Sao* and *Restaurant Hibiscus*, just north of Marché d'Adjougou. Hibiscus is on the main road along with *Restaurant Grand Canari*, *Bar Matita ô Bloqué*, *Restaurant les Voyageurs* and *Bar Safari Ambiance*. On the street running east-west along the south side of the market are a number of bars and restaurants, the most notable of which is *Bar-Restaurant Dicky*, which serves good bush meat for CFA 1000 a plate. Others along that street include *Bar la Source*, *Bar Confiance*, *Bar Beau Séjour*, coupé-coupé vendors, *Bar Énergie* and *Bar le Futbol Canon 120*, all of which serve food.

In the centre, *Hôtel Relais du Mvet* charges CFA 5000 for a full meal and less for à la carte selections and is one of the city's top two restaurants. The other is the *Restaurant Il Paradiso* run by a Belgian. It serves excellent meals (eg steak, cordon bleu, spaghetti) for around CFA 3000.

The city's other two hotels, which are to the south of the Shell station intersection including *Hôtel la Cabosse*, have less expensive restaurants, while prices at the relatively exclusive *Biliba Restaurant-Nightclub* nearby are on a par with the Mvet's. Between these places and the Shell station you'll find a bakery and the Supermarché Maxi-Centre.

On the northern side of town along the main drag you'll find, north to south, *Le Bambou Restaurant-Nightclub* (meals cost from CFA 500 to CFA 3000), coupé-coupé vendors, and three typical Senegalese restaurants with meals in the CFA 500 to CFA 1500 price range including *Restaurant Alimentation* and *Restaurant Moderne*. Further south but before the Grande Mosquée is a bakery.

For good chicken and fish à la braisse, head for *Bar-Restaurant Aquarium* on the western outskirts of town on the road to Mbomo. Nearby, there's a coupé-coupé vendor as well.

Entertainment

For drinks and dancing, the best top-end place is the *Biliba Restaurant-Nightclub*. Other nightclubs include the *no-name hotel-nightclub* nearby, *Le Balafon Nightclub* in the centre next to Cinéma le Woleu, and *Le Bambou Restaurant-Nightclub* on the northern outskirts of town.

Getting There & Away

Air Gabon, which has an office 300 metres south of the Shell station intersection, has flights to/from Libreville daily except Tuesday for CFA 25,600 (one way).

Minibuses plough the northern route to/from Bitam (CFA 2000) and the Cameroun border as well as the southern route to/from N'Djolé (CFA 9000 to CFA 10,000) and Libreville (CFA 10,000 to CFA 12,000 if you bargain, otherwise about CFA 15,000). Those to/from Libreville (frequently in bad condition) leave early in the morning from the gare routière and usually arrive in N'Djolé about eight hours later and in Libreville well after nightfall.

MAKOKOU

Some 610 km east of Libreville, Makokou (12,000 inhabitants) and the surrounding area, particularly **Bélinga** to the north-east, is one of the prettiest areas in Gabon, with rainforests and beautiful mountains. Those to the north-east around Bélinga (a mining camp built long ago by the Americans) and **Mékambo** are full of iron ore, so the government is seeking foreign aid for an extension of the Transgabonais to Makokou. However, world prices for iron ore have remained depressed for years and with no significant rises in sight, that dream is unlikely to be realised.

The city centre is fairly compact but the town is surprisingly sprawling, with a large number of West Africans. Don't look for a bank as there're none here but do drop by the gendarmerie as this is required.

If you're interested in woodcarvings, ask around for Thomas Issoko in Quartier M'Bolo Bas-Fond. He's the last Bakota who knows how to make the famous *masque du reliquaire*, a wooden statue covered in leather used as a shrine to the ancestors. Even his children have no interest in learning!

Places to Stay & Eat

The *Mission Catholique*, which is about half a km from the market, has bug-infested rooms for CFA 5000 and bathrooms with broken toilets. There's also a *Mission Protestante* which might be worth trying. For something more up-market, try *Les Merveilles de l'Ivindo*, which has bungalows in a garden next to the river. The city's top hotel used to be the 35-room, three-storey *Hôtel de l'Ivindo* (☎ 3069), but it is now closed, apparently for good.

For African food, try the popular *Relais de la Corniche* on Blvd Bongo, the main drag.

Entertainment

For dancing, there's the *Mbala* on the Alar Mitang road.

Getting There & Away

The easiest and quickest way by far to get here from Libreville is by air; Air Gabon has flights on Tuesdays and Saturdays (CFA 25,600 one way).

There are also minibuses every day headed to/from Booué (199 km), connecting with the Transgabonais; they charge CFA 5000 and the trip takes four hours. If you pay the driver the night before, he will come by your place the next morning to pick you up. For information on the route south to Okondja and Franceville, see the Getting There & Away section under Okondja.

AROUND MAKOKOU

Makokou is in the country's major Pygmy area. Their camps are scattered throughout the forests, and are difficult to get to; the nearest ones are a good 100 km to the east. For a small adventure, you could hire a pirogue and head for **Les Chutes de Loa-Loa** 10 km away on the Ivindo River.

Mongouli Waterfalls are much further away.

Gabon's forests in this area still harbour great numbers of forest elephants and a myriad of other species, but this area is still unprotected and accessible only by canoe. For a truly major adventure, consider hiring a pirogue and guides to take you northward up the Nouna River. You'll need a very knowledgeable guide or two because even finding the mouth to the river is quite difficult as there are many false channels leading nowhere.

The area up that river is literally filled with forest elephants. Because of the thick bush, you may not actually see so many elephants but you definitely will see their trails everywhere, facilitating passage through the dense forest. Unbashful chattering monkeys race through the treetops and in the evening you are likely to be entertained by throngs of parrots. And if you're real lucky, you might even come upon a family of lowland gorillas, which spend much of their daylight hours munching on fruit in the tall trees.

After visiting this area in 1989, the African Programme Director of the World Wide Fund for Nature (WWF) said 'it was like seeing Africa as it was during the 1890s, untouched and bursting with wildlife' – which is why the Fund has initiated efforts to help the government turn this area into a protected reserve.

BOOUÉ

On a beautiful site along the Ogooué River, 415 km east of Libreville and 12 km south of the equator, Booué is about the halfway

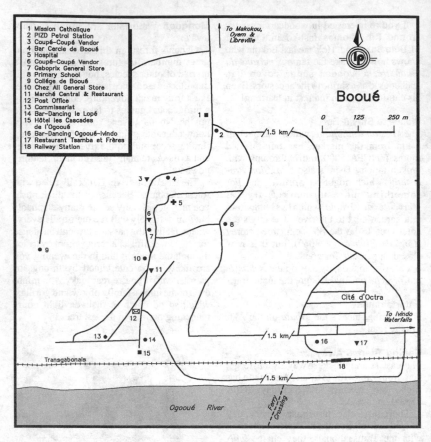

1 Mission Catholique
2 PIZD Petrol Station
3 Coupé-Coupé Vendor
4 Bar Cercle de Booué
5 Hospital
6 Coupé-Coupé Vendor
7 Gaboprix General Store
8 Primary School
9 Collège de Booué
10 Chez Ali General Store
11 Marché Central & Restaurant
12 Post Office
13 Commissariat
14 Bar-Dancing le Lopé
15 Hôtel les Cascades
     de l'Ogooué
16 Bar-Dancing Ogooué-Ivindo
17 Restaurant Tsamba et Frères
18 Railway Station

Booué

To Makokou,
Oyem &
Libreville

0   125   250 m

Cité d'Octra

To Ivindo
Waterfalls

Transgabonais

Ogooué   River

Ferry Crossing

point on the Transgabonais line to Franceville and in the centre of a principal logging
zone, with rolling hills in every direction.

The town is small but spread out, nevertheless nothing is out of walking distance,
including the railway station which is about
three km east of the central area. The older
part of town is on a hill overlooking the
rapids while the newer part around the
railway station consists of neatly lined
houses which all look the same except some
have TV antennas and others don't.

Other than fraternising with the locals,
about the only thing to do here is to take in

the beauty of the river and forests. For the
price of a couple of beers, you might be able
to find a local to give you a tour of the river
in his canoe. About 40 km east of town are
some waterfalls where the Ivindo River
meets the Ogooué but getting there by canoe
would take at least all day.

For tinned goods, try Gaboprix supermarket on the main drag near the market or Chez
Ali nearby.

Places to Stay

The French priest, Mr Sockeel, at the *Mission Catholique* on the northern outskirts of

town, likes company and has been known to put up one or two travellers for the night in his spare room, sometimes free of charge. You might also try your luck with the locals or one of the local Peace Corps volunteers. Your only remaining alternative is the 20-room *Hôtel les Cascades de l'Ogooué*, which is in the heart of town in a magnificent setting overlooking the river. Run by an eccentric French man who caters to expatriates, it's rather expensive, around CFA 10,000 for a room and CFA 4000 for a meal.

Places to Eat
You can get decent African fare at *Restaurant Tsamba et Frères*, near the railway station just east of the gare. In the centre you'll find a small place to eat at the market as well as good coupé-coupé a few minutes' walk north thereof on the main drag.

Entertainment
For drinks, good music and dancing, try *Bar Cercle de Booué* on the main drag between the market and the Mission Catholique, *Bar-Dancing le Lopé* further down the street near Hôtel les Cascades de l'Ogooué or, liveliest of all with dancing to dawn, *Bar-Dancing Ogooué-Ivindo*, which is just west of the railway station.

Getting There & Away
First-class/2nd-class seats on the train cost CFA 14,800/11,800 to Libreville and CFA 13,100/10,400 to Franceville. Minibuses to Makokou cost CFA 5000 and always meet the train coming from Libreville. Beer trucks headed north for Oyem are fairly frequent; other trucks headed west for Ndjolé and Libreville can also be found with some difficulty. The least travelled route is south towards Lastoursville. Occasionally, it's possible to find trucks headed that way; the cost is around CFA 5000 and the trip takes about six hours via Lopé.

RÉSERVE DE LA LOPÉ
If you're set on seeing some wildlife and don't mind roughing it a bit, the best place to head for is the Réserve de la Lopé adjoining

Parc National de l'Okanda and bordering the highway and railway, some 40 km west of Booué. Established in 1982, the reserve consists of open land with small but dense forests beside the creeks that run through the reserve. Unfortunately, most animals favour the forest except during the rainy season when there's water everywhere. So the rainy season is the best time to see many of the animals, especially large herds of buffalo. The other animals, including forest elephants, various types of antelope and lowland gorillas, are not easy to see even during the rainy season.

The main problem with visiting the reserve is that you require a vehicle and hiring one is expensive and problematic; the locals say the cost of hiring a vehicle is CFA 30,000. Inquire at the hotels as they may be able to arrange something or ask the game wardens if they'll take you around in their vehicle. There's also a park entrance fee of CFA 5000. The reserve was closed in mid-1992, so check to see if it has reopened before heading here.

Places to Stay & Eat
The park entrance is near the railway station; there you'll find an expensive hotel which is sometimes closed, as well as *Le Campement*, which has bungalows for CFA 8000 but no restaurant. For cheaper accommodation, head for *Au Nid des Routiers*, which is a small hotel at the eastern end of the village, opposite the grocery store. The basic rooms with clean sheets and mosquito coils cost CFA 3000. The shower and toilet are in a shack behind the hotel. Gustave, the friendly owner, also runs a small restaurant but you should order your meals in advance to be sure. There's also a rustic *case de passage* at the Eau et Forêt station in Lopé. Sleeping at the research centre in the reserve, however, is not permitted.

Getting There & Away
Lopé village is about five hours on the train from Libreville/Owendo, two stops before Booué.

The South-East

LASTOURSVILLE

While the Transgabonais was being constructed, Lastoursville, called 'Lozo' or 'Bonda' by the locals, was a boom town; now it's just another stop on the Transgabonais albeit still one of the better ones. It's also popular with truck drivers on their way to Franceville, in part perhaps because the local restaurants are relatively good and the lodging is cheaper than in many towns.

Named after the French general Lastours but now sometimes spelled Lastourville, the town is attractively located on the southern banks of the Ogooué River, with rolling hills all around. The heart of town is along Rue de Lastours which stretches 700 metres west along the river from the Rond-Point de la Préfecture where the post office is located to just beyond the Air Gabon office. The market and most small shops, bars and restaurants (but no banks) are located on or just off this strip. There are five roads branching out from the rond-point, including one to the north over the bridge, then east to the railway station seven km away, and one south (Blvd de l'Indépendance) past Cité Octra towards the airport and Moanda.

Things to See & Do

If you're interested in hiking, a good destination might be **Boundji Waterfalls**; just ask one of the small boys in town to guide you there. Another potential destination are the *grottes* (caves) outside town. The starting point is **Limbenga**, a village about four km from the centre on the road to the airport and Moanda. Ask someone there to guide you; you'll probably end up with five or 10 people accompanying you. The caves are at the escarpment of a mountain half an hour's walk from the village. They are not deep or large but they do have stalactites and stalagmites as well as bats. A torch is advisable although not absolutely required, and be prepared to pay as much as CFA 3000 for the opportunity to see the caves.

In town, if you go down to the Ogooué chances are you'll see someone fishing; however, taking a pirogue ride on the river is difficult as they have largely disappeared in this area.

Places to Stay

The *Mission Catholique* in the friendly village of **Bamboro**, four km west of the centre on the road to Libreville, is good value for money but it's an hour's walk from the centre. The French sisters there will gladly rent you one of the three spotless rooms for CFA 3000. There's also a small *Mission Protestante* about half a km up the hill from the Rond-Point on the road to the airport. It's run by an American pastor who may have a room to offer.

Chez Madame Nimbé, an unmarked home-like restaurant one block south of Sappol supermarket right in the town centre, is a very popular place. Madame Nimbé, who is a friendly Camerounian woman married to a Gabonese man, has about eight rooms for CFA 2500. This place has a wonderful, relaxing ambience and is highly recommended for both cheap lodging and good food. If her rooms are full, you may have to settle for a *no-name hotel*, 10-room dump one block to the west on Rue Guy Poncaille. It's about as bad as you'll find in Gabon, with filthy shared toilets and rooms for CFA 3000 (CFA 3500 with fan).

Hôtel Mulundu is closed except on special occasions, leaving *Hôtel Ngoombi Club* (☎ 254), an attractive place a short walk east of the Rond-Point, as the only 'hotel'. Overlooking the river, it has six decent air-con rooms for CFA 13,000 and a 1st-class restaurant.

Places to Eat

For good food and ambience, head for *Chez Madame Nimbé*, which is unmarked but conveniently located in the centre and one of the most popular places in town. In addition to tables with tablecloths, there are several sofas and a radio with music, all giving this place a relaxing home-like feeling. She can prepare all sorts of bush meat (antelope,

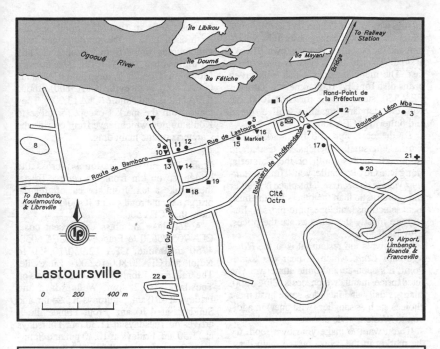

Lastoursville

0   200   400 m

1	Hôtel Mulundu	12	Sappol Supermarket
2	Hôtel Ngoombi Club	13	Bar
3	Lastours' Tomb	14	Restaurant Viande de Brousse
4	Restaurant Maman Débrouillard	15	Gaboprix General Store
5	Lively Bars	16	Coupé-Coupé Vendor & Shell Station
6	Post Office	17	School
7	Telecommunications Centre	18	No-Name Hotel
8	Stadium	19	Chez Madame Nimhé
9	Kasa Bar	20	Gendarmerie
10	Caféteria	21	Old Hospital
11	Air Gabon	22	Medical Centre (New)

porc-pic, etc) plus regular Gabonese and Camerounian dishes, most for CFA 1000. Her poisson avec sauce for CFA 1000 is truly outstanding, but she may not be able to offer you that or some of her other more exotic dishes unless you come in advance and tell her what you want.

Another good place for traditional African food is *Restaurant Maman Débrouillard*,

which is not far away. Look for the sign just west of the Air Gabon office; this rustic place is about 60 metres down a dirt path towards the river and fairly well marked. The friendly Ms Débrouillard can also prepare all kinds of bush meat, most for CFA 1000 a plate, but the ambience here is not quite up to Madame Nimbé's standards.

Nearby on Rue de Lastours, some 30

metres west of Air Gabon, is the *Caféteria*, which is a typical Senegalese-style restaurant and the best of this type in town. There's a small TV and the service is particularly fast. The menu includes a fish with green beans dish for CFA 1000, omelette garni for CFA 850, steak banane for CFA 1000, etc plus the standard breakfast (coffee, bread and butter) for CFA 300.

To the east, opposite the market, is a similar but smaller Senegalese restaurant. About 20 metres south of the Caféteria, along Rue Guy Poncaille, you'll find *Restaurant Viande de Brousse*. This place is smaller and more rustic than the others but the bush meat selections (antelope, porc-pic, sanglier, etc) are mostly the same as are the prices, CFA 1000 a plate.

The town's top restaurant is at the *Hôtel Ngoombi Club*, which is near the Rond-Point; it's open-air and quite attractive. The fixed price menu, which costs CFA 3500, changes daily and includes some bush meat choices such as sanglier (wild boar) in addition to Western-style dishes.

If you want to make your own food, try the market in the centre on the main drag, Gaboprix general store next door and Sappol supermarket about 200 metres to the west, next to Air Gabon. These supermarkets are the best you'll find, which isn't saying much. There's also coupé-coupé sold at the market, but it's likely to be as tough as leather.

Entertainment
For a lively bar with music blasting away, try the one opposite the market; it charges CFA 350 for a large Regab beer as does Chez Madame Nimbé, which has a more tranquil and comfortable setting for a drink. For dancing, head for *Kasa Bar* behind Air Gabon. It has a fairly large dancing floor and good music blasting away even during the day.

Getting There & Away
Air Air Gabon, on Rue de Lastours, has flights on Mondays and Fridays to/from Libreville; the one-way cost is CFA 32,500.

Minibus & Bush Taxi Most minibuses and bush taxis leave in the mornings and fares and journey times from Lastoursville are: Koulamoutou (CFA 1500, 1½ hours), Moundou (CFA 2500, three hours), Moanda (CFA 2800), Franceville (CFA 3800), Booué (CFA 6000), and Ndjolé (CFA 13,000). They leave from the market except for those to Koulamoutou which leave from outside the Caféteria on the main drag.

Train The railway station is across the bridge, seven km from the centre. To get there, take a taxi from the cut-off for the bridge near the rond-point; it should not cost more than CFA 500.

A 1st-class/2nd-class coach seat costs CFA 7050/5650 to Franceville, CFA 6050/4750 to Booué, CFA 12,950/10,350 to Ndjolé and CFA 20,800/16,600 to Libreville. The train from Libreville/Owendo arrives on Tuesdays at 5.25 pm, Wednesdays and Fridays at 4.10 am, Saturdays at 5.25 pm and Sundays at 4.10 am. From Franceville it arrives on Tuesdays at 11.30 pm, Thursdays at 11.50 am, Fridays at 10.30 pm and Saturdays, Sundays and holidays at 2 pm.

KOULAMOUTOU
Only 55 km south-west of the Lastoursville railway station, Koulamoutou is the provincial capital and one of the country's leading coffee and cocoa areas. The town is spread out along the banks of a river that runs through the middle of town. You might look around for one of the cubist-like *mvoudi* or *bodi* masks characteristic of the area, or climb 800-metre Mont Kondzo nearby. There are some *grottes* (caves) on the way up, but you'll miss them without a guide.

Places to Stay
For a cheap place to stay, try the *Mission Catholique* on top of the hill, called *Colline Mayi*, or the American-run *Mission Protestante*. If you can't get a bed at one of these places, your only alternative may be the 35-room *Hôtel la Bouenguidi* (☎ 655169; 733156, Libreville), which is a part of the

Relais Mulebi chain with rooms starting around CFA 8000.

Getting There & Away

A minibus to/from Lastoursville costs CFA 1500 and there's at least one a day. From there you can catch the Transgabonais.

MOANDA

Manganese, and lots of it, is the raison d'être of Moanda, 60 km west of Franceville by paved road. It's smaller and much more compact than Franceville, with most places within fairly easy walking distance of the centre, and thus more 'user friendly'. Moanda also has one of the larger French populations in the country and a few of the amenities that go with it, including a large supermarket stuffed with French goods.

The heart of this relatively new town is the Marché Municipal, which hops especially on weekends. Here you'll find most transport, cheap restaurants and several bars; the city's hotels, including one with a pool, are all within easy walking distance of it as is the BIPG bank. The latter has been known to change dollar-denominated travellers' cheques but must cable Libreville first for the rate.

The entire area is surrounded by verdant rolling hills. The mines are located on the top of them and just below are the relatively comfortable suburban homes of the company executives; then come the rows of company houses for the African miners. In the distance you can see the square-shaped Mt Moudinga, after which the city's top hotel is named.

Among the grocery stores, the biggest and best is Saen supermarket on the main drag opposite the taxi stand.

Places to Stay

The best value for money is the *Mission Catholique St-Dominique*, which charges CFA 4500 for its pleasant but sparse rooms with double beds, fresh sheets every day, air-con and moderately clean shared bathrooms. The French priest here is very friendly and welcomes travellers whole-heartedly. It's two blocks south of the market on the main drag; look for the steeple of the church next door.

If it's full or you prefer places with an African ambience, try *Hôtel Ampassi* (☎ 661329), which is unusually friendly. It's on the main drag, about 200 metres north of the market. The hotel's 10 rooms are fairly spacious and quite clean with fans and exterior bathrooms; they cost CFA 5000. There's an African restaurant next door.

Just north of the market on the main drag, the very popular old French-run *Auberge le Moulébé* (☎ 661038; telex 5568), has a very relaxing ambience and an attractive restaurant. It is highly recommended if you can afford the price – CFA 7000 to CFA 10,000 for an air-con room and CFA 4500 for the special full-course meal of the day. It's often full so reservations are advisable.

The city's top address, *Hôtel du Mont Moudinga* (☎ 661395; 733156 in Libreville), is an attractive modern place with a pool (CFA 1000 for nonguests) and palm trees in the centre and a bar-restaurant overlooking it. The hotel, part of the Relais Mulebi chain, is not far from the centre; it has 40 air-con singles/doubles for CFA 10,000/12,000.

Places to Eat

Moanda is renowned among Peace Corps volunteers for its coupé-coupé. The undisputed star is Youssouf, whose open-air grill faces the northern side of the market, on the same block as the Auberge. In all of Gabon you'll be hard pressed to find more delicious and tender meat. The secret is that his beef comes from France, which costs no more than the tough local meat.

There are also some typical Senegalese restaurants in the area, including *Restaurant Maison Lefouta-Toro* across the street and the rustic *Restaurant Touba* facing the Auberge. At the latter, all dishes, including manioc poisson, riz sauce and steak frites, are in the CFA 800 to CFA 1200 range except omelettes (CFA 650) and the standard breakfast of coffee, bread and butter (CFA 300).

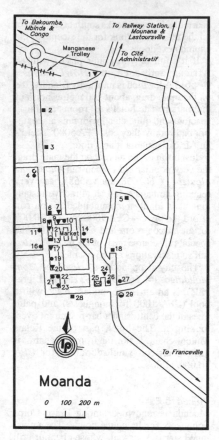

PLACES TO STAY

3   Hôtel Ampassi
5   Hôtel du Mont Moudinga
6   Auberge le Moulébé
18 Hôtel de Ville
28 Mission Catholique St-Dominique

PLACES TO EAT

1   Coupé-Coupé Vendor
3   Restaurant la Gargote
7   Coupé-Coupé Chez Youssou
8   Restaurant Touba
9   Restaurant Maison Lefouta-Toro
12 King's Restaurant
15 Coupé-Coupé de 3
17 Pâtisserie & Yoghurt Sellers
20 Restaurant Royal
24 Restaurant Porte de Masuku

OTHER

1   Bar-Club Dernière Souffle
2   Schóol
4   Mosque
10 Bar Hippo
11 Mobil Station
12 Hevula Nightclub
13 Taxis to Mounana, Lastoursville & Bakoumba
14 Bar-Dancing Masuku
16 Saen Supermarket
19 Gaboprix Supermarket
21 BIPG Bank & Alimentation SOFRIGAB Supermarket
22 Bar le Pippermint
23 Sodiex General Store
25 Post Office
26 Air Gabon
27 BICIG Bank
29 Shell Station & Gare Routière (Minibus to Franceville)

Restaurant la Gargote on the main drag next to Hôtel Ampassi is similar.

The best, however, is *Café Royal* on the main drag, a block north of the market. Freshly painted with a TV, spacious and quite clean, it's more restaurant-like than the others and its prices are roughly comparable, eg CFA 350 for the standard breakfast, CFA 800 for riz sauce viande, and CFA 900 for steak garni.

Two of the city's top three restaurants are at *Hôtel du Mont Moudinga* and, better, *Auberge le Moulébé* (CFA 4500 menu). The best for the price, however, is the *Porte de Masuku*, which is an attractive and breezy place with dining under thatched-roof paillotes just behind the post office near the centre. Most dishes cost CFA 2500 including braised fish, braised chicken, sanglier (wart hog), porc-pic and beef brochettes.

Facing the Saen supermarket is a bakery with pastries for around CFA 250 and outside the bakery there's a woman selling delicious yoghurt.

Entertainment

For a drink in clean surroundings, try *Bar le Pippermint* a block east of the market near Sodiex department store or the friendly well-kept *Bar Hippo* opposite Youssouf's grill. And for dancing there's the very African *Bar-Dancing Masuku* nearby, just down the hill from the market, next to *Coupé-Coupé de 3*.

Getting There & Away

Air & Train The easiest way to get here is by Air Gabon (☎ 661191), the local office for which is near the post office, or by train. The railway station is 15 km north-east of town, which costs CFA 500 by pick-up truck and CFA 1000 by taxi to reach.

For the Air Gabon flights and train schedules and fares, see the Getting There & Away section for Franceville, as Moanda shares the same airport as Franceville (it's between the two) and the train schedules and fares are similar (the train leaves/arrives in Franceville 32 minutes earlier/later).

Minibus & Bush Taxi Minibuses and bush taxis for Franceville leave from the Gare de Franceville at the Shell station near the post office; they fill up fast and cost CFA 1000 for the 50-minute trip. Vehicles for other destinations leave from the southern side of the market, not the gare routière.

Minibuses south to Bakoumba (86 km) cost CFA 1000, take about 1½ hours and most of them leave fairly early (before 9 am). The police at the immigration post in Bakoumba issue entry and exit stamps without hassle. From there, you can hitch a ride from the customs post to the Congo border post of Lékoko (45 km). The trip takes about 1½ hours and costs CFA 1500. The Gabonese border officials here are often drunk and may invent infractions so as to make you pay for their palm wine. After crossing the border you can continue seven km further to Mbinda where you can catch the daily train to Loubomo provided it's running again. Coming from the Congo, you may find minibus drivers demanding as much as CFA 4000 for the Lékoko-Moanda

trip. If so, you can save money by taking one just to Bakoumba and changing there for Moanda. There are also food-carrying trucks direct from the border to Franceville; the normal fare is CFA 3000.

The road north from Moanda to Lastoursville is laterite and in excellent condition during the dry season but sometimes in very bad condition during the rainy season. Minibuses from Moanda to Lastoursville cost CFA 2800 and most leave before 9 am. If you arrive later, rather than waiting for another minibus (possibly for hours), you could take a minibus to Mounana (CFA 300), which is about a 30-minute ride by paved road to the north, and try hitching a ride there (at the Hôtel de Ville police stop) to Lastoursville. Minibuses from this point to Lastoursville cost CFA 2500 and take about three hours during the dry season, while trucks usually cost the same and take much longer. Most of the minibuses continue on to Koulamoutou (CFA 1500).

FRANCEVILLE

Founded in 1880 by Savorgnan de Brazza and now the last stop on the Transgabonais railway, Franceville is a major town in large part because President Bongo, a Téké, was born in Bongoville (58 km to the east of Franceville). Why else would you find an Inter-Continental hotel in a town of 25,000 inhabitants? It's also important because the manganese and uranium mines are not far away.

The city, which is on an undulating plateau over 400 metres high, seems a little weird because it is so spread out, with lots of empty spaces. As a result, walking from one quarter to the next is nearly impossible, but fortunately there are lots of taxis and minibuses ploughing up and down the major streets, which are all paved.

There's nothing of great interest to see or do in the city, so take one of the excursions discussed in the Around Franceville section or, cheaper, content yourself with exploring the city's numerous bars, nightclubs and small restaurants, all of which are great places for meeting the locals. The city's hilly

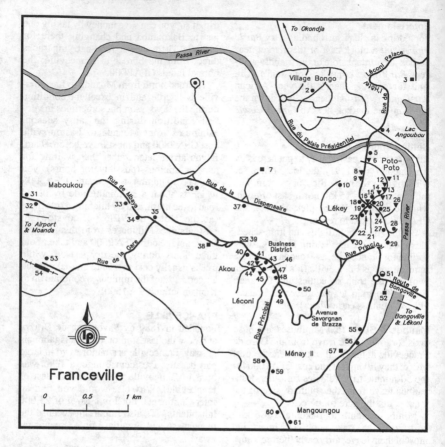

Franceville

0   0.5   1 km

location is attractive and the people can be quite friendly. Certainly the Peace Corps volunteers seem to thrive here. Chances are you may see several of them drinking in one of the local bars, which is how many of them and the locals pass the time. Travellers are rare so chances are the volunteers will welcome you wholeheartedly; buying a round or two of beer helps.

Orientation

Because Franceville is so hilly with ravines everywhere, the city's streets are winding and circuitous, resulting in a very confusing pattern. The two key sections of town are the market area in the Poto-Poto quarter near the Passa River and the business district, which rests on the edge of a plateau three km to the south-east. The former is where you'll find the Grand Marché (Marché du Poto-Poto), most cheap places to eat and drink, and the city's main intersection, while the latter has most of the major offices and establishments, eg the post office, all the banks, Air Gabon, etc. The Petit Marché, which is west of the business district and down the hill in a ravine, has a number of cheap bars and restaurants.

■ PLACES TO STAY

3	Hôtel Léconi Palace Inter-Continental
7	Hôtel Poubara
38	Hôtel le Masuku
52	Paroisse St-Hilaire
57	Motel Joumas

▼ PLACES TO EAT

5	Coupé-Coupé Vendor
6	Bar le Refuge
8	Bar de l'Amitié
9	Bar les Ailes
11	Caféteria (Senegalese)
12	Brochette Vendors
13	Restaurant Chez Tantine Rose
14	No-name Nigerian Restaurant
16	Fast Food le Parking & Boulangerie-Pâtisserie
17	Restaurant Moderne Bon Gôut
20	Street Food
22	Restaurant Étindi
23	Boulangerie Ékoufa
24	Restaurant la Délice & Coupé-Coupé
26	Bar-Restaurant Buké-Buké
30	Restaurant Supermenthe
42	Restaurant la Savane
44	Bar Repos du Combattant (Bar au Terminus)
45	Restaurant le Dialogue & Coupé-Coupé Vendor
51	Coupé-Coupé Vendor
60	Coupé-Coupé Vendor

OTHER

1	CIRMF (Centre International de Rescherches Médicals de Franceville)
2	Palais Présidentiel
4	City Market & Bar Cheri
5	Michelin du Pont
10	Hôpital Général
12	Bar Tommy
15	Grand Marché (Marché de Poto-Poto)
16	Galerie Altogovene Supermarket & Taxis to Moanda & Okondja
18	Cinéma du Gabon
19	Mobil Station
20	Cinéma M'Passa
21	Gaboprix General Store
22	Pharmacie Moderne & Sodiex General Store
25	Cheap Bars
27	Bar le Baobab
28	Bar-Dancing M'Passa
29	Tango Bar
30	Opépé Voyages Travel Agency
31	Université des Sciences et des Techniques de Masuku (USTM) & Presna Garage
32	Bar Masuku
33	Lycée d'État de Franceville
34	BEAC Bank & Banque du Gabon et du Luxembourg
35	Sogafric General Store
36	Palais de Justice
37	Dispensaire de la Caisse
38	Air Gabon & BGD Bank
39	Post Office & Total Station
40	Petit Marché & Hôtel de Ville
41	Boulangerie Franceville
42	Bar l'Escale
43	UGB Bank, Saen & Sogalivre Stores
46	Patience Bar
47	BICIG Bank
48	Commissariat
49	Mosque
50	Governor's Mansion
51	Taxis to Bongoville, Lékoni, Ngouoni & Akieni
53	Collége d'Enseignement Technique
54	Railway Station
55	Bar la Régina
56	Boulangerie & Moukoyi Bar
58	Gaboprix General Store
59	Bar au Zenith
61	Bar à la Campagne

Rue Principal, which is the main street connecting these two areas, winds southwards from the Grand Marché all the way to the Mangoungou quarter and then northwards up the plateau to the main business district, a distance of over five km. Most bush taxis and minibuses plough up and down on this route. There are also two other routes connecting these two districts, the shortest being Ave Savorgnan de Brazza, which cuts off about two km of the distance, and the wide Rue de la Dispensaire de la Caisse (or simply Rue de la Dispensaire).

From the main intersection in Poto-Poto (the Grand Marché is a stone's throw to the north), you can go north on the paved street past the Passa River towards the Hôtel Léconi or west towards Palais Présidentiel and out of town towards Okondja.

From the business district, you can either continue west on the paved road and turn left on Rue de la Gare which will take you to the railway station, or keep going straight on Rue de la Mbaya which will take you to Moanda (you'll pass the Université des Sciences et des Techniques de Masuku (USTM) on the right).

Information

Money The banks are all on the main drag in the business district including, from east to west, the BICIG, UGB, BGD and the Banque du Gabon et du Luxembourg. None of them seem to cash travellers' cheques denominated in US dollars, but most, including the BICIG but not the UGB, will cash those denominated in French francs. Banks here are open on weekdays from 7.45 to 11.30 am and 2.45 to 4.30 pm.

Markets The Grand Marché, which is just north of the main intersection in Poto-Poto, has a little bit of everything as does Sodiex, a general store 50 metres south of the intersection. For a supermarket, head for the modern Galerie Altogovene, which is 50 metres west of the intersection. It's a lot better than Gaboprix at the intersection.

Bookshop The town's only bookshop is Sogalivre, which is in the business district in the Saen building near the Mobil station; look for the 'Presse' sign. Magazines, the *Herald Tribune*, envelopes and recent books are all normally available.

Medical Services One of the better places to buy drugs is Pharmacie Moderne, which is about 70 metres south of the main intersection in Poto-Poto, next to Sodiex.

If you need a doctor, contact Dr Delmerre (☎ 677366) who is director of the Hôpital Général; he lives off the CIRMF road.

Swimming

The top-end hotels all have pools which are open to the public for CFA 1000.

Places to Stay – bottom end

The best value for money in this category is *Paroisse St-Hilaire* (☎ 677183), which is 1½ km east of the Grand Marché on the Route de Bongoville, just before the Passa River. The priests here are friendly and have 10 rooms ranging in price from CFA 4000 for a small room with a single bed, fan, private hot-water shower and basin (CFA 5000 with a large bed) to CFA 7500 to CFA 9000 for rooms with air-con.

If it's full, try *Motel Joumas* (☎ 677616), which is a km to the south on Rue Principal. At CFA 10,500 for an air-con room, it is way overpriced and definitely not recommended unless you can bargain down the price, which may be possible if business is slow. Regardless, for those attracted to hotels with popular nightclubs, it might be a good choice.

Places to Stay – top end

The city's top hotel is the modern *Hôtel Léconi Palace Inter-Continental* (☎ 677-416/7; fax 677419), which is ideally located on top of a hill overlooking Lac Angoubou, two km north of the Grand Marché. It has a pool, tennis court and rooms for CFA 21,000 and accepts all credit cards. If you talk to the friendly manager, he might offer you a reduced rate as the hotel has a low occupancy rate.

For value, I recommend the French-run *Hôtel Poubara* (☎ 677370), which is two km west of the Grand Marché and and is popular with travel agencies. Unlike the Hôtel Léconi Palace, it does not lack clients mainly because its air-con rooms are attractively priced (CFA 10,000) plus there's a tennis court, the best French restaurant in town and a pool surrounded by greenery for cooling off.

The nearby *Hôtel Beverly-Hills* is closed but the African-run *Hôtel le Masuku* (☎ 677-351/2), which is three km further south-west, past the business district is almost as good.

Singles/doubles with air-con cost CFA 10,500/12,600 plus there's a nice pool surrounded by thatched-roof paillotes and a terrace restaurant (good food) overlooking the pool and surrounding hillside.

Places to Eat

Poto-Poto Area The area around the Grand Marché has the highest concentration of cheap restaurants. On the road circling right around Poto-Poto, one of the first you'll come to is a tiny, blue, unmarked Nigerian restaurant. For CFA 500 you can get a filling plate of typical Nigerian fare including rice, beef and peas with a nice hot tomato sauce, riz sauce, foufou banane, ngname or, my favourite, foufou manioc with beef and gombo sauce. If you can't find it, ask around as the owner says he may change the location.

Restaurant Moderne Bon Goût, a Senegalese-style restaurant, is across the street. Dishes include manioc viande for CFA 700, omelette for CFA 600, riz poisson for CFA 700, poisson banane for CFA 800, plus the standard breakfast (coffee, bread and butter) for CFA 300.

A stone's throw further up the street on the other side are *Restaurant Chez Tantine Rose*, which definitely seems worth exploring, and *Bar Tommy*, which serves no food but at nights there are women outside grilling brochettes for CFA 200 each. Next in line is the *Caféteria*, a typical Senegalese-style restaurant with steak for CFA 500, omelettes for CFA 600, chicken for CFA 1000 and chicken rice or manioc for CFA 1300.

At night the main intersection in Poto-Poto is the best place for street food. The most popular snack food here and elsewhere in Gabon are the fried bread 'croquettes' (CFA 25); you'll also see some tiny fried shrimp which are quite tasty. On the dirt road leading east from the intersection is a coupé-coupé vendor whom the Peace Corps volunteers call 'Action Man'; when the big man asks you 'Where's the action, man?', you'll know you're there (minimum coupé-coupé purchase of CFA 300). Almost next door is the cheap *Restaurant la Délice* and

further, off the road, you may find with some difficulty *Bar-Restaurant Buké-Buké*, which has brochettes for CFA 1000 and, on occasion, bush meat, which is not cheap.

On the paved road leading north-west from the intersection are several other places. About 400 metres further north-west are *Bar de l'Amitié* and, next door, *Bar les Ailes*. The beer is more popular than the food, which suggests that these spacious open-air places are better for drinks than for food, which is not always available. About 100 metres further on the other side of the street is a coupé-couplé vendor and *Bar le Refuge*, which on occasion has poisson à la braisse and brochettes.

Business District The business district has only a few places to eat, most of which are in the Petit Marché, which is a block down the hill in a ravine. Two of the better ones are *Restaurant la Savane* and, nearby, *Restaurant le Dialogue*. The latter is a typical Senegalese-type restaurant with omelettes for CFA 500, riz poisson for CFA 800, steak frites for CFA 1200, etc. Or buy some coupé-coupé next door and take it to *Bar Repos du Combattant* (Bar au Terminus) nearby or across the street to *Bar l'Escale*. The latter has good music and large Regabs and Castels for CFA 275 and CFA 450, respectively. A tasty dish to be on the lookout for is nkoumu, which is a leafy vegetable in peanut sauce with manioc.

On the main drag in the business district near the Mairie you'll find *Boulangerie Franceville*, which is the best bakery in this area.

Up-Market Restaurants Some 100 metres south of the main intersection in Poto-Poto, next to Sodiex, is the cafeteria-like *Restaurant Étindi* (or Chez Miriam), which is one of the city's better mid-range restaurants. The selections are all in the CFA 800 to CFA 1800 range including omelette champignon for CFA 1000, riz Senegalais poisson for CFA 1000 and steak riz for CFA 1500. *Boulangerie Ékoufa* is next door and has nothing special.

Nearby, just east of the Galerie Alto-govene, is *Fast Food le Parking*, which is a popular (with expatriates) outdoor eatery with stools. It has five or six French selections all in the CFA 1500 to CFA 2000 range. Next door outside Altogovene is *Boulangerie Pâtisserie*, which is the best bakery in town.

Restaurant Supermenthe is half a km south of the Poto-Poto intersection. It has dishes in the CFA 500 to CFA 3000 range.

Restaurant Demba is a nice Italian-Gabonese restaurant with excellent food; a meal with drinks will cost around CFA 3000 to CFA 4000. It is near the well-known Garage M'Passa and is closed on Tuesdays.

Otherwise, your only choices for continental food are the restaurants at the top three hotels. The special menu of the day at all of them is around CFA 5000 (CFA 5500 at the Léconi Palace). Of these, the French restaurant at *Hôtel Poubara* is the best. Also, on Fridays nights there is a popular poolside buffet of grilled meats at the *Léconi Palace* for CFA 4900.

Entertainment

Nightclubs One of the liveliest nightclubs in the Poto-Poto area is *Bar Tommy*, which caters to the working person and is 100 metres north-east of the market; there's loud music and dancing virtually every night. I prefer the equally rustic *Bar-Dancing M'Passa*, which has comical paintings on the wall, good music, a more tranquil ambience and a fairly spacious area for drinks and dancing. It's roughly 500 metres south-east of the Grand Marché at the end of a dirt road starting at Gaboprix.

On the same street slightly closer to the centre are *Bar le Baobab* and *Tango Bar*, both of which are fairly tranquil and good for drinks. The nearby *Bar-Restaurant Buké-Buké*, listed under cheap eats and not so easy to find, is a good place to dance the night away as well as eat.

For dancing, the most up-market place in town is the *Bango* nightclub at Motel Joumas, which is open on Thursday, Friday and Saturday nights and has a cover charge

of CFA 2000 (includes a drink). You could also try the more rustic *Bar à la Campagne*, which is further south in Mangoungou and open only at night.

To meet the students out at the Université des Sciences et des Techniques de Masuku (USTM), take a minibus or taxi west towards Moanda and get off at *Bar Masuku*, which is across the street from the university. It's the best bar-dancing in the area.

Cinemas The best movie theatre in town is the Cinéma du Gabon, which is 100 metres west of the main intersection in Poto-Poto. It's a lot better than Cinéma M'Passa at the intersection.

Getting There & Away

Air Air Gabon, which is in the business district, has flights to Libreville (CFA 48,100 one way) every morning except Thursdays when there's no flight and Sundays when the plane leaves at 7.30 pm. The Monday and Saturday flights stop first in Port-Gentil.

Train The railway station, about six km from the Grand Marché, is on the south-western outskirts of town, past the business district. Trains depart on Tuesdays at 9.10 pm, Thursdays at 9.30 am, Fridays at 8.10 pm and Saturdays, Sundays and holidays at 12.30 pm. The trip to Owendo/Libreville is scheduled to take about 10½ hours but late arrivals are common. The trip to Booué and Owendo-Libreville costs CFA 13,100/27,600 1st class and CFA 10,400/22,100 2nd class, respectively. Getting a seat is virtually never a problem, so an early arrival is not required.

Bush Taxi Bush taxis headed west for Moanda and north to Okondja (and occasionally to Ngouoni, Akieni and Lékoni) leave from the Poto-Poto intersection. They're reliable, fast and reasonably priced (CFA 1000 to Moanda). Also, daily vans run between Franceville and Koulamoutou, stopping at Moanda and Lastoursville along the way.

Truck There are trucks ploughing every day

between Franceville and the Congo border via Moanda, carrying cheaper food from the Congo; the normal fare is CFA 3000. To find one, ask around the Grand Marché.

Getting Around
Taxis & Buses There are lots of shared taxis and blue and white minivans ploughing up and down the main streets, often starting at the main intersection in Poto-Poto; fares are between CFA 100 and CFA 200 depending on the distance.

Car Rental To rent a car call Avis (☎ 677172) or Translima, both at the airport.

AROUND FRANCEVILLE
The only tourist attractions are outside Franceville. One that is best forgotten is the president's *village natal*, **Bongoville**, some 58 km to the east. The other is **Poubara Falls** south of Franceville, at Mvengué, some 60 km by road from Franceville via the airport road. The falls are neither very exciting nor picturesque as there is a huge power plant next to them. To see the falls you must cross a foot bridge made of vines, which costs CFA 1000 and is not terribly exciting either. Most people going there hire a taxi as there is no regular bush taxi service; the standard fare is CFA 15,000.

Other half-day trips on the tourist circuit include **Ndjoumou Falls**, **Lac Souba** and the **Grand Canyon**.

OKONDJA
Some 136 km north of Franceville on the road to Makokou, Okondja is a good destination if you're looking for towns where foreigners rarely venture. It has no special attractions and indeed the frequently drunk gendarmes (you must report to them!), who have been known to hassle travellers (one because he didn't have a *certificat d'hérbergement*), can be a deterrent. Still, if you're looking for adventure, Okondja can be recommended but do report to the gendarmerie as it is apparently required.

Places to Stay & Eat
There are two places to stay, conveniently next to each other. The more expensive one is *L'Auberge* which has rooms with air-con for CFA 8000. The other is the town hall, *L'Assemblée*, which has two rooms for lodging in an adjacent house. The rooms, which cost CFA 4000, are spartan with mosquito coils, showers and outside toilets. The caretaker of the Assemblée will probably be asked to show you around, including leading you to a small restaurant in an unmarked shack a few blocks away as well as to the gendarmerie.

Getting There & Away
Air Gabon has a flight on Sundays to/from Libreville; the cost is CFA 36,500. Minibuses to/from Franceville cost CFA 3000 and finding one in the morning is fairly easy. If you're headed to Makokou (260 km), you will probably have to take two or more minibuses or bush taxis as very few vehicles travel the entire stretch. The trip normally takes about two days, and if you keep together with your fellow Gabonese travellers you'll probably be put up free for the night by the villagers or gendarmes. The road is in fairly bad condition, so try to avoid travelling on this route during the heavy rainy season. Apart from villages along the way you'll see nothing but rainforest and probably quite a few elephant tracks, perhaps a few animals as well.

São Tomé e Príncipe

A veritable paradise on earth awaits the visitor to these remote islands. With cloud-capped volcanoes, jungle greenery, and crystal-clear waters not yet discovered by the skin-diving crowd, São Tomé e Príncipe would undoubtedly be on almost every travellers' list of places to see, if they had ever heard of the country or knew that the country has recently opened itself wide to tourists.

São Tomé was cut off from the rest of the world for many years and the peoples' civil liberties were ignored, but all this has changed as the country is now well on its way to having the most opened democracy in the region. The days when you had to lie through your teeth and go through all sorts of shenanigans to get a visa are gone. Getting a tourist visa in Gabon is now a snap.

On a GNP basis the country is relatively poor, compared with some of the oil-rich Central African countries. It imports half its food, and doesn't have any flashy new airports and other 'show' projects, but don't let this fool you. The people are unquestionably the friendliest, the best-educated and the healthiest by far in Central Africa, and their towns look like picturesque little villages in Portugal, with multicoloured, well-kept houses on every block. On the United Nations' quality of life index, only two countries in West and Central Africa rank higher. You'll feel the difference the minute you arrive. Without massive foreign aid, however, conditions might be much worse.

If you get a charge out of being one of only a few travellers in a friendly country, exploring off-beat places, snorkelling in the clearest waters on the western coast of Africa, or camping on remote beaches still relatively unknown to the outside world, and you've got the wherewithal to get there, by all means go. I assure you, you won't be disappointed.

Facts about the Country

HISTORY
Having first spotted São Tomé in 1469, the Portuguese began settling the place 16 years later and quickly started amassing slaves, with the result that almost overnight São Tomé became the largest sugar-producing country in Africa. The sugar boom was short-lived, however – the slaves staged a successful revolt in 1530 and the plantation owners fled to less troublesome Brazil. However, because São Tomé served as the major staging post for the slave trade between the Congo and the USA, slaves remained critical to the economy.

In the 18th and 19th centuries, the Portuguese established large cocoa and coffee *roças* (plantations), which likewise depended on slavery. Although slavery was officially abolished by 1875, it was replaced by a system of forced contract labour. Revelations of the slavery-like nature of this

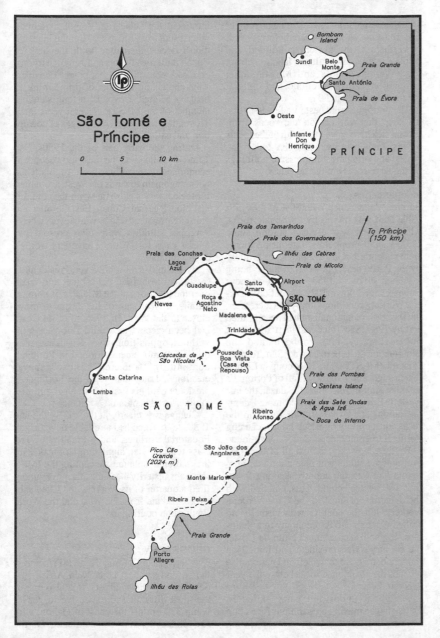

São Tomé e Príncipe

0   5   10 km

PRÍNCIPE

Bombom Island
Sundi
Belo Monte
Praia Grande
Santo António
Praia de Évora
Oeste
Infante Don Henrique

Praia dos Tamarindos
Praia dos Governadores
Ilhéu das Cabras
To Príncipe (150 km)
Praia das Conchas
Praia da Micolo
Lagoa Azul
Santo Amaro
Airport
Guadalupe
SÃO TOMÉ
Neves
Roça Agostino Neto
Madalena
Trinidade
Cascadas da São Nicolau
Pousada da Boa Vista (Casa de Repouso)
Praia das Pombas
Santana Island
Santa Catarina
Praia das Sete Ondas & Agua Izé
Lemba
Boca de Interno
SÃO TOMÉ
Ribeiro Afonso
Pico Cão Grande (2024 m)
São João dos Angolares
Monte Mario
Ribeira Peixe
Praia Grande
Porto Allegre
Ilhéu das Rolas

system resulted in an international boycott of São Tomé cocoa in the years before WW I. Nevertheless, the system continued and resulted in a massive influx of labourers from Cape Verde, Angola and Mozambique, bringing considerable ethnic and cultural diversity to the islands.

The Portuguese did bestow a few benefits. To keep the workers on the roças from getting sick, they gave the health of the locals a very high priority and even today the largest and often most impressive buildings on the large roças are the hospitals.

Independence
Before independence, over 80% of the cultivable land was owned by 28 private roças, while the rest was divided among some 11,000 small proprietors. Labour problems were endemic but always put down brutally by the Portuguese, the worst example being a labour strike in 1953 when Portuguese troops gunned down 1032 plantation workers. Working conditions improved thereafter, but the spirit of nationalism had been ignited and by 1960, São Tomé had its first modern political party, later to be named the Movimento de Libertação de São Tomé e Príncipe (MLSTP). The 1974 coup in Lisbon that brought about the downfall of Portugal's premier, António de Oliveira Salazar, the last western European dictator, prompted demonstrations and strikes in São Tomé on the roças and a mutiny by Black troops, causing Portugal to grant independence a year later.

By then, however, almost all of the 4000 Portuguese settlers and plantation administrators had fled the country, leaving fewer than 100 whites behind. This, coupled with the departure of most of the Cape Verdean workers, left the country with virtually no skilled workers and the economy in a shambles. It also forced Manuel Pinto da Costa, the country's first president and initially a moderate, to move to the left and nationalise most of the abandoned roças before the year was out.

A rightist opposition party exiled in Gabon began making preparations for a coup attempt. In 1978, with an invasion appearing imminent, the Cubans and Angolans, among others, sent troops to assist. But the invasion didn't occur; thereafter, with the help of Cuban military advisors and Angolan troops, da Costa consolidated his power considerably, abolishing the post of prime minister held by Miguel Trovoada, a long-standing member of the MLSTP. Several years later, Trovoada was arrested on charges of corruption and exiled to Portugal.

During the early part of the 1980s, São Tomé continued to be heavily dependent economically and militarily on Angola. This, not antagonism towards the West, accounted for the country's close ties with the communist bloc. Russian, Cuban, East German and North Korean advisors were everywhere. Angolan soldiers were also present but tourist visas for Western travellers weren't even available.

By the mid-1980s, however, President da Costa had reshuffled his cabinet and taken over the functions of the Ministry of Foreign Affairs, a clear sign of his desire to move closer to the West. In 1986, after da Costa had been elected to a third five-year term without opposition, two pro-democracy opposition movements formed in Portugal, demanding 'free and honest general elections'. Later that year, the Portuguese president paid his first official visit, promising increased economic assistance.

Change was clearly in the air. By the late 1980s, São Tomé had a reliable new airline, Equatorial Airlines, and a brand new, 1st-class tourist hotel, signalling its break with international isolation. Accepting the IMF's stringent austerity measures, the government fired a quarter of its workers and lifted subsidies, and aid from the West and the World Bank came pouring in.

GEOGRAPHY
The archipelago of São Tomé e Príncipe is the second-smallest country in Africa (the Seychelles is the smallest). It is also one of the most difficult and expensive to get to, being 320 km off the coast of Gabon, with few connections to the continent. Of the

islands' 115,000 inhabitants, a quarter live in the capital city, São Tomé.

Only two km north of the equator, the island of São Tomé is primarily dense mountainous rainforest and cacao plantations, capped by Pico Cão Grande (2024 metres) in the south, which is surrounded by a dozen other inactive volcanic cones all over 1000 metres high. The eastern slopes and coastal flatlands are covered by huge cocoa estates, formerly owned by Portuguese companies, along with a number of small farms. If you go inland from São Tomé past Trinidade and up into the mountains towards Pousada Boa Vista and São Nicolau waterfalls just beyond, you'll be passing through the heart of cocoa country. It's often cloudy and misty up there and refreshingly cool, as it is further north in Madalena and Roça Agostino Neto, a large, active cocoa plantation which is open to visitors.

As you approach the northern coast, the terrain gets drier, with rolling hills and baobab trees. The coast is protected there, which explains why Praia das Conchas has crystal clear waters and is the best place on the island for snorkelling. The more frequented beaches along the eastern side of the island are less protected, with rolling waves.

The island of Príncipe, some 150 km to the north-east and renowned for its parrots, is much smaller and flatter, with many fewer km of paved road and is connected to the main island by air and sea transport. The principal town is Santo António, in which live about 3000 of the island's some 8000 residents.

CLIMATE

Rain, not heat, is the major concern. October to May is the rainy season, with the heaviest rainfall in the south, and the north remaining relatively dry. Nevertheless, all year round except in July and August, you'll find high humidity and some rainfall, so come prepared.

GOVERNMENT

Perhaps the greatest recent changes have occurred in the political arena. In early 1990,

after massive pro-democracy demonstrations following the upheaval in Eastern Europe, da Costa announced that São Tomé would become a multiparty state and that there would be elections within two months. So confident was da Costa that he would retain his seat that he proposed himself as a candidate for the presidency of the Organisation of African Unity (OAU). Shortly thereafter, former Prime Minister Miguel Trovoada, an ex-crony of da Costa, returned after nine years in exile in France when da Costa gave assurances that he would not be arrested. Trovoada received immediate widespread expressions of popular support. Clearly worried, da Costa gave himself more time to prepare for the elections by calling first for a referendum for voters to endorse the new multiparty constitution, with elections to follow at the end of the year.

The strategy didn't work. Voters not only approved the referendum but in January 1991 voted Trovoada's opposition party, the Democratic Convergence Party (DCP), into office with 54% of the vote, much to Angola's disappointment. Trovoada then completed the removal of the remaining 400 Angolan troops and began moving the country even closer to the West with a quick trip to Portugal, France, Morocco and Angola, seeking investment and aid. Today, having joined the increasing ranks of African countries which have thrown out their dictators by peaceful electoral means, São Tomé is at the forefront in Central Africa of the pro-democracy movement in Africa. It has also joined the growing ranks of African countries, now 12 in all, to have abolished the death penalty.

ECONOMY

In the markets you'll see women tending wooden stalls with lots to offer, particularly fish, manioc, breadfruit, rice, tomatoes and pineapples. While this scene may be picturesque, it is really an African facade masking extensive foreign aid. The country imports about half of its food and about half of that is donated by foreign governments. Virtually all the rice, wheat, vegetable oil, dried milk and sugar, for example, is imported, and much is donated. Foreign aid is also behind the locally grown fresh vegetables – tomatoes, cabbage, radish, lettuce and eggplant – much of which comes from a demonstration farm in Mesquita financed by France's aid programme. This all seems pretty bleak until you realise that before independence 90% of the island's food had to be imported because of the lopsided dependence on cocoa.

Foreign aid accounts for over 40% of the country's GNP which is US$350 per capita (the only African countries with higher percentages are the Comoros and Cape Verde), and touches every sector of society. The French renovated the airport and are rebuilding telephone, water and electrical systems; the Germans renovated the port; the Spanish are building houses; and the Japanese are promoting fishery development. Portuguese, Swedes, Italians and Chinese help in the hospitals, and the Portuguese have financed the operations of the only functioning library and movie theatre. With so much foreign aid, competition among suitors has become inevitable – to São Tomé's advantage. When the Portuguese began building the country's television station, the French announced huge grants for media development.

The government's top priority is revitalising the cocoa and coffee plantations for generating foreign exchange. The African Development Bank, the World Bank and others are helping to rehabilitate some of the cocoa estates, which still account for about 90% of São Tomé's export earnings. Production is only up to half that of the pre-independence level of 10,000 tonnes per year. The government, which owned most of the plantations, now realises that it was in over its head, and so is selling off its cocoa plantations to private investors. It's also trying hard to diversify crop production, but with only modest success. The best hopes lie in fishing, petroleum and tourism, particularly the latter two. Oil exploration is now in full swing and the country's tourist potential is rapidly expanding, including a new hotel complex being developed on a secluded beach on Príncipe.

POPULATION & PEOPLE

The islands of São Tomé e Príncipe have only about 115,000 inhabitants – about the number of people in a good-sized suburb of Libreville (Gabon). With such a small, clustered population, mostly Catholics, the provision of services such as education and clean water are sometimes easier, which may be one of several reasons why São Tomé has the highest adult literacy rate in Central Africa (63%) and the third-highest life expectancy in all of Africa. Cape Verde, another former Portuguese colony in Africa, has a higher life expectancy, which suggests that the role of the Portuguese (especially their contributions to the health system) shouldn't be ignored – nor should the contributions of the country's socialist past to education.

There are five groups amongst the islands' inhabitants. The most powerful are the *filhos da terra*, the mixed-blooded, coffee-coloured descendants of imported slaves and Europeans (mostly Portuguese) who settled on the islands in the 16th and 17th centuries. Intermarriage has been common, but the influx of contract workers until 1950 tended to 're-Africanise' them. The *Angolares* are descendants of former castaway slaves from Angola who reputedly survived a shipwreck in 1540; they are now primarily fisherpeople. Then there are the *forros*, descendants of slaves freed when slavery was abolished in 1875. Finally, there are the *servicios* (migrant labourers) and the *tongas*, their children born on the island.

ARTS & CULTURE

The language, architecture, crafts and artistic expression of São Tomé are all Creole. There are more than 50 folkloric groups on the two islands which perform during the 28 principal festivals during the year between May and January. If you're lucky, you may get to see the *tchitoli*, a unique theatrical performance dating back to the time of Charlemagne, which was introduced by sailors from Madeira. Combining music, mime and dance of that era, it has been 'Africanised' over the years, especially in the music as well as the dance, which is performed by the Angolares.

LANGUAGE

Portuguese is the official language. Most people speak a creole language called *forro*.

Facts for the Visitor

VISAS & EMBASSIES
São Tomé

Everyone is required to have an entry visa. Tourist visas are now easily obtained at all of the country's diplomatic missions, of which there are now seven. The easiest place to get one is Libreville, in Gabon. The embassy there is open Monday to Friday from 8 am to noon and from 3 to 5 pm and issues visas the same day if you come in the morning with a passport, CFA 14,950 and two photos. Visas are valid for 120 days from the date of issue and permit stays of up to two weeks.

In the USA, you can contact the country's UN Mission (☎ (212) 687-8389), 801 2nd

Ave, Suite 1504, NY 10017-4704, and ask them to send you two forms, then return them with your passport, two photos, a copy of your International Health Certificate and a stamped return envelope. They'll issue you a visa (for free, in 24 hours) which is valid for 120 days and good for stays of up to two weeks.

In London, the São Tomé e Príncipe Consulate (☎ (071) 499-1995; fax 629-6460), 42 North Ordley St, London W1A 4PV, requires UK£20 and two photos and issues visas in 24 hours that are valid for three months and good for stays of two weeks. It may also still require that you send a letter confirming that you have a job in the UK and intend to return to it.

The embassy in Lisbon (☎ 638-242), Rua de Junqueira 2, P-1300 Lisbon, charges 5000 escudos and takes three days to issue visas. You can also get visas at the country's consulates in Montreal (☎ (514) 287-8563l; fax 287-8643), 85 St Catherine St, W, Suite 140, Montreal PQ H2X 3P4; and Brussels (☎ (2) 347-5375; fax 347-5408), Ave Brugman, B-1060 Brussels.

For visa extensions, see immigration at the Ministerio de Negocios Estrangeiros (☎ 22372; telex 211) on Largo Marcelo da Veiga in São Tomé. Regardless, if you over-extend your two-week stay, it seems unlikely that you'd have any major problems as the government policy is very pro-tourist and customs officials are exceptionally friendly. Indeed, my guess is that if you land here without a visa (I don't recommend it), you will probably be issued one right away so long as you look presentable and have a good excuse for not getting a visa earlier. The chances are strong, however, that you'll never be allowed to get on the plane to go there without proof of a visa.

São Tomé has diplomatic missions in Brussels, Libreville, Lisbon, London, Luanda, Montreal and New York.

Other Countries
Angola The Angolan Embassy, which is open on weekdays from 7.30 am to noon and from 2.30 to 5.30 pm, requires Db 6400 and

two photos for visas, which are good for 30-day stays. It's very doubtful that you will be issued a visa if you give 'tourism' as your reason for visiting. Getting an Angolan visa here is also very difficult because they will insist on your giving them a letter from your nearest embassy, plus a good reason why you didn't obtain a visa in your home country.

Gabon São Tomé is probably the easiest country in Africa, if not the world, in which to obtain a visa to Gabon. The embassy, which is open on weekdays from 7.30 am to noon and from 2.30 to 5.30 pm, requires only US$40 (or the equivalent in local currency), no photos, and gives same-day service. The visas are valid for one month.

For a list of foreign embassy addresses, see the São Tomé Information section.

DOCUMENTS
The only documents you need are a passport with a São Tomé visa and an International Health Certificate with proof of having received a yellow fever vaccination within the past 10 years.

CUSTOMS
Customs officials at the airport are extremely lax and usually do not ask to see anything even though, theoretically, there may be a limit on the amount of local currency that you may export.

MONEY
US$1	=	Db 370
UK£1	=	Db 675
CFA 1000	=	Db 1375

The unit of currency is the dobra (Db). It is no longer wildly over-valued but it is rapidly being devalued, so prices herein are quoted in CFA. Do not exchange much money – at least not at first – because most hotels insist upon payment in US dollars or CFA, and taxi drivers definitely prefer it. Restaurants, on the other hand, want dobra.

Many people exchange money on the black market. Depending on the last devaluation, rates there can vary anywhere from only marginally better than the bank, to 25% better or more, so check first. Regardless, it's certainly faster than the bank. CFA and US dollars are about equally preferred. In São Tomé, the black market is at the main market in town, on the street furthest from the ocean. Changing money there is generally not risky as the police definitely aren't zealous in controlling it. Nevertheless, you must still be discreet; negotiating inside a taxi is one way to do this.

The only bank for exchanging money and travellers' cheques is the Banco Nacional de São Tomé e Príncipe (BNSTP). The commission on travellers' cheques is only US$1 per transaction – just one more example of how receptive this country is to foreigners!

BUSINESS HOURS & HOLIDAYS
Business and government hours are weekdays from 8 am to noon and from 3 to 6 pm; Saturdays from 8 am to noon. Banking hours for changing money are weekdays from 7.30 to 11.30 am.

Public Holidays
1 January (New Year's Day)
3 February
1 May
12 July (Independence Day)
6 September
30 September
21 December
25-26 December (Christmas)

POST & TELECOMMUNICATIONS
The post office in São Tomé is very efficient, and issues beautifully designed stamps. A letter to anywhere in the world costs about CFA 125. It is also the best place for buying postcards (US$0.30), which is saying very little.

The telephone code for São Tomé is 23912. For telephone calls, try the post office or Hotel Miramar. Calling Príncipe is direct-dial and cheap.

TIME
Time in São Tomé is the same as GMT, so flying from Libreville you will gain an hour.

PHOTOGRAPHY

There is no photo permit system and taking photos is generally no longer a problem anywhere in the country. However, don't take photos of government buildings, the airport or the port without first checking to see if it's OK. There is one shop in São Tomé, Fotomé, that sells and develops film but the price of both is exorbitant.

HEALTH

A yellow fever vaccination is mandatory if you're coming from an infected area or will be staying more than two weeks; a cholera shot is mandatory if you've visited an infected area within the previous six months. Malaria here is of a particularly virulent type, often associated with cerebral malaria, and it is definitely chloroquine-resistant. If you get sick, try Hopital Ayres Menezes (☎ 21222) in São Tomé.

DANGERS & ANNOYANCES

São Tomé probably rates as the safest capital city in Africa and it's one of the few where you can walk around at night on the streets without fear. Nevertheless, thefts are not unknown and as the country continues to open up, conditions could gradually change. So don't let your guard down completely.

Getting There & Away

AIR

To/From Europe

From Europe, you could take one of the twice-weekly, 12-hour flights from Lisbon on TAP (Air Portugal), which stops in Dakar and Abidjan. You can also fly to São Tomé from Libreville (Gabon) on Equatorial International Airlines. The only other flights here are on TAAG (Angolan Airlines), which flies twice a week from Luanda to Lisbon via São Tomé. Travel agencies in Europe which can provide information on travel to São Tomé include VIP Travel Ltd (☎ (071) 499-4221) at Grosvenor Square in London; Wessel Tours (☎ (69) 239381/2) at Münchener

Strasse 7 in Frankfurt; and Falcon Travel (☎ (6) 6379011) at Via Pio IX in Rome.

To/From Gabon

The country is not impossibly expensive once you get there, but flying just from Gabon, 320 km to the east, costs about US$500 return. Fortunately, about every five days you can take a boat over for much less.

Many tourists arrive here by way of Libreville. Equatorial Airlines, which is 73% owned by an Irish group, has two 24-seater planes which are seemingly well maintained. There are return flights on Mondays, Tuesdays, Thursdays and Fridays.

The airline's agent in Libreville is Mistral Voyages (see the section on Libreville in the Gabon chapter) which offers some advantageous package tours, for trips of one to four nights. You should definitely inquire about them. For example, two people spending a three-night weekend trip pay CFA 160,000 per person (CFA 40,300 more than the airline ticket) and get three nights and nine meals at the Hotel Miramar – a saving of about CFA 50,000 compared with the same trip done independently and staying at the same hotel. Budget travellers, however, can still do better by buying the regular ticket and staying at inexpensive but decent hotels.

SEA

About every five days the *Solmar II* heads from Libreville to São Tomé. The boat starts filling up with people and goods around 7 am and finally leaves around noon, arriving at São Tomé about 22 hours later. It then stays a day or two in São Tomé and returns, stays one night, and then leaves Libreville again. To find out the exact day of departure you should call the São Tomé Embassy in Libreville because the boat company always wires the embassy as the vessel is leaving São Tomé. The one-way cost is about CFA 25,000. The boat is about 15 metres long and takes roughly 50 passengers. There is some shelter from the sun and some seats but not enough for everyone. If you can, get hold of some anti-seasickness pills at a pharmacy or the fishing shop in Libreville, because you'll be on the high seas and the boat can certainly bounce around. You must also bring all your food and water. For information in São Tomé on the boat, go to the Transcolmar office near the port or inquire at the port itself.

Transcolmar is also the agent for the *Pagué*, which plies once or twice a month in either direction between São Tomé and Douala (Cameroun). The cost is CFA 35,000 and the trip takes about 30 hours. For information in Douala, go to the main port.

About once a month the *Onangue* makes the round-trip circuit from São Tomé to Libreville, then Douala and back to São Tomé. São Tomé to Libreville costs CFA 25,000 and takes 24 hours, while the Libreville to Douala and Douala to São Tomé portions cost CFA 30,000 and CFA 35,000, respectively. The Turimar office, near the port in São Tomé, has information. Turimar is also responsible for much larger freighters going to Luanda, Bissau and Portugal but they don't have passenger service. Still, if you are headed in any of those directions, you could try your luck.

Getting Around

AIR
Equatorial International Airlines has flights to Príncipe on Mondays at 2.30 pm and Fridays at 8 am for CFA 16,250 one-way, payable only in hard currency. On weekends there's a round-trip special for CFA 27,500. The flight takes only 40 minutes and returns after a 40-minute stop.

BUS & TAXI
On São Tomé, the public transport system is reasonably good and cheap; you can take a minivan or *collectivo* (ie, shared) taxi on any day to just about anywhere on the island but there are no fixed schedules – they leave only when full. Hitching is also easy. Over half the 287 km of roads around the island of São Tomé are paved and they're still in fair condition despite numerous small potholes. The paved sections – and collectivos – go all the

way west from São Tomé to Santa Catarina and Lemba via Praia das Conchas in the north, and all the way south to São João Dos Angolares via Ribeiro Afonso. Fares are dirt cheap (CFA 335 from São Tomé to Ribeiro Afonso).

South of São Dos Angolares the road gets rough. There are collectivos twice weekly from São Tomé to Monte Mario (which is slightly further south than Dos Angolares) but not to Porto Allegre. Vehicles occasionally head through Angolares to Porto Allegre, but most people go by boat from São Tomé.

There is also a limited bus service on Príncipe, with short paved routes heading north, south and west from Santo António.

BOAT
The situation of the boats plying between São Tomé and Príncipe is in flux because rapidly rising fuel prices have virtually eliminated profits. Previously, both the *Bone de Joque* and Transcolmar's *Brizas do Mar* plied between São Tomé and Príncipe on regular schedules, about twice a week each. Now they have no schedules at all; instead, they leave when there's sufficient demand. The *Brizas do Mar* may even stop running this route altogether. The price is CFA 2500 and the trip takes 11 hours. Similarly, on Monday and Friday mornings the *Transcolmar* used to go from São Tomé to Porto Allegre, then across to Ilhéu das Rolas and back that night to São Tomé, but now the schedule is irregular, as the boat only leaves when full. For the latest information on both routes, listen to announcements on the radio or inquire at the port in São Tomé.

São Tomé

Sleepy and spotlessly clean are words frequently used to describe São Tomé, the capital city of some 35,000 inhabitants and the only town of any importance on the main island. Almost totally unaffected by modern influences, with buildings of pastel colours and wooden balconies, and a wide avenue bordered with fire-coloured *flamboyants* passing along the ocean and extending toward a 16th-century baroque cathedral and a 19th-century Portuguese fort, it is reminiscent of a small Portuguese town.

It is surely the prettiest town in Central Africa, if not the most active or the most interesting. A horseshoe-shaped harbour, where swimming is still possible and the passenger boat from Libreville docks, dominates the scenery. Colourful, freshly painted buildings, a colonial-era white wall along the beach road, uncongested clean streets with not a modern building in sight – certainly there's no other city in this area of the world even closely resembling it. Only at night when the bars and nightclubs come to life will you feel that you are indeed still in Africa.

Orientation

Coming from the airport, you'll pass along the wide Ave 12 Julho which extends eastward all around the harbour past the cathedral and the Presidential Palace to the port area, where it becomes Ave Marginal 12 Julho, and the old fort-museum, then abruptly heads southward along the water towards the deluxe new Miramar, the city's finest hotel, and the Palácio de Congresso. At that point it becomes the north-south coastal highway towards Praia das Pombas, the city's closest good beach, and all points south.

The town centre is between the Mercado Municipal, where most taxis and minibuses are stationed, and the old cathedral to the east. This area (half a km sq), which is bordered on the north by Ave 12 Julho and on the south by Ave Kwame Nkrumah, is where you'll find most cheap hotels, restaurants, bars and stores. The road inland for Trinidade starts here, with two converging routes to choose from.

Information

Tourist Office The Informoção Turismo office is on Ave 12 Julho next to the post office at the intersection with Rua Ponta

Mina. Somewhat surprisingly, the people here don't seem to know much, are indifferent and have little to offer. It does, however, have some local handicrafts that you might check out. They're unexceptional but may be the only handicraft souvenirs you'll find here.

Money The BNSTP (☎ 21301), which is open on weekdays between 7.30 and 11.30 am, is in the heart of town between the Praça Independência and Ave 12 Julho and accepts travellers' cheques but not credit cards. The major place for changing money on the street is on Ave Conceição alongside the market.

Foreign Embassies Except for the Spanish Consulate, which is in the town centre on Rua Patrice Lumumba just north of Praça Independência, all the diplomatic missions are on the eastern side of town: the Angolan Embassy (☎ 22376) on Ave Kwame Nkrumah, the Portuguese Embassy on Ave Marginal 12 Julho next to Hotel Miramar, the Gabonese Embassy (☎ 21043) on Rua Ponta Mina opposite the Ciné Imperio Roundabout, and the UN office (☎ 21814) a block away facing 3 de Fevereiro Roundabout. There's no US Embassy but the UN office acts as the liaison for the US Embassy in Libreville, which officially covers São Tomé and sends diplomats here periodically for consular work and other matters.

Supermarket The best supermarket and general store in town is Loja Franca (☎ 21555) on Rua Patrice Lumumba in the centre just off Ave 12 Julho, near Praça Independência. It's the best place for finding most essentials and some non-essentials, such as locally made shirts.

Maps There are reportedly plans for printing a tourist map of São Tomé, which will be available from the Tourist Office. Until then, your only hope of obtaining a map is to go to the Direcção de Planificação Física (Mapping Institute) which is on the 2nd floor of a building facing the eastern end of Praça Independência. It has a large, 30-year-old

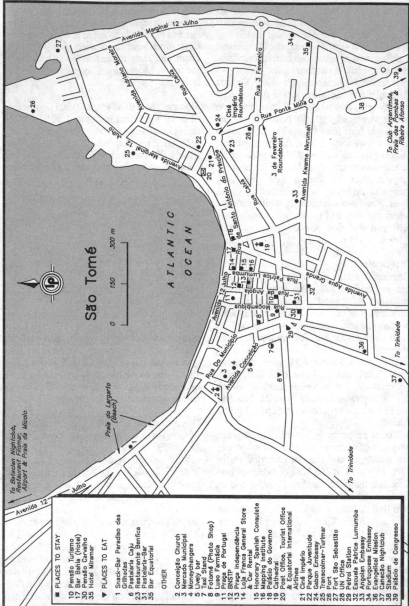

São Tomé

ATLANTIC OCEAN

0   150   300 m

PLACES TO STAY
10 Pensão Turismo
17 Bar Bahia (Hotel)
30 Pensão Carvalho
35 Hotel Miramar

PLACES TO EAT
1   Snack-Bar Paradiso das Grilhadas
6   Pastelaria Caju
23 Restaurante Benfica
31 Pastelaria-Bar
35 Bar Equatorial

OTHER
2   Conceição Church
4   Mercado Municipal
5   Moneychangers
7   Lively bar
8   Taxi Stand
9   Fotomã (Photo Shop)
9   Lusso Farmácia
11 Praça de Portugal
12 BNSTP
13 Praça Independência
14 Loja Franca General Store
15 Honorary Spanish Consulate
16 Mapping Institute
18 Palácio do Governo
19 Cathedral
20 Post Office, Tourist Office & Equatorial International Airlines
21 Ciné Império
22 Parque Juventude
25 Gabon Embassy
26 Transcolmar-Turimar
27 Fort São Sebastião
28 UN Office
29 Petrol Station
32 Escuela Patrice Lumumba
33 Angolan Embassy
34 Portuguese Embassy
36 Evangelical Mission
37 Canecão Nightclub
38 Stadium
39 Palácio de Congresso

map of the country; you can buy one if they have recently run off any copies.

Film The only place to buy and develop film is Fotomé, which is on Rua do Município just east of the market. It charges CFA 2500 for a roll of 36 Kodak film and CFA 7500 to develop it!

Things to See
For sightseeing, you could take a look at the baroque **cathedral** dating from the 16th century, and the **Presidential Palace** across the street, and then take a walk down the wide Ave Marginal 12 Julho for one km to **Fort São Sebastião**, overlooking the ocean.

The fort, built in 1578, is now the National Museum and contains a collection of furnishings and domestic objects from the 16th to the early 20th century. There are some 12 rooms in all, so a tour takes a minimum of one hour. On view are a wide selection of home furnishings made in both São Tomé and Portugal and dating from the 17th century, oil paintings of some of the Portuguese governors and early 19th-century plantation owners, a room on local culture including paintings of voodoo magic, and two rooms full of diningware from some of the wealthy Portuguese families who once ruled the island. Also included in the collection are Portuguese and Spanish religious art, including robes of some of the first bishops, old canons and statues of the nation's founders. Most memorable is the room dedicated to the infamous massacre in 1953 of the striking plantation workers; the gory photographs are unforgettable.

It's open on weekdays from 7 am to 3 pm and on Saturdays from 8 am to noon. It's free but they'll request a contribution and ask you to check the tourist souvenirs on sale in the office.

Activities
If you're interested in scuba diving, snorkelling or fishing, ask at the Hotel Miramar; it can put you in contact with a person in the business. The hotel also has the only pool, tennis court and squash court in town.

Places to Stay – bottom end
The cheapest hotel and the only one where you can pay in local currency is *Bar Bahia*, which charges the equivalent of CFA 4000 for a large, clean room with shared baths that have an irregular water supply and aren't very clean. There's no restaurant but there is a bar with cheap beers (CFA 150 per bottle) and snack food. It's in the town centre between the cathedral and the water.

A better place for money is *Pensão Carvalho*, which is near the town centre on Ave Kwame Nkrumah and charges CFA 5000 per room, payable in hard currency only. The rooms are small but have fans and a minibar, and the shared baths, which have tubs and fairly reliable running water, are quite decent and much better than at Bar Bahia. The Carvalho also has a restaurant and a pleasant street-side bar with cheap drinks.

Next in line is the nearby *Pensão Turismo* (☎ 22340) on Rua Caixa. A family-run pension, the friendly Turismo is quite popular and often full. The rooms, which cost CFA 6250/7500 for singles/doubles, have no fans but the shared baths have reliable running water and the restaurant is quite good.

Places to Stay – top end
The attractive, modern *Hotel Miramar* (☎ 22511; fax 21087; telex (967) 248) near the end of Ave Marginal 12 Julho, 1½ km from the centre and near the water, is Swiss-owned and the city's only tourist-class hotel. A very pleasant but overpriced hotel, it has 50 singles/doubles for US$92/124 including breakfast (US$10 for nonguests), a pool, billiard table, tennis and squash courts, and the best restaurant in town. You must pay in hard currency, travellers' cheques or by American Express credit card. It has no car rental agency but can arrange car rental for you.

Places to Eat
Unlike most hotels, restaurants accept only local currency – except Hotel Miramar, which also accepts foreign currency.

Cheap *petiscos* (snack food), such as

chocos (squid) and busios (sea snails) eaten with bread, is fairly easy to find in São Tomé. One of the better places for snacks is the *Paradiso das Grilhadas*, an open-air blue stall beneath the trees on Ave 12 Julho, half a km north-west of the market at Praia do Largarto. It's open only during the day and serves cheap meat-filled bocadillos as well as fish, squid, etc cooked on an oil-drum stove on the pavement. For drinks there are orange and lemon gassozas (soft drinks), cold beer and cheap Portuguese wine (CFA 250 a bottle).

There's no restaurant at *Bar Bahia* but you can get tasty meat-filled pastels (small pastries filled with meat) there for CFA 25 each. An excellent place for sweet pastries and bread is the popular new *Pastelaria Caju*, which is a good block behind the Mercado Municipal on one of the roads to Trinidade. It's open in the early evenings as well.

There are several restaurants with fixed menus catering for working-class people, where you can get a decent Portuguese-inspired meal for the equivalent of about CFA 900 plus beers for CFA 150, or cheaper gassozas. The meals are filling and good value. Typical dishes include kalilú, blá-blá, ijoga and barriage de peixe (fish). Three of the best are the family-run *Pensão Turismo* and the nearby *Pensão Carvalho*, both in the heart of town, and *Restaurant Benfica* (formerly Celestino), which is further east on Rua Caixa, just west of Ciné Imperio Roundabout. A beer at these places costs the equivalent of CFA 150.

For an inexpensive place with a nice ambience, try *Restaurant Filomar* (☎ 21908), which is open every night and is on the northern outskirts of town towards the airport, at the turn-off on your right to the Encogas complex, about three km from the town centre. You can eat inside or, better, outside on the terrace, which has a pleasant, breezy ambience. The menu is limited but prices are low, with most dishes in the CFA 500 to CFA 1000 range, including superb fish (barracuda, concon, etc) and meat dishes as well as soups. The beers, on the other hand, are all imported and double the price

of the local brew. Go early, as it is often full and reservations don't count for much.

If you're staying at Hotel Miramar, you can save considerably by eating at the popular *Bar Equatorial* next door. It has full Portuguese meals for CFA 1200 to CFA 1500 but also snack food for much less, including croquetes de carne for CFA 175, pasteles de bacalhau for CFA 150 and salgados. Eating at *Hotel Miramar*, which has the city's top restaurant, is very expensive – CFA 6250 for an overly filling four-course meal. Alternatively, try the much less expensive *Restaurante la Cabana* behind the hotel; the fish dishes there are excellent.

Entertainment
Bars A great place for a drink is the rustic, open-air terrace at Pensão Carvalho, which closes fairly late. A big bottle of Rosema (or 'cerveja nacional'), the local brew, courtesy of the former East Germans, costs the equivalent of CFA 150, as it does at most other bars in town, such as the lively bar on Ave Conceição just behind the market and Bar Bahia near the cathedral. Expatriates and tourists staying at Hotel Miramar tend to prefer the Bar Equatorial next door to the hotel. Beers there are twice as expensive, however; espresso coffee is also available.

Nightclubs São Tomé has some very decent and lively nightclubs, all of which are suitable for women, possibly even unaccompanied women. Beers at these places are usually imported and in small cans only (CFA 300). The city's top nightclub is *Bataclan*. It's on the northern outskirts of town, 2½ km from the centre, on the road to the airport, to your left a block. It's indoors and air-con, a variety of recorded music is played there, and there's a CFA 160 cover charge. It's open Wednesday to Friday from 9.30 pm to 1 am, Saturdays from 9.30 pm to 4 am, and Sundays from 8.30 pm to 1 am. On the south-western outskirts of town, off the road to Trinidade is another popular disco, the *Canecão*. It's open only on Friday and Saturday nights from around 9 pm, and on Sundays from around 3 pm.

Club Argentimôa (☎ 21908) has an informal African ambience and a big dance floor. This partially open-air place becomes lively from around 9.30 pm and it's open every night. The main problem is that it's four km south of the Palácio de Congresso, so you'll have to hitch a ride back into town or have a taxi wait for you.

The best place to hear live music is at the Parque Juventude (or Parque Populare) near the Ciné Imperio Roundabout. Every Saturday night starting around 9 pm and Sundays starting around 3 pm, bands perform free for the crowds. If you are lucky you may hear Conjunto Africana Negra, for years the country's best-known group. Other popular bands include Sangazuza, Dionense and Intues. These groups also perform occasionally at the Palácio Congresso but rarely anywhere else. For cassettes of their music, your best bet is the tiny music stand near the petrol station on Ave Conceição. They cost the equivalent of CFA 1250.

Cinema Ciné Império, which is on the eastern side of town at the intersection of Rua Caixa and Rua Ponta Mina, is the only movie theatre.

Getting There & Away
Air You can change money at the airport (☎ 151 for information) but there's no restaurant. For all flights other than those to Príncipe there's a departure tax at the airport of CFA 5000 (US$20), payable only in hard currency or travellers' cheques. The asking price for a taxi to the town centre is CFA 2500, but with hard bargaining you should be able to get one for half that. Hitching a ride into town usually isn't very difficult.

Equatorial International Airlines (☎ 21976, 21160; telex 216) has offices on Ave 12 Julho next to the post office and tourist information centre. All tickets are payable in hard currency only. The TAP office (☎ 22307, 21432) is in the town centre on Rua Patrice Lumumba near Praça Independência; TAAG (☎ 21794) is on Ave Giovani.

Bus & Taxi Minibuses and collectivos leave from the taxi park on Ave Conceição behind the market. They charge the equivalent of CFA 165 to Trinidade, Santana and Praia Pombas, CFA 335 to Ribeiro Afonso, and CFA 415 to Angolares, Praia das Conchas and Neves. All departures are between 6 am and 5 pm but there are no fixed schedules as they leave only when full. On Tuesdays and Saturdays there is also a collectivo as far south as Monte Mario.

Boat The two major shipping companies, Transcolmar (☎ 21839, 21840) and Turimar, are on Ave Marginal 12 Julho near the port, while Solmar (☎ 22273), which operates the *Solmar II* to Libreville, is on Ave Conceição near the market. The Solmar II does not have a fixed schedule but it is fairly regular, leaving about every five days. The cost is CFA 25,000 and the trip takes 24 hours. For boats to Príncipe (CFA 2500) and Porto Allegre, see Transcolmar or go to the port and ask around for other boats. None of them have regular schedules anymore.

Getting Around
Taxi Taxis are fairly plentiful in São Tomé but not elsewhere. Many of the drivers are part-time, trying to augment their incomes. During the day you can always find taxis at the taxi park, which is along Ave Conceição just behind the market. Finding them on the streets isn't so easy, so when you get one you may want to arrange future pick-ups. There's no cheap shared-taxi system but prices are still low despite high petrol prices (CFA 250 per litre). A short ride may cost the equivalent of CFA 200 to CFA 300, while one outside town to Praia das Pombas (nine km from the centre of town) costs about CFA 850. Hiring a taxi for the day costs CFA 12,500/US$50 including petrol; this price includes trips outside the city to places as far away as Praia das Conchas.

Car To rent a car or 4WD vehicle, see the owner of Loja Franca, Mr Leitao. He has a car and an all-terrain vehicle which he rents for CFA 12,500 per day plus petrol.

AROUND SÃO TOMÉ
Trinidade & Pousada da Boa Vista

Eight km inland from São Tomé, Trinidade is a pleasant little town with an attractive plaza, friendly people, various bars and a hotel. Rooms there aren't cheap, so it may be better to come for the day than to stay overnight.

Some seven km further up the mountain by a winding paved road, with cacao trees in every direction, is the old roça, La Casa de Repouso, which has been converted into a newly renovated hotel, La Pousada da Boa Vista. Even if you don't stay for the night, it's worth coming here just for the cool climate (the elevation is about 1000 metres) and wonderful views of the countryside and surrounding cacao farms.

Continuing two km further on the same road, which now becomes dirt, through the cacao farms you'll come to the well-known **Cascadas da São Nicolau**. These 25-metre high waterfalls are just off the road and surrounded by thick green vegetation which the sun can barely penetrate. There are some steps down to the pool below but few people swim here because the water is chilly and the site is hardly secluded.

Places to Stay & Eat Trinidade's only hotel is the two-storey *Hotel Me-Zoche* (☎ 71-561), which is just off the main square and has English-speaking staff. The seven rooms are carpeted and have tiled baths but the water supply is poor – at CFA 12,500 a room with breakfast (hard currency only) they're overpriced. The home-style restaurant, however, is a good place to eat and the fixed-menu meals are reasonably priced at CFA 1000. The wine selection is good but the beer is all foreign and relatively expensive. Meals are served from 12.30 to 2 pm and from 7.30 to 8.30 pm. There are no other restaurants in town but there are some bars where you can meet the locals.

La Pousada da Boa Vista was scheduled to reopen in early 1993 after a complete renovation. There are about 20 rooms and the place is charming, with panoramic views from the front terrace all the way down to the coast, but room prices are high and exceeded only by the Miramar's in São Tomé.

Getting There & Away Collectivos headed for Trinidade are stationed behind the market in São Tomé; the price is the equivalent of only CFA 165. To get to the Pousada or the waterfalls, however, you'll have to hitchhike or walk from Trinidade or rent a taxi in São Tomé.

Beaches to the North & West

São Tomé is famous for its white, sandy beaches and clear waters. Those to the north tend to have clearer waters, particularly around Praia das Conchas. Slightly north of the capital and a km or so offshore is a small, barren and uninhabited island, the **Ilhéu das Cabras**. There is reportedly a lovely beach on the side facing away from the mainland but the island is accessible by boat only at low tide.

The first good beach north of São Tomé by road is **Praia da Micolo**, which is about 12 km from town and beyond the airport. The only way to get there is to walk or take a taxi. Taxis will only go as far as Micolo because the road becomes incredibly rough beyond there.

If you walk along the beach westward from Micolo for a good hour you'll come to **Praia dos Governadores**, another beautiful white-sand beach that's even more secluded. By the old plantation jetty, just before reaching the beach, you'll come across an overgrown memorial to the workers gunned down in the 1953 massacre. Another hour's walk will bring you to **Praia dos Tamarindos**, which is one of the best beaches along the northern coast. You could camp on the beach there or walk back to Micolo where you could arrange for a taxi to pick you up.

The most famous beach is **Praia das Conchas**, which is further west and accessible by bus or collectivo. There's a small settlement of the same name somewhat inland, so to avoid confusion ask the bus driver to let you off at 'Praia da Praia das Conchas', which is not marked, then walk down the dirt drive to the beach. It's a small

Top :   Loading produce for transport to Malabo, Equatorial Guinea (HF)
Bottom :   Market in Malabo, Equatorial Guinea (HF)

Top :   Bioko Island village scene, Equatorial Guinea (HF)
Bottom :   Children, Equatorial Guinea (HF)

protected beach with no big waves, so the water is tranquil and clear – excellent for snorkelling.

An even better place for snorkelling, however, is **Lagoa Azul**, which is several km further west, just off the main road. It's a snorkelling paradise with calm, crystal clear water. Be careful with the coral, however, as it is being damaged despite the few people who come here. Further south-west you'll come to Neves and eventually to Santa Catarina and Lemba where the paved road ends and the buses stop.

An interesting side-trip which I highly recommend is one to **Roça Agostino Neto**, the turn-off to which is eight km or so before Praia das Conchas. It's a long walk south from the main road. This old plantation is open to the public, and the hospital and buildings here are a truly impressive architectural legacy of the colonial era.

Places to Stay You are unlikely to find lodging anywhere, but camping on the beaches is generally safe. Also, as you approach Praia das Conchas you'll pass some huts, not far from the beach. You might be able to rent one of them.

Getting There & Away Buses and collectivos headed for Praia das Conchas, Neves and Santa Catarina leave from behind the market in São Tomé. They cost the equivalent of CFA 415 to Neves and more to Santa Catarina.

Beaches to the South

The closest good beach to São Tomé is **Praia das Pombas**, which is seven km south of town and about 250 metres off the main north-south road. It's unmarked, so ask someone to point out the entrance. The beach, which is fairly isolated and pounded by some good-size waves, is some 200 metres long and lined with palm trees; off in the distance you'll see the tiny Santana Island just off the coast.

Five km or so further south is **Praia das Sete Ondas**, which is a better beach, and Agua Izé. Just south of Agua Izé is the **Boca de Inferno**, which is where the Atlantic swell is funnelled through a volcanic rock tunnel and explodes dramatically at the end, out of a blowhole. It's spectacular, so do try to get there. There are smaller versions around the island but most require a boat to get to them.

Further south is **São João Dos Angolares**, which is where the paved road and all public transport ends. Most notable here is a small but relatively expensive restaurant run by one of the few Portuguese who didn't flee the island in 1975. It is the house where Mario Soares, the current Portuguese president, stayed during his years of exile from the Salazar regime in Portugal. A signed photograph of him hangs proudly in the dining room.

The best and most isolated beaches of all are those south of Angolares, such as **Praia Grande**, but getting to them is difficult and generally requires a boat, as vehicles rarely go south of Angolares towards **Porto Allegre**, the southern tip of the island.

Getting There & Away Minibuses and collectivos leave daily from near the market in São Tomé. The cost to Angolares is the equivalent of CFA 415. None of them continue on to Porto Allegre, but it is possible to hitch a ride with the truck which takes kids from school in Angolares back to Porto Allegre on Friday afternoons, returning on Monday mornings. Otherwise you'll have to look for a boat from Angolares. If you're headed to Porto Allegre from São Tomé, the easiest way to get there is on the *Transcolmar*. The boat's schedule is erratic, so you'll have to inquire at Transcolmar or at the port in São Tomé about departures.

Ilhéu das Rolas

Ilhéu das Rolas (Rolas Island), east of Porto Allegre, is so small that it can be walked around comfortably in half a day. On the northern lip of a central volcanic cone, the highest point on the island, are the sad remains of an old lighthouse. The caretaker will be glad to show you around and explain how the Portuguese troops came in 1975 to remove the mercury which is needed to balance and support the heavy rotating mechanism. He still keeps that mechanism highly polished and greased.

Further down the slope, to the north, are the remains of a marble monument to Gago Coutinho (a Portuguese aviator) marking the equator. The commemorative plaque and visitor's book were removed long ago.

The island has only two beaches, one on the northern coast and one on the western coast. They are good places from which to view the impressive sunsets.

Places to Stay & Eat There is no lodging on the island, so you'll have to camp. Camping on the beaches is safe but you'll have to bring all of your food, and if you aren't careful some of the local children may walk away with it. You may also have to contend with some impressive rains, voracious mosquitoes and aggressive crabs which will try to eat your food at night.

Getting There & Away The only way to get there is on the *Transcolmar*, which heads from São Tomé to Porto Allegre, then to Ilhéu das Rolas, and back again that night to São Tomé. The boat stops there an hour, which is enough time to visit the monument and get back to the boat should you not wish to stay the night.

Príncipe

Much smaller than São Tomé island with only about 8000 inhabitants, Príncipe is a beautiful, flatter island with many birds, particularly parrots. The capital is Santo António, which has about 3000 inhabitants. Other than the crews of Russian trawlers which frequently visit the tuna processing plant, you'll probably be the only foreigner on the island. One correspondent spent the afternoon lying on the beach drinking vodka with a Russian trawler crew to celebrate the fact that they'd found a foreigner there – the first time, apparently, in 18 visits!

The island is small enough for most places

to be comfortably accessible by foot from Santo António, including **Praia Grande** to the north of the capital and **Praia de Évora** to the south. Two more remote places which you might head for are **Bombom Island** off the northern coast and **Praia Banana**, which is reportedly the best beach of all.

As you travel around the island be on the lookout for parrots. They used to be everywhere but today they are becoming increasingly scarce, as they're being exported from the island at an alarming rate. Flying back to São Tomé you may, sadly, see some in cages being packed inside the plane.

Places to Stay & Eat
For a bed in Santo António, if you're hurting for money look around the tuna processing factory. With luck you may find still standing the smelly old *Residencia Oficial*, which in years past has been the cheapest place by far to stay and eat. Otherwise head for *Pensão Residencial Palhota* (☎ 51060, 51079), which is owned and run by the governor of the island. A very decent double costs CFA 5000 (payable in hard currency only) and you can eat there as well for about CFA 700 for a fixed meal. Check your bill because the owner's maths is reportedly bad.

The town's top address is *Hotel Residencial Jardin* (☎ 22505), which charges CFA 11,250/15,000 for singles/doubles including breakfast. Another possibility is *Hotel Residencial Avenida* (☎ 22368). In the near future, first-class travellers will also be able to stay at an up-market hotel that is being built on a secluded beach near Bombom Island. You can easily reserve rooms at these places by calling ahead from São Tomé; telephone charges are very low and connections are excellent.

For drinks, you might try *Terraco Bar* on Rua dos Trabahadores; there's occasionally music there as well.

Getting There & Away
Equatorial International Airlines flies there on Mondays at 2.30 pm and Fridays at 8 am. The one-way cost is CFA 16,250 (hard currency only) and there's a weekend round-trip

special of CFA 27,500. Coming by boat (CFA 2500) is much cheaper but the boats have no schedules and leave only when full. Inquire at the port in São Tomé or at the Transcolmar offices nearby. Two of the boats that ply this route are Transcolmar's *Brizas do Mar* and *Bone de Joque*.

Getting Around
The island's road system is limited but there are taxis in Santo António. You can also get around the island and to secluded beaches, including such remote places as Bombom Island, by small boat, either as a passenger or by hiring one.

Zaïre

The former Belgian Congo is to Africa what the forests of Brazil are to South America. Many would think you are out of your mind to travel overland. Going from one end of the country to the other can take a month. The road system is probably Africa's worst. For part of the journey, you can travel by train or riverboat.

Indeed, a trip on the Zaïre River is the *sine qua non* of an adventure in Zaïre – absolutely not to be missed. You'll pass through some of the thickest rainforests in Africa. Fortunately, the famous Primus beer seems to make its way into every nook and cranny of the country. Travelling overland is not for everyone by a long shot. Those that do won't have any trouble coming up with stories for their grandchildren, including hunting with the Pygmies. Others simply fly.

The far eastern region, with Virunga park, Lake Kivu and the snowcapped Ruwenzori mountains, is considered by many to be the most spectacular area in all of Central and West Africa. It is also home to the incomparable mountain gorilla, and you can see them in their native habitat on the slopes of various volcanoes. Some of the other volcanoes which dot the landscape are active and you can even climb them. In the far south, there's the city of Lubumbashi, which has lush tropical surroundings and a relatively cool climate.

Kinshasa is just the opposite – huge and muggy, with an abnormally high crime rate stemming from the 1991 riots against the unpopular Mobutu. (See the following History section for more information.) Still, the former Leopoldville continues to have its admirers. No wonder – it's the music capital of Africa. Zaïre must surely produce more recording stars than any other country in Africa. No self-respecting traveller would fail to take in one of the *Zaïrois* bands in the lively Cité area, provided security conditions in the city return to normal. For the rugged traveller, however, Kinshasa is often merely

a starting point for a fantastic adventure into the hinterland.

Facts about the Country

HISTORY

As in all the thick rainforest areas of Central Africa, the first inhabitants were nomadic hunters and gatherers, some of them Pygmies. Basic communism was the order of the day. Men and women were equally responsible for finding food, and the few means of subsistence were shared by everyone. Those near the rivers found a life of fishing and farming less hostile and confining than in the forests.

Communities eventually arose along the rivers. The villagers relied on the Pygmies to supply meat and labour; the Pygmies relied on the villagers for iron implements, salt and some food. The villagers began acquiring possessions and improving their existence while the Pygmies did not. Eventually, village clans developed, with the wealthier ones dominating the source of labour.

Early Empires

The development of village clans created a social base for a major new phenomenon – the growth of empires in the savanna areas. Between the 13th century and the arrival of the Belgians in the late 19th century, numerous kingdoms arose. The first, the Kongo empire, extended over vast territories, each headed by a chief in charge of collecting taxes in goods, cloth or slaves (primarily criminals and prisoners of war).

When the Portuguese arrived in 1482, they converted the king to Christianity and for a brief period good relations existed. Soon, however, the Portuguese were demanding slaves. In the 16th century alone, they shipped some 60,000 slaves out of the Kongo empire. By the 17th century, the demand for slaves was more than the Kongo could provide. So the Portuguese initiated their own raiding parties. Eventually, their interests collided and war erupted in 1660. Outmatched, the Kongo lost. Their heyday was over.

By the 18th century, the two most powerful kingdoms were in the southern copper belt: the Luba in northern Katanga and the Landa further south. The kings had hundreds of wives and concubines, and court officials abounded. In 1906, a German explorer, Leo Frobenius, found magnificent towns with the principal streets lined on both sides for km on end with rows of palm trees, charmingly decorated houses, velvet and silk materials everywhere, and every man carrying intricate inlaid knives or other sumptuous weapons of iron or copper.

In the mid-19th century, Arabs from the island of Zanzibar in East Africa invaded eastern Zaïre and established equally magnificent towns and thriving plantations. Their fine houses had all the luxuries of urban life along the coast of East Africa – beds, furniture, coffee tables, elaborate doorways and European luxuries such as candles, sugar, matches, silver, glass goblets and decanters. Common soldiers slept on silk and satin mattresses, in carved beds with silk mosquito curtains! The most powerful Arab slave trader of the day, Tippu Tip, had some 50,000 guns at his command.

Colonial Period

European governments showed no interest in exploring the Congo. It took a British explorer and journalist, Stanley, to spark their interest. After Stanley's historic journey to Africa in the early 1870s to find Livingstone (he did at Lake Tanganyika), he made an equally historic voyage down the Congo River in 1874 – the first European to do so. Smallpox, starvation, crocodiles and battles with local tribes killed over half his men. Stanley proved that above the rapids on the lower Congo, there were thousands of km of navigable waters.

The British weren't interested. King Léopold II of Belgium was. Léopold envisioned a way to capture the trade of the entire lower Congo basin – build a railway around the rapids and launch steamers upcountry. So

King Léopold II

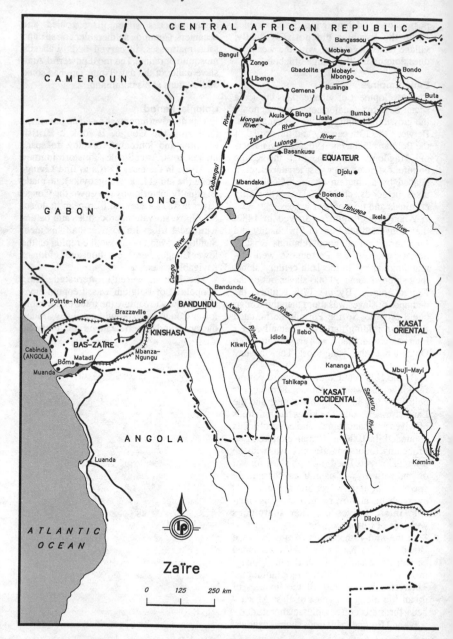

Zaïre

0   125   250 km

he hired Stanley to establish road and river communications from the river's mouth to Stanleyville (now Kisangani). The French saw Stanley as a threat, so in 1880 they sent Simon de Brazza to claim neighbouring Congo-Brazzaville (now the Congo). The European scramble for Africa was on; King Léopold had provided the spark.

The 'Congo Free State', awarded to King Léopold by the Berlin Conference of 1884-85, was neither free nor a colony. It was Léopold's own private estate and the most preposterous form of foreign domination Africa would ever know. Following the example of railway development in North and South America, he granted land and mineral rights to companies that would build railways. For an area almost twice the size of Luxembourg, one company built the line from Matadi on the sea to Léopoldville (now Kinshasa); others built those in the south. Léopold himself managed one of the operations, milking the Congo of its wealth.

A booming demand for rubber, following the development of rubber tyres, saved him from going broke. The only problem was that the operations needed labour. Slavery was the solution. Tribespeople who did not fulfill their quota of rubber for the bosses were maimed by the king's men. To prove that they had exacted the punishment, the gang bosses presented baskets of smoke cured human hands for inspection to their bosses. Such practices inspired Kurtz, the central figure in Joseph Conrad's short story *Heart of Darkness*, which was set in Zaïre, to exclaim: 'The horror! The horror!'

Europe eventually caught wind of Léopold's ghastly atrocities and an international scandal developed. Outraged and embarrassed, the Belgian government forced their king to cede the Congo to Belgium in 1908. In acquiring a colony, Belgium also acquired Léopold's huge debt from lavish spending on his palaces and other public buildings in Belgium. The debt at one time absorbed nearly 20% of the country's revenue.

Belgium did almost nothing to develop the Congo. Private companies moved in and began extracting copper, diamonds and other minerals from the rich fields in Shaba and elsewhere. Educating the masses was too much of a bother. Instead, the government left it to Catholic missionaries, agreeing only to subsidise primary schools. At independence, the Belgian Congo had a grand total of half a dozen African university graduates. Belgium did, however, build almost 50,000 km of roads and began the largest construction project in colonial Africa – the Inga dam on the lower Congo, with a capacity to supply half the electricity produced at the time in all of Western Europe!

Independence & Civil War

Politically, Belgium did absolutely nothing to prepare the Congo for independence. Political parties in West Africa began in 1915. In the Belgian Congo, they weren't allowed before 1955. For years the Belgians had simplified their rule by playing one African tribe off against another. For this reason and because the colony was so large, the political parties became almost entirely tribally oriented. In 1958 France made neighbouring Congo-Brazzaville self-governing, an event that ignited politics in the Belgian Congo.

A year later Belgium had to send troops to quell rioting in 'Léo'. Disturbances continued and more troops were required. Almost overnight, Belgium, never having seriously considered granting independence, made a 180° turn. Shocked African politicians were told they had six months to prepare for elections and independence.

Only two of the parties had any real loyalty to the idea of all-Congolese unity. One of them, headed by Patrice Lumumba, won the election. Lumumba became prime minister and his major rival, Kasavubu, became president. Six days later, the army mutinied. Five days thereafter, with backing from the Belgian-owned mining company, Moise Tshombe, the governor of Katanga province (now called Shaba) announced the secession of his province. With Katanga went the government's major source of revenue. Civil war was inevitable.

Lumumba pleaded for help from the UN and the UN began the most critical operation in its history. When the UN didn't do exactly what he wanted, Lumumba asked Russia for troops as well. This was the straw that broke the camel's back. Soon thereafter, Lumumba was overthrown by an alliance of the army, led by Joseph Mobutu (moh-BOU-tou), and regional politicians, headed by Kasavubu. They expelled the Russians and handed Lumumba over to Tshombe in Elizabethville (Lubumbashi), where he was murdered.

Civil war continued. With the aid of UN troops, the central government finally gained control of Katanga in 1963. But Russia, France and other countries refused to contribute any longer to the UN operation. Bankrupt, the UN withdrew. To keep Katanga from seceding again, Kasavubu had no choice but to accept Tshombe into the government.

Meanwhile, pro-Marxist troops took control of major parts of the east. The USA took note. Under Mobutu, the army went there to regain control and with the aid of US and Belgian paratroopers and about 1200 foreign mercenaries, they succeeded.

Mobutu

Within a year Mobutu, supported by the West and the CIA in particular, staged a bloodless coup. Luck was with him – copper prices started to skyrocket. A former journalist and a member of the tiny Ngbande tribe in the north around Gbadolite, Mobutu consolidated his power by returning power to the local chiefs, buying off his enemies, and turning his friends into millionaires. Corruption became a way of life, permeating the entire government bureaucracy.

His famous 'authenticity' campaign began in the early '70s. The Congo became Zaïre, Léopoldville became Kinshasa, Elizabethville became Lubumbashi, and Stanleyville became Kisangani. He then ordered all Zaïrois to replace their Christian names with African ones. Mobutu Joseph Desiré became Mobutu Sese Seko (his full name – Mobutu Sese Seko Koko Ngbendu wa za Banga – means 'the all-powerful warrior who, because of his endurance and inflexible will to win, will go from conquest to conquest leaving fire in his wake').

His portrait was everywhere and his words were propagated by slavish newspapers that placed his picture on every front page. To question him was to commit treason. Donning his now familiar leopard-skin hat and self-styled *abacos*, a blend of Mao jacket and pinstripe suit material, he forbade bureaucrats to wear Western attire, expropriated US$500 million in foreign enterprises, and threw out the important Asian business community.

Mobutu's extravagances were numerous and included various monuments to himself, stadiums, the World Trade Centre, the ultramodern Voice of Zaïre, and 11 palaces, some linked to the capital by four-lane highways. He even spent US$15 million to sponsor the world championship fight between Muhammed Ali and George Foreman in 1974, and his son was seen all over town driving his white Ferrari.

Mostly, however, in his megalomaniacal pursuit of wealth and power he used the money to amass a personal fortune of US$3 billion, primarily in foreign banks and real estate (several chateaux in Belgium and other homes in France, Switzerland, Italy, Senegal and the Côte d'Ivoire). Record copper prices financed most of it; huge loans from US banks supplied the rest.

Economic Collapse

In 1975, copper prices collapsed. The honeymoon was over. By 1977, the GNP had tumbled 14%, leaving Zaïre with the world's highest per-capita debt. The country was bankrupt. Neo-colonialism became the order of the day. New York banks and the International Monetary Fund (IMF) dictated economic policy which involved devaluations, import controls, wage restrictions, reductions in payrolls. By the early '80s, debt repayments were eating up 60% of export earnings; copper, cobalt and diamond prices were lower than ever. From 1965 to 1984, the average annual growth rate per capita was minus 1.6%!

Meanwhile, twice during the late '70s, some 5000 guerrilla troops from Angola invaded Shaba, capturing Kolwezi, an important mining town, and massacring European workers and missionaries.

In the face of the greatest threat to Zaïre since the Katanga secession, Zaïrois troops virtually refused to fight. 'Mobutisme' had become merely a way to justify absolute power by Mobutu's Ngbande tribe, which controlled the army. Several hundred thousand Zaïrois fled to Angola. The soldiers deeply resented the ethnic discrimination.

Only with the assistance of Moroccan troops and Belgian-French paratroopers (with aircraft and logistical support from the USA) did they recapture the area. Eventually, Mobutu and the Angolan rebel leaders came to an agreement – Mobutu wouldn't assist anti-guerrilla forces in Angola if the Angolan rebels withdrew from Shaba.

The 1980s

Throughout the '80s Zaïre's economy was in a real mess. Seemingly every year, the government rescheduled its debt with the International Monetary Fund (IMF). Rescheduling alone added about US$1 billion to the debt by the end of the decade. The country continued to import a shocking 50% of its food requirements; stores were stocked with South African products, from toilet-bowl cleaners to cocktail snacks (immediately prior to independence, the country was self-sufficient in food).

Mobutu had to eat humble pie on numerous occasions, by devaluing the currency, dissolving the state minerals marketing company, courting patronising Belgian industrialists and, upon the insistence of the World Bank, replacing the leadership of Gécamines, the all-important mining company.

Mobutu's political problems were almost as severe, and mutiny within the army was a constant threat. To keep abreast of his enemies, Mobutu maintained several competing intelligence agencies. No less than six countries – the USA, Belgium, France, China, Germany and Israel – all continuing to ignore Mobutu's incredible excesses, helped prop up the regime with military assistance.

Declaring 'We will do our best to prevent Soviet influence in Africa', Mobutu continued to receive US support, and he solidified this even more by allowing the USA to funnel aid to the National Union for the Total Independence of Angola (UNITA) through some sophisticated airstrips in Kamina (southern Zaïre) where the guerrilla group maintained bases. To his credit, at a summit of African leaders in Zaïre Mobutu helped broker a cease-fire in the Angolan war, which was signed in his home town, Gbadolite, in the presence of 18 African heads of state. As a result, in 1989 the USA rewarded the internationally criticised leader for what one US State Department official called his 'very positive attitude' with the honour of being the first African head of state to visit President Bush and a pledge of US$60 million in aid.

At the same time, however, US Congress was finally moving to put restrictions on aid to Zaïre in part because of financial discrepancies (some US$400 million in foreign exchange receipts couldn't be accounted for!) but mainly because of Mobutu's dismal human rights record. In 1977, for example, when the president's soldiers flew to the Bandundu region north-east of Kinshasa to confront members of an obscure sect who had turned against the government, they displayed their loyalty by mowing down some 800 of the sect members. World newspapers, however, barely took notice. According to Amnesty International, in 1982-83 police killed about 100 political prisoners, criminals and suspects in Zaïre's prisons.

Later, as reported by Sanford Ungar in *Africa: The People and Politics of an Emerging Country*, just after returning from a triumphant state visit in Washington with President Reagan, Mobutu found out that a US congressional delegation was meeting with 10 former members of parliament who had been jailed for advocating the establishment of a second political party. Furious, he sent police to attack and beat his audacious opponents as they left the hotel where they'd been meeting. US officials had to stand by and watch.

GEOGRAPHY

Zaïre is imposing. Just look at the Africa-wide statistics: with borders so long that they adjoin nine other African countries, it is the third-largest country after Sudan and Algeria (77 times as large as Belgium, its colonizer, and the same size as all of Western Europe), with the third-largest population (after Nigeria and Egypt), the third-highest mountain (Mt Stanley at 5109 metres), rainforests as extensive as those in the rest of Central Africa combined, and the second-longest river, the Zaïre, which is second only to the Amazon in water volume. (The name Zaïre comes from the Kongo word *nzere* meaning 'river'.)

The country's mineral resources are also impressive. Sixty percent of the world's cobalt, 90% of the world's small industrial diamonds, and a significant portion of the world's copper all come from southern Zaïre.

Exploiting these resources is a gargantuan task. As large as the USA east of the Mississippi, Zaïre has about 1750 km of asphalt highways in the countryside. The road system is so bad that virtually all overland travellers cross in the north-east corner, bypassing Kinshasa. There are trains from Kinshasa to Matadi and from Lubumbashi (Shaba) in the south-east to Ilebo, Kindu and Kalemie, but travelling from Kinshasa to Lubumbashi by road and rail still takes about two weeks.

While most of southern Zaïre is tropical grassland, with rolling hills around Lubumbashi, the northern half of Zaïre is mostly rainforested lowland, where the roads become incredibly muddy. Most travellers heading east from Kinshasa go via the Zaïre River (called the Congo River in the Congo), which curves through the country on a path that is even longer than the Mississippi. However, as with the Niger River in Mali (West Africa), a long series of rapids near the coast make it impossible for ocean-going ships to enter. Only from Kinshasa inland will you see Mississippi-style riverboats ploughing the Zaïre.

Zaïre's most beautiful area, the eastern border with Rwanda and Uganda, is also its most inaccessible. The main attractions here are Lake Kivu, the gorilla sanctuary near the lakeside town of Bukavu, and Virunga National Park north of the lake, which includes the snowcapped Ruwenzori (ROU-when-ZOR-ee) mountain range, active volcanoes and more gorillas. Garamba National Park in the far north-eastern corner of the country, bordering Sudan, is the last refuge of the northern white rhino and, unique in Africa, has domesticated elephants, but access to it is extremely difficult. Travellers in the north-east, however, often pass by Epulu, a major Pygmy area, where there's the newly created Parc National d'Okapis. Research is being carried on there to protect the elusive okapi.

Environmentally, the country's troubled economy and relatively low population pressure have combined to prevent any serious threat to the country's vast forest reserves which are likely to change little in the next 10 to 20 years. However, there are some huge logging operations, such as the two million acre concession of Danzer Corp (a German transnational company) at Lokuku some 2000 km up the Zaïre River, that are rapidly wiping out large areas of prime hardwood forests. This is of concern, in part because the logging roads these companies construct eventually attract new settlers who continue the process of clearing the land.

CLIMATE

About a third of Zaïre, including Kisangani, lies north of the equator, where it rains year-round, though less from December to February. In the rest of Zaïre, including Kinshasa, Lake Kivu and the Shaba area, there's a dry spell, with overcast days, from June to September. The heavy rain period is February to May. Despite its equatorial location, Zaïre is not one of Africa's hotter countries. Humidity, not high temperatures, is the problem.

GOVERNMENT

The advent of the 1990s has seen little change in Zaïre. When students at Lubumbashi University demonstrated in 1990, Mobutu sent in troops who proceeded to kill over 100 of them inside their dorms. With the end of the Cold War in the early '90s, however, came one significant change – Mobutu's political coffers became as bare as those of the state he had robbed, and virtually all aid from the West was cut off. With Mobutu left to his own resources and the economy in such a dismal state, conditions were ripe for overthrowing the widely hated president. Up against the wall, Mobutu proclaimed himself to be a great democrat and announced the legalisation of a multiparty system.

A few months later, in September 1991, all hell broke loose in Kinshasa. Army troops, once the bedrock of Mobutu's support, finally rebelled after many months of unpaid work. Rampaging and looting, they were soon joined by ordinary citizens, touching off the worst rioting in the city's history. Hundreds of major commercial establishments were stripped and destroyed. The attack on the General Motors assembly plant was typical of the catastrophic damage. As reported in the *International Herald Tribune*:

The first wave, a Zaïrian military unit based at the nearby airport, stole all the plant's vehicles. A second wave of rioters took all the assembly-line equipment and everything else that wasn't welded down. There wasn't much left for the third wave of looters, so they took the walls and the roof.

Belgium and France again sent commandos and paratroops to the rescue, gaining control of Kinshasa airport and the town centre. However, this time all they cared about was evacuating their kin and other foreigners including the Peace Corps, some 14,000 in all. Perched aboard his helicopter-equipped riverboat in the middle of the Zaïre River, the president watched four days of the deadly rioting before, under pressure from France and the USA, appointing opposition leader

Étienne Tshisekedi (from near Mbuji-Mayi in the Kasaï Occidental region) to form a coalition government. Mobutu sacked him within a week after he refused to swear an oath of allegiance.

In 1992, the rebellious National Assembly held a conference for more than six months during which delegates re-elected Tshisekedi as prime minister and made speeches all day long condemning Mobutu and his cronies. The public heard all this on the radio and prayed he would just take his money and run, but he did not. Mobutu continued to hold on to the purse strings and command of the army, thereby effectively refusing to give full authority to the transitional government.

In late 1992, soldiers in Kisangani went on a looting rampage, again for not having been paid. Soldiers in Kinshasa did the same a few months later when Mobutu tried to introduce a new five-million zaïre note which none of the shopkeepers would accept. Soldiers loyal to Tshisekedi and to Mobutu fought it out, which resulted in more than 1000 deaths, mostly of soldiers but also of the French ambassador who was accidentally hit by a stray bullet.

In December 1992, Mobutu sacked Tshisekedi, who was replaced as Prime Minister by Faustin Burundwa. One of his first challenges became trying to stop the ethnic fighting between native Zaïrians and Rwandan immigrants which had erupted in eastern Zaïre around Walikale as a result of longstanding land disputes, causing thousands of deaths and forcing tens of thousands of Rwandans to flee to their homeland.

In 1993, despite all privately owned newspapers being anti-Mobutu, he still had enough loyal supporters in the army, particularly his elite presidential division, to prevent the new Prime Minister and his coalition government supported by the National Assembly from pursuing the transition to democracy and ousting him. It is hardly surprising – there are now so many splintered and frail political groups that none can muster enough support to unseat Mobutu.

As long as the power struggle between Mobutu and the transitional government continues, conditions in Zaïre are likely to remain chaotic. Mobutu's incredibly strong patronage system could keep him in power indefinitely. Among African heads of state, only Houphouët Boigny of the Côte d'Ivoire has remained in power longer.

ECONOMY

On the economic front, per-capita incomes, standing at US$180 (eighth-lowest in the world), continue to plummet while Mobutu's personal wealth, now an estimated US$6 billion, and the country's foreign debt, up to US$12.5 billion, continue to grow.

Meanwhile, on the surface life in the cities looks fairly normal most of the time – hotels and restaurants open for business, taxis plough the streets, planes take off, market vendors sell food. But in reality, the chaos continues. The banks have virtually no money and doctors and teachers are on strike, so the capital's state-run hospitals and most schools, from first grade through to university level, are closed. With virtually no customs dues coming in, the government pays its bills by printing money. The notes are printed in Germany, then flown to Kinshasa and whisked away by helicopter to the yacht on the Zaïre River that has become Mobutu's refuge. He then dispenses all cash as he sees fit, making sure he meets the monthly payrolls of his key military units.

Mobutu's extravagances continue. As he has done since the early 1980s, he continues to have his European hair stylist flown in every two weeks to cut his hair, at an estimated cost of US$5000 each trip – a total of more than US$1 million by early 1993.

For the common person, life remains at the brink. A typical government worker's salary, if he or she receives it, barely amounts to the equivalent of US$30 to US$40 a month, or roughly the price of two sacks of cassava, the amount to feed a family of four for a month. How do people make ends meet? Police at roadblocks collect *matabiches* (bribes) from motorists. Telephone operators at the post office must be tipped, otherwise your call will never be made. If you send out international mail, postal workers are liable to remove and resell the stamps. Any foreigners walking down the streets of Kinshasa in broad daylight, even if they are not wearing a watch or jewellery, are likely to be robbed, possibly mugged as well.

POPULATION & PEOPLE

Zaïre has about 40 million people, with some 4.5 million in Kinshasa, 900,000 in Lubumbashi, 800,000 in Kananga, and 600,000 in both Kisangani and Mbuji-Mayi. However, about 60% of the population is rural, which is about par for Central Africa, with the highest concentrations in the central and southern parts of the country.

Ethnically, Zaïre is extremely varied, with some 250 tribes and clans. The most numerous people are the Kongo who live in the Kinshasa area; the people of Kwangu-Kwilu; the Mongo, who live in the great forests; the Luba in the south; the Bwaka; and the Zande in the north and north-east. Huge sections of the northern rainforests – Pygmy territory – are practically deserted. As long as the forests remain, the population there simply cannot increase.

With an adult literacy rate of around 70%, up from 44% in 1970, Zaïre has, amazingly, one of the highest literacy rates in all of Africa, thanks to the Catholic primary schools. This is despite the fact that the government spends a smaller percentage of its budget on education (less than 1%!) than any country in Africa except Somalia. Consequently, despite the high literacy rate, relatively few Zaïrians have university-level degrees.

ARTS & CULTURE

Zaïre has the greatest diversity of art in Africa and, unlike most African countries, the quality today is often still quite high, particularly the masks (*mbuya* in Lingala) and wooden statues, in large part because many areas remain relatively untouched by the outside world. If you go into the marketplace in Kinshasa, for example, your arm may be tugged again and again by vendors saying '*Mbuya, mbuya!*' and showing you

Basuku initiation mask

their wildly carved and painted wooden masks. Gold is almost never used in Zaïrian art and only a few tribes use ivory.

There are so many areas that are notable for their art that it's difficult to list them all without confusing the traveller. Ten of the more well-known styles/ethnic groups are the Kongo (Bakongo is the plural form), Pende (Bapende) and Yaka (Bayaka) in the west; Kuba (Bakuba) in the centre; Luba (Baluba) and Songye (Basongye) in the southern Shaba region; and Lega (Balega), Bembe (Babembe), Azande (Zande) and Mangbetu in the north and north-east. There are, however, many more major styles (Kongo, Mbun, Mbala and Kwésé in the west; Lele, Wongo, Lulua and Salampasu in the centre; and Mbole in the north).

Pende

The wooden masks of the Pende, often grotesque and comic, are characterised by heavy-lidded eyes and a triangular-shaped nose, head and coiffure, and were the inspiration for many of Picasso's paintings. The Pende are perhaps most famous, however, for their colourful all-body masks of woven raffia, leaves and feathers. If you were able to witness a *mukanda*, a puberty rite of the Pende who come from the Bandundu region east of Kinshasa, you'd see them for sure. Their creators – always male – are thought to have special powers and thus hold a place of honour in the village. When the circumcision ritual begins and the *minganji* dancers, covered from head to foot in their raffia costumes, enter the arena, the crowd draws back in deference to their powers. Then the dancing, sometimes erotic, sometimes comic but always mystical, begins and grows with intensity as the crowd, particularly the children, shriek from fear, delight and excitement, especially when the masked figures come running towards them.

Bakuba

The Bakuba, a tribe of virtuoso carvers, had a relatively powerful kingdom at one time and virtually all of their art during this period was made to serve the king, sometimes symbolising the cultural hero Woot who originated royalty. Once during each reign, one of the carvers was selected to carve the famous portrait statue of the king, and even today some of the masks may only be worn by men of royal descent. As a result, Kuba art is very decorative, whether in the form of surrealistic ladles for use in rituals, elaborately carved cups for ceremonial drinking of palm wine, or masks, of which there are a great variety. If you see a mask with geometric patterns and decorated with cowrie shells, beads and raffia cloth, chances are it's Kuba. Some masks can be rather crude-looking and made from straw; others are very elaborate and ornate. One among many is the colourful helmet mask used in boys' initiation rites. Kuba art also takes the form of charms, game boards, spoons, tobacco pipes, combs, three-legged stools, miniature hair ornaments, vessels and cosmetic boxes with geometric decorations.

Luba

Luba art was the first to be recognised internationally and today it's very difficult to find a really old example as they are virtually all in private collections. The style is relatively realistic with mostly correct proportions, and lots of attention to detail. The Luba are perhaps best known for the Kifwebe mask (shown in this chapter), which is used in ceremonies associated with chieftaincy, typically in a masked dance to celebrate the arrival of an important visitor or the death of a village dignitary. Painted black and white and decorated with curved grooves, the mask is hemispherical in structure with a protruding nose and mouth and is one of the most popular masks found in the markets and art shops not just in Zaïre but all over Black Africa. Most, however, are made expressly for the tourist market and therefore aren't authentic.

Luba (Kifwébe association) mask

Mangbetu

The Mangbetu, from the far north-east, were once admired for their centralised government and art. Today they are well known for a particular style of art – one that portrays the wrapped and elongated head fashionable for Mangbetu rulers at the turn of the century. When Europeans came onto the scene, they created a demand for anthropomorphic sculpture, with carved and sculpted heads being placed on pots, knife handles, the necks of harps, and many other utilitarian objects.

MUSIC

Zaïre's 'Congo' music is at the top of all the Central and West African 'pop' charts. The Latin influence is obvious; you may at first think you're listening to rumba music. Over the past 25 years, Congo music has exercised a profound influence over the musical development of the rest of Black Africa. Today, every bar in Central and West Africa seems to be playing it.

Two of the leading stars are Tabu Ley and Franco (recently deceased), while Kanda Bongo is one of Zaïre's wizards of soukous, a dance style introduced in the mid-1960s which became so popular that it later was adopted as a generic term for most Zaïrian music. Others are Samaguana, OK Jazz, Langa Langa, Bella Bella, M'Bongo, Papa Wemba, and female vocalists M'Bilia Bel, Tshala Muana and, deceased, M'Pongo Love. The Zaïrois honour their musicians by giving them titles. Tabu Ley is Seigneur Rochereau, the deceased Kasanda was called Docteur Nico, and Franco Luambo was Maître Franco. Some of the newer groups include Choc Stars, Empire, Anti-Choc and Zaïko. Another is Zap Mama, which is an extraordinary female group consisting of four Zaïrian women and Marie Daulne, the Belgian band leader and composer. Shunning musical instruments, they rely exclusively on voice and rhythmic clapping and get their inspiration from Pygmy songs.

Several famous Zaïrian singers have died from AIDS including Franco and M'Pongo Love. Franco, along with Hilarion Nguema of Gabon, took on the cause of AIDS before his death. One of his songs that hit number one some years back on the African hit parade warns, 'You, brothers and sisters, carriers of the virus, don't contaminate the others', and calls on students '...not to let themselves be attracted by any unknown person...', alluding to the widespread use of prostitutes by students in the large cities.

LANGUAGE

French is the official language. Of the 200-odd local languages and dialects, the major one is Lingala, spoken primarily in Kinshasa and along the rivers. You'll hear more Kikongo west of Kinshasa, Tshiluba in the south and central area, Kiswahili (Swahili) in the east and north-east including Goma and Bukavu and, to a lesser extent, Nandé in the area north of Goma.

Greetings & Civilities in Lingala

Good morning
   m-BOH-tay
Good evening
   m-BOH-tay
How are you?
   san-goh-BOH-nee?
I'm fine
   NAH-zah-lee MAH-lah-mou
Thank you
   MAY-lay-zee
Goodbye
   CAN-day MAH-lah-mou

Greetings & Civilities in Swahili

Good morning
   JHAM-boh
Good evening
   JHAM-boh
How are you?
   hah-BAR-ee?
I'm fine, thanks
   m-ZOU-ree
Thank you
   ah-SHAN-tay
Goodbye
   kwah-HER-ee

Greetings & Civilities in Nandé

Good morning
  wah-vous-KEE-ray
Good evening
  wah-see-BEE-ray
How are you?
  mhat-say-WAH-hay?
Thank you
  WAH-mou WAH-nee-ah
Goodbye
  mou-see-ah lay-YHAM-boh

Facts for the Visitor

VISAS & EMBASSIES
Zaïrian Visas
Visas are required for visitors of all nation-alities. Zaïrian visas, which are ridiculously expensive in Africa, are valid for one to three months, depending on how long you request, and the longer you stay, the more they cost. Some embassies require that you have an onward airline ticket, a letter of introduction *(note verbale* in French) from your embassy, an International Health Certificate, and proof of 'sufficient funds', typically US$500 in cash or travellers' cheques (US$250 for stays of less than 15 days).

In London, the Zaïrian Embassy (☎ (071) 235-6137/8) charges £18/27/45 for single-entry visas which are good for stays of one/two/three months, and requires three photos and proof of an onward airline ticket and sufficient funds. A one-month multiple-entry visa costs £21.

In Washington, the Zaïrian Embassy (☎ 234-7690/1) charges US$8 for an eight-day transit visa, and US$20/40/50 for multiple-entry visas which are good for stays of one/two/three months. The embassy requires three photos, and proof of yellow fever vaccination and an onward airline ticket.

The requirements of the Zaïrian embassies in Bonn (☎ (228) 34607), Ottawa (☎ (613) 236 7103) and Paris (☎ (1) 4225 5750/1) are similar.

In Africa, visas to Zaïre generally cost a fortune and, with the exception of Kenya where they are cheap (US$7.50 to US$16.50 depending on the length of stay), the embassy charges are fairly uniform – in most places from US$80 for a one-month single-entry visa to US$250 for a three-month mul-tiple-entry visa. In the CFA zone, for example, the fees charged by the Zaïrian Embassy in Libreville (Gabon) are typical: CFA 12,000 for transit visas, CFA 20,000/36,000/52,000 for single-entry visas good for stays of one/two/three months, and CFA 32,000/48,000/60,000 for multiple-entry visas.

Zaïre has embassies in most countries in West Africa and in every Central African country except São Tomé and Equatorial Guinea. In continental East Africa, it has embassies in every country except Somalia, and it's the only Central African country with an embassy in Nairobi (Kenya) or Dar es Salaam (Tanzania). In both Dar es Salaam and Nairobi, they are issued in 24 hours and require four photos, an International Health Certificate and a letter of introduction.

In Rwanda, you cannot get a visa at the border. The embassy on Rue Deputé Kamuzini in Kigali charges the same as in CFA countries and requires two photos and sometimes a letter from your embassy; visas are issued in 24 hours.

You can get a visa in all nine neighbouring countries except Sudan, but if there's a Zaïrian embassy in your country of resi-dence, you will probably save a considerable amount of money by getting one there.

The Zaïrian Embassy in Brazzaville (Congo) appears to be unique in that it gen-erally refuses to issue visas to travellers who are not residents of the Congo. A few travel-lers have gotten around the problem by pointing out (or fabricating a story) that they reside in a country without a Zaïrian embassy. While Zaïrian embassies in other countries generally don't impose this requirement, some, such as the one in Libre-ville (Gabon), require a letter of introduction from your nearest embassy. If there's a good chance you may enter Zaïre twice, get a multiple-entry visa.

Visa Extensions Obtaining visa extensions is time-consuming in Kinshasa, but in other cities, including Goma and Kisangani, immigration officials give same-day service without any hassles. Cities where this can be done outside Kinshasa include Lubumbashi, Goma, Kisangani and Bukavu. The cost is minimal and varies, for example US$3 in Goma and US$7 in Kisangani. You may also have to produce a photo but in Goma you don't have to do this or even sign any forms. In Kinshasa, on the other hand, the process takes four or five days. In addition to a note verbale/request from your embassy, the Agence Nationale d'Immigration (65 Blvd du 30 Juin near Ave des Huileries) will ask for two photos, an International Health Certificate (with a record of vaccinations) and a general medical certificate (to show you don't have any transmittable diseases). The certificate of 'good health' can be obtained from any small polyclinic without undergoing any test or examinations. As for the note verbale, if you write it yourself, many embassies will just stamp it. The British Embassy charges £5 for stamping a note verbale and, reportedly, much more if they write the letter themselves.

Re-Entry Visas For those travelling overland in far-eastern Zaïre between Bukavu and Uvira, there is a unique problem, one that is not encountered, for example, on the new, direct Bukavu to Bujumbura road. On the Bukavu to Uvira road, a single-entry visa theoretically won't suffice because the route from Bukavu is like a snake, passing into Rwanda then back into Zaïre. In practice this is not a problem for bus passengers as the Zaïrois border guards aren't supposed to stamp your passport – they don't consider you to be leaving because 25 km down the road you'll be winding back into Zaïre again. However, for those driving or hitching, there's no guarantee you'll be so lucky. Officials at the second border crossing have been known to hassle such travellers and either demand a *cadeau* (gift) or make them buy another visa. Even if this does happen, your total outlay for two single-entry visas prob-

ably won't be any more than what you would have paid for a multiple-entry visa. As for the short Rwandan leg of the journey, you can get a transit visa at the border.

If you will be travelling to/from Brazzaville (Congo) via the ferry at Kinshasa, you still need a visa to cross the river but no longer a *laissez-passer*, which is a special 'pass through' permit.

Other African Visas
Angola Visas to Angola are not issued at the embassy (which is next door to the Congolese Embassy) but at the Communate Angolaise au Zaïre (CAZ) at 12 Avenue de l'Action, a block east of the Marché Central in Kinshasa. It's open weekdays from 8 am to 2 pm, and requires two photos, US$35 (or the equivalent in CFA) and a note verbale from your embassy. Visas are usually issued in five or six days and are generally valid for 30 days, possibly longer if you ask. The scene at the CAZ is fairly chaotic, so look around for someone to help you.

Burundi Open every day except Sunday from 7.30 am to 2.30 pm (to 12.30 pm on Saturdays), the embassy of Burundi issues visas in 24 to 48 hours and requires US$20 (US dollars only) and two photos, but not a note verbale. Visas are valid for one month. You can also get visas to Burundi at the Burundi Consulate in Bukavu.

Cameroun Zaïre is one of the better places to get visas to Cameroun. The Camerounian Embassy is open for applications weekdays only from 11 am to 1 pm. Two photos and CFA 16,000 (no dollars) are required, but no note verbale, and 48-hour service is available. Visas are valid for three months from the date of issue.

The CAR The CAR Embassy, which is open weekdays from 8 am to 2 pm, issues visas in 48 hours and requires two photos and CFA 10,000/30,000 for one-month/three-month stays.

Chad The Chadian Embassy, towards the

south-western outskirts of town, requires CFA 5000 and two photos for a one-month visa, and usually gives same-day service.

Congo The Congolese Embassy, which is open weekdays from 8.30 am to 1 pm, takes only 48 hours to issue one-month visas. Bring two photos, CFA 10,000 or US$40 (zaïres not accepted) and a note verbale from your embassy.

Gabon To get a visa from the Gabonese Embassy, which is open weekdays from 9 am to 3 pm, you need CFA 20,000, two photos, a note verbale from your embassy and proof of sufficient funds (bring at least CFA 20,000). Visas are issued in 48 hours and are valid for stays of one to three months, depending on your request.

Kenya Open weekdays from 8 am to 2 pm, the Kenyan Embassy issues visas in 24 hours and requires only one photo and US$10 (no note verbale). Visas are valid for up to three months. People of certain nationalities, including Germans, Danes, the Irish, Swedes, Spaniards, Norwegians and, reportedly, Canadians, don't need visas.

If you won't be passing through Kinshasa, no sweat. You can get a two-week visa at Nairobi airport or at any border crossing, but at Nairobi airport they might ask to see an onward airline ticket or proof of sufficient funds, especially if you aren't dressed neatly. You can also get regular tourist visas for Kenya in the capital cities of Rwanda, Uganda and Burundi.

Namibia The Zambian Embassy issues visas to Namibia for free and gives 48-hour service. It receives visa applications on Mondays, Wednesdays and Fridays and requires a note verbale from your embassy, two photos, an onward airline ticket (one from elsewhere in Africa back home is usually acceptable) and proof of sufficient funds (US$2000 or the equivalent in travellers' cheques).

Nigeria The Nigerian Embassy, which is open weekdays from 9 am to noon, requires two photos, a note verbale, an onward airline ticket (unless you'll be travelling by road), and fees in zaïres ranging from the equivalent of US$4 for Americans to 10 times that amount for Britons. Visas are valid for three months from the date of issue.

Rwanda Bring two photos, the zaïre equivalent of CFA 2400 or US$10, and a note verbale from your embassy any weekday between 8 am and 3 pm to the Rwandan Embassy and it will issue you a three-month visa in 48 hours. If you'll be travelling overland in eastern Zaïre and won't be passing through Kinshasa, don't worry. While there's no consulate in either Goma or Bukavu, you can get a transit visa at either the Goma or Bukavu border posts (US$6) or a regular 30-day tourist visa for US$30. For details, see the later information sections under Goma and Bukavu.

South Africa The South African Embassy is on the outskirts of Kinshasa and issues multiple-entry visas for free, usually within three days.

Tanzania The Tanzanian Embassy takes 48 hours to issue visas and requires two photos, a note verbale from your embassy (not required if your country doesn't have a Zaïrian embassy) and fees ranging from US$11 for Americans and Canadians to US$26 for Britons; zaïres are not accepted. The embassy is open weekdays from 8 am to 2.30 pm and visas are valid for stays up to three months. Multiple-entry visas are also available.

Uganda The Ugandan Embassy in Kinshasa is open weekdays from 9 am to 2 pm and issues three-month visas in 24 hours. You need four photos, US$20 (dollars only) and a note verbale only if you reside in Zaïre. There is also a Ugandan Consulate in Goma; its requirements are virtually identical but visas are valid for only one month.

Zambia The Zambian Embassy issues visas

in 48 hours and requires two photos, a note verbale, your International Health Certificate and the equivalent in zaïres of about US$18/27 for single-entry/double-entry visas valid for three months. The embassy in Kinshasa is open weekdays from 8 am to 3 pm but receives visa applications only on Mondays, Wednesdays and Fridays. There's also a consulate in Lubumbashi which gives same-day service.

Zaïrian Embassies
Zaïre has embassies in Abidjan, Accra, Addis Ababa, Algiers, Athens, Bangui, Berlin, Berne, Bonn, Brasilia, Brazzaville, Brussels, Bujumbura, Cairo, Conakry, Cotonou, Dakar, Dar es Salaam, Geneva, The Hague, Harare, Kampala, Kigali, Lagos, Libreville, Lisbon, Lomé, London, Luanda, Lusaka, Luxembourg, Madrid, Maputo, Monrovia, Nairobi, Nouakchott, New Delhi, N'Djamena, New York, Ottawa, Paris, Rabat, Rome, Stockholm, Tokyo, Tunis, Vienna, Washington and Yaoundé. There is a consulate in Kigoma (Tanzania), but visas to Zaïre can take up to two weeks to process.

Foreign Embassies
See the Kinshasa section for the addresses and other details of foreign embassies in the capital.

DOCUMENTS
All travellers must have a valid passport and an International Health Certificate. Those driving their own vehicles also need a *carnet de passage en douane*, which is apparently obtainable at the border.

There is a special requirement for travel to the middle of Zaïre in the regions of Kasaï Oriental or Kasaï Occidental (particularly the cities of Mbuji-Mayi, Kabinda and Kananga) both of which are areas where precious minerals such as diamonds are mined. For either area you must first obtain a *permit de circulation* as otherwise the police will assume you are a smuggler. The only exception is for those travelling by train to/from Lubumbashi. In Kinshasa, these permits are issued by the Départment de l'Administration du Territoire (☎ 32098, 31984) at 41 Ave des Trois Z in Gombe. Because getting such a permit often takes a week or two, most travellers to these areas simply bribe their way through, but this can get quite expensive.

See the later Photography section for information on photo permits.

CUSTOMS
Importing and exporting zaïres in excess of about the equivalent of US$5 is strictly forbidden and you will probably be searched upon entering and leaving. Exchange rates are usually better in Zaïre in any event. If you feel compelled to bring zaïres into the country, be sure to hide them well.

Currency-declaration forms were eliminated in the mid-1980s and are generally not used. However, in 1992 they were back in use in Kinshasa although not elsewhere. Travellers entering Kinshasa at the airport or by ferry from Brazzaville were being issued currency-declaration forms and pressured to change an unspecified amount of money (usually around US$50). If this practice continues or spreads (which seems unlikely), ask customs officials for a form if they don't offer one, and be sure to keep your bank exchange receipts so that on leaving you can prove that you changed your money at the official rate. If you leave the country from Kinshasa without a form, you are fair game for being hassled by police who can barely make ends meet on their meagre government salaries.

MONEY
US$1	=	Z 1,000,000
UK£1	=	Z 1,500,000
CFA 1000	=	Z 4,000,000

The unit of currency is the *zaïre* (Z). Inflation is high; in late 1989 one US dollar was worth Z 441, but by mid-1992 the rate had soared to Z 265,000. Real prices, however, are fairly constant because the zaïre is constantly being devalued, which is why prices in this chapter are given in US dollars. Because most travellers change money on the black market, that rate has been used for prices in this chapter rather than the bank rate quoted earlier. The black-market rate is usually in the range of 15 to 60% better, depending on how recently the last devaluation occurred, and it usually improves the further you go from Kinshasa. The variation is incredible. One group of travellers reported receiving Z 185,000 for US$1 in Zongo, Z 350,000 in Kisangani and close to Z 480,000 in Goma!

If you have cash, the major advantage of changing money in small shops or on the street is the huge time-saving – a few minutes compared to an hour or more at the banks. However, don't let them load you up with small notes, otherwise you'll need a wheelbarrow to cart them away.

The operation of the black market is in great flux, and for many years has been wide open. By mid-1992, with no money in the banks, Mobutu's desperate government began cracking down on the black-market operations in major cities, forcing them to be conducted inside shops, through local merchants, instead of openly in the streets. As long as this continues, you should be extremely careful when changing money on the black market. Even if you're in an area with lots of moneychangers on the street, you could still easily run into problems with undercover police who could arrest you, or fake undercover police who could demand bribes.

It will also come as no real surprise to find that there is nothing even approaching a uniform black-market rate even in the same city. What merchants offer can vary greatly and from day to day, depending on how desperate a given one is for foreign currency, so you may have to shop around to get the best rate. European and Asian shopkeepers tend to be the most reliable and give the best rates.

The currency situation in Zaïre is in a total mess. In 1992, banks in Zaïre had very little cash and changing travellers' cheques was extremely difficult, often impossible, outside Kinshasa. This situation could last for some time so check the currency situation before going there; if it remains unchanged,

you should bring enough cash to allow you to avoid the banks altogether.

Most banks outside Kinshasa won't accept travellers' cheques. The few that do, charge commissions anywhere from 1 to 10%. Outside Kinshasa, the best bank for changing travellers' cheques is usually the Banque Commerciale Zaïroise (BCZ), in which Banque Belgolaise of Belgium has a major interest. Its commission is low, typically US$1.50 per transaction, and the service is faster, but with the scarcity of currency even the BCZ has been known to keep customers waiting for up to three hours to cash travellers' cheques. Other banks often won't cash travellers' cheques for an incredible variety of reasons, but mainly because of ignorance. For instance, many banks will not change your cheques if the signature on them differs from that on your passport, so make sure the two are the same.

Banks for changing money include four foreign banks with offices only in Kinshasa – Citibank, Barclays, Grindlays and Banque de Paris et des Pays-Bas – plus five local ones – the BCZ, the Banque Zaïroise du Commerce Extérieure (BZCE), the Banque Internationale pour l'Afrique au Zaïre (BIAZ), the Nouvelle Banque de Kinshasa and, worst of all, the Union Zaïroise des Banques (UZB).

BUSINESS HOURS & HOLIDAYS

Business hours are weekdays from 8 am to noon and 1 to 4.30 pm and Saturdays from 8 am to 12.30 pm. Government offices are open weekdays from 7.30 am to 3 pm. Banking hours for changing money are weekdays from 8 to 11.30 am. In Kinshasa, the Nouvelle Banque de Kinshasa at the Intercontinental is also open weekday afternoons and Saturday mornings.

Public Holidays
1 January (New Year's Day)
4 January (Day of the Martyrs for Independence)
1 May (Labour Day)
20 May (MPR Day)
24 June (Zaïre Day)

30 June (Independence)
1 August (Parents' Day)
14 October (President's Birthday)
27 October
17 November (Armed Forces Day)
24 November (Anniversary of the New Regime)
25 December (Christmas Day)

POST & TELECOMMUNICATIONS

The poste restante in Kinshasa is fairly reliable but if you mail out letters be sure you see the person cancel your stamps, otherwise they may be ripped off and resold.

International telephone connections are good and, for Africa, relatively cheap. In Kinshasa, you can call from the post office on Blvd du 30 Juin until late at night; the rate per minute to the UK is the equivalent of about US$2. Calls to the USA cost about 25% more. This compares to US$64 for a three-minute call to the USA from the Intercontinental Hotel in Kinshasa. The hotel's rates for sending telexes and faxes are equally outrageous.

TIME

Most of Zaïre is GMT plus one hour, so when it's noon in Kinshasa, it's 11 am in London and 7 am in New York. Add one hour during daylight-saving time. Eastern Zaïre and the southern Shaba area are one hour ahead of Kinshasa time, ie GMT plus two hours.

PHOTOGRAPHY

Photo permits are still required and are valid only in the region of issue, so a permit issued in Kinshasa is not valid for Kisangani. In Kinshasa, permits are issued weekday mornings for free and normally without any hassles at the headquarters of the Office National du Tourisme (ONT) at 11 Ave du 24 Novembre. Photo permits for Goma and Bukavu are issued by their respective ONT offices. In Kisangani permits are issued by the Voix de Zaïre while in the south they are issued by the Division de la Culture, Arts et Tourisme in Lubumbashi. The cost is very low, if not free, so if you're quoted a high figure you can be sure someone is just trying to make some quick money. In other regions, government officials rarely encounter anyone requesting a photo permit, so you'll probably be OK in those areas without one but exercise extreme caution in any case.

Even with a permit you must be extremely cautious in photographing anything in the cities as police are sure to question you and are likely to fabricate some rule you've violated. Moreover, taking photos of dams, government buildings, airports, bridges, ports (ie anything of military importance) and personnel is forbidden. Police have nabbed travellers for taking snapshots at markets, so be very careful.

HEALTH

A vaccination against yellow fever is required for Zaïre. Malaria is also particularly bad and the chloroquine-resistant variety is now found all over the country. Zaïre is also one of the two or three African countries worst hit by AIDS (Sida in French), so avoid prostitutes. If someone says a person est malade, there's a good chance that person is wasting away with the disease.

The quality of the hospitals is poor, which takes on added significance because of the major AIDS problem in Zaïre and Kinshasa in particular, so avoid injections. In Kinshasa, the clinics are generally better than the hospitals. The best is the Zaïre American Clinic at 1054 Ave Batétéla near the Intercontinental (the hotel has the most well-stocked pharmacy in town). Two of the largest clinics are the Centre Médical de Kinshasa at the corner of Avcs Wagenia and Chef Nkokina, and the Polyclinique de Kinshasa nearby at 12 Ave des Aviateurs.

DANGERS & ANNOYANCES

Because of the ongoing chaos in Zaïre, particularly since the rioting of mid-1991, security is a major problem throughout the country. The situation in Kinshasa is much worse than in towns such as Kisangani and the far eastern regions. In these latter areas, security remains a lesser concern, but the problem periodically swells and subsides, so consult your embassy for travel warnings and talk to other travellers returning from the area. If you find yourself in serious trouble with the police, try Mitchell, Friedlander & Gittleman (☎ 30659, 32031; fax 27730), a well-regarded US law firm at 128 Ave Uganda in the Gombe area of Kinshasa.

In terms of danger, Kinshasa is unrivalled in Central Africa, and not even Lagos (Nigeria) in West Africa comes close. Groups with knives and guns have attacked travellers in broad daylight, so even walking around Kinshasa during the daytime poses serious risk. The problem is theft and assault, occasionally murder. Foreigners have been dragged at gunpoint from their cars at major intersections and murdered. The area around the Hôtel Memling is particularly bad, as are major intersections, particularly that of Blvd du 30 Juin and Ave Shaba. Avoid wearing jewellery and carrying purses, keep your watch in your pocket, carry only enough money for your needs, and make sure you carry mostly large bills so your pockets don't bulge.

A common scam in Kinshasa faced by many many travellers (including myself) is being approached in broad daylight by two or three individuals in plain clothes flashing police ID cards and asking to see your passport and money. Travellers complying with such demands are invariably robbed. There are plain-clothes police in Kinshasa but they rarely approach people flashing their IDs. (As with most African police, they usually interrogate first, and only show their IDs if the interrogee expresses doubt about their identity.) So don't think for a moment that ID-flashing police are for real. If you're on the streets, head to any nearby store. If you're in a taxi, shut your windows immediately and drive off.

Try to avoid arriving at Kinshasa airport during the night. Just riding in a taxi from there to the city centre is very risky as you could easily be stopped along the way by bandits and robbed, if not killed. Several airlines run large buses to the city, so inquire about them before hiring a taxi.

Carry a copy of your passport with you at all times so as to keep potential problems with the police at a minimum. If you will be leaving Kinshasa on a night flight, don't sweat. You can catch one of the large, safe airport buses which leave periodically from the Hôtel Intercontinental as many airlines offer this service. When you reconfirm your flight, ask the airlines about the bus schedules.

Among the interior towns, Zongo (across the river from Bangui) is one of the worst in terms of theft. It has been called the 'biggest den of bandits in Africa'. Don't spend the night there. One group on an overland truck that camped there was raided by a group of about 40 locals who pinched everything in sight and left some nasty injuries. The incidents of theft between Zongo and Bumba is also extremely high, so travel in a group. If you're driving, pick up other foreign travellers.

FOOD

The national dish is *moambé*, a spicy sauce with peanuts, palm oil and meat (typically chicken) and rice. Don't miss trying *saka saka*, a stew of crushed manioc leaves, sort of like spinach; it's wonderful if you like greens. Other dishes include *soso* (a chicken stew), *ngombe* (beef), freshwater fish such as grilled *capitaine* (perch) and *maboké* (a local fish), and some exotic dishes such as *porc-pic* (porcupine), *phacochère* (wart hog), *gazelle* (antelope) and *singe* (monkey). Most of these dishes are served with *loso*, which is Zaïrian rice, or *fufu* or *kwanga*, which is a doughy-like glob of mashed manioc or yams.

Getting There & Away

AIR

From Europe, you can fly six days a week from Brussels on Sabena or Air Zaïre (the national airline); three days a week from Paris on Air France/UTA or Air Zaïre; and once a week from Zurich, Rome and Lisbon on Swissair, Air Zaïre and TAP (Air Portugal), respectively. Many short-term travellers take advantage of Sabena's 30-day excursion ticket from Brussels. If schedules to Kinshasa aren't convenient, check those to Brazzaville (Congo) as you could fly there instead and take the ferry across to Kinshasa.

There are no direct flights from New York. You could fly via Abidjan (Côte d'Ivoire) on Air Afrique, via Lagos (Nigeria) on Nigeria Airways or, better, via Europe.

The only East African cities with direct flights to Kinshasa are Nairobi (Kenya), Addis Ababa (Ethiopia), Kigali (Rwanda) and Bujumbura (Burundi). Fives days a week there are connections between Kinshasa and Nairobi on Ethiopian Airlines, Nigeria Airways, Cameroun Airlines and Air Zaïre, while twice a week Ethiopian Airlines has flights to/from Addis Ababa. You can also fly from Kinshasa to Bujumbura on Tuesdays on Cameroun Airlines and to Kigali on Thursdays on Air Zaïre.

The only Central African countries with direct air links to Kinshasa are Cameroun (via Cameroun Airlines) and Libreville (via Air Zaïre). Air Zaïre, Ethiopian Airlines and Nigeria Airways all offer services from Kinshasa to major cities in West Africa such as Lagos, Abidjan and Bamako.

LAND
Bus, Minibus & Truck
Most overland travellers from East Africa enter Zaïre via Bukavu, Goma or one of three crossings close to the Ugandan border (Kisoro, Ishasha or Kasindi). If you're going to East Africa and don't have visas, no sweat – you can get Ugandan visas in Goma, Burundi visas in Bukavu, and Rwandan visas at the border stations just outside both towns.

Crossing the border at either Bukavu or Goma is quite easy and fast. Afterwards, you can catch minibuses direct to Kigali (Rwanda) via asphalt roads – a half-day trip either way. If you're headed to Burundi, you'll find minibuses at the border just outside Bukavu headed for Bujumbura (150 km), about a three-hour trip by asphalt road. For details, see the chapters on Goma and Bukavu.

Car
Few people destined for Zaïre are willing to endure the hassle of getting there by vehicle; however, many travellers headed from Europe or northern Africa to East Africa go there via Central Africa and eastern Zaïre. The most frequently travelled route is via the Central African Republic (the CAR) and the north-eastern corner of Zaïre – from Bangui (the CAR) to Bukavu (about 2500 km) via Mobaye (the CAR), Lisala, Kisangani, Komanda, Butembo and Goma. Since the principal route is usually quite a challenge in itself, the alternate routes – Bangui to Kisangani via Zongo or Bangassou, and Kisangani to Bukavu via Walikale or Kindu – shouldn't be undertaken without a willingness to suffer considerable risk and delays. Whatever route you take, don't worry too much about finding petrol; while there are very few petrol stations between, for instance, Kisangani and Goma (1136 km), black-market petrol is sold everywhere, often around the market. Still, jerry cans can be quite useful.

You'll pass through three rainfall zones: the north around Bangui where there's a dry spell from November to February, the equator zone around Kisangani where it rains all year, and the area south of the equator where there's a heavy rainy season from February to May. Most of the route is north of the equator, so from December to February is a slightly better time to be travelling. When it rains, the muddy roads are as bad as you'll find anywhere in Africa. Getting stuck is guaranteed. The worst stretches are between Epulu and Komanda and, on the alternate more southerly route, between Lubutu and Bukavu. Even during the dry season you may average no more than 100 km a day on those sections. During the rainy season you could be stuck for days.

From Lake Kivu, you can head north-east to Uganda, east to Kenya via Rwanda, south-east to Burundi and Tanzania, or south to Lubumbashi and Zambia via the Lake Tanganyika steamer.

Getting to Kinshasa by car is no easy feat. You could drive south from Cameroun, passing through Gabon and the Congo, and take the ferry over from Brazzaville. The road is not paved for the most part, but it is passable all year, the worst sections being in the Congo. The straight driving time from Cameroun is one week of hard, all-day driving, a day or two more during the heavy rainy season, from February to May. Alternatively, you could take the Bangui to Brazzaville, or Kinshasa to Kisangani steamers (driving between these points is next to impossible); however, the cost of shipping a car on a steamer between these points is generally prohibitive – over US$1000.

If you'll be passing through Kinshasa, you should check out the local automobile association, Fédération Automobile du Zaïre, at 1 Ave des Citronniers.

SEA

A few wealthy souls come to Zaïre by way of freighter. Compagnie Maritime Belge (CMB) has two freighters with limited passenger accommodation ploughing between Hamburg and Matadi (Zaïre), calling at Rotterdam, Antwerp, Le Havre, Lisbon, Dakar and Abidjan, sometimes also stopping at Tema, Lagos, Douala and/or Pointe-Noire. There are departures every two weeks in either direction; the trip normally takes 15 days and the fare is 2000 Belgian francs (about US$60) per day (ie about US$ 900 total) for a single-berth crew cabin.

Compagnie Maritime Zaïroise (CMZ) operates a ship, the *Kananga*, with full passenger service on this route; the cheapest cabins cost 60,000 Belgian francs (about US$1700) per person. For information in Antwerp, contact CMB (☎ (03) 223-2111; telex 72304) at St Katelijnevest 61. Both CMB and CMZ also have offices in Kinshasa.

Getting Around

AIR

Most of the airlines offer a 30 to 40% student discount to those under 26 with student IDs; however, you must produce a *lettre d'attestation* from your university or embassy confirming your student status. Even then, many airline agents will refuse you the discount, saying that it's available only to Zaïrian students. Even though few foreign travellers have been able to take advantage of these discounts, it's still worth inquiring. Just be prepared to do a lot of talking and, in any event, to pay for your ticket in hard currency.

Air Zaïre has a bad reputation, and service has improved only marginally since 1986 when UTA started managing it. Air Zaïre has frequent flights to most major interior cities (as well as services to other African countries). Fares are not cheap; Kinshasa to Goma, for example, costs about US$300 one way.

Scibé-Airlift, Air Zaïre's major competitor within Zaïre, is now the country's top airline. In Brussels, tickets for Scibé-Airlift flights can be purchased in advance from Enzymase International (☎ (02) 647-0470).

For service between Kinshasa and the Shaba region, Shabair also offers reliable service and the most connections. Fares on all three airlines are virtually identical.

In addition, there are a number of much smaller airlines, including Air Charter Service (ACS), Travel Assistance Services (TAS), Bleu Airlines (BAL) and Katale. ACS, for example, has flights from Kinshasa to Lubumbashi and Bukavu among other cities, while BAL has regular flights from Kinshasa to Goma, Lubumbashi, Mbuji-Mayi and Kananga. These airlines generally have only one or two planes and offices only at the airport.

There are also some regional airlines which fly only between towns in a given region and not to/from Kinshasa. Virunga Air Charters (VAC), for example, has daily flights between Goma and Bukavu as well as weekly flights from Goma to Beni, Kindu and Kalemie. Scibé-Airlift, Swala, TMK Air Commuter and Broussair are four others that fly between Goma and Bukavu. In addition, Air Rwanda offers round-trip flights from Kigali to Goma on Saturdays.

MAJOR ROUTES

Travel overland by truck, bus or bush taxi can be tortuous in Zaïre not just because the roads are often in bad condition during the rainy season but also because the drivers often seem to have a death wish. The most dangerous routes are those that are in the best condition because the drivers can go faster. Gordon Glanz's observations on the paved Kinshasa to Kikwit route are telling:

Although I travelled most of the way from Lubumbashi to Kinshasa by truck, I would never do it again for one reason – it's dangerous. From Kikwit to Kinshasa, a 16-hour trip for me, I saw three over-turned trucks. Goods were all over the road, people were bandaged, the trucks were a mess. In the Land Rover in which I was squashed, one fellow had just been released from the hospital after treatment because the truck on which he was riding had over-turned.

I should have been forewarned when the fellow collecting the money said proudly, 'There has never been anyone like our driver, he is a demon.'

As soon as we started out I understood exactly what he had meant. The driver never seemed to touch his brakes. He didn't need a second thought. Encouraged by his cronies who shouted from the back of the truck, he tried to pass every vehicle on the road, including Land Rovers a fraction of the truck's size. Every time we passed a vehicle, a wild celebration broke out and people slapped each other on the back and made obscene gestures to the occupants of the more prudent vehicle behind.

The truck rolled like a ship in a storm and I thought we were going to tip over a hundred times.

So perhaps it's all for the best that most roads in Zaïre are in bad condition, requiring the drivers to go tortuously slow.

Bangui (the CAR) south-east to Goma and Bukavu (2503 km) via Kisangani, cutting across the north-eastern corner of Zaïre, is the major route connecting Central and East Africa and the one most travelled by over-landers. Those who can withstand the bumps, breakdowns and long waiting times on this arduous trip will be rewarded by the opportunity of seeing some of the most spectacular scenery in Africa, including Virunga National Park and the snowcapped Ruwenzori range. Take a week off and climb these mountains; you'll never forget it!

Most of the route is north of the equator, so the driest part of the year is from December to February. However, even then it rains, and most stretches of road are muddy. About halfway through Virunga National Park you'll cross the equator, south of which the rains fall heaviest from February to May. Not counting major stops along the way, the trip on the major route takes roughly 10 to 14 days – three weeks or more if it's raining heavily.

Details about this and the other major routes follow. One route that is so rarely used that it is not mentioned in this section is from eastern Zaïre to Kinshasa by truck or car. Bukavu to Kinshasa is a 2867-km trip by road via Kananga and takes four or five weeks, which is why almost everyone flies or takes the boat from Kinshasa to Kisangani (roughly two weeks) and trucks/buses from there to Lake Kivu (another week).

Bangui to Kisangani

Via Mobaye & Lisala The most well-travelled road is from Bangui east to Mobaye (the CAR), then south to Lisala and on to Kisangani. Getting from Bangui to Mobaye is no problem; by minibus you can make the trip in two days, with a change of buses and overnight in Bambari. There is a good camp ground near Mobaye (also in Businga, which is roughly halfway between Mobaye and Lisala). The ferry at Mobaye is quite reliable, operates every day and charges CFA 25,000 for vehicles, about half that for motorcycles and CFA 200 for passengers. In the rare event that it should not be operating, you could take a *pirogue* (canoe). From there south to Lisala the road is in good condition for the most part; trucks are fairly easy to find and they normally take about two days.

From Lisala or, much better, Buma, you can take the riverboat or a barge to Kisangani. There is only one riverboat operating and it passes about once a month in either direction, arriving in Lisala and Bumba seven or eight days after departing Kinshasa. From there, it's usually another three or four days to Kisangani. The ONATRA ferry people can tell you the location of the riverboat on its journey. For more details on the steamer, see the later Boat section.

As long as there is only one riverboat operating on the Kinshasa to Kisangani route, catching it can mean waiting for weeks. If you arrive at an inopportune time and can't wait long, you'll have to catch a truck east to Buta and another on to Kisangani or take one of the many barges that tugs pull up and down the river between Bumba and Kisangani. You'll have more breathing room than on the riverboats, but the barges are very slow and take a week or more to Kisangani.

Via Zongo & Lisala The major alternative route from Bangui to Kisangani is via Zongo and Lisala. A major disadvantage of taking this route is that you must pass through Zongo, which is notorious for its thieves and awful customs officials who demand stiff matabiches (bribes) and often delay travellers for hours on end. For more details, see the Zongo section. Another problem with this route is that while the road from Zongo to Lisala has been improved somewhat, it is still inferior to the one via Mobaye.

On the other hand, the Zongo route is shorter and at least as fast, and is more off the beaten track. In addition, you still have the option of catching the ONATRA riverboat from Lisala to Kisangani, which is surely one of the great highlights of any trip to Zaïre. (You'll need plenty of time though, as there is only one operating; see the later Boat section.)

You'll encounter rain year-round on this route except around Bangui, where there's a dry spell from November to February. There's a ferry from Bangui to Zongo every day except Sunday. Those driving should note that the load capacity of this ferry is markedly less than the one at Mobaye. Getting from Zongo to Lisala by a series of trucks can easily take three days.

Via Bangassou & Buta The third route from Bangui to Kisangani is via Bangassou and Buta. This used to be the most popular route but is now the least travelled due to its terrible condition. For those with vehicles, the ferry at Bangassou is very unreliable and usually not operating. Since this route does not pass along the Zaïre River at any point, it also means your missing out on the possibility of taking the riverboat to Kisangani, which is why I don't recommend it even for hitchhikers. Moreover, as this route is now the least popular, finding trucks is more of a problem than on the other two routes.

Bangui to Komanda
Another way to get from Bangui to East Africa is to head east from Buta to Isiro and Komanda, skipping Kisangani altogether. This way, however, you'll be missing an interesting city and the opportunity of getting lots of useful and up-to-date information from other overland travellers as Kisangani is the number-one hub for overland travellers on the Central Africa to East Africa route. If you do head towards Isiro, you should expect much greater difficulty in finding trucks as traffic is very light.

Kisangani to Bukavu
Via Goma The major route from Kisangani to East Africa is east to Epulu and Komanda, then south through the Virunga National Park to Goma. The section between Kisangani and Beni is infamous, the worst section by far being Epulu to Komanda. During the rainy season, travellers have reported taking 1½ weeks just from Epulu to Komanda because of broken bridges and 50 or more trucks stacked up in the muddiest sections. However, extremes such as these have become rare as the roads are gradually being improved. Three days for the Kisangani to Komanda section is typical (four to six days during the rainy season). I met one overland truck which had passed from Beni to Kisangani in four days in late April (the high rainy season) and was actually disappointed that conditions had been so good.

If you're without wheels, trucks are all you'll find between Kisangani and Beni. From Beni there are frequent taxi pick-up trucks to Butembo where, on Monday,

Tuesday, Thursday and Saturday mornings, you can take a large bus to Goma. The road from Beni to Goma and on to Bukavu is in excellent condition during the dry season and in fair-to-good condition the rest of the year. During the dry season, buses do the Butembo to Goma section in about 12 hours, and the Goma to Bukavu section in six hours.

From Goma to Bukavu most travellers take one of the three steamers, each of which makes one crossing a week. You can also take the thrice-weekly bus (six hours) or, for US$45, one of several daily flights. For details, see the Getting There & Away sections under Goma and Bukavu.

Via Lubutu The most recent change in the Eastern Zaïre road map is the new sealed road being constructed between Kisangani and Bukavu. The Chinese have been working on the eastern end and the Germans on the western end from Lubutu, but now only the Germans remain to finish the project, which should be completed by 1994 or so. As of mid-1992, only about 40 km remained unpaved but work is proceeding slowly because of the rough terrain. Already hitchhikers are taking this 708-km route and finding the week-long trip fascinating; until the project is completed, it involves walking in the jungle for many km. When complete, the trip should take as little as two long days in private vehicles and maybe three or four by truck. For more details, see the Kisangani to Bukavu section.

Via Kindu For more adventure, you could attempt the route to Bukavu (or Lubumbashi) via Kindu. From February to May, you are likely to encounter impassable sections. Just getting to Kindu takes a week, sometimes two, because the traffic between Lubutu (connected by an asphalt road to Kisangani) and Kindu is almost nonexistent. Here's what one traveller, John Kelly, had to say about it:

From Kisangani we headed to Bukavu via Lubutu. It was mid-March, a distance of 1200 km and it took us 10 days putting in at least 10 hours every day. Any

further into the wet season and we would have been stuck in Zaïre for some time.

It rates as the most desperate piece of road I've ever encountered. It should not be attempted by people not willing or equipped to dig themselves out of bogs above their wheel-arches up to five or six times a day. There are log bridges that will need rebuilding and a well-directed prayer before you can cross. A good winch would be your single most valuable possession, and even in the dry season if you need parts or service on your vehicle, it's going to take several weeks to get to either end and back. We spent five days in the middle without seeing another vehicle. Even when perfectly dry it would be a bloody horrible road because it is cut up so much. It was quite an achievement to get through it and is amongst my most vivid memories of Africa.

As for the towns along the way, Punia has very little of anything and is worth avoiding, especially since the Securité Nationale (security police) people are going to want to see you if you stay overnight and probably accuse you of being mercenaries.

Kindu is pretty reliable for petrol; get it at the depot downstream beside the river. But if the train hasn't been in for a while, you'll have to buy it off blokes in the street with 44 gallon drums for about US$1 per litre instead of US$0.40. There is a big Indian population here; these are the fellows to change money with and get information about the roads. Get as many different opinions on the road ahead in as many different places as you can. They'll all be different. The trick is to decide which ones are nearest the truth. We had to make several detours because of broken bridges.

Kamituga can be heaven if you're on this road and it's in the terrible condition it was for us. It's a mining town and signifies the last of the really bad road. It has a very reliable petrol supply. To find this go to 'The Club', the executive watering hole for the mining company. If nothing else you can get a terrific meal here of lamb chops and real vegetables with soup and dessert for US$2. There's cold beer and if you meet one of the expats, they'll probably offer to put you up in the company's guesthouse and line up petrol and a mechanic if you need one, as well as shout you drinks all night.

Instead of travelling by road from Kisangani to Kindu, you could take the Kisangani to Ubundu train, which departs once or twice weekly, and the Ubundu to Kindu steamer, which takes four to six days to reach Kindu. You're likely to end up waiting days for one or the other to depart, however. If there were one time to break down and buy an airline ticket, this would have to be it.

Kinshasa to Matadi

If you're headed west towards the coast to Matadi (362 km), you have the option of taking a SOTRAZ, the SNCZ train or bush taxis. The SOTRAZ buses leave every day at around 7 am, take about eight hours and cost US$5. The express train, which takes about nine hours, is scheduled to leave Kinshasa on Mondays, Wednesdays and Fridays at 7.15 am, and from Matadi on Tuesdays, Thursdays and Saturdays at the same hour, but departures are frequently an hour late. A deluxe cabin costs US$14; 2nd class costs US$3.50. There's no restaurant car but there are people who sell drinks and snacks on board.

Kinshasa to Lubumbashi

Travelling south-east from Kinshasa all the way to Lubumbashi (2916 km) usually takes about two weeks. It's an exhausting trip but logistically simple (unless you're driving) compared to the trip from Bangui to Bukavu through north-eastern Zaïre.

The trick is getting to Ilebo (932 km), because once you're there, you can take a twice-weekly train to Lubumbashi. The quickest way to Ilebo is by vehicle. Trucks direct to Ilebo leave Kinshasa every day and take a minimum of two days, usually more. Better still, take a large SOTRAZ bus to Kikwit; there are two departures daily from Kinshasa and the road is paved all the way. The trip takes about 12 hours. From there you'll find trucks heading towards Ilebo which is 405 km away.

The most painless way to get to Ilebo is by ONATRA riverboat. Under normal conditions, either the *Mudimbi* or the *Gungu* leaves Ilebo for Kinshasa every two weeks, taking about four days if there are no problems (the journey takes six days upriver). These boats are comparable to ONATRA's steamers to Kisangani, which have three cabin classes. Another possibility is to get a ride on one of the barges which plough very slowly up and down the Kasaï River; this is reportedly not too difficult.

From Ilebo, the ordinaire train is scheduled to depart for Lubumbashi on Tuesdays, and takes six days. The rapide, which has a dining car, leaves on Saturdays and, in principle, takes four days. From Lubumbashi, the ordinaire should leave on Saturdays and the rapide on Thursdays. However, because of the chaotic conditions in Zaïre, these schedules are rarely adhered to these days, so verify them at the railway station or ONATRA. Only Zaïrian students are entitled to the 50% student discount. These trains are in atrocious condition – among the worst in Africa. Even budget travellers recommend going 1st class if you're travelling the entire distance (about US$65 on the ordinaire and US$95 to US$120 on the rapide); 2nd class is bad news and 3rd class (about US$45 on the ordinaire) is an absolute nightmare. Nick North's description of this 'mobile slum' says it all:

The term '1st class' is something of a misnomer to say the least. The train could more accurately be described as a mobile slum. There was no water or electricity and none of the windows had glass in them. Our 1st-class compartment had no door and the table over the sink had disappeared. Everything was thickly coated with the grime of many years. The seats had huge holes in them from which the foam stuffing had been torn, the back of one seat (which would have formed the middle bunk) had been completely destroyed, leaving only the wooden frame. The top bunks were relatively intact, though at night you could hear rats running up and down what used to be the ventilation shafts along the roof.

Add to this such delights as a woman eating peanuts while watching her child go to the toilet on a cloth on her lap, and then seeing her simply fold the cloth up and put it to one side, and you get an idea of the quality of the journey. A man with a brush did come along occasionally and sweep up the peanut shells, sugar cane pulp, fruit peelings, children's urine, etc.

Notwithstanding all this, the journey itself was slightly disappointing, though some of the views during the latter part of the trip were excellent. There was quite a lot of food available up until the last day, but most of this food was fruit and therefore most likely seasonal – we were pleased we had taken extra supplies from Lubumbashi. We left at 1 pm on Saturday and arrived in Ilebo at 6 pm on Wednesday.

Lubumbashi to Bukavu

On the Lubumbashi to Bukavu route, most travellers take either the SNCZ train from

Lubumbashi to Kindu and trucks from there to Bukavu (580 km to the east on Lake Kivu), or the SNCZ train from Lubumbashi to Kalemie on Lake Tanganyika and a ferry north from there to Kigoma (Tanzania) and Uvira/Kalundu, which is 120 km south of Bukavu. You can catch the trains only once a week, however. In Kindu, the train departs on Fridays or Saturdays and takes about four or five days; from Lubumbashi it is supposed to leave on Wednesdays, with a change in Kabalo if you're headed to Kalemie. Fares from Lubumbashi to either Kalemie or Kindu range from about US\$48 in 3rd class to US\$173 in 1st class. Drunks and thieves are often a problem, so try to avoid travelling alone. As the Paul Simon song says, make an African friend – he'll be your bodyguard.

SNCZ operates a ferry from Kalemie north to Kigoma (Tanzania) and, further north, to Kulundu (near Uvira) and Bujumbura (Burundi). First class is a two-bed cabin with shower and costs about US\$36 to Kulundu; deck-class costs about US\$24. The schedule is fixed in principle but highly erratic in practice. How long the ferry stays at a port depends on how much cargo there is to load and unload. Moreover, it frequently breaks down. Even if it's operating, don't be surprised if it leaves much later, even days later, than scheduled. For what it's worth, the schedule is as follows:

	Arrive	Depart
Kalemie	—	4 pm Sun
Kigoma	7 am Mon	2 pm Mon
Kalundu	7 am Tues	9 am Tues
Bujumbura	10 am Tues	12 pm Tues
Kalundu	1 pm Tues	4 pm Tues
Kigoma	7 am Wed	4 pm Wed
Kalemie	7 am Thurs	—

For information and tickets in Kalemie, go to the SNCZ railway station there. You should also inquire in Kalemie about a private boat that ploughs between Kalemie and Uvira/Kalundu.

CAR

Taking a vehicle through Zaïre is an adventure in itself, so be prepared for the worst. Even on well-maintained roads, there are usually stretches that are simply terrible, so a 4WD vehicle or trail bike are essential – much more so than for crossing the Sahara.

Most people who decide to take a vehicle through Zaïre are on their way to Kenya and East Africa, and almost invariably take the route from Bangui (the CAR) to Lake Kivu via Kisangani. This is an extremely tough route and often very muddy, but the trip is done all the time by local truckers and by well-equipped overland trucks from London to Nairobi. The best (and driest) time for doing this stretch is from December to early February and June to September. (See the later sections on local transport for details on the condition of the roads on the major transport routes.) Forget about putting your vehicle on the steamer to Kisangani; the Lisala to Kisangani section alone costs more than US\$1000. By barge, however, the price is usually less than half that.

Driving from Kinshasa to Lubumbashi is feasible, but few people attempt it because the trip takes two weeks and the roads are bad, the worst section being from Idiofa to Mweka. Getting stuck after a rainfall is almost guaranteed. Still, there are overland companies from London that continue to travel from London to Johannesburg via this route without major problems. Finding petrol is generally no problem in Kikwit, Ilebo (black market), Kananga, Mbuji-Mayi, Kamina and Kolwezi as it is sold widely on the streets if not at petrol stations. However, several jerry cans can still come in useful for times when you can't find black-market petrol in smaller towns. There's a ferry at Ilebo but it's usually running and not a problem.

Car Rental

In Kinshasa, Eurocar, Avis, Hertz and Budget all have vehicles for hire. Avis and Budget are also represented in Lubumbashi. Most agencies will not allow you to take the car out of the city. Avis' rates are typical: US\$48 per day including insurance for a Renault 4TL (its cheapest car) plus US\$0.35

per km and 18% tax. A sizeable depost is required if you don't have a major credit card.

BOAT
Kinshasa to Kisangani Steamer
One of the great African adventures is taking the steam boat up the famous Zaïre (formerly Congo) River from Kinshasa to Kisangani or vice versa – a 1734-km trip. You'll pass by numerous villages and through some of the thickest rainforests in Africa. However, this trip is not for everyone. It's hot and muggy and far from tranquil. Over a thousand people will be floating along with you, most of them on the three or more barges tied to the steamer's bow.

The place is a floating zoo, with chickens cackling, pigs squealing, goats tied up anywhere and everywhere, and live crocodiles. There are also loads of dead monkeys and other wild animals piled on the deck along the way, waiting to be put under ice or dried. You'll find the smell of smoked fish everywhere, people sprawled all over the deck, radios blasting away, people joking, babies crying and Primus beer flowing – a good opportunity to make some Zaïrois friends.

Those travelling deck class will find that little 'quarters' develop and that you will become fast friends with those in your section. They will also guard your belongings when you want to wander about. In addition to sleeping gear, you should bring all of your food and cooking utensils unless you expect to live off the food provided. You should not have any problem finding someone in your section to cook you a meal but it'll cost double. All during the day women are pounding manioc into meal, and frying bananas and doughnuts for their families. On the more exotic side, chicks, baby crocodiles and snails are sometimes cooked and eaten as snacks; stewed monkey is also popular.

The prime entertainment on board is the thriving commerce. For many passengers, the trip is not a journey but a job, as many of them are actually merchants who have min-iature stalls on the deck and sell soap, matches, beer, black-market penicillin, malaria pills, etc. The barges are moving so slowly that there's commerce going on constantly during the trip. Day and night, men and women from villages along the river paddle out to the barge in dugout canoes (pirogues) filled with bananas, avocados, baskets of fish, monkeys, and sometimes live parrots for sale. At times as many as 100 canoes may be tied up to the barge. Once the villagers sell their goods, they come on board to purchase goods from the bazaars.

The main boats are operated by the government agency ONATRA and each has three classes of cabins. However, in 1993 only one was in operation. First-class includes two small bunk beds, a cabinet, private toilet and shower, and a large padlock. Each steamer also has one or two 1st-class deluxe cabins which are about 50% more expensive and have air-con; meals are served in the air-con dining room or your room.

Second class consists simply of three or four bunk beds; there is also a crude shared shower on the barge roof. Unless your group occupies an entire room, you won't be able to lock your cabin (note: thieves abound). Also, expect your cabin mates to stuff all manner of things inside the room.

Third class is the incredibly crowded deck, with loud music blasting 24 hours a day; finding space to sleep isn't easy. Make sure your ticket has a cabin number written on it; otherwise, you may find all the cabins full.

Fares downstream from Kisangani are about half those upstream from Kinshasa. Fares upstream/downstream per person (paid in zaïres) are approximately as follows: US$325/155 for 1st class (50% more for 1st-class deluxe), US$115/55 for 2nd class, and US$100/48 for 3rd class. Fares from Lisala to Kisangani are approximately 37% of these amounts. First class includes three meals (typically baked fish or roast beef with gravy, potatoes and carrots); 2nd and 3rd class include one filling meal a day, typically rice, beans and meat (frequently monkey).

Second-class passengers also have the option of eating in the 1st-class dining room (US$5 a meal) and drinking at the bar, but only beer is available. The water is not treated, so bring bottled water or purification tablets. You can buy food all along the way (sardines, fresh bread, rice, jungle meat, and occasionally fresh fruit).

As with the airlines, ONATRA offers a 30% student discount to those under 26 with a student ID and a *lettre d'attestation* from their embassy or university confirming their student status. These letters are also available in Kisangani, Lisala and Bumba from local education authorities; the port authorities can tell you where to go.

The length of the trip varies with the height of the river, and is shortest when the river is at its highest (from July to December). The average journey time is 11 to 12 days to Kisangani and seven days for the return (six days when the river is high). Under normal conditions there is one steamer about every two weeks heading upriver from Kinshasa and another heading downriver from Kisangani. Under today's tumultuous conditions, however, there is only one steamer a month. They stop at Bolobo, Mbandaka, Lisala, Bumba and Basoko. Going upriver, you should be at Mbandaka by day four, Bumba by day nine, and Kisangani by day 12. Don't be surprised if the boat is anywhere from several days to two weeks late departing from Kinshasa or Kisangani. Each day the ONATRA people radio the boat, so you can always find the location from them. Numerous travellers have reported waiting as much as two weeks and then just giving up. The boats seem to get stuck every other day on the sandy bottom, particularly during the months of January to May when the river is at its lowest level. A broken motor is also not an uncommon event. One traveller reported three children dying on the way, the steamer stopping for their funerals.

There are three ONATRA steamers which plough this course. The best is the *Colonel Kokolo*, followed by the *Colonel Tshatshi* and the *Colonel Ebeya*. As of 1992 only one

of them was operating, but this may change once conditions stabilise.

If there is no ONATRA steamer on the horizon, try getting a private barge. These consist of several barges tied together and hauled by a tug. These barges are usually cheaper if you bargain well and are not as crowded as the ONATRA steamers. However, they are slower, taking at least twice as long (six to 12 days from Kinshasa to Mbandaka compared to four days by steamer), and you must bring all of your food and water as there is no bar or restaurant. Plastic jerry cans for water and a charcoal burner for cooking meals are virtually indispensable. For information on making reservations in Kinshasa or Kisangani for a steamer or barge trip, see the Getting There & Away sections under those two cities.

Alternatively, for shorter trips such as that from Kisangani to Buma, you can hire motorised pirogues or larger motorised boats; however, you must usually hire the entire boat so they tend to be more expensive unless you are in a fairly large group, say 15 people or more. One group of 16 people reported hiring one for US$500 (US$31 per person) from Buma to Kisangani, which is slightly less than the 3rd-class fare on the steamer.

If you're limited for time, you could take the steamer from Kinshasa to, say, Mbandaka and fly back. Or, if you have lots of time, take it to Mbandaka and from there you can catch trucks or boats for Boende and Ikela. The advantages of this route are that it's so far off the beaten path that you are quite unlikely to see any other foreigners, and that people along the route tend to be extremely friendly to travellers. At any given point you could easily spend four days or so waiting for a truck to pick you up or even much longer for a boat. From Ikela it's possible to catch planes back to Kinshasa but you might have to wait up to a week.

Regardless of your destination, a good book to read during the journey is *The River Congo: the Discovery, Exploration and Exploitation of the World's Most Dramatic River* (1977) by Peter Forbath.

Kinshasa to Bangui If you're dead set on taking the riverboat, consider taking a trip on the Brazzaville to Bangui steamer as it operates twice monthly between July and December, is much more reliable than the ONATRA riverboats and follows the same route for part of the way. For details, see the Congo and Central African Republic chapters.

Western Zaïre

KINSHASA

Kinshasa is a vibrant city with both positive and negative qualities. On the one hand, it's huge (4½ million people), muggy and very dangerous, particularly since the riots of September 1991. On the other hand, with a few exceptions it's cheap compared to Brazzaville and the nightlife is as lively as anywhere else in Africa. Moreover, despite the widespread destruction during the riots, it still has a few modern shops and restaurants of some repute. Also, the city's layout, with one wide boulevard running parallel to the river, is more comprehensible than that of many African cities.

The pulse of the city is the Cité (see-TAY) – the vibrant African quarter where you'll find many cheap hotels, lively open-air bars, African food on the streets, and the Zaïrian musical groups on which the country stakes its reputation. Virtually any night of the week you can walk into the Vis-à-Vis Nightclub around midnight and hear a band. It's the home of OK Jazz, one of Zaïre's most famous groups, and they still perform there when not on tour in Europe. If you get tired of 'Congo' music, head for one of the many discos with European music. Since 1991, the music scene has lost much of its vibrancy as even the locals are afraid to go out at night; However, Kinshasa still reigns as the live music entertainment capital of Africa.

Orientation
No city in Africa has a street so dominating and impressive as the Blvd du 30 Juin, the Champs-Elysées of Africa. It is six lanes wide and runs almost the full length of the city, from the railway and SOTRAZ bus station near the Brazzaville ferry port (called 'le Beach') westward, parallel to the Zaïre River, for eight km towards the Cité de l'OUA, the seat of Mobutu's government. On the eastern end you'll find many of Kinshasa's major stores, banks and offices, the main post office (the heart of the modern city centre), the Galeries Présidentielles shopping centre (which was largely destroyed during the 1991 riots) and, just east thereof, the city's number-one landmark – the 22-storey SOZACOM building (the mineral marketing company). Another landmark, the Hôtel Memling, is just two blocks towards the Marché Central. Between it and the market is where much of the destruction took place during the 1991 riots.

The heart of the Cité is well south of the central area, three km beyond the Marché Central. The main artery from the centre is Ave Kasa-Vubu, which runs perpendicular to the Blvd du 30 Juin, starting at the post office. When you arrive at the Rond-Point Kasa-Vubu et Victoire, four km south along Kasa-Vubu, you'll be in the heart of the city's captivating nightlife – the Zone de Matonge (mah-tone-GAY).

Gombe (pronounced 'gomb'), the city's large chic residential area, is five km west of the centre along the Blvd du 30 Juin. This boulevard is punctuated by four rond-points starting with Place de Nelson Mandela where Ave du 24 November begins, and heads south towards the tourist office, Kinshasa Museum and beyond. Next is Rond-Point de Batétéla (bah-tay-TAY-lah), which is the turn-off for many embassies in the area as well as the Intercontinental (or 'l'Inter' as everyone calls it), which is far and away the city's best hotel and Gombe's major landmark.

Information
Tourist Office The Office National du Tourisme or ONT (☎ 33945; telex 21654), is headquartered at 11 Ave du 24 Novembre and is open weekdays from 8 am to 1 pm.

Top : Street scene in Trinidade, São Tomé (AN)
Bottom Left : Fort São Sebastião, São Tomé City, São Tomé (AN)
Bottom Right : President's palace, São Tomé City, São Tomé (AN)

Top : Nyamulagira & Nyiragongo volcanoes from Lake Kivu, Zaïre (GC)
Bottom : Gorilla, Zaïre (JL)

The people here are very friendly and may be a source of useful information. They are responsible for issuing photo permits, which are free and issued on the spot. ONT also has an office at the Intercontinental.

Money The best banks for changing money are Barclays (☎ 22356; telex 21113) at 191 Ave l'Equateur near Ave des Aviateurs; Citibank at the corner of Ave Col Lukusa and Longole; Banque de Paris et des Pays-Bas (telex 21020) on Ave Col Ebeya; Banque Commerciale Zaïroise or BCZ (telex 21127) on Blvd du 30 Juin one block north of the post office; and the Nouvelle Banque de Kinshasa, which has a branch at the Intercontinental and is the only one open on Saturdays. It's open weekdays from 9 to 11.30 am and 3 to 6.45 pm, and Saturdays from 9 am to noon.

Zaïrian banks, such as the Union Zaïroise des Banques (UZB) at the corner of Aviateurs and Nation, are slow in comparison to the black-market dealers, many of whom hang out on Ave de l'Hôtel in front of l'Edelweiss café, opposite the US Embassy.

Foreign Embassies Most embassies are in Gombe, including:

Algeria
    50 Ave Col Ebeya (☎ 22470/83)
Benin
    3990 Ave de Cliniques (☎ 30492)
Burundi
    4687 Ave de la Gombe (☎ 33353)
Cameroun
    Blvd du 30 Juin, east of Rond-Point Batétéla (☎ 34787)
Canada
    17 Ave Pumbu, near Rond-Point Batétéla (☎ 21801; telex 21403; fax from Canada (871) 156 0213)
CAR
    11 Ave Pumbu, near Rond-Point Batétéla (☎ 33571)
Congo
    Blvd du 30 Juin, east of Rond-Point Batétéla (☎ 34028)
Egypt
    Ave Ouganda, opposite the Kenyan Embassy

Gabon
    Blvd du 30 Juin, one km beyond Afrique Hôtel (☎ 50206; telex 21455)
Germany
    Ave des Trois Z (☎ 27720, 21529; telex 21110)
Greece
    72 Ave des Trois Z
India
    18 Ave Batétéla, near Ave de la Justice (☎ 30418)
Japan
    3668 Ave Mbuji-Mayi (☎ 22118, 24349; telex 21227)
Kenya
    5002 Ave Ouganda, near Rond-Point Petit Pont (☎ 33205)
Netherlands
    11 Ave Zongo-Ntolo (☎ 30638; telex 21126)
Nigeria
    Blvd du 30 Juin, west of Place de Nelson Mandela (☎ 33343)
Rwanda
    50 Ave de la Justice, near Rond-Point Batétéla (☎ 33080)
Switzerland
    Ave de Trois Z
Tanzania
    Blvd du 30 Juin, opposite the Place Royal (☎ 34364)
UK
    Ave des Trois Z (☎ 34775/6; fax 44903)

A few of the remaining diplomatic missions are in the centre, a block or two off Blvd du 30 Juin, including:

Angolan Consulate
    Communate Angolaise au Zaïre (CAZ), 12 Ave de l'Action, one block north of the Marché Central. (The embassy, which doesn't issue visas, is on Blvd du 30 Juin next door to the Congolese Embassy.)
Austria
    Galeries Présidentielles (☎ 22119)
Belgium
    Blvd du 30 Juin, next to Galeries Présidentielles Ave des Trois Z, near Ave Batétéla in Gombe (☎ 25525; telex 21114)
France
    3 Ave République du Tchad, just north of Hôtel Memling (☎ 22669; telex 21674)
Uganda
    Two blocks north of Ave Bokassa, between Aves Tombalbaye and du Haute Zaïre
USA
    310 Ave des Aviateurs, behind the SOZACOM building (☎ 25881/2/3; telex 21625)

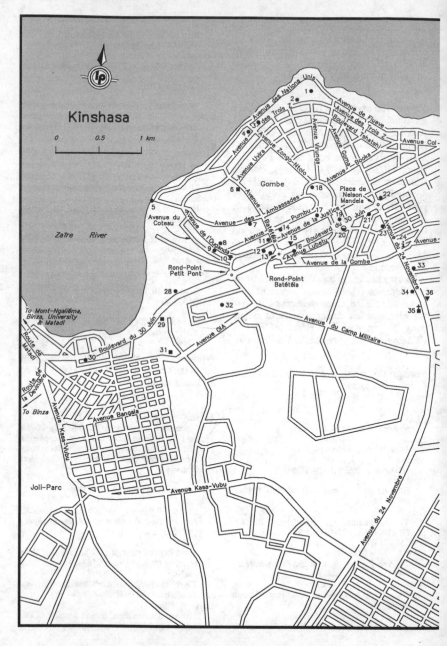

Kinshasa

0   0.5   1 km

Zaïre   River

Gombe

Avenue des Nations Unis

Avenue des Trois Z

Avenue de Flueve

Avenue des Trois Z

Boulevard Tshatshi

Avenue Col

Avenue Uvira

Avenue Zongo-Ntolo

Avenue Virunga

Avenue Goma-Boka

Place de
Nelson
Mandela

Avenue des Ambassades

Avenue du Coteau

Avenue de l'Ouganda

Avenue des

Avenue Batetela

Pumbu

Avenue de la Justice

Avenue du 30 Juin

Boulevard

Avenue Lubetu

Avenue de la Gombe

Rond-Point
Petit Pont

Rond-Point
Batétéla

To Mont-Ngaliéma,
Binza, University
& Matadi

Route de Matadi

Route de la Dewière

To Binza

Boulevard du 30 Juin

Avenue Kasa-Vubu

Avenue OIA

Avenue du Camp Militaire

Avenue Bangala

Joli-Parc

Avenue Kasa-Vubu

Avenue du 24 Novembre

Avenue du 24 Novembre

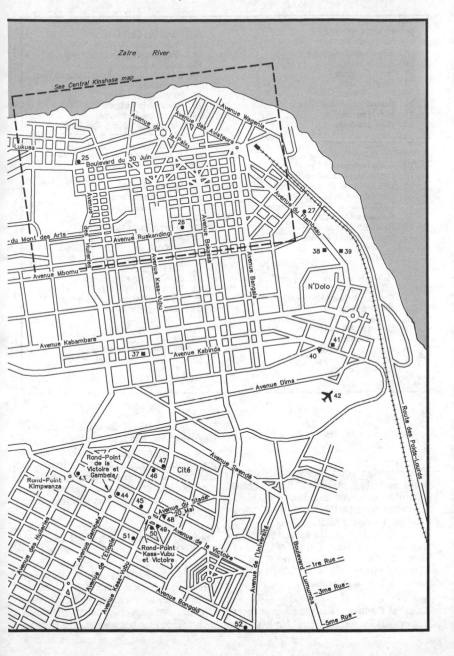

Zaïre River

See Central Kinshasa map

Lukusa

25
Boulevard du 30 Juin

Avenue de la Paix
Avenue des Aviateurs
Avenue Wagenia

- du Mont des Arts -

Avenue des Huileries

Avenue Ruakandingi

26

Avenue Bokassa

Avenue Mbomu

Avenue Kasa-Vubu

Avenue du Flambeau

27

38   39

N'Dolo

Avenue Bangala

Avenue Kabambare

37   Avenue Kabinda

41
40

Avenue Dima

42

Route des Poids-Lourds

Rond-Point
de la
Victoire et
Gambela

47
46   Cité

Avenue Swende

Rond-Point
Kimpwanza

43
44   45

Avenue du Stade

Avenue de l'Université

Avenue des Huileries

Avenue Gambela

Avenue de l'Étoile

Avenue Kasa-Vubu

48
49
50
51

Rond-Point
Kasa-Vubu et
Victoire

Avenue du 20 Mai

Avenue de la Victoire

Boulevard Lumumba

1re Rue

3me Rue

Avenue Bongola

5me Rue

52

- **PLACES TO STAY**

6	Hôtel Intercontinental
29	Afrique Hôtel
31	Hôtel Diplomat
37	Hôtel Kabinda
38	Hôtel Dibimbi
39	Guesthouse Hôtel
41	Hôtel Phenix
48	Hôtel Matonge

▼ **PLACES TO EAT**

10	Pizza Restaurant
15	Restaurant Coco Damus
28	UTEX Afrique Shopping Centre (Hamburger House Le Palmier, Le Chantilly & Netty's Supermarket)
36	Restaurant la Joker
40	Restaurant le Lotus
48	Bar-Restaurant Ali Baba

OTHER

1	Palais de la Nation
2	EC & Greek Embassy
3	German & Swiss Embassies
4	UK Embassy
5	La Raquette (River Observation Point)
7	Département de L'Environment et Conservation de la Nature
8	Egyptian Embassy
9	Kenyan Embassy
11	Indian Embassy

12	Canadian Embassy
13	Pharmacies
14	CAR Embassy
15	BCZ Bank
16	Congolese, Angolan & Camerounian Embassies
17	Rwandan Embassy
18	Place de la Victoire
19	Tanzanian Embassy
20	Place Royal (Bus & Taxi Stop)
21	Nigerian Embassy & Nigeria Airways
22	Institut Géographique (IGZA)
23	Polyclinique de la Gombe
24	ONT (Tourist Office)
25	Avis
26	Marché Central
27	Brasserie Bralima
30	Gabonese Embassy
32	Golf Course
33	Marché de 24 Novembre
34	Académie des Beaux-Arts & Musée de Kinshasa
35	Nôtre Dame Cathedral
42	Old N'Dolo Airport
43	Bar-Dancing Kimpwanza
44	Chez Kara Nightclub
45	Madison Square Bar-Dancing
46	Dancing Félicité
47	Music shop
49	Vis-à-Vis Nightclub
50	Hôtel la Creche
51	Bar-Dancing Vévé Centre
52	La Maison Blanche Nightclub

Zambia
54 Ave de l'École, near Col Ebeya intersection
(☎ 21802)

Other foreign embassies represented in Kinshasa include: Argentina, Brazil, Chad, Côte d'Ivoire (68 Ave de la Justice, Gombe), Ethiopia (Immeuble INSS, Blvd du 30 Juin), Guinea (7 Ave Lubefu), Italy (8 Ave Mongala), Liberia, Mauritania, Morocco, Portugal, South Africa (on the outskirts of town), Spain, Sudan (83 Ave des Trois Z, Gombe), Sweden (4854 Ave Col Lukusa, Gombe), Togo and Tunisia.

Cultural Centres The cultural centres of France (a block north of Hôtel Memling), the USA (just north of the railway station), Germany (Ave Équateur one block north of Blvd du 30 Juin) and Belgium (Les Galeries Présidentielles) are all close to one another and provide interesting programmes from time to time, plus you can catch up on the news from the newspapers and magazines they carry.

Travel Agencies The best travel agency by far is AMIZA (☎ 23390; fax 26927; telex 21027) at 600 Ave des Aviateurs, two blocks west of the US Embassy at the corner of Ave Équateur. For organised trips to eastern Zaïre, it may be your only choice. It offers five-and eight-day trips to Virunga park including treks to see gorillas. The five-day trip includes a one-day excursion to see gorillas and two full days in the park. The all-inclusive price per person from Goma including the US$210 park fee but not including the air fare to Goma (about US$650 return from Kinshasa) ranges from US$1359 (two people) down to US$1013 (six people); residents of Zaïre receive a reduced rate.

Three other notable travel agencies in the city centre are the long-standing Zaïre Travel Service (☎ 23232/88) at 11 Blvd du 30 Juin near the Hôtel Memling; Agence Sagres Voyages a block south of the Memling at 460 Ave Col Ebeya; and Acrep Voyages (☎ 20995), which is about five blocks west on Blvd du 30 Juin, a block beyond Ave Kasa-Vubu. Their bread and butter is making and reconfirming airline reservations. When conditions in Zaïre stabilise, Zaïre Travel Service might become involved again in package tours to eastern Zaïre.

Bookshops Kinshasa's best bookshop by far is the Librairie du Kioske at the Intercontinental. It has plenty of country maps including Michelin maps of Central Africa for US$15 but no city maps. Also available are postcards for US$1.75 (compared to US$0.15 outside the main post office), large expensive books of Zaïre, Congo, Gabon and other countries, and the *International Herald Tribune*, *Time* and *Newsweek*. Another bookshop possibly worth checking out is La Détente, which is not far away at 3 Ave Mbuji-Mayi, just off Ave de la Justice.

For city maps and maps of Zaïre, see the Institut Géographique (IGZA) on Blvd du 30 Juin just east of Place de Nelson Mandela. Its maps, which are quite old, cost about US$2.50 each.

For film and photo supplies, head for Tigre Photo in the city centre behind the Galeries Présidentielles.

Supermarkets Two of the city's largest supermarkets, Express Alimentation and Super Yaya, were destroyed during the riots of 1991, leaving the large Supermarché Select without any competitors in the city centre. It's directly behind the SOZACOM building and stocked with foreign goods. If you're out in the Gombe area, try the small new UTEX Afrique shopping centre on Blvd du 30 Juin, 300 metres or so beyond Rond-Point Petit Pont. The tiny Netty's Supermarket there carries cheeses, yoghurt, l'Eau Vive mineral water, etc. Next door is the modern Boucherie l'Ardennaise.

Pharmacies The best-stocked pharmacy is Internation Pharmacy at the Intercontinental. It's open Monday to Saturday from 9 am to 12.30 pm and 3 to 6 pm. In the centre, one of the best is the Pharmacie du Centre on Ave des Aviateurs opposite AMIZA.

La Cité

Kinshasa is a city to experience, not 'see'. If you spend much of your time in the Cité (short for 'La Cité Indigène'), fraternising with the locals, you will be experiencing far more than looking at Kinshasa's sights. Nightclubs here are frequently open-air, with large dance floors and all-African, mostly male clientele. Because of the security problem, most bars and some nightclubs liven up quite early, from about 5 pm onward. Other nightclubs, especially on weekends, continue the normal practice of opening much later.

Marché Central

As in most cities, the Grand Marché is fascinating; vendors sell everything from rice and fish to locusts and snakes. It's six blocks south of the Hôtel Memling towards the Cité. Go before 2 pm, when it starts closing down.

Musée de Kinshasa

The Kinshasa Museum and, next door, the Académie des Beaux-Arts, are on Ave du 24 Novembre, one km south of the Place de Nelson Mandela and four km south-west of the city centre. The main museum building has two large rooms. The one in front has a permanent collection of some superb masks, also high-quality wooden carvings including stools, pipes, statues and *fétiches*. The back room is a *sale d'exposition* where professors at the fine arts academy have frequent exhibitions of their work. The museum, which is closed on Tuesdays, is open from 9 am to 1 pm (10 am to noon on Sundays) and entry is free.

The fine arts academy in the same compound was started by the Jesuits in 1953 and is basically a huge workshop where you can observe students at work. On Sundays from 10 am to noon (and possibly other times as well) you can buy some of their pieces.

Cité de l'OUA

Some four km west of the Intercontinental along the Route de Matadi is the Mont-Ngaliéma quarter and the Cité de l'OUA, the site of the 1967 Organization of African Unity conference. Mobutu's government and the Presidential Palace are located here, so it's off-limits to the public. If you could visit, you'd see how extravagant African governments have been with such events – elegant houses for each head of state, a mammoth conference hall, restaurant and a huge swimming pool. And the conferences last only four days! Mobutu, however, clinging to his political life, has been forced into refuge aboard a yacht in the middle of the river, with a helicopter standing by.

Just beyond the Cité de l'OUA is the **Ile des Mimosas**, which is a good place to see some nearby rapids *(les rapides)*. When conditions in Kinshasa stabilise, it may again become possible to visit them.

Activities

For the use of its pool the Intercontinental charges nonguests US$8 on weekdays and US$17 on weekends, while for squash and tennis it charges everyone US$8 per session. For about US$7 more you can play tennis or squash with the club pro.

The Cercle de Kinshasa has an 18-hole golf course with sand greens and rough fairways. Nonmembers can play during specified hours. It borders Blvd du 30 Juin starting just after the turn-off for the Intercontinental.

The city's major private sporting club is

the Amicale Sportive de Kinshasa on Ave Ma Campagne in Joli-Parc, about five km southwest of the Intercontinental. It has lots of facilities and if you're a good tennis player, you may be able to get a game.

Places to Stay – bottom end

Cité The Cité has the highest concentration of cheap hotels but since the riots of 1991, the area's crime rate has soared. Until conditions change for the better, I strongly recommend staying elsewhere, especially since there are hotels outside the Cité that are just as cheap. Another factor to consider is noise. Some of the most popular and well-known hotels are at or near Rond-Point Kasa-Vubu et Victoire (Zone de Matonge), an area that's anything but tranquil. Moreover, on a busy night some proprietors may be reluctant to give you a room because these are used as brothels which brings in more money. Still, some of the rooms are quite tolerable and a tip may help you get one.

The long-standing, run-down *Hôtel Matonge* (☎ 60066), a block north of the rond-point at 23 Ave du Stade 20 Mai, has about 40 rooms and is quieter than most. The rooms, which cost the equivalent of about US$3, are large with marginally comfortable beds and private baths with tubs and running water. As in many hotels throughout Zaïre, two men aren't allowed to stay in the same room. Even if it's full, which is often the case, the popular shaded terrace in front is a super place for a drink. Many travellers prefer *Hôtel Yaki*, which is a stone's throw away at 28 Ave du Stade 20 Mai. It has similarly priced rooms, friendly management and good rooftop views.

The four-storey landmark *Hôtel le Creche* (☎ 60660), which is two blocks away, just south of the rond-point, is just as famous as the Matonge. It has rooms from US$3.50 to US$5; the least expensive ones are rarely available and the more expensive ones have fans and private baths. It's the noisiest hotel around, especially on weekends when a band plays on the top-floor terrace, filling the entire rond-point with music.

If you'd rather be closer to the centre,

check *Hôtel Kita Kita* on Ave Croix Rouge, which runs into Kasa-Vubu about eight blocks south of the central market, halfway between Blvd de 30 Juin and the rond-point. It has rooms for about US$2.

Other Areas My favourite cheap hotel is the 41-room *Afrique Hôtel*, which is at 4106 Blvd du 30 Juin, about six km west of the central area. Finding buses and taxis here, which pass directly in front, is a cinch and the area is quiet and relatively safe plus the room rates are low – about US$4 for a large clean room with air-con and a private bath with good showers. The main problem is that the rooms are infested with cockroaches. The hotel is run by a friendly Ethiopian woman who will safely guard your luggage and valuables, and there's an inexpensive restaurant next door.

Another place worth checking out is the *Guesthouse* (☎ 23490) on Ave du Flambeau in Quartier N'Dolo. It has rooms with shared bath for only US$2.50 (US$5 with private bath). The place is run-down but popular with Africans because of its low rates and good location. The hotel is three km from the centre on the main road heading towards the airport, with easy access to taxis and buses. There's also a decent courtyard restaurant with a TV and inexpensive food such as spaghetti for US$1.20, roast chicken for US$2.50 and a large Primus beer for US$0.60.

If it's full, forget about *Hôtel Dibindi* some 200 metres away as it's reportedly infested with thieves. Instead, try the large *Hôtel Phenix* (☎ 26627), which is 1½ km further out on the same road at the Ave Kabinda intersection. Its rooms are pricier at US$6/7.50 with fan/air-con, but are clean and have private baths (check if the water is running in your room) and the air-con restaurant is good. The 48-room *Hôtel de Presse* at the western end of Ave Kabinda at the Cité de la Voix du Zaïre is a slightly more expensive option.

If you can afford the higher cost, the friendly *Centre d'Accueil Protestante* or CAP (☎ 22852) is highly recommended. It's near the central area at 9 Ave Kalemie, a block west of Citibank towards the Casier Judiciaire, and is the best place for meeting overland travellers. Rates are US$8 per person for a spotless room with clean sheets and decent hot-water bath (some shared and some private). The rooms have two single beds and you may be asked to share a room if you're travelling alone as this place is very popular. There's also a large decent restaurant with TV that's open all day and serves a continental breakfast for US$0.90 and other meals such as steak frites (US$2.20) and grilled fish (US$2.50). Even though the CAP has many rooms, make sure you arrive early because by noon they may all be gone.

Places to Stay – middle
The best mid-range hotel in the centre is the small tranquil *Hôtel Estoril* (☎ 27790) on Ave du Flambeau, 400 metres south of the eastern end of Blvd du 30 Juin. This very pleasant, old-style hotel has room rates payable in zaïres (about US$26/40 at the street/official exchange rates) which are large and attractive with high ceilings, comfortable single beds, carpet, quiet air-con, a work table and a private tiled bathroom with a tub and hot water. The restaurant, which is known for its excellent Portuguese food, offers meals for under US$10 and there's a patio out the back which is good for food and drinks. The hotel is only a short walk to the heart of town. However, thieves have ambushed travellers walking in broad daylight in this and other areas of Kinshasa, so be extremely careful.

Some six km west of the central area just off Ave OIA (a main artery), behind the well-known Afrique Hotel, is an excellent new place, *Hôtel Diplomat* (☎ 50119). Highly recommended for the price, it has rooms payable in zaïres, equivalent to about US$18/27 at the street/official rate. The rooms are large and neat with air-con, desks, tile floors, and tile baths with reliable hot water. There's also an attractive bar and restaurant, and the very friendly hotel staff will find you a taxi whenever you ask.

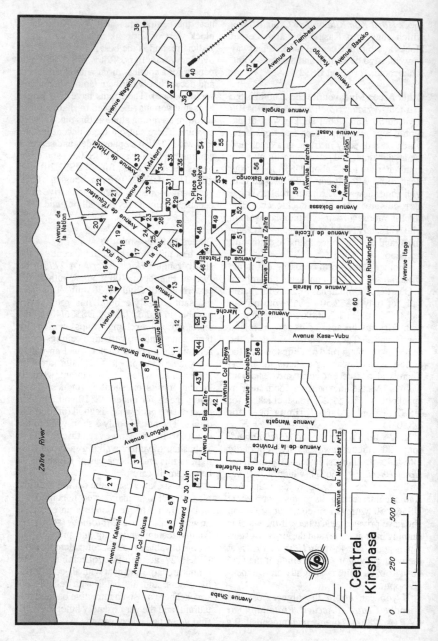

Central Kinshasa

■ PLACES TO STAY

3   Centre d'Accueil Protestante (CAP)
49 Hôtel Memling
57 Hôtel Estoril

▼ PLACES TO EAT

2   Restaurant Mama Kane
6   Sopic Plaisirs Snack-Bar
7   Restaurant le Surcouf
15 Restaurant Paradis de Shanghai
18 Restaurant Mona Lisa
23 Restaurant Sur le Pouch
24 Pâtisserie Nouvelle, Crème & Glacée
27 Restaurant le Relais, Brasserie
    l'Orangeraie & Big Steak
29 Restaurant Maxime
31 Pâtisserie New Aladin
34 Restaurant l'Edelweiss, Restaurant
    la Grande Muraille & Ice-Cream
    Shop
43 Au Coeur de Boeuf Snack-Bar
50 Restaurant la Botte
53 Restaurant les Délices

    OTHER

1   Le Grand Port
2   Casier Judicaire
4   Citibank
5   Avis
8   Shell Station
9   Maison d'Arts de l'Afrique Noir
10 Ethiopian Airlines
11 BMW Dealer-Garage
12 Cinéma Paladium, TAAG Angolan
    Airlines & Eurocar
13 Air Zaïre
14 Shabair (Branch Office)
16 Banque Zaïroise de Commerce
    Extérieur
17 BIAZ Bank

18 Cameroun Airlines
19 Pharmacie du Centre
20 Union Zaïroise des Banques (UZB) &
    CMZ Maritime Co
21 AMIZA Travel Agency
22 Barclay's Bank
25 German Cultural Centre
26 Delmas Voyages & Socopao
28 Air France/UTA
29 Galeries Présidentielles Shopping
    Centre
30 TAP (Air Portugal) & Tigre Photo
31 Belgian Embassy
32 Hertz
33 US Embassy & La Procure St Anne
34 Moneychangers
35 Supermarché Select
36 SOZACOM Building & Swiss Air
37 American Cultural Centre
38 Le Beach (Ferry Port for Brazzaville)
39 SOTRAZ Bus Station (Gare Centrale)
40 Railway Station
41 Immigration Office
42 Shabair (Main Office)
43 Acrep Voyages
44 Sabena
45 Post Office
46 Scibé-Airlift (Main Office)
47 Banque Commerciale Zaïroise (BCZ)
48 Budget Rent-A-Car & Zaïre Travel
    Service
51 Zambian Embassy
52 Agence Sagres Voyages
54 ONATRA (Riverboat Information)
55 Scibé-Airlift (Branch Office)
56 Ugandan Embassy
58 Hôpital Mama Yemo & City Bus Stop
59 Polyclinique Botte
60 Place de la Révolution
61 Marché Central
62 Communate Angolaise au Zaïre
    (Visa Service)

Places to Stay – top end

The 500-room *Hôtel Intercontinental* (☎ 20111; fax 20640/1; telex 21212) is in a league by itself. It has everything from squash, tennis courts and a huge pool to a bank, travel agency, casino, Avis agency and the city's best bookshop, pharmacy and clothing stores, and it accepts all major credit cards. The suburban location, about five km from the centre, is a drawback for some

travellers but the main problem is the extortionate price of a room – US$350/380 including 33% room tax for singles/doubles at the official exchange rate. However, if conditions in Kinshasa ever return to normal, check the room rates as they are likely to drop significantly.

A much better deal is the *Hôtel Memling* (telex 21654), which is in the heart of town at 5 Ave du République du Tchad. The burning of *Hôtel Okapi* during the riots of 1991 left it as the Intercontinental's only competitor. Run by Sabena, it has been completely renovated and was due to reopen in 1993. The hotel has some 325 rooms, which are likely to cost in excess of US$100, plus a pool, gym, a panoramic restaurant and taxis always waiting just outside.

Places to Eat

Finding cheap food in the Cité area is no problem, especially around Le Rond-Point Kasa-Vubu et Victoire. A bowl of beans and rice costs only about US$0.50. For a restaurant there, try *Bar-Restaurant Ali Baba* on Ave Victoire at the rond-point. It has hamburgers and brochettes-frites (kebabs-fries), for US$2 and steak frites for US$3.

Finding inexpensive food in the centre is not so difficult either. In the heart of town at the Galeries Présidentielles there's *Restaurant Maxime*, which is open Monday to Saturday from 7 am to 6 pm. Open-air and shady, it has beers for US$0.75, sandwiches for US$1.50, steak frites for US$2, and fried chicken for US$2.50. Nearby, a block or two south of the Hôtel Memling, is *Restaurant la Botte*, which is not as cheap – US$2.50 for steak frites and US$3.50 for fried chicken with frites.

Slightly to the west of the central area are three places all with relatively cheap non-African food. One is *Au Coeur de Boeuf Snack-Bar* on Blvd du 30 Juin, just beyond Sabena at Ave Bandundu. Open every day until 11 pm, it's a tiny outdoor place with a small menu – sandwiches are US$1.25 and hamburgers are US$2.50. Some five blocks further west and half a block north of the boulevard you'll find *Sopic Plaisirs* and, facing it, *Restaurant le Surcouf*. These simple outdoor snack-bars are virtually identical and offer sandwiches and omelettes for around US$2, steak frites for US$4 and draught beers for US$0.50.

Out in Gombe, try *Hamburger House 'Le Palmier'* at the UTEX shopping centre on Blvd du 30 Juin. Open every day from 10 am to 10 pm, this modern American-style hamburger place offers hot dogs for US$1.75,

hamburgers from US$2 to US$5, *croques messieurs* (a ham sandwich with egg) and draught beer for US$0.50. Finally, the extremely popular *Café l'Atrium* at the Intercontinental, which is open until 11 pm, is not so outrageously overpriced. If you go there in the early evening before 9 pm, you can have a drink and/or meal and be entertained by a live but subdued Zaïrian band. The menu includes spaghetti for US$5.50, roast chicken for US$6.25, croque messieurs for US$4.50 and large beers for US$1.65 (50% more if you change your money at the hotel or at the bank there).

African My favourite cheap African restaurant is the unmarked, open-air *Restaurant Mama Kane*. Near the central area, it's next door to the well-known Casier Judiciaire, 2½ blocks north of Blvd du 30 Juin and a block west of the Centre d'Accueil Protestante. From Monday to Saturday between 11 am and 4 pm you can get a very filling meal here; large beers cost US$0.70 and most dishes are in the US$1.25 to US$1.75 range including wonderful *saka saka* (manioc leaf stew), *gibier* (wild game), fufu (mashed manioc), *lembika*, grilled meats, fish stew, etc. This place is great – don't miss it.

If you're south-east of the central area, a good choice would be the similarly priced *Restaurant le Lotus* (☎ 26475) at the intersection of Aves du Flambeau and Kabinda, close to the Hôtel Phenix. The Chinese man who runs it is exceptionally friendly and offers saka saka (manioc leaves), soso (chicken stew), *biteku-teku*, ngombe (beef), *mbisi ya la mer* among other dishes, all accompanied by fufu or loso (rice). He also prepares continental food such as *entrecôte* (steak) with frites and Chinese food such as *poulet aux poivrons* (chicken with peppers) and *porc sauce piquante* (pork with hot sauce); most of these dishes are in the US$2.25 to US$3 range. The restaurant is open every day until midnight and you can eat inside with air-con or outside and watch the traffic.

In the streets of the Matonge area, especially around the Rond-Point Kasa-Vubu et Victoire, you'll find ordinary African food such as fufu of yams and manioc, maboké (fish), brochettes and all kinds of greens.

For a relatively fancy restaurant with aircon and moderately attractive décor, head for the *Restaurant Sur le Pouch*, which is 1½ blocks north of the Galeries Présidentielles. Most dishes, including crocodile, turtle, antelope and *poulet moambé* (the national dish, chicken in spicy peanut sauce), cost around US$8. Open every day and night, it also offers similarly priced French dishes. You can get moambé for one-third less at the *Hôtel Estoril* on Sundays when it's the speciality of the day.

Italian & Greek One of the city's top restaurants is the Greek-owned *Restaurant les Délices*, which is two blocks south of SOZACOM. Highly recommended and well patronised day and night, it's an open-air place with tables around a swimming pool. The most popular dish is pizza, which costs from US$7; large beers cost US$1.30. The menu also includes delicious Greek salads and other Greek selections as well as French food. You can also get similarly priced pizzas, a menu of the day for US$12 and other selections at the more informal *Restaurant le Relais* nearby on Blvd du 30 Juin, just west of the Galeries Présidentielles. It's open every day until 10 pm.

French & Belgian Virtually all of the major French restaurants closed after the 1991 riots, including *l'Étrier*, *Le Caf Conc*, *Kins' Inn* and *New Bistrot*. One that didn't is *Restaurant Mona Lisa* (☎ 24717) in the centre at 58 Ave du Port and south of Ave des Aviateurs. Most main dishes are in the US$5 to US$9 price range including capitaine fish, spaghetti and pork. You can also get cheaper dishes, including hamburgers for US$2.50 and steak sandwiches for US$3. Attractively decorated and open every day, it has air-con and is recommended for its good food, moderate prices and friendly management.

Another is the ever-popular, informal *Big Steak*, which has similarly priced French

meals and is recommended for its delicious steaks. It's nearby on Blvd du 30 Juin just east of the Ave de l'Équateur intersection. Next door is *Brasserie l'Orangeraie* (☎ 25556), one of the city's top Belgian restaurants. Closed Sundays, it offers Belgian specialities, mostly in the US$7.50 to US$11 range.

Chinese For Chinese food, there are still at least three options; two are in the centre – *Restaurant Paradis de Shanghai*, a block west of the Mona Lisa at the rond-point where Aves du Port and de la Paix intersect, and *Restaurant la Grande Muraille*, 500 metres to the east on Ave des Aviateurs. A third is *Coco Damus Chinese Restaurant* on Blvd du 30 Juin in Gombe, just east of Rond-Point Batétéla. All of them are in the medium price range.

Portuguese For Portuguese fare, head for *Hôtel Estoril* in the centre on Ave du Flambeau, 400 metres south of the railway station. Most dishes are in the US$4 to US$8 price range including numerous selections à la Portuguese – merou (fish), squid and sardines – as well as less expensive grilled steak and capitaine fish. You can eat inside in the pleasant dining room or on the back terrace.

Pastry Shops In the city centre, across from the US Embassy, is the ever-popular *l'Edelweiss*. It's open to 6 pm and offers ice cream for US$0.50 a scoop, espresso for US$0.75 and pastries for US$1.50. One of the city's fanciest pastry shops is *Pâtisserie New Aladin*, which is a block away, just east of the Galeries Présidentielles. The menu includes ice cream and Lebanese chawarma sandwiches for US$2.50, espresso for US$1 and full meals for US$6.50. A similar pastry shop in all respects is *Pâtisserie Nouvelle*, which is two blocks west on Ave de l'Équateur, next to the German cultural centre. Next door, at *Crème & Glacée*, the ice cream is far cheaper but it's also not very good. All of these places are closed on Sundays, and close at around 6 pm on other days.

In Gombe, the most popular places are the pâtisserie at the *Intercontinental* and, slightly less expensive, *Le Chantilly* at the UTEX shopping centre on Blvd du 30 Juin.

Entertainment

Bars In Matonge, around Rond-Point Kasa-Vubu et Victoire and all along Ave Victoire, especially to the west, there are innumerable open-air dancing bars known as *ngandas*, often with English names like *Harlem Dancing*, *Dolly Club* and *New York Disco Dancing*. One starting point could be *Club le Palmare* at the rond-point. Most of these places are just for drinking beer (US$0.70 for a large Primus), with recorded music blasting away. They are all very similar and virtually indistinguishable. Those that sometimes have live bands are listed under nightclubs.

For people-watching, head for *Big Steak*, which is on Blvd du 30 Juin just east of Ave de l'Équateur and has a street-side terrace and beers that are not so expensive. Some of the cheaper eateries and cafés also have draught beer *(pressions)*.

Nightclubs Nightspots with Zaïrian musicians are all in the Cité, mostly in the Matonge area. Because of security problems, on weekdays people tend to come here after work and leave by 9 pm; afterwards, the place continues to hum until midnight but not like in years past. On weekends, little appears to have changed on the surface but it's much harder to find places with orchestras, and some places have closed altogether.

Going to the Cité definitely involves some risk, especially at night, so if you decide to take the plunge, remove all valuables, even cheap watches, go with a friend if at all possible or make a Zaïrian friend once you get there, and don't stay out late. I stayed here far too late one night in 1992 exploring for this book and almost got killed, but a concealed knife that a Swiss friend was carrying and artfully used to fend off our attackers probably saved us.

With that sobering thought in mind, a good place to start on weekends is *Hôtel la Creche*, on the southern side of Rond-Point Kasa-Vubu et Victoire. It has a Zaïrian band playing on its rooftop terrace Thursdays to Saturdays. The band starts playing fairly early in the evening, and there's no cover charge.

One of the most well-known places – and my favourite – is the open-air *Vis-à-Vis* next door to Hôtel la Creche, where Viva la Musica and occasionally OK Jazz (which performed for the first time in 1956) play Fridays to Sundays from around midnight. Other groups often play during the rest of the week. The cover charge ranges from only US$0.50 to US$1.25.

During the week, an excellent place well worth trying is *Vévé Centre* (or Madison Square), which is on Ave de la Victoire, half a block west of the Rond-Point Kasa Vubu. It has a large open-air dancing area and frequently a band from around 5 to 9 pm.

If you continue west along Ave de la Victoire, you'll come to two more well-known dancing places that often have bands. The first is *Chez Kara*, near the Ave Gambela intersection. The second, which is at the next rond-point (Rond-Point Kimpwanza), is *Bar-Dancing Kimpwanza*. Another place with lots of dancing but usually no orchestra is *Dancing Félicité* (formerly Ngos Club), which is three blocks north of the Rond-Point de Kasa-Vubu et Victoire and just west of Kasa-Vubu.

Type Ka, at the corner of Ave de la Funa and Blvd Central, is where M'Bilia Bel got her start. *La Maison Blanche*, two km southeast of the rond-point at the intersection of Ave de l'Université and Bongolo, has the largest auditorium, which is why some of the city's most prestigious groups often perform there on weekends. The famous *Un-Deux-Trois*, on the other hand, has closed.

For dancing to recorded Zaïrian music, the common people head for places such as *Daïto Dancing Club*, on Ave du Stade du 20 Mai about 300 metres north-east of Rond-Point Kasa-Vubu et Victoire, and *Karmel* a block away. Both are usually packed.

Expatriates tend to prefer the flashy discos with Western music in 'their' area; most are closed on Sundays. Two that may still be around are *VIP* on Ave Mongala, a block behind the Palladium movie theatre on Blvd du 30 Juin, and *Jambo-Jambo* three blocks away on Ave du Bas-Zaïre, just behind the main post office. The latter is famous for *les femmes libres* (whores), who often don't show up until around 11 pm, but still the dancing is good there, particularly when there's a band. One of the flashiest nightclubs is *Le Privé* out in Binza; it's for members only but you can easily get in with a Zaïrian friend.

Cinemas The cinemas all have one showing nightly starting at 8.30 pm. The best is Cinéma Palladium on Blvd du 30 Juin opposite the post office; it's also used occasionally for concerts. In the Cité, there's Cinéma Venus at the Rond-Point Kasa-Vubu et Victoire.

Things To Buy

Artisan Goods One of the best places to buy Zaïrian art is the Maison d'Arts de l'Afrique Noir, which is a very small shop in the city centre at the intersection of Aves Col Lukusa and Bandundu, two short blocks north of Sabena. Open weekdays from 8 am to 5 pm and Saturdays from 8 am to 3 pm, it has lots of woodcarvings and masks (some quite small and portable), some of very good quality; moreover prices are very reasonable and the friendly owner is not pushy.

For modern oil paintings, metal sculptures, ceramics and wooden carvings by local artists, the best place by far is the city museum out on Ave du 24 Novembre. Open from 9 am to 1 pm except on Sundays (10 am to noon) and Tuesdays (closed), it has a sale d'exposition in the rear where art professors display their works; prices range from around US$20 to US$350. Also, at the Académie des Beaux-Arts next door you can purchase works by the students; Sunday from 10 am to noon is apparently the best time, but it's open all week.

Not far away, at the intersection of Aves Kisangani and Père Boka, is the Centre Culturel Boboto (☎ 30001), which offers a similar selection and is open from 9 am to noon every day and 4.30 to 6 pm from Monday to Thursday. For cheaper, souvenir-quality oil paintings and woodcarvings, try the Petit Marché in the city centre, a block south of SOZACOM building.

Malachite You don't have to buy ivory to come home with jewellery that's truly African. The beautiful dark green malachite from southern Zaïre is sold all over Africa and it's less expensive and less morally reprehensible than ivory. The Petit Marché is one of the cheaper places to buy malachite necklaces and other jewellery, as well as Zaïrian masks.

Nearby, across from the US Embassy, La Procure St Anne has a shop where you can buy malachite, as well as wood sculpture, carved chests, stationery and Zaïrois dolls. The church's shop is open weekdays from 10 am to noon and 3.30 to 5 pm, and Saturdays from 10 am to noon. For the finest, most beautifully carved malachite in town, head for L'Artiste Shabien on Ave de l'Equateur, three blocks from the US Embassy. Prices are high and fixed.

Music For cassettes and records, the music shop at the Intercontinental is clearly one of the best but prices there are very high. Other places to inquire about are Sedec on Ave Isiro, and Sansui on Ave de la Paix. In Matonge, you'll find an inexpensive music shop on Ave Kasa-Vubu, three blocks south of Ave de la Victoire.

Getting There & Away

Air Sabena, Swissair, Air France/UTA and TAP (Air Portugal) all provide direct connections with Europe (Brussels, Zurich, Paris, Rome and Lisbon), while Air Zaïre, Cameroun Airlines, Nigeria Airways and Ethiopian Airlines offer services to/from Nairobi five days a week as well as to cities along the Central and West African coast, including Libreville (Gabon), Douala (Cameroun), Lagos (Nigeria) and Abidjan (Côte d'Ivoire).

The two major internal carriers are Air Zaïre and, much better, Scibé-Airlift, which is open weekdays to 4 pm plus Saturdays from 8 am to noon and Sundays from 9 am to noon. Together they fly to most major cities within Zaïre including every day to Lubumbashi, Mbuji-Mayi and Kananga; four times weekly to Gbadolite, Gemena, Goma and Mbandaka; twice weekly to Kisangani, Isiro, Kindu, Matadi and Muanda; once weekly to Kikwit, Kalemie, Boende and Bandundu; and once a fortnight to Buta. Scibé-Airlift also provides a service from Goma to cities in the Kivu region including Beni, Bunia, Kindu and Lisala.

All flights on Shabair, which is closed on Sundays, are to points south, including to Lubumbashi and Mbuji-Mayi on Mondays, Tuesdays, Thursdays and Fridays; to Kananga three times a week; and to Kolwezi via Lubumbashi.

The smaller private airlines, including ACS, TAS and BAL, all have their offices at Kinshasa airport, not in the city centre. To make reservations you must see a travel agency or go to the airport. Each serves only a limited number of cities. BAL, for example, serves Goma, Lubumbashi, Mbuji-Mayi and Kananga among other cities, and ACS serves Bukavu, Kisangani and Lubumbashi. To reach really remote areas of the country, you might try catching a flight on Mission Aviation Fellowship, MAF (☎ 32941, 80569; telex 21435), which is normally reserved for people on church business.

Typical one-way fares from Kinshasa on any of the airlines are

Destination	Fare
Abidjan (Côte d'Ivoire)	US$900
Brussels (Belgium)	US$1938

Bukavu (Zaïre)	US$330
Goma (Zaïre)	US$300
Kalemie (Zaïre)	US$300
Kananga (Zaïre)	US$160
Kisangani (Zaïre)	US$230
Lagos (Nigeria)	US$572
Libreville (Gabon)	US$510
Lubumbashi (Zaïre)	US$300
Luanda (Angola)	US$335
Mbuji-Mayi (Zaïre)	US$190
Nairobi (Kenya)	US$908

Addresses of the major airlines follow; all of them except Nigeria Airways are in the city centre on, or a block or two off, Blvd du 30 Juin:

Air France/UTA
    Blvd du 30 Juin, just west of the Galeries Présidentielles
Air Portugal
    Ave de la Nation, just behind the Galeries Présidentielles
Air Zaïre
    4 Ave du Port, one block north of Blvd du 30 Juin (☎ 24286/7/8)
Cameroun Airlines
    Ave du Port, near Ave des Aviateurs (☎ 21268)
Ethiopian Airlines
    Ave du Port, one block north of Blvd du 30 Juin
Nigeria Airways
    Blvd du 30 Juin, at the Nigerian Embassy just beyond Place de Nelson Mandela in Gombe (☎ 33343)
Sabena
    Blvd du 30 Juin, a block west of Ave Kasa-Vubu
Scibé-Airlift
    Blvd du 30 Juin, two blocks east of the post office (☎ 25233, 26262; telex 21003)
Shabair
    98 Ave Col Ebeya, just east of Ave Wangata (☎ 45232)
    Ave de la Paix, at the eastern end of Ave Col Lukusa
Swissair
    Blvd du 30 Juin, near the SOZACOM building
TAAG Angolan Airlines
    Blvd du 30 Juin, just west of Ave du Port

Major Routes Getting to Kinshasa from elsewhere in Africa and beyond often involves a combination of overland and riverboat transport.

To/From Rwanda & Burundi There are good road connections from Rwanda and

Burundi to Goma and Bukavu, both on Lake Kivu. The most popular overland route from Lake Kivu to Kinshasa is by truck and bus to Butembo and Kisangani, and by riverboat from there to Kinshasa. You cannot travel overland from Kisangani to Kinshasa except by heading south all the way to Kananga. See the introductory Getting There & Away section for more details.

To/From Zambia The most popular overland route from Zambia to Kinshasa is by bus, bush taxi or train to Lubumbashi, by train from there to Ilebo (four to six days), by truck from there to Kikwit, and by bus from there to Kinshasa. Several times a month, you can also take a riverboat from Ilebo to Kinshasa.

Bus SOTRAZ has two inter-city bus routes, one to Kikwit and another to Boma via Matadi. The roads on both routes are paved all the way but are not in good condition. Nevertheless, many people prefer the bus to the train as it tends to stick to the schedule better. In Kinshasa the buses leave from the Gare Centrale (facing the train station). The daily bus for Boma leaves at around 7 am, arriving in Matadi around 3 pm and in Boma at around 6 pm; the fare is US$5 to Matadi and US$6.50 to Boma.

The SOTRAZ buses for Kikwit leave twice daily (at around 7 am and 2 pm) from the Gare Centrale; the trip takes about 12 hours. If you prefer an overnight trip, try SITAZ (in the Matété area), which has two buses (at around 3 and 5 pm) every day; the trip takes about 16 hours, with many stops along the way, and the buses are very crowded. Alternatively, you could take a minibus to Kikwit. They leave from the *gare routière* (bus station) in Ngaba, about seven km from the centre. All of these buses charge about US$5.

Train The express for Matadi leaves Mondays, Wednesdays and Fridays at around 8.30 am from Kinshasa's railway station, and usually arrives in Matadi at around 5 pm; it

then leaves Matadi the following day at 7.15 am to return to Kinshasa. The fare is US$3.50 in 2nd class, US$8 in 1st class, and US$14 for deluxe class. The ticket office is open weekdays from 6 am to 3 pm and Saturdays from 6 am to noon. There's no restaurant car but there are people who walk the aisles selling drinks and snacks.

Car You'll find Eurocar (telex 21530) on Blvd du 30 Juin opposite the post office; Avis (☎ 20770, 21185; fax 21012; telex 41040) one km further west on Blvd du 30 Juin and also at the Intercontinental; Hertz (☎ 23322, 24477; telex 21191) at 11 Ave des Aviateurs near the US Embassy; and Budget Rent-A-Car at 11 Blvd du 30 Juin next to the Zaïre Travel Service.

Boat Getting to/from Kinshasa can also involve river transport (ferry and steamer) or sea transport (freighter).

To/From Congo Between Kinshasa and Brazzaville (the Congo), there are ferries every hour punctually on the hour in either direction starting at 8 am; the last one departs at 4 pm. The schedule on Sunday is slightly different. The trip takes only 20 minutes, but you should get there about 45 minutes in advance to allow sufficient time to clear customs. There are two ferries, one Congolese and one Zaïrian which charge the same – CFA 6500 (US$26) from Brazzaville and the equivalent in zaïres at the official rate from Kinshasa.

From the Zaïre side you cannot import or export more than the equivalent of about US$5 in zaïres (from the Congo side the limit on exporting CFA is CFA 25,000) and you almost certainly will be questioned and searched on both sides. Regardless, the exchange rate for zaïres on the Congo side is generally quite poor.

If the ferry is extremely crowded (which is more likely at the 8 am departure), be very careful about the potential for theft as a number of travellers have been robbed under such circumstances. Upon arriving at 'le

Beach' (short for Beach Ngobila), which is the ferry port in Kinshasa, your passport will be collected and you will be ushered into customs and required to change some foreign currency at the bank there. The amount is unspecified but that could change; regardless, it's clear that a small amount like US$10 won't suffice. And don't throw away your exchange receipt!

Despite the large number of officials at the port, some travellers have still been robbed there. The risk is much greater, however, if you walk into town carrying all of your luggage, so definitely consider taking a taxi as they are plentiful at the port and not so expensive. Police there insisted on escorting me in my taxi to the hotel, but their main objective was clearly to obtain a small tip. If this happens, check the police booth in the parking area as you can verify there that they are in fact police. If you're extremely worried about security, consider asking the police to provide this escort service.

To/From Kisangani Unfortunately, as of 1992 only one ONATRA steamer was operating. For information and reservations in Kinshasa, go to the harbour or the Division des Tarifs on the 2nd floor of ONATRA (☎ 22109, 24761/4 ext 1136), opposite the landmark SOZACOM building. The office doesn't accept reservations by phone or telex, but will accept them from travel agencies. You have to be on the boat about two hours before departure. If not, forget your cabin. More tickets are sold than there are beds. See the introductory Getting There & Away section in this chapter for more details.

The best places to inquire about the private barges in Kinshasa are AVC and Nocafex, companies next to each other at the harbour behind the railway station. If there's a boat leaving, you can get on one by being friendly and buying the captain a few beers. If an official government authorisation is still required, the captain can and probably will get this for you.

If you can't find a private barge, think about taking the riverboat from Brazzaville to Bangui; it leaves roughly once a fortnight

between July and December and is much more reliable. For details, see the chapters on the Congo and the Central African Republic.

To/From Europe For a freighter from Matadi to points north including Europe, see Compagnie Maritime Belge (CMB) or Compagnie Maritime du Zaïre (CMZ), which is in the centre in the UZB bank building at the corner of Aves Aviateur and Équateur. Socopao, which is nearby, just behind the Galeries Présidentielles, may also have information.

Getting Around

To/From the Airport Kinshasa's N'Djili airport is 25 km south-east of the central area and has a bank, a restaurant, and Avis and Hertz car rentals. There is no longer an airport departure tax.

Because of the increased security problems in Kinshasa, there is now a bus that leaves from the Intercontinental about three hours before each international departure. It's free and the airlines can tell you the departure hour when you reconfirm your flight. You may be able to catch this going back to the city. If not, the cheapest way to get into town is by public bus. The No 16 passes by on the main highway in front of the airport every half hour. In the city centre you can catch this bus on Ave Kasa-Vubu next to the post office.

A taxi should cost no more than US$15 unless you arrive late at night when the rates are higher. A taxi from the city centre to the airport should be around half this rate on the street, but not at the hotels.

Bus The OTCZ national bus company collapsed in 1989, leaving SOTRAZ as the principal bus company. Its city buses are cheap (about US$0.10) and ply all the main routes, particularly Blvd du 30 Juin and Ave Kasa-Vubu, between 4 am and 9 pm. The main SOTRAZ station, 'la Gare Centrale', is opposite the railway station. Other starting/ending points in the central area are the Marché Central, Hôpital Mama Yemo on

Ave Kasa-Vubu, and Place Royal on Blvd du 30 Juin in Gombe. The major sections of town served by SOTRAZ buses include, to the south-east towards the airport, Kinkolé, Kingasani, Mikondo, N'Djili and, to the south and south-west, Kintambo, Lemba, Matété and Mbadal. Some of the more useful routes include:

Bus	Route
No 3	Matété via Ave du 24 Novembre to Place Royal
No 6	N'Djili via Ave Kasa-Vubu to Hôpital Mama Yemo
No 9	Pascual to Hôpital Mama Yemo
No 13	Kinkolé to Marché Central
No 16	Kingasani via airport and Cité to Marché Central
No 17	N'Djili via SECOMAF and Cité to Marché Central
No 22	Mikondo to Kinshasa University
No 23	Gare Central via Blvd du 30 Juin to Kintambo
No 24	Kingasani via Pascual and Petrol Zaïre to Marché Gambela
No 27	Matété via Cité to Kintambo

There are also some 30 or more huge white 'city train' buses connecting central Kinshasa with the suburbs. These locally built buses were introduced in 1990 and have fares similar to those of the SOTRAZ buses. The city trains are driven by huge DAF tractors and carry up to 400 passengers. Music blasts away continuously and powerful air horns signal their arrival.

Taxi Taxis do not have meters and are relatively inexpensive. A seat in a shared yellow cab or VW minibus costs the equivalent of about US$0.15. A 'charter' (taxi to yourself) costs a minimum of US$1, more if the ride exceeds about four km. Expect to pay about US$4 per hour and US$40 per day.

Because of the dangerous security situation in Kinshasa, taxis are next to impossible to find after 8 pm and rates at that time are at least double. The only places you can be sure of finding taxis at night are outside the Intercontinental and Memling hotels.

AROUND KINSHASA
Lac de Ma Vallée
To see some of the countryside, hire a taxi for the day in Kinshasa and head south-west along the road to Matadi. Some 30 km along the road you'll come to signs pointing to Le Lac de Ma Vallée. Located in **Kimwenza**, this small lake with scenic surroundings is the most popular weekend retreat near Kinshasa. The facilities here – paddle boats, thatched-roof *paillotes* (straw huts) for shade, and a restaurant – are relatively well maintained. Two km away there are some waterfalls where you can also swim.

Zongo Rapids
The Chutes de Zongo are spectacular rapids on the Zaïre River that could easily be combined with a trip to Lac de Ma Vallée. Well marked on the Michelin map, they are some 70 km west of Kinshasa, beyond Lac de Ma Vallée and well north of the main Matadi road.

Kisantu Botanical Gardens
Further on the road to Matadi, some 120 km south-west of Kinshasa, you'll come to Kisantu (also called Inkisi), and Les Jardins Botaniques de Kisantu, a well-maintained botanic garden with plants from all over the world. Started in 1900 by a Belgian priest, it's a vast place, with 225 hectares full of all kinds of plants including an arboretum with some 200 species of trees from the forests of Zaïre. Lined with tall conifer trees from Australia, the long entranceway gives a wonderful first impression. You can take leisurely walks along the many shaded paths, some of which follow the Inkisi River, and on Sundays and holidays the restaurant here is open for drinks and full meals.

Also, while you're in Kisantu, check out the cathedral. Built in 1926, it is the second or third largest in Africa, with seating for 4000 people.

MBANZA-NGUNGU
Some 34 km beyond Kisantu, the road to Matadi passes through Mbanza-Ngungu

(population 110,000). This was a resort area for the Belgians in colonial times because of its temperate climate. You could take the train or bus there.

The 24-room *Cosmopolite* is the city's best hotel and quite pleasant. Ask the kids to show you the prehistoric *grottes* (caves) five km away.

MATADI

Matadi, 352 km south-west of Kinshasa, is Zaïre's major port. Outside Matadi, you can see the village of **Palabala** with a great view of the river, the *cavernes* (large caves) inhabited by fisherpeople and, across the river, **Vivi**, the first capital of the Congo, where Stanley lived. Then climb **Mt Cambier** (502 metres) for a marvellous view of the Zaïre River, the Yelaba rapids, and the surrounding mountains.

Another major attraction is the huge **Inga dam**, the largest in Africa, 40 km upriver. In operation since 1974, the power station there is still under-utilised despite the spectacular but unnecessary 1725-km Inga-Shaba power line which is responsible for one-fifth of the country's total debt. The dam has so much excess capacity that feasibility studies are under way for connecting the dam's power grid with Egypt!

Places to Stay

The 31-room *Le Central* (☎ 2687), at 1 Ave Débarcadère, is one hotel, but there are probably cheaper ones. The city's finest is the intriguing six-storey *Le Métropole*, which has 63 rooms with air-con and hot-water private baths, a restaurant, and panoramic views of the port and river.

Getting There & Away

Scibé-Airlift has flights to/from Kinshasa on Monday and Friday, but most people take the train. The express leaves Kinshasa on Mondays, Wednesdays and Fridays at 8.30 am, and Matadi the following days at 7.15 am. The trip takes all day. Fares are US$3.50 in 2nd class, US$8 in 1st class, and US$14

deluxe. The SOTRAZ buses, however, are more comfortable than 2nd class on the train. They leave every day around 7 am in either direction, take about nine hours and cost US$5.

To get to Inga dam, head north across the river on the paved road to Boma; the dam will be on your right after 40 km.

BOMA

This town, 140 km west of Matadi, is a useful stopover if you're taking a SOTRAZ bus from Kinshasa to Muanda (see the next section). Hotels include the *Bel-Air*, *Hôtel du Port* and, most expensive, *Hôtel Boma* at 321 Ave Lumumba; two others are the *Ciné-Palace* at 376 Ave Mobutu and *Hôtel Excelsior* on Ave Makhuru. From Boma you can catch a bush taxi or minibus to Muanda.

MUANDA

Some 102 km west of Boma, Muanda is Zaïre's major beach resort but with so many foreigners having left Zaïre in recent years, it attracts few bathers these days. The main beach, **Tonde-Plage**, is eight km to the north; a lesser beach, Plage du Kumbi, is four km further north.

Places to Stay

The city's major hotel, the 32-room *Man-grove*, faces the ocean as does *Hôtel Beach Zaïre*. Cheaper places include *Hôtel de la Côte* and *Hôtel Makidi*.

Getting There & Away

The easiest way to get here from Kinshasa other than on Scibé-Airlift, which has flights on Mondays and Fridays via Matadi, is to take the daily SOTRAZ bus to Boma, where you stay overnight, then take a bush taxi or minibus to Muanda the next day. (See previous section.) All 594 km from Kinshasa are paved except the last 102-km stretch from Boma. For those with cars, the trip from Kinshasa can be done in one long day.

Central & Southern Zaïre

LUBUMBASHI

The capital of the southern, copper-rich Shaba province, Lubumbashi (formerly Elizabethville) is the country's second-largest city, with about 900,000 inhabitants. At an elevation of over 1000 metres with cool, dry air, it has one of Zaïre's most agreeable climates. Not many travellers make it this way but those that do will find that it and the surrounding area have the best rail connections in the country and the best links with adjacent countries, particularly Zambia.

Despite its remoteness from Kinshasa, Lubumbashi has not been spared the effects of the country's recent turmoil. In 1990, government troops gunned down about 100 rioting students at Lubumbashi University, and when Mobutu later refused to permit an impartial investigation Belgium responded by terminating its substantial aid programme to the country. A year later there were riots in Lubumbashi similar to those in Kinshasa, during which many shops, restaurants and other establishments were looted and burned. Many others simply closed their doors and haven't reopened. Consequently, the choice of places to eat and drink here is now much more limited than in the past.

Orientation

The city's main north-south drag is Ave Lumumba, which heads south from the roundabout intersecting with Blvd M'Siri (which goes to the airport and Kasenga) past two more major intersections (the Carrefour de la Synagogue and the Rond-Point de la Gare) and the SNCZ railway station to the market. Branching off it to the west is Ave Président Mobutu, which eventually becomes the road south to Kipushi and Zambia.

The heart of town is the area between the railway station and the post office two blocks to the west. From the Rond-Point de la Poste, Ave Mwepu heads diagonally north-west for

two blocks to the Cercle de Lubumbashi where you'll find several government buildings and, to the west of that roundabout, the cathedral, the regional governor's offices (the 'Gouvernorat') and, just beyond, the *jardin zoologique* (zoo). Blvd Kamanyola runs alongside the botanical gardens and if you follow it north-westward, it becomes the Route du Golf. This road passes by the Lac Municipal, into which the Lubumbashi River drains; the Hôtel Karavia, which is the city's finest hotel; and, just beyond it, the golf course.

Information

Tourist Office The Division de la Culture, Arts et Tourisme, not ONT (which has no office here), is responsible for issuing photo permits; they are free and good for the entire Shaba region. It's near the centre at Ave Ndjamena 1206, just west of Ave du 30 Juin. There are good maps of the city but if you can't get hold of one, try the Institut Géographique (IGZA) which is a block to the south of the Gouvernorat.

Money Most of the major banks have branches here. The best for changing money is the Banque Commerciale Zaïroise (BCZ), which is in the heart of town a block west of the railway station. To change money at the street rate, the surest place is the Café Mokador on Ave Mobutu.

Post & Telecommunications You can make telephone calls and send telexes from the main post office in the heart of town.

Travel Agencies As in most other major cities in Zaïre, the best travel agency is AMIZA (☎ 223103/7), which is between the BCZ and the Park Hôtel.

Cultural Centres The US cultural centre is closed but the French cultural centre, which is on Ave Président Mobutu, a block south of the Cercle de Lubumbashi, has interesting programmes. For cultural programmes you should also check out the Théâtre de Ville,

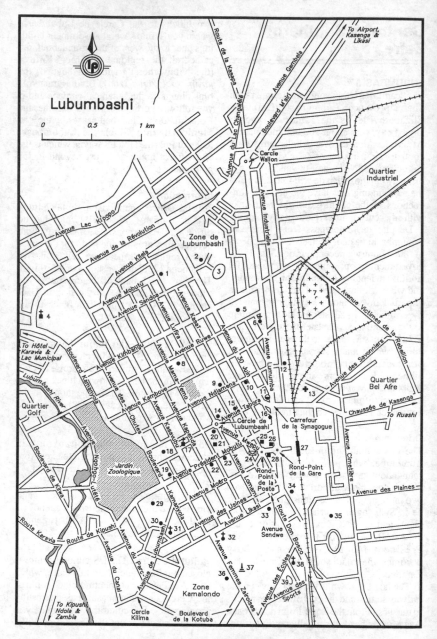

Lubumbashi

0   0.5   1 km

To Airport,
Kasenga &
Likasi

Route de la Kasapa

Avenue Gembela

Avenue du Lac Changalela

Boulevard M'siri

Cercle
Wallon

Avenue Industrielle

Quartier
Industriel

Avenue Lac Kipopo

Avenue de la Révolution

Zone de
Lubumbashi

Avenue Kilela

2

3

Avenue Mobutu

1

Avenue Sandoa

Avenue Lukasi

Avenue Kasaï

5

Avenue du 30 Juin

7

Avenue Victimes de la Rébellion

4

To Hôtel
Karavia &
Lac Municipal

Boulevard Kamanyola

Avenue Kimbangu

Avenue Ruwe

6

Avenue Lumumba

Avenue des Savonniers

Quartier
Bel Afre

Luhumbashi River

Avenue des Chutes

8

Avenue Mama Yemo

Avenue Ndjamena

9

10

11

12

Chaussée de Kasenga

To Ruashi

Quartier
Golf

Avenue Kambove

Avenue Kapenda

14

15

Avenue Tabora

16

13

Avenue Cimetière

Jardin
Zoologique

Avenue Kasavubu

Boulevard

18

17

Cercle de
Lubumbashi

20

21

Avenue Mwepu

23

24

25 26

Carrefour
de la Synagogue

Rond-Point
de la Gare

27

28

Avenue des Plaines

Quartier
Kamanyola

19

Avenue Président Mobutu

22

Avenue Moero

Rond-
Point
de la Poste

34

35

To Kipushi,
Ndola &
Zambia

Route Karavia

Route de Kipushi

29

Avenue du Parc

30

31

Avenue des Usines

Avenue Likasi

33

Avenue Don Bosco

Avenue Sendwe

32

Avenue Lomami

37

38

39

Avenue des Écoles

Avenue des Sports

36

Zone
Kamalondo

Cercle
Killma

Boulevard
de la Kotuba

Avenue Femmes Zaïroises

Avenue du Canal

Avenue de Lubumbashi

Avenue Ngobgo-Utété

■ PLACES TO STAY

21 Hôtel Shaba
25 Park Hôtel
26 Hôtel du Globe
28 Hôtel Belle-Vue

OTHER

1   Lubumbashi Museum & Theatre de la
    Ville
2   Public Pool
3   Stade Wpopo (Main Stadium)
4   St-Élizabeth Cathedral
5   Lycée Kiwélé
6   Greek Orthodox Church
7   Cemetery
8   Institut Imara & TV Antenna
9   Clinique Mama Mobutu
10 Division Culture, Art et Tourisme
11 Bus Stop
12 Brasimba Brewery
13 SNCZ Hospital
14 Hôtel de Ville
15 Gendarmerie
16 Fina Petrol Station
17 Cathedral
18 Gouvernorat
19 Institute Géographique
20 Palais de Justice
22 Café Mokador & Snackbar
23 Centre Culturel Français
24 Post Office
25 AMIZA Travel Agency & BCZ Bank
27 Railway Station
29 Gécamines Office (GCM)
30 GCM Clinic
31 St-Eboi Church
32 Methodist Church
33 Hôpital Sendwe
34 Market
35 Camp Militaire Major Vangu
36 Institut Technique Salama
37 Kimbanguiste Temple
38 St-Jean Church
39 Mazembe Stadium

which is 400 metres west of the main stadium, and the city museum next door.

Places to Stay – bottom end
Lubumbashi has quite a few bottom-end hotels. None of them are really cheap and any of them could easily close because of the country's continuing economic and political difficulties. Two of the cheapest are *Guest House Kabwehu* at 7829 Ave Mama-Yemo and, worse, *Hôtel de la Paix*, which is a real dive and close to Sendwe hospital (southwest of the market). Both charge about the same.

In the heart of town just west of the railway station and near the post office you'll find several others. One is the 34-room *Hôtel du Globe* (☎ 223612), which is at 247 Ave Mwepu in front of the railway station. It has decent rooms with private bath for about US$10 (a few with shared bath cost US$7) plus a restaurant and a bar. Nearby are two others with similarly priced rooms: *Hôtel Belle-Vue*, which is a block to the west towards the post office, and *Hôtel Silver House*, which is not far away.

Places to Stay – middle
Lubumbashi has two mid-range hotels which are still thriving despite the recession. One is the large, Belgian-run *Hôtel du Shaba* (☎ 223617), which is at 487 Ave Mama-Yemo, a block south-west of Lubumbashi Circle. It has 47 rooms with shared cold-water baths for US$20. The other is *Hôtel Macris*, which is not far away. Greek-run, it has clean rooms with private baths for about US$15 and one of the two best restaurants in town but it's not cheap.

Places to Stay – top end
The city's top address is still *Hôtel Karavia* (☎ 224512/5; fax 225011; telex 41049), formerly a Sheraton. Singles/doubles with breakfast cost about US$65/75 (US$15 more for a room facing the lake). Hot water is only available from 6.30 to 8.30 am and 6.30 to 8.30 pm. Some four km west of the central area via Blvd Kamanyola, the Karavia is a big hotel with 250 rooms, a pool, tennis court, Avis agency and a nearby golf course.

The best hotel in the centre is the old three-storey, 92-room *Park Hôtel* (☎ 222-351/2; telex 41011) which also survived the pillaging. It's in the very heart of town at 107 Ave Kasaï, just north of the post office, has no pool and is not particularly well maintained, but it is less expensive – about US$40 a room with breakfast.

Places to Eat
The city's most important address these days is *Café Mokador* at 702 Ave Mobutu in the central area. It's not only good for eating but also for meeting people, especially locals in the know as well as the occasional tourist, getting information and changing money. Next door is a new *Snack Bar*, which is the best place in town for having a leisurely breakfast, midday snack or coffee at any time, but expect to pay about what you would in Europe for the same.

For a cheap place to eat, including street food, try the central market just south of the railway station. For good continental meals, you will probably find your choices limited to Hôtel Macris near the centre and, more expensive and less convenient, Hôtel Karavia on the city's western outskirts; both are still open. For a cheaper place, check out the once-popular *Restaurant Zaïre* in the post office area. It may have closed, like most of the city's other major restaurants, such as the *St-Trop* on the Route du Golf.

Things to Buy
The best and cheapest places for malachite are the workshops (ateliers de malachite). A Swiss friend of mine involved in the malachite trade uses La Ruashi. You can catch a bus to it in the centre on Ave Lumumba at the Carrefour de la Synagogue. Malachite sales shops in the centre open and close with some frequency. Three that you might try are Arts et Cadeaux at the Park Hôtel, Home Comfort nearby at 42 Ave Mwepu, and Artiste Shabien.

Getting There & Away
Air The airport is on the northern outskirts of town, 6½ km from the centre. Shabair, Scibé-Airlift, Air Zaïre, Air Charter Services (ACS) and Bleu Airlines (BAL) all have flights from Kinshasa to Lubumbashi: Shabair flies every weekday except Wednesdays, with stops in Kananga and Mbuji-Mayi en route; and between Scibé-Airlift and Air

Zaïre there are flights every day. Fares for all airlines are about the same, typically US$300 one way (US$230 from Lubumbashi to Kananga). You can also fly from Lubumbashi to Kolwezi on Shabair three times a week.

Minibus & Truck If you're headed south to Zambia, you'll have to take a minibus or pick-up truck as the train to the border has no passenger cars. Trucks and minibuses leave from the south side of town out on Route de Kipushi, take up to five hours for the short trip (96 km) to the border (Kasumbalesa) and charge about US$3 (more for a shared taxi).

Train According to the schedule, the ordinaire and rapide depart Lubumbashi for Ilebo on Saturdays and Thursdays, respectively, and from Ilebo on Tuesdays and Saturdays, respectively. However, these schedules are as much fiction as reality, so you'll have to check and don't be surprised if one of the trains isn't even running. The

Wongo wooden palm wine cup

trip to Ilebo normally takes about four days on the rapide and six on the ordinaire. Fares from Lubumbashi to Ilebo on the rapide range from about US$65 for a 3rd-class seat to US$120 for a 1st-class seat in a twin-berth. Those on the ordinaire range from about US$45 (3rd class) to US$65 (1st class).

The train north-east to Kindu is scheduled to leave on Wednesdays; the trip typically takes three to five days and fares range from about US$48 (3rd class) to US$73 (1st class). For more information, see the introductory Getting Around section.

Car Rental Avis (☎ 223623; fax 225011; telex 41049) is at Hôtel Karavia, while Budget (☎ 222192) is at 8 Ave Changungu, a short street just east of the northernmost roundabout.

Getting Around
Bus The city buses cost about US$0.10 and are the cheapest way to get around town. The best place to catch them is along Ave Lumumba, particularly at the Carrefour de la Synagogue.

Taxi Taxis are plentiful and cost about US$0.15 for shared rides to most destinations and at least US$1 for a taxi to yourself.

KOLWEZI
The centre of the copper-mining region and 389 km north-west of Lubumbashi, Kolwezi made all the world newspapers in 1977-78 when it was captured by rebels from Angola. They killed a number of the city's 2000 Belgian residents, most of whom were rescued by Belgian paratroopers. Only a few Belgians have returned, so this important mining town is hardly as busy as it once was.

Orientation
Kolwezi is a planned city and fairly spread out, with the commercial zone on the western side of town, the main residential section on the eastern side, and the railway station, customs, post office and the city's top hotel in the centre, bordering the industrial zone. In the commercial area the main drag, running roughly east-west, is Ave Kasa-Vubu and its main intersection is with Ave des Lusangas, which heads north-east towards the railway station. Along Kasa-Vubu you'll find a number of establishments, including the market which is a block east of that intersection, and several banks (UZB and BCZ) slightly further east. Virtually all hotels and places to eat and drink are in this section as well as most churches, including the Mission Catholique, and the offices of the Gecamines mining company.

Places to Stay
For an inexpensive place to stay, try the 11-room *Air-Hôtel* (☎ 2697), which is on Ave Baobab, several blocks south-east of the main intersection in the commercial zone and parallel with Ave Kasa-Vubu. Two other bottom-end places are *Hôtel Pax* nearby on Ave Lukala, which is a block south and parallel with Ave Baobab, and *Hôtel Zaïre*. Other possibilities worth exploring if you're strapped for cash are the *Mission Catholique* on Ave de la Mission, which intersects Ave Kasa-Vubu a few blocks west of the main intersection, the *Gecamines Guesthouse* (two blocks north-west of the intersection), *Guesthouse Manika* (facing the intersection), and the *Paroisse St-Antoine*, which is half a km south-west of the intersection.

The city's top hotel and restaurant is the 28-room *Hôtel Impala* (☎ 2667), which is two blocks west of the railway station and a good way from the heart of the commercial zone, followed by the 10-room *Hôtel La Bonne Auberge* (☎ 2421), which is at 30 Ave Kajama, not far from Hôtel Pax.

Getting There & Away
The easiest way to get here is on Shabair, which has flights three times a week from Kinshasa to Kolwezi via Lubumbashi. The cheapest way is by minibus or truck; the 305-km road north-west from Lubumbashi is mostly paved and the trip usually takes a good day. You could also take the train from Lubumbashi for most of the way, but it is much more unreliable. For a minibus or truck

leaving for Lubumbashi or points north, ask around the market.

MBUJI-MAYI

A big diamond centre where mining is done both legally and illegally, Mbuji-Mayi (population 500,000) is in the centre of the country near Kananga. The area between Mbuji-Mayi and Tshikapa is full of diamond mines, primarily along the riverbeds. If you can get a permit to visit the area, it could be interesting to watch the thousands of families digging for diamonds in the dusty-red, dry riverbeds. However, if there's a government crackdown on diamond smugglers, getting a permit from the Département des Mines et Energie in town could be difficult.

Very few travellers pass this way because it's off the beaten path. Moreover, visitors are supposed to have a *permit de circulation* to visit the area and they're expensive and take a week or two to be issued. (See Documents in the Facts for the Visitor section for details.) If you come here without a permit, you'll have to give bribes left and right which can get expensive.

Places to Stay

For a cheap hotel, try *Hôtel Mukeba* on Ave Serpent near the post office, *Hôtel Mka-Kazadi* (☎ 903) on Rue Kabeya, or the *Guest House* (☎ 331) on Ave Tshilomba. For better quality accommodation, check out *Hôtel Tanko* or the 15-room *Hôtel Impala* (☎ 332) on Rue Mwene-Ditu.

Getting There & Away

There are flights every day to/from Kinshasa and at least four flights a week to/from Lubumbashi. Shabair has flights every weekday except Wednesdays from both Kinshasa and Lubumbashi while Scibé-Airlift has flights from Kinshasa on Tuesdays, Thursdays, Fridays and Sundays. Air Zaïre and BAL also have services from Kinshasa to Mbuji-Mayi. The one-way fare is US$190.

You can also get to Mbuji-Mayi via the Ilebo to Lubumbashi train as it is only about 150 km east of the line.

KANANGA

Some 163 km west of Mbuji-Mayi on the Ilebo to Lubumbashi railway line, Kananga (population 600,000) is another of Zaïre's largest cities. Blessed with a relatively sunny climate, it's in the dead centre of Zaïre, almost equal in distance from Kinshasa (1200 km), Lubumbashi (1200 km) and Kisangani (1255 km). Lined with the city's tallest buildings, Aves Mobutu and Lumumba form the main axes in the commercial and administrative district. The heart of town is the central plaza on Ave Lumumba, the favourite place for promenading. Overlooking the plaza is an old building housing the **Kananga Museum**.

As with Mbuji-Mayi, visitors (except those passing through by train) are supposed to have a *permit de circulation* to visit the area; see Documents in the earlier Facts about the Country section for details.

Places to Stay

For a cheap room, try the *Hôtel Kamina*, *Hôtel Palace* or *Le Cercle*; the latter two are in the heart of town not far from the railway station. Other bottom-end hotels include *Moderna Hôtel* (☎ 2334) on Ave du 20 Mai, *Hôtel Hocentshi* (☎ 2502) on Ave Muhona, and *Hôtel Musube* (☎ 2438) on Ave du Commerce. The 31-room *Hôtel Atlanta* (☎ 2828) on Ave Lumumba is the city's finest hotel.

Getting There & Away

Most travellers come here by way of the twice-weekly Ilebo to Lubumbashi train; fares from Lubumbashi range from US$45 for a 3rd-class seat on the ordinaire to US$120 for a 1st-class seat on the rapide.

You can also fly from Kinshasa or Lubumbashi; the one-way fare is US$160 and US$230, respectively. Between Scibé-Airlift and Air Zaïre there are flights every day to/from Kinshasa; Scibé's flights are on Tuesdays, Thursdays, Fridays and Sundays. BAL also provides a service to/from Kinshasa as does Shabair, which also has flights from Lubumbashi.

ILEBO

One tenth the size of Kananga, Ilebo is nevertheless an important commercial centre because it is at the point where the Kasaï River becomes navigable. Consequently, the train from Lubumbashi ends here and the Kinshasa to Ilebo steamers take over. You can reach Kinshasa sooner by hitching a ride in a truck to Kikwit and grabbing a bus from there. When you arrive here, you're supposed to register with immigration.

Places to Stay & Eat

The *Mission Catholique* three km south of town has clean rooms and is the best-value place to stay and eat; it also has a crafts shop which sells carvings at low prices. For a cheap hotel, try *Hôtel Frefima* or *Hôtel Machacador*. The best hotel is the 16-room *SNCZ Hôtel des Palmes*, which was built in the early 1920s for the visit of King Albert I of Belgium. One traveller said he was originally quoted a price of about US$9 for a room there with washing facilities (tap and bucket) but ended up paying only US$5.

Getting There & Away

The trip by bus and truck from Ilebo to Kinshasa via Kikwit takes two or three days. The trip involves crossing the Kasaï River by ferry and there are two round-trip crossings a day, the first departing from the Ilebo side at around 8 or 9 am and the second at around 2 or 3 pm. From there you'll have to hitch rides on trucks, and you may have to wait half a day or more to find one as there are very few passing this way.

To get to/from Lubumbashi, most travellers take the train, as going overland by truck is not only more time-consuming but is also more dangerous because of the truckers' penchant for reckless driving. According to the schedule, ordinaire and rapide trains leave for Lubumbashi on Tuesdays and Saturdays, respectively, but schedules are commonly disregarded.

Periodically, you'll also find steamers or barges in Ilebo headed for Kinshasa. Under normal conditions there is one three-class steamer leaving every two weeks, taking about four days downstream to Kinshasa, but this schedule has been rendered meaningless by the recent chaotic conditions in Zaïre.

KIKWIT

The main reference points in Kikwit, population 220,000, are the Kwilu River and Ave Mobutu, which runs from one end of the city to the other. The latter and Ave de la TSF lead to 'Le Plateau' where you'll find the market, stadium, most administrative buildings, the Mission Catholique and the finest residences. On holidays the stadium and Gungu Square are where most folkloric activities, including masked dances, are held.

Places to Stay

You'll find the city's major hotel, the 48-

Luba chief's stool

room *Hôtel Kwizu*, on Ave Motubu and a cheaper one, *Hôtel Mutashi*, nearby.

Getting There & Away
Scibé-Airlift has flights to/from Kinshasa on Thursdays. SOTRAZ also runs two buses a day (early morning and early afternoon) which cost about US$5 and take around 12 hours. SITAZ also provides a service between Kikwit and Kinshasa. It has two buses leaving in the late afternoon at around 3.30 and 5 pm, arriving in Kinshasa about 16 hours later, with many stops along the way. You must purchase your ticket in the morning and that can take up to an hour or more as conditions at the ticket office can be chaotic. There are also minibuses that ply this route (which is paved but full of potholes) as well as trucks, which often take no longer than the buses.

Taxi pick-up trucks between Kikwit and Idiofa usually leave early in the morning and take about four hours. On the Idiofa to Ilebo stretch you'll probably find only trucks; very few pass this way each day and the trip can easily take 24 hours, sometimes two full days. Before arriving at Ilebo you must cross the Kasaï River, and there are only two round-trip ferry crossings a day, one in the morning (leaving from the Ilebo side around 8 or 9 am) and one in the mid-afternoon (leaving from the Ilebo side at around 2 or 3 pm).

Northern Zaïre

GBADOLITE
Only 20 km south of the Oubangui River, Gbadolite, Mobutu's home town, is on the main overland route from the CAR (via the border towns of Mobaye and Mobayi-Mbongo) to eastern Zaïre. It's a 'must see' if you're headed that way, if nothing else just to see how badly Mobutu has ripped off the country. He has spared no expense in refurbishing his *village natal* making this small town of some 20,000 inhabitants a bizarre showcase.

After driving down a dirt track for less than an hour from the CAR border you'll be suddenly confronted with a multi-lane tarmac highway lined with lights and divided by a central flower bed. As you proceed to the town centre you'll see multistorey buildings, a bank, huge post office, supermarket, hospital and petrol station. The star attractions, however, are Mobutu's palace and the separate residences of his closest relatives and, off the road, a luxury hotel with a pool and swanky restaurants. There's even a large memorial to Mobutu's mother.

South of town is an international airport that receives large jets. With this set-up, it's no wonder Mobutu flies all of his international guests here, frequently to sign treaties as well as to take part in international meetings, such as the Angolan peace conference in 1989. However, when Mobutu is not here, the town is dead and weirder than ever.

Places to Stay & Eat
In addition to the modern commercial and residential sectors, Gbadolite also has a 'real' section, the Cité, which is where you'll find a cheap hotel or two, street food, local bars, dancing joints and a good market with huge quantities of snails from the nearby marshes. If you're driving, you'll find a *Mission Catholique* some 17 km south of town, where the paved road ends. You can camp there, possibly rent a room as well.

Getting There & Away
Air Zaïre has flights from Kinshasa to Gbadolite on Wednesdays and Saturdays, with onward connections to Kisangani. Scibé-Airlift also has two flights a week to/from Kinshasa.

Catching a truck south towards Lisala shouldn't be too difficult as the road is the major route connecting Kisangani with the CAR. It's in good condition between Gbadolite and Businga (157 km), in bad condition between Businga and Gumba (100 km), and in fair condition between Gumba and Lisala (104 km). By truck, the trip from Gbadolite to Lisala takes two days and costs US$12;

you'll find very little food en route, not even bananas.

If you're headed north towards Mobaye (the CAR), you'll find a minibus leaving from the market at 6 am sharp for the CAR border (US$0.50). Be prepared to pay CFA 25,000 per vehicle and CFA 1000 per person for the ferry crossing. The ferry there is much more reliable and has a much larger load capacity than ferries at other crossing points. The crossing here is fairly hassle-free, but CAR immigration officials may levy a small fee (about US$4 in zaïres, or the equivalent in CFA) for stamping your passport, which is probably a scam.

BUSINGA

Roughly halfway between Gbadolite and Lisala, Businga has a beautiful camping spot on the southern bank of the Mongala River, which flows east to west just south of town. Called *Pique Nique Camping*, it charges US$0.75 per person for camping and US$2.50 for a two-bed cabin. To get there, after passing southward over the river continue for 200 metres and turn left (east) at the signpost, then follow the tracks for 20 metres and turn left again. You can swim in the river as it's free of crocodiles, but watch out for the strong current.

ZONGO

Across the Oubangui River from Bangui (the CAR), Zongo used to be the major point for crossing the river. However, the thieves and crooked immigration officials in Zongo have become so notorious that most travellers now cross further east at Mobaye. Those with vehicles are subject to the greatest hassles by immigration officials. They will use any pretext to take hours searching vehicles. After that's done they will demand an 'entry tax', 'tourist tax' or whatever, usually in the order of CFA 2500 per person but sometimes as high as CFA 5000.

The main reason for crossing at Mobaye instead of Zongo, however, is that the Zongo to Lisala road is not in as good condition as the Mobaye to Lisala road; moreover, the ferry at Zongo has a low load capacity and,

unlike the one at Mobaye, it breaks down frequently.

If you cross at Zongo, you'll find a bank in town but most travellers find it easy to change money in the market. The rate here is generally not very good. Virtually any vendor in town will accept CFA francs as well as zaïres.

Places to Stay

The *Hôtel Zaïre* by the market has doubles for US$4.50 and very clean bathrooms with showers. If you have a vehicle, immigration officials won't let you camp near them, so the only place to camp will be on the outskirts of town and you are almost certain to get robbed there. For this reason, campers should try to arrive early in Zongo so as to avoid staying overnight there.

Getting There & Away

The Bangui to Zongo ferry, which operates from 8 am to 4 pm except on Sundays, charges CFA 1000 per passenger and CFA 25,000 per vehicle. If you are in a group, you can usually save money by taking a pirogue; the fare is quite variable depending on your bargaining skills – CFA 1000 for a pirogue to yourself, or CFA 200 to CFA 400 per person is typical.

If you're headed south-east to Gemena (259 km), you can expect trucks to charge about US$10 and take 10 to 12 hours. You'll find no restaurants on this stretch – only sardines, onions, smoked fish and occasionally crocodile in yukky red sauce.

GEMENA

Roughly halfway between Zongo and Lisala, Gemena is a frequent overnight stop for travellers passing this way. There's a bank in town which normally cashes travellers' cheques but, as in most of Zaïre, you are likely to be turned away.

Places to Stay & Eat

For convenience, you can't beat *Hôtel Papa Boualey*, which is close to the market and charges US$3/4 for singles/doubles. It's very basic with awful showers but the rooms are clean enough. The market is the best place to look for food as there are a number of food stalls there serving staples such as beans and rice.

Getting There & Away

Trucks leave from the market. If you're headed south-east towards Lisala, you should be able to make it there in about 16 hours. There is a ferry crossing en route and if the ferry is inoperational, you may have to take a pirogue across the river, which will prolong the trip by at least a day.

If you're headed north-west to Zongo, you should be able to make it there by truck in nine to 12 hours; the typical charge is US$10.

It's also possible to fly from Gemena to Kinshasa (four times weekly) or Kisangani with either Air Zaïre or Scibé-Airlift. Air Zaïre accepts zaïres but Scibé takes only hard currency – US$350 to Kisangani via Kinshasa!

BINGA

Some trucks from Gemena to Lisala stop over in Binga, which is off the Gemena to Lisala road; from Gemena to Binga by truck costs about US$7.

At a plantation village about two km outside of town on the Gemena road you'll find the *Grand Hôtel*, which is clean but very basic with singles for US$2; two people can stay in the same room. Nearby, at the palm oil factory, is the departure point for trucks headed to Lisala.

LISALA

Like Bumba 120 km to the east, Lisala is on the Zaïre River and is a potential transit point for those on the Kisangani to Bangui route who want to take the steamer. If you have to wait for the steamer, go on to Bumba where the accommodation is better, the food more plentiful, and the people not so aggressive. Also, the vehicle-loading facilities at Lisala are lousy.

Banks in Lisala will not change money or travellers' cheques, so go to the market where it's easy to change money.

Places to Stay

Two of the most popular hotels with travellers are the *Hôtel Nsele*, which is on the main drag in the centre of town, and the more expensive *Hôtel Cinquantenaire*, which is several blocks to the east next to the post office. Rooms at the Nsele cost only about US$2.50 and you can put three in a room, but there's no electricity or water. The Cinquantenaire has no singles, only doubles with private bath for US$6, and apartments for US$8. The latter have spacious sitting rooms and enormous bedrooms, and the hotel doesn't seem to mind having a few people in them. The private baths, however, have no running water, so you'll have to take bucket baths. There's also a pleasant bar with cold drinks but it's not always open.

The *Mission Catholique* doesn't take travellers, but the *Mission Protestante*, which is three km west of town on the road to Gemena, still lets travellers pitch tents there for free, and camping there is much safer than in town. It's not a camp site however, so you won't find showers or toilets.

Getting There & Away

Trucks headed north for Businga and Gbadolite leave from a tiny market north of the Mission Catholique on the road to Businga. The road is in good condition except for the stretch between Gumba and Businga; the trip to Gbadolite normally takes about two days by truck and costs US$12. For trucks northwest to Binga and Gemena, ask at the truck stop on the western side of town facing the market.

There's only one ONATRA riverboat operating now between Kinshasa and Kisangani with about one departure a month. Fares from Lisala to Kisangani have risen to US$119/42/38 in 1st/2nd/3rd class.

You can also fly to Lisala on Scibé-Airlift from Kinshasa on Saturdays; the one-way fare is about US$250.

BUMBA

For people travelling between Bangui (the CAR) and Kisangani, Bumba is a major transit point – where you get on or off the steamer. It's a much better place to wait for the steamer and barges than Lisala because it's a more comfortable and less aggressive town. However, be sure to report to immigration if you stay here for more than a day, and beware of a possible scam. Officials have been known to withhold passengers' tickets until the last moment so they can hurry them onto the steamer and ask for more money.

The centre of town is the intersection of the east-west Buta to Lisala road and the main north-south road, which heads north from the river past the ONATRA office and railway tracks to the intersection and further north to the market. Ave Manga, the road on which the port and BCZ bank are located, runs east-west along the river, intersecting with the north-south road.

Places to Stay & Eat

One of the most popular hotels with travellers is *Hôtel Dina*, which is a block off the river on the main north-south drag. It has large rooms and clean shared baths for US$2.50, a good laundry service, helpful staff and a lively bar but no restaurant.

If the Dina is full, try *Hôtel Modula*, which is nearby on the river-front road, east of the BCZ bank. It charges US$5 for a double and there's no problem if you want to squeeze three people into a room. The rooms have private baths with showers and sit-down toilets; the water supply, however, is erratic. *Hôtel de la Paix*, which is to the north, just before the market, has similarly priced clean rooms with showers. At either place you can get a meal if you order in advance. One of the few remaining places serving meals is the unmarked restaurant at the river end of the main north-south road. Finally, if you're camping, ask for the camp ground; it's decent and reasonably priced.

Getting There & Away

Truck There are trucks periodically from Bumba east to Buta and, more frequently, west to Lisala.

Boat There's only one ONATRA riverboat running now (the others have sunk or are inoperational) so catching it is extremely difficult unless you're prepared to wait, sometimes as much as two weeks. The trip upriver from Bumba to Kisangani takes three to four days; fares in 1st, 2nd and 3rd class have risen to US$95/34/31. The return (downriver) trip from Kisangani normally takes only half as long and fares are almost exactly half.

It is also possible to organise a trip from Bumba to Kisangani by private motorised pirogue or by barge; the length of the trip can vary considerably but five days is typical. One group of 16 recently reported paying a total of US$500 including fuel but not food. These barges often hit sand, prolonging the trip considerably. Also, don't expect to find any food en route except for fruit, bread and beer. And forget about shipping a vehicle as fares are sky-high – more than US$500 to Kisangani and US$1000 to Kinshasa.

BUTA

Some 321 km north of Kisangani, Buta is on the infrequently travelled Bangassou route to the Central African Republic. The town's best hotel appears to be *Hôtel Rubi* on the river's edge near the bridge. To save money, stay at the friendly, Norwegian-run *Mission Protestante* four km out of town. After finding your hotel, you should report to immigration. If you're headed to Isiro, you could inquire about the train, but don't get your hopes up as there's only about one departure a month these days. Every other week Air Zaïre has a flight to/from Kinshasa.

KISANGANI

Kisangani is more than 1700 km upstream from Kinshasa and one of Zaïre's largest cities, with some 600,000 people. For overland travellers, the former Stanleyville is a major hub. Some take the steamer west to Bumba or all the way to Kinshasa; others head north to the Central African Republic, east to Virunga park, Lake Kivu and East Africa, or south-east to Bukavu. Because of logistical problems, only a few head south (upstream) along the river.

The steamer stops here because for the

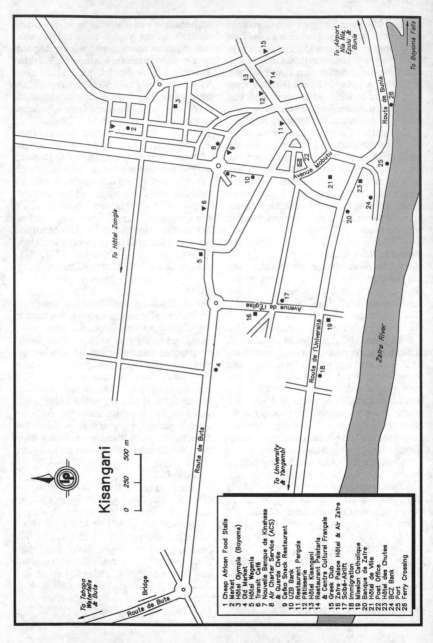

Kisangani

0 250 500 m

1   Cheap African Food Stalls
2   Market
3   Hôtel Olympia (Boyoma)
4   Old Market
5   Hôtel Wagenia
6   Transit Café
7   Nouvelle Banque de Kinshasa
8   Air Charter Service (ACS)
    & Guarde Civile
9   Cafko Snack Restaurant
10 UZB Bank
11 Restaurant Pergola
12 Pâtisserie
13 Hôtel Kisangani
14 Restaurant Pelastaria
    & Centre Culturel Français
15 Greek Club
16 Zaïre Palace Hôtel & Air Zaïre
17 Scibé-Airlift
18 Immigration
19 Mission Catholique
20 Banque de Zaïre
21 Hôtel de Ville
22 Post Office
23 Hôtel des Chutes
24 BCZ Bank
25 Port
26 Ferry Crossing

next 125 km upstream until Ubundu, there are seven major rapids, the closest to Kisangani being the famous Stanley Falls, now called Boyoma Falls. If you see any of Zaïre's tourist brochures, you're sure to see pictures of the city's major tourist attraction – the fishers of Wagenia, a village near the falls. They catch capitaine (perch) by suspending long conical basket traps from wooden scaffolds placed in the river at the falls – don't miss it.

Kisangani, like Kinshasa, was devastated by army looting in 1991, then again in late 1992 when soldiers in the army garrison went on a rampage after their pay was delayed, looting shops and homes and arresting the regional governor.

Orientation The heart of town is the post office on Ave Mobutu, which is the city's main thoroughfare. This road extends north-south from near the market past several rond-points, various banks and the old Hôtel des Chutes to the river and the port.

Information
Tourist Office ONT (☎ 2648) may still have an office on Ave de l'Église; if so, you can get free photo permits there which are good for the Kisangani region.

Money Kisangani has at least three banks for changing money. Normally, the best one is the Banque Commerciale Zaïroise (BCZ), which is in the port area. Its commissions are only about US$1.50 per transaction.

In 1992, the banks had almost no money, yet changing travellers' cheques was still possible and the rates weren't much lower than the black-market rate; the problem was that the process took three hours!

Warning Be very careful when changing money on the street. There are lots of moneychangers, particularly around the Hôtel Olympia, but this can lead to a false sense of security as a few of them are mainly in the business of staging 'set-ups'. Typically, one or two men pose as immigration officials and say they are going to arrest you, then one of the hustlers comes to the rescue and helps out the 'caught' traveller – for a fee.

Post Office The poste restante is quite reliable and efficient and costs US$0.30 per letter received.

Immigration The immigration office, which is on the western side of town on the road to the university, issues visa extensions, often on the same day. These are good for a 30-day period from the date of issue, not from the end of the original visa, and cost US$7 (compared to US$3 in Goma). Those with expired visas must pay a fine of US$2 for each excess day. If you're headed east, you won't be able to get a visa extension until Goma. However, in Beni you can get an 'attestation' from the police that you tried to get one there but only if your visa has expired or is within three days of expiring. With this attestation you won't be fined in Goma if you have overextended your stay.

Boyoma Falls

The former Stanley Falls, sometimes called Wagenia Falls, are located on the eastern edge of the city near **Wagenia village** and are the main tourist attraction. Hustlers around Hôtel Olympia will organise a pirogue trip to visit the falls and the famous fishers there; the trip takes only two to three hours. The going rate, payable in zaïres, is US$5 per person plus US$20 per group, which is supposedly for the village chief. Most overland travellers seem to think that the trip is well worth US$5 but that the US$20 group fee is a rip-off.

Places to Stay – bottom end

Hotels in Kisangani are generally run-down and often full. The long-standing, Greek-owned *Hôtel Olympia* (or Boyoma), near the market, continues to be the meeting place for overland travellers despite its worsening condition. It has three classes of doubles with showers and toilets, and prices range from US$2.50 to US$8. Camping costs only US$1 per person, US$0.30 per truck and US$0.15 per car. There are always lots of hustlers around the hotel and some thieves, so watch your gear.

To avoid the hustling scene at the Olympia, try *Hôtel Kisangani*, which is about a km north-east of the post office towards the Greek Club. It has a pleasant terrace for drinks, but travellers' descriptions of this hotel range from 'a flea pit' to 'nice and friendly'. A double with bath costs from US$3 to US$5. The similarly-priced *Hôtel Wagenia*, which is about a km north-west of the post office on a main road, has large rooms with fan and private bath from US$3.75 to US$5, and there's a good restaurant next door. If all of these places are full, try *Hôtel Baninga* in the Zone de Chopo.

Places to Stay – top end

The large *Zaïre Palace Hôtel* (☎ 2664/5), which is roughly a km west of the post office on Ave de l'Église, is a good place for the money. It has spacious, carpeted rooms with fresh linen, chairs, a writing desk and clean bath for US$10 a double, and apartments with air-con, mini-refrigerators and separate sitting rooms for US$14. The water supply, however, is erratic. The restaurant is spartan with slow service but the food is quite OK, with breakfast for US$2 and other meals from US$3.50 to US$6.

If it's full, try *Hôtel Zongia*, which is a 20-minute walk west of the market. It has clean doubles with private bath for US$13, which includes a light breakfast. The ramshackle, colonial-style *Hôtel des Chutes* (☎ 3498) near the port, is definitely not recommended. It has gone downhill considerably and is now as much a brothel as a hotel. The top rooms, which cost US$28, seem so overpriced that they must include a companion!

Places to Eat

For really cheap eats, mostly beans and rice (US$0.40 a plate) and beer, head for the stalls on the northern side of the market. The market is also a good place to stock up on supplies as it's one of the few good food markets in this part of Zaïre. For beans, rice and beer, you might also try the *Restaurant Amical*; it's around the corner from Hôtel Wagenia and may still be open. For good pastries, head for the *Pâtisserie* near Hôtel Kisangani and on the same side of the street.

Among the city's restaurants, the best is *Cafko Snack Restaurant*, which is roughly a km east of Hôtel Wagenia on the main drag, opposite the Guarde Civile military unit. Open from 7.30 am to 11 pm, it has air-con and an extensive menu, including salads, omelettes, steak, chicken, fish and pasta dishes. Prices range from US$0.85 for a salad to US$4.50 for steak or fish.

Both the *Olympia* and *Wagenia* hotels have good restaurants. Neither is cheap. At the Olympia, for example, prices start at US$2 for the set menu and rise to approximately US$3.50 to US$5 for steak & chips or capitaine fish & chips. The restaurant at the Wagenia, which is similar in all respects, has particularly good breakfasts, such as an omelette, bread and tea for US$1.50. Another alternative is the *Greek Club*, which is just a short walk east of Hôtel Kisangani.

It's very quiet with a limited menu but the food is OK and prices are almost identical to those at other restaurants.

Since the 1991 riots, lots of places have closed including the *Transit Café*, which is between the Wagenia and the Cafko. It used to be a good restaurant and a popular meeting place for travellers, with a blackboard showing air, boat and train arrivals, but in mid-1992 it was all boarded up and may not reopen. *Restaurant Psistaria* opposite the Hôtel Kisangani, and *Restaurant Pergola* between it and the post office, are standard priced restaurants and have been favourites in years past; hopefully they haven't suffered the same fate.

Getting There & Away
Air Air Zaïre, Scibé-Airlift and ACS all offer services to Goma and Kinshasa; the one-way fares are US$115 and US$224, respectively. Usually, only hard currency is accepted from foreigners. Air Zaïre is on Ave de l'Église at the Zaïre Palace Hôtel; Scibé is across the street; and ACS faces the Cafko restaurant.

Truck For trucks, ask around town, especially at the market. You can also find trucks at Kibibi, which is about six km from the centre, but you may have to wait a long time as the great majority will probably be full. Trucks north to Bengamisa (50 km) cost US$1.50, while south to Lubutu (248 km) they are US$4.25.

The main route to eastern Zaïre is via Epulu and Beni. The worst stretch on this road is between Epulu and Komanda. In years past it was not unusual to hear of stories where the trip took 11 days and travellers were stuck in a line of 54 trucks, each waiting its turn to drive up a muddy hillside. Now that section has been improved somewhat and travellers usually take just four days to do the Kisangani to Beni section (a day or two more if it's the rainy season or they stop in Epulu or Mt Hoyo).

By 1994 or so the new route heading south-east from Kisangani to Bukavu via Lubutu should be completely sealed, reducing travelling time to two or three days by private vehicle, and perhaps four by truck. See the Kisangani to Bukavu section for more details on this route and the towns along it.

Train If you're headed south to Kindu, good luck because whether you travel by road or train/steamer, the trip is likely to take up to two weeks. The train is supposed to leave Kisangani on Saturdays at 9 am, arriving in Ubundu at around 3 pm, but there are frequent cancellations because of derailings and other problems. You should purchase your ticket the day before from the SNTC railway agency in Kisangani. There are only 3rd-class seats and they cost about US$3 one way.

From Ubundu you can then try catching a barge or the three-class steamer headed to Kindu (typically four to five days) and points further south but be prepared for a long wait in Ubundu for the steamer, as its schedule is completely erratic.

Boat For many years there were two or three ONATRA riverboats ploughing the Zaïre River between Kinshasa and Kisangani; however, for some time only one of them has been in operation. It arrives in and departs from Kisangani about once a month to no fixed schedule. The trip downstream to Lisala normally takes about 2½ days by steamer and costs US$57/21/18 for 1st, 2nd and 3rd-class accommodation, about 20% less to Buma, and about US$155/55/48 to Kinshasa. Upstream from Lisala or Buma to Kisangani takes three or four days, and the fares are almost exactly double.

You can also organise trips from Kisangani to Bumba or Lisala by private motorised pirogue or larger boat. The length of the trip can vary considerably but four to six days is typical. One group of 16 travellers heading here from Bumba reported taking five days and negotiating a US$500 group rate (US$31 each).

Cheapest of all – and also the slowest – are the barges. The ONATRA port director can handle bookings and he has been known to do it in an orderly fashion, without any bribing of officials. One group heading from Kisangani to Lisala by barge reported taking 10 days and paying only US$8 a person. For more details on the riverboats and barges, see the introductory Getting Around section.

KISANGANI TO BUKAVU

More and more travellers headed for eastern Zaïre are using the new route from Kisangani to Bukavu via Lubutu. The 708-km route should be completely sealed by 1994. The Chinese were working on the Walikale (eastern) end but they have quit, leaving only the German company STRABAG, which is working eastward from Lubutu, to finish the road.

The first 248 km is on the old paved road from Kinshasa to Lubutu and is easy enough despite the road's poor condition but it will probably take you 12 to 16 hours by truck because of frequent stops. You'll cross the equator en route. In Kisangani, you can find trucks headed to Lubutu near the old market and the STRABAG office. STRABAG trucks are not supposed to take travellers but if you talk directly with the drivers instead of company officials you may find them amenable.

After Lubutu, you pass through Amisi (the first STRABAG camp), Burui, the second STRABAG camp, Ossukari, Walikale, Musenge, Hombo, Kahuzi-Biéga park and Bukavu, a total of 460 km. The first stretches paved were from Lubutu to Amisi and Ossukari to Walikale (26 km); Hombo to Bukavu was already paved. STRABAG trucks often carry hitchhikers from Lubutu to Amisi, where the main STRABAG camp is located, and on to the second STRABAG camp between Burui and Ossukari. Regardless, there's a good deal of traffic on this section, so hitching rides isn't so difficult.

On occasion, the Germans at these camps have invited travellers for meals and given them places to sleep, but a few travellers abused their hospitality, staying up to a full week, with the result that they are now reluctant to assist travellers. So if you should luck out and be offered a place to stay or invited to a meal at their canteen, don't overextend your welcome.

In **Walikale** you'll find a decent hotel a little off the main road with rooms for US$1.50; with a little persuasion the owners will let three people sleep in a room. There's also a small restaurant and market at the main intersection in town. In Walikale you have the choice of taking the road east to Goma, which is diabolical and not being improved, or continuing south-east to Bukavu on the improved road. When it's completed, you should have no problem making it from Walikale to Bukavu in a day. Also in **Hombo**, which is on that route, you'll have no problem finding trucks and minivans to Bukavu.

IKELA

Some 422 km south-east of Kisangani on the road to Kananga, Ikela, which was once a Belgian trading outpost, is a delightful town with a lovely riverside atmosphere. You can stay at the *Centre d'Accueil* at the hospital and get cold beers at a bar in the market which has a kerosene refrigerator. The Kisangani to Kananga road is worse than any of the major routes in the north-east, and hitchhiking can involve long waits.

Instead of continuing by road from Ikela, you could purchase a pirogue for about US$15 and paddle your way west to **Boende**, which takes about eight days. At night you can camp in forest clearings or at remote villages along the way. From Boende you could catch the once-a-month steamer to Kinshasa via Mbandaka, which altogether takes five to eight days. Like the ONATRA boat to Kisangani, this steamer has three classes of accommodation, but there are usually no foreigners on board.

MBANDAKA

The largest city on the Zaïre River between Kisangani and Kinshasa, Mbandaka is a major stop for riverboats and a great base for exploring areas where few travellers have trod. Despite its remoteness, it's a fairly typical town with a large post office and plenty of banks, bars and street vendors.

Places to Stay

The cheap hotels are in the Cité area around the market. One which charges US$2 a room is the *Hôtel Bokambro*. The *Hôtel Afrique* costs a little more but has essentially the same facilities, including electricity about four hours a night and water only sporadically.

Getting There & Away

Between Scibé-Airlift and Air Zaïre there are four flights a week to/from Kinshasa. You can also get to Mbandaka by barge or by an ONATRA riverboat from Kinshasa, one of which heads for Kisangani and another for Boende, both about once a month, stopping in Mbandaka. The steamers have three classes of accommodation, and the trip from Boende to Kinshasa typically takes five to eight days.

AROUND MBANDAKA

At the market you'll find pirogues heading up and down the river and to various tributaries. A trip upriver to **Ingende**, for example, can take three days and you'll be expected to chip in with the rowing. People are very friendly in small villages like Ingende, and even though you may have difficulty finding a beer, you won't have any problem finding palm wine.

Or take a pick-up truck south to **Bikoro** (134 km), which overlooks Lac Tumba; the trip takes about five hours. You can stay there at *Hôtel Jerusalem*, which charges US$2 for a deluxe double room. From Bikoro, which has a good market, you can take hikes or bike rides to nearby villages (for example: Mohele, Mbuli and Ntondo), including Bloc 6 which is a plantation village for Pygmies. There are frequent festivals in these villages and seeing one could be unforgettable. Getting back to Mbandaka is not a problem as there are two scheduled pick-up trucks a week leaving from the market, and probably others as well.

EPULU

A village on the route east from Kisangani to Virunga park, Epulu is definitely worth a stop. This is where you can see Pygmies and the extremely rare okapi, a doe-eyed creature resembling a zebra and a giraffe and closely related to the latter. It was discovered only in the early 20th century. There's a camp ground here where virtually all travellers stay. The facilities include two open cabins and a pit toilet and the price of camping is only US$0.10 a person; you can also buy ice-cold beers there.

Parc National d'Okapis

Since 1982, some Americans have been working here to delineate the boundaries of a park to protect the okapi. The park is now official and is supported by the Worldwide Fund for Nature. Inside it is a small zoo with about 10 okapis and a few young chimpanzees that travellers are allowed to play with. (If you're in Kinshasa, the Département de l'Environment et Conservation de la Nature on Ave de Cliniques in Gombe can give you some information.)

Warning There is an unfortunate scam in the Epulu area involving chimpanzees. Some of the local people hunt down chimpanzee families, murder the adults and take the babies away to the market. When a group of tourists arrives, the poacher tells them the baby chimp is a delicacy and will soon be eaten. The tourists get upset, buy the baby and look for a wildlife sanctuary to adopt it. Most sanctuaries, however, won't take the chimps because it is virtually impossible to reintroduce a lone chimp into the wild and they don't have the facilities to care for them. In the end, the chimp becomes neurotic, with the only solution being to kill it. Anyone who buys the live animals, no matter what the circumstances, is contributing to the poaching industry, so don't do it!

Pygmies

Near the park lodge you'll find an Efe Pygmy camp of tiny leaf huts where the inhabitants are friendly and enjoy offering travellers a puff on their metre-long pipes. Indeed, the Efe Pygmies are so addicted to tobacco that they will work three or four hours in a villager's field for a thumb's length of leaf tobacco. The exchange of tobacco for labour is just one component of the complex relationship between the Lese villagers and the Efe Pygmies. The Efe also hunt, fish and gather honey, building materials and medicines from the forest to trade for food, aluminum cooking pots, old clothes, soap, and metal to make knives. The Lese say the Pygmies are lazy, while the Pygmies say the Lese are miserly, and repeatedly cheat them out of their just rewards.

A US expert on Pygmies, Patrick Putman, lived and died here in the Ituri forests, studying the Pygmies. Traditionally, they have no chiefs. Instead, each age group has its own sphere of responsibility. The normal blood relationships of an individual family are recognised, but in every respect the 'family' is the whole band. All adults are called 'mother' and 'father' by children and everyone in the child's age group is a 'brother' or 'sister'. There is an overwhelming impression of very strong bonds existing within Pygmy bands.

In the villages, while the Pygmies may seem happy, they tend to adopt a rather servile attitude towards the Lese. In the forests, however, their servility disappears immediately, which is one reason you should try to go hunting with them. To the Pygmies, whose animal-tracking skills are legendary, hunting is the essence of their traditional livelihood even though gathering food is just as important.

Unlike those at Mt Hoyo to the east, the Epulu Pygmies hunt in large groups. Traditionally, a ritual fire is kindled at the start of the hunt; no one must kill more than is needed for food. They use a mixture of leaves, all with magical properties, to create smoke, then pass their bows and arrows over the ritual fire to enhance their chances of success. If a dog is nearby, it too may be passed through the smoke.

One of their techniques for catching animals is placing a series of nets on the ground, driving the animals into the mesh, then killing them with arrows or spears. Another is using poison-tipped arrows. The

Pygmies pound bark and exotic purple flowers in a heavy wooden mortar, then squeeze this pulp through a strainer until a black liquid drips into a bowl of leaves. The pin-shaped serrated wooden arrow tips are then dipped into the lethal liquid and hardened by fire.

If you take a 'grand tour' with the Pygmies, you will go hunting, sleeping and eating with them; you may even see a slaying of a black mamba snake or end up paddling in canoes with them down a river through the forest. Duiker and monkey are typical game animals hunted by Pygmies. If the Pygmies catch anything, you'll get to eat it with them. Frequently, however, all they return with is a few mushrooms, some giant snails, honey or wild yams, and sometimes fish.

Even if you don't go on a hunt, the Pygmies are so inundated with travellers on overland trucks that they will demand a tip just for sitting and talking and will beg for anything and everything. For this reason you should consider bypassing the Pygmies at Epulu and attempting instead to make contact with those living between Epulu and Mt Hoyo. Pygmies inhabit most of the Ituri forest region and few of them, except those near Epulu and Mt Hoyo, have ever encountered foreigners. (See the Mt Hoyo section later in this chapter.)

Fees Hunting or just visiting with the Pygmies is not difficult to arrange as all tours and hunts are handled through the park ranger's office. The fees per person include US$2 for park entry, US$5 for a three-hour bush walk with the Pygmies, and US$20 (plus US$8 per group which goes directly to the Pygmies) to go on a hunt; you must also pay a camera fee plus a small compulsory 'tip'. Payment can be in hard currency or zaïres.

ISIRO

Some 577 km north-east of Kisangani, Isiro is a possible stop if you're on your way to Garamba park, Sudan or eastern Zaïre. The *Mission Catholique* changes travellers' cheques and will even give you the money of your choice. They have also been known to let one or two travellers pitch a tent there, but groups are not welcome.

Places to Stay & Eat
For a cheap hotel, try the *Hôtel du Sport* near the football field. The best accommodation is at the 19-room *Hôtel Mangbetu*, which is a good block south of the main intersection, and the 26-room *Hôtel de l'Uélé*, which is on the northern side of town facing the hospital. Both have restaurants.

Getting There & Away
The 357-km trip east from Buta to Isiro can easily take four or five days as there is very little traffic on this route and you may have to wait several days for transport. If you were really lucky, you might be able to catch the Bumba to Isiro train but there are usually only one or two departures a month.

If you're headed to the Kivu region and you find a truck, you should anticipate the trip taking at least five days to Komanda; trucks from Isiro head there and further.

You can also fly to Isiro from Kinshasa on Scibé-Airlift, which has flights on Tuesdays and Sundays.

GARAMBA NATIONAL PARK
In the far north-eastern corner of the country bordering Sudan, and some 75 km west of the Ugandan border, Garamba park (492,000 hectares), established in 1938, is a fantastic, unheralded park that's well worth a visit if you're in north-eastern Zaïre. The main attractions are northern white rhinos and elephants. The park has a Land Rover which it rents to visitors for US$25 a day so that they can go looking for rhinos, giraffe and other animals.

Northern White Rhino
Fortunately, the rhinos are now being effectively protected and their numbers are increasing. Of the estimated 1300 northern white rhinos found in Zaïre in 1963, only 15 remained in 1984, making it one of the world's 12 most threatened animals. It was then that various conservation organisations began a concerted effort to save them. Kes Smith, who heads the effort, has set up an anti-poaching surveillance system combining poaching patrols on the ground with aerial surveillance, which she does from a Cessna. Chief park warden Mohindu Mesi says that the poachers have stopped hunting rhino altogether and switched their attention to buffalo (for meat). As a result, the rhino population has been increasing at a rate of about 10% per year, reaching 31 in 1992.

Elephant Project
The Garamba savannah park is the last habitat in the world of the white rhino and has been designated a World Heritage site. Equally unique is the elephant project here. The common belief worldwide is that the African elephant cannot be domesticated. This is false, as was proven long ago by the African elephant domestication centre here, the only one in the world, dating back to 1901. By independence in 1960, there were some 80 elephants in the Belgian-run centre, all trained as work animals, but with the ensuing civil war the project fell apart and the elephants returned to the bush. In recent years, the park has been rejuvenated with the help of the Worldwide Fund for Nature and the park staff have recaptured three 50-year-old females and a few of their youngsters. Remarkably, it is still possible to ride the old females!

Run by an English-speaking Belgian, Jean-Marc, the park is prepared to take visi-

White rhino

tors on a safari, riding the elephants as is done in Asia. One visitor who took the standard four-hour safari (US$50), and really enjoyed it, reported seeing a pack of wild dogs and fording a stream full of hippos. Jean-Marc also plans to offer three-day elephant safaris (in which the guests ride their own elephants), as well as trips with the locals to hunt small game. The park entrance fee is US$20.

Places to Stay & Eat
You can camp in the park for US$0.10 per tent or stay in an African-style hut for US$1. These may be paid for in zaïres; all other fees (park entrance, elephant safari and Land Rover hire) must be paid in hard currency. Plan on bringing most of your food as the park has very limited supplies, except for beer of which there is plenty.

Getting There & Away
Garamba is 335 km north-east of Isiro on the road to Aba (border post) and Juba (Sudan). The road is full of large holes and is often very muddy but it is no worse than the Kisangani to Bunia road. The trip from Isiro takes two days by private vehicle and much more if you're on local transport. The park entrance is at Nagero, not Gangala Na Bodio; the gate is four km north of the Dungu to Aba road. The park has no petrol or diesel to sell to visitors.

Eastern Zaïre

BUKAVU
On the southern edge of Lake Kivu, Bukavu (bou-kah-VOU), is one of the most picturesque cities in Zaïre. At an altitude of 1500 metres, and with a population of 250,000, it's also one of the most pleasant. Mobutu has a house here (one of many in Zaïre) and there are a number of schools including the Peace Corps training centre. (The centre was abandoned after the riots of 1991, but may reopen once conditions normalise.) Just below the training centre is a good place to take a dip in the lake. It's a beautiful lake and safe for swimming because the methane gas which seeps into the lake from beneath the lake bed kills off not only the fish but also the snails that carry bilharzia.

Since Bukavu became a separate province from Goma, and more and more traffic passes through Goma instead, the city's economy has been going downhill. However this could change with the completion of the direct road to Kisangani via the nearby Kahuzi-Biéga gorilla sanctuary. Meanwhile, as the economy suffers, so do the restaurants and nightclubs, which aren't so lively these days.

Orientation
The city's layout is easy to understand because many of the commercial establishments are along two major streets – Ave Président Mobutu, which winds south-eastward along the lake shore towards Kadutu, a major residential area for the working people, and Ave des Martyrs de la Révolution, which extends southward from Place du 24 Novembre near the centre for two km to Place Major Vangu. Most of the banks, major commercial establishments and pricier hotels plus the cathedral and the gorilla-booking office are along the former, while most of the cheap hotels, bars and restaurants, Marché Maman Mobutu (the main market) and truck parks are along the

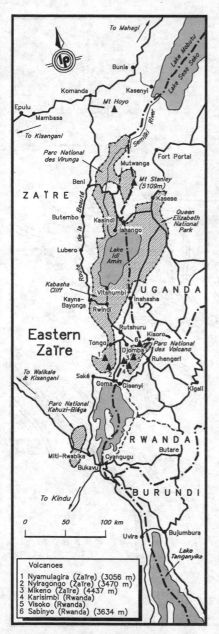

Eastern Zaïre

Volcanoes
1 Nyamulagira (Zaïre) (3056 m)
2 Nyiragongo (Zaïre) (3470 m)
3 Mikeno (Zaïre) (4437 m)
4 Karisimbi (Rwanda)
5 Visoko (Rwanda)
6 Sabinyo (Rwanda) (3634 m)

latter. The heart of the commercial district is just east of the Place du 24 Novembre.

Information
Money Like most places in Zaïre, banks in Bukavu are much more reluctant to cash travellers' cheques than in years past. Your best bet is the Banque Commerciale Zaïroise (BCZ), which is just north of the *carrefour* (intersection) on Ave Mobutu. Other banks to try are the UZB and the Banque du Peuple, both further south on the same street.

Foreign Consulates The Burundi Consulate is in the city centre at 184 Ave Mobutu; it accepts visa applications between 3 and 5 pm, Monday to Thursday. The process takes 24 hours. There's no Rwandan consulate but this is not a problem as you can get a 12-hour transit visa for US$6 or a full tourist visa for US$30 at the border.

Travel Agencies The two main travel agencies are AMIZA (☎ 2846/77), at 67 Ave Mobutu just south of the carrefour, and Somaco, which is 150 metres up the street at the Hôtel Résidence. Both agencies can arrange transport to Kahuzi-Biéga, but for bookings to see the gorillas you must go to the Institut Zaïrois pour la Conservation de la Nature (IZCN), which is two km further south-east at 185 Ave Mobutu, just beyond Place Mobutu.

Medical Services The Hôpital Général is on the road to Goma, half a km north of Place du 24 Novembre, and is staffed by US doctors. The cost of drugs and examinations is minimal.

One of the best pharmacies is Pharmakina (☎ 2073) at 186 Ave Mobutu, opposite the IZCN; another is Pharmacie Cophaza near AMIZA.

Places to Stay – bottom end
Most of the budget hotels, as well as the cheap bars and restaurants, are on Ave des Martyrs de la Révolution, which runs south from Place du 24 Novembre. It's a lively area, except when the electricity shuts down,

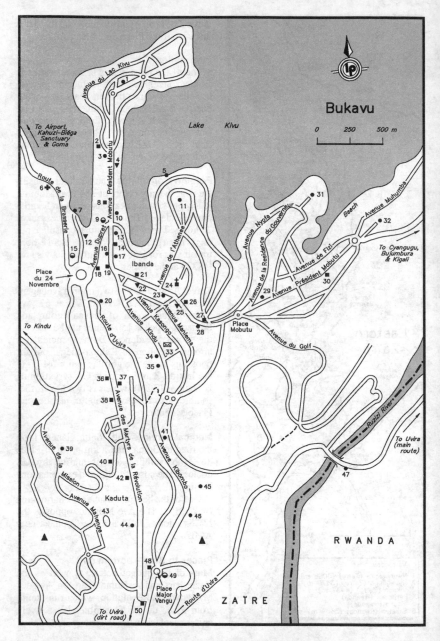

Bukavu

0   250   500 m

■ PLACES TO STAY

2 Hôtel Riviera
8 Hôtel Métropole & Hôtel Lolango I
14 Hôtel la Frégate
17 Hôtel Résidence
18 Hôtel Tchikoma
19 Hôtel Kéba
21 Hôtel Lolango II
26 Hôtel Belle-Vue
27 Hôtel Canadian
30 Nightclub du Tourist Hôtel
36 Hôtel Joli Logis
37 Hôtel Moderne
38 Hôtel Taifa
40 Hôtel de la Victoire
42 Hôtel Mondial
48 Hôtel Nambo
50 Ngerza Guesthouse

▼ PLACES TO EAT

2 Café Riviera
4 Pâtisserie du Kivu
12 Café du Peuple
14 Négrita Snackbar & Restaurant
22 Restaurant d'Éden
25 Restaurant Mama Na Bana
36 Restaurant ABC

OTHER

1 Hôtel de Ville
3 Le Coin des Artistes
4 Alimentation Moderne de Bukavu
5 Public Swimming Deck
6 Hôpital Général
7 Ferry Port
8 Scibé-Airlift
9 Taxi Stand
10 Banque Commerciale Zaïroise & Air Zaïre
11 Peace Corps Training Centre
12 Ferry Ticket Office
13 AMIZA Travel Agency, Pharmacie Cophaza & Bolingo General Store
15 Taxis to Kahuzi-Biéga Sanctuary
16 UZB Bank & Mobil Station
17 Somaco Voyages, Swala Airlines & VAC Airlines
18 Petrol Station
20 Prison
21 Banque du Peuple
22 Centre Culturel Français
23 Agetraf (Airline) & Alimentation Zaïre Supermarket
24 Nôtre Dame Cathedral
28 Burundi Consulate
29 Le Likimbé Artisan Shop & IZCN (Gorilla-Visit Bookings)
30 Nightclub du Tourist Hôtel
31 Résidence du Gouverneur
32 College Nôtre Dame
33 Post Office
34 TMK Air Commuter & Atelier de Sculpture Bois-Ivoire
35 Banque de Zaïre
39 Mission Catholique des Sœurs
41 Institut Superieur de Pédagogie (ISP)
43 Mobutu Stadium
44 Marché Maman Mobutu
45 Institut National des Mines
46 Voix de Zaïre
47 Ruzizi River Border Post
49 Buses to Uvira

which is much more frequent in this section than along Ave Mobutu. Starting about 800 metres south of the square there are a number of hotels. One that's very popular with travellers is *Hôtel Taifa*, which is one of the liveliest places in town, with good vibes and a large bar that's usually full of people. You can get a room with cold showers for US$2.50 and a meal for US$1.50. If you can take the noise and filthy shared toilets, it's highly recommended.

Hôtel Moderne (formerly Mareza), which is across the street and 50 metres north, is not recommended unless you can get one of the better rooms. It has a bar, which is dead in comparison to the Taifa's, and rooms for US$2.50, some of which are airy and fairly pleasant and others which are dingy and smelly without windows. Further south, and to the west on Ave de la Mission, you'll find *Hôtel de la Victoire*, which is a pretty dumpy place but better, with rooms for US$2.50 to US$3 and lively music. The rooms are well lit when there's electricity, and the sheets are clean but the bathrooms are fairly grubby.

Next in line is the friendly *Hôtel Mondial*, which is roughly half a km south of the Taifa on the same street and before the market. A large room with clean sheets and hot-water shower costs US$3.50. At the southern end of Ave des Martyrs de la Révolution is *Ngerza Guesthouse*, which is on a par with the Moderne. Nearby, facing Place Major Vangu you'll find still another cheapie, the cozy *Hôtel Nambo*. Despite being slightly remote and a bit more expensive than the others at US$4.75, it has much to recommend it – friendly staff, a quiet bar and restaurant, cold showers, reasonably clean communal toilets, large single beds, and clean, simple rooms that are safe for storing gear.

There are also several cheap hotels on Ave Mobutu. The best is the highly recommended *Hôtel Canadian* (☎ 2021), which is 200 metres east of the cathedral and opposite the Burundi Consulate. The hotel has nice views and a grass lawn, and most of the 10 rooms are in the US$6 to US$8 range. The more expensive rooms are large with two beds, private baths, and lounge chairs. One room costs only US$4 but it's invariably taken. Another is the poorly marked *Hôtel Kéba*, which is a single-storey, white building closer to the centre. A room with private bath costs US$6.50. As in many Zaïrian hotels, rates are higher for two men staying in the same room.

Places to Stay – middle

One of the best mid-range hotels is *Hôtel Joli Logis* (☎ 2487), on Ave des Martyrs de la Révolution before the Taifa. Well maintained, it has a central compound with ample parking space and a shaded area with grass, perfect for reading and relaxing. The 23 rooms range in price from US$5.50 to US$8. The cheapest have communal baths; the others have private baths and hot showers. All have clean sheets plus the staff is friendly and there's a bar but no restaurant; most important, it's reasonably quiet.

Closer to the centre, between Place du 24 Novembre and the carrefour on Ave Mobutu, is *Hôtel Tchikoma* (☎ 2977). The ambience is somewhat sterile but it has very tidy rooms for US$9.50 to US$12 plus a bar and restaurant. The more expensive rooms are spacious

and an excellent buy with balconies, two beds, clean tile baths and hot-water showers.

All the other mid-range hotels are on Ave Mobutu. Proceeding south along that avenue, the first is the relatively new *Hôtel Lolango I* (☎ 2907) and the much older three-storey *Hôtel Métropole* (☎ 2573); both are about 100 metres north of the carrefour. The Lolango has a restaurant and a more lively atmosphere than the Tchikoma. Clean rooms range in price from US$4.50 to US$30 but most are in the US$7.50 to US$15 category; those from US$12 have private baths and hot water. There's a 50% surcharge for two men in the same room. The Métropole, on the other hand, is poorly managed and not recommended. It has rooms with two beds and shared baths for US$7 (US$12 with private bath) and a popular bar but no restaurant.

Next in line is *Hôtel la Frégate*, which is close to the top-end Hôtel Résidence. The nicest feature of this old hotel is the courtyard out the back, which is filled with flowers, shrubbery and shade trees – perfect for drinks (there's no restaurant). Rooms range in price from US$7 to US$11; the most expensive ones have private baths. The rooms come with basins and lounge chairs but the beds are a little hard and the showers in the hallway bathrooms don't work, so you'll probably have to take a bucket bath.

About 100 metres further south is *Hôtel Lolango II*, which is similar to its sister hotel of the same name. Much further out at 260 Ave Mobutu you'll come to the *Guest House Tourist Hôtel Night-Club* (☎ 2445), which is better known as a nightclub than as a hotel, but apparently has rooms for rent.

Places to Stay – top end

The city's top hotel is the old 41-room *Hôtel Résidence* (☎ 2941; telex 41) in the centre of town at 89 Ave Mobutu. There are five classes of rooms ranging from US$30 to US$57 including breakfast. The rooms here are the nicest in town, but the hotel's ambience can be overly subdued. On the ground floor there's a travel agency, airline office, boutique, nightclub and a very good restaurant, the Bodega.

Personally, I prefer the *Hôtel Riviera* (☎ 2696) because the ambience is a little livelier, the restaurant is better, and there are good views of the lake from half of the 22 rooms. Also, the rooms are large, with comfortable chairs, ample closet space and clean baths; they are also slightly cheaper – US$28/41 for singles/doubles plus US$2.50 for breakfast. The more expensive singles/doubles (US$31/46) have telephones, and balconies overlooking the lake. Well managed by a friendly Italian woman married to a Zaïrian, it's popular with tour groups and properly maintained. It's just off the main drag at 67 Ave du Lac Kivu, a six-minute walk north of the carrefour.

For the lower price, I recommend *Hôtel Belle-Vue* (☎ 2266) which is on a hill and, as the name implies, has a superb view of the lake. Located at 143 Ave Mobutu just beyond the cathedral, a km south-east of the heart of town, it's well managed with 19 rooms. These are clean with spotless bathrooms, hot water, and comfortable chairs and cost US$20.

Places to Eat

A good place to look for cheap restaurants is along or near Ave des Martyrs de la Révolution but many of them close early, between 4 and 7 pm. *Restaurant ABC*, for example, which is next to the Hôtel Joli Logis, serves rice and beans for US$0.50 and steak & chips for US$1.25. The restaurant at *Hôtel Taifa* has similar fare and prices.

Another place open only during the day which travellers rave about is the *Café du Peuple*, which is behind the ferry port, near the small market there. The selection is limited, mostly omelettes, rice, potatoes, meat with sauce, and coffee, but the portions are large and the prices are rock-bottom.

Along Ave Mobutu, there are a number of places where you can get inexpensive food. There are two cheap restaurants near the cathedral; one is the friendly *Mama Na Bana*, which is about 70 metres east thereof. Open from 7 am to 8 pm, it serves excellent full meals for about US$1, including fufu (mashed yams), rice, ugali, omelettes and meat dishes. *Restaurant d'Édén*, which is about 200 metres closer to the centre on the same street, is similar in all respects. The popular *Négrita Snackbar & Restaurant*, which is at 81 Ave Mobutu just north of the Hôtel Résidence, is a workers' bar/restaurant and one of the best places for a beer and a light meal on Ave Mobutu, particularly Saturday nights when it really hops. It's open fairly late, which is unusual for Bukavu, and the speciality is grilled meat, served with soup, frites and salad (US$3 to US$4).

Much further north, about 250 metres beyond the Hôtel Métropole, are the town's best supermarket, *Alimentation Moderne de Bukavu*, and pastry shop, *Pâtisserie du Kivu*. The patisserie is a popular breakfast spot, with full breakfasts including eggs for around US$1.50. Across the street and next to Hôtel Riviera, is *Café Riviera*. It serves the best continental breakfast in town, with warm rolls and plenty of butter and jam; the cost is US$2.50. You can also get light meals there including sandwiches.

For continental food, try the hotels. The medieval décor at the *Bodega* in the Hôtel Résidence is quite attractive, but it's the food that makes this restaurant special. For about US$10, you can get a sumptuous three-course meal including drinks. For half that amount, you can get the Zaïrois special.

The city's best restaurant, however, is at the *Hôtel Riviera*. It has a large menu with similar prices; most main courses are in the US$4 to US$6 range. The restaurant at *Hôtel Belle-Vue* overlooks the lake and is not expensive, with most main dishes costing around US$4. For cheaper continental fare, try *Hôtel Lolango I* on Ave Mobutu; the meals there aren't bad and cost less.

Entertainment

Bukavu is full of small bars playing African music all night, especially along Ave des Martyrs de la Révolution. One of the better ones is the bar at *Hôtel Taifa*; like many of them it can get pretty wild as the night progresses.

For a brew on Ave Mobutu, head for the terrace of the *Hôtel Métropole* or the *Négrita*. They're about as lively as the bars get on that street and are quite unpretentious and inexpensive.

As for dancing, the choices are very slim these days. About the only time you'll find dancing is on the weekends. Your best bets are the nightclubs at *Hôtel Résidence* and *Hôtel Métropole*. You could also try *Club la Cave* at the Guest House Tourist Hôtel at 260 Ave Mobutu, well beyond the IZCN office.

For movies, some of the best are shown at the French cultural centre (☎ 2456) at 118 Ave Mobutu, a block north-west of the cathedral.

Things to Buy

Artisan Goods The best artisan shop by far is Le Coin des Artistes, which is 500 metres north of the main intersection on Ave Mobutu at the Ave du Lac Kivu junction. Run by the same people as the Hôtel Riviera next door, they sell excellent quality masks, statues and other artisan goods at very reasonable prices. Another shop with good-quality masks and other goods is Le Likimbé on Ave Mobutu, just beyond the IZCN office. There's also the Atelier de Sculpture Bois-Ivoire on Ave Kindu just north of the Banque de Zaïre on the same side of the street. You can watch the men carving, and then browse for possible purchases.

Lega wooden figurines

Music For cassettes of Zaïrian music, try Clip Inter on Ave Mahenge next to Stade Mobutu. It's open daily from 8 am to 9 pm.

Getting There & Away

Air Kuvumu airport is about 30 km north of town, where the paved road ends. The trip takes 40 minutes by taxi and costs US$15. Every day at 7.15 am and 2.15 pm, Somaco Voyages travel agency has a special bus from the Hôtel Résidence to the airport; the fare may be cheaper than a taxi.

There are various airlines serving Bukavu including Scibé-Airlift at 131 Ave Mobutu, 100 metres north of the carrefour; Air Zaïre (☎ 2162, 3162) at 59 Ave Mobutu, just north of the carrefour; Virunga Air Charters (VAC) and Swala, both at the Hôtel Résidence on Ave Mobutu; TMK Air Commuter on Ave Kindu, 800 metres south of the Hôtel Résidence; Air Charter Services (ACS); and Broussair. Reservations for ACS and Broussair can be made through the AMIZA and Somaco travel agencies on Ave Mobutu.

To/From Kinshasa Both ACS and Scibé-Airlift offer direct services between Bukavu and Kinshasa. ACS flights are on Mondays and Fridays, while Scibé flies on Sundays. The one-way fare to Kinshasa is US$335. If you can't get a seat on a direct flight to Kinshasa, fly via Goma.

ACS has three flights a week (Mondays, Thursdays, Fridays) from Kinshasa to Goma as does Scibé-Airlift (Wednesdays, Fridays, Sundays) and Air Zaïre (Tuesdays, Wednesdays and Saturdays).

To/From Goma The most popular destination from Bukavu is Goma; the one-way air fare is US$45. Scibé-Airlift, VAC, TMK, Swala and Broussair all provide services between the two cities. VAC and TMK offer a twice-daily service, while Swala provides a thrice-weekly service (Sundays, Wednesdays and Fridays) as does Scibé-Airlift (Mondays, Tuesdays and Thursdays). Most flights are full.

To/From Other Places As for other destinations, Swala has once-a-week flights to Kilembwe (Mondays), Kitutu (Tuesdays), Kama (Fridays) and Salamabila (Saturdays); while Broussair has flights to Beni, Bunia, Kisangani and other cities in the region. Similarly, Scibé-Airlift offers services on Mondays and Thursdays to Lubumbashi, Kongolo and Kalemie, and on Tuesdays to Kindu and Kisangani. All of these schedules are subject to frequent changes and, therefore, are illustrative only.

Bus & Truck While most travellers heading north to Goma (199 km) prefer to take the boat, you'll see the scenery at closer range going overland. There are two buses a week to Goma, leaving Bukavu on Tuesdays and Fridays and Goma on Wednesdays and Saturdays. The trip takes about six hours during the dry season and longer during the rainy season; the cost is about US$4. Buses leave at around 7 am from the Place du 24 Novembre.

The best place for catching trucks headed to Goma is at the BRALIMA brewery two km further north on the edge of Goma. The road is excellent and the scenery exhilarating.

By 1994, the new road connecting Bukavu and Kisangani should be completed, allowing you to travel to that city in about two days compared to up to two weeks via Goma.

If you're headed south to Uvira or Bujumbura, taxis and trucks leave from the Place Major Vangu at the southern end of Ave des Martyrs de la Révolution, two km south of the city centre. A minibus departs from there every day at around 7 am. (See the introductory Getting Around section regarding the visa complications for motorists or hitchhikers of crossing over into Rwanda on the way to Uvira.) Another place to look for trucks is Marché Maman Mobutu.

If you're headed to Kigali (Rwanda), after crossing the border at Cyangugu, you'll find minibuses waiting throughout the day to take you there. The cost is US$10 and the trip by paved road takes about five hours.

Boat Alternatively, you could take the ferry across Lake Kivu. There are three and none of them call at Rwandan ports. The best is the *Mulamba* which carries beer from the Primus brewery in Bukavu to Goma and has two classes. First-class seats are comfortable, not crowded and cost US$4 (US$8 during the high season), while those in 2nd-class are very crowded and cost US$2. Breakfast, which is included in the price of 1st-class tickets, and beer are available on board. The trip takes about 6½ hours. Tickets should be purchased not later than the morning of the preceding day; go to the port of the Primus brewery, which is two km north of town, or to ACT, which is on Ave Mobutu near the Hôtel Résidence.

The *Matadi* (better known as *La Vedette*), which is purely a passenger boat, also takes about 6½ hours. You must make a reservation at the main port near the city centre not later than the morning before; show up there before 9.30 am. The wait in the queue shouldn't take more than half an hour if you make your presence known. You'll need your passport and that of everyone for whom you'll be purchasing tickets. Once you get the ticket you will need to get it 'validated' at the customs office there as well – for a small fee. Seats are numbered and cost US$2. There's no restaurant but you can buy beer.

The much larger and slower *Karisimbi* (the *grand bateau* or big boat) carries cargo as well as passengers and the trip takes 10 hours. As with the Vedette, you should buy your ticket at the main port the morning of the preceding day; the price is the same. Similarly, there's plenty of Primus beer on board but no food.

The departure time for these boats is usually around 7 or 8 am. However, their schedules are constantly changing. Most recently the *Mulamba* was departing Bukavu on Thursdays, the *Karisimbi* on Wednesdays and Sundays, and the *Vedette* on Saturdays and Tuesdays. The schedule of the *Karisimbi* is particularly erratic and subject to frequent cancellations as departures depend in part on whether or not there's cargo.

You could also take the ferry on the Rwandan side (also called *La Vedette*) which ploughs twice weekly between Cyangugu (shan-GOU-gou), which is just across the border from Bukavu, and Gisenyi. For more information, see the Getting There & Away section under Gisenyi.

Getting Around

Taxis from the stand near the carrefour on Ave Mobutu cost US$1.25 to most destinations if you're by yourself, and much less if shared.

PARC NATIONAL DE KAHUZI-BIÉGA
The Gorillas

The gorillas in the Parc National de Kahuzi-Biéga are the major attraction. Don't miss the opportunity of seeing them, whatever it costs, because the experience is guaranteed to be worth 20 times that. Seeing a lion while you're protected in a vehicle is one thing; crawling through bamboo forest for several hours and finding a silver-back gorilla standing just a few metres in front of you is quite another. You'll never forget looking into a gorilla's brown, intelligent, curious eyes staring unblinking at you.

Parc logo

The species here is the eastern lowland gorilla, not the mountain gorilla found in Virunga park and Rwanda, and is more numerous, with an estimated 540 gorillas distributed among 20 families in the park area. Unlike the chimpanzee-like lowland gorillas found in Gabon, the CAR, Congo and other areas of Zaïre, the Kahuzi-Biéga gorillas are large (about the same size as the mountain gorilla), so you definitely won't be disappointed. Weighing up to 200 kg, one of these gorillas could seemingly kill you in seconds. Yet this is unlikely because they are not flesh-eaters, and couldn't care less about humans. Their favourite munchies are young bamboo and stalks of wild celery. All they care about other than food is protecting their young, which are accustomed to a lot of body contact. If you get too close, the unpredictable male may pound the ground with his huge fists, stand up and growl, rip down small trees and stare at you in a threatening manner.

A typical family group in this area has anywhere from six to 20 gorillas. The average family size in Kahuzi-Biéga is one dominant silver-back male, seven adults (males and females), five young gorillas and three babies. It is normal for female gorillas to transfer from their natal group into other groups or to join lone silver-backs, but it is rare for males to transfer to a new group. If the dominant silver-back coughs or grunts at the others, he is indicating displeasure or reprimanding them.

The park, which is in a mountainous jungle area, was the first in Africa – even before those in Rwanda – to allow viewing of gorilla families conditioned to humans. However, the park wasn't well managed and until the late 1980s any number of people could view the gorillas, even very closely, making them very susceptible to human disease, particularly measles and hook worm. Fortunately, the park management is now vastly improved and only eight people are allowed to see a family at any one time.

There are numerous gorilla families in the park as well as chimpanzees, monkeys, buffalo, antelope, and forest elephants, which you probably won't see. Only four of the gorilla families (No 1 Maheshe, No 2 Mushamuka, No 3 Mubalala and No 4 Mbayo) have been conditioned to accept human visitors. The groups range in size from about nine members in the Mbayo group to over 25 members in other groups. Sightings are not guaranteed, but the park wardens keep a daily watch on their family and know where they were last seen. Finding them normally takes one or two hours, so you may be back in Bukavu by early afternoon. Sometimes, however, it takes all day. Tipping the guide and trackers is customary.

Unless you go between June and mid-September, bring wet-weather gear as it'll be rainy and muddy. Also, be prepared for lots of tramping through thick jungle and up steep hillsides covered with vegetation, with lots of slipping and sliding along the way. Gloves can be useful since you'll be pulling on lots of vines as you climb up the slopes.

Other Attractions
Park visitors can also hire a guide at park headquarters to take them to the summit of **Mt Kahuzi** (3308 metres), which takes three hours from the base to the top, or to **Mt** Bugulumiza (2400 metres), which has a six-km road to the summit, or to a **Pygmy village** on the outskirts of the park. The Pygmies, who charge only US$1 per traveller to see their village, have been forced out of the park in order to protect the gorillas; instead of hunting, many of them now eke out an existence by farming. The most lucrative crop they grow is marijuana, which all of them smoke.

Bookings & Fees
For reservations, go to the national park office (IZCN) in Bukavu at 185 Ave Mobutu. The office is open weekdays from 8.30 am to 3 pm and Saturdays from 8.30 am to noon. If you don't have time to get one, you could try your luck showing up at the park by 8 or 8.30 am as it is occasionally still possible, especially during the week, to see them without a reservation since there are not many tourists in this area, at least compared to Rwanda. The park is open every day, even on holidays. Children under 15 are not allowed.

The park fee is US$120, which must be paid in hard currency or travellers' cheques; 25% goes to the park and 75% to the government. The fee for taking gorilla photos and videos is US$0.50 and US$20, respectively, and tipping the guides and trackers is customary. For cameras, bring ASA 1000 film or higher for best results, as the forest blocks much of the daylight.

Places to Stay & Eat
For a very small fee, you can camp at the park headquarters or stay at the hut there which has two rooms and six beds but no water. (There are plans to build tourist accommodation and a restaurant.) In addition, there is reportedly a camp site in the middle of the forest on the banks of the Musisi River, 10 km from the park headquarters by rough dirt road; inquire at the park headquarters for information. There's no food so you'll have to bring your own from Bukavu or buy some at the small market in **Miti**.

Getting There & Away

The sanctuary is 31 km north of Bukavu by paved road. Follow the asphalt road north towards Goma for 24 km until you come to Miti, a tiny village with a sign pointing to the left. The park entrance at Tshivanga Station is seven km up the hill. The cheapest way to get here from Bukavu is to take a truck or bus to Miti and hike from there. However, plan on taking two days because if you arrive after 9.30 pm, the guide will have departed. The simplest way is to arrange for transport through AMIZA or hire a taxi. If you bargain well, the one-way taxi fare shouldn't be more than US$15. The cost will quadruple if he waits. Getting a ride back is simple; almost anyone returning to Bukavu will take you. Also plenty of trucks pass through Miti. On the way back you will pass through **Moudaka** (mou-DAK-ah), which has a big market Sundays and Wednesdays – well worth a look.

GOMA

Goma (population 150,000) is the starting point for expeditions up the nearby volcanoes, Nyiragongo and Nyamulagira, and to see the gorillas and wild game in Virunga park, which begins only 13 km to the north. The city is nothing special but it is lively, especially at night when the bars and dancing joints get started. The people of Goma and elsewhere in eastern Zaïre are very open about political matters and not so suspicious of foreigners, so fraternising with them can be rewarding. Chances are they'll curse Mobutu and say let's drink to that.

At an altitude of 1500 metres, Goma's climate is ideal but the views of the lake don't compare to those in Bukavu and Gisenyi. The city's commercial district is over a km from the lake, so unlike in Bukavu or Gisenyi you'll rarely see it walking around town. To get a good view of it, the nearby volcanoes and lava fields, climb **Mt Goma** on the western outskirts of town – an easy three-hour trip up and down.

Orientation

The main drag, Ave Mobutu, heads north-west from the lake through the heart of town towards the airport on the northern outskirts. About one km inland on that avenue you'll come to the first of three roundabouts, Rond-Point de la Poste. The post office, four banks, the tourist information office and three hotels are at or just off this circle, which is the largest of the three. The main side street to the north-east, Ave du 20 Mai, leads to the airport while that to the west, Ave du Rond-Point, leads to the port. Proceeding further north on Ave Mobutu you'll pass various establishments, shops and restaurants. East and north-east of the second rond-point is where you'll find the market and most of the bottom-end hotels, while a km to the west you'll find the Cercle Sportif, which is the major camping ground.

Information

Tourist Office The Office National du Tourisme (ONT) is just north of the Rond-Point de la Poste, half a block north of the post office and a block east of Ave Mobutu. The people there are friendly and a good source of information; they are also responsible for issuing free photo permits good for this region only. One of the city's major travel agencies, Kivu Voyage, is next door.

Money Because of all the economic turmoil in Zaïre, banks are strapped for cash and are very reluctant to accept travellers' cheques. Even if they do accept yours, the amount they'll change may be very limited. The best bank to try is the Banque Commercial Zaïroise at the Rond-Point de la Poste; it's faster than the other banks and has very low commissions. Others at the rond-point include the Union Zaïroise des Banques (UZB); the Nouvelle Banque de Kinshasa (NBK) and the Banque Zaïroise du Commerce Extérieure (BZCE). The banks are open weekdays until 11.30 am but you must get there by 11 am if you have travellers' cheques. To avoid the banks, try the Masques Hôtel as it sometimes changes money, even for nonguests.

Consulates The Ugandan Consulate, which

is on Ave Mobutu and open weekdays from 10 am to 2 pm, charges US$20 for visas and issues them in 24 hours. Belgium no longer has a consulate here and there is no Rwandan consulate but at the border you can get a 12-hour transit visa to Rwanda for US$6 or a regular tourist visa for US$30. The main border post is on the south-eastern outskirts of town on the paved road to Gisenyi. The transit visa is theoretically good for only 12 hours but there's nothing on the stamp to indicate this, so some travellers have used the transit visas for much longer visits and experienced no problems when leaving. Visa extensions are obtainable from the immigration office in Kigali and cost about US$15. However, extending a cheap transit visa costs US$40 and is valid for only seven days.

Immigration Immigration issues Zaïrian visa extensions on the spot and charges only US$3 for one-month visa extensions (from the date of the extension, not from the expiration of the original visa) and requires no photos or forms to complete. Remember: if you overextend your visa, you'll be fined US$2 a day.

Travel Agencies The three principal travel agencies are AMIZA (☎ 23390) at 90 Ave Mobutu, one block south of the second rond-point; Kivu Voyage, next to ONT, a block north of the Rond-Point de la Poste; and Zaïre Safari (☎ 540) at the Masques Hôtel.

Gorilla Visits

For bookings to visit the gorillas, see the Institut Zaïroise pour la Conservation de la Nature (IZCN), which is on Ave Mobutu, a block south of the second rond-point and next to AMIZA. Kivu Voyage, IZCN and AMIZA are all good places to look for potential rides with other travellers to Djomba (three hours by private vehicle), the main starting point for seeing the gorillas.

All of the travel agencies in Bukavu rent minivans with chauffeurs for viewing the gorillas and visiting Virunga park. All-inclusive tours are more expensive – US$330 per person for a couple and US$225 per person

for groups of four. So the larger the group, the lower the cost per person.

Places to Stay – bottom end

Two of the best-value places are the *Mission Catholique* and the *Centre d'Accueil Protestante* (formerly the Hôtel Tuneko) next door. To get there from the Rond-Point de la Poste, go 400 metres west on Ave du Rond-Point; they'll be on your left, just off the road. The mission is in an unmarked yellow building and charges US$6/7.50 for tiny, spotlessly clean singles/doubles with basins and shared cold showers. It also has a library and you can get a meagre breakfast here for US$0.50. However, there are two big minuses – a 10 pm curfew, and a sister who rules the place with an iron fist, giving the place a very austere ambience.

I much prefer the Centre d'Accueil Protestante (☎ 549), which is friendly and popular but often full. It has 20 large singles/doubles for US$6/7.50 with shared hot-water showers and a very decent inexpensive restaurant, with English breakfasts for US$2.40 and slightly more expensive regular meals throughout the day.

Among the hotels, virtually all of them impose a 50% surcharge for two men sharing the same room. One of the most popular hotels with travellers on the cheap is *Hôtel Couboki* (formerly Hôtel Abki), which charges US$3 to US$4.75 for a room. The rooms are basic and dirty but the shared bucket baths are marginally clean and there's a cheap restaurant plus the people are friendly and will let you store gear while you climb the volcanoes. About 250 metres north-east of the second rond-point, this unmarked place is off the same north-south street as the market (50 metres off the street), so you may have to ask to find it.

If it's too dumpy, try the *Hôtel Touriste*, which is a simple hotel half a block to the south on the same street and on the opposite side, the friendly *Hôtel Amani*, which is another 250 metres further north-east, or *Hôtel Lumumba*, which is about half a km north-east of the Rond-Point de la Poste on the road to the airport. None of them have

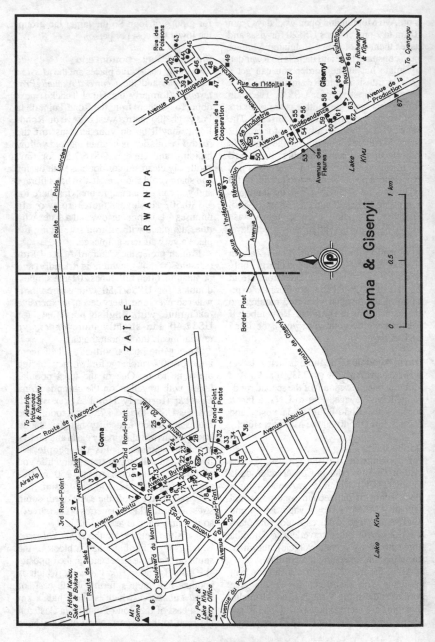

Goma & Gisenyi

■ PLACES TO STAY

4   Hôtel Amani
5   Hôtel Couboki
10 Hôtel Touriste
18 Jambo Hôtel
23 RIF Hôtel
28 Hotel Lumumba
29 Centre d'Accueil Protestante &
    Mission Catholique
32 Masques Hôtel
34 Hôtel des Grands Lacs
38 Hôtel Édelweiss
47 L'Auberge de Gisenyi
49 Centre d'Accueil de l'Église
    Presbytérienne
50 Hôtel Régina
60 Hôtel Palm Beach
62 Hôtel Izuba-Méridien

▼ PLACES TO EAT

2   Restaurant
9   Restaurant Afia Safi
13 Kairuza Rendez Vous Restaurant
17 Mapendo Salon de Thé
19 Bar Tora-Tina
21 Salon de Thé la Michaudiére
36 Le Nyira Restaurant
39 Restaurant Gar
40 Restaurant Bon Samaritan
41 Restaurant Pacifique
48 Restaurant Inyenyeli
67 Bar-Restaurant Bikini Tam-Tam

    OTHER

1   Mobil Station
3   Market
6   Cercle Sportif
7   Petrol Station
8   Fina Petrol Station
11 Artisan Shop
12 Air Zaïre

13 Small Grocery Store
14 Grocery Store
15 AMIZA Travel Agency & IZCN
    (Virunga Park & Gorilla-Visit
    Bookings)
16 Agetraf (Airline)
20 Feelings Club
22 Kivu Voyage, ONT Office & Pharmacy
23 Buses to Bukavu
24 SK Bar-Dancing
25 Hôtel de Ville
26 Banque Zaïroise du Commerce
    Extérieure (BZCE)
27 Post Office & Nouvelle Banque de
    Kinshasa (NBK)
29 Buses to Butembo
30 UZB Bank
31 Banque Commerciale Zaïroise (BCZ)
32 Virunga Air Charters (VAC) & Zaïre
    Safari
33 Scibé-Airlift
35 La Calabasse Night-Club
37 Club des Loisirs
42 Boulangerie & Grocery Store
43 Pharmacy
44 Market
45 Taxis
46 Gare Routière
47 Petrol Station
51 Post Office
52 Banque de Kigali
53 Ferry Port to Cyangugu
54 Banque Commerciale du Rwanda
55 Grocery Store
56 Papeterie
57 Hospital
58 Toyota-Mercedez Garage
59 Crafts Shop
61 La Boutik
63 Boulangerie
64 Petrol Station
65 Alimentation Dolly's
66 Fina Petrol Station

restaurants but all three places have clean rooms with good showers. At US$2.50 for a room, the Amani is the best deal. The Lumumba charges US$3 to US$4.50 for its rooms, while the Touriste, which is very scruffy with lots of resident families, charges US$4.50 for doubles (US$9 with private bath).

If price is your only concern, try *Hôtel Soto Toki*, which charges US$2.75 for a double and is conveniently located on the street behind the well-known, mid-range RIF Hôtel. *Chambres Aspro*, which may be closed, and *Hôtel Macho Kwa Macho* facing it are two others with similar rock-bottom prices but which are further from the centre. All three places are filthy dumps with bed-bugs but you won't find anywhere cheaper.

To get to these last two from the Rond-Point de la Poste, head north-east for about a km on the road to the airport (Ave du 20 Mai) and ask directions from there; the hotels are to your left down a side street.

You can also camp at the *Cercle Sportif* on the western outskirts of town for US$1 per person but during the June to September period it's frequently full. It has a cheap restaurant, but the facilities are filthy as the flush toilets are often not working and there's only one shower. Most important, there have been numerous instances of theft here, also serious muggings, and the guard, who appears to be in cahoots with the thieves, does nothing to stop it. So camping here is very risky and not recommended.

Places to Stay – middle & top end

Of the mid-range hotels, the cheapest is the *RIF Hôtel* (☎ 320), which faces the north-eastern side of the Rond-Point de la Poste. It has large singles/doubles with shared bath for US$9.50/15 and doubles with private bath for US$21. The baths are clean and have hot water but no shower attachments, and the restaurant is terrible, with few clients and awful breakfasts for US$2.25. The street-side terrace, however, is not bad for drinks and people-watching. The newly refurbished, 17-room *Jambo Hôtel* (formerly Hôtel Mont Goma) (☎ 559) has better rooms with two beds and good showers for US$27 but there's no hot water. It's a block west of the Rond-Point de la Poste, and has a bar and restaurant.

Next in line is the colonial-era *Hôtel des Grands Lacs* (☎ 308), which is on Ave Mobutu, 150 metres south of the Masques. Not well managed, it's a big, old hotel with 51 rooms and an empty pool out the back. The rooms in the older wing are large and frayed and cost US$21; those in the newer wing cost US$26 to US$33. The showers have hot water, and prices include breakfast. The bar and restaurant are attractive and popular, plus the nightclub, *La Calabasse*, is one of the two best in town.

Goma's top hotels are *Hôtel Karibu* and *Masques Hôtel* (☎ 540). Many travellers on package tours stay at the Karibu. It's eight km west of town on the lake's edge and has a pool and 100 rooms at US$50/68 a single/double including breakfast. You can get to know Goma better, however, if you stay at the Masques Hôtel, which is in the heart of town facing the Rond-Point de la Poste. It's a pleasant, well-managed hotel with a clean, medium-length pool, a travel agency, and 62 rooms for US$43/54 a single/double including breakfast. Even if you don't stay here, come here in the early evening for a drink as the popular open-air bar often has an orchestra.

Places to Eat

One of the most popular places with overland travellers is the *Tora-Tina*, which is 1½ blocks north of the Rond-Point de la Poste on Ave Mobutu. It's mainly a bar but it also serves decent food including grilled fish, steak, fries and beef brochettes. Another favourite is the *Salon de Thé la Michaudière* across the street. It's one of the best pastry shops in town but it's much more than a pastry shop as you can get relatively inexpensive full meals including hamburgers and decent coffee here as well. As with the Tora-Tina, there are tables outside facing the street. Both places are open late.

Also popular with overland travellers is the *Mapendo Salon de Thé*, which is a block further north. It's primarily a bakery and pastry shop but you can also get relatively expensive breakfasts here, as well as excellent meals similar to those at Tora-Tina.

One of the better inexpensive restaurants is the *Restaurant Yeneka* at the Centre d'Accueil Protestante. You can get a huge breakfast there for US$2.40 and full meals throughout the day for US$3 to $3.50 plus drinks.

Another place definitely worth checking out is the *Kairuza Rendez Vous Restaurant* (formerly Restaurant la Familia), which is two blocks east of the second rond-point. It's a family-run restaurant and you can have virtually anything you ask for including Zaïrian dishes. Next door is a small grocery which sells eggs and the famous Goma cheese (a favourite with travellers) which is reasonably priced. There's also a larger grocery store on Ave Mobutu, one block south of the same rond-point.

The city's top restaurant is *Le Nyira*, which is just south of Hôtel des Grands Lacs and 50 metres to the east down a sideroad. A typical meal there costs from US$10 to US$15. The restaurants at the nearby *Hôtel des Grands Lacs* and *Masques Hôtel* are quite decent but not cheap; a typical meal at either place costs at least US$10.

Entertainment
Bars A great place for a drink during the day or at night is *Tora-Tina*, a bar on Ave Mobutu, 1½ blocks north of the Rond-Point de la Poste, which is popular with Zaïrians and expatriates alike. Large Primus beers cost US$0.90 and you can also get brochettes there and other snacks. The *Michaudière* across the street is also popular for drinks and is open late.

The open-air bar at the Masques Hôtel usually has a Zaïrian band playing Tuesdays to Saturdays between 7 and 11 pm. There's no charge except for the beers, and whether you're interested in the music or not, it's a good place for a drink.

Nightclubs Two of the fancier dancing spots are *La Calabasse* across from the Hôtel des Grands Lacs and the *Feelings Club* across from the ONT office; both are very lively on Friday and Saturday nights. My favourite, however, is the *S K Bar & Dancing* a block behind the RIF Hôtel. There's a sizeable dance floor and the ambience is great, with large beers for less than US$1. It's for working people and really hops at night especially on weekends when it's very crowded; you can hear the music from a long way off so you shouldn't have any problem finding it.

Getting There & Away
Air The airport is on the northern outskirts of town, three km from the Rond-Point de la Poste. There's an airport tax of US$5 on all flights.

To/From Kinshasa ACS has three flights a week to/from Kinshasa (Mondays, Thursdays, Fridays) as does Scibé-Airlift (Wednesdays, Fridays, Sundays) and Air Zaïre (Tuesdays, Wednesdays, Saturdays); these airlines also provide services to Kisangani as does Agetraf (Thursdays via Bunia). BAL, which has no city office, also has flights to/from Kinshasa; inquire at the airport or at one of the travel agencies.

To/From Bukavu The most popular destination from Bukavu is Goma. Scibé-Airlift, Virunga Air Charter (VAC), TMK Air Commuter, Swala and Broussair all provide services between the two cities. VAC and TMK offer a twice-daily service, while Swala provides a thrice-weekly service (Sundays, Wednesdays and Fridays) as does Scibé-Airlift (Mondays, Tuesdays and Thursdays). Most flights are in the morning (at around 8 am) and again in the afternoon at around 4 pm; the cost is US$45.

To/From Elsewhere in Zaïre You can also fly from Goma to Beni, Bunia, Kindu and Isiro. Scibé-Airlift, VAC and Agetraf have flights to Beni on Sundays, Wednesdays and Fridays, respectively, while TMK has flights on Mondays, Wednesdays, Fridays and Sundays. Broussair also serves Beni. For flights to Bunia, try TMK (Mondays and Fridays), Agetraf (flights Thursdays and Fridays) or Broussair. Air Zaïre, Scibé Airlift and Agetraf have flights to Kindu as does Broussair, which also serves Isiro.

VAC and Scibé-Airlift are located just west of the Masques Hôtel, while Broussair, Air Zaïre and Agetraf are all on Ave Mobutu. Reservations for TMK and Swala flights can be made through Kivu Voyages. Typical one-way fares are US$70 to Kindu, US$115 to Kisangani, US$125 to Beni, US$145 to Bunia and US$300 to Kinshasa. Fares are usually payable in hard currency only.

To/From Rwanda You can also fly to Goma from Kigali in Rwanda on Saturdays with Air Rwanda.

Bus Travellers headed to Bukavu (199 km) usually take the boat but you'll see the scenery at closer range by taking a bus or truck. The road is in excellent condition during the dry season; during the rainy season you should inquire about the condition before taking a bus. There is one bus ploughing back and forth between the two cities and its schedule is constantly changing. Most recently it was leaving Goma on Wednesdays and Saturdays, and Bukavu on Tuesdays and Fridays. The trip takes about six hours during the dry season and longer during the rainy season. The bus costs US$4 and leaves between 7 and 8 am from the RIF Hôtel.

Bus connections to Butembo are provided by Butembo Bus Safari. Buses leave Goma at 5.30 am on Wednesdays, Thursdays, Saturdays and Sundays. The fare is US$6 and the departure point is the Accueil Protestante, three blocks west of the Rond-Point de la Poste. You must purchase your ticket no later than the morning of the preceding day, otherwise you'll never get a seat. Direct service to Beni and Bunia has been discontinued but could be revived; for information, ask at Butembo Bus Safari.

There are also daily buses to Rutshuru leaving Goma at around 2 pm and Rutshuru at 6.15 am. In Goma the bus departs from Le Bon Voyage Rutshuru; get there several hours ahead of time to get a seat. The 75-km trip takes up to four hours and the fare is US$2.50.

From Goma to Kigali (Rwanda) you can walk or take a taxi over to Gisenyi and then board one of the numerous minibuses connecting Gisenyi and Kigali, a three-hour trip.

Truck Two places to look for trucks headed north or south are the market and the third rond-point.

Car For viewing the gorillas or visiting Virunga park, you can rent a 10-seater van with driver for US$100 a day plus US$1 per km from AMIZA, Kivu Voyage or Zaïre Safari. Seeing the gorillas can be done in one

day but to see the Rwindi plains you need at least two days to cover most of the tracks.

Boat The port, which is a good 30-minute walk west from the central area, is where you buy tickets for the three boats connecting Goma with Bukavu. Purchase your ticket no later than the morning of the preceding day; you must bring your passport and that of everyone for whom you'll be purchasing tickets. The departure hour for these boats is usually between 7 and 8 am. Schedules are constantly changing, so those that follow are illustrative only: the *Mulamba* departs Bukavu on Thursdays and Goma on Saturdays; the *Karisimbi* departs Bukavu on Wednesdays and Sundays and Goma on the following days; and the *Vedette* departs Bukavu on Saturdays and Tuesdays and Goma on Sundays and Wednesdays. The *Karisimbi* is much more unreliable than the other two as sailings are often changed or cancelled for lack of cargo. For more details, see the Getting There & Away section under Bukavu.

Alternatively, you could take the Rwandan boat ploughing between Gisenyi and Cyangugu as the trip is equally pleasant and scenic. For details, see the Getting There & Away section under Gisenyi.

Getting Around
Taxis are fairly plentiful and cost about US$1.25 for most trips in town and less when shared. The normal fare to the airport is also US$1.25 but drivers will try to charge you triple that amount.

GISENYI
If you're in Goma and the idea of lying on the beach or visiting a small lake resort sounds appealing plus you have a multiple-entry visa to Zaïre, consider crossing the Rwandan border two km away and spending the day and/or night in Gisenyi. It's a delightful town right on the lake and half the size of Goma. You probably won't find taxis at the border, but Gisenyi is only a 30-minute walk from the border, which is open from 7 am to 6 pm for foreigners. Many travellers spend

the night here before visiting Rwanda's Volcans park, where you can see gorillas and climb more volcanoes.

Money

There are several banks in town for changing money including the Banque Commerciale du Rwanda, which is open weekdays from 7.45 to 11 am and 2 to 6 pm and Saturdays from 7.45 am to 1 pm. The black-market rate, however, is somewhat more favourable.

Activities

You could try your luck at renting a sailboard or Hobie cat from the Meridien although they are usually available only to guests at the hotel. The beach is accessible to everyone.

Places to Stay – bottom end

Gisenyi has two good inexpensive places to stay, both very near the market, a 10-minute walk to the beach. The most popular is the *Centre d'Accueil de l'Église Presbytérienne* (☎ 40397/522), which is a block south of the market. It charges US$3 per person in a four-bed dormitory room and US$5/8 for singles/doubles with shared bath (US$8/13 with private bath). The management is friendly and there is a spacious lawn for relaxing in the sun and talking to Africans who are here for church training.

If it's full, try the *L'Auberge de Gisenyi* (☎ 40620), which is a block to the north of the Centre d'Accueil. The rooms are tiny but they are very clean as are the attached baths with working showers. Singles/doubles cost US$10/15 including breakfast.

Places to Stay – middle & top end

My favourite mid-range hotel is the ever-popular *Hôtel Édelweiss* (☎ 40282), which is on the northern end of the main drag, 100 metres off the lake and a 10-minute walk from the centre. You can get clean rooms here with comfortable beds, private baths and hot water for US$15 to US$17. Run by a Belgian and his Zaïrian wife, this homey, family-run establishment resembles a Swiss chalet and has a great restaurant and a

delightful front veranda for drinks. On occasion the owners have allowed travellers with vehicles to camp out the back.

If the Édelweiss is full, try the African-run *Hôtel Régina* (☎ 40263), which is 250 metres south on Ave de la Révolution. It's not well managed and has a dreary ambience, but it's directly on the water, the rooms and bathrooms are clean, and the outdoor restaurant serves excellent grilled chicken and fish. Singles/doubles cost from US$15/20.

Next in line is the *Hôtel Palm Beach* (☎ 40304), which is four blocks south on the same street, a block before the Méridien. Overlooking the lake, it's the city's second-best hotel and has rooms (no singles) with hot-water private baths for US$26. This place is a hang-out for expats, particularly the bar, and the management seems to shun scruffy travellers.

The city's top hotel is the *Izuba-Méridien* (☎ 40381/2; fax 40605; telex 561). It's a block away in the heart of town on the beach and accepts all major credit cards except Visa. Singles/doubles cost US$70/85 at the official exchange rate; the facilities include a tiny bookshop, pool, tennis courts, and sailboards and Hobie cats for hire.

Places to Eat

The cheapest places to eat are all near the market. Many of them, including a small grocery store and bakery, are on Rue des Poissons, which runs along the northern side of the market. At *Restaurant Bon Samaritan* and *Restaurant GAR*, for example, you can get a meal, typically rice, beans and matoke, for US$1 to US$1.50.

Restaurant Inyenyeli, which is across the street from the Centre d'Accueil, is a notch up; full meals there cost from US$2. Still another in the same category is the restaurant at the *L'Auberge de Gisenyi*, which has full meals for US$4. For inexpensive food near the lake, head for the *Bar-Restaurant Bikini Tam-Tam*, which is on the southern end of town on Ave de la Production facing the water. You can get a decent meal there for US$5 plus drinks.

The food at *Hôtel Édelweiss* is good but a

meal will cost you US$10 to US$15 plus
drinks and the service is very slow. You'll do
much better eating at the paillote restaurant
behind it which serves grilled tilapia fish for
US$3.

At night on weekends, head for the *Club
des Loisirs*, where there's usually a band
playing. If you want, you can just hang out
at the bar without paying the cover charge.
It's only 100 metres west of the Hôtel Edelweiss on the dirt road to Goma. If you're just
looking for a beer, the cheapest places are
around the market but for a relaxing ambience you can't beat the front terrace of the
Édelweiss.

Things to Buy

La Boutik, which is next to the Hôtel Izuba-
Meridien, has a good selection of artisan
goods as does the crafts shop a block behind
it on the main drag, Ave de l'Indépendance.

Getting There & Away

Minibus & Taxi From Goma you have the
choice of walking or taking a taxi to the
border, but from there you will probably
have to walk for 30 minutes to Gisenyi as
there are frequently no taxis at the border.
The same goes when you travel from Gisyeni
to Goma.

Minibuses to Ruhengeri and Kigali depart
frequently from the gare routière at the
market.

Boat The *Nyungwe*, better known as 'La
Vedette', is a small boat with approximately
40 seats which ploughs twice-weekly between Gisenyi and Cyangugu, stopping at
Kirambo and Kibuye en route. As with the
Zaïre ferries, the schedule is constantly
changing. Most recently it was departing
Gisenyi on Wednesdays and Saturdays and
Cyangugu on Mondays and Thursdays, all at
around 6 am. The fare to Cyangugu is US$7
and the trip takes about 6½ hours. The boat
leaves from the main dock between the
Meridien and Hôtel Regina and you can buy
your ticket from the boat operator on the
morning of departure.

RUTSHURU

Some 75 km north of Goma by an excellent
dirt road, Rutshuru is a major hub on the
southern side of Virunga park. The Ugandan
border is 67 km to the north at **Inshasha** and
less than 30 km to the east. Djomba (for
gorilla viewing) and Tongo (for chimpanzee
viewing) are just 27 km to the south-east and
south-west, respectively, while the heart of
the Rwindi plains (for wildlife viewing) is 57
km to the west. Much closer to town, there
are two other tourist attractions – the **Chutes
de Rutshuru**, which are some waterfalls just
south-west of town, and the *sources d'eaux
chaudes* (warm springs) of **Mayi Ya Moto**,
which are about 15 km west of town towards
Rwindi. Both are popular stops on organised
tours.

Places to Stay & Eat

One of the cheapest hotels is *Hôtel Ba-
tungea*, which charges US$2 for a clean but
noisy room; you can also get good food
there. Another good-value place is *Hôtel
Gremafu*, which is on the main drag near the
truck park. It has singles/doubles with
private bath for US$3/4, a sporadic water
supply, electricity for a few hours at night, a
bar, and meals if you order in advance. You'll
also find a similarly-priced hotel on the main
drag on the western side of town (as well as
the *Concorde* restaurant in the centre). You
can stay at the friendly *Mission Catholique*,
for about US$6/8. It welcomes travellers and
has a guesthouse about four km outside
town; you can eat there as well and you may
be able to camp. The *Katata Hôtel* is still
another.

Getting There & Away

There are several minibuses a day between
Rutshuru and Goma. The 75-km trip south
to Goma can take up to four hours by minibus
and costs US$2.50. It's another four hours by
truck north to Inshasha and the Ugandan
border (closed Sunday); they leave around
5.30 am and typically charge US$2. The ride
is very bumpy but the scenery is great. In
Inshasha you'll find a cheap hotel near

customs, a restaurant in town as well as a market but little else.

BUTEMBO

As you're travelling north from the Rwindi plains to Butembo (165 km), you'll be passing through the Rift Valley and along the Route de la Beauté, which affords some really nice views. After crossing the Rwindi plains the road heads up the Kabasha Escarpment and is relatively busy because of all the coffee, tea and banana plantations which line the road starting at the top of the escarpment. About 20 km south of Butembo you'll see a marker on the side of the road indicating the equator.

Some 280 km north of Goma at an altitude of 1800 metres, Butembo is just west of Virunga park and the largest town in the park area, with some 50,000 inhabitants. The city is logistically simple as there's one long, unpaved north-south road, Ave Mobutu, through town with a large, open-air market in the centre. Many businesses line this street, including three banks which aren't very useful to travellers as they rarely, if ever, cash travellers' cheques. The city's other main commercial street runs east-west on the northern side of the market. You'll find numerous small shops there as well as cheap restaurants and hotels plus a cinema.

Places to Stay

There are at least three dirt-cheap hotels in the central area, all similarly priced dumps with bucket showers. One is the *Logement Spécial* in the centre of town just west of the market, across from the cinema. The accommodation is filthy but at US$3 a room you get what you pay for. Or try the nearby *Hôtel Apollo II*, 1½ blocks to the west. The prices are similar but it's pretty foul, with no electricity, tiny rooms and rotten toilets. The third is *Hôtel d'Ambiance*, which is seven blocks (a 10-minute walk) south of the market near the cathedral. It has singles/doubles for US$3/4. The beds are OK and there's electricity but the water supply for the showers in the shared baths is unreliable and,

despite the hotel's name, the ambience isn't great.

If you can afford to pay slightly more, I recommend staying at either the 25-room *Hôtel Semuliki*, which is near the northern entrance to town on Ave Mobutu, 1½ km (a 20-minute walk) from the centre, or *Hôtel Oasis*, which is on the same road but only a block north of the market. The Semuliki is slightly up-market with electricity, a restaurant and running water for the showers in the early morning and evening. Rooms with single beds and shared baths cost US$6.50 while those with private baths range in price from US$8.50 to US$13. The US$10 'apartments' have two dreary rooms, one barely big enough for a bed and another with a table and chair. The Semuliki has a bar, and a restaurant that serves fairly good food. The old Oasis has been completely renovated and now has a good restaurant, bar and large rooms of similar quality and price.

The city's top hotel used to be the 32-room *Hôtel Kikyo* (☎ 247), which is on a hill on the northern outskirts of town, a 45-minute walk from the centre. It has gone downhill considerably and seems likely to close, but until then it is still the city's second-best hotel. Top honours go to *L'Auberge de Butembo* (☎ 320), which is a lovely, tourist-class hotel somewhat remotely located on the top of a hill on the north-eastern side of town. A 20-minute walk from the centre, it's half a km east of the BCZ bank on the main drag. Opened in 1982 and run by a Zaïrois, this charming place is fairly large with four separate tile-roof buildings. It is immaculately maintained, with a large grass lawn and flowers in front, and a lovely restaurant. The 13 rooms, which are very clean and tastefully decorated, vary in price from US$27.50 to US$44, which includes breakfast.

Those wanting to camp should check out this auberge, as you can camp here for US$2.50 a person.

Places to Eat

A good place for cheap food in the centre is the *Restaurant Zoo*, which faces the north-

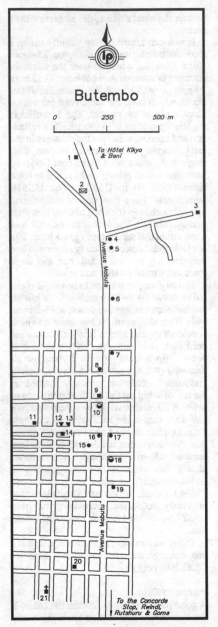

Butembo

0   250   500 m

To Hôtel Kikyo
& Beni

Avenue Mobutu

To Hôtel Kikyo & Beni

Avenue Nduru

To the Concorde
Stop, Rwindi,
Rutshuru & Goma

1   Hôtel Semuliki
2   Post Office
3   L'Auberge de Butembo
4   Agetraf (Airline)
5   Banque Commerciale Zaïroise
6   Boulangerie
7   AMIZA Travel Agency
8   Boulangerie
9   Hôtel Oasis
10 Taxi Stand & Minibuses to Beni
11 Hôtel Apollo II
12 Restaurant Tounane & Cinema
13 Restaurant Zoo
14 Logement Spécial
15 Market (Open-Air)
16 UZB Bank, Fina Petrol Station & TMK
    Air Commuter
17 Banque du Peuple
18 Butembo Safari Bus Station (Buses to
    Goma)
19 Music Shop
20 Hôtel d'Ambiance
21 Cathedral

western corner of the market. You can get a
decent Zaïrian meal there for US$1 as well
as at *Restaurant Tounane*, which is similar
and on the same block next to the cinema.
The owners know where you can get some
pombe, the local banana brew which is
popular throughout eastern Zaïre. You can
buy food at the central market, and bread at
the boulangerie a block north of the Hôtel
Oasis.

Both the Oasis and Semuliki hotels serve
good food. At the Semuliki, for example, you
can get a cheap omelette and bread, or the
US$4 menu, typically a tomato and onion
salad, steak, potatoes and delicious gravy.
Both places also have comfortable bars. The
restaurant with the best food and ambience
by far is the friendly, attractive *L'Auberge de
Butembo*. An entrée and main course will
cost you between US$7.50 and US$13, and
beers go for US$1.50.

Getting There & Away

Air Agetraf has an office on the main north-
south drag (just south of the post office) as
does TMK Air Commuter (north-eastern
corner of the market). To fly to Goma or

Bunia, you'll have to leave from Beni (55 km away), which has the closest airport.

Minibus & Truck The principal bus company serving Butembo and Goma is Butembo Safari Bus, which has offices on Ave Mobutu facing the south-eastern corner of the market. It has four buses a week to Goma (Mondays, Tuesdays, Thursdays and Saturdays) and four a week from Goma (Wednesdays, Thursdays, Saturdays and Sundays). Departures are supposed to be at 5.30 am, but 6.15 am is more typical; the fare is US$6 and the trip takes about 11½ hours during the dry season and more during the wet season. The buses are in fairly good condition and seating is guaranteed but seats are usually all booked by noon the previous day. The company also used to provide connections with Bunia but this service has been discontinued, as has that of Ika Massambe bus company. However, service could be revived, so it may be worth asking.

The departure point for minibuses and pick-up trucks to Beni is a block north of the market on Ave Mobutu. There are quite a few headed in that direction throughout the day, mostly in the morning; the fare is US$2 (more for a seat in the cabin). Trucks to Goma leave from the Concorde stop at the southern end of town.

BENI

In Beni (population 15,000), 55 km north of Butembo, you might get your first good view of the snowcapped Ruwenzori but more than likely they'll be covered in clouds.

The city is basically one long, north-south street, Ave Mobutu, with the market on the south side and the city's top hotel in the centre. The only rond-point is on the northern side and is the turn-off east for Ruwenzori, Kasindi and the northern shore of Lake Idi Amin. Virtually all shops and businesses, including three banks, line that street, with most housing behind. Most travellers find that the banks will not cash travellers' cheques.

The city lies at the eastern edge of the Ituri forest, which is a vast sea of green stretching westward to the horizon and noted for being the home of various Pygmy tribes. If you are headed for the forests, Beni will be the last town of any size you'll see for several days. The condition of the road north from here is not as good as the stretch southward; during the rainy season driving can be difficult but the route is not as treacherous as it once was.

To see Pygmies, head to **Oysha**, 25 km to the north on the main highway. Some of the overland trucks stop here, so the Pygmies there are quite accustomed to receiving visitors although you may find them all spaced out from smoking marijuana. If you have difficulty finding a guide to the Pygmy village, ask at the Mission Catholique; they have been known to arrange visits with local guides. You can exchange old T-shirts and other items for Pygmy handicrafts.

Places to Stay

The cheapest hotels are very near the rond-point, including *Hôtel Jumbo* 40 metres to the west, *Hôtel Isale* 50 metres to the north, and *Hôtel Sina Makosa*, which is 70 metres east of the rond-point and just a little off the road. The 12-room Jumbo has singles/doubles with shared African-style bucket showers for US$4/5 and a place for stored luggage. The Isale is similar in all respects, while the friendly Sina Makosa has rooms with single beds for US$4 and drinks available but no meals. You could also try *Restaurant Lualaba*, which is further east, about 150 metres from the rond-point. In the past it offered travellers cheap rooms with bucket showers and an area for stored luggage, but when I was last there it was only operating as a restaurant.

The city's top address, *Hôtel Beni*, which is in the heart of town on the main street, was renovated and expanded to 26 rooms in 1988. Most rooms cost US$30, which includes breakfast. There are also five rooms for US$18 and two for US$25 but they are usually taken. The rooms are very attractively designed with spotlessly clean tile baths but the hot-water supply is unreliable. The backyard is very pleasant, with tile-roof rooms overlooking a shaded grass centre

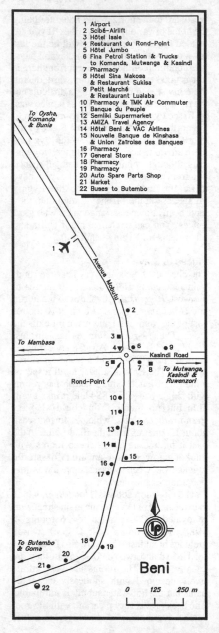

1 Airport
2 Scibé-Airlift
3 Hôtel Isale
4 Restaurant du Rond-Point
5 Hôtel Jumbo
6 Fina Petrol Station & Trucks
  to Komanda, Mutwanga & Kasindi
7 Pharmacy
8 Hôtel Sina Makosa
  & Restaurant Sukisa
9 Petit Marché
  & Restaurant Lualaba
10 Pharmacy & TMK Air Commuter
11 Banque du Peuple
12 Semliki Supermarket
13 AMIZA Travel Agency
14 Hôtel Beni & VAC Airlines
15 Nouvelle Banque de Kinshasa
   & Union Zaïroise des Banques
16 Pharmacy
17 General Store
18 Pharmacy
19 Pharmacy
20 Auto Spare Parts Shop
21 Market
22 Buses to Butembo

To Oysha,
Komanda
& Bunia

Avenue Mobutu

To Mambasa

Kasindi Road

To Mutwanga,
Kasindi &
Ruwenzori

Rond-Point

To Butembo
& Goma

Beni

0   125   250 m

yard. The restaurant is also agreeable, plus there's a street-side patio which is the top spot in town for watching all the action, but the drinks are not cheap.

Places to Eat
The area around the rond-point is also the best for cheap eats. The popular *Restaurant du Rond-Point* at the rond-point is a great place for cheap food including omelettes for around US$1 and full breakfasts for US$1.75. Another good place for cheap eats is *Restaurant Lualaba*, which is 150 metres to the east, next to the Petit Marché. It serves meat dishes, rice, beans and home-made bread among other things. The staff speaks English and the Somali owner will change money. Another place nearby for cheap African food is *Restaurant Sukisa*, which is next door to the Hôtel Sina Makosa.

The city's top restaurant is at the *Hôtel Beni*. It's quite attractive, with indoor and outdoor dining; expect to pay about US$2.50 for breakfast and US$7 for a meal plus drinks. At US$1.30 for a large Primus, beers are relatively expensive.

For stocking up on supplies, your best bets are the main market at the southern end of town, the much smaller Petit Marché at the northern end on Kasindi Rd, and the Greek-owned Semliki supermarket in the heart of town on the main drag. Semliki, for example, stocks the wonderful cheese made in this area. There are also some smaller general stores lining the main drag.

Getting There & Away
Air Various airlines connect Beni with Goma including TMK Air Commuter (Mondays, Wednesdays, Fridays, Sundays), Scibé-Airlift (Sundays), Virunga Air Charter (Wednesdays), Agetraf (Fridays), all of which have offices on the main drag. The normal one-way fare is US$125 but check Agetraf's fares as they may be much lower. A taxi from the airport to the centre costs US$2.50. Since the airport is only half a km north of the rond-point, walking is quite feasible.

Minibus Minibuses and pick-up trucks for Butembo leave from across the main market on the southern side of town. They generally leave between 7 am and 4 pm and take about 2½ hours due to frequent stops; the fare is US$2. Getting a minibus direct to Goma is next to impossible, so virtually everyone headed there goes to Butembo and catches a bus from there.

Large trucks and pick-ups headed north towards Komanda (an all-day trip) leave from the petrol station near the rond-point, as do those headed east to Mutwanga (the starting point for climbing Mt Stanley) and Kasindi (the turn-off for Ishango). The road to Kasindi is in bad condition, so the trip can take quite a few hours.

KASINDI

The road east from Beni to Kasindi is one of the major routes to Uganda, so hitching isn't difficult, especially on Thursdays when there's a market at Kasindi. There are several hotels in town including *Hôtel Kivu*, which is cheap with bucket showers and a restaurant. The Ugandan border is three km to the east and the first Ugandan town, **Mpondwe**, is another six km, to which you'll also have to walk as there are no taxis at the border.

KOMANDA

The worst stretch on the Kisangani to Goma road is that between Epulu and Komanda, though it has been slightly improved in recent years. During the dry season, vehicles pass through without problems but during the rainy season, travellers occasionally have significant problems. The major determining factor is how heavy the rains have been.

If you stay in Komanda, you'll find several cheap hotels and a restaurant near the main roundabout. From there to Beni is a day's trip by truck or, usually faster, by taxi pick-up.

BUNIA

Bunia is 75 km east of Komanda and the main town on the northernmost – and least travelled – route to Uganda. Regardless of where you're headed, since you're this far

north you shouldn't pass up the opportunity of seeing nearby **Lake Mobutu**. The fishing village of **Tshoma** is the place to head for. Even though you can't swim in the lake because of bilharzia, it's a lively village with 24-hour bars, excellent hospitality and inexpensive fresh fish, so chances are you won't be disappointed.

Places to Stay & Eat

There are lots of hotels in the US$2 to US$4 category including the popular *Hôtel Chez Tout Bunia* and, on the main drag, the *Hôtel Rubi*, the friendly *Hôtel Butembo II*, *Hôtel Semliki* and *Hôtel Ituri*. All of these places have restaurants serving decent food at reasonable prices.

Getting There & Away

There's no longer a direct minibus service south to Butembo, so you'll have to look for trucks. In Tshoma, for example, trucks haul fish from the lake to points south. You can also fly to Goma. TMK Air Commuter has flights on Mondays and Fridays; Agetraf on Thursdays and Fridays; and Broussair on Thursdays (continuing to Kisangani and back) and Fridays. The one-way fare is US$145. Fares may be payable only in hard currency.

Parc National des Virunga

Simply stated, Virunga National Park is the most spectacular park in Central Africa. Beginning 13 km north of Goma its 780,000 hectares stretch some 300 km north along the borders with Rwanda and Uganda – one of the most geologically active regions in all Africa. Established in 1925 to preserve the mountain gorilla, Virunga is also one of the oldest parks in Africa. It is contiguous with the Volcans National Park in Rwanda, which is a major gorilla sanctuary, and Uganda's Ruwenzori National Park. Lake Idi Amin, also called Lake Edward, is in the centre of

Virunga, with the world's largest concentration of hippos – an estimated 25,000.

Elsewhere in the park, you'll see volcanoes dominating marshy deltas, cool grassy plateaus and sun-baked plains filled with herds of antelope and other wild animals. Lava plains, deep equatorial forest, high-altitude glaciers and snowfields round out the picture. The park's altitude is equally varied, from 798 metres in the south to the huge Ruwenzori mountains north of the lake, Africa's highest range. Along the slopes of Mt Stanley, the tallest peak at 5109 metres, the rainfall measures more than 5000 mm (over 200 inches) annually. Bamboo grows up to a metre each day.

On a bright, fresh morning, the volcanoes may imbue you with a soaring sense of optimism, only to drop you into despair by the afternoon when they are generally masked by clouds. The best time for visiting and climbing is from December to January when the rains let up, and in June, the first month of the dry season. During the rest of the dry season (July to September) the skies are dusty, which spoils the views.

Don't overlook the possibility of combining a trip to Virunga with a trip to the Parc National des Volcans in Rwanda. Although not contiguous with it, Volcans is merely the Rwandan side of Virunga. The entrance is only about 100 km north-east of Goma via Gisenyi and Ruhengeri. Together, Virunga and Volcans offer the best hiking opportunities in all of Central and East Africa, and the only opportunity in the world for seeing the mountain gorilla.

Orientation

The park's main route, which is well maintained up to Beni, proceeds northward from Goma to Rutshuru (75 km); en route on your left will be Nyiragongo and Nyamulagira, the two volcanoes most frequently scaled by hikers. The road south-east from Rutshuru heads east to Djomba (or Jomba), the main centre for viewing gorillas. The road due north heads toward Uganda while the main road heading north-west, leads to the Rwindi plains, the centre for most of the wildlife viewing, with the park's main tourist lodge. Lake Idi Amin and Vitshumbi on its southern shore are about 20 km to the north via a rough dirt track. Continuing north-west over the plains on the main road you will eventually begin climbing Kabasha Escarpment, on top of which the road becomes lined with small farms. You'll pass Butembo, the largest town near the park, then Beni, which is the turn-off point for the Ruwenzori mountains and Ishango, a camping and bird-watching paradise on the lake's northern shore. The main road, however, continues northward towards Mt Hoyo, the principal Pygmy area.

Information

Park Fees Each area of the park has entrance permits, which are valid for seven days and vary in cost. The fees include the price of a guide where one is required and are payable only in hard currency or travellers' cheques; they are as follows:

1) Park entrance fee which includes Rwindi plains – US$60 plus US$5 tax
2) Nyiragongo and Nyamulagira volcanoes – US$30
3) Gorillas at Djomba – US$120
4) Ishango – US$30
5) Mt Ruwenzori – US$40
6) Mt Hoyo – US$20

There are fees for cameras (US$0.25), videos (US$1), gorilla videos (US$20), and camping or using the mountain huts (US$0.25 to US$0.50 per day). If you'll be going to several of these places, it may be worth purchasing the 'permis special Parc National des Virunga – touts sites compris', which costs US$240 and allows you to visit any area of the park during a one-month period. If you'll just be passing through the park by truck or public transport, no fee is levied.

Accommodation

The park is well prepared for tourism as there are four very decent, tourist-class lodges in the area. From south to north they are: *Hôtel de la Rwindi* at Km 130 on the Rwindi plains, *l'Auberge de Butembo* in Butembo, *Hôtel Beni* in Beni, and *l'Auberge du Mont Hoyo* at the northern edge of the park at Mt Hoyo. There are also numerous places to camp and cheap hotels in all of the small towns.

VOLCANO HIKES
Nyiragongo

The two major volcanoes for climbing – Nyiragongo and Nyamulagira – are both near Goma. The closest, Nyiragongo (3470 metres), last erupted in 1977, sending a wall of lava three metres high at 80 km/h into the valleys, killing 60 or 70 people, but stopping just north of Goma, whose inhabitants had fled across the Rwandan border. It could easily erupt again. Still, people climb it all the time except when there are warnings up, which occur now and then.

The starting point for Nyiragongo is the Camp des Guides at **Kibati** (1950 metres), 13 km north of Goma on the Rutshura road. The camp is an unmarked white building just inside the park entrance and within easy walking distance of the road. You can camp there, or if you booze it up with the friendly head guide he may allow you to sleep on the floor. The US$30 park fee, which includes a guide, is valid for seven days and can be used for climbing Nyamulagira as well. Make sure, however, that your permit includes climbing Nyamulagira, otherwise you may have to pay extra for it. A guide will be assigned to you at the camp and you can hire

a porter there as well for US$2 a day, but many hikers simply offer the guide US$2 a day extra for which he'll usually double as a porter. Bring all of your food and charcoal from Goma. Thieves have been known to steal petrol from vehicles parked outside the camp, so if you have one, consider paying someone to guard it.

The climb is steep but easy and takes four or five hours up (the guides will tell you three) and two to three hours down. No departures after 1 pm are allowed. On the way up you'll pass through rainforest to two bare tin cabins 25 minutes' walk before the crater rim. The cabins, which are quite basic, have beds and there is water nearby. From here, you may see huge clouds of sulphurous gas towering above you. When you climb up to the crater's lip, you'll see the black, smoking platform of volcanic ash below.

Many hikers used to stay overnight to see the volcano's impressive fires glowing in the dark, but those lava fires no longer exist as recent eruptions have drained the crater. Staying overnight is still recommended, however, as it allows you to be at the summit at dusk and in the early morning, the only times it's likely to be free of the cloudy mist which usually starts moving in at around 9 am. When visibility is good, the views of Lake Kivu and nearby volcanoes are spectacular.

If you climb during the rainy season, you are likely to find the peak socked in by clouds for days on end. It's especially cold then, so bring warm clothing. Even during the dry season, if you'll be staying overnight, be prepared for the cold at night and in the early morning.

Nyamulagira

Unlike Nyiragongo, Nyamulagira (3056 metres) hasn't had lava in recent memory and it's less active, but the view is better and if you're lucky you may see a variety of animals along the way, including forest elephants. The entire trip from Goma can be done in three days. The starting point is **Kakomero village** (1800 metres), which is 38 km north of Goma and two km south of

Lulenga. From Kakomero it's a two-hour hike west to the base of the volcano, passing through lovely rolling country dominated by the towering volcanoes. Bring a tent and all your food as the base camp has no accommodation. The nearest water is three km away, so pay a boy to bring you some.

The next day's hike takes five or six hours and is fairly gradual most of the way. First, you'll pass through lava fields supporting only lichens and small ferns, with occasional lava pools filled with inviting water. Next come dense forests with hundreds of different birds. You might also spot a herd of buffalo, antelope, maybe even chimpanzees, and if you're really lucky, a family of elephants.

Eventually, you'll arrive at a large rambling cabin at 2500 metres with numerous rooms and plenty of beds. There's no stove, but you can cook dinner on top of an oil drum in the centre. If you hear an animal scream it may be Bill de Bill, an old guide who died here and is said to still haunt the cabin.

The climb to the crater rim takes another two hours; the views are spectacular, clouds permitting. Descending into the 2½ km-wide crater you'll see lots of yellow sulphur deposits as well as a second tiny hut, which is a good place to brew some tea and wait out a possible hail storm. You can also camp there but it's extremely basic. Flowers, shrubs and ferns abound; you may even see a steam-heated orchid. On the floor of the volcano look for the huge blowhole. Descending from the lip of the crater to Kakomero takes five or six hours.

Park Fees The park fee for climbing Nyamulagira is US$30, which is payable in Goma at the IZCN office or at the Kibati Camp des Guides where you can also make arrangements for a guide. The permit is valid for seven days but you won't have to pay this if you purchased a permit for climbing Nyiragongo. The fee includes the cost of a guide, which is compulsory, but he'll expect a tip which is customary. Porters, which cost US$2 a day, are also available at Kibati or in Kakomero. For more information on both

climbs see the travel agencies in Goma; they can also arrange transport.

Mikeno

For a permit and information on climbing the Mikeno volcano on the Rwandan border, see the IZCN office in Goma. There are rock-climbing possibilities on Mikeno, so rock-climbers in particular should inquire there. Regardless, it's in an exceptionally scenic area, with tall hagenia forests like those on the slopes of the Ruwenzori, and there is a sturdy cabin apparently open to trekkers in the saddle connecting Mikeno and Karisimbi volcanoes.

VIRUNGA GORILLAS & CHIMPANZEES

Killing by poachers has made the mountain gorilla an endangered species. While 5000 to 15,000 were reportedly surviving in Central Africa in the 1960s, a census taken in 1989 showed only 310 mountain gorillas in 32 families roaming the Virunga mountains in Zaïre, Rwanda and Uganda. Of these, about 20 families reside primarily on the Zaïrian side – far more than in Rwanda. Fortunately, their numbers are now on the rise (from 278 in 1986) because of all the recent attention being paid to them in Rwanda and Zaïre. The mountain gorillas on the Rwandan side are easier to view because of their longer habituation to humans, but the ones on the Zaïre side can be viewed for longer periods of time, sometimes up to two hours because the park wardens permit longer viewing.

In recent years the Frankfurt Zoological Society has made major contributions to upgrading the protection of the gorillas on the Zaïrian side and the organisation of tourist visits to see them. To pay for this, park fees have risen to a level equal to those in Rwanda and, as in Rwanda, the maximum group size for viewing the gorillas is eight people.

There are now four groups open for viewing – Oscar (or Rugendo), Marcel (or Rugabo), Faida (or Rafiki) and Bukima (or Zunguruka). The starting point is near Djomba (26 km south-east of Rutshura) for the first three groups, and Rumangabo

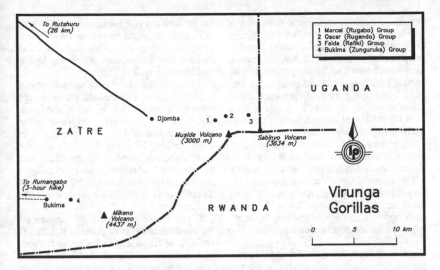

1 Marcel (Rugabo) Group
2 Oscar (Rugendo) Group
3 Faida (Rafiki) Group
4 Bukima (Zunguruka) Group

Virunga Gorillas

(between Rutshuru and Goma) for the fourth.

Djomba Gorilla Sanctuary

The gorillas near Djomba live on the nearby slopes of Sabinyo and Muside volcanoes bordering Rwanda. They aren't as tame as those in Rwanda, but contact is likely and getting a booking is normally easier. Moreover, with all the recent fighting in Rwanda, the Zaïrian gorillas were, as of mid-1993, the only ones that could be viewed. It is sometimes possible to get a reservation for the next day; but at peak periods you may have to wait four days or so.

The Oscar and Marcel groups are the easiest to see because they're in a flat plain, and the trekking is not tough. Marcel is often within an hour's walk while Oscar wanders around a bit more; finding that group can vary anywhere from one to five hours. The Faida group is higher up on Sabinyo volcano and involves much more difficult hiking; moreover, the group often wanders over into Uganda, making viewing impossible. When Dian Fossey initially began her gorilla research on the Zaïrian side, she worked further north, from Kibumba up the mountain to Kabara where there's still a cabin, reportedly now used by poachers.

Bookings & Fees The only places to make reservations are at the IZCN office in Goma and at the sanctuary headquarters in Djomba. If you can't get a reservation, see Zaïre Safari at the Masques Hôtel in Goma as they have group bookings and might not be completely full. Since the Faida group wanders back and forth between Zaïre and Uganda, advance reservations cannot be made for it. So if Faida is in Zaïre, the chances are good of your being able to book a place. If you don't have a reservation and go to Djomba, you can still join a group if they aren't full. Starting time is around 8 am.

The fee, which includes the guide, has risen to US$120 (UK£70 or FF 750), payable in hard currency or travellers' cheques, and tipping is expected. Use of a video camera costs another US$20. For many travellers seeing the gorillas is the highlight of their trip to Africa, so you can be virtually sure you won't regret paying.

Places to Stay & Eat The departure point is seven km up the hill from Djomba. The

Frankfurt Zoological Society maintains a park cabin there for visitors with dormitory bunk beds with mattresses, bedding, paraffin lamps and a kitchen with cooking and eating utensils for about US$4 per person. If you have a tent, you can camp outside for less than US$1 per person. Bring food from Djomba.

In Djomba itself you can bunk at the similarly priced *Mission Catholique* plus you can get meals there as well. Villagers will also sell you food – cooked if you like. There's also a US *Mission Baptiste*, but it's a few km out of town. The best accommodation is at *Djomba Camp*, a new tourist-class hotel run by Zaïre Safaris. It's a 30-minute walk uphill from Djomba towards the starting point for the gorilla-viewing walks.

Getting There & Away At a roundabout on the southern outskirts of Rutshuru you'll see a sign indicating the turn-off east for Djomba. The bus from Goma should drop you off there. Travel on this 26-km road is very light and you may not see vehicles passing for hours on end; Mondays and Fridays, which are market days in Djomba,

are the best days for hitching rides. The road is extremely rough, requiring 4WD, but is passable year-round. With luck, you can make it here from Goma in one day by bus and hitching.

Those driving from Goma should leave by 5.30 am because it's a three-hour trip and you need to be there by 8.30 am at the latest. Those travelling in a group with money can rent minibuses in Goma from AMIZA or Zaïre Safaris. If you're without a vehicle, you might find some other travellers with private vehicles headed that way by hanging around the IZCN office or AMIZA in Goma. There's a fabulous fruit and vegetable market en route.

If you're coming here from Uganda via the southernmost entry point at Kisoro (37 km east of Rutshuru) and want to try your luck arriving at Djomba without a prior booking, you can take a short cut south from the border, thereby avoiding Rutshuru. There's a restaurant about a km west of the border where you'll find a man who guides travellers on a path southwardly through several villages direct to the hut at the starting point, above Djomba. The hike takes

---

Gorilla Facts

The average silver-back male weighs about 170 kg compared to about 90 kg for the average female. The typical family size is around 10 – usually one silver-back, one male eight to 13 years old who isn't fully mature, four females, and four young under eight years of age.

The gorillas seem to feed on anything green around them but in fact their tastes are not catholic as they feed mainly on bamboo shoots when in season, bedstraw, wild celery, thistles, nettles and berries when in season. You won't see them drinking water as the vegetation provides all the water they need. Most of the eating is done in the early morning (two hours) and again in the late afternoon until around 5.30 pm when they go to sleep, generally for about 13 hours.

There are some common misconceptions concerning gorillas. One is that poachers want gorillas to sell their parts (feet, hands, testicles, etc) for fetishes and souvenirs. This was true at one time but today's poachers, who are often stoned from smoking grass, are almost invariably after other animals, mainly antelope and bush pig; what happens is that the gorillas get snared by, and often die from, the traps intended for these other animals. Also, the gorillas you see in zoos aren't mountain gorillas. Because of their threatened status, zoos today will accept only lowland gorillas, of which there are an estimated 2000 to 4000 in jungle lowland areas of Zaïre, Congo, Gabon, Cameroun and the CAR. They are smaller and more chimpanzee-like and spend much of their time in trees, so habituating them to do research is much more difficult. Sangha Reserve in the CAR is the one place where such research is being conducted.

The biggest problem of too many people viewing the gorillas and getting close to them is exposing them to human diseases. Some have died of measles, for example, which is why researchers in Rwanda are giving them measles vaccinations, spearing them with tiny spears with treated tips. ■

only about two hours and his fee is negotiable and usually very modest.

Rumangabo Gorilla Sanctuary
The fourth group, Bukima, is some distance away on the slopes of Mikeno volcano to the south of Djomba and requires an overnight stay; the starting point is Rumangabo, which is roughly halfway between Goma and Rutshuru and thus much easier to get to by public transport than Djomba. You must hike for about three hours from Rumangabo east to **Bukima village** and the base camp just beyond at the foot of Mikeno. You can sleep there at the park cabin, which is similar in all respects to the one at Djomba, or pitch a tent outside for a quarter the cost. Regardless, bring all your food and drink. The next morning at around 8 am you hike up the slopes looking for Bukima; the guide can usually find the group within one to three hours. Fees here are the same as at Djomba and bookings can be made in Goma or Djomba.

Getting There & Away Coming from Goma you should ask the bus driver to let you off at Rumangabo, which is 40 km north of Goma and marked by a triangular stone monument along the road. The sanctuary headquarters is just a short walk from the road. There you'll find a park guard who will escort you to the cabin, some three hours away.

Tongo Chimpanzee Sanctuary
Financed by the Swiss Fondacion Messerli and opened to tourists in 1990, the sanctuary at Tongo, just north of Nyamulagira Volcano, is the only one in Africa specifically for viewing chimpanzees in the wild. Looking for chimpanzee families is similar to looking for gorillas in that you must head off early in the morning and walk through the bush for three hours or so before spotting a group. On the way you may see baboons and monkeys, of which there are five species in the area including colobus and papio.

You have the choice of pitching a tent at the camp grounds here (showers and kitchen facilities are available) for about US$2 per person or taking a bed at the sanctuary's lodge (electricity, hot-water showers and a restaurant) for double or triple that.

Getting There & Away The turn-off for Tongo village is on the Goma to Rutshuru road at Kalangeera village, 10 km before Rutshuru. The village is 17 km south-west down a rough dirt track towards Nyamulagira volcano. Getting a lift is extremely difficult except on Friday mornings when there's a market in Tongo, so you may have to walk (four hours). The lodge is just above the village.

RWINDI PLAINS
A major attraction of Virunga park is the wildlife, and the principal viewing area is Rwindi, which is a large plain extending south from Lake Idi Amin towards Nyamulagira volcano.

Flora
Three animals that you will definitely see are kob and topi (antelope) and hippos. Every morning there's drama in the plains as male kobs, which are extremely territorial, clash in trials of strength or in disputes over the hornless females. In addition, hippos are so numerous that they literally clog all the streams. At the tourist lodge in Rwindi, for example, guests are occasionally awakened by the snorting and wailing of one of these two-tonne nocturnal feeders trying to satisfy its 60-kg-a-day eating habit. Other animals that you might see include lions, buffalo,

forest elephants, antelope, waterbuck, reedbuck, baboon, colobus monkeys, hyenas, jackal and wart hog.

The tree hyrax, a rabbit-size mammal that some Africans depend on for its meat and pelt, is virtually extinct in the lower valleys, as are the leopard and the duiker, a small antelope. Until very recently, forest elephants roamed the Rwindi plains in the thousands; today you're lucky to see one. In the evening when the elephants come out of hiding to feed, the poachers are there waiting. So are the park patrol officers, over 40 of whom have been killed since 1961 in armed struggles with poachers. In neighbouring Uganda, the situation has been just as bad or worse; during the '70s and '80s the elephant population fell from 30,000 to 2000!

Park Fees

The park fee for Rwindi is US$65 including tax, and all viewing requires a vehicle. This rule isn't a problem for those on tours or staying at the tourist lodge, but for overland travellers without vehicles or in huge unwieldy trucks it can be prohibitive. Your only hope is making friends with tourists at the lodge and, if you're lucky, going with them; in general, however, tourists are reluctant to make the offer. Alternatively, head for Ishango, where you can camp in an area with most of the same animals (see later in this chapter).

Viewing Routes

You have a choice of viewing routes. The most popular one follows the Rwindi River, which is literally packed with hippos, north for about 20 km to the fishing village of **Vitshumbi** on the southern shore of Lake Idi Amin and Mwiga Bay – hippo heaven. The lake's greatest concentration of hippos is found in that bay, which is also a paradise of aquatic birds, including egrets, white pelicans, ducks, and eagles perched on mud banks. You'll also see lots of marabou storks sitting vulture-like on top of the mud and thatched dwellings in Vitshumbi with bowed

heads and hunched shoulders waiting for scraps of food.

Another popular route is along the Rutshuru River, which also abounds with hippos. Three others are the Ishasa track which runs along the Ugandan border; the Kibirizi track, which leads westward towards the Kibasha Escarpment; and the nearby Muhaha River track which runs along the river of that name.

Places to Stay & Eat

You cannot camp inside the park in this area, but you can camp just outside at the park entrance at Mabenga, along the Rutshuru River. Nocturally grazing hippos can be very dangerous, so ask at the entrance where to camp.

The only hotel in this area of the park is *Hôtel de la Rwindi*, which is an attractive well-maintained tourist lodge in the heart of the plains and just off the Rutshuru to Butembo road, 57 km west of Rutshuru. It consists of a series of round white cabins, a central restaurant and bar, and a round pool circled by chairs. A room there costs about US$40 per person plus meals. For reservations, contact AMIZA or Zaïre Safaris in Goma.

Getting There & Away

If you're without a vehicle and heading south from Butembo or north from Goma, you could take a minibus for Goma or Butembo, respectively, and get off at the lodge.

ISHANGO

On the northern shore of Lake Idi Amin, some 103 km south-east of Beni and 76 km south of the entrance to Mt Ruwenzori at Mutwanga, Ishango is the loveliest spot in Virunga park for camping. You can camp by the lake, with no villages around, and during the day walk around looking for game (which you can't do in Rwindi). On a clear day you can see the glaciers of Mt Stanley. The area is also famous as a bird-watcher's paradise as the northern lake shore teems with birds including cormorants, herons, egrets, eagles, ibis, ducks, marabou storks and flocks of pelican, both white and pink.

The savannah grasslands here support most of the animals found south around Rwindi but in fewer numbers, including lions and antelope (such as topi and kob); elephants, on the other hand, are virtually nonexistent here. Hippos, up to two tonnes, lie submerged in the lake but at night they leave the lake to go grazing and can be quite dangerous – they are certainly responsible for more human deaths than any other animal in the park. If you scout along the Semliki River, which exits the 80 km-long Lake Idi Amin at Ishango and meanders northward toward Lake Mobutu, you may see some crocodiles as well. The old defunct lodge at Ishango, which is on top of a bluff, affords wonderful views of the river and lake.

The lake is free of bilharzia so you can swim in it, but wait five or 10 minutes to make sure there are no hippos submerged in the water as they are quite aggressive and will definitely attack swimmers.

The fee for visiting Ishango is US$30, which is steep if you're here mainly to camp rather than view animals. To avoid this fee, head for **Kiavinyonge**, a fishing village 10 km further down the road and outside the park. Rarely visited by travellers (you need a permit from customs in Kasindi to visit here), it's a wonderful place to fish, swim and watch birds and hippos while mingling with the friendly locals. The town is a lot like Vitshumbi, with marabou storks on every roof, but larger and more active, with all kinds of fascinating activities at the beach starting early in the morning when the fishers go out.

Places to Stay & Eat

In Kiavinyonge, you can stay at the *Lodgement Special* for about US$2 per room. There is a restaurant on the lake shore where you can have a breakfast of coffee and bread from early in the morning, and eat rice and delicious grilled tilapia, the local catch, during the day and early evening.

Getting There & Away

Kasindi, which is several km from the Ugandan border and some 40 km east of the Mt Stanley turn-off, is the road to Ishango. The park has a separate entrance here and it is three km south of Kasindi; Ishango itself is another 15 km or so south. Finding a truck headed in that direction is usually not too difficult as some of them transport fish from the lake. In Kiavinyonge, at around 8 am most days, you can catch a truck hauling fish west to Butembo. This is a fascinating four-hour journey over a winding back road (not the main Kasindi to Beni road).

RUWENZORI MOUNTAINS

The Ruwenzori mountain range, known since ancient times, is one of the most famous in Africa and it's the only one with glaciers. The range is about 110 km long and runs roughly north-south along the Zaïre-Uganda border, starting just barely north of the equator. The six tallest peaks are bunched together in an area less than 20 km long as the crow flies. The highest peak, and the one most often climbed, is Mt Stanley which is near the middle and straddles the border. The furthest north is Mt Emin on the Zaïrian side; the others are all slightly east of the border on the Ugandan side. The area is extremely wet however, and the mountains can remain hidden in the clouds for weeks on end. Rain frequently falls even during the dry season; after all, this is one of the two wettest areas in Africa (the other is Mt Cameroun).

The proximity of highly contrasting environments produces some unusual, almost mystical sights, with moss entangling yellowish vegetation and snow in the background. Hence, the nickname 'Mountains of the Moon'. This name dates back to the time of the Greek geographer Ptolemy who first named these mountains as the source of the Nile, based on stories relayed to him by travellers to distant locations. Ever since then the mountains were a source of intrigue to European geographers curious about the source of the Nile. Finally, in the late 19th century Henry Stanley became the first European to actually see them and it was he who gave them the name 'Ruwenzori' meaning 'the rainy hill'. Richard Burton's and John Speke's trip near here during the same period in search of the source of the Nile raised public awareness of the region as did, a century later, the 1989 motion picture *Mountains of the Moon* portraying that trip.

Flora & Fauna

What makes the Ruwenzori mountains possibly the most beautiful in Africa is the incredible vegetation. Shortly after starting out, you'll pass through dense rainforest, then a rocky area with twisted trees and yellow shrubs, followed by alpine meadows and, if you go high enough, snow. One of the glaciers, Elena Glacier, is almost black, looking like congealed lava, covered with white patches of newly fallen snow.

What is most amazing about the area is the remarkable plant and animal life, which is beautifully documented in Guy Yeoman's *Mountains of the Moon* (Universe Books,

New York). Unlike the nearby mountains to the south in Virunga park, the forests at the base of the Ruwenzori contain no gorillas. Yet other wildlife abounds, including forest elephants, chimpanzees, black-footed duikers, blue monkeys, l'Hoest's monkeys, colobus monkeys, Ruwenzori hyrax and 19 species of endemic forest birds including the red Ruwenzori turaco. The burgeoning human population in the area, however, has caused major environmental degradation including significant reductions in the elephant population and the total disappearance of leopards.

Higher up the Ruwenzori you'll enter a fantasy land of giant heather 'trees'. Heather, which seldom grows more than half a metre in Europe, grows to over six metres here and is enveloped in and distorted by mosses, lichens and ferns. You'll also see huge primeval trees 10 to 12 metres tall rise up from carpets of brilliantly coloured moss, covering the massive trunks and limbs in dense

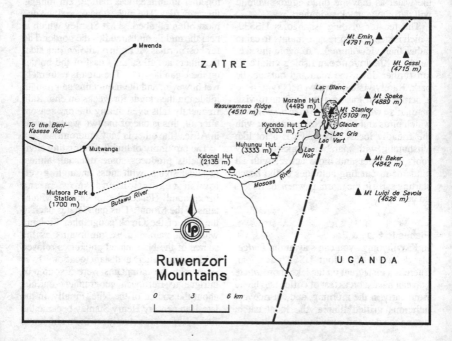

mounds of crimson, lemon yellow and emerald green, with small clusters of pinkish orchids standing almost a third of a metre high. And because of the cold temperatures from the high elevation, plants decay very slowly. The result is a labyrinth of broken trunks, limbs, roots and rock fragments covered with moss. Added to this is a forest floor which is water-soaked; hiking and stumbling through it can be truly exasperating – a false move will land you up to your knees in mire.

The alpine area above the tree line is where you'll encounter the most truly bizarre flora, including huge flowers that literally dwarf humans. Fast-growing blue lobelia plants, the kind that seldom reach a height of more than a few cm in most parts of the world, reach a height of three metres and more and their rosettes of leaves curl up at night to protect the plants from the cold. There are also giant slow-growing senecio groundsels whose leaves likewise open up only during the daytime. These plants have evolved their great size probably as a result of the high humidity and, more important, as a defence against the sometimes freezing night temperatures. And temperatures shift sharply. Every day here is like summer, and every night like winter.

Trail Conditions

Although Kilimanjaro is almost 850 metres higher, climbing it is a joke compared to climbing Mt Stanley. The last 800 metres is all snow, requiring a rope, ice axe and crampons, and the park rents none of this equipment except crampons. For this reason, most climbers don't attempt the summit.

Many people prefer climbing Mt Stanley on the Ugandan side (the starting point is Kasese at the Ruwenzori Mountain Club) as the climbing there is better organised, the ascent is more gradual, and there are more routes from which to choose, allowing you to climb up one way and descend another. However, on the Zaïrian side, which has only one route up and down, there is somewhat less rain and, consequently, the peaks aren't shrouded in clouds quite so often. Perhaps

most significantly, unlike the Ugandan routes, the Zaïrian trail avoids most of the maddening bogs that slow hiking to a crawl and often cause unprepared hikers without proper clothing to turn back.

Even if you don't attempt the summit, the weather can be freezing cold and wet. Because the humidity is so incredibly high, it frequently snows during the night at altitudes of 4500 metres or more. The best time to climb is June to mid-September and during the brief dry spell around Christmas, typically mid-December to mid-January. This latter, shorter period is not as ideal because it's still very wet then; on the other hand the skies aren't hazy as during the dry season. If you climb at other periods, you're likely to have a miserable time unless you have a very positive attitude and have the proper clothing and equipment.

Mutwanga, some 53 km east of Beni (13 km off the main Beni to Kasindi road), is at the foot of Mt Stanley and is the starting point for all climbs. Getting rides from Beni to Mutwanga and back is fairly easy as this is a major coffee-growing area and there are always trucks hauling coffee to Beni.

Equipment

Even during the four-month dry season, at a minimum you'll need warm clothing, a good sleeping bag and pad, rain gear or waterproof jacket (it occasionally rains even during the dry season), cooking utensils, a day pack if you use a porter and, for higher altitudes, a wool hat, maximum-protection sunscreen and warm, water-resistant gloves. Water-resistant boots are also strongly recommended as the ground is always very wet and muddy, but hiking up to the glacier can be done in tennis shoes with heavy wool socks if that's all you've got and you can tolerate hiking in water-soggy shoes; just be sure to have a second dry pair to put on at the end of each day.

To attempt the summit you must also have heavy boots and crampons, an ice axe, rope, and sunglasses which block out the ultraviolet rays and intense glare from the glaciers. And don't forget cigarettes for the porters;

they really enjoy a smoke after a hard day's climb.

A critical point – everything will get wet, so come prepared with plenty of spare dry clothes and wrap everything in plastic bags. Also, as some travellers recommend, the largest plastic bags can be used at night to cover up the huts' open windows – a super idea.

For more detailed logistical information, get a copy of Andrew Wielochowski's *Ruwenzori – Map & Guide*, listed in the Books section of the Facts for the Visitor chapter. Excellent and inexpensive, it's packed with all kinds of useful information and includes large maps of the hiking routes in Uganda and Zaïre as well as information on equipment, costs, flora & fauna, weather, etc.

Many climbers, like their guides and porters, purchase food at the Mutwanga market where all essentials (dried fish, vegetables, beer, etc) are available. However, I recommend stocking up in Beni or Butembo where you'll find a much wider selection.

Costs

The park fee, which you pay at the entrance, is US$40 (payable in hard currency or travellers' cheques) and quite reasonable compared to the price of seeing gorillas. Guides are compulsory and their fee is included in the price. The trail is fairly easy to follow but don't try to skip paying these fees as the money is responsible for the increased protection being given to the area in recent years.

You must purchase the guide's food (US$1 a day) and give him a tip at the end of the climb. As for porters, you'll need one per person; they are not included in the park fee and cost US$1.25 a day plus US$1 a day for food plus a tip at the end. Guides and porters bring their own equipment but you'll need an extra porter to carry the food and the guide's pack. There is another small fee for sleeping at each hut. Altogether you should budget for about US$4 per person per day plus your own food. The park office rents no

equipment except a pair of crampons (about US$3).

Accommodation

The best place to stay in Mutwanga is *Hôtel de la Niege*, which charges US$6 for a double. The hotel's restaurant, however, is not very good and the service is terribly slow. For only a bit more money you can eat much better at *Chez Patrick Engels*, a restaurant on the opposite side of town run by a Belgian man of that name. Meals there cost about US$4 but they're delicious and well worth the price.

There's also a grubby *case de passage* (a bare-minimum place with rooms only) in town with rooms for US1.50 but you definitely get what you pay for. In addition, you'll find an old, historic lodge, *Hôtel Ruwenzori*, alongside a stream about a km behind the market. Abandoned since the 1964-67 rebellion in the area (which caused Dian Fossey, who started her work on gorillas in this region, to change her venue permanently to Rwanda), this legendary place is unfurnished but you can camp there for free and take a dip in one of the cold pools. Be sure to tip the friendly caretaker; he'll bring you firewood for a fee. Others prefer camping at the *Camp des Guides* at the park entrance in Mutsora, four km up from Mutwanga; the cost per person is negligible.

Mt Stanley Climbing Route

Allow a minimum of five days for the climb and six or seven days if you'll be attempting the peak – three to five days up and two days down. On the way up, you'll find three unlocked cabins, all of which have fireplaces and hard bunk beds but no mattresses; the hiking time between each is roughly the same. There is also a fourth wooden shack higher up, at the glacier's edge, but it's rarely used for sleeping.

Mutsora Park to Kalongi Hut The climb starts at Mutsora Park Station and heads up the valley of the Butawu River through a dense scrub forest. The climb is gradual, from 1700 metres at Mutsora to 2135 metres at Hut 1 (called Kalongi), and normally takes about five hours. Kalongi hut, which sleeps 24 people, is relatively new, with water nearby.

Kalongi to Muhungu Hut The climb from Kalongi to Hut 2 (called Muhungu) through the giant heather wonderland is the toughest part and takes at least 5½ hours – all uphill to 3333 metres – through roots and vines, with wet ground. Moss blankets everything, so you are likely to stumble quite a bit. The hut can sleep 12 people; during the dry season you might find all the beds taken. Fresh water is two km away.

Muhungu to Kyondo Hut From Hut 2 to Hut 3 (called Kyondo) is another 970 metres; the latter sleeps 12 people and has water nearby. The trail, which progressively disintegrates on the way, passes through the fairyland-like region of the giant alpine flowers; the climb takes about 4½ hours. When you get to Kyondo hut, you'll see the beautiful Lac Noir below. It's very cold and windy at night here, with frequent snow flurries just above the hut, and wind blowing through the broken windows. If you bring plastic to cover the windows, this stone cabin will be much warmer. Some trekkers prefer returning the same day to Hut 2 so as to avoid the cold; if you do this, set out very early in the morning to give yourself enough time to arrive there before nightfall.

Kyondo to Moraine Hut The main trail from Hut 3 leads on for two km to Hut 4 (called Moraine). Easy to follow and rising only very gradually, it passes through a steep rocky area with only a metal cable to hang on to. This section is sufficiently risky that if you take this route, the park officer will require you to sign a waiver of liability. Shortly afterwards you will come to a chain of interconnecting lakes (first Lac Vert, then the much smaller lacs Gris and Blanc) and eventually Moraine hut, which is at the base of the summit. The large glacier surrounding Mt Stanley is just beyond, with Pic Margher-

ite (5109 metres), the mountain's highest point, and Pic Alexandra both in the distance.

The small wooden cabin is in such bad condition that most climbers attempting to scale Margherite make a direct assault from Hut 3. The climb is not difficult technically but anyone attempting it should have experience climbing at high altitudes and definitely must be equipped with crampons, ropes and ice axes. And make sure beforehand that your guide has no qualms about scaling it. If successful, you should be able to make it down to Hut 2 by nightfall (not to Hut 1!) and on to Mutwanga the following day.

Kyondo Hut to Wasuwameso Ridge Most hikers, however, don't attempt the summit; instead, from Hut 3 they hike over to Wasuwameso ridge, which is an hour's walk and 192 metres higher. From there you can get some spectacular, close-up views of Mt Stanley, clouds permitting. The crack of dawn is when the peaks are most often free of clouds, so plan accordingly. To get there you must take a side trail which your guide can point out; the route is fairly obvious.

MT HOYO

Some 126 km north of Beni, the area around Mt Hoyo (1450 metres), while not within the Virguna park boundaries, is in a national reserve and managed as though it were part of Virunga. It's at the northern end of the Ruwenzori range and at the eastern end of the Ituri forest. Pygmies are native to these tropical rainforests and the Mt Hoyo area is one of the best places to see them. Called Mbuti (or BaMbuti) in this region, the Pygmies live in a symbiotic relationship with the negroid Lese (or BaLese), who are primarily farmers and live in the villages. The Lese, who view themselves as masters of the Pygmies, sell them beer, cooking utensils, bananas, tobacco and metal for making knives and arrows in exchange for bush meat and ivory.

Unfortunately, as at Upulu, the Pygmies here have seen so many Westerners that meeting them has become an uninspired routine where they sell travellers Pygmy handicrafts and offer a staged dance performance for money while constantly pestering them for *cadeaux* (gifts), tobacco being their favourite (sugar and salt are also acceptable). It's all a little too touristy, but the dance performance and dealings with the Pygmies can nevertheless be enlightening, especially the interaction between them and the Lese. If you want to see a dance performance, consult the local Lese chief as he can arrange it; afterwards, the Pygmies may use your money to trade with the Lese.

As at Epulu, the most interesting thing to do with the Pygmies is going on a trip with them into the forest to gather food (mushrooms, honey, berries, roots, etc) and hunt small game (outside the reserve only). Instead of going with the Pygmies nearby, you might try looking for someone to take you to a more remote village where the experience might be more authentic. Half the fun is walking through the amazingly beautiful forests where they live. Some of the animals that you might see are blue monkey, white-nosed monkey, dwarf antelope, duiker and red dwarf buffalo.

Pygmies, however, are just one of the four attractions here. The others are several grottes (caves) with stalagmites, Mt Hoyo, and some waterfalls (pictured in many tourist brochures) called l'Escaliers de Venus (Venus Staircase) where *King Solomon's Mines* was filmed. The caverns, which are lit by paraffin lanterns, and nearby waterfalls are not of overwhelming interest, however they are within a short distance of the lodge and a tour takes only two hours.

Climbing Mt Hoyo takes two days and the trail is apparently overgrown, so few travellers attempt it.

For any of these excursions you must pay the park entrance fee, which is US$20. The Lese villagers will gladly act as guides to the Pygmy camps and any of these places including Mt Hoyo, just ask at the lodge. A visit to a Pygmy village costs about US$5 per group; the Pygmies will charge you for every photograph as well.

Places to Stay & Eat
Just outside the park entrance is the 30-room *Auberge du Mont Hoyo*, which has chalets for roughly US$30 as well as rooms for a fifth the price. There's also a camp ground next to it with toilets, showers and (sometimes) electricity. The camping fee is about US$2 a person. The restaurant at the lodge is expensive so bring food (you may be able to purchase fruit along the 13-km road leading here) or buy it from the Lese villagers.

Getting There & Away
A minibus from Beni north to Komanda, the crossroad for Bunia (75 km to the east) and Kisangani (631 km to the west), takes six or seven hours during the dry season (10 hours in a big truck) and often much longer during the rainy season. All along the way you'll see new farms being cut out of the once undisturbed equatorial forest. The turn-off for Mt Hoyo is 12 km south of Komanda, just north of the Loya River; the park entrance and lodge are 13 km to the east down a rough road. If you're walking and find a porter, he'll want about US$2 to carry your gear.

Index

ABBREVIATIONS

Cam – Cameroun
CAR – Central African
     Republic

Ch – Chad
Co – Congo
EG – Equatorial Guinea

G – Gabon
S&P – São Tomé e Príncipe
Z – Zaïre

MAPS

Abéché (Ch) 289
Around Mobaye (CAR) 238

Bafoussam (Cam) 170
Bambari (CAR) 237
Bamenda (Cam) 176
Bangui (CAR) 222
    Central Bangui 226
Bata (EG) 358
Beni (Z) 540
Bioko Island (EG) 349
Booué (G) 420
Bossembélé (CAR) 244
Bouar (CAR) 245
Brazzaville (Co) 308
    Central Brazzaville 312
Buea (Cam) 159
Bukavu (Z) 520
Butembo (Z) 538

Cameroun 107
    Northern Cameroun 183
Central Africa 12
Central African Republic 208
Chad 253
Congo 293
Douala (Cam) 138
    Central Douala 142

Dzanga-Sangha Reserve (CAR)
    248

Ebebiyin (EG) 363
Ebolowa (Cam) 154
Equatorial Guinea 339

Foumban (Cam) 167
Franceville (G) 428

Gabon 367
    Gabon Coast 398
Garoua (Cam) 190
Goma & Gisenyi (Z) 530

Kinshasa (Z) 482-83
    Central Kinshasa 488
Kisangani (Z) 510
Kribi (Cam) 151
Kumba (Cam) 163

Lambaréné (G) 408
Lastoursville (G) 423
Libreville (G) 382
    Around Libreville 397
    Central Libreville 386
Limbe (Cam) 156
Loubomo (Dolisie) (Co) 330
Lubumbashi (Z) 500

Malabo (EG) 350
Mamfé (Cam) 165
Maroua (Cam) 194
Moanda (G) 426

Mokolo (Cam) 200
Mora (Cam) 204
Moundou (Ch) 286

N'Dendé (G) 414
N'Djamena (Ch) 268-69
    Central N'Djamena 272
N'Gaoundéré (Cam) 184
Ndjolé (G) 407

Owando (Co) 335
Oyem (G) 416

Pointe-Noire (Co) 322
Port-Gentil (G) 400

Ruwenzori Mountains (Z) 550

São Tomé (S&P) 444
São Tomé e Príncipe 435
Sarh (Ch) 281
Sibut (CAR) 235

Virunga Gorillas (Z) 545

Yaoundé (Cam) 124
    Central Yaoundé 130

Zaïre (Z) 454-55
    Eastern Zaïre 519

TEXT

Map references are in **bold** type

Abéché (Ch) 288-289, **289**
Acalayong (EG) 361
adventure tours 104-105
AIDS 67
air travel
    to/from Central Africa 83-88
    within Central Africa 98-99
Ambam (Cam) 155

antiques 41
Arabs (Ch) 258-59

background reading 50-56
    art & culture 51-52
    ecology 53
    economics 53
    fiction 52-53
    history 50-51
    music 52

politics 53
travel 54
Bafang (Cam) 174
Bafoussam (Cam) 169-73, **170**
Bafut (Cam) 179
Bakuba art (Z) 462
Bali (Cam) 179
Bambari (CAR) 236-38, **237**
Bamboro (G) 422
Bamenda (Cam) 175-79, **176**

Bamiléké people 21
Bamingui-Bangoran National
    Park (CAR) 241-42
Bamoun people 21
Bangassou (CAR) 239
Bangem (Cam) 174
Bangui (CAR) 221-33, **222, 226**
Banyo (Cam) 182-83
bargaining 79
Barombi (Cam) 163
Bata (EG) 357-61, **358**
Batouri (Cam) 182
beaches
    Arena Blanca (EG) 356
    Cap Estérias (G) 396
    Cocotier Plage (Cam) 153
    Costa Blanca (Cam) 153
    Eboundja (Cam) 153
    Ekwata Beach (G) 396
    Londji (Cam) 153
    Mbini (EG) 361
    Mile Six Beach (Cam) 156
    Pointe Indienne (Co) 329
    Pointe-Dénis (G) 396
    Praia da Micolo (S&P) 448
    Praia das Conchas (S&P) 448
    Praia dos Governadores (S&P)
        448
beads 81
Befang (Cam) 179
begging 29
Bélinga (G) 418
Beni (Z) 539-41, **540**
Berbérati (CAR) 246-47
Bertoua (Cam) 181-82
Bikoro (Z) 515
bilharzia 66
Binga (Z) 508
Bioko Island (EG) 348-57, **349**
Birao (CAR) 242-43
Bitam (G) 415
black market 42-43
Boali Waterfalls (CAR) 233
Boca de Inferno (S&P) 449
Boende (Z) 514
Boma (Z) 498
Bomassa (Co) 336
books, see background reading
Booué (G) 419-21, **420**
Bossembélé (CAR) 243-44, **244**
Bouar (CAR) 244-46, **245**
Bouar megaliths (CAR) 246
Bouba Ndjida National Park
    (Cam) 188-89
Boula Ibib (Cam) 193
Boyoma Falls (Z) 512
Brazzaville (Co) 306-20, **308,
    312**
bribery 30

Buea (Cam) 159-62, **159**
Bukavu (Z) 518-26, **520**
Bumba (Z) 508-509
Bunia (Z) 541
Businga (Z) 507
Buta (Z) 509
Butembo (Z) 537-39, **538**

Cameroun 106-206, **107, 183**
Campo (Cam) 153
canoeing (CAR) 221, 234, (G)
    410, 419, (Z) 514
Cap Estérias (G) 396
carnet de passage 94
Carnot (CAR) 246
Cascades da São Nicolau (S&P)
    448
Central African Republic 207-
    50, **208**
Chad 251-91, **253**
Chefferie de Bandjoun (Cam)
    173
chimpanzees (Z) 544, 547
climate 14-17
Cocobeach (G) 405-406
Cogo (EG) 361
Congo 292-337, **293**
Congo/Zaïre riverboat, see
    Kisangani steamer
Congo River Rapids (Co) 311
credit cards 43
customs 41-42
cycling 73, 103, (Cam) 123, 179

dangers & annoyances 71-72
Diosso (Co) 329
Djambala (Co) 334
Djeno (Co) 324
Djingliya (Cam) 201-02
Djomba Gorilla Sanctuary (Z)
    545-47
Douala (Cam) 137-50, **138, 142**
Douguia (Ch) 279-80
Dschang (Cam) 174-75
Dzanga-Sangha Reserve (CAR)
    247-50, **248**

Ebebiyin (EG) 362-64, **363**
Ebolowa (Cam) 153-55, **154**
Eboundja (Cam) 153
economy 19-20
Ekom Waterfalls (Cam) 174
Ekwata Beach (G) 396
Elephant project (Z) 517
Epulu (Z) 515-17
Equatorial Guinea 338-64, **339**
Evinayong (EG) 362

Fada (Ch) 289

Fang people 21
Faya (Ch) 290
fishing 74
food 75-78
Foumban (Cam) 166-69, **167**
Franceville (G) 427-33, **428**
Fulani people 21

Gabon 365-433, **367, 398**
Gaoui (Ch) 278-79
Garamba National Park (Z) 517-
    18
Garoua (Cam) 189-93, **190**
Garoua-Boulaï 182
Gbadolite (Z) 506-507
Gemena (Z) 507-508
geography 14
gifts 29-30
Gisenyi (Z) 534, **530**
golf 74
Goma (Z) 528-534, **530**
gorillas (CAR) 249, (Z) 526-27,
    529, 544, 545, 547
government 18
Grands Lacs (G) 412
greetings 28-29

Hadide (Ch) 280
Hadjer el Hamis (Ch) 280
harmattan 17
health 58-71
hepatitis 65
hiking 72-73, see also trekking
hippos (Z) 547, 549
hitchhiking (across the Sahara)
    91-92
holidays & festivals 48-49
hunting (Cam) 189, (CAR) 224

Iguéla (G) 405
Ikela (Z) 514
Ilebo (Z) 505
immunisation 60-61
Impfondo (Co) 337
Ingende (Z) 515
Inshasha (Z) 536
Ishango (Z) 548-549
Isiro (Z) 516-17
Isla Corisco (EG) 362
Islam 34-35, 48
Islas Elobey (EG) 361

Jakiri (Cam) 181

Kabo (CAR) 240
Kaga Bandoro (CAR) 239-240
Kahuzi-Biéga National Park (Z)
    526-28

Kalamaloué National Park
(Cam) 206
Kananga (Z) 504
Kasindi (Z) 541
Kembé (CAR) 239
Kiavinyonge (Z) 549
Kikwit (Z) 505-506
Kill (Cam) 203
Kinkala (Co) 333
Kinshasa (Z) 480-97, **482-83,
488**
Kirdi people 22, (Cam) 201
Kisangani (Z) 509-514, **510**
Kisangani steamer (Z) 478, 513
Kisantu Botanical Gardens (Z)
497
Kolwezi (Z) 503
Komanda (Z) 541
Kongo 22
Korup National Park (Cam) 164-
65
Koulamoutou (G) 424-25
Koumra (Ch) 285
Kousseri (Cam) 206
Koza (Cam) 201-202
Kribi (Cam) 150-53, **151**
Kuba 22
Kumba (Cam) 162-64, **163**
Kumbo (Cam) 180

La Bénoué National Park (Cam)
188-89
Lac Bleu (Co) 321
Lac de Baleng (Cam) 173
Lac de Bamendjing (Cam) 174
Lac de Ma Vallé (Z) 497
Lac Evaro (G) 412
La Dent de Mindif (Cam) 199
Lake Barombi Mbo (Cam) 162
Lake Chad (Ch) 279
Lake Mobutu (Z) 541
Lake Nyos (Cam) 180
lake trips (Z) 525-26
Lake Wum (Cam) 180
Lambaréné (G) 407-12, **408**
language 35
Lastoursville (G) 422-24, **423**
Libreville (G) 381-396, **382,
386, 397**
Limbe (Cam) 155-59, **156**
Limbenga (G) 422
Linia (Ch) 279
Lisala (Z) 508
Loango (Co) 329
Lobé Falls (Cam) 153
Logone River (Cam) 200
Londji (Cam) 153
Loubomo (Dolisie) (Co) 329-33,
330

Loufoulakari Falls (Co) 320
Luba people 22, (EG) 355
Luba (EG) 355-56
Luba art (Z) 462
Lubumbashi (Z) 499-503, **500**

M'Baïki (CAR) 233-34
Mabas (Cam) 202
Madingo-Kayes (Co) 329
Maga (Cam) 199
Makari (Cam) 206
Makokou (G) 418
Makoua (Co) 335-36
Mala (Cam) 203
Malabo (EG) 348-55, **350**
malaria 68
Mamfé (Cam) 165-66, **165**
Mangbetu art (Z) 463
Maroua (Cam) 193-99, **194**
Matadi (Z) 498
Matoumbou (Co) 333
Mbandaka (Z) 514-15
Mbanza-Ngungu (Z) 497
Mbinda (Co) 333
Mbini (EG) 361
Mbuji-Mayi (Z) 504
Meiganga (Cam) 182
Mélong (Cam) 174
meningitis 66
Mikeno volcano (Z) 544
Mile Six Beach (Cam) 156
Moanda (G) 425-27, **426**
Moba (EG) 356
Mobaye (CAR) 238-39, **238**
Mokolo (Cam) 200-201, **200**
money 42-46
black market 42-43
credit cards 43
tipping 46
travellers' cheques 43-44
Mora (Cam) 203-204, **204**
Mouila (G) 413
Moundou (Ch) 285-88, **286**
mountain biking, see cycling
Moussoro (Ch) 290
Mpondwe (Uganda) (Z) 541
Mt Cambier (Z) 498
Mt Cameroun (Cam) 159-62
Mt Cameroun race (Cam) 160
Mt Goma (Z) 528
Mt Hoyo (Z) 553-54
Mt Manenguba (Cam) 174
Mt Oko (Cam) 181
Muanda (Z) 498
Mundemba (Cam) 164-65
music 23-28, 52, (Cam) 112-
113, (CAR) 213-14, (Ch)
259-60, (Z) 463
Afro-beat 27-28

Congo music 26
Juju 28
makossa 26-27
sahelian 27
Mutwanga (Z) 551

N'Délé (CAR) 242
N'Dendé (G) 413-14, **414**
N'Djamena (Ch) 267-78, **268-
69, 272**
N'Gaoundal (Cam) 182-83
N'Gaoundéré (Cam) 183-88, **184**
National Parks & Reserves 17-18
Bamingui-Bangoran (CAR)
241-42
Dzanga-Sangha Reserve (CAR)
247-50
Garamba National Park (Z) 517-
18
Kimbi River Game Reserve
(Cam) 180
Korup National Park (Cam)
164-65
Parc National d'Okapis (Z) 515
Parc National de Bouba Ndjida
(Cam) 188-89
Parc National de Kahuzi-Biéga
(Z) 526-28
Parc National de Kalamaloué
(Cam) 206
Parc National de la Bénoué
(Cam) 188-89
Parc National des Virunga (Z)
541-54
Réserve d'Iguéla (G) 405
Réserve de la Lopé (G) 421
St Floris National Park (CAR)
241-42
Waza National Park (Cam)
205-206
Zakouma National Park (Ch) 284
Ndjolé (G) 406-407, **407**
Ndop (Cam) 181
Ndu (Cam) 180
Nkambe (Cam) 180
Nyamulagira volcano (Z) 543-44
Nyanga (Co) 333
Nyiragongo volcano (Z) 543

Obala (Cam) 136
Oko (Cam) 181
Okondja (G) 433
Ouara (Ch) 289
Oudjilla (Cam) 204-205
Ouesso (Co) 336
overland travel
to/from CAF 88-96
Owando (Co) 334-35, **335**
Oyem (G) 415-18, **416**

Oyo (Co) 334
Oysha (Z) 539

Palabala (Z) 498
Palais du Lamido (Cam) 185-86
Palais Royal (Cam) 166-67
Pende art (Z) 461
Petits Lacs (G) 410
photography 56-58
Pico Malabo (EG) 355
Pitoa (Cam) 193
Pointe-Dénis (G) 396
Pointe-Noire (Co) 321-29, 322
Port-Gentil (G) 398-405, 400
Príncipe (S&P) 450-51,
Pygmies 22, (CAR) 233, (Co)
    336, 337, (Z) 515-16, 527,
    539, 553

religion 33-35
    Islam 34-35, 48
    traditional 33-34
Réserve de la Lopé (G) 421
Rey Bouba (Cam) 189
Ring Road (Cam) 179-81
Rio Benito (EG) 361
Rio Muni (EG) 357-64
riverboat trips (CAR) 232, (Co)
    304, 306, (G) 404, 407, (Z)
    478
Roça Agostino Neto (S&P) 449
rock-climbing 72-73, (Cam) 199
Rolas Island (Ilhéu das Rolas)
    (S&P) 449
Rumangabo Gorilla Sanctuary
    (Z) 547
Rumsiki (Cam) 202
Rutshuru (Z) 536-37
Ruwenzori Mountains (Z) 549,
    550
Rwindi Plains (Z) 547-48

safety, see dangers & annoyances
Sahara 90-96
São João Dos Angolares (S&P)
    449

São Tomé (S&P) 442-48, 444
São Tomé e Príncipe 434-51, 435
Sara people 23, (Ch) 259
Sarh (Ch) 280-84, 281
Setté Cama (G) 405
shopping 79-82
    beads 81
    gold 80-81
    gourds 82
    leather 82
    malachite jewellery 81
    painting 81
    silver 80-81
    woodcarvings 80
Sibiti (Co) 333
Sibut (CAR) 234-36, 235
Sido (CAR) 240, (Ch) 284
Sina (Cam) 203
Sport 32-33, 73
St Floris National Park (CAR)
    241-42
Sultan's Museum (Cam) 166

Tchibanga (G) 414
things to buy, see shopping
Tibati (Cam) 182-83
Tibesti mountains (Ch) 290-91
tipping 46
Tongo Chimpanzee Sanctuary
    (Z) 547
Toubo people 23, (Ch) 258
Tourou (Cam) 202
train travel 99-100
travellers' cheques 43-44
trekking
    Around Luba (EG) 356
    Mt Cameroun (Cam) 160
    Mt Kahuzi (Z) 527
    Mt Oko (Cam) 181
    Mt Stanley (Z) 552
    Pico Malabo (EG) 355
    Ring Road (Cam) 179
    volcanoes (Z) 543-44
Trinidade (S&P) 448
Tshoma (Z) 541
typhoid 65

Ureca (EG) 356

Virunga National Park (Z) 541-
    554, 545
visas 36-41
Vitshumbi (Z) 548
Vivi (Z) 498

Wagenia village (Z) 512
Walikale (Z) 514
waterfalls
    Boyoma (Wagenia) Falls (Z) 512
    Cascades da São Nicolau (S&P)
        448
    Chutes de Béla (Co) 320
    Chutes de la Lobé (Cam) 153
    Chutes de la Mouenkeu (Cam)
        174
    Chutes de Loufoulakari (Co) 320
    Chutes de Zongo (Z) 497
    Chutes du Tello (Cam) 188
    Ekom Waterfalls (Cam) 174
    Lambi Chutes (CAR) 244
    Les Chutes de Boali (CAR) 233
    Les Chutes de Loa-Loa (G) 419
    Nachtigal Falls (Cam) 136
Waza National Park (Cam) 205-
    206
white rhino (Z) 517
Wildlife Conservation Interna-
    tional (Co) 310
woodcarvings 80
Wum (Cam) 180

Yaoundé (Cam) 123-136, 124,
    130
yellow fever 69

Zaïre 452-554, 454-455, 519
Zinga (CAR) 234
Ziver (Cam) 202
Zongo (Z) 507
Zongo Rapids (Z) 497

Keep in touch!

We love hearing from you and think you'd like to hear from us.

The Lonely Planet Newsletter covers the when, where, how and what of travel. (AND it's free!)

When...is the right time to see reindeer in Finland?
Where...can you hear the best palm-wine music in Ghana?
How...do you get from Asunción to Areguá by steam train?
What...should you leave behind to avoid hassles with customs in Iran?

To join our mailing list just contact us at any of our offices. (details below)

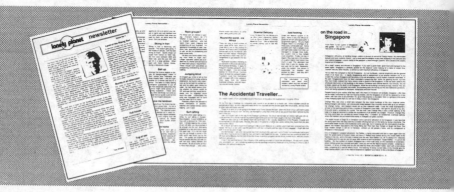

Every issue includes:

- a letter from Lonely Planet founders Tony and Maureen Wheeler
- travel diary from a Lonely Planet author - find out what it's really like out on the road
- feature article on an important and topical travel issue
- a selection of recent letters from our readers
- the latest travel news from all over the world
- details on Lonely Planet's new and forthcoming releases

Also available Lonely Planet T-shirts. 100% heavy weight cotton (S, M, L, XL)

LONELY PLANET PUBLICATIONS
Australia: PO Box 617, Hawthorn, 3122, Victoria (tel: 03-819 1877)
USA: Embarcadero West, 155 Filbert Street, Suite 251, Oakland, CA 94607 (tel: 510-893 8555)
UK: Devonshire House, 12 Barley Mow Passage, Chiswick, London W4 4PH (tel: 081-742 3161)

Guides to Africa

Africa on a shoestring
From Marrakesh to Kampala, Mozambique to Mauritania, Johannesburg to Cairo – this guidebook has all the facts on travelling in Africa. Comprehensive information on more than 50 countries.

East Africa - a travel survival kit
Detailed information on Kenya, Uganda, Rwanda, Burundi, eastern Zaïre and Tanzania. The latest edition includes a 32-page full-colour Safari Guide.

Egypt & the Sudan - a travel survival kit
This guide takes you into and beyond the spectacular and mysterious pyramids, temples, tombs, monasteries, mosques and bustling main streets of Egypt and the Sudan.

Kenya - a travel survival kit
This superb guide features a 32-page 'Safari Guide' with colour photographs, illustrations and information on East Africa's famous wildlife.

Morocco, Algeria & Tunisia - a travel survival kit
Reap the rewards of getting off the beaten track with this practical guide.

South Africa, Lesotho & Swaziland - a travel survival kit
Travel to southern Africa and you'll be surprised by its cultural diversity and incredible beauty. There's no better place to see Africa's amazing wildlife. All the essential travel details are included in this guide as well as information about wildlife reserves.

Trekking in East Africa
Practical, first-hand information for trekkers for a region renowned for its spectacular national parks and rewarding trekking trails. Covers treks in Kenya, Tanzania, Uganda, Malawi and Zambia.

West Africa - a travel survival kit
All the necessary information for independent travel in Benin, Burkino Faso, Cape Verde, Côte d'Ivoire, The Gambia, Ghana, Guinea, Guinea-Bissau, Liberia, Mali, Mauritania, Niger, Nigeria, Senegal, Sierra Leone and Togo.

Zimbabwe, Botswana & Namibia - a travel survival kit
Exotic wildlife, breathtaking scenery and fascinating people...this comprehensive guide shows a wilder, older side of Africa for the adventurous traveller. Includes a 32-page colour Safari Guide.

Also available:
Swahili phrasebook, *Arabic (Egyptian)* phrasebook & *Arabic (Moroccan)* phrasebook

Lonely Planet Guidebooks

Lonely Planet guidebooks cover every accessible part of Asia as well as Australia, the Pacific, South America, Africa, the Middle East, Europe and parts of North America. There are five series: *travel survival kits*, covering a country for a range of budgets; *shoestring guides* with compact information for low-budget travel in a major region; *walking guides*; *city guides* and *phrasebooks*.

Australia & the Pacific
Australia
Bushwalking in Australia
Islands of Australia's Great Barrier Reef
Fiji
Melbourne city guide
Micronesia
New Caledonia
New Zealand
Tramping in New Zealand
Papua New Guinea
Bushwalking in Papua New Guinea
Papua New Guinea phrasebook
Rarotonga & the Cook Islands
Samoa
Solomon Islands
Sydney city guide
Tahiti & French Polynesia
Tonga
Vanuatu
Victoria

South-East Asia
Bali & Lombok
Bangkok city guide
Myanmar (Burma)
Burmese phrasebook
Cambodia
Indonesia
Indonesia phrasebook
Malaysia, Singapore & Brunei
Philippines
Pilipino phrasebook
Singapore city guide
South-East Asia on a shoestring
Thailand
Thai phrasebook
Vietnam
Vietnamese phrasebook

North-East Asia
China
Mandarin Chinese phrasebook
Hong Kong, Macau & Canton
Japan
Japanese phrasebook
Korea
Korean phrasebook
Mongolia
North-East Asia on a shoestring
Seoul city guide
Taiwan
Tibet
Tibet phrasebook
Tokyo city guide

West Asia
Trekking in Turkey
Turkey
Turkish phrasebook
West Asia on a shoestring

Middle East
Arab Gulf States
Egypt & the Sudan
Arabic (Egyptian) phrasebook
Iran
Israel
Jordan & Syria
Yemen

Indian Ocean
Madagascar & Comoros
Maldives & Islands of the East Indian Ocean
Mauritius, Réunion & Seychelles

Mail Order

Lonely Planet guidebooks are distributed worldwide. They are also available by mail order from Lonely Planet, so if you have difficulty finding a title please write to us. US and Canadian residents should write to Embarcadero West, 155 Filbert St, Suite 251, Oakland CA 94607, USA; European residents should write to Devonshire House, 12 Barley Mow Passage, Chiswick, London W4 4PH; and residents of other countries to PO Box 617, Hawthorn, Victoria 3122, Australia.

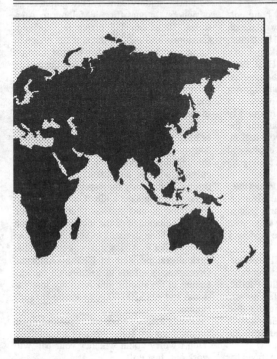

Indian Subcontinent
Bangladesh
India
Hindi/Urdu phrasebook
Trekking in the Indian Himalaya
Karakoram Highway
Kashmir, Ladakh & Zanskar
Nepal
Trekking in the Nepal Himalaya
Nepal phrasebook
Pakistan
Sri Lanka
Sri Lanka phrasebook

Africa
Africa on a shoestring
Central Africa
East Africa
Trekking in East Africa
Kenya
Swahili phrasebook
Morocco, Algeria & Tunisia
Arabic (Moroccan) phrasebook
South Africa, Lesotho & Swaziland
Zimbabwe, Botswana & Namibia
West Africa

Central America
Baja California
Central America on a shoestring
Costa Rica
La Ruta Maya
Mexico

North America
Alaska
Canada
Hawaii

South America
Argentina, Uruguay & Paraguay
Bolivia
Brazil
Brazilian phrasebook
Chile & Easter Island
Colombia
Ecuador & the Galápagos Islands
Latin American Spanish phrasebook
Peru
Quechua phrasebook
South America on a shoestring
Trekking in the Patagonian Andes

Europe
Dublin city guide
Eastern Europe on a shoestring
Eastern Europe phrasebook
Finland
Iceland, Greenland & the Faroe Islands
Italy
Mediterranean Europe on a shoestring
Mediterranean Europe phrasebook
Poland
Scandinavian & Baltic Europe on a shoestring
Scandinavian Europe phrasebook
Trekking in Spain
Trekking in Greece
USSR
Russian phrasebook
Western Europe on a shoestring
Western Europe phrasebook

The Lonely Planet Story

Lonely Planet published its first book in 1973 in response to the numerous 'How did you do it?' questions Maureen and Tony Wheeler were asked after driving, bussing, hitching, sailing and railing their way from England to Australia.

Written at a kitchen table and hand collated, trimmed and stapled, *Across Asia on the Cheap* became an instant local bestseller, inspiring thoughts of another book.

Eighteen months in South-East Asia resulted in their second guide, *South-East Asia on a shoestring*, which they put together in a backstreet Chinese hotel in Singapore in 1975. The 'yellow bible' as it quickly became known to backpackers around the world, soon became *the* guide to the region. It has sold well over half a million copies and is now in its 7th edition, still retaining its familiar yellow cover.

Today there are over 120 Lonely Planet titles in print – books that have that same adventurous approach to travel as those early guides; books that 'assume you know how to get your luggage off the carousel' as one reviewer put it.

Although Lonely Planet initially specialised in guides to Asia, they now cover most regions of the world, including the Pacific, South America, Africa, the Middle East and Europe. The list of *walking guides* and *phrasebooks* (for 'unusual' languages such as Quechua, Swahili, Nepalese and Egyptian Arabic) is also growing rapidly.

The emphasis continues to be on travel for independent travellers. Tony and Maureen still travel for several months of each year and play an active part in the writing, updating and quality control of Lonely Planet's guides.

They have been joined by over 50 authors, 54 staff – mainly editors, cartographers, & designers – at our office in Melbourne, Australia, 10 at our US office in Oakland, California and another three at our office in London to handle sales for Britain, Europe and Africa. In 1992 Lonely Planet opened an editorial office in Paris. Travellers themselves also make a valuable contribution to the guides through the feedback we receive in thousands of letters each year.

The people at Lonely Planet strongly believe that travellers can make a positive contribution to the countries they visit, both through their appreciation of the countries' culture, wildlife and natural features, and through the money they spend. In addition, the company makes a direct contribution to the countries and regions it covers. Since 1986 a percentage of the income from each book has been donated to ventures such as famine relief in Africa; aid projects in India; agricultural projects in Central America; Greenpeace's efforts to halt French nuclear testing in the Pacific and Amnesty International. In 1993 $100,000 was donated to such causes.

Lonely Planet's basic travel philosophy is summed up in Tony Wheeler's comment, 'Don't worry about whether your trip will work out. Just go!'